MANAGEMENT SCIENCE

ANDREW W. SHOGAN

University of California, Berkeley

Prentice Hall,
Englewood Cliffs, New Jersey 07632
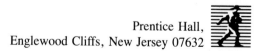

Library of Congress Cataloging-in-Publication Data

SHOGAN, ANDREW W.
    Management science / Andrew W. Shogan.
        p.   cm.
    Includes index.
    ISBN 0–13–551219–0
    1. Management science.   I. Title.
T56.S417 1988
658'.001'5197—dc19   87–32781

Editorial/production supervision: *Esther S. Koehn*
Interior design and cover design: *Lee Cohen*
Manufacturing buyer: *Barbara Kelly Kittle*

Cover art: *Josef Albers*. Homage to the Square: ''Ascending.'' *1953.*
Oil on composition board. 43¹/₂ x 43¹/₂ inches.
Collection of Whitney Museum of American Art. Purchase. 54.34

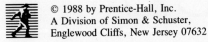
Printed in the United States of America
10 9 8 7 6 5 4 3 2 1

ISBN 0-13-551219-0

Prentice-Hall International (UK) Limited, *London*
Prentice-Hall of Australia Pty. Limited, *Sydney*
Prentice-Hall Canada Inc., *Toronto*
Prentice-Hall Hispanoamericana, S.A., *Mexico City*
Prentice-Hall of India Private Limited, *New Delhi*
Prentice-Hall of Japan, Inc., *Tokyo*
Prentice-Hall of Southeast Asia Pte. Ltd., *Singapore*
Editora Prentice-Hall do Brasil, Ltda., *Rio de Janeiro*

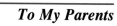
To My Parents

CONTENTS

PREFACE

This text is designed for a single course or a two-course sequence that introduces management science to undergraduate or graduate students studying business, economics, public policy, health care administration, or applied mathematics.

UNDERLYING PHILOSOPHY

The writing of this text was guided by the following philosophy:

- *Managerial Perspective*. A managerial perspective is maintained throughout the text. Examples are the discussion at the end of Section 4.3 of how to use a rolling planning process to implement the solution to a linear programming model of a production and inventory planning problem, the overview of inventory management in Sections 14.1–14.3, and the overview of queueing systems in Sections 16.1 and 16.2.

- *Innovative Examples*. The examples used to illustrate applications are not "toy problems" but realistic scenarios. These scenarios, many of which are simplified from recent journal articles, involve diverse applications, including applications in the public sector. Examples are Section 5.4's scenario involving the use of goal programming to allocate the budget of a state agency, Section 9.12's scenario involving the use of integer programming to perform cluster analysis for marketing research, and Section 17.6's scenario involving the use of simulation to improve a city's street-cleaning efforts.

- *Comprehensiveness.* Each topic is covered thoroughly, thereby eliminating the need for an instructor to supplement a topic with extra readings or notes. Within the coverage of each topic, there is an attention to detail that goes beyond that in other texts. This detail is not in the form of mathematical rigor but rather careful and patient explanations. While this approach demands more effort by the reader, it also leads to a greater understanding and appreciation of the topic.

- *Flexibility.* Despite their comprehensiveness, the chapters have been organized to provide maximum flexibility. Advanced material has been placed in separate chapters or in sections near the ends of chapters and can be omitted without loss of continuity. For example, a one-quarter survey course can omit the advanced topics in linear programming formulation in Chapter 5, the advanced topics in project management in Chapter 11, the advanced topics in decision analysis in Chapter 13, the coverage of material requirements planning in Section 14.7, and the coverage of the newsboy problem in Sections 15.8–15.12. Also, a course emphasizing modeling instead of solution techniques can omit the simplex method in Chapters 6 and 7 and the branch-and-bound method in Section 9.14. Additional flexibility is provided by the ability to cover the chapters in a sequence different from the order in which they appear. For more details on the text's flexibility, consult the accompanying Instructor's Manual.

- *Limited Prerequisites.* Despite its comprehensiveness, this text has as a prerequisite only a basic understanding of college algebra and elementary probability theory. Before a probability concept is used in the text, it is briefly reviewed. Statistics and calculus are not prerequisites.

PEDAGOGICAL CHOICES

In writing an introductory text, numerous choices must be made about the pedagogical approaches taken. Below is a summary of the most important choices made in this text.

- *Use of Computer Software Packages.* Because of the diversity of the software available and because of the lack of standardization, this text is not integrated with any particular software. However, in discussing linear programming and network optimization, two hypothetical software packages are used to introduce the reader to typical formats for input and output.

- *The Details of the Simplex Method.* This text accommodates both those instructors who do not wish to cover the simplex method and those who do. The former should omit Chapters 6 and 7, whereas the latter should cover at least Chapter 6 and possibly Chapter 7. In presenting the simplex method, these two chapters assume the reader does not want a ''cookbook'' approach and hence stress the relationship between geometry and algebra.

- *The Presentation of Goal Programming.* Instead of being treated as an isolated topic, goal programming is presented in Chapter 5 (along with piecewise linear programming and maximin or minimax objective functions) as one of several ''tricks'' for transforming an apparently nonlinear problem into a linear program.

- *Presentation of Network Optimization.* The topic of network optimization is presented under the unifying ''umbrella'' of the minimum cost network flow problem. This problem is introduced at the chapter's outset and other models are shown to be special cases.

- *Use of AOA or AON Project Networks.* Instead of using activity-on-arc project networks, this text uses activity-on-node project networks (the choice of almost every personal computer software package).

- *The Use of Bayes' Theorem in Decision Analysis.* A student's understanding of the value of imperfect information is greatly affected by his or her understanding of Bayes' Theorem. Instead of providing a direct statement and proof of Bayes' Theorem, this text uses a three-stage tabular approach that requires only an elementary knowledge of probability theory.

STUDENT LEARNING AIDS

The text has several learning aids that students will find useful as they read and then review a chapter. The most important learning aid is the summaries that are interspersed throughout every chapter. To facilitate quick identification, each summary is highlighted by a vertical line in color in the left margin. Besides the highlighted summaries, every chapter contains two other learning aids: a Checklist of important concepts and techniques and a Glossary of important terminology. For each item in the Checklist and Glossary, a reference to a specific section of the chapter indicates where the student can find more detail.

END-OF-CHAPTER EXERCISES

The text contains over 400 exercises. Several aspects of these exercises merit discussion:

- To ensure a student knows the purpose of each exercise, every exercise or set of similar exercises is introduced by a short learning objective. As examples of how useful the learning objectives can be, examine those that are interspersed throughout the exercises in Chapters 4 and 10. (Instructors will also find these learning objectives useful when they decide which exercises to assign to their students.)

- Each chapter's exercises have varying degrees of difficulty, ranging from requiring students simply to mimic similar examples in the chapter to requiring students to consider a concept or technique mentioned only briefly (if at all) in the chapter. For examples of the latter type of exercise, see Exercises 3.8–3.9, 6.20, 9.9, 10.11–10.12, 13.18–13.20, and 17.19.

- In the back of the text are abbreviated solutions to those exercises marked with an ''*'' in the left margin (approximately 30% of the exercises). Complete solutions to all exercises are in the Instructor's Manual described below.

SUPPLEMENTS

Accompanying this text are the following supplements:

- *Supplementary Chapters on Dynamic Programming and Heuristics.* Upon request, Prentice Hall will supply free to adopters of the text copies of chapters with comprehensive coverage of two topics excluded from the text: Supplementary Chapter A is on dynamic programming, and Supplementary Chapter B is on heuristics. These supplementary chapters may be duplicated and distributed to students. (Besides introducing an increasingly important topic, the chapter on heuristics has the added benefit of introducing an important class of decision problems—a routing problem involving several capacitated vehicles rendering service to several geographically dispersed locations.)

- *The Instructor's Manual.* The Instructor's Manual contains specific course outlines illustrating the text's flexibility, enlargements of selected artwork for use in making transparencies, and the complete solution (not just the final answer) to every exercise in every chapter. The manual also contains an appendix to Chapter 8 covering the solution of a transportation problem using the stepping-stone method.

- *Student's Solutions Manual.* Students may purchase a separate manual that provides the complete solutions to those exercises with abbreviated solutions in the back of the text.

- *Computer Software.* Prentice Hall will grant adopters of this text a free site license to the personal computer software package *Quantitative Systems for Business* (QSB), written by Y. Chang and R. S. Sullivan. Although QSB is not designed specifically for this text, it has modules that correspond to almost all the text's chapters. Students may purchase their own copies of QSB and its documentation.

For additional information on these supplements, contact your Prentice Hall representative.

ACKNOWLEDGMENTS

I could not have completed this text without the assistance of the following persons:

- At Prentice Hall, Dennis Hogan managed the project from beginning to end; Ray Mullaney supervised the development of the manuscript; Bob Lentz edited the manuscript; and Esther Koehn supervised the production process. These individuals and others at Prentice Hall deserve special thanks for their patience and flexibility in dealing with an author who was still writing portions of the textbook three months before it was printed.

- At the University of California at Berkeley, Gwen Cheeseburg typed much of the manuscript; Stephanie Lee provided a variety of secretarial services; Tom McCullough proofread the galleys and discovered errors that might otherwise have gone undetected; and many students suggested ways to improve the manuscript.

- At other colleges and universities, many professors reviewed portions of the manuscript and made helpful comments. Included among them are:

S. Christian Albright	Indiana University
James A. Bartos	Ohio State University
John P. Evans	University of North Carolina
Lori S. Franz	University of Missouri
George Heitman	The Pennsylvania State University
John W. Mamer	University of California, Los Angeles
Alan W. Neebe	University of North Carolina
Nancy V. Phillips	University of Texas
Gary R. Reeves	University of South Carolina
Laurence D. Richards	Old Dominion University
Daniel Samson	University of Melbourne
Daniel G. Shimshak	University of Massachusetts
Matthew J. Sobel	State University of New York, Stony Brook

A SPECIAL ACKNOWLEDGMENT

My wife JoAnn deserves special recognition. Besides serving as "Super Mom" to our three sons, she found time to read the manuscript from the perspective of a student and to proofread the galleys. More important than these tangible contributions were her love, patience, and understanding on the occasions when it would have been easier to be frustrated and angry.

January 1988   *Andrew W. Shogan*

AN OVERVIEW OF MANAGEMENT SCIENCE

1.1 INTRODUCTION

Welcome to the field of *management science!* Briefly stated,

> **Management science** is a body of knowledge that employs scientific methods to aid a manager's decision making.

In this definition we should stress the word *aid*. Management science does not relieve the manager from making a decision. It only aids the decision making by giving the manager a *quantitative perspective* on the decision problem. When the manager combines this perspective with the qualitative perspective obtained from personal experience, common sense, and intuition, the outcome almost always is a better decision.

In this chapter we survey the field of management science. We discuss

- The nature of management science.
- The evolution of management science.
- The status of management science today.
- Some recent "success stories" achieved through management science.
- Some guidelines for avoiding the misapplication of management science.
- The role of this text.

1.2 THE NATURE OF MANAGEMENT SCIENCE

Fundamental to management science are the concepts of a *decision problem* and a *mathematical model* of a decision problem. A decision problem is simply a problem requiring a manager to make a decision. Let us illustrate a mathematical model, in terms of the following decision problem:

Graham Krackers is the product distribution manager of Gramma's Biscuit Company (GBC), a national manufacturer and distributor of cookies, cakes, and crackers. As illustrated in Figure 1.1, GBC has three plants (in Pittsburgh, Memphis, and Omaha) and five regional warehouses (in Newark, Chicago, Atlanta, Dallas, and Los Angeles). For distribution purposes, GBC uses the hundredweight, CWT (1 CWT = 100 lb), as the unit of measurement. Every CWT shipped from a plant to a warehouse consists of a standard assortment of GBC's baked goods.

Table 1.1 summarizes the data for the decision problem confronting Graham Krackers this month. The table consists of a rectangular array (3 rows by 5 columns) of "cells." Row i corresponds to plant i, column j corresponds to warehouse j, and the cell at the intersection of row i and column j corresponds to shipments between plant i and warehouse j. In particular,

- The data appearing in Table 1.1's right margin are the plants' supplies; for example, plant 2 (Memphis) has 280 CWT available for shipment this month.

- The data appearing in the table's bottom margin are the warehouses' demands; for example, GBC has allocated warehouse 4 (Dallas) 80 CWT as its share of this month's total production. (Observe that total supply equals total demand; that is,

$$180 + 280 + 150 = 120 + 100 + 160 + 80 + 150 = 610 .)$$

- The data appearing in the upper-left corners of the cells are the unit freight costs between all plant-warehouse pairs. For example, the cell at the intersection

Figure 1.1 Locations of GBC's plants and warehouses

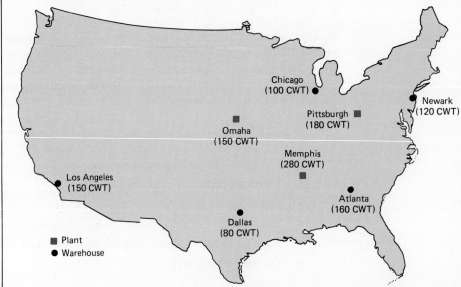

TABLE 1.1 Data for Graham Krackers' Decision Problem

	Warehouse 1 (Newark)	Warehouse 2 (Chicago)	Warehouse 3 (Atlanta)	Warehouse 4 (Dallas)	Warehouse 5 (Los Angeles)	Supplies
Plant 1 (Pittsburgh)	4	6	5	12	19	180 CWT
Plant 2 (Memphis)	10	4	8	5	14	280 CWT
Plant 3 (Omaha)	13	9	3	6	10	150 CWT
Demands	120 CWT	100 CWT	160 CWT	80 CWT	150 CWT	

of row 2 and column 4 indicates that the freight cost between plant 2 (Memphis) and warehouse 4 (Dallas) is $5 per CWT.

Given the data in Table 1.1 and an objective of minimizing total freight costs, Graham must now determine how many CWT each plant should ship to each warehouse.

A Trial-and-Error Approach

Let us imagine how Graham might solve his decision problem without the aid of management science. He would probably rely on a trial-and-error approach something like this:

1. Attempting to take advantage of low-cost shipping routes as much as possible, Graham initially proposes the distribution plan displayed in Table 1.2(a), where the **boldfaced** numbers in the cells' lower-right corners represent the shipments between the various plant-warehouse pairs. For example, the table's second row indicates that this distribution plan calls for plant 2 to distribute its supply of 280 CWT by making shipments to warehouses 1, 2, 3, 4, and 5 of 0, 100, 0, 80, and 100 CWT, respectively. The proposal is feasible, since each row sums to the supply in the row's right margin and each column sums to the demands in the column's bottom margin. The total freight cost is obtained by multiplying the two numbers in each of the 15 cells (i.e., the unit freight cost times the total CWT shipped) and summing the resulting products. For this proposal, the sum of the nonzero products (row by row) is

$$(4)(120) + (5)(10) + (19)(50) + (4)(100) + (5)(80)$$

$$+ (14)(100) + (3)(150) = 4130.$$

2. When Graham shows his initial proposal to his colleagues, someone proposes the distribution plan displayed in Table 1.2(b), thereby avoiding the high-cost shipping route between Pittsburgh and Los Angeles. This proposal's total freight cost is

$$(4)(120) + (5)(60) + (4)(100) + (5)(30) + (14)(150)$$

$$+ (3)(100) + (6)(50) = 4030,$$

a savings of 100 over Graham's initial proposal.

TABLE 1.2 Proposed Distribution Plans for Graham's Problem

(a) Initial Proposal

	Warehouse 1 (Newark)	Warehouse 2 (Chicago)	Warehouse 3 (Atlanta)	Warehouse 4 (Dallas)	Warehouse 5 (Los Angeles)	Supplies
Plant 1 (Pittsburgh)	4 120	6 0	5 10	12 0	19 50	180 CWT
Plant 2 (Memphis)	10 0	4 100	8 0	5 80	14 100	280 CWT
Plant 3 (Omaha)	13 0	9 0	3 150	6 0	10 0	150 CWT
Demands	120 CWT	100 CWT	160 CWT	80 CWT	150 CWT	

Total Freight Cost = $4130.

(b) Second Proposal

	Warehouse 1 (Newark)	Warehouse 2 (Chicago)	Warehouse 3 (Atlanta)	Warehouse 4 (Dallas)	Warehouse 5 (Los Angeles)	Supplies
Plant 1 (Pittsburgh)	4 120	6 0	5 60	12 0	19 0	180 CWT
Plant 2 (Memphis)	10 0	4 100	8 0	5 30	14 150	280 CWT
Plant 3 (Omaha)	13 0	9 0	3 100	6 50	10 0	150 CWT
Demands	120 CWT	100 CWT	160 CWT	80 CWT	150 CWT	

Total Freight Cost = $4030.

(c) Third Proposal

	Warehouse 1 (Newark)	Warehouse 2 (Chicago)	Warehouse 3 (Atlanta)	Warehouse 4 (Dallas)	Warehouse 5 (Los Angeles)	Supplies
Plant 1 (Pittsburgh)	4 120	6 50	5 10	12 0	19 0	180 CWT
Plant 2 (Memphis)	10 0	4 50	8 0	5 80	14 150	280 CWT
Plant 3 (Omaha)	13 0	9 0	3 150	6 0	10 0	150 CWT
Demands	120 CWT	100 CWT	160 CWT	80 CWT	150 CWT	

Total Freight Cost = $3980.

3. When Graham shows the second proposal to his colleagues, someone proposes the distribution plan in Table 1.2(c). This proposal, with its total freight cost of

$$(4)(120) + (6)(50) + (5)(10) + (4)(50) + (5)(80)$$

$$+ (14)(150) + (3)(150) = 3980,$$

represents a savings of 50 over the second proposal.

The trial-and-error approach ends when no one can suggest a distribution plan with lower total freight cost. The danger here is that there may well be a lower-cost plan that no one can see. (Can you find one?)

The Management Science Approach

Now let us describe the management science approach to Graham's decision problem. Graham has 15 decisions to make. For each of the $3 \times 5 = 15$ possible combinations of plant i and warehouse j he must decide how much to ship from plant i to warehouse j. Therefore, we define the following *decision variables:*

$$x_{ij} = \text{CWT shipped from plant } i \text{ to warehouse } j.$$

For example, $x_{24} = 80$ denotes that plant 2 ships 80 CWT to warehouse 4.

Using these decision variables and the format of Table 1.2, we can develop a mathematical model of Graham's problem. In Table 1.2 we displayed a proposed distribution plan by writing the amounts shipped between each plant-warehouse pair in the lower-right corners of the table's 15 cells. We can now do the same using the decision variables in place of specific numbers, thereby obtaining Table 1.3. To obtain the total freight cost incurred for shipments from plant i to warehouse j, we simply look in the cell in Table 1.3's ith row and jth column and multiply the unit shipping cost in the cell's upper-left corner times x_{ij}. For example, the total freight cost incurred for shipments between plant 2 and warehouse 4 is $5x_{24}$. Applying this reasoning to each of the 15 plant-warehouse pairs, we can mathematically express Graham's objective of minimizing total freight cost as

$$
\begin{aligned}
\text{Minimize} \quad & 4x_{11} + 6x_{12} + 5x_{13} + 12x_{14} + 19x_{15} \\
+ \; & 10x_{21} + 4x_{22} + 8x_{23} + 5x_{24} + 14x_{25} \\
+ \; & 13x_{31} + 9x_{32} + 3x_{33} + 6x_{34} + 10x_{35}
\end{aligned}
$$

Graham cannot assign just any values to the decision variables. Their values must satisfy certain relationships called *constraints*. An obvious set of constraints requires that each decision variable must assume a nonnegative value. Graham cannot ship a negative quantity! Besides these *nonnegativity constraints,* Graham notes that the decision variables must satisfy the following two sets of constraints:

- In Table 1.3, the sum of the decision variables in each row must equal the supply in the row's right margin. That is, the following three equations must hold:

TABLE 1.3 Developing the Mathematical Model for Graham's Problem

	Warehouse 1 (Newark)	Warehouse 2 (Chicago)	Warehouse 3 (Atlanta)	Warehouse 4 (Dallas)	Warehouse 5 (Los Angeles)	Supplies
Plant 1 (Pittsburgh)	4 x_{11}	6 x_{12}	5 x_{13}	12 x_{14}	19 x_{15}	180 CWT
Plant 2 (Memphis)	10 x_{21}	4 x_{22}	8 x_{23}	5 x_{24}	14 x_{25}	280 CWT
Plant 3 (Omaha)	13 x_{31}	9 x_{32}	3 x_{33}	6 x_{34}	10 x_{35}	150 CWT
Demands	120 CWT	100 CWT	160 CWT	80 CWT	150 CWT	

$$x_{11} + x_{12} + x_{13} + x_{14} + x_{15} = 180$$
$$x_{21} + x_{22} + x_{23} + x_{24} + x_{25} = 280$$
$$x_{31} + x_{32} + x_{33} + x_{34} + x_{35} = 150$$

■ In Table 1.3, the sum of the decision variables in each column must equal the demand in the column's bottom margin. That is, the following five equations must hold:

$$x_{11} + x_{21} + x_{31} = 120$$
$$x_{12} + x_{22} + x_{32} = 100$$
$$x_{13} + x_{23} + x_{33} = 160$$
$$x_{14} + x_{24} + x_{34} = 80$$
$$x_{15} + x_{25} + x_{35} = 150$$

To summarize, Graham has transformed the verbal statement of his problem into the mathematical statement displayed in Figure 1.2. This mathematical statement is an example of a special type of mathematical model known as a *linear program*. We will study linear programs extensively in Chapters 2–7, and we will return to Graham's problem in Section 4.5. We will learn that the distribution plan that minimizes total freight costs is not the one in Table 1.2(c) but rather the one displayed in Table 1.4.

The transformation of the verbal description of Graham's problem into a mathematical model is known as the *formulation phase* of the management science approach. The formulation phase often presents the management scientist with a dilemma. On one hand, he wants the mathematical model to be sufficiently complex that it accurately reflects the real decision problem. On the other hand, he wants it to be sufficiently simple that it is *mathematically tractable*—that is, it can be analyzed using "off-the-shelf" techniques (or slight modifications of them). He usually compromises by making assumptions that result in a mathematical model that only approximates the real decision problem. If the management scientist and

---

Among all nonnegative values for $x_{11}, x_{12}, \ldots, x_{35}$ that satisfy the system of equations

$$\begin{array}{rcl}
x_{11} + x_{12} + x_{13} + x_{14} + x_{15} & = & 180 \\
x_{21} + x_{22} + x_{23} + x_{24} + x_{25} & = & 280 \\
x_{31} + x_{32} + x_{33} + x_{34} + x_{35} & = & 150 \\
x_{11} + x_{21} + x_{31} & = & 120 \\
x_{12} + x_{22} + x_{32} & = & 100 \\
x_{13} + x_{23} + x_{33} & = & 160 \\
x_{14} + x_{24} + x_{34} & = & 80 \\
x_{15} + x_{25} + x_{35} & = & 150
\end{array}$$

determine values for the decision variables that

minimize $\quad 4x_{11} + 6x_{12} + 5x_{13} + 12x_{14} + 19x_{15}$
$\qquad + 10x_{21} + 4x_{22} + 8x_{23} + 5x_{24} + 14x_{25}$
$\qquad + 13x_{31} + 9x_{32} + 3x_{33} + 6x_{34} + 10x_{35}$

Figure 1.2 The mathematical model for Graham's problem

TABLE 1.4 Minimal-Cost Distribution Plan for Graham's Problem

	Warehouse 1 (Newark)		Warehouse 2 (Chicago)		Warehouse 3 (Atlanta)		Warehouse 4 (Dallas)		Warehouse 5 (Los Angeles)		Supplies
Plant 1 (Pittsburgh)	4	**120**	6	**0**	5	**60**	12	**0**	19	**0**	180 CWT
Plant 2 (Memphis)	10	**0**	4	**100**	8	**0**	5	**80**	4	**100**	280 CWT
Plant 3 (Omaha)	13	**0**	9	**0**	3	**100**	6	**0**	10	**50**	150 CWT
Demands	120 CWT		100 CWT		160 CWT		80 CWT		150 CWT		

Total Freight Cost = $3780.

the manager clearly understand these assumptions, the mathematical model is still useful.

In general, then,

> A **mathematical model** is a mathematical representation of a decision problem or an acceptable approximation of it.

As illustrated in Figure 1.3, two additional phases follow the formulation phase: the analysis phase and the implementation phase.

In the *analysis phase*, the management scientist uses mathematical computations (usually performed by a computer software package) to convert the mathematical model into numerical output on which to base the decision. The *implementation phase* translates this numerical output into a recommendation about the real decision problem. The difficulties encountered in the implementation phase are proportional to the number of assumptions made in the formulation phase. In other words, the greater degree of accuracy achieved in the mathematical model's representation of the real decision problem, the easier the implementation phase is.

It may happen that the recommendation produced by the mathematical model does not conform to the manager's expectations. In such a case, the management scientist should determine whether unwarranted or erroneous assumptions have been made in the formulation phase. If so, as indicated by the dashed line in Figure 1.3, the mathematical model should be revised and the three phases repeated. If not, the management scientist must argue persuasively that the recommendation, while not conforming to the manager's expectations, deserves serious consideration. After all, if mathematical models always produced recommendations that were similar to the manager's expectations, they would have little value!

Figure 1.3 The three phases of the management science approach

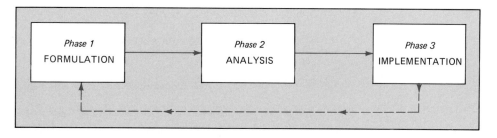

To summarize,

The management science approach to a decision problem consists of the following three phases (which may need to be repeated):

1. **Formulation phase.** This phase begins with the description of the decision problem (including the relevant data) and ends with a mathematical model of the decision problem.

2. **Analysis phase.** This phase employs mathematical analysis (usually executed by a computer software package) to convert the mathematical model into numerical data on which the manager can base a decision.

3. **Implementation phase.** This phase translates the analysis phase's numerical output into a recommendation about the decision problem.

Deterministic Models versus Stochastic Models

We should distinguish here between two types of mathematical models. The mathematical model for Graham's problem is a *deterministic model*. There is no uncertainty about the model's data, or else the uncertainty is sufficiently low that the management scientist can accurately estimate each piece of data by a single number. For example, Graham feels confident using 12 for the unit freight cost between Pittsburgh and Dallas. He believes that, if this cost is not exactly equal to 12, it will be very close to it. He is equally confident about his estimates for the model's other unit freight costs, as well as those for the supplies available at the plants and the demands allocated to the warehouses.

Because there is no uncertainty about a deterministic model's data, there is also no uncertainty about the consequences of a decision. For example, if Graham decides to ship 80 CWT from Pittsburgh to Dallas, he is certain that all units are available at Pittsburgh, all units will be used at Dallas, and the total freight cost will be $(12)(80) = 960$.

The opposite of a deterministic model is a *stochastic model*.[1] A management scientist must use a stochastic model when the decision problem involves at least one piece of data about which there is considerable uncertainty. As examples, consider the following:

- When you buy an insurance policy, you are uncertain whether the hazard you are insuring against will or will not occur, and, if it occurs, you are uncertain about the dollar amount of the financial loss you will sustain.

- When a corporation introduces a new product into the marketplace, it is uncertain about the market share the new product will ultimately attain.

- When a department store's buyer orders a new fashion item, she is uncertain about the demand for the item.

- When a portfolio manager invests in a particular security, she is uncertain about the annual return on investment.

- When an oil company bids for the rights to drill for oil at a particular site, it is uncertain about the quantity of oil (if any) it will discover.

---

[1] Some instructors, textbooks, and computer software packages refer to a stochastic model as a *probabilistic model* or a *random model*.

In these examples it is inappropriate to estimate each uncertain datum by a single number. Instead, the estimate should take the form of a probability distribution. For example, in the department store buyer's problem, a management scientist might assume the demand for a particular fashion item has a normal probability distribution with a mean of 1000 and a variance of 200.

Because there is uncertainty about a stochastic model's data, there is also uncertainty about the consequences of a decision. For example, if the buyer orders 1200 items, her uncertainty about the total consumer demand for the item translates into uncertainty about the store's eventual total profit from the 1200 items.

To summarize,

- In a deterministic model, there is little uncertainty about the model's data and, therefore, about the consequences of a decision.

- In a stochastic model, there is much uncertainty about the model's data and, therefore, about the consequences of a decision.

In the chapters that follow, we will encounter many examples of both types of mathematical models.

1.3 THE EVOLUTION OF MANAGEMENT SCIENCE

Relatively speaking—as compared, say, with the field of mathematics—management science is "young." Most of the fundamental concepts and techniques of calculus, probability, and statistics are centuries old. For example, Sir Isaac Newton developed the concept of a derivative in the late seventeenth century. In contrast, almost all concepts and techniques of management science are less than 50 years old.

As illustrated in Table 1.5, the roots of management science can be traced to the early 1900s. However, management science did not emerge as a field until World War II.

TABLE 1.5 Three Early Scientific Approaches to Management

DATE	NAME	SCIENTIFIC APPROACH TO MANAGEMENT
1900	H. L. Gantt	The use of charts to efficiently schedule jobs on machines. (This was the first application of a subfield of management science now known as *project management.*
1915	F. W. Harris	The derivation of a mathematical formula for the most economic quantity of an item to order from a vendor. (This was the first application of a subfield of management science now known as *inventory management,*
1917	A. K. Erlang	The derivation of mathematical formulae for analyzing the problems encountered by callers to an automated telephone switchboard. (This was the first application of a subfield of management science now known as *queueing analysis.*

The war effort created urgent problems in such areas as the allocation of scarce resources, production planning and scheduling, inventory control, quality control, and transportation of personnel, equipment, and supplies. To address these problems, Great Britain in 1937 assembled a team of scientists, engineers, mathematicians, and military analysts. Because this team conducted research on (military) operations, its activities were called *operational research* or *operations research*.[2] Spurred on by the success of the British, the American military management assembled similar operations research teams.

After the war, some of those who conducted military operations research applied similar approaches and techniques to related industrial problems. Others went to universities or research centers to work on new approaches and techniques.

In 1947, a significant breakthrough occurred. While working for the Air Force, George Dantzig developed a method to solve a linear program.[3] Important in its own right, Dantzig's research also motivated others to extend and complement his work or to emulate it in other areas. Consequently, Dantzig is among the best known "pioneers" of management science.

By the early 1950s, the number of persons working in management science was sufficiently large to lead to the establishment of two professional societies: the Operations Research Society of America (ORSA) and The Institute of Management Sciences (TIMS). The formation of TIMS led to the use of the term *management science* as a synonym for what had previously been called operations research. Other synonyms also have emerged, such as *systems analysis* and *decision science*.

Management science's rapid growth in the 1950s would have been confined to theoretical advances were it not for the concurrent development of the electronic digital computer and its increasing commercial availability. Before the computer, management science applications were limited to those that could be analyzed with manual computations. The computer enabled management scientists to begin applying their knowledge to complex problems.

By the end of the 1950s, most of the fundamental tools of management science (i.e., the ones discussed in an introductory text such as this) had been developed. However, the applications of management science were still limited primarily to the military and to industrial organizations such as the oil companies.

This state of affairs changed in the early 1960s with the establishment of formal academic programs in management science. As graduates of these programs attained positions of responsibility, they introduced management science to all types of organizations.

By the end of the 1960s, many organizations had begun to form staff groups consisting of individuals with academic training in management science and computer usage. Management science's applied side was now enjoying the same rapid growth as its theoretical side.

This rapid growth of applications almost came to a halt in the late 1960s and early 1970s. An increasing number of "horror stories" began to circulate among upper management about how the use of management science had led to disastrous results. On examination, it became apparent that these disasters were due to a fundamental deficiency in most academic programs in management science. In the early years of these programs, education focused primarily on the theoretical aspects of the field. Neglected were the equally important applied aspects, such as how management scientists must explain, interpret, and justify their recommenda-

---

[2] The term *management science* would not be coined until over a decade later.

[3] Recall that a linear program is a special type of mathematical model, an example of which was provided in Section 1.2's discussion of Graham's problem.

tions to management or how management scientists cannot expect to help solve managerial problems unless they understand not only management science but also economics, finance, accounting, marketing, and so on. In the eyes of management scientists, managers were mathematically unsophisticated and unwilling to use anything they could not fully understand. In the eyes of managers, management scientists were persons with solutions looking for nonexistent problems.

Fortunately, in the mid 1970s, educators put management science back "on track" by making necessary changes in the curriculum. Both management scientists and managers began to gain a more realistic view of the potential and the limitations of management science. There is, however, still room to improve the communication between management scientists and managers. Many would say it is the most important problem facing the field today.

1.4 THE STATUS OF MANAGEMENT SCIENCE TODAY

When the deficiencies of the early 1970s were recognized and corrected, management science once again enjoyed rapid growth. Today, management science is "everywhere"!

For example:

- Colleges and universities offer management science courses in programs in business, engineering, health management, public policy, and so on.
- ORSA and TIMS (the previously mentioned professional societies) each have about 7000 members. Both societies publish journals. ORSA publishes *Operations Research* and *Operations Research Letters,* TIMS publishes *Management Science* and *Marketing Science,* and ORSA and TIMS jointly publish *Mathematics of Operations Research, Interfaces,* and *OR/MS Today.* Together, these journals contain well over 5000 pages per year reporting new research and applications. ORSA and TIMS are only the "tip of the iceberg." Other professional societies and/or journals exist not only in the United States but also in Canada, England, France, West Germany, The Netherlands, India, and Japan. Indeed, the International Federation of Operations Research Societies (IFORS) has over 30 professional societies as members.
- Most major businesses (e.g., manufacturers, airlines, banks) and most major not-for-profit organizations (e.g., government agencies, public utilities, hospitals) have at least one staff group of persons with management science training. Organizations not large enough to have an in-house staff can obtain the benefits of management science by retaining the services of a consulting firm. To illustrate the diversity of the demand for management scientists, Figure 1.4 displays job ads from recent issues of *OR/MS Today.*

Let us look now at some recent management science "success stories."

1.5 SOME MANAGEMENT SCIENCE "SUCCESS STORIES"

TIMS annually honors excellence in the practice of management science through the Edelman Award for Management Science Achievement. Established in 1972, the award is named in honor of the late Franz Edelman, who was responsible at

Figure 1.4 Examples of job ads in management science

RCA for some of the earliest applications of management science to business problems. Our survey below of six award winners illustrates the contribution management science makes toward solving decision problems in both private and public organizations.

Tree-Stem Cutting at Weyerhaeuser

A 1985 award went to M. R. Lembersky and U. H. Chi for their improvement of timber profits at Weyerhaeuser. Since forest products is primarily a commodity industry, there is little control over the prices realized from sales. Consequently, it is imperative that Weyerhaeuser make the most profitable use of each of the 15 million trees cut each year. After a tree is felled, delimbed, and possibly topped, a worker (either a logger in the field or a machine operator in a mill) must decide how to cut the resulting tree stem into several logs, keeping in mind that length, curvature, diameter, and knots are factors in the value of a particular log. Each log is then allocated to a market (e.g., export to Japan or sale domestically) or to a company manufacturing facility (e.g., a lumber mill, a plywood mill, or a paper products mill). With the goal of improving the decisions of the workers who cut a stem into several logs, Lembersky and Chi designed a video-game-like computer system called VISION to train woods and mill personnel, as well as company managers and top executives. The computer presented the "player" with a tree stem having a particular set of characteristics. After the player cut the stem into logs, his results were compared with those of the computer, whose decisions were based on the technique of *dynamic programming*. Weyerhaeuser estimates that, during the period 1977–1985, VISION increased annual profits by a total of at least $100 million. VISION was paid the ultimate complement by a logger who said that, if VISION were placed in his favorite tavern, he and his co-workers would pay to play it!

Manpower Planning at United Airlines

Another 1985 award went to T. J. Holloran and J. E. Byrn of United Airlines for their design and implementation of a computerized manpower planning system for scheduling shift work at reservation offices and airports. Cost control is essential to competing successfully in the airline industry. An important cost-cutting measure is improving work scheduling and manpower utilization. In 1985, United employed on a full-time to part-time basis over 4000 reservation sales representatives (RSRs) and support personnel at 11 reservation offices and over 1000 customer service agents (CSAs) at its 10 largest airports. Preparation of the work shift schedules for RSRs and CSAs was complicated by two factors: (1) personnel requirements that varied widely from day to day and from hour to hour and (2) work rules governing length of work shift, length of meal periods, length of rest breaks, and number and frequency of days off. These complexities made it virtually impossible to manually prepare low-cost work schedules. Consequently, Holloran and Byrn designed and implemented a computerized station manpower planning system called SMPS, whose decisions were based on the techniques of *linear programming, network optimization, integer linear programming,* and *heuristics.* Using the work shift schedules produced by SMPS, United significantly reduced labor costs, realizing savings in direct salary and benefits costs of $6 million annually. Furthermore, there were unquantifiable benefits such as additional revenue generated by improved customer service and benefits from the use of SMPS in contract negotiations.

Cleaning Streets in New York City

Yet another 1985 award went to L. J. Riccio, J. Miller, and A. Litke of New York City's Department of Sanitation for their design and implementation of a program to improve the cleanliness of the streets and the efficiency of the department ("polishing the Big Apple" in their words). In 1980, New York City had fewer street cleaners than in 1975 (800 versus 2500) and, according to a street cleanliness rating system, had significantly dirtier streets (53% of its streets acceptably clean versus 72%). In 1981, Riccio, Miller, and Litke began analyzing the street cleaning problem from a management science perspective. Using the technique of *simulation* and statistical regression, they designed and implemented procedures that resulted not only in five consecutive years of improved cleanliness ratings but also in a 1985 rating that was close to the record set in 1975. These improved ratings were accomplished with 400 fewer street cleaners than were employed in 1975, a number equivalent in financial terms to $12 million a year in salaries and fringe benefits.

Inventory Management at Pfizer

A 1984 award went to P. P. Kleutghen and J. C. McGcc of Pfizer Incorporated for their design and implementation of a computer system to manage inventories in its United States pharmaceutical business. Pfizer is a vertically integrated company that manufactures key intermediates or chemicals used in its finished products (called dosages). Pfizer's supply chain can be summarized in three steps:

1. Pfizer produces the active pharmaceutical ingredients through fermentation or organic synthesis. (In 1984, there were two organic synthesis plants.)
2. Pfizer combines these ingredients with other raw materials to obtain the dosages. (In 1984, there were four dosage plants.)
3. Pfizer distributes the finished product to its customers.

Thus, Pfizer accumulates inventories of raw materials, active pharmaceutical ingredients, and dosages. In 1984, a combination of high interest rates, rapid growth in the pharmaceutical business, and historically high inventories necessitated a better approach to managing inventories. Using the techniques of *inventory management*, Kleutghen and McGee designed and implemented a computer-based inventory management system that was credited over a three-year period with reducing inventories by $23.9 million and back orders by 95%.

Designing the Emergency Medical Service System in Austin

Another 1984 award went to D. J. Eaton (of the University of Texas, Austin), M. S. Daskin (of Northwestern University), D. Simmons (of the City of Austin), B. Bullock (of Nash, Phillips-Copus Company), and G. Jansma (of Jansma Consulting, Inc.) for their redesign of the operations of Austin's emergency medical service

(EMS) system. The EMS system was to consist of two types of vehicles housed at two types of facilities. The vehicle types were:

1. Advanced life-support vehicles staffed by highly trained paramedics and dispatched to life-threatening calls.

2. Basic life-support vehicles of lower cost staffed by personnel with less training and dispatched to non-life-threatening calls.

These vehicles would be housed in two types of facilities:

1. Existing fire stations.

2. Newly built EMS-only stations.

Using the techniques of *integer linear programming* and *heuristics*, Eaton and his co-workers developed a plan that called for four advanced life-support vehicles and eight basic life-support vehicles to operate from ten shared-use fire stations and two EMS-only stations. The plan's implementation in 1984 reduced average response time (despite an upsurge in calls for service) and, in comparison with the existing plan, saved $3.3 million in construction costs and $1.2 million per year in operating costs.

Faster Service at Burger King

A 1981 award went to W. Stewart and L. Donno of Burger King Corporation for their improvement of efficiency, productivity, and sales in more than 3000 restaurants worldwide. The introduction of drive-thru service and new menu items had transformed a once simple operation into a sophisticated production process. For Burger King (as for most fast-food companies) an effective way to increase sales revenue is to increase the number of customers served. The faster the service, the more people can be served, and the higher the restaurant's potential sales revenue. Therefore, as the principal evaluation criterion for any suggested change in restaurant operations, Burger King used the change's impact on speed of service. To enable Burger King to perform the evaluation, Stewart and Donno used the techniques of *queueing analysis* and *simulation* to build a comprehensive model capable of analyzing any restaurant type currently in the Burger King system as well as any potential design for a new restaurant. Using this model, Burger King was able to analyze issues such as

- The operational impact of adding a second drive-thru window to a restaurant.
- The operational impact of introducing a new product.
- Determining for a specific location the best size for a restaurant and the best configuration of the restaurant's kitchen and service facilities.
- Determining how many crew members a restaurant should have, where in the restaurant to position them, and how to divide the labor among them. (These decisions depend on such factors as the restaurant's configuration, its product mix, the percentage of its business that is drive-thru, and so on.)

Better decision making for each of the above issues translated into multimillion-dollar increases in systemwide profits. For example, it was estimated that using the model to address the last issue stated above increased systemwide profits by over $32 million annually.

TABLE 1.6 A Survey of Recent Applications of Management Science

---

PRIVATE

Finance and Banking

- capital budgeting
- management of cash inflows and outflows
- portfolio management
- municipal bond underwriting
- government bond trading
- phasing the construction of income-producing real estate
- planning the number and location of check-processing centers to serve the branches of a bank
- procedures for deciding whether to grant credit

Marketing

- selection of advertising media
- allocation of shelf space across merchandise to be displayed
- allocation of page space across merchandise to be pictured in a catalog
- design of sales districts and management of sales personnel
- number and location of regional warehouses and distribution of products from these warehouses to customers

Manufacturing

- plant design
- raw materials procurement
- inventory management
- production planning and scheduling
- manpower planning
- number and location of plants and distribution of products from these plants to regional warehouses
- selection of pollution control equipment

Operations

- planning an airline's operations, including the routing and scheduling of aircraft, fuel purchasing, and scheduling of flight and ground personnel
- evaluating proposed changes to a fast-food restaurant's operations
- planning the expansion of a railroad system's track
- operation of an electrical utility's hydroelectric system
- routing of delivery vehicles (e.g., trucks delivering fuel to service stations or trucks delivering parcels to customers)
- management of the overbooking of a hotel's rooms or an aircraft's seats
- management of a rental car agency's fleet of cars
- blending of feedstuffs that comprise the diet of cattle
- sports strategy and management, including the planning of a baseball team's batting order, selecting gymnasts to compete in the all-around portion of a meet, and designing a league's schedule for an entire season

---

A Survey of Other Management Science Applications

Space constraints preclude our continuing to describe successful applications of management science. Interested readers are encouraged to go to a library and browse through recent issues of *Interfaces*, the joint publication of ORSA and TIMS. Table 1.6 on pages 16-17 summarizes the applications of management science reported in recent issues of *Interfaces*, as well as other related journals.

TABLE 1.6 (Continued).

PUBLIC

Health Management
- hospital staffing
- menu planning for a hospital's patients
- inventory control of human blood
- location and type of vehicles to provide a city's emergency medical service

Military
- search and rescue efforts
- reliability analysis of complex equipment
- manpower planning

Educational
- assigning a university's classes to the available classrooms
- scheduling of an education district's school busses
- achieving racial balance in an education district by reassigning students to other schools
- consolidation of an education district's students into fewer schools

Government
- maintenance policies for a state's highway system
- courtroom scheduling
- number and location of fire stations or police stations
- routing and scheduling of vehicles (e.g., for mail delivery, public transit, refuse collection, street cleaning, or snow removal)
- water and air pollution control
- analysis of the toll collection facilities for a toll bridge or a toll road
- allocation of federal funds across various state agencies
- political redistricting
- designing flight plans for an aerial spray pest control program

1.6 SOME GUIDELINES FOR AVOIDING THE MISAPPLICATION OF MANAGEMENT SCIENCE

We would be remiss not to mention that management science has often been misapplied. For obvious reasons these misapplications have not been well documented.[4] This is unfortunate, since there may be as much to learn from a misapplication as from a successful application.

Below are some guidelines for avoiding the misapplication of management science. If you are ever a management scientist, you should follow them. Or, if you are ever a manager having a management scientist work for you, you should not only expect the management scientist to follow these guidelines but also do your best to facilitate their being followed.

- **Management science does not make decisions; it helps make decisions.** Management science does not relieve the manager from making a decision. It only helps the manager make the decision by giving him or her a quantitative perspective on the decision problem. When the manager combines this with the qualitative perspective obtained from personal experience, common sense, and intuition, a better decision almost always results.

---

[4] Most of the limited documentation that does exist may be found in the journal *Interfaces*, which regularly publishes feature articles entitled "Misapplication Reviews" and "20/30 Hindsight."

- **Management science is not a set of concepts and techniques looking for problems to solve**. A successful application of management science should almost always begin with a real managerial problem. A management scientist should not even begin to think about how to solve the problem until he fully understands it, and he should consider himself lucky if he can solve the problem using an "off-the-shelf" technique.

- **A management scientist cannot solve a decision problem in the office**. For example, consider Section 1.5's Weyerhaeuser "success story." This successful application required the management scientists to spend many hours interviewing managers, loggers, and machine operators and many hours simply watching them at work. Many management scientists have lost credibility (to say nothing of jobs!) because their recommendations made it obvious they had not gone where they had to go to fully understand the real problem.

- **A management scientist must convey his recommendations to management in a way that can be understood and appreciated**. It is not enough for a management scientist to know the optimal solution to a problem; he or she must also convince management. This means presenting recommendations in a way that can be understood and appreciated. For example, management cannot be expected to read or listen to a report filled with mathematical detail or technical jargon. The report should contain "executive summaries" that concisely state the problem, highlight the management science approach to it, present clear recommendations, and document potential benefits if the recommendations are implemented.

- **The end-users of a management science application must believe in the recommendations**. To illustrate, consider again the Weyerhaeuser "success story." The success was achieved partly by the use of a video-game-like computer system that challenged the loggers or machine operators to do better. After seeing they could not beat the computer, they were much more willing to trust the management scientists' recommendations about how to cut tree stems into logs. Without this trust, they might have ignored those recommendations and simply cut tree stems the way they always had. Worse, they might have attempted to discredit the recommendations by pretending to follow them while actually cutting logs in ways they knew were foolish.

- **Where possible, a management science approach should not overlook qualitative issues, such as the opinions and personalities of key decision makers or organizational politics and policies**. This doesn't mean telling management what it wants to hear. For example, a management scientist analyzing where to build a new plant should not exclude a potential site from consideration just because the company's president opposes it. However, it would be unfortunate not to learn of the president's opposition until after making a recommendation to use the site. Before conducting the analysis, the management scientist must ask the right questions about the problem's qualitative issues as well as quantitative ones. Then, if the analysis dictates the selection of the site the president opposes, the management scientist will be prepared to be especially convincing when presenting and defending the recommendation to management.

Following these guidelines does not ensure a successful application, but failing to follow them usually leads to a misapplication.

1.7 CONCLUDING REMARKS — THE ROLE OF THIS TEXT

In your managerial careers, you will encounter management science in one of two ways: as a "seller" or a "buyer." As a seller, you may be either an employee of an organization's in-house management science group or an employee of a consulting firm. As a buyer, you may be a manager working to solve a decision problem with the help of a management scientist.

For those of you (probably the minority) who intend to become management scientists, this text represents your first step. It gives you a foundation in management science. Later, you will probably read entire texts devoted to topics that are surveyed here in one or two chapters.

Those of you who do not become management scientists will probably (at least once in your careers) work with a management scientist to solve a decision problem. For you, this text is analogous to one in music appreciation: such a text does not make you capable of writing a symphony, but it helps you distinguish a good performance of a symphony from a bad one. Similarly, when you finish this text, you should be able to "applaud" good management science applications and "hiss" bad ones!

1.8 CHAPTER CHECKLIST AND GLOSSARY

Quickly review this chapter by rereading the material highlighted by a vertical line in the left margin. You should then be familiar with the concepts, techniques, and terminology in the Checklist and Glossary that follow. If you need "help" with a particular item, consult the section or sections indicated for a more detailed discussion. (*Note*: The Glossary is arranged chronologically, not alphabetically; that is, the terms appear in the approproximate order in which we encountered them in the chapter.)

Checklist of Concepts and Techniques

☐ The nature of a mathematical model. [1.2]

☐ The three phases (formulation, analysis, and implementation) in the management science approach to a decision problem. [1.2]

☐ The distinction between a deterministic model and a stochastic model. [1.2]

☐ The evolution of management science. [1.3]

☐ The status of management science today. [1.4]

☐ Some examples of the application of management science to real decision problems. [1.5]

☐ Some guidelines for avoiding the misapplication of management science. [1.6]

☐ The role of this text. [1.7]

Management science.   A body of knowledge that employs scientific methods to aid a manager's decision making. [1.1]

Decision problem.   A problem requiring a manager to make a decision. [1.2]

Mathematical model.   A mathematical representation of a decision problem or an acceptable approximation of it. [1.2]

Formulation phase.   The phase of the management science approach that begins with a description of the decision problem (including the relevant data) and ends with a mathematical model of the decision problem. [1.2]

Analysis phase.   The phase of the management science approach that employs mathematical analysis (usually executed by a computer software package) to convert the formulation phase's mathematical model into numerical data on which the manager can base a decision. [1.2]

Implementation phase.   The phase of the management science approach that translates the analysis phase's numerical output into a recommendation about the decision problem. [1.2]

Deterministic model.   A mathematical model in which there is little uncertainty about the model's data and, therefore, about the consequences of a decision. [1.2]

Stochastic model.   A mathematical model in which there is much uncertainty about the model's data and therefore, about the consequences of a decision. [1.2]

Operations research.   A synonym for management science; others are *operational research*, *systems analysis*, and *decision science*. [1.3]

EXERCISES

These exercises require you to go to your library and browse through issues of the journal *Interfaces*.

1.1. Select three applications reported in *Interfaces* and summarize each in a manner similar to that used for Section 1.5's six "success stories." For each application, note the volume, number, and pages where it appears.

1.2. By categorizing applications reported in *Interfaces*, add new entries to the applications summarized in Table 1.6. For each entry, note the volume, number, and pages where it appears.

2

LINEAR PROGRAMMING: CONCEPTS AND GRAPHICAL ILLUSTRATIONS

2.1 INTRODUCTION

In this chapter we introduce the subject of linear programming. You will learn what a linear program (LP) is and how to solve graphically a two-variable LP.

Linear programming has a special importance within the field of management science. This importance is due to two facts mentioned in Chapter 1. First, management science really did not exist until George Dantzig provided the impetus with his development of linear programming in 1947. Second, surveys of business, industry, and government consistently rank linear programming among the most frequently employed quantitative methods. It can be "guaranteed" that, whatever career path you follow, you will encounter applications of linear programming. Either you will apply linear programming yourself, or you will interact with someone who applies it.

If George Dantzig were to rename linear programming today, perhaps he would call it "linear optimizing." This would eliminate the common and mistaken assumption that linear programming is closely related to computer programming. Although computers are used to solve linear programs, an LP itself is not a list of instructions to a computer. Instead, it is a mathematical model whose solution provides a decision maker with an optimal plan to follow. The adjective "linear" refers to the use of linear (i.e., straight-line) equations and inequalities in formulating the mathematical model.

The examples and exercises of this and subsequent chapters will illustrate the numerous and diverse applications of linear programming. As a sample of this diversity, consider the following four scenarios:

- **Production planning.** Given limited availabilities of resources such as labor and machinery, how much of each of a firm's products should be produced this month to maximize total profit?

- **Investment planning.** Given limited availabilities of cash for each of the next 12 months and given government-imposed or self-imposed regulations that must be complied with, how much money should a portfolio manager invest each month in each of a variety of stocks and bonds to maximize the portfolio's annual return on investment?

- **Product distribution.** Given the monthly production capacities of a set of geographically dispersed plants and given the monthly demands of a set of geographically dispersed customers, how much should each plant ship each month to each customer to minimize the total transportation costs?

- **Personnel planning.** Given the hourly workforce requirements for a service facility or system (e.g., a hospital or a public transit system) that operates 24-hours-a-day 7-days-a-week, how many employees should be assigned to each of a variety of alternative workshifts to minimize the total payroll costs?

Despite their diversity, these four decision problems have three elements in common: a set of interrelated *decisions,* an *objective* to maximize or minimize, and a set of *constraints* that impose restrictions on the decisions. Table 2.1 summarizes these three common elements.

TABLE 2.1 The Three Elements Common to All Linear Programming Applications

APPLICATION	DECISIONS	OBJECTIVE	EXAMPLES OF CONSTRAINTS
Production planning	How much to produce of each product.	Maximize total profit.	For each scarce resource, the total amount consumed during production of all products cannot exceed the resource's availability.
Investment planning	How much to invest each month in each stock or bond.	Maximize annual return on investment.	(a) In each month, the total amount invested in all stocks and bonds cannot exceed the month's cash availability. (b) In each month, no more than, say, 30% of the portfolio can be invested in a specified set of "risky" stocks. (This may be a government-imposed or a self-imposed restriction.)
Product distribution	How much each plant should ship to each customer.	Minimize total transportation costs.	(a) For each plant, the total shipments from the plant to all customers cannot exceed the plant's capacity. (b) For each customer, the total shipments to the customer from all plants must equal the customer's demand.
Personnel planning	How many employees to assign to each workshift.	Minimize total payroll costs.	For each one-hour period in the workweek, the total number of employees assigned to all workshifts spanning the hour must equal or exceed the hour's requirement.

In terms of these common elements we can define linear programming as follows:

> Linear programming is a quantitative method for making an optimal set of *decisions* (e.g., decisions that achieve an *objective* of maximal profit or minimum cost) that are interrelated by *constraints* on resources the decisions jointly consume and/or on goals to which the decisions jointly contribute.

2.2 LINEAR EQUATIONS AND LINEAR INEQUALITIES

In a linear program both the objective and the constraints are expressed in the form of linear functions, linear equations, or linear inequalities. Let us see what concepts and principles linearity involves.

A basic building block of linear equations is an expression called a *linear function*. An example of a *linear function* involving four variables is $5x_1 - x_2 + 7x_3 + 2x_4$. The function is linear because each of its four terms contains a single variable that has an (unwritten) exponent of 1. The function would be nonlinear if it contained a term in which a variable had an exponent different than 1 (e.g., $7x_3^5$ or $7x_3^{-\frac{1}{2}}$) or a term in which there was a "crossproduct" of variables (e.g., $4x_1x_3$ or $4x_1^2x_4^{-\frac{1}{2}}$).

A linear equation is simply a linear function set equal to a constant. An example of a *linear equation* involving four variables is $5x_1 - x_2 + 7x_3 + 2x_4 = 60$.

When a linear equation involves only two variables, its two dimensional graph is a straight line. To illustrate, consider the linear equation $3x_1 + 2x_2 = 18$. Let us rewrite it in what is known as its *slope intercept form:*

$$3x_1 + 2x_2 = 18 \;\rightarrow\; 2x_2 = -3x_1 + 18 \;\rightarrow\; x_2 = -\frac{3}{2}x_1 + 9.$$

In this rewritten form, it is easy to see the following:

- When $x_1 = 0$, $x_2 = (-3/2)(0) + 9 = 9$; that is, the equation's graph intersects the x_2 axis at the x_2 *intercept* $(0, 9)$.

- The coefficient of x_1, $-3/2$, indicates that every 1 unit increase in x_1 *always* results in a decrease in x_2 of 3/2; that is, the equation's *slope* is $-3/2$.

Consequently, we conclude that the graph of the linear equation $3x_1 + 2x_2 = 18$ is a straight line passing through the point $(x_1, x_2) = (0, 9)$ and having a slope of $-3/2$. Knowing the line's x_2 intercept and its slope permits us to quickly determine other points on the line. In particular, if $(0, 9)$ is a point on the line, then the point

$$(x_1, x_2) = (0 + \Delta, 9 - \tfrac{3}{2}\Delta)$$

is on the line for any value of Δ. For example, setting $\Delta = 2$ yields that $(x_1, x_2) = (2, 6)$ is on the line. We now know two points on the line: $(0, 9)$ and $(2, 6)$. Plotting these two points and connecting them with a straight line produces the graph displayed in Figure 2.1.

There is an easier way to graph the linear equation if we are not concerned with computing its slope. We simply find any two points on the line as quickly as possible and connect them by a straight line. Usually, the quickest points to find

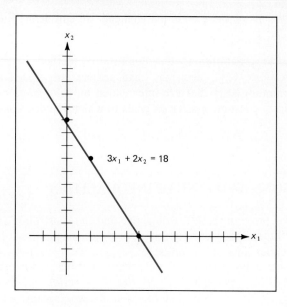

Figure 2.1 Graph of $3x_1 + 2x_2 = 18$

are those at which the line intersects the x_1 axis and the x_2 axis—the line's x_1 intercept and x_2 intercept, respectively. To find the two intercepts, we alternately set one variable to 0 and solve for the corresponding value of the other. For example, we calculate the two intercepts for $3x_1 + 2x_2 = 18$ as follows:

$$x_1 \text{ intercept: } x_2 = 0 \rightarrow 3x_1 + 2(0) = 18 \rightarrow x_1 = \frac{18}{3} = 6 \rightarrow (x_1, x_2) = (6, 0).$$

$$x_2 \text{ intercept: } x_1 = 0 \rightarrow 3(0) + 2x_2 = 18 \rightarrow x_2 = \frac{18}{2} = 9 \rightarrow (x_1, x_2) = (0, 9).$$

To graph the equation, we simply plot the intercepts (6, 0) and (0, 9) and connect them by a straight line, thereby obtaining the graph in Figure 2.1 faster than before.

Now let us add 6 to the right-hand side (18 + 6 = 24) and graph the linear equation $3x_1 + 2x_2 = 24$. We calculate the two intercepts as follows:

$$x_1 \text{ intercept: } x_2 = 0 \rightarrow 3x_1 + 2(0) = 24 \rightarrow x_1 = \frac{24}{3} = 8 \rightarrow (x_1, x_2) = (8, 0).$$

$$x_2 \text{ intercept: } x_1 = 0 \rightarrow 3(0) + 2x_2 = 24 \rightarrow x_2 = \frac{24}{2} = 12 \rightarrow (x_1, x_2) = (0, 12).$$

Figure 2.2 displays the graphs of both $3x_1 + 2x_2 = 18$ and $3x_1 + 2x_2 = 24$. Observe that the lines are *parallel* to each other because changing an equation's right-hand side does not change the line's slope, only its intercepts. We can see this by rewriting the equation $3x_1 + 2x_2 = 24$ in its slope intercept form as follows:

$$3x_1 + 2x_2 = 24 \rightarrow 2x_2 = -3x_1 + 24 \rightarrow x_2 = -\frac{3}{2}x_1 + 12.$$

The slope, $-3/2$, is identical to that previously calculated for $3x_1 + 2x_2 = 18$. This example illustrates that changing only the right-hand side of a linear equation will simply result in a parallel linear equation, that is, one with the same slope but different intercepts.

To summarize the concepts illustrated by our examples, consider a "generic" linear equation

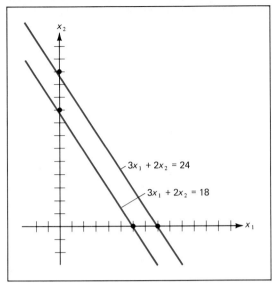

Figure 2.2 Graphs of $3x_1 + 2x_2 = 18$
and $3x_1 + 2x_2 = 24$

$$a_1x_1 + a_2x_2 = b,$$

where a_1, a_2, and b are *known* constants. (For the linear equation $3x_1 + 2x_2 = 18$, for example, $a_1 = 3$, $a_2 = 2$, and $b = 18$.) Our examples have illustrated the following general principles and concepts:

- For any specified values of a_1, a_2, and b, the graph of $a_1x_1 + a_2x_2 = b$ is a straight line.

- The easiest method for graphing the straight line is to first find the line's x_1 intercept and x_2 intercept as follows:

$$x_1 \text{ intercept } (x_2 = 0): a_1x_1 + a_2(0) = b \rightarrow x_1 = \frac{b}{a_1} \rightarrow (x_1, x_2) = (\frac{b}{a_1}, 0).$$

$$x_2 \text{ intercept } (x_1 = 0): a_1(0) + a_2x_2 = b \rightarrow x_2 = \frac{b}{a_2} \rightarrow (x_1, x_2) = (0, \frac{b}{a_2}).$$

Then plot the two intercepts $(b/a_1, 0)$ and $(0, b/a_2)$ and connect them by a straight line.

- The slope intercept form of the linear equation $a_1x_1 + a_2x_2 = b$ is

$$x_2 = -\frac{a_1}{a_2}x_1 + \frac{b}{a_2},$$

where $-a_1/a_2$ is the slope and b/a_2 is the value at which the x_2 axis is intercepted. A change in b, the equation's right-hand side, does not change the slope, so the new equation it creates is parallel with the first one.

Armed with our understanding of linear equations, let us now examine linear inequalities. Two examples of linear inequalities are $5x_1 - x_2 - 7x_3 + 2x_4 \geqslant 60$ and $3x_1 + 2x_2 \leqslant 18$. We see that a *linear inequality* is simply a linear equation with the $=$ sign replaced by a $\geqslant$ or $\leqslant$ sign.

When a linear inequality involves only two variables, we can depict it graphically using a three-step procedure. Consider the inequality $3x_1 + 2x_2 \leqslant 18$.

1. **Convert inequality to equation.** We convert the linear inequality to a linear equation by replacing the $\leqslant$ or $\geqslant$ sign with an $=$ sign. We call the resulting linear equation the linear inequality's *boundary equation*. In our example, the boundary equation of $3x_1 + 2x_2 \leqslant 18$ is $3x_1 + 2x_2 = 18$.

2. **Graph the boundary equation.** Using the method discussed earlier, we graph the boundary equation $3x_1 + 2x_2 = 18$. Figure 2.3 displays the result. Figure 2.3 shows that the boundary equation divides the plane into two *half-planes*. The shaded half-plane consists of the points on or below the boundary equation, and the unshaded half-plane consists of points on or above the boundary equation. (Note that the boundary equation belongs to both half-planes.)

3. **Determine which half-plane satisfies the inequality.** Since the $\leqslant$ includes $=$, all points on the boundary equation clearly satisfy the inequality. The question now is whether the other points satisfying the inequality lie in the shaded or the unshaded half-plane. There is a simple way to answer this question. We choose a point on the graph and ask whether it satisfies the inequality. Consider, for example, the origin—the point where both x_1, and $x_2 = 0$. Substituting the values $x_1 = 0$ and $x_2 = 0$ into the linear inequality $3x_1 + 2x_2 \leqslant 18$, we see that

$$\underset{\substack{\text{[inequality's left-hand side} \\ \text{when } (x_1, x_2) = (0, 0)]}}{3(0) + 2(0) = 0} \quad < \quad \underset{\text{[inequality's right-hand side]}}{18}$$

In other words, the point $(x_1, x_2) = (0, 0)$ satisfies the inequality. Consequently, the other points satisfying the inequality are the points located in the *same* half-plane as $(0, 0)$—that is, the shaded half-plane in Figure 2.3. If you are not convinced of this, try a few points on either side of the boundary equation and verify that only those in the shaded region satisfy the inequality.

Suppose, by way of comparison, that the inequality under consideration had been $3x_1 + 2x_2 \geqslant 18$ instead of $\leqslant 18$. Because, $3(0) + 2(0) = 0 < 18$, the origin violates (i.e., does not satisfy) this inequality. Consequently, all other points in the shaded half-plane containing the origin violate the inequality. Instead, the

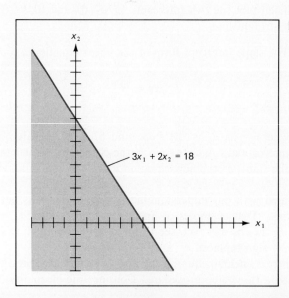

Figure 2.3 Graph of $3x_1 + 2x_2 \leqslant 18$

inequality is satisfied by the points in the unshaded half-plane in Figure 2.3 (including those on the boundary equation).

We can summarize the general procedure as follows:

> In order to determine the half-plane that contains all points satisfying an inequality,
>
> - Graph the inequality's boundary equation.
>
> - Select a so-called *trial point* located anywhere except on the boundary equation. Usually the origin is the most convenient trial point.
>
> - Substitute the trial point into the inequality's left-hand side, and determine whether it satisfies the inequality. If it does, then all points satisfying the inequality reside in the half-plane containing the trial point. However, if the trial point violates the inequality, then all points satisfying the inequality reside in the half-plane *not* containing the trial point.

In order to avoid jumping to conclusions when graphing linear inequalities, let us consider an additional example. Consider the following four inequalities:

$$3x_1 - 2x_2 \leqslant 18,$$

$$3x_1 - 2x_2 \geqslant 18,$$

$$-3x_1 + 2x_2 \leqslant -18,$$

$$-3x_1 + 2x_2 \geqslant -18.$$

The first two inequalities have the common boundary equation $3x_1 - 2x_2 = 18$. The last two have the common boundary equation $-3x_1 + 2x_2 = -18$, an equation that we can convert (by multiplying both sides by -1) into $3x_1 - 2x_2 = 18$. Hence, all four inequalities have the *same* boundary equation, which is graphed in Figure 2.4. We might be tempted here to assume that the graphs of the first and third inequalities lie in the same half-plane, because both are $\leqslant$ inequalities. Let us, however, apply our systematic procedure. Substituting the origin $(x_1, x_2) = (0, 0)$ into the left-hand sides of the four inequalities, we see that the origin satisfies the first and last inequalities but violates the second and third ine-

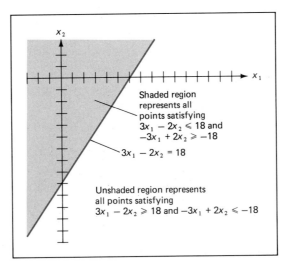

Figure 2.4 Graph of $3x_1 - 2x_2 \leqslant$
18, $3x_1 - 2x_2 \geqslant 18$,
$-3x_1 + 2x_2 \leqslant -18$,
$-3x_1 + 2x_2 \geqslant -18$

qualities. Consequently, the shaded half-plane in Figure 2.4 is the graph of all points satisfying the first and last inequalities, and the unshaded region is the graph of all points satisfying the second and third inequalities. Note that the shaded half-plane is the correct graph for a $\leqslant$ inequality and a $\geqslant$ inequality, and the same is true for the unshaded region. The lesson here is that we should always graph an inequality with care. An impression such as "All points satisfying a $\leqslant$ inequality lie on or below the boundary equation," for example, is correct under some conditions and incorrect under others.

2.3 ORANGE MICROCOMPUTER CORPORATION'S PRODUCT MIX PROBLEM

We are now ready to learn how to apply linear programming. As our first example, consider the following scenario:

Mildred Sekend (Millie, for short) has the responsibility of planning production for the Orange Microcomputer Corporation (OMC). OMC manufactures two models of microcomputers: the Orange, a desk-top microcomputer with dual disk drives, and the Tangerine, a portable version having only a single disk drive.

Among the resources consumed in the manufacture of these microcomputers, Millie expects that those in limited supply this quarter will be disk drives, assembly labor, and quality assurance labor. After consulting with the appropriate department managers, she has estimated that the monthly availability of these resources for the upcoming quarter will be as follows: disk drives, 20,000 units; assembly labor, 32,000 hours; quality assurance labor, 88,000 hours. Consumption of these three scarce resources occurs as follows:

- Manufacture of each Orange consumes 2 disk drives, 4 hours of assembly labor, and 2 hours of quality assurance labor.

- Manufacture of each Tangerine consumes 1 disk drive, 1 hour of assembly labor, and 7 hours of quality assurance labor. (The higher amount of quality assurance labor is necessary because of problems stemming from the Tangerine's portability.)

Using the accounting department's current data on selling prices and production costs, Millie has estimated that the sale of each Orange contributes $900 to OMC's profit and the sale of each Tangerine contributes $600. The marketing department has assured her that OMC can sell all its production of microcomputers, regardless of how much it produces of each.

Millie's problem, then, is to determine the monthly production quantities for the two models of microcomputers that will maximize the total contribution to OMC's profit without violating the constraints imposed on production by the limited resource availabilities. To aid her analysis, Millie has summarized the data she has gathered as shown in Table 2.2.

TABLE 2.2 Data for OMC's Product Mix Problem

	Resource Consumption per Unit Produced		Resource Availabilities
	Orange	Tangerine	
Disk Drives	2	1	20,000 units
Assembly Labor	4	1	32,000 hours
Quality Assurance Labor	2	7	88,000 hours
Unit Profit	$900	$600	

Millie's problem exemplifies in simple form a general class of decision problems common to firms that manufacture more than a single product: it is a *product mix problem*. In a general product mix problem, where *n* products "compete" for *m* scarce resources, the following data are the "inputs" to the decision-making process:

- The unit profit for each of the *n* products. In OMC's problem, Table 2.2's last row provides the unit profits for each of the *n* = 2 products.

- The availability of each of the *m* scarce resources during the problem's *planning horizon*.[1] In OMC's problem, Table 2.2's last column provides the availability of each of the *m* = 3 scarce resources during each month of the three-month planning horizon.

- The so-called *technology matrix*—that is, a rectangular (*m* rows, *n* columns) array of numbers in which the number in row *i* and column *j* is the amount of resource *i* consumed by the manufacture of each unit of product *j*. In OMC's problem, the technology matrix is the three-row, two-column array of numbers surrounded by a box in Table 2.2. For example, the number 2 in row 3 and column 1 of the matrix indicates that 2 units of resource 3 (quality assurance labor) are consumed by the manufacture of each unit of product 1 (the Orange).

Given these data, the decision problem is to determine the optimal *product mix*. That is, subject to the constraints limiting the consumption of each resource to at most the resource's availability, the decision problem is to determine how much to produce of each product during the planning horizon in order to maximize total profit.

Before we solve OMC's problem, pretend for a moment that you are Millie Sekend. Using common sense, intuition, and trial-and-error, decide how many Oranges and Tangerines OMC should produce each month. Write your recommendation in the boxes below (or on a piece of scratch paper). Later, after we have determined the optimal solution via linear programming, you can compare the optimal solution to your recommendation. You may be surprised at how much "extra" profit linear programming earns for OMC. Or, if your recommendation yields a closely similar total profit, you will at least be impressed with the efficiency of the linear programming approach.

	Your Recommended Production Quantities		Total Profit of Your Product Mix
	Oranges	Tangerines	
	7K	4K	8.7M

2.4 FORMULATION OF OMC'S PRODUCT MIX PROBLEM AS AN LP

Any application of linear programming begins with a *formulation phase*. Here the verbal description of the decision problem is translated (formulated) into a mathematical model of the problem, the LP.

---

[1] The planning horizon is the period of time over which the decision problem is defined.

In Section 2.1 we learned that every decision problem amenable to a linear programming approach has three elements in common: (1) a set of interrelated *decisions,* (2) an *objective* to maximize or minimize, and (3) a set of *constraints* that impose restrictions on the decisions. Formulation of an LP, accordingly, entails the following three steps:

1. Translate the verbal description of each of the interrelated decisions into a *decision variable.*

2. Translate the verbal description of the decision problem's objective into a maximization or minimization of a linear function of the decision variables.

3. Translate the verbal description of each constraint imposing a restriction on the decisions into a linear inequality or equation involving the decision variables.

Let us illustrate by translating OMC's product mix problem into an LP.

Definition of the Decision Variables

Millie Sekend must make two decisions: how many Oranges to produce each month and how many Tangerines to produce each month. We can think of Millie's decisions as assigning values to the following two decision variables:

$$x_1 = \text{the production quantity for product 1, the Orange}$$
$$x_2 = \text{the production quantity for product 2, the Tangerine.}$$

For example, a product mix of $(x_1, x_2) = (7000, 3000)$ corresponds to a decision by Millie to produce 7000 Oranges and 3000 Tangerines.

Writing the Objective as a Linear Function

Millie's objective is to maximize OMC's total monthly profit. OMC derives its profit from two sources: the production of x_1 Oranges and the production of x_2 Tangerines. Since Table 2.2's last row indicates that OMC earns a profit of $900 from *each* Orange, its total profit from Oranges is $900x_1$. Similarly, since OMC earns a profit of $600 from *each* Tangerine, its total profit from Tangerines is $600x_2$. Combining these two terms, we can express OMC's total profit from both sources as the following linear function:

$$900x_1 + 600x_2.$$

Consequently, a mathematical representation of Millie's objective is

$$\text{Maximize } 900x_1 + 600x_2.$$

In the terminology of linear programming, we have just written the *objective function* for the linear programming formulation of OMC's product mix problem. This function expresses Millie's objective: to assign values to x_1 and x_2 in such a way as to maximize the value of the function $900x_1 + 600x_2$.

What are the implications of our expressing OMC's total profit as the linear function $900x_1 + 600x_2$? Consider the Orange, product 1. Our expressing OMC's total profit from x_1 Oranges as $900x_1$ has two implications:

- **Product independence.** The total profit OMC derives from x_1 Oranges is independent of x_2, the production quantity of Tangerines; that is, it is always $900x_1$ regardless of the value of x_2. In the terminology of microeconomics, Tangerines are neither *supplements* nor *complements* for Oranges. If this is not true, then our expressing OMC's total profit as $900x_1 + 600x_2$ is inaccurate.

- **Constant marginal revenue and constant marginal cost.** The unit profit that OMC derives from Oranges is $900, regardless of the value of x_1; that is, the 1000th Orange OMC produces earns the same $900 as the first Orange produced. Economists describe such a situation as *constant marginal profit* (or constant returns to scale). Since profit equals revenue minus cost, constant marginal profit in turn implies *constant marginal revenue* and *constant marginal cost*. In other words, OMC receives the same revenue and incurs the same production cost from the 5000th Orange as it does for the first. Sometimes the assumptions of constant marginal revenue and constant marginal cost are unrealistic. For example, if OMC must lower the Orange's selling price as it increases x_1, then the Orange's marginal revenue decreases rather than remains constant. Or, if OMC must use more and more overtime as it increases x_1, then the Orange's marginal cost increases rather than remains constant. In either instance it would be inaccurate for OMC to assume that Orange's unit profit is $900 regardless of the value of x_1.

To summarize, our expression of OMC's total profit as the linear function $900x_1 + 600x_2$ is accurate only insofar as we can validly assume product independence and constant marginal revenue and constant marginal cost. For now, let us suppose that these assumptions are valid and postpone until later a discussion of what Millie must do if they are invalid.

Writing the Constraints as Linear Inequalities

Millie's assignment of values to x_1 and x_2 is constrained by the limited availabilities of three scarce resources: disk drives, assembly labor, and quality control labor. Let us first consider the constraint arising from the availability of no more than 20,000 disk drives. OMC consumes disk drives in two ways: production of x_1 Oranges and production of x_2 Tangerines. As indicated in Table 2.2's first row, each Orange consumes 2 disk drives, and each Tangerine 1 disk drive. Consequently, with a product mix of (x_1, x_2), OMC's total consumption of disk drives is the linear function

$$2x_1 + x_2.$$

We can now translate the verbal statement that "OMC's total consumption of disk drives must be less than or equal to 20,000" into the linear inequality

$$2x_1 + x_2 \leqslant 20{,}000.$$

The limitation of 32,000 hours of assembly labor also imposes a constraint on the values Millie can assign to x_1 and x_2. Table 2.2's second row indicates that *each* Orange consumes 4 hours of assembly labor and *each* Tangerine consumes 1 hour of assembly labor. Consequently, if OMC produces x_1 Oranges and x_2 Tangerines, its total consumption of assembly labor is the linear function

$$4x_1 + x_2.$$

We can now translate the verbal statement that "OMC's total consumption of assembly labor must be less than or equal to 32,000 hours" into the linear inequality

$$4x_1 + x_2 \leqslant 32,000.$$

Observe that our expressing OMC's total consumption of assembly labor as the linear function $4x_1 + x_2$ requires the following two assumptions:

- Each product's total consumption of assembly labor is independent of the production quantity of the *other* product.

- During production, there is constant marginal resource consumption by each product. That is, OMC does not experience any economies or diseconomies of scale such that the assembly labor required by the 1000th unit of either product differs from that required by the first unit.

You should now be ready to express the constraint imposed by the limited availability of quality control labor. After looking at Table 2.2's third row, convince yourself that the constraint is the linear inequality

$$2x_1 + 7x_2 \leqslant 88,000.$$

We must be careful not to overlook two other constraints: OMC cannot produce a negative quantity of Oranges or of Tangerines. Consequently, x_1 and x_2 must satisfy the two inequalities

$$x_1 \geqslant 0 \text{ and } x_2 \geqslant 0.$$

These two constraints ensure that x_1 and x_2 take on nonnegative (i.e., 0 or positive) values. For this reason, we refer to them as the *nonnegativity constraints*. Any constraint that is not a nonnegativity constraint is a *structural constraint*. Such terminology reflects the fact that, while $2x_1 + x_2 \leqslant 20,000$ and $x_1 \geqslant 0$ are both constraints, the former has much more structure (substance) than the latter.

Putting the Pieces Together

Through the formulation process, we have restated OMC's product mix problem as that of finding the values of x_1 and x_2 that make the linear objective function $900x_1 + 600x_2$ as large as possible without violating any of the five constraints (three structural and two nonnegativity) that x_1 and x_2 are subject to (i.e., must satisfy). More specifically, we have translated the lengthy verbal description of OMC's product mix problem into the following concise mathematical statement:

Maximize $900x_1 + 600x_2$			(total profit)	← **objective function**
subject to	$2x_1 +$	$1x_2 \leqslant 20,000$	(disk drives)	← **structural constraint**
	$4x_1 +$	$1x_2 \leqslant 32,000$	(assembly)	← **structural constraint**
	$2x_1 +$	$7x_2 \leqslant 88,000$	(quality assurance)	← **structural constraint**
and $x_1 \geqslant 0, x_2 \geqslant 0$				← **nonnegativity constraints.**

This is an example of a two-variable, three-constraint linear program (LP). "Three-constraint" here refers to the three structural constraints. We need not explicitly acknowledge the presence of the two nonnegativity constraints, since, unless otherwise noted, it is customary to assume that there is a nonnegativity constraint for each of the LP's decision variables. Unlike OMC's product mix LP, a general LP may involve any number of decision variables, may involve either maximizing or minimizing a linear objective function, and may involve a set of constraints that are a mixture of linear inequalities of the $\leq$ type, linear inequalities of the $\geq$ type, and linear equations. We will encounter LP's more general than OMC's later in this chapter and throughout Chapters 3, 4, and 5. For now, however, we restrict our attention to OMC's "simple" two-variable, three-constraint LP.

2.5 RESCALING OMC'S LP

It is often convenient or necessary to *rescale* a linear program—that is, to change the units of measurement of the LP's variables and data. By rescaling OMC's LP, we eliminate the need to continually write numbers that end in two or three zeros. As a first step, we redefine x_1 and x_2 to represent the number of *thousands* of Oranges and Tangerines produced instead of the number of single units. (For example, $x_1 = 3$ now represents a decision to produce 3000 Oranges, not three.) As a consequence of this revaluing of x_1 and x_2, keeping our mathematical expressions correct requires us to multiply all coefficients of x_1 and x_2 by 1000, thereby producing the following transformation of our original LP:

$$\text{Maximize } 900x_1 + 600x_2 \qquad \rightarrow \text{Maximize } 900{,}000x_1 + 600{,}000x_2$$

$$
\begin{array}{llll}
\text{subject to} & 2x_1 + 1x_2 \leq 20{,}000 & \rightarrow \text{subject to} & 2000x_1 + 1000x_2 \leq 20{,}000 \\
& 4x_1 + 1x_2 \leq 32{,}000 & \rightarrow & 4000x_1 + 1000x_2 \leq 32{,}000 \\
& 2x_1 + 7x_2 \leq 88{,}000 & \rightarrow & 2000x_1 + 7000x_2 \leq 88{,}000
\end{array}
$$

$$\text{and } x_1 \geq 0, x_2 \geq 0 \qquad \rightarrow \qquad \text{and } x_1 \geq 0, x_2 \geq 0.$$

If you are not clear on why we multiply the coefficients by 1000, think it through step by step. For each 1000 Oranges produced, the profit will be $900,000, and so on.

So far we have added extra zeros to our LP, not eliminated them! However, we can now eliminate all zeros by rescaling the objective function and the structural constraints. In particular, dividing the revised objective function by 100,000 changes its unit of measurement from $1 to $100,000, and dividing both sides of each of the three structural constraints by 1000 changes their units of measurement from single units to units of 1000—that is, units of 1000 disk drives, units of 1000 hours of assembly labor, and units of 1000 hours of quality assurance labor. Our rescaling of the LP's objective function and structural constraints produces the following transformation of our revised LP:

(Unit of Measurement)

$$
\begin{array}{ll}
\text{Maximize } 9x_1 + 6x_2 & \text{(hundred-thousands of dollars)} \\[4pt]
\text{subject to } 2x_1 + 1x_2 \leq 20 & \text{(thousands of disk drives)} \\
\quad\quad\quad\quad 4x_1 + 1x_2 \leq 32 & \text{(thousands of hours)} \\
\quad\quad\quad\quad 2x_1 + 7x_2 \leq 88 & \text{(thousands of hours)} \\[4pt]
\text{and } x_1 \geq 0, x_2 \geq 0 & \text{(thousands of microcomputers)}
\end{array}
$$

It is this rescaled LP that we will solve in the next section.

Although we rescaled OMC's LP for our convenience, rescaling is sometimes necessary rather than optional. In particular, if the LP will be solved using a computer, the so-called *round-off error* will usually be kept to minimum if rescaling is performed to achieve the following goals:

1. The absolute value of all the variables' coefficients and all the constraints' right-hand sides should fall somewhere in the interval between 0.0001 and 100,000.

2. The coefficients of each variable should be of approximately the same magnitude, and the constraints' right-hand sides should be of approximately the same magnitude. For example, it would be unwise to keep the assembly constraint's unit of measurement as single hours while at the same changing the quality assurance constraint's unit of measurement to 1000 hours, thereby resulting in the pair of constraints

$$4000x_1 \;+\; 1000x_2 \;\leqslant\; 32{,}000 \quad \text{(in units of hours)}$$
$$2x_1 \;+\; 7x_2 \;\leqslant\; 88 \quad \text{(in units of 1000 hours)}$$

The resulting imbalance in the magnitudes of the constants in the two constraints would probably cause significant round-off error.

2.6 SOLVING OMC'S LP USING THE GRAPHICAL METHOD

Before solving OMC's LP, we need to introduce some solution terminology. Normally, one thinks of a solution as the final answer to a problem. However, we call *any* (not just the final) assignment of values to an LP's decision variables a *solution* for the LP. For example, $(x_1, x_2) = (7, 4)$ and $(x_1, x_2) = (4, 13)$ are both solutions to OMC's two-variable LP. A *feasible solution* for an LP is an assignment of values that satisfies *all* the LP's constraints (both the structural and the nonnegativity constraints). In contrast, an *infeasible solution* violates (i.e., does not satisfy) *at least one* of the LP's constraints.

As examples in the context of OMC's LP, consider once again the solutions $(x_1, x_2) = (7, 4)$ and $(x_1, x_2) = (4, 13)$. To determine their feasibility or infeasibility we must substitute them into the LP's constraints as follows:

CONSTRAINT	DOES (7,4) SATISFY CONSTRAINT?	DOES (4,13) SATISFY CONSTRAINT?
$2x_1 + 1x_2 \leqslant 20$	Is $2(7) + 1(4) \leqslant 20$? *Yes!*	Is $2(4) + 1(13) \leqslant 20$? *No!*
$4x_1 + 1x_2 \leqslant 32$	Is $4(7) + 1(4) \leqslant 32$? *Yes!*	Is $4(4) + 1(13) \leqslant 32$? *Yes!*
$2x_1 + 7x_2 \leqslant 88$	Is $2(7) + 7(4) \leqslant 88$? *Yes!*	Is $2(4) + 7(13) \leqslant 88$? *No!*
$x_1 \geqslant 0$	Is $7 \geqslant 0$? *Yes!*	Is $4 \geqslant 0$? *Yes!*
$x_2 \geqslant 0$	Is $4 \geqslant 0$? *Yes!*	Is $13 \geqslant 0$? *Yes!*

Since (7, 4) satisfies all five constraints, it is a feasible solution to OMC's LP. In contrast, (4, 13) is an infeasible solution, since it violates two of the LP's five constraints.

Given a particular feasible solution, we compute its *objective value* by substituting the values of the decision variables into the LP's objective function. For example, having determined that $(x_1, x_2) = (7, 4)$ is a feasible solution for OMC's LP, we compute its objective value by substituting as follows:

$$9x_1 + 6x_2 = 9(7) + 6(4) = 63 + 24 = 87 \,.$$

To solve OMC's LP, we must find the assignment of values to (x_1, x_2) that satisfies all the LP's five constraints and simultaneously maximizes the LP's objective function. That is, we seek *the feasible solution with the maximal objective value.* We call such a solution the LP's *optimal solution,* and we call the optimal solution's objective value the LP's *optimal objective value.*

There are three ways we can find an LP's optimal solution:

- **Graphically.** If the LP has only two variables, we can solve it graphically (regardless of the number of constraints) using the method we will discuss shortly.

- **With manual computations.** If the LP has only a few variables and constraints (say, at most five variables and five structural constraints), we can solve the LP in a reasonable amount of time by manually executing the so-called *simplex method,* a sequence of numerical computations discussed in Chapters 6 and 7.

- **With a computer.** If the LP has many variables or structural constraints, none of us would have the patience or the time to solve it manually. Instead, we must use a computer program that quickly and accurately performs the extensive computations required by the simplex method. We discuss such a computer program in Chapter 3.

An LP encountered in the "real world" (as distinct from the simplified world of this and other textbooks) will almost always have enough decision variables or constraints so that we need a computer to find the optimal solution. Why, then, do we bother to learn the graphical method? The answer is that our graphical solution of two-variable LPs gives us insight and intuition, establishing a foundation on which to build our understanding of the more abstract concepts in subsequent chapters.

We begin our graphical solution of OMC's LP by developing a representation of the LP's *feasible region*—that is, the set of all feasible solutions. Recall from Section 2.2 that the general method for graphing an inequality is to first graph the inequality's boundary equation and then use a trial point to determine which half-plane contains all points satisfying the inequality. Owing to their simplicity, we do not need to employ the general method to graph the two nonnegativity constraints $x_1 \geq 0$ and $x_2 \geq 0$. As indicated by the shaded region in Figure 2.5(a), only those points in the so-called *nonnegative quadrant* simultaneously satisfy both nonnegativity constraints. Graphing the three structural constraints does, however, require us to use the general method. Let us first consider $2x_1 + x_2 \leq 20$, the structural constraint on disk drive consumption. We calculate the two intercepts of the constraint's boundary equation $2x_1 + x_2 = 20$:[2]

$$x_1 \text{ intercept:} \quad 2x_1 + \cancel{1x_2} = 20 \rightarrow (x_1, x_2) = (10, 0)$$
$$x_2 \text{ intercept:} \quad \cancel{2x_1} + 1x_2 = 20 \rightarrow (x_1, x_2) = (0, 20)$$

Connecting these two intercepts with a straight line results in the graph displayed in Figure 2.5(b). Using $(x_1, x_2) = (0, 0)$ as the trial point, we note that $2(0) + 1(0) = 0 < 20$; that is, the half-plane that is shaded in Figure 2.5(b), including the boundary equation, is the one that contains all points satisfying the constraint $2x_1 + x_2 \leq 20$. You should verify for yourself that the half-planes that are shaded in Figures 2.5(c) and 2.5(d) are the ones that contain all points satisfy-

---

[2] The crossing out ($\cancel{}$) of a term indicates it has a value of 0.

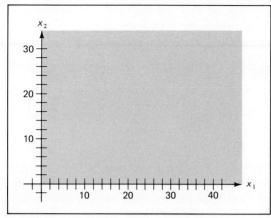

Figure 2.5(a) Graph of $x_1 \geqslant 0$ and $x_2 \geqslant 0$

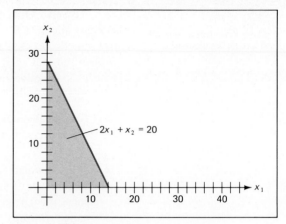

Figure 2.5(b) Graph of $2x_1 + x_2 \leqslant 20$

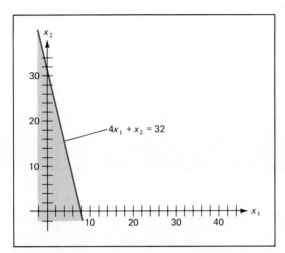

Figure 2.5(c) Graph of $4x_1 + x_2 \leqslant 32$

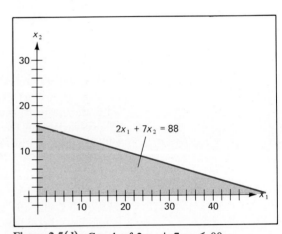

Figure 2.5(d) Graph of $2x_1 + 7x_2 \leqslant 88$

ing, respectively, the assembly constraint $4x_1 + x_2 \leqslant 32$ and the quality assurance constraint $2x_1 + 7x_2 \leqslant 88$.

The LP's feasible region—the set of all feasible solutions—consists of all solutions that simultaneously satisfy the LP's two nonnegativity constraints and three structural constraints. We can graphically represent the feasible region by superimposing the four shaded regions in Figure 2.5 on a single graph. Figure 2.6 is the result. Observe that Figure 2.6's shaded region contains only those (x_1, x_2) that lie within or on the boundary of all four shaded regions in Figures 2.5(a)-(d). For example, earlier we verified that $(7, 4)$ is a feasible solution because it satisfies all five constraints, and that $(4, 13)$ is an infeasible solution because it violates both the disk drive constraint $2x_1 + x_2 \leqslant 20$ and the quality assurance constraint $2x_1 + 7x_2 \leqslant 88$. We can graphically confirm $(7, 4)$'s feasibility and $(4, 13)$'s infeasibility by noting that $(7, 4)$ lies within Figure 2.6's shaded region and $(4, 13)$ does not.

We must now determine which of the infinite number of feasible solutions in Figure 2.6's shaded region is the optimal solution. For example, we can see that both $(7, 4)$ and $(4, 11)$ are feasible solutions. Substituting each of these points into the objective function $9x_1 + 6x_2$, we see that $(7, 4)$'s objective value is $9(7) + 6(4) = 63 + 24 = 87$ and $(4, 11)$'s objective value is $9(4) + 6(11) = 36 + 66$

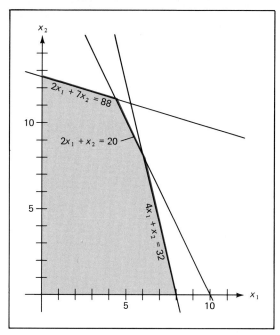

Figure 2.6 Feasible region for OMC's linear program

= 102. Thus, a product mix of 4 thousand Oranges and 11 thousand Tangerines earns OMC a profit that is $102 - 87 = 15$ hundred thousand dollars greater than the profit earned with a product mix of 7 thousand Oranges and 4 thousand Tangerines. At this point, we know that $(4, 11)$ is a better product mix than $(7, 4)$. However, is there a feasible solution with a higher objective value? If so, how do we find it? With an infinite number of feasible solutions, it would be fruitless to keep arbitrarily selecting a feasible solution and evaluating its objective value. There would always be one more feasible solution to select, and it might well be the optimal one!

Let us try a different approach. We arbitrarily select a particular objective value and ask which feasible solutions (if any) have this objective value. For example, which feasible solutions (if any) have an objective value of 54? Since the objective function is $9x_1 + 6x_2$, this question is mathematically equivalent to asking "Does the equation $9x_1 + 6x_2 = 54$ intersect the feasible region?" To answer this question, we need only graph the equation $9x_1 + 6x_2 = 54$ on a graph that also displays the LP's feasible region. We determine the two intercepts for $9x_1 + 6x_2 = 54$ as follows:

$$x_1 \text{ intercept:} \quad 9x_1 + \cancel{6x_2} = 54 \rightarrow (x_1, x_2) = (6, 0)$$
$$x_2 \text{ intercept:} \quad \cancel{9x_1} + 6x_2 = 54 \rightarrow (x_1, x_2) = (0, 9).$$

Figure 2.7 illustrates graphically that the straight line passing through $(6, 0)$ and $(0, 9)$ does intersect the feasible region. In fact, each of the infinite number of points along the line segment between $(6, 0)$ and $(0, 9)$ is a feasible solution with an objective value of 54. The straight line $9x_1 + 6x_2 = 54$ is an *isoprofit line,* because all points on it have the same ("iso" in Greek) profit.

Now that we know that OMC can earn a total profit of 54 hundred thousand dollars (i.e., 5.4 million dollars), we can get "greedier" and seek a total profit first of 72 and then of 90. To do so, we must determine if the isoprofit lines $9x_1 + 6x_2 = 72$ and $9x_1 + 6x_2 = 90$ intersect the feasible region. The numbers of 72 and 90 are convenient choices (as was our former choice of 54) because both are

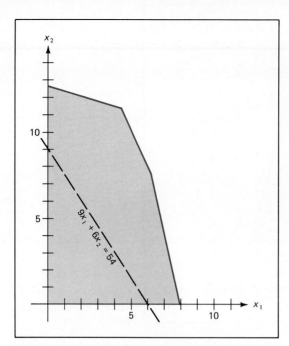

Figure 2.7 Checking for feasible solutions having an objective value of 54

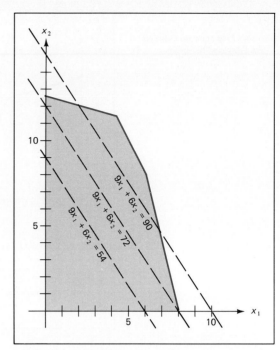

Figure 2.8 Checking for feasible solutions having an objective value of 72 or 90

multiples of both 9 and 6, thereby ensuring integer values in the following calculations of the isoprofit lines' intercepts:

	TOTAL PROFIT OF 72	TOTAL PROFIT OF 90
x_1 intercept:	$9x_1 + 6x_2 = 72 \rightarrow (x_1, x_2) = (8, 0)$	$9x_1 + 6x_2 = 90 \rightarrow (x_1, x_2) = (10, 0)$
x_2 intercept:	$9x_1 + 6x_2 = 72 \rightarrow (x_1, x_2) = (0, 12)$	$9x_1 + 6x_2 = 90 \rightarrow (x_1, x_2) = (0, 15)$

Figure 2.8 illustrates graphically that the line segments between (8, 0) and (0, 12) and between (10, 0) and (0, 15) both intersect the feasible region. Even though not all points on the line segments lie within the feasible region, there are still an infinite number of points that do. Thus, there are an infinite number of product mixes that will earn OMC a total profit of 72 or 90.

Observe in Figure 2.8 that the three isoprofit lines are parallel to each other. This is not a coincidence! As we discussed earlier, changing the right-hand side of a linear equation but leaving the variables' coefficients unchanged affects only the equation's intercepts, not its slope. Therefore, $9x_1 + 6x_2 = 54$, $9x_1 + 6x_2 = 72$, $9x_1 + 6x_2 = 90$ form a sequence of parallel isoprofit lines that progressively shift in a northeast direction (i.e., upward and to the right). This observation eliminates the need to keep graphing specific isoprofit lines. Instead, we use a straight edge (e.g., a ruler or the edge of a piece of paper) to serve as an isoprofit line. Placing the straight edge along one of the three isoprofit lines in Figure 2.8, we start sliding the straight edge in a northeast direction, keeping it parallel to the three isoprofit lines. We stop sliding it when any further movement to the northeast would cause it to no longer intersect the feasible region. Figure 2.9 displays the "last" isoprofit line to intersect the feasible region. Observe that the intersection occurs at a single point, a so-called *point of tangency*. This point of tangency is the optimal solution to OMC's LP.

Although we have graphically identified the optimal solution, we do not yet know its exact coordinates and the corresponding optimal objective value. Looking at Figure 2.9, we see that the optimal solution's x_1-coordinate is between 4 and 5 (but closer to 4) and its x_2-coordinate is between 11 and 12 (but closer to 11). The key to finding the exact coordinates is to note that the optimal solution occurs at the intersection of two boundary equations, the disk drive boundary equation $2x_1 + x_2 = 20$ and the quality assurance boundary equation $2x_1 + 7x_2 = 88$. Consequently, the optimal solution is the simultaneous solution to the system of equations

$$2x_1 + 1x_2 = 20$$
$$2x_1 + 7x_2 = 88$$

There are a variety of methods one can use to simultaneously solve a system of equations. When two variables are involved, a method that works just as well as any other is known as the *method of substitution*. The method begins by arbitrarily selecting one of the two equations and then using this equation to solve for either one of the variables in terms of the other. In the case at hand, let us select the system's "top" equation, $2x_1 + x_2 = 20$, and solve for x_1 in terms of x_2:

$$2x_1 + x_2 = 20 \;\rightarrow\; 2x_1 = 20 - x_2 \;\rightarrow\; x_1 = \frac{20 - x_2}{2} \;\rightarrow\; x_1 = 10 - \frac{x_2}{2}$$

We next substitute this expression for x_1 into the system's "bottom" equation, $2x_1 + 7x_2 = 88$, and solve the resulting one-variable equation for x_2; the computations proceed as follows:

$$
\begin{aligned}
2x_1 + 7x_2 = 88 \;\;\rightarrow\;\; & 2\left(10 - \tfrac{x_2}{2}\right) + 7x_2 && = 88 \\
\rightarrow\;\; & (20 - x_2) + 7x_2 && = 88 \\
\rightarrow\;\; & 6x_2 && = 68 \\
\rightarrow\;\; & x_2 && = \frac{68}{6} = 11\tfrac{2}{6} = 11\tfrac{1}{3}\,.
\end{aligned}
$$

Knowing that $x_2 = 11\frac{1}{3}$ and $x_1 = 10 - \dfrac{x_2}{2}$, we can now easily solve for x_1 as follows:

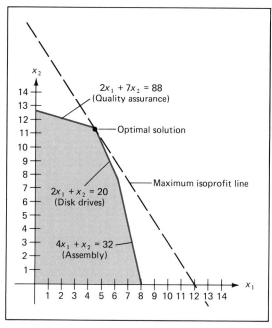

Figure 2.9 Optimal solution of OMC's product mix problem

$$x_1 = 10 - \frac{x_2}{2} \rightarrow x_1 = 10 - \frac{11\frac{1}{3}}{2} = 10 - \frac{\frac{34}{3}}{2} = 10 - \frac{34}{6} = 10 - 5\frac{4}{6} = 4\frac{1}{3}.$$

Hence, the exact coordinates of the optimal solution are $(x_1, x_2) = (4\frac{1}{3}, 11\frac{1}{3})$. To obtain the LP's optimal objective value, we simply substitute the optimal values of x_1 and x_2 into the LP's objective function:

$$9x_1 + 6x_2 = 9(4\frac{1}{3}) + 6(11\frac{1}{3}) = 39 + 68 = 107.$$

To summarize, we have determined that the optimal solution to OMC's LP is $(x_1, x_2) = (4\frac{1}{3}, 11\frac{1}{3})$ and the corresponding optimal objective value is 107.

2.7 IMPLEMENTING THE OPTIMAL SOLUTION TO OMC'S LP

Although we have solved the linear programming formulation of OMC's product mix problem, have we really solved OMC's *actual* product mix problem? This question raises the issue of *implementation*. In Chapter 1 we discussed in detail that the optimal solution to a mathematical model of a decision problem is rarely the final solution to the actual decision problem. We can illustrate this point in the context of OMC's product mix problem.

The optimal solution to OMC's LP is $(x_1, x_2) = (4\frac{1}{3}, 11\frac{1}{3})$, and the corresponding optimal objective value is 107. This corresponds to an optimal product mix of $4333\frac{1}{3}$ Oranges and $11,333\frac{1}{3}$ Tangerines and an optimal total profit of 10.7 million dollars (i.e., 107 hundred thousand dollars).[3] If we were to recommend this product mix to Millie Sekend, she would probably ask us how OMC can produce (let alone sell!) $\frac{1}{3}$ of an Orange or Tangerine.

The optimal solution to OMC's LP illustrates a fundamental limitation of linear programming:

> The optimal solution to an LP may have fractional values for one or more of the decision variables, even in cases where all the LP's data (i.e., the variables' coefficients and constraints' right-hand sides) are integer-valued.

That the optimal solution to OMC's LP has fractional values does not imply that our analysis has been in vain. Depending on the actual situation faced by OMC, Millie can implement the optimal solution in one of two ways:

- Millie can interpret the $\frac{1}{3}$ of an Orange or Tangerine as *work in progress*. That is, during the upcoming three-month period, OMC should produce $(4333\frac{1}{3}) \times 3 = 13,000$ Oranges and $(11,333\frac{1}{3}) \times 3 = 34,000$ Tangerines.

- The work-in-progress interpretation would be inappropriate if OMC required (as it might for a variety of reasons) that the monthly production quantities of each of its products be integer multiples of 1000. In this case, a recommendation for a monthly product mix of $(x_1, x_2) = (4\frac{1}{3}, 11\frac{1}{3})$ would be unacceptable. To represent production quantities that are multiples of 1000, both x_1 and x_2 must assume integer values. An LP with the added restriction that some or all of its decision variables must assume integer values is called an *integer linear program* (abbreviated hereafter by ILP). Is the optimal solution to OMC's LP helpful in finding the optimal solution to the ILP? It is tempting to conclude that we can solve the ILP by simply rounding the

---

[3] How does this compare to the recommendation you made at the end of Section 2.3?

LP's optimal solution to the nearest integer values — that is, to conclude that the ILP's optimal solution is $(x_1, x_2) = (4, 11)$. Unfortunately, the rounded solution is rarely optimal. However, it may be acceptably close to optimal.

Let us examine the rounded solution $(4, 11)$ more carefully. Observe in Figure 2.6 that $(4, 11)$ lies within the feasible region. Also, note that $(4, 11)$'s objective value is $9(4) + 6(11) = 102$. Consequently, $(4, 11)$ is a feasible solution to the ILP having an objective value of 102. Although we will shortly see that $(4, 11)$ is not the ILP's optimal solution, we can demonstrate that it is a close-to-optimal solution. The ILP is simply the LP with the added restriction that x_1 and x_2 must assume integer values. Since adding more constraints can never lead to increased total profit, the ILP's optimal objective value can never exceed the LP's optimal objective value. In other words, knowing that the LP's optimal solution $(4\frac{1}{3}, 11\frac{1}{3})$ has an optimal objective value of 107, we can conclude that 107 is an upper bound on the ILP's optimal objective value. Therefore, with its objective value of 102, the rounded solution $(4, 11)$ is within $107 - 102 = 5$ hundred thousand dollars of being the ILP's optimal solution. Stated in percentage terms, $(4, 11)$ is within

$$\frac{107 - 102}{107} \times 100\% = 4.67\%$$

of optimality for the ILP.

Managers faced with an ILP have two reasons to be happy when linear programming discovers a feasible solution guaranteed to be within 5% of optimality:

1. Given that the decision problem's data (e.g., a product's unit profit or a resource's availability) may be accurate only to within 5%, a solution that is within 5% of optimality should suffice. Why ask more of the solution than you do of the data?

2. As we will see in Chapter 9's discussion of integer linear programs, finding an ILP's optimal solution is significantly more time-consuming and costly than solving the corresponding LP and rounding its optimal solution.

Consequently, if Millie requires integer values for x_1 and x_2, she could implement a product mix of $(4, 11)$, recognizing that it is within 5% of optimality.

Although rounding the LP's optimal solution produces an acceptable integer-valued solution for OMC's product mix problem, we will see in Chapter 9 that rounding is not always so successful. In particular, we will see that the rounded solution may be infeasible or, even when it is feasible, cannot always be guaranteed to be within 5% of optimality. Chapter 9 will also show that the optimal solution to the ILP version of OMC's product mix problem is not $(4, 11)$ but $(5, 10)$. Observe that $(5, 10)$'s objective value is $9(5) + 6(10) = 105$, 3 hundred thousand dollars higher than the objective value for the rounded solution $(4, 11)$. However, it is interesting to note that $(4, 11)$'s actual percentage error, in contrast to the guaranteed maximal percentage error of 4.67%, is

$$\frac{105 - 102}{105} \times 100\% = 2.86\% .$$

This illustrates the general phenomenon that a rounded solution's guaranteed maximal percentage error is a "worst-case" percentage. The actual percentage error is usually lower, sometimes significantly lower.[4]

---

[4] If you are intrigued by this strategy of rounding, you may wish to digress for a moment and read the more detailed discussion in Sections 9.1–9.5, especially if you will not cover these sections later in your course.

We have used the ILP version of OMC's product mix problem to illustrate the following general principle:

> Before resorting to the more time-consuming and costlier methods used to solve integer linear programs, it is worthwhile to ignore the integer restrictions on the decision variables, solve the resulting linear program, and round its optimal solution in an attempt to discover a feasible solution for the integer linear program that is acceptably close to optimality.

In this section we have seen how fractional values for the decision variables may complicate the implementation of an LP's optimal solution. In Section 2.15 we will see that there may be other obstacles to overcome.

2.8 SLACK VARIABLES AND BINDING CONSTRAINTS

In the previous section we determined that OMC maximizes its total profit with a product mix of $4\frac{1}{3}$ thousand Oranges and $11\frac{1}{3}$ thousand Tangerines. Millie will probably also want answers to the following questions:

1. How many of the available 20 thousand disk drives are *not* consumed by the optimal product mix?

2. How much of the available 32 thousand hours of assembly labor is *not* consumed by the optimal product mix?

3. How much of the available 88 thousand hours of quality assurance labor is *not* consumed by the optimal product mix?

The answers provide insight into how scarce the so-called scarce resources really are.

Let us illustrate the general method of answering these questions by considering question 2. In our formulation of OMC's product mix problem, we expressed the limitation on the consumption of assembly labor as

$$4x_1 + x_2 \leqslant 32 .$$

Recall that this constraint's right-hand side is the available assembly labor and its left-hand side is the total consumption of assembly labor by the product mix (x_1, x_2). Consequently, the available assembly labor *not* consumed by the product mix (x_1, x_2) is the constraint's right-hand side minus its left-hand side:

$$32 - (4x_1 + x_2) .$$

We call $32 - (4x_1 + x_2)$ the *slack* for the constraint $4x_1 + x_2 \leqslant 32$. We denote the constraint's slack by the *slack variable* S_2 (using S for slack and the subscript 2 because we are dealing with the LP's *second* constraint). To summarize,

$$S_2 = 32 - (4x_1 + x_2) .$$

Using this linear equation for S_2, we can now easily compute the unconsumed assembly labor for any specific product mix by substituting the values of x_1 and x_2. Consider the following three examples:

PRODUCT MIX (x_1, x_2)	SLACK VARIABLE S_2	= =	AVAILABLE 32	− −	CONSUMED $[4x_1 + 1x_2]$		
(5, 3)	S_2	=	32	−	$[4(5) + 1(3)]$	=	5
(6, 8)	S_2	=	32	−	$[4(6) + 1(8)]$	=	0
(9, 14)	S_2	=	32	−	$[4(9) + 1(14)]$	=	−18

Our first observation concerns the *sign* of the slack variable. The *nonnegative* values of the slack variable for the product mixes (5, 3) and (6, 8) indicate that both consume no more assembly labor than is available. However, the *negative* slack of $S_2 = -18$ for the product mix (9, 14) indicates that it would consume 18 thousand *more* hours of assembly labor than is available. In other words, $(x_1, x_2) = (9, 14)$ is an infeasible product mix, since it violates the assembly constraint $4x_1 + x_2 \leqslant 32$.

Figure 2.10 illustrates these three examples. The shaded region is the half-plane containing all points satisfying the constraint $4x_1 + x_2 \leqslant 32$. As illustrated, a point such as (6, 8) having a slack of 0 satisfies the constraint and lies on the constraint's boundary equation, a point such as (5, 3) having a positive slack also satisfies the constraint but lies in the shaded region off the boundary equation, and a point such as (9, 14) having a negative slack violates the constraint and lies in the unshaded region. Figure 2.10 illustrates the following general principle:

> An assignment of values to the decision variables satisfies a $\leqslant$ constraint if and only if the constraint's slack variable assumes a nonnegative value.

At this point we need to introduce an additional bit of terminology. As illustrated by our three examples, whenever a constraint's left-hand side evaluated for a particular assignment of values to the decision variables equals the constraint's

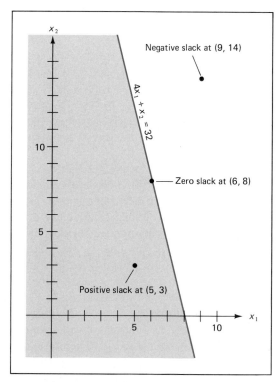

Figure 2.10 Graphical illustration of slack for constraint $4x_1 + 1x_2 \leqslant 32$

right-hand side, the constraint's slack variable assumes a value of 0. In such a case, we say that the constraint is *binding* for that particular assignment of values to the decision variables.[5] For example, in computing the respective values of the slack variable at the points $(5, 3)$, $(6, 8)$, and $(9, 14)$, we saw that only $(6, 8)$ had a slack of 0. Therefore, we say that the constraint $4x_1 + x_2 \leqslant 32$ is binding at the point $(6, 8)$ and *nonbinding* at the points $(5, 3)$ and $(9, 14)$. The concept of binding versus nonbinding can be explained graphically. As illustrated in Figure 2.10, the slack variable S_2 equals 0 only for those values of (x_1, x_2) satisfying the constraint's boundary equation $4x_1 + x_2 = 32$. In general, then,

> A $\leqslant$ constraint is *binding* for a particular assignment of values to the decision variables if and only if the constraint's slack variable assumes a value of 0. In two dimensions, a constraint is binding at a point if and only if the point lies on the constraint's boundary equation.

We can now answer the questions asked at the beginning of the section about the resources consumed by OMC's optimal product mix. For each of the three resource constraints, we define a slack variable equal to the constraint's right-hand side minus its left-hand side. In particular, besides the previously defined slack variable S_2 for the second resource constraint, we define slack variables S_1 and S_3 for the first and third resource constraints, respectively:

Slack variable for disk drive constraint:	$S_1 = 20 - (2x_1 + 1x_2)$
Slack variable for assembly constraint:	$S_2 = 32 - (4x_1 + 1x_2)$
Slack variable for quality assurance constraint:	$S_3 = 88 - (2x_1 + 7x_2)$.

Observe the convention of using S for slack and a subscript equal to the number of the constraint (e.g., S_2 for the second constraint). Using these linear equations for S_1, S_2, and S_3, we compute how much (if any) of each of the three scarce resources is not consumed by the optimal product mix $(x_1, x_2) = (4\frac{1}{3}, 11\frac{1}{3})$:

RESOURCE	SLACK VARIABLE = RESOURCE *not* CONSUMED
Disk drives	$S_1 = 20 - [2(4\frac{1}{3}) + 1(11\frac{1}{3})] = 20 - 20 = 0$
Assembly	$S_2 = 32 - [4(4\frac{1}{3}) + 1(11\frac{1}{3})] = 32 - 28\frac{2}{3} = 3\frac{1}{3}$
Quality assurance	$S_3 = 88 - [2(4\frac{1}{3}) + 7(11\frac{1}{3})] = 88 - 88 = 0$

Thus, the optimal product mix entirely consumes the available disk drives and the available quality assurance labor but leaves unconsumed $S_2 = 3\frac{1}{3}$ thousand hours of assembly labor.

With a little thought, we can predict that the slack variables S_1 and S_3 both equal 0, thereby avoiding their time-consuming calculations. How can we make such a prediction? Recall that, after graphically locating the optimal solution in Figure 2.9, we noted that the optimal solution lay at the intersection of two boundary equations, the boundary equation for the disk drive constraint $2x_1 + x_2 \leqslant 20$ and the boundary equation for the quality assurance constraint $2x_1 + 7x_2 \leqslant 88$. We then proceeded to simultaneously solve the two boundary equations $2x_1 + x_2 = 20$ and $2x_1 + 7x_2 = 88$ to determine the exact coordinates of the optimal solution. Since the optimal solution $(4\frac{1}{3}, 11\frac{1}{3})$ satisfies the boundary equations for the constraints $2x_1 + x_2 \leqslant 20$ and $2x_1 + 7x_2 \leqslant 88$, these constraints are binding at $(4\frac{1}{3}, 11\frac{1}{3})$, and we can conclude that the constraints' slack variables, S_1 and S_3, must both equal 0. Therefore, our earlier computations of S_1

---

[5] Some instructors or textbooks use the terminology *tight* or *active*.

and S_3 were unnecessary. In contrast, however, observe in Figure 2.9 that, although the optimal solution satisfies the constraint $4x_1 + x_2 \leqslant 32$, it does not lie on the constraint's boundary equation; that is, the constraint $4x_1 + x_2 \leqslant 32$ is nonbinding at the optimal solution. Consequently, although we can predict that the slack variable S_2 is positive, we can determine its exact value only by substituting, as we did earlier, $(4\frac{1}{3}, 11\frac{1}{3})$ into the expression $32 - (4x_1 + x_2)$. In general, then,

> We need only calculate the values of those slack variables corresponding to nonbinding constraints; all others must equal 0.

2.9 PETE MOSS'S BLENDING PROBLEM

As a second example of applying linear programming, consider the following scenario:

Pete Moss is the production manager for a company that supplies fertilizers to its customers on a make-to-order basis. When placing an order, a customer specifies a triple of percentages *N-P-K*, where *N* is the desired percentage of nitrogen in the fertilizer, *P* the desired percentage of phosphorus, and *K* the desired percentage of potassium. For example, in a 20-10-5 fertilizer, 20% of the fertilizer's weight is nitrogen, 10% is phosphorus, and 5% is potassium; the remaining 65% of the weight is due to inert compounds. The *N-P-K* values vary from order to order, depending on the requirements dictated by each customer's soil conditions.

For some customers, the *N-P-K* values represent percentages from which there can be no deviations. However, for other customers, the *N-P-K* values represent minimum percentages. The latter is the case for an order Pete has just received for 1000 pounds of a 17-14-10 fertilizer. The customer wants at least 17% of the fertilizer's weight to be nitrogen, at least 14% to be phosphorus, and at least 10% to be potassium. (Note that, although we will refer to this order as a 17-14-10 fertilizer, you should keep in mind that the *N-P-K* values represent minimum percentages.)

To satisfy a customer's order, Pete blends appropriate amounts of "stock" fertilizers that he purchases from a wholesaler in 100-pound bags. To satisfy the current order for 1000 pounds of 17-14-10 fertilizer, Pete intends to blend three types of stock fertilizers. Type 1 is a 50-20-5 fertilizer, type 2 a 0-15-20 fertilizer, and type 3 a 10-10-10 fertilizer. (Note that, for these stock fertilizers, the *N-P-K* values represent exact pecentage compositions.)

Pete's decision problem is to determine a minimal-cost "recipe" for the 1000 pounds of 17-14-10 fertilizer; that is, he must determine the least expensive way to blend the three stock fertilizers to obtain 1000 pounds of 17-14-10 fertilizer. To aid his analysis, Pete has summarized his decision problem's data as shown in Table 2.3.

The decision problem Pete faces is a simple instance of a general class of decision problems known as *blending problems*. In such problems, the decision maker seeks a minimal-cost "recipe" for blending several ingredients into a final product that meets certain specifications. As indicated in Table 2.4, these problems arise in the blending of such diverse final products as steel, gasoline, animal feed, and sausage.

Before we use linear programming to solve Pete Moss's blending problem, pretend for a moment you are Pete Moss. Use common sense, intuition, and trial-and-error to recommend a "recipe" for blending 1000 pounds of 17-14-10 fertilizer from 100-pound bags of the three stock fertilizers. Write your recommendation in

TABLE 2.3 Data for Pete Moss's Blending Problem

	Composition of 100-pound Bags			Minimum Permissible Pounds in 1000 lb of 17-14-10
	50-20-5	0-15-20	10-10-10	
Pounds of Nitrogen in a 100-pound Bag	50 lb	0 lb	10 lb	170 lb
Pounds of Phosphorus in a 100-pound Bag	20 lb	15 lb	10 lb	140 lb
Pounds of Potassium in a 100-pound Bag	5 lb	20 lb	10 lb	100 lb
Cost per 100-pound Bag	$90	$20	$30	

TABLE 2.4 Examples of Blending Problems

FINAL PRODUCT	INGREDIENTS	LOWER AND/OR UPPER LIMITS ON SUCH THINGS AS . . .
Fertilizer	"Stock" fertilizers with differing chemical compositions	Nitrogen content Phosphorus content Potassium content
Steel	Pig iron Alloys Silicons "Stock" steels with differing characteristics	Strength Melting point Resistance to rust
Gasoline	Butane Heavy naptha Catalytic reformate	Octane Volatility Vapor pressure
Animal feed	Alfalfa Cornmeal Soybean meal	Grams (per serving size) of protein, fats, carbohydrates, and various vitamins and minerals
Sausage	Various grades of beef Various grades of pork Various grades of lamb Some other things you really don't want to know	Beef content Pork content Lamb content Fat content "Eye appeal" (e.g., coloring and texture)

the boxes below. Later you can compare the cost of your recipe to the minimal-cost recipe we discover via linear programming.

Your Recommendation
for the Number of 100-pound Bags
of Each Stock Fertilizer
to Be Used to Blend 1000 Pounds
of 17-14-10 Fertilizer

Total Cost of
Your Recipe

50-20-5	0-15-20	10-10-10

Formulation of Pete Moss's Blending Problem as a Linear Program

The first step in the formulation process is to define a decision variable to represent each decision Pete must make. We define the following three decision variables:

x_1 = the number of 100-pound bags of 50-20-5 fertilizer used to blend the order for 1000 pounds of 17-14-10 fertilizer

x_2 = the number of 100-pound bags of 0-15-20 fertilizer used to blend the order for 1000 pounds of 17-14-10 fertilizer

x_3 = the number of 100-pound bags of 10-10-10 fertilizer used to blend the order for 1000 pounds of 17-14-10 fertilizer.

The second step in the formulation process is to express Pete's objective of minimizing total cost as a linear function of the variables x_1, x_2, and x_3. Using the costs per 100-pound bag given in Table 2.3's bottom row, we can express Pete's objective as

$$\text{Minimize } 90x_1 + 20x_2 + 30x_3.$$

The third and final step of the formulation process is to write the linear inequalities and equations that constrain the values of x_1, x_2, and x_3. Since the 1000 pound order for 17-14-10 fertilizer is a blend of 100-pound bags of the three stock fertilizers, Pete must use *exactly* ten 100-pound bags; that is, one of the LP's constraints must be the linear equation:

$$x_1 + x_2 + x_3 = 10.$$

Not all values of x_1, x_2, and x_3 that sum to 10 result in a blend that has sufficient nitrogen, phosphorus, and potassium. To illustrate, consider the phosphorus content of a blend of x_1 100-pound bags of 50-20-5 fertilizer, x_2 100-pound bags of 0-15-20 fertilizer, and x_3 100-pound bags of 10-10-10 fertilizer. Using the data in Table 2.3's *second* row, we see that the total pounds of phosphorus in such a blend is

$$
\underbrace{20x_1}_{\begin{pmatrix}\text{Pounds of phosphorus}\\ \text{in } x_1 \text{ bags of}\\ \text{50-20-5 fertilizer}\end{pmatrix}} + \underbrace{15x_2}_{\begin{pmatrix}\text{Pounds of phosphorus}\\ \text{in } x_2 \text{ bags of}\\ \text{0-15-20 fertilizer}\end{pmatrix}} + \underbrace{10x_3}_{\begin{pmatrix}\text{Pounds of phosphorus}\\ \text{in } x_3 \text{ bags of}\\ \text{10-10-10 fertilizer}\end{pmatrix}}
$$

Consequently, to ensure that the phosphorus content of the 1000-pound blend is at least 140 pounds (i.e., 14% of 1000), x_1, x_2, and x_3 must satisfy the linear inequality

$$20x_1 + 15x_2 + 10x_3 \geqslant 140.$$

You should convince yourself, using Table 2.3's first and third rows of data, that the linear inequalities

$$
\begin{aligned}
50x_1 + 0x_2 + 10x_3 &\geqslant 170 \quad \text{(nitrogen content)}\\
5x_1 + 20x_2 + 10x_3 &\geqslant 100 \quad \text{(potassium content)}
\end{aligned}
$$

ensure that the 1000-pound blend has sufficient nitrogen and potassium, respectively.

Besides the single equation and the three $\geqslant$ inequalities, we must not forget to include the three nonnegativity constraints

$$x_1 \geqslant 0, \ x_2 \geqslant 0, \text{ and } x_3 \geqslant 0.$$

Although these seem so obvious that you may wonder about the need to include them, keep in mind that nothing can be taken for granted. The LP "knows" only what we "tell" it. Just as we must include the structural constraint $x_1 + x_2 + x_3 = 10$, we must also include the nonnegativity constraints to ensure that no decision variable assumes a negative value.

Putting together the pieces, we have formulated Pete Moss's blending problem as the LP

Minimize $90x_1 + 20x_2 + 30x_3$	(total cost)
subject to $\quad x_1 + \quad x_2 + \quad x_3 = \quad 10$	(use ten 100-pound bags)
$\quad 50x_1 + \quad 0x_2 + 10x_3 \geqslant 170$	(nitrogen content)
$\quad 20x_1 + 15x_2 + 10x_3 \geqslant 140$	(phosphorus content)
$\quad 5x_1 + 20x_2 + 10x_3 \geqslant 100$	(potassium content)
and $x_1 \geqslant 0, x_2 \geqslant 0, x_3 \geqslant 0$	(nonnegativity)

Observe that, in contrast to our formulation of OMC's product mix problem, the objective function involves minimization (rather than maximization), and the structural constraints consist of a linear equation and three $\geqslant$ linear inequalities (rather than three $\leqslant$ inequalities).

Solving the Blending LP Graphically

At first glance, it appears that we cannot graphically solve our linear programming formulation of Pete Moss's blending problem because it involves three variables. However, because one of the constraints is the equation $x_1 + x_2 + x_3 = 10$, we can convert the three-variable LP into an equivalent two-variable LP. To do so, we rewrite the equation $x_1 + x_2 + x_3 = 10$ as

$$x_3 = 10 - x_1 - x_2$$

and then substitute this expression for x_3 into the objective function and all constraints, *including the nonnegativity constraints*. The substitution proceeds as follows:

Minimize $90x_1 + 20x_2 + 30(10-x_1-x_2)$	$\rightarrow$	Minimize $60x_1 - 10x_2 + 300$
subject to $x_1 + x_2 + (10-x_1-x_2) = 10$	$\rightarrow$	subject to $\quad 10 \quad = 10$
$50x_1 + 0x_2 + 10(10-x_1-x_2) \geqslant 170$	$\rightarrow$	$40x_1 - 10x_2 \geqslant 70$
$20x_1 + 15x_2 + 10(10-x_1-x_2) \geqslant 140$	$\rightarrow$	$10x_1 + 5x_2 \geqslant 40$
$5x_1 + 20x_2 + 10(10-x_1-x_2) \geqslant 100$	$\rightarrow$	$-5x_1 + 10x_2 \geqslant 0$
and $x_1 \geqslant 0$	$\rightarrow$	and $x_1 \geqslant 0$
$x_2 \geqslant 0$	$\rightarrow$	$x_2 \geqslant 0$
$(10-x_1-x_2) \geqslant 0$	$\rightarrow$	$x_1 + x_2 \leqslant 10.$

Observe that

1. The constraint $x_1 + x_2 + (10-x_1-x_2) = 10$ reduces to $10 = 10$, an equation that is always satisfied and can therefore be ignored.

2. The constant 300 appearing in the revised objective function $60x_1 - 10x_2 + 300$ is a "sunk cost" that is incurred regardless of the values

of x_1 and x_2. Consequently, we can temporarily ignore the \$300 and consider the objective function to be $60x_1 - 10x_2$. However, to recover the optimal blend's actual total cost, we must remember to add \$300 to the optimal objective value obtained by using $60x_1 - 10x_2$ as the objective function.

Having made these two observations, we have established the equivalence of our original three-variable LP and the following two-variable LP:

$$\text{Minimize} \quad 60x_1 - 10x_2$$

$$
\begin{aligned}
\text{subject to} \quad & x_1 + x_2 \leqslant 10 \\
& 40x_1 - 10x_2 \geqslant 70 \\
& 10x_1 + 5x_2 \geqslant 40 \\
& -5x_1 + 10x_2 \geqslant 0
\end{aligned}
$$

$$\text{and } x_1 \geqslant 0, x_2 \geqslant 0 \,.$$

After solving this LP, we subtract the optimal values of x_1 and x_2 from 10 to obtain the optimal value of x_3, and we add \$300 to our two-variable LP's optimal objective value to obtain the actual minimal cost of the 1000-pound blend of 17-14-10 fertilizer.

To graphically solve our two-variable linear programming formulation of Pete Moss's blending problem, we proceed exactly as we did for OMC's product mix problem. First, we graph each of the four structural constraints by graphing its boundary equation and determining which half-plane contains all points that satisfy the inequality. Figures 2.11 (a)-(d) contain the four graphs. Figure 2.11(d) deserves special comment because it exhibits a certain "pathological" situation that occurs when a constraint's right-hand side equals 0. Observe that the boundary equation $-5x_1 + 10x_2 = 0$ has only a single intercept, since both the x_1 intercept and the x_2 intercept are the same point, the origin. Consequently, to graph the boundary equation, we need to determine another point on the line. As indicated in Figure 2.11(d), by arbitrarily assuming $x_1 = 6$, we can compute that $x_2 = 3$ must hold; that is, $(x_1, x_2) = (6, 3)$ is a second point on the boundary equation. The pathology persists when we attempt to determine which half-plane contains all points satisfying the inequality $-5x_1 + 10x_2 \geqslant 0$. Because $(0, 0)$ is a point on the boundary equation, we cannot use it as the trial point. Instead, we must choose another point, say, $(1, 1)$. Arbitrarily substituting $(1, 1)$ into the inequality, we see that

$$-5x_1 + 10x_2 = -5(1) + 10(1) = 5 > 0 \,.$$

Consequently, the half-plane containing $(1, 1)$ also contains all other points satisfying the inequality. Before proceeding, you should verify that Figures 2.11(a)–(c) correctly display the graphs of the inequalities $x_1 + x_2 \leqslant 10$, $4x_1 + 10x_2 \geqslant 70$, and $10x_1 + 5x_2 \geqslant 40$, respectively.

Figure 2.12 displays the LP's feasible region, the result of superimposing the shaded regions of Figures 2.11(a)-(d) on a single graph's nonnegative quadrant (remember the nonnegativity constraints!). The shaded region of Figure 2.12 (including the boundary) contains all points that simultaneously satisfy the LP's four structural and two nonnegativity constraints.

As a first step in determining the LP's optimal solution, we arbitrarily choose two "trial" objective values, say, 180 and 300, and determine which feasible points (if any) have such objective values by graphing the parallel *isocost lines*

$$
\begin{aligned}
60x_1 - 10x_2 &= 180 \\
60x_1 - 10x_2 &= 300.
\end{aligned}
$$

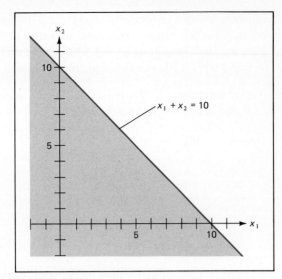

Figure 2.11(a) Graph of $x_1 + x_2 \leqslant 10$

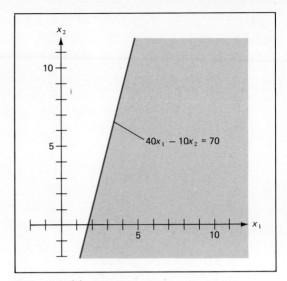

Figure 2.11(b) Graph of $40x_1 - 10x_2 \geqslant 70$

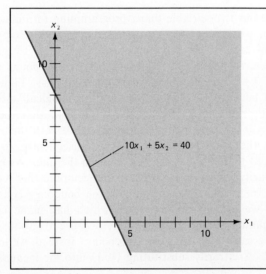

Figure 2.11(c) Graph of $10x_1 + 5x_2 \geqslant 40$

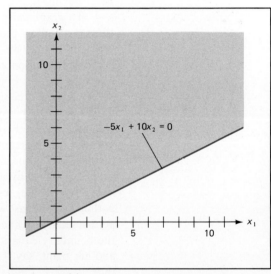

Figure 2.11(d) Graph of $-5x_1 + 10x_2 \geqslant 0$

As indicated in Figure 2.13, these two isocost lines do intersect the feasible region. Actually, this fact itself is unimportant. What is important is the observation that the isocost line with the lower objective value, $60x_1 - 10x_2 = 180$, lies to the northwest (i.e., upward and to the left) of the isocost line with the higher objective value, $60x_1 + 10x_2 = 300$. In other words, lowering the objective value corresponds to northwesterly and parallel shifts in the isocost lines.[6] Graphically, then, we place a straight edge along either of the two isocost lines in Figure 2.13 and slide the straight edge to the northwest, keeping it parallel to the two already graphed isocost lines. As indicated in Figure 2.14, the "last" isocost line to inter-

---

[6] This is not a general conclusion. Lowering the objective value in a minimization LP can, depending on the objective function, correspond to not only northwesterly but also northeasterly, southeasterly, or southwesterly shifts in the isocost lines. A similar statement applies to raising the objective value in a maximization LP.

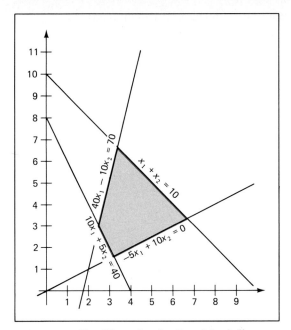

Figure 2.12 Feasible region for Pete Moss's linear program

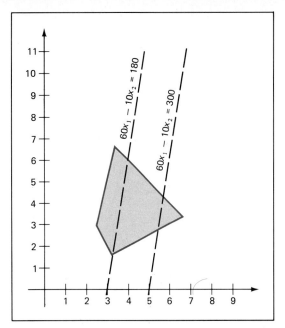

Figure 2.13 Checking for feasible solutions having an objective value of 180 or 300

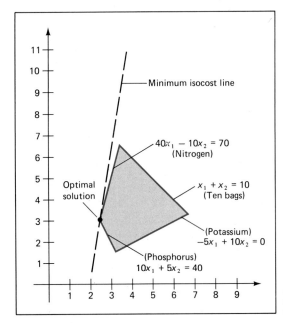

Figure 2.14 Optimal solution of Pete Moss's blending problem

sect the feasible region does so at the point lying at the intersection of the two boundary equations

$$40x_1 - 10x_2 = 70$$
$$10x_1 + 5x_2 = 40.$$

From the graph, it appears that the exact coordinates of this optimal point are $(x_1, x_2) = (2.5, 3.0)$, a fact you may verify by simultaneously solving the above system of equations. Substituting $(2.5, 3.0)$ into the objective function $60x_1 - 10x_2$, we obtain

51

as the optimal objective value. That is, the equation of the isocost line in Figure 2.14 that intersects the feasible region at the optimal solution $(2.5, 3.0)$ is $60x_1 - 10x_2 = 120$.

We now know that the optimal solution to the two-variable LP is $(2.5, 3.0)$ and that the corresponding optimal objective value is 120. To obtain the optimal solution to our original three-variable LP, we proceed as follows:

- Recalling our substitution of $x_3 = 10 - x_1 - x_2$, we recover the optimal value of x_3 by subtracting from 10 the optimal values of x_1 and x_2; that is,

$$x_3 = 10 - 2.5 - 3.0 = 4.5.$$

- Recalling that we temporarily ignored the sunk cost of $300, we note that the actual optimal objective value is not 120 but $120 + 300 = 420$.

To summarize, the optimal solution to our linear programming formulation of Pete Moss's blending problem is

$$(x_1, x_2, x_3) = (2.5, 3.0, 4.5),$$

and the corresponding optimal objective value is 420. In other words, to obtain 1000 pounds of 17-14-10 fertilizer at the minimal cost of $420, Pete Moss should blend 2.5 100-pound bags of 50-20-5 fertilizer, 3.0 100-pound bags of 0-15-20 fertilizer, and 4.5 100-pound bags of 10-10-10 fertilizer.[7]

Like that for OMC's product mix problem, the optimal solution for Pete Moss's blending problem is not integer-valued, even though all the LP's data (i.e., the variables' coefficients and the constraints' right-hand sides) are integer-valued. If Pete does not mind storing partially filled bags of fertilizer for use in filling future orders, the noninteger values of x_1 and x_3 in the optimal solution cause no difficulty. However, if Pete requires that a bag of fertilizer, once opened, must be used immediately, then x_1, x_2, and x_3 must assume integer values; that is, Pete's blending problem is actually an integer linear program.

We have solved for the optimal "recipe" for *1000 pounds* of 17-14-10 fertilizer. Suppose Pete's next order is for 800 pounds of the same type of fertilizer. Since the optimal percentage compositions of the three stock fertilizers in the 1000-pound blend are $(2.5/10) \times 100\% = 25\%$, $(3.0/10) \times 100\% = 30\%$, and $(4.5/10) \times 100\% = 45\%$, respectively, we may conclude that the same percentage compositions are optimal for an order of any amount of 17-14-10 fertilizer. In particular, the optimal "recipe" for 800 pounds is

$$(x_1, x_2, x_3) = (25\% \text{ of } 8, 30\% \text{ of } 8, 45\% \text{ of } 8) = (2.0, 2.4, 3.6).$$

2.10 SURPLUS VARIABLES AND BINDING CONSTRAINTS

In the previous section we determined Pete Moss's optimal "recipe" for 1000 pounds of 17-14-10 fertilizer. Besides the optimal "recipe," Pete will probably want to know the answers to the following questions:

---

[7] How does this compare to the recommendation you made at the beginning of this section?

1. By how much does the nitrogen content of the optimal blend exceed the minimal requirement of 170 pounds?

2. By how much does the phosphorus content of the optimal blend exceed the minimal requirement of 140 pounds?

3. By how much does the potassium content of the optimal blend exceed the minimal requirement of 100 pounds?

As we will see, the answers to these questions are provided by the values of the *surplus variables*. A surplus variable is a variable associated with a $\geqslant$ constraint in a manner analogous to the association of a slack variable with a $\leqslant$ constraint.

To illustrate, consider the potassium content of the optimal blend. In the fourth constraint of the LP formulation of Pete Moss's blending problem, we expressed the requirement that the optimal blend must have at least 100 pounds of potassium as

$$5x_1 + 20x_2 + 10x_3 \geqslant 100 .$$

Consequently, the surplus (i.e., excess) potassium in a blend (x_1, x_2, x_3) is the result obtained by subtracting the constraint's right-hand side from its left-hand side; that is,

$$(5x_1 + 20x_2 + 10x_3) - 100 .$$

We call $(5x_1 + 20x_2 + 10x_3) - 100$ the *surplus variable* for the constraint $5x_1 + 20x_2 + 10x_3 \geqslant 100$. It would be natural to denote this surplus variable by S_4 (S for surplus and the subscript 4 because we are dealing with the LP's fourth constraint). However, since we have already used S as our notation for slack variables, we will avoid confusion by using the notation E_4 (E for excess). To summarize,

$$E_4 = (5x_1 + 20x_2 + 10x_3) - 100 .$$

Using the above linear equation for E_4, we can now easily compute the surplus potassium in a specific blend by substituting the values of x_1, x_2, and x_3. Consider the following three examples:

BLEND (x_1, x_2, x_3)	SURPLUS VARIABLE E_4	=	ACTUAL CONTENT $[5x_1 + 20x_2 + 10x_3]$	−	REQUIRED CONTENT 100		
(3, 4, 3)	E_4	=	[5(3) + 20(4) + 10(3)]	−	100	=	25
(6, 3, 1)	E_4	=	[5(6) + 20(3) + 10(1)]	−	100	=	0
(4, 1, 5)	E_4	=	[5(4) + 20(1) + 10(5)]	−	100	=	−10

The *nonnegative* values of the surplus variable for the blends (3, 4, 3) and (6, 3, 1) indicate that both blends satisfy the requirement that the blend have a potassium content of at least 100 pounds. Note, however, that (3, 4, 3)'s surplus of $E_4 = 25$ indicates that this blend's potassium content exceeds the 100-pound minimum requirement by 25 pounds, whereas (6, 3, 1)'s surplus of $E_4 = 0$ indicates that this blend's potassium content exactly equals the 100-pound minimal requirement (i.e., the surplus is 0). Using the terminology introduced in Section 2.8, we say the constraint $5x_1 + 20x_2 + 10x_3 \geqslant 100$ is *nonbinding* for the blend (3, 4, 3) and *binding* for the blend (6, 3, 1). In contrast to the nonnegative surpluses of the blends

(3, 4, 3) and (6, 3, 1), (4, 1, 5)'s *negative* surplus of $E_4 = -10$ indicates that this blend is infeasible because its potassium content is 10 pounds *below* the 100-pound minimal requirement. In other words, the blend (4, 1, 5) violates the constraint $5x_1 + 20x_2 + 10x_3 \geqslant 100$.

Surplus variables have a graphical interpretation similar to that of slack variables. Recall that, to graphically solve the three-variable linear programming formulation of Pete Moss's blending problem, we converted it into a two-variable LP by substituting for every occurrence of x_3 the expression $10 - x_1 - x_2$. In particular, we converted the three-variable constraint $5x_1 + 20x_2 + 10x_3 \geqslant 100$ into the two-variable constraint $-5x_1 + 10x_2 \geqslant 0$. In the two-variable LP, the surplus variable E_4 still equals the constraint's left-hand side minus its right-hand side; that is,

$$E_4 = (-5x_1 + 10x_2) - 0.$$

Let us recompute the surplus variable E_4 for each of our three example blends, this time using the equation $E_4 = (-5x_1 + 10x_2) - 0$ instead of the equation $E_4 = (5x_1 + 20x_2 + 10x_3) - 100$:

BLEND (x_1, x_2, x_3)	$E_4 = [-5x_1 + 10x_2] - 0$	
(3, 4, 3)	$E_4 = [-5(3) + 10(4)] - 0 =$	25
(6, 3, 1)	$E_4 = [-5(6) + 10(3)] - 0 =$	0
(4, 1, 5)	$E_4 = [-5(4) + 10(1)] - 0 =$	-10

These are the identical values we previously computed for E_4, a consequence of equivalence between the two-variable LP and the original three-variable LP. Consequently, we can graphically illustrate the surplus in the constraint $5x_1 + 20x_2 + 10x_3 \geqslant 100$ through its equivalence to the two-variable constraint $-5x_1 + 10x_2 \geqslant 0$. Figure 2.15 displays the graph of the inequality $-5x_1 + 10x_2 \geqslant 0$, where the shaded region is the half-plane containing all points

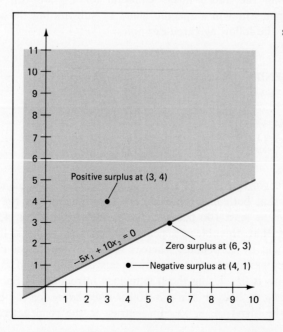

Figure 2.15 Graphical illustration of surplus for constraint $-5x_1 + 10x_2 \geqslant 0$

satisfying the inequality. (This is the same graph as Figure 2.11(d).) Our three example blends are plotted on the graph by simply ignoring the value of x_3. These three points illustrate that a point such as (6, 3) having a surplus of 0 not only satisfies the constraint but also lies on the constraint's boundary equation (i.e., the constraint is binding at the point), a point such as (3, 4) having a positive surplus also satisfies the constraint but lies within the shaded region off the boundary equation, and a point such as (4, 1) having a negative surplus violates the constraint and lies in the unshaded region. These three examples illustrate the following general principles:

- An assignment of values to the decision variables satisfies a $\geq$ constraint if and only if the constraint's surplus variable assumes a nonnegative value.

- A $\geq$ constraint is binding for an assignment of values to the decision variables if and only if the constraint's surplus variable assumes a value of 0. In two dimensions, a constraint is binding at a point if and only if the point lies on the constraint's boundary equation.

We can now answer the questions asked at the beginning of the section about the nitrogen, phosphorus, and potassium content of the optimal blend for 1000 pounds of 17-14-10 fertilizer. For each blending constraint, we define a surplus variable equal to the constraint's left-hand side minus its right-hand side. In particular, besides the previously defined surplus variable E_4 for the LP's fourth constraint, we define surplus variables E_2 and E_3 for the LP's second and third constraints, respectively; that is,

Surplus variable for nitrogen constraint:	$E_2 = (50x_1 + 0x_2 + 10x_3) - 170$
Surplus variable for phosphorus constraint:	$E_3 = (20x_1 + 15x_2 + 10x_3) - 140$
Surplus variable for potassium constraint:	$E_4 = (5x_1 + 20x_2 + 10x_3) - 100.$

Using these linear equations for E_2, E_3, and E_4, we compute the surplus amounts (i.e., amounts in excess of the minimal requirements) of nitrogen, phosphorus, and potassium in the optimal blend (2.5, 3.0, 4.5) as follows:

ELEMENT	SURPLUS VARIABLE = EXCESS AMOUNT IN BLEND (2.5, 3.0, 4.5)
Nitrogen	$E_2 = [50(2.5) + 0(3.0) + 10(4.5)] - 170 = 170 - 170 = 0$
Phosphorus	$E_3 = [20(2.5) + 15(3.0) + 10(4.5)] - 140 = 140 - 140 = 0$
Potassium	$E_4 = [5(2.5) + 20(3.0) + 10(4.5)] - 100 = 117.5 - 100 = 17.5$

Thus, whereas the nitrogen and phosphorus contents of the optimal blend exactly equal the respective minimal requirements, the optimal blend's potassium content is 17.5 pounds in excess of the minimum requirement.

As was the case in Section 2.8 with a slack variable assuming a value of 0, our calculation of $E_2 = 0$ and $E_3 = 0$ was unnecessary. By looking at Figure 2.14, we can see the optimal blend (2.5, 3.0) lies at the intersection of the boundary equations for the nitrogen and phosphorus constraints, thereby implying that these are binding constraints at the optimal solution and that both E_2 and E_3 must equal 0. In contrast, however, observe in Figure 2.14 that, although the optimal blend satisfies the potassium constraint, it does not lie on the constraint's boundary equation. Consequently, although we can use the fact that the potassium constraint is nonbinding at the optimal blend to predict that the surplus variable E_4 is positive, we can determine its exact value only by the computations summarized above.

To summarize the concepts of slack and surplus:

- If an LP's ith constraint is a $\leqslant$ constraint, we associate with it a slack variable S_i equal to the constraint's right-hand side minus its left-hand side. The slack variable serves as a "signpost" that indicates whether a particular assignment of values to the decision variables satisfies or violates the constraint. A nonnegative slack indicates the constraint is satisfied, with a slack of 0 further indicating that the constraint is binding. In contrast, a negative slack indicates the constraint is violated.

- If the LP's ith constraint is a $\geqslant$ constraint, we associate with it a surplus variable E_i equal to the constraint's left-hand side minus its right-hand side. The surplus variable serves as a "signpost" that indicates whether a particular assignment of values to the decision variables satisfies or violates the constraint. A nonnegative surplus indicates the constraint is satisfied, with a surplus of 0 further indicating that the constraint is binding. In contrast, a negative surplus indicates the constraint is violated.

- If the LP's ith constraint is an $=$ constraint (such as $x_1 + x_2 + x_3 = 10$ in Pete's blending LP), then any feasible solution must have no slack or surplus; that is, the $=$ constraint must always be binding at a feasible solution. Consequently, we associate neither a slack variable nor a surplus variable with an $=$ constraint.

In concluding this section we should note that, although our formulation of OMC's product mix problem had $\leqslant$ constraints but no $\geqslant$ constraints and our formulation of Pete Moss's blending problem had $\geqslant$ constraints but no $\leqslant$ constraints, both $\leqslant$ and $\geqslant$ constraints may be present in the same LP.

2.11 THE RELATIONSHIP BETWEEN CORNER-POINT SOLUTIONS AND AN LP'S OPTIMAL SOLUTION

Look again at Figures 2.9 and 2.14, the figures displaying the optimal solutions to OMC's product mix problem and Pete Moss's blending problem, respectively. Observe that the optimal solution to each of the LP's occurs at a "corner" of its respective feasible region, not at a point located in the feasible region's interior and not at a point located on a "edge" of the feasible region between two "corners." We call the feasible solutions that correspond to "corners" of the feasible region *corner-point solutions*.[8] The occurrence in both Figures 2.9 and 2.14 of the optimal solution at a corner-point solution is not a coincidence but rather a graphical illustration of the following general principle:

In searching for an LP's optimal solution, it is sufficient to look only at corner-point solutions.

Before providing additional illustrations of this general principle, it is worthwhile to consider its significance. Observe in Figures 2.9 and 2.14 that, although the feasible regions contain an infinite number of feasible solutions, only a finite number of the feasible solutions are corner-point solutions. In particular, there are five corner-point solutions in Figure 2.9 and four corner-point solutions in Figure

---

[8] Some instructors or textbooks call corner-point solutions *extreme-point solutions*.

2.14. Consequently, in searching for an LP's optimal solution, if we can restrict our attention to corner-point solutions, we need to search only among a finite number of feasible solutions and can ignore the infinite number of other feasible solutions. This fact, we will see later, makes it possible to design an efficient solution method for solving an LP, even one having thousands of variables and constraints.

To provide additional illustrations of the above general principle, let us graphically solve OMC's product mix problem for several alternative objective functions. In particular, consider the following four:

$$\text{Maximize } 1x_1 + 9x_2$$
$$\text{Maximize } 9x_1 + 6x_2$$
$$\text{Maximize } 9x_1 + 3x_2$$
$$\text{Maximize } 9x_1 + 1x_2$$

The second objective function is the one we used in our original formulation of OMC's product mix problem. Its coefficients, 9 and 6, are the respective unit profits of Oranges and Tangerines. The other objective functions might arise if the unit profits for Oranges and Tangerines were other than 9 and 6, respectively. Observe that, as you move down the list, the ratio of the unit profits of Oranges to Tangerines changes from $\frac{1}{9} = 0.111$ to $\frac{9}{6} = 1.5$ to $\frac{9}{3} = 3$ to $\frac{9}{1} = 9$. In other words, Oranges become more and more profitable relative to Tangerines. It is unlikely that the same product mix (x_1, x_2) is optimal for all four objective functions. Intuitively, as we move down the list, we expect the optimal solution's x_1-component (Oranges) to increase and its x_2-component (Tangerines) to decrease.

Figure 2.16 will permit us to use the same graph to solve four LPs, one for each of the alternative objective functions. The figure displays the feasible region common to all four LPs (the same feasible region shown in Figure 2.9). The figure also displays one isoprofit line for each of the four alternative objective functions. In particular, the figure displays the following nonoptimal isoprofit lines:

$$1x_1 + 9x_2 = 9 \text{ for the objective function "Maximize } 1x_1 + 9x_2\text{"}$$
$$9x_1 + 6x_2 = 54 \text{ for the objective function "Maximize } 9x_1 + 6x_2\text{"}$$
$$9x_1 + 3x_2 = 36 \text{ for the objective function "Maximize } 9x_1 + 3x_2\text{"}$$
$$9x_1 + 1x_2 = 9 \text{ for the objective function "Maximize } 9x_1 + 1x_2\text{."}$$

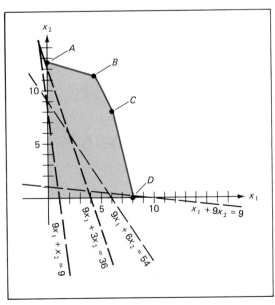

Figure 2.16 Illustration that the optimal solution is always a corner-point solution

You should verify that these isoprofit lines are correctly graphed in Figure 2.16. Now, placing a straight edge along the isoprofit line $x_1 + 9x_2 = 9$, make parallel shifts to the north-northeast until you reach a "point of tangency" at the corner-point solution labeled A. Repeat this general procedure for each of the other three isoprofit lines until you have convinced yourself of the following:

OBJECTIVE FUNCTION	OPTIMAL SOLUTION
Maximize $1x_1 + 9x_2$	Corner-point solution A having exact coordinates $(0 , 12\frac{4}{7})$
Maximize $9x_1 + 6x_2$	Corner-point solution B having exact coordinates $(4\frac{1}{3} , 11\frac{1}{3})$
Maximize $9x_1 + 3x_2$	Corner-point solution C having exact coordinates $(6 , 8)$
Maximize $9x_1 + 1x_2$	Corner-point solution D having exact coordinates $(8 , 0)$

Although each objective function results in a different optimal solution, the optimal solution is always a corner-point solution. Observe that as you move down the list of objective functions and corresponding optimal solutions, the x_1-component increases and the x_2-component decreases, thereby confirming our earlier intuition. Also, observe that the first and fourth objective functions result in optimal solutions in which OMC produces only one type of microcomputer. This illustrates that, contrary to the intuition of some first-time students of linear programming, the optimal values of one or more decision variables may be 0.

There is an important phenomenon not illustrated in Figure 2.16. Consider an objective function for OMC's product mix problem of

$$\text{Maximize } 8x_1 + 4x_2.$$

As illustrated in Figure 2.17 by the parallel isoprofit lines $8x_1 + 4x_2 = 40$, $8x_1 + 4x_2 = 60$, and $8x_1 + 4x_2 = 80$, the "last" isoprofit line to intersect the feasible region intersects at a "line of tangency," not a "point of tangency." Consequently, when the objective function is $8x_1 + 4x_2$, there are an *infinite* number of optimal solutions to OMC's LP, namely the two corner-point solutions labeled B

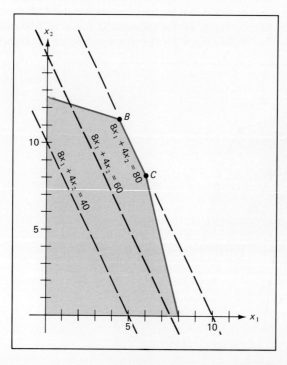

Figure 2.17 Multiple optimality

and C and all points on the line segment between them. This phenomenon is called *multiple optimality*. Multiple optimality is the exception, not the rule. However, when it occurs, it is a "luxury" for the decision maker, because she can employ some secondary criterion not included in the LP to select from among the multiple optimal solutions. For example, if Millie Sekend encounters the multiple optimality illustrated in Figure 2.17, she may choose corner-point solution B, corner-point solution C, or any solution on the line segment between B and C. All yield the same total profit of 80 hundred thousand dollars. Suppose Millie feels that the market for Oranges is stronger than that for Tangerines, despite the Marketing Department's optimism that OMC can sell all the Oranges and Tangerines it can make. Then Millie should implement the product mix corresponding to corner-point solution C, because, among all the multiple optimal solutions, this one produces the most Oranges and the fewest Tangerines.

The examples of this section have illustrated the following general principle:

If an LP has an optimal solution, then one of the following two cases must occur:

1. **Unique optimality.** The LP has a unique (i.e., exactly one) optimal solution, and it occurs at a corner-point solution.

2. **Multiple optimality.** The LP has an infinite number of optimal solutions, but at least two of them are corner-point optimal solutions.

You may be wondering about the need to preface this general principle with the phrase "If an LP has an optimal solution, ..." How can an LP fail to have an optimal solution? The answer to this question is the subject of the next section.

2.12 INFEASIBILITY AND UNBOUNDEDNESS

Infeasibility

Not all LPs have optimal solutions. Consider an LP with some unspecified objective function and the following set of constraints:

$$
\begin{aligned}
1x_1 - 2x_2 &\geq 4 \\
-3x_1 + 1x_2 &\geq 3
\end{aligned}
$$

$$\text{and } x_1 \geq 0, x_2 \geq 0 .$$

Figure 2.18 displays a graph of the boundary equations $x_1 - 2x_2 = 4$ and $-3x_1 + x_2 = 3$. At first glance, it is tempting to conclude that the shaded region in Figure 2.18 is the LP's feasible region. Note, however, that the origin $(0, 0)$ *violates* both of the LP's structural constraints. Consequently, the half plane containing all points satisfying the inequality $x_1 - 2x_2 \geq 4$ is not the one containing the origin but the unshaded one to the *southeast* of the boundary equation $x_1 - 2x_2 = 4$. Similarly, the half plane containing all points satisfying the inequality $-3x_1 + x_2 \geq 3$ is the unshaded one to the *northwest* of the boundary equation $-3x_1 + x_2 = 3$. A feasible solution, then, must be located in the nonnegative quadrant to the southeast of the boundary equation $x_1 - 2x_2 = 4$ *and* to the northwest of the boundary equation $-3x_1 + x_2 = 3$. Clearly, no such point exists! Our example LP is said to be *infeasible*. Infeasibility, then, occurs when the feasible region does not exist.

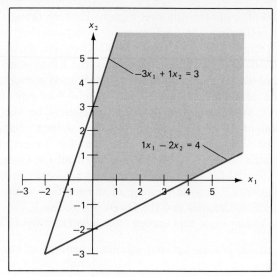

Figure 2.18 A graph used to illustrate infeasibility and unboundedness

In the "real world", infeasible LPs arise in one of three ways:

1. The decision problem is not well posed. For example, the problem's constraints may be so restrictive that no feasible solution exists. In such a case, the constraints must be made less restrictive by raising the right-hand side of one or more $\leqslant$ constraints, lowering the right-hand side of one or more $\geqslant$ constraints, or deleting one or more constraints.

2. The decision problem is well posed, but an error is made in formulating the problem as an LP. Perhaps the verbal description of a particular constraint is incorrectly translated into a linear inequality.

3. The LP is correctly formulated, but, in preparing the input for a computer program to solve the LP, a typing error is made. For example, perhaps a $\leqslant$ constraint's right-hand side is misentered as 100 instead of 1000, thereby making it impossible for a solution to simultaneously satisfy this constraint and the other structural constraints.

Note that whether an LP is infeasible depends solely on its constraints. Changing an infeasible LP's objective function will never overcome infeasibility. Another point worth noting is that infeasibility, although "pathological," is not easily diagnosed. In most instances (such as our example), you cannot recognize by sight that an LP is infeasible. An LP's infeasibility becomes apparent only during an attempt to solve it.

Unboundedness

By slightly modifying the structural constraints of the preceding example, we can illustrate another "pathology" resulting in an LP 's having no optimal solution. In particular, let us change the $\geqslant$ signs in our example's two structural constraints to $\leqslant$ signs. The set of constraints, then, is

$$1x_1 - 2x_2 \leqslant 4$$
$$-3x_1 + 1x_2 \leqslant 3$$

$$\text{and } x_1 \geqslant 0, x_2 \geqslant 0.$$

Observe that the constraint's boundary equations remain unchanged, but now the origin $(0, 0)$ *satisfies* both structural inequalities. Consequently, Figure 2.18's shaded region, extending indefinitely to the northeast, is the LP's feasible region. Although the feasible region exists, it has a characteristic that has the potential to preclude the existence of an optimal solution. Compare Figure 2.18's shaded region to those encountered previously in Figures 2.6 and 2.12. Do you see an important difference? Feasible regions such as those of Figures 2.6 and 2.12 are said to be *closed* because they have finite area. In contrast, a feasible region such as Figure 2.18's shaded region is said to be *open* because it has an infinite area.

When an LP's feasible region is open, it is *possible* (not necessary) that the LP has no optimal solution. To illustrate, consider the following two LP's:

Maximize	$2x_1 - 8x_2$	
subject to	$1x_1 - 2x_2 \leqslant 4$	
	$-3x_1 + 1x_2 \leqslant 3$	
and $x_1 \geqslant 0, x_2 \geqslant 0$.		

Maximize $2x_1 - 1x_2$

subject to $1x_1 - 2x_2 \leqslant 4$
                  $-3x_1 + 1x_2 \leqslant 3$

and $x_1 \geqslant 0, x_2 \geqslant 0$.

Observe that the only difference between the LPs is that the objective function coefficient of x_2 is -8 in the "left-hand" LP and -1 in the "right-hand" LP. As illustrated by the graphing of several parallel isoprofit lines in Figure 2.19(a), the

Figure 2.19(a) An optimal solution exists

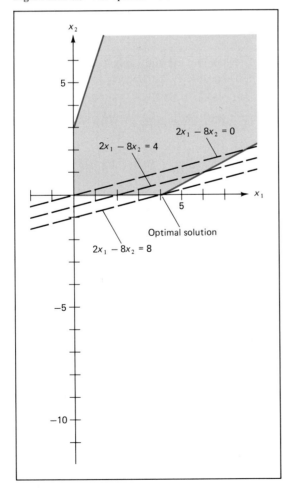

Figure 2.19(b) Unboundedness

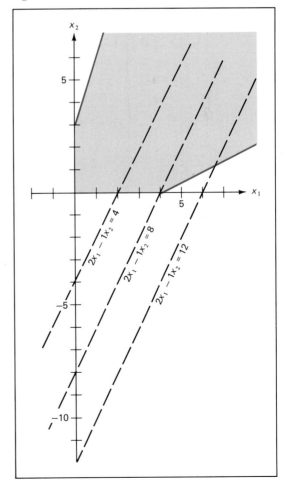

"left-hand" LP's optimal solution is $(x_1, x_2) = (4, 0)$, and the corresponding optimal objective value is 8. In contrast, the graphing of several isoprofit lines in Figure 2.19(b) indicates we can continue indefinitely the process of "sliding" the isoprofit line in a parallel and southeasterly direction. As we continue to do so, we discover feasible solutions with higher and higher objective values. Consequently, we can make the "right-hand" LP's objective value infinitely positive. The "right-hand" LP is said to be *unbounded*. Our two example LPs illustrate the following general principle:

An unbounded LP always has an open feasible region, but an LP with an open feasible region is not always unbounded.

Like an infeasible LP, an unbounded LP is not easily recognized by sight. Our two example LP's illustrate that something as minor as changing an 8 to 1 can change an LP with an optimal solution into an unbounded LP.

In "real-world" problems, unboundedness arises for the same three reasons given above for infeasibility, with one exception. The exception is that, in reason 1, the decision problem is ill posed not because too many constraints have been included but because some important ones have been excluded, thereby resulting in an open feasible region. Once the "missing" constraints are identified and added to the LP, the feasible region will be closed, and the LP will have an optimal solution.

We can summarize our discussions in this and the previous sections as follows:

In attempting to solve an LP, one of the following four cases will occur:

1. **Infeasibility.** The LP has no optimal solution because it has no feasible solution.

2. **Unboundedness.** The LP has no optimal solution because the objective value can be made infinitely positive (i.e., approaching ∞) if maximizing or infinitely negative (i.e., approaching $-\infty$) if minimizing.

3. **Unique Optimality.** The LP has an optimal solution, and it occurs at a corner-point solution.

4. **Multiple Optimality.** The LP has an infinite number of optimal solutions, but at least two are corner-point solutions.

Thus, an LP has either 0, 1, or an infinite number of optimal solutions. There is no such thing as an LP with exactly 2 or exactly 10 optimal solutions.

2.13 REDUNDANT CONSTRAINTS

Before concluding this chapter, we graphically illustrate one last "pathology" of linear programming: a *redundant constraint*. Formally,

A redundant constraint is one whose deletion leaves the feasible region unchanged.

By returning to Figures 2.6 and 2.12, you should convince yourself that neither OMC's product mix LP nor Pete Moss's blending LP contained a redundant constraint. The deletion of any constraint from either of these two LPs increases the area of the LP's feasible region.

Suppose, however, we slightly modify OMC's product mix problem by increasing the availability of assembly labor from 32 to 44 thousand hours. This

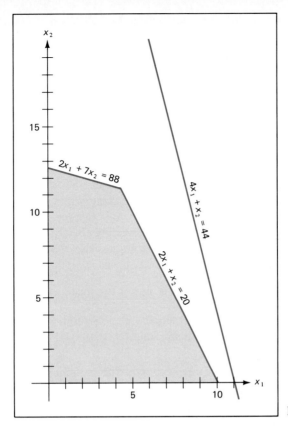

Figure 2.20 A redundant constraint

has the effect of changing the LP's assembly labor constraint from $4x_1 + x_2 \leqslant 32$ to $4x_1 + x_2 \leqslant 44$. Figure 2.20 depicts the feasible region of this revised LP. Observe that changing the right-hand side of the assembly labor constraint from 32 to 44 causes the constraint's boundary equation to shift in a parallel and northeasterly direction. As a result, the half plane containing all points satisfying the inequality $4x_1 + x_2 \leqslant 44$ now includes *as a subset* the revised LP's feasible region. Whereas the assembly labor constraint played a role in determining the feasible region when it was $4x_1 + x_2 \leqslant 32$, deletion of the revised assembly labor constraint $4x_1 + x_2 \leqslant 44$ has no effect on the LP's feasible region. In other words, simply changing the availability of assembly labor from 32 to 44 thousand hours causes the assembly labor constraint to become redundant. This example illustrates an important aspect about redundant constraints:

> Even in a two-variable LP, it is virtually impossible to recognize which, if any, constraints are redundant.

Consequently, although redundant constraints can *in theory* be deleted from an LP without altering the feasible region, *in practice* a redundant constraint usually goes unrecognized.

2.14 A SUMMARY OF THE GRAPHICAL METHOD FOR SOLVING AN LP

We can summarize the steps of the graphical method for solving an LP as follows:

1. Identify the LP's feasible region by superimposing the graph of each of the structural and nonnegativity constraints on the same graph. If the feasible

region does not exist, then the LP is *infeasible* and, consequently, has no optimal solution.

2. If the feasible region exists, then arbitrarily select at least two objective values and graph the corresponding isoprofit lines if the LP involves maximization or the corresponding isocost lines if the LP involves minimization. This establishes not only the slope of every isoprofit or isocost line but also the direction of movement in the isoprofit or isocost line that will improve the objective value.

3. Placing a straight edge (real or imaginary) along one of the isoprofit or isocost lines graphed in Step 2, slide the straight edge in the direction that improves the objective value, maintaining the same slope throughout the sliding process. Stop when any further shift of the straight edge would result in its no longer intersecting the feasible region. If stopping is never called for (i.e., the sliding process can continue indefinitely), then the LP is *unbounded* and, consequently, has no optimal solution.

4. If stopping is called for, one of two cases occurs:

   - The "last" intersection of the straight edge with the feasible region is a single corner-point solution; that is, the LP has a *unique optimal solution.*

   - The "last" intersection of the straight edge with the feasible region is a line segment between two corner-point solutions; that is, the LP has *multiple optimal solutions.* Both corner-point solutions, as well as the infinite number of points on the line segment between them, are optimal solutions.

   Regardless of which case occurs, the exact coordinates of the optimal corner-point solution(s), if they cannot be accurately read directly from the graph, can be determined by simultaneously solving the two boundary equations that intersect at the optimal corner-point solution(s).

5. Obtain the optimal objective value by substituting the decision variables' optimal values into the objective function.

6. For each ≤ constraint, obtain the associated slack variable's value by substituting the decision variables' optimal values into the constraint's left-hand side and subtracting the result from the constraint's right-hand side.

   For each ≥ constraint, obtain the associated surplus variable's value by substituting the decision variables' optimal values into the constraint's left-hand side and subtracting from this result the constraint's right-hand side.

You will gain additional experience with the graphical method while working the exercises at the end of the chapter.

2.15 CONCLUDING REMARKS: THE LIMITATIONS OF LINEAR PROGRAMMING

In some situations a decision maker should not employ linear programming or, if she does, should at least recognize the implications of doing so. A linear programming formulation of a decision problem is most accurate when the following three assumptions are valid:

1. **Linearity.** In an LP, the objective function and the constraint's left-hand sides are linear functions. In Section 2.4, in the context of OMC's product mix problem, we discussed in detail the assumptions underlying the use of a linear objective function and linear constraints. We can summarize these assumptions as follows:

   - **Product independence.** The total profit derived from a particular product is solely a function of the production quantity of that product; that is, the production quantities of the other products are irrelevant.

   - **Constant marginal profit and resource consumptions.** In producing a particular product, there are no economies or diseconomies of scale; consequently, each product's marginal profit remains constant, and each product's marginal consumption of each resource remains constant.

   Even if the LP under consideration is not a product mix LP, similar assumptions underlie the use of a linear objective function and linear constraints. In some instances when these assumptions are not valid, it is still possible to formulate an accurate linear program by using an advanced formulation technique known as *piecewise linear programming,* a technique we will discuss in detail in Chapter 5. In other instances, however, the only alternative will be the use of a nonlinear function to express the objective function or a constraint's left-hand side, thereby resulting in a *nonlinear program,* a subject beyond the scope of this textbook.

2. **Divisibility.** As we saw with both OMC's product mix problem and Pete Moss's blending problem, an LP's optimal solution may have noninteger values for one or more of the decision variables, even when the LP's data are all integer-valued. Consequently, an underlying assumption of linear programming is that the decision variables represent activities that are divisible; that is, there is a meaningful physical interpretation to a decision variable's assuming a noninteger value. If it is physically impossible to implement a solution with noninteger values for one or more decision variables, two courses of action are open to the decision maker:

   - Ignore the integer restrictions on the decision variables, solve the resulting linear program, and round its optimal solution. This rounding strategy will hopefully produce a feasible solution to the integer linear program that can be guaranteed to be acceptably close to optimality. (We illustrated this rounding strategy in Section 2.7 in the context of OMC's product mix problem.)

   - If the rounding strategy is unsuccessful, the decision maker must resort to the more time-consuming and costlier methods for solving integer linear programs.

   Chapter 9 discusses both of the above alternatives.

3. **Deterministic data.** The "output" from an LP consists of the optimal values of the decision variables. This output is only as reliable as the data that serve as "input," namely, the variables' coefficients and the constraints' right-hand sides. For example, in OMC's product mix problem, we illustrated with Figure 2.16 that use of an objective function of $9x_1 + 3x_2$ instead of $9x_1 + 6x_2$ results in an optimal solution of $(x_1, x_2) = (6, 8)$ instead of $(x_1, x_2) = (4\frac{1}{3}, 11\frac{1}{3})$. Consequently, if OMC mistakenly uses 3 instead of 6 for the Tangerine's unit profit, it will solve the "wrong" LP and mistakenly believe that its optimal product mix is $(6, 8)$. This is an example of the following general principle:

An LP's optimal solution does not necessarily remain optimal if changes are made to the LP's data.

We encountered another example of this general principle in Section 2.12, where the change of a single coefficient in the objective function resulted in an LP's becoming unbounded. In formulating an LP, then, we must exercise great care in estimating or computing the constants that serve as the variables' coefficients and the constraints' right-hand sides. Under ideal conditions, we know the LP's data with complete certainty. Such data are said to be *deterministic data.* Unfortunately, ideal conditions are rare. In the "real world," an LP's data are usually *stochastic data* (also called probabilistic data or random data). We cannot specify stochastic data with certainty. Instead, we must estimate or forecast the data, using either rigorous statistical analysis or subjective "guesstimates." By their very nature, estimates and forecasts are not 100% reliable. This uncertainty about the LP's data translates into uncertainty about the LP's optimal solution, uncertainty leading to questions such as, "Is the LP's optimal solution still optimal if the estimate of x_7's objective function coefficient is 10% too high or if the estimate of the third constraint's right-hand side is 5% too low?" The answer to such questions is provided by *sensitivity analysis,* a technique that is introduced in the next chapter. As we will see, sensitivity analysis provides insight into the degree to which an LP's optimal solution is "sensitive" to (i.e., changes in response to) changes in the LP's data.

We can summarize this section's caveats as follows:

Before applying linear programming, a decision maker should ask the following questions:

1. Is it accurate to express the objective function and the constraints' left-hand sides as linear functions?

2. Is an optimal solution with noninteger values acceptable?

3. Are the LP's data deterministic?

To the extent the answer to one or more of these question is "NO!", the decision maker should proceed with caution or possibly even consider abandoning a linear programming approach.

2.16 CHAPTER CHECKLIST AND GLOSSARY

Quickly review this chapter by rereading the material highlighted by a vertical line in the left margin. You should then be familiar with the concepts, techniques, and terminology in the Checklist and Glossary that follow. If you need "help" with a particular item, consult the section or sections indicated for a more detailed discussion.

Checklist of Concepts and Techniques

☐ Graphing linear equations and linear inequalities. [2.2]

☐ The three steps to formulating a decision problem as an LP: (1) defining the decision variables, (2) expressing the objective function as a linear function of the decision variables, and (3) expressing the constraints as linear inequalities or equations. [2.4]

☐ Formulating a product mix problem as an LP. [2.4]

☐ Formulating a blending problem as an LP. [2.9]

☐ Rescaling an LP. [2.5]

☐ Graphically solving a two-variable LP. [2.6, 2.9, 2.14]

☐ Converting a three-variable LP containing an equality constraint into a two-variable LP, thereby permitting a graphical solution. [2.9]

☐ Given the optimal solution that results from ignoring the integer restrictions on the decision variables of an integer linear program, how to round the LP's optimal solution and to compute the rounded solution's guaranteed maximal percentage error. [2.7]

☐ Given values for an LP's decision variables, how to compute the value of the slack variable associated with each $\leq$ constraint and the surplus variable associated with each $\geq$ constraint. [2.8, 2.10]

☐ The usual outcome when solving an LP: a unique optimal solution that is a corner-point solution. [2.11]

☐ The "pathological" outcomes when solving an LP: multiple optimality, infeasibility, and unboundedness. [2.11, 2.12]

☐ The three assumptions underlying the formulation of a decision problem as an LP: (1) linearity, (2) divisibility, and (3) deterministic data. [2.15]

Glossary

Linear function. A mathematical expression in which each term contains a single variable that has an (unwritten) exponent of 1. [2.2]

Linear equation. A mathematical relationship requiring a linear function to equal a constant. [2.2]

Linear inequality. A mathematical relationship requiring a linear function to be either $\leq$ or $\geq$ a constant. [2.2]

Boundary equation. The linear equation that results from replacing a linear inequality's $\leq$ or $\geq$ sign with an $=$ sign. [2.2]

Formulation. The process of translating a verbal statement of a decision problem into an LP. [2.4]

Linear program (LP). A mathematical model seeking values for decision variables that maximize or minimize a linear function while simultaneously satisfying a set of linear constraints. [2.4]

Decision variables. The variables in a LP that represent the decisions that must be made. [2.4]

Objective function. The portion of an LP that specifies the linear function to be maximized or minimized. [2.4]

Nonnegativity constraints. The portion of an LP that specifies that each decision variable must assume a nonnegative value. [2.4]

Structural constraints. The portion of an LP that (besides the nonnegativity constraints) specifies the linear equations and linear inequalities that any assignment of values to the decision variables must satisfy. [2.4]

Product mix LP. An LP seeking the production quantities for a product line that maximize total profit subject to constraints on scarce resources. [2.3]

Blending LP. An LP seeking a minimal-cost "recipe" for blending several ingredients into a final product subject to certain specifications. [2.9]

Integer linear program. An LP with the added requirement that some or all the decision variables must assume integer values. [2.7]

Rescaling. Converting an LP into an equivalent LP having different units of measurement for the decision variables, the objective function, and the constraints. [2.5]

Solution. Any assignment of values to an LP's decision variables. [2.6]

Feasible solution. An assignment of values to an LP's decision variables that satisfies all the LP's structural and nonnegativity constraints. [2.6]

Infeasible solution. An assignment of values to an LP's decision variables that violates at least one of the LP's structural or nonnegativity constraints. [2.6]

Feasible region. The set of all feasible solutions for an LP. [2.6]

Objective value. The value obtained by substituting the values of the decision variables into the objective function. [2.6]

Optimal solution. The feasible solution for an LP that has the best objective value. [2.6]

Optimal objective value. The optimal solution's objective value. [2.6]

Isoprofit (isocost) line. Graphically in two dimensions, a straight line representing the set of all combinations of values for (x_1, x_2) having the same profit (cost). [2.6, 2.9]

Slack variable. Associated with a $\leq$ constraint, a slack variable equals the constraint's right-hand side minus its left-hand side. (In a product mix LP, each slack variable can be interpreted as the amount of a resource that is unconsumed.) [2.8, 2.10]

Surplus variable. Associated with a $\geq$ constraint, a surplus variable equals the constraint's left-hand side minus its right-hand side. (In a blending LP, each surplus variable can be interpreted as the amount by which a minimal requirement is exceeded.) [2.10]

Binding constraint (for a particular assignment of values to the decision variables). A constraint for which, when evaluated at the values of the decision variables, the left-hand side equals the right-hand side (i.e., the constraint's slack or surplus variable equals 0). Graphically in two dimensions, a constraint is binding at a point (x_1, x_2) if (x_1, x_2) lies on the constraint's boundary equation. [2.8, 2.10]

Nonbinding constraint. A constraint that is not binding. Consequently, the constraint's slack or surplus variable is nonzero. [2.8, 2.10]

Corner-point solution. Graphically in two dimensions, a corner-point solution is a feasible solution located at a "corner" of the feasible region — that is, at a point where two boundary equations intersect. [2.11]

Unique optimality. When solving an LP, the one of four possible outcomes in which the LP has exactly one optimal solution. (It will always be a corner-point solution.) [2.11]

Multiple optimality. When solving an LP, the one of four possible outcomes in which the LP has an infinite number of optimal solutions. (At least two will always be corner-point solutions.) [2.11]

Infeasibility. When solving an LP, the one of four possible outcomes in which the LP has no optimal solution because it has no feasible solutions. [2.12]

Unboundedness. When solving an LP, the one of four possible outcomes in which the LP has no optimal solution because the objective value can be made infinitely positive when maximizing or infinitely negative when minimizing. [2.12]

Redundant constraint. A constraint whose removal from the LP leaves the feasible region unchanged. [2.13]

EXERCISES

Exercises 2.1 through 2.7 test your ability to graphically solve a linear program.

2.1. Consider the following LP:

$$\text{Maximize} \quad 3x_1 + 5x_2$$

$$\text{subject to} \quad \begin{aligned} x_1 \quad & \leqslant 4 \\ 2x_2 & \leqslant 12 \\ 3x_1 + 2x_2 & \leqslant 18 \end{aligned}$$

$$\text{and} \quad x_1 \geqslant 0, x_2 \geqslant 0$$

(a) Graph the LP's feasible region.
(b) How many corner points does the feasible region have?
(c) Determine the LP's optimal solution and optimal objective value.
(d) Using the optimal solution's location on the feasible region's graph, determine which of the constraints are binding at the optimal solution and which are nonbinding.
(e) For each structural constraint, determine the optimal value of the slack or surplus variable.

*2.2. Redo Exercise 2.1, this time using the following LP:

$$\text{Maximize} \quad 5x_1 + 10x_2$$

$$\text{subject to} \quad \begin{aligned} -x_1 + 2x_2 & \leqslant 25 \\ x_1 + x_2 & \leqslant 20 \\ 5x_1 + 3x_2 & \leqslant 75 \end{aligned}$$

$$\text{and} \quad x_1 \geqslant 0, x_2 \geqslant 0$$

2.3. Redo Exercise 2.1, this time using the following LP:

$$\text{Minimize} \quad 3x_1 + 5x_2$$

$$\text{subject to} \quad \begin{aligned} x_1 + 5x_2 & \geqslant 20 \\ -3x_1 + 2x_2 & \leqslant 6 \\ x_1 + x_2 & \geqslant 8 \end{aligned}$$

$$\text{and} \quad x_1 \geqslant 0, x_2 \geqslant 0$$

2.4. Redo Exercise 2.1, this time using the following LP:

$$\text{Minimize} \quad 30x_1 + 20x_2$$

$$\text{subject to} \quad \begin{aligned} x_1 \quad & \geqslant 4 \\ 2x_1 + x_2 & = 20 \\ x_1 + 2x_2 & \geqslant 19 \end{aligned}$$

$$\text{and} \quad x_1 \geqslant 0, x_2 \geqslant 0$$

(*Hint*: The feasible region is a line segment.)

2.5. Redo Exercise 2.1, this time using the following LP:

$$\text{Maximize} \quad 3x_1 + 2x_2$$

$$\text{subject to} \quad \begin{aligned} 2x_1 + 4x_2 & \leqslant 22 \\ -x_1 + 4x_2 & \leqslant 10 \\ 2x_1 - x_2 & \leqslant 7 \\ x_1 - 2x_2 & \leqslant 2 \end{aligned}$$

$$\text{and} \quad x_1 \geqslant 0, x_2 \geqslant 0$$

*2.6. Redo Exercise 2.1, this time using the following LP:

$$\text{Maximize} \quad 5x_1 + 4x_2$$

$$\text{subject to} \quad \begin{aligned} 10x_1 + 15x_2 & \leqslant 150 \\ 20x_1 + 20x_2 & \geqslant 100 \\ 20x_1 + 10x_2 & \leqslant 160 \\ -3x_1 + x_2 & \leqslant 3 \end{aligned}$$

$$\text{and} \quad x_1 \geqslant 0, x_2 \geqslant 0$$

2.7. Redo Exercise 2.1, this time using the following LP:

$$\text{Maximize} \quad 10x_1 + 20x_2$$

$$\text{subject to} \quad \begin{aligned} x_1 + 6x_2 & \leqslant 54 \\ x_1 + x_2 & \leqslant 19 \\ -x_1 + x_2 & \leqslant 2 \\ 2x_1 + x_2 & \geqslant 8 \\ 2x_1 - 3x_2 & \leqslant 18 \end{aligned}$$

$$\text{and} \quad x_1 \geqslant 0, x_2 \geqslant 0$$

The following exercise tests your ability to solve a three-variable LP having a structural constraint of the = type by transforming the LP into an equivalent two-variable LP.

2.8. Consider the following LP:

$$\text{Maximize} \quad 40x_1 + 190x_2 + 60x_3$$

$$\text{subject to} \quad \begin{aligned} 3x_1 + x_2 + 2x_3 & \leqslant 18 \\ 3x_1 + 5x_2 + 4x_3 & \geqslant 18 \\ x_1 + 4x_2 + 2x_3 & = 12 \end{aligned}$$

$$\text{and} \quad x_1 \geqslant 0, x_2 \geqslant 0, x_3 \geqslant 0$$

(a) Convert this three-variable LP into an equivalent two-variable LP by: (1) using the third structural constraint to express x_3 in terms of x_1 and x_2 and (2) substituting this expression for x_3 into the objective function and all constraints, including the nonnegativity constraints.

(b) Graphically solve the equivalent two-variable LP.

(c) Use the optimal solution to the equivalent two-variable LP to determine the optimal solution to the original LP.

(d) Redo parts (a)–(c), this time using an objective function of $40x_1 + 130x_2 + 60x_3$.

(e) Redo parts (a)–(c), this time using an objective function of $20x_1 + 130x_2 + 60x_3$.

Exercises 2.9 through 2.16 test your understanding of multiple optimality, infeasibility, and unboundedness.

*2.9. For the LP below, one of the following four cases will occur: (1) unique optimality, (2) multiple optimality, (3) infeasibility, or (4) unboundedness. After solving the LP graphically, specify which case has occurred.

$$\text{Maximize} \quad 5x_1 + 3x_2 \; = 15$$
$$\text{subject to} \quad 2x_1 + 2x_2 \leqslant 10$$
$$-x_1 + x_2 \geqslant 8$$
$$\text{and} \quad x_1 \geqslant 0, x_2 \geqslant 0 \qquad x_1 - x_2 \leqslant 8$$

2.10. Redo Exercise 2.9, this time using the following LP:

$$\text{Maximize} \quad x_1 + x_2$$
$$\text{subject to} \quad -6x_1 + 3x_2 \leqslant 12$$
$$x_1 - x_2 \leqslant 3$$
$$\text{and} \quad x_1 \geqslant 0, x_2 \geqslant 0$$

2.11. Redo Exercise 2.9, this time using the following LP:

$$\text{Maximize} \quad -5x_1 + 2x_2$$
$$\text{subject to} \quad -6x_1 + 3x_2 \leqslant 12$$
$$x_1 - x_2 \leqslant 3$$
$$\text{and} \quad x_1 \geqslant 0, x_2 \geqslant 0$$

(Note that this LP's feasible region is identical to that of the LP in Exercise 2.10.)

2.12. Redo Exercise 2.9, this time using the following LP:

$$\text{Maximize} \quad 9x_1 + 6x_2$$
$$\text{subject to} \quad x_1 \qquad \leqslant 4$$
$$2x_2 \leqslant 12$$
$$3x_1 + 2x_2 \leqslant 18$$
$$\text{and} \quad x_1 \geqslant 0, x_2 \geqslant 0$$

(Note that this LP's feasible region is identical to that of the LP in Exercise 2.1.)

*2.13. Redo Exercise 2.9, this time using the following LP:

$$\text{Maximize} \quad 5x_1 - 2x_2$$
$$\text{subject to} \quad 2x_1 - x_2 \leqslant 10$$
$$-4x_1 + x_2 \leqslant 8$$
$$x_1 - 2x_2 \leqslant 2$$
$$\text{and} \quad x_1 \geqslant 0, x_2 \geqslant 0$$

2.14. Redo Exercise 2.9, this time using the following LP:

$$\text{Maximize} \quad 3x_1 - 2x_2$$
$$\text{subject to} \quad 2x_1 - x_2 \leqslant 10$$
$$-4x_1 + x_2 \leqslant 8$$
$$x_1 - 2x_2 \leqslant 2$$
$$\text{and} \quad x_1 \geqslant 0, x_2 \geqslant 0$$

(Note that this LP's feasible region is identical to that of the LP in Exercise 2.13.)

2.15. Redo Exercise 2.9, this time using the following LP:

$$\text{Maximize} \quad 4x_1 + 6x_2$$
$$\text{subject to} \quad 10x_1 + 15x_2 \leqslant 150$$
$$20x_1 + 20x_2 \geqslant 100$$
$$20x_1 + 10x_2 \leqslant 160$$
$$-3x_1 + x_2 \leqslant 3$$
$$\text{and} \quad x_1 \geqslant 0, x_2 \geqslant 0$$

(Note that this LP's feasible region is identical to that of the LP in Exercise 2.6.)

2.16. Redo Exercise 2.9, this time using the following LP:

$$\text{Minimize} \quad 2x_1 + 5x_2$$
$$\text{subject to} \quad 3x_1 + 2x_2 \leqslant 12$$
$$x_1 - 2x_2 \geqslant 10$$
$$\text{and} \quad x_1 \geqslant 0, x_2 \geqslant 0$$

Exercises 2.17 through 2.19 test your understanding of the geometrical interpretation of slack and surplus variables.

*2.17. The shaded portion of the accompanying figure displays the feasible region for an unspecified LP having two nonnegative decision variables x_1 and x_2 and having three structural constraints whose respective boundary equations are labeled 1 through 3.

70

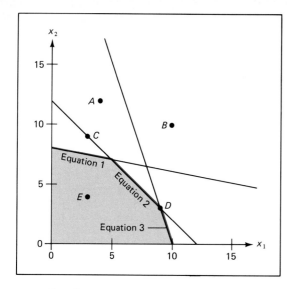

Let $E_1 =$ the surplus variable for the first structural constraint

$E_2 =$ the surplus variable for the second structural constraint.

(a) From the location of point A, determine the sign of each surplus variable (i.e., whether the variable is positive, zero, or negative).
(b) Redo part (a), this time for point B.
(c) Redo part (a), this time for point C.
(d) Redo part (a), this time for point D.
(e) Redo part (a), this time for point E.

2.19. The shaded portion of the accompanying figure displays the feasible region for an unspecified LP having two nonnegative decision variables x_1 and x_2 and having five structural constraints whose respective boundary equations are labeled 1 through 5.

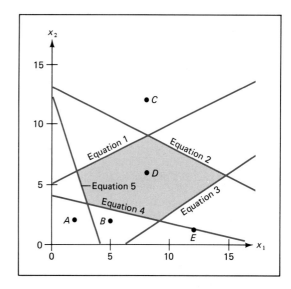

Let $S_1 =$ the slack variable for the first structural constraint

$S_2 =$ the slack variable for the second structural constraint

$S_3 =$ the slack variable for the third structural constraint

$E_4 =$ the surplus variable for the fourth structural constraint

$E_5 =$ the surplus variable for the fifth structural constraint.

(a) From the location of point A, determine the sign of each slack and surplus variable (i.e., whether the variable is positive, zero, or negative).
(b) Redo part (a), this time for point B.
(c) Redo part (a), this time for point C.
(d) Redo part (a), this time for point D.
(e) Redo part (a), this time for point E.

Let $S_1 =$ the slack variable for the first structural constraint

$S_2 =$ the slack variable for the second structural constraint

$S_3 =$ the slack variable for the third structural constraint.

(a) From the location of point A, determine the sign of each slack variable (i.e., whether the variable is positive, zero, or negative).
(b) Redo part (a), this time for point B.
(c) Redo part (a), this time for point C.
(d) Redo part (a), this time for point D.
(e) Redo part (a), this time for point E.

2.18. The shaded portion of the accompanying figure displays the feasible region for an unspecified LP having two nonnegative decision variables x_1 and x_2 and having two structural constraints whose respective boundary equations are labeled 1 and 2.

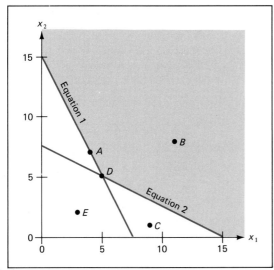

Exercises 2.20 through 2.22 illustrate the concept that an LP's optimal solution always occurs at a corner-point solution.

*2.20. This exercise assumes you have already worked Exercise 2.2. In that exercise, the LP's objective was $5x_1 + 10x_2$. In this exercise, you will resolve the LP with a series of different objective functions and observe that, although the optimal solution changes, it still occurs at a corner-point solution.

(a) Using the graph of the LP's feasible region you drew in Exercise 2.2, locate the corner-point solution that was optimal in Exercise 2.2 when the objective function was $5x_1 + 10x_2$. Label this corner-point solution A. Then, proceeding in a *clockwise* direction, label the remaining corner-point solutions B, C, and so on.

(b) What is the label of the corner-point solution that is optimal when the objective function changes to $15x_1 + 10x_2$?

(c) What is the label of the corner-point solution that is optimal when the objective function changes to $20x_1 + 10x_2$?

(d) Determine a maximizing objective function for which the corner-point solution E is optimal.

2.21. This exercise assumes you have already worked Exercise 2.3. In that exercise, the LP's objective function was $3x_1 + 5x_2$. In this exercise, you will resolve the LP with a series of different objective functions and observe that, although the optimal solution changes, it still occurs at a corner point.

(a) Using the graph of the LP's feasible region you drew in Exercise 2.3, locate the corner-point solution that was optimal in Exercise 2.3 when the objective function was $3x_1 + 5x_2$. Label this corner-point solution A. Then, proceeding in a *counterclockwise* direction, label the remaining corner-point solutions B and C.

(b) What is the label of the corner-point solution that is optimal when the objective function changes to $3x_1 + 2x_2$?

(c) What is the label of the corner-point solution that is optimal when the objective function changes to $x_1 + 6x_2$?

2.22. This exercise assumes you have already worked Exercise 2.7. In that exercise, the LP's objective function was $10x_1 + 20x_2$. In this exercise, you will resolve the LP with a series of different objective functions and observe that, although the optimal solution changes, it still occurs at a corner point.

(a) Using the graph of the LP's feasible region you drew in Exercise 2.7, locate the corner-point solution that was optimal in Exercise 2.7 when the objective function was $10x_1 + 20x_2$. Label this corner-point solution A. Then, proceeding in a *clockwise* direction, label the remaining corner-point solutions B, C, and so on.

(b) What is the label of the corner-point solution that is optimal when the objective function changes to $20x_1 + 10x_2$?

(c) What is the label of the corner-point solution that is optimal when the objective function changes to $10x_1 + 80x_2$?

(d) Determine a maximizing objective function for which the corner-point solution E is optimal.

(e) Determine a maximizing objective function for which the corner point C is optimal.

Exercises 2.23 and 2.24 illustrate that, when integer values are required for all decision variables, solving the LP and rounding the optimal solution may or may not lead to a good approximation to the integer linear program's true optimal solution.

*2.23. Consider the following LP:

$$\text{Maximize} \quad 9x_1 + 7x_2$$
$$\text{subject to} \quad 2x_1 + x_2 \leqslant 10$$
$$4x_1 + 5x_2 \leqslant 40$$
$$\text{and} \quad x_1 \geqslant 0, x_2 \geqslant 0$$

(a) Graph the LP's feasible region.

(b) Determine the LP's optimal solution and the optimal objective value, and observe that the optimal values of x_1 and x_2 are noninteger.

(c) Suppose integer values for x_1 and x_2 are required. Consider the rounded solution obtained by examining the LP's optimal solution and rounding both x_1 and x_2 *upward* to the nearest integer. Verify that this rounded solution is infeasible.

(d) Now consider the rounded solution obtained by examining the LP's optimal solution and rounding x_1 *upward* to the nearest integer and x_2 *downward* to the nearest integer. After verifying that this rounded solution is feasible, compute its maximum percentage error.

(e) Does the rounded solution appear to be a good approximation of the integer linear program's true optimal solution?

2.24. Redo Exercise 2.23, this time using the following LP:

$$\text{Maximize} \quad 10x_1 + 36x_2$$
$$\text{subject to} \quad -4x_1 + 7x_2 \leqslant 3$$
$$2x_1 + 7x_2 \leqslant 18$$
$$\text{and} \quad x_1 \geqslant 0, x_2 \geqslant 0$$

Exercises 2.25 and 2.26 test your ability to rescale an LP.

*2.25. Rescale the following LP so that the variables'

coefficients and the structural constraints' right-hand sides all have approximately the same order of magnitude (i.e., the same number of digits):

Maximize $5000x_1 + 3000x_2$

subject to

$$x_1 + 2x_2 \leqslant 40{,}000$$
$$2x_1 + x_2 \leqslant 25{,}000$$
$$3x_1 + 2x_2 \leqslant 30{,}000$$

and $x_1 \geqslant 0, x_2 \geqslant 0$.

2.26. Redo Exercise 2.25, this time using the following LP:

Maximize $500x_1 + 800x_2$

subject to

$$0.03x_1 + 0.02x_2 \leqslant 240$$
$$200x_1 + 200x_2 \leqslant 2{,}000{,}000$$
$$4x_1 + x_2 \leqslant 32{,}000$$

and $x_1 \geqslant 0, x_2 \geqslant 0$.

Exercises 2.27 through 2.32 test your ability to formulate product mix linear programs and blending linear programs.

*2.27. The Stuffed Animal Division of Coleeko Toy Company (CTC) produces stuffed hawks and doves. Under present market conditions, CTC sells hawks at a profit of $4 and doves at a profit of $2. Hawk skins are tougher and take longer to make than dove skins; in particular, the machine that produces skins must be used for 15 seconds to make a hawk skin and 10 seconds to make a dove skin. On the other hand, hawks require less time to stuff than doves; in particular, the stuffing machine must be used for 10 seconds to stuff a hawk and 15 seconds to stuff a dove. The daily availabilities of the skin machine and the stuffing machine are each 28,800 seconds. Hawks go through a final beak sharpening machine that can process at most 1680 hawks per day; dove beaks are not sharpened. A final constraint arises because CTC's president has a fondness for doves and has specified that at least 720 doves must be produced each day.

(a) Formulate an LP for determining the product mix that maximizes total profit subject to the constraints.
(b) Graph the LP's feasible region.
(c) Determine the LP's optimal solution and optimal objective value.
(d) Using the optimal solution's location on the feasible region's graph, determine which of the constraints are binding at the optimal solution and which are nonbinding.
(e) Which (if any) of the three machines are being used for less time than available?
(f) Is the constraint requiring a minimum dove production binding at the optimal solution?

(g) Resolve the LP assuming the unit profit of doves increases by $0.50. (Assume all other data remain unchanged.)
(h) Resolve the LP assuming the unit profit of doves increases by $1.00. (Assume all other data remain unchanged.)

2.28. The Big Bang Novelty Company makes three basic types of noise-makers: Toot, Wheet, and Honk. A Toot can be made in 30 minutes and has a feather attached to it. A Wheet requires 20 minutes, has two feathers, and is sprinkled with 0.5 ounces of sequin powder. The Honk requires 30 minutes, three feathers, and 1 ounce of sequin powder. The unit profits are $0.45 per Toot, $0.55 per Wheet, and $0.70 per Honk. The following resources are available: 4800 minutes of labor, 90 ounces of sequin powder, and 360 feathers. Formulate an LP for determining the product mix that maximizes total profit subject to the resource constraints.

2.29. A firm is about to introduce a new product. Mark Etting is responsible for planning the advertising campaign during the product's introductory month. Mark has been given a budget of $100,000 for the advertising campaign.

Mark is considering three types of ads: radio ads during the morning commute hours of 6:30 a.m. to 8:30 a.m., TV ads during the prime time hours of 8:00 p.m. to 10:00 p.m., and daily newspaper ads. The firm's advertising agency has provided the following data:

	Advertising Medium		
	Radio	TV	Newspaper
Cost per ad	$1900	$3000	$1400
Number of potential customers exposed to product per ad	35000	70000	50000
Number of units sold per ad	3000	8000	5000

In addition to meeting the $100,000 budget, Mark wants to ensure that the advertising campaign will satisfy several other criteria. In particular,
- A total of 2,500,000 potential customers must be exposed to the product across all media.
- At least 5 ads should appear in each medium.
- No more than 30 ads should appear in any single medium.

(a) Formulate the LP Mark should solve to determine the advertising mix that maximizes total sales subject to the constraints on the advertising campaign.
(b) What aspects of a real-world advertising mix problem are not taken into account in the LP?

2.30. Pittsburgh Iron Company (PIC) is a cast-iron foundry with a contract to produce 10-pound castings whose manganese content is at least 3.6% and whose silicon content is at most 1.7%. To produce the castings, PIC blends two types of pig iron, A and B. The table below provides the composition and cost per pound of each type of pig iron:

	Pig Iron A	Pig Iron B
Percent manganese	6	3
Percent silicon	2	1
Cost per pound	3 cents	2 cents

Assume that unlimited quantities of pig iron A and pig iron B are available to PIC at the indicated costs.

(a) Formulate an LP for determining the blend that satisfies PIC's product requirements at minimum cost.

(b) Graph the LP's feasible region. (*Hint*: The feasible region is a line segment.)

(c) Determine the LP's optimal solution and optimal objective value.

(d) Using the optimal solution's location on the graph of the feasible region, determine which of the constraints are binding at the optimal solution and which are nonbinding.

(e) Does the optimal blend's manganese content exceed the minimum acceptable percentage of 3.6%?

(f) Does the optimal blend's silicon content fall short of the maximum acceptable percentage of 1.7%?

(g) Resolve the LP assuming the cost per pound of pig iron A decreases by 0.5 cents. (Assume all other data remain unchanged.)

(h) Resolve the LP assuming the cost per pound of pig iron A decreases by 1.5 cents. (Assume all other data remain unchanged.)

*2.31 The Hot Dawg Company (HDC) must determine the quantities of beef, chicken, and lamb to use in blending 100 pounds of its Super Sausage. In blending the Super Sausage, HDC must meet the following four product requirements:

- The percentage of the sausage's weight that is protein must be at least 12%.
- The percentage of the sausage's weight that is fat must be at most 24%.
- The percentage of the sausage's weight that is water must be at most 64%.
- The percentage of the sausage's weight that is lamb must be at least 30%.

The table below provides the composition and cost per pound of each type of meat:

	Beef	Chicken	Lamb
Percent protein	20	15	15
Percent fat	20	15	25
Percent water	60	70	60
Cost per pound	$1.00	$0.50	$0.70

Assume that spices and casings contribute an insignificant amount to the total sausage weight and that unlimited quantities of beef, chicken, and lamb are available to HDC at the indicated costs. Formulate an LP for determining the blend that satisfies HDC's product requirements at minimum cost.

2.32. The Harrus Feeding Company (HFC) operates a feedlot to which cattle are brought for the final fattening process. Since HFC's cattle population averages 100,000, it is important for HFC to feed the cattle in a way that meets their nutritional requirements at minimum cost.

The mixture HFC feeds the cattle is a blend of four feedstuffs: corn, wheat, barley, and hay. The table below provides the relevant dietary and cost information per pound of each feedstuff, along with a steer's daily nutritional requirement. For example, for each pound of corn a steer consumes, it receives 2 grams of fat, 20 grams of protein, 4 milligrams of iron, and 200 calories.

(a) Assuming a steer must consume exactly 24 pounds of feedstuffs per day, formulate an LP for determining the dietary blend that satisfies HFC's daily requirements at minimum cost.

(b) How would you modify your formulation if there were no daily limit to the total poundage of feedstuffs a steer must consume?

(c) Can the formulations for parts (a) and (b) lead to distinct optimal solutions? Can you anticipate a potential problem with the optimal solution to part (b)'s LP?

Nutrient	Units of Nutrient per Pound of Feedstuff				Minimum Daily Requirement	Maximum Daily Requirement
	Corn	Wheat	Barley	Hay		
Fat (g)	2	1	3	4	25 g	100 g
Protein (g)	20	15	15	10	400 g	no limit
Iron (mg)	4	7	6	5	125 mg	no limit
Calories	200	400	300	500	6,000	no limit
Cost per pound	60 cents	40 cents	35 cents	5 cents		

3

LINEAR PROGRAMMING: GRAPHICAL SENSITIVITY ANALYSIS AND INTERPRETING COMPUTER OUTPUT

3.1 INTRODUCTION

A "real world" LP usually has so many decision variables and structural constraints that determining the optimal solution requires a computer software package. In this chapter we will discuss how to input data into an LP software package and how to interpret the resulting output.

Organizations wishing to purchase or lease an LP software package have a wide variety to choose from. Table 3.1 summarizes the characteristics typical of the two "extreme" types of LP software packages—those designed primarily for personal computers and those designed primarily for mainframe computers. Today, most LP software packages are of one of these extreme types. However, future advances in computer hardware and software will undoubtedly bring the two extremes closer together. Soon, a user will not need to choose between, say, a personal computer software package's interactive command structure and a mainframe software package's capability to solve extremely large LPs. Both characteristics will be available in a single package.

Commercially available software packages all have one thing in common: they all solve an LP by a sequence of numerical computations known as the *simplex method*. We will discuss the details of the simplex method in a later chapter; for the moment we simply regard it as a "black box" into which we input the LP's data and out of which we receive the LP's optimal solution. We should note that each of the simplex method's computations involves only the basic operations of addition, subtraction, multiplication, and division. The need for a computer arises, then, not because each computation involves complex mathematics but because there are just too many computations to perform manually. For example, even an

TABLE 3.1 Characteristics of LP Software Packages

TYPICAL CHARACTERISTICS OF SOFTWARE PACKAGES FOR PERSONAL COMPUTERS	TYPICAL CHARACTERISTICS OF SOFTWARE PACKAGES FOR MAINFRAME COMPUTERS
Designed for individuals or small businesses.	Designed for large organizations (e.g., oil companies and airlines)
Limited to solving an LP with no more than, say, 500 decision variables and 250 structural constraints.	Capable of solving a very large LP with up to, say, 10,000 decision variables and 5000 structural constraints.
Purchase cost is usually under $1000 for a single-machine license and under $5000 for a site license.	Leasing cost often exceeds $25,000 annually.
Package is "user-friendly" in the sense that it is designed for an LP novice.	User must be an LP expert to fully utilize the package.
Package has *interactive command structure*. The user and the computer "converse" in the sense that the user issues commands one at a time, each time waiting for an on-screen response by the computer before issuing the next command.	Package has *batch command structure*. The user specifies all commands at the start, and the computer then executes these commands without permitting interruption or modification by the user.

LP having only ten decision variables and five structural constraints usually requires thousands of simple numerical computations. Even if a human had the time and patience to perform the computations manually, it is unlikely she would perform them with 100% accuracy.

After we have input the LP's data, a typical personal computer software package automatically displays the LP's optimal objective value and the optimal values of the decision variables, the slack variables, and the surplus variables. Then the software package performs *sensitivity analysis*,[1] which provides insight into how the LP's optimal solution is affected by changes in the LP's data (i.e., the decision variables' objective-function coefficients, the decision variables' constraint coefficients, and the structural constraints' right-hand sides).

The LP's data are only estimates of numerical values that may undergo changes (planned or unplanned) after the LP has been solved. If changes are made in the LP's data, the LP's optimal solution may also change. Consequently, we need to understand how changes in the LP's data affect the LP's optimal solution. For example, suppose that we use a value of 20 as our best estimate of a particular decision variable's objective-function coefficient. If this estimate were to change, would the LP's optimal solution remain the same or would it change? The answer to this and similar questions affects the "credibility" of the LP's optimal solution. We could not confidently implement a solution knowing that it would no longer be optimal if the data were to change slightly. Fortunately, the sensitivity analysis portion of an LP software package provides insight into how the LP's optimal solution is affected by changes in the LP's data. In the "real world," where the changing of data is routine, sensitivity analysis is just as important as the LP's optimal solution.

---

[1] Some instructors, textbooks, and software packages use the terminology *postoptimality analysis*.

We will devote much of the chapter to the topic of sensitivity analysis. Our goal is to illustrate that, for a two-variable LP, we can graphically duplicate the sensitivity analysis performed automatically by an LP software package. Unfortunately, it is impossible to avoid some "messy" algebra. If at times it seems a bit too messy, be patient! Your reward will be a clear understanding of the sensitivity analysis portion of the output of an LP software package.

To graphically illustrate the concepts of sensitivity analysis, we will use Chapter 2's product mix LP for the Orange Microcomputer Corporation (OMC). Recall that, after rescaling, OMC's product mix LP is

$$\text{Maximize} \quad 9x_1 + 6x_2 \qquad \text{(profit)}$$

$$\text{subject to} \quad \begin{aligned} 2x_1 + x_2 &\leqslant 20 \quad \text{(disk drives)} \\ 4x_1 + x_2 &\leqslant 32 \quad \text{(assembly labor)} \\ 2x_1 + 7x_2 &\leqslant 88 \quad \text{(quality assurance labor)} \end{aligned}$$

$$\text{and} \quad x_1 \geqslant 0, x_2 \geqslant 0,$$

where x_1 and x_2 respectively denote the production quantities (in units of 1000) of Oranges and Tangerines.[2] For easier reference, Figure 3.1 reproduces the graphical solution of OMC's LP, displayed previously in Figure 2.9. Observe that the LP's optimal solution is $(x_1, x_2) = (4\frac{1}{3}, 11\frac{1}{3})$ with an optimal objective value of 107.

---

[2] If your memory of OMC's product mix LP is "fuzzy," you should quickly review Sections 2.3–2.6.

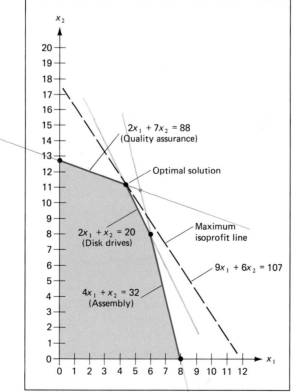

Figure 3.1 Graphical solution of OMC's product mix LP

3.2 SENSITIVITY ANALYSIS OF AN OBJECTIVE-FUNCTION COEFFICIENT

As our first example of sensitivity analysis, let us consider OMC's objective function $9x_1 + 6x_2$ and ask how changes in its coefficients of 9 and 6 affect the optimal solution. (Throughout this section, we assume that there are no changes to the LP's remaining data—that is, the coefficients appearing on the constraints' left-hand sides and the constants appearing on the constraints' right-hand sides.)

Let us denote the objective-function coefficients of x_1 and x_2 by c_1 and c_2, respectively ("c" for coefficient). Currently, with $c_1 = 9$ and $c_2 = 6$, the LP's optimal solution is $(x_1, x_2) = (4\frac{1}{3}, 11\frac{1}{3})$. Of course we should not expect this to be the LP's optimal solution for all values of c_1 and c_2. Intuitively, as c_1 *increases* from its current value of 9 and/or c_2 *decreases* from its current value of 6 (i.e, the Orange's unit profit increases and/or the Tangerine's unit profit decreases), the optimal solution should eventually shift from $(x_1, x_2) = (4\frac{1}{3}, 11\frac{1}{3})$ to a new corner-point solution in which x_1 has increased and x_2 has decreased (i.e., more Oranges and less Tangerines). Similarly, as c_1 *decreases* from its current value of 9 and/or c_2 *increases* from its current value of 6, the optimal solution should eventually shift from $(x_1, x_2) = (4\frac{1}{3}, 11\frac{1}{3})$ to a new corner-point solution in which x_1 has decreased and x_2 has increased.

Although it is possible to analyze the effect of simultaneously changing more than one objective-function coefficient, we (like most software packages) will restrict our attention to the analysis of the effect of changing one objective-function coefficient while holding all others constant at their current values. We will comment briefly on simultaneous changes in Section 3.11.

Throughout our discussion we will make repeated use of the following property of a linear equation $a_1x_1 + a_2x_2 = b$, where a_1, a_2, and b are known constants:

The straight line $a_1x_1 + a_2x_2 = b$ has a slope of

$$\frac{-(\text{coefficient of } x_1)}{(\text{coefficient of } x_2)} = \frac{-a_1}{a_2},$$

regardless of the value of b.

For example, the straight lines $9x_1 + 6x_2 = 54$ and $9x_1 + 6x_2 = 72$ both have a slope of $\frac{-9}{6} = -1.5$. If you are puzzled by this property, you should review Section 2.2.

Sensitivity Analysis of the Objective-Function Coefficient of x_1

Let us first consider the effect on the LP's optimal solution of either increasing or decreasing c_1 from its current value of 9, while holding c_2 constant at its current value of 6. The question we wish to answer is:

If c_2 is held constant at 6, within what range can c_1 vary such that the LP's current optimal solution, $(x_1, x_2) = (4\frac{1}{3}, 11\frac{1}{3})$, remains optimal?

The answer to this question is called c_1's *range of optimality*. We can find c_1's range of optimality using graphical analysis.

Consider first the effect of increasing c_1 from its current value of 9, while holding c_2 constant at its current value of 6. Figure 3.2 (a)–(d) depict the graphical solution of OMC's LP for four increasing values of c_1: $c_1 = 9$ (its current

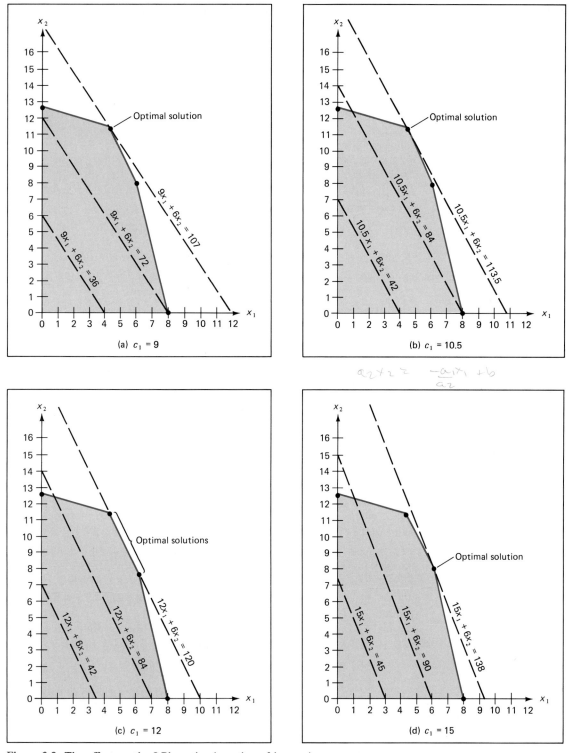

Figure 3.2 The effect on the LP's optimal soution of increasing c_1

value), $c_1 = 10.5$, $c_1 = 12$, and $c_1 = 15$. Each figure displays three parallel isoprofit lines for the objective function $c_1x_1 + 6x_2$, with the most northeast of the isoprofit lines being the optimal one. In each figure the slope of the parallel isoprofit lines is given by

79

$$\text{slope} = \frac{-c_1}{6} = \begin{cases} -1.50 & \text{when } c_1 = 9 & \text{in Figure 3.2(a)} \\ -1.75 & \text{when } c_1 = 10.5 & \text{in Figure 3.2(b)} \\ -2.00 & \text{when } c_1 = 12 & \text{in Figure 3.2(c)} \\ -2.50 & \text{when } c_1 = 15 & \text{in Figure 3.2(d).} \end{cases}$$

Observe that, as c_1 increases from 9 to 10.5 to 12 to 15, the slopes of the isoprofit lines *decrease* (i.e., become more negative), thereby causing the isoprofit lines to rotate in a clockwise direction. This clockwise rotation in the isoprofit lines has the following effect on the LP's optimal solution:

- When $c_1 = 10.5$ in Figure 3.2(b), the clockwise rotation of the isoprofit lines is sufficiently small that the LP's optimal solution is the same as in Figure 3.2(a), $(x_1, x_2) = (4\frac{1}{3}, 11\frac{1}{3})$.

- When $c_1 = 12$ in Figure 3.2(c), the isoprofit lines have rotated the exact amount necessary for them to be parallel to the disk drive boundary equation $2x_1 + x_2 = 20$, thereby creating multiple optimality. The corner-point solutions $(x_1, x_2) = (4\frac{1}{3}, 11\frac{1}{3})$ and $(x_1, x_2) = (6, 8)$ are both optimal, as well as all points on the line segment between them.

- When $c_1 = 15$ in Figure 3.2(d), the clockwise rotation of the isoprofit lines is so great that $(x_1, x_2) = (4\frac{1}{3}, 11\frac{1}{3})$ is no longer an optimal solution. Instead, the LP's optimal solution has "jumped" to $(x_1, x_2) = (6, 8)$.

Figure 3.2(c), then, depicts the maximum permissible clockwise rotation of the isoprofit lines such that the solution $(x_1, x_2) = (4\frac{1}{3}, 11\frac{1}{3})$ remains optimal.

Based on Figure 3.2, we can conclude that, for $9 \leqslant c_1 \leqslant 12$, $(x_1, x_2) = (4\frac{1}{3}, 11\frac{1}{3})$ remains the LP's optimal solution (although, when $c_1 = 12$, multiple optimality exists). When $c_1 > 12$, that solution is no longer optimal. Observe that, although the (x_1, x_2)-coordinates of the LP's optimal solution do not change as c_1 increases from 9 to 12, the LP's optimal objective value does change by an amount equal to the product of the change in c_1 and the optimal value of x_1. For example, if c_1 increases from 9 to 11, the optimal values of the decision variables remain $(4\frac{1}{3}, 11\frac{1}{3})$, but the optimal objective value increases from its current value of 107 by an amount equal to $(11 - 9)(4\frac{1}{3}) = 8\frac{2}{3}$.

Let us now consider the effect of decreasing c_1, while holding c_2 constant at its current value of 6. Figure 3.3 (a)–(d) depict the graphical solution of OMC's LP for four decreasing values of c_1: $c_1 = 9$ (its current value), $c_1 = 6$, $c_1 = 1\frac{5}{7}$, and $c_1 = 1$. Each figure displays three parallel isoprofit lines for the objective function $c_1 x_1 + 6x_2$, with the most northeast of the isoprofit lines being the optimal one. In each figure, the slope of the parallel isoprofit lines is given by

$$\text{slope} = \frac{-c_1}{6} = \begin{cases} -1.5 & \text{when } c_1 = 9 & \text{in Figure 3.3(a)} \\ -1 & \text{when } c_1 = 6 & \text{in Figure 3.3(b)} \\ -\frac{2}{7} & \text{when } c_1 = 1\frac{5}{7} & \text{in Figure 3.3(c)} \\ -\frac{1}{6} & \text{when } c_1 = 1 & \text{in Figure 3.3(d).} \end{cases}$$

Observe that, as c_1 decreases from 9 to 6 to $1\frac{5}{7}$ to 1, the slopes of the isoprofit lines *increase* (i.e., become less negative), thereby causing the isoprofit lines to rotate in a counterclockwise direction. This counterclockwise rotation in the isoprofit lines has the following effect on the LP's optimal solution:

- When $c_1 = 6$ in Figure 3.3(b), the counterclockwise rotation of the isoprofit lines is sufficiently small that the LP's optimal solution is the same as in Figure 3.3(a), $(x_1, x_2) = (4\frac{1}{3}, 11\frac{1}{3})$.

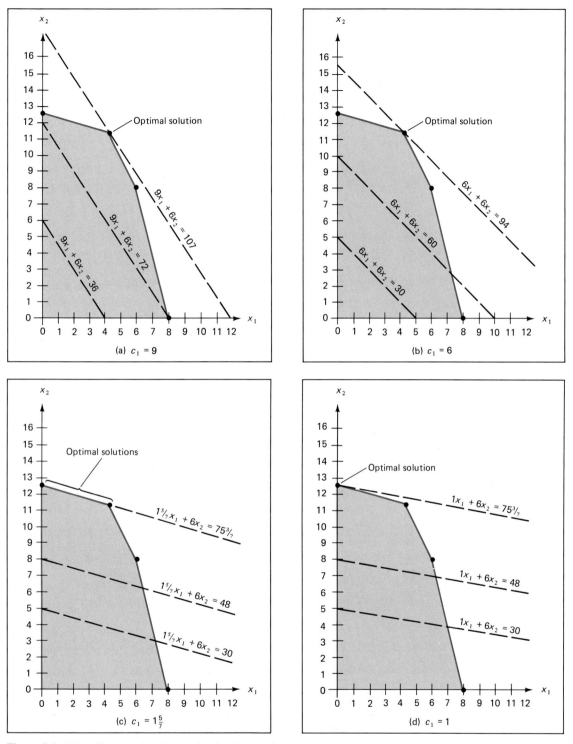

Figure 3.3 The effect on the LP's optimal solution of c_1

- When $c_1 = 1\frac{5}{7}$ in Figure 3.3(c), the isoprofit lines have rotated the exact amount necessary for them to be parallel to the quality assurance boundary equation $2x_1 + 7x_2 = 88$, thereby creating multiple optimality. The corner-point solutions $(x_1, x_2) = (4\frac{1}{3}, 11\frac{1}{3})$ and $(x_1, x_2) = (0, 12\frac{4}{7})$ are both optimal, as well as all points on the line segment between them.

■ When $c_1 = 1$ in Figure 3.3(d), the counterclockwise rotation of the isoprofit lines is so great that $(x_1, x_2) = (4\frac{1}{3}, 11\frac{1}{3})$ is no longer an optimal solution. Instead, the LP's optimal solution has "jumped" to $(x_1, x_2) = (0, 12\frac{4}{7})$.

Figure 3.3(c), then, depicts the maximum permissible counterclockwise rotation of the isoprofit lines such that $(x_1, x_2) = (4\frac{1}{3}, 11\frac{1}{3})$ remains the LP's optimal solution.

Based on Figure 3.3, we can conclude that, for $1\frac{5}{7} \leqslant c_1 \leqslant 9$, $(x_1, x_2) = (4\frac{1}{3}, 11\frac{1}{3})$ remains the LP's optimal solution (although, when $c_1 = 1\frac{5}{7}$, multiple optimality exists). When $c_1 < 1\frac{5}{7}$, $(x_1, x_2) = (4\frac{1}{3}, 11\frac{1}{3})$ is no longer optimal.

Combining the results obtained from Figures 3.2 and 3.3, we see that c_1's range of optimality is $1\frac{5}{7} \leqslant c_1 \leqslant 12$; that is, if c_2 is held constant at its current value of 6, c_1 can vary anywhere in the interval $1\frac{5}{7} \leqslant c_1 \leqslant 12$ without altering the optimality of $(x_1, x_2) = (4\frac{1}{3}, 11\frac{1}{3})$. A range of optimality for c_1 from $1\frac{5}{7} = 1.7143$ to 12 corresponds to a range on the Orange's unit profit from \$171.43 to \$1200.[3] Consequently, when the Orange's unit profit is at least \$171.43 but at most \$1200 (and the LP's other data remain unchanged), OMC's optimal product mix will remain constant at $4\frac{1}{3}$ thousand Oranges and $11\frac{1}{3}$ thousand Tangerines.

Figures 3.2 and 3.3 together illustrate the following general principle:

> Changing a decision variable's objective-function coefficient causes the parallel isoprofit lines to rotate in either a clockwise or counterclockwise direction. If this rotation is sufficiently large, the LP's optimal solution will change.

Now that we understand this general principle, we can simplify the process of computing c_1's range of optimality. In particular, we can let Figure 3.4 do the "work" of Figures 3.2 and 3.3. As Figure 3.4 illustrates, $(x_1, x_2) = (4\frac{1}{3}, 11\frac{1}{3})$ remains

---

[3] Recall that our rescaling of OMC's LP resulted in the objective-function coefficients having a unit of measurement of \$100,000 profit per 1000 computers.

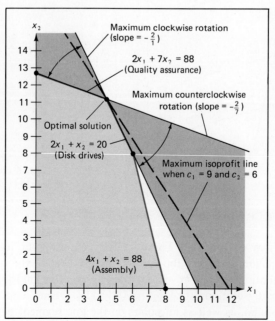

Figure 3.4 Maximum clockwise and counterclockwise rotations in the optimal isoprofit line that do not affect the LP's optimal solution

optimal when the optimal isoprofit line's rotation remains in the figure's light-colored region. In other words, $(x_1, x_2) = (4\frac{1}{3}, 11\frac{1}{3})$ remains optimal when

$$\begin{pmatrix} \text{slope of} \\ \text{disk drive} \\ \text{boundary equation} \\ 2x_1 + x_2 = 20 \end{pmatrix} \leqslant \begin{pmatrix} \text{slope of} \\ \text{optimal isoprofit line} \\ \text{for objective function} \\ c_1 x_1 + 6x_2 \end{pmatrix} \leqslant \begin{pmatrix} \text{slope of} \\ \text{quality assurance} \\ \text{boundary equation} \\ 2x_1 + 7x_2 = 88 \end{pmatrix}$$

Using the fact that the straight line $a_1 x_1 + a_2 x_2 = b$ has a slope of $-a_1/a_2$, the above verbal expression is equivalent to the following mathematical expression:

$$\frac{-2}{1} \leqslant \frac{-c_1}{6} \leqslant \frac{-2}{7}.$$

To simplify this expression, we divide it into two inequalities and solve each individually:[4]

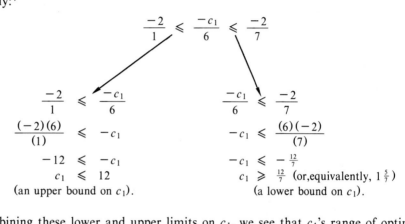

$$\frac{-2}{1} \leqslant \frac{-c_1}{6} \leqslant \frac{-2}{7}$$

$$\frac{-2}{1} \leqslant \frac{-c_1}{6} \qquad\qquad \frac{-c_1}{6} \leqslant \frac{-2}{7}$$

$$\frac{(-2)(6)}{(1)} \leqslant -c_1 \qquad\qquad -c_1 \leqslant \frac{(6)(-2)}{(7)}$$

$$-12 \leqslant -c_1 \qquad\qquad -c_1 \leqslant -\frac{12}{7}$$

$$c_1 \leqslant 12 \qquad\qquad c_1 \geqslant \frac{12}{7} \ (\text{or, equivalently, } 1\frac{5}{7})$$

(an upper bound on c_1). \qquad\qquad (a lower bound on c_1).

Combining these lower and upper limits on c_1, we see that c_1's range of optimality is $1\frac{5}{7} \leqslant c_1 \leqslant 12$, the same as we previously determined using Figures 3.2 and 3.3.

Sensitivity Analysis of the Objective-Function Coefficient of x_2

In computing c_1's range of optimality, we held c_2 constant while investigating the effect of varying c_1. Now let us compute c_2's range of optimality; that is, let us answer the following question:

If c_1 is held constant at 9, within what range can c_2 vary such that the LP's current optimal solution, $(x_1, x_2) = (4\frac{1}{3}, 11\frac{1}{3})$, remains optimal?

Using Figure 3.4, we can find c_2's range of optimality in a manner similar to that employed for c_1. Observe the following:

- The slope of the parallel isoprofit lines for an objective function of "Maximize $9x_1 + c_2 x_2$" is

$$\text{slope} = \frac{-(\text{coefficient of } x_1)}{(\text{coefficient of } x_2)} = \frac{-9}{c_2}.$$

With c_2 equal to its current value of 6, the slope equals $\frac{-9}{6} = \frac{-3}{2}$.

---

[4] Remember that, when solving an inequality, if we multiply both sides by -1, we must also "flip" a $\leqslant$ to a $\geqslant$, or a $\geqslant$ to a $\leqslant$. For example, after multiplying both sides of $-c \leqslant 4$, the inequality becomes $c \geqslant -4$.

- As c_2 increases from its current value of 6, the slope $-9/c_2$ increases (i.e., becomes less negative), thereby causing the parallel isoprofit lines to rotate in a counterclockwise direction.

- As c_2 decreases from its current value of 6, the slope $-9/c_2$ decreases (i.e., becomes more negative), thereby causing the parallel isoprofit lines to rotate in a clockwise direction.

Consequently, using Figure 3.4, we see that $(x_1, x_2) = (4\frac{1}{3}, 11\frac{1}{3})$ remains optimal when the optimal isoprofit line's rotation remains in the figure's crosshatched region, a region bounded by the disk drive's boundary equation with its slope of -2 and the quality assurance boundary equation with its slope of $\frac{-2}{7}$. Mathematically, $(x_1, x_2) = (4\frac{1}{3}, 11\frac{1}{3})$ remains optimal when

$$\frac{-2}{1} \leqslant \frac{-9}{c_2} \leqslant \frac{-2}{7}.$$

As we did when computing c_1's range of optimality, we simplify the above expression by dividing it into two parts and solving each individually:

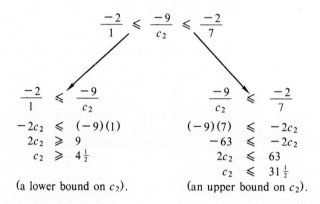

$$\frac{-2}{1} \leqslant \frac{-9}{c_2} \leqslant \frac{-2}{7}$$

$\dfrac{-2}{1} \leqslant \dfrac{-9}{c_2}$	$\dfrac{-9}{c_2} \leqslant \dfrac{-2}{7}$
$-2c_2 \leqslant (-9)(1)$	$(-9)(7) \leqslant -2c_2$
$2c_2 \geqslant 9$	$-63 \leqslant -2c_2$
$c_2 \geqslant 4\frac{1}{2}$	$2c_2 \leqslant 63$
	$c_2 \leqslant 31\frac{1}{2}$
(a lower bound on c_2).	(an upper bound on c_2).

Combining the above lower and upper limits on c_2, we see that c_2's range of optimality is $4\frac{1}{2} \leqslant c_2 \leqslant 31\frac{1}{2}$.

Applications of the Ranges of Optimality

To summarize, we have determined that the ranges of optimality for c_1 and c_2 are

Range of optimality for c_1: $1\frac{5}{7} \leqslant c_1 \leqslant 12$

Range of optimality for c_2: $4\frac{1}{2} \leqslant c_2 \leqslant 31\frac{1}{2}$.

Given current values for c_1 and c_2 of 9 and 6, respectively, an equivalent format for summarizing these ranges of optimality is displayed in Table 3.2. As we will illustrate in a later section, LP software packages often use Table 3.2's format.

Let us use Table 3.2 to analyze three scenarios that illustrate applications of the ranges of optimality. Before reading the discussion that follows each scenario, try to use Table 3.2 to analyze the scenario yourself.

Scenario 1. After solving OMC's product mix LP with $c_1 = 9$ and $c_2 = 6$ and obtaining an optimal solution of $(x_1, x_2) = (4\frac{1}{3}, 11\frac{1}{3})$, OMC decides to increase the Orange's selling price from \$900 to \$1100. Can OMC use Table 3.2 to determine the effect this increase has on the optimal product mix?

TABLE 3.2 Sensitivity Analysis of Objective-Function Coefficients

DECISION VARIABLE	CURRENT VALUE OF COEFFICIENT	MAXIMUM ALLOWABLE INCREASE	MAXIMUM ALLOWABLE DECREASE
x_1	9	3	$7\frac{2}{7}$
x_2	6	$25\frac{1}{2}$	$1\frac{1}{2}$

Analysis: An increase in the Orange's selling price from \$900 to \$1100 corresponds to a change in c_1 from 9 to 11. This 2-unit increase in c_1 is less than the maximum allowable increase specified in Table 3.2's third column. Consequently, $(x_1, x_2) = (4\frac{1}{3}, 11\frac{1}{3})$ remains the LP's optimal solution. Observe that, although the decision variables' optimal values remain unchanged, the optimal objective value does change. The reason is that the former optimal objective value of 107 was based on $c_1 = 9$. With c_1 now increased from 9 to 11 and with x_1's optimal value remaining at $4\frac{1}{3}$, the optimal objective value increases by $(11-9)(4\frac{1}{3}) = 8\frac{2}{3}$.

Scenario 2. After solving OMC's product mix LP with $c_1 = 9$ and $c_2 = 6$ and obtaining an optimal solution of $(x_1, x_2) = (4\frac{1}{3}, 11\frac{1}{3})$, OMC decides to decrease the Tangerine's selling price from \$600 to \$400. Can OMC use Table 3.2 to determine the effect this decrease has on the optimal product mix?

Analysis: A decrease in the Tangerine's selling price from \$600 to \$400 corresponds to a change in c_2 from 6 to 4. This 2-unit decrease in c_2 is more than the maximum allowable decrease specified in Table 3.2's fourth column. Consequently, $(x_1, x_2) = (4\frac{1}{3}, 11\frac{1}{3})$ is no longer the LP's optimal solution. To determine the new optimal solution, OMC must re-solve the LP with c_2 changed from 6 to 4.

Scenario 3. After solving OMC's product mix LP with $c_1 = 9$ and $c_2 = 6$ and obtaining an optimal solution of $(x_1, x_2) = (4\frac{1}{3}, 11\frac{1}{3})$, OMC decides to simultaneously increase the Orange's selling price from \$900 to \$1100 and decrease the Tangerine's selling price from \$600 to \$500. Can OMC use Table 3.2 to determine the effect these simultaneous changes have on the optimal product mix?

Analysis: The answer is "No!", even though c_1's 2-unit increase is less than Table 3.2's maximum allowable increase and c_2's 1-unit decrease is less than Table 3.2's maximum allowable decrease. (Were you fooled?) Remember, we held c_2 constant when computing c_1's range of optimality, and we held c_1 constant when computing c_2's range of optimality. Consequently, we cannot use Table 3.2 to analyze simultaneous changes in the objective-function coefficients. Instead, we must re-solve the LP with c_1 changed from 9 to 11 and c_2 changed from 6 to 5.[5]

A Summary

The following is a summary of the range of optimality of c_j, the objective-function coefficient of x_j:

- The range of optimality of c_j consists of a lower limit on the value of c_j and an upper limit on the value of c_j. (The lower limit may equal $-\infty$ or the upper limit may equal ∞.)

---

[5] As we will discuss in Section 3.11, there exist advanced sensitivity analysis techniques for analyzing simultaneous changes in an LP's data. However, these techniques are beyond the scope of this text.

- If, after solving the LP, the value of c_j changes (and this is the only change in the LP's data), it is unnecessary to re-solve the LP when c_j's new value falls within c_j's range of optimality. The current optimal values of the decision variables will remain optimal, and the optimal objective value will change by the product of the change in c_j and the still-optimal value of x_j.

- Most LP software packages provide us with c_j's range of optimality in a format that is similar to Table 3.2. However, when the LP involves only two decision variables, we can graphically compute the ranges of optimality of c_1 and c_2 by determining the maximum amount the optimal isoquant line can rotate in a clockwise or counterclockwise direction without causing the LP's optimal solution to "jump" to a new corner-point solution.

In closing, we should note that graphically computing a range of optimality can sometimes be a bit more "tricky" than it was for OMC's LP. In particular, Exercises 3.2, 3.4, and 3.5 will illustrate the need for caution when the region of permissible rotation of the optimal isoquant line contains an isoquant line with a slope of 0 or ∞ (i.e., a horizontal or a vertical line).

3.3 SENSITIVITY ANALYSIS OF THE RIGHT-HAND SIDE OF A BINDING CONSTRAINT

We focus now on the effect on the optimal solution of changing the right-hand side of a single structural constraint. We will see that the nature of our sensitivity analysis depends on whether the constraint under consideration is binding or nonbinding at the LP's optimal solution. Recall from Section 2.8 that a structural inequality constraint is binding at a point if and only if the point satisfies the constraint's boundary equation, or, equivalently, the constraint's slack or surplus variable equals 0. Looking at Figure 3.1, we see that the optimal solution to OMC's LP lies at the intersection of the disk drive boundary equation $2x_1 + x_2 = 20$ and the quality assurance boundary equation $2x_1 + 7x_2 = 88$. Thus, at the LP's optimal solution, there are two binding structural constraints, the disk drive constraint and the quality assurance constraint, and one nonbinding structural constraint, the assembly constraint. In this and the next three sections, we will learn how to perform sensitivity analysis first on a binding constraint's right-hand side and then on a nonbinding constraint's right-hand side.

As our first example, let us perform sensitivity analysis on the right-hand side of the binding disk drive constraint $2x_1 + x_2 \le 20$; that is, let us analyze the effect on the LP's optimal solution of changing the availability of disk drives from its current value of 20 thousand. To avoid continually repeating the phrase "the right-hand side of the disk drive constraint," we will use instead the notation RHS_1 (RHS for right-hand side and the subscript 1 because the disk drive constraint is the LP's first structural constraint). Also, we will use the notation Δ to denote the as-yet-unspecified change in the value of RHS_1; that is, RHS_1 will change from its current value of 20 to a new value of $20 + \Delta$. For example, $\Delta = 1$ corresponds to RHS_1 increasing by 1 from 20 to 21, and Δ equals -2 corresponds to RHS_1 decreasing by 2 from 20 to 18. Our sensitivity analysis answers the question:

What is the effect on the LP's optimal solution of changing RHS_1 from 20 to $20 + \Delta$ (assuming all the LP's other data remain unchanged)? [6]

---

[6] Although we will not always add the parenthetic phrase "assuming all the LP's other data remain unchanged," keep in mind that it applies throughout our sensitivity analysis.

For now, let us assume that Δ can only take on values close to 0 (e.g., $\Delta = 0.5$ or $\Delta = -0.5$). Later, we will determine the extent to which our sensitivity analysis remains valid for values of Δ not close to 0.

Sensitivity Analysis Assuming a Small Change in RHS_1

Figures 3.5(a)–(c) depict the graphical solution of OMC's LP for three different values of Δ: $\Delta = 0$ corresponding to no change in RHS_1, $\Delta = 0.5$ corresponding to a small increase in RHS_1, and $\Delta = -0.5$ corresponding to a small decrease in RHS_1. Observe that, since we have not changed the objective-function coefficients, the slope of the optimal isoprofit line (shown only in Figure 3.5(a)) is the same in all three figures. Differing from figure to figure, however, are the coordinates of the LP's optimal solution. In particular, observe the following:

- In Figure 3.5(a) when RHS_1 equals its current value of 20, the LP's optimal solution lies at point A, the intersection of the disk drive boundary equation $2x_1 + x_2 = 20$ and the quality assurance boundary equation $2x_1 + 7x_2 = 88$. In other words, the disk drive constraint and the quality assurance constraint are the binding constraints at the LP's optimal solution.

- In Figure 3.5(b) when RHS_1 increases from its current value of 20 by a small amount, the LP's feasible region expands as the disk drive boundary equation shifts in a parallel and northeast direction. As the equation shifts to the northeast, its intersection with the stationary quality assurance boundary equation "slides" to the southeast. Consequently, the LP's optimal solution "slides down" the stationary quality assurance boundary equation from point A to point B.

- In Figure 3.5(c) when RHS_1 decreases from its current value of 20 by a small amount, the LP's feasible region contracts as the disk drive boundary equation shifts in a parallel and southwest direction. As the equation shifts to the southwest, its intersection with the stationary quality assurance boundary equation "slides" to the northwest. Consequently, the LP's optimal solution "slides up" the stationary quality assurance boundary equation from point A to point C.

To summarize, Figure 3.5(a)–(c) together illustrate the following general principle:

> A small change in a binding constraint's right-hand side causes the constraint's boundary equation to shift slightly in a parallel direction, thereby resulting in the LP's optimal solution "sliding" a small distance to the new point of intersection of the binding constraints' boundary equations.

In the particular case of the disk drive constraint, changing its right-hand side by a small amount Δ causes a parallel shift in the disk drive boundary equation, thereby resulting in the LP's optimal solution "sliding" to the new point of intersection of the shifting disk drive boundary equation $2x_1 + x_2 = 20 + \Delta$ and the stationary quality assurance boundary equation $2x_1 + 7x_2 = 88$. Mathematically, then, when Δ is close to 0, the LP's optimal solution is the simultaneous solution to the system of equations

$$2x_1 + x_2 = 20 + \Delta \quad \text{(shifted disk drive boundary equation)}$$
$$2x_1 + 7x_2 = 88 \quad \text{(stationary quality assurance boundary equation)}.$$

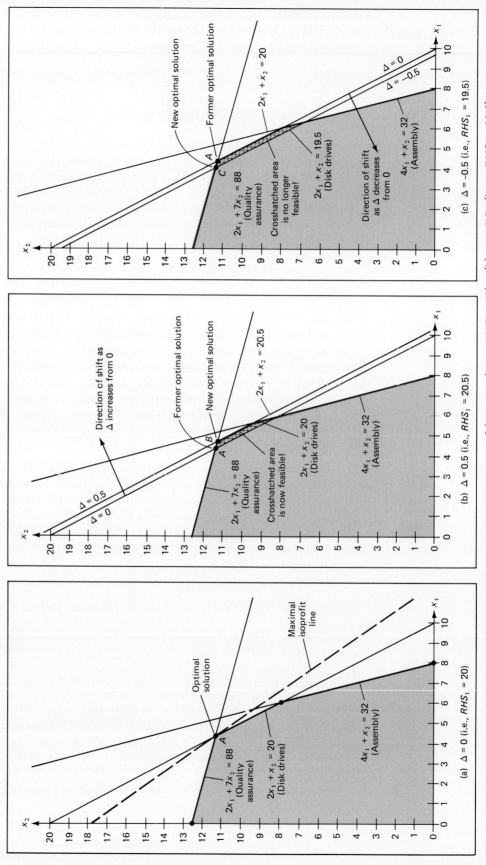

Figure 3.5 The effect on the LP's optimal solution if a small change in RHS_1: (a) $\Delta = 0$ (i.e., $RHS_1 = 20$), (b) $\Delta = 0.5$ (i.e., $RHS_1 = 20.5$), (c) $\Delta = -0.5$ (i.e., $RHS_1 = 19.5$)

For example, if $\Delta = 0.5$, the LP's optimal solution is the simultaneous solution to

$$2x_1 + x_2 = 20.5$$
$$2x_1 + 7x_2 = 88,$$

or, if $\Delta = -0.5$, the LP's optimal solution is the simultaneous solution to

$$2x_1 + x_2 = 19.5$$
$$2x_1 + 7x_2 = 88.$$

We do not need to know the specific value of Δ before solving the system of equations. Instead, we can use the method of substitution (introduced in Section 2.6) to solve

$$2x_1 + x_2 = 20 + \Delta$$
$$2x_1 + 7x_2 = 88$$

for values of x_1 and x_2 expressed in terms of Δ. The computations (a bit "messy"!) proceed as follows:

1. First, we select the system's "top" equation, $2x_1 + x_2 = 20 + \Delta$, and solve for x_1 in terms of x_2 and Δ:

$$2x_1 + x_2 = 20 + \Delta \rightarrow 2x_1 = 20 + \Delta - x_2$$
$$\rightarrow x_1 = 10 + \tfrac{1}{2}\Delta - \tfrac{1}{2}x_2$$

2. Next, we substitute this expression for x_1 into the system's "bottom" equation, $2x_1 + 7x_2 = 88$, and then solve for x_2 in terms of Δ:

$$2x_1 + 7x_2 = 88 \rightarrow 2(10 + \tfrac{1}{2}\Delta - \tfrac{1}{2}x_2) + 7x_2 = 88$$
$$\rightarrow 20 + \Delta - x_2 + 7x_2 = 88$$
$$\rightarrow 6x_2 = 68 - \Delta$$
$$\rightarrow x_2 = 11\tfrac{1}{3} - \tfrac{1}{6}\Delta$$

3. Finally, we substitute this expression for x_2 into Step 1's expression for x_1 and solve for x_1 in terms of Δ:

$$x_1 = 10 + \tfrac{1}{2}\Delta - \tfrac{1}{2}x_2 \rightarrow x_1 = 10 + \tfrac{1}{2}\Delta - \tfrac{1}{2}(11\tfrac{1}{3} - \tfrac{1}{6}\Delta)$$
$$\rightarrow x_1 = 10 + \tfrac{1}{2}\Delta - 5\tfrac{2}{3} + \tfrac{1}{12}\Delta$$
$$\rightarrow x_1 = 4\tfrac{1}{3} + \tfrac{7}{12}\Delta.$$

Hence, from the results obtained in Steps 2 and 3, we see that the LP's optimal solution expressed in terms of Δ is

$$(x_1, x_2) = (4\tfrac{1}{3} + \tfrac{7}{12}\Delta, 11\tfrac{1}{3} - \tfrac{1}{6}\Delta).$$

Let us now compute in terms of Δ the optimal objective value and the optimal values of the structural constraints' slack variables. First we substitute $x_1 = 4\tfrac{1}{3} + \tfrac{7}{12}\Delta$ and $x_2 = 11\tfrac{1}{3} - \tfrac{1}{6}\Delta$ into the LP's objective function $9x_1 + 6x_2$. The computations proceed as follows:

$$9x_1 + 6x_2 = 9(4\tfrac{1}{3} + \tfrac{7}{12}\Delta) + 6(11\tfrac{1}{3} - \tfrac{1}{6}\Delta)$$
$$= 39 + \tfrac{21}{4}\Delta + 68 - \Delta$$
$$= 107 + \tfrac{17}{4}\Delta.$$

To obtain the optimal values of the constraints' slack variables, recall from Section 2.8 that the slack variable for a particular $\leqslant$ constraint equals the constraint's right-hand side minus its left-hand side; that is,

$$\text{Disk drive constraint's slack variable:} \quad S_1 = (20 + \Delta) - (2x_1 + x_2)$$
$$\text{Assembly constraint's slack variable:} \quad S_2 = 32 - (4x_1 + x_2)$$
$$\text{Quality assurance constraint's slack variable:} \quad S_3 = 88 - (2x_1 + 7x_2) .$$

To determine the values of S_1, S_2, and S_3, we could substitute $x_1 = 4\frac{1}{3} + \frac{7}{12}\Delta$ and $x_2 = 11\frac{1}{3} - \frac{1}{6}\Delta$ into the above expressions. However, with a little thought, we can predict that both $S_1 = 0$ and $S_3 = 0$, thereby saving some "messy" algebra. Do you see why? The reason is that, since we computed $(x_1, x_2) = (4\frac{1}{3} + \frac{7}{12}\Delta, 11\frac{1}{3} - \frac{1}{6}\Delta)$ as the simultaneous solution to the disk drive boundary equation $2x_1 + x_2 = 20 + \Delta$ and the quality assurance boundary equation $2x_1 + 7x_2 = 88$, the disk drive constraint and the quality assurance constraint are binding constraints and, therefore, their corresponding slack variables must equal 0. Since the assembly constraint is nonbinding, we can determine the value of its slack variable only by substituting $x_1 = 4\frac{1}{3} + \frac{7}{12}\Delta$ and $x_2 = 11\frac{1}{3} - \frac{1}{6}\Delta$ into the above expression for S_2. The computations proceed as follows:

$$S_2 = 32 - [(4)(4\frac{1}{3} + \frac{7}{12}\Delta) + (1)(11\frac{1}{3} - \frac{1}{6}\Delta)]$$
$$= 32 - 17\frac{1}{3} - \frac{7}{3}\Delta + 11\frac{1}{3} - \frac{1}{6}\Delta$$
$$= 3\frac{1}{3} - \frac{13}{6}\Delta .$$

Table 3.3 (temporarily ignore the first three columns) summarizes our sensitivity analysis of RHS_1 for values of Δ close to 0. Given such a value, Table 3.3 permits us to immediately update the LP's optimal solution without having to re-solve the LP. To obtain the new optimal solution, we simply substitute the value of Δ into the table's last six columns and simplify. For example, if $\Delta = \frac{1}{2}$, the LP's new optimal solution is

$$
\begin{aligned}
x_1 &= 4\frac{1}{3} + \frac{7}{12}(\frac{1}{2}) = 4\frac{5}{8} \\
x_2 &= 11\frac{1}{3} - \frac{1}{6}(\frac{1}{2}) = 11\frac{1}{4} \\
S_1 &= \qquad\qquad\quad = 0 \\
S_2 &= 3\frac{1}{3} - \frac{13}{6}(\frac{1}{2}) = 2\frac{1}{4} \\
S_3 &= \qquad\qquad\quad = 0 \\
\text{Objective value} &= 107 + \frac{17}{4}(\frac{1}{2}) = 109\frac{1}{8}
\end{aligned}
$$

Let us now determine the extent to which our sensitivity analysis of RHS_1 is valid for values of Δ that are not close to 0. In particular, let us determine a positive upper limit on Δ and a negative lower limit on Δ such that our sensitivity analysis remains valid when Δ is between these two limits.

Our sensitivity analysis is based on the observation that, despite the shifts in the disk drive constraint, the LP's optimal solution continues to lie at the "sliding"

TABLE 3.3 Sensitivity Analysis of RHS_1

RHS_1's CURRENT VALUE	RHS_1's MAXIMUM ALLOWABLE INCREASE	RHS_1's MAXIMUM ALLOWABLE DECREASE	OPTIMAL VALUES					
			x_1	x_2	S_1	S_2	S_3	OBJECTIVE VALUE
20	$1\frac{7}{13}$	$7\frac{3}{7}$	$4\frac{1}{3} + \frac{7}{12}\Delta$	$11\frac{1}{3} - \frac{1}{6}\Delta$	0	$3\frac{1}{3} - \frac{13}{6}\Delta$	0	$107 + \frac{17}{4}\Delta$

intersection of the shifting disk drive boundary equation and the stationary quality assurance boundary equation, and, therefore, is the solution to the system of equations

$$2x_1 + x_2 = 20 + \Delta \quad \text{(shifted disk drive boundary equation)}$$
$$2x_1 + 7x_2 = 88 \qquad \text{(stationary quality assurance boundary equation)}.$$

In other words, despite the shifts in the disk drive boundary equation, the disk drive constraint and the quality assurance constraint continue to be binding at the LP's optimal solution. When this observation remains true, our sensitivity analysis remains valid. Hence, we must answer the following question:

> *Within what range of values can Δ vary such that the constraints that are currently binding at the LP's optimal solution continue to be binding?*

The answer to this question is known as the *range of validity* for the sensitivity analysis of RHS_1. In the next two subsections we will compute the upper and lower limits of the range of validity.

Determining the Range of Validity's Upper Limit

How positive can Δ get without invalidating our sensitivity analysis? Figure 3.6 can help us answer this question. To see how, observe the following aspects of the figure:

- When $\Delta = 0$, the disk drive boundary equation is in Position 0. Now imagine Δ increasing from 0 to the as-yet-unknown positive value that results in the disk drive boundary equation shifting in a parallel and northeast direction to Position 1. As the equation shifts to Position 1, the LP's optimal solution "slides" southeast from Point A to Point B, always lying at the intersection of the shifting disk drive boundary equation $2x_1 + x_2 = 20 + \Delta$ and the stationary quality assurance boundary equation $2x_1 + 7x_2 = 88$. In other words, as the disk drive boundary equation shifts from Position 0 to Position 1, the disk drive constraint and the quality assurance constraint continue to be binding at the LP's optimal solution. Thus, when Δ does not exceed the as-yet-unknown positive value corresponding to Position 1 of the disk drive boundary equation, our sensitivity analysis remains valid.

- Now imagine Δ increasing further to a value that results in the disk drive boundary equation shifting to Position 2. The LP's optimal solution does not slide from Point B to Point C but instead remains stationary at Point B. The reason is that, once the disk drive boundary equation shifts to the northeast of Position 1, its intersection with the stationary quality assurance boundary equation is no longer optimal because it now lies outside the feasible region. The up-to-now binding disk drive constraint is now nonbinding, and the up-to-now nonbinding assembly constraint has replaced the disk drive constraint as one of the two binding constraints. Consequently, when Δ exceeds the as-yet-unknown value corresponding to Position 1, our sensitivity analysis becomes invalid.

To summarize, the range of validity's upper limit is the as-yet-unknown positive value of Δ that makes the disk drive boundary equation $2x_1 + x_2 = 20 + \Delta$ shift to Position 1, thereby passing through Point B.

There are several ways to compute this value of Δ. The easiest way is to observe in Figure 3.6 that, during its southeast "slide" from Point A to Point B, the

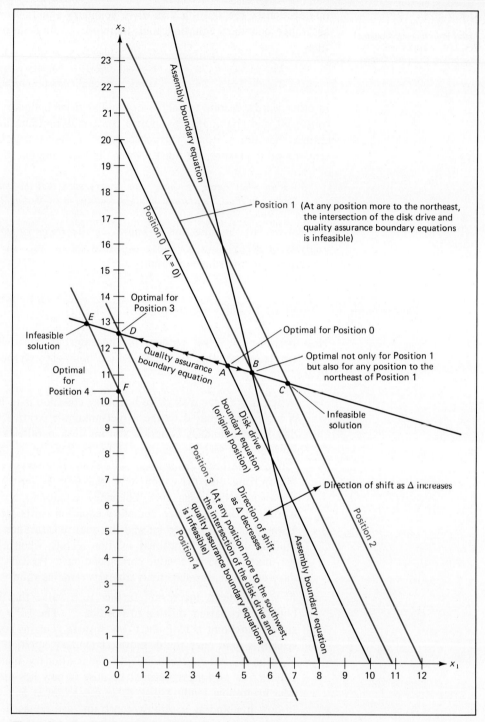

Figure 3.6 The effect changing RHS_1 has on the LP's optimal solution

optimal solution gets closer and closer to the assembly boundary equation $4x_1 + x_2 = 32$, and, when it reaches Point B, the optimal solution actually lies on the assembly boundary equation. In other words, the assembly constraint's slack variable S_2 gets smaller and smaller and finally assumes a value of 0. This graphical observation is borne out algebraically by Table 3.3, which indicates that $S_2 = 3\frac{1}{3} - \frac{13}{6}\Delta$, an expression that decreases toward 0 as Δ increases from 0.

Hence, the range of validity's upper limit is that positive value of Δ that results in S_2 assuming a value of 0. To find this value of Δ, we need only set $S_2 = 3\frac{1}{3} - \frac{13}{6}\Delta$ equal to 0 and solve for Δ. The computations proceed as follows:

$$3\tfrac{1}{3} - \tfrac{13}{6}\Delta = 0 \quad \rightarrow \quad \tfrac{13}{6}\Delta = \tfrac{10}{3} \quad \rightarrow \quad \Delta = 1\tfrac{7}{13} \approx 1.538 \,.$$

Thus, when $0 \leqslant \Delta \leqslant 1\frac{7}{13}$, our sensitivity analysis remains valid. Any value of Δ greater than $1\frac{7}{13}$ invalidates the sensitivity analysis because it results in a negative value of S_2 and, therefore, an infeasible solution.

Determining the Range of Validity's Lower Limit

How negative can Δ get without invalidating our sensitivity analysis? To answer this question, return to Figure 3.6 and observe the following:

- When $\Delta = 0$, the disk drive boundary equation is in Position 0. Now imagine Δ decreasing from 0 to the as-yet-unknown negative value that results in the disk drive boundary equation shifting in a parallel and southwest direction to Position 3. As the equation shifts to Position 3, the LP's optimal solution "slides" northwest from Point A to Point D, always lying at the intersection of the shifting disk drive boundary equation $2x_1 + x_2 = 20 + \Delta$ and the stationary quality assurance boundary equation $2x_1 + 7x_2 = 88$. In other words, the disk drive constraint and the quality assurance constraint continue to be binding at the LP's optimal solution. Thus, when Δ is less negative than the as-yet-unknown negative value corresponding to Position 3 of the disk drive boundary equation, our sensitivity analysis remains valid.

- Now imagine Δ decreasing to a value that results in the disk drive boundary equation shifting to Position 4. The LP's optimal solution does not "slide" from Point D to Point E but instead "turns the corner" and then "slides" down from Point D to Point F. The reason is that, once the disk drive boundary equation shifts to the southwest of Position 3, its intersection with the stationary quality assurance boundary equation is no longer optimal because it now lies outside the feasible region. The up-to-now binding quality assurance constraint is now nonbinding, and the up-to-now nonbinding nonnegativity constraint on x_1 has replaced the quality assurance constraint as one of the two binding constraints. Consequently, when Δ is more negative than the as-yet-unknown value corresponding to Position 3, our sensitivity analysis becomes invalid.

To summarize, the range of validity's lower limit is the as-yet-unknown negative value of Δ that makes the disk drive boundary equation $2x_1 + x_2 = 20 + \Delta$ shift to Position 3, thereby passing through Point D.

The easiest way to compute this value of Δ is to observe in Figure 3.6 that, during its northwest "slide" from Point A to Point D, the optimal solution gets closer and closer to the boundary equation $x_1 = 0$, and, when it reaches Point D, the optimal solution actually lies on the boundary equation $x_1 = 0$. In other words, the decision variable x_1 gets smaller and smaller and finally assumes a value of 0. This graphical observation is borne out algebraically by Table 3.3, which indicates that $x_1 = 4\frac{1}{3} + \frac{7}{12}\Delta$, an expression that decreases toward 0 as Δ decreases from 0. Hence, the range of validity's lower limit is that negative value of Δ that results in x_1 assuming a value of 0. To find this value of Δ, we need only set $x_1 = 4\frac{1}{3} + \frac{7}{12}\Delta$ equal to 0 and solve for Δ. The computations proceed as follows:

$$4\tfrac{1}{3} + \tfrac{7}{12}\Delta = 0 \quad \rightarrow \quad \tfrac{7}{12}\Delta = -\tfrac{13}{3} \quad \rightarrow \quad \Delta = -7\tfrac{3}{7} \approx -7.429 \,.$$

Thus, when $-7\frac{3}{7} \leqslant \Delta \leqslant 0$, our sensitivity analysis remains valid. Any value of Δ more negative than $-7\frac{3}{7}$ invalidates the sensitivity analysis because it results in a negative value of x_1 and, therefore, an infeasible solution.

Applications

Returning to Table 3.3, we see that the first three columns summarize the range of validity for our sensitivity analysis of RHS_1. Let us now use Table 3.3 to analyze two scenarios that illustrate applications of our sensitivity analysis. Before reading the analysis that follows each scenario, you should attempt to use Table 3.3 to analyze the scenario yourself.

Scenario 1. After we have solved OMC's product mix LP and obtained an optimal solution of $(x_1, x_2) = (4\frac{1}{3}, 11\frac{1}{3})$ and an optimal objective value of 107, we learn that the number of available disk drives has decreased from 20,000 to 18,500. Can we use Table 3.3 to determine the LP's new optimal solution?

Analysis: A decrease in disk drive availability from 20,000 to 18,500 corresponds to a decrease in the disk drive constraint's right-hand side from 20 to $18\frac{1}{2}$, a decrease of $1\frac{1}{2}$. This decrease is well below the maximum allowable decrease indicated in Table 3.3's third column. Consequently, using Table 3.3's last six columns, we see that the LP's new optimal solution is

$$
\begin{aligned}
x_1 &= 4\tfrac{1}{3} + \tfrac{7}{12}\left(-\tfrac{3}{2}\right) &=& \ 3\tfrac{11}{24} \\
x_2 &= 11\tfrac{1}{3} - \tfrac{1}{6}\left(-\tfrac{3}{2}\right) &=& \ 11\tfrac{7}{12} \\
S_1 &= &=& \ 0 \\
S_2 &= 3\tfrac{1}{3} - \tfrac{13}{6}\left(-\tfrac{3}{2}\right) &=& \ 6\tfrac{7}{12} \\
S_3 &= &=& \ 0 \\
\text{Objective value} &= 107 + \tfrac{17}{4}\left(-\tfrac{3}{2}\right) &=& \ 100\tfrac{5}{8}
\end{aligned}
$$

Scenario 2. After we have solved OMC's product mix LP and obtained an optimal solution of $(x_1, x_2) = (4\frac{1}{3}, 11\frac{1}{3})$ and an optimal objective value of 107, we learn that the number of available disk drives has increased from 20,000 to 22,000. Can we use Table 3.3 to determine the LP's new optimal solution?

Analysis: An increase in disk drive availability from 20,000 to 22,000 corresponds to an increase in the disk drive constraint's right-hand side from 20 to 22, an increase of 2. This increase exceeds the maximum allowable increase indicated in Table 3.3's second column. Consequently, we cannot use Table 3.3 to determine the LP's new optimal solution. Instead, we must re-solve the LP with the disk drive constraint's right-hand side now equal to 22.

3.4 THE SHADOW PRICE OF A CONSTRAINT

A most important application of sensitivity analysis of a resource constraint's right-hand side is that it enables us to determine the maximum unit price that we should pay to acquire additional units of the resource. To illustrate, consider the following scenario:

An opportunity arises for OMC to obtain additional disk drives beyond the current availability of 20,000. What is the maximum unit price OMC should pay for additional disk drives?

To answer this question, we need to understand the concept of the *shadow price* of a constraint, a concept defined as follows:[7]

> The *shadow price* of a constraint is the rate of improvement in the LP's optimal objective value per unit increase in the constraint's right-hand side. (*Note*: The "rate of improvement" in the optimal objective value is the "rate of increase" in an LP involving maximization and the "rate of decrease" in an LP involving minimization.)

Can you use the sensitivity analysis summarized in Table 3.3 to determine the shadow price of the disk drive constraint? The answer is $\frac{17}{4}$, the coefficient of Δ in the $107 + \frac{17}{4}\Delta$ appearing in Table 3.3's last column. The expression $107 + \frac{17}{4}\Delta$ indicates that the optimal objective value improves from 107 at the rate of $\frac{17}{4} = 4.25$ per unit increase in RHS_1. Recall that OMC's objective-function value is measured in units of \$100,000 and that RHS_1 is measured in units of 1000 disk drives. Hence, a shadow price of 4.25 implies that OMC's optimal objective value increases at the rate of \$425,000 per additional 1000 disk drives or, equivalently, at the rate of \$425 per additional disk drive.

Since the shadow price of \$425 represents the rate of improvement in the optimal objective value per additional disk drive, it is tempting to conclude that \$425 is the maximum unit price OMC should pay for additional disk drives. However, the correct price is the sum of two terms, the shadow price of \$425 plus the unit price of disk drives already accounted for in the objective function. In other words, the shadow price is the maximum unit price OMC should pay over and above the unit price already accounted for in the unit profits of the Orange and Tangerine microcomputers. To illustrate, consider the following two possibilities relating to the status of the original 20,000 disk drives available to OMC:

> **Case 1.** OMC has a contract with a disk drive vendor to purchase up to 20,000 disk drives at a unit price of \$300, with the exact purchase quantity not specified until after OMC has decided on its production plan. Under such a contract, OMC's disk drive acquisition cost is a *variable cost*—that is, a cost dependent on its production plan. Consequently, when OMC computes the unit profit of the dual-drive Orange, it must include (2)(\$300) as a portion of the variable cost subtracted from the Orange's selling price. Similarly, when OMC computes the unit profit of the single-drive Tangerine, it must include \$300 as a portion of the variable cost subtracted from the Tangerine's selling price. Since the unit price of disk drives is included in the computations of the unit profits of the Orange and Tangerine, the LP's objective value represents OMC's net profit after the acquisition of any necessary disk drives at a unit price of \$300. Therefore, when the disk drive constraint's shadow price of \$425 indicates that the optimal objective value will rise by \$425 per additional disk drive, the \$425 represents a net figure that already accounts for paying \$300 for each additional disk drive. From the \$425 figure must be deducted only the amount paid in excess of the \$300 already accounted for; that is, the increase in net profit is given by
>
> $$(\text{increase in net profit}) = (\text{shadow price of \$425}) - \begin{pmatrix} \text{amount by which} \\ \text{actual unit price} \\ \text{exceeds the \$300} \\ \text{already accounted for in} \\ \text{the objective function} \end{pmatrix}$$
>
> Hence, OMC's net profit will increase when it pays a premium for additional disk drives of less than \$425 over and above the \$300 unit price already accounted for in

---

[7] In place of *shadow price*, some instructors, textbooks, or LP software packages use the terminology *dual price*.

the objective function. For example, suppose OMC pays $650 per additional disk drive, a premium of $350 more than the $300 unit price already accounted for. Then the increase in net profit is

$$
\text{(increase in net profit)} = \text{(shadow price)} - \left(\begin{array}{l} \text{amount by which the} \\ \text{actual unit price} \\ \text{exceeds the \$300} \\ \text{already accounted for in} \\ \text{the objective function} \end{array}\right)
$$

$$
= \quad \$425 \ - \quad (\$650 - \$300)
$$
$$
= \quad \$75
$$

To summarize Case 1, the disk drive constraint's shadow price of $425 is the maximum unit price OMC should pay over and above the unit price already accounted for in the objective function. (When OMC pays a premium of exactly $425, the increase in net profit is zero. At this point OMC neither gains nor loses by making the buy and is *indifferent* as to whether it buys or not. Customarily we assume that it will buy.)

Case 2. OMC has a contract with the disk drive vendor to purchase exactly 20,000 disk drives at a unit price of $300, regardless of the number of disk drives required by OMC's production plan. Under such a contract, OMC's disk drive acquisition cost is a *sunk cost*—that is, a cost independent of its production plan. Consequently, when OMC computes the unit profits of Oranges and Tangerines, the unit price of disk drives will play no role. Instead, after determining the objective value of the LP's optimal production plan, OMC will compute its net profit by subtracting its sunk costs. Since the unit price of disk drives is not included in the computation of the unit profits of Oranges and Tangerines, the LP's objective value represents a gross profit before the acquisition of any disk drives at a unit price of $300. Therefore, when the disk drive constraint's shadow price of $425 indicates that the optimal objective value will rise by $425 per additional disk drive, the $425 is only a gross figure that neglects the entire cost of disk drive acquisition. From this $425 figure must be deducted the entire unit cost of an additional disk drive; that is, the increase in net profit is

$$
\text{(increase in net profit)} = \$425 - \text{(entire unit price)} .
$$

Hence, OMC's net profit will increase when it pays less than $425 per additional disk drive. To summarize Case 2, the disk drive constraint's shadow price of $425 is the maximum unit price OMC should pay to acquire additional disk drives. Observe that it is still correct to say that the shadow price represents the maximum unit price OMC should pay over and above the unit price already accounted for in the objective function, because the unit price already accounted for is 0!

Although Cases 1 and 2 are quite different, we can summarize them with a common general principle:

In an LP involving the maximization of profit, the shadow price of a resource-availability constraint is the maximum unit price over and above the unit price already accounted for in the objective function that should be paid to acquire additional units of the resource. The increase in net profit per additional unit of the resource is

$$
\left(\begin{array}{l} \text{increase in net profit} \\ \text{per additional unit} \\ \text{of the resource} \end{array}\right) = \left(\begin{array}{l} \text{resource's} \\ \text{shadow} \\ \text{price} \end{array}\right) - \left(\begin{array}{l} \text{amount by which the actual unit price} \\ \text{exceeds the unit price already accounted} \\ \text{for in the objective function} \end{array}\right) .
$$

Portions of subsequent sections will be devoted to expanding our understanding of shadow prices. At this point we should stress that the disk drive constraint's shadow price of $425 applies only to an increase in disk drive availability of no more than $1\frac{7}{13}$ thousand disk drives, the maximum allowable increase specified in Table 3.3. For example, suppose OMC were offered 2 thousand additional disk drives at a unit price of $350 over and above that already included in the objective function. Unfortunately, we cannot use the shadow price of $425 to quickly decide if the acquisition of the 2 thousand disk drives will yield an increase in net profit. Our sensitivity analysis guarantees only that the first $1\frac{7}{13}$ thousand disk drives will yield an increase in net profit of $425 - $350 = $75 per additional disk drive. We can say nothing about the profitability of acquiring disk drives beyond the first $1\frac{7}{13}$ thousand. To determine if it is profitable to acquire the entire 2 thousand disk drives, OMC's only alternative is to re-solve its LP with RHS_1 increased from 20 to 22 and compare the resulting increase in the optimal objective value with the incremental cost of acquiring the additional 2 thousand disk drives.

3.5 MORE ON SENSITIVITY ANALYSIS OF A BINDING CONSTRAINT'S RIGHT-HAND SIDE

Let us now proceed with sensitivity analysis of the quality assurance constraint $2x_1 + 7x_2 \leqslant 88$. As we perform this analysis, note its similarity with that performed in Section 3.3 for the disk drive constraint $2x_1 + x_2 \leqslant 20$. At the end of this section we will summarize a general procedure for performing sensitivity analysis of the right-hand side of a constraint that is binding at optimality.

Since the quality assurance constraint is the LP's third structural constraint, we will denote its right-hand side by RHS_3, and we will denote by Δ the change in RHS_3 from its current value of 88. The question we wish to answer with our sensitivity analysis is:

What is the effect on the LP's optimal solution of changing RHS_3 from 88 to 88 $+ \Delta$ (assuming all the LP's other data remain unchanged)? [8]

As we did with our sensitivity analysis of the disk drive constraint, let us first make the assumption that Δ can only take on values close to 0 and then subsequently determine the extent to which our sensitivity analysis remains valid for values of Δ not close to 0.

Determination of the Optimal Solution's Coordinates in Terms of Δ

Figures 3.7(a)–(c) depict the graphical solution of OMC's LP for three different values of Δ: $\Delta = 0$ corresponding to no change in RHS_3, $\Delta = 0.5$ corresponding to a small increase in RHS_3, and $\Delta = -0.5$ corresponding to a small decrease in RHS_3. (Since the maximal isoprofit line is shown only in Figure 3.7(a), you will have to imagine it in the other two figures.) Figures 3.7(a)–(c) are similar to Figures 3.5(a)–(c), except that the changes in Δ now cause the quality assurance boundary equation to shift instead of the disk drive boundary equation. In particular, observe the following:

---

[8] Although we will not always add the parenthetic phrase "assuming all the LP's other data remain unchanged," keep in mind that it applies throughout our sensitivity analysis.

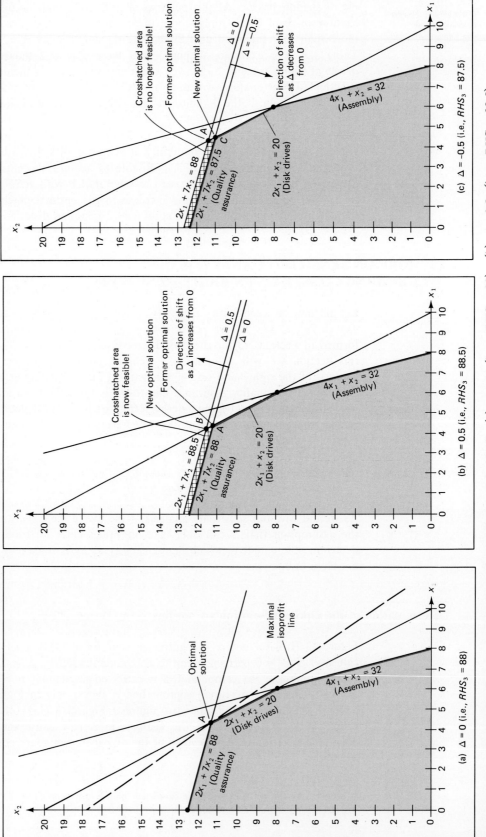

Figure 3.7 The effect on the LP's optimal solution of a small change in RHS_3: (a) $\Delta = 0$ (i.e., $RHS_3 = 88$), (b) $\Delta = 0.5$ (i.e., $RHS_3 = 88.5$), (c) $\Delta = -0.5$ (i.e., $RHS_3 = 87.5$).

- In Figure 3.7(a) when RHS_3 equals its current value of 88, the LP's optimal solution lies at Point A, the intersection of the disk drive boundary equation $2x_1 + x_2 = 20$ and the quality assurance boundary equation $2x_1 + 7x_2 = 88$. In other words, the disk drive constraint and the quality assurance constraint are the binding constraints at the LP's optimal solution.

- In Figure 3.7(b) when RHS_3 increases from its current value of 88 by a small amount, the LP's feasible region expands as the quality assurance boundary equation shifts in a parallel and northeast direction. As the equation shifts, its intersection with the stationary disk drive boundary equation "slides" to the northwest. Consequently, the LP's optimal solution "slides up" the stationary disk drive boundary equation from Point A to Point B.

- In Figure 3.7(c) when RHS_3 decreases from its current value of 88 by a small amount, the LP's feasible region contracts as the quality assurance boundary equation shifts in a parallel and southwest direction. As the equation shifts, its intersection with the stationary disk drive boundary equation "slides" to the southeast. Consequently, the LP's optimal solution "slides down" the stationary disk drive boundary equation from Point A to Point C.

To summarize Figure 3.7(a)–(c), changing RHS_3 by a small amount Δ causes a parallel shift in the quality assurance boundary equation, thereby resulting in the LP's optimal solution "sliding" to the new point of intersection of the shifting quality assurance boundary equation $2x_1 + 7x_2 = 88 + \Delta$ and the stationary disk drive boundary equation $2x_1 + x_2 = 20$. Mathematically, then, when Δ is close to 0, we can determine the LP's optimal solution by solving the simultaneous system of equations

$$2x_1 + x_2 = 20 \qquad \text{(stationary disk drive boundary equation)}$$
$$2x_1 + 7x_2 = 88 + \Delta \qquad \text{(shifted quality assurance boundary equation)}$$

for x_1 and x_2 in terms of Δ. Using the method of substitution, you can verify for yourself that the simultaneous solution to this system of equations is

$$(x_1, x_2) = (4\tfrac{1}{3} - \tfrac{1}{12}\Delta, 11\tfrac{1}{3} + \tfrac{1}{6}\Delta).$$

Determination of the Optimal Values of the Slack Variables

Since the disk drive constraint and the quality assurance constraint remain binding when Δ is close to 0, their slack variables S_1 and S_3 retain their values of 0. Thus we need only compute the value of S_2, the slack variable of the assembly constraint that remains nonbinding at the LP's optimal solution (for small values of Δ). To compute S_2 in terms of Δ, we substitute $x_1 = 4\tfrac{1}{3} - \tfrac{1}{12}\Delta$ and $x_2 = 11\tfrac{1}{3} + \tfrac{1}{6}\Delta$ into the assembly constraint's left-hand side and subtract the result from the constraint's right-hand side. The computations proceed as follows:

$$\begin{aligned} S_2 &= 32 - [(4)(4\tfrac{1}{3} - \tfrac{1}{12}\Delta) + (1)(11\tfrac{1}{3} + \tfrac{1}{6}\Delta)] \\ &= 32 - 17\tfrac{1}{3} + \tfrac{1}{3}\Delta - 11\tfrac{1}{3} - \tfrac{1}{6}\Delta \\ &= 3\tfrac{1}{3} + \tfrac{1}{6}\Delta . \end{aligned}$$

Determination of the Optimal Objective Value

To determine the LP's optimal objective value in terms of Δ, we simply substitute $x_1 = 4\tfrac{1}{3} - \tfrac{1}{12}\Delta$ and $x_2 = 11\tfrac{1}{3} + \tfrac{1}{6}\Delta$ into the LP's objective function $9x_1 + 6x_2$.

TABLE 3.4 Sensitivity Analysis of RHS_3

RHS_3's CURRENT VALUE	RHS_3's MAXIMUM ALLOWABLE INCREASE	RHS_3's MAXIMUM ALLOWABLE DECREASE	OPTIMAL VALUES					
			x_1	x_2	S_1	S_2	S_3	OBJECTIVE VALUE
88	52	20	$4\frac{1}{3} - \frac{1}{12}\Delta$	$11\frac{1}{3} + \frac{1}{6}\Delta$	0	$3\frac{1}{3} + \frac{1}{6}\Delta$	0	$107 + \frac{1}{4}\Delta$

The computations proceed as follows:

$$
\begin{aligned}
9x_1 + 6x_2 &= 9(4\tfrac{1}{3} - \tfrac{1}{12}\Delta) + 6(11\tfrac{1}{3} + \tfrac{1}{6}\Delta) \\
&= 39 - \tfrac{3}{4}\Delta + 68 + \Delta \\
&= 107 + \tfrac{1}{4}\Delta .
\end{aligned}
$$

Table 3.4 (temporarily ignore the first three columns) summarizes our sensitivity analysis of RHS_3 for values of Δ close to 0. Given such a value, Table 3.4 permits us to immediately update the LP's optimal solution without having to re-solve the LP. To obtain the new optimal solution, we simply substitute the value of Δ into the table's last six columns and simplify.

Determination of the Range of Validity's Upper Limit

Let us now determine the extent to which our sensitivity analysis of RHS_3 is valid for values of Δ that are not close to 0. That is, we wish to determine the sensitivity analysis's range of validity.

Our sensitivity analysis is based on the observation that, despite the shifts in the quality assurance boundary equation, the LP's optimal solution continues to lie at the "sliding" intersection of the shifting quality assurance boundary equation and the stationary disk drive boundary equation, and, therefore, is the solution to the system of equations

$$
\begin{aligned}
2x_1 + \ \ x_2 &= 20 \qquad \text{(stationary disk drive boundary equation)}\\
2x_1 + 7x_2 &= 88 + \Delta \qquad \text{(shifted quality assurance boundary equation)}.
\end{aligned}
$$

In other words, despite the shifts in the quality assurance boundary equation, the disk drive constraint and the quality assurance constraint continue to be binding at the LP's optimal solution. When this observation remains true, our sensitivity analysis remains valid. Hence, we must answer the following question:

Within what range of values can Δ vary such that the constraints that are currently binding at the LP's optimal solution continue to be binding?

Let us first compute the range of validity's upper limit. How positive can Δ get without invalidating our sensitivity analysis? Figure 3.8 can help us answer this question. To see how, observe the following aspects of the figure:

- When $\Delta = 0$, the quality assurance boundary equation is in Position 0. Now imagine Δ increasing from 0 to the as-yet-unknown positive value that results in the quality assurance boundary equation shifting in a parallel and northeast direction to Position 1. As the equation shifts, the LP's optimal solution "slides" northwest from Point A to Point B, always lying at the intersection of

100

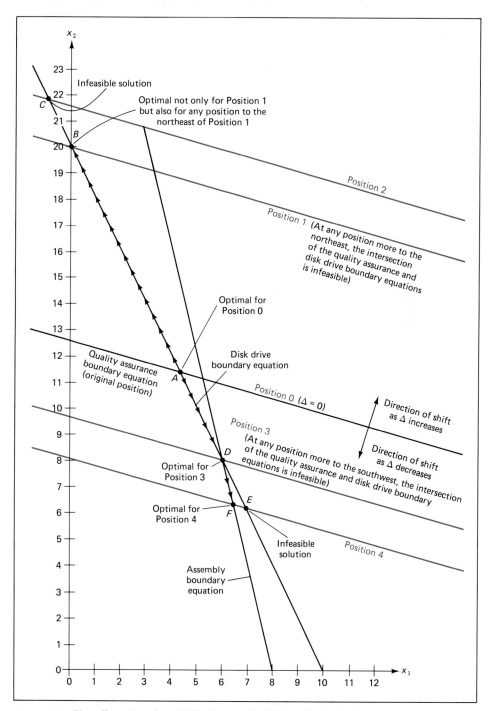

Figure 3.8 The effect changing RHS_3 has on the LP's optimal solution

the shifting quality assurance boundary equation $2x_1 + 7x_2 = 88 + \Delta$ and
the stationary disk drive boundary equation $2x_1 + x_2 = 20$. In other words,
the quality assurance constraint and the disk drive constraint continue to be
binding at the LP's optimal solution. Thus, when Δ does not exceed the value
corresponding to Position 1 of the quality assurance boundary equation, our
sensitivity analysis remains valid.

- Now imagine Δ increasing further to a value that results in the quality assurance boundary equation shifting to Position 2. Although the equation shifts, the LP's optimal solution does not slide from Point B to Point C but instead remains stationary at Point B. The reason is that, once the quality assurance boundary equation shifts to the northeast of Position 1, its intersection with the stationary disk drive boundary equation is no longer optimal because it now lies outside the feasible region. The up-to-now binding quality assurance constraint is now nonbinding, and the up-to-now nonbinding nonnegativity constraint on x_1 has replaced the quality assurance constraint as one of the two binding constraints. Consequently, when Δ exeeds the value corresponding to Position 1, our sensitivity analysis becomes invalid.

To summarize, the range of validity's upper limit is the as-yet-unknown positive value of Δ that makes the quality assurance boundary equation $2x_1 + 7x_2 = 88 + \Delta$ shift to Position 1, thereby passing through Point B.

The easiest way to compute this value of Δ is to observe in Figure 3.8 that, during its northwest "slide" from Point A to Point B, the optimal solution gets closer and closer to the boundary equation $x_1 = 0$, and, when it reaches Point B, the optimal solution actually lies on the boundary equation $x_1 = 0$. In other words, the decision variable x_1 gets smaller and smaller and finally assumes a value of 0. This graphical observation is borne out algebraically by Table 3.4, which indicates that $x_1 = 4\frac{1}{3} - \frac{1}{12}\Delta$, an expression that decreases toward 0 as Δ increases from 0. Hence, the range of validity's upper limit is that positive value of Δ that results in x_1 assuming a value of 0. To find this value of Δ, we need only set $x_1 = 4\frac{1}{3} - \frac{1}{12}\Delta$ equal to 0 and solve for Δ. The computations proceed as follows:

$$4\tfrac{1}{3} - \tfrac{1}{12}\Delta = 0 \quad \rightarrow \quad \tfrac{1}{12}\Delta = 4\tfrac{1}{3} \quad \rightarrow \quad \Delta = 52 .$$

Thus, when $0 \leqslant \Delta \leqslant 52$, our sensitivity analysis remains valid. Any value of Δ greater than 52 invalidates the sensitivity analysis because it results in a negative value of x_1 and, therefore, an infeasible solution.

Determining the Range of Validity's Lower Limit

How negative can Δ get without invalidating our sensitivity analysis? To answer this question, return to Figure 3.8 and observe the following:

- When $\Delta = 0$, the quality assurance boundary equation is in Position 0. Now imagine Δ decreasing from 0 to the as-yet-unknown negative value that results in the quality assurance boundary equation shifting in a parallel and southwest direction to Position 3. As the equation shifts, the LP's optimal solution "slides" southeast from Point A to Point D, always lying at the intersection of the shifting quality assurance boundary equation $2x_1 + 7x_2 = 88 + \Delta$ and the stationary disk drive boundary equation $2x_1 + x_2 = 20$. In other words, the disk drive constraint and the quality assurance constraint continue to be binding at the LP's optimal solution. Thus, when Δ is less negative than the value corresponding to Position 3 of the quality assurance boundary equation, our sensitivity analysis remains valid.

- Now imagine Δ decreasing further to a value that results in the quality assurance boundary equation shifting to Position 4. The LP's optimal solution does not "slide" from Point D to Point E but instead "turns the corner" and then "slides" down from Point D to Point F. The reason is that, once the quality assurance boundary equation shifts to the southwest of Position 3, its intersection with the stationary disk drive boundary equation is no longer optimal because it now lies outside the feasible region. The up-to-now binding disk drive constraint is now nonbinding, and the up-to-now nonbinding assembly constraint $4x_1 + x_2 \leqslant 32$ has replaced the disk drive constraint as one of the two binding constraints. Consequently, when Δ is more negative than the value corresponding to Position 3, our sensitivity analysis becomes invalid.

To summarize, the range of validity's lower limit is the as-yet-unknown negative value of Δ that makes the quality assurance boundary equation $2x_1 + 7x_2 = 88 + \Delta$ shift to Position 3, thereby passing through Point D.

The easiest way to compute this value of Δ is to observe in Figure 3.8 that, during its downward "slide," the optimal solution gets closer and closer to the assembly boundary equation $4x_1 + x_2 = 32$, and, when it reaches Point D, the optimal solution actually lies on the assembly boundary equation. In other words, the assembly constraint's slack variable S_2 gets smaller and smaller and finally assumes a value of 0. This graphical observation is borne out algebraically by Table 3.4, which indicates that $S_2 = 3\frac{1}{3} + \frac{1}{6}\Delta$, an expression that decreases toward 0 as Δ decreases from 0. Hence, the range of validity's lower limit is that negative value of Δ that results in S_2 assuming a value of 0. To find this value of Δ, we need only set $S_2 = 3\frac{1}{3} + \frac{1}{6}\Delta$ equal to 0 and solve for Δ. The computations proceed as follows:

$$3\tfrac{1}{3} + \tfrac{1}{6}\Delta = 0 \;\; \rightarrow \;\; \tfrac{1}{6}\Delta = -3\tfrac{1}{3} \;\; \rightarrow \;\; \Delta = -20.$$

Thus, when $-20 \leqslant \Delta \leqslant 0$, our sensitivity analysis remains valid. Any value of Δ more negative than -20 invalidates the sensitivity analysis because it results in a negative value of S_2 and, therefore, an infeasible solution.

Returning to Table 3.4, we see that the first three columns summarize the range of validity for our sensitivity analysis of RHS_3. When the change in RHS_3 remains within that range, we can use Table 3.4 to quickly determine the effect on the LP's optimal solution of changes in the quality assurance constraint's right-hand side. For example, an increase in RHS_3 from 88 to 124 (i.e., $\Delta = 36$) is well within the range of validity. Hence, instead of re-solving the LP, we can simply substitute $\Delta = 36$ into the expressions in Table 3.4's last six columns, thereby obtaining the new optimal solution of

$$
\begin{aligned}
x_1 &= & 4\tfrac{1}{3} &- \tfrac{1}{12}(36) &=& 1\tfrac{1}{3} \\
x_2 &= & 11\tfrac{1}{3} &+ \tfrac{1}{6}(36) &=& 17\tfrac{1}{3} \\
S_1 &= & & &=& 0 \\
S_2 &= & 3\tfrac{1}{3} &+ \tfrac{1}{6}(36) &=& 9\tfrac{1}{3} \\
S_3 &= & & &=& 0 \\
\text{Objective value} &= & 107 &+ \tfrac{1}{4}(36) &=& 116.
\end{aligned}
$$

The Shadow Price of the Quality Assurance Constraint

A "by-product" of our sensitivity analysis is the shadow price of the quality assurance constraint $2x_1 + 7x_2 \leqslant 88$. Recall that this shadow price is the rate of improvement in the LP's optimal objective value per unit increase in the constraint's right-hand side. From the coefficient of Δ in Table 3.4's expression for the optimal objective value, we see that this rate of improvement is $\frac{1}{4} = 0.25$. Since OMC's objective-function value is measured in units of $100,000$ and RHS_3

is measured in units of 1000 hours of available quality assurance labor, a shadow price of 0.25 implies that OMC's optimal objective value increases at the rate of $25,000 per additional 1000 hours of quality assurance labor or, equivalently, at the rate of $25 per additional hour of quality assurance labor. Consequently, given an opportunity to acquire additional hours of quality assurance labor, $25 is the maximum unit price OMC should pay over and above the unit price already accounted for in the objective function.

We can improve our understanding of shadow prices by contrasting the shadow price of the disk drive constraint, $425 per additional disk drive, and the shadow price of the quality assurance constraint, $25 per additional hour of quality assurance labor. Does this difference in the shadow prices mean that acquiring additional disk drives is more profitable than acquiring more quality assurance labor? The answer is "Not necessarily!" To illustrate, suppose OMC has a choice between obtaining one additional disk drive or one additional hour of quality assurance labor at respective unit prices of $410 and $5 over and above the respective unit prices already accounted for in the objective function. Given the shadow prices stated previously, OMC's choice is between the following two increases in net profits:

$$\text{(shadow price)} - \begin{pmatrix} \text{amount by which the} \\ \text{actual unit price} \\ \text{exceeds the unit price} \\ \text{already accounted for in} \\ \text{the objective function} \end{pmatrix} = \text{(increase in net profit)}$$

	(shadow price)	−	(amount exceeding)	=	(increase in net profit)
For 1 additional disk drive:	$425	−	$410	=	$15
For 1 additional hour of quality assurance labor:	$25	−	$5	=	$20

Thus, OMC should choose the additional hour of quality assurance labor. Even though its shadow price is $400 less, it increases net profits by $5 more than one additional disk drive. Now suppose the alternatives are 1000 (not 1) additional disk drives versus 500 (not 1) additional hours of quality assurance labor.[9] OMC's choice is now between the following two increases in net profit:

$$\left[\begin{pmatrix} \text{resource's} \\ \text{shadow} \\ \text{price} \end{pmatrix} - \begin{pmatrix} \text{amount by which the} \\ \text{actual unit price} \\ \text{exceeds the unit price} \\ \text{already accounted for in} \\ \text{the objective function} \end{pmatrix} \right] \times \begin{pmatrix} \text{number of} \\ \text{additional units} \\ \text{of the resource} \\ \text{to be acquired} \end{pmatrix} = \begin{pmatrix} \text{total increase} \\ \text{in} \\ \text{net profit} \end{pmatrix}$$

	[resource's shadow price	−	amount exceeding]	×	number additional	=	total increase
For 1000 additional disk drives:	[$425	−	$410]	×	1000	=	$15,000
For 500 additional hours of quality assurance labor:	[$25	−	$5]	×	500	=	$10,000

Thus, 1000 additional disk drives is a more profitable choice than 500 additional hours of quality assurance labor. These two examples illustrate the following general principle:

---

[9] Observe from Tables 3.3 and 3.4 that the increases of 1 thousand disk drives and 0.5 thousand hours of quality assurance labor are less than the maximum allowable increases over which the shadow prices apply.

Just because the shadow price of one resource constraint is greater than the shadow price of another resource constraint, it does *not* follow that the acquisition of additional units of the first resource is more profitable than the acquisition of additional units of the second resource. Which is more profitable depends not only on the resources' shadow prices but also on their actual unit prices and acquisition quantities. In particular, the profitability of each alternative can be evaluated and compared using the following formula:

$$\begin{pmatrix} \text{total increase} \\ \text{in} \\ \text{net profit} \end{pmatrix} = \left[\begin{pmatrix} \text{resource's} \\ \text{shadow} \\ \text{price} \end{pmatrix} - \begin{pmatrix} \text{amount by which the} \\ \text{actual unit price} \\ \text{exceeds the unit price} \\ \text{already accounted for in} \\ \text{the objective function} \end{pmatrix} \right] \times \begin{pmatrix} \text{number of} \\ \text{additional units} \\ \text{of the resource} \\ \text{to be acquired} \end{pmatrix}$$

A Summary

We have twice illustrated a procedure for graphical sensitivity analysis of the right-hand side of a constraint that is binding at the LP's optimal solution, once in Section 3.3 for the binding disk drive constraint and once again in this section for the binding quality assurance constraint. We can summarize the general procedure as follows:

A General Procedure for Graphical Sensitivity Analysis of the Right-hand Side of a Binding Constraint

1. Let Δ denote the change in the value of the constraint's right-hand side and assume initially that Δ only takes on values close to 0.

2. When $\Delta = 0$, the LP's optimal solution lies at the intersection of two boundary equations, one corresponding to the constraint undergoing sensitivity analysis and the other corresponding to another of the LP's constraints. As Δ changes, the boundary equation of the constraint undergoing sensitivity analysis shifts its position and the other boundary equation remains stationary. Consequently, when Δ increases or decreases slightly, the coordinates of the LP's optimal solution "slide" a small distance to the new point of intersection between the two boundary equations. In other words, when Δ increases or decreases slightly from 0, the currently binding constraints remain binding. Assuming, then, that Δ takes on values close to 0,

    a. We can determine the (x_1, x_2)-coordinates of the LP's optimal solution in terms of Δ by finding the simultaneous solution to the two boundary equations intersecting at the LP's optimal solution. (Remember to add Δ to the right-hand side of the boundary equation corresponding to the constraint undergoing sensitivity analysis.)

    b. The optimal value of the slack or surplus variables of every structural constraint that is *binding* at the LP's optimal solution is 0. To compute the optimal value in terms of Δ of the slack or surplus variable of each *nonbinding* structural constraint, we substitute the optimal (x_1, x_2)-coordinates into the constraint's left-hand side and, for a slack variable, subtract the result from the constraint's right-hand side or, for a surplus variable, subtract the constraint's right-hand side from the result.

    c. To determine the optimal objective value in terms of Δ, we substitute the optimal (x_1, x_2)-coordinates in terms of Δ into the objective function.

    d. In Step 2c's expression for the optimal objective value, the coefficient of

Δ is the constraint's shadow price, provided the sign of the shadow price is properly interpreted to reflect the rate of *improvement* (not rate of increase) in the optimal objective value. For example, suppose the optimal objective value in terms of Δ is $100 + 7\Delta$, thereby indicating that the optimal objective value increases at the rate of 7 units per unit increase in the constraint's right-hand side. If the LP involves maximization, an increase of 7 is an improvement in the optimal objective value, hence the shadow price is +7. If the LP involves minimization, an increase of 7 is a worsening (i.e., a negative improvement) of the optimal objective value, hence the shadow price equals -7. Now suppose the optimal objective value in terms of Δ is $100 - 7\Delta$, thereby indicating that the optimal objective value decreases at the rate of 7 units per unit increase in the constraint's right-hand side. If the LP involves maximization, a decrease of 7 is a worsening of the optimal objective value, hence the shadow price is -7. If the LP involves minimization, a decrease of 7 is an improvement in the optimal objective value, hence the shadow price equals $+7$.[10]

3. The final step is to compute the sensitivity analysis's range of validity—that is, a positive upper limit and a negative lower limit on Δ such that Step 2's sensitivity analysis remains valid when Δ remains within these limits. Step 2's computations are based on the observation that, despite the shift in the boundary equation of the constraint undergoing sensitivity analysis, there is no change in the constraints that are binding at the LP's optimal solution. When this observation remains true, Step 2's analysis remains valid. Consequently, the easiest way to calculate the range of validity's upper limit or lower limit is to graphically observe which currently positive decision variable, slack variable, or surplus variable will decrease to 0 as Δ is increased from 0 (for the upper limit) or decreased from 0 (for the lower limit) to the point where the any further change would cause the variable to take on a negative value, thereby implying the infeasibility of the (x_1, x_2)-coordinates determined in Step 2a and a change in the binding constraints. After observing which variable will decrease to 0, determine the limiting value of Δ by first setting Step 2's expression for the variable in terms of Δ equal to 0 and then solving for Δ.

Now that you have read the general procedure, you might find it instructive to review our sensitivity analysis of the disk drive constraint and the quality assurance constraint and observe how we followed the general procedure.

3.6 SENSITIVITY ANALYSIS OF A NONBINDING CONSTRAINT'S RIGHT-HAND SIDE

We have completed sensitivity analysis of the right-hand sides of the two structural constraints that are binding at the optimal solution to OMC's LP, the disk drive

---

[10] In the definition of shadow price, some instructors, textbooks, and LP software packages replace "rate of *improvement* in the optimal objective value" with "rate of *increase* in the optimal objective value." When the LP involves minimization, this alternative definition results in the shadow prices of all constraints having the opposite sign (i.e., + instead of −, or − instead of +) from what they would have under our definition. However, with proper interpretation, this alternative definition and our definition lead to the same conclusion regarding the change in the optimal objective value per unit increase in the constraint's right-hand side.

constraint and the quality assurance constraint. Let us now conduct sensitivity analysis of the right-hand side of the structural constraint that is nonbinding at the LP's optimal solution, the assembly constraint $4x_1 + x_2 \leqslant 32$. As we will see, sensitivity analysis of a nonbinding constraint is considerably simpler than for a binding constraint.

Since the quality assurance constraint is the LP's second structural constraint, we will denote its right-hand side by RHS_2, and we will denote by Δ the change in RHS_2 from its current value of 32. The question we wish to answer with our sensitivity analysis is:

What is the effect on the LP's optimal solution of changing RHS_2 from 32 to 32 $+\Delta$ (assuming all the LP's other data remain unchanged)? [11]

As before, let us first make the assumption that Δ can only take on values close to 0 and then subsequently determine the extent to which our sensitivity analysis remains valid for values of Δ not close to 0.

Determination of the Optimal Solution's Coordinates in Terms of Δ

Figures 3.9(a)–(c) depict the graphical solution of OMC's LP for three different values of Δ: $\Delta = 0$ corresponding to no change in RHS_2, $\Delta = 0.5$ corresponding to a small increase in RHS_2, and $\Delta = -0.5$ corresponding to a small decrease in RHS_2. (Since the maximal isoprofit line is shown only in Figure 3.9(a), you will have to imagine it in the two others.) Figures 3.9(a)–(c) are similar to Figures 3.5(a)–(c) and Figures 3.7(a)–(c), except that the changes in Δ now cause the assembly boundary equation to shift instead of the disk drive boundary equation or the quality assurance boundary equation. In particular, observe the following:

- In Figure 3.9(a) when RHS_2 equals its current value of 32, the LP's optimal solution lies at Point A, the intersection of the disk drive boundary equation $2x_1 + x_2 = 20$ and the quality assurance boundary equation $2x_1 + 7x_2 = 88$. In other words, the disk drive constraint and the quality assurance constraint are the binding constraints at the LP's optimal solution.

- In Figure 3.9(b) when RHS_2 increases from its current value of 32 by a small amount, the LP's feasible region expands as the assembly boundary equation shifts in a parallel and northeast direction. Despite the assembly boundary equation's shift to the northeast, the LP's optimal solution remains stationary at Point A.

- In Figure 3.9(c) when RHS_2 decreases from its current value of 32 by a small amount, the LP's feasible region contracts as the assembly boundary equation shifts in a parallel and southwest direction. Despite the assembly boundary equation's shift to the southwest, the LP's optimal solution remains stationary at Point A.

To summarize Figures 3.9(a)–(c), although changing RHS_2 by a small amount Δ causes a parallel shift in the assembly boundary equation, it has no effect whatsoever on the optimal (x_1, x_2)-coordinates and, therefore, on the optimal objective value. What about the effect on the slack variables S_1, S_2, and S_3? As we observed in Figure 3.9, a small change in RHS_2 does not alter the fact that the disk drive constraint and the quality assurance constraint are binding at the LP's

---

[11] Although we will not always add the parenthetic phrase "assuming all the LP's other data remain unchanged," keep in mind that it applies throughout our sensitivity analysis.

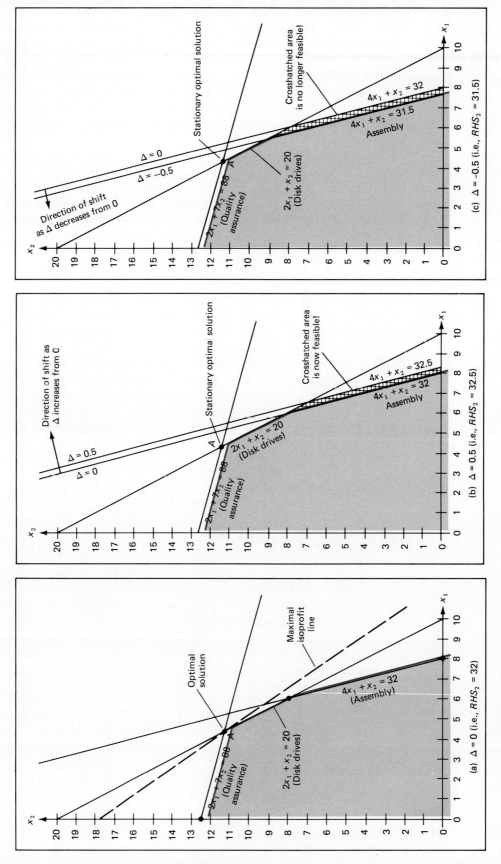

Figure 3.9 The effect on the LP's optimal solution of a small change in RHS_2: (a) $\Delta = 0$ (i.e., $RHS_2 = 32$), (b) $\Delta = 0.5$ (i.e., $RHS_2 = 32.5$), (c) $\Delta = -0.5$ (i.e., $RHS_2 = 31.5$).

108

optimal solution. Consequently, for small changes in RHS_2, the slack variables for these two binding constraints, S_1 and S_3, retain their optimal values of 0. The optimal value of the nonbinding assembly constraint's slack variable S_2, however, does change. To see why, observe that, since the LP's optimal solution remains stationary at $(x_1, x_2) = (4\frac{1}{3}, 11\frac{1}{3})$, the amount of assembly labor consumed by the optimal production plan remains constant at

$$4x_1 + x_2 = (4)(4\tfrac{1}{3}) + (1)(11\tfrac{1}{3}) = 17\tfrac{1}{3} + 11\tfrac{1}{3} = 28\tfrac{2}{3}.$$

With assembly labor availability at its original value of 32 when $\Delta = 0$, the unconsumed assembly labor represented by the slack variable S_2 is $32 - 28\frac{2}{3} = 3\frac{1}{3}$. However, when the availability of assembly labor is changed to $32 + \Delta$ at the same time assembly labor consumption remains constant at $28\frac{2}{3}$, S_2 simply changes from its former value of $3\frac{1}{3}$ to $3\frac{1}{3} + \Delta$.

Table 3.5 (temporarily ignore the first three columns) summarizes our sensitivity analysis of RHS_2 for values of Δ close to 0. The only effect of a small change in RHS_2 is a change in the assembly constraint's slack variable. Table 3.5 illustrates the following general principle:

> Although a small change in the right-hand side of a constraint that is non-binding at the LP's optimal solution causes a slight expansion or contraction of the feasible region, the only effect on the optimal values of the decision variables, the slack and surplus variables, and the objective value is a small change in the slack or surplus variable of the constraint undergoing sensitivity analysis.

Determination of the Range of Validity

Let us now determine the extent to which our sensitivity analysis of RHS_2 is valid for values of Δ that are not close to 0. That is, let us determine its range of validity. Our sensitivity analysis is based on the observation that, despite the shifts in the assembly boundary equation, the LP's optimal solution remains stationary at the intersection of the stationary disk drive boundary equation and the stationary quality assurance boundary equation. In other words, the disk drive constraint and the quality assurance constraint continue to be binding at the LP's optimal solution. When this observation remains true, our sensitivity analysis remains valid. Hence, we must answer the following question:

> *Within what range of values can Δ vary such that the constraints that are currently binding at the LP's optimal solution continue to be binding?*

TABLE 3.5 Sensitivity Analysis of RHS_2

RHS_2's CURRENT VALUE	RHS_2's MAXIMUM ALLOWABLE INCREASE	RHS_2's MAXIMUM ALLOWABLE DECREASE	OPTIMAL VALUES					
			x_1	x_2	S_1	S_2	S_3	OBJECTIVE VALUE
32	∞	$3\frac{1}{3}$	$4\frac{1}{3}$	$11\frac{1}{3}$	0	$3\frac{1}{3} + \Delta$	0	107

Figure 3.10 provides a graphical answer to this question. Observe the following aspects of the figure:

- When $\Delta = 0$, the assembly boundary equation is in Position 0, and the LP's optimal solution is at Point A. Now imagine Δ increasing from 0 to a positive value that results in the assembly boundary equation shifting in a parallel and northeast direction to Position 1. Throughout the equation's shift, the optimal

Figure 3.10 The effect changing RHS_2 has on the LP's optimal solution

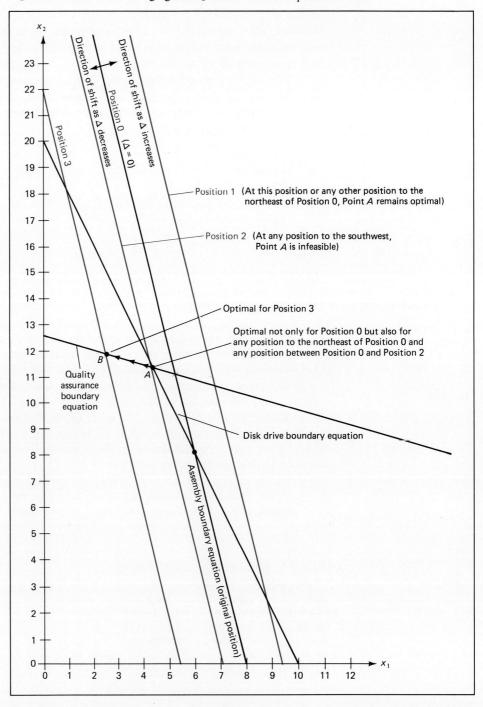

solution remains stationary at Point A. In fact, regardless of how far the assembly boundary equation shifts to the northeast of Position 0, the optimal solution remains stationary at Point A. Thus, our sensitivity analysis's range of validity has no upper limit, or, equivalently, has an upper limit of ∞.

- Now imagine Δ decreasing from 0 to the as-yet-unknown negative value that results in the assembly boundary equation shifting in a parallel and southwest direction to Position 2. Throughout the equation's shift, the LP's optimal solution remains stationary at Point A. Thus, decreasing Δ from 0 to the value corresponding to Position 2 has no effect whatsoever on the LP's optimal solution. In other words, the disk drive constraint and the quality assurance constraint continue to be binding at the LP's optimal solution. Thus, when Δ is less negative than the value corresponding to Position 2 of the assembly boundary equation, our sensitivity analysis remains valid. Now imagine Δ decreasing further to a value that results in the assembly boundary equation shifting to Position 3. As the equation shifts, the LP's optimal solution no longer remains stationary at Point A but instead begins "sliding" northwest from Point A toward Point B. The reason is that, once the assembly boundary equation shifts to the southwest of Position 2, the intersection at Point A of the stationary disk drive boundary equation and the stationary quality assurance boundary equation is no longer optimal because it now lies outside the feasible region. The up-to-now binding disk drive constraint is now nonbinding, and the up-to-now nonbinding assembly constraint has replaced the disk drive constraint as one of the two binding constraints. Consequently, when Δ is more negative than the value corresponding to Position 2, our sensitivity analysis becomes invalid.

To summarize, the range of validity's upper limit is ∞ and its lower limit is the as-yet-unknown negative value of Δ that makes the quality assurance boundary equation $2x_1 + 7x_2 = 88 + \Delta$ shift to Position 2, thereby passing through Point A.

The easiest way to compute Δ's lower limit is to observe in Figure 3.10 that, as the assembly boundary equation shifts southwest, it gets closer and closer to the stationary optimal solution at Point A, and, when it reaches Position 2, it actually passes through Point A. In other words, the assembly constraint's slack variable S_2 gets smaller and smaller and finally assumes a value of 0. This graphical observation is borne out algebraically by Table 3.5, which indicates that $S_2 = 3\frac{1}{3} + \Delta$, an expression that decreases toward 0 as Δ decreases from 0. Hence, the range of validity's lower limit is that negative value of Δ that results in $S_2 = 3\frac{1}{3} + \Delta$ assuming a value of 0. Clearly, this occurs when $\Delta = -3\frac{1}{3}$, the negative of the original optimal value of S_2 (i.e., when RHS_2 equals its original value of 32). This is an intuitive result. In words, it states that a currently nonbinding $\leqslant$ constraint becomes binding when its right-hand side decreases by an amount equal to the current value of its slack variable.

To summarize, our sensitivity analysis's range of validity is $-3\frac{1}{3} \leqslant \Delta < \infty$.

Returning to Table 3.5, we see that the first three columns summarize the range of validity for our sensitivity analysis of RHS_2. When the change in RHS_2 remains within the specified range of validity, there is no effect on the decision variables' optimal values or on the optimal objective value (although the value of the assembly constraint's slack variable changes).

The Shadow Price of the Assembly Constraint

What is the shadow price of the nonbinding assembly constraint? Recall that this shadow price is the rate of improvement in the LP's optimal objective value per unit increase in the constraint's right-hand side. From Table 3.5's last column, we see that this rate of improvement is 0! A shadow price of 0 for a nonbinding constraint is not surprising. After all, when $\Delta = 0$, the constraint is nonbinding because the LP's optimal solution does not consume $S_2 = 3\frac{1}{3}$ thousand of the available 32 thousand hours of assembly labor. Hence, increasing the availability of assembly labor beyond its current value of 32 thousand hours does not improve the optimal objective value but only increases the unconsumed portion of the available labor. In general, then,

> Only constraints that are binding at the LP's optimal solution have nonzero shadow prices. A constraint that is nonbinding at the LP's optimal solution always has a shadow price of 0.

A Summary

Our sensitivity analysis of the assembly constraint illustrates the following general procedure for conducting sensitivity analysis of the right-hand side of a structural constraint that is nonbinding at the LP's optimal solution:

A General Procedure for Sensitivity Analysis of the Right-hand Side of a Nonbinding Constraint

When conducting sensitivity analysis of the right-hand side of a constraint that is nonbinding at the LP's optimal solution, no computations are necessary because:

1. Determining the sensitivity analysis's range of validity requires no computation. If the constraint is a $\leqslant$ constraint (as was the assembly constraint), the maximum allowable increase always equals ∞, and the maximum allowable decrease always equals the optimal value of the constraint's slack variable. If the constraint is a $\geqslant$ constraint (as we will encounter in Section 3.8), the maximum allowable increase always equals the optimal value of the constraint's surplus variable, and the maximum allowable decrease is always ∞.

2. Within the sensitivity analysis's range of validity, no computations are necessary to determine the precise effect changing the constraint's right-hand side has on the LP's optimal solution. The optimal values of the decision variable, the slack and surplus variables, and the optimal objective value remain unchanged, except for a change in the optimal value of the slack or surplus variable of the constraint undergoing sensitivity analysis.

3. No computations are required to determine the constraint's shadow price. Since the LP's optimal objective value does not change as the constraint's right-hand side is increased, the shadow price of the nonbinding constraint is 0.

3.7 COMPUTER ANALYSIS OF OMC'S PRODUCT MIX LP

In Chapter 2 we graphically solved OMC's product mix LP, and in previous sections of this chapter we performed graphical sensitivity analysis of the decision variables' objective-function coefficients and the constraints' right-hand sides. In this section we will illustrate how to use a computer to obtain the same results.

Figure 3.11 displays the input to and output from a hypothetical LP software package we will call LINPRO.[12] While the LP software package available at your computer facility may be different, the differences will be ones of form rather than substance. That is, your software package may use slightly different formats to request the same input and provide the same output.

Typical of LP software packages designed for use on a personal computer, LINPRO has an interactive command structure in which the user issues a command or inputs data and then waits for an on-screen response from the computer before issuing the next command or inputting more data. In Figure 3.11, the user's input is unshaded and the computer's response is shaded. The following observations are more detailed discussions of the correspondingly-numbered comments appearing in Figure 3.11's right margin:

1. The " > " is the operating system's *prompt*—that is, the symbol displayed to indicate the computer's readiness to execute an operating system command.

2. In response to the " > " prompt, the user requests the execution of the LINPRO software package by simply typing "linpro".

3. LINPRO is now activated and, to indicate its readiness to accept the first command, LINPRO displays its own command-level prompt, the ":".

4. The user now inputs the LP. Observe the following aspects of the input process:

   a. As an abbreviation for "maximize", LINPRO accepts "max". (Similarly, LINPRO accepts "min" for "minimize".)

   b. After the user completes each line of input (by hitting the RETURN or ENTER key), LINPRO displays a "?" as a prompt for additional data. LINPRO continues to display the "?" as a prompt for additional data until the user signals the completion of the LP's data input by typing "end". In response to "end", LINPRO reverts to its command-level prompt of ":".

   c. When inputting the LP, the user must give the decision variables names of from one to eight alphanumeric characters. In Figure 3.11, we chose the names "x1" and "x2" to conform with our original formulation of OMC's LP. However, we could have chosen the names "orange" and "tanger". Since each decision variable name must be typed several times during input, there is a trade-off between shorter names and longer, but more descriptive names.

   d. The user must type the line "subject to" as a signal to LINPRO that the entry of the LP's objective function is complete and that the entry of the constraints is about to begin.

   e. When inputting a constraint, LINPRO provides the user with the option of associating with the constraint a name of from one to eight alphanumeric characters. As indicated in Figure 3.11, the user names a constraint by preceding the constraint by its name, followed by a ")" and at least one blank space. For example, we have given the name "assembly" to the assembly constraint. User-supplied names facilitate the interpretation of LINPRO's output. If the user fails to name the constraints, LINPRO provides default names of "1), 2), 3)" and so on.

   f. During the inputting of the constraints, LINPRO is "friendly" enough to interpret " < " and " > " as " ≤ " and " ≥ ", two keys not usually

---

[12] The input and output displayed is very similar to that of the LINDO software package developed by Professor Linus E. Schrage of the University of Chicago.

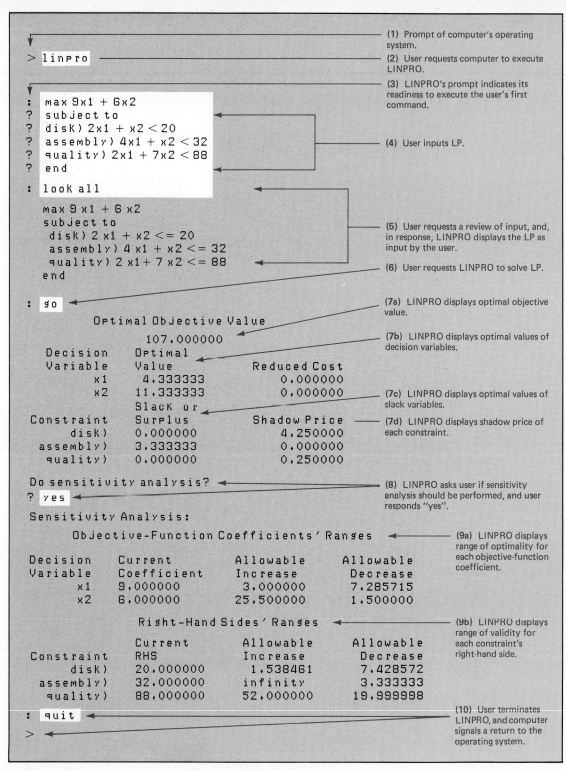

Figure 3.11 Using LINPRO to solve OMC's product mix LP

present on the computer's keyboard. (Some "less friendly" LP software packages require the two-key sequences " < =" and " > =".)

g. LINPRO automatically assumes that all decision variables are constrained to nonnegative, thereby eliminating the need for the user to

114

type the nonnegativity constraints. This time-saving feature of LINPRO creates a problem when the initial formulation of the LP involves decision variables that can assume negative as well as nonnegative values or decision variables that have nonzero lower bounds. In Sections 3.9 and 3.10 we will discuss methods for dealing with these two situations.

5. After the user has input the LP and LINPRO has returned the prompt of ":" to indicate its readiness to accept another command, the user inputs the command "look all". Although this command is optional, it is highly recommended, because LINPRO responds to the command by displaying the user's actual input, which may differ somewhat from the user's intended input.

6. If (as in Figure 3.11) the LP displayed in response to the "look all" command agrees with what the user intended to input, the user may then request LINPRO to solve the LP by typing the command "go". However, if a review of the displayed input uncovers an error, the user's next command would be "alter", a command that permits the user to change one or more aspects of the LP's input.

7. In response to the 'go" command, LINPRO uses the simplex method discussed in Chapters 6 and 7 to solve the LP and then displays the following output:

   a. The optimal objective value.

   b. The optimal values of the decision variables named "x1" and "x2".[13]

   c. The optimal values of the slack variables for the structural constraints named "disk", "assembly", and "quality".

   d. The shadow prices of the structural constraints named "disk", "assembly", and "quality". (The range of validity for these shadow prices appears later.)

   Observe that these values are identical to those we determined graphically when solving OMC's LP in Chapter 2 and conducting sensitivity analysis earlier in this chapter.

8. LINPRO next asks the user if it should perform sensitivity analysis. A user response of "no" would return LINPRO to the command level. In Figure 3.11, however, the user's response is "yes".

9. In response to the user's request for sensitivity analysis, LINPRO displays the following output:

   a. The first portion of the output contains the ranges of optimality for the sensitivity analysis of the objective-function coefficients of x_1 and x_2. Observe that the format of the output is identical to Table 3.2's summary of our graphical determination of the ranges of optimality (except for the use of decimal values instead of fractional values). As a review of the interpretation of these ranges of optimality, consider the range of optimality for x_1's objective-function coefficient. The output indicates that the currently optimal solution of $(x_1, x_2) = (4.33, 11.33)$ remains optimal even if x_1's current objective-function coefficient of 9 increases by as much as 3 or decreases by as much as 7.29 (assuming all the LP's other data remain unchanged). Remember that, although the optimal values of x_1 and x_2 do not change, the optimal objective value will

---

[13] For now, ignore the output to the right of the optimal values of "x1" and "x2", under the heading of "Reduced Cost". We will explain this portion of the output after discussing the simplex method in Chapter 6.

change. For example, if x_1's objective-function coefficient decreases by 2, the optimal objective value will decrease by 2 times the still-optimal value of x_1.

b. The second portion of the output contains the ranges of validity for the sensitivity analysis of the right-hand sides of the structural constraints named "disk", "assembly", and "quality". Observe that these ranges of validity are identical to those appearing in the first three columns of Tables 3.3, 3.4, and 3.5, the tables summarizing our graphical sensitivity analysis of the the constraints' right-hand sides. As a review of the interpretation of these ranges of validity, consider the range of validity of the "quality" constraint. The computer output indicates that the constraint's shadow price, specified in item 7d of the output as 0.25, is valid even if the constraint's current right-hand side of 88 increases by as much as 52 or decreases by as much as 20.[14] Recall that a constraint's range of validity applies not only to the shadow price (which is the rate of improvement in the objective value) but also to the rates of change in the optimal values of the decision variables and the slack variables. These rates of change were computed during our graphical sensitivity analysis and are summarized in Tables 3.3, 3.4, and 3.5. Unfortunately, as part of its normal output, LINPRO (like many other software packages designed for a personal computer) provides only the shadow prices and not the rates of change in the variables' optimal values. However, as we will discuss in Chapter 7, this "missing information" is available from LINPRO to users who understand the simplex method.

10. After displaying the sensitivity analysis output, LINPRO requests a new command with the prompt of ":". In Figure 3.11, the user responded with the "quit" command, thereby exiting from LINPRO and returning to the computer's operating system. Alternatively, the user could have elected to remain in LINPRO and solve another LP.

In using LINPRO to solve OMC's product mix LP, we have illustrated only a small portion of LINPRO's capabilities. Other LINPRO commands can save an LP's input on disk, retrieve an LP's previously saved input from disk, and alter an LP's input. Although the LP software package available at your computer facility may not be identical in all respects to LINPRO, it should have enough similarities that you should have little difficulty adapting to it.

3.8 COMPUTER ANALYSIS OF PETE MOSS'S BLENDING PROBLEM

As a second example of using an LP software package, let us return to Pete Moss's fertilizer blending problem from Chapter 2. Recall that we formulated this problem as the following LP:

$$\text{Minimize } 90x_1 + 20x_2 + 30x_3 \qquad \text{(total cost)}$$

$$
\begin{array}{llllllll}
\text{subject to} & x_1 & + & x_2 & + & x_3 & = & 10 & \text{(demand)} \\
& 50x_1 & + & & & 10x_3 & \geqslant & 170 & \text{(nitrogen content)} \\
& 20x_1 & + & 15x_2 & + & 10x_3 & \geqslant & 140 & \text{(phosphorus content)} \\
& 5x_1 & + & 20x_2 & + & 10x_3 & \geqslant & 100 & \text{(potassium content)}
\end{array}
$$

and $x_1 \geqslant 0, x_2 \geqslant 0, x_3 \geqslant 0,$

---

[14] Observe that LINPRO actually displays the maximum allowable decrease as 19.999998 instead of 20, owing to the round-off error that sometimes "creeps" into numerical calculations on a computer.

where x_1, x_2, and x_3 denote respectively the number of 100-pound bags of 50-20-5 fertilizer, 0-15-20 fertilizer, and 10-10-10 fertilizer used to blend the order for 1000 pounds of 17-14-10 fertilizer. (If your memory of Pete Moss's blending problem is "fuzzy," you may wish to quickly review Sections 2.9 and 2.10.) In Chapter 2 we graphically determined that the LP's optimal solution is:

x_1	x_2	x_3	E_2	E_3	E_4	OBJECTIVE VALUE
2.5	3.0	4.5	0	0	17.5	420

where E_2, E_3, and E_4 respectively denote the surplus variables for the constraints on the blended fertilizer's nitrogen, phosphorous, and potassium content. (Since the LP's first constraint is an equality constraint, it has no slack or surplus variable associated with it.)

Figure 3.12 displays the input to and output from the use of LINPRO to analyze Pete Moss's blending problem. Observe in LINPRO's output that the optimal values of the decision variables, the surplus variables, and the objective value are identical to those we determined graphically in Chapter 2.

The shadow-price portion of LINPRO's output merits discussion. In contrast to OMC's production planning LP, where all three structural constraints had nonnegative shadow prices, all four constraints in Pete Moss's blending LP have nonpositive shadow prices. The reason is that, whereas the structural constraints in OMC's LP are of the $\leq$ type, the structural constraints in Pete Moss's LP are of the $=$ and $\geq$ type.

To understand the effect of the constraint's type, let us first consider a $\leq$ constraint. Increasing the right-hand side always "loosens" the constraint—that is, makes it easier to satisfy. For example, it is easier to satisfy the constraint $2x_1 + x_2 \leq 21$ than to satisfy $2x_1 + x_2 \leq 20$. Since a $\leq$ constraint is easier to satisfy after an increase in its right-hand side, not only do all formerly feasible solutions (including the former optimal solution) remain feasible, but also some formerly infeasible solutions become newly feasible. In other words, the LP's new feasible region includes as a subset the former feasible region. Because the former optimal solution remains feasible, the new optimal objective value will always either improve or remain the same. More specifically, if the best objective value among the newly feasible solutions is better than the former optimal solution, then the new optimal objective value will be an improvement over the former optimal objective value, thereby resulting in a positive shadow price. On the other hand, if the best objective value among the newly feasible solutions is no better than the former optimal objective value, then the new optimal objective value will remain the same as it was, thereby resulting in a shadow price of 0. To summarize, then, the shadow price of a $\leq$ constraint is always nonnegative.

Now consider a $\geq$ constraint. Increasing the right-hand side always "tightens" the constraint—that is, makes it harder to satisfy than before. For example, it is harder to satisfy the constraint $2x_1 + x_2 \geq 21$ than to satisfy $2x_1 + x_2 \geq 20$. Since a $\geq$ constraint is harder to satisfy after an increase in its right-hand side, some formerly feasible solutions (including perhaps the former optimal solution) become infeasible and, furthermore, no formerly infeasible solutions become feasible. In other words, the LP's new feasible region is included as a subset in the former feasible region. Because no formerly infeasible solutions become feasible, the new optimal objective value will always either worsen or remain the same. More specifically, if the former optimal solution is among the formerly feasible but now infeasible solutions, then the optimal objective value will be worse than the former optimal objective value, thereby resulting in a negative shadow price (i.e., a negative improvement). On the other hand, if the former optimal solution remains

```
:   min 90x1 + 20x2 + 30x3
?   subject to
?   demand) x1 + x2 + x3 = 10
?   nitro) 50x1 + 10x3 > 170
?   phos) 20x1 + 15x2 + 10x3 > 140
?   pot) 5x1 + 20x2 + 10x3 > 100
?   end


:   go


              Optimal Objective Value

                 420.000000
    Decision     Optimal
    Variable     Value              Reduced Cost
         x1      2.500000               0.000000
         x2      3.000000               0.000000
         x3      4.500000               0.000000

                 Slack or
  Constraint     Surplus            Shadow Price
    demand)      0.000000             -10.000000
     nitro)      0.000000              -1.333333
      phos)      0.000000              -0.666667
       pot)     17.500000               0.000000


Do sensitivity analysis?
?  yes


Sensitivity Analysis:

        Objective-Function Coefficients' Ranges
    Decision     Current        Allowable        Allowable
    Variable     Coefficient    Increase         Decrease
         x1      90.000000      infinity         20.000000
         x2      20.000000      39.999996         5.000000
         x3      30.000000       4.000000        79.999985


              Right-Hand Sides' Ranges
                 Current        Allowable        Allowable
  Constraint     RHS            Increase         Decrease
    demand)      10.000000       3.000000         1.800000
     nitro)     170.000000      42.000000       149.999985
      phos)     140.000000      27.000000        15.000001
       pot)     100.000000      17.500000         infinity
```

Figure 3.12 Using LINPRO to solve Pete Moss's blending problem

feasible, then it will remain optimal and the new optimal objective value will remain the same as it was, thereby resulting in a shadow price of 0. To summarize, then, the shadow price of a $\geq$ constraint is always nonpositive.

Now consider an $=$ constraint. A $\leq$ constraint's nonnegative shadow price is a consequence of the fact that increasing the constraint's right-hand side only "adds to" the feasible region. Similarly, a $\geq$ constraint's nonpositive shadow price is a consequence of the fact that increasing the constraint's right-hand side only "subtracts from" the feasible region. In contrast, increasing an = constraint's right-hand side results in an entirely new feasible region, since all formerly feasible solutions (including of course the former optimal solution) become infeasible. For example, no values of x_1 and x_2 that satisfy the constraint $2x_1 + x_2 = 20$ can also satisfy $2x_1 + x_2 = 21$. Since an increase in an = constraint's right-hand side creates an entirely new feasible region, it is impossible to predict the effect on the LP's optimal objective value. It may improve, stay the same, or worsen, depending on whether the best objective value in the entirely new feasible region is better, the same, or worse than the former optimal objective value. Consequently, the shadow price of an = constraint may be either positive, 0, or negative.

We can summarize the last three paragraphs as follows:

Regardless of whether an LP involves maximization or minimization,

1. The shadow price of a $\leqslant$ constraint is always nonnegative, because increasing the right-hand side always results in the optimal objective value's improving or remaining the same.

2. The shadow price of a $\geqslant$ constraint is always nonpositive, because increasing the right-hand side always results in the optimal objective value's worsening or remaining the same.

3. The shadow price of an = constraint may be positive, zero, or negative, because increasing the right-hand side has an unpredictable effect on the optimal objective value.

Now that we understand the reason for the nonpositive shadow prices, let us analyze four scenarios that illustrate applications of the shadow price portion and sensitivity analysis portion of Figure 3.12's display of LINPRO's output. Before reading the discussion that follows each scenario, try to use LINPRO's output to analyze the scenario yourself.

Scenario 1. After Pete Moss has solved his blending LP but before his implementation of the optimal solution, he learns that his supplier is substantially raising the price of 0-15-20 fertilizer (represented in the LP by x_2) from its current price of $20 per 100-pound bag to a new price of $50 per 100-pound bag. Can Pete Moss use LINPRO's output to determine this price increase's effect on the minimal-cost blending "recipe" (assuming all the LP's other data remain unchanged)?

Analysis: The price increase corresponds to an increase in x_2's objective-function coefficient from 20 to 50, an increase that is less than the maximum allowable increase of 40 specified in the "range of optimality portion" of LINPRO's output. Consequently, the minimal-cost blending "recipe," $(x_1, x_2, x_3) = (2.5, 3.0, 4.5)$, remains optimal. Of course, since x_2's optimal value is 3.0 and its objective-function coefficient has increased by $30, the minimal blending cost increases by $(3)($30) = 90.

Scenario 2. After Pete Moss has solved his blending LP but before his implementation of the optimal solution, the customer that placed the order calls Pete to ask how much less it would cost to change the 1000-pound order from a 17-14-10 blend to a 15-14-10 blend—that is, a blend with a minimum nitrogen content of only 15% instead of 17%. Can Pete Moss use LINPRO's output to quickly answer the customer's question (assuming all the LP's other data remain unchanged)?

Analysis: The change in nitrogen content from at least 17% to at least 15% corresponds to decreasing the right-hand side of the LP's second structural constraint (named "nitro" in LINPRO's input) from 170 to 150. Because (as indicated by LINPRO's output) the optimal value of the constraint's surplus variable is 0, the constraint is binding at the LP's optimal solution. Hence, we expect a decrease in the constraint's right-hand side to have an effect on the LP's optimal solution. This effect can be quickly determined via the constraint's shadow price, if the proposed change is within the shadow price's range of validity. LINPRO's output confirms our expectation by indicating a shadow price of $-1\frac{1}{3}$ and also indicating that the shadow price is valid for decreases in the constraint's right-hand side of up to 150. Since the customer's proposed decrease is only 20, the constraint's shadow price of $-1\frac{1}{3}$ is valid for the entire decrease. Hence, the LP's optimal objective value improves by

$$\text{(shadow price)} \times \text{(right-hand side's increase)} = \left(-1\tfrac{1}{3}\right)(-20) = 26\tfrac{2}{3}$$

—that is, the LP's optimal objective value will improve by \$26.67 from its previous minimum of \$420 to a new minimum of \$393.33. To summarize, in comparison with the minimal cost of blending 1000 pounds of 17-14-10 fertilizer, the minimal cost of blending the same amount of 15-14-10 fertilizer is lower by \$26.67.[15]

Scenario 3. After Pete Moss has solved his blending LP but before his implementation of the optimal solution, the customer that placed the order calls Pete to ask how much more it would cost to change the 1000-pound order from a 17-14-10 blend to a 17-14-11 blend—that is, a blend with a minimum potassium content of 11% instead of only 10%. Can Pete Moss use LINPRO's output to quickly answer the customer's question (assuming all the LP's other data remain unchanged)?

Analysis: The change in potassium content from at least 10% to at least 11% corresponds to increasing the right-hand side of the LP's last structural constraint (named "pot" in LINPRO's input) from 100 to 110. Because (as indicated by LINPRO's output) the optimal value of the constraint's surplus variable is 17.5, the constraint is nonbinding at the LP's optimal solution; that is, the current blend already has 17.5 more pounds of potassium than is required. Hence, we expect an increase in the constraint's right-hand side to have no effect on the LP's optimal solution, if the proposed increase is less than the constraint's surplus variable of 17.5. LINPRO's output confirms our expectation by indicating a shadow price of 0 and also indicating that the shadow price is valid for increases in the constraint's right-hand side of up to 17.5 (the exact value of the surplus variable).[16] Since the customer's proposed increase is only 10, the constraint's shadow price of 0 is valid for the entire decrease. Hence, the LP's optimal objective value improves by

$$\text{(shadow price)} \times \text{(right-hand side's increase)} = (0)(10) = 0;$$

—that is, the LP's optimal objective value will remain unchanged at its current minimum of \$420. To summarize, the minimal cost of blending 1000 pounds of 17-14-10 fertilizer and the minimal cost of blending the same amount of 17-14-11 fertilizer are equal.[17]

Scenario 4. After Pete Moss has solved his blending LP but before his implementation of the optimal solution, the customer that placed the order for 1000 pounds of 17-14-10 fertilizer calls Pete to ask how much more it would cost to increase the order

---

[15] Note that the LINPRO output displayed in Figure 3.12 only permits us to determine the change in the optimal objective value. Using "advanced" LINPRO commands that cannot be explained until we have learned the details of the simplex method in Chapter 6, it is possible to determine the changes in the optimal values of the decision variables and the surplus variables without re-solving the LP.

[16] The equality of the maximum allowable increase and constraint's surplus variable illustrates part 1 of the summary given at the end of Section 3.6 for a general procedure for sensitivity analysis of a nonbinding constraint's right-hand side.

[17] In Section 3.6's summary of a general procedure for sensitivity analysis of the right-hand side of a constraint that is nonbinding at the LP's optimal solution, we indicated that the only effect of a change of Δ in a $\geq$ constraint's right-hand side (within the range of validity) is that the constraint's surplus variable will change by Δ. Hence, in Scenario 3, we do not need "advanced" LINPRO commands to determine the new optimal values of the decision variables and the surplus variables. All remain unchanged, except for a decrease in the "pot" constraint's surplus variable from 17.5 to 7.5.

size from 1000 pounds to 1100 pounds. Can Pete Moss use LINPRO's output to quickly answer the customer's question?

Analysis: At first glance, we may be tempted to conclude that the change in demand from 1000 pounds to 1100 pounds corresponds only to increasing the right-hand side of the LP's first structural constraint (named "demand" in LINPRO's output) from 10 to 11. However, we would be forgetting that, whereas the minimum nitrogen content in 1000 pounds of 17-14-10 fertilizer is 170 pounds, the minimum nitrogen content in 1100 pounds is 187 pounds. Similar comments apply to the minimum phosphorus content and the minimum potassium content. Thus, changing the demand corresponds to changing the right-hand sides of all four structural constraints. Since LINPRO's sensitivity analysis output is valid only when one right-hand side changes and the others remain unchanged, determining the effect of a change in demand requires the LP to be re-solved, this time using the new values for the four right-hand sides.

3.9 DECISION VARIABLES THAT ARE UNCONSTRAINED IN SIGN

As discussed in Section 3.7, many LP software packages automatically assume that all decision variables are constrained to be nonnegative, thereby eliminating the need for the user to input the nonnegativity constraints. This time-saving feature creates a problem when the initial formulation of an LP includes decision variables that are unconstrained (in sign) — that is, can assume negative as well as nonnegative values. For example, an LP involving financial planning might include a variable representing a cash inflow when the variable is positive but a cash outflow when the variable is negative.

Fortunately, there is a simple "trick" that enables us to convert an LP with unconstrained decision variables into an equivalent LP with all nonnegative variables. The validity of the trick rests on the following general observation:

> For every assignment of values to the n unconstrained decision variables x_1, $x_2, \ldots, x_n$ there exists an assignment of values to the $n + 1$ nonnegative decision variables $y_1, y_2, \ldots, y_n$ and w such that
>
> $$x_j = y_j - w \text{ for } j = 1, 2, \ldots, n.$$
>
> To find one such an assignment, let w equal the absolute value of the most negative value among $x_1, x_2, \ldots, x_n$ (let $w = 0$ if there is no negative value) and then let $y_j = w + x_j$ for $j = 1, 2, \ldots, n$.

For example, suppose

$$x_1 = 5, \ x_2 = -7, \ x_3 = 0, \ x_4 = 9, \text{ and } x_5 = -2.$$

Since $x_2 = -7$ is the most negative value, $w = |-7| = 7$. Then, using the formula $y_j = w + x_j$, we compute $y_1, y_2, \ldots, y_5$ as follows:

$$
\begin{aligned}
y_1 &= x_1 + w = 5 + 7 = 12 \\
y_2 &= x_2 + w = -7 + 7 = 0 \\
y_3 &= x_3 + w = 0 + 7 = 7 \\
y_4 &= x_4 + w = 9 + 7 = 16 \\
y_5 &= x_5 + w = -2 + 7 = 5.
\end{aligned}
$$

Note that the values of $y_1, y_2, \ldots, y_n,$ and w are all nonnegative and that, for $j = 1, 2, \ldots, n, x_j = y_j - w$; that is,

$$
\begin{array}{l}
x_j = y_j - w \\
\text{For } x_1: \quad 5 = 12 - 7 \\
\text{For } x_2: \;-7 = \;\;0 - 7 \\
\text{For } x_3: \quad 0 = \;\;7 - 7 \\
\text{For } x_4: \quad 9 = 16 - 7 \\
\text{For } x_5: \;-2 = \;\;5 - 7
\end{array}
$$

To illustrate how the above observation leads to a procedure for converting an LP having unconstrained decision variables into an equivalent LP having all non-negative decision variables, consider the following LP:

$$
\text{Maximize } 2x_1 - x_2 - 3x_3
$$

$$
\begin{array}{rrrrl}
\text{subject to } 6x_1 & - & 3x_2 & + & x_3 & \leqslant & 38 \\
2x_1 & + & x_2 & - & 5x_3 & \leqslant & 28 \\
x_1 & - & 4x_2 & - & x_3 & \leqslant & 53
\end{array}
$$

and x_1, x_2, x_3 unconstrained in sign.

We obtain an equivalent LP with all nonnegative decision variables by first defining the four nonnegative decision variables y_1, y_2, y_3, and w and then substituting $y_1 - w$ for x_1, $y_2 - w$ for x_2, and $y_3 - w$ for x_3. The result is

$$
\text{Maximize } 2(y_1 - w) - (y_2 - w) - 3(y_3 - w)
$$

$$
\begin{array}{rrrl}
\text{subject to } 6(y_1 - w) & - & 3(y_2 - w) & + & (y_3 - w) & \leqslant & 38 \\
2(y_1 - w) & + & (y_2 - w) & - & 5(y_3 - w) & \leqslant & 28 \\
(y_1 - w) & - & 4(y_2 - w) & - & (y_3 - w) & \leqslant & 53
\end{array}
$$

and $y_1 \geqslant 0, y_2 \geqslant 0, y_3 \geqslant 0, w \geqslant 0$,

which, after the collection in each row of all terms involving w into a single term, simplifies to

$$
\text{Maximize } 2y_1 - y_2 - 3y_3 + 2w
$$

$$
\begin{array}{rrrrl}
\text{subject to } 6y_1 & - & 3y_2 & + & y_3 & - & 4w & \leqslant & 38 \\
2y_1 & + & y_2 & - & 5y_3 & + & 2w & \leqslant & 28 \\
y_1 & - & 4y_2 & - & y_3 & + & 4w & \leqslant & 53
\end{array}
$$

and $y_1 \geqslant 0, y_2 \geqslant 0, y_3 \geqslant 0, w \geqslant 0$.

The optimal solution to this equivalent LP is

y_1	y_2	y_3	w	OBJECTIVE VALUE
13	0	4	11	36

corresponding to an optimal solution of the original LP of

$x_1 = y_1 - w$	$x_2 = y_2 - w$	$x_3 = y_3 - w$	OBJECTIVE VALUE
2	−11	−7	36

The above example illustrates the following general procedure:

To convert an LP with unconstrained variables into an equivalent LP having all nonnegative decision variables,

1. Define new nonnegative decision variables $y_1, y_2, \ldots, y_n$, and w.

2. In the objective function and in each structural constraint, substitute $y_j - w$ for x_j for $j = 1, 2, \ldots, n$ and then collect all terms involving w into a single term.

3. After solving the equivalent LP, obtain the optimal solution of the original LP using the formula $x_j = y_j - w$.

3.10 DECISION VARIABLES THAT HAVE NONZERO LOWER BOUNDS

LINPRO's time-saving feature of automatically assuming all decision variables are constrained to be nonnegative also causes a problem when the LP's initial formulation includes decision variables that have nonzero lower bounds. To illustrate, suppose the LP's initial formulation includes among its constraints

$$x_1 \geqslant -50 \quad \text{and} \quad x_2 \geqslant 800.$$

The latter constraint, for example, might arise in a product mix LP where at least 800 units of product 2 must be produced to satisfy contractual commitments. Given the constraint $x_1 \geqslant -50$, LINPRO's automatic nonnegativity constraint $x_1 \geqslant 0$ is too restrictive, and, given the constraint $x_2 \geqslant 800$, LINPRO's automatic nonnegativity constraint $x_2 \geqslant 0$ is redundant (i.e., unnecessary). Consequently, LINPRO should not be used to solve this LP as it was originally formulated.

Fortunately, there is a "trick" for converting an LP with decision variables having nonzero lower bounds into an equivalent LP with all decision variables having lower bounds of 0, thereby making correct LINPRO's automatic nonnegativity constraints. The validity of this trick rests on the following simple observation:

> If the decision variable x_j is always greater than or equal to a specified value v, then $x_j - v$ is always nonnegative. For example, if $x_1 \geqslant -50$, then $x_1 + 50$ is always nonnegative, and, if $x_2 \geqslant 800$, then $x_2 - 800$ is always nonnegative.

To illustrate how this observation leads to a procedure for converting an LP having decision variables with nonzero lower bounds into an equivalent LP having all nonnegative decision variables, consider the following LP:

$$\text{Minimize} \quad 7x_1 + 5x_2$$

$$\text{subject to} \quad x_1 + x_2 \geqslant 1750$$
$$-4x_1 + x_2 \leqslant 1900$$

$$\text{and} \quad x_1 \geqslant -50, x_2 \geqslant 800 .$$

We obtain an equivalent LP with all nonnegative decision variables by first defining the two nonnegative decision variables

$$y_1 = x_1 + 50 \quad \text{(or, equivalently, } x_1 = y_1 - 50)$$
$$y_2 = x_2 - 800 \quad \text{(or, equivalently, } x_2 = y_2 + 800)$$

We then substitute $y_1 - 50$ for x_1 and $y_2 + 800$ for x_2 in the objective function and every constraint. The result is

$$\text{Minimize} \quad 7(y_1 - 50) + 5(y_2 + 800)$$

$$\text{subject to} \quad (y_1 - 50) + (y_2 + 800) \geqslant 1750$$
$$-4(y_1 - 50) + (y_2 + 800) \leqslant 1900$$

$$\text{and} \quad (y_1 - 50) \geqslant -50, (y_2 + 800) \geqslant 800 .$$

Next, we simplify this LP by the collection in each row of all constants into a single constant, thereby obtaining

$$\text{Minimize} \quad 7y_1 + 5y_2 + 3650$$
$$\text{subject to} \quad y_1 + y_2 \geq 1000$$
$$-4y_1 + y_2 \leq 900$$

$$\text{and } y_1 \geq 0, y_2 \geq 0.$$

In solving this equivalent LP, we may ignore the constant of 3650 appearing at the end of the objective function and simply remember to add 3650 to the resulting LP's optimal objective value. If we ignore the objective function's constant and use LINPRO to solve the resulting LP, the optimal solution is

y_1	y_2	OBJECTIVE VALUE (ignoring constant of 3650)
20	980	5040

corresponding to an optimal solution of the original LP of

$x_1 = y_1 - 50$	$x_2 = y_2 + 800$	OBJECTIVE VALUE (including constant of 3650)
−30	1780	8690

The above example illustrates the following general procedure:

To convert an LP with decision variables having nonzero lower bounds into an equivalent LP having all nonnegative decision variables,

1. If x_j is a decision variable having a nonzero lower bound of v_j (i.e., $x_j \geq v_j$), then define the new nonnegative decision variable y_j equal to $x_j - v_j$. Since the relationship $y_j = x_j - v_j$ is equivalent to the relationship $x_j = y_j + v_j$, we obtain an equivalent LP by substituting $y_j + v_j$ for x_j in the objective function and every constraint.

2. After performing Step 1 for every decision variable with a nonzero lower bound, simplify the resulting LP by collecting all constants in each row into a single constant.

3. Temporarily ignore the constant appearing in the objective function and solve the resulting LP to obtain the optimal values of the y_j decision variables. Then, to obtain the original LP's optimal objective value, add the temporarily ignored constant to the equivalent LP's optimal objective value and, to obtain the optimal values of the original LP's x_j decision variables, use the formula $x_j = y_j + v_j$.

3.11 CONCLUDING REMARKS

In this chapter we have seen how to input data into an LP software package and how to interpret the resulting output. If you wish to learn how the software package employs the simplex method to convert your input into its output, you will have to continue to Chapters 6 and 7. Don't feel guilty, however, if you are willing to trust that an LP software package knows what it is doing, your curiosity having been sufficiently satisfied by Chapter 2's graphical solution procedure and this chapter's graphical sensitivity analysis.

We have used OMC's two-variable, three-constraint LP to illustrate how sensitivity analysis can potentially save time and money that would otherwise be spent to re-solve an LP after a change in a single decision variable's objective-function coefficient or a single constraint's right-hand side. For a large LP the savings in time and money can be dramatic. For example, suppose that, after we have just run up a large computer bill solving a product mix LP involving 5000 variables and 1000 constraints, we discover that the objective-function coefficient of x_{317} should be changed from $c_{317} = 500$ to $c_{317} = 400$. The change may be necessitated by a computer input error (i.e., we mistakenly typed 5 when we meant 4) or perhaps by an actual change in x_{317}'s unit profit. Regardless of the reason behind it, if the size of the change is within c_{317}'s range of optimality, we can quickly determine that there is no need to re-solve the LP because the current optimal solution remains optimal.

One additional application deserves mention. We can use sensitivity analysis to identify those objective-function coefficients or constraint right-hand sides that deserve closer scrutiny before our implementation of the LP's optimal solution. To illustrate, suppose that, in a product mix LP, the objective-function coefficient of a particular decision variable, say x_7, has an estimated value of $c_7 = \$350$. After solving the LP, suppose we determine that c_7's range of optimality is $349 \leqslant c_7 \leqslant 500$. With the current estimate of c_7 only \$1 above the range of optimality's lower limit, it would be wise to delay implementing the LP's optimal solution until we have carefully reestimated c_7, this time spending more time and/or money to obtain a more accurate estimate. If the new estimate falls within c_7's range of optimality, we can implement the LP's optimal solution. If not, we should re-solve the LP using the new estimate of c_7. To summarize,

> Prior to implementing an LP's optimal solution, we should carefully reestimate the following data:
>
> **1.** Any objective-function coefficient whose current estimate is close to the lower or upper limit of the coefficient's range of optimality,
>
> **2.** Any constraint right-hand side whose current estimate is close to the lower or upper limit of the right-hand side's range of validity.

In closing, we should point out that this chapter's coverage of sensitivity analysis has only "scratched the surface." The treatment here was limited to instances where a single decision variable's objective-function coefficient or a single structural constraint's right-hand side changes, *and all the LP's other data remain unchanged.* A more advanced treatment (beyond the scope of this text) would discuss procedures for determining the effect on the LP's optimal solution of such things as

1. simultaneous changes in two or more decision variables' objective-function coefficients,

2. simultaneous changes in two or more constraints' right-hand sides,

3. simultaneous changes in two or more decision variables' constraint coefficients,

4. combinations of items 1–3,

5. the addition to the LP of a new variable (with specified coefficients in the objective function and structural constraints),

6. the addition to the LP of a new constraint.

These more advanced forms of sensitivity analysis are useful in the "real world," where it is rare that only one datum changes and all other data remain unchanged.

3.12 CHAPTER CHECKLIST AND GLOSSARY

Quickly review this chapter by rereading the material highlighted by a vertical line in the left margin. You should then be familiar with the concepts, techniques, and terminology in the Checklist and Glossary that follow. If you need "help" with a particular item, consult the section or sections indicated for a more detailed discussion.

Checklist of Concepts and Techniques

☐ Performing graphical sensitivity analysis on a decision variable's objective-function coefficient. [3.2]

☐ Performing graphical sensitivity analysis on the right-hand side of a structural constraint that is binding at the LP's optimal solution. [3.3, 3.4, 3.5]

☐ Performing graphical sensitivity analysis on the right-hand side of a structural constraint that is nonbinding at the LP's optimal solution. [3.6]

☐ Using an LP software package and, in particular, interpreting the sensitivity-analysis portion of the output. [3.7, 3.8]

☐ Converting an LP with unconstrained decision variables into an equivalent LP with all nonnegative decision variables. [3.9]

☐ Converting an LP with decision variables having nonzero lower bounds into an equivalent LP with all nonnegative decision variables. [3.10]

Glossary

Sensitivity analysis. A collection of techniques for determining the effect changes in the LP's data have on the LP's optimal solution. [3.1, 3.11]

Range of optimality. For sensitivity analysis of a decision variable's objective-function coefficient, the range of optimality is the range of values over which the coefficient can vary (assuming all the LP's other data remain unchanged) without causing a change in the optimal values of the decision variables. [3.2]

Range of validity. For sensitivity analysis of a structural constraint's right-hand side, the range of validity is the range of values over which the right-hand side can vary (assuming all the LP's other data remain unchanged) without causing a change in the set of constraints that are binding at the LP's optimal solution. For changes within the range of validity, it is possible to compute the rates of change (per unit change in the constraint's right-hand side) in the optimal values of the decision variables, the slack and surplus variables, and the objective value. [3.3]

Shadow Price. A "by-product" of sensitivity analysis of a structural constraint's right-hand side, the shadow price is the rate of improvement in the LP's optimal objective value per unit increase in the constraint's right-hand side. [3.4]

EXERCISES

Exercises 3.1 through 3.7 test your ability to conduct graphical sensitivity analysis on a decision variables's objective-function coefficient or a structural constraint's right-hand side.

3.1. Consider the following LP:

$$\text{Maximize} \quad 3x_1 + 5x_2$$

$$\text{subject to} \quad x_1 \qquad\qquad \leqslant 4$$
$$2x_2 \leqslant 12$$
$$3x_1 + 2x_2 \leqslant 18$$

$$\text{and} \quad x_1 \geqslant 0, x_2 \geqslant 0.$$

(a) Graphically determine the optimal values of the decision variables, the slack and/or surplus variables, and the objective function. Note that, if you have worked Exercise 2.1, then you have already done part (a).

(b) Conduct graphical sensitivity analysis of each decision variable's objective-function coefficient by determining its range of optimality. Summarize your sensitivity analysis in a format similar to that of Table 3.2.

(c) Conduct graphical sensitivity analysis of each structural constraint's right-hand side by (1) letting Δ denote the change in the value of the right-hand side, (2) determining expressions involving Δ for the optimal values of the decision variables, the slack and/or surplus variables, and the objective function, (3) determining the shadow price of the constraint's right-hand side, and (4) determining the sensitivity analysis's range of validity. Summarize your sensitivity analysis in a format similar to that of Tables 3.3–3.5.

(d) Use an available software package to solve the LP and verify that your graphical analysis has produced the same information as the computer.

3.2. Redo Exercise 3.1, this time using the following LP:

$$\text{Maximize} \quad 5x_1 + 10x_2$$

$$\text{subject to} \quad -x_1 + 2x_2 \leqslant 25$$
$$x_1 + x_2 \leqslant 20$$
$$5x_1 + 3x_2 \leqslant 75$$

$$\text{and} \quad x_1 \geqslant 0, x_2 \geqslant 0.$$

Note that you have already done part (a) if you have worked Exercise 2.2. Also, note in part (b) that you should proceed with caution when graphi-

cally determining each objective-function coefficient's range of optimality because the region of permissible rotation of the optimal isoquant lines contains an isoquant line with a slope of 0 (i.e., a horizontal line).

3.3. Redo Exercise 3.1, this time using the following LP:

$$\text{Minimize} \quad 3x_1 + 5x_2$$

$$\text{subject to} \quad x_1 + 5x_2 \geqslant 20$$
$$-3x_1 + 2x_2 \leqslant 6$$
$$x_1 + x_2 \geqslant 8$$

$$\text{and} \quad x_1 \geqslant 0, x_2 \geqslant 0.$$

Note that you have already done part (a) if you have worked Exercise 2.3.

3.4. Redo Exercise 3.1, this time using the following LP:

$$\text{Minimize} \quad 30x_1 + 20x_2$$

$$\text{subject to} \quad x_1 \qquad\qquad \geqslant 4$$
$$2x_1 + x_2 = 20$$
$$x_1 + 2x_2 \geqslant 19$$

$$\text{and} \quad x_1 \geqslant 0, x_2 \geqslant 0.$$

Note that you have already done part (a) if you have worked Exercise 2.4. Also, note in part (b) that you should proceed with caution when graphically determining each objective-function coefficient's range of optimality because the region of permissible rotation of the optimal isoquant line contains an isoquant line with a slope of 0 (i.e., a horizontal line).

3.5. Redo Exercise 3.1, this time using the following LP:

$$\text{Maximize} \quad 3x_1 + 2x_2$$

$$\text{subject to} \quad 2x_1 + 4x_2 \leqslant 22$$
$$-x_1 + 4x_2 \leqslant 10$$
$$2x_1 - x_2 \leqslant 7$$
$$x_1 - 2x_2 \leqslant 2$$

$$\text{and} \quad x_1 \geqslant 0, x_2 \geqslant 0.$$

Note that you have already done part (a) if you have worked Exercise 2.5. Also, note in part (b) that you should proceed with caution when graphically determining each objective-function coefficient's range of optimality because the region of permissible rotation of the optimal isoquant line contains an isoquant line with a slope of ∞ (i.e., a vertical line).

* 3.6. Redo Exercise 3.1, this time using the following LP:

$$\text{Maximize} \quad 5x_1 + 4x_2$$

$$\text{subject to} \quad \begin{aligned} 10x_1 + 15x_2 &\leqslant 150 \\ 20x_1 + 20x_2 &\geqslant 100 \\ 20x_1 + 10x_2 &\leqslant 160 \\ -3x_1 + x_2 &\leqslant 3 \end{aligned}$$

$$\text{and} \quad x_1 \geqslant 0, x_2 \geqslant 0.$$

Note that you have already done part (a) if you have worked Exercise 2.6.

3.7. Redo Exercise 3.1, this time using the following LP:

$$\text{Maximize} \quad 10x_1 + 20x_2$$

$$\text{subject to} \quad \begin{aligned} x_1 + 6x_2 &\leqslant 54 \\ x_1 + x_2 &\leqslant 19 \\ -x_1 + 10x_2 &\leqslant 2 \\ 2x_1 + x_2 &\geqslant 8 \\ 2x_1 - 3x_2 &\leqslant 18 \end{aligned}$$

$$\text{and} \quad x_1 \geqslant 0, x_2 \geqslant 0.$$

Note that you have already done part (a) if you have worked Exercise 2.7.

Exercises 3.8 through 3.10 test your understanding of how to calculate the objective-function coefficients for a product mix LP.

3.8. Andrew and Jonathan are arguing about how to formulate the objective function for a product mix linear program faced by their employer, The Gadget Company (TGC). The relevant information is as follows:

- TGC manufactures two products: widgets and thingamabobs.
- TGC sells widgets for $30 each and thingamabobs for $40 each.
- Three resources used in the production of widgets and thingamabobs are available in limited quantities this week. In particular, TGC has purchased 400 units of resource 1 at a cost of $2 per unit, 130 units of resource 2 at a cost of $3 per unit, and 450 units of resource 3 at a cost of $4 per unit. Unused units can neither be returned to the supplier nor sold to another manufacturer.
- The production of each widget consumes 4 units of resource 1, 1 unit of resource 2, and 1 unit of resource 3.
- The production of each thingamabob consumes 1 unit of resource 1, 1 unit of resource 2, and 5 units of resource 3.
- The variable unit production costs are $5 for widgets and $10 for thingamabobs. (These unit costs exclude the total cost of resources 1, 2, and

3 consumed in producing one widget or one thingamabob.)

Andrew and Jonathan both agree that product mix LP's constraints are

$$\begin{aligned} 4x_1 + x_2 &\leqslant 400 \\ x_1 + x_2 &\leqslant 130 \\ x_1 + 5x_2 &\leqslant 450 \end{aligned}$$

$$\text{and} \quad x_1 \geqslant 0, x_2 \geqslant 0.$$

However, they disagree over the objective function. Andrew wants to calculate the decision variables' objective-function coefficients as follows:

	Andrew's Computation of a Widget's Unit Profit		Andrew's Computation of a Thingamabob's Unit Profit
30	(selling price)	40	(selling price)
−5	(variable production cost)	−10	(variable production cost)
−8	(cost of 4 units of resource 1 at $2 per unit)	−2	(cost of 1 unit of resource 1 at $2 per unit)
−3	(cost of 1 unit of resource 2 at $3 per unit)	−3	(cost of 1 unit of resource 2 at $3 per unit)
−4	(cost of 1 unit of resource 3 at $4 per unit)	−20	(cost of 5 units of resource 3 at $4 per unit)
10	(unit profit)	5	(unit profit)

Thus, Andrew believes the LP's objective function should be to maximize $10x_1 + 5x_2$.

Jonathan disagrees! He wants to eliminate from Andrew's calculation of each unit profit the last three subtractions (i.e., the total cost of resources 1, 2, and 3 consumed by one widget or one thingamabob). Hence, Jonathan believes the unit profit should be $30 - 5 = 25$ for a widget and $40 - 10 = 30$ for a thingamabob, thereby leading to an objective function of maximizing $25x_1 + 30x_2$.

Whom do you agree with—Andrew, who proposes an objective function of $10x_1 + 5x_2$, or Jonathan, who proposes an objective function of $25x_1 + 30x_2$?

3.9 Reconsider Exercise 3.8. Andrew insists he can prove his objective function is correct. He states that he has solved both the following LP's:

	Andrew's LP		Jonathan's LP
Maximize	$10x_1 + 5x_2$	Maximize	$25x_1 + 30x_2$
subject to	$4x_1 + x_2 \leqslant 400$	subject to	$4x_1 + x_2 \leqslant 400$
	$x_1 + x_2 \leqslant 130$		$x_1 + x_2 \leqslant 130$
	$x_1 + 5x_2 \leqslant 450$		$x_1 + 5x_2 \leqslant 450$
and	$x_1 \geqslant 0, x_2 \geqslant 0$	and	$x_1 \geqslant 0, x_2 \geqslant 0.$

Andrew says that the optimal objective value for his LP is $440 higher than the value obtained by subtracting from the optimal objective value for Jonathan's LP the total purchase cost of all resources. In what follows, you will be asked to verify Andrew's statements and discuss whether his logic is correct.

(a) Graphically solve Andrew's LP to verify that the optimal product mix is $(x_1, x_2) = (90, 40)$ and the optimal objective value is $1100.

(b) Graphically solve Jonathan's LP to verify that the optimal product mix is $(x_1, x_2) = (50, 80)$ and the optimal objective value is $3650.

(c) Andrew and Jonathan agree that, since Jonathan's objective-function coefficients exclude the resources' costs, Jonathan's optimal objective value must be reduced by the total purchase cost of all resources, that is, by

$$(400 \times 2) + (130 \times 3) + (450 \times 4) = \$2990.$$

Thus, Andrew claims that, whereas his optimal product mix of $(x_1, x_2) = (90, 40)$ yields a total profit of $1100, Jonathan's optimal product mix yields a total profit of only $3650 - $2990 = $660, $440 less than Andrew's. Is Andrew correct? If not, what is the fallacy in his logic?

3.10. Reconsider Exercise 3.8. Now assume that the resource availabilities of 400 units for resource 1, 130 for resource 2, and 450 for resource 3 are not units that The Gadget Company (TGC) has already purchased. Instead, assume that each resource availability represents the maximum supply TGC can obtain from the resource's vendor. TGC does not need to purchase the maximum supply, only the exact amount required by TGC's product mix. For example, TGC can purchase up to 400 units of resource 1; however, if its optimal product mix consumes only 300 units of resource 1, TGC need not purchase the remaining 100 units. (Alternatively, you may assume that TGC first purchases all 400 units and the supplier subsequently repurchases any unused units at the same price paid by TGC.) Under this new assumption, whom do you agree with—Andrew, who proposes an objective function of $10x_1 + 5x_2$, or Jonathan, who proposes an objective function of $25x_1 + 30x_2$?

Exercises 3.11 and 3.12 test your understanding of the interpretation of a shadow price associated with a resource constraint in a product mix LP.

3.11. You have just used a software package to solve a product mix LP in which the first of the scarce resources has an availability of 200 and a unit cost of $2. On reviewing the software package's output, you observe that resource 1 has a shadow price of $6 for increases in its availability up to a maximum

of 30 units and decreases in its availability up to a maximum of 20 units. Now suppose you receive a phone call from a vendor offering you 10 additional units of the resource at a cost of $7 each (a unit cost that is $5 more than the $2 unit cost of the 200 units currently available).

(a) Assume that, when calculating each decision variable's objective-function coefficient, it was incorrect to subtract the cost of the amount of resource 1 consumed by the manufacturer of 1 unit of product 1 and, hence, you did not perform the subtraction. Under this assumption, what would be the change in total profit if you purchase the additional 10 units of resource 1 at a cost of $7 each? Do you recommend the purchase?

(b) Assume that, when calculating each decision variable's objective-function coefficient, it was correct to subtract the cost of the amount of resource 1 consumed by the manufacturer of 1 unit of product 1 and, hence, you did perform the subtraction. Under this assumption, what would be the change in total profit if you purchase the additional 10 units of resource 1 at a cost of $7 each? Do you recommend the purchase?

(c) Discuss the general principle illustrated by parts (a) and (b).

3.12. You have just used a software package to solve a product mix LP. On reviewing the software package's output, you observe that
- The first of the scarce resources has a shadow price of $10 for increases in its availability up to a maximum of 50 units and decreases in its availability up to a maximum of 20 units.
- The second of the scarce resources has a shadow price of $5 for increases in its availability up to a maximum of 40 units and decreases in its availability up to a maximum of 30 units.

(a) Suppose you must choose one of the following two options:

(1) Acquire 1 additional unit of resource 1 at a unit cost that is $7 over and above that which has already been accounted for in the objective function.

(2) Acquire 1 additional unit of resource 2 at a unit cost that is $1 over and above that which has already been accounted for in the objective function.

Which option would you choose and why?

(b) Redo part (a), this time assuming option 1 involves 3 (not 1) additional units of resource 1 and option 2 involves 2 (not 1) additional units of resource 2.

129

(c) Discuss the general principle illustrated by parts (a) and (b).

Exercises 3.13 through 3.19 test your ability to use sensitivity analysis information. An exercise consists of parts (a)–(g), each requesting you to analyze the effect of a change in a decision variable's objective-function coefficient or a structural constraint's right-hand side. Regard each part as independent of the others. In some parts, sensitivity analysis may provide insufficient information to allow you to answer, in which case you should state "Insufficient information!"

3.13. (*Note*: If you have not already done so, read the above comments.) This exercise assumes you have already performed the graphical sensitivity analysis requested in Exercise 3.1. Using this graphical sensitivity analysis, answer the following questions:

(a) Within what range can x_1's objective-function coefficient vary such that the current optimal solution remains optimal?

(b) If x_2's objective-function coefficient changes from 5 to 7, what are the optimal values of x_1 and x_2 and what is the optimal objective value?

(c) If x_2's objective-function coefficient changes from 5 to 1, what are the optimal values of x_1 and x_2 and what is the optimal objective value?

(d) Within what range can the third structural constraint's right-hand side vary such that the constraints that are currently binding at the LP's optimal solution remain binding?

(e) If the first structural constraint's right-hand side changes from 4 to 5, what are the optimal values of the decision variables, the slack variables, and the objective function?

(f) If the second structural constraint's right-hand side changes from 12 to 9, what are the optimal values of the decision variables, the slack variables, and the objective function?

(g) If the third structural constraint's right-hand side changes from 18 to 25, what are the optimal values of the decision variables, the slack variables, and the objective function?

*3.14. (*Note*: If you have not already done so, read the comments preceding Exercise 3.13.) This exercise assumes you have already performed the graphical sensitivity analysis requested in Exercise 3.2. Using this graphical sensitivity analysis, answer the following questions:

(a) Within what range can x_2's objective-function coefficient vary such that the current optimal solution remains optimal?

(b) If x_1's objective-function coefficient changes from 5 to 9, what are the optimal values of x_1 and x_2 and what is the optimal objective value?

(c) If x_1's objective-function coefficient changes from 5 to 11, what are the optimal values of x_1 and x_2 and what is the optimal objective value?

(d) Within what range can the first structural constraint's right-hand side vary such that the constraints that are currently binding at the LP's optimal solution remain binding?

(e) If the first structural constraint's right-hand side changes from 25 to 31, what are the optimal values of the decision variables, the slack variables, and the objective function?

(f) If the second structural constraint's right-hand side changes from 20 to 22, what are the optimal values of the decision variables, the slack variables, and the objective function?

(g) If the third structural constraint's right-hand side changes from 75 to 72, what are the optimal values of the decision variables, the slack variables, and the objective function?

3.15. (*Note*: If you have not already done so, read the comments preceding exercise 3.13.) This exercise assumes you have already performed the graphical sensitivity analysis requested in Exercise 3.3. Using this graphical sensitivity analysis, answer the following questions:

(a) Within what range can x_1's objective-function coefficient vary such that the current optimal solution remains optimal?

(b) If x_2's objective-function coefficient changes from 5 to 4, what are the optimal values of x_1 and x_2 and what is the optimal objective value?

(c) If x_2's objective-function coefficient changes from 5 to 1, what are the optimal values of x_1 and x_2 and what is the optimal objective value?

(d) Within what range can the second structural constraint's right-hand side vary such that the constraints that are currently binding at the LP's optimal solution remain binding?

(e) If the second structural constraint's right-hand side changes from 6 to 1, what are the optimal values of the decision variables, the slack variables, and the objective function?

(f) If the first structural constraint's right-hand side changes from 20 to 35, what are the optimal values of the decision variables, the slack variables, and the objective function?

(g) If the third structural constraint's right-hand side changes from 8 to 18, what are the optimal values of the decision variables, the slack variables, and the objective function?

3.16. (*Note*: If you have not already done so, read the comments preceding Exercise 3.13.) This exercise assumes you have already performed the graphical sensitivity analysis requested in Exercise 3.4. Using this graphical sensitivity analysis, answer the following questions:

(a) Within what range can x_2's objective-function coefficient vary such that the current optimal solution remains optimal?

(b) If x_1's objective-function coefficient changes from 30 to 35, what are the optimal values of x_1 and x_2 and what is the optimal objective value?

(c) If x_2's objective-function coefficient changes from 20 to 18, what are the optimal values of x_1 and x_2 and what is the optimal objective value?

(d) Within what range can the second structural constraint's right-hand side vary such that the constraints that are currently binding at the LP's optimal solution remain binding?

(e) If the second structural constraint's right-hand side changes from 20 to 26, what are the optimal values of the decision variables, the slack variables, and the objective function?

(f) If the first structural constraint's right-hand side changes from 4 to 8, what are the optimal values of the decision variables, the slack variables, and the objective function?

(g) If the third structural constraint's right-hand side changes from 19 to 13, what are the optimal values of the decision variables, the slack variables, and the objective function?

3.17. (*Note*: If you have not already done so, read the comments preceding Exercise 3.13.) This exercise assumes you have already performed the graphical sensitivity analysis requested in Exercise 3.5. Using this graphical sensitivity analysis, answer the following questions:

(a) Within what range can x_1's objective-function coefficient vary such that the current optimal solution remains optimal?

(b) If x_2's objective-function coefficient changes from 2 to 5, what are the optimal values of x_1 and x_2 and what is the optimal objective value?

(c) If x_2's objective-function coefficient changes from 2 to 7, what are the optimal values of x_1 and x_2 and what is the optimal objective value?

(d) Within what range can the third structural constraint's right-hand side vary such that the constraints that are currently binding at the LP's optimal solution remain binding?

(e) If the third structural constraint's right-hand side changes from 7 to 8, what are the optimal values of the decision variables, the slack variables, and the objective function?

(f) If the second structural constraint's right-hand side changes from 10 to 8, what are the optimal values of the decision variables, the slack variables, and the objective function?

(g) If the first structural constraint's right-hand side changes from 22 to 20, what are the optimal values of the decision variables, the slack variables, and the objective function?

*3.18. (*Note*: If you have not already done so, read the

comments preceding Exercise 3.13.) This exercise assumes you have already performed the graphical sensitivity analysis requested in Exercise 3.6. Using this graphical sensitivity analysis, answer the following questions:

(a) Within what range can x_2's objective-function coefficient vary such that the current optimal solution remains optimal?

(b) If x_2's objective-function coefficient changes from 4 to 3, what are the optimal values of x_1 and x_2 and what is the optimal objective value?

(c) If x_1's objective-function coefficient changes from 5 to 2, what are the optimal values of x_1 and x_2 and what is the optimal objective value?

(d) Within what range can the first structural constraint's right-hand side vary such that the constraints that are currently binding at the LP's optimal solution remain binding?

(e) If the first structural constraint's right-hand side changes from 150 to 130, what are the optimal values of the decision variables, the slack variables, and the objective function?

(f) If the second structural constraint's right-hand side changes from 100 to 200, what are the optimal values of the decision variables, the slack variables, and the objective function?

(g) If the third structural constraint's right-hand side changes from 160 to 350, what are the optimal values of the decision variables, the slack variables, and the objective function?

3.19. (*Note*: If you have not already done so, read the comments preceding Exercise 3.13.) This exercise assumes you have already performed the graphical sensitivity analysis requested in Exercise 3.7. Using this graphical sensitivity analysis, answer the following questions:

(a) Within what range can x_1's objective-function coefficient vary such that the current optimal solution remains optimal?

(b) If x_1's objective-function coefficient changes from 10 to 5, what are the optimal values of x_1 and x_2 and what is the optimal objective value?

(c) If x_2's objective-function coefficient changes from 20 to 5, what are the optimal values of x_1 and x_2 and what is the optimal objective value?

(d) Within what range can the third structural constraint's right-hand side vary such that the constraints that are currently binding at the LP's optimal solution remain binding?

(e) If the third structural constraint's right-hand side changes from 2 to 5, what are the optimal values of the decision variables, the slack variables, and the objective function?

(f) If the first structural constraint's right-hand side changes from 54 to 49, what are the optimal values of the decision variables, the slack variables, and the objective function?

(g) If the second structural constraint's right-hand side changes from 19 to 20, what are the optimal values of the decision variables, the slack variables, and the objective function?

Exercises 3.20 through 3.25 test your ability to interpret the sensitivity analysis portion of computer output.

3.20. This exercise assumes you have already worked Exercise 2.27. That exercise requested you to formulate an LP for the product mix decision problem of Coleeko Toy Company (CTC). Your formulation should be similar to the following LP:

$$\text{Maximize} \quad 4x_H + 2x_D$$

$$\text{subject to} \quad 15x_H + 15x_D \leqslant 28{,}800$$
$$10x_H + 15x_D \leqslant 28{,}800$$
$$x_H \leqslant 1{,}680$$
$$x_D \geqslant 720$$

$$\text{and} \quad x_H \geqslant 0, x_D \geqslant 0.$$

where x_H and x_D denote the daily production quantities of hawks and doves, respectively. Solving the above LP with LINPRO results in the output displayed here. Parts (a)–(f) below request you to use the computer output to analyze the effect of a change in a decision variable's objective-function coefficient or a structural constraint's right-hand side. Regard each part as being independent of the other parts. In some parts, the computer output may provide insufficient information to allow you to answer, in which case you should state "Insufficient information!"

Exercise 3.20

```
            OPTIMAL OBJECTIVE VALUE

                 7200.00000
    DECISION     OPTIMAL
    VARIABLE     VALUE          REDUCED COST
         XH      1440.000000       .000000
         XD       720.000000       .000000

                 SLACK OR
    CONSTRAINT   SURPLUS        SHADOW PRICE
       SKIN)       .000000        .266667
       STUFF)   3600.000000        .000000
       SHARP)    240.000000        .000000
       DOVES)      .000000       -.666667


              SENSITIVITY ANALYSIS

        OBJECTIVE-FUNCTION COEFFICIENTS' RANGES
    DECISION    CURRENT       ALLOWABLE      ALLOWABLE
    VARIABLE    COEFFICIENT   INCREASE       DECREASE
         XH     4.000000      INFINITY       1.000000
         XD     2.000000       .666667       INFINITY


            RIGHT-HAND SIDES' RANGES
                 CURRENT       ALLOWABLE      ALLOWABLE
    CONSTRAINT   RHS           INCREASE       DECREASE
       SKIN)   28800.000000   3600.000000    21600.000000
       STUFF)  28800.000000   INFINITY        3600.000000
       SHARP)   1680.000000   INFINITY         240.000000
       DOVES)    720.000000    432.000000      360.000000
```

(a) CTC anticipates a change in market conditions that would increase the unit profit of doves from $2.00 to $2.50. If this increase occurs, what are the optimal values of the decision variables, and what is the optimal objective value?

(b) CTC anticipates a change in market conditions that would decrease the unit profit of hawks from $4.00 to $2.50. If this decrease occurs, what are the optimal values of the decision variables, and what is the optimal total profit?

(c) If the availability of the skin machine increases from 28,800 to 30,600 seconds, what is the optimal total profit?

(d) If the availability of the stuffing machine increases from 28,800 to 30,600 seconds, what is the optimal total profit?

(e) If CTC's president were to reduce the minimum dove production from 720 to 600, how would CTC's total profit change?

(f) If CTC's president were to reduce the minimum dove production from 720 to 350, how would CTC's total profit change?

3.21. This exercise assumes you have already worked Exercise 2.28. That exercise requested you to formulate an LP for the product mix decision problem of the Big Bang Novelty Company (BBNC). Your formulation should be similar to the following LP:

$$\text{Maximize} \quad 0.45x_T + 0.55x_W + 0.70x_H$$

$$\text{subject to} \quad 30x_T + 20x_W + 30x_H \leqslant 4800$$
$$0.5x_W + x_H \leqslant 90$$
$$x_T + 2x_W + 3x_H \leqslant 360$$

$$\text{and} \quad x_T \geqslant 0, x_W \geqslant 0, x_H \geqslant 0.$$

where x_T, x_W, and x_H denote the daily production quantities of Toots, Wheets, and Honks, respectively, Solving the above LP with LINPRO results in the output displayed here. Parts (a)–(g) below request you to use the computer output to analyze the effect of a change in a decision variable's objective-function coefficient or a structural constraint's right-hand side. Regard each part as independent of the other parts. In some parts, the computer output may provide insufficient information to allow you to answer, in which case you should state "Insufficient information!"

(a) If the unit profit of a Toot decreases from $0.45 to $0.30, what are the optimal values of the decision variables, and what is the optimal total profit?

(b) If the unit profit of a Honk increases from $0.70 to $0.80, what are the optimal values of the decision variables, and what is the optimal total profit?

132

```
            OPTIMAL OBJECTIVE VALUE

                109.500000
   DECISION      OPTIMAL
   VARIABLE      VALUE            REDUCED COST
      XT         60.000000           .000000
      XW        150.000000           .000000
      XH           .000000           .125000

                 SLACK OR
   CONSTRAINT    SURPLUS          SHADOW PRICE
    LABOR)          .000000          .008750
    SEQUINS)      15.000000          .000000
    FEATHERS)       .000000          .187500


             SENSITIVITY ANALYSIS

       OBJECTIVE-FUNCTION COEFFICIENTS' RANGES
   DECISION    CURRENT      ALLOWABLE    ALLOWABLE
   VARIABLE    COEFFICIENT  INCREASE     DECREASE
      XT        .450000      .375000      .175000
      XW        .550000      .350000      .083333
      XH        .700000      .125000     INFINITY


            RIGHT-HAND SIDES' RANGES
               CURRENT      ALLOWABLE    ALLOWABLE
   CONSTRAINT  RHS          INCREASE     DECREASE
    LABOR)     4800.000000  6000.000000  1200.000000
    SEQUINS)     90.000000  INFINITY       15.000000
    FEATHERS)   360.000000    40.000000    200.000000
```

Exercise 3.21

```
            OPTIMAL OBJECTIVE VALUE

                294.333300
   DECISION      OPTIMAL
   VARIABLE      VALUE            REDUCED COST
      XR          5.000000           .000000
      XT         16.166670           .000000
      XN         30.000000           .000000

                 SLACK OR
   CONSTRAINT    SURPLUS          SHADOW PRICE
    BUDGET)         .000000         2.666667
    EXPOSE)      306.666700          .000000
    RMIN)           .000000        -2.066667
    TMIN)         11.166670          .000000
    NMIN)         25.000000          .000000
    RMAX)         25.000000          .000000
    TMAX)         13.833330          .000000
    NMAX)           .000000         1.266667


             SENSITIVITY ANALYSIS

       OBJECTIVE-FUNCTION COEFFICIENTS' RANGES
   DECISION    CURRENT      ALLOWABLE    ALLOWABLE
   VARIABLE    COEFFICIENT  INCREASE     DECREASE
      XR       3.000000      2.066667    INFINITY
      XT       8.000000      2.714286     3.263158
      XN       5.000000     INFINITY      1.266667


            RIGHT-HAND SIDES' RANGES
               CURRENT      ALLOWABLE    ALLOWABLE
   CONSTRAINT  RHS          INCREASE     DECREASE
    BUDGET)    100.000000     41.500000    13.142860
    EXPOSE)   2500.000000    306.666700   INFINITY
    RMIN)        5.000000     17.631580     5.000000
    TMIN)        5.000000     11.166670    INFINITY
    NMIN)        5.000000     25.000000    INFINITY
    RMAX)       30.000000    INFINITY      25.000000
    TMAX)       30.000000    INFINITY      13.833330
    NMAX)       30.000000     23.928570    17.692310
```

Exercise 3.22

(c) If the availability of labor decreases from 4800 to 4000 hours, what is the optimal total profit?

(d) BBNC has the opportunity to purchase 10 additional ounces of sequin powder. What is the maximum unit price BBNC should be willing to pay?

(e) BBNC has the opportunity to purchase 30 additional feathers at a unit price that is $0.15 over and above the unit price already accounted for in the products' unit profits. Should BBNC make the purchase?

(f) Redo part (e), this time assuming that 50 additional feathers (instead of 30) are available.

(g) Redo part (e), this time assuming that the unit price of the additional 30 feathers is $0.20 over and above the unit price already accounted for in the products' unit profits.

3.22. This exercise assumes you have already worked Exercise 2.29. That exercise requested you to formulate an LP for the advertising mix decision problem of Mark Etting. Your formulation should be similar to the following LP:

$$\text{Maximize} \quad 3x_R + 8x_T + 5x_N$$

$$
\begin{aligned}
\text{subject to} \quad 1.9x_R + 3.0x_T + 1.4x_N &\leq 100 \\
35x_R + 70x_T + 50x_N &\geq 2500 \\
x_R &\geq 5 \\
x_T &\geq 5 \\
x_N &\geq 5 \\
x_R &\leq 30 \\
x_T &\leq 30 \\
x_N &\leq 30
\end{aligned}
$$

and $x_R \geq 0, x_T \geq 0, x_N \geq 0$.

where x_R, x_T, and x_N denote the number of ads on radio, on TV, and in the newspaper, respectively. Solving the above LP with LINPRO results in the output displayed here. Parts (a)–(h) below request you to use the computer output to analyze the effect of a change in a decision variable's objective-function coefficient or a structural constraint's right-hand side. Regard each part as independent of the other parts. In some parts, the computer output may provide insufficient information to allow you to answer, in which case you should state "Insufficient information!"

(a) If the number of units sold per radio ad increases from 3000 to 5000, what are the optimal values of the decision variables, and what is the maximum total sales?

(b) If the number of units sold per TV ad decreases from 8000 to 4000, what are the optimal values of the decision variables, and what is the maximum total sales?

(c) If the budget increases from $100,000 to $120,000, what is maximum total sales?

(d) If the required number of potential customers that must be exposed to the product across all media decreases from 2,500,000 to 2,000,000, what is the maximum total sales?

(e) If there were no minimum requirement for radio ads, what would be the maximum total sales?

(f) If there were no maximum requirement for TV ads, what would be the maximum total sales?

(g) If the maximum requirement for newspaper ads were to increase to 50, what would be the maximum total sales?

(h) If there were no maximum requirement for newspaper ads, what would be the maximum total sales?

3.23. This exercise assumes you have already worked Exercise 2.30. That exercise requested you to formulate an LP for the blending decision problem of the Pittsburgh Iron Company (PIC). Your formulation should be similar to the following LP:

$$\text{Minimize} \quad 3x_A + 2x_B$$

$$\text{subject to} \quad x_A + x_B = 10$$
$$0.06x_A + 0.03x_B \geq 0.36$$
$$0.02x_A + 0.01x_B \leq 0.17$$

$$\text{and} \quad x_A \geq 0, x_B \geq 0.$$

where x_A and x_B denote the respective pounds of pig iron A and pig iron B used to blend a 10-pound casting. Solving the above LP with LINPRO results in the output displayed here. Parts (a)–(h) below request you to use the computer output to analyze the effect of a change in a decision variable's objective-function coefficient or a structural constraint's right-hand side. Regard each part as independent of the other parts. In some parts, the computer output may provide insufficient information to allow you to answer, in which case you should state "Insufficient information!"

Exercise 3.23

```
         OPTIMAL OBJECTIVE VALUE

              22.0000000
DECISION      OPTIMAL
VARIABLE      VALUE              REDUCED COST
    XA        2.000000              .000000
    XB        8.000000              .000000

              SLACK OR
CONSTRAINT    SURPLUS             SHADOW PRICE
  DEMAND)     .000000            -1.000000
   MANG)      .000000           -33.333340
 SILICON)     .050000              .000000


              SENSITIVITY ANALYSIS

      OBJECTIVE-FUNCTION COEFFICIENTS' RANGES
DECISION    CURRENT      ALLOWABLE      ALLOWABLE
VARIABLE    COEFFICIENT  INCREASE       DECREASE
   XA       3.000000     INFINITY       1.000000
   XB       2.000000     1.000000       INFINITY


              RIGHT-HAND SIDES' RANGES
            CURRENT      ALLOWABLE      ALLOWABLE
CONSTRAINT  RHS          INCREASE       DECREASE
  DEMAND)   10.000000    2.000000       4.000000
   MANG)    .360000      .150000        .060000
 SILICON)   .170000      INFINITY       .050000
```

(a) If the cost per pound of pig iron A decreases from 3 cents to 2.5 cents, what are the optimal values of the decision variables, and what is the minimum total cost?

(b) If the cost per pound of pig iron B increases from 2 cents to 3.5 cents, what are the optimal values of the decision variables, and what is the minimum total cost?

(c) If the minimum manganese content increases from 3.6% to 4.0%, what is the minimum total cost?

(d) If the minimum manganese content decreases from 3.6% to 3.1%, what is the minimum total cost?

(e) If the minimum manganese content decreases from 3.6% to 2.9%, what is the minimum total cost?

(f) If the maximum silicon content increases from 1.7% to 2.0%, what is the minimum total cost?

(g) If the maximum silicon content decreases from 1.7% to 1.0%, what is the minimum total cost?

(h) If the casting's total weight were to increase from 10 pounds to 11 pounds, what would be the minimum total cost?

*3.24. This exercise assumes you have already worked Exercise 2.31. That exercise requested you to formulate an LP for the blending decision problem of the Hot Dawg Company (HDC). Your formulation should be similar to the following LP:

$$\text{Minimize} \quad 1.0x_B + 0.5x_C + 0.7x_L$$

$$\text{subject to} \quad x_B + x_C + x_L = 100$$
$$0.20x_B + 0.15x_C + 0.15x_L \geq 12$$
$$0.20x_B + 0.15x_C + 0.25x_L \leq 24$$
$$0.60x_B + 0.70x_C + 0.60x_L \leq 64$$
$$x_L \geq 30$$

$$\text{and} \quad x_B \geq 0, x_C \geq 0, x_L \geq 0.$$

where x_B, x_C, and x_L denote the respective pounds of beef, chicken, and lamb used to blend the 100 pounds of Super Sausage. Solving the above LP with LINPRO results in the output displayed here. Parts (a)–(g) below request you to use the computer output to analyze the effect of a change in a decision variable's objective-function coefficient or a structural constraint's right-hand side. Regard each part as independent of the other parts. In some parts, the computer output may provide insufficient information to allow you to answer, in which case you should state "Insufficient information!"

(a) If the cost per pound of beef decreases from $1.00 to $0.75, what are the optimal values of the decision variables and the minimum total cost?

```
              OPTIMAL OBJECTIVE VALUE

                    62.0000000
    DECISION       OPTIMAL
    VARIABLE        VALUE              REDUCED COST
         XB         .000000              .300000
         XC       39.999990              .000000
         XL       60.000010              .000000

                    SLACK OR
    CONSTRAINT      SURPLUS            SHADOW PRICE
    DEMAND)         .000000             -1.900000
    PROTEIN)       3.000000              .000000
    FAT)           2.999998             .000000
    WATER)          .000000             2.000001
    LAMB)         30.000010              .000000


                SENSITIVITY ANALYSIS

         OBJECTIVE-FUNCTION COEFFICIENTS' RANGES
    DECISION     CURRENT       ALLOWABLE      ALLOWABLE
    VARIABLE    COEFFICIENT    INCREASE       DECREASE
         XB     1.000000       INFINITY        .300000
         XC      .500000        .200000       INFINITY
         XL      .700000        .300000        .200000


              RIGHT-HAND SIDES' RANGES
                 CURRENT       ALLOWABLE      ALLOWABLE
    CONSTRAINT    RHS          INCREASE       DECREASE
    DEMAND)     100.000000     3.529409       4.285715
    PROTEIN)     12.000000     3.000000       INFINITY
    FAT)         24.000000     INFINITY       2.999998
    WATER)       64.000000     3.000000       2.999997
    LAMB)        30.000000    30.000010       INFINITY
```

Exercise 3.24

(b) Redo part (a), this time assuming the cost per pound of beef decreases to $0.65.

(c) If the cost per pound of lamb increases from $0.70 to $0.90, what are the optimal values of the decision variables and the minimum total cost?

(d) If the minimum protein content increases from 12% to 14%, what is the minimum total cost?

(e) If the maximum fat content decreases from 24% to 20%, what is the minimum total cost?

(f) If the maximum water content decreases from 64% to 62%, what is the minimum total cost?

(g) If HDC must blend 90 pounds of Super Sausage instead of 100 pounds, what is the minimum total cost?

3.25. This exercise assumes you have already worked Exercise 2.32. That exercise requested you to formulate an LP for the blending decision problem of the Harrus Feeding Company. Your formulation should be similar to the following LP:

$$\text{Minimize} \quad 60x_B + 40x_C + 35x_L + 5x_H$$

$$
\begin{aligned}
\text{subject to} \quad 2x_C + x_W + 3x_B + 4x_H &\geqslant 25 \\
2x_C + x_W + 3x_B + 4x_H &\leqslant 100 \\
20x_C + 15x_W + 15x_B + 10x_H &\geqslant 400 \\
4x_C + 7x_W + 6x_B + 5x_H &\geqslant 125 \\
200x_C + 400x_W + 300x_B + 500x_H &\geqslant 6000 \\
x_C + x_W + x_B + x_H &= 24
\end{aligned}
$$

and $x_C \geqslant 0, x_W \geqslant 0, x_B \geqslant 0, x_H \geqslant 0$.

where x_C, x_W, x_B, and x_H denote the respective pounds of corn, wheat, barley, and hay used to blend the 24 pounds of feedstuffs that comprise a steer's daily food ration. Solving the above LP with LINPRO results in the output displayed here. Parts (a)–(i) below request you to use the computer output to analyze the effect of a change in a decision variable's objective-function coefficient or a structural constraint's right-hand side. Regard each part as independent of the other parts. In some parts, the computer output may provide insufficient information to allow you to answer, in which case you should state "Insufficient information!"

(a) If the cost per pound of wheat decreases from 40 cents to 37 cents, what are the optimal values of the decision variables, and what is the minimum total cost?

(b) Redo part (a), this time assuming the cost per pound of wheat decreases to 35 cents.

(c) If the cost per pound of hay increases from 5 cents to 8 cents, what are the optimal values of the decision variables, and what is the minimum total cost?

(d) If the minimum fat requirement increases from 25 to 55 grams, what is the minimum total cost?

(e) If the maximum fat requirement decreases from 100 to 60 grams, what is the minimum total cost?

Exercise 3.25

```
              OPTIMAL OBJECTIVE VALUE

                    1035.00000
    DECISION
    VARIABLE       VALUE              REDUCED COST
         XC        9.000000            .000000
         XW         .000000           3.333332
         XB       14.000000            .000000
         XH        1.000000            .000000

                    SLACK OR
    CONSTRAINT      SURPLUS            SHADOW PRICE
    FATMIN)        39.000000           .000000
    FATMAX)        36.000000           .000000
    PROTEIN)        .000000          -5.666667
    IRON)           .000000          -1.666667
    CALORIES)     500.000000           .000000
    DEMAND)         .000000          60.000000


                SENSITIVITY ANALYSIS

         OBJECTIVE-FUNCTION COEFFICIENTS' RANGES
    DECISION     CURRENT       ALLOWABLE      ALLOWABLE
    VARIABLE    COEFFICIENT    INCREASE       DECREASE
         XC     60.000000      5.000001       9.999991
         XW     40.000000      INFINITY       3.333332
         XB     35.000000      1.999999       2.500001
         XH      5.000000      5.000001       9.999991


              RIGHT-HAND SIDES' RANGES
                 CURRENT       ALLOWABLE      ALLOWABLE
    CONSTRAINT    RHS          INCREASE       DECREASE
    FATMIN)      25.000000     39.000000      INFINITY
    FATMAX)     100.000000     INFINITY       36.000000
    PROTEIN)    400.000000      7.500000     135.000000
    IRON)       125.000000      3.000000      21.000000
    CALORIES)  6000.000000    500.000000      INFINITY
    DEMAND)      24.000000      3.500000       .250000
```

135

(f) If the minimum protein requirement increases from 400 to 410 grams, what is the minimum total cost?

(g) If the minimum iron requirement decreases from 125 milligrams to 110 milligrams, what is the minimum total cost?

(h) If the minimum calorie requirement increases from 6000 to 6250 calories, what is the minimum total cost?

(i) If a steer's daily consumption increases from 24 pounds to 27 pounds, what is the minimum total cost?

Exercises 3.26 through 3.30 test your ability to solve an LP having decision variables that are unconstrained in sign or have nonzero lower bounds.

*3.26. Consider the following LP:

$$\text{Maximize} \quad 2x_1 + 3x_2$$
$$\text{subject to} \quad x_1 + 2x_2 \leq 12$$
$$x_1 - 4x_2 \leq 24$$
$$x_1 - x_2 \geq 1$$

and x_1 and x_2 unconstrained in sign.

(a) Convert this LP into an equivalent LP having all nonnegative decision variables.

(b) Solve the equivalent LP using an available software package.

(c) Use the equivalent LP's optimal solution to determine the original LP's optimal solution.

3.27. Redo Exercise 3.26, this time using the following LP:

$$\text{Maximize} \quad 5x_1 + 2x_2 + x_3$$
$$\text{subject to} \quad x_1 - x_2 + 3x_3 \leq 5$$
$$x_1 + 2x_2 - x_3 \leq 10$$
$$x_1 \leq 25$$

and x_1 and x_2 and x_3 unconstrained in sign.

3.28. Redo Exercise 3.26, this time using the following LP:

$$\text{Maximize} \quad 5x_1 + 2x_2 + x_3$$
$$\text{subject to} \quad x_1 - x_2 + 3x_3 \leq 5$$
$$x_1 + 2x_2 - x_3 \leq 10$$
$$x_1 \leq 25$$

and x_1 unconstrained in sign
$x_2 \geq 0$
x_3 unconstrained in sign.

(Note that this LP is identical to the LP in Exercise 3.27 except that x_2 is now constrained to be nonnegative.)

*3.29. Redo Exercise 3.26, this time using the following LP:

$$\text{Maximize} \quad 2x_1 + 3x_2$$
$$\text{subject to} \quad x_1 + 2x_2 \leq 12$$
$$x_1 - x_2 \geq 1$$

and $x_1 \geq 3, x_2 \geq -2$.

3.30. Redo Exercise 3.26, this time using the following LP:

$$\text{Maximize} \quad 5x_1 + 2x_2 + x_3$$
$$\text{subject to} \quad x_1 - x_2 + 3x_3 \leq 5$$
$$x_1 + 2x_2 - x_3 \leq 10$$
$$x_1 \leq 25$$

and $x_1 \geq 15, x_2 \geq -10, x_3 \geq -5$.

4

LINEAR PROGRAMMING: APPLICATIONS

4.1 INTRODUCTION

This chapter focuses on formulating LPs—that is, translating verbal statements of decision problems into LPs. Recall from Chapter 2 that the formulation process consists of three steps:

1. Defining a decision variable to represent each decision.

2. Expressing the decision problem's objective as maximizing or minimizing a linear function of the decision variables.

3. Expressing each constraint on the decisions as a linear inequality or linear equation involving the decision variables.

Formulating an LP from a verbal statement of a decision problem is more an art than a science. A good analogy is the so-called "word problems" encountered during high school algebra. Do you remember the various classes of problems? There were the "age" problems ("Two years from now, John will be three times as old as Mary will be then . . ."), the "work" problems ("Working together, two painters can paint a house in 8 hours . . ."), the "mixture" problems ("How many quarts of pure alcohol must be added to 5 quarts of a 40% alcohol solution . . ."), and others. Each class of word problems required different insight and creativity. However, once your instructor showed you how to work one or two "age" problems, the next ones you encountered were not so intimidating.

In much the same way, you will encounter various classes of LP formulations, with members of the same class having characteristics that make their formulations similar. We saw two such classes in Chapter 2: product mix LPs and blending LPs.

This chapter provides examples of five other classes of LP formulations, and the end-of-chapter exercises introduce you to several more. Careful study of the examples should enable you to formulate other LPs of these same classes but having a slightly different "twist." Of course, a particular LP may not fit precisely into a single class; it may share characteristics of several classes or belong in a class by itself.

In this chapter we consider examples of five classes of decision problems:

- A *make-or-buy problem* faced by a manufacturer who can fill contracted orders only by supplementing "in-house" production with purchases from "outside" suppliers.

- A *production and inventory planning problem* faced by a manufacturer using forecasts of demand to plan production and inventory levels for the next six months.

- A *financial planning problem* faced by a firm intending to use a variety of investment opportunities to help meet a schedule of required payments over the next six months.

- A *transportation problem* faced by a manufacturer who must plan the distribution of its product from three geographically dispersed plants to five geographically dispersed warehouses.

- A *personnel scheduling problem* faced by a hospital administrator who must assign registered nurses to alternative weekly work schedules.

To conserve space (and your time!) our examples will be smaller in scale than similar "real-world" problems. For example, our financial planning problem involves only 12 investment opportunities instead of the hundreds that might be available, and our transportation problem involves only three plants and five warehouses instead of, say, 7 plants and 20 warehouses. Despite their small scale, the examples are sufficiently realistic to illustrate the approach to similar large-scale problems.

This chapter's five examples (as well as the many end-of-chapter exercises) will serve two purposes. First, their diversity should convince you that linear programming is an extremely useful managerial "tool" applicable to a wide variety of important decision problems. Second, familiarity with the techniques used here will enable you during your managerial career either to formulate an LP yourself or to interact intelligently with someone who formulates an LP for you.

In presenting the examples we will adhere to the following format:

1. We will provide a concise verbal statement of the decision problem. (Keep in mind that this is a luxury enjoyed only in textbooks. In the "real world," obtaining a concise verbal statement of a problem, including all required data, is usually a time-consuming task—and perhaps a costly one.)

2. You will be asked to pause for a moment and use common sense, intuition, and trial-and-error to propose a solution to the decision problem. (Later, you can compare your recommendation to the optimal solution. If your recommendation is almost as good, ask yourself whether your methods would work equally as well on a large-scale version of the problem.)

3. We will formulate the decision problem as an LP.

4. We will discuss the LP's optimal solution, including any associated implementation issues. (You will have to accept "on faith" that this is the LP's optimal solution. In Chapter 3 we discussed how to use a computer as a "black box" to find an LP's optimal solution, and in Chapters 6 and 7 you will learn what is inside the "black box" when we discuss the simplex method, the method used by computers to solve LPs.)

Now, let us turn to our first example.

4.2 A MAKE-OR-BUY-PROBLEM

A *make-or-buy problem* arises when a firm experiencing rapid growth finds itself with insufficient production capacity to fill its customers' orders. Although the long-run solution may be to expand the production capacity, the short-run solution usually consists of meeting demand with a combination of "in-house" production and "outside" purchases from vendors having excess capacity.

Problem Statement

To illustrate a make-or-buy problem, consider the following scenario:

DuPunt, Inc. manufactures three types of chemicals. For the upcoming month, DuPunt has contracted to supply the following amounts of the three chemicals:

CHEMICAL	CONTRACTED SALES
	(lb)
1	2000
2	3500
3	1800

DuPunt's production is limited by the availability of processing time in two chemical reactors. Each chemical must be processed first in reactor 1 and then in reactor 2. The following table provides the hours of processing time available next month for each reactor and the processing time required in each reactor per pound of each chemical:

	Reactor Processing Times (hr per lb)			Reactor
	Chemical			
	1	2	3	Availabilities
Reactor 1	0.05	0.04	0.01	200 hours
Reactor 2	0.02	0.06	0.03	150 hours

.67   .⦁   .04

Owing to the limited availability of reactor processing time, DuPunt has insufficient capacity to meet its demand with in-house production. Consequently, DuPunt must purchase some chemicals from vendors having excess capacity and resell them to its own customers. The following table provides each chemical's in-house production cost and outside purchase cost:

CHEMICAL	IN-HOUSE PRODUCTION COST ($ per lb)	OUTSIDE PURCHASE COST ($ per lb)
1	2.50	2.80
2	1.75	2.50
3	2.90	3.25

Diↄ
.3
.75 ←
.35

DuPunt's objective is to fill its customers' orders with the cheapest combination of in-house production and outside purchases. In short, DuPunt must decide how much of each chemical to produce in-house and how much of each chemical to purchase outside.

Your Recommendation

Before we formulate DuPunt's make-or-buy problem as an LP and discuss its optimal solution, pause for a moment and use common sense, intuition, and trial-and-error to develop a solution to the problem. Write your recommendation in the spaces below:

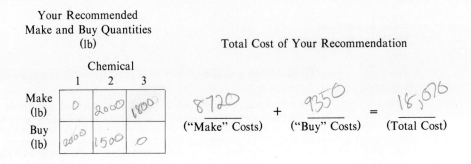

Your Recommended
Make and Buy Quantities
(lb)

Total Cost of Your Recommendation

Chemical

	1	2	3
Make (lb)	0	2000	1800
Buy (lb)	2000	1500	0

$$\underline{8720} \quad + \quad \underline{9350} \quad = \quad \underline{15,670}$$
("Make" Costs) ("Buy" Costs) (Total Cost)

Definition of the LP's Decision Variables

For each of its three products, DuPunt must make two decisions: how much to make and how much to buy. Consequently, let us define the following six decision variables:

m_1 = the pounds of chemical 1 DuPunt makes in-house,
b_1 = the pounds of chemical 1 DuPunt buys from outside vendors,

m_2 = the pounds of chemical 2 DuPunt makes in-house,
b_2 = the pounds of chemical 2 DuPunt buys from outside vendors,

m_3 = the pounds of chemical 3 DuPunt makes in-house,
b_3 = the pounds of chemical 3 DuPunt buys from outside vendors.

We could have used the notation $x_1, x_2, \ldots, x_6$ for our six decision variables. However, using mnemonic notation—"m" for the "make" decisions and "b" for the "buy" decisions—has the advantage of making our LP formulation easier for us and others to understand.[1] This illustrates the following formulation guideline:

> In defining an LP's decision variables, use mnemonic notation; that is, use notation suggestive of what the decision variables represent.

Formulating the LP's Objective Function

DuPunt's objective is to minimize the total cost of its in-house production and outside purchases. Using the production and purchase costs given in the problem statement, we can express DuPunt's total cost as

$$\text{Minimize } 2.50m_1 + 2.80b_1 + 1.75m_2 + 2.50b_2 + 2.90m_3 + 3.25b_3.$$

---

[1] As we saw in Chapter 3, using mnemonic decision variables also facilitates the interpretation of computer output.

Besides the six nonnegativity constraints on the six decision variables, DuPunt's make-or-buy LP requires two groups of structural constraints. The first group ensures that each chemical's demand is met by some combination of in-house production and outside purchases. Consider, for example, chemical 1. DuPunt needs 2000 pounds of chemical 1. Since DuPunt can only obtain chemical 1 by in-house production and outside purchases, the following linear equation must hold:

$$m_1 + b_1 = 2000.$$

[handwritten: $m_2 + b_2 = 3500$; $m_3 + b_3 = 1600$]

Such a constraint is called a *demand constraint*. In general,

A demand constraint has the form

$$\left(\begin{array}{l} \text{summation of decision variables} \\ \text{representing the alternative ways} \\ \text{to satisfy demand} \end{array} \right) \leqslant, =, \text{or} \geqslant \left(\begin{array}{l} \text{a constant equal to} \\ \text{the demand that} \\ \text{must be satisfied} \end{array} \right)$$

The choice of $\leqslant$, $=$, or $\geqslant$ is dictated by the nature of the decision problem.

Our make-or-buy example requires the $=$ form of the demand constraint. You will encounter the $\leqslant$ and $\geqslant$ forms in the end-of-chapter exercises.

Besides the demand constraint for chemical 1, there are two similar demand constraints for chemicals 2 and 3. You should attempt to write these two demand constraints and check them against those appearing below in the LP's complete formulation.

The second group of structural constraints are *resource constraints* similar to those we formulated in Chapter 2 for OMC's product mix LP. In general,

A resource constraint has the form

$$\left(\begin{array}{l} \text{summation of terms representing} \\ \text{each decision variable's} \\ \text{resource consumption} \end{array} \right) \leqslant \left(\begin{array}{l} \text{a constant equal to} \\ \text{the resource's} \\ \text{availability} \end{array} \right)$$

In DuPunt's make-or-buy problem, the scarce resources are the chemical reactors. For each chemical reactor, it is necessary to ensure that the mix of chemicals DuPunt produces in-house does not require more reactor processing time than is available. For example, consider reactor 1. An in-house product mix of m_1 pounds of chemical 1, m_2 pounds of chemical 2, and m_3 pounds of chemical 3 requires (using the data given in the problem statement)

$$0.05m_1 + 0.04m_2 + 0.01m_3$$

total hours of reactor 1 processing time. Since only 200 hours of reactor 1 processing time are available, the following resource constraint must hold:

$$0.05m_1 + 0.04m_2 + 0.01m_3 \leqslant 200.$$

A similar resource constraint must hold for reactor 2. You should attempt to write this resource constraint, then check it against the one appearing below in the LP's complete formulation.

[handwritten: $.02m_1 + .06m_2 + .03m_3$]

The LP's Complete Formulation

The complete formulation of DuPunt's make-or-buy problem is the following six-variable, five-constraint LP:

Minimize $2.50m_1 + 2.80b_1 + 1.75m_2 + 2.50b_2 + 2.90m_3 + 3.25b_3$ (total cost)

subject to

$$
\begin{array}{llll}
m_1 + b_1 & & & = 2000 \\
& m_2 + b_2 & & = 3500 \quad \text{(demand constraints)} \\
& & m_3 + b_3 & = 1800
\end{array}
$$

$$
\begin{array}{llll}
0.05m_1 & + 0.04m_2 & + 0.01m_3 & \leqslant 200 \\
0.02m_1 & + 0.06m_2 & + 0.03m_3 & \leqslant 150
\end{array}
\quad \text{(resource constraints)}
$$

and $m_1 \geqslant 0, b_1 \geqslant 0, m_2 \geqslant 0, b_2 \geqslant 0, m_3 \geqslant 0, b_3 \geqslant 0.$ (nonnegativity constraints)

The LP's Optimal Solution

By using a software package such as the one we discussed in Chapter 3, DuPunt would discover that the optimal solution to its make-or-buy problem is

Optimal Make and Buy Quantities
(lb)

	Chemical 1	Chemical 2	Chemical 3
Make (lb)	$m_1 = 2000$	$m_2 = 1833\frac{1}{3}$	$m_3 = 0$
Buy (lb)	$b_1 = 0$	$b_2 = 1666\frac{2}{3}$	$b_3 = 1800$

Optimal Total Cost

$$\$8208\tfrac{1}{3} + \$10{,}016\tfrac{2}{3} = \$18{,}225$$
("Make" Costs)   ("Buy" Costs)   (Total Cost)

How does this compare to your recommendation? Are you surprised by the optimal solution calling for DuPunt to buy so much of chemical 2? In making your recommendation, which of the following two bits of logic did you employ? Did you incorrectly conclude that you should minimize the buying of chemical 2 because it cost $0.75 per pound more to buy than to make (compared to figures of $0.30 more and $0.35 more for chemicals 1 and 3, respectively)? Or did you correctly conclude that DuPunt should pay the high premium to purchase chemical 2 from an outside supplier because of chemical 2's relatively high reactor 2 processing time (0.06 hours per pound)? Although the latter logic is correct given the LP's current data, a small change in the data can make the former logic correct. For example, if chemical 2's outside purchase price increases by $0.20 (and all other data remain unchanged), the revised LP's optimal solution calls for DuPunt to devote all its in-house production capacity to chemical 2. This illustrates the value of linear programming. Linear programming can simultaneously take into consideration all a decision problem's data, make the necessary "trade-offs" in an unbiased fashion, and provide the optimal solution.

Before turning to another example, we should comment on the noninteger values assumed by two of the decision variables, m_2 and b_2. While this may be fine with a divisible commodity measured in pounds (such as chemicals) or gallons (such as gasolines), some manufacturers produce indivisible items. If our example make-or-buy problem had dealt with a semiconductor manufacturer producing memory chips for microcomputers, the noninteger values for m_2 and b_2 would preclude direct implementation of the LP's optimal solution. Fortunately, when a make-or-buy problem requires integer values for the decision variables, rounding will almost always produce an acceptable close-to-optimal solution. Simply round each product's "make" variable *down* to the next lowest integer and round each product's "buy" variable *up* to the next highest integer. Such a rounding always maintains feasibility and usually has an acceptable maximum percentage error.

4.3 A PRODUCTION AND INVENTORY PLANNING PROBLEM

A widespread application of linear programming is *production and inventory planning*. The primary "inputs" to the production and inventory planning process are the demand forecasts for the next several time periods (e.g., the next six months). The primary "outputs" are the planned production and inventory levels for each of the upcoming time periods that will satisfy the forecasted demand in the most economical way. What makes production and inventory planning so important is that its "outputs" are in turn the "inputs" to many other plans (e.g., raw materials procurement, personnel scheduling, and cash management).

Problem Statement

To illustrate a production and inventory planning problem, consider the following scenario:

The Suny Corporation, a manufacturer of VCRs (video cassette recorders), wants to plan its production and inventory levels for the next six months. Its demand forecasts for the next six months are given in the second column of Table 4.1. Suny desires a plan that satisfies this demand with no backlogging; that is, all demand must be met in the month it occurs.

Owing to fluctuations in the costs of such things as raw materials and utilities, a VCR's unit cost of production will vary from month to month. Table 4.1's third column specifies Suny's forecasts of each month's unit production costs.

Suny's maximum production level also fluctuates from month to month, owing to such things as differences in each month's required maintenance and number of working days. It is Suny's policy not to change its workforce size from month to month. Consequently, to prevent excessive idleness, Suny has set the minimum monthly production level at 50% of the maximum monthly production level. Table 4.1's fourth and fifth columns contain each month's maximum and minimum production levels, respectively.

TABLE 4.1 Data for Suny's Production and Inventory Problem

MONTH	DEMAND FORECAST	UNIT PRODUCTION COST	MAXIMUM PRODUCTION LEVEL	MINIMUM PRODUCTION LEVEL	MAXIMUM INVENTORY LEVEL	MINIMUM INVENTORY LEVEL
1	1000	$460	7000	3500	7000	2500
2	4000	$470	5000	2500	7000	2500
3	6000	$480	4000	2000	7000	2500
4	5000	$500	8000	4000	7000	2500
5	3000	$500	6000	3000	7000	2500
6	2000	$490	3000	1500	7000	2500

Suny currently has 3500 VCRs in inventory. To ensure sufficient safety stock,[2] Suny has specified 2500 VCRs as the minimum permissible inventory level at the end of any month. Given the available storage space, Suny's maximum permissible inventory level at the end of any month is 7000 VCRs. Table 4.1's next-to-last and last columns contain each month's maximum and minimum inventory levels, respectively.

Suny's accounting department has estimated that it costs $8 per month to hold a VCR in inventory, including the opportunity cost of forgone interest.[3] Furthermore, the accounting department recommends that Suny compute each month's inventory costs by multiplying the $8 per month figure by the average of the month's starting and ending inventory levels.

Given the above data, Suny's goal is to find production and inventory levels for each month that will minimize the total cost (total production costs plus total inventory costs) of satisfying forecasted demand with no backlogging.

Production and inventory problems are members of a broader class of decision problems known as *multiperiod planning problems*. (The financial planning problem we consider in the next section is also a multiperiod planning problem.) Such problems involve decisions that span several time periods, in contrast to problems (such as OMC's product mix problem, Pete Moss's blending problem, and DuPunt's make-or-buy problem) where the decisions pertain to a single point in time. In multiperiod planning problems, the decisions pertaining to a particular time period are "linked" (i.e., related) to decisions made in previous time periods. In production and inventory planning problems, this linkage occurs because a particular time period's starting inventory level is the preceding period's ending inventory level. In particular, the following so-called *material balance equation* must hold for each time period:

$$\begin{pmatrix} \text{this time period's} \\ \text{starting inventory level} \\ \text{(which equals the} \\ \text{previous time period's} \\ \text{ending inventory level)} \end{pmatrix} + \begin{pmatrix} \text{this time period's} \\ \text{production} \end{pmatrix} = \begin{pmatrix} \text{this time period's} \\ \text{demand} \end{pmatrix} + \begin{pmatrix} \text{this time period's} \\ \text{ending inventory level} \end{pmatrix}$$

This material balance equation ensures that a time period's two "sources" of items (i.e., the starting inventory level and new production) are in balance with the time period's two "uses" of items (i.e., satisfying demand and the ending inventory level). As we will soon see, each time period's material balance equation results in a constraint in the LP formulation.

Your Recommendation

Before we formulate Suny's production and inventory planning problem as an LP and discuss its optimal solution, pause for a moment and use common sense, intuition, and trial-and-error to develop your own solution. In making your recommendation, keep in mind that your decisions must satisfy each month's material balance equation. Write your recommendation in the spaces below.

---

[2] Safety stock is inventory held as "insurance" against such things as demand forecasts that turn out to be too low or unanticipated loss of production (e.g., labor strikes or raw material shortages). A more detailed explanation is given in Chapter 15.

[3] When a VCR that costs $500 to produce sits in inventory for one month, Suny has essentially placed $500 in inventory instead of in a one-month, interest-bearing account. Consult Chapter 14 for a detailed explanation of the various components of inventory costs, including the opportunity cost of forgone interest.

Your Recommended Production and Inventory Levels   Total Cost of Your Recommendation

Month

	1	2	3	4	5	6
Production Level						
Ending Inventory Level						

$$\left(\overline{\text{Production Costs}}\right) \;+\; \left(\overline{\text{Inventory Costs}}\right) \;=\; \left(\overline{\text{Total Cost}}\right)$$

Defining the LP's Decision Variables

Suny has two decisions each month: the month's production level and the month's ending inventory level. Let us use "p" for production decisions and "i" for inventory decisions. In particular, for month t ($t = 1, 2, \ldots, 6$), let

p_t = the production level for month t
i_t = the inventory level at the end of month t (and, of course, at the start of month $t + 1$).

Thus, our LP formulation will contain 12 decision variables, six representing the monthly production levels and six representing the monthly ending inventory levels.

Formulating the LP's Objective Function

Suny's objective is to minimize its total production and inventory costs. Using the data in Table 4.1's third column, it is easy to express Suny's total production cost as

$$460p_1 + 470p_2 + 480p_3 + 500p_4 + 500p_5 + 490p_6.$$

Expressing Suny's total inventory costs is not as straightforward. The inventory level fluctuates daily as production adds to inventory and demand depletes inventory. To simplify the bookkeeping, however, an estimate of each month's inventory costs is obtained by multiplying the inventory cost per item per month by the average of the month's starting and ending inventory levels. In terms of our decision variables, then, an estimate of Suny's inventory cost for month t is

$$\begin{pmatrix}\text{inventory cost} \\ \text{per VCR} \\ \text{per month}\end{pmatrix} \times \left[\frac{\begin{array}{l}(\text{month } t\text{'s starting inventory level}) \\ + \ (\text{month } t\text{'s ending inventory level})\end{array}}{2}\right] = (8)\left[\frac{i_{t-1} + i_t}{2}\right].$$

To express Suny's total inventory costs, we simply sum the individual month's inventory costs, thereby obtaining

$$(8)\left[\frac{3500 + i_1}{2}\right] + (8)\left[\frac{i_1 + i_2}{2}\right] + (8)\left[\frac{i_2 + i_3}{2}\right] + (8)\left[\frac{i_3 + i_4}{2}\right] + (8)\left[\frac{i_4 + i_5}{2}\right] + (8)\left[\frac{i_5 + i_6}{2}\right],$$

where the "3500" in the first term's numerator is Suny's current inventory level (as specified in the problem's statement). Simplifying this expression yields

$$(8)\left[\frac{(3500 + i_1) + (i_1 + i_2) + (i_2 + i_3) + (i_3 + i_4) + (i_4 + i_5) + (i_5 + i_6)}{2}\right] = (8)\left[\frac{3500 + 2i_1 + 2i_2 + 2i_3 + 2i_4 + 2i_5 + i_6}{2}\right]$$

$$= (8)\,[1750 + i_1 + i_2 + i_3 + i_4 + i_5 + \frac{i_6}{2}].$$

Consequently, Suny's total inventory costs are

$$14,000 + 8i_1 + 8i_2 + 8i_3 + 8i_4 + 8i_5 + 4i_6.$$

Observe that the expression's first term, the constant 14,000, is a "sunk cost" that Suny incurs regardless of the values the decision variables assume. Therefore, in formulating the LP's objective function, we can temporarily ignore the $14,000 sunk cost and express Suny's objective of minimizing total production and inventory costs as

$$\text{Minimize } 460p_1 + 470p_2 + 480p_3 + 500p_4 + 500p_5 + 490p_6 + 8i_1 + 8i_2 + 8i_3 + 8i_4 + 8i_5 + 4i_6.$$

After obtaining the LP's optimal objective value, we can recover Suny's actual total cost by adding $14,000.

Formulating the LP's Constraints

Besides the 12 nonnegativity constraints on the 12 decision variables, our LP formulation of Suny's problem must contain three groups of structural constraints. The first group ensures that each month's production level assumes a value between the month's minimum and maximum production levels (as specified in Table 4.1). For example, for month 1, the pair of inequalities

$$p_1 \geqslant 3500$$
$$p_1 \leqslant 7000$$

ensures a production level p_1 in the interval [3500, 7000]. For obvious reasons, we refer to such constraints as a *lower bound constraint* and an *upper bound constraint,* respectively. Similar lower and upper bound constraints are required for the decision variables p_2, p_3, . . . , and p_6. You should attempt to write these constraints, then check them against those appearing below in the LP's complete formulation.

A second group of structural constraints ensures that each month's ending inventory level assumes a value between the month's minimum and maximum inventory levels (as specified in Table 4.1). For example, for month 1, the pair of inequalities

$$i_1 \geqslant 2500$$
$$i_1 \leqslant 7000$$

ensure an ending inventory level i_1 in the interval [2500, 7000]. Similar lower and upper bound constraints are required for the decision variables i_2, i_3, . . . , and i_6. You should attempt to write these constraints, then check them against those appearing below in the LP's complete formulation.

The third and final group of structural constraints ensures that the decision variables satisfy each month's material balance equation. Using our decision variables and Table 4.1's demand forecasts, we can express each month's material balance equation as follows:

	MONTH t's STARTING INVENTORY LEVEL	+	MONTH t's PRODUCTION LEVEL	=	MONTH t's DEMAND	+	MONTH t's ENDING INVENTORY LEVEL
Month 1	3500	+	p_1	=	1000	+	i_1
Month 2	i_1	+	p_2	=	4000	+	i_2
Month 3	i_2	+	p_3	=	6000	+	i_3
Month 4	i_3	+	p_4	=	5000	+	i_4
Month 5	i_4	+	p_5	=	3000	+	i_5
Month 6	i_5	+	p_6	=	2000	+	i_6

This formulation of the material balance equations facilitates their interpretation and is entirely appropriate for the LP's "first draft." However, in the final version of an LP's formulation, it is customary to rewrite (if necessary) a constraint so that its left-hand side contains all terms involving the decision variables and its right-hand side consists of a single constant. Rewriting the six material balance equations to conform to this convention, we obtain

$$
\begin{aligned}
\text{Month 1:} \quad & p_1 - i_1 = -2500 \\
\text{Month 2:} \quad & i_1 + p_2 - i_2 = 4000 \\
\text{Month 3:} \quad & i_2 + p_3 - i_3 = 6000 \\
\text{Month 4:} \quad & i_3 + p_4 - i_4 = 5000 \\
\text{Month 5:} \quad & i_4 + p_5 - i_5 = 3000 \\
\text{Month 6:} \quad & i_5 + p_6 - i_6 = 2000
\end{aligned}
$$

In general, then,

> The LP formulation of a production and inventory planning problem contains, for each time period t, a material balance equation of the form
>
> $$
> \underset{\substack{\text{the time period's} \\ \text{starting inventory level}}}{i_{t-1}} \quad + \quad \underset{\substack{\text{the time period's} \\ \text{production level}}}{p_t} \quad = \quad \underset{\substack{\text{the time period's} \\ \text{demand}}}{(\text{month } t\text{'s demand})} \quad + \quad \underset{\substack{\text{the time period's} \\ \text{ending inventory level}}}{i_t}
> $$
>
> In the final version of the LP, this material balance equation is rewritten as
>
> $$
> i_{t-1} + p_t - i_t = (\text{month } t\text{'s demand}).
> $$

In some production and inventory problems (though not Suny's), the product has a property that necessitates multiplying the material balance equation's first term, i_{t-1}, by a specified constant. For example, if 10% of the inventory spoils from month to month (e.g., a food product), month t's material balance equation must be

$$
0.9 i_{t-1} + p_t - i_t = (\text{month } t\text{'s demand}),
$$

thereby reflecting the fact that only 90% of the previous month's ending inventory level is usable at the start of month t. How would you modify month t's material balance equation if items in inventory "reproduced" from month to month (e.g., rabbits!) in the ratio of one "offspring" for every five items in inventory?

The LP's Complete Formulation

The complete formulation of Suny's production and inventory planning problem is the following 12-variable, 30-constraint LP:

$$\text{Minimize} \quad 460p_1 + 470p_2 + 480p_3 + 500p_4 + 500p_5 + 490p_6$$
$$+ 8i_1 + 8i_2 + 8i_3 + 8i_4 + 8i_5 + 4i_6 \quad \text{(total cost)}$$

subject to

$$
\begin{aligned}
p_1 &\geqslant 3500 \\
p_1 &\leqslant 7000 \\
p_2 &\geqslant 2500 \\
p_2 &\leqslant 5000 \\
p_3 &\geqslant 2000 \quad \text{(lower and upper bound} \\
p_3 &\leqslant 4000 \quad \text{constraints on} \\
p_4 &\geqslant 4000 \quad \text{production levels)} \\
p_4 &\leqslant 8000 \\
p_5 &\geqslant 3000 \\
p_5 &\leqslant 6000 \\
p_6 &\geqslant 1500 \\
p_6 &\leqslant 3000
\end{aligned}
$$

$$
\begin{aligned}
i_1 &\geqslant 2500 \\
i_1 &\leqslant 7000 \\
i_2 &\geqslant 2500 \\
i_2 &\leqslant 7000 \\
i_3 &\geqslant 2500 \quad \text{(lower and upper bound} \\
i_3 &\leqslant 7000 \quad \text{constraints on} \\
i_4 &\geqslant 2500 \quad \text{inventory levels)} \\
i_4 &\leqslant 7000 \\
i_5 &\geqslant 2500 \\
i_5 &\leqslant 7000 \\
i_6 &\geqslant 2500 \\
i_6 &\leqslant 7000
\end{aligned}
$$

$$
\begin{aligned}
p_1 - i_1 &= -2500 \\
i_1 + p_2 - i_2 &= 4000 \\
i_2 + p_3 - i_3 &= 6000 \quad \text{(material} \\
i_3 + p_4 - i_4 &= 5000 \quad \text{balance} \\
i_4 + p_5 - i_5 &= 3000 \quad \text{equations)} \\
i_5 + p_6 - i_6 &= 2000
\end{aligned}
$$

and $p_1 \geqslant 0, p_2 \geqslant 0, p_3 \geqslant 0, p_4 \geqslant 0, p_5 \geqslant 0, p_6 \geqslant 0$ (nonnegativity
$i_1 \geqslant 0, i_2 \geqslant 0, i_3 \geqslant 0, i_4 \geqslant 0, i_5 \geqslant 0, i_6 \geqslant 0.$ constraints)

Observe that the nonnegativity constraints are redundant, owing to the lower bound constraints on the decision variables. Despite this redundancy, it is customary to include the nonnegativity constraints in the LP's formulation.

The LP's Optimal Solution

By using a software package such as the one discussed in Chapter 3, Suny would discover that the optimal solution to its production and inventory planning problem is:[4]

[4] How does this compare to your recommendation?

Month

	1	2	3	4	5	6			

Production
Level

Inventory
Level

$p_1 = 4500$	$p_2 = 4000$	$p_3 = 2500$	$p_4 = 4000$	$p_5 = 3000$	$p_6 = 2000$
$i_1 = 7000$	$i_2 = 7000$	$i_3 = 3500$	$i_4 = 2500$	$i_5 = 2500$	$i_6 = 2500$

$$\$9,630,000 \ + \ \$190,000 \ = \ \$9,820,000$$
$$\begin{pmatrix}\text{Production}\\\text{Costs}\end{pmatrix} \quad \begin{pmatrix}\text{Inventory}\\\text{Costs}\end{pmatrix} \quad \begin{pmatrix}\text{Total}\\\text{Cost}\end{pmatrix}$$

Remember that we must add $14,000 to the LP's optimal objective value to account for the sunk cost we temporarily ignored when formulating the LP's objective function.

It is *not* a coincidence that the optimal values of the decision variables are all integer-valued. Although we have stressed repeatedly that an LP's optimal solution may have decision variables with noninteger values (even when the LP's constraints' data are integer-valued), the following is a theorem:

> A production and inventory planning LP having the characteristics of Suny's LP (including constraint data that are integer-valued) *always* has an optimal solution in which all decision variables assume integer values.

Consequently, Suny will never have to resort to rounding or integer linear programming to obtain integer values for the decisions. The proof of this theorem is well beyond the scope of this text. It consists of showing that, although there exist feasible solutions to the LP in which the decision variables assume noninteger values, every corner-point solution, and, therefore, the optimal solution, has the property that all decision variables assume integer values. Care must be taken not to apply this theorem to all production and inventory planning LPs. Suny's problem has the following characteristics:

1. A single product.
2. Integer-valued demand forecasts.
3. Integer-valued lower and upper bounds on production levels.
4. Integer-valued lower and upper bounds on inventory levels.

An LP formulation of a production and inventory problem having different characteristics (such as one involving several products sharing common production and/or inventory facilities) may have an optimal solution in which one or more decision variables assume noninteger values.

Suny's implementation of the LP's optimal solution merits discussion. The LP's optimal solution calls for production levels for the next six months of 4500, 4000, 2500, 4000, 3000, and 2000, respectively. The only portion of this optimal solution requiring immediate implementation, however, is month 1's production level of 4500. Suny uses the subsequent months' production levels for planning purposes only, recognizing that new information will undoubtedly necessitate revisions. One month from now, while it is implementing month 1's production level of 4500 VCRs, Suny will solve another LP identical in format to the one we formulated but having different data. Rather than using data for months 1–6, the second LP's data will pertain to months 2–7. Undoubtedly, new information obtained during the month 1 will result in Suny's revising the data (e.g., demand forecasts) for months 2–6. To the revised data for months 2–6, Suny will add the data for month 7 and solve the appropriate new LP. One month later, then, this new LP's optimal solution provides Suny with a production level to implement in month 2 and planned production levels for months 3–7. Suny repeats this process each month, always looking ahead six months to obtain a "firm" production level for the next month and planned production levels for the subsequent five months. This is known as a *rolling planning process,* terminology reflecting that each successive plan results from "rolling" the planning horizon ahead one month and re-solving a similar LP.

We should comment on one other characteristic of the optimal solution to Suny's LP, namely, the variability of its production levels. Observe that the LP's optimal solution calls for production levels that change from month to month by amounts of -500, -1500, $+1500$, -1000, and -1000, respectively. Frequent changes in the production level may well be costly, especially if each increase is accompanied by new hiring and each decrease is accompanied by layoffs. In such a case, it may be optimal to have "smooth" production levels (i.e., levels with little or no variability). To consider such a possibility, it is necessary to formulate an LP that takes into account three cost components: (1) production costs, (2) inventory costs, (3) changes-in-production-level costs. We will formulate such an LP when we discuss advanced formulation techniques in the next chapter.

4.4 A FINANCIAL PLANNING PROBLEM

Linear programming can be used to address financial planning problems. Such problems are faced not only by organizations whose primary business is cash management (e.g., banks, credit unions, mutual funds, or insurance companies) but also by nonfinancial organizations (e.g., manufacturers or public utilities) that invest "idle" cash or set up so-called *sinking funds* whose principal and interest will be used in the future to make a capital expenditure.

Problem Statement

To illustrate a financial planning problem, consider the following scenario:

Anne Alyze is the investments manager for an organization that has just signed a contract to purchase some new equipment costing $750,000. The contract calls for payment of $150,000 two months from now and payment of the balance six months from now when the equipment will be delivered.

To meet this schedule of payments, Anne intends to immediately set up a sinking fund. Because the available investments will generate additional cash before the scheduled payments are due, Anne knows she can start the sinking fund with less than the full purchase price of $750,000. How much less depends on the quality of the investment opportunities available.

Anne has decided to focus on the 12 investment opportunities summarized in Table 4.2. For example, Table 4.2's third row indicates the following:

- Investment C is available twice, once at the beginning of month 1 and once again at the beginning of month 4.

- Every dollar invested in C at either of these two times matures 3 months later, yielding a return of $1.06. The $1.06 is available for immediate reinvestment at the beginning of the month in which it is returned (as is the case for all other investments).

- Anne assesses the riskiness of investment C as 9 on a scale of 1 to 10, with 1 indicating the lowest risk and 10 the highest risk.

TABLE 4.2 Data for Anne Alyze's Financial Planning Problem

INVESTMENT OPPORTUNITY	AVAILABLE AT THE BEGINNING OF . . .	MONTHS TO MATURITY	YIELD AT MATURITY	RISK INDEX
A	Months 1, 2, 3, 4, 5, and 6	1	1.5%	1
B	Months 1, 3, and 5	2	3.5%	4
C	Months 1 and 4	3	6.0%	9
D	Month 1	6	11.0%	7

Given the available investment opportunities and the required schedule of payments, Anne's goal is to develop an investment strategy that minimizes the amount of cash she must initially place in the fund. In developing her strategy, Anne must also ensure she meets the following two self-imposed guidelines pertaining to risk and liquidity:

1. During each month, the average risk index of invested funds cannot exceed 6.
2. At the beginning of each month (after any new investments have been made), the average months to maturity of invested funds cannot exceed 2.5 months.

To aid her analysis, Anne has developed Table 4.3, illustrating the timing of each investment's cash inflow and outflow. For example, the eighth row of data indicates that every dollar invested in B at the beginning of month 3 results in a cash inflow of $1.035 at the beginning of month 5 (in time for immediate reinvestment).

Like Suny's, Anne Alyze's is a multiperiod planning problem. Her investment decisions span 6 time periods (months), across which they are "linked" to each other because the cash available to invest at the start of a particular time period depends on investment decisions made in previous time periods. More specifically, the following so-called *cash balance equation* must hold at the beginning of each time period:

$$\begin{pmatrix} \text{cash inflow at} \\ \text{beginning of} \\ \text{time period} \\ \text{from investments} \\ \text{made in previous} \\ \text{time periods} \end{pmatrix} + \begin{pmatrix} \text{cash inflow at} \\ \text{beginning of} \\ \text{time period} \\ \text{from funds} \\ \text{made available} \\ \text{for first time} \end{pmatrix} = \begin{pmatrix} \text{cash outflow} \\ \text{required at} \\ \text{beginning of} \\ \text{time period} \\ \text{to meet} \\ \text{scheduled payments} \end{pmatrix} + \begin{pmatrix} \text{cash outflow} \\ \text{required at} \\ \text{beginning of} \\ \text{time period} \\ \text{for investments} \end{pmatrix}$$

TABLE 4.3 A Summary of the Investments' Cash Outflows and Cash Inflows

	BEGINNING OF MONTH						
INVESTMENT	1	2	3	4	5	6	7
A in Month 1:	$1.00 →	$1.015					
A in Month 2:		$1.00 →	$1.015				
A in Month 3:			$1.00 →	$1.015			
A in Month 4:				$1.00 →	$1.015		
A in Month 5:					$1.00 →	$1.015	
A in Month 6:						$1.00 →	$1.015
B in Month 1:	$1.00 →	→	→ $1.035				
B in Month 3:			$1.00 →	→	→ $1.035		
B in Month 5:					$1.00 →	→	→ $1.035
C in Month 1:	$1.00 →	→	→	→	→ $1.060		
C in Month 4:				$1.00 →	→	→	→ $1.060
D in Month 1:	$1.00 →	→	→	→	→	→	→ $1.110

Analogous to the material balance equation in production and inventory planning problems, this cash balance equation ensures a balance between a time period's cash inflow and cash outflow. We will soon see that each time period's cash balance equation results in a constraint in our LP formulation.

Your Recommendation

Before we formulate Anne's financial planning problem as an LP and discuss its optimal solution, pretend for a moment that you are Anne and use common sense, intuition, and trial-and-error to develop an appropriate investment strategy. In developing your strategy, keep in mind each month's cash balance equation as well as the restrictions on risk and liquidity. Write your recommendation in the spaces below:

Initially, place $_____ in the sinking fund.

At the beginning of Month 1 invest $_____ in A,
    invest $_____ in B,
    invest $_____ in C, and
    invest $_____ in D.

At the beginning of Month 2 invest $_____ in A.

At the beginning of Month 3 invest $_____ in A and
    invest $_____ in B.

At the beginning of Month 4 invest $_____ in A and
    invest $_____ in C.

At the beginning of Month 5 invest $_____ in A and
    invest $_____ in B.

At the beginning of Month 6 invest $_____ in A.

Defining the LP's Decision Variables

Anne has 13 decisions. The first one is the initial size of the sinking fund, and the subsequent 12 are how much to invest in each of the 12 investment alternatives. Accordingly, let us define the following 13 decision variables:

I = initial size of the sinking fund (i.e., at the beginning of month 1)

$A_1, A_2, A_3, A_4, A_5, A_6$ = dollars invested in investment A at the beginning of months 1, 2, 3, 4, 5, and 6, respectively

B_1, B_3, B_5 = dollars invested in investment B at the beginning of months 1, 3, and 5, respectively

C_1, C_4 = dollars invested in investment C at the beginning of months 1 and 4, respectively

D_1 = dollars invested in investment D at the beginning of month 1.

Formulating the LP's Objective Function

Anne's objective is to minimize the initial size of the sinking fund, an objective expressed quite simply as

Do not be concerned over the simple nature of the objective function. It is unnecessary for all (or even most) decision variables to appear in the objective function.

Formulating the LP's Constraints

Besides the 13 nonnegativity constraints on the 13 decision variables, our LP formulation of Anne's problem requires three groups of structural constraints. The first group ensures that the decision variables satisfy each month's cash balance equation. We can use Table 4.3 to assist us in writing a particular month's cash balance equation. In the column of Table 4.3 that corresponds to the month under consideration, all entries that equal 1 (expressed as $1.00) indicate the month's cash outflows for current investment opportunities, and all entries greater than 1 indicate the month's cash inflows from previous investments. Using Table 4.3 as a guideline, then, we can express each month's cash balance equation as follows:

$$
\begin{pmatrix}
\text{Cash Inflow at} \\
\text{Beginning of} \\
\text{Month } t \\
\text{From Investments} \\
\text{Made in Previous} \\
\text{Time Periods}
\end{pmatrix}
+
\begin{pmatrix}
\text{Cash Inflow at} \\
\text{Beginning of} \\
\text{Month } t \\
\text{From Funds} \\
\text{Made Available} \\
\text{for First Time}
\end{pmatrix}
=
\begin{pmatrix}
\text{Cash Outflow} \\
\text{Required at} \\
\text{Beginning of} \\
\text{Month } t \\
\text{to Meet} \\
\text{Scheduled Payments}
\end{pmatrix}
+
\begin{pmatrix}
\text{Cash Outflow} \\
\text{Required at} \\
\text{Beginning of} \\
\text{Month } t \\
\text{for Investments}
\end{pmatrix}
$$

Month 1	0	$+$	I	$=$	0	$+ \quad A_1 + B_1 + C_1 + D_1$
Month 2	$1.015A_1$	$+$	0	$=$	0	$+ \quad A_2$
Month 3	$1.015A_2 + 1.035B_1$	$+$	0	$=$	$150{,}000$	$+ \quad A_3 + B_3$
Month 4	$1.015A_3 + 1.060C_1$	$+$	0	$=$	0	$+ \quad A_4 + C_4$
Month 5	$1.015A_4 + 1.035B_3$	$+$	0	$=$	0	$+ \quad A_5 + B_5$
Month 6	$1.015A_5$	$+$	0	$=$	0	$+ \quad A_6$
Month 7	$1.015A_6 + 1.035B_5$ $+ 1.060C_4 + 1.110D_1$	$+$	0	$=$	$600{,}000$	$+ \quad 0$

To conform to the convention that a constraint's left-hand side contain all terms involving decision variables and its right-hand side consist of a single constant, we rewrite these seven cash balance equations as follows:

Month 1: $I - A_1 - B_1 - C_1 - D_1$ $= \quad 0$

Month 2: $1.015A_1 - A_2$ $= \quad 0$

Month 3: $1.015A_2 + 1.035B_1 - A_3 - B_3$ $= \quad 150{,}000$

Month 4: $1.015A_3 + 1.060C_1 - A_4 - C_4$ $= \quad 0$

Month 5: $1.015A_4 + 1.035B_3 - A_5 - B_5$ $= \quad 0$

Month 6: $1.015A_5 - A_6$ $= \quad 0$

Month 7: $1.015A_6 + 1.035B_5 + 1.060C_4 + 1.110D_1 = 600{,}000$

In general, then,

The LP formulation of a financial planning problem contains, for each time period t, a cash balance equation of the form

$$
\begin{pmatrix}
\text{cash inflow at} \\
\text{beginning of} \\
\text{time period} \\
\text{from investments} \\
\text{made in previous} \\
\text{time periods}
\end{pmatrix}
+
\begin{pmatrix}
\text{cash inflow at} \\
\text{beginning of} \\
\text{time period} \\
\text{from funds} \\
\text{made available} \\
\text{for first time}
\end{pmatrix}
=
\begin{pmatrix}
\text{cash outflow} \\
\text{required at} \\
\text{beginning of} \\
\text{time period} \\
\text{to meet} \\
\text{scheduled payments}
\end{pmatrix}
+
\begin{pmatrix}
\text{cash outflow} \\
\text{required at} \\
\text{beginning of} \\
\text{time period} \\
\text{for investments}
\end{pmatrix}
$$

In the final version of the LP, this cash balance equation is rewritten so that its left-hand side contains all terms involving decision variables and its right-hand side consists of a single constant.

The second group of structural constraints ensures that, during each month, the average risk index of invested funds cannot exceed 6. In words, this restriction states that, during each month,

$$\frac{\text{total risk index of invested funds}}{\text{total invested funds}} \leqslant 6 \, .$$

To illustrate how to express this constraint mathematically for a particular month, let us consider month 4. What are the investments in effect during month 4? Table 4.3 again provides assistance. Looking down the column for month 4 and checking for either an "$\rightarrow$" (indicating an investment in progress) or a "$\$1.00$" (indicating a new investment), we see that there are four investments in effect during month 4: A_4, B_3, C_4, and D_1. The average risk index of these four investments is simply the investments' total risk index divided by the total dollars invested, namely,

$$\frac{1A_4 + 4B_3 + 9C_4 + 7D_1}{A_4 + B_3 + C_4 + D_1} \, .$$

Hence, to ensure that the average risk index of investments in effect during month 4 does not exceed 6, our LP formulation must include the following constraint:

$$\frac{1A_4 + 4B_3 + 9C_4 + 7D_1}{A_4 + B_3 + C_4 + D_1} \leqslant 6 \, .$$

In its present form, with decision variables in both the numerator and denominator, this is a nonlinear constraint. However, we can "linearize" it by multiplying both sides of the constraint by the denominator. (Note that the $\leqslant$ remains unchanged because the nonnegativity constraints ensure the nonnegativity of the demoninator.) The result is

$$1A_4 + 4B_3 + 9C_4 + 7D_1 \leqslant 6 \, (A_4 + B_3 + C_4 + D_1) \, .$$

Then, to conform to the convention that a constraint's left-hand side contain all terms involving decision variables and its right-hand side consist of a single constant, we rewrite the constraint in its final form as

$$-5A_4 - 2B_3 + 3C_4 + 1D_1 \leqslant 0 \, .$$

We have used month 4 to illustrate the process of writing an average risk constraint. Similar constraints are required for months 1, 2, 3, 5, and 6. You should attempt to write these five constraints, then check them against those appearing below in the LP's complete formulation.

The third group of structural constraints ensures that, during each month, the average months to maturity of invested funds cannot exceed 2.5. Because they also pertain to averages, these constraints are similar to the average risk constraints. In words, the average maturity constraint states that, during each month,

$$\frac{\text{total months to maturity of invested funds}}{\text{total invested funds}} \leqslant 2.5 \, .$$

Let us again use month 4 to illustrate the process of expressing this constraint mathematically. As we saw earlier, the investments in effect during month 4 are A_4, B_3, C_4, and D_1. The average months to maturity of these four investments is simply the investments' total months to maturity divided by the total dollars invested:

$$\frac{1A_4 + 1B_3 + 3C_4 + 3D_1}{A_4 + B_3 + C_4 + D_1}.$$

Observe that the coefficients in the numerator are the investments' *remaining* months to maturity, not the original months to maturity. To ensure that the average months to maturity of funds invested during month 4 does not exceed 2.5, our LP formulation must include the following constraint:

$$\frac{1A_4 + 1B_3 + 3C_4 + 3D_1}{A_4 + B_3 + C_4 + D_1} \leqslant 2.5.$$

After "clearing" the denominator to linearize the constraint, we obtain

$$1A_4 + 1B_3 + 3C_4 + 3D_1 \leqslant 2.5\,(A_4 + B_3 + C_4 + D_1),$$

and, after collecting all terms involving decision variables on the constraint's left-hand side, we obtain

$$-1.5A_4 - 1.5B_3 + 0.5C_4 + 0.5D_1 \leqslant 0$$

as the final form of month 4's average maturity constraint.

Similar constraints are required for months 1, 2, 3, 5, and 6. You should attempt to write these five constraints, then check them against those appearing below in the LP's complete formulation. In writing your constraints, keep in mind that an investment's remaining months to maturity decrease by one each month. For example, investment C_1 has 3 months to maturity at the beginning of month 1, 2 months to maturity at the beginning of month 2, and 1 month to maturity at the beginning of month 3.

The average risk constraints and the average maturity constraints are examples of *ratio constraints*. In general,

A ratio constraint has the form

$$\frac{\left(\begin{array}{l}\text{total value of some attribute} \\ \text{possessed by a group of decision variables}\end{array}\right)}{(\text{summation of the group of decision variables})} \quad \leqslant,\ =,\ \geqslant \quad \text{(a specified constant).}$$

The choice of $\leqslant$, $=$, or $\geqslant$ is dictated by the nature of the decision problem. A ratio constraint's final form is obtained by "clearing" the denominator and rearranging terms.

The LP's Complete Formulation

The complete formulation of Anne's financial planning problem is the following 13-variable, 19-constraint LP:

Minimize I (fund's initial size)

subject to

$$I - A_1 - B_1 - C_1 - D_1 = 0$$
$$1.015A_1 - A_2 = 0$$
$$1.015A_2 + 1.035B_1 - A_3 - B_3 = 150{,}000 \quad \text{(cash}$$
$$1.015A_3 + 1.060C_1 - A_4 - C_4 = 0 \quad \text{balance}$$
$$1.015A_4 + 1.035B_3 - A_5 - B_5 = 0 \quad \text{equations)}$$
$$1.015A_5 - A_6 = 0$$
$$1.015A_6 + 1.035B_5 + 1.060C_4 + 1.110D_1 = 600{,}000$$

$$-5A_1 - 2B_1 + 3C_1 + 1D_1 \leqslant 0$$
$$-5A_2 - 2B_1 + 3C_1 + 1D_1 \leqslant 0$$
$$-5A_3 - 2B_3 + 3C_1 + 1D_1 \leqslant 0 \quad \text{(average}$$
$$-5A_4 - 2B_3 + 3C_4 + 1D_1 \leqslant 0 \quad \text{risk}$$
$$-5A_5 - 2B_5 + 3C_4 + 1D_1 \leqslant 0 \quad \text{constraints)}$$
$$-5A_6 - 2B_5 + 3C_4 + 1D_1 \leqslant 0$$

$$-1.5A_1 - 0.5B_1 + 0.5C_1 + 3.5D_1 \leqslant 0$$
$$-1.5A_2 - 1.5B_1 - 0.5C_1 + 2.5D_1 \leqslant 0$$
$$-1.5A_3 - 0.5B_3 - 1.5C_1 + 1.5D_1 \leqslant 0 \quad \text{(average}$$
$$-1.5A_4 - 1.5B_3 + 0.5C_4 + 0.5D_1 \leqslant 0 \quad \text{maturity}$$
$$-1.5A_5 - 0.5B_5 - 0.5C_4 - 0.5D_1 \leqslant 0 \quad \text{constraints)}$$
$$-1.5A_6 - 1.5B_5 - 1.5C_4 - 1.5D_1 \leqslant 0$$

and $A_1 \geqslant 0, A_2 \geqslant 0, A_3 \geqslant 0, A_4 \geqslant 0, A_5 \geqslant 0, A_6 \geqslant 0,$
$B_1 \geqslant 0, B_3 \geqslant 0, B_5 \geqslant 0,$ (nonnegativity
$C_1 \geqslant 0, C_4 \geqslant 0,$ constraints)
$D_1 \geqslant 0.$

Observe that the last two average maturity constraints are redundant. They will always be satisfied, because the nonnegativity constraints ensure that the decision variables assume nonnegative values. Consequently, we may remove these two constraints from our formulation. Of course, failing to recognize this redundancy will not lead to an incorrect optimal solution.

The LP's Optimal Solution

By using a software package such as the one discussed in Chapter 3, Anne would discover that the optimal solution to her LP (rounded to two decimal places) is:[5]

Initially, place I = \$683,176.44 in the sinking fund.

At the beginning of Month 1 A_1 = \$ 0,
B_1 = \$461,836.69,
C_1 = \$221,339.78, and
D_1 = \$ 0.

At the beginning of Month 2 A_2 = \$ 0.

At the beginning of Month 3 A_3 = \$ 2672.49 and
B_3 = \$325,328.44

At the beginning of Month 4 A_4 = \$ 7667.67 and
C_4 = \$229,665.08

At the beginning of Month 5 A_5 = \$ 0 and
B_5 = \$344,497.62

At the beginning of Month 6 A_6 = \$ 0.

---

[5] How does this compare to your recommendation?

Thus, by initially placing $I = \$683,176.44$ in the sinking fund and following the investment strategy indicated by the LP's optimal solution, Anne will ensure that sufficient funds are available to meet the scheduled payments and that, furthermore, the restrictions on average risk and average maturity are satisfied.

Although the noninteger optimal values for some of the decision variables do not present a problem for Anne, some financial planning problems require integer-valued decision variables. For example, a bond usually requires a total investment that is a multiple of $1000, and a stock selling for $50 per share requires a total investment that is a multiple of $50. Such situations necessitate rounding the LP's optimal solution in an attempt to find an acceptable close-to-optimal solution or, if this fails, resorting to the integer linear programming techniques discussed in Chapter 9.

Another aspect of implementing the LP's optimal solution merits discussion. Anne may choose to implement a "rolling" planning process similar to that discussed for Suny's production and inventory planning. In particular, at the beginning of each month, Anne could solve a new LP incorporating any new information (e.g., new yields or even new investment opportunities). Using the new LP's optimal solution, Anne would implement the investments called for in the current month and use the subsequent months' investments for planning purposes only, recognizing that these plans will probably change when the LP is revised and re-solved next month.

We should also notice that financial planning problems may differ in the nature of the objective function. In Anne's problem, the given information is a schedule of required payments and the objective is to minimize the initial cash investment. In some financial planning problems, the given information is an initial investment budget (and perhaps some scheduled budget augmentations at the start of some subsequent time periods) and the objective is to maximize the cash inflow occurring at the end of the last time period.

4.5 A TRANSPORTATION PROBLEM

Any manufacturer with geographically dispersed supply centers (e.g., plants) and geographically dispersed demand centers (e.g., regional warehouses or retail outlets) faces the so-called *transportation problem*. The data for a transportation problem are:

1. The available supply of some commodity at each of the supply centers (hereafter called *sources*).

2. The required demand for the commodity at each of the demand centers (hereafter called *sinks*).

3. The unit freight cost between every possible source-sink pair.

The objective is to minimize the total freight costs incurred in transporting the commodity from the sources to the sinks.

Problem Statement

To illustrate a transportation problem, consider the following scenario:

Graham Krackers is the product distribution manager of Gramma's Biscuit Company (GBC), a national manufacturer and distributor of cookies, cakes, and crackers. As

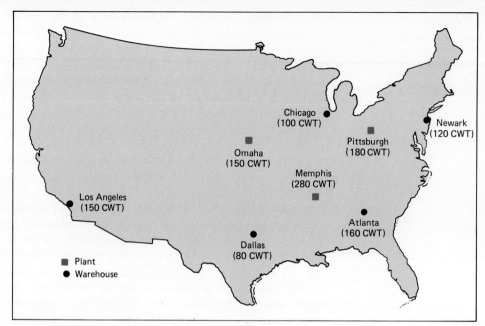

Figure 4.1 Location of GBC's plants and warehouses

illustrated in Figure 4.1 by the three squares and five circles, GBC has plants in Pittsburgh, Memphis, and Omaha and regional warehouses in Newark, Chicago, Atlanta, Dallas, and Los Angeles. For distribution purposes, GBC uses CWT (1 CWT = 100 lb) as the unit of measurement. Every CWT shipped from a plant to a warehouse consists of a standard assortment of GBC's baked goods.

Table 4.4 summarizes the data for the transportation problem confronting Graham Krackers this month. The table consists of a rectangular array (3 rows by 5 columns) of "cells." Row i of the table corresponds to plant i, column j corresponds to warehouse j, and the cell at the intersection of row i and column j corresponds to shipments between plant i and warehouse j. In particular,

- The data appearing in Table 4.4's right margin are the plants' supplies; for example, plant 2 (Memphis) has 280 CWT available for shipment this month.
- The data appearing in the table's bottom margin are the warehouses' demands; for example, GBC has allocated warehouse 4 (Dallas) 80 CWT as its share of this month's total production. (Observe that total supply equals total demand; that is,

$$180 + 280 + 150 = 120 + 100 + 160 + 80 + 150 = 610.$$

TABLE 4.4 Data for Graham Kracker's Transportation Problem

	Warehouse 1 (Newark)	Warehouse 2 (Chicago)	Warehouse 3 (Atlanta)	Warehouse 4 (Dallas)	Warehouse 5 (Los Angeles)	Supplies
Plant 1 (Pittsburgh)	4	6	5	12	19	180 CWT
Plant 2 (Memphis)	10	4	8	5	14	280 CWT
Plant 3 (Omaha)	13	9	3	6	10	150 CWT
Demands	120 CWT	100 CWT	160 CWT	80 CWT	150 CWT	

Because total supply equals total demand, this is a *balanced transportation problem*. We will consider unbalanced transportation problems later in this section.)

■ The data appearing in the upper-left corners of the cells are the unit freight costs between all plant-warehouse pairs; for example, the cell at the intersection of row 2 and column 4 indicates that the freight cost between plant 2 (Memphis) and warehouse 4 (Dallas) is $5 per CWT.

Given the data in Table 4.4 and an objective of minimizing total freight costs, Graham must now determine how many CWT each plant should ship to each warehouse.

Besides providing a concise way of displaying the problem's data, Table 4.4 provides a concise way of displaying a proposed distribution plan. In particular, Graham can simply write the proposed number of CWT plant i should ship warehouse j in the lower-right corner of the cell in row i and column j. Consider, for example, the following distribution plan:

	Warehouse 1 (Newark)	Warehouse 2 (Chicago)	Warehouse 3 (Atlanta)	Warehouse 4 (Dallas)	Warehouse 5 (Los Angeles)	Supplies
Plant 1 (Pittsburgh)	4 **120**	6 **50**	5 **10**	12 **0**	19 **0**	180 CWT
Plant 2 (Memphis)	10 **0**	4 **50**	8 **0**	5 **80**	14 **150**	280 CWT
Plant 3 (Omaha)	13 **0**	9 **0**	3 **150**	6 **0**	10 **0**	150 CWT
Demands	120 CWT	100 CWT	160 CWT	80 CWT	150 CWT	

where the boldfaced numbers in the cells' lower-right corners represent the shipments between the various plant-warehouse pairs. For example, the table's second row indicates that plant 2 will distribute its supply of 280 CWT by making shipments to warehouses 1, 2, 3, 4, and 5 of 0, 50, 0, 80, and 150 CWT, respectively. Observe how the table's structure makes it easy to verify the feasibility of any proposed distribution plan. Graham needs to verify only that each row sums to the supply in the row's right margin and that each column sums to the demands in the column's bottom margin. The table also facilitates computing any proposal's total freight costs. Graham needs only to multiply the two numbers in each of the 15 cells (i.e., the unit freight cost times the total CWT shipped) and sum the resulting products. For our example proposal, summing the nonzero products (row by row) yields total freight costs of

$$(4)(120) + (6)(50) + (5)(10) + (4)(50) + (5)(80) + (14)(150) + (3)(150) = 3980.$$

Your Recommendation

Before we formulate Graham Krackers transportation problem as an LP and discuss its optimal solution, pretend for a moment that you are Graham and use common sense, intuition, and trial-and-error to propose a distribution plan. Summarize your proposal in the table below. In developing your proposal, keep in mind each of the table's rows must sum to the supply in the row's right margin and each of the table's columns must sum to the demand in the column's bottom margin.

	Warehouse 1 (Newark)	Warehouse 2 (Chicago)	Warehouse 3 (Atlanta)	Warehouse 4 (Dallas)	Warehouse 5 (Los Angeles)	Supplies
Plant 1 (Pittsburgh)	4	6	5	12	19	180 CWT
Plant 2 (Memphis)	10	4	8	5	14	280 CWT
Plant 3 (Omaha)	13	9	3	6	10	150 CWT
Demands	120 CWT	100 CWT	160 CWT	80 CWT	150 CWT	

Total freight costs of your recommendation = _____

Defining the LP's Decision Variables

We have already seen that Graham has 15 decisions. For each of the $3 \times 5 = 15$ possible combinations of plant i and warehouse j, Graham must decide how much to ship from plant i to warehouse j. Since each decision has two attributes (a plant and a warehouse), it is convenient to formulate an LP with doubly subscripted decision variables. In particular, for each of the 15 combinations of i and j, let

$$x_{ij} = \text{CWT shipped from plant } i \text{ to warehouse } j.$$

For example, $x_{24} = 75$ denotes that plant 2 ships 75 CWT to warehouse 4.

Formulating the LP's Objective Function

The format of Table 4.4 provides a convenient starting point for formulating our LP. Earlier, we used this format to display a proposed distribution plan by writing the amounts shipped between each plant-warehouse pair in the lower-right corners of the table's 15 cells. We can now do the same using the decision variables in place of specific numbers, thereby obtaining Table 4.5. To obtain the total freight cost incurred for shipments from plant i to warehouse j, we simply look in the cell in Table 4.5's ith row and jth column and multiply the unit shipping cost in the cell's upper-left corner times x_{ij}. For example, the total freight cost incurred for shipments between plant 2 and warehouse 4 is $5x_{24}$. Applying this reasoning to

TABLE 4.5 Formulating Graham Kracker's Transportation Problem

	Warehouse 1 (Newark)	Warehouse 2 (Chicago)	Warehouse 3 (Atlanta)	Warehouse 4 (Dallas)	Warehouse 5 (Los Angeles)	Supplies
Plant 1 (Pittsburgh)	4 x_{11}	6 x_{12}	5 x_{13}	12 x_{14}	19 x_{15}	180 CWT
Plant 2 (Memphis)	10 x_{21}	4 x_{22}	8 x_{23}	5 x_{24}	14 x_{25}	280 CWT
Plant 3 (Omaha)	13 x_{31}	9 x_{32}	3 x_{33}	6 x_{34}	10 x_{35}	150 CWT
Demands	120 CWT	100 CWT	160 CWT	80 CWT	150 CWT	

each of the 15 plant-warehouse pairs, we can mathematically express Graham's objective of minimizing total freight costs as

$$
\begin{aligned}
\text{Minimize} \quad & 4x_{11} + 6x_{12} + 5x_{13} + 12x_{14} + 19x_{15} \\
& + 10x_{21} + 4x_{22} + 8x_{23} + 5x_{24} + 14x_{25} \\
& + 13x_{31} + 9x_{32} + 3x_{33} + 6x_{34} + 10x_{35}
\end{aligned}
$$

Formulating the LP's Constraints

Besides the 15 nonnegativity constraints on the 15 decision variables, the LP formulation of Graham's transportation problem contains 8 structural constraints. Just as Table 4.5 proved useful in expressing the LP's objective function, it also facilitates formulating the structural constraints. To ensure that Table 4.5 represents a feasible distribution plan, the decision variables in each row must sum to the supply in the row's right margin, and the decision variables in each column must sum to the demand in the column's bottom margin.

To illustrate the three "row constraints," consider plant 2. To ensure that the sum of amounts shipped from plant 2 to the five warehouses equals plant 2's supply, we simply set the sum of the decision variables in Table 4.5's second row equal to the supply in the row's right margin, thereby obtaining the following constraint:

$$x_{21} + x_{22} + x_{23} + x_{24} + x_{25} = 280.$$

We refer to such a constraint as a *supply constraint*. In general,

A supply constraint has the form

$$
\begin{pmatrix}
\text{summation of decision variables} \\
\text{representing the alternative ways} \\
\text{to use the supply}
\end{pmatrix}
\leqslant \text{ or } =
\begin{pmatrix}
\text{a constant equal to} \\
\text{the available supply}
\end{pmatrix}
$$

The choice of $\leqslant$ or $=$ is dictated by the nature of the decision problem.

Similar supply constraints are required for plants 1 and 3. You should attempt to write these two supply constraints, then check them against those appearing below in the LP's complete formulation.

To illustrate the five "column constraints", consider warehouse 4. To ensure that the sum of the amounts shipped from the three plants to warehouse 4 equals warehouse 4's demand, we simply set the sum of the decision variables in Table 4.5's fourth column equal to the demand in the column's bottom margin, thereby obtaining the following constraint:

$$x_{14} + x_{24} + x_{34} = 80.$$

This constraint, with its left-hand side consisting of alternative ways to satisfy the demand specified on its right-hand side, is an example of a *demand constraint,* a general class of constraints we first encountered when formulating DuPunt's make-or-buy problem. Similar demand constraints are required for warehouses 1, 2, 3, and 5. You should attempt to write these four demand constraints, then check them against those appearing below in the LP's complete formulation.

The LP's Complete Formulation

The complete formulation of Graham Kracker's transportation problem is the following 15-variable, 8-constraint LP:

$$\text{Minimize} \quad 4x_{11} + 6x_{12} + 5x_{13} + 12x_{14} + 19x_{15} \quad \text{(total}$$
$$+ \ 10x_{21} + 4x_{22} + 8x_{23} + 5x_{24} + 14x_{25} \quad \text{freight}$$
$$+ \ 13x_{31} + 9x_{32} + 3x_{33} + 6x_{34} + 10x_{35} \quad \text{costs)}$$

$$\text{subject to} \qquad x_{11} + x_{12} + x_{13} + x_{14} + x_{15} = 180 \quad \text{(supply}$$
$$x_{21} + x_{22} + x_{23} + x_{24} + x_{25} = 280 \quad \text{constraints)}$$
$$x_{31} + x_{32} + x_{33} + x_{34} + x_{35} = 150$$

$$x_{11} + x_{21} + x_{31} = 120$$
$$x_{12} + x_{22} + x_{32} = 100$$
$$x_{13} + x_{23} + x_{33} = 160 \quad \text{(demand}$$
$$x_{14} + x_{24} + x_{34} = \ \ 80 \quad \text{constraints)}$$
$$x_{15} + x_{25} + x_{35} = 150$$

and $x_{ij} \geqslant 0$ for all i-j pairs. \qquad (nonnegativity constraints)

The LP's Optimal Solution

Using a software package such as the one discussed in Chapter 3, Graham would discover that the optimal solution to his LP (displayed in the format of Table 4.5) is:

Optimal Distribution Plan

	Warehouse 1 (Newark)	Warehouse 2 (Chicago)	Warehouse 3 (Atlanta)	Warehouse 4 (Dallas)	Warehouse 5 (Los Angeles)	Supplies
Plant 1 (Pittsburgh)	4 **120**	6 **0**	5 **60**	12 **0**	19 **0**	180 CWT
Plant 2 (Memphis)	10 **0**	4 **100**	8 **0**	5 **80**	14 **100**	280 CWT
Plant 3 (Omaha)	13 **0**	9 **0**	3 **100**	6 **0**	10 **50**	150 CWT
Demands	120 CWT	100 CWT	160 CWT	80 CWT	150 CWT	

Optimal total freight costs = $3780.

It is interesting to note that the optimal solution ships only $x_{33} = 100$ CWT from plant 3 to warehouse 3 (the route with the lowest unit freight cost) and ships $x_{25} = 100$ CWT from plant 2 to warehouse 5 (the route with the second highest unit freight cost). How does this compare with your recommendation?

As was the case with Suny's LP, it is *not* a coincidence that the optimal decision variables are all integer-valued. The following is a theorem:

A transportation problem having the characteristics of Graham's (including integer-valued supplies and demands) *always* has an optimal solution in which all decision variables assume integer values.

Consequently, when decision makers face transportation problems similar to Graham Kracker's, they may employ linear programming without worrying that they

162

will have to round the LP's optimal solution or resort to integer linear programming.

Formulating More Complex Transportation Problems

Before concluding our discussion of the transportation problem, we will discuss how to formulate transportation problems that are similar to Graham's but have a few added "wrinkles." In particular, we consider the following three complications:

1. An unbalanced transportation problem.
2. Upper and lower bounds on a decision variable.
3. Prohibition of a shipping route.

An unbalanced transportation problem with total supply greater than total demand. There are two types of unbalanced transportation problems: total supply may be greater than, or it may be less than, total demand. Let us consider the former type first. When total supply exceeds total demand, at least one source will not ship all its supply. Therefore, we create a so-called *fictitious sink*[6] whose demand exactly equals the excess of total supply over total demand. For example, if total supply is 800 units and total demand is 610 units, we set the fictitious sink's demand equal to 190 units.

A shipment from a source to the fictitious sink is itself fictitious. It represents undistributed units of the source's supply. For example, a shipment of 100 units from a source to the fictitious sink implies that 100 units of the source's supply are undistributed. Undistributed supply has two interpretations: (1) inventory remaining at the source or (2) unused production capacity at the source. In the former case, the unit freight cost from a source to the fictitious sink should be set equal to the unit inventory cost at the source. The latter case arises when a decision maker is solving the transportation problem before the actual production of the product. Here, the goal is to use the LP to determine the production level at each source as well as how much to ship between each source-sink pair. Consequently, the unit freight cost from a source to the fictitious sink should be set equal to the unit cost of unused production capacity (e.g., layoff costs). Furthermore, if the unit production costs differ across the sources, each source's unit production cost should be added to the unit freight costs from the source to all *nonfictitious* sinks; that is,

$$\begin{pmatrix} \text{revised unit freight cost} \\ \text{from plant } i \text{ to} \\ \text{nonfictitious sink } j \end{pmatrix} = \begin{pmatrix} \text{unit production cost} \\ \text{at source } i \end{pmatrix} + \begin{pmatrix} \text{unit freight cost} \\ \text{from plant } i \text{ to} \\ \text{warehouse } j \end{pmatrix}$$

Having created the fictitious sink and appropriately specified the unit cost of "shipping" to it, we are now faced with a balanced transportation problem, one that we may formulate as an LP exactly as we did Graham's transportation problem. The only differences are ones of interpretation. In particular, the LP's objective function includes not only actual freight costs but additional costs "disguised" as freight costs incurred for shipping to the fictitious sink. Similarly, the decision variables represent not only actual shipments but also inventory or unused production capacity "disguised" as shipments to the fictitious sink. (Exercise 4.7 involves an unbalanced transportation problem requiring the creation of a fictitious sink.)

---

[6] Sometimes called *artificial sink, pseudosink,* or *dummy sink.*

Unbalanced transportation problems with total supply less than total demand.
When total supply is less than total demand, at least one sink will not have its demand satisfied. Therefore, we proceed in a manner similar to the excess supply case. This time, however, instead of creating a fictitious sink, we create a fictitious source whose supply equals the amount by which total supply falls short of total demand. For example, if total supply is 500 units and total demand is 610 units, we set the fictitious source's supply equal to 110 units.

A shipment from the fictitious source to a sink is itself fictitious. (Think of it as the fictitious source shipping empty boxes!) A shipment of, say, 50 units from the fictitious source to a sink actually means 50 units of the sink's demand are not satisfied. Consequently, we should set the unit freight cost from the fictitious source to a sink equal to the sink's unit penalty cost for unsatisfied demand. A sink's unit penalty cost may equal, for example, the incremental cost of filling unsatisfied demand with purchases from "outside" suppliers.

Our creation of the fictitious source results in a balanced transportation problem, one that we may formulate as an LP exactly as we did Graham's transportation problem. The only differences are ones of interpretation. In particular, the LP's objective function includes not only actual freight costs but also penalty costs "disguised" as freight costs. Similarly, the decision variables represent not only actual shipments but also unsatisfied demand "disguised" as shipments from the fictitious source. (Exercise 4.8 involves an unbalanced transportation problem requiring the creation of a fictitious source.)

Upper and lower bounds on a decision variable. Some situations require upper and/or lower bounds to be placed on the total amount shipped between a particular source-sink pair. Using Graham's transportation problem as an example, suppose the capacity of the mode of transportation between plant 2 and warehouse 4 limits the total amount shipped to 50 CWT. Then Graham must add to his LP the upper bound constraint

$$x_{24} \leqslant 50 \, .$$

To illustrate a lower bound constraint, suppose Graham has to ensure that his distribution plan meets the terms of a contract with the freight carrier calling for a shipment of at least 25 CWT between plant 2 and warehouse 4. Then Graham must add to his LP the lower bound constraint

$$x_{24} \geqslant 25 \, .$$

It is important to understand that this lower bound constraint guarantees that x_{24} will never assume a value below 25 CWT. It does *not* say, "If x_{24} does not equal 0, it will be at least 25 CWT." Such a constraint can be dealt with only by using an integer linear programming formulation technique, as discussed in Chapter 9.

Prohibition of a shipping route. Some situations require the prohibition of any shipments whatsoever between a particular source-sink pair. Using Graham's transportation problem to illustrate, suppose that shipments between plant 2 and warehouse 4 are unacceptable, perhaps because of a lack of a suitable freight carrier. To resolve this complication, Graham has two choices for guaranteeing that the LP's optimal solution will not call for x_{24} to assume a positive value:

1. He may eliminate the decision variable x_{24} from the LP formulation.

2. He may set the unit freight cost between plant 2 and warehouse 4 to some arbitrarily large number, say \$1000 per CWT. This creates an exorbitant penalty for shipments between plant 2 and warehouse 4, a penalty that will be avoided in the LP's optimal solution by having $x_{24} = 0$.

The latter method is preferred, especially when the LP has already been formulated without the prohibition of the route or when the prohibition of the route might subsequently be dropped.

A Final Comment on the Transportation Problem

Transportation problems are members of a broader class of decision problems amenable to an LP approach, a class known as *network flow problems*. They are so named because they involve the "flow" of some commodity through a "network" of locations interconnected by distribution routes. Network flow problems are so important that we devote almost all of Chapter 8 to them. In case your course does not include that chapter, Exercise 4.17 will introduce you to a network flow problem different from the transportation problem.

4.6 A PERSONNEL SCHEDULING PROBLEM

Many service facilities (e.g., a hospital or a toll bridge) or service systems (e.g., a public transit system or a police force) operate 24 hours a day and/or 7 days a week. In a personnel scheduling problem, a manager of such a service facility or system must decide how to assign personnel to each of a variety of alternative work schedules so as to meet workforce requirements at minimal payroll costs.

Problem Statement

To illustrate a personnel scheduling problem, consider the following scenario:

Among his personnel scheduling duties as administrator at St. Andrew's Nursing Home for Retired MBAs, Regis Tiered is responsible for scheduling the workshifts of St. Andrew's registered nurses (RNs). The scheduling problem currently confronting Regis involves the scheduling of RNs for the "swing" shift (3:00 to 11:00 P.M.). The following table provides the minimal daily requirements for swing-shift RNs:

Sunday	Monday	Tuesday	Wednesday	Thursday	Friday	Saturday
22 RNs	17 RNs	13 RNs	21 RNs	16 RNs	14 RNs	20 RNs

St. Andrew's contract with the RNs calls for each to have 2 consecutive days off each week and to work the remaining 5 days. Consequently, Regis must assign an RN to one of the seven work schedules listed in Table 4.6. Regis computed the table's weekly salaries from the contract terms, which call for an RN working the swing shift to receive a daily salary of $100 for any weekday, $150 for Saturday, and $175 for Sunday. For example, since schedules 2–5 all call for two weekdays off, an RN with either of these schedules earns $100 for the three weekdays, $150 for Saturday, and $175 for Sunday, for a total of

$$(3)(\$100) + \$150 + \$175 = \$625 \text{ per week.}^7$$

---

[7] You should verify the weekly salaries of the remaining three schedules.

TABLE 4.6 Alternative Work Schedules for Regis's Personnel
Scheduling Problem

SCHEDULE	DAYS OFF	WEEKLY SALARY
1	Sunday and Monday	$550
2	Monday and Tuesday	$625
3	Tuesday and Wednesday	$625
4	Wednesday and Thursday	$625
5	Thursday and Friday	$625
6	Friday and Saturday	$575
7	Saturday and Sunday	$500

Given the daily swing-shift requirements and given the salaries associated with each of the seven alternative work schedules, Regis's goal is to decide on an assignment of RNs to work schedules that will meet the daily requirements with the minimal weekly payroll costs.

Your Recommendation

Before we formulate Regis's personnel scheduling problem as an LP and discuss its optimal solution, pretend for a moment that you are Regis and use common sense, intuition, and trial-and-error to develop a personnel schedule. Write your recommendation in the spaces below.

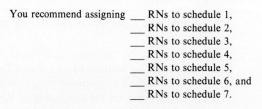

You recommend assigning ___ RNs to schedule 1,
___ RNs to schedule 2,
___ RNs to schedule 3,
___ RNs to schedule 4,
___ RNs to schedule 5,
___ RNs to schedule 6, and
___ RNs to schedule 7.

Total payroll costs of your recommendation are $___.

Defining the LP's Decision Variables

We have already seen that Regis has seven decisions, namely, how many RNs to assign to each of the seven alternative work schedules. Consequently, for $i = 1, 2, \ldots, 7$, we define the following seven decision variables:

x_i = the number of RNs assigned to the ith work schedule.

Formulating the LP's Objective Function

Regis's objective is to minimize St. Andrew's weekly payroll costs. Using the weekly salaries provided in Table 4.6, we can express this objective function as

$$\text{Minimize } 550x_1 + 625x_2 + 625x_3 + 625x_4 + 625x_5 + 575x_6 + 500x_7.$$

Observe that this objective function minimizes the weekly payroll costs, not necessarily the total number of RNs on the payroll. In some personnel scheduling problems, the salaries associated with the alternative work schedules are identically equal. In these problems, an objective of minimizing the total number of employees on the payroll also minimizes the total payroll costs. For example, if an RN's daily salary at St. Andrew's did not vary according to the day of the week, Regis's objective would be

$$\text{Minimize } x_1 + x_2 + x_3 + x_4 + x_5 + x_6 + x_7.$$

Formulating the LP's Constraints

Besides the seven nonnegativity constraints on the seven decision variables, the LP formulation of Regis's personnel scheduling problem requires seven structural constraints. All these structural constraints are so-called *minimal requirement constraints*. In general,

A minimal requirement constraint has the form

$$\begin{pmatrix} \text{summation of terms representing} \\ \text{each decision variable's contribution} \\ \text{to meeting the requirement} \end{pmatrix} \geqslant \begin{pmatrix} \text{a constant equal to} \\ \text{the} \\ \text{minimal requirement} \end{pmatrix}$$

We previously encountered minimal requirement constraints in Pete Moss's blending LP in Chapter 2, where three such constraints were necessary to ensure that the blended fertilizer contained sufficient nitrogen, phosphorus, and potassium.

In Regis's personnel scheduling problem, the seven minimal requirement constraints are necessary to ensure that a sufficient number of RNs are on duty each of the seven days of the week. Consider Wednesday, for example. In Table 4.6, Wednesday appears in the "days-off" column twice, once for schedule 3 and once again for schedule 4. This implies that the RNs on duty on Wednesday are those *not* working schedule 3 or 4, that is, those RNs working schedules 1, 2, 5, 6, or 7. Therefore, to ensure the number of on-duty RNs on Wednesday is at least as large as Wednesday's minimal requirement of 21, the LP must include the following constraint:

$$x_1 + x_2 + x_5 + x_6 + x_7 \geqslant 21.$$

Because the optimal assignment of RNs to work schedules may result in more RNs on duty on Wednesday than the minimum required, we use a $\geqslant$ constraint.

A similar minimal requirement constraint must hold for each of the remaining six days of the week. You should attempt to write these six constraints, then check them against those appearing below in the LP's complete formulation.

The LP's Complete Formulation

The complete formulation of Regis's personnel scheduling problem is the following 7-variable, 7-constraint LP:

$$\text{Minimize } 550x_1 + 625x_2 + 625x_3 + 625x_4 + 625x_5 + 575x_6 + 500x_7 \qquad \text{(total payroll costs)}$$

$$
\begin{array}{llllllllll}
\text{subject to} & & x_2 + & x_3 + & x_4 + & x_5 + & x_6 & & \geqslant 22 & \text{(Sunday)} \\
& & & x_3 + & x_4 + & x_5 + & x_6 + & x_7 & \geqslant 17 & \text{(Monday)} \\
& x_1 & & + & x_4 + & x_5 + & x_6 + & x_7 & \geqslant 13 & \text{(Tuesday)} \\
& x_1 + & x_2 & & + & x_5 + & x_6 + & x_7 & \geqslant 21 & \text{(Wednesday)} \\
& x_1 + & x_2 + & x_3 & & + & x_6 + & x_7 & \geqslant 16 & \text{(Thursday)} \\
& x_1 + & x_2 + & x_3 + & x_4 & & + & x_7 & \geqslant 14 & \text{(Friday)} \\
& x_1 + & x_2 + & x_3 + & x_4 + & x_5 & & & \geqslant 20 & \text{(Saturday)}
\end{array}
$$

and $x_1 \geqslant 0, x_2 \geqslant 0, \ldots, x_7 \geqslant 0.$ 　　　　　　　　　(nonnegativity constraints)

The LP's Optimal Solution

Using a software package such as the one discussed in Chapter 3, Regis would discover that his LP's optimal solution is the one displayed in the first row of Table 4.7. (Temporarily ignore the table's second and third rows.) Owing to the noninteger values of x_2, x_3, x_5, and x_7, Regis cannot implement the LP's optimal solution. Fortunately, for personnel scheduling problems there exists a rounding strategy that often provides an acceptable close-to-optimal solution. The rounding strategy simply rounds any decision variable with a noninteger value to the next *highest* integer. This "rounding up" strategy always maintains feasibility because it only increases the summations of decision variables appearing on the left-hand sides of the minimal requirement constraints, thereby ensuring that the constraints remain satisfied. Application of the "rounding up" strategy to the LP's optimal solution appearing in Table 4.7's first row yields the rounded solution displayed in the table's second row. This rounded solution calls for a staff of 26 RNs to be divided among five of the seven alternative work schedules.

To compute the rounded solution's maximum percentage error, we proceed as we did in OMC's product mix problem in Chapter 2. Since an LP's optimal objective value provides a lower bound (when minimizing) on the integer linear program's optimal objective value, the rounded solution's maximum percentage error is

$$\frac{(\text{rounded solution's objective value}) - (\text{LP's optimal objective value})}{(\text{LP's optimal objective value})} \times 100\% =$$

$$\frac{15{,}775 - 14{,}983\frac{1}{3}}{14{,}983\frac{1}{3}} \times 100\% = 5.28\%$$

Regis would probably find this an acceptable maximum percentage error. If not, he would have to turn to the integer linear programming solution techniques discussed in Chapter 9. Regis would then discover that the actual optimal solution to his problem is the one displayed in Table 4.7's third row, a solution calling for a

TABLE 4.7 Solutions to Regis's Personnel Scheduling Problem

SOLUTION	VALUES OF DECISION VARIABLES							TOTAL PAYROLL COSTS	$x_1 + x_2 + \cdots + x_7$ (Sum of decision variables)
	x_1	x_2	x_3	x_4	x_5	x_6	x_7		
LP's optimal solution	0	$7\frac{2}{3}$	$3\frac{2}{3}$	0	$8\frac{2}{3}$	2	$2\frac{2}{3}$	$\$14{,}983\frac{1}{3}$	$24\frac{2}{3}$
Rounded solution	0	8	4	0	9	2	3	$\$15{,}775$	26
Actual optimal solution	0	7	4	0	9	2	3	$\$15{,}150$	25

staff of 25 RNs to be divided among five of the seven alternative work schedules.[8] It is interesting to note that, in contrast to the rounded solution's maximum percentage error of 5.28%, its actual percentage error is only

$$\frac{(\text{rounded solution's objective value}) - (\text{actual optimal objective value})}{(\text{actual optimal objective value})} \times 100\% =$$

$$\frac{15{,}775 - 15{,}150}{15{,}150} \times 100\% = 4.13\%$$

This illustrates the general phenomenon (also observed in OMC's product mix problem) that a rounded solution's actual percentage error is usually lower than the maximal (i.e., worst-case) percentage error.

Research by Bartholdi, Orlin, and Ratliff [9] actually shows that, for some personnel scheduling problems (including Regis's), finding the optimal solution does not require resorting to integer linear programming solution techniques. Instead, all that is required is the solution of two additional LPs, each of which is the original LP plus one additional structural constraint. In particular, the solution procedure proposed by Bartholdi, Orlin, and Ratliff consists of four steps:

1. Sum the decision variables' values in the LP's optimal solution, and denote this sum by V. For example, as indicated in Table 4.7's last column, the decision variables in the optimal solution of Regis's LP sum to $V = 24\frac{2}{3}$.

2. Let $\lceil V \rceil$ denote the smallest integer greater than or equal to V, and let $\lfloor V \rfloor$ denote the largest integer less than or equal to V. For example, given $V = 24\frac{2}{3}$ in Regis's problem,

$$\lceil V \rceil = 25 \text{ and } \lfloor V \rfloor = 24.$$

3. Formulate two modified LPs, one by adding to the original LP the constraint

$$(\text{summation of all decision variables}) = \lceil V \rceil$$

and one by adding to the original LP the constraint

$$(\text{summation of all decision variables}) = \lfloor V \rfloor.$$

For example, for Regis's LP, one modified LP is the original LP we formulated with the added constraint

$$x_1 + x_2 + x_3 + x_4 + x_5 + x_6 + x_7 = 25$$

and the other is the original LP with the added constraint

$$x_1 + x_2 + x_3 + x_4 + x_5 + x_6 + x_7 = 24.$$

4. Solve the two modified LPs, both of which are guaranteed to have optimal solutions in which the decision variables all assume integer values. The modified LP with the lower optimal objective value provides the optimal solu-

---

[8] How does this compare to your recommendation?

[9] J.J. Bartholdi III, J.B. Orlin, and H.D. Ratliff, "Cyclic Scheduling via Integer Programs with Circular Ones," *Operations Research*, **28**: 5 (Sept.–Oct. 1980), pp. 1074–1085.

tion to the personnel scheduling problem. For example, for Regis's problem, the modified LP with the added constraint whose right-hand side is 25 provides the optimal solution in Table 4.7's third row.

Proof of the validity of this four-step solution procedure is well beyond the scope of this text. However, if you encounter a personnel scheduling problem later in your managerial career, keep this procedure in mind. It could save you much time and money that might otherwise be spent using integer linear programming solution techniques. As we will see in Chapter 9, solving three LPs is usually much faster than solving one integer linear program of the same size.

We conclude our discussion of Regis's personnel scheduling problem with a final observation on implementation. To illustrate, consider the optimal solution in Table 4.7's third row, a solution calling for a staff of 25 RNs. The values of the decision variables only indicate how many (not who) of the staff of 25 RNs should be assigned to each of the alternative work schedules. There is nothing to prevent Regis from periodically (say, monthly) shifting the names of the RNs among the alternative work schedules so that, for example, every RN on the staff is assigned to schedule 7 (weekends off) an approximately equal number of weeks during the calendar year.

4.7 CONCLUDING REMARKS

As summarized in Table 4.8, we have formulated examples of five classes of decision problems amenable to a linear programming approach. The end-of-chapter exercises not only provide additional examples from these five classes but also introduce you to several other classes. In formulating these decision problems (or those that you may encounter later in your managerial career), follow these guidelines:

1. After carefully reading the verbal statement of the decision problem, make a list that verbally describes each decision you would have to make if this were your decision problem. Then define a decision variable to represent each decision on your list.

2. Verbally express the decision problem's objective. Then, mathematically express the objective function as a linear function of the decision variables.

3. Verbally express each constraint on the decisions. Then, mathematically express the constraint as a linear inequality or linear equation involving the decision variables.

After following the above guidelines to obtain a "first draft" of the LP, there are several ways of checking your work. The first recommended self-check is to reread the statement of the decision problem. As you reread each sentence and table, ask yourself if you have "captured" its content somewhere in your LP's decision variables, objective function, or constraints. If not, make the necessary corrections.

A second self-check involves verifying the consistency of the units of measurement in the objective function and each constraint. For example, suppose the intent of a constraint is to ensure that no more than 10,000 hours of a scarce resource are consumed during the manufacture of two products. Also suppose that the manufacture of each unit of product 1 consumes 2 hours of the resource, whereas the manufacture of each unit of product 2 consumes 7 hours of the resource. If x_1

TABLE 4.8 A Summary of Five Classes of Decision Problems

PROBLEM TYPE	DECISION VARIABLES	OBJECTIVE FUNCTION	STRUCTURAL CONSTRAINTS	Will optimal values of decision variables *always* be integers (assuming LP's constraints' data are integer-valued)?
Make-or-Buy (involving n products and m resources)	$2n$ decision variables, n for the "make" decisions and n for the "buy" decisions.	Minimize total costs of making and buying.	$n + m$ constraints, n demand constraints and m resource constraints.	No.
Production and Inventory Planning (involving m time periods)	$2m$ decision variables, one for each time period's production level and one for each time period's inventory level.	Minimize total costs of production and inventory.	$5m$ constraints, one material balance equation for each time period, one lower bound constraint and one upper bound constraint on each time period's production level, and one lower bound constraint and one upper bound constraint on each time period's inventory level.	Yes.
Financial Planning (involving m time periods and n investments)	n decision variables, one for each investment (plus one additional decision variable when the initial budget is also a decision)	When given information is a schedule of required payments, the objective is to minimize the initial cash investment; When given information is an initial investment budget (and possibly a schedule of subsequent budget augmentations), the objective is to minimize the cash inflow at the end of the last time period.	$m + 1$ constraints, one cash balance equation for the beginning of each time period (plus possibly some ratio constraints on such things as risk and time to maturity).	No.
Transportation (involving m sources and n sinks)	mn decision variables, one for each source-sink pair.	Minimize total freight costs.	$m + n$ constraints, one supply constraint for each source and one demand constraint for each sink (plus possibly some lower and/or upper bound constraints on one or more decision variables).	Yes.
Personnel Scheduling (involving m time periods and n work schedules)	n decision variables, one for each alternative work schedule.	When the payroll costs of the alternative work schedules are different, the objective is to minimize the total payroll costs. When the payroll costs of the alternative work schedules are identically equal, the objective is to minimize the number of employees on the payroll.	m constraints, one minimal requirement constraint to ensure sufficient on-duty personnel for each time period.	No.

and x_2 represent the number of units manufactured of products 1 and 2, respectively, you may express the resource constraint in either of the following two forms:

$$\left(2 \frac{\text{hours}}{\text{unit}}\right)(x_1 \text{ units}) + \left(7 \frac{\text{hours}}{\text{unit}}\right)(x_2 \text{ units}) \leqslant 10,000 \text{ hours}$$

$$\left(0.002 \frac{\text{thousand hours}}{\text{unit}}\right)(x_1 \text{ units}) + \left(0.007 \frac{\text{thousand hours}}{\text{unit}}\right)(x_2 \text{ units}) \leqslant 10 \text{ thousand hours}$$

By verifying the consistency of your units of measurement, you might discover you had inadvertently mixed units and expressed the resource constraint as, say,

$$2x_1 + 7x_2 \leqslant 10$$

(Units are hours)   (Units are thousands of hours)

A third and final check of your formulation occurs when you solve your LP. As we discussed in Section 2.12, if you discover the LP is infeasible, it usually means one or more of its constraints is too restrictive. If you discover your LP has an unbounded objective value, it usually means you have inadvertently omitted one or more important constraints. Even if the LP has an optimal solution, a close examination may disclose a decision variable with a "suspicious-looking" value, thereby providing a clue to a potential formulation error.

In closing, we should reiterate the two primary differences between the decision problems you encounter in this chapter and those you may encounter in the "real world."

1. In the real world, you will rarely enjoy the luxury of a concise problem statement. Instead, you will most likely encounter a "fuzzy" problem statement, perhaps with missing data.

2. Real-world decision problems usually have much larger scale than those of this chapter. Their LP formulations may involve hundreds and even thousands of decision variables and structural constraints.

Despite these differences in conciseness and scale, careful study of this chapter's examples and exercises will prepare you well for the applications of linear programming you will undoubtedly encounter later in your managerial career.

The next chapter focuses on several advanced LP formulation techniques. Owing to constraints on time, your course may not include that chapter. If so, keep it in mind for self-study if you should ever need to add to your "tool kit" of formulation techniques.

4.8 CHAPTER CHECKLIST AND GLOSSARY

Quickly review this chapter by rereading the material highlighted by a vertical line in the left margin and Table 4.8. You should then be familiar with the concepts, techniques, and terminology in the Checklist and Glossary that follow. If you need help with a particular item, consult the section or sections indicated for a more detailed discussion.

Checklist of Concepts and Techniques

- ☐ Formulating as an LP the following classes of decision problems:
  - ☐ make-or-buy problems [4.2],
  - ☐ production and inventory planning problems [4.3],
  - ☐ financial planning problems [4.4],
  - ☐ transportation problems (both balanced and unbalanced) [4.5],
  - ☐ personnel planning problems [4.6].

- ☐ Formulating the following types of constraints:
  - ☐ resource constraints [4.2],
  - ☐ demand constraints [4.2, 4.5],
  - ☐ material balance constraints [4.3],
  - ☐ lower and upper bound constraints [4.3, 4.5],
  - ☐ cash balance constraints [4.4],
  - ☐ ratio constraints [4.4],
  - ☐ supply constraints [4.5],
  - ☐ minimum requirement constraints [4.6].

Glossary

Make-or-buy problem.   A decision problem faced by a manufacturer who can fill customers' orders only by supplementing "in-house" production with purchases from "outside" suppliers. [4.2]

Demand constraint.   A constraint ($\leqslant$, $=$, or $\geqslant$) whose right-hand side is a specified demand and whose left-hand side is the summation of alternative ways of satisfying that demand. [4.2, 4.5]

Resource constraint.   A $\leqslant$ constraint ensuring that the planned consumption of a scarce resource does not exceed the resource's availability. [4.2]

Multiperiod planning problem.   A decision problem involving decisions that span several time periods. [4.3, 4.4]

Production and inventory planning problem.   A decision problem faced by a manufacturer who uses demand forecasts to plan production and inventory levels for the next several time periods. [4.3]

Material balance equation.   A constraint ensuring equality between the "sources" of a commodity during some time period and the "uses" of the commodity during the same time period. [4.3]

Lower bound constraint.   A constraint requiring a single decision variable to be greater than or equal to a specified constant. [4.3, 4.5]

Upper bound constraint.   A constraint requiring a single decision variable to be less than or equal to a specified constant. [4.3, 4.5]

Rolling planning process.   A multiperiod planning process in which a similar LP is solved at the start of each successive time period, thereby obtaining the decisions to implement in the current time period and the planned (but revisable) decisions for all subsequent periods. [4.3, 4.4]

Financial planning problem. A decision problem involving the selection from a variety of investment opportunities. [4.4]

Cash balance equation. A constraint ensuring equality at some point in time between the cash inflow and cash outflow. [4.4]

Ratio constraint. A constraint ensuring that the average value of some attribute of a group of activities meets a specified criterion. [4.4]

Transportation problem. A decision problem faced by an organization that must distribute some commodity from several supply centers called *sources* to several demand centers called *sinks*. [4.5]

Balanced transportation problem. A transportation problem in which total supply equals total demand. [4.5]

Unbalanced transportation problem. A transportation problem in which total supply does *not* equal total demand. [4.5]

Fictitious sink. Given an unbalanced transportation problem with total supply greater than total demand, we create a balanced transportation problem by adding a fictitious sink (whose demand equals the excess supply). [4.5]

Fictitious source. Given an unbalanced transportation problem with total supply less than total demand, we create a balanced problem by adding a fictitious source (whose supply equals the excess demand). [4.5]

Personnel planning problem. A decision problem involving the meeting of staffing requirements by assigning employees to alternative work schedules. [4.6]

Minimum requirement constraint. A $\geq$ constraint ensuring that the total value of some attribute possessed by a group of decision variables does not fall below a specified minimum value. [4.6]

EXERCISES

The exercises that follow test your ability to formulate a linear program. Exercises 4.1–4.10 involve scenarios that closely resemble those discussed in the chapter. Exercises 4.11–4.24 illustrate a variety of other applications of linear programming. As you formulate each LP, you may encounter a situation where a decision variable's interpretation implies it should have an integer value. Do not worry that, in general, there is no guarantee of an integer value when using a linear program. Assume integer values will be subsequently obtained by rounding the linear program's optimal solution or by using integer linear programming, as discussed in Chapter 9. Also, if you have access to a computer package, you should use it to solve your linear program. A close examination of the optimal solution may reveal a flaw in your formulation that would otherwise go undetected.

4.1 *Make-or-Buy.* The California Kettle Company (CKC) is experiencing tremendous growth in the demand for its two types of outdoor barbeque grills: a charcoal grill and a gas grill. CKC has contracted to supply its customers each week with a total of 20,000 charcoal grills and 10,000 gas grills.

CKC's production is limited by the availability of processing time in three departments: Production, Assembly, and Packaging. The following table provides the hours of processing time available per week in each department and the processing time required in each department by each type of grill:

	Processing Times (hours per grill)		Processing Availability (hours per week)
	Charcoal Grill	Gas Grill	
Production Department	0.10	0.20	2500
Assembly Department	0.15	0.25	4000
Packaging Department	0.05	0.05	2000

Owing to this limited availability of processing time, CKC cannot meet its demand with in-house production. Consequently, CKC has been negotiating with

174

another manufacturer who currently has excess production capacity. This manufacturer has agreed to supply CKC with any combination of charcoal and gas grills at a unit cost of $50 per charcoal grill and $100 per gas grill. These unit costs exceed CKC's in-house unit production costs by $10 per charcoal grill and $15 per gas grill. CKC's objective is to meet its demand with the cheapest combination of in-house production and outside purchases. Formulate an appropriate linear program.

4.2. *Production and Inventory Planning.* The Specific Motors Company (SMC), which manufactures only one model of car, wants to plan its production and inventory levels for the next four months. The following table provides the relevant data for each month, where the inventory levels in the last two columns refer to the levels at the end of the month:

Month	Demand	Unit Production Cost	Maximum Production Level	Minimum Production Level	Maximum Inventory Level	Minimum Inventory Level
1	10,000	$10,800	25,000	3000	15,000	2000
2	15,000	$11,100	35,000	3000	15,000	2000
3	25,000	$11,000	30,000	3000	15,000	2000
4	20,000	$11,300	10,000	3000	15,000	2000

Other relevant information is:
- SMC estimates that the cost to hold one car in inventory for one month is $150. To estimate a month's inventory costs, SMC multiplies the average of the month's starting and ending inventory levels by $150.
- SMC currently has an inventory level of 3000 cars.
- SMC wants to meet its demand with no backlogging; that is, all demand must be met in the month it occurs.

Formulate a linear program SMC can use to minimize its total production and inventory costs.

*4.3. *Financial Planning.* In Anne Alyze's financial planning problem in Section 4.4, the given information is a schedule of required payments and the objective is to minimize the initial investment budget. Now suppose Anne has no financial obligations to meet. Instead, assume she has $500,000 available to invest at the beginning of month 1 and her goal is to use the investment opportunities summarized in Table 4.2 to maximize the cash available at the end of six months.
(a) To account for this new scenario, what modifications would you make to the LP formulated in Section 4.4?
(b) Now assume that, besides the $500,000 available to invest at the beginning of month 1, Anne expects to have an additional $250,000 available to invest at the beginning of month 4.

What additional modifications to the LP does this new assumption necessitate?

4.4. *Financial Planning.* The table below describes five projects which are competing for a company's investment dollars. The table displays the cash flow that will result from investing one dollar. Project A is a two-year investment available at the beginning of 1990 which pays $0.30 per dollar invested at the end of the first year and returns an additional dollar per dollar invested at the end of the second. At most, $500,000 can be invested in Project A. Project B is identical to Project A, except that it is available a year later. Project C is a one-year investment available only at the beginning of 1990 which pays $1.10 per dollar invested at the end of that year. Project D is a three-year investment available at the beginning of 1990 which pays $1.75 per dollar invested at the beginning of 1993. Project E will become available at the beginning of 1992 and will, after a year, pay $1.40 per dollar invested. Project E is limited to a maximum investment of $750,000. The cash received from any of these projects may be reinvested in others which are available at the time. In addition, the company can obtain 6 percent via short-term bank accounts for any money not invested in a given year.

Cash Flow Per Dollar Invested

	Project				
	A	B	C	D	E
1990	−1.00	0	−1.00	−1.00	0
1991	+0.30	−1.00	+1.10	0	0
1992	+1.00	+0.30	0	0	−1.00
1993	0	+1.00	0	+1.75	+1.40
Limit	$500,000	$500,000	None	None	$750,000

The company has $1 million to invest and wishes to maximize the amount of money it can accumulate by January 1, 1993. Formulate an appropriate linear program.

4.5. *Financial Planning.* The controller of McCullough's department store is conducting her financial planning for the next six months, September through February. The table below summarizes the estimated financial data for these six months (in millions of dollars):

	Sept.	Oct.	Nov.	Dec.	Jan.	Feb.
Accounts Receivable Balance (at beginning of month)	1.4	1.0	1.4	2.4	2.0	1.0
Planned Payments of Purchases	1.6	1.8	2.0	1.2	0.8	1.0
Cash Needs for Operations	–	0.6	1.2	1.8	–	–
Cash Surplus from Operations	0.4	–	–	–	0.6	3.0

To meet McCullough's needs, the controller has three sources of short-term funds:

1. *Borrow Against Accounts Receivable.* On a month-by-month basis, a local bank will lend McCullough's up to 80% of its accounts receivable balance at the beginning of a month. The interest on this loan is 1.5% per month, payable at the beginning of the following month.

2. *Delay Payment of Purchases.* McCullough's suppliers permit it to delay payment of purchases for one month. For example, McCullough's can delay the $2 million of planned payments for November until December, using the funds instead to meet its cash needs in November. When McCullough's delays a payment, it loses the 3% discount it normally receives for prompt payment.

3. *Use a Six-Month Loan.* On a six-month basis, the same local bank is willing to lend McCullough's any amount from $1 million to $2 million. McCullough's would take out the loan in full at the beginning of September and pay back the loan in full at the end of February. During the six months, McCullough's could not add to the loan or pay off part of the loan. The interest on this loan is 1.0% per month, payable at the beginning of each month.

During any month, McCullough's can invest its excess funds in one-month government securities that return 0.5% per month. The controller's objective is to minimize the net interest cost McCullough's incurs in meeting its cash requirements. Formulate an appropriate linear program.

4.6. *A Transportation Problem.* The Hurtz Rent-a-Car Company has eight outlets in a metropolitan area. Hurtz operates under a policy that calls for a specific "target" percentage of all available cars to be located at each outlet at the start of each day. These percentages are summarized by the following table:

Outlet	1	2	3	4	5	6	7	8
Percentage	20	10	20	5	10	20	5	10

For example, if 500 cars are available, 100 should be at outlet 1 at the start of the day. At the end of a day, if the current distribution of cars does not comply with the targets, Hurtz employees drive the cars overnight from outlet to outlet so that the new distribution meets the specified targets. (For simplicity, assume that no cars are driven from an outlet with a deficit or driven to an outlet with a surplus.) The distance between each pair of outlets is given by the following table:

		To Outlet							
		1	2	3	4	5	6	7	8
From Outlet	1	–	8	6	7	3	5	4	2
	2	8	–	6	5	8	4	6	7
	3	6	6	–	8	3	4	7	4
	4	7	5	8	–	9	5	3	7
	5	3	8	3	9	–	5	6	2
	6	5	4	4	5	5	–	3	3
	7	4	6	7	3	6	3	–	4
	8	2	7	4	7	2	3	4	–

Suppose that at the end of a particular day Hurtz finds that the 100 cars currently available are distributed at the outlets as follows:

Outlet	1	2	3	4	5	6	7	8
Cars	4	14	5	17	22	7	10	21

(a) Given this distribution of cars, formulate a linear program for minimizing the total distance traveled during the overnight redistribution of the cars.

(b) Discuss how the linear program would change from day to day.

4.7. *A Transportation Problem with Excess Supply.* Reconsider Graham Kracker's transportation problem in Section 4.5. Now suppose the supply at Plant 1 has increased from 180 to 200 CWT, thereby creating an excess of total supply over total demand.

(a) Assume that the following table provides the cost incurred at each plant for storing each CWT of supply that is not shipped to a warehouse.

Plant	Storage Cost per CWT of Unused Supply
1	$0.15
2	$0.20
3	$0.10

As described in Section 4.5, convert this unbalanced problem into a balanced one by adding a column to Table 4.4 corresponding to a fictitious warehouse. Then use the modified table to formulate the now-balanced transportation problem as a linear program.

(b) What modifications would you make to the LP in part (a) if the unit production cost varied by plant according to the following table:

Plant	Production Cost per CWT
1	$0.90
2	$0.75
3	$0.80

176

*4.8. *A Transportation Problem with Excess Demand.* Reconsider Graham Kracker's transportation problem in Section 4.5. Now suppose the supply at plant 2 has decreased from 280 to 250, thereby creating an excess of total demand over total supply. Assume that the following table provides the cost per CWT Gramma's Biscuit Company incurs for not satisfying the demand at each warehouse:

Warehouse	1	2	3	4	5
Cost per CWT of Unsatisfied Demand	$0.15	$0.10	$0.25	$0.20	$0.05

The costs are incurred because of penalties built into Gramma's contracts with the customers served by each warehouse. As described in Section 4.5, convert this unbalanced problem into a balanced one by adding a row to Table 4.4 corresponding to a fictitious plant. Then use the modified table to formulate the now-balanced transportation problem as a linear program.

4.9. *Personnel Scheduling.* The following table summarizes how the Centerville police department's requirements for on-duty police officers varies according to the time of day:

Time	Minimum Number of Officers Required
2:00 A.M. – 6:00 A.M.	22
6:00 A.M. – 10:00 A.M.	55
10:00 A.M. – 2:00 P.M.	88
2:00 P.M. – 6:00 P.M.	110
6:00 P.M. – 10:00 P.M.	44
10:00 P.M. – 2:00 A.M.	33

Officers report for duty at the start of each of the above six time periods and remain on-duty for eight consecutive hours.

(a) Formulate a linear program Centerville can use to minimize the total number of police officers it must hire to meet its needs throughout the day.

(b) Experts have proved that the LP for a personnel scheduling problem having the characteristics of this problem (including an *even* number of time periods) always has an optimal solution in which all decision variables have integer values. Illustrate this fact by solving your linear program using a computer package.

4.10. *Personnel Scheduling* (continued). Reconsider Exercise 4.9. Now suppose Centerville can schedule an officer to work overtime by staying four hours beyond the normal quitting time. (For simplicity, assume that, if an officer works overtime, it must be for exactly four hours.) For example, an officer re-

porting for duty at 2:00 A.M. can work overtime by working the normal eight-hour shift from 2:00 A.M. to 10:00 A.M. and then staying on-duty for an additional four hours until 2:00 P.M. Officers working overtime receive a 50% wage premium per hour of overtime. Formulate a linear program Centerville can use to minimize the total payroll costs of the police officers it must hire.

The next two exercises illustrate how a firm can use linear programming to coordinate two or more types of decisions (for example, production and advertising).

*4.11. *Coordinating Production and Advertising.* The Huntz Company purchases cucumbers and makes two kinds of pickles: sweet and dill. Huntz has made it a policy that at least 30%, but no more than 60%, of the pickles it produces be sweet.

Huntz wants to produce up to, but not more than, the demand for each product. The marketing manager estimates that the demand for sweet pickles is 5000 jars plus an additional 3 jars for each $1 spent on advertising, and the demand for dill pickles is 4000 jars plus an additional 5 jars for every $1 spent on advertising.

Sweet pickles sell for $1.45 per jar, while dill pickles sell for $1.75 per jar. It costs $0.60 to produce a jar of sweet pickles and $0.85 to produce a jar of dill pickles.

Huntz has $16,000 to spend on producing and advertising pickles. It wants to know how many units of each product to produce and how much to spend on advertising for each product to maximize profit. Formulate an appropriate linear program.

4.12. *Coordinating Production, Advertising, and Capacity Expansion.* The engineering staff of a corporation has developed a promising new product. Management now must make three decisions for each of the next two years: how much money to spend on expanding production capacity, how many units to produce, and how much money to spend on promoting the product in order to increase demand. Management wants to make these six decisions in such a way that the total profits over the two years will be maximized.

Since this is a new product, the current annual production capacity is 0. However, every $30 spent at the beginning of the first year will immediately increase the annual production capacity by one unit. Since it is expected that the cost of the required technology will decrease with time, every $20 spent at the beginning of the second year will immediately increase the annual production capacity by one unit. The corporation desires to end the second year with an annual production capacity of at least 9000 units.

It is estimated that if no money is spent at

the beginning of the first year promoting the product, the annual demand will be 600 units. However, every \$15 spent at the beginning of the first year on promotion will immediately increase the annual demand by one unit. It is also estimated that, if no money is spent on promotion at the beginning of the second year, the demand during the second year will be 75% of the demand during the first year. However, every \$10 spent at the beginning of the second year on promotion will immediately increase the annual demand by one unit.

Profits for the first year will be \$100 per unit sold minus the cost of capacity expansion and promotion, and profits for the second year will be \$120 per unit sold minus the cost of capacity expansion and promotion. Because of annual changes in the industry, units produced during the first year cannot be sold during the second year.

At the beginning of the first year, the corporation has \$80,000 available to finance capacity expansion and product promotion. Funds available to finance capacity expansion and product promotion at the beginning of the second year include both unspent funds from the first year and funds obtained by the sale of units during the first year.

Formulate the corporation's two-year decision problem as a linear program.

In some industries (for example, the oil industry), a production process produces two or more products jointly (that is, simultaneously). The next two exercises involve a joint production process.

*4.13. *Joint Production.* A company uses cardboard to produce artificial flowers. The company buys cardboard in units of 1 square yard and stamps (cuts) each unit into one of three different patterns. Pattern 1 produces 70 roses and 20 carnations. Pattern 2 produces 60 roses and 60 carnations. Pattern 3 produces 23 roses and 117 carnations. The only variable cost in these stamping processes is the cost of the cardboard, which is \$10 per square yard. The company sells two types of floral arrangements. Arrangement 1 requires 8 roses and 4 carnations. Arrangement 2 requires 3 roses and 12 carnations. Arrangement 1 has a unit profit of \$7, and arrangement 2 has a unit profit of \$5. (Note: Each unit profit equals revenue minus all variable costs except the cost of cardboard.) The company must produce all the flowers it uses in the floral arrangements. Cardboard supply is limited to 1000 units. During the coming period, the company has agreed to sell at least 40 units of floral arrangement 1, and it knows that it cannot sell more than 200 units of each floral arrangement. The company has also decided to follow a policy that limits the production of arrangements of type 1 to no more than 40% of the total production of arrangements of both types. As-

suming the objective is to maximize total profit, formulate an appropriate linear program.

4.14. *Joint Production.* A company processes a raw material X in Department 1 with a *joint* yield of 3 units of product A and 2 units of product B for every unit of raw material processed in Department 1; that is, 1 unit of raw material X processed in Department 1 *simultaneously* produces 3 units of product A and 2 units of product B. Products A and B cannot be identified as separate products until after they are processed in Department 1. This is called the *split-off point.*

The variable operating costs in Department 1 total \$2.00 per unit of material X processed (including the cost of the material). Product A can either be sold at the split-off point for \$8.00 per unit or be processed further in Department 2 at a cost of \$6.00 per unit and then sold at a price of \$15 per unit. Product B can be sold at \$7.00 per unit at the split-off point or sold at \$10.00 after additional processing in Department 3 at a cost of \$4.00 per unit.

A particular kind of skilled labor is used in each of the three departments. The available amount of this labor is limited to 80,000 hours per week. To process 1 unit of material X in Department 1 requires 1.5 hours of the skilled labor. If product A is processed further in Department 2, 3 hours of skilled labor per unit are needed, and if product B is processed further in Department 3, 1 hour per unit is required. Material X can be acquired up to a maximum quantity of 40,000 units per week.

Using the following diagram as a guide, formulate a linear program the company can solve to maximize its profits.

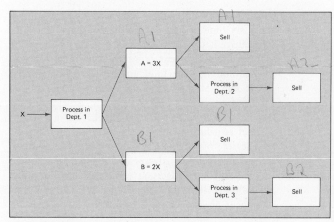

Exercise 4.14

In some industries (for example, the lumber industry or the sausage industry), a raw material of a higher quality may be "downgraded" and used in place of a raw material

178

of a lower quality. The next exercise illustrates how to incorporate downgrading into a product mix linear program.

4.15. *Downgrading of Raw Materials.* A firm uses two raw materials (A and B) to manufacture four products (1, 2, 3, and 4). Both raw materials are inspected and graded as either "choice" or "standard." Choice material of either type can be downgraded to standard material (that is, used in its place) at no cost. The table below displays the unit profit per pound of each product, the already-purchased supply (in pounds) of each grade of each raw material, and the pounds of each grade of each raw material that make up one pound of each product (assuming no downgrading):

| | | Product | | | | Raw Material |
		1	2	3	4	Availability
	Choice A	0.6	0.3	0.0	0.1	60
Raw	Standard A	0.0	0.2	0.0	0.6	90
Material	Choice B	0.4	0.3	0.8	0.0	200
	Standard B	0.0	0.2	0.2	0.3	75
	Unit Profit:	$10	$6	$8	$4	

For example, one pound of product 4 consists of 0.1 pounds of choice A, 0.6 pounds of standard A (some of which may be downgraded choice A), and 0.3 pounds of standard B (some of which may be downgraded choice B).

Assuming that unused raw material of any type can be sold for $0.50 per pound, formulate a linear program to determine the optimal product mix and the optimal amounts of raw materials to downgrade.

Linear programming has applications to farm management. The blending problem in Exercise 2.32 illustrated one application. The next exercise illustrates another.

4.16. *Farm Management.* A farmer has 100 acres that can be used for growing corn or wheat. His yield is 90 bushels per acre per year of corn or 60 bushels per acre per year of wheat. He can devote any fraction of the 100 acres to growing either crop. Labor requirements are 4 hours *per acre* per year, plus 0.70 hours *per bushel* of corn and 0.15 hours *per bushel* of wheat. Cost of seed, fertilizer, and so on is $0.25 per bushel of corn and $0.40 per bushel of wheat. The farmer can sell corn for $1.90 per bushel and wheat for $3.50 per bushel. He can purchase corn for $3.00 per bushel and wheat for $5.00 per bushel.

In addition, the farmer may raise pigs or calves. He sells the pigs or calves when they reach the age of one year. A pig sells for $80, and a calf for $160. One pig requires 20 bushels of corn or 25 bushels of wheat, plus 25 hours of labor and 25 square feet of floor space. One calf requires 50 bushels of corn or 20 bushels of wheat, 80 hours of

labor, and 30 square feet of floor space. (Note: Although a pig or calf can be raised on either corn or wheat but not both, the farmer can have some raised on one and some raised on the other.)

The farmer has 10,000 square feet of floor space. He has available per year 2000 hours of his own time and another 4000 hours from his family. He can also hire labor at $3.00 per hour. However, for each hour of hired labor, 0.15 hours of the farmer's time is required for supervision.

Assuming the farmer wants to maximize profits, formulate a linear program the farmer can use to determine how many acres to devote to corn and to wheat, how many bushels of corn and wheat to purchase and sell, how many pigs and calves to raise on corn and wheat, and how many hours of labor to hire. (*Hint*: One correct formulation has six structural constraints.)

As we will discuss in greater detail in Chapter 8, the transportation problem is a special case of a class of decision problems known as *minimum-cost network flow problems*. The next exercise illustrates such a problem.

*4.17. *A Network Flow Problem.* Consider a firm that, for simplicity, produces a single product. The firm has three plants (A, B, and C), two warehouses (Y and Z), and four customers (1, 2, 3, and 4) geographically dispersed across the United States. As diagrammed in the figure below, the firm ships its product from a plant to a warehouse and then on to a customer:

Exercise 4.17

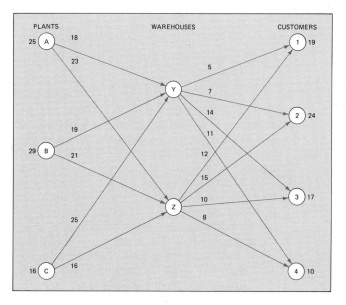

179

In this figure,

- The number to the left of each plant represents the plant's supply of the product.
- The number to the right of each customer represents the customer's demand for the product. (Note that total supply equals total demand.)
- The number written along an arrow drawn from a plant to a warehouse or from a warehouse to a customer is the corresponding unit shipping cost. For example, the shipping cost from plant C to warehouse Y is $25 per unit.

The firm wants to distribute its product at the minimum cost.

(a) Formulate an appropriate linear program.

(b) How would you modify your LP if the supply at plant C were increased to 20, thereby creating an excess supply?

(c) How would you modify your LP if the amount shipped between plant B and warehouse Y had to be at least 7 but at most 12?

The *assignment problem* is a classic management science problem that involves a number of tasks that must be assigned to an equal number of agents (for example, people or machines) subject to the provision that each task must be assigned to exactly one agent. The next exercise is an example. Section 8.6 discusses the assignment problem in greater detail.

4.18. *An Assignment Problem.* A university has four jobs to fill and exactly four job candidates to fill them. The university has given each candidate an aptitude test for each job. The table below displays the percentage of *wrong* answers for each candidate on the test for each job:

	Job 1	Job 2	Job 3	Job 4
Dick	13	15	5	17
Jane	16	29	7	21
Sally	12	23	10	25
Tom	11	20	6	14

Jobs

Harry   18   14   9   16

Given these scores, the university wants to find the assignment of candidates to jobs that minimizes the total percentage of questions missed by the candidates on the tests for the jobs to which they are assigned. For example, if the university assigns Dick to job 3, Jane to job 1, Sally to job 4, and Tom to job 2, the total percentage of wrong answers is 5 + 16 + 25 + 20 = 66.

(a) Formulate the university's problem as a linear program. (*Hint*: This problem is a special case of the transportation problem, where each candidate is a "supply" of one person, each job is a "demand" for one person, and assigning a can-

didate to a job is "transporting" an employee to a job.)

(b) Now suppose that there are five candidates for the four jobs, with Harry being the name of the fifth candidate. Harry's percentages of wrong answers on the tests are 18 for job 1, 14 for job 2, 9 for job 3, and 16 for job 4. Since there are five candidates for only four jobs, one person will remain unemployed. Formulate this revised version of the problem as a linear program. (*Hint*: Create a fictitious job.)

(c) Suppose in part (b) that Harry must not be the individual who remains unemployed (for example, Harry is the university president's nephew). What modifications would you make to your linear program to guarantee Harry gets one of the four jobs?

The next exercise illustrates an application of linear programming to the leasing of a commodity that is temporarily in short supply.

4.19. *Temporary Leasing.* A firm has just discovered that, for the next five months, it will have an insufficient supply of warehouse space. The additional space requirements for the next five months are

Month	Additional Space Requirement (in 1000 sq. ft.)
1	25
2	10
3	20
4	5
5	15

To meet its requirements, the firm plans to lease additional space on a short-term basis. At the beginning of each month, the firm can lease any amount of square feet for any number of months. Separate leases can be taken out for different amounts of space and/or different lengths of time. For example, it might lease 5000 square feet for 2 months and another 10,000 square feet for 3 months. Also, new leases may be taken out before old ones expire. The costs per thousand square feet for leases of various lengths are given by

Length of Lease (months)	1	2	3	4	5
Cost per 1000 square feet	280	450	600	730	840

Formulate a linear program whose solution will provide a leasing policy that satisfies the space requirements at minimum cost. (*Hint*: You will need 15 decision variables, one for each possible combination of the month in which the lease originates and the month in which the lease expires.)

Linear programming is useful in planning how to select and distribute the cargo for a ship, a train, an airplane, or a spacecraft. The next exercise is an example.

*4.20. *Cargo Loading.* A ship has three cargo holds: forward, center, and rear. The capacity limits are:

Hold	Weight Capacity (tons)	Volume Capacity (cubic feet)
Forward	3000	155,000
Center	4000	185,000
Rear	2500	145,000

Because of balance considerations, the weight in the forward hold must be within 5% of the weight in the rear hold; the weight in the center hold must be at least 30% greater than the weight in the forward hold, at least 30% greater than the weight in the rear hold, and at most 90% of the sum of the weights in the forward and rear holds.
The following cargoes are offered:

Commodity	Amount Offered (tons)	Volume per ton (cubic feet)	Profit per ton ($)
1	5000	60	6
2	3000	50	8
3	1000	25	5
4	1500	40	7

The shipowner may accept all or any part of each commodity. (Assume, for example, the commodities are grains and/or liquids.) The shipowner wishes to find the number of tons of each commodity which should be placed in each hold in order to maximize profits. Formulate an appropriate linear program.

School districts have used linear programming to reallocate students to achieve better racial balance. The next exercise involves a simplified example in which a student is considered to be either white or nonwhite. A more realistic model would have several classifications.

4.21. *Reallocating Students to Achieve Racial Balance.* To comply with recent judicial guidelines on racial composition, a school district must reallocate its white and nonwhite high school students to its five schools. This reallocation will be achieved by busing students. At present, all students attend the school in their neighborhood, giving rise to the racial imbalance. The school district's Board of Education (BOE) has compiled the following data on the enrollment of the five schools and the district as a whole:

School	Present Enrollment	Present Nonwhite Enrollment	Present White Enrollment	% White
1	1000	200	800	80
2	800	200	600	75
3	500	50	450	90
4	1200	900	300	25
5	500	450	50	10
Entire District	4000	1800	2200	55

In addition, the BOE has computed the distance (in miles) between every pair of schools. The following table summarizes these distances:

		To School			
	1	2	3	4	5
1	–	3	5	2	2
2	3	–	1	4	2
From School 3	5	1	–	5	3
4	2	4	5	–	1
5	2	2	3	1	–

In devising a busing plan, the BOE must conform to the following guidelines:
1. The proportion of white students in any school must fall within 10% of the proportion of white high school students in the entire city (i.e., 55%).
2. The enrollment in any school cannot increase by more than 5% nor decrease by more than 15% of the present enrollment.
3. White students can be assigned only to their present school or to a school that is currently predominantly nonwhite, and nonwhite students can be assigned only to their present school or to a school that is currently predominantly white.
4. The objective is to minimize the total distance traveled by the bused students (as measured by the distance from a student's former school to his or her new one).

Formulate a linear program that the BOE can use to determine an acceptable busing plan.

In many industries (e.g., paper, textile, steel, and lumber), a product is first manufactured in a large economically produced size. This large size is subsequently cut into a variety of smaller sizes, depending upon customer orders. How to minimize product waste when cutting the larger size into smaller sizes is called the *trim loss* (or *cutting stock*) *problem.* The next exercise is a simplified version of such a problem.

181

4.22. *Trim Loss (or Cutting Stock).* Pittsburgh Paper Products (PPP) produces reels of paper having a standard width of 60 inches. PPP stacks these rolls in a warehouse where they wait to be sliced into rolls of smaller width, depending on the orders to be filled. To cut a standard roll into smaller-sized rolls, PPP transports the roll into the cutting room and mounts it on the cutting machine. This device unrolls the 60-inch roll, slices the roll into smaller widths using prepositioned blades, and collects the smaller widths into rolls at the other end of the machine. For example, the picture below illustrates the cutting of a 60-inch roll into three 15-inch rolls, one 10-inch roll, and one 5-inch roll.

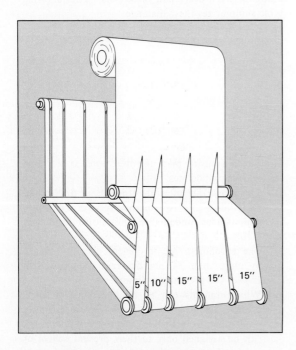

Exercise 4.22

For today, PPP has received the following orders:

Width (inches)	Number of Rolls Ordered
28	30
20	60
15	48

PPP wants to fill these orders by slicing standard 60-inch rolls in a way that minimizes the total waste. There are two sources of waste:

- *Trim Loss.* Trim loss results from a roll of paper that has a width other than 28, 20, or 15 inches (the widths in today's orders). For exam-

ple, if PPP positions the cutting machines blades so as to slice a 60-inch roll into one 28-inch roll and two 15-inch rolls, the trim loss will be a roll having a width of $60-28-15-15 = 2$ inches. (In reality, trim loss might have some value; however, for simplicity, consider it as waste.)

- *Surplus Rolls.* Because the slicing of a standard size roll simultaneously creates several smaller-sized rolls, there is a likelihood that PPP will end the day with surplus rolls of the ordered widths. For example, if PPP ends the day with 50 rolls of the 15-inch rolls, 2 rolls would be considered as waste since only 48 rolls were ordered. (In reality, a surplus roll might have some value; however, for simplicity, consider it has waste.)

There are seven different patterns PPP can use to slice a 60-inch roll. We have already illustrated that one pattern slices a 60-inch roll into one 28-inch roll, two 15-inch rolls, and a one 2-inch roll defined as trim loss. Enumerate the other six patterns PPP can use to slice a 60-inch roll into rolls of the ordered widths. Using a decision variable for each of the seven patterns, formulate an LP that PPP can use to decide how to fill today's orders with the minimum total waste.

Motivated by rapidly escalating fuel prices during the world oil crisis in 1973, the airline companies developed and continue to use linear programming to determine how much fuel an airplane should load at each stop, given the price of the fuel at the stop and the nature of the plane's next flight segment. The next exercise involves a simplified version of this application.

4.23. *Airplane Refueling.* Trans Global Airlines (TGA) wants to optimize its purchases of jet fuel at the cities its serves around the world. Since the fuel efficiency of an airplane is related to its weight, an airplane carrying more fuel than needed to reach its destination will waste fuel. This fact suggests that a plane should take off with just enough fuel to reach its next destination. However, since fuel prices vary from city to city, a policy of minimal fuel purchases may be more costly than filling the plane to capacity at the inexpensive cities.

To illustrate TGA's problem, consider an airplane that each day flies a so-called *rotation* that consists of the following four flight segments:

New York → Los Angeles → San Francisco → Seattle → New York

Upon its arrival in New York, the airplane repeats the rotation. For each flight segment, the table below displays the minimum and maximum fuel levels at takeoff, a linear function that relates fuel consumption to the fuel level at takeoff, and the fuel prices at the departure city.

Flight Segment	City of Departure	City of Arrival	Minimal Fuel Level at Takeoff (1000 gals.)	Maximum Fuel Level at Takeoff (1000 gals.)	Fuel Consumption during Flight Given a Fuel Level of G at Takeoff (1000 gals.)	Price per Gallon of Fuel at City of Departure
1	New York	Los Angeles	23	33	2.90+0.40G	82¢
2	Los Angeles	San Francisco	8	19	1.60+0.05G	75¢
3	San Francisco	Seattle	19	33	4.75+0.25G	77¢
4	Seattle	New York	25	33	1.75+0.45G	89¢

To illustrate the table's next-to-the-last column, suppose that, for flight segment 1, the airplane departs New York with 25 thousand gallons of fuel. Then it will arrive in Los Angeles with 2.9+(0.40)(25) = 12.9 thousand gallons of fuel. Formulate a linear program TGA can use to determine how much fuel to purchase at each of the four cities the airplane visits during its rotation. (*Hint*: This problem is similar to a production and inventory planning problem, with the flight segments analogous to time periods, fuel purchases analogous to production, and fuel on board at the end of a flight analogous to inventory. Also, you will need a constraint that ensures that the fuel on board when the plane lands in New York at the end of the rotation is equal to the amount on board at the start of the rotation before the purchase of fuel.)

Linear programming can be used to plan the economy of a country. The next exercise provides a simplified example.

4.24. The country of Utopia has a newly appointed Minister of International Trade. She has decided that Utopia's welfare (as well as her popularity) can be served best in the upcoming year by maximizing the net dollar value of Utopia's exports (that is, the dollar value of the exports minus the cost of the materials imported to produce the exports). The relevant information is:

- Utopia produces only three products: steel, heavy machinery, and trucks. For the coming year, the minister feels Utopia can sell all it can produce of these three items at the existing world market prices of $900 per unit of steel, $2500 per unit of machinery, and $3000 per unit of trucks.
- To produce one unit of steel, it takes 0.05 units of machinery, 0.08 units of trucks, 0.5 person-years of labor, and imported materials costing $300. Utopia's steel mills have the capacity to produce up to 300,000 units per year.
- To produce one unit of machinery, it takes 0.75 units of steel, 0.12 units of trucks, 5 person-years of labor, and imported materials costing $150. Utopia's machinery plants have the capacity to produce up to 50,000 units per year.
- To produce one unit of trucks, it takes 1 unit of steel, 0.1 units of machinery, 3 person-years of labor, and imported materials costing $500. Utopia's truck plants have the capacity to produce up to 550,000 units per year.
- The pool of labor in Utopia is equivalent to 1,200,000 person-years.

Assuming Utopia cannot import steel, machinery, or trucks, formulate a linear program to determine the optimal production quantities and export quantities for steel, machinery, and trucks. (*Hint*: Among your structural constraints should be a balance equation for each of the three products.)

5

LINEAR PROGRAMMING: ADVANCED APPLICATIONS, INCLUDING GOAL PROGRAMMING

5.1 INTRODUCTION

Sometimes a decision problem possesses a nonlinear characteristic that precludes its formulation as an LP, thereby necessitating the use of nonlinear programming (a topic beyond the scope of this text). At other times, however, the nonlinear characteristic is simply a "cleverly disguised" linear characteristic. In these cases, it is possible to employ advanced techniques to "unmask" the linearity, thereby permitting an LP formulation. In this chapter we focus on three advanced techniques that enable us to "linearize" an apparently nonlinear decision problem:

1. *Piecewise linear programming.*
2. Use of *deviation variables,* including their use in *goal programming.*
3. *Maximin* (or *minimax) objective functions.*

Owing to the complexity of these three formulation techniques, we will discuss each in detail before attempting to provide a concise overview.

5.2 PIECEWISE LINEAR PROGRAMMING

An Introduction to Piecewise Linear Functions

To illustrate the technique of piecewise linear programming, let us reconsider OMC's product mix problem. (You should reread the problem statement in Section 2.3.) We formulated OMC's objective function (before its rescaling in Section 2.5) as

$$\text{Maximize } 900x_1 + 600x_2.$$

Recall that x_1 and x_2 denote the respective production quantities of product 1 (Oranges) and product 2 (Tangerines), and that the variables' coefficients in the objective function, 900 and 600, are the respective contributions to profit of every Orange and every Tangerine. When we formulated OMC's objective function as $900x_1 + 600x_2$, we stressed that the accuracy of this linear function was directly related to the validity of an assumption economists refer to as *constant marginal profits*.

Let us use product 1 (Oranges) to examine more closely the assumption of constant marginal profits. Figure 5.1 is a graph of the function $900x_1$, the total profit OMC earns from producing x_1 Oranges. Of course, the graph is linear, and its constant slope of 900 implies that OMC earns the same $900 profit from every Orange it produces. In other words, OMC's marginal (i.e., incremental) profit from successive Oranges is constant at $900 per Orange.

Let us now consider a revised version of OMC's product mix problem, in which we assume that Millie Sekend's most accurate estimate of OMC's total profit from producing x_1 Oranges is the nonlinear function depicted in Figure 5.2. (We continue to assume that OMC's total profit from Tangerines is the linear function $600x_2$.) The difference between the linear and the nonlinear total profit functions is that, while both increase as x_1 increases, the linear function increases at the same constant rate of 900 whereas the nonlinear function increases at a *decreasing* rate.

Figure 5.1 Original total profit function for Oranges

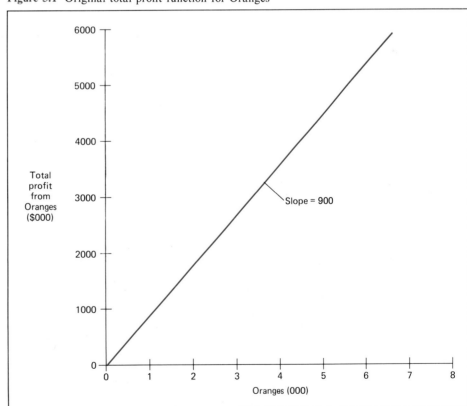

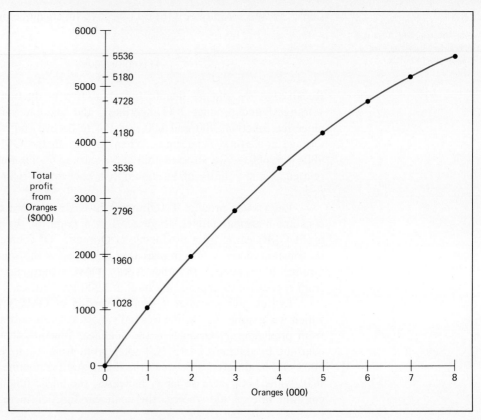

Figure 5.2 Revised total profit function for Oranges

In other words, the function depicted in Figure 5.2 has the property that successive one unit increases in x_1 result in correspondingly smaller and smaller increases in the value of the function. Mathematicians call such a function a *concave function,* and economists refer to a concave total profit function as one having *decreasing marginal profits.*[1] Since profit equals revenue minus cost, decreasing marginal profits may result from one or both of the following two circumstances:

- Decreasing marginal revenues (For example, suppose OMC must lower the Orange's selling price as x_1 increases.)

- Increasing marginal costs. (For example, suppose OMC must rely on increasingly expensive suppliers of disk drives as x_1 increases.)

Let us not take the time here to develop an explicit scenario to account for the Orange's decreasing marginal profits. (One of the exercises will ask you to do this.)

Given the Orange's nonlinear total profit function, how can we formulate OMC's product mix problem as an LP? One alternative is to approximate the nonlinear function with a linear function, say, $900x_1$, and then formulate the LP as we did in Chapter 2. However, as illustrated in Figure 5.3, this approximation is so poor that we would have little confidence in the LP's optimal solution. Fortunately, there is a "trick" that enables us to formulate OMC's revised product mix problem

---

[1] Formally, $f(x)$, a function of a single variable, is concave if and only if the function's first derivative (i.e., its slope) always decreases as x increases, or, equivalently, the function's second derivative (i.e., the slope's rate of change) always assumes a nonpositive value.

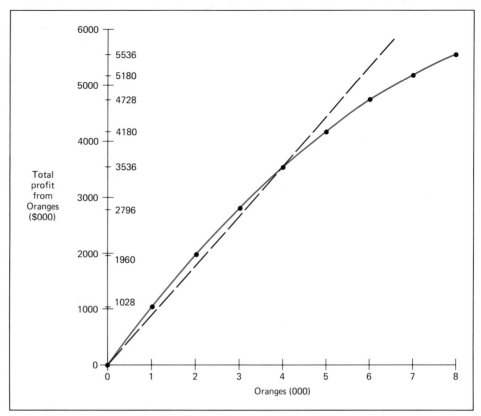

Figure 5.3 A poor approximation

as an LP. Instead of approximating the Orange's nonlinear total profit function by a single linear function, we approximate it with a *piecewise linear concave function* —that is, a function consisting of "pieces" from a sequence of different linear functions whose respective slopes decrease as x_1 increases. Figures 5.4(a) and (b) depict two examples of a piecewise linear approximation to the Orange's nonlinear total profit function. Observe that each approximation is a concave function because the slopes of the successive linear functions decrease as x_1 increases. The points at which there is a change in the linear function used to approximate the nonlinear function are called *breakpoints*.

Before proceeding, let us notice two aspects of the approximations depicted in Figures 5.4(a) and (b). First, both approximations "stop" at $x_1 = 8000$. The reason is that, as illustrated graphically by Figure 2.6, there is no feasible product mix in which x_1 assumes a value greater than 8000. Consequently, we need only concern ourselves with values of x_1 less than or equal to 8000. Second, for both approximations the intervals between breakpoints may have unequal lengths. For example, in Figure 5.4(a), the first interval has a length of 2000, whereas the second and third intervals have lengths of 3000. This illustrates a common approach to improving the accuracy of a piecewise linear approximation to a concave funtion. In particular, when x_1 is small and the function is increasing at a rapid rate, an accurate approximation requires closely spaced breakpoints. Then, as x_1 increases and the function's rate of increase slows, accuracy is not sacrificed by having more widely spaced breakpoints.

Which approximation, Figure 5.4(a) or Figure 5.4(b), is more accurate? Clearly, the answer is Figure 5.4(b), because it possesses many more breakpoints. However, as we will soon see, more breakpoints lead not only to greater accuracy

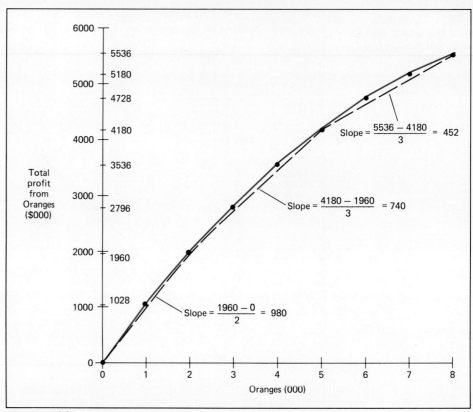

Figure 5.4(a) A piecewise linear approximation having three "pieces"

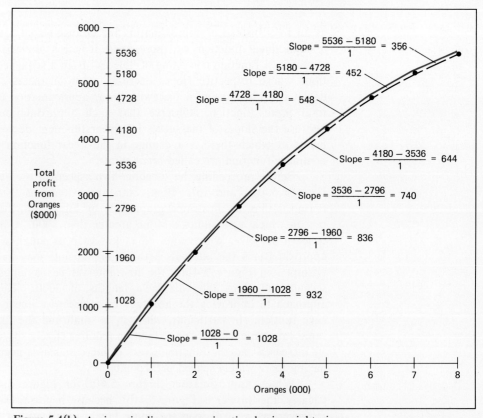

Figure 5.4(b) A piecewise linear approximation having eight pieces

but also to an LP with more decision variables and more constraints. If this were a "real-world" decision problem, we would probably choose the higher accuracy at the expense of a larger LP. However, since the technique of piecewise linear programming proceeds in the same manner regardless of the number of breakpoints, we may as well conserve time and space here by choosing the approximation with fewer breakpoints, Figure 5.4(a). Observe that Figure 5.4(a)'s approximation consists of "pieces" of three linear functions. The figure shows that the Orange's marginal profit is $980 in the interval $[0,2000]$, $740 in the interval $[2000,5000]$, and $452 in the interval $[5000,8000]$. In other words, each of the first 2000 Oranges contributes $980 to OMC's profit, each of the next 3000 Oranges contributes $740, and each of the next 3000 contributes $452.

Formulating the LP

We now proceed as follows:

1. Define the Interval Variables. In our original formulation we denoted the production of Oranges by the single decision variable x_1. This was sufficient, because each Orange contributed the same amount to OMC's profit. Now, however, there are three distinct contributions to profit by the Orange, one for each of the three intervals $[0,2000]$, $[2000,5000]$, and $[5000,8000]$. Consequently, we "split" x_1, the total production of Oranges, into the sum of the following three *interval variables:*

x_{11} = the number of Oranges produced in the interval $[0,2000]$,
x_{12} = the number of Oranges produced in the interval $[2000,5000]$,
x_{13} = the number of Oranges produced in the interval $[5000,8000]$,

where each variable's first subscript (always 1) denotes product 1 and each variable's second subscript denotes the interval (i.e., 1 for the first interval $[0,2000]$, 2 for the second interval $[2000,5000]$, and 3 for the third interval $[5000,8000]$). Mathematically, then,

$$x_1 = x_{11} + x_{12} + x_{13}.$$

Figure 5.5 graphically depicts the three interval variables.

2. Formulate the Upper Bound Constraints on the Interval Variables. To ensure that no interval variable assumes a value greater than the length of its corresponding interval, our LP must contain the following three upper bound constraints:

$$x_{11} \leqslant 2000$$
$$x_{12} \leqslant 3000$$
$$x_{13} \leqslant 3000.$$

Note that the constraints' right-hand sides are the intervals' lengths, not the intervals' ending breakpoints. For example, the upper bound constraint for x_{12}, the interval variable corresponding to the interval $[2000,5000]$, is $x_{12} \leqslant 3000$, not $x_{12} \leqslant 5000$. In some applications of piecewise linear programming the last interval variable has no ending breakpoint; that is, the "last piece" of the piecewise linear function continues indefinitely. In such cases, there is no upper bound constraint for the last interval variable.

3. Formulate the LP's Structural Constraints. In our original formulation the structural constraints were the following resource constraints:

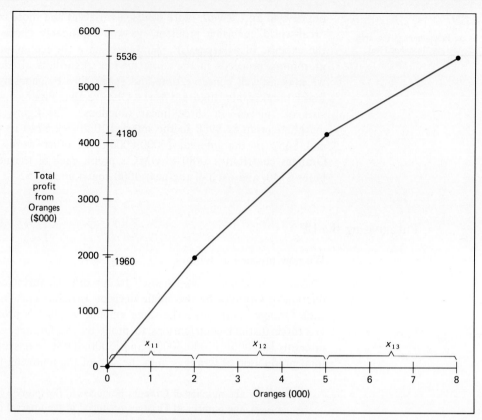

Figure 5.5 Graphical depiction of interval variables

$$2x_1 + 1x_2 \leqslant 20{,}000$$
$$4x_1 + 1x_2 \leqslant 32{,}000$$
$$2x_1 + 7x_2 \leqslant 88{,}000 \, .$$

Now, however, the total production of Oranges is $x_{11} + x_{12} + x_{13}$, not x_1. Consequently, we can easily obtain the revised resource constraints by substituting $x_{11} + x_{12} + x_{13}$ for x_1. This substitution proceeds as follows:

$$2x_1 + 1x_2 \leqslant 20{,}000 \quad \rightarrow \quad 2(x_{11} + x_{12} + x_{13}) + 1x_2 \leqslant 20{,}000 \quad \rightarrow \quad 2x_{11} + 2x_{12} + 2x_{13} + 1x_2 \leqslant 20{,}000$$
$$4x_1 + 1x_2 \leqslant 32{,}000 \quad \rightarrow \quad 4(x_{11} + x_{12} + x_{13}) + 1x_2 \leqslant 32{,}000 \quad \rightarrow \quad 4x_{11} + 4x_{12} + 4x_{13} + 1x_2 \leqslant 32{,}000$$
$$2x_1 + 7x_2 \leqslant 88{,}000 \quad \rightarrow \quad 2(x_{11} + x_{12} + x_{13}) + 7x_2 \leqslant 88{,}000 \quad \rightarrow \quad 2x_{11} + 2x_{12} + 2x_{13} + 7x_2 \leqslant 88{,}000 \, .$$

4. Formulate the LP's Objective Function. In our original formulation the objective function was

$$\text{Maximize } 900x_1 + 600x_2 \, .$$

The term $900x_1$ is no longer valid since each Orange's contribution to profit is no longer constant at \$900. To account for the changes from interval to interval in the Orange's contribution to profit, we substitute for $900x_1$

$$980x_{11} + 740x_{12} + 452x_{13,}$$

thereby obtaining the objective function

$$\text{Maximize } 980x_{11} + 740x_{12} + 452x_{13} + 600x_2 \, .$$

The LP's Complete Formulation

The complete formulation of OMC's revised product mix problem is the following four-variable, six-constraint LP:

$$\text{Maximize } 980x_{11} + 740x_{12} + 452x_{13} + 600x_2$$

$$
\begin{aligned}
\text{subject to} \quad 2x_{11} + 2x_{12} + 2x_{13} + 1x_2 &\leqslant 20{,}000 \\
4x_{11} + 4x_{12} + 4x_{13} + 1x_2 &\leqslant 32{,}000 \\
2x_{11} + 2x_{12} + 2x_{13} + 7x_2 &\leqslant 88{,}000 \\
x_{11} &\leqslant 2000 \\
x_{12} &\leqslant 3000 \\
x_{13} &\leqslant 3000
\end{aligned}
$$

and $x_{11} \geqslant 0$, $x_{12} \geqslant 0$, $x_{13} \geqslant 0$, $x_2 \geqslant 0$.

In Chapter 2 we rescaled our formulation to facilitate graphically solving the LP. Because the four decision variables in our present formulation preclude a graphical solution, we will not rescale the LP.

The LP's Optimal Solution

Using a software package such as the one discussed in Chapter 3, OMC would discover that the optimal solution to its revised product mix problem is:[2]

Oranges	Tangerines	Total Profit
$x_{11} = 2000$, $x_{12} = 2333\frac{1}{3}$, $x_{13} = 0$	$x_2 = 11{,}333\frac{1}{3}$	$10,486,666.67

Of course, the answer to the question "How many Oranges should OMC produce?" is simply

$$x_{11} + x_{12} + x_{13} = 2000 + 2333\tfrac{1}{3} + 0 = 4333\tfrac{1}{3}.$$

The Fill Restrictions

Our LP formulation of OMC's revised product mix problem lacks something that, at first glance, appears to raise doubts about the LP's correctness. Nowhere did we require the LP to "fill" x_{11} to its upper bound of 2000 before starting to "fill" x_{12} or to "fill" x_{12} to its upper bound of 3000 before starting to "fill" x_{13}. Stated mathematically, nowhere did we require the LP's optimal solution to satisfy the following so-called *fill restrictions:*

$$
\begin{aligned}
x_{12} > 0 \quad &\rightarrow \quad x_{11} = 2000 \\
x_{13} > 0 \quad &\rightarrow \quad x_{12} = 3000.
\end{aligned}
$$

A solution not satisfying both these fill restrictions makes no sense, because it calls for production in an interval before exhausting production in the immediately

---

[2] OMC can deal with the noninteger values in the LP's optimal solution in the same manner we discussed in detail in Section 2.7 (i.e., interpreting as work in progress, rounding, or integer linear programming).

preceding interval. For example, consider the following assignment of values to the decision variables:

Oranges	Tangerines
$x_{11} = 1500$, $x_{12} = 1000$, $x_{13} = 2000$	$x_2 = 8000$

You should verify that this is a feasible solution to our LP by substituting the decision variables in the LP's three resource constraints and three upper bound constraints. Although feasible, this solution makes no practical sense, since it calls for production in the second interval when the first interval's production is still 500 below its upper bound of 2000, and it calls for production in the third interval when the second interval's production is still 2000 below its upper bound of 3000.

Do the existence of feasible solutions that violate the fill restrictions invalidate our LP? The answer is "No!" Our LP remains valid because, given a feasible solution that violates the fill restrictions, it's always possible to transform the solution into another feasible solution that not only satisfies the fill restrictions but also has a better objective value. Consequently, a feasible solution that violates the fill restrictions can never be the LP's optimal solution. To illustrate this transformation process, reconsider our previous example of a feasible solution not satisfying the fill restrictions, namely,

Solution 1: $x_{11} = 1500$, $x_{12} = 1000$, $x_{13} = 2000$, $x_2 = 8000$.

Since x_{11} is 500 below its upper bound of 2000, let us "shift" 500 from x_{12} to x_{11}, thereby obtaining the solution:

Solution 2: $x_{11} = 2000$, $x_{12} = 500$, $x_{13} = 2000$, $x_2 = 8000$.

Given the feasibility of Solution 1, Solution 2 must also be feasible because, in shifting 500 from x_{12} to x_{11}, we continue to satisfy the upper bound constraints, and we have not changed the value of $x_{11} + x_{12} + x_{13}$ (thereby ensuring the resource constraints remain satisfied). Besides being feasible, Solution 2 has a higher objective value because the 500 Oranges shifted from x_{12} to x_{11} were previously contributing $740 to profit but are now contributing $980 to profit. Therefore, Solution 2's objective value is $(980 - 740)(500) = 120,000$ higher than Solution 1's. Although we have maintained feasibility and improved the objective value, we have not yet satisfied the fill restrictions because $x_{13} > 0$ but x_{12} is 2500 less than its upper bound of 3000. To satisfy the fill restrictions, however, we need only "shift" x_{13}'s entire amount of 2000 to x_{12}, thereby obtaining the solution:

Solution 3: $x_{11} = 2000$, $x_{12} = 2500$, $x_{13} = 0$, $x_2 = 8000$.

For the same reason used in transforming Solution 1 into Solution 2, the transformation of Solution 2 into Solution 3 maintains feasibility and improves the objective value, this time by $(740 - 452)(2000) = 576,000$.

By transforming Solution 1 into Solution 3, we have illustrated that, given a feasible solution that violates the fill restrictions, we can always transform the solution into another feasible solution that not only satisfies the fill restrictions but also has a better objective value. Consequently, we need not worry about feasible solutions that violate the fill restrictions. One will never be the LP's optimal solution.

It is important to realize that the transformation process we just employed is valid because of two facts:

TABLE 5.1 When Piecewise Linear Programming Can Be Applied

| Objective | Type of Piecewise Linear Function | |
| Function | Concave | Convex |
Type	(i.e., slopes decrease)	(i.e., slopes increase)
Maximize	Yes!	No!
Minimize	No!	Yes!

1. The objective function is of the *maximization* type.

2. Owing to the concavity of the piecewise linear approximation, the objective function coefficients of x_{11}, x_{12}, and x_{13} *decrease* from 980 to 740 to 452.

These two facts are critical to the argument that the objective value improves when we shift Oranges first from x_{12} to x_{11} and then from x_{13} to x_{12}. If the objective function coefficients of x_{11}, x_{12}, and x_{13} had *increased* (e.g., from 750 to 900 to 1000) or had *oscillated* (e.g., from 900 down to 750 and then up to 1000), the LP's optimal solution might violate the fill restrictions. Therefore, as summarized by Table 5.1's first row, if the decision problem under consideration involves maximization, we can apply the technique of piecewise linear programming only if the piecewise linear approximation is *concave*—that is, if the slopes of the successive linear pieces *decrease* from interval to interval.

The same logic applies also to a decision problem involving minimization. Here, as summarized by Table 5.1's second row, we can apply the technique of piecewise linear programming only if the piecewise linear approximation is *convex* —that is, if slopes of the successive linear pieces *increase* from interval to interval.[3] Figure 5.6 depicts a piecewise linear convex approximation to a nonlinear convex function.

---

[3] Formally, $f(x)$, a function of a single variable, is convex if and only if the function's first derivative (i.e., its slope) always increases as x increases, or, equivalently, the function's second derivative (i.e., the slope's rate of change) always assumes a nonnegative value.

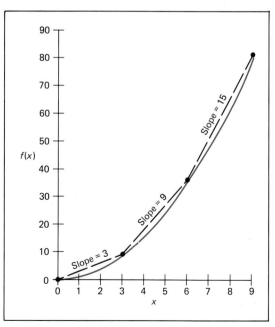

Figure 5.6 A piecewise linear convex approximation

Before summarizing, we should make two observations. First, although this section's example involved only a single piecewise linear approximation, an LP may involve several (e.g., one for Oranges and one for Tangerines). Faced with such a decision problem, we simply treat each piecewise linear approximation individually, first defining interval variables for each and then proceeding as we did in this section's example. Second, although our example's piecewise linear function was an approximation to a more general nonlinear function, this need not always be the case. In some decision problems the piecewise linear function is not an approximation but the true representation of a total profit function or total cost function.

We can summarize our study of piecewise linear programming as follows:

Piecewise linear programming is applicable only in the following two cases:

- If the decision problem involves maximization, the piecewise linear function must be concave, that is, the slopes of the successive linear pieces must decrease.

- If the decision problem involves minimization, the piecewise linear function must be convex, that is, the slopes of the successive linear pieces must increase.

Given a piecewise linear function spanning n intervals and having successive slopes of s_{i1}, s_{i2}, . . ., s_{in} (where the subscript i refers to the ith decision variable), we proceed as follows:

1. We define n interval variables x_{i1}, x_{i2}, . . ., x_{in}, where x_{ij} corresponds to the jth interval for the ith decision variable.

2. We formulate an upper bound constraint for each interval variable having the form

$$x_{ij} \leqslant \text{(the length of the } j\text{th interval)}.$$

3. In formulating the LP's other structural constraints, we use the summation $x_{i1} + x_{i2} + \cdots + x_{in}$ as if it were a single decision variable.

4. In formulating the LP's objective function, we include the expression

$$s_{i1}x_{i1} + s_{i2}x_{i2} + \cdots + s_{in}x_{in}$$

to reflect the fact that each interval variable contributes differently to the objective value.

5.3 USE OF DEVIATION VARIABLES

A Revision of Suny's Production and Inventory Planning Problem

Deviation variables are very helpful formulation "tools." To illustrate their use, we consider a revised version of Suny's production and inventory planning problem we formulated in Section 4.3. Our problem now takes into account three cost components: (1) production costs, (2) inventory costs, and (3) changes-in-production costs. In Section 4.3 we took into account only the first two costs.

Returning to the statement of Suny's problem at the beginning of Section 4.3 (you should reread it at this point), we make the following revision:

> It is Suny's policy to respond to month-to-month changes in its production level by laying off employees when it decreases its production level and by recalling former employees (or hiring new ones) when it increases its production level. After considering the costs associated with laying off and recalling employees, Suny has estimated that each one unit change in the production level from one month to the next costs $2, regardless of whether the change is an increase or a decrease.[4] Suny's current production level is 4000.

Two "extreme" strategies usually surface in managerial debates about how to plan production and inventory levels. Owing to their desire for "smooth" (i.e., stable) utilizations of machines and labor, the production manager and the personnel manager usually advocate a so-called *constant production level plan*. Such a plan calls for a production level that does not change from month to month. While it has the advantage of smooth utilization of machines and labor, it has the disadvantages of unnecessarily high inventory levels in months having low demand and dangerously low inventory levels (perhaps even a backlog) in months having high demand.[5] High inventory levels do not please the controller, who could be earning interest on the capital "tied up" in inventory, and low inventory levels worry the marketing manager, who likes to promise customers prompt delivery. Therefore, the controller and the marketing manager usually are proponents of a so-called *chase demand plan*. This plan calls for each month's production level to be set at the lowest level necessary to satisfy the month's demand or safety stock requirement, whichever is more stringent that month. Consequently, the production level "chases" demand in the sense that it rises as demand rises and falls as demand falls. While this plan has the advantage of low inventory costs, it has the disadvantage of changing the production level every month, thereby leading to uneven utilization of machines and labor. Rarely is either of the two extreme plans optimal. Usually, the optimal plan is a compromise between the constant production level plan (with its high inventory costs but low changes-in-production costs) and the chase demand plan (with its low inventory costs but high changes-in-production costs).

Recall that, in our formulation of Suny's original problem, the objective function was

Minimize $\quad 460p_1 + 470p_2 + 480p_3 + 500p_4 + 500p_5 + 490p_6$ (production costs)
$\quad\quad\quad\quad + \quad 8i_1 + \quad 8i_2 + \quad 8i_3 + \quad 8i_4 + \quad 8i_5 + \quad 4i_6$ (inventory costs)

where p_t and i_t denote month t's production level and inventory level, respectively. We now want to add to this objective function a third component, the total cost of changing the production level from month $t - 1$ to month t. We can express this cost as $2 times the absolute value of the difference between the two months' production levels:

$$2|p_t - p_{t-1}| .$$

---

[4] At the close of this section, we will see that it is possible to have the cost of each unit increase in the production level differ from the cost of each unit decrease in the production level.

[5] This latter disadvantage can be eliminated by setting a sufficiently high constant production level, but this leads to even higher inventory levels, thereby increasing the magnitude of the former disadvantage.

We can then express the objective function for Suny's revised problem as

Minimize $\quad 460p_1 + 470p_2 + 480p_3 + 500p_4 + 500p_5 + 490p_6 \quad$ (production costs)
$\quad + \quad 8i_1 + \quad 8i_2 + \quad 8i_3 + \quad 8i_4 + \quad 8i_5 + \quad 4i_6 \quad$ (inventory costs)
$\quad + \quad 2|p_1 - 4000| + 2|p_2 - p_1| + 2|p_3 - p_2| \quad$ (changes-in-production
$\quad + \quad 2|p_4 - p_3| + 2|p_5 - p_4| + 2|p_6 - p_5| \quad$ costs)

However, this is a nonlinear objective function, owing to the nonlinearity of the absolute value function.

An Introduction to Deviation Variables

Fortunately, there is a "trick" that enables us to "linearize'" Suny's revised objective function. Its validity rests on the following property:

> Any numerical value v can be expressed as the difference between two *nonnegative* numerical values, at least one of which is 0.

Consider the following examples:

$v =$	$\left(\begin{array}{c}\text{First Nonnegative}\\\text{Numerical Value}\end{array}\right)$	$-$	$\left(\begin{array}{c}\text{Second Nonnegative}\\\text{Numerical Value}\end{array}\right)$
15 =	15	−	0
4 =	4	−	0
0 =	0	−	0
−8 =	0	−	8
−23 =	0	−	23

Observe that the number under the heading "First Nonnegative Numerical Value" is always the amount by which v deviates from 0 in the positive direction, whereas the number under the heading "Second Nonnegative Numerical Value" is always the amount by which v deviates from 0 in the negative direction. This observation enables us to formally restate the property of any numerical value as follows:

> Any numerical value v can be expressed as $v^+ - v^-$, where v^+ is v's deviation from 0 in the positive direction and v^- is v's deviation from 0 in the negative direction.

How can it help to replace a single value v by the difference between two other values? The answer is that we can now replace the nonlinear expression $|v|$ with the linear expression $v^+ + v^-$. Consider the following examples:

$v = v^+ - v^-$			$\|v\| = v^+ + v^-$		
15 = 15 − 0			$\|15\|$ = 15 + 0		
4 = 4 − 0			$\|4\|$ = 4 + 0		
0 = 0 − 0			$\|0\|$ = 0 + 0		
−8 = 0 − 8			$\|-8\|$ = 0 + 8		
−23 = 0 − 23			$\|-23\|$ = 0 + 23		

Note that, whereas v is the *difference* between v^+ and v^-, $|v|$ is the *sum* of v^+ and v^-.

Let us now apply this reasoning to the six terms in Suny's revised objective function that involve the absolute value function. Consider, for example, the term $|p_4 - p_3|$. The expression within the absolute value signs, $p_4 - p_3$ is simply a "place-holder" for some unknown numerical value. Therefore, applying the same reasoning as we did earlier, we can express the unknown value of $p_4 - p_3$ as the difference between two nonnegative variables at least one of which assumes a value of 0. In particular, define the following nonnegative decision variables:

d_4^+ = the deviation of $p_4 - p_3$ from 0 in the *positive* direction
     (i.e., the *increase* in the production level from month 3 to month 4)

d_4^- = the deviation of $p_4 - p_3$ from 0 in the *negative* direction
     (i.e., the *decrease* in the production level from month 3 to month 4)

Because they measure an expression's deviation from a constant (in this case, 0), we refer to d_4^+ and d_4^- as a *positive deviation variable* and a *negative deviation variable,* respectively. Our earlier relationships of $v = v^+ - v^-$ and $|v| = v^+ + v^-$ are analogous to

$$p_4 - p_3 = d_4^+ - d_4^- \quad \text{and} \quad |p_4 - p_3| = d_4^+ + d_4^- \ .$$

The following examples illustrate the above two relationships for several alternative values of p_3 and p_4.

p_3	p_4	$p_4 - p_3 = d_4^+ - d_4^-$	$|p_4 - p_3| = d_4^+ + d_4^-$
2000	3000	$3000 - 2000 = 1000 - 0$	$|3000 - 2000| = 1000 + 0$
5000	5000	$5000 - 5000 = 0 - 0$	$|5000 - 5000| = 0 + 0$
7000	3000	$3000 - 7000 = 0 - 4000$	$|3000 - 7000| = 0 + 4000$

If necessary, "invent" some other values for p_3 and p_4, then determine values for d_4^+ and d_4^-, and finally observe that $|p_4 - p_3| = d_4^+ + d_4^-$.

By defining the deviation variables d_4^+ and d_4^- and adding to the LP's structural constraints the constraint

$$p_4 - p_3 = d_4^+ - d_4^- \ ,$$

we can replace the nonlinear expression $2|p_4 - p_3|$ in Suny's revised objective function by the linear expression $2(d_4^+ + d_4^-)$ or, equivalently, $2d_4^+ + 2d_4^-$. You may be wondering what in our LP prevents a "nonsensical" situation where d_4^+ and d_4^- both assume positive values (i.e., there is a positive and negative deviation at the same time!). The answer is that, while such a solution may be feasible, it will never be optimal because it will always have a worse objective value than a feasible solution in which either d_4^+ or d_4^- equals 0. The following table illustrates that, although there are many combinations of values for d_4^+ and d_4^- that satisfy the structural constraint $p_4 - p_3 = d_4^+ - d_4^-$, the combination in which either d_4^+ or d_4^- equals 0 always has the best objective value:

Case	p_3	p_4	$p_4 - p_3 =$	$d_4^+ - d_4^-$	$2d_4^+ + 2d_4^-$
					Contribution to Objective Function
				$9000 - 8000$	$18{,}000 + 16{,}000 = 34{,}000$
				or	
I	2000	3000	$3000 - 2000 =$	$5000 - 4000$	$10{,}000 + 8000 = 18{,}000$
				or	
				$1000 - 0$	$2000 + 0 = 2000$
				$9000 - 9000$	$18{,}000 + 18{,}000 = 36{,}000$
				or	
II	5000	5000	$5000 - 5000 =$	$4000 - 4000$	$8000 + 8000 = 16{,}000$
				or	
				$0 - 0$	$0 + 0 = 0$
				$5000 - 9000$	$10{,}000 + 18{,}000 = 28{,}000$
				or	
III	7000	3000	$3000 - 7000 =$	$1000 - 5000$	$2000 + 10{,}000 = 12{,}000$
				or	
				$0 - 4000$	$0 + 8000 = 8000$

We proceed in a similar fashion for each of the other five expressions in Suny's revised objective function that involve the absolute–value function. In particular, for month t, we define the following two deviation variables:[6]

d_t^+ = the deviation of $p_t - p_{t-1}$ from 0 in the *positive* direction (i.e., the *increase* in the production level from month $t-1$ to month t)

d_t^- = the deviation of $p_t - p_{t-1}$ from 0 in the *negative* direction (i.e., the *decrease* in the production level from month $t-1$ to month t)

The LP's Complete Formulation

We may now formulate Suny's revised production and inventory planning problem as the following 24-variable, 36-constraint LP:

$$
\begin{aligned}
\text{Minimize} \quad & 460p_1 + 470p_2 + 480p_3 + 500p_4 + 500p_5 + 490p_6 && \text{(production costs)} \\
+ \ & 8i_1 + 8i_2 + 8i_3 + 8i_4 + 8i_5 + 4i_6 && \text{(inventory costs)} \\
+ \ & 2d_1^+ + 2d_1^- + 2d_2^+ + 2d_2^- + 2d_3^+ + 2d_3^- && \text{(changes-in-production} \\
+ \ & 2d_4^+ + 2d_4^- + 2d_5^+ + 2d_5^- + 2d_6^+ + 2d_6^- && \text{costs)}
\end{aligned}
$$

subject to

$$
\begin{aligned}
p_1 - 4000 &= d_1^+ - d_1^- \\
p_2 - p_1 &= d_2^+ - d_2^- \\
p_3 - p_2 &= d_3^+ - d_3^- \\
p_4 - p_3 &= d_4^+ - d_4^- \\
p_5 - p_4 &= d_5^+ - d_5^- \\
p_6 - p_5 &= d_6^+ - d_6^-
\end{aligned}
\qquad \text{(deviation constraints)}
$$

and   the 30 structural constraints that appeared in our original formulation of Suny's problem in Section 4.3 (i.e., 12 lower and upper bound constraints on the monthly production levels, 12 lower and upper bound constraints on the monthly inventory levels, and 6 material balance equations).

and $p_1 \geqslant 0, p_2 \geqslant 0, p_3 \geqslant 0, p_4 \geqslant 0, p_5 \geqslant 0, p_6 \geqslant 0,$
$i_1 \geqslant 0, i_2 \geqslant 0, i_3 \geqslant 0, i_4 \geqslant 0, i_5 \geqslant 0, i_6 \geqslant 0,$
$d_1^+ \geqslant 0, d_1^- \geqslant 0, d_2^+ \geqslant 0, d_2^- \geqslant 0, d_3^+ \geqslant 0, d_3^- \geqslant 0,$ (nonnegativity constraints)
$d_4^+ \geqslant 0, d_4^- \geqslant 0, d_5^+ \geqslant 0, d_5^- \geqslant 0, d_6^+ \geqslant 0, d_6^- \geqslant 0.$

Observe that the six deviation constraints require rewriting to conform to the convention that a constraint's left-hand side contains all terms involving decision variables and its right-hand side consists of a single constant. For example, we would rewrite the first deviation constraint as

$$ p_1 - d_1^+ + d_1^- = 4000 . $$

The LP's Optimal Solution

Using a software package such as the one discussed in Chapter 3, Suny would discover that the optimal solution to its production and inventory planning problem is:[7]

---

[6] When $t = 1$, we need to slightly alter this definition by replacing p_0 with Suny's current production level of 4000.

[7] It is only a coincidence that all decision variables assume integer values. In contrast to Chapter 4's LP, there is no guarantee that our revised LP's optimal solution will have integer values for all decision variables.

Optimal Values of the Decision and Deviation Variables

	Month 1	Month 2	Month 3	Month 4	Month 5	Month 6
Production Level	$p_1 = 4000$	$p_2 = 3500$	$p_3 = 3500$	$p_4 = 4000$	$p_5 = 3000$	$p_6 = 2000$
Inventory Level	$i_1 = 6500$	$i_2 = 6000$	$i_3 = 3500$	$i_4 = 2500$	$i_5 = 2500$	$i_6 = 2500$
Increase From Previous Month's Production Level	$d_1^+ = 0$	$d_2^+ = 0$	$d_3^+ = 0$	$d_4^+ = 500$	$d_5^+ = 0$	$d_6^+ = 0$
Decrease From Previous Month's Production Level	$d_1^- = 0$	$d_2^- = 500$	$d_3^- = 0$	$d_4^- = 0$	$d_5^- = 1000$	$d_6^- = 1000$

Optimal Total Cost

$$\begin{array}{ccccc} \$9{,}645{,}000 & + & \$178{,}000 & + & \$6000 & = & \$9{,}829{,}000 \\ \text{(production)} & & \text{(inventory)} & & \text{(changes-in-production)} & & \text{(total)} \end{array}$$

Note from the optimal values of the deviation variables that the month-to-month changes in the production level (given the current production level of 4000) are 0, -500, 0, $+500$, -1000, and -1000. Thus, although Suny's production levels are not constant from month to month, they are considerably "smoother" than in Chapter 4, when neglecting the costs of changing the production level resulted in month-to-month changes of $+500$, -500, -1500, $+1500$, -1000, and -1000.

A Summary

Before summarizing, we need to make one additional observation. To simplify our earlier discussion, we assumed that Suny incurs a cost of $2 for each unit change in its production level, regardless of whether the change is an increase or a decrease. What if Suny incurs a cost of $2 for each one unit increase in its production level but incurs a cost of $3 for each one unit decrease? Can we continue to employ deviation variables to formulate an appropriate LP? Yes, we can. In the objective function, we simply "attach" the cost of a one-unit increase to the positive deviation variables and the cost of a one-unit decrease to the negative deviation variables, thereby obtaining the following objective function:

$$\begin{array}{lllllll} \text{Minimize} & 460p_1 + & 470p_2 + & 480p_3 + & 500p_4 + & 500p_5 + & 490p_6 & \text{(production costs)} \\ & +\ 8i_1 + & 8i_2 + & 8i_3 + & 8i_4 + & 8i_5 + & 4i_6 & \text{(inventory costs)} \\ & +\ 2d_1^+ + & 3d_1^- + & 2d_2^+ + & 3d_2^- + & 2d_3^+ + & 3d_3^- & \text{(changes-in-production} \\ & +\ 2d_4^+ + & 3d_4^- + & 2d_5^+ + & 3d_5^- + & 2d_6^+ + & 3d_6^- & \text{costs)} \end{array}$$

In general, then,

> A positive deviation variable and its associated negative deviation variable may have different coefficients in the objective function.

We can summarize the use of deviation variables as follows:

> Let $f(x_1, x_2, \ldots, x_n)$ denote a linear function (e.g., $3x_1 - x_2 + 2x_3 - 10$). Suppose that a known cost of c^+ is incurred for each unit the function deviates from 0 in the positive direction and a known cost of c^- is incurred for each unit the function deviates from 0 in the negative direction. Then, to account for these deviation costs in the objective function, we proceed as follows:
>
> **1.** We define two deviation variables, d^+ and d^-, equal to the amount by

which the function deviates from 0 in the positive direction or the negative direction, respectively.

2. Besides including d^+ and d^- in the LP's nonnegativity constraints, we include as one of the LP's structural constraints the equation

$$f(x_1, x_2, \ldots, x_n) = d^+ - d^-$$

(e.g., $3x_1 - x_2 + 2x_3 - 10 = d^+ - d^-$). In the LP's final version, we rewrite this constraint to conform to the convention that a constraint's left-hand side contains all terms involving decision variables and its right-hand side consists of a single constant (e.g., $3x_1 - x_2 + 2x_3 - d^+ + d^- = 10$).

3. We include in the objective function the expression

$$c^+ d^+ + c^- d^- \ .$$

5.4 GOAL PROGRAMMING, A SPECIALIZED USE OF DEVIATION VARIABLES

An Overview of Multicriterion Decision Problems

A increasingly important topic in management science is *multicriterion decision problems*—problems that involve not one but several objective functions. There are two primary reasons for this development.

1. Members of the business community are increasingly aware of disadvantages in focusing solely on the maximization of profit (or the minimization of cost). Such "myopia" frequently has an adverse effect on secondary objectives, be they economic objectives such as modernizing production facilities, social objectives such as increasing employee safety, or environmental objectives such as reducing pollution.

2. In cases where the business community has been slow to respond to social and environmental concerns, government regulatory agencies, consumer groups, minority groups, and labor unions have been increasingly strident in their demands that the decision-making process includes issues such as pollution control, equal opportunity employment, and employee and consumer safety.

Recognizing the need to include multiple objectives in the decision-making process is much easier than actually doing so. Two "obstacles" impede the solution of a multicriterion decision problem:

1. **Conflicting objectives.** Two objectives are in *conflict* when improving one has an adverse effect on the other. For example, to increase a portfolio's annual return, a portfolio manager usually has to make more risky investments. Consequently, a portfolio manager's objectives of maximizing return and minimizing risk are in conflict.

2. **Incommensurate objectives.** Two objectives are *incommensurate* when they are measured in different units. For example, a monetary objective such as profit may be measured in dollars, a social objective such as consumer safety may be measured in the number of fatalities, and an environmental objective

such as pollution may be measured in units reflecting damage to surrounding vegetation or wildlife. Few decision makers feel comfortable comparing dollars, human lives, and trees!

How can a manager overcome the obstacles of conflicting and incommensurate objectives? One approach is the so-called *penalty approach*. To illustrate it, let us use metaphorical "apples," "oranges," and "pears" in place of more meaningful items. Consider a manager who must select one of several bushels of fruit, each of which contains different quantities of apples, oranges, and pears. Because the manager does not like all fruits equally, his selection of a bushel of fruit involves conflicting and incommensurate objectives. To provide a common basis for comparison, the manager can assign each fruit a *penalty* that reflects his dislike for the fruit. The higher the penalty, the more he dislikes the fruit. For example, on a scale ranging from 0 to 100, assigning penalties of 90 to apples, 30 to oranges, and 5 to pears reflects a strong dislike of apples, a moderate dislike of oranges, and almost no dislike of pears. The manager can now select a bushel of fruit using the single objective function of minimizing the total penalties, that is,

$$Minimize \ \ 90 \begin{bmatrix} \text{number of apples} \\ \text{in the bushel} \end{bmatrix} + 30 \begin{bmatrix} \text{number of oranges} \\ \text{in the bushel} \end{bmatrix} + 5 \begin{bmatrix} \text{number of pears} \\ \text{in the bushel} \end{bmatrix}.$$

The important characteristic of the penalties is not the range of the penalty scale (which is arbitrary) but the ratios of the penalties to each other. For example, the following three assignments of penalties are equivalent, since the ratios are the same, namely 18:6:1.

Range of Penalty Scale	Penalties		
	Apples	Oranges	Pears
0 – 1	0.90	0.30	0.05
0 – 100	90	30	5
0 – 1000	900	300	50

Clearly, the penalties that serve as the objective function coefficients are *subjective* rather than *objective*. They are based on personal preferences and beliefs. If several individuals within an organization are asked to independently assign penalties to apples, oranges, and pears, their responses will vary greatly. Even if the organization agrees to let a single individual act as its "conscience," that individual will still agonize over such things as whether the ratio of his dislike for apples to his dislike for oranges is 4:1 or 3:1. How, then, can the diverse personal preferences of many individuals in an organization be combined into a single assignment of penalties? The answer is, "Not very easily!" The assignment of penalties may generate much debate, a debate that may end with a decision to first solve the decision problem several times, each with a different set of penalties, and then debate the merits of the alternative "optimal" solutions. Despite the dilemma created by the subjectivity of the penalties, there are a growing number of organizations, especially in the public sector, that are applying the penalty approach to multicriterion decision problems.

Let us now consider *goal programming,* a method that incorporates the penalty approach into the format of linear programming. To apply goal programming, we first set a *target value* (i.e., a goal) for each of the multiple criteria. Then, since it is unlikely that we can simultaneously satisfy all goals, we subjectively assign a penalty for each unit of deviation from the target value in the positive direction (i.e., overachievement of the goal) and a penalty for each unit of deviation from the target value in the negative direction (i.e., underachievement of the goal). Finally, we use deviation variables to formulate an LP whose optimal solution comes "as close as possible" to achieving our goals in the sense that it minimizes the total of the penalties incurred for overachieving or underachieving the goals.

Problem Statement

The majority of the applications of goal programming that have appeared in academic and professional journals are public-sector applications. In light of this, we illustrate goal programming with the following public-sector scenario:[8]

Al Lokation is an administrator for a state's Public Health Department. One of his current decision problems involves the allocation of $1,200,000 received under a federally funded program designed to provide nutritious food supplements during the upcoming fiscal year to three categories of individuals: (1) pregnant or breastfeeding women, (2) infants (under 1 year old), (3) children (1–4 years old).

For simplicity, assume the state is divided into only five counties. Al intends to allocate the funds among these five counties, with each county receiving at least 10% of the budget. Al has requested each county to consider its current "mix" of public health programs and agencies and inform him how the county would use each $1000 of allocated funds to provide food supplements during the fiscal year to each of the three categories of individuals. Table 5.2 summarizes each county's response. For example, Table 5.2's third column indicates that county 3 would use every $1000 it receives to provide food supplements to 0.5 women, 2.0 infants, and 1 child. With a total allocation of, say, $400,000, county 3 would provide food supplements to $(400)(0.5) = 200$ women, $(400)(2.0) = 800$ infants, and $(400)(1) = 400$ children.

Al's allocation of the $1,200,000 budget is complicated by the absence of a single objective Al can maximize or minimize. Instead, Al has identified several goals he would like to achieve and has assigned each goal to one of three priority levels, where priority level 1 has the highest priority. Al has summarized his goals as follows:

- **Priority level 1.** Although the federal government gives the state considerable flexibility in allocating the funds, there is one federal regulation to which Al's allocation must conform. This federal regulation specifies (somewhat vaguely) that a state "must make an effort" to "concentrate" its budget allocation in the

---

[8] This example is based on K. M. Tingley and J. S. Liebman, "A Goal Programming Example in Public Health Resource Allocation," *Management Science,* **30**: 3 (March 1984), pp. 279–289.

TABLE 5.2 Data for Al's Goal Program

Number of Women, Infants, and Children Each County Will Provide with Food Supplements per $1000 of Allocated Funds					
	County				
	1	2	3	4	5
Women	1.0	1.0	0.5	0.0	1.5
Infants	1.0	2.0	2.0	2.0	0.0
Children	1.0	0.0	1.0	2.0	1.0

40% of its counties that are most in need, where a county's "need" is measured by an index that simultaneously takes into account health status indicators (such as a county's infant mortality rate and incidence of low birth weight) and economic indicators (such as a county's unemployment rate and the percentage of its population with income below the national poverty level). Based on Al's computation of each county's need index, the two counties (40% of 5) with the highest indices are counties 3 and 4. To comply with the federal regulation, Al has decided to interpret "make an effort" as "have as his highest priority" and to interpret "concentrate" as "allocate at least 50% of the budget." Consequently, Al's primary goal is to allocate at least 50% of the budget to counties 3 and 4.

- **Priority level 2.** Although Al has made complying with the federal regulation his primary goal, he has a secondary goal of equity between urban and rural counties. Counties 1, 2, and 3 are predominantly urban counties containing 75% of the state's population, whereas counties 4 and 5 are predominantly rural counties containing the remaining 25% of the state's population. Consequently, to achieve his secondary goal of equity between urban and rural counties, Al wants the total allocation to counties 1, 2, and 3 to be close to 75% of the total budget.

- **Priority level 3.** Al has three tertiary goals. In particular, he has set the following "target values" for the total number of individuals in each category who are to be provided with food supplements during the fiscal year:

Category	Target Value
Women	1500 women
Infants	1800 infants
Children	800 children

Al recognizes that, given his primary and secondary goals, it may be impossible for him to allocate the budget in a manner that will serve exactly 1500 women, 1800 infants, and 800 children. He regards these target values as desirable goals.

Given his primary, secondary, and tertiary goals, Al must now decide how much of the $1,200,000 budget to allocate to each of the five counties.

Let us formulate Al's allocation problem as a special type of linear program known as a *goal program*.

Defining the Goal Program's Decision Variables

Al has five decisions, namely, how many dollars to allocate to each of the five counties. Consequently, for $j = 1, 2, \ldots, 5$, we define the decision variables

x_j = the amount of Al's allocation to county j, measured in *thousands* of dollars.

Formulating the Goal Program's Structural Constraints

To ensure the allocation of Al's total budget of 1200 thousand dollars, our goal program must contain the following budget constraint:

$$x_1 + x_2 + x_3 + x_4 + x_5 = 1200.$$

Our goal program must also contain the lower bound constraints

$$x_1 \geqslant 120$$
$$x_2 \geqslant 120$$
$$x_3 \geqslant 120$$
$$x_4 \geqslant 120$$
$$x_5 \geqslant 120$$

to ensure that each county receives at least 10% of the budget.

Formulating the Goal Program's Primary Goal

Recall that Al's primary goal is to allocate at least 50% of the total budget (i.e., 600 thousand dollars) to counties 3 and 4. If Al wanted to be 100% sure that counties 3 and 4 received at least 600 thousand dollars, we would include

$$x_3 + x_4 \geqslant 600$$

among the goal program's structural constraints. However, Al regards a total allocation of 600 thousand dollars to counties 3 and 4 as a goal, not a requirement.

We can employ deviation variables to formulate Al's goal of having $x_3 + x_4$ at least as large as 600. In particular, we define the following pair of deviation variables:

d_1^+ = the deviation of $x_3 + x_4$ from 600 in the *positive* direction (i.e., the *overachievement* of the target value)

d_1^- = the deviation of $x_3 + x_4$ from 600 in the *negative* direction (i.e., the *underachievement* of the target value)

To ensure that d_1^+ and d_1^- assume values in accordance with their definitions, our goal program's structural constraints must include the following deviation constraint:

$$x_3 + x_4 - 600 = d_1^+ - d_1^- .$$

As we indicated in our overview, a goal program's objective function is to minimize the penalties incurred for not achieving the goals. Consequently, Al must assign values to the following penalties:

p_1^+ = the penalty for each unit $x_3 + x_4$ deviates from 600 in the *positive* direction (i.e., the penalty for each unit of *overachievement* of the target value)

p_1^- = the penalty for each unit $x_3 + x_4$ deviates from 600 in the *negative* direction (i.e., the penalty for each unit of *underachievement* of the target value)

The penalties p_1^+ and p_1^- serve as the respective objective function coefficients of d_1^+ and d_1^-; that is, a portion of the goal program's objective function is

$$p_1^+ d_1^+ + p_1^- d_1^- .$$

Until we have formulated the entire goal program, let us leave the values of p_1^+ and p_1^- unspecified. Keep in mind, however, that Al must assign values to p_1^+ and p_1^- before the goal program can be solved.

Formulating the Goal Program's Secondary Goal

Recall that Al's secondary goal is equity between urban and rural counties, a goal that he has expressed as counties 1, 2, and 3 receiving approximately 900 thousand dollars (i.e., 75% of the total budget). If Al wanted absolute equity, we would include

$$x_1 + x_2 + x_3 = 900$$

among the goal program's structural constraints. However, since urban-rural equity is only a goal, not a requirement, we proceed in a manner similar to that for the primary goal. In particular, we proceed as follows:

1. We define the following pair of deviation variables:

    d_2^+ = the deviation of $x_1 + x_2 + x_3$ from 900 in the *positive* direction (i.e., the *overachievement* of the target value)

    d_2^- = the deviation of $x_1 + x_2 + x_3$ from 900 in the *negative* direction (i.e., the *underachievement* of the target value)

    Then, to ensure that d_2^+ and d_2^- assume values in accordance with their definitions, we include the deviation constraint

    $$x_1 + x_2 + x_3 - 900 = d_2^+ - d_2^-$$

    among the goal program's structural constraints.

2. We request Al to assign values to the following penalties:

    p_2^+ = the penalty for each unit $x_1 + x_2 + x_3$ deviates from 900 in the *positive* direction (i.e., the penalty for each unit of *overachievement* of the target value)

    p_2^- = the penalty for each unit $x_1 + x_2 + x_3$ deviates from 900 in the *negative* direction (i.e., the penalty for each unit of *underachievement* of the target value)

    Then we include

    $$p_2^+ d_2^+ + p_2^- d_2^-$$

    as a portion of the goal program's objective function.

Formulating the Goal Program's Tertiary Goals

Recall that Al's tertiary goals are to provide food supplements during the fiscal year to 1500 women, 1800 infants, and 800 children. Let us formulate the first of these tertiary goals, providing food supplements to 1500 women. Using the data in Table 5.2's first row, we can express the total number of women who receive food supplements as

$$1.0x_1 + 1.0x_2 + 0.5x_3 + 0.0x_4 + 1.5x_5.$$

If Al wanted to provide food supplements to exactly 1500 women, we would include

205

among the goal program's structural constraints. However, since providing food supplements to 1500 women is only a goal, not a requirement, we proceed in a manner similar to that for the primary and secondary goals. The following table summarizes the procedure:

Tertiary Goal	Deviation Variables		Structural Constraint	Unit Penalties		Portion of Objective Function
	Over	Under		Over	Under	
1500 women	d_3^+	d_3^-	$1.0x_1 + 1.0x_2 + 0.5x_3 + 0.0x_4 + 1.5x_5 - 1500 = d_3^+ - d_3^-$	p_3^+	p_3^-	$p_3^+ d_3^+ + p_3^- d_3^-$

Similar deviation variables, structural constraints, and portions of the objective function are required for the two remaining tertiary goals of providing food supplements to 1800 infants and 800 children. You should attempt to formulate the two remaining tertiary goals and check your formulations with those summarized in the following table:

Tertiary Goal	Deviation Variables		Structural Constraint	Unit Penalties		Portion of Objective Function
	Over	Under		Over	Under	
1800 infants	d_4^+	d_4^-	$1.0x_1 + 2.0x_2 + 2.0x_3 + 2.0x_4 + 0.0x_5 - 1800 = d_4^+ - d_4^-$	p_4^+	p_4^-	$p_4^+ d_4^+ + p_4^- d_4^-$
800 children	d_5^+	d_5^-	$1.0x_1 + 0.0x_2 + 1.0x_3 + 2.0x_4 + 1.0x_5 - 800 = d_5^+ - d_5^-$	p_5^+	p_5^-	$p_5^+ d_5^+ + p_5^- d_5^-$

The Goal Program's Complete Formulation

The complete formulation of Al's allocation problem is the following 15-variable, 10-constraint goal program:

Minimize $p_1^+ d_1^+ + p_1^- d_1^- + p_2^+ d_2^+ + p_2^- d_2^- + p_3^+ d_3^+ + p_3^- d_3^-$ (total

$\qquad + p_4^+ d_4^+ + p_4^- d_4^- + p_5^+ d_5^+ + p_5^- d_5^-$ penalty)

subject to $\qquad\qquad\qquad\qquad x_1 + x_2 + x_3 + x_4 + x_5 = 1200$ (budget)

$\qquad\qquad\qquad\qquad\qquad\qquad x_1 \geqslant 120$

$\qquad\qquad\qquad\qquad\qquad\qquad x_2 \geqslant 120$ (lower

$\qquad\qquad\qquad\qquad\qquad\qquad x_3 \geqslant 120$ bound

$\qquad\qquad\qquad\qquad\qquad\qquad x_4 \geqslant 120$ constraints)

$\qquad\qquad\qquad\qquad\qquad\qquad x_5 \geqslant 120$

$\qquad\qquad\qquad\qquad x_3 + x_4 - 600 = d_1^+ - d_1^-$ (primary goal)

$\qquad\qquad\qquad x_1 + x_2 + x_3 - 900 = d_2^+ - d_2^-$ (secondary goal)

$1.0x_1 + 1.0x_2 + 0.5x_3 + 0.0x_4 + 1.5x_5 - 1500 = d_3^+ - d_3^-$

$1.0x_1 + 2.0x_2 + 2.0x_3 + 2.0x_4 + 0.0x_5 - 1800 = d_4^+ - d_4^-$ (tertiary goal)

$1.0x_1 + 0.0x_2 + 1.0x_3 + 2.0x_4 + 1.0x_5 - 800 = d_5^+ - d_5^-$

and $x_1 \geqslant 0, x_2 \geqslant 0, x_3 \geqslant 0, x_4 \geqslant 0, x_5 \geqslant 0,$

$\qquad d_1^+ \geqslant 0, d_1^- \geqslant 0,$

$\qquad d_2^+ \geqslant 0, d_2^- \geqslant 0,$ (nonnegativity

$\qquad d_3^+ \geqslant 0, d_3^- \geqslant 0,$ constraints)

$\qquad d_4^+ \geqslant 0, d_4^- \geqslant 0,$

$\qquad d_5^+ \geqslant 0, d_5^- \geqslant 0.$

Observe that the five deviation constraints require rewriting to conform to the convention that a constraint's left-hand side contains all terms involving decision variables and its right-hand side consists of a single constant. For example, we would rewrite the first goal deviation constraint as

$$x_3 + x_4 - d_1^+ + d_1^- = 600 .$$

Solving the Goal Program

Before solving the goal program, Al must assign values to the ten unit penalties that serve as the coefficients in the objective function. The assignment of values to the penalties may generate much debate among Al and his colleagues, a debate that may end with a decision to solve the goal program several times, each time with a different set of penalties. Table 5.3 summarizes the results of using a software package such as the one discussed in Chapter 3 to solve the goal program three times, each time with a different set of penalties. Note the following characteristics of the three sets of penalties:

- The unit penalties for overachieving and underachieving a target value may be unequal. In fact, one of the two may equal 0. To illustrate, consider the primary goal. In all three cases in Table 5.3, Al has assigned a value of 0 to p_1^+, the penalty for $x_3 + x_4$ exceeding the goal's "target value" of 600. Assigning p_1^+ a value of 0 is consistent with Al's stated goal of assigning *at least* 600 thousand dollars to counties 3 and 4. In other words, there is no penalty for allocating counties 3 and 4 *more than* 600 thousand dollars.

- In all three cases in Table 5.3, the following property holds:

$$\begin{bmatrix} \text{unit penalty for} \\ \text{underachieving primary goal} \\ \text{(i.e., } p_1^-) \end{bmatrix} \geqslant \begin{bmatrix} \text{unit penalties for} \\ \text{deviating from secondary goal} \\ \text{(i.e., } p_2^+ \text{ and } p_2^-) \end{bmatrix} \geqslant \begin{bmatrix} \text{unit penalties for} \\ \text{deviating from tertiary goals} \\ \text{(i.e., } p_3^+ , p_3^- , p_4^+ , p_4^- , p_5^+ , p_5^-) \end{bmatrix} .$$

TABLE 5.3 Optimal Solution for Three Different Penalty Assignments

| Case | Assigned Penalties | | | | | | | | | |
| | Primary Goal | | Secondary Goal | | Tertiary Goals | | | | | |
	p_1^+	p_1^-	p_2^+	p_2^-	p_3^+	p_3^-	p_4^+	p_4^-	p_5^+	p_5^-
1	0	100	10	10	1	1	1	1	1	1
2	0	25	15	10	1	1	2	2	3	3
3	0	1	1	1	1	1	1	1	1	1

| Case | Optimal Values of Decision Variables | | | | | | | | | | | | | | | |
| | County Allocations | | | | | Primary Goal | | Secondary Goal | | Tertiary Goals | | | | | |
	x_1	x_2	x_3	x_4	x_5	d_1^+	d_1^-	d_2^+	d_2^-	d_3^+	d_3^-	d_4^+	d_4^-	d_5^+	d_5^-
1	240	180	480	120	180	0	0	0	0	0	570	0	0	340	0
2	120	300	480	120	180	0	0	0	0	0	570	120	0	220	0
3	240	520	140	120	180	0	340	0	0	0	400	0	0	0	0

In particular, observe in Case 1 that Al has assigned a unit penalty of $10^2 = 100$ to underachieving his primary goal, a unit penalty of $10^1 = 10$ to deviating in either direction from his secondary goal, and unit penalties of $10^0 = 1$ to deviating in either direction from all three tertiary goals. With such divergent penalties for the primary, secondary, and tertiary goals, Al hopes to ensure that, if the goal program's optimal solution satisfies only one goal, it is his primary goal, and, if the optimal solution satisfies two goals, they are the primary and secondary goals.

Case 1 in Table 5.3 illustrates what is known in goal programming terminology as a *preemptive assignment of penalties*. When assigning preemptive penalties, it is common (though not necessary) to use decreasing powers of 10 (or 2). Table 5.3's last ten columns indicate that Case 1's preemptive assignment of penalties has the desired effect. We see that, under Case 1's preemptive assignment of penalties, the only deviation variables with nonzero optimal values are two deviation variables associated with the tertiary goals. In other words, the only unachieved goals are the tertiary goals of providing food supplements to 1500 women and 800 children, with the former goal underachieved by $d_3^- = 570$ women and the latter goal overachieved by $d_5^+ = 340$ children.

Case 3 in Table 5.3 illustrates the other extreme of assigning penalties, a so-called *uniform assignment of penalties* in which all nonzero unit penalties have the identical value of 1. Under this uniform assignment of penalties, Table 5.3 indicates that the primary goal is now underachieved by an amount of $d_1^- = 340$ thousand dollars.

Case 2 in Table 5.3 illustrates an assignment of penalties that is neither preemptive nor uniform.

- Besides being neither preemptive nor uniform, Case 2 also illustrates another aspect of assigning penalties. In particular, observe that Case 2's unit penalties for the three tertiary goals are not identical. Instead, Al has chosen to differentiate among the tertiary goals by slightly varying their unit penalties. Such goals are called *differentiated subgoals*.

The three "optimal" solutions given in Table 5.3 illustrate that there is no truly optimal solution to Al's allocation problem. Goal programming provides the optimal solution only for a specific set of penalties. Al and his colleagues must now debate which of Table 5.3's three sets of penalties and their corresponding optimal solutions are most "defensible" to others (such as the federal government or county administrators) who might ask how the allocations were made.

A Summary

We can summarize the formulation of a goal program as follows:

Let $f(x_1, x_2, \ldots, x_n)$ denote a linear function having a specified target value of v (e.g., suppose $3x_1 - x_2 + 2x_3$ has a target value of 10). To incorporate this goal into the format of linear programming, we proceed as follows:

1. We define the following pair of deviation variables:

$d^+ = $ the amount by which $f(x_1, x_2, \ldots, x_n)$ deviates from the target value in the *positive* direction (i.e., the *overachievement* of the target value)

$d^- = $ the amount by which $f(x_1, x_2, \ldots, x_n)$ deviates from the target value in the *negative* direction (i.e., the *underachievement* of the target value)

2. Besides including d^+ and d^- in the goal program's nonnegativity constraints, we include among the goal program's structural constraints the deviation constraint

$$f(x_1, x_2, \ldots, x_n) - v = d^+ - d^-$$

(e.g., $3x_1 - x_2 + 2x_3 - 10 = d^+ - d^-$). In the goal program's final version, we rewrite this constraint to conform to the convention that a constraint's left-hand side contains all terms involving decision variables and its right-hand side consists of a single constant (e.g., $3x_1 - x_2 + 2x_3 - d^+ + d^- = 10$).

3. We include as a portion of the goal program's objective function the expression

$$p^+ d^+ + p^- d^-,$$

where p^+ and p^- are constants equal to the respective unit penalties for positive deviation (i.e, overachievement) and negative deviation (i.e., underachievement) from the goal's target value. The following table summarizes the assignment of values to p^+ and p^- for the three different cases of the desired relationship between $f(x_1, x_2, \ldots, x_n)$ and the target value v:

Case	p^+	p^-
Goal is to exactly equal the target value.	$p^+ > 0$	$p^- > 0$
Goal is to equal or exceed the target value.	$p^+ = 0$	$p^- > 0$
Goal is to equal or fall below the target value.	$p^+ > 0$	$p^- = 0$

In assigning penalties, the various goals are usually grouped into priority levels, with level 1 having the highest priority and, therefore, the highest unit penalties. Under a preemptive assignment of penalties, the nonzero unit penalties decrease significantly from priority level to priority level (e.g., by a factor of 10 or 2). Under a uniform assignment of penalties, the nonzero unit penalties all equal 1, effectively "collapsing" all priority levels into a single level. Within a particular priority level, there may be differentiated subgoals—that is, goals with slightly different unit penalties.

This concludes our introduction to goal programming. Our discussion has only "scratched the surface," as evidenced by the existence of entire books devoted solely to goal programming.

5.5 A MAXIMIN (OR MINIMAX) OBJECTIVE FUNCTION

In this section we illustrate one last "trick" for converting an apparently nonlinear problem into an LP. In particular, we consider a decision problem with a *maximin objective function*—that is, an objective function involving the maximization of the minimum of several linear functions. We also discuss how the "mirror image" of the trick for a maximin objective function can be used for a decision problem with a *minimax objective function,* that is, an objective function involving the minimization of the maximum of several linear functions.

TABLE 5.4 Data for Coleeko's Production Problem

	Production Rate (units per minute)			Available Production Time (minutes)
	Part 1	Part 2	Part 3	
Production Line 1	8	7	6	5600
Production Line 2	2	10	4	7500

Problem Statement

Consider the following scenario:

A product of Coleeko, a toy manufacturer, is the Pumpkin Patch Doll, a doll assembled from three different parts. Assembly of each doll requires the following parts list:

Part 1	Part 2	Part 3
4 units	1 unit	2 units

Coleeko has two production lines, both of which have the capability to manufacture all three parts. However, owing to differences in age and design, each production line produces each part at a different rate. Table 5.4 summarizes each production line's production rate for each part as well as the total number of minutes available this week on each production line. Given these data and an objective of maximizing this week's production of the Pumpkin Patch Dolls, Coleeko must now decide how many minutes each production line should devote to the manufacture of each part.

Defining the LP's Decision Variables

Coleeko has six decisions. For each of the 2×3 possible combinations of production line i and part j, Coleeko must decide how many minutes production line i should devote to part j. Since each decision has two attributes (a production line and a part), it is convenient to define doubly subscripted decision variables. For each of the six combinations of i and j, let

x_{ij} = the total minutes production line i devotes to part j.

For example, $x_{23} = 1500$ denotes that production line 2 devotes 1500 minutes to the manufacture of part 3.

Formulating the LP's Structural Constraints

As we will see, the LP's objective function is the most difficult part to formulate. Therefore, let us postpone consideration of the objective function until we have formulated the LP's structural constraints.

To ensure that the total minutes production line 1 devotes to all three parts does not exceed the 5600 available minutes, our LP must include the following structural constraint:

$$x_{11} + x_{12} + x_{13} \leqslant 5600 .$$

Our LP must also include a similar constraint for production line 2, namely

$$x_{21} + x_{22} + x_{23} \leqslant 7500.$$

Formulating the LP's Objective Function

Coleeko's objective is to maximize this week's production of Pumpkin Patch Dolls. Although easily stated verbally, this objective is not as easily formulated mathematically. To see why, suppose that Coleeko's two production lines together manufacture a total of 60,000 units of part 1, 20,000 units of part 2, and 20,000 units of part 3. How many dolls can Coleeko assemble with such part availabilities? To answer this question, we must compute the different limitation on assembly imposed by each part's availability. First, since each doll requires 4 of the 60,000 available units of part 1, Coleeko can assemble at most 60,000/4 = 15,000 dolls. Next, since each doll requires 1 of the 20,000 available units of part 2, Coleeko can assemble at most 20,000/1 = 20,000 dolls. Finally, since each doll requires 2 of the 20,000 available units of part 3, Coleeko can assemble at most 20,000/2 = 10,000 dolls. Given the three limitations imposed by the part availabilities, we can express the number of dolls Coleeko can assemble as the *minimum* of the three limitations:

$$\text{minimum of } [15,000; \ 20,000; \ 10,000] \ = \ 10,000.$$

In general, then, the number of dolls Coleeko can assemble equals

$$\text{minimum of } \left[\frac{\text{total production of part 1}}{4}, \ \frac{\text{total production of part 2}}{1}, \ \frac{\text{total production of part 3}}{2} \right]$$

Let us now replace the above expression's "verbal numerators" with mathematical expressions. First, consider part 1. As indicated in Table 5.4's first column, production lines 1 and 2 manufacture part 1 at the rates of 8 and 2 units per hour, respectively. Consequently, the total production of part 1 is the linear function

$$8x_{11} + 2x_{21}.$$

Similarly, using Table 5.4's second and third columns, we can express the total production of parts 2 and 3, respectively, as following linear functions:

$$7x_{12} + 10x_{22} \quad \text{and} \quad 6x_{13} + 4x_{23}.$$

Substituting these three linear functions for our earlier "verbal numerators," we can now express the total number of dolls Coleeko can assemble as

$$\text{minimum of } \left[\frac{8x_{11} + 2x_{21}}{4}, \ \frac{7x_{12} + 10x_{22}}{1}, \ \frac{6x_{13} + 4x_{23}}{2} \right].$$

Thus, Coleeko's objective of maximizing its production of dolls is equivalent to the following objective function:

$$\textit{Maximize} \text{ the minimum of } \left[\frac{8x_{11} + 2x_{21}}{4}, \ \frac{7x_{12} + 10x_{22}}{1}, \ \frac{6x_{13} + 4x_{23}}{2} \right].$$

Such an objective function, which involves the maximization of the minimum of several linear functions, is called a *maximin objective function.*

To "linearize" this objective function, we proceed as follows:

1. We define a new decision variable z equal to the minimum of the three linear functions

$$\frac{8x_{11} + 2x_{21}}{4}, \quad \frac{7x_{12} + 10x_{22}}{1}, \quad \text{and} \quad \frac{6x_{13} + 4x_{23}}{2}.$$

2. To ensure that z assumes a value in accordance with its definition, we add to the LP's structural constraints the three constraints:

$$\frac{8x_{11} + 2x_{21}}{4} \geqslant z$$

$$\frac{7x_{12} + 10x_{22}}{1} \geqslant z$$

$$\frac{6x_{13} + 4x_{23}}{2} \geqslant z$$

and we use as our objective function

$$\text{Maximize } z.$$

Because the added constraints require z to be less than or equal to all three of the linear functions and because the objective function maximizes z, z will always equal the minimum of the three linear functions.

The LP's Complete Formulation

The complete formulation of Coleeko's decision problem is the following seven-variable, five-constraint LP:

$$\text{Maximize } z$$

$$
\begin{aligned}
\text{subject to} \quad & \frac{8x_{11} + 2x_{21}}{4} && \geqslant && z \\
& \frac{7x_{12} + 10x_{22}}{1} && \geqslant && z \\
& \frac{6x_{13} + 4x_{23}}{2} && \geqslant && z \\
& x_{11} + x_{12} + x_{13} && \leqslant && 5600 \\
& x_{21} + x_{22} + x_{23} && \leqslant && 7500
\end{aligned}
$$

$$
\text{and} \quad x_{11} \geqslant 0, x_{12} \geqslant 0, x_{13} \geqslant 0,
$$
$$
x_{21} \geqslant 0, x_{22} \geqslant 0, x_{23} \geqslant 0.
$$

Observe that we must rewrite the first three structural constraints to conform to the convention that a constraint's left-hand side contains all terms involving decision variables and its right-hand side consists of a single constant. For example, we would rewrite the first structural constraint as follows:

$$\frac{8x_{11} + 2x_{21}}{4} \geqslant z \rightarrow 8x_{11} + 2x_{21} \geqslant 4z \rightarrow 8x_{11} + 2x_{21} - 4z \geqslant 0.$$

The LP's Optimal Solution

Using a software package such as the one discussed in Chapter 3, Coleeko would discover that the LP's optimal solution is

Coleeko's Optimal Solution

	Part 1	Part 2	Part 3	
Production Line 1	x_{11} = 5600 hours	x_{12} = 0 hours	x_{13} = 0 hours	and $z = 11{,}500$ dolls
Production Line 2	x_{21} = 600 hours	x_{22} = 1150 hours	x_{23} = 5750 hours	

With the above allocation of production line minutes to parts, then, Coleeko can produce 11,500 Pumpkin Patch Dolls this week.

A Summary

To summarize the approach to a maximin objective function, consider the following brief example:

> Suppose the original formulation of a decision problem results in the following maximin objective function:
>
> Maximize the minimum of $[5x_1 + 9x_2 + 6x_3, 4x_1 + 2x_3 + 1x_3, 3x_1 + 7x_2 + 4x_3]$.
>
> To "linearize" this objective function, we proceed as follows:
>
> **1.** We define a new decision variable z equal to the minimum of the three linear functions in the maximin's objective function.
>
> **2.** To ensure that z assumes a value in accordance with its definition, we use an objective function of
>
> $$\text{Maximize } z,$$
>
> and we include the following among the LP's structural constraints:
>
> $$5x_1 + 9x_2 + 6x_3 \geqslant z$$
> $$4x_1 + 2x_2 + 1x_3 \geqslant z$$
> $$3x_1 + 7x_2 + 4x_3 \geqslant z.$$
>
> In the LP's final version, we rewrite these constraints with z on the left-hand sides, thereby leaving a constant of 0 for the constraints' right-hand sides.

How can we proceed if we are faced with a minimax objective function—that is, an objective function involving the minimization of the maximum of several linear functions? The answer is that we simply employ the "mirror image" of the procedure for maximin objective functions. In particular,

> If the original formulation of a decision problem results in minimax objective function, we modify the maximin procedure as follows:
>
> **1.** In the definition of z, we replace "minimum" by "maximum."
>
> **2.** In the objective function, we replace "minimize" by "maximize"
>
> **3.** In the structural constraints, we replace "$\geqslant z$" by "$\leqslant z$".

5.6 CONCLUDING REMARKS

In this chapter we have introduced several "tricks" by which an apparently non-linear problem can be formulated as a linear program. Two concluding remarks are in order:

> This chapter's "tricks" can be used together. For example, Exercise 5.25 requires you to combine the techniques of piecewise linear programming and goal programming to formulate a goal program in which the *total penalty* incurred for deviating from a particular goal's target value does not increase at a constant rate but instead increases at an increasing rate as the deviation gets larger and larger.

> Some nonlinear decision problems cannot be "linearized" and, consequently, can be solved only by the techniques of nonlinear programming, a topic beyond the scope of this text.

5.7 CHAPTER CHECKLIST AND GLOSSARY

Quickly review this chapter by rereading the material highlighted by a vertical line in the left margin. You should then be familiar with the concepts, techniques, and terminology in the Checklist and Glossary that follow. If you need "help" with a particular item, consult the section or sections indicated for a more detailed discussion.

Checklist of Concepts and Techniques

☐ The use of interval variables in piecewise linear programming. [5.2]

☐ The use of deviation variables, including their use in goal programming. [5.3, 5.4]

☐ Maximin or minimax objective functions. [5.5]

Glossary

Concave function. A function of a single variable x is concave if its slope decreases as x increases—that is, if successive one unit increases in x result in correspondingly smaller and smaller increases in the value of the function. If the function is a total profit function, concavity is equivalent to decreasing marginal profits. [5.2]

Convex function. A function of a single variable x is convex if its slope increases as x increases—that is, if successive one unit increases in x result in correspondingly larger and larger increases in the value of the function. If the function is a total cost function, convexity is equivalent to increasing marginal costs. [5.2]

Piecewise linear function. A function consisting of "pieces" from a sequence of different linear functions. [5.2]

Piecewise linear concave function. A piecewise linear function for which the slopes of the successive linear pieces decrease. [5.2]

Piecewise linear convex function. A piecewise linear function for which the slopes of the successive linear pieces increase. [5.2]

Breakpoint. A point at which a piecewise linear function changes its slope. [5.2]

214

Interval variable. A decision variable associated with the interval between two breakpoints of a piecewise linear function. [5.2]

Piecewise linear programming. A formulation technique that employs interval variables to "linearize" a piecewise linear function. [5.2]

Positive deviation variable. A decision variable that measures a linear function's deviation in the positive direction from a specified "target value." In the context of goal programming, a positive deviation variable represents the overachievement of a target value. [5.3, 5.4]

Negative deviation variable. A decision variable that measures a linear function's deviation in the negative direction from a specified "target value." In the context of goal programming, a negative deviation variable represents the underachievement of a target value. [5.3, 5.4]

Conflicting objectives. Objectives that cannot be attained simultaneously because improving one has an adverse affect on the other. [5.4]

Incommensurate objectives. Objectives that are difficult to compare because they have different units of measurement. [5.4]

Multicriterion decision problem. A decision problem involving several conflicting and incommensurate objectives. [5.4]

Penalty approach. An approach to a multicriterion decision problem in which the objectives' different units of measurement are all assigned corresponding penalties on some scale (e.g., 0 to 100). [5.4]

Goal programming. A formulation technique that employs pairs of deviation variables to minimize the total penalties incurred for overachievement or underachievement of the specified target values. [5.4]

Preemptive assignment of penalties. Assignment such that the nonzero unit penalties used as a goal program's objective-function coefficients decrease significantly (e.g., by a factor of 10) from one priority level to the next. [5.4]

Uniform assignment of penalties. Assignment such that the nonzero unit penalties used as a goal program's objective function coefficients all equal 1. [5.4]

Differentiated subgoals. Goals belonging to the same priority level but having different unit penalties in the goal program's objective function. [5.4]

Maximin objective function. An objective function involving the maximization of the minimum of several linear functions. [5.5]

Minimax objective function. An objective function involving the minimization of the maximum of several linear functions. [5.5]

EXERCISES

Before beginning the exercises below, you should reread the comments at the beginning of the exercises for Chapter 4. They apply to the exercises below as well.

Exercises 5.1-5.7 test your understanding of piecewise linear programming.

5.1. Reconsider Section 5.2's piecewise linear programming formulation of OMC's product mix problem. Suppose someone claims that the optimal solution to this linear program is

$$x_{11} = 500$$
$$x_{12} = 1500$$
$$x_{13} = 3000$$
$$x_2 = 10{,}000$$

Show that this is impossible by transforming the solution into another solution with the following properties:
1. The transformed solution is feasible.
2. The transformed solution satisfies the so-called fill restrictions that require $x_{11} = 2000$ if $x_{12} > 0$ and $x_{12} = 3000$ if $x_{13} > 0$.

3. The transformed solution has a higher objective value.

*5.2. Reconsider the product mix problem in Exercise 2.27. In that exercise, we assumed that the unit profit for hawks was $4 and the unit profit for doves was $2. We now assume that the unit profits for hawks and doves do not remain constant but instead decrease as their respective daily production quantities increase. In particular, we assume the following:

- If x_H hawks are produced per day, the total profit is $8x_H - 0.002x_H^2$ dollars.
- If x_D doves are produced per day, the total profit is $5x_D - 0.001x_D^2$ dollars.

(a) Graph the total profit for hawks as a function of x_H for $0 \leqslant x_H \leqslant 2000$.

(b) Graph the total profit for doves as a function of x_D for $0 \leqslant x_D \leqslant 2000$.

(c) Describe two scenarios (one relating to revenue and one relating to cost) that could account for the shape of the graphs in parts (a) and (b).

(d) Using two equally spaced intervals, approximate the graph in part (a) with a piecewise linear function. Then do the same for the graph in part (b).

(e) Using the approximations in part (d), formulate this product mix problem as a piecewise linear program.

(f) Repeat part (d), this time using four equally spaced intervals.

(g) Repeat part (e), this time using the approximations in part (f).

(h) Which linear program—the one in part (e) or the one in part (g)—will yield more accurate results? Why?

5.3. Reconsider the product mix problem in Exercise 2.28. In that exercise, we assumed that the unit profit for a Wheet was $0.55. Now assume that a Wheet's unit profit is $0.65 for the first 75 units, $0.55 for the next 50 units, and $0.50 thereafter.

(a) Graph the total profit from Wheets as a function of the number produced.

(b) Describe two scenarios (one relating to revenue and one relating to cost) that could account for the shape of the graph in part (a).

(c) Formulate this product mix problem as a piecewise linear program.

(d) Solve the linear program in part (c) with a computer package. Use the optimal solution to determine the optimal production quantity for Wheets.

(e) Now assume that a Wheet's unit profit is $0.50 for the first 75 units, $0.55 for the next 50 units, and $0.65 thereafter. Can the product mix problem still be formulated as a piecewise linear program? Why?

5.4. Reconsider the blending problem in Exercise 2.30. In that exercise, we assumed that the unit cost of pig iron A was 3 cents per pound and the unit cost of pig iron B was 2 cents per pound. We now assume that the unit costs for pig irons A and B increase as their respective purchase quantities increase. In particular, we assume the following:

- If x_A pounds of pig iron A are purchased for use in the blend, the total cost is $0.5x_A^2$ cents.
- If x_B pounds of pig iron B are purchased for use in the blend, the total cost is $0.3x_B^2$ cents.

(a) Graph the total cost for pig iron A as a function of x_A for $0 \leqslant x_A \leqslant 10$.

(b) Graph the total cost for pig iron B as a function of x_B for $0 \leqslant x_B \leqslant 10$.

(c) Describe a scenario that could account for the shape of the graphs in parts (a) and (b).

(d) Using two equally spaced intervals, approximate the graph in part (a) with a piecewise linear function. Then do the same for the graph in part (b).

(e) Using the approximations in part (d), formulate this blending problem as a piecewise linear program.

(f) Repeat part (d), this time using four equally spaced intervals.

(g) Repeat part (e), this time using the approximations in part (f).

(h) Which linear program—the one in part (e) or the one in part (g)—will yield more accurate results? Why?

*5.5. Reconsider the blending problem in Exercise 2.32. In that exercise, we assumed that the unit cost of barley was 35 cents per pound. Now assume that barley costs 30 cents per pound for the first 5 pounds used in the blend, 35 cents per pound for the next 10 pounds used in the blend, and 45 cents per pound used in the blend thereafter.

(a) Graph the total cost for barley as a function of the pounds purchased.

(b) Describe a scenario that could account for the shape of the graph in part (a).

(c) Formulate this blending problem as a piecewise linear program.

(d) Solve part (c)'s linear program with a computer package. Use the optimal solution to determine the optimal amount of barley to use in the dietary blend.

(e) Now assume that corn costs 45 cents per pound for the first 5 pounds, 35 cents per pound for the next 10 pounds, and 30 cents per pound thereafter. Can the blending problem still be formulated as a piecewise linear program? Why?

5.6. Reconsider the make-or-buy problem in Exercise 4.1. In that exercise, we assumed that CKC could purchase charcoal grills from another manufacturer at a unit cost of $50. Now assume that CKC's unit cost for charcoal grills purchased from the manufacturer is $40 for the first 9000 grills, $45 for the next 6000 grills, and $55 thereafter. Formulate this revised problem as a piecewise linear program.

5.7. Reconsider the economic planning problem in Exercise 4.24. In that exercise, we assumed Utopia could sell all the trucks it could produce at the existing world market price of $3000 per unit. Now assume the unit price at which Utopia can sell trucks decreases as the quantity sold increases. In particular, assume that Utopia can sell trucks at $4000 per unit for the first 50,000 units, $3500 per unit for the next 25,000 units, $3000 per unit for the next 75,000 units, and $2700 per unit thereafter. Formulate this revised problem as a piecewise linear program.

Exercises 5.8–5.11 test your understanding of how to use deviation variables in contexts other than goal programming.

5.8. Reconsider the production and inventory planning problem in Exercise 4.2. In that exercise, we implicitly assumed there was no cost associated with changing the production level from month to month. Now assume that, if the production level changes from one month to the next, SMC incurs a cost of $90 per car, regardless of whether the change is an increase or a decrease.

(a) Assuming SMC's current production level is 15,000 cars, revise the linear program you formulated in Exercise 4.2 to account for the cost associated with changing the production level.

(b) Modify your formulation in part (a) assuming the cost of increasing the production level from one month to the next is $90 per car but that the cost of decreasing the production level is $70 per car.

(c) Using a computer package, solve the linear programs you formulated in Exercise 4.2 and in part (a) of this exercise. For each optimal solution, compute and compare the month-to-month changes in the production levels.

*5.9. The city of Fairville wants to build a new fire station that will serve four new housing developments (A, B, C, and D) that are located along a straight stretch of road. The diagram below is a map of road, with each unit representing one mile:

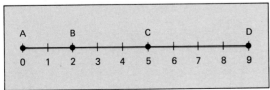

The following table provides the map coordinate of each housing development and the number of houses that will eventually be built in the development:

Housing Development	Map Coordinate	Number of Houses
A	0	100
B	2	400
C	5	200
D	9	300

Fairville believes that the best location for the fire station is the one that minimizes the sum of the products obtained by multiplying each housing development's size by the development's distance from the fire station. For example, if the fire station were built at map coordinate 4, the sum of products would be

$$100|4-0| + 400|4-2| + 200|4-5| + 300|4-9| = 2900$$

Formulate a linear program Fairville can use to determine where to locate the fire station.

5.10. (This exercise is a two-dimensional version of the previous exercise.) The city of Squaretown wants to build a recreation center for senior citizens who live in three low-income apartment buildings (A, B, and C). The diagram below is a map of Squaretown's streets, with each unit representing one city block.

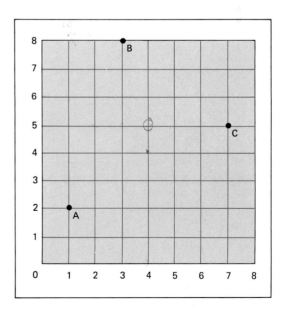

The table below provides the map coordinates of each apartment building and the number of senior citizens in each building:

217

Apartment Building	Map Coordinates (x, y)	Number of Senior Citizens
A	(1, 2)	100
B	(3, 8)	300
C	(7, 5)	200

Squaretown believes that the best location for the senior citizens center is the one that minimizes the sum of products obtained by multiplying each apartment building's senior citizen population by the building's distance from the center (as measured by the number of city blocks). For example, if the center were built at map coordinates (4, 5), the sum of products would be

$$100(|4-1| + |5-2|) + 300(|4-3| + |5-8|)$$
$$+ 200(|4-7| + |5-5|) = 2400$$

Formulate a linear program that Squaretown can use to determine where to locate the senior citizens center.

5.11. A classic problem in the field of statistics is the *linear regression problem*. Broadly speaking, this problem involves determining the equation of the straight line that "best fits" statistical data represented by n points–(x_1, y_1), (x_2, y_2), ..., (x_n, y_n)–on a graph. For simplicity, we will assume there are only the following five data points:

i	(x_i, y_i)
1	(1, 40)
2	(3, 50)
3	(5, 80)
4	(8, 90)
5	(10, 100)

If we denote the straight line by $y = ax + b$, we can define the error associated with the *i*th data point as the difference between the observed value y_i and its predicted value $ax_i + b$; that is, the error for the *i*th data point is $[(ax_i + b) - y_i]$. For example, the error associated with the third of the above five data points is $[(5a + b) - 80]$.

Before we can determine the values of a and b, we must define what we mean by the straight line that "best fits" the data. The most common definition of "best fit" is to find the values of a and b that minimize the sum of the squared errors. Given our five data points, this means minimizing

$$(1a+b-40)^2 + (3a+b-50)^2 + (5a+b-80)^2$$
$$+ (8a+b-90)^2 + (10a+b-100)^2$$

For this definition of "best fit," there are well-known formulae we can use to determine the values of a and b.

Although the most common by far, the above definition of "best fit" is not the only one. Another definition useful in some contexts is to minimize the sum of the errors' absolute values. Given our five data points, this means minimizing

$$|1a+b-40| + |3a+b-50| + |5a+b-80|$$
$$+ |8a+b-90| + |10a+b-100|$$

For this definition of "best fit," there are no formulae for determining the values of a and b. However, we can do so by using linear programming.

(a) For the five data points given above, formulate a linear program whose solution provides values for a and b that minimize the sum of the errors' absolute values. (Note: For simplicity, you may assume a and b are nonnegative.)

(b) Why do you think that minimizing the sum of squared errors is a much more common definition of "best fit" than minimizing the sum of the errors' absolute values?

Exercises 5.12–5.19 test your understanding of goal programming.

5.12. Consider a goal program in which the fourth goal (in decreasing order of priority) is to make $3x_1 + 2x_2$ as close to 18 as possible. Then the goal program would contain the following constraint:

$$3x_1 + 2x_2 - d_4^+ + d_4^- = 18,$$

where d_4^+ and d_4^- denote the goal's deviation variables. Explain why it would be impossible to obtain an optimal solution to the goal program in which $d_4^+ = 5$ and $d_4^- = 2$.

*5.13. Suppose we have the following goals (in decreasing order of priority):

1. Minimize the amount by which $3x_1 + 2x_2$ deviates (either underachievement or overachievement) from a target value of 60.
2. Minimize the amount by which $2x_1 + x_2$ underachieves a target value of 44.
3. Minimize the amount by which $7x_1 + 3x_2$ overachieves a target value of 84.

Formulate an appropriate goal program.

The next exercise illustrates the changes that take place in a goal program if each goal is restated in terms of the *percentage* of underachievement and/or overachievement instead of the amount of underachievement and/or overachievement.

5.14. Reconsider Exercise 5.13. Suppose the goals are as stated there, except that "amount" has been replaced in each goal with "percentage." Formulate a revised goal program.

The next exercise illustrates how to incorporate into a goal program a goal of maximizing or minimizing some function of the decision variables.

5.15 Reconsider Exercise 5.13.
    (a) Assume a fourth goal is to maximize the value of $x_1 + 2x_2$. Modify the goal program to take this goal into account. (*Hint*: Use an extremely large target value.)
    (b) Instead of the assumption in part (a), assume the fourth goal is to minimize the value of $x_1 + 2x_2$. Modify the goal program to take this goal into account.

5.16. Reconsider the school busing problem in Exercise 4.21. In that exercise, we assumed the objective was to minimize the total distance traveled by bused students. Now assume that, although minimizing the total distance traveled is the Board of Education's primary goal, a secondary goal is to minimize the number of bused students. Formulate an appropriate goal program.

5.17. A hospital administrator is reviewing departmental requests prior to the design of a new emergency room. At issue is the number of beds for each department. The current plans call for a 15,000-square-foot facility and a budget of $300,000. The following table summarizes other relevant data:

Type of Bed	Number of Beds Requested	Cost per Bed (including equipment)	Area per Bed (square feet)	Peak Requirements (maximum number of patients at one time)
Major Trauma	5	$12,600	474	3
Surgical	20	5,400	542	18
Medical	20	8,600	438	15

The hospital board has established the following four goals (in decreasing order of priority):
1. Devise a plan that requires at most 15,000 square feet.
2. Meet or exceed peak requirements (Surgical and Medical can be interchanged, but Major Trauma patients cannot use other facilities).
3. Spend no more than the $300,000 budget.
4. Meet or exceed the departmental requests.

    (a) Formulate a goal program the hospital administrator can use to decide how many beds each department should have in the new emergency room.
    (b) What modifications to your goal program are necessary if the third goal were restated as "Minimize the cost of the new emergency room"?
    (c) What modifications to your goal program are necessary if a fifth goal is added stating that "If the first goal is not achieved, the amount above 15,000 square feet should be at most 1000"?

5.18. The Midtown City Council is reviewing housing proposals for a new development area. There is some dispute among various interest groups as to what goals should be sought. The Zoning Committee has recommended three types of housing: one-family houses, deluxe condominiums, and apartments. There are 50 acres available for zoning.

The Zoning Committee has compiled the following data for each type of housing:

	Housing Type		
	One-Family	Deluxe Condo	Apartment
Land Usage (acres per unit)	.25	.20	.125
Families Housed per Unit	1	4	6
Tax Base Generated per Unit	$50,000	$100,000	$150,000
Taxes Required for City Services per Unit	$4,000	$8,000	$10,000

The City Council hired a public-opinion survey company to assess the priorities of the citizens. Using this survey, the City Council has established the following goals (in decreasing order of priority):
1. Provide housing for at least 500 families.
2. Establish at least $5,000,000 worth of new tax base.
3. Taxes for city services should be limited to $250,000.
4. Reserve at least 5 acres for a neighborhood park area.

    (a) Formulate a goal program the City Council can use to decide how to zone the new development area.
    (b) What modifications to your goal program are necessary if the second goal were restated as "Maximize the worth of the new tax base"?
    (c) What modifications to your goal program are necessary if a fifth goal is added stating that "If the first goal is not achieved, the amount of underachievement should not exceed 25 families"?

*5.19. Because of new tax laws, a state's Franchise Tax Board (FTB) must expand its staff. The FTB needs to fill 50 managerial positions and 200 clerical positions.

The cost to recruit a nonminority male is $900 for a managerial position and $400 for a clerical position. Recruiting a female increases these costs by 10%, and recruiting a minority increases these costs by 20%. Thus, for example, the cost of recruiting a minority female to a managerial position is 900 + 90 + 180 = 1170.

The FTB has set the following goals (in decreasing order of priority):

1. Females should constitute at least 40% of the new hirings.
2. Minorities should constitute at least 25% of the new hirings.
3. The recruiting budget should not exceed $175,000.
4. Minorities should constitute at most 60% of the new hirings to clerical positions.
5. Females should constitute at most 75% of the new hirings to clerical positions.

Formulate a goal program the FTB can use to plan its recruiting.

Exercises 5.20–5.23 test your understanding of a maximin (or minimax) objective function.

5.20. Consider an optimization problem with two nonnegative decision variables x_1 and x_2, several linear constraints involving x_1 and x_2, and the following objective function:

Maximize the minimum of $[3x_1 + 2x_2, x_1 + 4x_2]$

If we use the technique discussed in Section 5.5 to convert the problem into a linear program, the objective function will be

Maximize z

and two of the structural constraints will be

$$3x_1 + 2x_2 - z \geqslant 0$$
$$x_1 + 4x_2 - z \geqslant 0.$$

Suppose someone claims the optimal solution to the linear program is $x_1 = 20$, $x_2 = 10$, and $z = 50$. Explain why this is impossible. (You should assume the values of x_1 and x_2 satisfy the linear program's other structural constraints.)

5.21. Reconsider Squaretown's location problem in Exercise 5.10. Now assume the objective is to minimize

the maximum distance between the senior citizens center and any of the three apartment buildings.
(a) Explain in words what Squaretown is trying to do with this new objective.
(b) Formulate a linear program Squaretown can use to achieve this objective.

*5.22. Reconsider the linear regression problem in Exercise 5.11. In that exercise the objective was to minimize the sum of the errors' absolute values. Now assume the objective is to minimize the maximum of the errors' absolute values; that is, to minimize the maximum of

$$|1a + b - 40|, |3a + b - 50|, |5a + b - 80|, |8a + b - 90|,$$
$$\text{and } |10a + b - 100|$$

Formulate an appropriate linear program.

5.23. Three businesses (A, B, and C) share the same office building. Each business wants to have its offices painted. A painting contractor has made the following proposal:
- If he paints A's offices only, the cost will be $3000.
- If he paints B's offices only, the cost will be $3500.
- If he paints C's offices only, the cost will be $2500.
- If he paints the offices of A and B only, the total cost will be $5800.
- If he paints the offices of A and C only, the total cost will be $4800.
- If he paints the offices of B and C only, the total cost will be $5200.
- If he paints all three offices, the total cost will be $7500.

The businesses have decided to hire the painter but are having trouble deciding how to share the total cost of $7500. For example, when B proposed that they share the total cost equally, A and C pointed out that this would be unfair because their total payment of $5000 would be more than the $4800 bid the painter submitted to paint the offices of A and C only. After some thought, A, B, and C decided to define a "fair" division of the total cost of $7500 as one with the following characteristics:
1. No business pays more than the painter would charge to paint only the business's offices.
2. No pair of businesses pays more than the painter would charge to paint only the pair's offices.
3. Subject to items 1 and 2, the maximum payment among the three businesses is as low as possible.

Formulate a linear program whose solution provides the businesses with a fair division of payments (according to their definition).

The previous exercises have required you to use exactly one of the techniques we have discussed in this chapter–either piecewise linear programming, deviation variables, or a maximin (or a minimax) objective function. In the next three exercises, you will need to use two of these techniques together.

5.24. Reconsider the production and inventory planning problem in Exercise 5.8 In that exercise, we assumed that if the production level changed from one month to the next, SMC incurred a cost of $90 per car, regardless of whether the change was an increase or a decrease. Now assume that the cost to change (increase or decrease) the production level from one month to the next is $50 per car for the first 4000 cars of change, $90 per car for the next 6000 cars of change, and $125 per car for changes thereafter. Formulate an appropriate linear program.

*5.25. Reconsider Exercise 5.17. Now suppose the unit penalty for deviating from the first goal does not remain constant but increases as the amount of the deviation increases. In particular, assume that we want to assign a unit penalty of 10 for the first 500 square feet in excess of 15,000, a unit penalty of 15 for the next 1000 square feet, and a unit penalty of 25 for each square foot thereafter. Assume constant unit penalties of 5, 3, and 1 for the second, third, and fourth goals, respectively. What modifications does this new penalty structure necessitate to the goal program you formulated in Exercise 5.17?

5.26 In a goal program, it is customary to assume that the objective is to minimize the sum of the penalties incurred for deviating from the goals. An alternative objective is to minimize the maximum among the deviations from the goals. Using this objective, reconsider Exercise 5.13 and formulate an appropriate goal program.

LINEAR PROGRAMMING: THE SIMPLEX METHOD

6.1 INTRODUCTION

In earlier chapters we made repeated reference to the *simplex method,* the algebraic method used to solve linear programs. In this chapter we will learn the details of the simplex method.[1] Three characteristics of this method facilitate our learning it:

1. The simplex method consists of three basic steps that are repeated over and over until the LP's optimal solution is identified. For this reason, we describe the simplex method as an *iterative* method, and we call each repetition of the three basic steps an *iteration.* Although every iteration of the simplex method involves different numerical computations, the framework for carrying out these computations is identical from iteration to iteration. To understand the simplex method, then, we really have to understand only how to perform one iteration.

2. The numerical computations required by each iteration of the simplex method involve only the basic mathematical operations of addition, subtraction, multiplication, and division. Consequently, when the LP involves, say, less than five decision variables and five structural constraints, we can manually solve it using the simplex method. (Larger LPs require the use of a software package

---

[1] Some instructors, textbooks, and LP software packages refer to the simplex method as the *simplex algorithm.* In mathematical contexts, "algorithm" is frequently used as a synonym for a systematic procedure.

only because manual computation would be too time-consuming and error-prone.)

3. When the LP involves only two decision variables, the numerical computations required by an iteration of the simplex method can be illustrated using a graph of the LP's feasible region.

We will begin our study of the simplex method in the context of Chapter 2's product mix LP for the Orange Microcomputer Corporation (OMC). Recall that, after rescaling, OMC's product mix LP is

$$\text{Maximize } 9x_1 + 6x_2$$

$$\text{subject to } \begin{aligned} 2x_1 + x_2 &\leqslant 20 \\ 4x_1 + x_2 &\leqslant 32 \\ 2x_1 + 7x_2 &\leqslant 88 \end{aligned}$$

$$\text{and } x_1 \geqslant 0, x_2 \geqslant 0$$

where x_1 and x_2 respectively denote the production quantities (in thousands) of Oranges and Tangerines. By first considering OMC's two-variable LP, we not only can keep the numerical computations to manageable proportions but we can also illustrate the computations using a graph of the feasible region.

Our discussion will be greatly simplified if we initially restrict our attention to LPs that, like OMC's product mix LP, have the following characteristics:

- The objective function involves maximization.
- All structural constraints are of the $\leqslant$ type with nonnegative constants appearing on their right-hand sides.
- All decision variables are subject to nonnegativity constraints.

Hereafter, we refer to such an LP as a *standard LP*. After learning in this chapter how to solve a standard LP, we will extend our understanding in Chapter 7 to a *nonstandard LP*—that is, an LP having an objective function involving minimization, a mixture of $\leqslant$, $\geqslant$, and $=$ structural constraints, or decision variables that are unconstrained in sign or have nonzero lower bounds.

6.2 TRANSFORMING OMC'S LP INTO EQUALITY FORM

The simplex method is designed to work with structural constraints that are expressed as equations, not inequalities. Therefore, before solving OMC's LP, we must transform it into an equivalent LP in which the three $\leqslant$ structural constraints have been replaced by three equations. Fortunately, the concept of a slack variable provides a means of accomplishing this task.

Consider the LP's first structural constraint, $2x_1 + x_2 \leqslant 20$. In Section 2.8 we defined the slack variable S_1 as the constraint's right-hand side minus its left-hand side—that is,

$$S_1 = 20 - (2x_1 + x_2)$$

An equivalent way of writing this definition is

$$2x_1 + x_2 + S_1 = 20$$

Putting this into words, S_1 is the amount that must be added to the constraint's left-hand side, $2x_1 + x_2$, to make it equal to the constraint's right-hand side of 20. To illustrate, consider the following three examples:

(x_1, x_2)	$2x_1 + x_2 +$	S_1	$= 20$
(7,6)	20 +	0	= 20
(5,8)	18 +	2	= 20
(6,12)	24 +	(−4)	= 20

Observe in all three examples that S_1 is the amount that must be added to the constraint's left-hand side of $2x_1 + x_2$ to make it equal to the constraint's right-hand side of 20. Observe also that only two of the three cases correspond to values of (x_1, x_2) that satisfy the constraint $2x_1 + x_2 \leqslant 20$. By looking at the value of S_1, can you quickly identify which two? The answer is Cases 1 and 2, the cases in which S_1 assumes a nonnegative value. When $2x_1 + x_2 = 20$ (as in Case 1), $S_1 = 0$; when $2x_1 + x_2 < 20$ (as in Case 2), $S_1 > 0$; when $2x_1 + x_2 > 20$ (as in Case 3), $S_1 < 0$. Figure 6.1 provides a graphical illustration of the three cases.

Our examples illustrate the following general principle (first illustrated in Section 2.8):

> An assignment of values to the decision variables satisfies a structural constraint of the $\leqslant$ type if and only if the constraint's slack variable assumes a nonnegative value. Furthermore, when the slack variable equals 0, the constraint's left-hand side is exactly equal to the constraint's right-hand side.

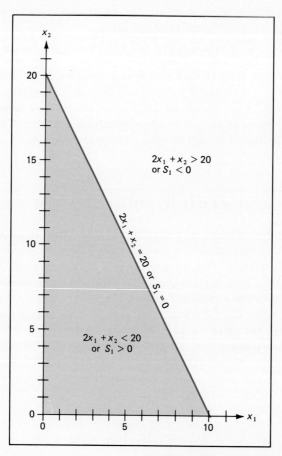

Figure 6.1 Graphical illustration of a slack variable

Recall that our goal is to transform OMC's LP into an equivalent LP in which the three $\leqslant$ structural constraints have been replaced by three equations. Because of the above general principle, we can replace the LP's first structural constraint, $2x_1 + x_2 \leqslant 20$, with the structural equation

$$2x_1 + x_2 + S_1 = 20$$

if we also add the nonnegativity constraint $S_1 \geqslant 0$. Note that the nonnegativity constraint on S_1 is necessary to ensure that $2x_1 + x_2$ does not exceed 20.

We can perform similar replacements for the second and third structural constraints, thereby obtaining the following transformation of OMC's LP, a transformation known as the *LP in equality form:*

Maximize $9x_1 + 6x_2$

$$
\begin{aligned}
\text{subject to } 2x_1 + x_2 + S_1 &= 20 \\
4x_1 + x_2 + S_2 &= 32 \\
2x_1 + 7x_2 + S_3 &= 88
\end{aligned}
$$

and $x_1 \geqslant 0, x_2 \geqslant 0,$
$ S_1 \geqslant 0, S_2 \geqslant 0, S_3 \geqslant 0.$

It is the LP in equality form that the simplex method is designed to solve.

To summarize:

In transforming an LP into equality form, we replace a structural constraint of the $\leqslant$ type with two constraints:

1. An equality constraint obtained from the $\leqslant$ constraint by adding a slack variable to the constraint's left-hand side and changing the $\leqslant$ sign to an $=$ sign.

2. A nonnegativity constraint on the slack variable.

6.3 THE CORRESPONDENCE BETWEEN GEOMETRY AND ALGEBRA

We now focus our attention on the three structural equations of OMC's LP in equality form—that is,

$$
\begin{aligned}
2x_1 + x_2 + S_1 &= 20 \\
4x_1 + x_2 + S_2 &= 32 \\
2x_1 + 7x_2 + S_3 &= 88.
\end{aligned}
$$

Hereafter, for ease of reference, we call the above system of equations *OMC's equality form system of equations.*

Our next goal is to recall the geometrical concepts we encountered when learning to solve an LP graphically and to demonstrate that they are equivalent to certain algebraic concepts, which we can describe in terms of solutions to the LP's equality form system of equations. This correspondence between geometry and algebra is the "foundation" on which we will "build" our understanding of the simplex method.

An important aid to our discussion will be Figure 6.2, which displays the feasible region of OMC's LP. We have labeled the feasible region's five corner

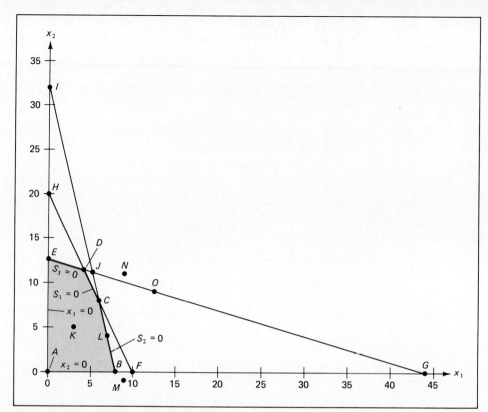

Figure 6.2 The feasible region for OMC's LP

points A, B, C, D, and E, and we have also identified ten other points we will subsequently refer to (points F, G, H, I, J, K, L, M, N, and O). Another important aspect of Figure 6.2 is the labels attached to the five boundary equations. Since two of the boundary equations correspond to the x_1-axis and the x_2-axis, their respective labels of $x_2 = 0$ and $x_1 = 0$ are self-explanatory. However, the boundary equations labeled $S_1 = 0$, $S_2 = 0$, and $S_3 = 0$ require a brief explanation.

Consider first the boundary equation labeled $S_1 = 0$. In Figure 6.2, the line labeled $S_1 = 0$ is actually the equation $2x_1 + x_2 = 20$, the boundary equation for the structural constraint $2x_1 + x_2 \leqslant 20$. However, as we illustrated in Figure 6.1, any point lying on the boundary equation $2x_1 + x_2 = 20$ has the property that $S_1 = 0$; that is, $2x_1 + x_2 = 20$ is equivalent to $S_1 = 0$. Similarly, $4x_1 + x_2 = 32$ is equivalent to $S_2 = 0$, and $2x_1 + 7x_2 = 88$ is equivalent to $S_3 = 0$. Thus, the boundary equations' labels of $S_1 = 0$, $S_2 = 0$, and $S_3 = 0$ are merely "abbreviations" for the labels of $2x_1 + x_2 = 20$, $4x_1 + x_2 = 32$, and $2x_1 + 7x_2 = 88$.

An Infinite Number of Solutions

Let us now demonstrate that OMC's equality form system of equations has an infinite number of solutions. If you haven't solved too many systems of equations since your high-school algebra days, you may have forgotten that solving a system of m linear equations involving n variables will have one of three outcomes:

1. The system of equations may have a unique (i.e., one) solution.
2. The system of equations may have no solutions.
3. The system of equations may have an infinite number of solutions.

When the system has fewer equations than variables (i.e., $m < n$), only outcomes 2 and 3 are possible, with outcome 3 being the most likely.

Since OMC's equality form system of equations has $m = 3$ equations and $n = 5$ variables, we expect it to have an infinite number of solutions. The easiest way to illustrate the correctness of this expectation is to demonstrate that each of the infinite number of points in Figure 6.2 corresponds to a solution to OMC's equality form system of equations. To see this, we rearrange the equations as follows:

$$
\begin{array}{llll}
2x_1 + x_2 & + S_1 & = 20 & \quad S_1 = 20 - 2x_1 - x_2 \\
4x_1 + x_2 & \quad + S_2 & = 32 \;\;\rightarrow & \quad S_2 = 32 - 4x_1 - x_2 \\
2x_1 + 7x_2 & \quad\quad + S_3 & = 88 & \quad S_3 = 88 - 2x_1 - 7x_2.
\end{array}
$$

In this rearranged form, it is clear that, given any assignment of values to x_1 and x_2, we can determine a solution to OMC's equality form system of equations by substituting the values of x_1 and x_2 into the right-hand sides of the rearranged form of the equations, thereby obtaining values for S_1, S_2, and S_3. For example, consider point K in Figure 6.2, a point having coordinates $(x_1, x_2) = (3,5)$. Substituting $x_1 = 3$ and $x_2 = 5$ into the rearranged form of the equations, we obtain

$$S_1 = 9, S_2 = 15, \text{ and } S_3 = 47.$$

Thus, the point K in Figure 6.2 is equivalent to the solution of OMC's equality form system of equations given by

$$(x_1, x_2, S_1, S_2, S_3) = (3, 5, 9, 15, 47).$$

Table 6.1 summarizes the correspondence between six points in Figure 6.2 and the values of $(x_1, x_2, S_1, S_2, S_3)$ in the corresponding solution of OMC's equality form system of equations. We have already verified the table's first point. Before proceeding, you should verify for yourself the table's remaining five points. Table 6.1 illustrates the following general principle:

> The geometrical notion of a point in Figure 6.2 corresponds to the algebraic notion of values for $(x_1, x_2, S_1, S_2, S_3)$ that satisfy OMC's equality form system of equations
>
> $$
> \begin{array}{lllll}
> 2x_1 + & x_2 + & S_1 & & = 20 \\
> 4x_1 + & x_2 & & + S_2 & = 32 \\
> 2x_1 + & 7x_2 & & & + S_3 = 88
> \end{array}
> $$

TABLE 6.1 Selected Points in Figure 6.2 and the Corresponding Values of $(x_1, x_2, S_1, S_2, S_3)$

Point in Figure 6.2	Corresponding Solution to OMC's Equality Form System of Equations $(x_1,$ $x_2,$ $S_1,$ $S_2,$ $S_3)$				
Point K having coordinates $(3,5)$	$(3,$	$5,$	$9,$	$15,$	$47)$
Point L having coordinates $(7,4)$	$(7,$	$4,$	$2,$	$0,$	$46)$
Point C having coordinates $(6,8)$	$(6,$	$8,$	$0,$	$0,$	$20)$
Point J having coordinates $(5\frac{3}{13}, 11\frac{1}{13})$	$(5\frac{3}{13},$	$11\frac{1}{13},$	$-1\frac{7}{13},$	$0,$	$0)$
Point M having coordinates $(9, -1)$	$(9,$	$-1,$	$3,$	$-3,$	$77)$
Point N having coordinates $(9,11)$	$(9,$	$11,$	$-9,$	$-15,$	$-7)$

Just as there are an infinite number of points in Figure 6.2, there are an infinite number of solutions to OMC's equality form system of equations.

Algebraically Identifying Feasible Solutions

Observe that, of the six points listed in Table 6.1, the first three (K, L, and C) lie within Figure 6.2's feasible region, while the last three (J, M, and N) lie outside the feasible region. Looking at the values of $(x_1, x_2, S_1, S_2, S_3)$ in Table 6.1, can you detect the characteristic that differentiates the feasible points K, L, and C from the infeasible points J, M, and N? The answer is that, for the three feasible points, all the variables $x_1, x_2, S_1, S_2,$ and S_3 assume nonnegative values. In contrast, for the three infeasible points, at least one of the variables x_1, x_2, S_1, S_2, and S_3 assumes a negative value. Recall that the constraints of the LP in equality form consist not only of OMC's equality form system of equations but also of the five nonnegativity constraints. Whereas the values for $x_1, x_2, S_1, S_2,$ and S_3 for all six points in Table 6.1 satisfy OMC's equality form system of equations, only the values of $x_1, x_2, S_1, S_2,$ and S_3 for the points K, L, and C also satisfy the five nonnegativity constraints. For points J, M, and N, at least one of the variables assumes a negative value. A negative value for x_1 or x_2 is a clear violation of the nonnegativity constraint $x_1 \geqslant 0$ or $x_2 \geqslant 0$, and (from our discussion in Section 6.2) a negative value for S_1, S_2, or S_3 indicates a violation of the structural constraint $2x_1 + x_2 \leqslant 20$, $4x_1 + x_2 \leqslant 32$, or $2x_1 + 7x_2 \leqslant 88$. For example, in Table 6.1, there are two indications that point M, with coordinates $(9, -1)$, is infeasible:

1. $x_2 = -1$, thereby indicating a violation of the nonnegativity constraint $x_2 \geqslant 0$.

2. $S_2 = -3$, thereby indicating a violation of the second structural constraint.

Hereafter, given values for $(x_1, x_2, S_1, S_2, S_3)$ that are a solution to OMC's equality form system of equations, we will use the term *nonnegative solution* if all variables assume nonnegative values, and we will use the term *negative solution* if at least one variable assumes a negative value. We can now summarize as follows the general principle illustrated by the contrast between Table 6.1's first three and last three points.

The geometrical notion of a point in Figure 6.2 lying within the feasible region corresponds to the algebraic notion of a *nonnegative solution* to OMC's equality form system of equations.

Algebraically Identifying a Corner Point

An important subset of the feasible points in Figure 6.2 are the five so-called *corner points*, those points labeled A, B, C, D, and E. In Section 2.11 we demonstrated that, regardless of the LP's objective function, we can restrict our search for the best of the infinite number of feasible points to the finite set of corner points. It is easy to graphically identify the five corner points, since, as their name suggests, they lie at the "corners" of the feasible region. What is the algebraic equivalent to the geometrical notion of a corner point? To answer this question, we need to understand the concept of a *basic solution* to a system of equations.

To illustrate this concept, consider OMC's equality form system of equations, a system of three equations involving five variables. If we arbitrarily set any two of the five variables equal to 0, the system of equations simplifies to a "square" system—that is, a system of three equations involving only the three variables not set equal to 0. For example, suppose we arbitrarily decide to set x_1 and x_2 equal to 0. The LP's equality form system of equations simplifies to the following square system of three equations involving the three variables S_1, S_2, and S_3 (where the columns corresponding to the variables x_1 and x_2 are shaded to indicate they are to be ignored):

$$
\begin{array}{rcrcrcrcrcl}
2x_1 & + & x_2 & + & S_1 & & & & & = & 20 \\
4x_1 & + & x_2 & & & + & S_2 & & & = & 32 \\
2x_1 & + & 7x_2 & & & & & + & S_3 & = & 88.
\end{array}
$$

The solution is immediately evident as $S_1 = 20$, $S_2 = 32$ and $S_3 = 88$.

To summarize, by setting x_1 and x_2 equal to 0 and then solving for S_1, S_2, and S_3, we have identified

$$(x_1, x_2, S_1, S_2, S_3) = (0, 0, 20, 32, 88)$$

as a solution to OMC's equality form system of equations. A solution such as this one is known as a *basic solution*. The variables set equal to 0 (i.e., x_1 and x_2 in the example) are known as the *nonbasic variables,* and the remaining variables (i.e., S_1, S_2, and S_3 in the example) are known as the *basic variables.* In general,

> Consider a system of m equations involving n variables, with $m < n$. A *basic solution* is a solution obtained by arbitrarily setting $n - m$ of the variables equal to 0 and then solving the resulting square system of m equations involving the remaining m variables. The $n - m$ variables set equal to 0 are called the *nonbasic variables* and the remaining m variables are called the *basic variables.*

In OMC's equality form system of equations, $m = 3$ and $n = 5$. By choosing x_1 and x_2 as the $n - m = 5 - 3 = 2$ nonbasic variables to set equal to 0 and then solving the resulting square system of equations for the values of the $m = 3$ basic variables S_1, S_2, and S_3, we earlier identified

$$(x_1, x_2, S_1, S_2, S_3) = (0, 0, 20, 32, 88)$$

as one basic solution to OMC's equality form system of equations. Let us now find another basic solution. This time, let us choose x_2 and S_1 as the nonbasic variables, thereby leaving x_1, S_2, and S_3 as the basic variables. With $x_2 = 0$ and $S_1 = 0$, OMC's equality form system of equations simplifies to the following system of three equations involving the three variables x_1, S_2, and S_3:

$$
\begin{array}{rcrcrcrcrcl}
2x_1 & + & x_2 & + & S_1 & & & & & = & 20 \\
4x_1 & + & x_2 & & & + & S_2 & & & = & 32 \\
2x_1 & + & 7x_2 & & & & & + & S_3 & = & 88
\end{array}
$$

Looking at the first equation, we can easily see that $x_1 = \frac{20}{2} = 10$. Then, substituting $x_1 = 10$ into the second and third equations, we determine $S_2 = -8$ and $S_3 = 68$. Thus, we have identified

$$(x_1, x_2, S_1, S_2, S_3) = (10, 0, 0, -8, 68)$$

as another basic solution to OMC's equality form system of equations. Observe from the negative value of S_2 that a basic solution need not be nonnegative.

With a little thought, we can easily predict the point in Figure 6.2 to which a basic solution will correspond. For example, consider the second basic solution we discussed,

$$(x_1, x_2, S_1, S_2, S_3) = (10, 0, 0, -8, 68)$$

Our choice of x_2 and S_1 as the nonbasic variables to set equal to 0 is geometrically equivalent in Figure 6.2 to requiring a point to simultaneously lie on the two boundary equations $x_2 = 0$ and $S_1 = 0$. For this to occur, the point must lie at the intersection of these two boundary equations, the precise location of point F in Figure 6.2.

Let us now consider several points in Figure 6.2 that do not lie at the intersection of two boundary equations and see that they cannot correspond to basic solutions. First, consider points such as K and N that lie on none of the five boundary equations. Such points cannot correspond to basic solutions (where two variables equal 0) because the corresponding values of x_1, x_2, S_1, S_2, and S_3 are all nonzero. Next, consider points such as L and O that lie on exactly one of the five boundary equations. Such points cannot correspond to basic solutions because all except one of the corresponding values of x_1, x_2, S_1, S_2, and S_3 are nonzero. By example, then, we have illustrated the following general principle:

> The geometrical notion of a point in Figure 6.2 that lies at the intersection of two boundary equations corresponds to the algebraic notion of a basic solution to OMC's equality form system of equations—that is, a solution in which exactly two of the five variables equal 0 and the remaining three variables are nonzero.

With this principle, we have almost arrived at our goal of finding the algebraic equivalent to the geometric concept of a corner point of the feasible region in Figure 6.2. Observe that the five corner points in Figure 6.2's feasible region all lie at the intersection of two boundary equations and, therefore, correspond to basic solutions of OMC's equality form system of equations—basic solutions in which the two nonbasic variables correspond to the two intersecting boundary equations. Unfortunately, as we have already illustrated with point F, other points besides the feasible region's corner points lie at the intersection of two boundary equations and, therefore, correspond to basic solutions.

Looking at Figure 6.2, we can count ten points that lie at the intersection of two boundary equations, the points labeled A through J. Observe that, of these ten points, the five labeled A through E are corner points in Figure 6.2's feasible region, and the remaining five are infeasible points. Table 6.2 displays the ten points in Figure 6.2 that lie at the intersection of two boundary equations and the basic solutions to which these ten points correspond. We have already discussed several of these ten points.[2]

Looking in Table 6.2, can you identify a characteristic of the variables' values that distinguishes those basic solutions that correspond to corner points (the first five) from those that do not (the last five)?[3] The answer is that the first five basic solutions are all nonnegative solutions, indicating that the corresponding points in Figure 6.2 are feasible points. In contrast, Table 6.2's last five basic solutions are all negative solutions, indicating that the corresponding points in Figure 6.2 are

---

[2] If you are still confused by the concept of a basic solution, you should spend some time verifying the other entries in Table 6.2.

[3] *Hint*: Recall the concept of a nonnegative solution.

TABLE 6.2 The Ten Points in Figure 6.2 That Lie at the Intersection of Two Boundary Equations and the Corresponding Basic Solutions

Point in Figure 6.2 That Lies at the Intersection of Two Boundary Equations	Corresponding Basic Solution $(x_1,\quad x_2,\quad S_1,\quad S_2,\quad S_3)$				
Point A having coordinates $(0,0)$	$(0,$	$0,$	$20,$	$32,$	$88)$
Point B having coordinates $(8,0)$	$(8,$	$0,$	$4,$	$0,$	$72)$
Point C having coordinates $(6,8)$	$(6,$	$8,$	$0,$	$0,$	$20)$
Point D having coordinates $(4\frac{1}{3},11\frac{1}{3})$	$(4\frac{1}{3},$	$11\frac{1}{3},$	$0,$	$3\frac{1}{3},$	$0)$
Point E having coordinates $(0,12\frac{4}{7})$	$(0,$	$12\frac{4}{7},$	$7\frac{3}{7},$	$19\frac{3}{7},$	$0)$
Point F having coordinates $(10,0)$	$(10,$	$0,$	$0,$	$-8,$	$68)$
Point G having coordinates $(44,0)$	$(44,$	$0,$	$-68,$	$-144,$	$0)$
Point H having coordinates $(0,20)$	$(0,$	$20,$	$0,$	$12,$	$-52)$
Point I having coordinates $(0,32)$	$(0,$	$32,$	$-12,$	$0,$	$-136)$
Point J having coordinates $(5\frac{3}{13},11\frac{1}{13})$	$(5\frac{3}{13},$	$11\frac{1}{13},$	$-1\frac{7}{13},$	$0,$	$0)$

infeasible points. Based on these observations about Table 6.2, we conclude that, for a solution to OMC's equality form system of equations to correspond to a corner point in Figure 6.2, the solution must be not only a basic solution but also a nonnegative solution. The requirement that the solution be a basic solution ensures that it corresponds to a point in Figure 6.2 that lies at the intersection of two boundary equations. The further requirement that it be a nonnegative solution ensures that it lies within the feasible region. A solution that is both basic and nonnegative is known as a *basic feasible solution*. A solution that is basic but not nonnegative is known as a *basic infeasible solution*.

To summarize:

> The geometric notion of a corner point in Figure 6.2 is equivalent to the algebraic notion of a special type of solution to OMC's equality form system of equations, a solution that is not only a basic solution but also a nonnegative solution. Such a solution is known as a *basic feasible solution*.

A Finite Number of Basic Feasible Solutions

We observe now that the equality form system of equations for any LP can have only a finite number of basic feasible solutions. For LPs whose feasible region we can graph (such as OMC's), we can see that there are only a finite number of basic feasible solutions by simply counting the always finite number of corner points. However, for LPs whose feasible regions we cannot graph, we need a way to algebraically demonstrate that there are only a finite number of basic feasible solutions. To accomplish this, recall that a basic solution to OMC's equality form system of equations is obtained by first choosing two of the five variables to be the nonbasic variables to set equal to 0 and then solving the resulting system of three equations involving the three basic variables. Thus, the number of basic solutions can never exceed the number of distinct ways there are to choose the two nonbasic variables from the five variables. Clearly, this is a finite number. In fact, from your high-school algebra days, you may recall that the number of distinct ways to choose two objects out of five objects is given by the formula:[4]

$$\frac{5!}{2!\ 3!} = 10$$

This is precisely the number of basic solutions contained in Table 6.2. In general,

> If an LP's equality form system of equations involves m equations and n variables (where $m < n$), the number of basic solutions is limited by the number of distinct ways to choose the $n - m$ nonbasic variables from the entire set of n variables, a number given by the formula
>
> $$\frac{n!}{(n-m)!\ m!}$$

We should note that this formula does not always give an exact value for the number of basic solutions. Sometimes it gives only an upper bound, because some choices of the nonbasic variables lead to a system of equations involving the basic variables that has no solution. For example, consider an LP for which $x_1 \leq 10$ is the first structural constraint in the LP's original formulation. When the LP is converted to equality form, the inequality $x_1 \leq 10$ becomes the equation $x_1 + S_1 = 10$, where S_1 is the slack variable for the original constraint. With $x_1 + S_1 = 10$ being one equation in the LP's equality form system of equations, it is impossible to select x_1 and S_1 to simultaneously be among the set of nonbasic variables. The reason is that substituting $x_1 = 0$ and $S_1 = 0$ into $x_1 + S_1 = 10$ leads to the impossible result that $0 + 0 = 10$.

Since we have established that there are only a finite number of basic solutions, and since we know that the basic feasible solutions are a subset of the basic solutions, we can conclude that the number of basic feasible solutions is finite. In general, then,

> Just as a graphical search for an LP's optimal solution can be restricted to the finite number of corner points of the feasible region, an algebraic search for an LP's optimal solution can be restricted to the finite number of basic feasible solutions to the LP's equality form system of equations.

This general principle is the "foundation" on which we will "build" our understanding of the simplex method.

6.4 A VERBAL "PREVIEW" OF THE SIMPLEX METHOD

The general principle stated above suggests the following three-step procedure for solving an LP:

---

[4] The factorial symbol ! is defined by $n! = (n)(n-1) \cdots (2)(1)$, where, by convention, $0! = 1$.

TABLE 6.3 The Five Basic Feasible Solution to OMC's Equality Form System of Equations

Corner Point in Figure 6.2's Feasible Region	Corresponding Basic Feasible Solution $(x_1,$ $x_2,$ $S_1,$ $S_2,$ $S_3)$					Objective Value $(9x_1 + 6x_2)$
Point A having coordinates $(0,0)$	(0,	0,	20,	32,	88)	0
Point B having coordinates $(8,0)$	(8,	0,	4,	0,	72)	72
Point C having coordinates $(6,8)$	(6,	8,	0,	0,	20)	102
Point D having coordinates $(4\frac{1}{3}, 11\frac{1}{3})$	$(4\frac{1}{3},$	$11\frac{1}{3},$	0,	$3\frac{1}{3},$	0)	107
Point E having coordinates $(0, 12\frac{4}{7})$	(0,	$12\frac{4}{7},$	$7\frac{3}{7},$	$19\frac{3}{7},$	0)	$75\frac{3}{7}$

1. Suppose the LP's equality form system of equations consists of m equations involving n variables. Find the number of basic solutions to the LP's equality form system of equations by considering each of the $n!/[(n-m)!\, m!]$ distinct ways to choose the $(n-m)$ nonbasic variables. For each choice of the nonbasic variables, set the nonbasic variables equal to 0 and then determine the solution (if one exists) to the square system of m equations involving the m basic variables.

2. Delete from the list of basic solutions compiled in Step 1 those which are also negative solutions, thereby retaining on the list only the basic feasible solutions.

3. For each of the basic feasible solutions, compute its objective value. The LP's optimal solution is given by the basic feasible solution with the best objective value.

Table 6.3 illustrates the application of this procedure to OMC's LP. Its rows are simply the first five rows of Table 6.2—the table in which we previously summarized all basic solutions to OMC's equality form system of equations. (Recall that only Table 6.2's first five rows contain basic feasible solutions.) Table 6.3's last column summarizes the objective value of each basic feasible solution. Looking at these objective values, we see that the basic feasible solution with the highest objective value is

$$(x_1, x_2, S_1, S_2, S_3) = (4\tfrac{1}{3}, 11\tfrac{1}{3}, 0, 3\tfrac{1}{3}, 0),$$

corresponding to point D in Figure 6.3. This is the same optimal solution we identified during Chapter 2's graphical solution of OMC's LP.

Solving an LP by enumerating all basic feasible solutions is a time-consuming procedure, even for a small LP. Fortunately, the simplex method is much more efficient; it identifies the optimal basic feasible solution by considering only a small subset of the basic feasible solutions.

Adjacent Basic Feasible Solutions

A concept we need at this point is that of adjacent basic feasible solutions. To aid our discussion, we will refer to Figure 6.3, a graphical illustration of Table 6.3

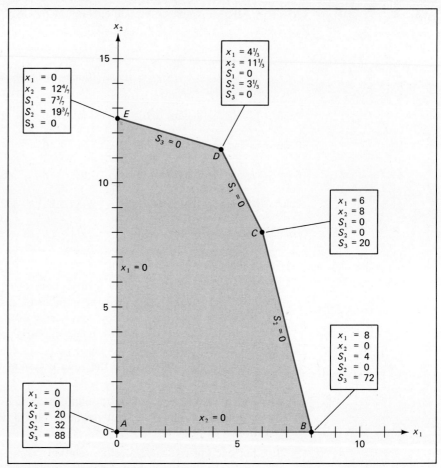

Figure 6.3 Feasible region for OMC's LP illustrating the correspondence between corner points and basic feasible solutions

which displays each of the five basic feasible solutions next to its corresponding corner point of the feasible region.

Looking at Figure 6.3, it is easy to see that every corner point has two adjacent corner points. For example, corner point A's two adjacent corner points are B and E, and corner point C's two adjacent corner points are B and D. In general, then,

> When an LP's feasible region has a two-dimensional graph, every corner point has two adjacent corner points.

Let us now investigate the algebraic significance of two corner points being adjacent. To illustrate, consider in Figure 6.3 the adjacent corner points A and B and observe the following:

- Since A lies at the intersection of the boundary equations $x_1 = 0$ and $x_2 = 0$, the corresponding basic feasible solution's nonbasic variables (i.e., those equal to 0) and basic variables are given by

Set of Nonbasic Variables at Point A	Set of Basic Variables at Point A
x_1, x_2	S_1, S_2, S_3

- Since B lies at the intersection of the boundary equations $x_2 = 0$ and $S_2 = 0$, the corresponding basic feasible solution's nonbasic variables and basic variables are given by

Set of Nonbasic Variables at Point B	Set of Basic Variables at Point B
x_2, S_2	x_1, S_1, S_3

Note that the two sets of nonbasic variables differ by exactly one variable, and the two sets of basic variables differ by exactly one variable. This illustrates the following general principle:

> When two corner points are adjacent, their corresponding basic feasible solutions will have respective sets of nonbasic variables and basic variables that both differ by exactly one variable.

As an additional example of this general principle, consider in Figure 6.3 the two corner points C and E, two that are not adjacent to each other. Observe the following:

- Since C lies at the intersection of the boundary equations $S_1 = 0$ and $S_2 = 0$, the corresponding basic feasible solution's nonbasic variables (i.e., those equal to 0) and basic variables are given by

Set of Nonbasic Variables at Point C	Set of Basic Variables at Point C
S_1, S_2	x_1, x_2, S_3

- Since E lies at the intersection of the boundary equations $x_1 = 0$ and $S_3 = 0$, the corresponding basic feasible solution's nonbasic variables (i.e., those equal to 0) and basic variables are given by

Set of Nonbasic Variables at Point E	Set of Basic Variables at Point E
x_1, S_3	x_2, S_1, S_2

Note that the two sets of nonbasic variables and the two sets of basic variables both differ by more than one variable.

Hereafter, whenever two basic feasible solutions have respective sets of nonbasic variables and basic variables that both differ by exactly one variable, we will say that they are *adjacent basic feasible solutions*. We will use this terminology even when it is impossible to graph the LP's feasible region.

Let us deepen our understanding by geometrically investigating how moving from a basic feasible solution to an adjacent one affects the set of nonbasic variables and basic variables. Imagine that we are located in Figure 6.2 at corner point A (the origin) and wish to "walk east" along the feasible region's boundary to the adjacent corner point B. In walking from A to B, what changes take place in the set of nonbasic variables and the set of basic variables? Let us divide the answer to this question into two parts:

- **Nonbasic variables.** Corner point A lies at the intersection of the boundary equations $x_1 = 0$ and $x_2 = 0$, thereby indicating that x_1 and x_2 are the nonbasic variables at point A. As we walk from A to B, we never leave the boundary equation $x_2 = 0$, thereby indicating that x_2 maintains its value of 0 throughout the walk. Consequently, x_2 is a nonbasic variable at both A and B. In contrast, as we walk from A to B, we leave the boundary equation $x_1 = 0$ and walk in a direction that increases x_1 from 0 to increasingly positive values. Consequently, whereas x_1 is a nonbasic variable at point A, it is a basic variable at point B.

- **Basic variables.** Since corner point A lies on none of the boundary equations $S_1 = 0$, $S_2 = 0$, and $S_3 = 0$, the values of the slack variables are positive, thereby indicating that S_1, S_2, and S_3 are the basic variables at point A. As we walk from A to B, we get closer and closer to the boundary equations $S_1 = 0$, $S_2 = 0$, and $S_3 = 0$, and, consequently, the positive values of the slack variables all get closer and closer to 0. In fact, when we finally arrive at point B, we have "bumped into" the boundary equation $S_2 = 0$, thereby indicating that S_2 has decreased from its positive value at point A to a value of 0 at point B. Consequently, whereas S_2 was a basic variable at point A, it is a nonbasic variable at point B. In contrast, S_1 and S_2, which are basic variables at A, are still basic variables at B (though, because B is closer to the boundary equations $S_1 = 0$ and $S_3 = 0$, S_1 and S_3 will have decreased positive values).

Figure 6.4 diagrams the net effect the above changes have on the set of nonbasic variables and the set of basic variables. Observe that, as indicated by the arrows, the net effect is an exchange of "roles" between the two variables x_1 and S_2. Whereas x_1 is a nonbasic variable at A, it is a basic variable at B; whereas S_2 is a basic variable at A, it is a nonbasic variable at B. Since, in moving from A to B, x_1 enters the set of basic variables and S_2 leaves the set of basic variables, we refer to x_1 as the *entering basic variable* and S_2 as the *leaving basic variable*.[5]

We have just seen a geometrical illustration of the following general principle:

> After a move from one basic feasible solution to an adjacent basic feasible solution, there has been a one-for-one trade between the set of basic variables and the set of nonbasic variables. More specifically,
>
> - One member of the former set of nonbasic variables has increased from 0 to a positive value, thereby becoming a member of the set of basic variables.
>
> - One member of the former set of basic variables has decreased from a positive value to 0, thereby becoming a member of the set of nonbasic variables.
>
> These two variables are known respectively as the *entering basic variable* and the *leaving basic variable*.

This general principle will be extremely important when we learn how to algebraically move from one basic feasible solution to another. To check your understanding, you should attempt to geometrically identify the entering basic variable and the leaving basic variable when moving in Figure 6.3 from corner point B to corner point C. As diagrammed in Figure 6.5, the entering basic variable is x_2 and the

---

[5] Alternatively, we could refer to x_1 as the *leaving nonbasic variable* and S_2 as the *entering nonbasic variable*. However, it is customary to describe the exchange between the set of nonbasic variables and the set of basic variables in terms of what "leaves" and what "enters" the set of basic variables.

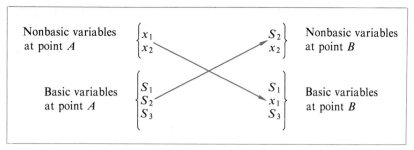

Figure 6.4 The one-for-one trade between the set of nonbasic variables and the set of basic variables when moving from A to B

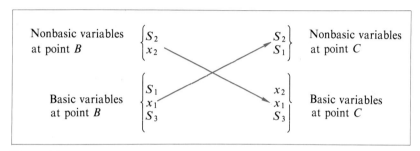

Figure 6.5 The one-for-one trade between the set of nonbasic variables and the set of basic variables when moving from B to C

leaving basic variable is S_1. (If you obtained a different answer you should reread this subsection.)

A Verbal "Preview" of the Simplex Method

Now that we understand the concept of adjacent basic feasible solutions, we can give the following verbal "preview" of how the simplex method solves an LP:

The simplex method is an algebraic method of moving from one basic feasible solution to an adjacent basic feasible solution. Each successive movement is known as an *iteration* of the simplex method. Each iteration makes progress toward identifying the optimal basic feasible solution, because the simplex method guarantees that movement is always from a basic feasible solution with a lower objective value to an adjacent basic feasible solution with a higher objective value. Thus the simplex method can never move to a basic feasible solution that it has previously "visited." Since each iteration visits a new basic feasible solution with an improved objective value, and since there are only a finite number of basic feasible solutions, the simplex method will terminate in a finite number of iterations at the optimal basic feasible solution.

Over the course of the next three sections, we will learn how to algebraically perform what is verbally described in the above preview.

Let us illustrate (using Figure 6.3) the geometrical implications of the fact that successive basic feasible solutions visited by the simplex method are adjacent. Suppose the simplex method starts its search for the LP's optimal solution at the basic feasible solution corresponding in Figure 6.3 to corner point A (the origin). Since the successive solutions visited by the simplex method are adjacent, the corresponding successive corner points in Figure 6.3 must also be adjacent. In Figure

6.3, there are only two possible sequences of adjacent corner points the simplex method can take from the origin at point A to the optimal solution at point D:

$$A \rightarrow B \rightarrow C \rightarrow D$$

$$A \rightarrow E \rightarrow D.$$

Whichever sequence the simplex method takes, it will be illustrative of the following general principle:

> The successive adjacent basic feasible solutions "visited" by the simplex method correspond geometrically to a "walk" along the feasible region's boundary that "visits" adjacent corner point after adjacent corner point until finally stopping at the optimal corner point.

6.5 MOVING FROM ONE BASIC FEASIBLE SOLUTION TO AN ADJACENT BASIC FEASIBLE SOLUTION

The key to understanding the simplex method is understanding how it moves from one basic feasible solution to an adjacent one with an improved objective value. In this section we have the more limited goal of understanding how to move from one basic feasible solution to an adjacent one without regard for whether the adjacent basic feasible solution has an improved objective value.

Transforming a System of Equations Using Elementary Equation Operations

As a first step, we must understand how to employ so-called *elementary equation operations* to transform a system of equations into an equivalent system of equations. In particular, we will employ the following two types of elementary equation operations:

1. **Multiplying a particular equation by a nonzero constant.** For example, Figure 6.6(a) displays a simple transformation of the equality form system of equa-

Figure 6.6 Examples of elementary equation operations

	Original System of Equations		Transformed System of Equations
(a)	$2x_1 + x_2 + S_1 \qquad\qquad = 20$ $4x_1 + x_2 \qquad + S_2 \qquad = 32$ $2x_1 + 7x_2 \qquad\qquad + S_3 = 88$	$\rightarrow$ $\rightarrow$ $\rightarrow$	$2x_1 + x_2 + S_1 \qquad\qquad\qquad = 20$ $4x_1 + x_2 \qquad\qquad + S_2 \qquad = 32$ $4x_1 + 14x_2 \qquad\qquad + 2S_3 = 176$
(b)	$2x_1 + x_2 + S_1 \qquad\qquad = 20$ $4x_1 + x_2 \qquad + S_2 \qquad = 32$ $2x_1 + 7x_2 \qquad\qquad + S_3 = 88$	$\rightarrow$ $\rightarrow$ $\rightarrow$	$2x_1 + x_2 + S_1 \qquad\qquad\qquad = 20$ $4x_1 + x_2 \qquad\qquad + S_2 \qquad = 32$ $-4x_1 + 4x_2 - 3S_1 \qquad\qquad + S_3 = 28$
(c)	$2x_1 + x_2 + S_1 \qquad\qquad = 20$ $4x_1 + x_2 \qquad + S_2 \qquad = 32$ $2x_1 + 7x_2 \qquad\qquad + S_3 = 88$	$\rightarrow$ $\rightarrow$ $\rightarrow$	$10x_1 + 3x_2 + S_1 + 2S_2 \qquad\qquad = 84$ $2x_1 + \frac{1}{2}x_2 \qquad + \frac{1}{2}S_2 \qquad = 16$ $-4x_1 + 4x_2 - 3S_1 \qquad\qquad + S_3 = 28$

tions for OMC's LP, in which we leave the first and second equations unchanged but multiply both sides of the third equation by 2.

2. **Replacing a particular equation by a new equation obtained by adding to or subtracting from the equation a specified multiple of another equation.** For example, Figure 6.6(b) displays a simple transformation of OMC's equality form system of equations in which we leave the first and second equations unchanged but replace the third equation by a new one obtained by subtracting from the third equation a multiple of three times the first equation. The computations proceed as follows:

$$
\begin{array}{lrcrcrcrcrcr}
\text{Third equation:} & 2x_1 & + & 7x_2 & + & 0S_1 & + & 0S_2 & + & 1S_3 & = & 88 \\
-3(\text{First equation}): & -3\,(2x_1 & + & 1x_2 & + & 1S_1 & + & 0S_2 & + & 0S_3 & = & 20) \\
\hline
\text{Transformed third equation:} & -4x_1 & + & 4x_2 & - & 3S_1 & + & 0S_2 & + & 1S_3 & = & 28
\end{array}
$$

To enable us to concisely describe a series of elementary equation operations, let us use the Roman numerals I, II, III, and so on, to identify equations in the current system of equations, and let us use the primed Roman numerals I', II', III', and so on, to identify the revised system of equations resulting from a series of elementary equation operations. Using this notation, for example, we can concisely describe Figure 6.6(b)'s transformation as

$$
\begin{aligned}
I' &= I \\
II' &= II \\
III' &= III - 3I
\end{aligned}
$$

In contrast to Figure 6.6(a) and Figure 6.6(b), which display transformations that change only one equation, Figure 6.6(c) displays a transformation in which elementary equation operations are employed to revise all three equations. In particular, the transformation employs the following three elementary equation operations

$$
\begin{aligned}
I' &= I + 2II \\
II' &= \tfrac{1}{2}II \\
III' &= III - 3I
\end{aligned}
$$

We verified above the algebra involved in the transformation of equation III. Before proceeding, you should verify the algebra involved in the transformation of equations I and III.

From your high-school algebra days, you may recall the following general principle:

> Although employing a series of elementary equation operations does alter the appearance of the system of equations (by changing the variables' coefficients and the equations' right-hand sides), the transformed system of equations is equivalent to the original system in the sense that both have exactly the same set of solutions.

To convince yourself of the validity of this general principle, reconsider Table 6.1 and Table 6.2, which display some solutions to the equality form system of equations for OMC's LP. Verify that each solution also satisfies Figure 6.6(c)'s transformed system of equations. (To verify, simply substitute the values for a solution in Table 6.1 or 6.2 into the left-hand sides of the transformed equations in Figure 6.6(c).)

Moving from One Basic Solution to Another by Employing Elementary Equation Operations

Consider now OMC's equality form system of equations. Recall that, to identify a basic feasible solution, we first choose two of the five variables to be the nonbasic variables, then set these nonbasic variables equal to 0, and finally solve the resulting system of three equations involving the three basic variables. Given the format of OMC's equality form system of equations, there is one basic solution that is much easier to identify than all the others. To illustrate, Figure 6.7 contains, for each of three distinct choices for the two nonbasic variables, the resulting system of three equations involving the three basic variables (where the columns corresponding to the nonbasic variables are shaded to indicate they are to be ignored). Which of Figure 6.7's three systems of equations is easiest to solve? The answer is clearly the system corresponding to choice 1. Solving it requires no computational effort whatsoever. It is immediately evident that the values of the basic variables S_1, S_2, and S_3 equal the values appearing on the equations' right-hand sides; that is,

- S_1 equals equation I's right-hand side of 20,
- S_2 equals equation II's right-hand side of 32,
- S_3 equals equation III's right-hand side of 88.

In contrast, some computational effort is required to solve the system of equations corresponding to either choice 2 or choice 3. You can verify for yourself that every other choice for the nonbasic variables leads to a system of equations that, like those corresponding to choices 2 and 3, require computational effort to solve.

Why in Figure 6.7 does choice 1 for the nonbasic variables lead to an immediate identification of the basic variables' values, whereas choices 2 and 3 do not? We can provide a precise answer to this question by adopting the following terminology:

Choice 1: Nonbasic Variables are x_1 and x_2

$$
\begin{aligned}
2x_1 + x_2 + S_1 \quad\quad\quad &= 20 \\
4x_1 + x_2 \quad\quad + S_2 \quad\quad &= 32 \\
2x_1 + 7x_2 \quad\quad\quad + S_3 &= 88
\end{aligned}
$$

Choice 2: Nonbasic Variables are x_2 and S_2

$$
\begin{aligned}
2x_1 + x_2 + S_1 \quad\quad\quad &= 20 \\
4x_1 + x_2 \quad\quad + S_2 \quad\quad &= 32 \\
2x_1 + 7x_2 \quad\quad\quad + S_3 &= 88
\end{aligned}
$$

Choice 3: Nonbasic Variables are S_1 and S_2

$$
\begin{aligned}
2x_1 + x_2 + S_1 \quad\quad\quad &= 20 \\
4x_1 + x_2 \quad\quad + S_2 \quad\quad &= 32 \\
2x_1 + 7x_2 \quad\quad\quad + S_3 &= 88
\end{aligned}
$$

Figure 6.7 The square system of equations resulting from three alternative choices for the nonbasic variables

Given a system of m linear equations involving n variables (with $m < n$):

- A variable is said to be an *isolated variable* in a particular equation if its coefficient in that equation equals 1 and its coefficient in every other equation equals 0.

- A set of m variables is said to be an *isolated set of variables* if each of the m variables is an isolated variable in a different one of the m equations.

In the equality form system of equations for OMC's LP,

$$\begin{array}{rrrrrrr} 2x_1 & + & x_2 & + & S_1 & & & & = & 20 \\ 4x_1 & + & x_2 & & & + & S_2 & & = & 32 \\ 2x_1 & + & 7x_2 & & & & & + & S_3 & = & 88, \end{array}$$

S_1 is an isolated variable in equation I, S_2 is an isolated variable in equation II, and S_3 is an isolated variable in equation III; that is, each of the three variables is an isolated variable in a different one of the three equations. Hence, $\{S_1, S_2, S_3\}$ is an isolated set of variables. This isolation of the variables S_1, S_2, and S_3 is what makes it so easy to identify their values in choice 1 of Figure 6.7, when x_1 and x_2 are chosen as the nonbasic variables. In contrast, observe that, when S_1 and S_2 are chosen as the nonbasic variables in choice 3 of Figure 6.7, the only isolated variable among the basic variables x_1, x_2, and S_3 is S_3. Figure 6.7, in conjunction with the concept of an isolated variable, illustrates the following general principle:

Consider a system of m linear equations involving n variables (with $m < n$). For a given choice of the $(n-m)$ nonbasic variables to set equal to 0, immediate identification of the basic variables' values is possible if the basic variables are an isolated set of variables. More specifically, the value of a basic variable isolated in a particular equation equals the equation's right-hand side.

Now that we understand how isolating the set of basic variables in the system of equations makes their values readily apparent, we can begin to explain how to move from one basic feasible solution to an adjacent one. To illustrate, let us "visit" two adjacent basic feasible solutions for OMC's equality form system of equations. We begin our "visitations" at the basic solution

$$(x_1, x_2, S_1, S_2, S_3) = (0, 0, 20, 32, 88)$$

—the basic solution that we observed to be so easily identified because of the isolation of basic variables S_1, S_2, and S_3 in OMC's equality form system of equations. This basic solution corresponds in Figure 6.3 to point A. Let us now see how to move algebraically to the adjacent basic feasible solution corresponding to point B. Recall that this movement involves the one-for-one trade between the set of nonbasic variables and the set of basic variables that is diagramed in Figure 6.4. In particular, the entering basic variable is x_1 and the leaving basic variable is S_2. Consequently, the set of basic variables changes from $\{S_1, S_2, S_3\}$ at A to $\{S_1, x_1, S_3\}$ at B. At the basic solution corresponding to point B, one way to find the basic variables' values would be to perform the work necessary to solve the system of equations displayed in Figure 6.7 under choice 2. Instead, however, let us employ elementary equation operations to transform the system of equations

$$\begin{array}{rrrrrrr} 2x_1 & + & x_2 & + & S_1 & & & & = & 20 \\ 4x_1 & + & x_2 & & & + & S_2 & & = & 32 \\ 2x_1 & + & 7x_2 & & & & & + & S_3 & = & 88 \end{array}$$

into an equivalent system in which the new set of basic variables is an isolated set of variables, thereby making their values readily apparent when the nonbasic variables are set equal to 0.

We will illustrate the process by referring to Figure 6.8. Figure 6.8(a) displays OMC's equality form system of equations using the Roman numerals *I*, *II*, and *III* to identify the equations. Keep in mind that our goal is to make $\{S_1, x_1, S_3\}$, the set of basic variables at point *B*, an isolated set of variables. Looking at Figure 6.8(a), observe that two members of the set of basic variables, S_1 and S_3, are already isolated variables because they are also basic variables at point *A*. In particular, S_1 is isolated in equation *I*, and S_3 is isolated in equation *III*. The only basic variable that is not isolated is the entering basic variable x_1. Hence, in transforming the system of equations into an equivalent system of equations in which the new set of basic variables is isolated, our goal is to preserve the existing isolation of S_1 in equation *I* and S_3 in equation *III* while simultaneously isolating the entering basic variable x_1 in equation *II*, in which the leaving basic variable S_2 is now isolated. We can achieve this goal by employing a special type of transformation of the system of equations, in which specific rules govern the transformation's elementary equation operations. A transformation governed by these special rules is known as a *pivot*. Described below is a pivot that transforms the system of equations in Figure 6.8(a) using specific rules that preserve the existing isolation of S_1 in equation *I* and S_3 in equation *III* while simultaneously isolating x_1 in equation *II*:

1. **Identification of a pivot variable and a pivot equation.** To perform a pivot, we must first identify a *pivot variable* and a *pivot equation*. The pivot variable is always the entering basic variable, and the pivot equation is always the equation in which the leaving basic variable is now an isolated variable or, equivalently, the equation in which the entering basic variable is to become an isolated variable. In our example, the pivot variable is the entering basic variable x_1, and the pivot equation is equation *II*, in which the leaving basic variable S_2 is now isolated and in which the entering basic variable x_1 is to become isolated. Our goal in the pivot's subsequent steps is to isolate the pivot variable x_1 in equation *II* while simultaneously preserving the existing isolation of S_1 in equation *I* and S_3 in equation *III*.

Figure 6.8 A summary of the first pivot

$$
\begin{array}{llll}
 & I & : & 2x_1 + 1x_2 + 1S_1 + 0S_2 + 0S_3 = 20 \\
(a) & II & : & 4x_1 + 1x_2 + 0S_1 + 1S_2 + 0S_3 = 32 \\
 & III & : & 2x_1 + 7x_2 + 0S_1 + 0S_2 + 1S_3 = 88
\end{array}
$$

$$
\begin{array}{llll}
 & I & : & 2x_1 + 1x_2 + 1S_1 + 0S_2 + 0S_3 = 20 \\
(b) & II' = \tfrac{1}{4} II & : & 1x_1 + \tfrac{1}{4}x_2 + 0S_1 + \tfrac{1}{4}S_2 + 0S_3 = 8 \\
 & III' & : & 2x_1 + 7x_2 + 0S_1 + 0S_2 + 1S_3 = 88
\end{array}
$$

$$
\begin{array}{llll}
 & I' = \; I - 2II' & : & 0x_1 + \tfrac{1}{2}x_2 + 1S_1 - \tfrac{1}{2}S_2 + 0S_3 = 4 \\
(c) & II' & : & 1x_1 + \tfrac{1}{4}x_2 + 0S_1 + \tfrac{1}{4}S_2 + 0S_3 = 8 \\
 & III & : & 2x_1 + 7x_2 + 0S_1 + 0S_2 + 1S_3 = 88
\end{array}
$$

$$
\begin{array}{llll}
 & I' & : & 0x_1 + \tfrac{1}{2}x_2 + 1S_1 - \tfrac{1}{2}S_2 + 0S_3 = 4 \\
(d) & II' & : & 1x_1 + \tfrac{1}{4}x_2 + 0S_1 + \tfrac{1}{4}S_2 + 0S_3 = 8 \\
 & III' = \; III - 2II' & : & 0x_1 + \tfrac{13}{2}x_2 + 0S_1 - \tfrac{1}{2}S_2 + 1S_3 = 72
\end{array}
$$

2. **Transforming the pivot equation so that the pivot variable's coefficient equals 1.** Isolation of x_1 in equation *II* requires that x_1 have a coefficient of 1 in equation *II* and coefficients of 0 in equations *I* and *III*. In this step we concern ourselves with x_1's coefficient in equation *II*. Given that the pivot equation, equation *II*, is

$$4x_1 + 1x_2 + 0S_1 + 1S_2 + 0S_3 = 32,$$

we can easily transform the equation into an equivalent one in which x_1's coefficient is 1 by the elementary equation operation $II' = \frac{1}{4} II$; that is, we multiply both sides of the equation by $\frac{1}{4}$, thereby obtaining

$$1x_1 + \tfrac{1}{4}x_2 + 0S_1 + \tfrac{1}{4}S_2 + 0S_3 = 8.$$

Figure 6.8(b) displays the status of the system of equations after the transformation of the pivot equation.

3. **Transformation of the other equations so that the pivot variable's coefficient equals 0.** Our goal here is to use elementary equation operations to transform equations *I* and *III* into equivalent equations in which x_1's coefficients are both 0. According to the rules of a pivot, we achieve this goal by elementary equation operations that replace equations *I* and *III* with transformed equations obtained by subtracting from equation *I* and *III* appropriate multiples of the transformed pivot equation, equation *II'*. To illustrate, first consider equation *I*. Listed below are equations *I* and *II'*, with equation *I* on top:

$$
\begin{array}{lllllll}
I: & 2x_1 + & 1x_2 + & 1S_1 + & 0S_2 + & 0S_3 = & 20 \\
II': & 1x_1 + & \tfrac{1}{4}x_2 + & 0S_1 + & \tfrac{1}{4}S_2 + & 0S_3 = & 8
\end{array}
$$

Can you determine what multiple of equation *II'* must be subtracted from equation *I* to obtain a transformed equation *I* in which x_1's coefficient equals 0? The answer is 2, the coefficient of the pivot variable x_1 in equation *I*. The algebra proceeds as follows:

$$
\begin{array}{lllllll}
I: & 2x_1 + & 1x_2 + & 1S_1 + & 0S_2 + & 0S_3 = & 20 \\
-2II': & -2(1x_1 + & \tfrac{1}{4}x_2 + & 0S_1 + & \tfrac{1}{4}S_2 + & 0S_3 = & 8) \\
\hline
I': & 0x_1 + & \tfrac{1}{2}x_2 + & 1S_1 - & \tfrac{1}{2}S_2 + & 0S_3 = & 4
\end{array}
$$

Figure 6.8(c) displays the status of the system of equations after the transformation of equation *I*. Let us now focus our attention on equation *III*. Listed below are equations *III* and *II'*, with equation *III* on top:

$$
\begin{array}{lllllll}
III: & 2x_1 + & 7x_2 + & 0S_1 + & 0S_2 + & 1S_3 = & 88 \\
II': & 1x_1 + & \tfrac{1}{4}x_2 + & 0S_1 + & \tfrac{1}{4}S_2 + & 0S_3 = & 8
\end{array}
$$

Can you determine what multiple of equation *II'* must be subtracted from equation *III* to obtain a transformed equation *I* in which x_1's coefficient equals 0? The answer (coincidentally) is again 2, the coefficient of the pivot variable x_1 in equation *III*. The algebra proceeds as follows:

$$
\begin{array}{lllllll}
III: & 2x_1 + & 7x_2 + & 0S_1 + & 0S_2 + & 1S_3 = & 88 \\
-2II': & -2(1x_1 + & \tfrac{1}{4}x_2 + & 0S_1 + & \tfrac{1}{4}S_2 + & 0S_3 = & 8) \\
\hline
III': & 0x_1 + & \tfrac{13}{2}x_2 + & 0S_1 - & \tfrac{1}{2}S_2 + & 1S_3 = & 72
\end{array}
$$

The transformation of equation *III* completes the pivot. Figure 6.8(d) displays the status of the system of equations after the completion of the pivot.

Observe in Figure 6.8(d) that the transformation of the system of equations has achieved the goal of preserving the isolation of S_1 and S_3 in equations I' and III' while simultaneously isolating the entering basic variable x_1 in equation II'.

Given the system of equations obtained by the pivot in Figure 6.8, we can immediately identify the basic variables' values after setting the nonbasic variables equal to 0. In particular, setting the nonbasic variables x_2 and S_2 equal to 0 results in the following system of equations (where the columns corresponding to the nonbasic variables are shaded to indicate they are to be ignored):

$$
\begin{array}{lrcccccccccc}
I': & 0x_1 & + & \tfrac{1}{2}x_2 & + & 1S_1 & - & \tfrac{1}{2}S_2 & + & 0S_3 & = & 4 \\
II': & 1x_1 & + & \tfrac{1}{4}x_2 & + & 0S_1 & + & \tfrac{1}{4}S_2 & + & 0S_3 & = & 8 \\
III': & 0x_1 & + & \tfrac{13}{2}x_2 & + & 0S_1 & - & \tfrac{1}{2}S_2 & + & 1S_3 & = & 72
\end{array}
$$

It is immediately evident that the basic variables' values are equal to the equations' right-hand sides; that is,

$$
\begin{array}{rcl}
S_1 & = & 4 \\
x_1 & = & 8 \\
S_3 & = & 72
\end{array}
$$

Thus, Figure 6.8(d)'s transformed system of equations enables us to immediately identify the basic feasible solution

$$(x_1, x_2, S_1, S_2, S_3) = (8, 0, 4, 0, 72).$$

This basic feasible solution corresponds geometrically in Figure 6.3 to point *B*. Hence, the pivot summarized in Figure 6.8 has moved us from the basic feasible solution corresponding in Figure 6.3 to point *A* to the adjacent basic feasible solution corresponding to point *B*.

A Summary

Figure 6.9 summarizes our movement from the basic feasible solution corresponding in Figure 6.3 to point *A* to the adjacent basic feasible solution corresponding to point *B*. Observe the following aspects:

- The figure's first two columns diagram the one-for-one trade between the set of nonbasic variables and the set of basic variables that initiates the movement from one basic feasible solution to the next.

- The figure's third column is simply a condensation of the pivot displayed earlier in Figure 6.8(a)–(d).

- The figure's fourth column is the basic feasible solution immediately identified when the nonbasic variables are set equal to 0.

- The figure's last column is the point in Figure 6.3's graph of OMC's feasible region that corresponds to the basic feasible solution. (The point's (x_1, x_2) coordinates are obtained from simply reading the values of x_1 and x_2 from the figure's fourth column.)

Set of Nonbasic Variables	Set of Basic Variables	System of Equations		Variables' Values $(x_1, x_2, S_1, S_2, S_3)$	Corresponding Corner Point in Figure 6.3's Feasible Region
$x_1 \quad x_2$	$S_1 \; S_2 \; S_3$	I :	$2x_1 + 1x_2 + 1S_1 + 0S_2 + 0S_3 = 20$	$(0, 0, 20, 32, 88)$	A
		II :	$4x_1 + 1x_2 + 0S_1 + 1S_2 + 0S_3 = 32$		
		III :	$2x_1 + 7x_2 + 0S_1 + 0S_2 + 1S_3 = 88$		
$S_2 \quad x_2$	$S_1 \; x_1 \; S_3$	$I' = I - 2II'$:	$0x_1 + \frac{1}{2}x_2 + 1S_1 - \frac{1}{2}S_2 + 0S_3 = 4$	$(8, 0, 4, 0, 72)$	B
		$II' = \frac{1}{4}II$:	$1x_1 + \frac{1}{4}x_2 + 0S_1 + \frac{1}{4}S_2 + 0S_3 = 8$		
		$III' = III - 2II'$:	$0x_1 + \frac{13}{2}x_2 + 0S_1 - \frac{1}{2}S_2 + 1S_3 = 72$		

Figure 6.9 A summary of the pivot

Figure 6.9 illustrates the following general principle:

To move from one basic feasible solution to an adjacent one, we must first specify the entering basic variable and the leaving basic variable; that is, we must first specify a current nonbasic variable to become a basic variable and a current basic variable to become a nonbasic variable. (In this section, we have identified the entering basic variable and the leaving basic variable from geometrical observations made in Section 6.4. In subsequent sections, we will learn how to algebraically select the entering basic variable and the leaving basic variable.) We next perform a *pivot*, a transformation of the system of equations that preserves the existing isolation of those current basic variables that will remain basic while simultaneously isolating the entering basic variable in the equation in which the leaving basic variable is now isolated. The pivot consists of the following steps:

1. **Identification of the pivot variable and the pivot equation.** The pivot variable is the entering basic variable. The pivot equation is the equation that now contains the leaving basic variable as an isolated variable or, equivalently, the equation in which the entering basic variable is to become an isolated variable.

2. **Transformation of the pivot equation so that the pivot variable's coefficient equals 1.** We employ here the following elementary equation operation:

$$\text{transformed pivot equation} = \frac{1}{c}\,(\text{current pivot equation}),$$

where c is a constant equal to the pivot variable's coefficient in the pivot equation.

3. **Transformation of every other equation so that the pivot variable's coefficient equals 0.** To transform every other equation into an equivalent equation in which the pivot variable's coefficient equals 0, we perform the following elementary equation operation:

$$\text{transformed equation} = \text{current equation} - k\,(\textit{transformed} \text{ pivot equation}),$$

where k is a constant equal to the pivot variable's current coefficient in the equation undergoing transformation.

At the conclusion of the pivot, the basic variables' values can be determined immediately from the transformed equations' right-hand sides. In particular, the value of the basic variable isolated in a particular equation equals the equation's right-hand side. Of course, the nonbasic variables' values are 0.

6.6 ALGEBRAICALLY SELECTING THE ENTERING BASIC VARIABLE AND THE LEAVING BASIC VARIABLE

We have thus far relied on Figure 6.3's geometry to identify the entering basic variable and the leaving basic variable. In this section we will learn how to algebraically select the entering basic variable and the leaving basic variable in a way that guarantees movement not only to an adjacent basic feasible solution but also to one with an improved objective value.

Let us consider the transformation of OMC's equality form system of equations displayed at the bottom of Figure 6.9.[6] This system of equations enables immediate identification of the basic feasible solution

$$(x_1, x_2, S_1, S_2, S_3) = (8, 0, 4, 0, 72),$$

in which the nonbasic variables are x_2 and S_2 and the basic variables are x_1, S_1, and S_3. To move to an adjacent basic feasible solution, we follow the general principle introduced in the previous section; that is, we

1. Select one of the nonbasic variables x_2 and S_2 to be the entering basic variable.

2. Select one of the basic variables x_1, S_1, and S_3 to be the leaving basic variable.

3. Transform the system of equations by performing the appropriate pivot.

In executing this procedure, however, we will introduce specific rules for choosing the entering basic variable and leaving basic variable—rules that guarantee a move to an adjacent basic feasible solution that has an improved objective value.

Constructing a Simplex Tableau

The numerical calculations we will perform to select the entering basic variable and the leaving basic variable involve some "messy" algebra. We will be able to perform this algebra faster and with fewer errors if we organize the data in a tabular format known as a *simplex tableau*. Figure 6.10 displays six copies of the simplex tableau corresponding to the transformed system of equations displayed at the bottom of Figure 6.9, with each copy having a different portion of the tableau shaded in color. The contents of each highlighted portion is as follows:

Portion of Simplex Tableau Shaded in Figure 6.10(a). This shaded portion displays the system of equations with the variables "detached" from their coefficients. Within the shaded portion, a vertical bar plays the role of =, separating each

---

[6] We use this transformation of OMC's equality form system of equations instead of the original system because it better illustrates the concepts we learn in this section.

Equation	Basic Variable	c_j / c_B	9 x_1	6 x_2	0 S_1	0 S_2	0 S_3	RHS
$I' = I - 2II'$	S_1	0	0	$\frac12$	1	$-\frac12$	0	4
$II' = \frac14 II$	x_1	9	1	$\frac14$	0	$\frac14$	0	8
$III' = III - 2II'$	S_3	0	0	$\frac{13}{2}$	0	$-\frac12$	1	72
		z_j						$OV = 72$
		$c_j - z_j$						

(a)

Equation	Basic Variable	c_j / c_B	9 x_1	6 x_2	0 S_1	0 S_2	0 S_3	RHS
$I' = I - 2II'$	S_1	0	0	$\frac12$	1	$-\frac12$	0	4
$II' = \frac14 II$	x_1	9	1	$\frac14$	0	$\frac14$	0	8
$III' = III - 2II'$	S_3	0	0	$\frac{13}{2}$	0	$-\frac12$	1	72
		z_j						$OV = 72$
		$c_j - z_j$						

(b)

Equation	Basic Variable	c_j / c_B	9 x_1	6 x_2	0 S_1	0 S_2	0 S_3	RHS
$I' = I - 2II'$	S_1	0	0	$\frac12$	1	$-\frac12$	0	4
$II' = \frac14 II$	x_1	9	1	$\frac14$	0	$\frac14$	0	8
$III' = III - 2II'$	S_3	0	0	$\frac{13}{2}$	0	$-\frac12$	1	72
		z_j						$OV = 72$
		$c_j - z_j$						

(c)

Equation	Basic Variable	c_j / c_B	9 x_1	6 x_2	0 S_1	0 S_2	0 S_3	RHS
$I' = I - 2II'$	S_1	0	0	$\frac12$	1	$-\frac12$	0	4
$II' = \frac14 II$	x_1	9	1	$\frac14$	0	$\frac14$	0	8
$III' = III - 2II'$	S_3	0	0	$\frac{13}{2}$	0	$-\frac12$	1	72
		z_j						$OV = 72$
		$c_j - z_j$						

(d)

Equation	Basic Variable	c_j / c_B	9 x_1	6 x_2	0 S_1	0 S_2	0 S_3	RHS
$I' = I - 2II'$	S_1	0	0	$\frac12$	1	$-\frac12$	0	4
$II' = \frac14 II$	x_1	9	1	$\frac14$	0	$\frac14$	0	8
$III' = III - 2II'$	S_3	0	0	$\frac{13}{2}$	0	$-\frac12$	1	72
		z_j						$OV = 72$
		$c_j - z_j$						

(e)

Equation	Basic Variable	c_j / c_B	9 x_1	6 x_2	0 S_1	0 S_2	0 S_3	RHS
$I' = I - 2II'$	S_1	0	0	$\frac12$	1	$-\frac12$	0	4
$II' = \frac14 II$	x_1	9	1	$\frac14$	0	$\frac14$	0	8
$III' = III - 2II'$	S_3	0	0	$\frac{13}{2}$	0	$-\frac12$	1	72
		z_j						$OV = 72$
		$c_j - z_j$						

(f)

Figure 6.10 The six portions of a simplex tableau

equation's right-hand-side (abbreviated by *RHS*) from its left-hand-side coefficients. For example, equation II',

$$1x_1 + \tfrac14 x_2 + 0S_1 + \tfrac14 S_2 + 0S_3 = 8,$$

is represented in the tableau as

x_1	x_2	S_1	S_2	S_3	RHS
1	$\frac14$	0	$\frac14$	0	8

Portion of Simplex Tableau Shaded in Figure 6.10(b). This shaded portion is the tableau's first column. Under the heading "Equation" the first column simply identifies the equations with the Roman numerals I', II', and III'. We will use these Roman numerals not only to refer to the equations but also to describe elementary equation operations. For example, the notation $II' = II - \frac{1}{4}I'$ indicates that the transformed equation II equals the former equation II minus $\frac{1}{4}$ times the transformed equation I.

Portion of the Simplex Tableau Shaded in Figure 6.10(c). This shaded portion is the tableau's second column. Under the heading "Basic Variable" the second column displays for each equation the basic variable that is isolated in that equation. (Recall that each basic variable is isolated in a different one of the three equations.) For example, since x_1's coefficients in equations I', II', and III' are respectively 0, 1, and 0, the tableau's second column indicates that x_1 is the basic variable isolated in equation II'. The Basic Variable column, in conjunction with the RHS column, enables immediate identification of the variables' current values. In particular, any variable that does not appear in the Basic Variable column is a nonbasic variable and, by definition, has a value of 0. Furthermore, owing to the nonbasic variables' values of 0 and the basic variables' isolation, the basic variables equal the values appearing in the tableau's RHS column. For example, looking at Figure 6.10(c)'s Basic Variable column and the RHS column, we can immediately identify the values of the basic variables S_1, x_1, and S_3 as 4, 8, and 72, respectively. Furthermore, given the absence of x_2 and S_2 from the Basic Variable column, we can immediately identify their values as 0.

Portion of Simplex Tableau Shaded in Figure 6.10(d). This shaded portion consists of two distinct parts:

1. a row of numbers appearing in the tableau's top row to the right of the heading "c_j" and

2. a column of numbers appearing in the tableau's third column under the heading "c_B".

To explain the contents of the c_j row and the c_B column, let

$$c_j = \text{the } j\text{th variable's objective-function coefficient;}$$

that is, let c_1 and c_2 denote the objective-function coefficient of the decision variables x_1 and x_2, and let c_3, c_4, and c_5 denote the objective-function coefficient of the slack variables S_1, S_2, and S_3. Since OMC's objective-function is to "Maximize $9x_1 + 6x_2$," $c_1 = 9$, $c_2 = 6$, $c_3 = 0$, $c_4 = 0$, and $c_5 = 0$. Observe that these objective-function coefficients are precisely the contents of Figure 6.10(d)'s highlighted c_j row. The c_B column contains a subset of the objective-function coefficients appearing in the c_j row. In particular, the c_B column displays the objective-function coefficients corresponding to the basic variables listed in the Basic Variable column. For example, since x_1 appears in the Basic Variable column as equation II's basic variable, its objective-function coefficient appears to the right in the c_B column.[7] You may be wondering why we include the c_B column, since the same information is available in the c_j row. We will soon see that, despite its redundancy, the c_B column is useful.

Portion of the Simplex Tableau Shaded in Figure 6.10(e). This shaded portion contains the current basic feasible solution's objective value (abbreviated by OV). In computing the objective value, we need only consider the basic variables' values, since the nonbasic variables equal 0. The basic variables' objective-function coefficients are listed in the simplex tableau's c_B column, and the basic variables'

---

[7] The c_B column's heading was chosen as a reminder that its contents are the objective-function coefficients of the basic variables ("c" stands for "coefficient," and the subscript "B" stands for "Basic").

values are listed in the simplex tableau's *RHS* column. To compute the objective value, then, we need only multiply the corresponding values in the c_B column and the *RHS* column and sum each of the products. These computations are summarized as follows:

Basic Variable's Objective-Function Coefficient As Given By the Simplex Tableau's c_B Column		Basic Variable's Value As Given By the Simplex Tableau's *RHS* Column		Product
0	×	4	=	0
9	×	8	=	72
0	×	72	=	0
				72 ← Sum of products

After computing the objective value as diagramed above, we display it in the simplex tableau's *OV* portion, as illustrated in Figure 6.10(e).

Portion of the Simplex Tableau Shaded in Figure 6.10(f). This shaded portion consists of two distinct parts:

1. a blank row appearing in the tableau's next-to-the-last row to the right of the heading z_j, and

2. a blank row appearing in the tableau's last row to the right of the heading $c_j - z_j$.

The z_j row and the $c_j - z_j$ row are used to summarize calculations required to select the entering basic variable. Consequently, we will postpone discussion of these two rows until the next subsection.

Selection of the Entering Basic Variable

Our goal in this subsection is to learn how to use the simplex tableau to select the entering basic variable in a way that guarantees that the new basic feasible solution will have an improved objective value. When changing from a nonbasic variable to a basic variable, the entering basic variable's value will change from 0 to a nonzero value. Although we do not yet know the specific nonzero value the entering basic variable will take on, we know with certainty that the nonzero value will be positive (since a basic feasible solution must have nonnegative values for all variables).

Let us examine the effects that increasing the entering basic variable from its current value of 0 has on the basic variables' value. Consider Figure 6.11, in which the coefficients of the nonbasic variables x_2 and S_2 are shaded to enable us to quickly identify them. Figure 6.11's top portion is simply a copy of the system of equations displayed in Figure 6.10's simplex tableau, with the variables' coefficients reattached to the variables. Figure 6.11's middle portion displays the system of equations obtained by transferring to the equations' right-hand sides all terms involving the nonbasic variables x_2 and S_2. Figure 6.11's bottom portion displays the two systems of equations obtained as follows:

- **Bottom-left portion.** If we select x_2 as the entering basic variable, S_2 will remain a nonbasic variable and, hence, will maintain its current value of 0. Consequently, we can delete from the system of equations in Figure 6.11's middle portion all terms involving S_2, thereby obtaining the system of equations displayed in Figure 6.11's bottom-left portion.

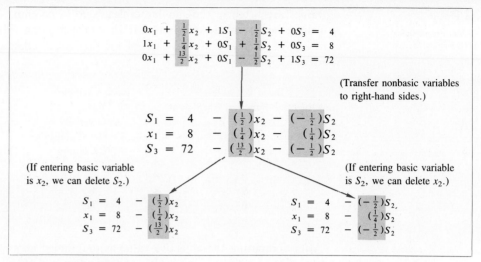

Figure 6.11 The effect that increasing a nonbasic variable has on the basic variables' values

- **Bottom-right portion.** If we select S_2 as the entering basic variable, x_2 will remain a nonbasic variable and, hence, will maintain its current value of 0. Consequently, we can delete from the system of equations in Figure 6.11's middle portion all terms involving x_2, thereby obtaining the system of equations displayed in Figure 6.11's bottom-right portion.

Figure 6.11's bottom-left and bottom-right portions enable us to easily determine the effect the choice of the entering basic variable has on the current basic variables' values.

Suppose we select x_2 as the entering basic variable. The system of equations in Figure 6.11's bottom-left portion makes it evident that, as the entering basic variable x_2 increases from its current value of 0, the current basic variables' values change as follows:

- S_1 decreases from its current value of 4 at the rate of $\frac{1}{2}$ per unit increase in x_2.

- x_1 decreases from its current value of 8 at the rate of $\frac{1}{4}$ per unit increase in x_2.

- S_3 decreases from its current value of 72 at the rate of $\frac{13}{2}$ per unit increase in x_2.

Observe from the shading in Figure 6.11 that these rates of decrease for S_1, and x_1, and S_3 are precisely the coefficients of x_2 in Figure 6.10's simplex tableau.

Suppose we select S_2 as the entering basic variable. The system of equations in Figure 6.11's bottom-right portion makes it evident that, as the entering basic variable S_2 increases from its current value of 0, the current basic variables' values change as follows:

- S_1 decreases from its current value of 8 at the rate of $-\frac{1}{2}$ per unit increase in x_2 (i.e., S_1 increases at the rate of $\frac{1}{2}$).

- x_1 decreases from its current value of 72 at the rate of $\frac{1}{4}$ per unit increase in x_2.

- S_3 decreases from its current value of 12 at the rate of $-\frac{1}{2}$ per unit increase in x_2 (i.e., S_3 increases at the rate of $\frac{1}{2}$).

Observe from the shading in Figure 6.11 that these rates of decrease for S_1, and x_1, and S_3 are precisely the coefficients of S_2 in Figure 6.10's simplex tableau.

We have just illustrated the following general principle:

> As the entering basic variable increases, the rates of decrease in the current basic variables' values equal the entering basic variable's coefficients in the simplex tableau. (Note that a negative rate of, say, -2 corresponds to a rate of increase of 2.)

This general principle is extremely useful, because it will save us time as we subsequently explain the details of selecting the entering basic variable. In particular, many occasions will arise in which we need to answer the question, "What are the current basic variables' rates of decrease per unit increase in the entering basic variable?" If we had to answer this question without knowledge of the above general principle, we would have to repeatedly go through algebra similar to that displayed in Figure 6.11. Fortunately, the general principle enables us to answer the question immediately by simply looking at the entering basic variable's coefficients in the simplex tableau. (Because of the importance of this general principle, make sure you understand it before proceeding.)

Now we can put our knowledge to use. Suppose for the moment that we choose x_2 as the entering basic variable. What is the rate of increase in the objective value per unit increase in x_2? Since the LP's objective function is "Maximize $9x_1 + 6x_2$," it is tempting to answer that every unit increase in x_2 results in an increase in the objective value of 6, the objective-function coefficient of x_2 appearing in the c_j row of Figure 6.11's simplex tableau. Such an answer is incorrect, however, because it fails to account for any decrease in the objective value resulting from the decreases in the basic variables necessary to compensate for the increase in the entering basic variable x_2. More specifically, we observed earlier that, as x_2 increases, the basic variables S_1, x_1, and S_3 decrease according to the rates given by the entering basic variable's coefficients in the simplex tableau; that is,

$$S_1\text{'s rate of decrease} = \begin{pmatrix} \text{entering basic variable } x_2\text{'s} \\ \text{simplex tableau coefficient} \\ \text{in equation } I' \end{pmatrix} = \frac{1}{2}$$

$$x_1\text{'s rate of decrease} = \begin{pmatrix} \text{entering basic variable } x_2\text{'s} \\ \text{simplex tableau coefficient} \\ \text{in equation } II' \end{pmatrix} = \frac{1}{4}$$

$$S_3\text{'s rate of decrease} = \begin{pmatrix} \text{entering basic variable } x_2\text{'s} \\ \text{simplex tableau coefficient} \\ \text{in equation } III' \end{pmatrix} = \frac{13}{2}$$

These decreases in the basic variables result in a decrease in the objective value—a decrease we will have to compute and then subtract from the entering basic variable's objective function coefficient in order to determine the net rate of increase in the objective value per unit increase in the entering basic variable.

To summarize, we have identified the following two effects that increasing the entering basic variable x_2 has on the objective value:

1. Since x_2's objective function coefficient is 6, the objective value will *increase* at the rate of 6 per unit increase in x_2.

2. Owing to the adjustment in the basic variables' values necessary to compensate for the increase in x_2, the objective value will *decrease* at a yet-to-be determined rate per unit increase in x_2.

Hereafter, we refer to item 1's rate as the objective value's *direct rate of increase* and to item 2's rate as the objective value's *indirect rate of decrease*.[8]

To determine the objective value's *net rate of increase* per unit increase in the entering basic variable x_2, we simply subtract the indirect rate of decrease from the direct rate of increase; that is,

$$\begin{pmatrix} \text{objective value's} \\ \text{net rate of increase} \\ \text{per unit increase in} \\ \text{the entering basic variable} \end{pmatrix} = \begin{pmatrix} \text{objective value's} \\ \text{direct rate of increase} \\ \text{per unit increase in} \\ \text{the entering basic variable} \end{pmatrix} - \begin{pmatrix} \text{objective value's} \\ \text{indirect rate of decrease} \\ \text{per unit increase in} \\ \text{the entering basic variable} \end{pmatrix}$$

Let us use Figure 6.12 to demonstrate that the simplex tableau's format makes it easy to compute the quantities involved in the above formula. Observe the following:

- As illustrated in Figure 6.12(a) by the circular shading near the top of the simplex tableau, the objective value's direct rate of increase per unit increase in x_2 already appears in the simplex tableau because we have listed in the c_j row the objective-function coefficients of all variables.

- Although the objective value's indirect rate of decrease per unit increase in x_2 does not yet appear in the simplex tableau, the two shaded columns in Figure 6.12(a) provide all the information necessary to compute it. In particular, since the x_2 column contains the basic variables' rates of decrease per unit increase in x_2, and since the c_B column contains the basic variables' objective-function coefficients, we compute the objective value's indirect rate of decrease per unit increase in x_2 by multiplying the corresponding numbers in the c_B column and the x_2 column and then summing the resulting products. The computations proceed as follows:

Basic Variable's Objective-Function Coefficient As Given By the Simplex Tableau's c_B Column		Basic Variable's Rate of Decrease As Given By the Simplex Tableau's x_2 Column		Product
0	×	$\frac{1}{2}$	=	0
9	×	$\frac{1}{4}$	=	$\frac{9}{4}$
0	×	$\frac{13}{2}$	=	0
				$\frac{9}{4}$ ← Sum of products

- After the computation of the objective value's indirect rate of decrease per unit increase in x_2, the circular shading near the bottom of Figure 6.12(b)'s simplex tableau illustrates that we record this value in the z_j row and the x_2 column. This illustrates the purpose of the z_j row—namely, to record for

---

[8] The use of the adjectives "direct" and "indirect" is a reminder that the direct rate of increase is a direct result of x_2's increase in the sense that it equals x_2's objective-function coefficient, whereas the indirect rate of decrease is the indirect result of x_2's increase in the sense that it results from the adjustments to the basic variables' values.

Equation	Basic Variable	c_j	9	6	0	0	0	
		c_B	x_1	x_2	S_1	S_2	S_3	RHS
$I' = I - 2II'$	S_1	0	0	$\frac{1}{2}$	1	$-\frac{1}{2}$	0	
$II' = \frac{1}{4} II$	x_1	9	1	$\frac{1}{4}$	0	$\frac{1}{4}$	0	8
$III' = III - 2II'$	S_3	0	0	$\frac{13}{2}$	0	$-\frac{1}{2}$	1	72
		z_j						$OV = 72$
		$c_j - z_j$						

(a)

Equation	Basic Variable	c_j	9	6	0	0	0	
		c_B	x_1	x_2	S_1	S_2	S_3	RHS
$I' = I - 2II'$	S_1	0	0	$\frac{1}{2}$	1	$-\frac{1}{2}$	0	4
$II' = \frac{1}{4} II$	x_1	9	1	$\frac{1}{4}$	0	$\frac{1}{4}$	0	8
$III' = III - 2II'$	S_3	0	0	$\frac{13}{2}$	0	$-\frac{1}{2}$	1	72
		z_j		$\frac{9}{4}$				$OV = 72$
		$c_j - z_j$						

(b)

Equation	Basic Variable	c_j	9	6	0	0	0	
		c_B	x_1	x_2	S_1	S_2	S_3	RHS
$I' = I - 2II'$	S_1	0	0	$\frac{1}{2}$	1	$-\frac{1}{2}$	0	4
$II' = \frac{1}{4} II$	x_1	9	1	$\frac{1}{4}$	0	$\frac{1}{4}$	0	8
$III' = III - 2II'$	S_3	0	0	$\frac{13}{2}$	0	$-\frac{1}{2}$	1	72
		z_j		$\frac{9}{4}$				$OV = 72$
		$c_j - z_j$		$\frac{15}{4}$				

(c)

Figure 6.12 Computation of x_2's z_j value and $c_j - z_j$ value

each nonbasic variable the objective value's indirect rate of decrease if the nonbasic variable were chosen as the entering basic variable.[9]

- With the objective value's direct rate of increase per unit increase in x_2 appearing in the c_j row as 6, and with the objective value's indirect rate of decrease per unit increase in x_2 now recorded in the z_j row as $\frac{9}{4}$, we can quickly compute the objective value's net rate of increase per unit increase in x_2 as

$$\begin{pmatrix} \text{objective value's} \\ \text{net rate of increase} \\ \text{per unit decrease in } x_2 \end{pmatrix} = (x_2\text{'s } c_j \text{ value}) - (x_2\text{'s } z_j \text{ value}) = 6 - \frac{9}{4} = \frac{15}{4}.$$

---

[9] You might be wondering what the "z" stands for in the heading z_j. The answer is, "Nothing!" We chose the letter "z" simply because someone else arbitrarily chose it long ago and most instructors, textbooks, and LP software packages have continued to use it.

■ As illustrated by the circular shading in Figure 6.12(c)'s simplex tableau, we record this value in the $c_j - z_j$ row. As its name suggests, then, the $c_j - z_j$ row is used to record for each nonbasic variable the objective value's net rate of increase if the nonbasic variable were chosen as the entering basic variable.

We have just determined that, if we select x_2 as the entering basic variable, the objective value will increase at the net rate of $\frac{15}{4}$ per unit increase in x_2. If we perform a similar calculation for the alternative of selecting S_2 as the entering basic variable, we can base our selection of the entering basic variable (x_2 or S_2) on which selection will result in the faster rate of increase in the objective value. You should verify that s_2's c_j value is 0 and its z_j value is $\frac{9}{4}$, thereby resulting in a $c_j - z_j$ value of $-\frac{9}{4}$. Thus, we see that the objective value's net rate of increase per unit increase in S_2 is $-\frac{9}{4}$. This negative rate of increase indicates that the objective value actually decreases by $\frac{9}{4}$ per unit increase in S_2.

Figure 6.13 displays the simplex tableau after we have computed and recorded the z_j values and $c_j - z_j$ values for x_2 and S_2, the two candidates for the entering basic variable. Note that it is necessary to compute a z_j value and a $c_j - z_j$ value only for the nonbasic variables, since only these variables are the candidates for the entering basic variable. To emphasize this, we place asterisks in every column of the z_j row and $c_j - z_j$ row that correspond to a basic variable.[10]

The $c_j - z_j$ row of Figure 6.13's simplex tableau provides us with sufficient information to select either x_2 or S_2 as the entering basic variable. In particular, according to the values in the $c_j - z_j$ row, we must choose between the following two alternatives:

1. If we select x_2 as the entering basic variable, the objective value's net rate of increase per unit increase in x_2 will be $\frac{15}{4}$.

2. If we select S_2 as the entering basic variable, the objective value's net rate of increase per unit increase in x_2 will be $-\frac{9}{4}$.

These two alternatives illustrate the following general principle:

■ If a nonbasic variable's $c_j - z_j$ value is positive, selecting it as the entering basic variable will result in the objective value increasing.

■ If a nonbasic variable's $c_j - z_j$ value equals 0, selecting it as the entering basic variable will result in the objective value remaining constant.

[10] Some instructors, textbooks, and LP software packages compute z_j values and $c_j - z_j$ values for the basic variables as well as the nonbasic variables, even though the computations for the basic variables are meaningless and always result in (as you can verify in Figure 6.13) $c_j - z_j$ values of 0. Instead of cluttering our simplex tableau with meaningless zeroes, we will use the asterisk symbol for the entries in the columns of the z_j row and $c_j - z_j$ row that correspond to basic variables.

Equation	Basic Variable	c_j c_B	9 x_1	6 x_2	0 S_1	0 S_2	0 S_3	RHS
$I' = I - 2II'$	S_1	0	0	$\frac{1}{2}$	1	$-\frac{1}{2}$	0	4
$II' = \frac{1}{4}II$	x_1	9	1	$\frac{1}{4}$	0	$\frac{1}{4}$	0	8
$III' = III - 2II'$	S_3	0	0	$\frac{13}{2}$	0	$-\frac{1}{2}$	1	72
		z_j	*	$\frac{9}{4}$	*	$\frac{9}{4}$	*	
		$c_j - z_j$	*	$\frac{15}{4}$	*	$-\frac{9}{4}$	*	OV = 72

Figure 6.13 The simplex tableau after computation of the nonbasic variables' $c_j - z_j$ values

■ If a nonbasic variable's $c_j - z_j$ value is negative, selecting it as the entering basic variable will result in the objective value decreasing.

Given our desire to maximize the objective function, we select x_2 as the entering basic variable. That is, we select as the entering basic variable the nonbasic variable with a positive $c_j - z_j$ value or, equivalently, the alternative that results in an increase in the objective value.

Before summarizing the procedure for selecting the entering basic variable, we should make the following observations:

■ If the $c_j - z_j$ values of x_2 and S_2 had both been positive, then we could choose either nonbasic variable as the entering basic variable. In such a case, it is customary to select the nonbasic variable with the most positive $c_j - z_j$ value, thereby being "greedy" in the sense that we select the nonbasic variable whose increase results in the objective value's increasing at the fastest rate.[11] In selecting the entering basic variable, unless we explicitly state otherwise, we will always follow this "greedy" rule. However, we will illustrate later that being greedy does *not* guarantee that we will find the LP's optimal solution with less computational effort than if we arbitrarily chose from among the nonbasic variables with positive $c_j - z_j$ values.

■ If the $c_j - z_j$ values of x_2 and S_2 had both been nonpositive, then no choice for the entering basic variable would result in an increase in the objective value. In such a case, we can conclude that the basic feasible solution identified by the current simplex tableau is optimal.

Thus, by examining the values in the simplex tableau's $c_j - z_j$ row, we can decide if the current basic feasible solution is optimal, and, if not, we can then select the entering basic variable in a way that guarantees that the next basic feasible solution we "visit" will have an improved objective value.

Our selection of x_2 as the entering basic variable illustrates the following general procedure:[12]

Procedure for Selecting the Entering Basic Variable (assuming the LP involves maximization)

1. Using the formula below, compute and record in the simplex tableau each nonbasic variable's z_j value:

   Nonbasic variable's z_j value = sum of products obtained by multiplying each basic variable's objective-function coefficient (as specified in the simplex tableau's c_B column) by its rate of decrease per unit increase in the nonbasic variable (as specified in the simplex tableau column that contains the nonbasic variable's coefficients

2. Compute and record in the simplex tableau each nonbasic variable's $c_j - z_j$ value by subtracting the z_j value computed in Step 1 from the c_j value that already appears at the top of the simplex tableau in the c_j row.

3. Examine the $c_j - z_j$ values computed in Step 2. If every nonbasic variable

---

[11] Ties are broken arbitrarily.

[12] We will delay until Section 7.2 a complete discussion of the selection of the entering basic variable when the LP's objective function involves minimization. However, given our discussion thus far, you might have already guessed that, when minimizing, the entering basic variable is chosen as the nonbasic variable with the most *negative* $c_j - z_j$ value.

has a nonpositive $c_j - z_j$ value, there is no need to select an entering basic variable because the current basic feasible solution is optimal. Otherwise, select as the entering basic variable that nonbasic variable with the most positive $c_j - z_j$ value, thereby selecting that nonbasic variable whose increase will increase the objective value at the fastest rate.

Before concluding our present discussion let us use Figure 6.3 to investigate the geometrical significance of our algebraic procedure for selecting the entering basic variable. Our current basic feasible solution,

$$(x_1, x_2, S_1, S_2, S_3) = (8, 0, 4, 0, 72),$$

corresponds to being located in Figure 6.3 at corner point B. Looking at Figure 6.3, observe the following:

- Selecting x_2 as the entering basic variable means that the value of x_2 will increase while the value of S_2, which remains a nonbasic variable, will maintain its value of 0. This corresponds to "walking" away from point B by moving northwest along the boundary equation $S_2 = 0$, that is, moving in the direction indicated in Figure 6.14(a). Observe that moving in this direction ultimately leads to the adjacent corner point C.

- Selecting S_2 as the entering basic variable means that the value of S_2 will increase while the value of x_2, which remains a nonbasic variable, will maintain its value of 0. This corresponds to "walking" away from point B by moving west along the boundary equation $x_2 = 0$, that is, moving in the direction indicated in Figure 6.14(b). Observe that moving in this direction ultimately leads to the adjacent corner point A.

Consequently, selecting one of the two nonbasic variables (x_2 or S_2) as the entering basic variable is geometrically equivalent to selecting one of the two

Figure 6.14 Geometric interpretation of selecting the entering basic variable

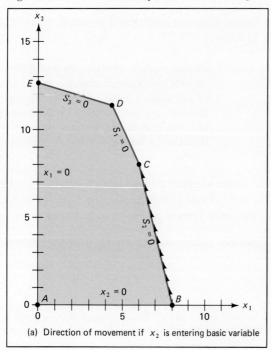

(a) Direction of movement if x_2 is entering basic variable

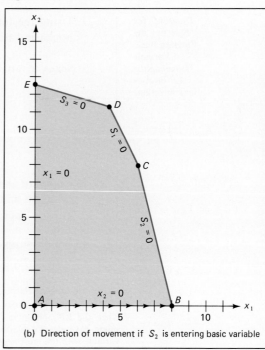

(b) Direction of movement if S_2 is entering basic variable

directions at corner point B that lead to adjacent corner points (Figure 6.14(a)'s direction or Figure 6.14(b)'s direction). Although either direction will lead to an adjacent corner point, we do not want to move to just any adjacent corner point. We want to move to an adjacent corner point with an improved objective value. If we choose Figure 6.14(a)'s direction, x_2's $c_j - z_j$ value indicates that the objective value increases at the rate of $\frac{15}{4}$ per unit increase in x_2, thereby ensuring an improved objective value when we stop our walk at adjacent corner point C. If we choose Figure 6.14(b)'s direction, S_2's $c_j - z_j$ value indicates the objective value increases as the rate of $-\frac{9}{4}$ per unit increase in S_2, thereby ensuring a worsened objective value when we stop our walk at adjacent corner point A. Given the two alternatives, we choose to walk in Figure 6.14(a)'s direction, thereby ensuring the adjacent corner point we are walking toward has an improved objective value.

We can summarize the foregoing as follows:

> The algebraic procedure of selecting the entering basic variable is geometrically equivalent to choosing a direction of movement away from the current corner point that will lead not only to an adjacent corner point but to one with an improved objective value.

Selecting the Leaving Basic Variable

Let us now focus our attention on the selection of the leaving basic variable. We would like to increase the entering basic variable x_2 as much as possible, because every unit increase in x_2 results in a net increase in the objective value of $\frac{15}{4}$, x_2's $c_j - z_j$ value. Remember, however, that this net increase in the objective value results not only from the increase in x_2's value but also from the changes in the current basic variables' values necessary to compensate for the increase in x_2. As we will soon see, these changes in the basic variables' values prevent us from increasing x_2 indefinitely and thereby enable us to select the leaving basic variable.

To begin our discussion, recall that, as the entering basic variable x_2 increases, the basic variables' currently positive values decrease at rates equal to x_2's coefficients in the simplex tableau. Looking at Figure 6.13's simplex tableau, we see that the x_2 column is

$$x_2$$

$$\frac{1}{2}$$

$$\frac{1}{4}$$

$$\frac{13}{2}$$

Because all the coefficients in the x_2 column are positive, every basic variable decreases toward 0 as x_2 increases. Observe that we must stop increasing the entering basic variable x_2 when one of the decreasing basic variables becomes the first to decrease to a value of 0. The reason for stopping is twofold:

1. If we stop increasing x_2 after one of the basic variables has decreased below 0 to a negative value, we will no longer have a feasible solution, since feasibility requires all variables to be nonnegative.

2. If we stop increasing x_2 before one of the basic variables becomes the first to decrease to a value of 0, there will be no leaving basic variable, since, by definition, the leaving basic variable becomes a nonbasic variable with a value of 0.

Consequently, when one of the basic variables becomes the first to decrease to a value of 0, we must stop increasing the entering basic variable x_2 and select as the leaving basic variable the basic variable that was the first to decrease to 0.

To summarize:

> The leaving basic variable is that basic variable that is the first to decrease to 0 as the entering basic variable increases.

How can we identify which basic variable is the first to decrease to 0 as the entering basic variable increases? It is *not* the basic variable with the fastest rate of decrease! When a basic variable reaches 0 depends not only on its rate of decrease but also on its current value. For example, suppose a basic variable has a current value of 10 but decreases at a rate of 2 per unit increase in the entering basic variable x_2. When will such a variable decrease to a value of 0? It will do so when $x_2 = \frac{10}{2} = 5$, the ratio of the basic variable's current value to its rate of decrease. In general, then,

> The value of the entering basic variable at which a basic variable decreases to 0 equals the ratio of the basic variable's current value to its rate of decrease per unit increase in the entering basic variable.

This general principle, in conjunction with the simplex tableau, enables us to easily identify which basic variable is the first to decrease to 0 as the entering basic variable increases. To illustrate, let us focus our attention on the two shaded columns in the simplex tableau that follows:

Equation	Basic Variable	c_j / c_B	9 / x_1	6 / x_2	0 / S_1	0 / S_2	0 / S_3	RHS
$I' = I - 2II'$	S_1	0	0	$\frac{1}{2}$	1	$-\frac{1}{2}$	0	4
$II' = \frac{1}{4}II$	x_1	9	1	$\frac{1}{4}$	0	$\frac{1}{4}$	0	8
$III' = III - 2II'$	S_3	0	0	$\frac{13}{2}$	0	$-\frac{1}{2}$	1	72
	z_j		*	$\frac{9}{4}$	*	$\frac{9}{4}$	*	$OV = 72$
	$c_j - z_j$		*	$\frac{15}{4}$	*	$-\frac{9}{4}$	*	

We know from our earlier discussion that the numbers in the highlighted x_2 column equal the basic variables' rates of decrease per unit increase in x_2 and that the numbers in the highlighted *RHS* column equal the basic variables' current values. Hence, to obtain the values of x_2 at which the basic variables decrease to 0, we simply compute the ratio of the values in the *RHS* column to the values in the x_2 column. The computations proceed as follows:

Basic Variable	Simplex Tableau's x_2 Column	Simplex Tableau's RHS Column	Ratio = $\dfrac{\text{number in } RHS \text{ column}}{\text{number in } x_2 \text{ column}}$	
S_1	$\frac{1}{2}$	4	$\dfrac{4}{\frac{1}{2}} =$	8
x_1	$\frac{1}{4}$	8	$\dfrac{8}{\frac{1}{4}} =$	32
S_3	$\frac{13}{2}$	72	$\dfrac{72}{\frac{13}{2}} =$	$11\frac{1}{13}$

Observe that the minimum of these ratios occurs for the basic variable S_1. Thus, S_1 will be the first basic variable to decrease to 0 as x_2 increases, thereby indicating we should select S_1 as the leaving basic variable.

At this point we need to make an additional observation. When a particular basic variable's rate of decrease per unit increase in the entering basic variable is 0 or negative, we can exclude this basic variable from consideration when selecting the leaving basic variable. To see why, suppose that the simplex tableau's x_2 column is

$$\begin{pmatrix} \dfrac{x_2}{} \\[2pt] 5 \\[4pt] -3 \\[4pt] 0 \end{pmatrix} \quad \text{instead of} \quad \begin{pmatrix} \dfrac{x_2}{} \\[2pt] \frac{1}{2} \\[4pt] \frac{1}{4} \\[4pt] \frac{13}{2} \end{pmatrix}$$

Given the above x_2 column, we can conclude the following about how the basic variables' values change as x_2 increases:

- Equation I'''s basic variable decreases toward 0 at the rate of 5 per unit increase in x_2.
- Equation II'''s basic variable decreases toward 0 at the rate of -3 or, equivalently, increases away from 0 at the rate of 3.
- Equation III'''s basic variable decreases toward 0 at the rate of 0 or, equivalently, does not change in value.

Since equation II'''s and equation III'''s basic variables do not decrease toward 0, neither can be the basic variable that decreases to 0 first as the entering basic variable x_2 increases. Hence, in selecting the leaving basic variable, we can exclude these variables from consideration.

We can now summarize the general procedure for selecting the leaving basic variable:

The Minimum Ratio Procedure for Selecting the Leaving Basic Variable

1. For each equation in the simplex tableau that has a *positive entry* in the entering basic variable's column, compute the ratio of the number in the equation's *RHS* column to the number in the entering basic variable's column. This ratio equals the value of the entering basic variable at which the equation's basic variable decreases to 0. (No ratio is computed for equations with nonpositive numbers in the entering basic variable's column, because such numbers indicate that the equation's basic variable increases or remains constant as the entering basic variable increases.)

2. After computing the ratios in Step 1, select as the leaving basic variable that basic variable corresponding to the equation with the *minimum ratio.*

Before concluding our discussion let us return to Figure 6.3's graph of the OMC's feasible region and discuss the geometrical significance of our algebraic procedure for selecting the leaving basic variable. We previously noted that the geometrical significance of increasing the entering basic variable x_2 was to move from our current location in Figure 6.3 at corner point B and "walk" in the direction indicated by the arrows in Figure 6.14(a). Notice that, the further we walk, the closer we get to each of the boundary equations $S_1 = 0$, $x_1 = 0$, and $S_3 = 0$, and, consequently, the closer the values of S_1, x_1, and S_3 get to 0. This is a geometric confirmation of our earlier algebraic determination (through the simplex tableau's x_2 column) that the basic variables S_1, x_1, and S_3 all decrease toward 0 as the entering basic variable x_2 increases. To avoid leaving the feasible region as we walk in the direction indicated by the arrows in Figure 6.14(a), we must stop walking the first time we "bump into" one of the boundary equations. The first time this occurs is at corner point C, when we "bump into" the boundary equation $S_1 = 0$. This is a geometric confirmation of our earlier algebraic determination (through the minimum-ratio procedure) that S_1 is the first basic variable to decrease to 0 as the entering basic variable x_2 increases.

We can summarize the foregoing as follows:

> The minimum ratio procedure for selecting the leaving basic variable (as the basic variable that is the first to decrease to 0 as the entering basic variable increases) is equivalent to geometrically identifying which boundary equation is the first we "bump into" as we leave the current corner point and walk along the feasible region's boundary in the direction indicated by the selection of the entering basic variable.

Pivoting to Obtain the Adjacent Basic Feasible Solution

In the previous two subsections we have selected the entering basic variable as x_2 and the leaving basic variable as S_1. To algebraically identify the adjacent corner point to which we are moving, we must transform the system of equations into an equivalent system of equations in which the new set of basic variables is isolated. To accomplish this, we perform a pivot, with the pivot variable being the entering basic variable x_2 and the pivot equation being the equation I', in which the leaving basic variable S_1 is now isolated. Such a pivot preserves the existing isolation of x_1 and S_3 (the current basic variables that remain basic variables) while simultaneously isolating the entering basic variable x_2 in equation I', in which the leaving basic variable S_1 is now isolated. (Before proceeding, you may wish to review the steps of a pivot as summarized at the conclusion of Section 6.5.)

Figure 6.15 summarizes the steps involved in the pivot. Observe the following aspects:

- Figure 6.15(a), a copy of Figure 6.13, displays the current simplex tableau. As can be seen from the tableau, the leaving basic variable S_1 is the basic variable now isolated in equation I', thereby identifying equation I' as the pivot equation. Of course, the entering basic variable x_2 is the pivot variable.

- In preparation for the upcoming pivot, we make three modifications in the simplex tableau that give it the appearance shown in Figure 6.15(b). Our first step is to "erase" the numbers that appear in the tableau's z_j row, $c_j - z_j$ row, and OV portion. We no longer need this information because it pertains to the current basic feasible solution, not the new basic feasible solution. Later, we will enter revised numbers into these portions of the tableau. Our second step is to replace the leaving basic variable S_1 with the entering basic variable x_2 in the equation I' of the tableau's Basic Variable column. In the c_B column, we also replace S_1's objective-function coefficient of 0 with x_2's objective-function coefficient of 6. Our final step is to circle the coefficient of the pivot variable x_2 in the pivot equation, I'. This circled number of $\frac{1}{2}$ serves as a visual reminder that the pivot variable is x_2 and the pivot equation is equation I'.

- With the simplex tableau appearing as displayed in Figure 6.15(b), we are now ready to begin the pivot. (Because Section 6.5 provided a detailed illus-

| Equation | Basic Variable | c_j | 9 | 6 | 0 | 0 | 0 | |
		c_B	x_1	x_2	S_1	S_2	S_3	RHS
I'	S_1	0	0	$\frac{1}{2}$	1	$-\frac{1}{2}$	0	4
II'	x_1	9	1	$\frac{1}{4}$	0	$\frac{1}{4}$	0	8
III'	S_3	0	0	$\frac{13}{2}$	0	$-\frac{1}{2}$	1	72
	z_j		*	$\frac{9}{4}$	*	$\frac{9}{4}$	*	$OV = 72$
	$c_j - z_j$		*	$\frac{15}{4}$	*	$-\frac{9}{4}$	*	

(a)

| Equation | Basic Variable | c_j | 9 | 6 | 0 | 0 | 0 | |
		c_B	x_1	x_2	S_1	S_2	S_3	RHS
I'	x_2	6	0	$\left(\frac{1}{2}\right)$	1	$-\frac{1}{2}$	0	4
II'	x_1	9	1	$\frac{1}{4}$	0	$\frac{1}{4}$	0	8
III'	S_3	0	0	$\frac{13}{2}$	0	$-\frac{1}{2}$	1	72
	z_j							$OV =$
	$c_j - z_j$							

(b)

| Equation | Basic Variable | c_j | 9 | 6 | 0 | 0 | 0 | |
		c_B	x_1	x_2	S_1	S_2	S_3	RHS
$I'' = 2I'$	x_2	6	0	(1)	2	-1	0	8
II'	x_1	9	1	$\frac{1}{4}$	0	$\frac{1}{4}$	0	8
III'	S_3	0	0	$\frac{13}{2}$	0	$-\frac{1}{2}$	1	72
	z_j							$OV =$
	$c_j - z_j$							

(c)

| Equation | Basic Variable | c_j | 9 | 6 | 0 | 0 | 0 | |
		c_B	x_1	x_2	S_1	S_2	S_3	RHS
$I'' = 2I'$	x_2	6	0	(1)	2	-1	0	8
$II'' = II' - \frac{1}{4}I''$	x_1	9	1	0	$-\frac{1}{2}$	$\frac{1}{2}$	0	6
$III'' = III' - \frac{13}{2}I''$	S_3	0	0	0	-13	6	1	20
	z_j							$OV =$
	$c_j - z_j$							

(d)

| Equation | Basic Variable | c_j | 9 | 6 | 0 | 0 | 0 | |
		c_B	x_1	x_2	S_1	S_2	S_3	RHS
$I'' = 2I'$	x_2	6	0	(1)	2	-1	0	8
$II'' = II' - \frac{1}{4}I''$	x_1	9	1	0	$-\frac{1}{2}$	$\frac{1}{2}$	0	6
$III'' = III' - \frac{13}{2}I''$	S_3	0	0	0	-13	6	1	20
	z_j							$OV = 102$
	$c_j - z_j$							

(e)

Figure 6.15 A summary of the pivot with an entering basic variable of x_2 and a leaving basic variable of S_1

tration of a pivot, we will give here only a brief description of the algebra involved in the pivot.) The pivot's first goal is to transform equation I', the pivot equation, into an equation in which the now-circled coefficient of x_2, the pivot variable, changes from its current value of $\frac{1}{2}$ into a new value of 1. To accomplish this, we perform the elementary equation operation $I'' = 2I'$. After this transformation, the simplex tableau appears as displayed in Figure 6.15(c). Observe that in the tableau's Equation column we have recorded the elementary equation operation used to transform equation I'.

- With the simplex tableau now appearing as in Figure 6.15(c), we are ready to achieve the pivot's second goal of transforming equations II' and III' so that the coefficients of the pivot variable x_2 have changed from their current respective values of $\frac{1}{4}$ and $\frac{13}{2}$ into new values of 0. To transform x_2's coefficient in equation II' into 0, we perform the elementary equation operation $II'' = II' - \frac{1}{4} I''$, where the multiple of the transformed pivot equation I'' that we subtract from equation II' equals $\frac{1}{4}$, the pivot variable x_2's current coefficient in equation II'. Similarly, to transform x_2's coefficient in equation III' into 0, we perform the elementary equation operation $III'' = III' - \frac{13}{2} I''$, where the multiple of the transformed pivot equation I'' that we subtract from equation III' equals $\frac{13}{2}$, the pivot variable x_2's current coefficient in equation III'. After this transformation, the simplex tableau appears as displayed in Figure 6.15(d). Observe that in the tableau's Equation column we have recorded the elementary equation operations used to transform equations II' and III'. This completes the pivot's elementary equation operations. The pivot has preserved the existing isolation of x_1 and S_3 (the current basic variables that remain basic variables) while simultaneously isolating the entering basic variable x_2 in equation I', the equation in which the leaving basic variable S_1 was formerly isolated. Looking at Figure 6.15(d)'s simplex tableau and focusing our attention on the Basic Variable column and the *RHS* column, we can immediately identify the basic variables' values. In particular,

$$\begin{aligned} x_2 &= 8 &&\text{(from equation } I'') \\ x_1 &= 6 &&\text{(from equation } II'') \\ S_3 &= 20 &&\text{(from equation } III'') \end{aligned}$$

The variables not appearing in the tableau's Basic Variable column are the nonbasic variables, which, by definition, have values of 0. The new basic feasible solution, then, is

$$(x_1, x_2, S_1, S_2, S_3) = (6, 8, 0, 0, 20).$$

- To compute the new basic feasible solution's objective value, look at Figure 6.15(d)'s simplex tableau and sum the products obtained by multiplying the corresponding numbers in the tableau's c_B column and *RHS* column. The resulting sum of products is

Basic Variable's Objective-Function Coefficient As Given By the Simplex Tableau's c_B Column		Basic Variable's Value As Given By the Simplex Tableau's *RHS* Column		Product
6	×	8	=	48
9	×	6	=	54
0	×	20	=	0
				102 ← Sum of products

We record this sum in the simplex tableau's *OV* portion. The simplex tableau now appears as displayed in Figure 6.15(e). By comparing the *OV* portions of the simplex tableaux in Figures 6.15(a) and 6.15(e), we see that the new basic feasible solution's objective value is an improvement of $102 - 72 = 30$.

We have now completed the algebraic move from the basic feasible solution

$$(x_1, x_2, S_1, S_2, S_3) = (8, 0, 4, 0, 72)$$

to the basic feasible solution

The latter is not only an adjacent basic feasible solution but also one with an improved objective value.

Although we will not do so now, we could determine whether the new basic feasible solution is optimal. To do so, we would compute z_j values and $c_j - z_j$ values for the new set of nonbasic variables (now S_1 and S_2 instead of x_2 and S_2) and record these values in the now-empty z_j row and $c_j - z_j$ row in Figure 6.15(e)'s simplex tableau. If $c_j - z_j$ values for S_1 and S_2 were both nonpositive, the new basic feasible solution would be optimal. If not, we would move to yet another adjacent basic feasible solution with an improved objective value by repeating the procedure illustrated in this section—that is, by

1. selecting as the entering basic variable that nonbasic variable with the most positive $c_j - z_j$ value,

2. selecting the leaving basic variable using the minimum ratio procedure, and

3. performing the appropriate pivot to enable identification of the new basic feasible solution.

These three steps are known as an *iteration* of the simplex method. If we perform as many iterations of the simplex method as necessary, we eventually obtain the optimal basic feasible solution.

As you gain practice with the simplex method, you will find it unnecessary to summarize an iteration in as much detail as displayed in Figure 6.15. Probably you will simply "jump" from Figure 6.15's top tableau to its bottom tableau.

6.7 A SUMMARY OF THE SIMPLEX METHOD

In this section we will summarize the simplex method's steps. In the next section we will employ the simplex method to solve OMC's LP. We continue to assume that the LP we wish to solve has the following characteristics:

-   The objective function is of the maximization type.

-   All structural constraints are of the $\leqslant$ type with nonnegative constants appearing on the right-hand sides.

-   All decision variables are subject to nonnegativity constraints.

The following is a summary of how to use the simplex method to solve an LP with the above characteristics:[13]

A Summary of
the Simplex
Method

1. **Identifying the initial basic feasible solution.** To identify the initial basic feasible solution, we proceed as follows:

    a. Using slack variables (as described in Section 6.2), we convert the initial formulation of the LP into an LP in equality form.

    b. Because the slack variables are already an isolated set of variables, we choose them as the initial set of basic variables and, therefore,

---

[13] After reading the summary, do not be concerned if you have some questions. Proceed to the next section's solution of OMC's LP, where you will find numerical examples of each of the simplex method's steps. These examples should answer your questions.

choose the decision variables as the initial set of nonbasic variables. The initial basic feasible solution, then, is the one in which the decision variables all equal 0, and each slack variable equals the right-hand side of its corresponding structural constraint.

c. Construct the simplex tableau corresponding to the initial basic feasible solution, leaving blank for now the tableau's z_j and $c_j - z_j$ row.

2. **Selection of the entering basic variable.** The entering basic variable is the nonbasic variable whose increase improves the objective function's value at the fastest rate. To determine the entering basic variable, we use the procedure summarized on pages 255–56.

3. **Selection of the leaving basic variable.** The leaving basic variable is the basic variable that is the first to decrease to 0 as the entering basic variable increases. To select the leaving basic variable, we perform the minimum-ratio procedure summarized on page 259.

4. **The pivot.** To identify the new basic feasible solution and the new objective value, we proceed as follows:

a. Perform a pivot (as summarized on page 245) in which the pivot variable is the entering basic variable and the pivot equation is the equation in which the leaving basic variable is now an isolated variable.

b. After performing the pivot, we can immediately identify the variables' values. In particular, any variable appearing in the simplex tableau's Basic Variable column equals the corresponding number appearing in the tableau's *RHS* column, and any variable not appearing in the tableau's Basic Variable column is, of course, a nonbasic variable, which, by definition, equals 0.

c. We compute the new basic feasible solution's objective value as the sum of products obtained by multiplying the corresponding values in the simplex tableau's c_B column and the *RHS* column. After computing the objective value, we enter it into the simplex tableau's *OV* portion and return to Step 2.

As indicated in the summary, the simplex method repeats Steps 2, 3, and 4 until the optimal basic feasible solution has been found. Each repetition of Steps 2–4 is called an *iteration* of the simplex method. At the conclusion of each iteration, we have identified a new basic feasible solution—one that not only is adjacent to the previous basic feasible solution but also has an improved objective value. This is geometrically equivalent to having walked from one of the feasible region's corner points to an adjacent corner point with an improved objective value.

6.8 USING THE SIMPLEX METHOD TO SOLVE OMC'S LP

In this section we provide a detailed summary of how to use the simplex method to solve OMC's LP. Throughout the summary, we will make reference to Figure 6.16, which displays the sequence of simplex tableaux that we construct as we execute the simplex method.

(a)

Equation	Basic Variable	c_j → c_B	9 x_1	6 x_2	0 S_1	0 S_2	0 S_3	RHS
I	S_1	0	2	1	1	0	0	20
II	S_2	0	(4)	1	0	1	0	32
III	S_3	0	2	7	0	0	1	88
	z_j		0	0	*	*	*	$OV = 0$
	$c_j - z_j$		9	6	*	*	*	

(b)

Equation	Basic Variable	c_j → c_B	9 x_1	6 x_2	0 S_1	0 S_2	0 S_3	RHS
$I' = I - 2II'$	S_1	0	0	$(\tfrac{1}{2})$	1	$-\tfrac{1}{2}$	0	4
$II' = \tfrac{1}{4}II'$	x_1	9	1	$\tfrac{1}{4}$	0	$\tfrac{1}{4}$	0	8
$III' = III - 2II'$	S_3	0	0	$\tfrac{13}{2}$	0	$-\tfrac{1}{2}$	1	72
	z_j		*	$\tfrac{9}{4}$	*	$\tfrac{9}{4}$	*	$OV = 72$
	$c_j - z_j$		*	$\tfrac{15}{4}$	*	$-\tfrac{9}{4}$	*	

(c)

Equation	Basic Variable	c_j → c_B	9 x_1	6 x_2	0 S_1	0 S_2	0 S_3	RHS
$I'' = 2I'$	x_2	6	0	1	2	-1	0	8
$II'' = II' - \tfrac{1}{4}I''$	x_1	9	1	0	$-\tfrac{1}{2}$	$\tfrac{1}{2}$	0	6
$III'' = III' - \tfrac{13}{2}I''$	S_3	0	0	0	-13	(6)	1	20
	z_j		*	*	$\tfrac{15}{2}$	$-\tfrac{3}{2}$	*	$OV = 102$
	$c_j - z_j$		*	*	$-\tfrac{15}{2}$	$\tfrac{3}{2}$	*	

(d)

Equation	Basic Variable	c_j → c_B	9 x_1	6 x_2	0 S_1	0 S_2	0 S_3	RHS
$I''' = I'' + III'''$	x_2	6	0	1	$-\tfrac{1}{6}$	0	$\tfrac{1}{6}$	$\tfrac{34}{3}$
$II''' = II'' - \tfrac{1}{2}III'''$	x_1	9	1	0	$\tfrac{7}{12}$	0	$-\tfrac{1}{12}$	$\tfrac{13}{3}$
$III''' = \tfrac{1}{6}III''$	S_2	0	0	0	$-\tfrac{13}{6}$	1	$\tfrac{1}{6}$	$\tfrac{10}{3}$
	z_j		*	*	$\tfrac{17}{4}$	*	$\tfrac{1}{4}$	$OV = 107$
	$c_j - z_j$		*	*	$-\tfrac{17}{4}$	*	$-\tfrac{1}{4}$	

Figure 6.16 Sequence of simplex tableaux for OMC's LP

Identifying an Initial Basic Feasible Solution

In Section 6.2 we converted the original formulation of OMC's LP into the following LP in equality form:

$$\text{Maximize } 9x_1 + 6x_2$$

$$
\begin{aligned}
\text{subject to } 2x_1 + x_2 + S_1 &= 20 \\
4x_1 + x_2 \quad\quad + S_2 &= 32 \\
2x_1 + 7x_2 \quad\quad\quad + S_3 &= 88
\end{aligned}
$$

and $x_1 \geqslant 0, x_2 \geqslant 0, S_1 \geqslant 0, S_2 \geqslant 0, S_3 \geqslant 0$.

In the LP's equality form system of equations, the slack variables are an isolated set of variables. Consequently, we can choose the slack variables as the initial set of basic variables and the decision variables as the initial set of nonbasic variables, thereby identifying

$$(x_1, x_2, S_1, S_2, S_3) = (0, 0, 20, 32, 88)$$

as the initial basic feasible solution, a solution whose objective value is 0. Starting the simplex method at this basic feasible solution has the geometric interpretation of starting in Figure 6.3 at the origin—that is, corner point A. The simplex tableau corresponding to this initial basic feasible solution is identical to Figure 6.16(a)'s tableau, except that there is no circle around the "4" that appears as x_1's

265

coefficient in equation II, and the z_j row and $c_j - z_j$ row are now blank. (Filling in these rows will be the next thing we do.)

The First Iteration

Selection of the Entering Basic Variable. The candidates for the entering basic variable are the current nonbasic variables x_1 and x_2. From these two candidates, we must select the entering basic variable as the nonbasic variable whose increase improves the objective value at the fastest rate. Our first step is to compute each nonbasic variable's z_j value and $c_j - z_j$ value. After we enter these values into the simplex tableau, its appearance is identical to that in Figure 6.16(a), except that we have yet to circle the "4" that appears as x_1's coefficient in equation II. In Figure 6.16(a)'s simplex tableau, the most positive $c_j - z_j$ value occurs in the x_1 column. Consequently, we select x_1 as the entering basic variable. This selection is geometrically equivalent to determining that the objective value will increase at the faster rate if in Figure 6.3 we leave corner point A and "walk" in the direction of corner point B (instead of corner point E).

Selection of the Leaving Basic Variable. Looking at the x_1 column in Figure 6.16(a)'s simplex tableau, we see that the entering basic variable x_1 has a positive coefficient in equations I, II, and III, thereby indicating that the basic variables for these equations (S_1, S_2, and S_3) are the candidates for the leaving basic variable. Focusing our attention on the x_1 column and the RHS column in Figure 6.16(a)'s simplex tableau, we compute respective ratios for equations I, II, and III of 10, 8, and 44. Since the minimum of these ratios is 8, we select S_2, (the basic variable in equation II) as the leaving basic variable. This selection is algebraic confirmation of the geometric observation that as we "walk" in Figure 6.3 from corner point A toward corner point B, the first boundary equation we "bump into" is $S_2 = 0$.

The Pivot. The pivot variable is the entering basic variable x_1, and the pivot equation is equation II, in which the leaving basic variable S_2 is now isolated. To emphasize this, we circle the number "4" that appears in Figure 6.16(a)'s simplex tableau as x_1's coefficient in equation II. The goal of the pivot is to transform this circled number into a 1 and to transform every number above and below it into a 0. To achieve this goal, we perform the following elementary equation operations:

$$II' = \tfrac{1}{4} II, \, I' = I - 2II', \text{ and } III' = III - 2II'.$$

To update the simplex tableau, we

1. Record the transformed equations resulting from the above elementary equation operations. (Before proceeding, you should verify for yourself the algebra involved.)

2. Update the simplex tableau's Basic Variable column and the c_B column by replacing in equation II the leaving basic variable S_2 and its objective function coefficient of 0 with the entering basic variable x_1 and its objective function coefficient of 9.

3. Compute the new basic feasible solution's objective value as 72 and record this value in the simplex tableau's OV portion.

After these three steps have been performed, the appearance of the simplex tableau is identical to that in Figure 6.16(b), except that there is no circle around the "$\tfrac{1}{2}$" that appears as x_2's coefficient in equation I', and the z_j and the $c_j - z_j$ row are blank, awaiting the recording of new numbers at the start of the next iteration. Focusing our attention on the Basic Variable column and the *RHS* column in Figure 6.16(b)'s simplex tableau, we see that the values of the basic variables S_1, x_1, and S_3 equal respectively 4, 8, and 72. Of course, the values of the nonbasic variables x_2 and S_2 equal 0. Hence, Figure 6.16(b)'s simplex tableau identifies the new basic feasible solution

$$(x_1, x_2, S_1, S_2, S_3) = (8, 0, 4, 0, 72),$$

for which the objective value is 72. With $x_1 = 8$ and $x_2 = 0$, the new basic feasible solution corresponds geometrically in Figure 6.3 to corner point *B*.

Thus, in performing the first iteration of the simplex method, we have "walked" in Figure 6.3 from corner point *A* to the adjacent corner point *B*. We are now ready to check whether the new basic feasible solution is optimal and, if not, to move to yet another basic feasible solution.

The Second Iteration

Selection of the Entering Basic Variable. The candidates for the entering basic variable are the current nonbasic variables x_2 and S_2. From these two candidates, we must select the entering basic variable as the nonbasic variable whose increase improves the objective value at the fastest rate. Our first step is to compute each nonbasic variable's z_j value and $c_j - z_j$ value. After we enter these z_j values and $c_j - z_j$ values into the simplex tableau, its appearance is identical to that in Figure 6.16(b), except that we have yet to circle the number "$\frac{1}{2}$" that appears as x_2's coefficient in equation I'. In Figure 6.16(b)'s simplex tableau, the most positive $c_j - z_j$ value occurs in the x_2 column. Consequently, we select x_2 as the entering basic variable. This selection is geometrically equivalent to determining that the objective value will increase at the faster rate if in Figure 6.3 we leave corner point *B* and "walk" in the direction of corner point *C* (instead of back to corner point *A*).

Selection of the Leaving Basic Variable. Looking at the x_2 column in Figure 6.16(b)'s simplex tableau, we see that the entering basic variable x_2 has a positive coefficient in equations I', II', and III', thereby indicating that the basic variables for these equations (S_1, x_1, and S_3) are the candidates for the leaving basic variable. Focusing our attention on the x_2 column and the *RHS* column, we compute respective ratios for equations I', II', and III' of 8, 32, and $11\frac{1}{13}$. Since the minimum of these ratios is 8, we select S_1 (the basic variable in equation I') as the leaving basic variable. This selection is algebraic confirmation of the geometric observation that as we "walk" in Figure 6.3 from corner point *B* toward corner point *C*, the first boundary equation we "bump into" is $S_1 = 0$.

The Pivot. The pivot variable is the entering basic variable x_2, and the pivot equation is equation I', in which the leaving basic variable S_1 is now isolated. To emphasize this, we circle the number "$\frac{1}{2}$" that appears in Figure 6.16(b)'s simplex tableau as x_2's coefficient in equation I'. The goal of the pivot is to transform this circled number into a 1 and to transform every other number below it into a 0. To achieve this goal, we perform the following elementary equation operations:

$$I'' = 2I', II'' = II' - \frac{1}{4}I'', \text{ and } III'' = III' - \frac{13}{2}I''$$

To update the simplex tableau, we

1. Record the transformed equations resulting from the above elementary equation operations. (Before proceeding, you should verify for yourself the algebra involved.)

2. Update the simplex tableau's Basic Variable column and the c_B column by replacing in equation *II* the leaving basic variable S_2 and its objective-function coefficient of 0 with the entering basic variable x_2 and its objective-function coefficient of 6.

3. Compute the new basic feasible solution's objective value as 102 and record this value in the simplex tableau's *OV* portion.

After these three steps have been performed the appearance of the simplex tableau is identical to that in Figure 6.16(c), except that there is no circle around the "6" that appears as S_2's coefficient in equation *III″*, and the z_j row and the $c_j - z_j$ row are blank, awaiting the recording of new numbers at the start of the next iteration. Focusing our attention on the Basic Variable column and the *RHS* column in Figure 6.16(c)'s simplex tableau, we see that the values of the basic variables x_2, x_1, and S_3 equal respectively 8, 6, and 20. Of course, the values of the nonbasic variables S_1 and S_2 equal 0. Hence, Figure 6.16(c)'s simplex tableau identifies the new basic feasible solution

$$(x_1, x_2, S_1, S_2, S_3) = (6, 8, 0, 0, 20),$$

for which the objective value is 102. With $x_1 = 6$ and $x_2 = 8$, the new basic feasible solution corresponds geometrically in Figure 6.3 to corner point *C*.

Thus, in performing the second iteration of the simplex method, we have "walked" in Figure 6.3 from corner point *B* to the adjacent corner point *C*. We are now ready to check whether the new basic feasible solution is optimal and, if not, to move to yet another basic feasible solution.

The Third Iteration

Selection of the Entering Basic Variable. The candidates for the entering basic variable are the current nonbasic variables S_1 and S_2. From these two candidates, we must select the entering basic variable as the nonbasic variable whose increase improves the objective value at the fastest rate. Our first step is to compute each nonbasic variable's z_j value and $c_j - z_j$ value. After we enter these values into the simplex tableau, its appearance is identical to that in Figure 6.16(c), except that we have yet to circle the number 6 that appears as S_2's coefficient in equation *III″*. In Figure 6.16(c)'s simplex tableau, the most positive $c_j - z_j$ value occurs in the S_2 column. Consequently, we select S_2 as the entering basic variable. This selection is geometrically equivalent to determining that the objective value will increase at the faster rate if in Figure 6.3 we leave corner point *C* and "walk" in the direction of corner point *D* (instead of back to corner point *B*).

Selection of the Leaving Basic Variable. Looking at the S_2 column in Figure 6.16(c)'s simplex tableau, we see that the entering basic variable S_2 has a positive coefficient in equations *II″* and *III″*, thereby indicating that the basic variables for these equations (x_1 and S_3) are the candidates for the leaving basic variable. Focusing our attention on the S_2 column and the *RHS* column, we compute respective ratios for equations *II″* and *III″* of 12 and $3\frac{1}{3}$. Since the minimum of these ratios is $3\frac{1}{3}$, we select S_3 (the basic variable in equation *III″*) as the leaving basic variable. This selection is algebraic confirmation of the geometric observation that as we "walk" in Figure 6.3 from corner point *C* toward corner point *D*, the first boundary equation we "bump into" is $S_3 = 0$.

The Pivot. The pivot variable is the entering basic variable S_2, and the pivot equation is equation III'', in which the leaving basic variable S_3 is now isolated. To emphasize this, we circle the number "6" that appears in Figure 6.16(c)'s simplex tableau as S_2's coefficient in equation III''. The goal of the pivot is to transform this circled number into a 1 and to transform every number above it into a 0. To achieve this goal, we perform the following elementary equation operations:

$$III'' = \tfrac{1}{6} III', I''' = I'' + III''', \text{ and } II''' = II'' - \tfrac{1}{2} III'''.$$

To update the simplex tableau, we

1. Record the transformed equations resulting from the above elementary equation operations. (Before proceeding, you should verify for yourself the algebra involved.)

2. Update the simplex tableau's Basic Variable column and the c_B column by replacing in equation II the leaving basic variable S_3 and its objective-function coefficient of 0 with the entering basic variable S_2 and its objective-function coefficient of 0.

3. Compute the new basic feasible solution's objective value as 107, and record this value in the simplex tableau's OV portion.

After these three steps have been performed, the appearance of the simplex tableau is identical to that in Figure 6.16(d), except that the z_j row and the $c_j - z_j$ row are blank, awaiting the recording of new numbers at the start of the next iteration. Focusing our attention on the Basic Variable column and the RHS column in Figure 6.16(d)'s simplex tableau, we see that the values of the basic variables x_2, x_1, and S_2 equal respectively $11\tfrac{1}{3}$, $4\tfrac{1}{3}$, and $3\tfrac{1}{3}$. Of course, the values of the non-basic variables x_2 and S_2 equal 0. Hence, Figure 6.16(d)'s simplex tableau identifies the new basic feasible solution

$$(x_1, x_2, S_1, S_2, S_3) = (4\tfrac{1}{3}, 11\tfrac{1}{3}, 0, 3\tfrac{1}{3}, 0),$$

for which the objective value is 107. With $x_1 = 4\tfrac{1}{3}$ and $x_2 = 11\tfrac{1}{3}$, the new basic feasible solution corresponds geometrically in Figure 6.16(d) to corner point D.

Thus, in performing the third iteration of the simplex method, we have "walked" in Figure 6.3 from corner point C to the adjacent corner point D. We are now ready to check whether the new basic feasible solution is optimal, and, if not, to move to yet another basic feasible solution.

The Fourth (and Last) Iteration

Selection of the Entering Basic Variable. The candidates for the entering basic variable are the current nonbasic variables S_1 and S_3. From these two candidates, we must select the entering basic variable as the nonbasic variable whose increase improves the objective value at the fastest rate. Our first step is to compute each nonbasic variable's z_j value and $c_j - z_j$ value. After we enter these values into the simplex tableau, its appearance is identical to that in Figure 6.16(d). Since all numbers in this tableau's $c_j - z_j$ row are nonpositive, we conclude that the current basic feasible solution is optimal, and we terminate execution of the simplex method. Since we terminate it early in the fourth iteration, it is customary not to count this iteration when stating the total number of iterations performed. Thus, we say we have solved the LP in three (not four) iterations of the simplex method.

Figure 6.17 displays the geometrical route we have followed in solving the LP,

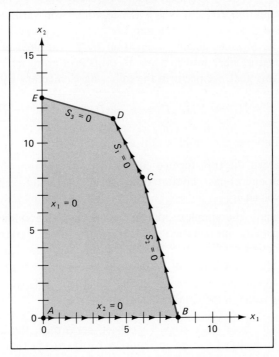

Figure 6.17 The route followed to the optimal solution of OMC's LP

illustrating that each iteration of the simplex method is geometrically equivalent to moving from the current corner point to an adjacent corner point. Observe in Figure 6.17 that there exists another route to the optimal solution at corner point D, namely,

$$A \to E \to D.$$

This route, in contrast to route $A \to B \to C \to D$, requires only two iterations of the simplex method instead of three. In Exercise 6.14, you will be asked to demonstrate that this alternative route would have been the one we followed if, during the simplex method's first iteration, we had selected x_2 instead of x_1 as the entering basic variable, thereby ignoring the fact that x_1's positive $c_j - z_j$ value was more positive than x_2's positive $c_j - z_j$ value. This illustrates the following general principle:

> There are many "routes" to the LP's optimal solution. By "greedily" selecting as the entering basic variable the nonbasic variable with the most positive $c_j - z_j$ value (thereby "greedily" selecting the nonbasic variable whose increase improves the objective value at the fastest rate), we do *not* guarantee that we will follow the route to the optimal solution requiring the fewest iterations of the simplex method. Unfortunately, there is no way to select the entering basic variable to obtain such a guarantee. The only guarantee we can obtain is that, if at each iteration we select the entering basic variable from among those nonbasic variables with positive $c_j - z_j$ values, we will follow one of the routes to the optimal solution.

Despite this general principle, it is customary to "greedily" select the entering basic variable as the nonbasic variable with the most positive $c_j - z_j$ value. Hereafter, unless we explicitly state otherwise, we will follow this custom.

6.9 DEGENERACY

As its sinister-sounding name suggests, *degeneracy* is a phenomenon that can cause difficulties in the execution of the simplex method. A basic feasible solution is said to be a *degenerate basic feasible solution* whenever one or more of the basic variables has a value of 0. A *nondegenerate basic feasible solution* is defined as a basic feasible solution in which all basic variables have positive values. Until now, we have encountered only nondegenerate basic feasible solutions when executing the simplex method. To verify this, look at all simplex tableaux displayed in Figure 6.16 and observe that a value of 0 never appears in the *RHS* columns.

In this section, we will illustrate difficulties that can arise in the execution of the simplex method when we encounter a degenerate basic feasible solution. As an example, we will use the following modification of OMC's LP:

$$\text{Maximize } 9x_1 + 6x_2$$

$$
\begin{aligned}
\text{subject to } 2x_1 + x_2 &\leqslant 20 \\
4x_1 + x_2 &\leqslant 32 \\
2x_1 + 7x_2 &\leqslant 88 \\
6x_1 + 2x_2 &\leqslant 52
\end{aligned}
$$

$$\text{and } x_1 \geqslant 0, x_2 \geqslant 0.$$

This modification consists of the added structural constraint $6x_1 + 2x_2 \leqslant 52$, whose slack variable we will denote by S_4. After converting the LP to equality form, we obtain the following LP:

$$\text{Maximize } 9x_1 + 6x_2$$

$$
\begin{aligned}
\text{subject to } 2x_1 + x_2 + S_1 \phantom{{}+ S_2 + S_3 + S_4} &= 20 \\
4x_1 + x_2 \phantom{{}+ S_1} + S_2 \phantom{{}+ S_3 + S_4} &= 32 \\
2x_1 + 7x_2 \phantom{{}+ S_1 + S_2} + S_3 \phantom{{}+ S_4} &= 88 \\
6x_1 + 2x_2 \phantom{{}+ S_1 + S_2 + S_3} + S_4 &= 52
\end{aligned}
$$

$$
\begin{aligned}
\text{and } &x_1 \geqslant 0, x_2 \geqslant 0, \\
&S_1 \geqslant 0, S_2 \geqslant 0, S_3 \geqslant 0, S_4 \geqslant 0.
\end{aligned}
$$

To graph the LP's feasible region, we need only determine the effect adding the constraint $6x_1 + 2x_2 \leqslant 52$ has on Figure 6.3's graph of the feasible region of OMC's LP. As displayed in Figure 6.18, there is no effect. The constraint $6x_1 + 2x_2 \leqslant 52$ is redundant, although its boundary equation intersects the feasible region of OMC's LP at the corner point C.[14]

A Graphical Illustration of Degeneracy

Corner point C in Figure 6.18 provides a two-dimensional graphical illustration of a degenerate basic feasible solution. To see why, first note that, the LP's equality form system of equations consists of $m = 4$ equations involving $n = 6$ variables. A

---

[14] Recall from Section 2.13 that a redundant constraint is one whose deletion leaves the feasible region unchanged.

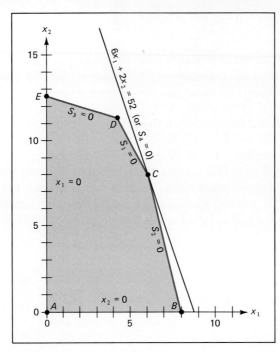

Figure 6.18 The effect on OMC's feasible region of adding the structural constraint $6x_1 + 2x_2 \leqslant 52$

basic feasible solution consists, by definition, of $n - m = 6 - 4 = 2$ nonbasic variables (whose values equal 0) and four basic variables (whose values are nonnegative). Hence, in our example, a basic feasible solution can only be degenerate if the number of variables equal to 0 exceeds two, the number of nonbasic variables. This is precisely what occurs at corner point C, where S_1, S_2, and S_3 all must equal 0 because the point C lies at the intersection of the three boundary equations $S_1 = 0$, $S_2 = 0$, and $S_4 = 0$. Thus, corner point C corresponds to a degenerate basic feasible solution. Each of the remaining four corner points in Figure 6.18's feasible region corresponds to a nondegenerate basic feasible solution, because each lies at the intersection of exactly two boundary equations. In a moment, we will see what happens during the execution of the simplex method when we encounter the degenerate basic feasible solution that corresponds to corner point C. First, however, let us discuss a potential misconception.

From our two-dimensional example, it may seem that degeneracy must always be accompanied by redundancy. While this is true in two dimensions, it need not be true in three dimensions. As illustrated by Exercise 6.19, when the LP's original formulation involves three or more decision variables, a degenerate basic feasible solution may occur even if no constraint is redundant.

Solving the Modification of OMC's LP

Let us see what happens when we use the simplex method to solve the modification to OMC's LP. At the outset of the section, we saw that the LP's equality form system of equations is

$$
\begin{array}{rcrcrcrcrcr}
2x_1 &+& x_2 &+& S_1 & & & & & & = 20 \\
4x_1 &+& x_2 & & &+& S_2 & & & & = 32 \\
2x_1 &+& 7x_2 & & & & &+& S_3 & & = 88 \\
6x_1 &+& 2x_2 & & & & & & &+& S_4 = 52
\end{array}
$$

By selecting the four slack variables as the initial set of basic variables and the two decision variables as the initial set of nonbasic variables, we can immediately identify

$$(x_1, x_2, S_1, S_2, S_3, S_4) \;=\; (0, 0, 20, 32, 88, 52)$$

as an initial basic feasible solution, which corresponds geometrically in Figure 6.18 to corner point A (i.e., the origin). The corresponding simplex tableau is displayed at the top of Figure 6.19, which then goes on to display the entire sequence of simplex tableaux generated during the execution of the simplex method. The following is a commentary on each iteration:

- **First iteration.** The first iteration is routine. The entering basic variable is x_1, and the leaving basic variable is S_2. You should verify for yourself that the appropriate pivot results in Figure 6.19's second tableau. This tableau identifies the basic feasible solution

$$(x_1, x_2, S_1, S_2, S_3, S_4) \;=\; (8, 0, 4, 0, 72, 4),$$

which corresponds geometrically in Figure 6.18 to corner point B. Thus, the simplex method's first iteration has moved us in Figure 6.18 from corner point A to corner point B.

- **Second iteration.** The "excitement" begins when we try to leave corner point B by performing a second iteration of the simplex method. After selecting x_2 as the entering basic variable, we begin the selection of the leaving basic variable using the minimum-ratio procedure. Looking at Figure 6.19's second simplex tableau, verify for yourself that there is a tie for the minimum ratio of 8 between the ratios for equations I' and IV', in which S_1 and S_4 are basic variables. The algebraic implication of this tie is that, as the entering basic variable x_2 increases, S_1 and S_4 tie for the first basic variable to decrease to 0. The geometric interpretation of this tie, as we will soon see, is that the selection of x_2 as the entering basic variable is moving us in the direction of a corner point that corresponds to a degenerate basic feasible solution. Despite the tie for the minimum ratio, we cannot select both S_1 and S_4 as the leaving basic variable, since the trade between the set of nonbasic variables and the set of basic variables must be on a one-for-one basis. Since we must make a selection, let us arbitrarily decide to select S_4 as the leaving basic variable, thereby keeping S_1 as a basic variable. Although it will remain a basic variable, S_1's tie with the leaving basic variable S_4 during the minimum-ratio procedure implies that S_1 will have a value of 0 in the next basic feasible solution, thereby indicating that the next basic feasible solution will be degenerate. Having selected x_2 as the entering basic variable and S_4 as the leaving basic variable, we can complete the simplex method's second iteration by performing the appropriate pivot. You should verify for yourself that the pivot results in Figure 6.19's third simplex tableau. From the 0 that appears in the tableau's *RHS* column, we see that the tableau, as predicted, identifies a degenerate basic feasible solution in which the basic variable S_1 has a value of 0. In particular, the tableau identifies the degenerate basic feasible solution

$$(x_1, x_2, S_1, S_2, S_3, S_4) \;=\; (6, 8, 0, 0, 20, 0),$$

which corresponds geometrically in Figure 6.18 to corner point C. Thus, the simplex method's second iteration has moved us in Figure 6.18 from corner point B to corner point C, a corner point corresponding to a degenerate basic feasible solution.

Equation	Basic Variable	c_j	9 x_1	6 x_2	0 S_1	0 S_2	0 S_3	0 S_4	RHS
		c_B							
I	S_1	0	2	1	1	0	0	0	20
II	S_2	0	(4)	1	0	1	0	0	32
III	S_3	0	2	7	0	0	1	0	88
IV	S_4	0	6	2	0	0	0	1	52
		z_j	0	0	*	*	*	*	$OV = 0$
		$c_j - z_j$	9	6	*	*	*	*	

Equation	Basic Variable	c_j	9 x_1	6 x_2	0 S_1	0 S_2	0 S_3	0 S_4	RHS
		c_B							
$I' = I - 2II'$	S_1	0	0	$\frac{1}{2}$	1	$-\frac{1}{2}$	0	0	4
$II' = \frac{1}{4} II$	x_1	9	1	$\frac{1}{4}$	0	$\frac{1}{4}$	0	0	8
$III' = III - II'$	S_3	0	0	$\frac{13}{2}$	0	$-\frac{1}{2}$	1	0	72
$IV' = IV - 6II'$	S_4	0	0	$\left(\frac{1}{2}\right)$	0	$-\frac{3}{2}$	0	1	4
		z_j	*	$\frac{9}{4}$	*	$\frac{9}{4}$	*	*	$OV = 72$
		$c_j - z_j$	*	$\frac{15}{4}$	*	$-\frac{9}{4}$	*	*	

Equation	Basic Variable	c_j	9 x_1	6 x_2	0 S_1	0 S_2	0 S_3	0 S_4	RHS
		c_B							
$I'' = I' - \frac{1}{2} IV''$	S_1	0	0	0	1	(1)	0	-1	0
$II'' = II' - \frac{1}{4} IV''$	x_1	9	1	0	0	1	0	$-\frac{1}{2}$	6
$III'' = III' - \frac{13}{2} IV''$	S_3	0	0	0	0	19	1	-13	20
$IV'' = 2IV'$	x_2	6	0	1	0	-3	0	2	8
		z_j	*	*	*	-9	*	$\frac{15}{2}$	$OV = 102$
		$c_j - z_j$	*	*	*	9	*	$-\frac{15}{2}$	

Equation	Basic Variable	c_j	9 x_1	6 x_2	0 S_1	0 S_2	0 S_3	0 S_4	RHS
		c_B							
$I''' = 1I''$	S_2	0	0	0	1	1	0	-1	0
$II''' = II'' - 1I'''$	x_1	9	1	0	-1	0	0	$\frac{1}{2}$	6
$III''' = III'' - 19I'''$	S_3	0	0	0	-19	0	1	(6)	20
$IV''' = IV'' + 3I'''$	x_2	6	0	1	3	0	0	-1	8
		z_j	*	*	9	*	*	$-\frac{3}{2}$	$OV = 102$
		$c_j - z_j$	*	*	-9	*	*	$\frac{3}{2}$	

Figure 6.19 Sequence of simplex tableaux for example LP illustrating degeneracy

Equation	Basic Variable	c_j c_B	9 x_1	6 x_2	0 S_1	0 S_2	0 S_3	0 S_4	RHS
$I''''=I'''+1III''''$	S_2	0	0	0	$-\frac{13}{6}$	1	$\frac{1}{6}$	0	$\frac{10}{3}$
$II''''=II'''-\frac{1}{2}III''''$	x_1	9	1	0	$\frac{7}{12}$	0	$-\frac{1}{12}$	0	$\frac{13}{3}$
$III''''=\frac{1}{6}III'''$	S_4	0	0	0	$-\frac{19}{6}$	0	$\frac{1}{6}$	1	$\frac{10}{3}$
$IV''''=IV'''+1III''''$	x_2	6	0	1	$-\frac{1}{6}$	0	$\frac{1}{6}$	0	$\frac{34}{3}$
		z_j	*	*	$\frac{17}{4}$	*	$\frac{1}{4}$	*	$OV=107$
		$c_j-.z_j$	*	*	$-\frac{17}{4}$	*	$-\frac{1}{4}$	*	

Figure 6.19 (continued)

- **Third iteration.** The "excitement" continues when we try to leave corner point C by performing a third iteration of the simplex method. After selecting S_2 as the entering basic variable, we begin the selection of the leaving basic variable using the minimum-ratio procedure. Looking at Figure 6.19's third simplex tableau, verify for yourself that the minimum ratio occurs in equation II'' and has a value of 0, thereby indicating the leaving basic variable is S_1, equation I''''s current basic variable. Since this is our first encounter with a minimum ratio of 0, some explanation is required. Recall from Section 6.6 that the minimum ratio equals the value of the entering basic variable at which the leaving basic variable's value decreases to 0. Usually, some increase in the nonbasic variable is necessary before one of the basic variables becomes the first to decrease to a value of 0, thereby becoming the leaving basic variable. However, owing to the degeneracy of the current basic feasible solution, the leaving basic variable S_1 already has a value of 0! Any increase whatsoever in the entering basic variable S_2 will immediately result in the leaving basic variable decreasing to a negative value, thereby indicating infeasibility. In brief, it is impossible to increase the entering basic variable S_1. If we cannot increase the entering basic variable, the current basic variables' values will remain unchanged, and we will not be able to move one to a new basic feasible solution! We appear to be "stalled" at the degenerate basic feasible solution corresponding in Figure 6.18 to corner point C. Instead of quitting, let us "have faith" in the simplex method and perform the appropriate pivot for our selection of S_2 as the entering basic variable and S_1 as the leaving basic variable. You should verify for yourself that the pivot results in Figure 6.19's fourth simplex tableau. This tableau identifies the basic feasible solution

$$(x_1, x_2, S_1, S_2, S_3, S_4) = (6, 8, 0, 0, 20, 0),$$

the same degenerate basic feasible solution identified by the previous tableau. The difference is that S_2 instead of S_1 is the basic variable that has the value of 0. Thus, as predicted, we are "stalled" at the degenerate basic feasible solution corresponding in Figure 6.18 to corner point C. Again, instead of quitting, let us "keep the faith" and perform another iteration of the simplex method.

- **Fourth iteration.** Our persistence is finally rewarded, because, as we will soon see, the fourth iteration is routine and leads to the LP's optimal solution.

After selecting S_4 as the entering basic variable, nothing unusual occurs (i.e., a tie for the minimum ratio or a minimum ratio of 0) during the selection of S_3 as the leaving basic variable. You should verify for yourself that the appropriate pivot results in Figure 6.19's fifth simplex tableau. This tableau identifies the new basic feasible solution

$$(x_1, x_2, S_1, S_2, S_3, S_4) = (4\tfrac{1}{3}, 11\tfrac{1}{3}, 0, 3\tfrac{1}{3}, 0, 3\tfrac{1}{3}),$$

which corresponds geometrically in Figure 6.18 to corner point D. Thus, in the simplex method's fourth iteration, we have "broken away" from the degenerate basic feasible solution corresponding in Figure 6.18 to corner point C and moved to the adjacent corner point D. Observe in Figure 6.19's fifth simplex tableau that the $c_j - z_j$ row contains only nonpositive numbers, thereby indicating that the current basic feasible solution is optimal.

Our example has illustrated only part of the difficulties that can arise during the execution of the simplex method when we encounter a degenerate basic feasible solution. In our example, although we "stalled" at a degenerate basic feasible solution for one iteration, we were able to "break away" from it and move on to the optimal basic feasible solution. Unfortunately, experts have constructed example linear programs that demonstrate that something worse than "stalling" can happen. As illustrated by the four-variable, three-constraint LP in Exercise 6.20, it is possible to get "stuck" at a degenerate basic feasible solution in the sense that the simplex method repeats the same sequence of iterations over and over without ever leaving the degenerate basic feasible solution. The experience of practitioners who solve real-world LPs suggests that this is an extremely rare occurrence.[15] For this reason, we will not worry about getting "stuck" at a degenerate basic feasible solution. Thus, when a tie arises during the use of the minimum-ratio procedure to select the leaving basic variable, we will break the tie arbitrarily (e.g., by flipping a coin).

Although we will not use them, special tie-breaking rules have been devised for breaking a tie that arises when using the minimum ratio procedure to select the leaving basic variable. One such rule is introduced in Exercise 6.20. Use of one of these special tie-breaking rules guarantees that the simplex method will never get "stuck" at a degenerate basic feasible solution. For our purposes, however, these tie-breaking rules are "overkill," and we will simply break the ties arbitrarily.

We can summarize our discussion of degeneracy as follows:

Degeneracy occurs at a basic feasible solution when one or more of the basic variables has a value of 0. When executing the simplex method, the "signal" that the next basic feasible solution will be degenerate is a tie when using the minimum ratio procedure to select the leaving basic variable. Theoretically, a tie should be broken using one of the special tie-breaking rules devised to guarantee that the simplex method will not get "stuck" at a degenerate basic feasible solution. However, to break a tie we will select the leaving basic variable arbitrarily.

---

[15] Note that degenerate basic feasible solutions are not rare. What is rare is getting "stuck" at a degenerate basic feasible solution. For a discussion of how frequently getting "stuck" occurs in practice, consult the following: S.I. Gass, "Comments on the Possibility of Cycling with the Simplex Method," *Operations Research*, **20**, 4, July-August 1979, pp. 848-852.

6.10 CONCLUDING REMARKS

In this chapter, we have learned how the simplex method solves an LP in standard form, that is, an LP whose objective function involves maximization, whose structural constraints are all of the $\leqslant$ type with nonnegative constants appearing on their right-hand sides, and whose decision variables are all subject to nonnegativity constraints. Knowing how to solve a standard LP may satisfy your curiosity about the simplex method. If not, you should proceed to Chapter 7, where the topics include how the simplex method solves a nonstandard LP, how the simplex method recognizes infeasibility, unboundedness, and multiple optimality, and how the optimal simplex tableau serves as a starting point for sensitivity analysis. (Chapter 7 also includes an introduction to a topic known as *duality*.)

6.11 CHAPTER CHECKLIST AND GLOSSARY

Quickly review this chapter by rereading the material highlighted by a vertical line in the left margin. You should then be familiar with the concepts, techniques, and terminology in the Checklist and Glossary that follow. If you need "help" with a particular item, consult the section or sections indicated for a more detailed discussion.

Checklist of Concepts and Techniques

☐ Using slack variables to transform into equality form an LP whose structural constraints are all of the $\leqslant$ type with nonnegative right-hand sides. [6.2]

☐ Understanding how the geometrical notion of a corner point is equivalent to the algebraic notion of a basic feasible solution. [6.3]

☐ Understanding how the geometric notion of two adjacent corner points is equivalent to the algebraic notion of two basic feasible solutions whose respective sets of nonbasic variables and basic variables both differ by exactly one variable. [6.4]

☐ Given the choices for the entering basic variable and the leaving basic variable, understanding how to perform a pivot that enables identification of the new basic feasible solution. [6.5]

☐ Constructing a simplex tableau. [6.6]

☐ Algebraically selecting the entering basic variable by computing each nonbasic variable's $c_j - z_j$ value. [6.6]

☐ The geometrical significance of the algebraic selection of the entering basic variable. [6.6]

☐ Algebraically selecting the leaving basic variable by performing the minimum ratio procedure. [6.6]

☐ The geometrical significance of the algebraic selection of the leaving basic variable. [6.6]

☐ Execution of the simplex method to solve a standard LP, that is, an LP whose objective function involves maximization, whose structural constraints are all of the ≤ type with nonnegative right-hand sides, and whose decision variables are all subject to nonnegativity constraints. [6.7, 6.8]

☐ Understanding the implication of encountering a degenerate basic feasible solution during the execution of the simplex method. [6.9]

Glossary

Simplex method. An algebraic procedure for solving an LP. [6.1, 6.4, 6.7]

Standard LP. An LP whose objective function involves maximization, whose structural constraints are all of the ≤ type with nonnegative constants appearing on their right-hand sides, and whose decision variables are all subject to nonnegativity constraints. [6.1]

Nonstandard LP. An LP lacking at least one of the characteristics of a standard LP.

LP in equality form. The LP obtained from the original LP by (1) adding a nonnegative slack variable to the left-hand side of each structural constraint. [6.2]

LP's equality form system of equations. The system of equations that comprise the structural constraints of the LP in equality form. [6.2]

Solution. Any assignment of values to the variables that satisfies the LP's equality form system of equations. [6.3]

Nonnegative solution. A solution in which all variables have nonnegative values. [6.3]

Basic solution. Given an equality form system of equations with m equations involving n variables (with $m < n$), a basic solution is obtained by arbitrarily setting $n - m$ of the variables equal to 0 and then determining the unique solution (if one exists) to the resulting square system of m equations involving the remaining m variables. [6.3]

Nonbasic variable. A variable that must equal 0 in a basic solution. [6.3]

Basic variable. A variable that need not equal 0 in a basic solution. [6.3]

Basic feasible solution. A solution that is both a basic solution and a nonnegative solution. A basic feasible solution is the algebraic equivalent of the geometric notion of a corner point of the LP's feasible region. [6.3]

Adjacent basic feasible solutions. Two basic feasible solutions whose respective sets of nonbasic variables and basic variables both differ by exactly one variable. [6.4]

Entering basic variable. That currently nonbasic variable that is selected to become a basic variable during the move to an adjacent basic feasible solution. At the completion of the move, the entering basic variable's value will have increased from its former value of 0 to a positive value (except possibly in the case of degeneracy, when the entering basic variable might end with a value of 0). [6.4]

Leaving basic variable. That currently basic variable that is selected to become a nonbasic variable during the move to an adjacent basic feasible solution. At the completion of the move, the leaving basic variable will have decreased from its former positive value to a value of 0 (except possibly in the case of degeneracy, when the leaving basic variable might already have a value of 0). [6.4]

Elementary equation operations. Algebraic operations performed on a system of equations that alter the appearance of the system of equations but do not alter the set of solutions to the system of equations. [6.5]

Transformed system of equations. The equivalent system of equations that results from applying one or more elementary equation operations to the original system of equations. [6.5]

Isolated variable. A variable is isolated in a particular equation if its coefficient is 1 in that equation and 0 in every other equation. [6.5]

Isolated set of variables. A set of m variables is an isolated set of variables in a system of m equations if each of the m variables is isolated in a different one of the m equations. [6.5]

Pivot. A transformation of the current system of equations governed by specific rules that preserve the existing isolation of the basic variables that will remain basic while simultaneously isolating the pivot variable (the entering basic variable) in the pivot equation (the equation in which the leaving basic variable is now isolated). Performing a pivot is the algebraic equivalent of the geometric notion of "walking" from a corner point to an adjacent corner point. [6.5]

Simplex tableau. A tabular representation of the current system of equations that facilitates the performance of the algebra required to select the entering basic variable, select the leaving basic variable, and perform the pivot that enables identification of the next basic feasible solution. [6.6]

c_j value. A nonbasic variable's c_j value is the objective value's direct rate of increase per unit increase in the nonbasic variable. A nonbasic variable's c_j value equals its objective-function coefficient. [6.6]

z_j value. A nonbasic variable's z_j value is the objective value's rate of decrease per unit increase in the nonbasic variable. A nonbasic variable's z_j value equals the sum of products obtained by multiplying each basic variable's objective-function coefficient (as specified in the simplex tableau's c_B column) by its rate of decrease per unit increase in the nonbasic variable (as specified in the simplex tableau column that contains the nonbasic variable's coefficients). [6.6]

$c_j - z_j$ value. A nonbasic variable's $c_j - z_j$ value is the objective value's net rate of increase per unit increase in the nonbasic variable. A nonbasic variable's $c_j - z_j$ value equals its c_j value minus its z_j value. The entering basic variable is selected as that nonbasic variable with the most positive $c_j - z_j$ value when maximizing or the most negative $c_j - z_j$ value when minimizing. [6.6]

Minimum ratio procedure. The procedure used to select the leaving basic variable on the basis of which basic variable is the first to decrease to a value of 0 as the entering basic variable is increased. [6.6]

Iteration. An iteration of the simplex method consists of three parts: (1) selection of the entering basic variable, (2) selection of the leaving basic variable, and (3) performance of the pivot that enables identification of an adjacent basic feasible solution with an improved objective value. [6.7]

Degenerate basic feasible solution. A basic feasible solution in which one or more of the basic variables has a value of 0. [6.10]

Nondegenerate basic feasible solution. A basic feasible solution in which all basic variables have positive values. [6.10]

EXERCISES

Exercises 6.1 and 6.2 test your understanding of the correspondence between geometry and algebra.

*6.1. Consider an LP whose feasible region corresponds to

the shaded region in Figure 6.20. In this graph, each of the feasible region's boundary equations is labeled with the variable that equals 0 at all points lying on the boundary equation, where x_j denotes

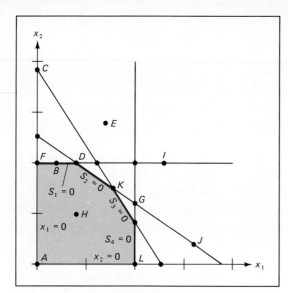

Figure 6.20 Graph for Exercise 6.1

the jth decision variable and S_i denotes the slack variable for the ith structural constraint. Also labeled on the graph are the twelve points A through L.

(a) Which of the labeled points correspond to solutions of the LP's equality form system of equations?

(b) Which of the labeled points correspond to nonnegative solutions to the LP's equality form system of equations?

(c) Which of the labeled points correspond to basic solutions of the LP's equality form system of equations?

(d) Which of the labeled points correspond to basic feasible solutions of the LP's equality form system of equations?

(e) For each of the points identified in part (d) as corresponding to basic feasible solutions, specify the set of nonbasic variables and the set of basic variables.

(f) Imagine we are located at point A and start walking along the feasible region's boundary toward point F.

    1. As we walk, specify for each nonbasic variable in the basic feasible solution corresponding to point A whether the variable's value is increasing or remaining constant at 0.

    2. As we walk, specify for each basic variable in the basic feasible solution corresponding to point A whether the variable's value is increasing, decreasing, or remaining constant at 0.

3. Which of the basic variables in part (2) is the first to reach the value of 0 when we finally arrive at point F?

4. Using the format of Figure 6.4, diagram the one-for-one trade between the set of basic variables and the set of nonbasic variables that takes place when we move from point A to point F.

(g) Redo part (f), this time assuming we are located at point D and start walking along the feasible region's boundary toward the point K.

6.2. Redo Exercise 6.1, this time using the graph in Figure 6.21.

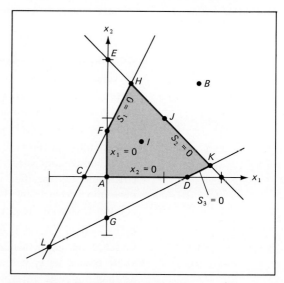

Figure 6.21 Graph for Exercise 6.2

Exercises 6.3 through 6.6 illustrate that it is possible (though inefficient) to solve an LP by explicitly enumerating every basic solution, then identifying those that are basic feasible solutions, and finally identifying the basic feasible solution with the best objective value.

6.3. Consider the following LP:

$$\text{Maximize} \quad 3x_1 + 5x_2$$

$$\text{subject to} \quad \begin{aligned} x_1 \quad\quad &\leqslant\ 4 \\ 2x_2 &\leqslant 12 \\ 3x_1 + 2x_2 &\leqslant 18 \end{aligned}$$

$$\text{and} \quad x_1 \geqslant 0,\, x_2 \geqslant 0$$

(a) Graph the LP's feasible region, and (in a manner similar to Figure 6.2) assign the labels A, B, C, and so on to each point on the graph corresponding to a basic solution. Note: If you have worked Exercise 2.1 or 3.1, you have already graphed the LP's feasible region.

(b) Using S_1, S_2, and S_3 to denote the respective slack variables for the first, second, and third structural constraints, write the LP's equality form system of equations.

(c) How many nonbasic variables are there in a basic solution to part (b)'s system of equations?

(d) For each of the distinct ways to choose the set of nonbasic variables from x_1, x_2, S_1, S_2, and S_3, set the nonbasic variables equal to 0 and then determine the solution (if one exists) to the square system of equations involving the basic variables. By summarizing your results in a table similar to Table 6.2, relate each basic solution you determine to a specific point in part (a)'s graph of the feasible region.

(e) Delete basic solutions from your table in part (d) until only basic feasible solutions remain. For each of these, substitute the variables' values into the objective function to obtain the corresponding objective value. Summarize your results in a table similar to Table 6.3.

(f) Using part (e)'s table, identify the LP's optimal solution.

(g) Why is it much more efficient to determine the LP's optimal solution using the simplex method instead of the procedure followed in parts (b)–(f)?

*6.4. Redo Exercise 6.3, this time using the following LP:

$$\text{Maximize} \quad 5x_1 + 10x_2$$

$$\text{subject to} \quad \begin{array}{rcrcr} -x_1 &+& 2x_2 &\leqslant& 25 \\ x_1 &+& x_2 &\leqslant& 20 \\ 5x_1 &+& 3x_2 &\leqslant& 75 \end{array}$$

$$\text{and} \quad x_1 \geqslant 0, x_2 \geqslant 0$$

Note: If you have worked Exercise 2.2 or 3.2, you have already graphed the LP's feasible region.

6.5. Redo Exercise 6.3, this time using the following LP:

$$\text{Maximize} \quad 4x_1 + 3x_2 + 6x_3$$

$$\text{subject to} \quad \begin{array}{rcrcrcr} 3x_1 &+& x_2 &+& 3x_3 &\leqslant& 30 \\ 2x_1 &+& 2x_2 &+& 3x_3 &\leqslant& 40 \end{array}$$

$$\text{and} \quad x_1 \geqslant 0, x_2 \geqslant 0, x_3 \geqslant 0$$

Note that, because the LP involves three decision variables, you need not graph its feasible region.

6.6. Consider an LP that has 10 nonnegative decision variables and 20 structural constraints.

(a) Using the formula provided at the end of Section 6.3, compute an upper bound on the

number of basic solutions to the LP's equality form system of equations.

(b) Explain why part (a)'s answer is only an upper bound instead of an exact answer.

(c) Explain why we expect it to be much more efficient to determine the LP's optimal solution using the simplex method instead of explicitly enumerating every basic solution.

Exercises 6.7 through 6.13 test your ability to use the simplex method to solve a standard LP.

6.7. Consider the following LP:

$$\text{Maximize} \quad 5x_1 + 4x_2$$

$$\text{subject to} \quad \begin{array}{rcrcr} x_1 & & &\leqslant& 4 \\ & & 2x_2 &\leqslant& 12 \\ 3x_1 &+& 2x_2 &\leqslant& 18 \end{array}$$

(a) Graph the LP's feasible region. Note that, if you have worked Exercise 2.1, 3.1, or 6.3, then you have already graphed the LP's feasible region (even though the objective function is different).

(b) Use the simplex method to solve the LP.

(c) What are the optimal values of the decision variables, the slack variables, and the objective function?

(d) Using part (a)'s graph of the feasible region, identify the sequence of corner points to which your sequence of simplex tableaux correspond.

*6.8. Redo Exercise 6.7, this time using the following LP:

$$\text{Maximize} \quad 5x_1 + 10x_2$$

$$\text{subject to} \quad \begin{array}{rcrcr} -x_1 &+& 2x_2 &\leqslant& 25 \\ x_1 &+& x_2 &\leqslant& 20 \\ 5x_1 &+& 3x_2 &\leqslant& 75 \end{array}$$

$$\text{and} \quad x_1 \geqslant 0, x_2 \geqslant 0$$

Note that you have already done part (a) if you have worked Exercise 2.2, 3.2, or 6.4.

6.9. Redo Exercise 6.7, this time using the following LP:

$$\text{Maximize} \quad 3x_1 + 2x_2$$

$$\text{subject to} \quad \begin{array}{rcrcr} 2x_1 &+& 4x_2 &\leqslant& 22 \\ -x_1 &+& 4x_2 &\leqslant& 10 \\ 2x_1 &-& x_2 &\leqslant& 7 \\ x_1 &-& 2x_2 &\leqslant& 2 \end{array}$$

$$\text{and} \quad x_1 \geqslant 0, x_2 \geqslant 0$$

Note that you have already done part (a) if you have worked Exercise 2.5 or 3.5.

*6.10. Redo Exercise 6.7, this time using the following LP:

$$\text{Maximize} \quad 5x_1 + 4x_2$$

$$\text{subject to} \quad 10x_1 + 15x_2 \leqslant 150$$
$$20x_1 + 10x_2 \leqslant 160$$
$$-3x_1 + x_2 \leqslant 3$$

$$\text{and} \quad x_1 \geqslant 0, x_2 \geqslant 0$$

Note that you have *almost* done part (a) if you have worked Exercise 2.6 or 3.6; you have only to modify your graph to account for the structural constraint of the $\geqslant$ type that is missing from this exercise's LP.

6.11. Redo Exercise 6.7, this time using the following LP:

$$\text{Maximize} \quad 10x_1 + 20x_2$$

$$\text{subject to} \quad x_1 + 6x_2 \leqslant 54$$
$$x_1 + x_2 \leqslant 19$$
$$-x_1 + x_2 \leqslant 2$$
$$2x_1 - 3x_2 \leqslant 18$$

$$\text{and} \quad x_1 \geqslant 0, x_2 \geqslant 0$$

Note that you have *almost* done part (a) if you have worked Exercise 2.7 or 3.7; you have only to modify your graph to account for the structural constraint of the $\geqslant$ type that is missing from this exercise's LP.

6.12. Use the simplex method to solve the following LP:

$$\text{Maximize} \quad 4x_1 + 3x_2 + 6x_3$$

$$\text{subject to} \quad 3x_1 + x_2 + 3x_3 \leqslant 30$$
$$2x_1 + 2x_2 + 3x_3 \leqslant 40$$

$$\text{and} \quad x_1 \geqslant 0, x_2 \geqslant 0, x_3 \geqslant 0$$

6.13. Use the simplex method to solve the following LP:

$$\text{Maximize} \quad 7x_1 + 5x_2 + 9x_3 + 10x_4$$

$$\text{subject to} \quad 2x_1 + x_2 + 3x_3 + x_4 \leqslant 9$$
$$x_1 + x_2 + 2x_3 + 2x_4 \leqslant 10$$
$$3x_1 + 2x_2 + x_3 + 4x_4 \leqslant 21$$

$$\text{and} \quad x_1 \geqslant 0, x_2 \geqslant 0, x_3 \geqslant 0, x_4 \geqslant 0$$

Exercises 6.14 and 6.15 illustrate that "greedily" selecting as the entering basic variable the nonbasic variable with the most positive $c_j - z_j$ value does *not* guarantee the fewest iterations of the simplex method.

*6.14. When solving OMC's LP in Section 6.8, we "greedily" selected as the entering basic variable that nonbasic variable with the most positive $c_j - z_j$ value. This selection criterion led to the optimal solution in

three iterations of the simplex method—iterations that corresponded to the geometrical route to the optimal solution displayed in Figure 6.17.

Now reconsider the initial simplex tableau displayed in Figure 6.16(a). This time, ignore the fact that x_1's $c_j - z_j$ value is more positive than x_2's $c_j - z_j$ value and select x_2 as the entering basic variable. Then continue executing the simplex method until you obtain the optimal solution.

(a) How many iterations did you perform?
(b) In Figure 6.17, to what geometrical route to the optimal solution do your iterations correspond?
(c) What general principle does this exercise illustrate?

6.15. This exercise assumes you have already worked Exercise 6.7, where you "greedily" selected as the entering variable that nonbasic variable with the most positive $c_j - z_j$ value. This selection criterion led to the optimal solution in three iterations of the simplex method.

Now reconsider your initial simplex tableau. This time, ignore the fact that x_1's $c_j - z_j$ value is more positive than x_2's $c_j - z_j$ value and select x_2 as the entering basic variable. Then continue executing the simplex method until you obtain the optimal solution.

(a) How many iterations did you perform?
(b) Using your graph of the LP's feasible region from Exercise 6.7, identify the geometrical route to the optimal solution to which your iterations correspond.
(c) What general principle does this exercise illustrate?

The next exercise illustrates what happens when the leaving basic variable is incorrectly identified because of a mistake when applying the minimum ratio procedure.

6.16 Reconsider the initial simplex tableau for OMC's LP, as displayed in Figure 6.16. Suppose that, when applying the minimum ratio procedure during the first iteration of the simplex method, the leaving basic variable was incorrectly identified as S_1 instead of S_2.

(a) By performing the pivot with x_1 as the entering basic variable and S_1 as the leaving basic variable, determine the tableau that would be obtained instead of Figure 6.16's second tableau.
(b) Explain whether part (a)'s tableau corresponds to a basic feasible solution.
(c) Using Figure 6.2, provide a geometrical interpretation of what happened because of the incorrect identification of the leaving basic variable.

The next exercise involves three misconceptions sometimes held by first-time students of the simplex method.

6.17. Each of the following three statements is *false*. In a concise but explicit manner, explain why each statement is false, and illustrate your explanation using a graph of the feasible region for a two-variable LP of your own choosing.

(a) In the optimal solution to a linear program, every slack variable must equal 0.

(b) When using the simplex method to solve an LP, a variable can never be a basic variable in one tableau, then a nonbasic variable in a later tableau, and then a basic variable again in an even later tableau.

(c) When using the simplex method to solve an LP, the next-to-the-last simplex tableau always corresponds to the basic feasible solution that has the second-highest objective value.

Working Exercises 6.18 through 6.20 will improve your understanding of degeneracy.

6.18 Consider the following LP:

$$\text{Maximize} \quad 5x_1 + 4x_2$$
$$\text{subject to} \quad x_1 \qquad\qquad \leqslant 4$$
$$2x_2 \leqslant 12$$
$$3x_1 + 2x_2 \leqslant 18$$
$$2x_1 + x_2 \leqslant 11$$
$$\text{and} \quad x_1 \geqslant 0, x_2 \geqslant 0$$

Let S_1, S_2, S_3, and S_4 denote the respective slack variables for the first through fourth structural constraints.

(a) Graph the LP's feasible region and (in a manner similar to Figure 6.3) label each boundary equation with the variable that equals 0 at all points lying on the boundary equation. Note that, if you have already worked Exercise 6.7, you have only to modify your graph to account for the added constraint $2x_1 + x_2 \leqslant 11$.

(b) For each corner point in part (a)'s feasible region, specify which variables equal 0.

(c) Using your answer to part (b), determine which of the corner points in part (a)'s feasible region corresponds to a degenerate basic feasible solution. Why?

(d) Verify that constructing the initial simplex tableau and performing one iteration of the simplex method generates the tableau displayed in Figure 6.22.

(e) Looking at Figure 6.22's tableau, how can you tell that the next iteration of the simplex method will lead to a tableau corresponding to the degenerate basic feasible solution?

Equation	Basic Variable	c_j c_B	5 x_1	4 x_2	0 S_1	0 S_2	0 S_3	0 S_4	RHS
I' = 1I	x_1	5	1	0	1	0	0	0	4
II' = II − 0I'	S_2	0	0	2	0	1	0	0	12
III' = III − 3I'	S_3	0	0	2	−3	0	1	0	6
IV' = IV −2I'	S_4	0	0	1	−2	0	0	1	3
	z_j		*	0	5	*	*	*	OV=20
	$c_j - z_j$		*	4	−5	*	*	*	

Figure 6.22 Simplex tableau after one iteration for Exercise 6.18's LP

(f) In Figure 6.22's tableau, arbitrarily break the tie between S_3 and S_4 for the leaving basic variable by selecting S_4. Then continue executing the simplex method until you obtain the optimal solution. Did you temporarily "stall" at the degenerate basic feasible solution (i.e., did two or more successive tableaux correspond to the same basic feasible solution)?

(g) Reconsider Figure 6.22's tableau and, this time, select S_3 instead of S_4 as the entering basic variable. Then continue executing the simplex method until you obtain the optimal solution. Did you temporarily "stall" at the degenerate basic feasible solution?

(h) Using your answers to parts (f) and (g), comment on the validity of the following statement:

When the simplex method encounters a degenerate basic feasible solution, a temporary "stall" will always occur.

(i) Suppose at the first iteration of the simplex method that, instead of selecting x_1 as the entering basic variable and thereby obtaining Figure 6.22's tableau, you select x_2 as the entering basic variable. Using only part (a)'s graph of the feasible region, determine whether a subsequent simplex tableau will correspond to a degenerate basic feasible solution.

(j) Using your answer to part (i), comment on the validity of the following statement:

If a degenerate basic feasible solution exists, it will always correspond to one of the sequence of the simplex tableaux generated when using the simplex method to solve the LP.

6.19. Consider the following LP:

$$\text{Maximize} \quad 20x_1 + 30x_2 + 10x_3$$
$$\text{subject to} \quad x_1 + x_2 \qquad\qquad \leqslant 5$$
$$3x_2 + 5x_3 \leqslant 15$$
$$\text{and} \quad x_1 \geqslant 0, x_2 \geqslant 0, x_3 \geqslant 0$$

283

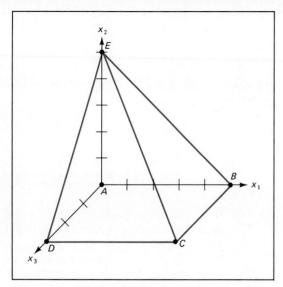

Figure 6.23 Three-dimensional example of degeneracy

Let S_1 and S_2 denote the respective slack variables for the first and second structural constraints. As you will verify below, Figure 6.23 is a three-dimensional representation of the LP's feasible region. The feasible region has the shape of a pyramid with two vertical walls and two slanted walls. The feasible region has five corner points labeled $A - E$ and five faces, which we will refer to as faces ADE, $ABCD$, ABE, BCE, and CDE.

(a) Verify that Figure 6.23 represents the LP's feasible region by convincing yourself of the following: (1) faces ADE, $ABCD$, and ABE correspond respectively to the boundary equations for the nonnegativity constraints $x_1 \geqslant 0$, $x_2 \geqslant 0$, and $x_3 \geqslant 0$ and (2) faces BCE and CDE correspond respectively to the boundary equations for the structural constraints $x_1 + x_2 \leqslant 5$ and $3x_2 + 5x_3 \leqslant 15$.

(b) Use your answer to part (a) to complete the following table:

Face	Decision Variable or Slack Variable That Equals 0 at All Points Lying on the Face
ADE	
ABCD	
ABE	
BCE	
CDE	

(c) Use your answer to part (b) to complete the following table:

Corner Point	Variables That Equal 0 in the Basic Feasible Solution to Which the Corner Point Corresponds
A	
B	
C	
D	
E	

(d) Using your answer to part (c), determine which corner point in Figure 6.23's feasible region corresponds to a degenerate basic feasible. Why?

(e) Does the LP contain any redundant constraints?

(f) Using your answers to parts (d) and (e), comment on the validity of the following statement:

When an LP has a degenerate basic feasible solution, there is always a redundant constraint.

6.20. Consider the following LP:

$$\text{Maximize} \quad \tfrac{3}{4}x_1 - 20x_2 + \tfrac{1}{2}x_3 - 6x_4$$

$$\text{subject to} \quad \tfrac{1}{4}x_1 - 8x_2 - x_3 + 9x_4 \leqslant 0$$
$$\tfrac{1}{2}x_1 - 12x_2 - \tfrac{1}{2}x_3 + 3x_4 \leqslant 0$$
$$x_3 \leqslant 1$$

$$\text{and} \quad x_1 \geqslant 0, x_2 \geqslant 0, x_3 \geqslant 0, x_4 \geqslant 0$$

Let S_1, S_2, and S_3 denote the respective slack variables for the first, second, and third structural constraints.

(a) Assume we use the following criteria for selecting the entering basic variable and leaving basic variable:

Criterion for selecting the entering basic variable: In the usual manner, select as the entering basic variable that nonbasic variable with the most positive $c_j - z_j$ value. Break ties arbitrarily.

Criterion for selecting the leaving basic variable: In the usual manner, select the leaving basic variable using the minimum-ratio procedure. Break ties by selecting the basic variable for the lowest-numbered equation (e.g., if there is a tie for the minimum-ratio between equations I and III, select equation I's basic variable as the leaving basic variable).

Using these criteria, verify that constructing the initial simplex tableau and performing five iterations of the simplex method generates the sequence of tableaux displayed in Figure 6.24. (You need *not* verify the algebra of the pivots; just verify the selection of the entering basic variable and the leaving basic variable.)

(b) To what values of x_1, x_2, x_3, x_4, S_1, S_2, and S_3 do all six tableaux displayed in Figure 6.24 correspond?

(c) What phenomenon accounts for the fact that, after five iterations, we are "stalled" at the same basic feasible solution?

(d) Starting from the last tableau in Figure 6.24, perform one iteration of the simplex method. What do you observe when you compare the resulting tableau with Figure 6.24's initial tableau?

(e) Assuming we continued to use the selection criterion in part (a), what would happen if we continued to execute the simplex method?

(f) Now assume that, instead of part (a)'s selection criterion, we use the following:

Criterion for selecting the entering basic variable. Select as the entering basic variable that nonbasic variable having a positive $c_j - z_j$ value and appearing leftmost in the tableau (e.g., if x_2, x_4, and S_3 are the nonbasic with positive $c_j - z_j$ values, select x_2).

Criterion for selecting the leaving basic variable. In the usual manner, select the leaving basic variable using the minimum ratio procedure. Break ties by selecting the basic variable appearing leftmost in the tableau (e.g., if the tie for the minimum ratio

Figure 6.24 Sequence of simplex tableaux for Exercise 6.20's LP

Equation	Basic Variable	c_B	$\frac{3}{4}$ x_1	-20 x_2	$\frac{1}{2}$ x_3	-6 x_4	0 S_1	0 S_2	0 S_3	RHS
I	S_1	0	$\frac{1}{4}$	-8	-1	9	1	0	0	0
II	S_2	0	$\frac{1}{2}$	-12	$-\frac{1}{2}$	3	0	1	0	0
III	S_3	0	0	0	1	0	0	0	1	1
	z_j		0	0	0	0	$*$	$*$	$*$	$OV = 0$
	$c_j - z_j$		$\frac{3}{4}$	-20	$\frac{1}{2}$	-6	$*$	$*$	$*$	

Equation	Basic Variable	c_B	$\frac{3}{4}$ x_1	-20 x_2	$\frac{1}{2}$ x_3	-6 x_4	0 S_1	0 S_2	0 S_3	RHS
I′	x_1	$\frac{3}{4}$	1	-32	-4	36	4	0	0	0
II′	S_2	0	0	4	$\frac{3}{2}$	-15	-2	1	0	0
III′	S_3	0	0	0	1	0	0	0	1	1
	z_j		$*$	-24	-3	27	3	$*$	$*$	$OV = 0$
	$c_j - z_j$		$*$	4	$\frac{7}{2}$	-33	-3	$*$	$*$	

Equation	Basic Variable	c_B	$\frac{3}{4}$ x_1	-20 x_2	$\frac{1}{2}$ x_3	-6 x_4	0 S_1	0 S_2	0 S_3	RHS
I″	x_1	$\frac{3}{4}$	1	0	8	-84	-12	8	0	0
II″	x_2	-20	0	1	$\frac{3}{8}$	$-\frac{15}{4}$	$-\frac{1}{2}$	$\frac{1}{4}$	0	0
III″	S_3	0	0	0	1	0	0	0	1	1
	z_j		$*$	$*$	$-\frac{3}{2}$	12	1	1	$*$	$OV = 0$
	$c_j - z_j$		$*$	$*$	2	-18	-1	-1	$*$	

Equation	Basic Variable	c_j	$\frac{3}{4}$	-20	$\frac{1}{2}$	-6	0	0	0	
		c_B	x_1	x_2	x_3	x_4	S_1	S_2	S_3	RHS
I''''	x_3	$\frac{1}{2}$	$\frac{1}{8}$	0	1	$-\frac{21}{2}$	$-\frac{3}{2}$	1	0	0
II''''	x_2	-20	$-\frac{3}{64}$	1	0	$\boxed{\frac{3}{16}}$	$\frac{1}{16}$	$-\frac{1}{8}$	0	0
III''''	S_3	0	$-\frac{1}{8}$	0	0	$\frac{21}{2}$	$\frac{3}{2}$	-1	1	1
		z_j	1	*	*	-9	-2	3	*	OV = 0
		$c_j - z_j$	$-\frac{1}{4}$	*	*	3	2	-3	*	

Equation	Basic Variable	c_j	$\frac{3}{4}$	-20	$\frac{1}{2}$	-6	0	0	0	
		c_B	x_1	x_2	x_3	x_4	S_1	S_2	S_3	RHS
I'''''	x_3	$\frac{1}{2}$	$-\frac{5}{2}$	56	1	0	$\boxed{2}$	-6	0	0
II'''''	x_4	-6	$-\frac{1}{4}$	$\frac{16}{3}$	0	1	$\frac{1}{3}$	$-\frac{2}{3}$	0	0
III'''''	S_3	0	$\frac{5}{2}$	-56	0	0	-2	6	1	1
		z_j	$\frac{1}{4}$	-4	*	*	-1	1	*	OV = 0
		$c_j - z_j$	$\frac{1}{2}$	-16	*	*	1	-1	*	

Equation	Basic Variable	c_j	$\frac{3}{4}$	-20	$\frac{1}{2}$	-6	0	0	0	
		c_B	x_1	x_2	x_3	x_4	S_1	S_2	S_3	RHS
I''''''	S_1	0	$\frac{5}{4}$	28	$\frac{1}{2}$	0	1	-3	0	0
II''''''	x_4	-6	$\frac{1}{6}$	-4	$-\frac{1}{6}$	1	0	$\frac{1}{3}$	0	0
III''''''	S_3	0	0	0	1	0	0	0	1	1
		z_j	-1	24	1	*	*	-2	*	OV = 0
		$c_j - z_j$	$\frac{7}{4}$	-44	$-\frac{1}{2}$	*	*	2	*	

Figure 6.24 (continued)

occurs in equations in which x_2 and S_1 are currently the basic variables, select x_2 as the leaving basic variable).

R. G. Bland has proved that using these criteria guarantees the simplex method will never become "stuck" at a degenerate basic feasible solution (i.e., will never repeat the same sequence of iterations over and over without ever leaving the degenerate basic feasible solution). Illustrate that Bland's criteria work by doing the following: (1) Note that their application to this exercise's LP generates the first five tableaux displayed in Figure 6.24. (2) Starting from Figure 6.24's fifth tableau, perform two more iterations of the simplex method to obtain a tableau corresponding to the optimal solution (instead of Figure 6.24's last tableau).

LINEAR PROGRAMMING: THE SIMPLEX METHOD CONTINUED, SENSITIVITY ANALYSIS, AND DUALITY

7.1 INTRODUCTION

We will begin this chapter by discussing how to modify the simplex method to solve a nonstandard LP. Next, we will learn how, during the execution of the simplex method, to recognize infeasibility, unboundedness, and multiple optimality. Then we will see how the optimal simplex tableau serves as a starting point for sensitivity analysis. Finally, we introduce *duality*.

7.2 MODIFYING THE SIMPLEX METHOD TO SOLVE A NONSTANDARD LINEAR PROGRAM

Until now, we have assumed that the LP we wish to solve is a standard LP, that is, an LP with the following characteristics:

- The LP's objective function is of the maximization type.
- All structural constraints are of the ⩽ type with nonnegative constants appearing on the constraints' right-hand sides.
- All decision variables are subject to nonnegativity constraints.

In this section, we will discuss modifications to the simplex method that enable it to solve a nonstandard LP, that is, an LP that lacks one or more of the above characteristics.

Solving an LP That Involves Minimization

To solve an LP involving minimization, we need only modify the simplex method's criterion for selection of the entering basic variable. Recall that a nonbasic variable's $c_j - z_j$ value equals the objective value's rate of *increase* per unit increase in the nonbasic variable. Consequently, to improve the objective value when maximizing, we limit our selection of the entering basic variable to those nonbasic variables with positive $c_j - z_j$ values, thereby guaranteeing an increase in the objective value. However, when the LP involves minimization, improvement in the objective value requires the objective value to decrease, not increase. Therefore, when minimizing, we limit our selection of the entering basic variable to those nonbasic variables with negative $c_j - z_j$ values. For example, if we select as the entering basic variable a nonbasic variable with a $c_j - z_j$ value of -7, the objective value's rate of increase per unit increase in the entering basic variable is -7, equivalent to a rate of decrease of 7.

We can summarize the selection of the entering basic variable when the LP involves minimization as follows:

Modification to the Procedure for Selecting the Entering Basic Variable When the LP Involves Minimization

To select the entering basic variable when minimizing, we first compute each nonbasic variable's $c_j - z_j$ value in the usual manner. Then, if every nonbasic variable has a nonnegative $c_j - z_j$ value, the current basic feasible solution is optimal, so we may terminate execution of the simplex method. Otherwise, we select as the entering basic variable any nonbasic variable with a negative $c_j - z_j$ value. To have a definite rule to follow, we will select as the entering basic variable that nonbasic variable with the most negative $c_j - z_j$ value, although (as was the case when maximizing) being "greedy" does not guarantee we will find the LP's optimal solution in the fewest iterations of the simplex method.

Solving an LP When Some Decision Variables Lack Nonnegativity Constraints

In Sections 3.9 and 3.10, we discussed respectively how to solve an LP involving unconstrained decision variables and how to solve an LP with decision variables having nonzero lower bounds. Consequently, we can omit here a detailed discussion of how to proceed when not all the LP's decision variables are subject to nonnegativity constraints. To summarize,

A Procedure for Solving an LP When Some Decision Variables Lack Nonnegativity Constraints

1. Use the "tricks" discussed in Sections 3.9 and 3.10 to convert the LP into an equivalent LP with all nonnegative decision variables.

2. Use the simplex method to obtain the equivalent LP's optimal solution.

3. Using the equivalent LP's optimal solution, determine the original LP's optimal solution in the manner described in Sections 3.9 and 3.10.

Eliminating Negative Right-Hand Sides from Structural Constraints

At this point, we only know how to solve an LP whose structural constraints are all of the $\leq$ type with nonnegative right-hand sides. We now wish to learn how to solve an LP having one or both of the following characteristics:

1. One or more structural constraints has a negative right-hand side.

2. The structural constraints are a mixture of the $\leqslant$, $\geqslant$, and $=$ types.

When faced with a structural constraint with a negative right-hand side, we simply replace the constraint with the equivalent constraint obtained by first multiplying both sides of the constraint by -1 and then, if it is an inequality, reversing its sense (i.e., change $\leqslant$ to $\geqslant$, change $\geqslant$ to $\leqslant$, and leave $=$ unchanged). Three examples follow.

Original Structural Constraint	Equivalent Structural Constraint
$3x_1 - x_2 + 2x_3 \leqslant -40$	$-3x_1 + x_2 - 2x_3 \geqslant 40$
$-2x_1 + 5x_2 - 3x_3 = -60$	$2x_1 - 5x_2 + 3x_3 = 60$
$-4x_1 + 2x_2 - 7x_3 \geqslant -50$	$4x_1 - 2x_2 + 7x_3 \leqslant 50$

Solving an LP Containing Structural Constraints of the $\geqslant$ Type or $=$ Type

Now let us learn how to solve an LP containing structural constraints of the $\geqslant$ type or $=$ type. As an example, consider the following LP:

$$\text{Maximize } 30x_1 - 10x_2 + 20x_3 - 8x_4$$

$$\text{subject to } \quad \begin{aligned} x_1 - 2x_2 + 4x_3 + x_4 &\leqslant 7 \\ 4x_1 - x_2 + 3x_3 - 2x_4 &\leqslant -3 \\ 2x_1 \quad\quad + x_3 - x_4 &= -1 \\ x_1 + 2x_2 + 3x_3 + x_4 &\geqslant 12 \end{aligned}$$

and $x_1 \geqslant 0, x_2 \geqslant 0, x_3 \geqslant 0, x_4 \geqslant 0$.

As the first step, we eliminate the negative right-hand sides of the second and third structural constraints by multiplying the constraints by -1 and reversing the sense of the inequality in the second constraint. The resulting LP is

$$\text{Maximize } 30x_1 - 10x_2 + 20x_3 - 8x_4$$

$$\text{subject to } \quad \begin{aligned} x_1 - 2x_2 + 4x_3 + x_4 &\leqslant 7 \\ -4x_1 + x_2 - 3x_3 + 2x_4 &\geqslant 3 \\ -2x_1 \quad\quad - x_3 + x_4 &= 1 \\ x_1 + 2x_2 + 3x_3 + x_4 &\geqslant 12 \end{aligned}$$

and $x_1 \geqslant 0, x_2 \geqslant 0, x_3 \geqslant 0, x_4 \geqslant 0$.

Our next step is to convert this LP into equality form. From our previous examples, we already know how to use slack variables to transform the first structural constraint into equality form. Also, the third structural constraint is already an equation and, thus, requires no attention. Hence, the only obstacle to our converting the LP into equality form are the two structural constraints of the $\geqslant$ type, the second and fourth structural constraints. To convert these constraints into equality form, we proceed in a manner similar to that for a $\leqslant$ structural constraint, except that, in place of adding a nonnegative slack variable to the constraint's left-hand side, we subtract a nonnegative surplus variable. In Section 2.10 we defined the surplus variable for a $\geqslant$ structural constraint as the constraint's left-hand side minus its right-hand side. Consequently, if we denote the respective surplus variables for the second and fourth structural constraints by E_2 and E_4,[1] then

$$\begin{pmatrix} \text{constraint's} \\ \text{surplus} \\ \text{variable} \end{pmatrix} = \begin{pmatrix} \text{constraint's} \\ \text{left-hand side} \end{pmatrix} - \begin{pmatrix} \text{constraint's} \\ \text{right-hand side} \end{pmatrix}$$

$$
\begin{aligned}
E_2 &= (-4x_1 + x_2 - 3x_3 + 2x_4) - 3 \\
E_4 &= (x_1 + 2x_2 + 3x_3 + x_4) - 12
\end{aligned}
$$

An equivalent way of writing the above is

$$\begin{pmatrix} \text{constraint's} \\ \text{left-hand side} \end{pmatrix} - \begin{pmatrix} \text{constraint's} \\ \text{surplus} \\ \text{variable} \end{pmatrix} = \begin{pmatrix} \text{constraint's} \\ \text{right-hand side} \end{pmatrix}$$

$$
\begin{aligned}
-4x_1 + x_2 - 3x_3 + 2x_4 - E_2 &= 3 \\
x_1 + 2x_2 + 3x_3 + x_4 - E_4 &= 12
\end{aligned}
$$

In words, this states that a surplus variable is the amount that must be subtracted from the constraint's left-hand side to make it equal to the constraint's right-hand side. Since an assignment of values to x_1, x_2, x_3, and x_4 satisfies a $\geqslant$ structural constraint if and only if the constraint's surplus variable is nonnegative, we can replace the second structural constraint with the following structural equation and nonnegativity constraint:

$$-4x_1 + x_2 - 3x_3 + 2x_4 - E_2 = 3 \text{ and } E_2 \geqslant 0.$$

Similarly, we can replace the fourth structural constraint with the following structural equation and nonnegativity constraint:

$$x_1 + 2x_2 + 3x_3 + x_4 - E_4 = 12 \text{ and } E_4 \geqslant 0.$$

To summarize:

In transforming an LP into equality form, we replace a $\geqslant$ structural constraint with two constraints:

1. A structural equation obtained from the $\geqslant$ constraint by subtracting a surplus variable from the constraint's left-hand side and changing the $\geqslant$ to an $=$.

2. A nonnegativity constraint on the surplus variable.

Applying this general principle and the analogous general principle for a $\leqslant$ structural constraint, we obtain the following LP in equality form:

Maximize $30x_1 - 10x_2 + 20x_3 - 8x_4$

$$
\begin{aligned}
\text{subject to} \quad x_1 - 2x_2 + 4x_3 + x_4 + S_1 \quad\quad &= 7 \\
-4x_1 + x_2 - 3x_3 + 2x_4 \quad - E_2 \quad\quad &= 3 \\
-2x_1 \quad - x_3 + x_4 \quad\quad &= 1 \\
x_1 + 2x_2 + 3x_3 + x_4 \quad\quad - E_4 &= 12
\end{aligned}
$$

$$
\begin{aligned}
\text{and } &x_1 \geqslant 0, x_2 \geqslant 0, x_3 \geqslant 0, x_4 \geqslant 0, \\
&S_1 \geqslant 0, E_2 \geqslant 0, E_4 \geqslant 0.
\end{aligned}
$$

---

[1] Since we use S as our notation for a slack variable, we avoid confusion by using E as our notation for a surplus variable (E for "excess"). We use the subscripts "2" and "4" because constraints involved are the second and fourth constraints.

Our next task is to identify an initial basic feasible solution from which we can start the simplex method. Before doing so, let us recall how we identified an initial basic feasible solution for the LP in Section 6.8. For this LP, each equation in the LP's equality form system of equations contained an isolated slack variable and had a nonnegative right-hand side. Consequently, we could immediately identify an initial basic feasible solution by setting each decision variable equal to 0 and each slack variable equal to the corresponding equation's right-hand side. Let us see what happens if we proceed in an analogous fashion for the current equality form system of equations, stated above.

Setting the decision variables x_1, x_2, x_3 and x_4 equal to 0 results in the following system of equations (where the columns corresponding to the decision variables are shaded to indicate they are to be ignored):

$$
\begin{array}{rcrcrcrcrcrcrcr}
x_1 & - & 2x_2 & + & 4x_3 & + & x_4 & + & S_1 & & & & & = & 7 \\
-4x_1 & + & x_2 & - & 3x_3 & + & 2x_4 & & & - & E_2 & & & = & 3 \\
-2x_1 & & & - & x_3 & + & x_4 & & & & & & & = & 1 \\
x_1 & + & 2x_2 & + & 3x_3 & + & x_4 & & & & & - & E_4 & = & 12 \\
\end{array}
$$

This system of equations clearly has no solution, since the third equation cannot be satisfied when all decision variables equal 0. Thus, setting the decision variables equal to 0 and solving for the values of slack and surplus variables cannot be used to identify a basic feasible solution.

We have just illustrated the following general principle:

> We can identify an initial basic feasible solution by setting all decision variables equal to 0 and then solving for the values of the remaining variables only when all the LP's structural constraints are of the $\leqslant$ type with nonnegative right-hand sides.

How, then, can we identify an initial basic feasible solution for our current LP? To resolve this dilemma, we will consider a slight modification known as the *artificial equality form system of equations,* displayed below.

Original Equality Form
System of Equations

$$
\begin{array}{rcrcrcrcrcrcrcr}
x_1 & - & 2x_2 & + & 4x_3 & + & x_4 & + & S_1 & & & & & = & 7 \\
-4x_1 & + & x_2 & - & 3x_3 & + & 2x_4 & & & - & E_2 & & & = & 3 \\
-2x_1 & & & - & x_3 & + & x_4 & & & & & & & = & 1 \\
x_1 & + & 2x_2 & + & 3x_3 & + & x_4 & & & & & - & E_4 & = & 12 \\
\end{array}
$$

Artificial Equality Form
System of Equations

$$
\begin{array}{rcrcrcrcrcrcrcrcr}
x_1 & - & 2x_2 & + & 4x_3 & + & x_4 & + & S_1 & & & & & & & = & 7 \\
-4x_1 & + & x_2 & - & 3x_3 & + & 2x_4 & & & - & E_2 & & & + & A_2 & & & = & 3 \\
-2x_1 & & & - & x_3 & + & x_4 & & & & & & & + & A_3 & & & = & 1 \\
x_1 & + & 2x_2 & + & 3x_3 & + & x_4 & & & & & - & E_4 & & & + & A_4 & = & 12 \\
\end{array}
$$

Note that, to obtain the artificial equality form system, we add nonnegative variables A_2, A_3, A_4 to the left-hand sides of the second, third, and fourth equations (the equations that arose from the $\geqslant$ and $=$ structural constraints). Unlike decision variables, slack variables, and surplus variables, A_2, A_3, and A_4 have no physical meaning in the context of the original LP (e.g., a production quantity or the unconsumed amount of a resource). Consequently, we refer to these new variables as *artificial variables,* and we denote each by the letter "A" (A for "artificial") with a subscript equal to the number of the equation the variable has been added to (e.g., A_3 for the third equation's artificial variable).

You are probably wondering what we gain by this approach. The answer is provided by the following observation:

> If we can find a basic feasible solution to the artificial equality form system of equations in which all artificial variables equal 0, we can obtain a basic feasible solution to the original equality form system of equations by simply ignoring the artificial variables. For example, if a basic feasible solution to the artificial equality form system of equations is

x_1	x_2	x_3	x_4	S_1	E_2	E_4	A_2	A_3	A_3
0	$\frac{11}{2}$	0	1	17	$\frac{9}{2}$	0	0	0	0

> then a basic feasible solution to the original equality form system of equations is

x_1	x_2	x_3	x_4	S_1	E_2	E_4
0	$\frac{11}{2}$	0	1	17	$\frac{9}{2}$	0

Thus, we have transformed the task of finding a basic feasible solution to the original equality form system of equations into the task of finding a special type of basic feasible solution to the artificial equality form system of equations, one in which all artificial variables equal 0. As we will now demonstrate, this latter task is much easier.

To see why it is easier, observe that stating that all artificial variables equal 0 is equivalent (since they are nonegative variables) to stating that their sum, $A_2 + A_3 + A_4$, equals 0. This suggests that, to find a basic feasible solution to the artificial equality form system of equations in which all artificial variables equal 0, we can temporarily ignore the original objective function of "Maximize $30x_1 - 10x_2 + 20x_3 - 8x_4$" and use in its place the objective function "Minimize $A_2 + A_3 + A_4$." That is, we solve the so-called *artificial LP*

Minimize $A_2 + A_3 + A_4$

$$
\begin{aligned}
\text{subject to} \quad & x_1 - 2x_2 + 4x_3 + x_4 + S_1 && && = 7 \\
& -4x_1 + x_2 - 3x_3 + 2x_4 - E_2 + A_2 && && = 3 \\
& -2x_1 - x_3 + x_4 + A_3 && && = 1 \\
& x_1 + 2x_2 + 3x_3 + x_4 - E_4 + A_4 && && = 12
\end{aligned}
$$

and $x_1 \geqslant 0, x_2 \geqslant 0, x_3 \geqslant 0, x_4 \geqslant 0,$
$S_1 \geqslant 0, E_2 \geqslant 0, E_4 \geqslant 0,$
$A_2 \geqslant 0, A_3 \geqslant 0, A_4 \geqslant 0.$

If the minimal objective value equals 0, then all artificial variables equal 0, thereby identifying a basic feasible solution to the original equality form system of equations (though not necessarily the optimal one).[2]

The solution to the artificial LP is straightforward because the variables S_1, A_2, A_3, and A_4 are an isolated set of variables in the artificial equality form system of equations

---

[2] It is possible that the artificial LP's minimal objective value equals a positive value rather than 0. As we will discuss in detail in the next section, this special case indicates that the LP has no feasible solution, let alone an optimal one.

$$\begin{aligned}
x_1 - 2x_2 + 4x_3 + x_4 + S_1 &= 7 \\
-4x_1 + x_2 - 3x_3 + 2x_4 - E_2 + A_2 &= 3 \\
-2x_1 - x_3 + x_4 + A_3 &= 1 \\
x_1 + 2x_2 + 3x_3 + x_4 - E_4 + A_4 &= 12
\end{aligned}$$

Consequently, we can immediately construct the initial simplex tableau

Equation	Basic Variable	c_j → c_B	0 x_1	0 x_2	0 x_3	0 x_4	0 S_1	0 E_2	0 E_4	1 A_2	1 A_3	1 A_4	RHS
I	S_1	0	1	-2	4	1	1	0	0	0	0	0	7
II	A_2	1	-4	1	-3	2	0	-1	0	1	0	0	3
III	A_3	1	-2	0	-1	1	0	0	0	0	1	0	1
IV	A_4	1	1	2	3	1	0	0	-1	0	0	1	12
		z_j											
		$c_j - z_j$											$OV = 16$

This tableau identifies

x_1	x_2	x_3	x_4	S_1	E_2	E_4	A_2	A_3	A_3
0	0	0	0	7	0	0	3	1	12

as the initial basic feasible solution to the artificial equality form system of equations, a solution whose objective value is 16. Note that, owing to the positive values of A_2, A_3, and A_4, this is not a basic feasible solution to the original equality form system of equations; we have not identified such a solution until all artificial variables have values of 0.

Figure 7.1 displays the complete sequence of simplex tableaux obtained by using the simplex method to solve the artificial LP. As you verify for yourself the correctness of the tableaux, keep in mind that, since the artificial LP involves minimization, we select the entering basic variable as that nonbasic variable with the *most negative* $c_j - z_j$ value.[3] Observe from Figure 7.1's final simplex tableau that the artificial LP's optimal solution is

x_1	x_2	x_3	x_4	S_1	E_2	E_4	A_2	A_3	A_3
0	$2\frac{1}{2}$	$1\frac{1}{2}$	$2\frac{1}{2}$	$3\frac{1}{2}$	0	0	0	0	0

—a solution in which the artificial variables A_2, A_3, and A_4 all equal 0. Hence, the final simplex tableau identifies

x_1	x_2	x_3	x_4	S_1	E_2	E_4
0	$2\frac{1}{2}$	$1\frac{1}{2}$	$2\frac{1}{2}$	$3\frac{1}{2}$	0	0

as a basic feasible solution to the original equality form system of equations.

---

[3] During the second iteration, there is a three-way tie for the entering basic variable among x_1, x_2, and x_3 (all of which have $c_j - z_j$ values of -3). The tie has been arbitrarily broken by choosing x_2 as the entering basic variable.

Equation	Basic Variable	c_j → c_B	x_1	x_2	x_3	x_4	S_1	E_2	E_4	A_2	A_3	A_4	RHS
			0	0	0	0	0	0	0	1	1	1	
I	S_1	0	1	−2	4	1	1	0	0	0	0	0	7
II	A_2	1	−4	1	−3	2	0	−1	0	1	0	0	3
III	A_3	1	−2	0	−1	①	0	0	0	0	1	0	1
IV	A_4	1	1	2	3	1	0	0	−1	0	0	1	12
		z_j	−5	3	−1	4	*	−1	−1	*	*	*	OV = 16
		$c_j - z_j$	5	−3	1	−4	*	1	1	*	*	*	

Equation	Basic Variable	c_j → c_B	x_1	x_2	x_3	x_4	S_1	E_2	E_4	A_2	A_3	A_4	RHS
			0	0	0	0	0	0	0	1	1	1	
$I' = I - 1III'$	S_1	0	3	−2	5	0	1	0	0	0	−1	0	6
$II' = II - 2III'$	A_2	1	0	①	−1	0	0	−1	0	1	−2	0	1
$III' = 1III$	x_4	0	−2	0	−1	1	0	0	0	0	1	0	1
$IV' = IV - 1III'$	A_4	1	3	2	4	0	0	0	−1	0	−1	1	11
		z_j	3	3	3	*	*	−1	−1	*	−3	*	OV = 12
		$c_j - z_j$	−3	−3	−3	*	*	1	1	*	4	*	

Equation	Basic Variable	c_j → c_B	x_1	x_2	x_3	x_4	S_1	E_2	E_4	A_2	A_3	A_4	RHS
			0	0	0	0	0	0	0	1	1	1	
$I'' = I' + 2II''$	S_1	0	3	0	3	0	1	−2	0	2	−5	0	8
$II'' = 1II'$	x_2	0	0	1	−1	0	0	−1	0	1	−2	0	1
$III'' = III' - 0II''$	x_4	0	−2	0	−1	1	0	0	0	0	1	0	1
$IV'' = IV' - 2II''$	A_4	1	3	0	⑥	0	0	2	−1	−2	3	1	9
		z_j	3	*	6	*	*	2	−1	−2	3	*	OV = 9
		$c_j - z_j$	−3	*	−6	*	*	−2	1	3	−2	*	

Equation	Basic Variable	c_j → c_B	x_1	x_2	x_3	x_4	S_1	E_2	E_4	A_2	A_3	A_4	RHS
			0	0	0	0	0	0	0	1	1	1	
$I''' = I'' - 3IV'''$	S_1	0	$\frac{3}{2}$	0	0	0	1	−3	$\frac{1}{2}$	3	$-\frac{13}{2}$	$-\frac{1}{2}$	$\frac{7}{2}$
$II''' = II'' + 1IV'''$	x_2	0	$\frac{1}{2}$	1	0	0	0	$-\frac{2}{3}$	$-\frac{1}{6}$	$\frac{2}{3}$	$-\frac{3}{2}$	$\frac{1}{6}$	$\frac{5}{2}$
$III''' = III'' + 1IV'''$	x_4	0	$-\frac{3}{2}$	0	0	1	0	$\frac{1}{3}$	$-\frac{1}{6}$	$-\frac{1}{3}$	$\frac{3}{2}$	$\frac{1}{6}$	$\frac{5}{2}$
$IV''' = \frac{1}{6} IV''$	x_3	0	$\frac{1}{2}$	0	1	0	0	$\frac{1}{3}$	$-\frac{1}{6}$	$-\frac{1}{3}$	$\frac{1}{2}$	$\frac{1}{6}$	$\frac{3}{2}$
		z_j	0	*	*	*	*	0	0	0	0	0	OV = 0
		$c_j - z_j$	0	*	*	*	*	0	0	1	1	1	

Figure 7.1 Sequence of simplex tableaux for artificial LP

Figure 7.1's final simplex tableau not only identifies a basic feasible solution to the original equality form system of equations but also, after some modifications, provides a starting point for our search for the original LP's optimal solution. The modifications are necessary because the artificial LP's objective function of "Minimize $A_2 + A_3 + A_4$" has served its purpose; that is, it has enabled us to identify a basic feasible solution to the original equality form system of equations. To proceed from this initial basic feasible solution to the optimal basic feasible solution, we must now "discard" the artificial objective function of "Minimize $A_2 + A_3 + A_4$" and replace it with the original objective function of "Maximize $30x_1 - 10x_2 + 20x_3 - 8x_4$." To reflect this change in the objective function, we proceed as described below and as illustrated in Figure 7.2 (where the portions of the tableau that change are shaded):

1. We change the c_j row and the c_B column in Figure 7.1's final simplex tableau so that they now contain the values for the original objective function rather than the artificial objective function.

2. Based on these new values in the tableau's c_j row and c_B column, we then recompute new values for the tableau's z_j row, the $c_j - z_j$ row, and the OV portion.

Since the objective function now involves maximization and since the tableau's $c_j - z_j$ row contains some positive values, the tableau does not correspond to the LP's optimal solution. To find the optimal solution, we simply execute the simplex method in the usual manner, with one important exception. The exception is that, in selecting the entering basic variable, we ignore the artificial variables, regardless

Figure 7.2 Transition from artificial LP to the original LP

| Equation | Basic Variable | c_j | 0 | 0 | 0 | 0 | 0 | 0 | 0 | 1 | 1 | 1 | |
		c_B	x_1	x_2	x_3	x_4	S_1	E_2	E_4	A_2	A_3	A_4	RHS
$I''' = I'' - 3IV'''$	S_1	0	$\frac{3}{2}$	0	0	0	1	-3	$\frac{1}{2}$	3	$-\frac{13}{2}$	$-\frac{1}{2}$	$\frac{7}{2}$
$II''' = II'' + 1IV'''$	x_2	0	$\frac{1}{2}$	1	0	0	0	$-\frac{2}{3}$	$-\frac{1}{6}$	$\frac{2}{3}$	$-\frac{3}{2}$	$\frac{1}{6}$	$\frac{5}{2}$
$III''' = III'' + 1IV'''$	x_4	0	$-\frac{3}{2}$	0	0	1	0	$\frac{1}{3}$	$-\frac{1}{6}$	$-\frac{1}{3}$	$\frac{3}{2}$	$\frac{1}{6}$	$\frac{5}{2}$
$IV''' = \frac{1}{6} IV''$	x_3	0	$\frac{1}{2}$	0	1	0	0	$\frac{1}{3}$	$-\frac{1}{6}$	$-\frac{1}{3}$	$\frac{1}{2}$	$\frac{1}{6}$	$\frac{3}{2}$
	z_j		0	*	*	*	*	0	0	0	0	0	$OV = 0$
	$c_j - z_j$		0	*	*	*	*	0	0	1	1	1	

| Equation | Basic Variable | c_j | 30 | -10 | 20 | -8 | 0 | 0 | 0 | 0 | 0 | 0 | |
		c_B	x_1	x_2	x_3	x_4	S_1	E_2	E_4	A_2	A_3	A_4	RHS
$I''' = I'' - 3IV'''$	S_1	0	$\frac{3}{2}$	0	0	0	1	-3	$\frac{1}{2}$	3	$-\frac{13}{2}$	$-\frac{1}{2}$	$\frac{7}{2}$
$II''' = II'' + 1IV'''$	x_2	-10	$\frac{1}{2}$	1	0	0	0	$-\frac{2}{3}$	$-\frac{1}{6}$	$\frac{2}{3}$	$-\frac{3}{2}$	$\frac{1}{6}$	$\frac{5}{2}$
$III''' = III'' + 1IV'''$	x_4	-8	$-\frac{3}{2}$	0	0	1	0	$\frac{1}{3}$	$-\frac{1}{6}$	$-\frac{1}{3}$	$\frac{3}{2}$	$\frac{1}{6}$	$\frac{5}{2}$
$IV''' = \frac{1}{6} IV''$	x_3	20	$\frac{1}{2}$	0	1	0	0	$\frac{1}{3}$	$-\frac{1}{6}$	$-\frac{1}{3}$	$\frac{1}{2}$	$\frac{1}{6}$	$\frac{3}{2}$
	z_j		17	*	*	*	*	$\frac{32}{3}$	$-\frac{1}{3}$	$-\frac{32}{3}$	13	$\frac{1}{3}$	$OV = -15$
	$c_j - z_j$		13	*	*	*	*	$-\frac{32}{3}$	$\frac{1}{3}$	$\frac{32}{3}$	-13	$-\frac{1}{3}$	

Equation	Basic Variable	c_j / c_B	30 x_1	-10 x_2	20 x_3	-8 x_4	0 S_1	0 E_2	0 E_4	0 A_2	0 A_3	0 A_4	RHS
I	S_1	0	$(\frac{3}{2})$	0	0	0	1	-3	$\frac{1}{2}$	3	$-\frac{13}{2}$	$-\frac{1}{2}$	$\frac{7}{2}$
II	x_2	-10	$\frac{1}{2}$	1	0	0	0	$-\frac{2}{3}$	$-\frac{1}{6}$	$\frac{2}{3}$	$-\frac{3}{2}$	$\frac{1}{6}$	$\frac{5}{2}$
III	x_4	-8	$-\frac{3}{2}$	0	0	1	0	$\frac{1}{3}$	$-\frac{1}{6}$	$-\frac{1}{3}$	$\frac{3}{2}$	$\frac{1}{6}$	$\frac{5}{2}$
IV	x_3	20	$\frac{1}{2}$	0	1	0	0	$\frac{1}{3}$	$-\frac{1}{6}$	$-\frac{1}{3}$	$\frac{1}{2}$	$\frac{1}{6}$	$\frac{3}{2}$
	z_j		17	*	*	*	*	$\frac{32}{3}$	$-\frac{1}{3}$	$-\frac{32}{3}$	13	$\frac{1}{3}$	$OV = -15$
	$c_j - z_j$		13	*	*	*	*	$-\frac{32}{3}$	$\frac{1}{3}$	$\frac{32}{3}$	-13	$-\frac{1}{3}$	

Equation	Basic Variable	c_j / c_B	30 x_1	-10 x_2	20 x_3	-8 x_4	0 S_1	0 E_2	0 E_4	0 A_2	0 A_3	0 A_4	RHS
$I' = \frac{2}{3}I$	x_1	30	1	0	0	0	$\frac{2}{3}$	-2	$\frac{1}{3}$	2	$-\frac{13}{3}$	$-\frac{1}{3}$	$\frac{7}{3}$
$II' = II - \frac{1}{2}I'$	x_2	-10	0	1	0	0	$-\frac{1}{3}$	$\frac{1}{3}$	$-\frac{1}{3}$	$-\frac{1}{3}$	$\frac{2}{3}$	$\frac{1}{3}$	$\frac{4}{3}$
$III' = III + \frac{3}{2}I'$	x_4	-8	0	0	0	1	1	$-\frac{8}{3}$	$\frac{1}{3}$	$\frac{8}{3}$	-5	$-\frac{1}{3}$	6
$IV' = IV - \frac{1}{2}I'$	x_3	20	0	0	1	0	$-\frac{1}{3}$	$(\frac{4}{3})$	$-\frac{1}{3}$	$-\frac{4}{3}$	$\frac{8}{3}$	$\frac{1}{3}$	$\frac{1}{3}$
	z_j		*	*	*	*	$\frac{26}{3}$	$-\frac{46}{3}$	4	$\frac{46}{3}$	$-\frac{130}{3}$	-4	$OV = \frac{46}{3}$
	$c_j - z_j$		*	*	*	*	$-\frac{26}{3}$	$\frac{46}{3}$	-4	$-\frac{46}{3}$	$\frac{130}{3}$	4	

Equation	Basic Variable	c_j / c_B	30 x_1	-10 x_2	20 x_3	-8 x_4	0 S_1	0 E_2	0 E_4	0 A_2	0 A_3	0 A_4	RHS
$I'' = I' + 2IV''$	x_1	30	1	0	$\frac{3}{2}$	0	$\frac{1}{6}$	0	$-\frac{1}{6}$	0	$-\frac{1}{3}$	$\frac{1}{6}$	$\frac{17}{6}$
$II'' = II' - \frac{1}{3}IV''$	x_2	-10	0	1	$-\frac{1}{4}$	0	$-\frac{1}{4}$	0	$-\frac{1}{4}$	0	0	$\frac{1}{4}$	$\frac{5}{4}$
$III'' = III' + \frac{8}{3}IV''$	x_4	-8	0	0	2	1	$\frac{1}{3}$	0	$-\frac{1}{3}$	0	$\frac{1}{3}$	$\frac{1}{3}$	$\frac{20}{3}$
$IV'' = \frac{3}{4}IV'$	E_2	0	0	0	$\frac{3}{4}$	0	$-\frac{1}{4}$	1	$-\frac{1}{4}$	-1	2	$\frac{1}{4}$	$\frac{1}{4}$
	z_j		*	*	$\frac{63}{2}$	*	$\frac{29}{6}$	*	$\frac{1}{6}$	0	$-\frac{38}{3}$	$-\frac{1}{6}$	$OV = \frac{115}{6}$
	$c_j - z_j$		*	*	$-\frac{23}{2}$	*	$-\frac{29}{6}$	*	$-\frac{1}{6}$	0	$\frac{38}{3}$	$\frac{1}{6}$	

Figure 7.3 Sequence of simplex tableaux for the original LP

of their $c_j - z_j$ values. Thus, the artificial variables, which are all currently non-basic variables in Figure 7.2's bottom simplex tableau, will remain nonbasic variables throughout all subsequent iterations of the simplex method. This guarantees that all artificial variables maintain values of 0 throughout all subsequent iterations of the simplex method, thereby ensuring that all subsequent simplex tableaux identify feasible solutions to the original equality form system of equations.[4]

Figure 7.3 displays the complete sequence of simplex tableaux generated by starting with Figure 7.2's bottom simplex tableau and executing the simplex

---

[4] If no sensitivity analysis is planned for later, a preferred alternative to ignoring the artificial variables is to simply remove their corresponding columns from the simplex tableau. However, as discussed in Section 7.5, subsequent performance of sensitivity analysis requires that we now retain the columns in the simplex tableau corresponding to the artificial variables.

method (subject to the already noted exception of ignoring all artificial variables when selecting the entering basic variable). You should verify for yourself the correctness of Figure 7.3's simplex tableaux. From the final tableau, observe that the LP's optimal solution is

x_1	x_2	x_3	x_4	S_1	E_2	E_4
$2\frac{5}{6}$	$1\frac{1}{4}$	0	$6\frac{2}{3}$	0	$\frac{1}{4}$	0

and the optimal objective value is $19\frac{1}{6}$.[5]

The procedure we used to solve our example LP was sufficiently complex that it merits a detailed summary. First, however, we should observe that we can divide our solution of the example LP into two phases. In Phase I, we identified an initial basic feasible solution to the original equality form system of equations by solving the artificial LP. In Phase II, after replacing the artificial LP's objective function with the original LP's objective function, we proceeded from Phase I's initial basic feasible solution to the LP's optimal basic feasible solution. Thus, we hereafter refer to the procedure as the *two-phase simplex method*. A summary of this method is provided by the following:

A Summary of
the Two-Phase
Simplex Method

1. **Elimination of negative right-hand sides from the structural constraints.** Replace any structural constraint with a negative right-hand side with the equivalent constraint obtained by first multiplying both sides of the constraint by -1 and then, if it is an inequality, reversing its sense (i.e., change $\leqslant$ to $\geqslant$, change $\geqslant$ to $\leqslant$, and leave $=$ unchanged).

2. **Converting the LP into equality form.** To convert the LP to equality form, add a nonnegative slack variable to the left-hand side of each $\leqslant$ structural constraint, subtract a nonnegative surplus variable from the left-hand side of each $\geqslant$ structural constraint, and replace all $\leqslant$ and $\geqslant$ with $=$.

3. **Using Phase I to identify an initial basic feasible solution.** The goal of Phase I is to identify an initial basic feasible solution to the LP's equality form system of equations. To do so, we first formulate the artificial LP by making the following modifications to the LP in equality form:

   a. We add a nonnegative artificial variable to the left-hand side of each equation in the equality form system of equations, *except those equations that contain slack variables.*

   b. We replace the LP's original objective function with the artificial objective function of minimizing the sum of the artificial variables.

Owing to the isolation of all slack variables and all artificial variables in the artificial equality form system of equations, we can construct the initial simplex tableau by selecting the decision variables and the surplus variables as the initial set of nonbasic variables and by selecting the slack variables and the artificial variables as the initial set of basic variables. After constructing the initial simplex tableau, we solve the artificial LP by executing the simplex method in the usual manner, remembering that, since we are minimizing, we select the entering basic variable as that nonbasic variable with the most negative $c_j - z_j$ value. If the artificial LP has an optimal objective value of 0, the

---

[5] You may be wondering why this tableau identifies the optimal solution, even though A_2's and A_3's $c_j - z_j$ values are positive. Remember that, to maintain feasibility, we must ignore the artificial variables when selecting the entering basic variable.

tableau identifies a basic feasible solution to the original equality form system of equations. However, if the artificial LP's optimal objective value is positive, we terminate execution of the simplex method because the LP has no feasible solution. (This latter special case will be discussed in detail in the next section).

4. **Transition from Phase I to Phase II.** Before using the final simplex tableau from Phase I to begin Phase II, we "discard" the artificial objective function of minimizing the sum of the artificial variables and replace it with the LP's original objective function. To reflect this change, we first revise the c_j row and c_B column in Phase I's final simplex tableau and then recompute new values for the z_j row, the $c_j - z_j$ row, and the OV portion.

5. **Using Phase II to identify the LP's optimal solution.** The goal of Phase II is to start from the initial basic feasible solution identified at the end of Phase I and proceed to the LP's optimal solution. To do so, we start with Phase I's final simplex tableau (modified as described in Step 4) and execute the simplex method in the usual manner, except that, in selecting the entering basic variable, we ignore the artificial variables, regardless of their $c_j - z_j$ values. Thus, we have identified the LP's optimal solution when the simplex method generates a tableau for which all nonbasic variables (except the artificial variables) have nonpositive $c_j - z_j$ values when the LP involves maximization and all nonnegative $c_j - z_j$ values when the LP involves minimization.

We should briefly mention here a potential (but unlikely) difficulty that might arise at the termination of Phase I. It is possible that the optimal solution to the artificial LP is a degenerate basic feasible solution. If so, then it is also possible that, although all artificial variables have values of 0 in Phase I's final tableau, one or more of them is a basic variable with a value of 0. Although such a tableau would still identify an initial basic feasible solution to the original equality form system of equations, special provisions (omitted here) must be made to ensure that no artificial variable that is a basic variable with a value of 0 at the conclusion of Phase I subsequently becomes a basic variable with a positive value in Phase II.

7.3 RECOGNIZING INFEASIBILITY, UNBOUNDEDNESS, AND MULTIPLE OPTIMALITY

In Chapter 2 we illustrated geometrically that, when attempting to solve an LP, one of the following four cases occurs:

1. **Infeasibility.** The LP has no optimal solution because it has no feasible solution.

2. **Unboundedness.** The LP has no optimal solution because the objective value can be made infinitely positive (i.e., approaching ∞) if maximizing or infinitely negative (i.e., approaching $-\infty$) if minimizing.

3. **Unique optimality.** The LP has an optimal solution, and it occurs at a corner-point solution.

4. **Multiple optimality.** The LP has an infinite number of optimal solutions, but at least two are corner-point solutions.

In this section we will learn how to recognize, as we execute the simplex method, which of these cases has occurred.

Recognizing Infeasibility

Infeasibility occurs when the LP has no feasible solution— that is, when there is no assignment of values to the variables that simultaneously satisfies the LP's structural constraints and nonnegativity constraints. In Section 2.12 we illustrated that, when the LP's formulation involves two decision variables, we can graphically identify the phenomenon of infeasibility when the attempt to graph the LP's feasible region ends with the observation that the feasible region is an empty set. Now we will learn how to recognize infeasibility during the execution of the simplex method.

As an example, we use the following LP:

$$\text{Maximize } 20x_1 + 50x_2 + 30x_3$$

$$\text{subject to } \quad 2x_1 + 3x_2 + 2x_3 \leq 10$$
$$x_1 + x_2 + x_3 \geq 6$$
$$3x_1 + 2x_2 + x_3 \geq 9$$

$$\text{and } x_1 \geq 0, x_2 \geq 0, x_3 \geq 0.$$

Converting this LP to equality form using the slack variable S_1 and the surplus variables E_2 and E_3, we obtain the following:

$$\text{Maximize } 20x_1 + 50x_2 + 30x_3$$

$$\text{subject to } \quad 2x_1 + 3x_2 + 2x_3 + S_1 = 10$$
$$x_1 + x_2 + x_3 - E_2 = 6$$
$$3x_1 + 2x_2 + x_3 - E_3 = 9$$

$$\text{and } x_1 \geq 0, x_2 \geq 0, x_3 \geq 0,$$
$$S_1 \geq 0, E_2 \geq 0, E_3 \geq 0.$$

Because the original LP involved $\geq$ structural constraints, we must solve the LP using the two-phase simplex method, where we use Phase I to identify an initial basic feasible solution and Phase II to proceed from Phase I's initial basic feasible solution to the optimal basic feasible solution. As we saw in Section 7.2, Phase I is an attempt to identify an initial basic feasible solution by solving the artificial LP. To obtain the artificial LP, we modify the LP in equality form as follows:

1. We add the nonnegative artificial variables A_2 and A_3 to the left-hand sides of the second and third equations.

2. We temporarily replace the LP's original objective function of "Maximize $20x_1 + 50x_2 + 30x_3$" with the artificial objective function of "Minimize $A_2 + A_3$."

The result is the following artificial LP:

$$\text{Minimize } A_2 + A_3$$

$$\text{subject to } 2x_1 + 3x_2 + 2x_3 + S_1 = 10$$
$$x_1 + x_2 + x_3 - E_2 + A_2 = 6$$
$$3x_1 + 2x_2 + x_3 - E_3 + A_3 = 9$$

$$\text{and } x_1 \geq 0, x_2 \geq 0, x_3 \geq 0,$$
$$S_1 \geq 0, E_2 \geq 0, E_3 \geq 0.$$
$$A_2 \geq 0, A_3 \geq 0.$$

299

Equation	Basic Variable	c_j c_B	0 x_1	0 x_2	0 x_3	0 S_1	0 E_2	0 E_3	1 A_2	1 A_3	RHS
I	S_1	0	2	3	2	1	0	0	0	0	10
II	A_2	1	1	1	1	0	-1	0	1	0	6
III	A_3	1	③	2	1	0	0	-1	0	1	9
		z_j	4	3	2	*	-1	-1	*	*	$OV = 15$
		$c_j - z_j$	-4	-3	-2	*	1	1	*	*	

Equation	Basic Variable	c_j c_B	0 x_1	0 x_2	0 x_3	0 S_1	0 E_2	0 E_3	1 A_2	1 A_3	RHS
$I' = I - 2III'$	S_1	0	0	$\frac{5}{3}$	$\frac{4}{3}$	1	0	$\frac{2}{3}$	0	$-\frac{2}{3}$	4
$II' = II - 1III'$	A_2	1	0	$\frac{1}{3}$	$\frac{2}{3}$	0	-1	$\frac{1}{3}$	1	$-\frac{1}{3}$	3
$III' = \frac{1}{3}III$	x_1	0	1	$\frac{2}{3}$	$\frac{1}{3}$	0	0	$-\frac{1}{3}$	0	$\frac{1}{3}$	3
		z_j	*	$\frac{1}{3}$	$\frac{2}{3}$	*	-1	$\frac{1}{3}$	*	$-\frac{1}{3}$	$OV = 3$
		$c_j - z_j$	*	$-\frac{1}{3}$	$-\frac{2}{3}$	*	1	$-\frac{1}{3}$	*	$\frac{4}{3}$	

Equation	Basic Variable	c_j c_B	0 x_1	0 x_2	0 x_3	0 S_1	0 E_2	0 E_3	1 A_2	1 A_3	RHS
$I'' = \frac{3}{4}I'$	x_3	0	0	$\frac{5}{4}$	1	$\frac{3}{4}$	0	$\frac{1}{2}$	0	$-\frac{1}{2}$	3
$II'' = II' - \frac{2}{3}I''$	A_2	1	0	$-\frac{1}{2}$	0	$-\frac{1}{2}$	-1	0	1	0	1
$III'' = III' - \frac{1}{3}I''$	x_1	0	1	$\frac{1}{4}$	0	$-\frac{1}{4}$	0	$-\frac{1}{2}$	0	$\frac{1}{2}$	2
		z_j	*	$-\frac{1}{2}$	*	$-\frac{1}{2}$	-1	0	*	0	$OV = 1$
		$c_j - z_j$	*	$\frac{1}{2}$	*	$\frac{1}{2}$	1	0	*	1	

Figure 7.4 Sequence of simplex tableaux for example LP illustrating infeasibility

Figure 7.4 displays the sequence of simplex tableaux generated during Phase I's solution of the artificial LP. (Before proceeding, you should verify the correctness of the tableaux.)[6] Looking at Figure 7.4's final simplex tableau, we see that the $c_j - z_j$ row contains only nonnegative values, thereby indicating that the tableau provides the artificial LP's optimal solution. From the tableau's Basic Variable column and the *RHS* column, we can identify the artificial LP's optimal solution as

x_1	x_2	x_3	S_1	E_2	E_3	A_2	A_3
2	0	3	0	0	0	1	0

—a solution with an optimal objective value of 1. Since the artificial variable A_2 has a positive optimal value, we can conclude that the original LP has no feasible solution. Otherwise, it would be possible to obtain an optimal solution to the

---

[6] As you do so, remember that, since Phase I's objective function involves minimization, we select the entering basic variable as that nonbasic variable with the most *negative* $c_j - z_j$ value.

artificial LP in which all artificial variables had values of 0 (as was the case in Section 7.2's example LP).

Our example has illustrated the following general principle for recognizing infeasibility:

> When the optimal solution to Phase I's artificial LP has nonzero values for one or more of the artificial variables, we terminate execution of the two-phase simplex method and conclude that the original LP has no optimal solution because of infeasibility.

The following observations are of interest here:

- Infeasibility can never occur if the LP's structural constraints are all of the $\leqslant$ type with nonnegative right-hand sides. The reason is that, for such an LP, the origin (i.e., all decision variables equal to 0) is always a feasible solution.

- As discussed more fully in Section 2.12, infeasibility usually indicates that we have made an error before starting the execution of the simplex method. Perhaps we have not formulated the LP correctly from the verbal statement of the decision problem, or perhaps we have simply made a clerical error in transcribing the LP's data.

- When using an LP software package to solve an LP for which infeasibility occurs, the package will terminate execution not with an optimal solution but with an error message such as

"The linear program is infeasible!"

Recognizing Unboundedness

Unboundedness occurs when the LP's objective value can be made infinitely positive (i.e., approaching ∞) when maximizing or infinitely negative (i.e., approaching $-\infty$) when minimizing. In Section 2.12 we illustrated how to graphically identify the phenomenon of unboundedness when the LP's formulation involves two decision variables. Now we will learn how to recognize unboundedness during the execution of the simplex method.

As an example, we use the following LP:

$$\text{Maximize } 6x_1 + 2x_2 + 10x_3 + 8x_4$$

$$
\begin{aligned}
\text{subject to } 3x_1 - 3x_2 + 2x_3 + 8x_4 &\leqslant 25 \\
5x_1 + 6x_2 - 4x_3 - 4x_4 &\leqslant 20 \\
4x_1 - 2x_2 + x_3 + 3x_4 &\leqslant 10
\end{aligned}
$$

$$\text{and } x_1 \geqslant 0, x_2 \geqslant 0, x_3 \geqslant 0, x_4 \geqslant 0.$$

Converting this LP to equality form by using the slack variables S_1, S_2, and S_3, we obtain the following:

$$\text{Maximize } 6x_1 + 2x_2 + 10x_3 + 8x_4$$

$$
\begin{aligned}
\text{subject to } 3x_1 - 3x_2 + 2x_3 + 8x_4 + S_1 \qquad\qquad\quad &= 25 \\
5x_1 + 6x_2 - 4x_3 - 4x_4 \qquad + S_2 \qquad &= 20 \\
4x_1 - 2x_2 + x_3 + 3x_4 \qquad\qquad + S_3 &= 10
\end{aligned}
$$

$$\text{and } x_1 \geqslant 0, x_2 \geqslant 0, x_3 \geqslant 0, x_4 \geqslant 0,$$
$$S_1 \geqslant 0, S_2 \geqslant 0, S_3 \geqslant 0.$$

Figure 7.5 displays the sequence of simplex tableaux generated by two iterations of the simplex method. (Before proceeding, you should verify the correctness of the tableaux.) Let us focus our attention on the S_3 column of Figure 7.5's final simplex tableau. Given that S_3's $c_j - z_j$ value is 34, we know that the selection of S_3 as the entering basic variable will increase the objective value at the rate of 34 per unit increase in S_3. If we now try to select the leaving basic variable using the minimum ratio procedure, we see that there are no ratios to compute because no number in the tableau's S_3 column is positive. To understand the implication of this, recall (from Section 6.6) that the numbers in the tableau's S_3 column provide the rates of decrease in the basic variables' values per unit increase in S_3. We can conclude then that, as the entering basic variable S_3 increases, the following changes take place in the basic variables' values per unit increase in S_3:

- Equation I''''s basic variable x_2 decreases at the rate of -2 per unit increase in S_3 or, equivalently, increases at the rate of 2. The resulting new value for x_2 is $x_2 = 5 + 2S_3$.

- Equation II''''s basic variable S_2 decreases at the rate of 0 per unit increase in S_3 or, equivalently, remains unchanged.

- Equation III''''s basic variable x_3 decreases at the rate of -3 per unit increase

Figure 7.5 Sequence of simplex tableaux for example LP illustrating unboundedness

| Equation | Basic Variable | c_j | 6 | 2 | 10 | 8 | 0 | 0 | 0 | |
		c_B	x_1	x_2	x_3	x_4	S_1	S_2	S_3	RHS
I	S_1	0	3	-3	2	8	1	0	0	25
II	S_2	0	5	6	-4	-4	0	1	0	20
III	S_3	0	4	-2	①	3	0	0	1	10
	z_j		0	0	0	0	*	*	*	$OV=0$
	c_j-z_j		6	2	10	8	*	*	*	

| Equation | Basic Variable | c_j | 6 | 2 | 10 | 8 | 0 | 0 | 0 | |
		c_B	x_1	x_2	x_3	x_4	S_1	S_2	S_3	RHS
$I' = I - 2III'$	S_1	0	-5	①	0	2	1	0	-2	5
$II' = II + 4III'$	S_2	0	21	-2	0	8	0	1	4	60
$III' = 1III$	x_3	10	4	-2	1	3	0	0	1	10
	z_j		40	-20	*	30	*	*	10	$OV=100$
	c_j-z_j		-34	22	*	-22	*	*	-10	

| Equation | Basic Variable | c_j | 6 | 2 | 10 | 8 | 0 | 0 | 0 | |
		c_B	x_1	x_2	x_3	x_4	S_1	S_2	S_3	RHS
$I'' = 1I'$	x_2	2	-5	1	0	2	1	0	-2	5
$II'' = II' + 2I''$	S_2	0	11	0	0	12	2	1	0	70
$III'' = III' + 2I''$	x_3	10	-6	0	1	7	2	0	-3	20
	z_j		-70	*	*	-74	22	*	-34	$OV=210$
	c_j-z_j		76	*	*	-66	-22	*	34	

in S_3 or, equivalently, increases at the rate of 3. The resulting new value for x_3 is $x_3 = 20 + 3S_3$.

Consequently, as the entering basic variable S_3 increases, no basic variable will eventually block any further increase by becoming the first basic variable to decrease to a value of 0. Thus, we can continue "forever" to increase the objective value at the rate of 34 (S_3's $c_j - z_j$ value). Having discovered how to make the LP's objective value approach ∞, we conclude that the LP has no optimal solution because of unboundedness.

Our example has illustrated the following general principle:

We may terminate execution of the simplex method and conclude that, owing to unboundedness, the LP has no optimal solution whenever the current simplex tableau contains a nonbasic variable (excluding artificial variables, if any) with the following properties:

1. The nonbasic variable's $c_j - z_j$ value is positive if the LP involves maximization or negative if the LP involves minimization. (This implies that the objective value improves as the nonbasic variable increases.)

2. The numbers in the nonbasic variable's column in the simplex tableau are all nonpositive. (This implies that none of the basic variables' values decreases toward 0 as the nonbasic variable increases, thereby permitting the nonbasic variable to be increased indefinitely.)

Observe that the nonbasic variable that "signals" unboundedness need not be the one with the most positive $c_j - z_j$ value when maximizing or the most negative $c_j - z_j$ value when minimizing. In our example, we were able to recognize unboundedness even though the nonbasic variable S_3 did not have the most positive $c_j - z_j$ value.[7]

Two further observations are of interest here:

■ As discussed more fully in Section 2.12, unboundedness is usually an indication that we have made an error before starting execution of the simplex method. Perhaps we have neglected to include an important structural constraint in the LP's formulation, or perhaps we have simply made a clerical error when transcribing the LP's data.

■ When using an LP software package to solve an LP for which unboundedness occurs, the package will terminate execution not with an optimal solution but with an error message such as

"The linear program is unbounded!"

Recognizing Multiple Optimality

Multiple optimality occurs when the LP, instead of having a unique optimal solution, has an infinite number of optimal solutions. In Section 2.11 we learned how to graphically identify the phenomenon of multiple optimality when the LP involves two decision variables. In particular, we saw that, when multiple optimality occurs for an LP with a two-dimensional feasible region, the infinite number of optimal solutions consist of two corner points and the entire line segment between them.

---

[7] In Exercise 7.14 you will be asked to demonstrate that if we had ignored the unboundedness "signaled" by S_3 in Figure 7.5's final simplex tableau and had instead selected x_1 as the entering basic variable, our recognition of unboundedness would simply have been delayed for several iterations.

Equation	Basic Variable	c_j / c_B	x_1	x_2	x_3	S_1	S_2	S_3	S_4	RHS
			30	15	45	0	0	0	0	
I	S_1	0	2	1	3	1	0	0	0	30
II	S_2	0	1	0	0	0	1	0	0	5
III	S_3	0	0	1	0	0	0	1	0	8
IV	S_4	0	0	0	(1)	0	0	0	1	6
	z_j		0	0	0	*	*	*	*	$OV=0$
	$c_j - z_j$		30	15	45	*	*	*	*	

Equation	Basic Variable	c_j / c_B	x_1	x_2	x_3	S_1	S_2	S_3	S_4	RHS
			30	15	45	0	0	0	0	
$I' = I - 3IV'$	S_1	0	2	1	0	1	0	0	−3	12
$II' = II - 0IV'$	S_2	0	(1)	0	0	0	1	0	0	5
$III' = III - 0IV'$	S_3	0	0	1	0	0	0	1	0	8
$IV' = IV$	x_3	45	0	0	1	0	0	0	1	6
	z_j		0	0	*	*	*	*	45	$OV=270$
	$c_j - z_j$		30	15	*	*	*	*	−45	

Equation	Basic Variable	c_j / c_B	x_1	x_2	x_3	S_1	S_2	S_3	S_4	RHS
			30	15	45	0	0	0	0	
$I'' = I' - 2II''$	S_1	0	0	(1)	0	1	−2	0	−3	2
$II'' = II'$	x_1	30	1	0	0	0	1	0	0	5
$III'' = III' - 0II''$	S_3	0	0	1	0	0	0	1	0	8
$IV'' = IV' - 0II''$	x_3	45	0	0	1	0	0	0	1	6
	z_j		*	0	*	*	30	*	45	$OV=420$
	$c_j - z_j$		*	15	*	*	−30	*	−45	

Equation	Basic Variable	c_j / c_B	x_1	x_2	x_3	S_1	S_2	S_3	S_4	RHS
			30	15	45	0	0	0	0	
$I''' = I''$	x_2	15	0	1	0	1	−2	0	−3	2
$II''' = II'' - 0I'''$	x_1	30	1	0	0	0	1	0	0	5
$III''' = III'' - 1I'''$	S_3	0	0	0	0	−1	2	1	3	6
$IV''' = IV'' - 0I'''$	x_3	45	0	0	1	0	0	0	1	6
	z_j		*	*	*	15	0	*	0	$OV=450$
	$c_j - z_j$		*	*	*	−15	0	*	0	

Figure 7.6 Sequence of simplex tableaux for example LP illustrating multiple optimality

Now we will learn how to recognize multiple optimality when executing the simplex method.

As an example, we use the following LP:

$$\text{Maximize } 30x_1 + 15x_2 + 45x_3$$

$$\begin{array}{rrrrcl}
\text{subject to} \quad 2x_1 + & x_2 + & 3x_3 & \leqslant & 30 \\
x_1 & & & \leqslant & 5 \\
& x_2 & & \leqslant & 8 \\
& & x_3 & \leqslant & 6
\end{array}$$

$$\text{and } x_1 \geqslant 0, x_2 \geqslant 0, x_3 \geqslant 0.$$

You should verify for yourself that converting the LP into equality form, constructing the initial simplex tableau, and performing three iterations of the simplex method leads to the sequence of simplex tableaux displayed in Figure 7.6. Looking at Figure 7.6's final simplex tableau and focusing our attention on the Basic Variable column and *RHS* column, we see that the tableau corresponds to the basic feasible solution displayed in Table 7.1's first row. Now focus your attention at the tableau's $c_j - z_j$ row and observe that it contains only nonpositive numbers, thereby indicating that the basic feasible solution displayed in Table 7.1's first row is an optimal solution. To see that there are other optimal solutions, note that S_2's $c_j - z_j$ value and S_4's $c_j - z_j$ value both equal 0. Consequently, the objective value will remain unchanged if we move to a new basic feasible solution by selecting either S_2 or S_4 as the entering basic variable, selecting the appropriate leaving basic variable for the choice of the entering basic variable, and performing the appropriate pivot. To see this in more detail, consider Figure 7.7, which displays the simplex tableaux that result from selecting S_2 or S_4 as the entering basic variable. Observe the following aspects of these tableaux:

- If we perform the pivot initiated by the selection of S_2 as the entering basic variable, we obtain the simplex tableau displayed in Figure 7.7's bottom-left portion. From the tableau's Basic Variable column and *RHS* column, we see that the tableau corresponds to the basic feasible solution displayed in Table 7.1's second row This basic feasible solution's objective value (as indicated by the tableau's *OV* portion) is 450. As predicted, the objective value has not changed, thereby confirming that the basic feasible solution displayed in Table 7.1's second row is also an optimal solution.

TABLE 7.1 The Three Optimal Basic Feasible Solutions for the Example LP Illustrating Multiple Optimality

	Basic Feasible Solution $(x_1, x_2, x_3, S_1, S_2, S_3, S_4)$						
1.	(5,	2,	6,	0,	0,	6,	0)
2.	(2,	8,	6,	0,	3,	0,	0)
3.	(5,	8,	4,	0,	0,	0,	2)

Equation	Basic Variable	c_j	30	15	45	0	0	0	0	
		c_B	x_1	x_2	x_3	S_1	S_2	S_3	S_4	RHS
$I''' = I''$	x_2	15	0	1	0	1	-2	0	-3	2
$II''' = II'' - 0I'''$	x_1	30	1	0	0	0	1	0	0	5
$III''' = III'' - 1I''$	S_3	0	0	0	0	-1	2	1	3	6
$IV''' = IV'' - 0I'''$	x_3	45	0	0	1	0	0	0	1	6
		z_j	*	*	*	15	0	*	0	$OV = 450$
		$c_j - z_j$	*	*	*	-15	0	*	0	

S_2 is entering basic variable. S_4 is entering basic variable.

Equation	Basic Variable	c_j	30	15	45	0	0	0	0	
		c_B	x_1	x_2	x_3	S_1	S_2	S_3	S_4	RHS
$I'''' = I''' + 2III''''$	x_2	15	0	1	0	0	0	1	0	8
$II'''' = II''' - 1III''''$	x_1	30	1	0	0	$\frac{1}{2}$	0	$-\frac{1}{2}$	$-\frac{3}{2}$	2
$III'''' = \frac{1}{2} III'''$	S_2	0	0	0	0	$-\frac{1}{2}$	1	$\frac{1}{2}$	$\frac{3}{2}$	2
$IV'''' = IV''' - 0III''''$	x_3	45	0	0	1	0	0	0	1	6
		z_j	*	*	*	15	*	0	0	$OV = 450$
		$c_j - z_j$	*	*	*	-15	*	0	0	

Equation	Basic Variable	c_j	30	15	45	0	0	0	0	
		c_B	x_1	x_2	x_3	S_1	S_2	S_3	S_4	RHS
$I'''' = I''' + 3III''''$	x_2	15	0	1	0	0	0	1	0	8
$II'''' = II''' - 0III''''$	x_1	30	1	0	0	0	1	0	0	5
$III'''' = \frac{1}{3} III'''$	S_4	0	0	0	0	$-\frac{1}{3}$	$\frac{2}{3}$	$\frac{1}{3}$	1	2
$IV'''' = IV''' - 1III''''$	x_3	45	0	0	1	$\frac{1}{3}$	$-\frac{2}{3}$	$-\frac{1}{3}$	0	4
		z_j	*	*	*	15	0	0	*	$OV = 450$
		$c_j - z_j$	*	*	*	-15	0	0	*	

Figure 7.7 Pivoting to find other optimal basic feasible solutions

- If we perform the pivot initiated by the selection of S_4 as the entering basic variable, we obtain the simplex tableau displayed in Figure 7.7's bottom-right portion. From the tableau's Basic Variable column and *RHS* column, we see that the tableau corresponds to the basic feasible solution displayed in Table 7.1's third row. This basic feasible solution's objective value (as indicated by the tableau's *OV* portion) is 450. As predicted, the objective value has not changed, thereby confirming that the basic feasible solution displayed in Table 7.1's third row is also an optimal solution.

To summarize, the three simplex tableaux displayed in Figure 7.7 indicate that the three basic feasible solutions displayed in Table 7.1 are optimal solutions.

Our example has illustrated the following general principle for distinguishing between the cases of unique optimality and multiple optimality:

> Whenever the optimal simplex tableau's $c_j - z_j$ row contains all negative values when maximizing and all positive values when minimizing, we conclude that the LP has a unique optimal solution. However, whenever the optimal simplex tableau's $c_j - z_j$ row contains one or more values of 0, we conclude that the LP has multiple optimal solutions. To determine an alternative optimal basic feasible solution, we perform the pivot initiated by selecting as the entering basic variable a nonbasic variable whose $c_j - z_j$ value is 0. (Note that, in the preceding statements, the $c_j - z_j$ values for artificial variables, if any, are ignored.)

Three further observations are appropriate here:

306

- In Section 2.11 we stated a general principle that, when multiple optimality occurs, *at least* two of the infinite number of optimal solutions correspond geometrically to corner points. Using only an LP with a two-dimensional feasible region, it is impossible to illustrate the need for the italicized *at least* because, when multiple optimality occurs for such an LP, there are always *exactly* two optimal solutions that correspond to corner points, namely, the two corner points at the end of the line segment that is the intersection of the optimal isoprofit line and the feasible region. In contrast, when the LP has a three-dimensional feasible region, the intersection of the optimal isoprofit plane and the feasible region will be one of the following three cases:

1. The intersection of the optimal isoprofit plane and the feasible region consists of exactly one of the feasible region's corner points. Such an intersection corresponds to unique optimality.

2. The intersection of the optimal isoprofit plane and the feasible region consists of one of the feasible region edges. Such an intersection corresponds to multiple optimality with exactly two optimal corner points (as well as an infinite number of optimal solutions that are not corner points).

3. The intersection of the optimal isoprofit plane and the feasible region consists of one of the feasible region faces. Such an intersection corresponds to multiple optimality with at least three optimal corner points (as well as an infinite number of optimal solutions that are not corner points). For example, if the intersection of the optimal isoprofit plane and the feasible region were to consist of an octagon, there would be eight optimal corner points.

In general, then, when multiple optimality occurs, there will always be *at least* two optimal basic feasible solutions.

■ As discussed more fully in Section 2.11, multiple optimality is a "luxury" for the decision maker because it permits some secondary criterion not included in the LP to be used to select from among the multiple optimal solutions.

■ When using an LP software package to solve an LP, the package will terminate execution the first time it generates an optimal simplex tableau. After printing the corresponding optimal solution, a well-written software package will check for multiple optimality and, if found, will print a message such as

"Multiple optimality has occurred!"

A package capable of displaying such a message usually has a command structure that permits an "expert user" to perform the additional iterations of the simplex method necessary to identify other alternative optimal solutions.

7.4 SENSITIVITY ANALYSIS OF AN OBJECTIVE-FUNCTION COEFFICIENT

In Chapter 3 we saw that LP software packages provide a range of optimality for each decision variable's objective-function coefficient—that is, a range of values within which the coefficient can vary such that the LP's current optimal solution remains optimal. We also saw how to graphically determine an objective-function coefficient's range of optimality when the LP involves only two decision variables. In this section we will learn how to use the optimal simplex tableau to determine an objective-function coefficient's range of optimality.

As an example we use the following LP from Section 7.2:

$$\text{Maximize} \quad 30x_1 - 10x_2 + 20x_3 - 8x_4$$

$$\text{subject to} \quad \begin{array}{rcrcrcrcl} x_1 & - & 2x_2 & + & 4x_3 & + & x_4 & \leqslant & 7 \\ -4x_1 & + & x_2 & - & 3x_3 & + & 2x_4 & \geqslant & 3 \\ -2x_1 & & & - & x_3 & + & x_4 & = & 1 \\ x_1 & + & 2x_2 & + & 3x_3 & + & x_4 & \geqslant & 12 \end{array}$$

and $x_1 \geqslant 0, x_2 \geqslant 0, x_3 \geqslant 0, x_4 \geqslant 0$.

Figure 7.8 displays the output when LINPRO, the hypothetical LP software package introduced in Chapter 3, is used to solve the LP. For ease of reference, Figure 7.9 displays the optimal simplex tableau (the last tableau in Figure 7.3).

Figure 7.8 LINPRO output for example LP

```
              OPTIMAL OBJECTIVE VALUE
                  19.1666660

   Decision.    Optimal
   Variable     Value            Reduced Cost
        x1      2.833333           0.000000
        x2      1.250000           0.000000
        x3      0.000000          11.500001
        x4      6.666667           0.000000


                Slack/
   Constraint   Surplus          Shadow Price
        1)      0.000000           4.833333
        2)      0.250000           0.000000
        3)      0.000000         -12.666667
        4)      0.000000          -0.166667


Do sensitivity analysis?
?yes


Sensitivity Analysis:

               Objective-Function Coefficients' Ranges
   Decision     Current         Allowable        Allowable
   Variable     Coefficient     Increase         Decrease
        x1      30.000000        1.000000         7.666667
        x2     -10.000000        0.666667         infinity
        x3      20.000000       11.500001         infinity
        x4      -8.000000        0.500000         5.750000


                  Right-Hand Sides' Ranges
                Current         Allowable        Allowable
   Constraint   RHS             Increase         Decrease
        1)       7.000000        1.000000        16.999998
        2)       3.000000        0.250000         infinity
        3)       1.000000        8.499999         0.125000
        4)      12.000000        infinity         1.000000
```

Basic Variable	c_j / c_B	30 / x_1	-10 / x_2	20 / x_3	-8 / x_4	0 / S_1	0 / E_2	0 / E_4	0 / A_2	0 / A_3	0 / A_4	RHS
x_1	30	1	0	$\frac{3}{2}$	0	$\frac{1}{6}$	0	$-\frac{1}{6}$	0	$-\frac{1}{3}$	$\frac{1}{6}$	$\frac{17}{6}$
x_2	-10	0	1	$-\frac{1}{4}$	0	$-\frac{1}{4}$	0	$-\frac{1}{4}$	0	0	$\frac{1}{4}$	$\frac{5}{4}$
x_4	-8	0	0	2	1	$\frac{1}{3}$	0	$-\frac{1}{3}$	0	$\frac{1}{3}$	$\frac{1}{3}$	$\frac{20}{3}$
E_2	0	0	0	$\frac{3}{4}$	0	$-\frac{1}{4}$	1	$-\frac{1}{4}$	-1	2	$\frac{1}{4}$	$\frac{1}{4}$
z_j		*	*	$\frac{63}{2}$	*	$\frac{29}{6}$	*	$\frac{1}{6}$	0	$-\frac{38}{3}$	$-\frac{1}{6}$	$OV=\frac{115}{6}$
$c_j - z_j$		*	*	$-\frac{23}{2}$	*	$-\frac{29}{6}$	*	$-\frac{1}{6}$	0	$\frac{38}{3}$	$\frac{1}{6}$	

Figure 7.9 Optimal simplex tableau for Section 7.1's example LP

The Range of Optimality for a Nonbasic Variable's Objective-Function Coefficient

We first learn how to compute the range of optimality for the objective-function coefficient of a decision variable that is a nonbasic variable in the optimal simplex tableau, a task that (as we will see) is considerably easier than for a basic variable. In Figure 7.9's optimal simplex tableau, the only nonbasic variable that is a decision variable is x_3. Let us now compute the range of optimality for x_3's objective-function coefficient. We will use the notation Δ to denote the change in x_3's objective-function coefficient; that is, it will change from 20 to $20 + \Delta$. For example, $\Delta = 1$ corresponds to an increase from 20 to 21, and $\Delta = -2$ corresponds to a decrease from 20 to 18. The question we wish to answer with our sensitivity analysis is

Assuming all the LP's other data remain unchanged, within what range of values can Δ vary such that the LP's current optimal solution remains optimal?

If x_3's objective-function coefficient is no longer 20 but $20 + \Delta$, what numbers in Figure 7.9's simplex tableau change? The answer is provided by the two shaded numbers in the x_3 column of the tableau displayed in Figure 7.10. Observe that the two shaded changes result from first changing x_3's objective-function coefficient in the tableau's c_j row from 20 to $20 + \Delta$ and then recomput-

Figure 7.10 Revised simplex tableau for sensitivity analysis of x_3's objective-function coefficient

Basic Variable	c_j / c_B	30 / x_1	-10 / x_2	$20 + \Delta$ / x_3	-8 / x_4	0 / S_1	0 / E_2	0 / E_4	0 / A_2	0 / A_3	0 / A_4	RHS
x_1	30	1	0	$\frac{3}{2}$	0	$\frac{1}{6}$	0	$-\frac{1}{6}$	0	$-\frac{1}{3}$	$\frac{1}{6}$	$\frac{17}{6}$
x_2	-10	0	1	$-\frac{1}{4}$	0	$-\frac{1}{4}$	0	$-\frac{1}{4}$	0	0	$\frac{1}{4}$	$\frac{5}{4}$
x_4	-8	0	0	2	1	$\frac{1}{3}$	0	$-\frac{1}{3}$	0	$\frac{1}{3}$	$\frac{1}{3}$	$\frac{20}{3}$
E_2	0	0	0	$\frac{3}{4}$	0	$-\frac{1}{4}$	1	$-\frac{1}{4}$	-1	2	$\frac{1}{4}$	$\frac{1}{4}$
z_j		*	*	$\frac{63}{2}$	*	$\frac{29}{6}$	*	$\frac{1}{6}$	0	$-\frac{38}{3}$	$-\frac{1}{6}$	$OV=\frac{115}{6}$
$c_j - z_j$		*	*	$-\frac{23}{2} + \Delta$	*	$-\frac{29}{6}$	*	$-\frac{1}{6}$	0	$\frac{38}{3}$	$\frac{1}{6}$	

ing x_3's $c_j - z_j$ value. For Figure 7.10's revised tableau to remain optimal, x_3's revised $c_j - z_j$ value must remain nonpositive; that is, the following relationship must hold:

$$-\frac{23}{2} + \Delta \leqslant 0.$$

If this relationship did not hold, it would be possible to improve the objective value by performing the pivot initiated by selecting x_3 as the entering basic variable. Simplifying the above relationship, we have

$$-\frac{23}{2} + \Delta \leqslant 0 \rightarrow \Delta \leqslant \frac{23}{2} \rightarrow \Delta \leqslant 11\tfrac{1}{2}.$$

Observe that this upper limit on Δ equals the absolute value of x_3's $c_j - z_j$ value in Figure 7.9's optimal simplex tableau. Thus, we have determined that

- The maximum allowable increase in x_3's objective-function coefficient is $11\tfrac{1}{2}$, the absolute value of x_3's $c_j - z_j$ value in Figure 7.9's optimal simplex tableau.

- The maximum allowable decrease in x_3's objective-function coefficient is ∞.

Observe that these are precisely the values given in Figure 7.8's LINPRO output. Our example has illustrated the following general principle:

> When the LP involves maximization, no extensive computations are required to compute the range of optimality for the objective-function coefficient of a nonbasic variable in the optimal simplex tableau. In particular,
>
> - The objective-function coefficient's maximum allowable increase equals the absolute value of the nonbasic variable's $c_j - z_j$ value in the optimal simplex tableau.
>
> - The objective-function coefficient's maximum allowable decrease equals ∞.

In several of the end-of-chapter exercises you will illustrate the following "companion" general principle:

> When the LP involves minimization, no extensive computations are required to compute the range of optimality for the objective-function coefficient of a nonbasic variable in the optimal simplex tableau. In particular,
>
> - The objective-function coefficient's maximum allowable increase equals ∞.
>
> - The objective-function coefficient's maximum allowable decrease equals the nonbasic variable's $c_j - z_j$ value in the optimal simplex tableau.[8]

The Range of Optimality for a Basic Variable's Objective-Function Coefficient

We must expend considerably more computational effort to determine the range of optimality for the objective-function coefficient of a decision variable that is a basic

---

[8] It is unnecessary to say "the absolute value of" the $c_j - z_j$ value, since, when minimizing, all $c_j - z_j$ values are nonnegative.

variable in the optimal simplex tableau. In Figure 7.9's optimal tableau, the basic variables that are decision variables are x_1, x_2, and x_4. Let us first compute the range of optimality for x_1's objective-function coefficient. Once again, we will use Δ to denote the change in x_1's objective-function coefficient; that is, it will change from its current value of 30 to $30 + \Delta$.

If x_1's objective-function coefficient is $30 + \Delta$, what numbers in Figure 7.9's simplex tableau change? In contrast to the case for a nonbasic variable where only two numbers change, the shaded numbers in the tableau displayed in Figure 7.11 indicate that many numbers change. Observe that the shaded changes result from the new value of $30 + \Delta$ for x_1's objective-function coefficient replacing its former value of 30 not only in the tableau's c_j row but also the c_B column. Since the c_B column has changed, we must recompute every nonbasic variable's z_j value and, hence, every nonbasic variable's $c_j - z_j$ value.[9] For Figure 7.11's revised tableau to remain optimal, every number in the revised $c_j - z_j$ row (except those for the artificial variables) must remain nonpositive; that is, the following three relationships must hold:

$$x_3\text{'s revised } c_j - z_j \text{ value:} \qquad -\frac{23}{2} - \frac{3}{2}\Delta \leqslant 0$$

$$S_1\text{'s revised } c_j - z_j \text{ value:} \qquad -\frac{29}{6} - \frac{1}{6}\Delta \leqslant 0$$

$$E_4\text{'s revised } c_j - z_j \text{ value:} \qquad -\frac{1}{6} + \frac{1}{6}\Delta \leqslant 0$$

After simplification, each of the above relationships provides either a positive upper limit or a negative lower limit on Δ. The computation of these limits proceeds as follows:

		Negative Lower Limit on Δ	Positive Upper Limit on Δ
$-\frac{23}{2} - \frac{3}{2}\Delta \leqslant 0 \quad \rightarrow$	$-\frac{23}{2} \leqslant \frac{3}{2}\Delta \rightarrow$	$-\frac{23}{3} \leqslant \Delta$	
$-\frac{29}{6} - \frac{1}{6}\Delta \leqslant 0 \quad \rightarrow$	$-\frac{29}{6} \leqslant \frac{1}{6}\Delta \rightarrow$	$-29 \leqslant \Delta$	
$-\frac{1}{6} + \frac{1}{6}\Delta \leqslant 0 \quad \rightarrow$	$\frac{1}{6}\Delta \leqslant \frac{1}{6} \rightarrow$		$\Delta \leqslant 1$

[9] Also note that the objective value changes.

Figure 7.11 Revised simplex tableau for sensitivity analysis of x_1's objective-function coefficient

Basic Variable	c_j	$30 + \Delta$	-10	20	-8	0	0	0	0	0	0	
	c_B	x_1	x_2	x_3	x_4	S_1	E_2	E_4	A_2	A_3	A_4	RHS
x_1	$30 + \Delta$	1	0	$\frac{3}{2}$	0	$\frac{1}{6}$	0	$-\frac{1}{6}$	0	$-\frac{1}{3}$	$\frac{1}{6}$	$\frac{17}{6}$
x_2	-10	0	1	$-\frac{1}{4}$	0	$-\frac{1}{4}$	0	$-\frac{1}{4}$	0	0	$\frac{1}{4}$	$\frac{5}{4}$
x_4	-8	0	0	2	1	$\frac{1}{3}$	0	$-\frac{1}{3}$	0	$\frac{1}{3}$	$\frac{1}{3}$	$\frac{20}{3}$
E_2	0	0	0	$\frac{3}{4}$	0	$-\frac{1}{4}$	1	$-\frac{1}{4}$	-1	2	$\frac{1}{4}$	$\frac{1}{4}$
	z_j	*	*	$\frac{63}{2} + \frac{3}{2}\Delta$	*	$\frac{29}{6} + \frac{1}{6}\Delta$	*	$\frac{1}{6} - \frac{1}{6}\Delta$	0	$-\frac{38}{3} - \frac{1}{3}\Delta$	$-\frac{1}{6} + \frac{1}{6}\Delta$	$OV = \frac{115}{6} + \frac{17}{6}\Delta$
	$c_j - z_j$	*	*	$-\frac{23}{2} - \frac{3}{2}\Delta$	*	$-\frac{29}{6} - \frac{1}{6}\Delta$	*	$-\frac{1}{6} + \frac{1}{6}\Delta$	0	$\frac{38}{3} + \frac{1}{3}\Delta$	$\frac{1}{6} - \frac{1}{6}\Delta$	

For Δ to simultaneously satisfy the upper limit and the two lower limits, it must satisfy the upper limit and the most restrictive of the two lower limits (i.e., the *maximum* of $-\frac{23}{3}$ and -29, or, equivalently, the least negative of the two values). Consequently, for all $c_j - z_j$ values in Figure 7.11's revised tableau to remain nonpositive, Δ must satisfy

$$-\frac{23}{3} \leqslant \Delta \leqslant 1.$$

The above limits on Δ are equivalent to the following:

- The maximum allowable increase in x_1's objective-function coefficient is 1.
- The maximum allowable decrease in x_1's objective-function coefficient is $7\frac{2}{3}$.

Observe that these are precisely the values in Figure 7.8's LINPRO output.

Our example has illustrated the following general procedure:

A General
Procedure for
Computing the
Range of
Optimality for
the Objective-
Function
Coefficient of a
Basic Variable in
the Optimal
Simplex Tableau

1. Add Δ to the basic variable's objective-function coefficient in the optimal simplex tableau's c_j row and c_B column.

2. Recompute each nonbasic variable's z_j value and $c_j - z_j$ value. (Also recompute the objective value.)

3. Since the revised $c_j - z_j$ values must all be nonpositive if maximizing or nonnegative if minimizing, the revised $c_j - z_j$ values imply that Δ must satisfy a system of inequalities (e.g., if we are maximizing and one of the revised $c_j - z_j$ values is $-3 - \Delta$, then one of the inequalities is $-3 - \Delta \leqslant 0$). On simplification, each inequality provides either a positive upper limit or a negative lower limit on Δ. To simultaneously satisfy all upper limits and all lower limits, Δ must satisfy

$$\begin{pmatrix} maximum \text{ of the} \\ \text{negative lower limits} \\ \text{on } \Delta \end{pmatrix} \leqslant \Delta \leqslant \begin{pmatrix} minimum \text{ of the} \\ \text{positive upper limits} \\ \text{on } \Delta \end{pmatrix}$$

The above limits on Δ are equivalent to

$$\begin{pmatrix} \text{maximum allowable increase} \\ \text{in the basic variable's} \\ \text{objective-function coefficient} \end{pmatrix} = \begin{pmatrix} minimum \text{ of the} \\ \text{positive upper limits} \\ \text{on } \Delta \end{pmatrix}$$

$$\begin{pmatrix} \text{maximum allowable decrease} \\ \text{in the basic variable's} \\ \text{objective-function coefficient} \end{pmatrix} = \begin{pmatrix} \text{absolute value of the} \\ maximum \text{ of the} \\ \text{negative lower limits} \\ \text{on } \Delta \end{pmatrix}$$

Before proceeding, you should check your understanding of this subsection by computing range of optimality for either x_2's objective-function coefficient or x_4's objective-function coefficient (or both) and comparing your answer to that given in Figure 7.8's LINPRO output.

Continuing on to Optimality When the Change in an Objective-Function Coefficient Is Too Large

When a change in an objective-function coefficient results in a revised coefficient outside the range of optimality, we can determine the LP's new optimal solution by using the formerly optimal simplex tableau as a starting point. To illustrate, suppose that x_1's objective-function coefficient decreases from 30 to 18. Since this decrease of 12 exceeds the previously computed maximum allowable decrease of $7\frac{2}{3}$, the currently optimal solution is no longer optimal. To determine the LP's new optimal solution, we could resolve the LP "from scratch." However, we will now demonstrate that our search for the LP's new optimal solution can start from the simplex tableau corresponding to the formerly optimal simplex tableau. To see how, note that a decrease in x_1's objective-function coefficient from 30 to 18 corresponds to $\Delta = -12$. Substituting $\Delta = -12$ into Figure 7.11's simplex tableau, we obtain the following simplex tableau:

Basic Variabl	c_j	18	-10	20	-8	0	0	0	0	0	0	
	c_B	x_1	x_2	x_3	x_4	S_1	E_2	E_4	A_2	A_3	A_4	RHS
x_1	18	1	0	$\frac{3}{2}$	0	$\frac{1}{6}$	0	$-\frac{1}{6}$	0	$-\frac{1}{3}$	$\frac{1}{6}$	$\frac{17}{6}$
x_2	-10	0	1	$-\frac{1}{4}$	0	$-\frac{1}{4}$	0	$-\frac{1}{4}$	0	0	$\frac{1}{4}$	$\frac{5}{4}$
x_4	-8	0	0	2	1	$\frac{1}{3}$	0	$-\frac{1}{3}$	0	$\frac{1}{2}$	$\frac{1}{3}$	$\frac{20}{3}$
E_2	0	0	0	$\frac{3}{4}$	0	$-\frac{1}{4}$	1	$-\frac{1}{4}$	-1	2	$\frac{1}{4}$	$\frac{1}{4}$
	z_j	*	*	$\frac{27}{2}$	*	$\frac{17}{6}$	*	$\frac{13}{6}$	0	$-\frac{26}{3}$	$-\frac{13}{6}$	$OV=-\frac{89}{6}$
	$c_j - z_j$	*	*	$\frac{13}{2}$	*	$-\frac{17}{6}$	*	$-\frac{13}{6}$	0	$\frac{26}{3}$	$\frac{13}{6}$	

To determine the LP's new optimal solution, we can use this tableau as a starting point and perform an iteration of the simplex method that begins by selecting x_3 as the entering basic variable.[10] Note that there is no guarantee that only one iteration of the simplex method will be required to identify the LP's new optimal solution. However, the expectation is that fewer iterations will be required if we begin at the formerly optimal simplex tableau instead of resolving the LP "from scratch."

To summarize:

> When a change in a decision variable's objective-function coefficient results in a revised coefficient outside the range of optimality, we can determine the LP's new optimal solution by using the formerly optimal simplex tableau as a starting point (after recomputing the $c_j - z_j$ values).

7.5 SENSITIVITY ANALYSIS OF A STRUCTURAL CONSTRAINT'S RIGHT-HAND SIDE

In Chapter 3 we saw that LP software packages provide a shadow price and an associated range of validity for each structural constraint's right-hand side. We also saw how to graphically determine a structural constraint's shadow price and its associated range of validity when the LP involves only two decision variables. In this section we will learn how to use the optimal simplex tableau to determine a

[10] You will be asked to do this in Exercise 7.21.

structural constraint's shadow price and its associated range of validity. As an example, we continue to use the example introduced in Section 7.4.

Sensitivity Analysis of the Right-Hand Side of a Binding Constraint

We will first learn how to conduct sensitivity analysis on the right-hand side of a structural constraint that is binding at optimality, a task that (as we will see) is considerably more difficult than when the structural constraint is nonbinding. In Figure 7.9's optimal simplex tableau, S_1 and E_4 have values of 0, thereby indicating that the first and fourth structural constraints are binding constraints at the LP's optimal solution. Of course, because the third structural constraint is an equality, it must also be binding. Thus, the following structural constraints are binding at the LP's optimal solution:

$$
\begin{array}{llrrrrrrr}
\text{First structural constraint:} & x_1 & - & 2x_2 & + & 4x_3 & + & x_4 & \leqslant & 7 \\
\text{Third structural constraint:} & -2x_1 & & & - & x_3 & + & x_4 & = & 1 \\
\text{Fourth structural constraint:} & x_1 & + & 2x_2 & + & 3x_3 & + & x_4 & \geqslant & 12
\end{array}
$$

Let us first conduct sensitivity analysis on the right-hand side of the first structural constraint, $x_1 - 2x_2 + 4x_3 + x_4 \leqslant 7$. Since this is the LP's first structural constraint, we will denote its right-hand side by RHS_1, and we will denote by Δ the change in RHS_1 from its current value of 7 (i.e., RHS_1 will change from 7 to $7 + \Delta$). The question we wish to answer with our sensitivity analysis is

> Assuming all the LP's other data remain unchanged, what is the effect on the LP's optimal solution of changing RHS_1 from 7 to $7 + \Delta$?

As we did in Chapter 3's graphical sensitivity analysis, let us first make the assumption that Δ can only take on a value close to 0 (e.g., $\Delta = 0.01$ or $\Delta = -0.01$) and then subsequently determine the extent to which our sensitivity analysis remains valid for values of Δ not close to 0.

A formally conducted sensitivity analysis of RHS_1 is beyond the scope of this text. Instead, we will justify our sensitivity analysis with the following intuitive observation:

> Increasing RHS_1 from 7 to $7 + \Delta$ is equivalent to keeping RHS_1 at its current value of 7 but instead decreasing the lower bound on the constraint's slack variable S_1 from 0 to $-\Delta$. For example, increasing RHS_1 from 7 to 10 is equivalent to keeping RHS_1 at 7 but instead decreasing the lower bound on S_1 from 0 to -3.

Given this observation, we can determine the effect on the LP's optimal solution of increasing RHS_1 from 7 to $7 + \Delta$ by answering the following question:

> Assuming the LP's other data remain unchanged, what is the effect on the LP's optimal solution of decreasing the lower bound on S_1 from 0 to $-\Delta$?

Fortunately, we already know how to answer this question.

Let us first determine the effect decreasing S_1's lower bound has on the optimal objective value. Looking at Figure 7.9's optimal simplex tableau, we see that S_1's $c_j - z_j$ value is $-\frac{29}{6}$. This implies that the optimal objective value *decreases* at the rate of $\frac{29}{6}$ per unit *increase* in S_1, or, equivalently, that the optimal objective value *increases* at the rate of $\frac{29}{6}$ per unit *decrease* in S_1. Thus, decreasing S_1 from 0 to $-\Delta$ has the following effect on the optimal objective value:

revised optimal objective value $= \dfrac{115}{6} + \dfrac{29}{6}\Delta$

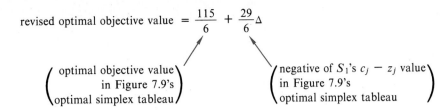

$\begin{pmatrix} \text{optimal objective value} \\ \text{in Figure 7.9's} \\ \text{optimal simplex tableau} \end{pmatrix}$ $\begin{pmatrix} \text{negative of } S_1\text{'s } c_j - z_j \text{ value} \\ \text{in Figure 7.9's} \\ \text{optimal simplex tableau} \end{pmatrix}$

From the coefficient of Δ, we see that RHS_1's shadow price is $\frac{29}{6} = 4\frac{5}{6}$.[11] Observe that this is precisely the shadow price displayed in Figure 7.8's LINPRO output.

Having determined the effect that decreasing S_1 from 0 to $-\Delta$ has on the optimal objective value, let us now look at the effect on the optimal values of the variables. Recall from Section 6.6 that S_1's simplex tableau coefficients represent the rate of *decrease* in the basic variables' current values per unit *increase* in S_1. This is equivalent to saying that S_1's simplex tableau coefficients represent the rate of *increase* in the basic variables' current values per unit *decrease* in S_1. Thus, decreasing S_1 from 0 to $-\Delta$ has the following effect on the basic variables' optimal values:

$$x_1 = \frac{17}{6} + \frac{1}{6}\Delta$$

$$x_2 = \frac{5}{4} - \frac{1}{4}\Delta$$

$$x_4 = \frac{20}{3} + \frac{1}{3}\Delta$$

$$E_2 = \frac{1}{4} - \frac{1}{4}\Delta$$

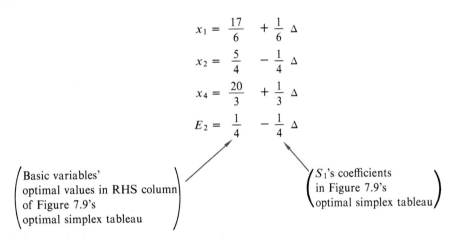

$\begin{pmatrix} \text{Basic variables'} \\ \text{optimal values in RHS column} \\ \text{of Figure 7.9's} \\ \text{optimal simplex tableau} \end{pmatrix}$ $\begin{pmatrix} S_1\text{'s coefficients} \\ \text{in Figure 7.9's} \\ \text{optimal simplex tableau} \end{pmatrix}$

To summarize, by investigating the effect decreasing S_1 has on the basic variables' optimal values, we have determined that, if RHS_1 changes from 7 to $7 + \Delta$, the LP's optimal simplex tableau changes from that displayed in Figure 7.9 to that displayed in Figure 7.12.

For the above sensitivity analysis to remain valid, the basic variables' revised optimal values must all remain nonnegative; otherwise, the revised solution is no longer feasible, let alone optimal. Thus, the sensitivity analysis remains valid as long as

$$x_1\text{'s revised value:} \quad \frac{17}{6} + \frac{1}{6}\Delta \geqslant 0$$

$$x_2\text{'s revised value:} \quad \frac{5}{4} - \frac{1}{4}\Delta \geqslant 0$$

$$x_4\text{'s revised value:} \quad \frac{20}{3} + \frac{1}{3}\Delta \geqslant 0$$

$$E_2\text{'s revised value:} \quad \frac{1}{4} - \frac{1}{4}\Delta \geqslant 0$$

---

[11] Recall from Chapter 3 that a constraint's shadow price is the rate of *improvement* in the optimal objective value per unit increase in the right-hand side.

Basic Variable	c_j	30	-10	$20 + \Delta$	-8	0	0	0	0	0	0	
	c_B	x_1	x_2	x_3	x_4	S_1	E_2	E_4	A_2	A_3	A_4	RHS
x_1	30	1	0	$\frac{3}{2}$	0	$\frac{1}{6}$	0	$-\frac{1}{6}$	0	$-\frac{1}{3}$	$\frac{1}{6}$	$\frac{17}{6} + \frac{1}{6}\Delta$
x_2	-10	0	1	$-\frac{1}{4}$	0	$-\frac{1}{4}$	0	$-\frac{1}{4}$	0	0	$\frac{1}{4}$	$\frac{5}{4} - \frac{1}{4}\Delta$
x_4	-8	0	0	2	1	$\frac{1}{3}$	0	$-\frac{1}{3}$	0	$\frac{1}{3}$	$\frac{1}{3}$	$\frac{20}{3} + \frac{1}{3}\Delta$
E_2	0	0	0	$\frac{3}{4}$	0	$-\frac{1}{4}$	1	$-\frac{1}{4}$	-1	2	$\frac{1}{4}$	$\frac{1}{4} - \frac{1}{4}\Delta$
z_j		*	*	$\frac{63}{2}$	*	$\frac{29}{6}$	*	$\frac{1}{6}$	0	$-\frac{38}{3}$	$-\frac{1}{6}$	$OV = \frac{115}{6} + \frac{29}{6}\Delta$
$c_j - z_j$		*	*	$-\frac{23}{2} + \Delta$	*	$-\frac{29}{6}$	*	$-\frac{1}{6}$	0	$\frac{38}{3}$	$\frac{1}{6}$	

Figure 7.12 Revised simplex tableau for sensitivity analysis of RHS_1

After simplification, each of the above relationships provides either a positive upper limit or a negative lower limit on Δ. The computation of these limits proceeds as follows:

		Negative Lower Limit on Δ	Positive Upper Limit on Δ

$$\frac{17}{6} + \frac{1}{6}\Delta \geqslant 0 \quad \rightarrow \quad -\frac{17}{6} \leqslant \frac{1}{6}\Delta \quad \rightarrow \quad -17 \leqslant \Delta$$

$$\frac{5}{4} - \frac{1}{4}\Delta \geqslant 0 \quad \rightarrow \quad \frac{1}{4}\Delta \leqslant \frac{5}{4} \quad \rightarrow \quad \Delta \leqslant 5$$

$$\frac{20}{3} + \frac{1}{3}\Delta \geqslant 0 \quad \rightarrow \quad -\frac{20}{3} \leqslant \frac{1}{3}\Delta \quad \rightarrow \quad -20 \leqslant \Delta$$

$$\frac{1}{4} - \frac{1}{4}\Delta \geqslant 0 \quad \rightarrow \quad \frac{1}{4}\Delta \leqslant \frac{1}{4} \quad \rightarrow \quad \Delta \leqslant 1$$

For Δ to simultaneously satisfy the two upper limits and the two lower limits, it must satisfy the most restrictive of the two upper limits (i.e., the *minimum* of 5 and 1) and the most restrictive of the two lower limits (i.e., the *maximum* of -17 and -20 or, equivalently, the *least negative*). Consequently, the sensitivity analysis's range of validity is

$$-17 \leqslant \Delta \leqslant 1.$$

The above limits on Δ are equivalent to the following:

- RHS_1's maximum allowable increase is 1.
- RHS_1's maximum allowable decrease is 17.

Observe that these are precisely the values in Figure 7.8's LINPRO output.

We have just illustrated sensitivity analysis of a $\leqslant$ constraint. The procedure for a $\geqslant$ constraint or an $=$ constraint is similar, the difference being that, if the constraint undergoing sensitivity analysis is a $\geqslant$ or $=$ constraint, the artificial variable added to the constraint during Phase I of the simplex method plays the role that the slack variable plays during sensitivity analysis of a $\leqslant$ constraint. More specifically, to determine the shadow price and the rates of increase in the basic variables' optimal values per unit increase in Δ, we look in the column of the optimal simplex tableau corresponding to the artificial variable added to the constraint during Phase I of the simplex method.

We will now summarize the general procedure for conducting sensitivity analysis on the right-hand side of a constraint that is binding at the LP's optimal solution. Within the summary, we will illustrate the procedure's steps by conducting sensitivity analysis of another one of our example LP's binding structural constraints, the third structural constraint $-2x_1 - x_3 + x_4 = 1$. Following the usual notation, we will denote the third structural constraint's right-hand side by RHS_3.

1. **Determining the constraint's shadow price.** A constraint's shadow price is determined using Table 7.2. For example, since A_3 is the artificial variable added to the constraint $-2x_1 - x_3 + x_4 = 1$ during Phase I of the simplex method, the negative of its $c_j - z_j$ value in Figure 7.9's optimal simplex tableau (i.e., $-\frac{38}{3} = -12\frac{2}{3}$) equals the constraint's shadow price. Observe that this is precisely the shadow price specified in Figure 7.8's LINPRO output.

2. **Determining the rates of increase in the basic variables' optimal values per unit increase in the constraint's right-hand side.** The rates of increase in the basic variables' optimal values per unit increase in Δ equal the column of coefficients in the optimal simplex tableau corresponding to the slack or artificial variable associated with the constraint. For example, looking at Figure 7.9's optimal simplex tableau, we see the following columns:

Column of Coefficients Corresponding to the Artificial Variable A_3	RHS Column
$-\dfrac{1}{3}$	$\dfrac{17}{6}$
0	$\dfrac{5}{4}$
$\dfrac{1}{3}$	$\dfrac{20}{3}$
2	$\dfrac{1}{4}$

Thus, the basic variables x_1, x_2, x_4, and E_2 have respective revised values

TABLE 7.2 How to Use the Optimal Simplex Tableau to Determine the Shadow Price of a Binding Structural Constraint

Type of Structural Constraint	If the LP involves *maximization* then the constraint's shadow price can be determined from the optimal simplex tableau as...	If the LP involves *minimization*, then the constraint's shadow price can be determined from the optimal simplex tableau as...
$\leqslant$	the negative of the $c_j - z_j$ value for the *slack variable* associated with the constraint.	the $c_j - z_j$ value for the *slack variable* associated with the constraint.
$=$	the negative of the $c_j - z_j$ value for the *artificial variable* associated with the constraint.	the $c_j - z_j$ value for the *artificial variable* associated with the constraint.
$\geqslant$	the negative of the $c_j - z_j$ value for the *artificial variable* associated with the constraint.	the $c_j - z_j$ value for the *artificial variable* associated with the constraint.

$$x_1\text{'s revised value:}\quad \frac{17}{6} \;-\; \frac{1}{3}\Delta$$

$$x_2\text{'s revised value:}\quad \frac{5}{4} \;+\; 0\Delta$$

$$x_4\text{'s revised value:}\quad \frac{20}{3} \;+\; \frac{1}{3}\Delta$$

$$E_2\text{'s revised value:}\quad \frac{1}{4} \;+\; 2\Delta$$

By substituting a particular value of Δ into the basic variables' revised optimal values, we can immediately update the LP's optimal solution (provided the value of Δ lies within the range of validity computed below in Step 3).

3. **Determining the sensitivity analysis's range of validity.** Since the basic variables' revised optimal values must all be nonnegative to maintain feasibility, the basic variables' revised optimal values in terms of Δ imply that Δ must satisfy a system of inequalities. For the basic variables' revised optimal values given at the end of Step 2, the system of inequalities is

$$\frac{17}{6} \;-\; \frac{1}{3}\,\Delta \;\geqslant\; 0$$

$$\frac{5}{4} \;+\; 0\,\Delta \;\geqslant\; 0$$

$$\frac{20}{3} \;+\; \frac{1}{3}\,\Delta \;\geqslant\; 0$$

After simplification, each of the inequalities provides either a positive upper limit or a negative lower limit on Δ. For Δ to simultaneously satisfy all upper limits and all lower limits, it must satisfy the most restrictive of the upper limits (i.e., the *minimum*) and the most restrictive of the lower limits (i.e., the *maximum* or, equivalently, the *least negative*). For the example system of inequalities given above, you should verify that the most restrictive limits on Δ are

$$-\frac{1}{8} \;\leqslant\; \Delta \;\leqslant\; 8\frac{1}{2}$$

corresponding to a maximum allowable increase in RHS_3 of $8\frac{1}{2}$ and a maximum allowable decrease in RHS_3 of $\frac{1}{8}$. Observe that these are precisely the values specified in Figure 7.8's LINPRO output.

Before proceeding, you should test your understanding of the above general procedure by conducting sensitivity analysis on our example LP's fourth structural constraint: $x_1 + 2x_2 + 3x_3 + x_4 \geqslant 12$. You can check your analysis using Figure 7.8's LINPRO output.

We should note here that (as illustrated by Figure 7.8's LINPRO output) the output of most LP software packages provides a constraint's shadow price and its associated range of validity but does not provide Step 2's rates of increase in the basic variables' optimal values per unit increase in the constraint's right-hand side. Without this latter information, it is very difficult to revise the LP's optimal solution for a revised right-hand side within the range of validity. Fortunately, most LP software packages have a command that enables "expert" users to view the optimal simplex tableau. As summarized in Step 2, using the appropriate column from this optimal simplex tableau, the user can determine the rates of increase in the basic variables' optimal values per unit increase in the constraint's right-hand side.

Sensitivity Analysis of the Right-Hand Side of a Nonbinding Constraint

Conducting sensitivity analysis on the right-hand side of a structural constraint that is nonbinding at optimality requires us to expend considerably less computational effort than when the constraint is binding. In Figure 7.9's optimal simplex tableau, the surplus variable E_2 has a value of $\frac{1}{4}$, thereby indicating that the second structural constraint, $-4x_1 + x_2 - 3x_3 + 2x_4 \geqslant 3$, is a nonbinding constraint at the LP's optimal solution. Let us now conduct sensitivity analysis on this constraint's right-hand side. Since this is the LP's second structural constraint, we will denote its right-hand side by RHS_2, and we will denote by Δ the change in RHS_2. The question we wish to answer with our sensitivity analysis is

Assuming all the LP's other data remain unchanged, what is the effect on the LP's optimal solution of changing RHS_2 from 3 to $3 + \Delta$?

A formally conducted sensitivity analysis is beyond the scope of this text. Instead, we will justify our sensitivity analysis with the following two intuitive observations:

- Regardless of its size, a decrease in the right-hand side of a nonbinding $\geqslant$ constraint has no effect on the variables' optimal values, except for a compensating increase in the optimal value of the constraint's surplus variable (e.g., if the right-hand side decreases by 2, the constraint's surplus variable increases by 2, but all other variables remain unchanged).

- Unless the size of the increase exceeds the surplus variable's current optimal value, an increase in the right-hand side has no effect on the variables' optimal values, except for a compensating decrease in the constraint's surplus variable.

Analogues of these two intuitive observations for a $\leqslant$ structural constraint were graphically illustrated in Section 3.6.

Based on the above two observations, we can conduct sensitivity analysis on the RHS_2 without any computational effort. In particular, we can conclude the following:

1. The sensitivity analysis's range of validity is given by

$$-\infty \leqslant \Delta \leqslant \frac{1}{4}$$

   Observe that this is precisely the range of validity specified in Figure 7.8's LINPRO output.

2. For changes in RHS_2 falling within the range of validity, the rates of increase in the variables' optimal values per unit increase in RHS_2 are all 0, except that the constraint's surplus variable E_2 has a rate of decrease in its optimal value equal to the rate of increase in RHS_2.

3. Since the decision variables' optimal values remain unchanged for changes in RHS_2 falling within the range of validity, the optimal objective value also remains unchanged. Hence, the constraint's shadow price is 0. Observe that this is precisely the shadow price displayed in Figure 7.8's LINPRO output.

Our sensitivity analysis of the nonbinding constraint $-4x_1 + x_2 - 3x_3 + 2x_2 \geqslant 3$ has illustrated the following general procedure:

A General
Procedure for
Conducting
Sensitivity
Analysis on the
Right-Hand Side
of a Nonbinding
Constraint

When conducting sensitivity analysis on the right-hand side of a structural constraint that is nonbinding at the LP's optimal solution, no extensive computations are necessary. In particular,

1. **Determining the sensitivity analysis's range of validity.** If the constraint is a $\leqslant$ constraint, the maximum allowable increase always equals ∞, and the maximum allowable decrease always equals the associated slack variable's current optimal value. If the constraint is a $\geqslant$ constraint, the maximum allowable increase always equals the associated surplus variable's current optimal value, and the maximum allowable decrease always equals ∞.

2. **Determining the constraint's shadow price.** The shadow price of a nonbinding constraint is always 0.

3. **Determining the rates of increase in the basic variables' optimal values per unit increase in the constraint's right-hand side.** The rates of increase in the basic variables' optimal values per unit increase in the constraint's right-hand side are all 0, except for the slack or surplus variable associated with the nonbinding constraint undergoing sensitivity analysis. If a $\leqslant$ constraint is undergoing sensitivity analysis, the associated slack variable's optimal value *increases* at a rate equal to the rate of increase in the constraint's right-hand side. If a $\geqslant$ constraint is undergoing sensitivity analysis, the associated surplus variable's optimal value *decreases* at a rate equal to the rate of increase in the constraint's right-hand side.

We should note that the above general procedure makes no mention of an $=$ constraint because such a constraint is always binding at optimality.

7.6 DUALITY

In this section we shall learn that every linear program has an associated linear program called the *dual.* Referring to the linear program's original formulation as the *primal,* we will first learn how to convert the primal LP into its associated dual LP. Then we will discuss several important relationships between the primal and dual LPs, the most important being that the optimal simplex tableau for any one of the two LPs (primal or dual) provides the optimal solution to both LPs. Hence, when there is a significant difference in the computational effort required, we can choose to solve the easier LP.

Converting the Primal LP Into the Dual LP

In learning how to convert the primal LP into the dual LP, we initially assume that the primal has one of the following two formats:

1. The objective-function type is maximize, all structural constraints are of the $\leqslant$ type with nonnegative right-hand sides, and all decision variables are subject to nonnegativity constraints.

2. The objective-function type is minimize, all structural constraints are of the

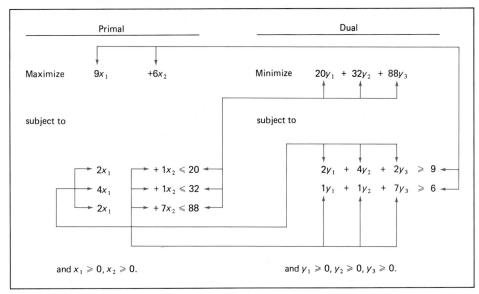

Figure 7.13 Construction of dual of OMC's LP

$\geqslant$ type with nonnegative right-hand sides, and all decision variables are subject to nonnegativity constraints.

We refer to the former type as a *max-$\leqslant$-nonnegative LP* and to the latter type as a *min-$\geqslant$-nonnegative LP*. In a subsequent subsection we will learn how to construct the dual of an LP that has neither of these two formats.

To illustrate the conversion to the dual LP, assume the primal LP is OMC's LP, which is displayed in Figure 7.13's left half. Observe that OMC's LP is a max-$\leqslant$-nonnegative LP. The dual of OMC's LP is displayed in Figure 7.13's right half.[12] As emphasized by Figure 7.13's arrows, the dual is a "mirror image" of the primal that is constructed according to the following general procedure:

A General Procedure for Constructing the Dual When the Primal is a Max-$\leqslant$-Nonnegative LP or a Min-$\geqslant$-Nonnegative LP

1. **Number of constraints and number of variables in the dual.** If the primal has n nonnegative decision variables and m structural constraints of the $\leqslant$ type, the dual has m nonnegative decision variables and n constraints of the $\geqslant$ type. Similarly, if the primal has n nonnegative decision variables and m structural constraints of the $\geqslant$ type, the dual has m nonnegative decision variables and n constraints of the $\leqslant$ type. (In Figure 7.13, the primal has $n=2$ nonnegative decision variables and $m=3$ structural constraints of the $\leqslant$ type. Consequently, the dual has $m=3$ nonnegative decision variables and $n=2$ structural constraints of the $\geqslant$ type.)

2. **Dual's objective-function type.** If the primal's objective-function type is maximization, the dual's is minimization. Conversely, if the primal's objective-function type is minimization, the dual's is maximization. (In Figure 7.13, the primal's objective-function type is maximization, so the dual's is minimization.)

3. **Objective-function coefficients of the dual's decision variables.** To obtain the objective-function coefficients of the dual's decision variables, use the

---

[12] To avoid confusion, it is customary to use different notation for the decision variables in the primal and dual (i.e., x in one and y in the other).

right-hand sides of the primal's structural constraints. More specifically, the objective-function coefficient of the ith dual variable equals the right-hand side of the ith primal constraint. (In Figure 7.13, the right-hand sides of the primal's three structural constraints are 20, 32, and 88. Consequently, the dual's three decision variables have objective-function coefficients of 20, 32, and 88.)

4. **Right-hand sides of dual's structural constraints.** To obtain the right-hand sides of the dual's structural constraints, use the objective-function coefficients of the primal's decision variables. More specifically, the right-hand side of the jth dual structural constraint equals the objective-function coefficient of the jth primal decision variable. (In Figure 7.13, the primal's two decision variables have objective-function coefficients of 9 and 6. Consequently, the dual's two structural constraints have right-hand sides of 9 and 6.)

5. **Constraint coefficients of the dual's decision variables.** The constraint coefficients of the decision variables in the jth dual structural constraint equal the constraint coefficients of the jth primal decision variable. (In Figure 7.13, the first primal decision variable x_1 has constraint coefficients of 2, 4, and 2. Consequently, the first dual constraint's left-hand side is $2y_1 + 4y_2 + 2y_3$. Similarly, since the second primal decision variable x_2 has constraint coefficients of 1, 1, and 7, the second dual constraint's left-hand side is $1y_1 + 1y_2 + 7y_3$.)

Observe that the above procedure establishes a 1–1 correspondence between the jth primal decision variable and the jth dual structural constraint and a 1–1 correspondence between the ith primal structural constraint and the ith dual decision variable. For this reason, we hereafter refer to the jth dual structural constraint as the dual structural constraint *associated with* the jth primal decision variable, and we refer to the ith dual decision variable as the dual decision variable *associated with* the ith primal structural constraint. For example, in Figure 7.13,

Dual Decision Variable	Associated Primal Structural Constraint
y_1	$2x_1 + x_2 \leqslant 20$
y_2	$4x_1 + x_2 \leqslant 32$
y_3	$2x_1 + 7x_2 \leqslant 88$

Dual Structural Constraint	Associated Primal Decision Variable
$2y_1 + 4y_2 + 2y_3 \geqslant 9$	x_1
$y_1 + y_2 + 7y_3 \geqslant 6$	x_2

To test your understanding of the general procedure for constructing a dual, try to construct the dual of the following LP:

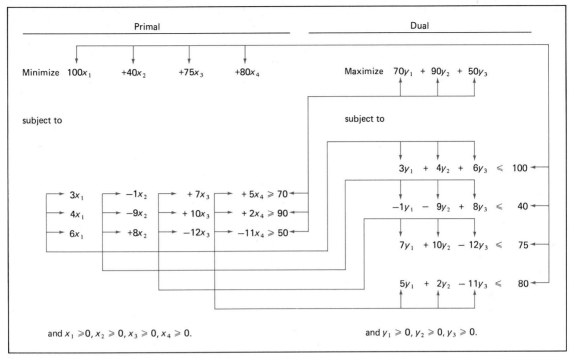

Figure 7.14 Construction of dual of "test" LP

$$\text{Minimize } 100x_1 + 40x_2 + 75x_3 + 80x_4$$

$$
\begin{aligned}
\text{subject to} \quad 3x_1 &- x_2 + 7x_3 + 5x_4 \geqslant 70 \\
4x_1 &- 9x_2 + 10x_3 + 2x_4 \geqslant 90 \\
6x_1 &+ 8x_2 - 12x_3 - 11x_4 \geqslant 50
\end{aligned}
$$

$$\text{and } x_1 \geqslant 0, x_2 \geqslant 0, x_3 \geqslant 0, x_4 \geqslant 0.$$

You will find the dual displayed in Figure 7.14.

As a final test of your understanding of the general procedure for constructing the dual, you should reverse the roles of primal and dual in Figure 7.13; that is, assume that the LP displayed on Figure 7.13's right half is the primal and construct the dual. The resulting dual should be the LP displayed on Figure 7.13's left half, thereby illustrating the first of four primal-dual relationships we will encounter in this section:

Primal-Dual Relationship 1 | If the primal is a max-$\leqslant$-nonnegative LP or a min-$\geqslant$-nonnegative LP, the dual of the primal's dual is the primal.

Other Primal-Dual Relationships

In this subsection we will examine three additional primal-dual relationships. We can best illustrate them by comparing the optimal simplex tableau for OMC's LP with the optimal simplex tableau for its dual. The optimal simplex tableau for OMC's LP (obtained originally in Section 6.8) is displayed in Figure 7.15's left half. To obtain the optimal simplex tableau for the dual of OMC's LP (displayed in Figure 7.15's right half), we proceed as follows:

Primal's Optimal Simplex Tableau

Equation	Basic Variable	c_j / c_B	x_1	x_2	S_1	S_2	S_3	RHS
			9	6	0	0	0	
I'''	x_2	6	0	1	$-\frac{1}{6}$	0	$\frac{1}{6}$	$\frac{34}{3}$
II'''	x_1	9	1	0	$\frac{7}{12}$	0	$-\frac{1}{12}$	$\frac{13}{3}$
III'''	S_2	0	0	0	$-\frac{13}{6}$	1	$\frac{1}{6}$	$\frac{10}{3}$
	z_j		*	*	$\frac{17}{4}$	*	$\frac{1}{4}$	$OV=107$
	c_j-z_j		*	*	$-\frac{17}{4}$	*	$-\frac{1}{4}$	

Dual's Optimal Simplex Tableau

Equation	Basic Variable	c_j / c_B	y_1	y_2	y_3	E_1	E_2	A_1	A_2	RHS
			20	32	88	0	0	0	0	
I	y_1	20	1	$\frac{13}{6}$	0	$-\frac{7}{12}$	$\frac{1}{6}$	$\frac{7}{12}$	$-\frac{1}{6}$	$\frac{17}{4}$
II	y_3	88	0	$-\frac{1}{6}$	1	$\frac{1}{12}$	$-\frac{1}{6}$	$-\frac{1}{12}$	$\frac{1}{6}$	$\frac{1}{4}$
	z_j		*	$\frac{86}{3}$	*	$-\frac{13}{3}$	$-\frac{34}{3}$	$\frac{13}{3}$	$\frac{34}{3}$	$OV=107$
	c_j-z_j		*	$\frac{10}{3}$	*	$\frac{13}{3}$	$\frac{34}{3}$	$-\frac{13}{3}$	$-\frac{34}{3}$	

Figure 7.15 Optimal simplex tableaux for OMC's LP and its dual

1. We convert the dual to equality form by subtracting nonnegative surplus variables from the structural constraints' left-hand sides and by changing the $\geqslant$ to $=$. This conversion results in the following LP in equality form:

$$\text{Minimize } 20y_1 + 32y_2 + 88y_3$$

$$
\begin{aligned}
\text{subject to} \quad 2y_1 + 4y_2 + 2y_3 - E_1 \quad\quad &= 9 \\
y_1 + y_2 + 7y_3 \quad\quad - E_2 &= 6
\end{aligned}
$$

$$\text{and } y_1 \geqslant 0, y_2 \geqslant 0, y_3 \geqslant 0,$$
$$E_1 \geqslant 0, E_2 \geqslant 0.$$

2. We find an initial basic feasible solution for the above LP by solving the following artificial LP:

$$\text{Minimize } A_1 + A_2$$

$$
\begin{aligned}
\text{subject to} \quad 2y_1 + 4y_2 + 2y_3 - E_1 \quad\quad + A_1 \quad\quad &= 9 \\
y_1 + y_2 + 7y_3 \quad\quad - E_2 \quad\quad + A_2 &= 6
\end{aligned}
$$

$$\text{and } y_1 \geqslant 0, y_2 \geqslant 0, y_3 \geqslant 0,$$
$$E_1 \geqslant 0, E_2 \geqslant 0,$$
$$A_1 \geqslant 0, A_2 \geqslant 0.$$

3. After determining the optimal simplex tableau for the artificial LP, we determine the optimal simplex tableau for the original LP by replacing the artificial objective function with the original objective function of "Minimize $20y_1 + 32y_2 + 88y_3$" and then continuing to apply the simplex method.

As you will be asked to verify in an end-of-chapter exercise, the resulting optimal tableau is the one displayed in Figure 7.15's right half.

Let us now compare the primal's optimal simplex tableau and the dual's optimal simplex tableau. Looking at Figure 7.15, observe the following:

- The optimal objective values displayed in the primal's optimal simplex tableau and the dual's optimal simplex tableau have the identical value of 107.

- From the primal's optimal simplex tableau, we can identify the optimal values of the primal's decision variables and slack variables as

x_1	x_2	S_1	S_2	S_3
$4\frac{1}{3}$	$11\frac{1}{3}$	0	$3\frac{1}{3}$	0

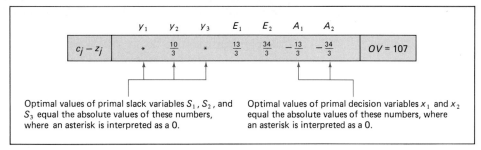

Figure 7.16(a) How to determine the primal's optimal solution from the dual's optimal simplex tableau

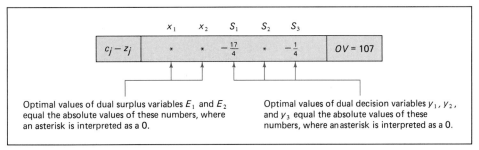

Figure 7.16(b) How to determine the dual's optimal solution from the primal's optimal simplex tableau

As diagrammed in Figure 7.16(a), these values also appear in the $c_j - z_j$ row of the dual's optimal simplex tableau, provided we interpret the asterisk in the $c_j - z_j$ row as signifying a value of 0. Thus, the primal's optimal solution can be determined from the $c_j - z_j$ row of the dual's optimal simplex tableau.

■ From the dual's optimal simplex tableau, we can identify the optimal values of the dual's decision variables and surplus variables as

$$\frac{y_1 \quad y_2 \quad y_3 \quad E_1 \quad E_2}{4\frac{1}{4} \quad 0 \quad \frac{1}{4} \quad 0 \quad 0}$$

As diagrammed in Figure 7.16(b), these values also appear in the $c_j - z_j$ row of the primal's optimal simplex tableau, provided we once again interpret the asterisk in the $c_j - z_j$ row as signifying a value of 0. Thus, the dual's optimal solution can be determined from the $c_j - z_j$ row of the primal's optimal simplex tableau.[13]

These three observations illustrate the following primal-dual relationship:

Primal-Dual Relationship 2

If we have an optimal simplex tableau for either the primal or the dual LP, we can determine the optimal solution of both LPs. In particular, the optimal objective values for the primal and dual are equal. Furthermore, if we solve the primal LP, we can use Table 7.3 to determine the dual variables' optimal

---

[13] If you recall Section 7.5's discussion of the sensitivity analysis of the right-hand side of a structural constraint, you may have noticed that the shadow prices of the primal's binding structural constraints are obtained in a similar manner to the dual variables' optimal values. In a subsequent subsection, we will examine the relationship between the value of the dual variable associated with a primal structural constraint and the shadow price of the same primal structural constraint.

values from the primal's optimal simplex tableau. (Temporarily ignore Table 7.3's last row, which pertains to a dual variable associated with a primal structural constraint of the = type. We will discuss this row in a subsequent subsection.) Conversely, if we solve the dual LP, we can determine the primal variables' optimal values from the dual's optimal simplex tableau by using a table similar to Table 7.3 except that every occurrence of "primal" and "dual" is interchanged.

Given this primal-dual relationship, if we need to solve an LP, we have two alternatives. We can solve the LP directly, or we can solve the LP's dual and obtain the primal's optimal solution from the dual's optimal simplex tableau. Since each alternative leads to the same optimal solution, which is better? A partial answer is provided by empirical evidence gathered by practitioners who for decades have been solving large-scale LPs with computer implementations of the simplex method. They have found that the computational effort required to solve a large-scale LP depends much more on the number of structural constraints than on the number of decision variables. Thus, as a "rule of thumb," we should base our decision on whether the primal or the dual LP has the fewer structural constraints. For example, if the primal LP has 100 decision variables and 1000 structural constraints, the dual should be easier to solve because, although it has 1000 decision variables, it has only 100 structural constraints. There are important exceptions to this "rule of thumb," but constraints on space preclude our discussing them here. For our purposes, it is sufficient to understand the following general principle:

The dual may require less computational effort to solve than the primal. In deciding which LP to solve, experts in the area of linear programming consider which one has the fewer structural constraints as well as other more technical criteria.

TABLE 7.3 How to Use the Primal's Optimal Simplex Tableau to Determine the Dual Variables' Optimal Values

Type of Dual Variable	Regardless of whether the primal LP involves maximization or minimization, the dual variables' optimal values can be determined from the primal's optimal simplex tableau as...
Dual variable associated with a primal structural constraint of the $\leqslant$ type.	The absolute value of the $c_j - z_j$ value for the associated primal constraint's slack variable, where a "*" is interpreted as a 0.
Dual variable associated with a primal structural constraint of the $\geqslant$ type.	The absolute value of the $c_j - z_j$ value for the associated primal constraint's artificial variable, where a "*" is interpreted as a 0.
Dual Slack or Surplus Variable For a Dual Structural Constraint Associated with a Primal Decision Variable	The absolute value of the $c_j - z_j$ value for the associated primal decision variable, where a "*" is interpreted as a 0.
Dual variable associated with a primal structural constraint of the = type.	The negative of the $c_j - z_j$ value for the associated primal constraint's artificial variable, where a "*" is interpreted as a 0.

We can use the optimal solutions to OMC's LP and its associated dual to illustrate another primal-dual relationship. To do so, let us display the optimal solutions in the following manner:

$$\text{Primal decision variables} \left\{ \begin{array}{ll} x_1 = 4\frac{1}{3} & E_1 = 0 \\ x_2 = 11\frac{1}{3} & E_2 = 0 \end{array} \right\} \text{Dual decision variables}$$

$$\text{Primal slack variables} \left\{ \begin{array}{ll} S_1 = 0 & y_1 = 4\frac{1}{4} \\ S_2 = 3\frac{1}{3} & y_2 = 0 \\ S_3 = 0 & y_3 = \frac{1}{4} \end{array} \right\} \text{Dual decision variables}$$

Observe that the product of each row's primal and dual variable is 0; that is,

$$\begin{array}{lll} x_1 E_1 = & (4\frac{1}{3})(0) & = 0 \\ x_2 E_2 = & (11\frac{1}{3})(0) & = 0 \end{array}$$

$$\begin{array}{lll} S_1 y_1 = & (0)(4\frac{1}{4}) & = 0 \\ S_2 y_2 = & (3\frac{1}{3})(0) & = 0 \\ S_3 y_3 = & (0)(\frac{1}{4}) & = 0 \end{array}$$

This is no coincidence. Experts in the area of linear programming can prove that such primal-dual relationships always hold.

To understand the implications of these five relationships, recall first that stating that a structural constraint's slack or surplus variable has an optimal value of 0 is equivalent to stating that the structural constraint is binding at optimality; furthermore, stating that a structural constraint's slack or surplus variable has a positive optimal value is equivalent to stating that the structural constraint is nonbinding at optimality. Thus, the relationship $x_1 E_1 = 0$ precludes the simultaneous occurrence of the events that the first primal decision variable x_1 has a positive optimal value and the first dual structural constraint is nonbinding at optimality (i.e., $E_1 > 0$). Similarly, the relationship $S_2 y_2 = 0$ precludes the simultaneous occurrence of the events that the second primal constraint is nonbinding at optimality (i.e., $S_2 > 0$) and the second dual decision variable y_2 has a positive optimal value.

The above five relationships, requiring a primal variable and its associated dual variable to have a product of 0, are examples of the following primal-dual relationship:

**Primal-Dual
Relationship 3**

- If a primal structural constraint is nonbinding at optimality, the associated dual decision variable has an optimal value of 0. Conversely, if a dual decision variable has a positive optimal value, the associated primal structural constraint is binding at optimality.

- If a primal decision variable has a positive optimal value, the associated dual structural constraint is binding at optimality. Conversely, if a dual structural constraint is nonbinding at optimality, the associated primal decision variable has an optimal value of 0.

This primal-dual relationship is known as *the principle of complementary slackness.*

We conclude this subsection with one last primal-dual relationship. Before we state it, recall that an LP does not always have an optimal solution. The phenomena of infeasibility or unboundedness may occur.[14] Thus, in solving an LP, one of the following three outcomes will occur:

---

[14] These two phenomena were discussed in Section 2.11 and also in Section 7.3.

1. The LP has an optimal solution. (This includes the case of unique optimality as well as the case of multiple optimality.)

2. The LP has no optimal solution because of infeasibility.

3. The LP has no optimal solution because of unboundedness.

Hence, if we solved a primal LP and also solved its associated dual LP, we might expect there would be $3 \times 3 = 9$ possible outcomes. However, experts in the area of linear programming have proven that, of the nine possible outcomes, only four can actually occur. These are summarized by the following primal-dual relationship:

Primal-Dual Relationship 4

When a primal LP and its associated dual LP are solved, one of the following four outcomes must occur:

1. The primal and dual both have optimal solutions, and, furthermore, their optimal objective values are equal.

2. The primal has no optimal solution because of infeasibility, and the dual has no optimal solution because of unboundedness.

3. The primal has no optimal solution because of unboundedness, and the dual has no optimal solution because of infeasibility.

4. Both the primal and dual have no optimal solution because of infeasibility.

OMC's LP and its associated dual provide an example of outcome 1. The remaining three outcomes will be illustrated in the end-of-chapter exercises.

The Dual of More General LPs

We have been assuming that the primal was either a max- $\leqslant$ -nonnegative LP or a min- $\geqslant$ -nonnegative LP. Now we will relax this assumption and permit the primal to have simultaneously structural constraints of all types ($\leqslant$, $\geqslant$, and $=$) and decision variables that are not all subject to nonnegative constraints.

When the primal is neither a max- $\leqslant$ -nonnegative LP nor a min- $\geqslant$ - nonnegative LP, the procedure for constructing the dual is as follows:

A General Procedure for Constructing the Dual When the Primal Is Neither a Max- $\leqslant$ - Nonnegative LP nor a Min- $\geqslant$ - Nonnegative LP

1. If the primal involves maximization, transform every $\geqslant$ structural constraint into a $\leqslant$ structural constraint by multiplying both sides of the inequality by -1, and transform every $=$ structural constraint with a negative right-hand side into an $=$ structural constraint with a positive right-hand side by multiplying both sides of the equality by -1. (Note that it is permissible for the transformed LP to have a $\leqslant$ structural constraint with a negative right-hand side.)

OR

If the primal involves minimization, transform every $\leqslant$ structural constraint into a $\geqslant$ structural constraint by multiplying both sides of the inequality by -1, and transform every $=$ structural constraint with a negative right-hand side into an $=$ structural constraint with a positive right-hand side by multiplying both sides of the equality by -1. (Note that it is permissible for the transformed LP to have a $\geqslant$ structural constraint with a negative right-hand side.)

2. Construct the dual of the transformed primal according to the procedure (given earlier in this section) for a max-$\leqslant$-nonnegative LP or a min-$\geqslant$-nonnegative LP, subject to the following modifications:

- If a primal structural constraint is of the $=$ type, the associated dual variable is unconstrained in sign (i.e., not subject to a nonnegativity constraint).

- If a primal decision variable is unconstrained in sign, then the associated dual structural constraint is of the $=$ type.

Let us employ this procedure to construct the dual of the following LP:

$$\text{Maximize} \quad 70x_1 + 100x_2 + 30x_3$$

$$
\begin{array}{rrrrrr}
\text{subject to} & 7x_1 & - & x_2 & - & 10x_3 & \geqslant & 50 \\
& 3x_1 & + & 11x_2 & - & 5x_3 & \leqslant & 75 \\
& 8x_1 & + & 4x_2 & - & 11x_3 & = & -10 \\
& -2x_1 & + & 6x_2 & + & 12x_3 & \geqslant & 40
\end{array}
$$

and $x_1 \geqslant 0, x_3 \geqslant 0$
(Note that x_2 is unconstrained in sign.)

Executing Step 1 of the procedure, we multiply both sides of the first and fourth structural constraints by -1 to transform them into $\leqslant$ constraints, and we multiply the third structural constraint by -1 to transform it into an $=$ constraint with a positive right-hand side. This results in the following transformed primal:

$$\text{Maximize} \quad 70x_1 + 100x_2 + 30x_3$$

$$
\begin{array}{rrrrrr}
\text{subject to} & -7x_1 & + & x_2 & + & 10x_3 & \leqslant & -50 \\
& 3x_1 & + & 11x_2 & - & 5x_3 & \leqslant & 75 \\
& -8x_1 & - & 4x_2 & + & 11x_3 & = & 10 \\
& 2x_1 & - & 6x_2 & - & 12x_3 & \leqslant & -40
\end{array}
$$

and $x_1 \geqslant 0, x_3 \geqslant 0$
(Note that x_2 is unconstrained in sign.)

Figure 7.17 diagrams the construction of the dual of the transformed primal. Note that the only modifications to the procedure for constructing a dual of a max-$\leqslant$-nonnegative LP are the following:

- Since the primal's third structural constraint is of the $=$ type, the dual's third decision variable is unconstrained in sign.
- Since the primal's second decision variable is unconstrained in sign, the dual's second structural constraint is of the $=$ type.

To test your understanding, try constructing the dual of the following LP:

$$\text{Minimize } 100x_1 + 40x_2 + 75x_3 + 80x_4$$

$$\text{subject to} \quad
\begin{aligned}
3x_1 - x_2 + 7x_3 + 5x_4 &\geqslant 70 \\
-4x_1 + 9x_2 - 10x_3 - 2x_4 &= -90 \\
-6x_1 - 8x_2 + 12x_3 + 11x_4 &\leqslant -50
\end{aligned}$$

and $x_1 \geqslant 0, x_2 \geqslant 0, x_4 \geqslant 0$.
(Note that x_3 is unconstrained in sign.)

You will find the dual displayed in Figure 7.18.

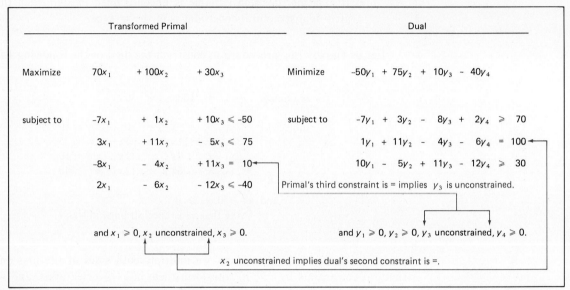

Figure 7.17 Construction of dual of the example LP

Figure 7.18 Construction of dual of "test" LP

	Transformed Primal				Dual	
Minimize	$100x_1$	$+ 40x_2$	$+ 75x_3$	$+ 80x_4$	Maximize	$70y_1 + 90x_2 + 50y_3$
subject to	$3x_1$	$- 1x_2$	$+ 7x_3$	$+ 5x_4 \geqslant 70$	subject to	$3y_1 + 4y_2 + 6y_3 \leqslant 100$
	$4x_1$	$- 9x_2$	$+ 10x_3$	$+ 2x_4 = 90$		$-1y_1 - 9y_2 + 8y_3 \leqslant 40$
	$6x_1$	$+ 8x_2$	$- 12x_3$	$- 11x_4 \geqslant 50$		$7y_1 + 10y_2 - 12y_3 = 75$
						$5y_1 + 2y_2 - 11y_3 \leqslant 80$

Primal's second constraint is = implies y_2 is unconstrained.

and $x_1 \geqslant 0, x_2 \geqslant 0, x_3$ unconstrained, $x_4 \geqslant 0$.   and $y_1 \geqslant 0, y_2$ unconstrained, $y_3 \geqslant 0$.

x_3 unconstrained implies dual's third constraint is =.

We conclude this subsection by discussing the previously ignored last row of Table 7.3, which summarizes how to determine a dual variable's optimal value from the primal's optimal simplex tableau when the dual variable is associated with a primal structural constraint of the = type. Since such a dual decision variable is unconstrained in sign, its optimal value may be positive, 0, or negative (unlike a dual decision variable associated with a primal structural constraint of the $\leqslant$ or $\geqslant$ type, which must have a nonnegative optimal value). Table 7.3's last row summarizes how to determine the optimal value of a dual decision variable associated with a primal structural constraint of the = type. Note that we do not take the absolute value of the artificial variable's $c_j - z_j$ value.

Let us illustrate how to employ Table 7.3 to determine the dual variables' optimal values from the primal's optimal simplex tableau by using as our example the primal and dual displayed in Figure 7.19. In Section 7.2, we solved the primal with the two-phase simplex method. The $c_j - z_j$ row from the optimal simplex tableau displayed at the bottom of Figure 7.3 is reproduced below:

$$\begin{array}{c|ccccccccccc} & x_1 & x_2 & x_3 & x_4 & S_1 & E_2 & E_4 & A_2 & A_3 & A_4 & \\ \hline c_j - z_j & * & * & -\frac{23}{2} & * & -\frac{29}{6} & * & -\frac{1}{6} & 0 & \frac{38}{3} & \frac{1}{6} & OV = \frac{115}{6} \end{array}$$

Employing Table 7.3 to determine the dual variables' optimal values, we obtain

$$\begin{aligned} y_1\text{'s optimal value} &= \text{absolute value of } S_1\text{'s } c_j - z_j \text{ value} = \tfrac{29}{6} = 4\tfrac{5}{6} \\ y_2\text{'s optimal value} &= \text{absolute value of } A_2\text{'s } c_j - z_j \text{ value} = 0 \\ y_3\text{'s optimal value} &= \text{negative of } A_3\text{'s } c_j - z_j \text{ value} = -\tfrac{38}{3} = -12\tfrac{2}{3} \\ y_4\text{'s optimal value} &= \text{absolute value of } A_4\text{'s } c_j - z_j \text{ value} = \tfrac{1}{6} \end{aligned}$$

Figure 7.19 Primal from Section 7.2 and its dual

Primal (before transformation)		Dual	
Maximize $30x_1 - 10x_2 + 20x_3 - 8x_4$		Minimize $7y_1 - 3y_2 + 1y_3 - 12y_4$	
subject to $1x_1 - 2x_2 + 4x_3 + 1x_4 \leqslant 7$		subject to $1y_1 + 4y_2 - 2y_3 - 1y_4 \geqslant 30$	
$-4x_1 + 1x_2 - 3x_3 + 2x_4 \geqslant 3$		$-2y_1 - 1y_2 + 0y_3 - 2y_4 \geqslant -10$	
$-2x_1 + 0x_2 - 1x_3 + 1x_4 = 1$		$4y_1 + 3y_2 - 1y_3 - 3y_4 \geqslant 20$	
$1x_1 + 2x_2 + 3x_3 + 1x_4 \geqslant 12$		$1y_1 - 2y_2 + 1y_3 - 1y_4 \leqslant -8$	
and $x_1 \geqslant 0, x_2 \geqslant 0, x_3 \geqslant 0, x_4 \geqslant 0.$		and $y_1 \geqslant 0, y_2 \geqslant 0, y_3$ unconstrained, $y_4 \geqslant 0.$	

Thus, the dual's optimal solution is

$$
\begin{array}{cccc}
y_1 & y_2 & y_3 & y_4 \\
\hline
4\frac{5}{6} & 0 & -12\frac{2}{3} & \frac{1}{6}
\end{array}
$$

and the dual's optimal objective value is $\frac{115}{6}$.[15]

An Economic Interpretation of the Dual

When the primal has the interpretation of a product mix LP, the dual has an interesting economic interpretation. To illustrate, consider a firm called ABC that manufactures four products that compete for three scarce resources. Table 7.4 summarizes the relevant data. Letting x_1, x_2, x_3, and x_4 denote the respective monthly production quantities of products 1, 2, 3, and 4, ABC can determine its optimal product mix by solving the following LP:

$$\text{Maximize } 50x_1 + 20x_2 + 30x_3 + 40x_4$$

$$
\begin{array}{rrrrrr}
\text{subject to} & 3x_1 + & 11x_2 + & 9x_3 + & x_4 & \leqslant 95 \\
& 10x_1 + & 7x_2 + & 4x_3 + & 8x_4 & \leqslant 72 \\
& 2x_1 + & 5x_2 + & 12x_3 + & 6x_4 & \leqslant 81
\end{array}
$$

and $x_1 \geqslant 0, x_2 \geqslant 0, x_3 \geqslant 0, x_4 \geqslant 0$.

Suppose that another firm called XYZ wishes to "buy out" ABC; that is, XYZ wishes to purchase all ABC's resources for its own use. Let us investigate how XYZ can use linear programming to determine a "fair" offer to submit to ABC.

Let the decision variables y_1, y_2, and y_3 denote the nonnegative unit prices XYZ will pay ABC for resources 1, 2, and 3, respectively. Since resources 1, 2, and 3 have respective availabilities of 95, 72, and 81, the total payment XYZ will make to ABC is

$$95y_1 + 72y_2 + 81y_3.$$

---

[15] To confirm this, you may wish to: (1) substitute the decision variables' values into the dual's structural constraints and verify that the solution is feasible and (2) substitute the decision variables' values into the dual's objective function and verify that the resulting objective value is $\frac{115}{6}$ (the same as the primal's).

TABLE 7.4 Data for ABC's Product Mix Problem

	Resource Consumption per Unit Produced				Resource
	Product 1	Product 2	Product 3	Product 4	Availabilities
Resource 1	3	11	9	1	95
Resource 2	10	7	4	8	72
Resource 3	2	5	12	6	81
Unit Profit	$50	$20	$30	$40	

Naturally, XYZ wants this total payment to be as small as possible. Thus, XYZ's objective is to

$$\text{Minimize } 95y_1 + 72y_2 + 81y_3.$$

The constraints on the decision variables arise because XYZ must be able to convince ABC that its offer is fair. To illustrate, consider product 1. Looking at Table 7.4, we see that each unit of product 1 ABC manufactures consumes 3 units of resource 1, 10 units of resource 2, and 2 units of resource 3. Thus, the total payment ABC will receive from XYZ for all resources consumed by manufacturing one unit of product 1 is

$$3y_1 + 10y_2 + 2y_3.$$

Since the unit profit ABC earns from product 1 is 50, ABC will insist that

$$3y_1 + 10y_2 + 2y_3 \geqslant 50.$$

Otherwise, ABC will conclude that selling its resources to XYZ is less profitable than continuing to manufacture product 1. Thus, to convince ABC that its offer is fair, XYZ must include

$$3y_1 + 10y_2 + 2y_3 \geqslant 50.$$

as one of the LP's structural constraints. Similarly, to ensure that ABC does not conclude that selling its resources to XYZ is less profitable than continuing to manufacture products 2, 3, and 4, the LP's structural constraints must include the following:

$$\begin{aligned} 11y_1 + 7y_2 + 5y_3 &\geqslant 20 \\ 9y_1 + 4y_2 + 12y_3 &\geqslant 30 \\ y_1 + 8y_2 + 6y_3 &\geqslant 40. \end{aligned}$$

To summarize, XYZ can formulate the problem of determining a fair offer to ABC as the following LP:

$$\text{Minimize } 95y_1 + 72y_2 + 81y_3$$

$$\begin{aligned} \text{subject to} \quad 3y_1 + 10y_2 + 2y_3 &\geqslant 50 \\ 11y_1 + 7y_2 + 5y_3 &\geqslant 20 \\ 9y_1 + 4y_2 + 12y_3 &\geqslant 30 \\ y_1 + 8y_2 + 6y_3 &\geqslant 40 \end{aligned}$$

$$\text{and } y_1 \geqslant 0, y_2 \geqslant 0, y_3 \geqslant 0.$$

This is precisely the dual of ABC's product mix LP.

We have just illustrated the following general principle:

When the primal has the interpretation of a product mix LP, the dual has the interpretation of determining "fair" unit prices for the resources—fair in the sense that the firm will not conclude that it is less profitable to sell all its resources at these prices than it is to continue to manufacture its products.

The Relationship Between a Structural Constraint's Shadow Price and the Constraint's Associated Dual Variable

A structural constraint's shadow price and the constraint's associated dual decision variable are closely related, as suggested by the following observations:

- When the primal is a product mix LP, the previous section's economic interpretation of the dual variables is similar to the interpretation of the primal constraints' shadow prices.

- Table 7.2 (which summarizes how to use the primal's optimal simplex tableau to determine primal structural constraints' shadow prices) is similar to Table 7.3 (which summarizes how to use the primal's optimal simplex tableau to determine the dual's optimal solution).

In fact, when the primal LP is a max-$\leqslant$-nonnegative LP , a primal structural constraint's shadow price is exactly equal to the optimal value of the constraint's associated dual decision variable.[16]

Unfortunately, a source of confusion for first-time students of linear programming is that a primal structural constraint's shadow price is not always exactly equal to the optimal value of the constraint's associated dual decision variable. More specifically,

> A primal constraint's shadow price and the constraint's associated dual variable always have the same absolute values but may differ in sign.

To illustrate, consider Figure 7.19's primal and dual LPs. In Section 7.5 we determined the structural constraints' shadow prices, and earlier in this section we determined the dual variables' optimal values. This is summarized by the following table:

Primal Structural Constraint	Primal Structural Constraint's Shadow Price (as determined in Section 7.5 using Table 7.2)	Optimal Value of the Dual Variable Associated with the Primal Structural Constraint (as determined earlier in this section using Table 7.3)
$x_1 - 2x_2 + 4x_3 + x_4 \leqslant 7$	$4\frac{5}{6}$	$4\frac{5}{6}$
$-4x_1 + x_2 - 3x_3 + 2x_4 \geqslant 3$	0	0
$-2x_1 - x_3 + x_4 = 1$	$-12\frac{2}{3}$	$-12\frac{2}{3}$
$x_1 + 2x_2 + 3x_3 + 1x_4 \geqslant 12$	$-\frac{1}{6}$	$\frac{1}{6}$

Notice that the numbers in the second and third columns have the same absolute values but differ in sign in the last row.

7.7 CONCLUDING REMARKS

Given the effort required to manually solve this chapter's LPs, you can appreciate that practitioners routinely employ LP software packages to solve (using only seconds of computer CPU time) LPs involving thousands of variables and hundreds

---

[16] This is the reason that some instructors, textbooks, and LP software packages use the terminology *dual price* instead of *shadow price*.

of constraints. Practitioners who for decades have been solving large-scale LPs with computer implementations of the simplex method have gathered empirical evidence suggesting that, on average, the number of iterations of the simplex method necessary to solve an LP depends much more on the number of structural constraints than on the number of variables. According to this "empirical folklore," solving an LP involving m structural constraints will require approximately m to $3m$ iterations of the simplex method. Keep in mind that this estimate of the number of iterations is only a "rule of thumb." In fact, theoreticians have constructed a "pathological" LP with only 50 decision variables that would require *years* of computer CPU time to solve. Fortunately, no one has ever encountered such an LP in practice.

7.8 CHAPTER CHECKLIST AND GLOSSARY

Quickly review this chapter by rereading the material highlighted by a vertical line in the left margin. You should then be familiar with the concepts, techniques, and terminology in the Checklist and Glossary that follow. If you need "help" with a particular item, consult the section or sections indicated for a more detailed discussion.

Checklist of Concepts and Techniques

- ☐ Modifications to the simplex method's procedure for selecting the entering basic variable when the LP involves minimization. [7.2]

- ☐ Solving an LP when some of the decision variables are not subject to nonnegativity constraints. [7.2]

- ☐ Eliminating negative right-hand sides from structural constraints. [7.2]

- ☐ Using slack and surplus variables to transform into equality form an LP whose structural constraints include a mixture of the ⩽ type and ⩾ type. [7.2]

- ☐ Using artificial variables to transform into an artificial LP an LP that, before its transformation into equality form, contained structural constraints of the ⩾ type and = type. [7.2]

- ☐ Using the two-phase simplex method to solve an LP that, before its transformation into equality form, contained structural constraints of the ⩾ type and = type. [7.2]

- ☐ Recognizing infeasibility during the execution of the two-phase simplex method. [7.3]

- ☐ Recognizing unboundedness during the execution of the simplex method. [7.3]

- ☐ Recognizing multiple optimality during the execution of the simplex method. [7.3]

- ☐ Conducting sensitivity analysis on a decision variable's objective-function coefficient. [7.4]

- ☐ Conducting sensitivity analysis on a structural constraint's right-hand side. [7.5]

- ☐ Constructing the dual of a primal LP. [7.6]

☐ Identifying the dual's optimal solution from the primal's optimal simplex tableau, and vice versa. [7.6]

☐ The economic interpretation of the dual when the primal has the interpretation of a product mix LP. [7.6]

☐ The relationship between a primal structural constraint's shadow price and the constraint's associated dual variable. [7.6]

Glossary

Artificial variable. When a structural constraint of the original LP is of the $\geq$ type or = type (after the elimination of any negative right-hand side), an artificial variable is added to the constraint's left-hand side after the LP is transformed into equality form. [7.2]

Artificial LP. When the original LP contains one or more structural constraints of the $\geq$ type or = type (after the elimination of any negative right-hand sides), the addition of artificial variables results in the artificial LP (with its objective function of minimizing the sum of the artificial variables). The solution of the artificial LP identifies an initial basic feasible solution to the original LP. [7.2]

Two-phase simplex method. The modification of the "basic" simplex method that is used to solve an LP that contains one or more structural constraints of the $\geq$ type or = type (after the elimination of any negative right-hand sides). [7.2]

Primal. The original LP. [7.6]

Dual. A "mirror image" of the original LP constructed according to a specific set of rules. [7.6]

Dual variable. A variable in the dual LP. [7.6]

EXERCISES

Exercises 7.1 through 7.6 test your ability to solve a non-standard LP using the two-phase simplex method. For each LP, besides displaying the sequence of tableaux generated by the two-phase simplex method, specify the feasible solution identified by Phase I's final tableau and the optimal solution identified by Phase II's final tableau.

7.1.   Minimize $3x_1 + 2x_2$

   subject to $x_1 + x_2 = 10$
   $x_1 \geq 4$

   and $x_1 \geq 0, x_2 \geq 0$

7.2.   Maximize $2x_1 + 3x_2$

   subject to $5x_1 + 4x_2 \leq 40$
   $11x_1 - 4x_2 = 0$
   $4x_1 - 5x_2 \leq -10$

   and $x_1 \geq 0, x_2 \geq 0$

*7.3.   Minimize $30x_1 + 20x_2$

   subject to $x_1 \geq 4$
   $2x_1 + x_2 = 20$
   $x_1 + 2x_2 \geq 19$

   and $x_1 \geq 0, x_2 \geq 0$

7.4.   Maximize $3x_1 + 5x_2 + 2x_3$

   subject to $-2x_2 + x_3 \geq 2$
   $x_1 + 4x_2 + 2x_3 = 5$

   and $x_1 \geq 0, x_2 \geq 0, x_3 \geq 0$

7.5.   Maximize $3x_1 - x_2 - x_3$

   subject to $x_1 - 2x_2 + x_3 \leq 11$
   $-4x_1 + x_2 + 2x_3 \geq 3$
   $2x_1 - x_3 = -1$

   and $x_1 \geq 0, x_2 \geq 0, x_3 \geq 0$

7.6.   Minimize $20y_1 + 32y_2 + 88y_3$
       subject to $\quad 2y_1 + 4y_2 + 2y_3 \geqslant 9$
       $\qquad\qquad\quad\; y_1 + \;\; y_2 + 7y_3 \geqslant 6$

       and $\; y_1 \geqslant 0, y_2 \geqslant 0, y_3 \geqslant 0$

(Note that this LP is the dual of OMC's LP. In this exercise, you are verifying the correctness of Figure 7.15's optimal simplex tableau.)

Exercises 7.7 and 7.8 test your ability to use the simplex method, in conjunction with the "tricks" of Sections 3.9 and 3.10, to solve an LP having decision variables not subject to nonnegativity constraints.

*7.7. Use the simplex method to solve the following LP with unconstrained decision variables:

   Maximize $2x_1 + \quad 3x_2$

   subject to $\quad x_1 + \;\; 2x_2 \leqslant \quad 12$
   $\qquad\qquad\; x_1 - \;\; 4x_2 \leqslant \quad 24$
   $\qquad\qquad\; x_1 - \;\;\; x_2 \geqslant \qquad 1$

   and x_1 and x_2 unconstrained in sign

7.8. Use the simplex method to solve the following LP *with decision variables having nonzero lower bounds*:

   Maximize $2x_1 + 3x_2$

   subject to $\quad x_1 + 2x_2 \leqslant 12$
   $\qquad\qquad\; x_1 - \;\; x_2 \geqslant 1$

   and $x_1 \geqslant 3, x_2 \geqslant -2$

This exercise illustrates that the simplex method can be used to solve a system of linear equations.

7.9. Consider the following system of equations:

   $$x_1 - 2x_2 + x_3 = 8$$
   $$3x_1 + 5x_2 + 7x_3 = 6$$
   $$2x_1 - 3x_2 - 5x_3 = 7$$

   (a) Suppose you want to find nonnegative values for x_1, x_2, and x_3 that simultaneously satisfy each equation in the system. Formulate (but do not solve) an LP for finding such values for x_1, x_2, and x_3 or determining that no such values exist.
   (b) Redo part (a), this time assuming that a variable may take on a negative value.

The next exercise illustrates that knowledge of the simplex method enables you to anticipate a potential problem in implementing an LP's optimal solution.

7.10. Suppose you have been hired as a consultant to a manufacturing firm that has produced positive amounts of 100 distinct products in every month of the past five years. Your assignment is to determine the firm's optimal product mix for the upcoming month. After much work, you formulate a linear program with 100 decision variables (one for each product) and 60 structural constraints.

   (a) Why is the firm likely to object to implementing the optimal solution to your LP?
   (b) How will you react to the firm's objection?

Exercises 7.11 through 7.14 test your understanding of how, during the execution of the simplex method, to recognize infeasibility, unboundedness, and multiple optimality.

*7.11. Below are three LPs labeled LP 1, LP 2, LP 3.

   LP 1: Maximize $\quad 2x_1 - \;\; x_2$

       subject to $\quad x_1 - 2x_2 \leqslant 4$
       $\qquad\qquad -3x_1 + \;\; x_2 \leqslant 3$

       and $x_1 \geqslant 0, x_2 \geqslant 0$

   LP 2: Maximize $\quad 3x_1 + 2x_2$

       subject to $\quad 2x_1 + \;\; x_2 \leqslant 2$
       $\qquad\qquad\; 3x_1 + 4x_2 \geqslant 12$

       and $x_1 \geqslant 0, x_2 \geqslant 0$

   LP 3: Maximize $\quad 9x_1 + 6x_2$

       subject to $\quad x_1 \qquad\qquad \leqslant 4$
       $\qquad\qquad\qquad\quad 2x_2 \leqslant 12$
       $\qquad\qquad\; 3x_1 + 2x_2 \leqslant 18$

       and $x_1 \geqslant 0, x_2 \geqslant 0$

Accept as a fact that Figure 7.20 displays for each LP a simplex tableau that we would obtain after introducing the necessary slack, surplus, and artificial variables and performing several iterations of the simplex method. After examining each tableau, specify which of the following is true of the corresponding LP:

   (a) The LP has no optimal solution because of infeasibility.
   (b) The LP has no optimal solution because of unboundedness.
   (c) The LP has multiple optimal solutions.

If case (c) occurs, identify the optimal solution corresponding to the current simplex tableau, perform one more iteration of the simplex method, and identify the additional optimal solution corresponding to the new tableau.

Equation	Basic Variable	c_j	2 $\ $ -1 $\ $ 0 $\ $ 0	RHS
		c_B	x_1 $\ x_2$ $\ S_1$ $\ S_2$	
I	x_1	2	1 $\ $ -2 $\ $ 1 $\ $ 0	4
II	S_2	0	0 $\ $ -5 $\ $ 3 $\ $ 1	15
		z_j	* $\ $ -4 $\ $ 2 $\ $ *	OV = 8
		$c_j - z_i$	* $\ $ 3 $\ $ -2 $\ $ *	

(a) Tableau for LP 1

Equation	Basic Variable	c_j	40 $\ $ 45 $\ $ 25 $\ $ 0 $\ $ 0	RHS
		c_B	x_1 $\ x_2$ $\ x_3$ $\ S_1$ $\ S_2$	
I	x_2	45	0 $\ $ 1 $\ $ $-\frac{1}{3}$ $\ $ 1 $\ $ $-\frac{2}{3}$	20
II	x_1	40	1 $\ $ 0 $\ $ 1 $\ $ -1 $\ $ 1	20
		z_j	* $\ $ * $\ $ 25 $\ $ 5 $\ $ 10	OV = 1700
		$c_j - z_j$	* $\ $ * $\ $ 0 $\ $ -5 $\ $ -10	

(a) Tableau for LP 1

Equation	Basic Variable	c_j	0 $\ $ 0 $\ $ 0 $\ $ 0 $\ $ 1	RHS
		c_B	x_1 $\ x_2$ $\ S_1$ $\ E_2$ $\ A_2$	
I	x_2	0	2 $\ $ 1 $\ $ 1 $\ $ 0 $\ $ 0	2
II	A_2	1	-5 $\ $ 0 $\ $ -4 $\ $ -1 $\ $ 1	4
		z_j	-5 $\ $ * $\ $ -4 $\ $ -1 $\ $ *	OV = 4
		$c_j - z_j$	5 $\ $ * $\ $ 4 $\ $ 1 $\ $ *	

(b) Tableau for LP 2

Equation	Basic Variable	c_j	0 $\ $ 0 $\ $ 0 $\ $ 0 $\ $ 1 $\ $ 1	RHS
		c_B	x_1 $\ x_2$ $\ E_1$ $\ E_2$ $\ A_1$ $\ A_2$	
I	A_1	1	$-\frac{1}{2}$ $\ $ 0 $\ $ -1 $\ $ $-\frac{1}{2}$ $\ $ 1 $\ $ $\frac{1}{2}$	$\frac{5}{2}$
II	x_2	0	$-\frac{3}{2}$ $\ $ 1 $\ $ 0 $\ $ $-\frac{1}{2}$ $\ $ 0 $\ $ $\frac{1}{2}$	$\frac{5}{2}$
		z_j	$-\frac{1}{2}$ $\ $ * $\ $ -1 $\ $ $-\frac{1}{2}$ $\ $ * $\ $ $\frac{1}{2}$	OV = $\frac{5}{2}$
		$c_j - z_j$	$\frac{1}{2}$ $\ $ * $\ $ 1 $\ $ $\frac{1}{2}$ $\ $ * $\ $ $\frac{1}{2}$	

(b) Tableau for LP 2

Equation	Basic Variable	c_j	9 $\ $ 6 $\ $ 0 $\ $ 0 $\ $ 0	RHS
		c_B	x_1 $\ x_2$ $\ S_1$ $\ S_2$ $\ S_3$	
I	x_1	9	1 $\ $ 0 $\ $ 1 $\ $ 0 $\ $ 0	4
II	S_2	0	0 $\ $ 0 $\ $ 3 $\ $ 1 $\ $ -1	6
III	x_2	6	0 $\ $ 1 $\ $ $-\frac{3}{2}$ $\ $ 0 $\ $ $\frac{1}{2}$	3
		z_j	* $\ $ * $\ $ 0 $\ $ * $\ $ 3	OV = 54
		$c_j - z_j$	* $\ $ * $\ $ 0 $\ $ * $\ $ -3	

(c) Tableau for LP 3

Figure 7.20 Simplex tableaux for Exercise 7.11's LPs

Equation	Basic Variable	c_j	1 $\ $ 1 $\ $ 0 $\ $ 0 $\ $ 0 $\ $ 0 $\ $ 0	RHS
		c_B	x_1 $\ x_2$ $\ E_1$ $\ S_2$ $\ E_3$ $\ A_1$ $\ A_3$	
I	x_2	1	0 $\ $ 1 $\ $ $-\frac{1}{3}$ $\ $ 0 $\ $ $\frac{4}{3}$ $\ $ $\frac{1}{3}$ $\ $ $-\frac{4}{3}$	$\frac{4}{3}$
II	S_2	0	0 $\ $ 0 $\ $ -1 $\ $ 1 $\ $ 6 $\ $ 1 $\ $ -6	6
III	x_1	1	1 $\ $ 0 $\ $ 0 $\ $ 0 $\ $ -1 $\ $ 0 $\ $ 1	2
		z_j	* $\ $ * $\ $ $-\frac{1}{3}$ $\ $ * $\ $ $\frac{1}{3}$ $\ $ $\frac{1}{3}$ $\ $ $-\frac{1}{3}$	OV = $\frac{10}{3}$
		$c_j - z_j$	* $\ $ * $\ $ $\frac{1}{3}$ $\ $ * $\ $ $-\frac{1}{3}$ $\ $ $-\frac{1}{3}$ $\ $ $\frac{1}{3}$	

(c) Tableau for LP 3

Figure 7.21 Simplex tableaux for Exercise 7.12's LPs

7.12. Redo Exercise 7.11, this time using the three LPs below and the simplex tableaux displayed in Figure 7.21:

LP 1: Maximize $\quad 40x_1 + 45x_2 + 25x_3$

subject to
$$2x_1 + 3x_2 + x_3 \leqslant 100$$
$$3x_1 + 3x_2 + 2x_3 \leqslant 120$$

and $\quad x_1 \geqslant 0, x_2 \geqslant 0, x_3 \geqslant 0$

LP 2: Maximize $\quad 3x_1 + 7x_2$

subject to
$$x_1 - x_2 \geqslant 0$$
$$-3x_1 + 2x_2 \geqslant 5$$

and $\quad x_1 \geqslant 0, x_2 \geqslant 0$

LP 3: Maximize $\quad x_1 + x_2$

subject to
$$4x_1 + 3x_2 \geqslant 12$$
$$2x_1 - 3x_2 \leqslant 6$$
$$x_1 \geqslant 2$$

and $\quad x_1 \geqslant 3, x_2 \geqslant 0$

7.13. Consider a linear program having an objective function involving maximization, having nonnegative decision variables x_1 and x_2, and having three structural constraints with respective slack variables S_1, S_2, and S_3. Suppose that after a number of iterations of the simplex method the following tableau is reached, where a_1 and a_2 are symbolic representations of actual numbers:

338

Equation	Basic Variable	c_j / c_B	3 / x_1	2 / x_2	0 / S_1	0 / S_2	0 / S_3	RHS
I	x_1	3	1	0	3	-1	0	2
II	x_2	2	0	1	4	a_1	0	2
III	S_3	0	0	0	1	a_2	1	6
	z_j		*	*	17	$-3+2a_1$	*	OV = 10
	$c_j - z_j$		*	*	-17	$3-2a_1$	*	

For each of the following cases, explicitly discuss how many optimal solutions (if any) there are to the linear program.

(a) $a_1 = -2$ and $a_2 = 0$.

(b) $a_1 = 2$ and $a_2 = -1$.

(c) $a_1 = \frac{3}{2}$ and $a_2 = 1$.

7.14. Reconsider Figure 7.5's sequence of simplex tableaux for the example LP illustrating unboundedness.

(a) Suppose we ignore the unboundedness "signalled" by S_3 in Figure 7.5's final simplex tableau and instead select x_1 as the entering basic variable. Continue executing the simplex method until you obtain another tableau that "signals" unboundedness.

(b) What general principle does this exercise illustrate?

Exercises 7.15 through 7.21 test your understanding of the use of an LP's optimal simplex tableau to conduct sensitivity analysis.

7.15. Assuming you have already worked Exercise 6.12, this exercise requests you to use the optimal simplex tableau for Exercise 6.12's LP to conduct sensitivity analysis.

(a) For each objective-function coefficient, determine the range of optimality. Summarize your analysis in a table having the format of Table 3.2.

(b) For each structural constraint, determine the shadow price and its associated range of validity. Summarize your analysis in a table having the format of Tables 3.3–3.5.

*7.16. Redo Exercise 7.15, this time using the LP in Exercise 7.3 and the optimal simplex tableau you obtained in that exercise.

7.17. Redo Exercise 7.15, this time using the LP in Exercise 7.4 and the optimal simplex tableau you obtained in that exercise.

7.18. This exercise assumes you have already worked Exercise 2.28. That exercise requested you to formu-

late an LP for the product mix decision problem of the Big Bang Novelty Company (BBNC). Your formulation should be similar to the following LP:

Maximize $\quad 0.45X_T + 0.55X_W + 0.70X_H$

subject to
$$30X_T + 20X_W + 30X_H \leqslant 4800$$
$$0.5X_W + X_H \leqslant 90$$
$$X_T + 2X_W + 3X_H \leqslant 360$$

and $\quad X_T \geqslant 0, X_W \geqslant 0, X_H \geqslant 0$

where X_T, X_W, and X_H denote the daily production quantities of Toots, Wheets, and Honks, respectively. Accept as a fact that use of the simplex method to solve this LP results in the optimal tableau displayed in Figure 7.22, where S_1, S_2, and S_3 denote the respective slack variables for the structural constraints.

Equation	Basic Variable	c_j / c_B	$\frac{9}{20}$ / x_T	$\frac{11}{20}$ / x_W	$\frac{7}{10}$ / x_H	0 / S_1	0 / S_2	0 / S_3	RHS
I	x_T	$\frac{9}{20}$	1	0	0	$\frac{1}{20}$	0	$-\frac{1}{2}$	60
II	S_2	0	0	0	$\frac{1}{4}$	$\frac{1}{80}$	1	$-\frac{3}{8}$	15
III	x_W	$\frac{11}{20}$	0	1	$\frac{3}{2}$	$-\frac{1}{40}$	0	$\frac{3}{4}$	150
	z_j		*	*	$\frac{33}{40}$	$\frac{7}{800}$	*	$\frac{3}{16}$	OV = $\frac{219}{2}$
	$c_j - z$		*	*	$-\frac{1}{8}$	$-\frac{7}{800}$	*	$-\frac{3}{16}$	

Figure 7.22 Optimal simplex tableau for Exercise 7.18's LP

(a) For each objective-function coefficient, determine the range of optimality. Summarize your analysis in a table having the format of Table 3.2.

(b) For each structural constraint, determine the shadow price and its associated range of validity. Summarize your analysis in a table having the format of Tables 3.3–3.5.

(c) Using your analysis in part (a), determine the LP's optimal solution and the optimal total profit if the unit profit of a Toot decreases from $0.45 to $0.35.

(d) Using your analysis in part (b), determine the LP's optimal solution and the optimal total profit if the availability of labor increases from 4800 to 6800 hours.

*7.19. This exercise assumes you have already worked Exercise 2.31. That exercise requested you to formulate an LP for the blending decision problem of the Hot Dawg Company (HDC). Your formulation should be similar to the following LP:

$$\text{Minimize} \quad 1.0X_B + 0.5X_C + 0.7X_L$$

$$\text{subject to} \quad \begin{aligned} X_B + X_C + X_L &= 100 \\ 0.20X_B + 0.15X_C + 0.15X_L &\geq 12 \\ 0.20X_B + 0.15X_C + 0.25X_L &\leq 24 \\ 0.60X_B + 0.70X_C + 0.60X_L &\leq 64 \\ X_L &\geq 30 \end{aligned}$$

$$\text{and} \quad X_B \geq 0,\, X_C \geq 0,\, X_L \geq 0$$

where X_B, X_C, and X_L denote the respective pounds of beef, chicken, and lamb used to blend the 100 pounds of Super Sausage. Accept as a fact that use of the simplex method to solve the LP results in the optimal tableau displayed in Figure 7.23, where E_2, S_3, S_4, E_5, A_1, A_2, and A_5 denote the slack, surplus, and artificial variables for the structural constraints.

(a) First for the objective-function coefficient of X_B and then for the objective-function coefficient of X_L, determine the range of optimality. Summarize your analysis in a table having the format of Table 3.2.

(b) First for the structural constraint corresponding to maximum fat content and then for the structural constraint corresponding to maximum water content, determine the shadow price and its associated range of validity. Summarize your analysis in a table having the format of Tables 3.3–3.5.

(c) Using your analysis in part (a), determine the LP's optimal solution and the minimum total cost if the cost per pound of beef decreases from $1.00 to $0.80.

(d) Using your analysis in part (b), determine the LP's optimal solution and the minimum total cost if maximum water content increases from 64% to 66%.

7.20. This exercise assumes you have already worked Exercise 2.32. That exercise requested you to formulate an LP for the blending decision problem of the Harrus Feeding Company. Your formulation should be similar to the following LP:

$$\text{Minimize} \quad 60X_C + 40X_W + 35X_B + 5X_H$$

$$\text{subject to} \quad \begin{aligned} 2X_C + X_W + 3X_B + 4X_H &\geq 25 \\ 2X_C + X_W + 3X_B + 4X_H &\leq 100 \\ 20X_C + 15X_W + 15X_B + 10X_H &\geq 400 \\ 4X_C + 7X_W + 6X_B + 5X_H &\geq 125 \\ 200X_C + 400X_W + 300X_B + 500X_H &\geq 6000 \\ X_C + X_W + X_B + X_H &= 24 \end{aligned}$$

$$\text{and} \quad X_C \geq 0,\, X_W \geq 0,\, X_B \geq 0,\, X_H \geq 0$$

where X_C, X_W, X_B, and X_H denote the respective pounds of corn, wheat, barley, and hay used to blend the 24 pounds of feedstuffs that comprise a steer's daily food ration. Accept as a fact that the use of the simplex method to solve the LP results in the optimal tableau displayed in Figure 7.24, where E_1, S_2, E_3, E_4, E_5, A_1, A_3, A_4, A_5 and A_6 denote the slack, surplus, and artificial variables for the structural constraints.

(a) First for the objective-function coefficient of X_C and then for the objective-function coefficient of X_W, determine the range of optimality. Summarize your analysis in a table having the format of Table 3.2.

(b) First for the structural constraint corresponding to minimum calorie consumption and then for structural constraint requiring a steer to consume exactly 24 pounds per day, determine the shadow price and its associated range of validity. Summarize your analysis in a table having the format of Tables 3.3–3.5.

(c) Using your analysis in part (a), determine the LP's optimal solution and the minimum total cost if the cost per pound of wheat decreases from 40 to 38 cents.

(d) Using your analysis in part (b), determine the LP's optimal solution and the minimum total cost if a steer's daily consumption increases from 24 to 26 pounds. Provide an intuitive explanation of why minimum total cost decreases.

Figure 7.23 Optimal simplex tableau for Exercise 7.19's LP

Equation	Basic Variable c_B	c_j	1 X_B	$\frac{1}{2}$ X_C	$\frac{7}{10}$ X_L	0 E_2	0 S_3	0 S_4	0 E_5	0 A_1	0 A_2	0 A_5	RHS
I	E_5	0	1	0	0	0	0	-10	1	7	0	-1	30
II	X_C	$\frac{1}{2}$	0	1	0	0	0	10	0	-6	0	0	40
III	S_3	0	$-\frac{1}{20}$	0	0	0	1	1	0	$-\frac{17}{20}$	0	0	3
IV	E_2	0	$-\frac{1}{20}$	0	0	1	0	0	0	$\frac{3}{20}$	-1	0	3
V	X_L	$\frac{7}{10}$	1	0	1	0	0	-10	0	7	0	0	60
	z_j		$\frac{7}{10}$	$*$	$*$	$*$	$*$	-2	$*$	$\frac{19}{10}$	0	0	$OV = 62$
	$c_j - z_j$		$\frac{3}{10}$	$*$	$*$	$*$	$*$	2	$*$	$-\frac{19}{10}$	0	0	

340

Equation	Basic Variable	c_B	x_C	x_W	x_B	x_H	E_1	S_2	E_3	E_4	E_5	A_1	A_3	A_4	A_5	A_6	RHS
		c_j	60	40	35	5	0	0	0	0	0	0	0	0	0	0	
I	x_C	60	1	$-\frac{1}{3}$	0	0	0	0	$-\frac{1}{15}$	$\frac{1}{3}$	0	0	$\frac{1}{15}$	$-\frac{1}{3}$	0	1	9
II	S_2	0	0	-2	0	0	0	1	$-\frac{1}{5}$	0	0	0	$\frac{1}{5}$	0	0	-6	36
III	E_1	0	0	2	0	0	1	0	$\frac{1}{5}$	0	0	-1	$-\frac{1}{5}$	0	0	6	39
IV	E_5	0	0	$-\frac{400}{3}$	0	0	0	0	$\frac{100}{3}$	$\frac{100}{3}$	1	0	$-\frac{100}{3}$	$-\frac{100}{3}$	-1	1000	500
V	x_B	35	0	$\frac{5}{3}$	1	0	0	0	$-\frac{1}{15}$	$-\frac{2}{3}$	0	0	$\frac{1}{15}$	$\frac{2}{3}$	0	-4	14
VI	x_H	5	0	$-\frac{1}{3}$	0	1	0	0	$\frac{2}{15}$	$\frac{1}{3}$	0	0	$-\frac{2}{15}$	$-\frac{1}{3}$	0	4	1
	z_j		*	$\frac{110}{3}$	*	*	*	*	$-\frac{17}{3}$	$-\frac{5}{3}$	*	0	$\frac{17}{3}$	$\frac{5}{3}$	0	-60	OV = 1035
	$c_j - z_j$		*	$\frac{10}{3}$	*	*	*	*	$\frac{17}{3}$	$\frac{5}{3}$	*	0	$-\frac{17}{3}$	$-\frac{5}{3}$	0	60	

Figure 7.24 Optimal simplex tableau for Exercise 7.20's LP

7.21. For Section 7.4's example LP, we saw in Section 7.4's last subsection that decreasing x_1's objective-function coefficient from 30 to 16 resulted in a nonoptimal simplex tableau.

(a) Determine the LP's new optimal solution by starting from this nonoptimal simplex tableau and performing as many iterations of the simplex method as necessary.

(b) Explain why the computational effort required in part (a) is likely to be significantly less than that required to resolve the LP "from scratch."

Exercises 7.22 and 7.23 test your understanding of the construction of the dual LP and of Primal-Dual Relationship 1.

*7.22. Reconsider the LP in Exercise 6.9.

(a) Construct the dual of this primal LP.

(b) Construct the dual of the primal's dual.

(c) What general principle does this exercise illustrate?

7.23. Redo Exercise 7.22, this time using the following LP:

$$\text{Maximize } 5x_1 + 3x_2 + 2x_3$$

$$\text{subject to } \quad 2x_1 + 3x_2 + x_3 \geqslant 10$$
$$4x_1 \qquad - x_3 \geqslant 5$$

$$\text{and } \quad x_1 \geqslant 0,\, x_2 \geqslant 0,\, x_3 \geqslant 0$$

Exercises 7.24 through 7.26 test your understanding of the construction of the dual LP and of Primal-Dual Relationships 2 and 3.

7.24. This exercise assumes you have already worked Exercise 6.12.

(a) Using Exercise 6.12's LP as the primal LP, construct the dual LP.

(b) Using Exercise 6.12's optimal simplex tableau and Table 7.3, illustrate Primal-Dual Relationship 2 by determining the dual LP's optimal solution (including any slack and surplus variables) and optimal objective value.

(c) Illustrate Primal-Dual Relationship 3 by computing the following products of pairs of variables:

1. For each primal structural constraint, compute the product of the optimal value of the constraint's slack or surplus variable and the optimal value of the associated dual decision variable.

2. For each primal decision variable, compute the product of the optimal value of the primal decision variable and the optimal value of the associated dual structural constraint's slack or surplus variable.

*7.25. Redo Exercise 7.24, this time using the LP in Exercise 7.3 and the optimal simplex tableau you obtained in that exercise.

7.26. Redo Exercise 7.24, this time using the LP in Exercise 7.4 and the optimal simplex tableau you obtained in that exercise.

The next exercise illustrates the second and third possibilities listed in Primal-Dual Relationship 4, namely that the primal LP has no optimal solution because of infeasibility while the dual LP has no optimal solution because of unboundedness and vice versa.

7.27. (a) Reconsider Exercise 2.9, where you determined graphically that the exercise's LP has no optimal solution because of infeasibility. (If you haven't already done this, do it now.) Construct the LP's dual and verify graphically that it has no optimal solution because of unboundedness.

(b) Reconsider Exercise 2.10, where you deter-

341

mined graphically that the exercise's LP has no optimal solution because of unboundedness. (If you haven't already done this, do it now.) Construct the LP's dual and verify graphically that it has no optimal solution because of infeasibility.

The next exercise illustrates the fourth possibility listed in Primal-Dual Relationship 4, namely that both the primal and dual LPs have no optimal solution because of infeasibility.

7.28. Consider the following LP:

$$\text{Maximize} \quad x_1 + x_2$$

$$\text{subject to} \quad x_1 - x_2 \geq 1$$
$$-x_1 + x_2 \geq 1$$

$$\text{and} \quad x_1 \geq 0, x_2 \geq 0$$

(a) Explain why this LP has no feasible solution. (Note that you can do this without solving the LP by simply examining the structural constraints.)

(b) Construct this LP's dual. (Note that you must first transform each $\geq$ structural constraint into a $\leq$ structural constraint by multiplying both sides of the constraint by -1.)

(c) Explain why the dual LP has no feasible solution. (Note once again that you can do this without solving the LP.)

Exercises 7.29 and 7.30 illustrate the correspondence between a structural constraint's shadow price and the optimal value of the constraint's associated dual variable.

*7.29. This exercise assumes you have already worked Exercises 7.16 and 7.25.

(a) Using your answers to these exercises, develop a table (similar to the one appearing at the end of Section 7.6) that displays, for Exercise 7.3's LP, each structural constraint, the constraint's shadow price, and the optimal value of the constraint's associated dual variable.

(b) What general principle does this exercise illustrate?

7.30. Redo Exercise 7.29, this time using your answers to Exercises 7.17 and 7.26.

342

NETWORK OPTIMIZATION PROBLEMS

This chapter considers in detail a special class of decision problems known as *network optimization problems*. We will look first at a specific example, which will prepare us for the next section's general overview of network decision problems.

8.1 AN EXAMPLE OF A NETWORK OPTIMIZATION PROBLEM

To introduce the concept of a network optimization problem, consider the following scenario:

Mike's TV (MTV) is a large retailer of televisions. Although the televisions it sells bear the MTV brand logo, MTV does not actually manufacture them. Instead, MTV purchases televisions from three original equipment manufacturers (OEMs), who manufacture them according to MTV's specifications and then place the MTV brand logo on them before shipment to MTV. Figure 8.1 depicts the various stages in the flow of televisions from their point of manufacture to their point of sale. Some details of this flow are as follows:

- MTV purchases televisions from three OEMs located in Tokyo, Taipei, and Hong Kong.

- After purchase, MTV contracts with a Seattle based shipping company and a Los Angeles-based shipping company to transport the televisions in large containers (each holding 1000 units) from the OEMs to port facilities in Seattle and Los Angeles.

- On arrival in Seattle or Los Angeles, the containers are removed from the boats

343

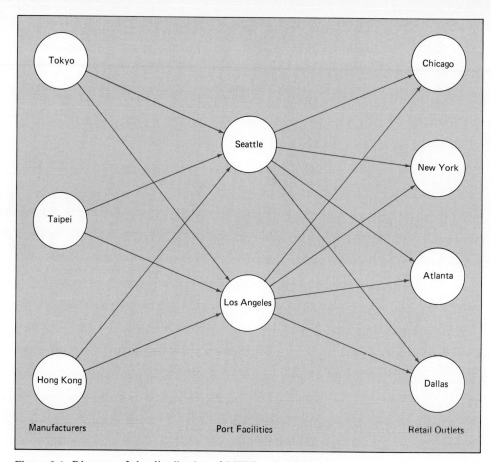

Figure 8.1 Diagram of the distribution of MTV's televisions

and transferred to trucks that transport them to MTV's four retail outlets in Chicago, New York, Atlanta, and Dallas.

Ned Wurk, the MTV logistics manager, has the responsibility for determining the most cost-effective way to satisfy the demand for televisions at MTV's four retail outlets. For planning purposes, Ned divides the year into four three-month periods. He is currently planning the logistics for an upcoming three-month period with the following data:

- Each OEM has notified MTV of the maximum number of containers of televisions it can manufacture during the three-month period. Table 8.1(a) displays these data. For example, the Tokyo OEM can supply MTV with at most 25 containers of televisions.

- Contracts with each of the two container shipping firms specify three pieces of data for each shipping route: (1) a shipping cost per container, (2) an upper bound on the number of containers that can be shipped, and (3) a lower bound on the number of containers that can be shipped. Table 8.1(b) displays these data, where the symbol "~" indicates the absence of a contractual upper or lower bound. For example, for shipments from Taipei to Seattle, the contract specifies a cost per container of $19,000 and that the number of containers shipped along this route during the three-month period must be at least 10 but at most 25.

TABLE 8.1 Data for Ned's Decision Problem

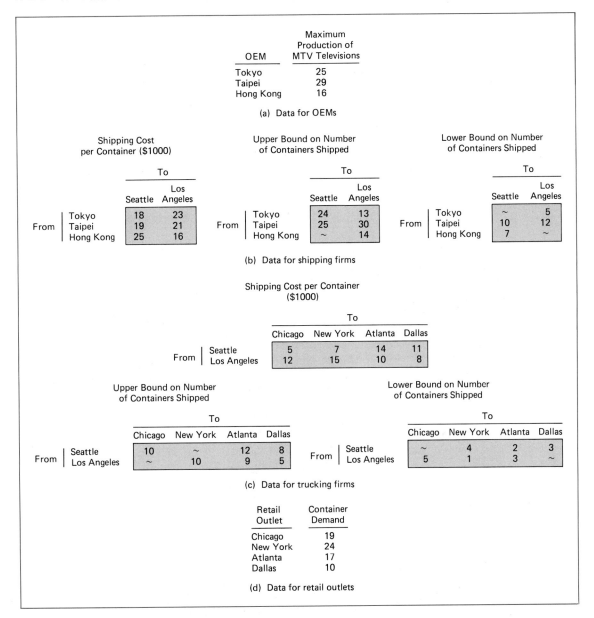

(a) Data for OEMs

OEM	Maximum Production of MTV Televisions
Tokyo	25
Taipei	29
Hong Kong	16

Shipping Cost per Container ($1000)

From \ To	Seattle	Los Angeles
Tokyo	18	23
Taipei	19	21
Hong Kong	25	16

Upper Bound on Number of Containers Shipped

From \ To	Seattle	Los Angeles
Tokyo	24	13
Taipei	25	30
Hong Kong	~	14

Lower Bound on Number of Containers Shipped

From \ To	Seattle	Los Angeles
Tokyo	~	5
Taipei	10	12
Hong Kong	7	~

(b) Data for shipping firms

Shipping Cost per Container ($1000)

From \ To	Chicago	New York	Atlanta	Dallas
Seattle	5	7	14	11
Los Angeles	12	15	10	8

Upper Bound on Number of Containers Shipped

From \ To	Chicago	New York	Atlanta	Dallas
Seattle	10	~	12	8
Los Angeles	~	10	9	5

Lower Bound on Number of Containers Shipped

From \ To	Chicago	New York	Atlanta	Dallas
Seattle	~	4	2	3
Los Angeles	5	1	3	~

(c) Data for trucking firms

Retail Outlet	Container Demand
Chicago	19
New York	24
Atlanta	17
Dallas	10

(d) Data for retail outlets

- Contracts with the various trucking firms that transport the containers from Seattle or Los Angeles to MTV's retail outlets specify data similar to that specified by the two shipping firms. Table 8.1(c) displays these data.

- The demand during the three-month period for containers of televisions for MTV's four retail outlets are displayed in Table 8.1(d). For example, the New York retail outlet's demand is 24 containers. Note that the total supply available from the OEMs (25 + 29 + 16 = 70) equals the total demand at the retail outlets (19 + 24 + 17 + 10 = 70).[1]

---

[1] In Section 8.4, we will consider an extension of this problem in which total supply exceeds total demand.

Given Table 8.1's data, Ned's task is to determine the most cost-effective answers to the following related questions:

1. How many containers of televisions should MTV ship from each of the three OEMs to each of the two port facilities?

2. How many containers of televisions should MTV ship from each of the two ports to each of the four retail outlets?

Representing Ned's Decision Problem as a Network

In the next subsection we will formulate Ned Wurk's decision problem as a linear program. This task will be facilitated by Figure 8.2, which is the *network representation* of Ned's decision problem. Observe the following characteristics of Figure 8.2:

- The nine cities involved are represented by nine circles. These circles are called *nodes*.[2] For ease of identification, the nine nodes have been labeled with reference numbers from 1 through 9. For example, we refer to the node representing Los Angeles as node 5.

- The 14 transportation routes between the various pairs of cities are represented by 14 arrows. These arrows are called *arcs*.[3] We refer to a particular arc by the labels of the nodes it connects. For example, arc 5-8, is the arc originating at node 5 (Los Angeles) and terminating at node 8 (Atlanta).

- Adjacent to all but two of Figure 8.2's nodes is a number in parentheses that indicates the node's supply of televisions, where a negative supply indicates a demand for televisions and where the absence of a number in parentheses indicates the absence of supply or demand. For example, Taipei's supply of 29 containers is indicated by the "(29)" adjacent to node 2, Dallas's demand for ten containers is indicated by the "(-10)" adjacent to node 9, and the absence of any supply or demand at Seattle is indicated by the absence of any number adjacent to node 4. In network terminology, a node with a positive supply is called a *source node,* a node with negative supply (i.e., a demand) is called a *sink node,* and a node with neither supply nor demand is called a *transshipment node.* Thus, Figure 8.2 contains three source nodes, four sink nodes, and two transshipment nodes.

- Adjacent to each of Figure 8.2's arcs are three numbers with labels of c, u, and l. These three numbers represent respectively the arc's unit transportation cost, the upper bound on the amount that can be transported along the arc, and the lower bound on the amount that can be transported along the arc.[4] For example, adjacent to arc 2-5 is "$c = 21, u = 30, l = 12$," indicating that MTV's contract with the Los-Angeles-based shipping firm specifies that every container shipped between Taipei and Los Angeles costs \$21,000 and that the maximum and minimum number of containers that can be shipped are 30 and 12, respectively. For arcs in which no upper bound has been expli-

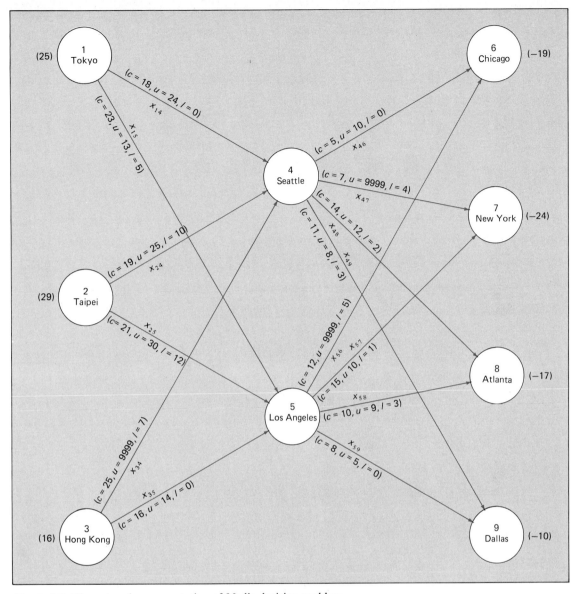

Figure 8.2 The network representation of Ned's decision problem

citly specified by the firm (e.g., arc 3-4), Figure 8.2 specifies an arbitrarily large upper bound of $u = 9999$.[5]

■ Also adjacent to each of Figure 8.2's arcs is a decision variable whose two subscripts correspond to the pair of nodes connected by the arc. For example, adjacent to arc 4-7 is the decision variable x_{47}. The decision variable x_{47} represents an as-yet-unknown integer equal to the number of containers that will be shipped from node 4 to node 7 along the route represented by arc 4-7. Similar definitions apply to the other decision variables. In network terminology, the number of containers shipped along arc 4-7 is the *flow* on arc i-j.

---

[5] Since node 3's supply is 16, the amount transported along arc 3-4 can never exceed 16. However, instead of using $u = 16$ as arc 3-4's upper bound, we use $u = 9999$ to enable us to quickly identify that the upper bound is meaningless.

Figure 8.2's network representation is a pictorial illustration of the verbal statement of Ned Wurk's decision problem. It is a useful visual aid when Ned discusses the problem with his colleagues. In addition, we will now show that it facilitates the formulation of Ned's problem as a linear program.

Formulation of Ned's Decision Problem as a Linear Program

The LP's 14 nonnegative decision variables (written adjacent to Figure 8.2's 14 arcs) have already been defined as

$$x_{ij} = \text{the flow of containers on arc } i\text{-}j.$$

The LP's objective is to minimize total cost of all flows. The cost of the flow on arc $i\text{-}j$ is obtained by multiplying x_{ij} by the arc's unit flow cost. For example, given Figure 8.2's specification of a unit flow cost for arc 2-5 of $c = 21$, the cost of the flow on arc 2-5 is simply $21x_{25}$. Thus, we can express the LP's objective of minimizing the total cost of all flows as

$$\text{Minimize } 18x_{14} + 23x_{15} + 19x_{24} + 21x_{25} + 25x_{34} + 16x_{35} + 5x_{46} + 7x_{47}$$

$$+ 14x_{48} + 11x_{49} + 12x_{56} + 15x_{57} + 10x_{58} + 8x_{59}$$

What are the LP's structural constraints? Some of them are simple. For example, given Figure 8.2's specification for arc 2-5 of $u = 30$ and $l = 12$, the following structural constraints must hold:

$$x_{25} \leq 30$$
$$x_{25} \geq 12.$$

Hereafter, we refer to such constraints as an *upper bound constraint* and a *lower bound constraint*. Similar bounding constraints hold for the remaining decision variables. Note, however, when the arc's upper bound is $u = 9999$, the upper bound constraint may be omitted, since it is meaningless, and when the arc's lower bound is 0, the lower bound constraint may be omitted, since it duplicates the decision variable's nonnegativity constraint.

The LP also includes structural constraints of another type. The purpose of these constraints is to ensure a balance of flow at each of the network's nodes. Consequently, these constraints are known as the nodes' *flow balance equations*. In words, a node's flow balance equation states the following:

$$\left(\begin{array}{c} \text{flow on arcs} \\ \text{out of the node} \end{array} \right) - \left(\begin{array}{c} \text{flow on arcs} \\ \text{into the node} \end{array} \right) = \left(\begin{array}{c} \text{node's} \\ \text{supply} \end{array} \right)$$

For example, consider the transshipment node 4, which has a supply of 0. Looking at Figure 8.2, we see that the arcs originating at node 4 are arcs 4-6, 4-7, 4-8, and 4-9, and the arcs terminating at node 4 are arcs 1-4, 2-4, and 3-4. Thus, to ensure a balance of flow at node 4, the LP's structural constraints must include the following flow balance equation for node 4:

$$\left(\begin{array}{c} \text{flow on arcs} \\ \text{out of node 4} \end{array} \right) - \left(\begin{array}{c} \text{flow on arcs} \\ \text{into node 4} \end{array} \right) = \left(\begin{array}{c} \text{node 4's} \\ \text{supply} \end{array} \right)$$

$$(x_{46} + x_{47} + x_{48} + x_{49}) \quad - \quad (x_{14} + x_{24} + x_{34}) \quad = \quad 0$$

Now consider the source node 2, which has a supply of 29. Looking at Figure 8.2, we see that the arcs originating at node 2 are arcs 2-4 and 2-5, and that there are no arcs terminating at node 2. Thus, to ensure a balance of flow at node 2, the LP's structural constraints must include the following flow balance equation for node 2:

$$
\begin{pmatrix} \text{flow on arcs} \\ \text{out of node 2} \end{pmatrix} - \begin{pmatrix} \text{flow on arcs} \\ \text{into node 2} \end{pmatrix} = \begin{pmatrix} \text{node 2's} \\ \text{supply} \end{pmatrix}
$$

$$
(x_{24} + x_{25}) \quad - \quad (0) \quad = \quad 29
$$

Finally, consider the sink node 9, which has a demand of 10, equivalent to a supply of -10. Looking at Figure 8.2, we see that there are no arcs originating at node 9, and that the arcs terminating at node 9 are arcs 4-9 and 5-9. Thus, to ensure a balance of flow at node 9, the LP's structural constraints must include the following flow balance equation for node 9:

$$
\begin{pmatrix} \text{flow on arcs} \\ \text{out of node 9} \end{pmatrix} - \begin{pmatrix} \text{flow on arcs} \\ \text{into node 9} \end{pmatrix} = \begin{pmatrix} \text{node 9's} \\ \text{supply} \end{pmatrix}
$$

$$
(0) \quad - \quad (x_{49} + x_{59}) \quad = \quad -10
$$

On multiplying both sides of this equation by -1, we obtain the equation $x_{49} + x_{59} = 10$. This is a more direct statement of the fact that node 9's demand of 10 units must be met by shipments from node 4 and node 5. However, to conform to the generic format of the flow balance equation, we will continue to use the constraint $-x_{49} - x_{59} = -10$.

To summarize, the complete LP formulation of Ned's decision problem is the 14-variable, 42-constraint LP shown on the following page.

The Special Structure of Ned's Network LP

The LP on page 350 has a special structure that is revealed by displaying the LP's data in a tabular format known as the *node-arc incidence matrix*. Figure 8.3 displays the node-arc incidence matrix for Ned's problem.

Looking column-by-column at Figure 8.3's shaded portion, we see that each column corresponds to one of the LP's decision variables and contains the variable's coefficients in the nine flow balance equations (where a blank denotes a coefficient of 0), the variable's lower and upper bounds, and the variable's objective-function coefficient. Figure 8.3's last column contains the supplies at each of the nine nodes.

Looking row-by-row at Figure 8.3's shaded portion, we see that each row corresponds to one of the nine flow balance equations and contains the nonzero coefficients of the decision variables. Figure 8.3's last three rows contain respectively the decision variables' lower bound, upper bound, and objective-function coefficient.

The LP's special structure is exhibited by the shaded portion of Figure 8.3's node-arc incidence matrix. Observe that each shaded column contains exactly two nonzero coefficients, one a $+1$ and the other a -1. This is a consequence of the fact that the decision variable x_{ij} corresponds to the arc that transports flow out of node i and into node j. Consider, for example, x_{35}. Because the arc represented by x_{35} transports flow out of node 3, x_{35} appears with a coefficient of $+1$ in node 3's

$$\text{Minimize } 18x_{14} + 23x_{15} + 19x_{24} + 21x_{25} + 25x_{34} + 16x_{35} + 5x_{46} + 7x_{47} + 14x_{48} + 11x_{49} + 12x_{56} + 15x_{57} + 10x_{58} + 8x_{59}$$

subject to

$$
\begin{aligned}
x_{14} + x_{15} &= 25 \\
x_{24} + x_{25} &= 29 \\
x_{34} + x_{35} &= 16 \\
-x_{14} - x_{24} - x_{34} + x_{46} + x_{47} + x_{48} + x_{49} &= 0 \\
-x_{15} - x_{25} - x_{35} + x_{56} + x_{57} + x_{58} + x_{59} &= 0 \\
-x_{46} - x_{56} &= -19 \\
-x_{47} - x_{57} &= -24 \\
-x_{48} - x_{58} &= -17 \\
-x_{49} - x_{59} &= -10
\end{aligned}
$$

$$
\begin{aligned}
x_{14} &\leq 24 & x_{14} &\geq 0 \\
x_{15} &\leq 13 & x_{15} &\geq 5 \\
x_{24} &\leq 25 & x_{24} &\geq 10 \\
x_{25} &\leq 30 & x_{25} &\geq 12 \\
x_{34} &\leq 9999 & x_{34} &\geq 7 \\
x_{35} &\leq 14 & x_{35} &\geq 0 \\
x_{46} &\leq 10 & x_{46} &\geq 0 \\
x_{47} &\leq 9999 & x_{47} &\geq 4 \\
x_{48} &\leq 12 & x_{48} &\geq 2 \\
x_{49} &\leq 8 & x_{49} &\geq 3 \\
x_{56} &\leq 9999 & x_{56} &\geq 5 \\
x_{57} &\leq 10 & x_{57} &\geq 1 \\
x_{58} &\leq 9 & x_{58} &\geq 3 \\
x_{59} &\leq 5 & x_{59} &\geq 0
\end{aligned}
$$

and $x_{ij} \geq 0$ for all 14 i-j combinations.

	Arc														Node's Supply
	x_{14}	x_{15}	x_{24}	x_{25}	x_{34}	x_{35}	x_{46}	x_{47}	x_{48}	x_{49}	x_{56}	x_{57}	x_{58}	x_{59}	
Node 1	+1	+1													25
Node 2			+1	+1											29
Node 3					+1	+1									16
Node 4	−1		−1		−1		+1	+1	+1	+1					0
Node 5		−1		−1		−1					+1	+1	+1	+1	0
Node 6							−1				−1				−19
Node 7								−1				−1			−24
Node 8									−1				−1		−17
Node 9										−1				−1	−10
Arc's lower bound:	0	5	10	12	7	0	0	4	2	3	5	1	3	0	
Arc's upper bound:	24	13	25	30	9999	14	10	9999	12	8	9999	10	9	5	
Arc's unit flow cost:	18	23	19	21	25	16	5	7	14	11	12	15	10	8	

Figure 8.3 Node-arc incidence matrix for Ned's problem

flow balance equation; because the arc represented by x_{35} transports flow into node 5, x_{35} appears with a coefficient of −1 in node 5's flow balance equation; and because the arc represented by x_{35} is involved only with nodes 3 and 5, x_{35} does not appear in the flow balance equations for nodes other than 3 and 5. Similar statements are true for the remaining decision variables.

8.2 AN OVERVIEW OF DECISION PROBLEMS HAVING A NETWORK REPRESENTATION

Before discussing the solution to Ned's decision problem, let us pause for a overview of decision problems having a network representation. Ned Wurk's decision problem is an example of what we will call a *minimum-cost network flow problem,* and our LP formulation of Ned's problem is a special type of LP known as a *network LP.*[6] We can summarize a minimum-cost network flow problem and its associated network LP as follows:

A decision problem is a *minimum-cost network flow problem* when it can be represented pictorially as the flow of a commodity through a network of nodes interconnected by arcs. The network representation has the following characteristics:

- Associated with each node is a supply of the commodity, where a negative supply indicates a demand. Depending on whether a node's supply is positive, negative, or 0, the node is classified respectively as a *source node,* a *sink node,* or a *transshipment node.*

- Associated with each arc are three numbers representing the unit cost for flow on the arc, an upper bound for flow on the arc, and a lower bound for flow on the arc.

To formulate a minimum-cost network flow problem as special type of linear program known as a network LP, we proceed as follows:

- There is one decision variable for each arc. More specifically, we denote the flow from node i to node j on arc i-j by the decision variable x_{ij}.

351

[6] Some refer to a minimum-cost network flow problem as a *capacitated transshipment problem.*

- Among the LP's structural constraints is one flow balance equation for each node. A node's flow balance equation ensures that the flow out of the node minus the flow into the node equals the node's supply. In particular, node i's flow balance equation has a left-hand side consisting of the sum of the decision variables corresponding to arcs originating at node i minus the sum of the decision variables corresponding to arcs terminating at node i; the equation's right-hand side is the node's supply.

- The remaining structural constraints simply specify upper and lower bounds on the decision variables.

All network LPs possess a special structure. More specifically, if the decision variables' lower and upper bound constraints are ignored, each decision variable appears exactly twice in the remaining structural constraints, once with a coefficient of $+1$ and once with a coefficient of -1. This special structure is a direct consequence of the fact that each arc connects exactly two nodes; hence, the corresponding decision variable appears in exactly two flow balance equations, once with a coefficient of $+1$ for the node at which the arc originates and once with a coefficient of -1 for the node at which the arc terminates.

Ned Wurk's decision problem involves the flow of containers of televisions along transportation routes over water first and land subsequently. As we will see in this chapter's examples, networks arise in a variety of other contexts. Table 8.2 summarizes some applications having network representations.

Before proceeding, we should comment on one potential characteristic of an arc of a network that did not arise in our example. An arc is either a *directed arc* or an *undirected arc*. In drawing the network, we distinguish between the two types of arcs by the presence or absence of an arrow tip at the end of the arc. As we illustrated in Figure 8.2, we draw a directed arc from node i to node j as

The arrow tip emphasizes that the flow on the arc must be oriented from node i to node j. In contrast, we draw an undirected arc between nodes i and j as

TABLE 8.2 Some Applications Having Network Representations

Application	Commodity Flowing through Network	Nodes Represent	Arcs Represent
Product distribution	Units of a product	Plants, warehouses, and retail outlets	Transportation routes
Urban transportation	Vehicles	Intersections	Roads
Airline transportation	Aircraft	Airports	Air lanes
Rail transportation	Freight or passenger cars	Railroad stations and and switching junctions	Rail tracks
Water distribution	Water	Lakes, reservoirs, and pumping stations	Pipelines, canals, and rivers
Oil or gas distribution	Oil or gas	Oil or gas fields and pumping stations	Pipelines
Communication systems	Messages	Communcation centers relay stations, and satellites	Communication channels

The absence of an arrow tip indicates that the flow on the arc can be in either direction, and, furthermore, that the same unit flow cost, upper bound on flow, and lower bound on flow apply for both directions. Of course, we can also indicate the possibility of flow between nodes i and j in either direction as

Such a representation is necessary in cases when the unit flow cost, upper bound on flow, or lower bound on flow depend on the direction of the flow. For example, the cost of traveling from node i to node j may differ from the cost of traveling from node j to node i (as is the case for an airplane that consumes less fuel traveling from west to east versus east to west, owing to the direction of the air currents). A network with all directed arcs is called a *directed network,* and a network with all undirected arcs is called an *undirected network.* Ned's network is a directed network; we will encounter undirected networks in subsequent examples in this chapter.

Network LPs are among the most widely used types of LPs. Network representations similar to that for Ned's decision problem have enabled large firms to save millions of dollars per year in transportation costs. The usefulness of network LPs stems from three attributes:

1. A network LP has a pictorial representation that facilitates describing the problem to others, especially given the multicolor graphics capabilities of today's computers.

2. If the nodes' supplies and demands and the arcs' upper and lower bounds all have integer values, then a network LP is guaranteed to have an optimal solution in which all decision variables have integer values.[7] Although its proof is well beyond the scope of this text, the importance of this property is easily explained. In particular, since a network LP almost always involves the flow of an indivisible commodity, a decision variable's taking on a noninteger value has no meaningful physical interpretation. If this event were to occur, we would need to round to a not-necessarily-optimal integer value or employ the more time-consuming and more expensive solution methods of integer linear programming. Not to worry! Faced with a network LP with all-integer data (with the possible exception of the unit flow costs), we can always employ an LP software package and be guaranteed of an all-integer optimal solution.

3. Although we can always solve a network LP with a general-purpose LP software package (such as Chapter 3's LINPRO), there exist special-purpose network software packages that will solve the same problems from 100 to 200 times faster. These packages employ solution procedures that experts have developed by exploiting the special structure of network LPs. (Space constraints preclude us from discussing these special-purpose solution procedures.) A state-of-the-art network software package running on one of today's mainframe computers can routinely solve a network LP with tens of thousands of nodes and hundreds of thousands of arcs. In fact, the Internal

---

[7] Recall from Chapter 2 that, for a general LP, all-integer data does not guarantee an all-integer optimal solution (as was illustrated by OMC's product mix LP).

Revenue Service has reported solving a network LP involving 50,000 nodes and 63,000,000 arcs in less than one hour of computing time!

To summarize:

> The widespread use of network LPs is a consequence of:
>
> **1.** The ability to represent the decision problem pictorially.
>
> **2.** The guarantee of an all-integer optimal solution.
>
> **3.** The existence of highly efficient special-purpose network solution procedures.

8.3 USING A NETWORK SOFTWARE PACKAGE

This section illustrates the solution of Ned's minimum-cost network flow problem using a hypothetical interactive network software package we will call NETOPT.[8] You should have no difficulty adapting to the actual network software package available at your computer facility, even if there are slight differences in the input and/or output formats.

Figure 8.4 displays the input to and output from NETOPT when used to solve Ned's minimum cost network flow problem. Figure 8.4's unshaded portions contain NETOPT's prompts and requests, while the shaded portions contain the user's commands and data input. Observe the following aspects of Figure 8.4:

- NETOPT's execution is initiated by the user's keying in "netopt" in response to the operating system's prompt of ":"

- NETOPT's execution begins with its own prompt of " > " thereby indicating its readiness to accept a command from the user.

- The user's first command is the CREATE command, whose function is to input the network's data. After keying in "create" the user provides a network name of "nedsnet" and specifies by typing "dir" that the network to be input is a directed network. The network's name will be used for identification purposes if the network's input is saved on disk storage for subsequent recall. The specification that the network is a directed network means that each arc permits travel only in the specified direction. If the user had typed "undir" in place of "dir" NETOPT would have assumed that all arcs permitted travel in either direction.

- When the user hits the ENTER (or RETURN) key after typing the CREATE command, NETOPT requests a name and a supply for each node and requests the user to terminate the node data with a blank line (i.e., simply hitting the ENTER key at the start of the line). A node name can be from one to eight characters in length. Although the user may choose short node names such as $1, 2, 3, \ldots$ or $A, B, C, \ldots$, this user has chosen mnemonic names of "Tokyo," "Taipei,", . . . , "Dallas."

- After the user terminates the node data with a blank line, NETOPT requests the user to input the arc data and to terminate the arc data with a blank line.

---

[8] NETOPT is similar to an actual network software package called NETSOLVE, a package marketed by DISTINCT Management Consultants, 10750 Hickory Ridge Road, Suite 108, Columbia, MD 21044.

The arc data have five fields: FROM, TO, COST, UPPER, LOWER. The FROM and TO fields contain respectively the node at which the arc originates and the node at which the arc terminates.[9] The COST, UPPER, and LOWER fields contain respectively the arc's unit flow cost, upper bound on

[9] If the user had typed "undir" in the CREATE command, it would make no difference which nodes the user typed in the FROM and TO fields. NETOPT would automatically assume that the arc is undirected.

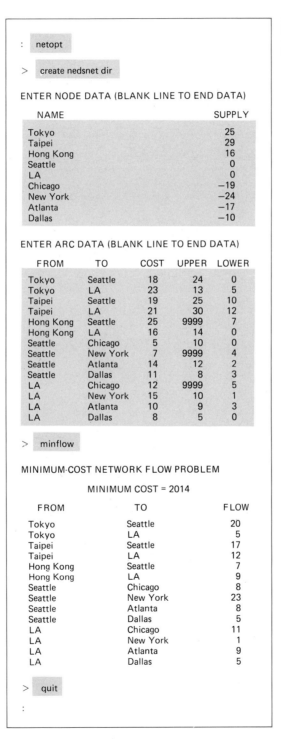

Figure 8.4 Input to and output from NETOPT when used to solve Ned's decision problem

```
:    netopt

>    create nedsnet dir

ENTER NODE DATA (BLANK LINE TO END DATA)

        NAME                        SUPPLY

     Tokyo                            25
     Taipei                           29
     Hong Kong                        16
     Seattle                           0
     LA                                0
     Chicago                         −19
     New York                        −24
     Atlanta                         −17
     Dallas                          −10

ENTER ARC DATA (BLANK LINE TO END DATA)

     FROM        TO       COST   UPPER   LOWER

     Tokyo       Seattle    18      24       0
     Tokyo       LA         23      13       5
     Taipei      Seattle    19      25      10
     Taipei      LA         21      30      12
     Hong Kong   Seattle    25    9999       7
     Hong Kong   LA         16      14       0
     Seattle     Chicago     5      10       0
     Seattle     New York    7    9999       4
     Seattle     Atlanta    14      12       2
     Seattle     Dallas     11       8       3
     LA          Chicago    12    9999       5
     LA          New York   15      10       1
     LA          Atlanta    10       9       3
     LA          Dallas      8       5       0

>    minflow

MINIMUM-COST NETWORK FLOW PROBLEM

          MINIMUM COST = 2014

     FROM              TO            FLOW

     Tokyo             Seattle         20
     Tokyo             LA               5
     Taipei            Seattle         17
     Taipei            LA              12
     Hong Kong         Seattle          7
     Hong Kong         LA               9
     Seattle           Chicago          8
     Seattle           New York        23
     Seattle           Atlanta          8
     Seattle           Dallas           5
     LA                Chicago         11
     LA                New York         1
     LA                Atlanta          9
     LA                Dallas           5

>    quit

:
```

flow, and lower bound on flow. Note that the user does not need to input the flow balance equations, as would be the case if the problem were being solved using an LP software package. NETOPT infers the flow balance equations from the data provided in the CREATE command.

- After the user terminates the arc data, NETOPT signals its readiness to accept a new command by the ">" prompt. At this point, the user can check the input by a LIST NODES command followed by a LIST ARCS command. Any detected input errors can be corrected using the CHANGE command. To conserve space, Figure 8.4 omits this portion of the computer session. In Figure 8.4, the user's response to NETOPT's prompt is the MIN-FLOW command. This command invokes the execution of a special-purpose solution method for a minimum cost network flow problem. After solving the problem, NETOPT outputs the optimal objective value of 2014 as well as the optimal flows (when nonzero). Figure 8.5 summarizes the optimal flows directly on the network by writing the flows adjacent to each arc (e.g., "9"

Figure 8.5 The optimal flows for Ned's decision problem

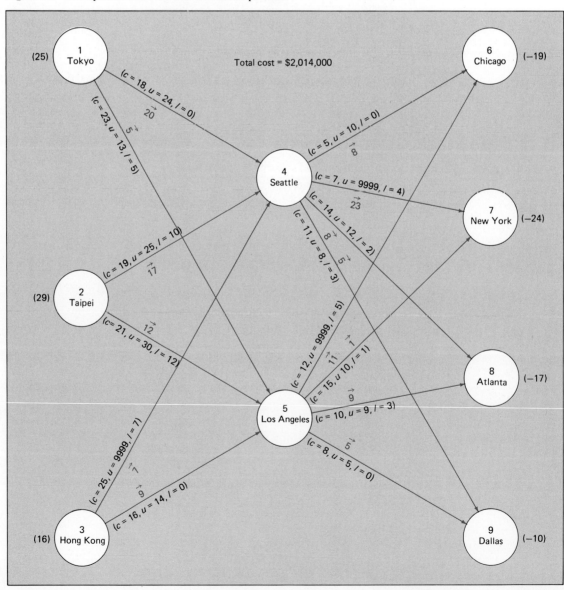

for arc 3-5). NETOPT's output enables Ned to answer the two questions posed at the end of Section 8.1's statement of Ned's decision problem. For example, Tokyo's supply of 25 is divided into shipments of 20 to Seattle and 5 to Los Angeles. Also, the total shipments of 26 into Los Angeles (5 from Tokyo, 12 from Taipei, and 9 from Hong Kong) are sent to Chicago, New York, Atlanta, and Dallas in respective quantities of 11, 1, 9, and 5.

- After displaying the optimal solution, NETOPT indicates its readiness to accept a new command with its ">" prompt. At this point, the user in Figure 8.4 terminates NETOPT's execution with the QUIT command and receives the operating system's ":" prompt.

8.4 EXCESS SUPPLY

A frequent occurrence in network decision problems is that the total supply at the source nodes exceeds the total demand at the sink nodes. Fortunately, there is a simple procedure for transforming a network with excess supply into an equivalent network where total supply equals total demand. As an example, let us return to Ned Wurk's decision problem and modify the respective supplies at Tokyo, Taipei, and Hong Kong from 25, 29, and 16 to 31, 36, and 23. These new supplies represent upper bounds on the number of containers of televisions MTV can purchase from the OEMs. Total supply is now $31 + 36 + 23 = 90$, an excess of 20 over the total demand of 70. If our goal were only to solve this excess-supply version of Ned's problem with an LP software package, we would simply replace the flow balance equations of the three source nodes with three inequalities. The replacement would proceed as follows:

$$
\text{Replace} \quad
\begin{array}{l}
x_{14} + x_{15} = 25 \\
x_{24} + x_{25} = 29 \\
x_{34} + x_{35} = 16
\end{array}
\quad \text{with} \quad
\begin{array}{l}
x_{14} + x_{15} \leq 31 \\
x_{24} + x_{25} \leq 36 \\
x_{34} + x_{35} \leq 23
\end{array}
$$

Former supplies ↑   Modified supplies ↑

However, let us assume our goal is to solve the excess-supply version with a network software package that requires total supply equal to total demand. To achieve this goal, we must proceed as summarized below and as diagrammed in Figure 8.6:

1. We first add to the network a *fictitious sink node* whose demand equals the excess supply of 20.[10] As indicated in Figure 8.6, this is equivalent to a negative supply of -20.

2. We then add to the network three arcs, one directed from each of the three source nodes to the fictitious sink node. As indicated in Figure 8.6, the data for each added arc's unit flow cost, upper bound on flow, and lower bound on flow are $c = 0$, $u = 9999$, and $l = 0$.

Thus, the fictitious sink node will receive at no cost from the source nodes a total of 20 containers, an amount equal to the excess supply. We interpret any shipment to the fictitious sink node not as an actual shipment but as the amount of the available supply at an OEM that MTV does not need.[11]

---

[10] Some refer to a fictitious sink node as an *artificial sink node* or a *dummy sink node*.

[11] The assumption that there is no cost to "ship" to the fictitious sink node is not always valid. Some end-of-chapter exercises involve scenarios where the assumption is invalid.

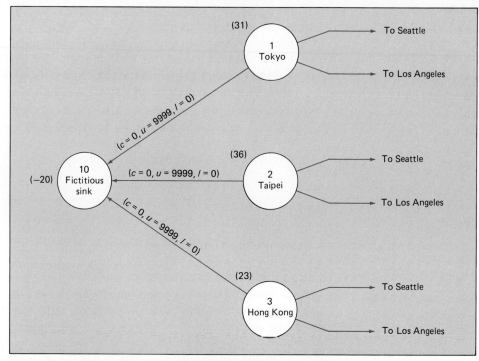

Figure 8.6 Using a fictitious sink node when there is excess supply

Figure 8.7 The optimal flows for Ned's decision problem with excess supply

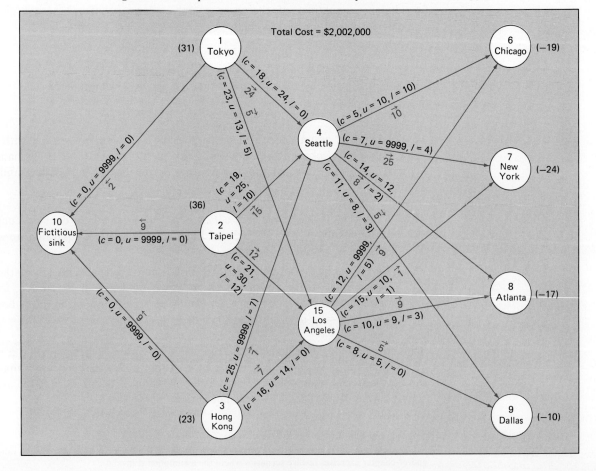

Figure 8.7 displays the optimal solution we would obtain using NETOPT to solve the excess-supply version of Ned's decision problem. The respective shipments of 2, 9, and 9 from Tokyo, Taipei, and Hong Kong to the fictitious sink node indicate that, of the supplies available from the OEMs, MTV purchases $31 - 2 = 29$ from Tokyo, $36 - 9 = 27$ from Taipei, and $23 - 9 = 14$ from Hong Kong.

We can summarize this section as follows:

When total supply exceeds total demand, we transform the network as follows:

1. We add to the network a fictitious sink node whose demand equals the excess supply.

2. We add to the network an arc directed from each source node to the fictitious sink node. The arc's unit flow cost, upper bound on flow, and lower bound on flow are $c = 0$, $u = 9999$, and $l = 0$.

In the transformed network, we interpret any shipment from a source node to the fictitious sink node as unused supply at the source node.

When total demand exceeds total supply, Exercise 8.3 illustrates that we transform the network in a similar manner, using a *fictitious source node* instead of a fictitious sink node.

8.5 COSTS AND BOUNDS ASSOCIATED WITH THE TOTAL FLOW ON A SUBSET OF ARCS THAT ORIGINATE (OR TERMINATE) AT A NODE

As we have seen, each arc has associated with it a unit flow cost, an upper bound on the flow on the arc, and a lower bound on the flow on the arc. A frequent occurrence in network decision problems is a situation in which the total flow on a subset of arcs that originate (or terminate) at a particular node also has associated with it a unit cost, an upper bound, and a lower bound.[12] As an example, consider the excess-supply version of Ned's decision problem with the following additional modification:

MTV has a different contract with each OEM. Each contract specifies a unit cost to MTV per container of televisions and upper and lower bounds on the number of containers MTV can purchase. Table 8.3 summarizes these data. For example, MTV's contract with the Hong Kong OEM specifies a unit cost of $160,000 per container and a purchase quantity that is at least 18 and at most 23. Note that this minimum purchase requirement is violated by the solution displayed in Figure 8.7, in which a total of only $7 + 7 = 14$ containers are sent from Hong Kong to Seattle and Los Angeles.

TABLE 8.3 Data for Contracts with MTV's OEMs

OEM	Cost per Container ($1000)	Upper Bound on Quantity Purchased	Lower Bound on Quantity Purchased
Tokyo	140	31	20
Taipei	170	36	25
Hong Kong	160	23	18

---

[12] The subset of arcs may include all arcs originating (or terminating) at the node.

If our only goal were to solve this additional modification of Ned's decision problem with an LP software package, we could make some simple modifications to our LP formulation. In particular, looking at Figure 8.7, we can express MTV's total purchases from each of the OEMs as the sum of the flow on the arcs directed from the OEM to Seattle and Los Angeles; that is,

$$
\begin{aligned}
\text{Total purchases from Tokyo} &= x_{14} + x_{15} \\
\text{Total purchases from Taipei} &= x_{24} + x_{25} \\
\text{Total purchases from Hong Kong} &= x_{34} + x_{35}
\end{aligned}
$$

Thus, we need to make the following modifications to our LP:

- To account for the purchase costs, we add to the LP's objective function the terms

$$
\underbrace{(\text{Tokyo cost})}_{} \quad + \quad \underbrace{(\text{Taipei cost})}_{} \quad + \quad \underbrace{(\text{Hong Kong cost})}_{}
$$

$$
\underbrace{140x_{14} + 140x_{15}}_{} + \underbrace{170x_{24} + 170x_{25}}_{} + \underbrace{160x_{34} + 160x_{35}}_{}
$$

- To ensure satisfying the bounds on MTV's purchases from each OEM, we add to the LP the following structural constraints:

$$
\left.\begin{aligned}
x_{14} + x_{15} &\leqslant 31 \\
x_{14} + x_{15} &\geqslant 20
\end{aligned}\right\} \text{(bounds for Tokyo OEM)}
$$

$$
\left.\begin{aligned}
x_{24} + x_{25} &\leqslant 36 \\
x_{24} + x_{25} &\geqslant 25
\end{aligned}\right\} \text{(bounds for Taipei OEM)}
$$

$$
\left.\begin{aligned}
x_{34} + x_{35} &\leqslant 23 \\
x_{34} + x_{35} &\geqslant 18
\end{aligned}\right\} \text{(bounds for Hong Kong OEM)}
$$

However, let us assume our goal is to solve the modified problem with a network software package. Then, we must resort to some "trickery" by proceeding as summarized below and diagrammed in Figure 8.8:

We add to the network three of a special type of transshipment node called a *collection node*. The purpose of the three collection nodes is to "collect" the flow of televisions out of each OEM before it is divided into two portions, one going to Seattle and the other to Los Angeles. To illustrate, consider the Hong Kong OEM. In Figure 8.8, the Hong Kong OEM node (node 3) is connected by arc 3-13 to the Hong Kong collection node (node 13), which in turn is connected by arcs 13-4 and 13-5 to Seattle and Los Angeles. Hence, every television from the Hong Kong OEM that is destined for Seattle or Los Angeles must first "travel" on the arc 3-13 connecting the Hong Kong OEM to its collection node. Consequently, the specifications of MTV's contract with the Hong Kong OEM can be associated with arc 3-13 in Figure 8.8. In particular, since MTV's contract with the Hong Kong OEM specifies a unit cost of \$160,000 per container and a purchase quantity of at least 18 and at most 23, arc 3-13's unit flow cost, upper bound, and lower bound equal $c = 160$, $u = 23$, and $l = 18$. Similar comments apply to the use of collection nodes with the other OEMs.

Before we proceed with a summary of the use of collection nodes, let us test your understanding by yet another modification to Ned's decision problem. In particular, let us add to the problem the following additional modification:

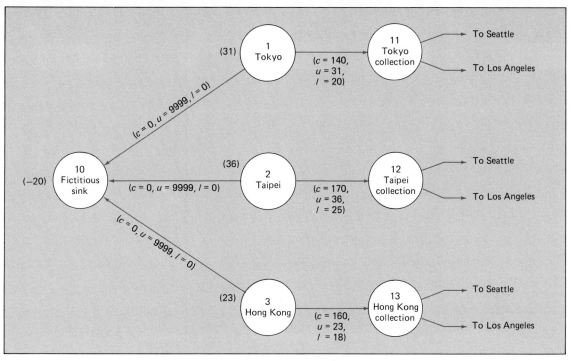

Figure 8.8 Using collection nodes associated with the OEMs

MTV also has different contracts with the Seattle-based shipping firm and the Los Angeles-based shipping firm. Each contract specifies upper and lower bounds on the containers that MTV can ship to the firm's home port. Table 8.4 summarizes these data. For example, MTV's contract with the Los Angeles firm calls for a flow of containers into Los Angeles of at least 30 but at most 50. Note that the lower bound on the flow into Los Angeles is violated by the solution displayed in Figure 8.7, in which Los Angeles receives from the three OEMs a total of only 5 + 12 + 7 = 24. Also note in Figure 8.7 that the upper bounds on the arcs terminating at Los Angeles add to 13 + 30 + 14 = 57, a sum that is not sufficiently restrictive to guarantee that at most 50 containers will flow into Los Angeles.

How can collection nodes be used to obtain a network representation of this new modification?[13] The answer is diagrammed in Figure 8.9, where, for example, the Seattle collection node "collects" the flow on the arcs into Seattle from the three OEMs before "passing it on" to the Seattle node. Observe that every television destined for Seattle must first travel on arc 14-4, the arc directed from the Seattle

TABLE 8.4 Data for Contracts with MTV's Shipping Firms

Shipping Firm's Home Port	Upper Bound on Containers MTV Ships to Home Port	Lower Bound on Containers MTV Ships to Home Port
Seattle	45	20
Los Angeles	50	30

---

[13] Here's a hint! MTV's contract with the Seattle shipping firm pertains to the sum of the flow on all arcs terminating in Figure 8.7 at Seattle. A similar comment applies to MTV's contract with the Los Angeles firm.

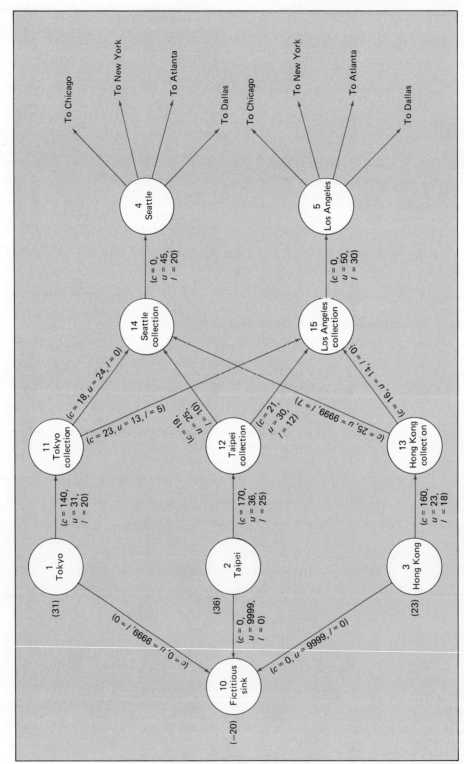

Figure 8.9 Using collection nodes associated with the shipping firms

collection node to the Seattle node. Consequently, the contractual bounds on the total flow into Seattle are associated with arc 14-4. The Los Angeles collection node performs a similar function for the total flow destined for Los Angeles.

Figure 8.10 displays the network representation of the fully modified version of Ned's decision problem, including the optimal solution we would obtain using NETOPT to minimize total *purchase and transportation costs*. Observe that the optimal solution permits Ned to answer the following five types of questions:

1. How many televisions does MTV purchase from each OEM? For example, the flow in Figure 8.10 on arc 3-13 indicates MTV purchases 18 containers from the Hong Kong OEM, an amount that satisfies the contractual bounds.

2. How many televisions does MTV ship from each of the three OEMs to each of the port cities of Seattle and Los Angeles? For example, the flows in Figure 8.10 on arcs 13-14 and 13-15 indicate that MTV divides its purchase of 18 containers from the Hong Kong OEM into respective shipments to Seattle and Los Angeles of 7 and 11.

3. How many televisions does MTV ship into each of the port cities of Seattle and Los Angeles? For example, the flow in Figure 8.10 on arc 14-4 indicates that MTV ships 40 containers into Seattle, an amount that satisfies the contractual bounds.

4. How many televisions does MTV ship from each of the port cities of Seattle and Los Angeles to each of MTV's four retail outlets? For example, the flows in Figure 8.10 on arcs 4-6, 4-7, 4-8, and 4-9 indicate that MTV divides the total shipments of 40 into Seattle into respective shipments to Chicago, New York, Atlanta, and Dallas of 4, 23, 8, and 5.

5. How many televisions does each of MTV's four retail outlets receive from each of the port cities of Seattle and Los Angeles? For example, the flows in Figure 8.10 on arcs 4-8 and 5-8 indicate that Atlanta's demand of 17 is satisfied with respective shipments from Seattle and Los Angeles of 8 and 9.

We can summarize the use of collection nodes as follows:

Suppose a cost and upper and lower bounds are associated with the total flow on a subset of arcs that originate (or terminate) at node *i*. Then we transform the network as follows:

- We add to the network a collection node associated with node *i*.

- If we are concerned about the total flow on a subset of arcs *originating* at node *i*, we force any flow on this subset of arcs to first "travel" on an arc *directed from node i into the collection node*. (This was the case in our example for the collection nodes used with the OEMs.) However, if we are concerned about the total flow on a subset of arcs *terminating* at node *i*, we force any flow on this subset of arcs to first "travel" on an arc *directed from the collection node into node i*. (This was the case in our example for the collection nodes used with the shipping firms.)

- Regardless of whether the collection node follows or precedes node *i*, the arc connecting node *i* and the collection node is given the unit cost and upper and lower bounds that apply to the total flow on the subset of arcs that previously originated or terminated at node *i* and now originate or terminate at the collection node.

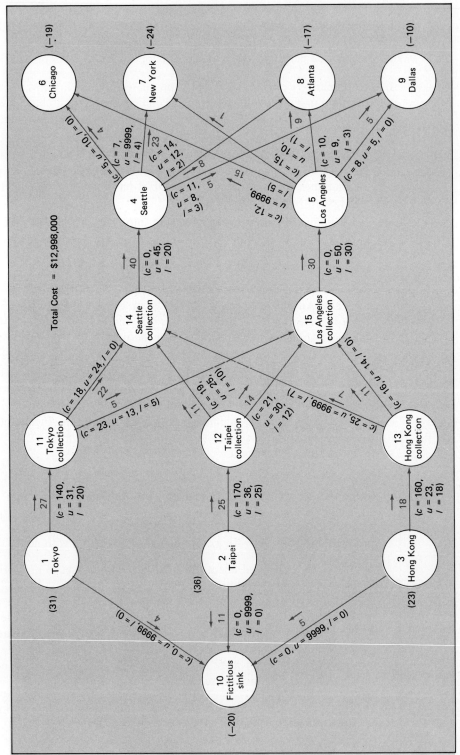

Figure 8.10 The optimal flows for the fully modified version of Ned's decision problem

364

In this and the preceding section, we have learned some "tricks" to keep a decision problem within the framework of a minimum-cost network flow problem. The end-of-chapter exercises will not only review these "tricks" but also introduce others.

8.6 FOUR SPECIAL CASES OF THE MINIMUM COST NETWORK FLOW PROBLEM

In this section we will consider four distinct classes of network optimization problems. We will demonstrate that each class has a network representation that is a special case of the minimum cost network flow problem.

For each class, three options exist for determining an optimal solution:

1. Given the network representation, we can formulate the corresponding network LP and employ a general-purpose LP software package (such as Chapter 3's hypothetical LINPRO).

2. As a more effective alternative, we can employ a special-purpose network software package designed for solving a minimum-cost network flow problem (such as this chapter's hypothetical NETOPT).

3. There is an even more effective alternative. Because each class of decision problems is a special case of the minimum-cost network flow problem, experts have devised special-purpose solution methods for each class of problems, methods significantly more efficient than the solution methods for the minimum-cost network flow problem. Software packages specially designed for each of the four classes of decision problems are widely available. Such special-purpose software packages not only require less computing effort to determine an optimal solution but also have simplified input and output that are specially tailored for the class of decision problems.

Space constraints preclude a detailed discussion of option 3. Consequently, in this section we will employ option 2, which is illustrated by the hypothetical NETOPT.

The Transportation Problem

As we learned in Section 4.5, the *transportation problem* concerns the optimal shipment of a commodity from a set of supply centers to a set of demand centers. As an example we introduced Graham Kracker's transportation problem. Before proceeding, you should quickly review Section 4.5's verbal statement of Graham's transportation problem and its subsequent formulation as an LP.

Our present goal is to develop a network representation of Graham's problem.

Figure 8.11 displays the appropriate network representation. Observe the following aspects of Figure 8.11:

- On the network's extreme left, a vertical column of three source nodes represent the plants, and on the network's extreme right a vertical column of five sink nodes represent the warehouses.

- To denote direct shipments from a plant to a warehouse, a directed arc connects each plant-warehouse combination. Only the unit flow cost appears

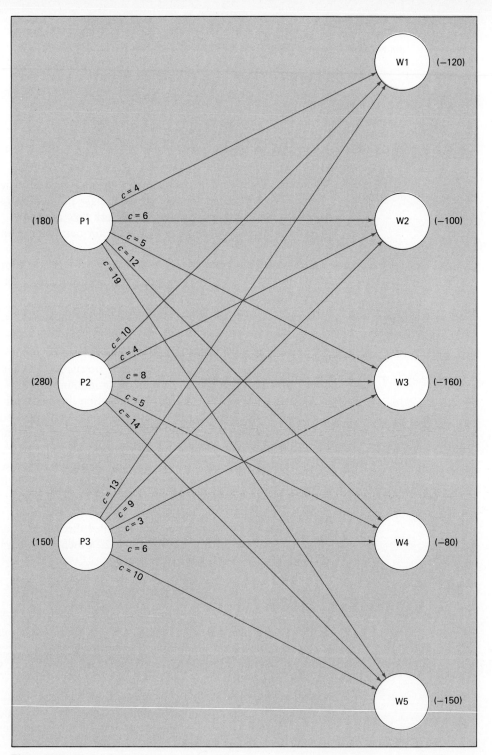

Figure 8.11 Network representation of Graham's transportation problem

adjacent to each arc. The upper and lower bounds have been omitted, because all arcs have upper bounds of $u = 9999$ and lower bounds of $l = 0$.

Figure 8.11 illustrates the following general principle:

A transportation problem is a special case of the minimum-cost network flow problem with the following three characteristics:

```
MINIMUM COST NETWORK FLOW PROBLEM

MINIMUM COST = 3780

    FROM            TO          FLOW

     P1             W1           120
     P1             W3            60
     P2             W2           100
     P2             W4            80
     P2             W5           100
     P3             W3           100
     P3             W5            50
```

Figure 8.12 NETOPT's output for the minimum-cost network flow problem equivalent to Graham's transportation problem

1. The network's nodes consist only of source nodes and sink nodes (i.e., no transshipment nodes exist).

2. Each of the network's arcs originates at a source node and terminates at a sink node (i.e., no shipments are possible from a source node to another source node, from a sink node to another sink node, or from a sink node to a source node).

3. Each of the network's arcs has upper and lower bounds of $u = 9999$ and $l = 0$, respectively.

Figure 8.12 displays the output from using NETOPT to solve the minimum-cost network flow problem equivalent to Graham's transportation problem.

Two further observations are of interest here:

- When total supply exceeds total demand in a transportation problem, we need to employ a fictitious sink node as we did in Section 8.4's excess-supply version of Ned Wurk's decision problem. (Similarly, if total demand exceeds total supply, we need to employ a fictitious source node.)

- If we wish to preclude shipments between a particular source-sink combination, we can either remove the corresponding arc from the network or else set the arc's unit flow cost to an arbitrarily large number, such as $c = 9999$.

The Assignment Problem

The *assignment problem* involves a number of tasks that must be assigned in an optimal way to an equal number of agents (e.g., people or machines), subject to the provision that each task must be assigned to exactly one agent. As an example of the assignment problem, consider the following scenario:

Moe T. Vator is the vice-president of sales for a firm that is planning to begin to market its products internationally. Moe has decided to organize his international sales staff into six major sales districts:

- Mexico, with district headquarters in Mexico City
- Canada, with district headquarters in Montreal
- South America, with district headquarters in Rio de Janeiro
- Europe, with district headquarters in Paris
- Middle East, with district headquarters in Cairo
- Far East, with district headquarters in Hong Kong

TABLE 8.5 Data for Moe's Assignment Problem: Percentage of Wrong Answers for Each Employee on Each Test

		SALES DISTRICT					
		Mexico (Mexico City)	Canada (Montreal)	South America (Rio de Janeiro)	Europe (Paris)	Middle East (Cairo)	Far East (Hong Kong)
EMPLOYEE	Jane	28	43	34	8	14	21
	Sally	39	12	23	47	53	18
	Mary	46	16	20	36	22	33
	Tom	21	47	13	29	19	26
	Dick	11	25	9	37	42	12
	Harry	15	23	51	11	10	19

Moe has been considering six employees—Jane, Sally, Mary, Tom, Dick, and Harry—as the sales managers for the six international sales districts. Moe must now decide how to assign the six employees to the six positions of district sales managers. Although several factors influence Moe's decision, he has decided the most important one is the employees' various familiarities with the dominant languages and cultures in the international sales districts. To measure this factor, Moe has administered to each employee a language and culture test for each sales district. Table 8.5 displays the percentage of *wrong* answers for each employee on each test. For example, Tom missed 29% of the questions on the European test. Given these scores, Moe wants to find the assignment of employees that minimizes the total percentage of test questions missed by the employees on the tests for the sales district to which they are assigned.

Moe can use Table 8.5 to evaluate any particular assignment of employees to sales districts. For example, suppose Moe chooses the assignment below, where each sales district is represented by its headquarters:

Employee		Assigned Headquarters	Employee's Percentage of Wrong Answers on Test for Corresponding Sales District
Jane	→	Paris	8
Sally	→	Montreal	12
Mary	→	Hong Kong	33
Tom	→	Mexico City	21
Dick	→	Rio de Janeiro	9
Harry	→	Cairo	10
			—
			93

The total percentage of wrong answers is 93.

One way to find the optimal solution to Moe's assignment problem is to explicitly enumerate all possible alternatives, compute the objective value for each, and select the best alternative. However, given that there are $6 \times 5 \times 4 \times 3 \times 2 \times 1 = 720$ possible alternatives, explicit enumeration would be a time-consuming and error-prone process.[14]

---

[14] The number of alternatives is obtained by noting that Moe has 6 choices for the Mexican position. Once he makes this choice, he has 5 choices for the Canadian position, then 4 choices for the South American position, and so on.

We can construct a network representation of Moe's assignment problem by imagining individuals "flowing" through a network, where each employee is represented by a source node with a supply of one individual, and each district headquarters is represented by a sink node with a demand for one individual. Figure 8.13 displays the network representation. Observe the following aspects of Figure 8.13:

- On the network's extreme left, a vertical column of six source nodes represent the six employees. As indicated by each source node's supply of 1, each employee is a "supply" of one individual capable of meeting the "demand" for one individual at any one of the six district headquarters.

- On the network's extreme right, a vertical column of six sink nodes represent

Figure 8.13 Network representation of Moe's assignment problem

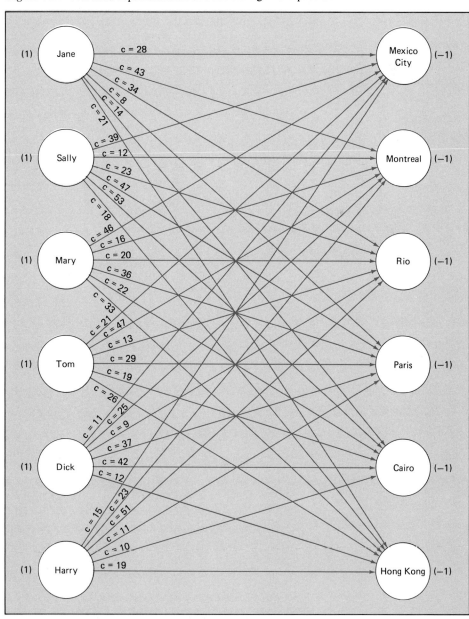

the six district headquarters. As indicated by each sink node's demand of 1, each headquarters has a "demand" for one individual.

■ To denote the alternative assignments of employees to headquarters, a directed arc connects each employee-headquarters combination. The unit flow costs adjacent to the arcs are not actual costs but instead are the percentages of wrong answers contained in Table 8.5. The arcs' upper and lower bounds do not appear adjacent to the arcs because all upper bounds equal $u = 9999$ and all lower bounds equal $l = 0$.

Since each arc is a direct connection between a source node with a supply of 1 and a sink node with a demand of 1, each arc will carry an optimal flow of either 0 or 1.[15] An optimal flow of 1 on the arc connecting a particular employee-headquarters combination indicates the combination is part of the optimal assignment; an optimal flow of 0 indicates otherwise.

You may have noticed that Figure 8.13's network representation of Moe's assignment problem has the same format as Figure 8.11's network representation of Graham's transportation problem. The only difference is that, in the network representation of the assignment problem, all supplies and demands equal 1. This illustrates the following general principle:

> An assignment problem is a special case of the transportation problem in which the supply at each source node and the demand at each sink node equal 1.

Figure 8.14 displays the output from using NETOPT to solve the minimum-cost network flow problem equivalent to Moe's assignment problem. We see that the optimal assignment has a total percentage of wrong test answers of 76 and consists of the following assignments:

Employee		Assigned Headquarters	Employee's Percentage of Wrong Answers on Test for Corresponding Sales District
Jane	→	Paris	8
Sally	→	Hong Kong	18
Mary	→	Montreal	16
Tom	→	Rio de Janeiro	13
Dick	→	Mexico City	11
Harry	→	Cairo	10
			—
			76

Two observations are of interest at this point:

■ When an assignment problem involves m agents and n tasks with $m > n$ (i.e., supply exceeds demand), we can add to the network $m - n$ fictitious sink nodes (each with a demand of 1) to represent $m - n$ fictitious tasks. A flow of 1 from a particular agent's source node to any of the fictitious sink nodes would indicate that the agent is not assigned to perform an actual task. Consequently, an arc directed from any agent's source node to any fictitious sink node should have a unit flow cost of $c = 0$.

---

[15] Recall from Section 8.2 that the optimal arc flows are guaranteed to have integer values.

MINIMUM-COST NETWORK FLOW PROBLEM

MINIMUM COST = 76

FROM	TO	FLOW
Jane	Paris	1
Sally	Hong Kong	1
Mary	Montreal	1
Tom	Rio	1
Dick	Mex. City	1
Harry	Cairo	1

Figure 8.14 NETOPT's output for the minimum-cost network flow problem equivalent to Moe's assignment problem

- If we wish to preclude the assignment of a particular agent to a particular task, we can either remove the corresponding arc from the network or, alternatively, we can set the arc's unit flow cost to an arbitrarily large number such as $c = 9999$. Note that this "trick" can be used when the number of agents exceeds the number of tasks and we wish to guarantee that a particular agent is assigned to an actual task. To obtain such a guarantee, we would simply set the unit flow costs equal to $c = 9999$ on all arcs directed from the agent's source node to the fictitious sink nodes (which represent fictitious tasks).

The Shortest-Path Problem

The *shortest-path problem* involves determining how to travel in a network from one specified node to another with the goal of minimizing either total cost, total distance, or total time. As an example, consider the following scenario:

> Dale Mation is the dispatcher at a fire station located in a large city. Figure 8.15 displays a network representing a portion of the city's intersections (nodes) and streets (arcs). Note that some streets are two-way, while others are one-way. The fire station's location is at node 1, and Dale has just received a report of a fire at node 9. The numbers adjacent to Figure 8.15's arcs represent current estimates of the travel times (in minutes) between the various intersections. These estimates are based on a

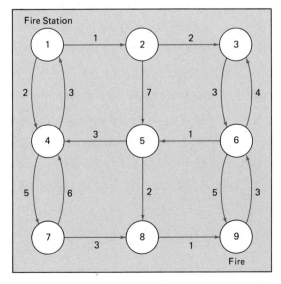

Figure 8.15 Dale's shortest-path problem

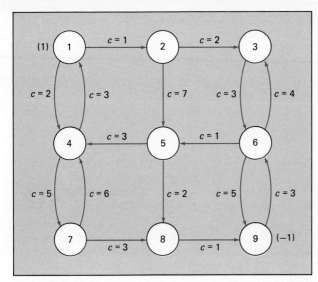

Figure 8.16 Network representation of Dale's shortest-path problem

computer program that periodically updates travel times according to current traffic and weather conditions. Note that, owing to different conditions, the travel time on arc i-j does not necessarily equal the travel time on arc j-i. Given an objective of minimizing the fire station's response time, Dale must now determine the path to follow from the fire station to the fire.

To convert Figure 8.15 into a network representation on Dale's shortest-path problem, we proceed as summarized below and as diagrammed in Figure 8.16:

- We regard node 1, the location of the fire station, as a source node with a supply of 1.
- We regard node 9, the location of the fire, as a sink node with a demand of 1.
- We regard the remaining seven nodes as transshipment nodes.
- We regard each arc's travel time as its unit flow cost. The arc's upper and lower bounds are omitted in Figure 8.16 because all upper bounds equal 9999 and all lower bounds equal 0.

When Figure 8.16's minimum-cost network flow problem is solved, the sequence of arcs followed by the 1 unit of flow from node 1 to node 9 will identify the "fastest" path from the fire station to the fire.

Figure 8.17 displays the output from using NETOPT to solve the minimum-

Figure 8.17 NETOPT's output for the minimum-cost network flow problem equivalent to Dale's shortest- path problem

MINIMUM-COST NETWORK FLOW PROBLEM

MINIMUM COST = 10

FROM	TO	FLOW
Node 1	Node 2	1
Node 2	Node 3	1
Node 3	Node 6	1
Node 6	Node 5	1
Node 5	Node 8	1
Node 8	Node 9	1

cost network flow problem equivalent to Dale's shortest-path problem. We see that the minimum response time to the fire is 10 minutes, achieved by the following path:

$$\text{node } 1 \rightarrow \text{node } 2 \rightarrow \text{node } 3 \rightarrow \text{node } 6 \rightarrow \text{node } 5 \rightarrow \text{node } 8 \rightarrow \text{node } 9.$$

Of course, Dale's problem is simple enough that you can probably solve it by explicitly enumerating every alternative path from node 1 to node 9. However, shortest-path problems arising in practice may involve hundreds, or even thousands, of nodes. Given a problem of this size, explicitly enumerating all paths is too time-consuming and error-prone.

To summarize:

> Given a network whose arcs have associated with them a distance (or cost or time), we can determine the shortest path (or cheapest path or fastest path) between a specified pair of nodes by solving a minimum-cost network flow problem obtained as follows:
>
> - Regard the node at which the path begins as a source node with a supply of 1.
>
> - Regard the node at which the path ends as a sink node with a demand of 1.
>
> - Regard all other nodes as transshipment nodes.
>
> - Regard the distance (or cost or time) associated with each arc as the arc's unit flow cost.
>
> After solving the minimum cost network flow problem, the shortest (or cheapest or fastest) path consists of those arcs with optimal flows of 1.

There are several variations of the shortest-path problem:

- Determining the shortest path from one specified node to another (the variation we have considered).
- Determining the shortest path from one specified node to every other node in the network.
- Determining the shortest path between all pairs of nodes in the network.

Experts have devised special-purpose solution methods for each variation.[16]

The Maximum-Flow Problem

In all network optimization problems considered thus far, our goal was to *minimize* the total value of the flow in the network, where the value was measured in terms of cost, distance, or time. Now, we consider a network optimization problem where our goal is to *maximize* the flow per unit time from one specified node to another.

---

[16] The efficiency of these special-purpose solution methods is lower if some arcs have negative costs and/or the network contains at least one cycle, where a cycle is a path from a node back to itself.

This is known as a *maximum-flow problem.* As an example, consider the following scenario:

> Gus Oline is the logistics manager of an oil company with an oil field in Texas. The crude oil from this field is pumped through a network of pumping stations and pipelines to an oil refinery in Louisiana. Figure 8.18 diagrams the network of pumping stations and pipelines that transport the oil from the field at node 1 to the refinery at node 10. The number adjacent to an arc is an upper bound on the oil flow in the pipeline the arc represents (where the flow is measured in thousands of gallons per minute). The upper bounds differ among the arcs because of varying pipe diameters, geographies, and other factors. Gus wants to determine the maximum oil flow per minute that can be pumped from the oil field to the oil refinery.

Gus's problem does not fit the standard framework of the minimum-cost network flow problem because it does not involve a specified supply of oil at node 1 (the oil field) that should flow through the network at minimum cost to satisfy a specified demand at node 10 (the refinery). Instead, no costs are involved, and the objective is to maximize the flow per minute from node 1 to node 10.

Fortunately, there is a "trick" that transforms Gus's maximum-flow problem into an equivalent minimum-cost network flow problem. This trick is diagrammed in Figure 8.19 and summarized below:

- To begin, we associate with node 1 (the oil field) an arbitrarily large supply of 9999, and we associate with node 10 (the refinery) an equal demand of 9999. Of course, given the arcs' upper bounds, it is impossible to have a flow of 9999 from node 1 to node 10.

- To circumvent this difficulty, we next add to the network a fictitious arc directed from node 1 to node 10 and having an upper bound of $u = 9999$.

Figure 8.18 Gus's maximum-flow problem

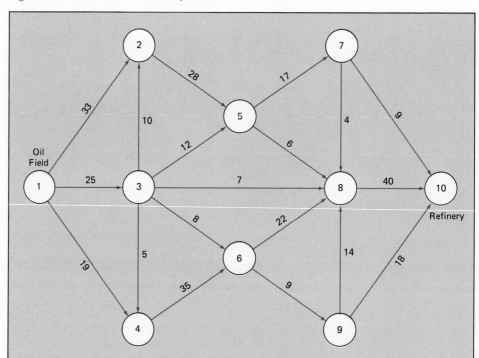

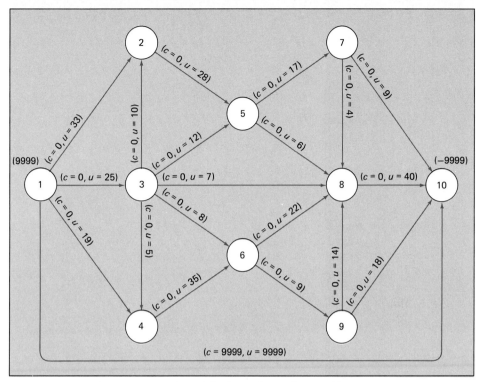

Figure 8.19 Network representation of Gus's maximum-flow problem

This fictitious arc will not carry an actual flow of oil but instead will carry a fictitious oil flow to artificially satisfy the portion of node 10's demand of 9999 that is unable to be satisfied by actual flows through the network's original arcs.

- To ensure that, to the extent possible, node 10's demand is met by actual flow rather than artificial flow, we associate with the fictitious arc an arbitrarily large unit flow cost of $c=9999$, and we associate with all other arcs a unit flow cost of $c=0$. Given the fictitious arc's extremely high unit flow cost, the oil flow will avoid the fictitious arc to the extent possible, thereby maximizing the oil flow through the network's original arcs. Of course, any flow above the maximum will be forced to travel on the fictitious arc. Observe in Figure 8.19 that the arcs' lower bounds have been omitted because they are all 0.

Once we have solved the equivalent minimum-cost network flow problem, we can easily determine the optimal solution for the original maximum-flow problem. The maximum flow is simply

$$9999 - \text{(the flow on the fictitious arc)}.$$

Figure 8.20 displays the output from using NETOPT to solve the minimum-cost network flow problem equivalent to Gus's maximum-flow problem. From the output's optimal flow of 9942 on the fictitious arc (arc 1-10), we compute the maximum flow as

$$9999 - \text{(flow on fictitious arc 1-10)} = 9999 - 9942 = 57.$$

The output also displays the optimal flow on each arc (when it is nonzero).

```
MINIMUM-COST NETWORK FLOW PROBLEM

MINIMUM COST = 99,410,058

    FROM          TO          FLOW

    Node 1       Node 2         19
    Node 1       Node 3         19
    Node 1       Node 4         19
    Node 1       Node 10      9942
    Node 2       Node 5         19
    Node 3       Node 4          5
    Node 3       Node 6          7
    Node 3       Node 8          7
    Node 4       Node 6         24
    Node 5       Node 7         13
    Node 5       Node 8          6
    Node 6       Node 8         22
    Node 6       Node 9          9
    Node 7       Node 8          4
    Node 7       Node 10         9
    Node 8       Node 10        39
    Node 9       Node 10         9
```

Figure 8.20 NETOPT's output for the minimum-cost network flow problem equivalent to Gus's maximum-flow problem

To summarize:

To transform a maximum-flow problem into an equivalent minimum-cost network flow problem, we proceed as follows:

- We associate with the node at which the flow originates an arbitrarily large supply of 9999, and we associate with the node at which the flow terminates an equal demand of 9999.

- We add to the network a fictitious arc directed from the source node to the sink node and having an upper bound of $u = 9999$.

- We associate with the fictitious arc an arbitrarily large unit flow cost of 9999, and we associate with every other arc a unit flow cost of 0. (We associate with all arcs lower bounds on flow of 0.)

After solving this equivalent minimum-cost network flow problem, we determine the maximum flow by subtracting from 9999 the flow on the fictitious arc.

Concluding Remarks

In this section we have seen the versatility of the minimum-cost network flow problem. More specifically, we have learned how to transform the transportation problem, the assignment problem, the shortest-path problem, and the maximum-flow problem into equivalent minimum-cost network flow problems.

376

8.7 THE MINIMUM-SPANNING-TREE PROBLEM

This section discusses a decision problem known as the *minimum-spanning-tree problem*. A problem of this sort arises during the design of a network that will interconnect a set of nodes at minimum cost. Unlike every other network optimization problem encountered in this chapter, the minimum-spanning-tree problem is *not* equivalent to a minimum-cost network flow problem. Nevertheless, we discuss it here because it is a common network design problem and because most network software packages include an option for solving a minimum-spanning-tree problem.

As an example, consider the following scenario:

> Stan Fird is the operations manager of a university's computer facilities. One of Stan's current decision problems concerns the creation of a campus wide electronic mail system. Installation of such a system entails linking the campus's various computers with underground communication cables. In the network displayed in Figure 8.21, each node represents the location of a computer, and each undirected arc represents a *potential* (not an existing) two-way connection between two computers via underground cable. The number adjacent to each arc is the cost (in thousands of dollars) of laying the underground cable along the route the arc represents (based on such factors as the distance and terrain involved). Stan's decision problem is to determine how to link the campus's computers at minimum cost.

While constructing all the potential arcs in Figure 8.21 would solve Stan's problem, such a solution clearly would not minimize costs. The solution must be a so-called *subnetwork* of Figure 8.21's network—that is, a portion of the entire network. The subnetwork must possess certain properties. To illustrate these properties, consider the three subnetworks indicated in **boldface** in Figures 8.22(a)–(c). Can you identify why none of them can be the optimal solution to Stan's problem? The reasons are as follows:

- Figure 8.22(a)'s subnetwork cannot be optimal because it does not include all the network's nodes. For example, node 7 does not belong to it. In network terminology, it is not a *spanning subnetwork*.

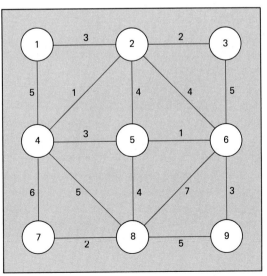

Figure 8.21 Stan's minimum-spanning-tree problem

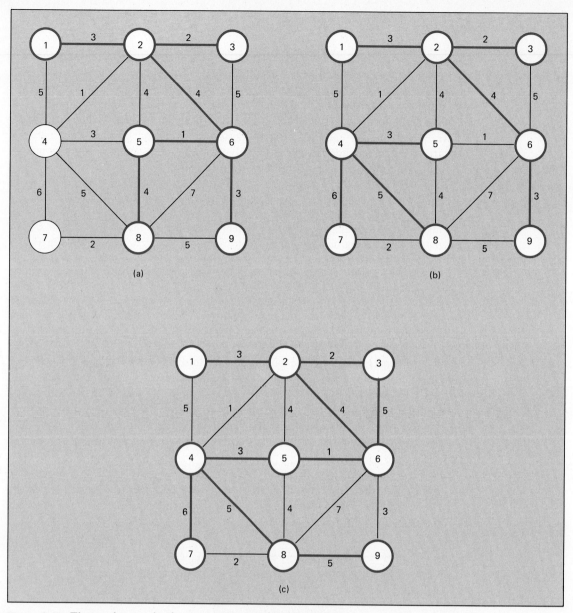

Figure 8.22 Three subnetworks that cannot be the optimal solution

- Figure 8.22(b)'s subnetwork cannot be optimal because, although it is a spanning subnetwork, there is not a communication path between every pair of nodes. For example, nodes 4 and 9 cannot communicate. In network terminology, it is not a *connected subnetwork*.

- Figure 8.22(c)'s subnetwork cannot be optimal because, although it is a connected spanning subnetwork, it contains a cycle among the nodes 2, 3, and 6.[17] By deleting any of the cycle's arcs from the subnetwork, we can reduce total cost and retain a connected spanning subnetwork. In network terminology, it is not an *acyclic subnetwork*.

---

[17] As defined in an earlier footnote, a cycle is a path from a node back to itself.

Figure 8.22's three subnetworks illustrate that the solution to Stan's problem must be a *connected, acyclic, spanning subnetwork*. Such a subnetwork is known as a *spanning tree*. Figure 8.23 displays one of the many spanning-tree solutions to Stan's problem. Observe that the spanning tree is connected and acyclic and spans the network's nodes. Also observe that the spanning tree contains nine nodes and eight arcs, thereby illustrating the following general principle:

| If a network contains n nodes, any spanning tree contains $n - 1$ arcs.

Stan cannot solve his problem by finding just any spanning tree. He must find the so-called *minimum spanning tree* — that is, the spanning tree with the lowest total construction costs. For example, the total construction cost for Figure 8.26's spanning tree is the sum of the costs adjacent to the **boldface** arcs — namely, $3 + 2 + 5 + 3 + 1 + 4 + 2 + 5 = 25$. As we will soon see, Figure 8.23's spanning tree is not the minimum spanning tree.

The solution procedure for determining the minimum spanning tree is one of the simplest in all of management science. Its simplicity stems from the fact that we obtain the optimal solution by being "greedy" at each step of the procedure. This provides a rare exception to the general principle that being greedy in the early stages of a solution procedure typically leads to unattractive alternatives in the later stages of the solution procedure, thereby resulting in a nonoptimal solution.

The minimum-spanning-tree problem's solution procedure is easily summarized as follows:

To solve a minimum-spanning-tree problem involving n nodes, begin with a subnetwork consisting of one arbitrarily selected node and no arcs and then perform $n - 1$ repetitions of the following iterative step:

- Add to the current subnetwork the cheapest arc that connects any node within the current subnetwork to any node outside the current subnetwork. (If there is a tie for the cheapest arc, break the tie arbitrarily.)

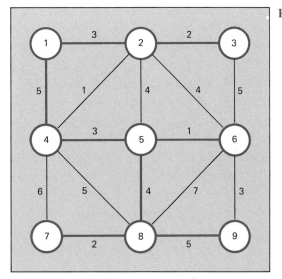

Figure 8.23 A spanning tree

Let us employ this procedure to solve Stan Fird's minimum-spanning-tree problem:

- **Iteration 1.** We arbitrarily select as the starting subnetwork the subset consisting of node 1 and no arcs, thereby beginning with the **boldface** subnetwork displayed in Figure 8.24(a). We see that the arcs that connect the nodes within the subnetwork (only node 1) to the nodes outside the subnetwork (all nodes except node 1) are

Arc	Cost
1-2	3
1-4	5

The cheaper of these is arc 1-2. After arc 1-2 is added, the subnetwork appears as displayed in boldface in Figure 8.24(b).

Figure 8.24 Finding the minimum spanning tree

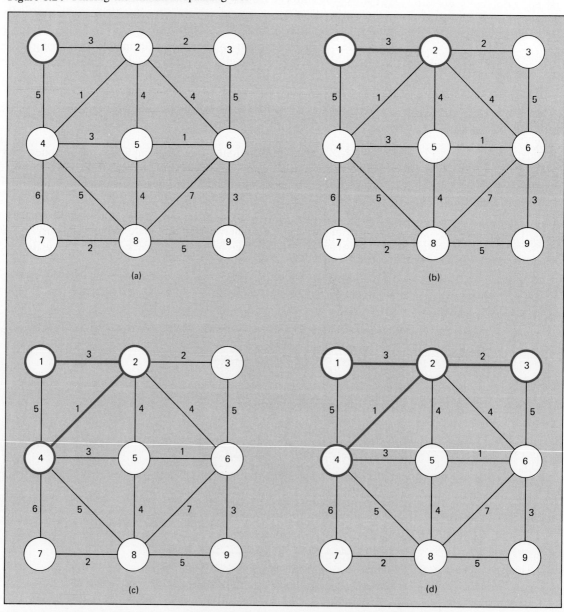

■ **Iteration 2.** Looking at Figure 8.24(b), we see that the arcs that connect a node within the subnetwork (node 1 or 2) to a node outside the subnetwork (nodes 3 through 9) are

Arc	Cost
1-4	5
2-3	2
2-4	1
2-5	4
2-6	4

The cheapest of these is arc 2-4. After arc 2-4 is added, the subnetwork appears as displayed in boldface in Figure 8.24(c).

■ **Iteration 3.** Looking at Figure 8.24(c), we see that the arcs that connect a node within the subnetwork (node 1, 2, or 4) to a node outside the subnetwork (node 3 or nodes 5 through 9) are

Arc	Cost
2-3	2
2-5	4
2-6	4
4-5	3
4-7	6
4-8	5

The cheapest of these is arc 2-3. After arc 2-3 is added, the subnetwork appears as displayed in boldface in Figure 8.24(d).

■ **Iterations 4 through 8.** You should verify for yourself that the remaining five iterations successively add the following arcs to the subnetwork:

Iteration	Added Arc
4	4-5
5	5-6
6	6-9
7	5-8
8	8-7

After eight iterations, then, we obtain the spanning tree displayed in boldface in Figure 8.25. Note that Figure 8.25's spanning tree has a total cost of $3 + 2 + 1 + 3 + 1 + 3 + 4 + 2 = 19$, an amount less than Figure 8.23's spanning tree.

The proof that the above procedure results in the minimum spanning tree is beyond the scope of this text. However, to intuitively convince yourself that Figure 8.25's spanning tree is optimal, do the following:

■ Arbitrarily select any arc that is not a member of Figure 8.25's spanning tree.

■ Add this arc to the spanning tree, thereby creating a cycle. Delete any arc from the cycle (except the newly added arc), thereby obtaining a new spanning tree.

■ Note that this new spanning tree has a higher total cost because the added arc's cost exceeds the deleted arc's cost.

For example, the addition of arc 1-4 to Figure 8.25's spanning tree creates a cycle that can be broken by deleting arc 1-2 or arc 2-4. Regardless of which arc is

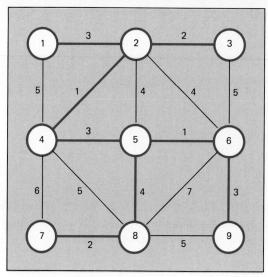

Figure 8.25 The minimum spanning tree

deleted, the new spanning tree has an increased total cost, since the added arc's cost of 5 exceeds the cost of the deleted arc, either 3 or 1.

You can test your understanding of how to determine a minimum spanning tree by resolving Stan's problem. Recall that the choice of the node at which the solution procedure begins is arbitrary. As indicated in Figure 8.24(a), we chose to begin at node 1. You can now make a different choice and verify that, regardless of your choice, you obtain the minimum spanning tree displayed in boldface in Figure 8.25.

We conclude this section by noting that Stan's minimum-spanning-tree problem involved cost. In other applications, the number associated with each potential arc might not represent the cost of constructing the arc but instead might represent the distance traversed in constructing the arc or the time required to construct the arc. In such applications, the minimum-spanning-tree's solution procedure determines the minimum-distance spanning tree or the minimum-time spanning tree.

8.8 CONCLUDING REMARKS

Our discussion of network optimization problems has just "scratched the surface" of this topic. Entire textbooks have been written about it, and there are consulting firms that deal exclusively with network optimization problems. Some important classes of network optimization problems we were unable to consider in this chapter include the following:

- **Dynamic network optimization problems.** We considered only *static network optimization problems* — that is, ones in which all flows occurred during a single time period. In many practical applications, the flows occur over several time periods. Such network optimization problems are known as *dynamic network optimization problems*. In dynamic network optimization problems, a different node represents a particular geographical location in each time period. For example, if it takes two days to ship from Boston to Dallas, a portion of the network might appear as displayed in Figure 8.37. The flow on the arc directed from node B6 to node D8 (or from B7 to D9) represents a shipment that leaves Boston on day 6 (or day 7) and arrives two

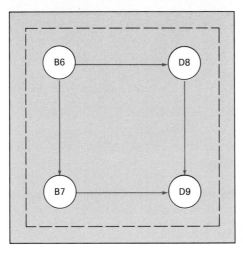

Figure 8.26 A portion of a dynamic network

days later in Dallas, whereas the flow on the arc directed from node B6 to node B7 represents inventory held over in Boston from day 6 to day 7.

- **Networks having arcs with flow loss or gain.** In the networks we considered, if 10 units of flow left node i on arc i-j, 10 units of flow arrived at node j. In some applications, flow traveling on an arc undergoes a loss or a gain. Associated with each arc then is the arc's loss or gain factor. For example, arcs with loss factors arise in water distribution networks, where flow is lost due to evaporation or seepage. Arcs with gain factors occur in dynamic networks arising in financial planning, where nodes i and j represent different time periods and, thus, the cash flow leaving node i on arc i-j has earned interest by the time it arrives at node j. Given a loss factor for arc i-j of, say, 0.9, if 10 units of flow leave node i on arc i-j, only 9 units of flow arrive at node j. Similarly, given a gain factor for arc i-j of, say, 1.1, if 10 units of flow leave node i on arc i-j, 11 units of flow arrive at node j.

- **Multicommodity network optimization problems.** We considered only *single-commodity network optimization problems* — that is, ones in which only a single commodity was flowing through the network. As its name suggests, a *multicommodity network optimization problem* arises when several commodities flow through the same network. In a multicommodity network, each node has associated with it a supply or demand for each commodity, and each arc has associated with it the following data:

  1. A unit flow cost for each commodity.

  2. An upper bound and a lower bound for each commodity's flow on the arc.

  3. An upper bound and lower bound on the total flow on the arc for all commodities.

  Multicommodity networks arise in communication networks, urban traffic networks, rail networks, and multiproduct distribution networks.

- **Optimal vehicle routing in a network.** In many decision problems, a fleet of vehicles must render a service at minimal cost to the nodes or the arcs of a network. As an example of a service to a network's nodes, consider a fleet of school busses picking up children at designated bus stops and delivering them to a school. As an example of a service to a network's arcs, consider a fleet of street sweepers (or snow removal vehicles) cleaning the streets of a city.

8.9 CHAPTER CHECKLIST AND GLOSSARY

Quickly review this chapter by rereading the material highlighted by a vertical line in the left margin. You should then be familiar with the concepts, techniques and terminology in the Checklist and Glossary that follow. If you need "help" with a particular item, consult the section or sections indicated for a more detailed discussion.

Checklist of Concepts and Techniques

- ☐ Given a verbal statement of a network optimization problem, construct the corresponding network representation. [8.1, 8.2]

- ☐ Given the network representation of a decision problem, formulate the corresponding network linear program. [8.1, 8.2]

- ☐ Given a network representation, construct the corresponding node-arc incidence matrix, and, given a node-arc incidence matrix, construct the corresponding network representation. [8.1, 8.2, 8.7]

- ☐ The three primary reasons the minimum cost network flow problem is so widely-used. [8.2]

- ☐ Using a network software package. [8.3]

- ☐ Using a fictitious sink node to transform a network with excess supply into an equivalent network in which total supply equals total demand. [8.4]

- ☐ Using a collection node when the total flow on a subset of arcs originating (or terminating) at a particular node has associated with it a unit cost, an upper bound, and a lower bound. [8.5]

- ☐ How to formulate the following network optimization problems as special cases of the minimum-cost network flow problem: the transportation problem, the assignment problem, the shortest-path problem, and the maximum-flow problem. [8.6]

- ☐ Solving a minimum-spanning-tree problem. [8.7]

Glossary

Network. A set of nodes interconnected by a set of arcs. [8.1]

Source node. A node with a supply of the commodity flowing through the network. [8.1]

Sink node. A node with a demand for the commodity flowing through the network. [8.1]

Transshipment node. A node with neither a supply of nor a demand for the commodity flowing through the network. [8.1]

Network linear program. A linear program having the special structure that, if the decision variables' upper and lower bound constraints are ignored, each decision variable appears exactly twice in the remaining structural constraints, once with a coefficient of $+1$ and once with a coefficient of -1. [8.1]

Flow balance equations. The fundamental constraints in a network linear program that ensure that, for each node, the flow on the arcs originating at the node minus the flow on the arcs terminating at the node equals the node's supply. [8.1]

Node-arc incidence matrix. A tabular representation of a network linear program. [8.1]

384

Minimum-cost network flow problem. This chapter's most general network optimization problem, in which the objective is to minimize the total cost of the flow of some commodity from the source nodes to the sink nodes, subject to a flow balance constraint at each node and upper and lower bounds constraints on the flow on each arc. [8.1]

Directed arc. An arc between two nodes that permits flow only in the specified direction. [8.2]

Undirected arc. An arc between two nodes that permits travel in both directions. [8.2]

Fictitious node. A node added to the network not because it represents a real geographical location but because it enables a decision problem to have a network representation (e.g., when total supply exceeds total demand). [8.4]

Collection node. A node added to a network when the total flow on a subset of arcs originating (or terminating) at a particular node has associated with it a unit cost, an upper bound, and a lower bound. [8.5]

Transportation problem. A network optimization problem whose objective is to minimize the total cost of direct shipments from a set of source nodes to a set of sink nodes. [8.6]

Assignment problem. A network optimization problem whose objective is to identify the best assignment of agents to tasks. [8.6]

Path. A sequence of arcs leading from one node to another. [8.6]

Cycle. A path from a node back to itself. [8.6]

Shortest-path problem. A network optimization problem whose objective is to minimize the total distance, total cost, or total time required to travel from one specified node to another specified node. [8.6]

Maximum-flow problem. A network optimization problem whose objective is to maximize the flow through a network from one specified node to another specified node. [8.6]

Subnetwork. A network consisting of a portion of the nodes and arcs of the original network. [8.7]

Spanning subnetwork. A subnetwork that includes all the nodes of the original network [8.7]

Connected network. A network in which every pair of nodes has at least one path between them. [8.7]

Acyclic network. A network containing no cycles. [8.7]

Spanning tree. A connected, acyclic, spanning subnetwork of the original network. [8.7]

Minimum-spanning-tree problem. A network optimization problem whose objective is to find the cheapest spanning tree within a given network. [8.7]

EXERCISES

In the exercises below, you will repeatedly encounter a sentence similar to "Draw a network representation of the decision problem." This means to formulate the problem as a minimum-cost network flow problem not only by drawing the network's nodes and arcs, but also by labeling each node with a supply or demand (if any) and each arc with a unit flow cost, an upper bound on flow on the arc, and a lower bound on flow on the arc.

Exercises 8.1–8.7 test your ability to formulate a decision problem as a minimum-cost network flow problem.

8.1. A manufacturer of a single product has 3 plants, 2 warehouses, and 3 customers geographically dispersed throughout the country. The tables below display the production capacity at each plant and the demand by each customer for the upcoming month:

Plant	1	2	3
Capacity	300	200	500

Customer	1	2	3
Demand	300	600	100

Note that total capacity equals total demand. The table below displays the unit transportation cost (in dollars) between each plant-warehouse combination and between each warehouse-customer combination.

	Warehouse	
	1	2
Plant 1	1	5
Plant 2	6	2
Plant 3	3	4

	Customer		
	1	2	3
Warehouse 1	6	4	3
Warehouse 2	2	5	1

The manufacturer wants to distribute its product from the plants to the warehouses and then on to the customers at minimum cost. (Note that a plant never ships directly to a customer.)

(a) Draw the network representation of the manufacturer's decision problem.

(b) Formulate the corresponding linear program, and then display the LP's data in a node-arc incidence matrix.

(c) Now assume that the contracts with the trucking firms the manufacturer uses to transport the product contain the following stipulations:

1. The amount shipped from plant 2 to warehouse 1 must be at least 50 units and at most 125 units.

2. The amount shipped from warehouse 2 to customer 3 must be at least 25 units and at most 75 units.

Make the necessary modifications to part (a)'s network.

(d) Besides the assumption in part (c), now assume that the production capacity at plant 2 is 400 instead of 200, thereby causing total production capacity to exceed total demand. Make the necessary modifications to part (c)'s network, assuming the manufacturer is indifferent about which plants produce at less than capacity.

(e) Besides the assumptions in parts (c) and (d), now assume that each plant has associated with it a unit production cost and a minimum production quantity. The following table summarizes these data for the upcoming month:

Plant	Unit Production Cost	Minimum Production Quantity
1	13	100
2	15	150
3	11	125

Make the necessary modifications to part (d)'s network, assuming that the objective is now to minimize the total production and transportation costs.

(f) Besides the assumptions in parts (c)–(e), now assume that the manufacturer wants each warehouse to process approximately the same amount of product. In particular, of the total of 1000 units that must be shipped to the customers, no warehouse should ship more than 60% of the total. Make the necessary modifications to part (e)'s network.

(g) Besides the assumptions in parts (c)–(f), now assume that the contracts with the trucking firms stipulate that the total amount shipped into warehouse 2 from plants 1 and 2 must be at least 200 and at most 500. Make the necessary modifications to part (f)'s network.

8.2. Reconsider Exercise 8.1, ignoring the additional assumptions made in parts (c)–(g). Now assume that the production capacities specified in the exercise represent supplies of units that have already been produced rather than units that could be produced if needed. Also assume that the supply at plant 2 is 400 instead of 200, thereby causing total supply to exceed total demand. This means that, after shipments have been made to the warehouses, one or more plants will have units remaining in inventory. The following table displays the estimated unit cost the manufacturer incurs for storing a unit for one month at each plant:

Plant	1	2	3
Unit Storage Cost per Month	5	3	4

The manufacturer wants to minimize the total transportation and storage costs incurred in the upcoming month for satisfying its customers' demands. Draw the network representation of the manufacturer's problem.

8.3. Reconsider Exercise 8.1, ignoring the additional assumptions made in parts (c)–(g). Now assume that the production capacity at plant 2 is 100 instead of 200, thereby causing total demand to exceed total production capacity. This means that the demand at one or more customers cannot be fully satisfied.

According to contracts with the customers, the manufacturer must pay a customer a penalty for each unit of unsatisfied demand. The table below displays these penalties:

Customer	1	2	3
Unit Penalty Cost	5	3	4

The manufacturer wants to minimize the total transportation and penalty costs if each plant produces and ships at capacity.

(a) Draw the network representation of the manufacturer's problem.

(b) What modifications to part (a)'s network are necessary if there are no unit penalty costs associated with unsatisfied demand?

*8.4. Oil in the amount of 25 million barrels must be transported from Kuwait to the ports of Rotterdam, Marseille, and Naples in Europe. The respective demands at these ports are 6, 14, and 5 million barrels. The oil may travel along any of the following three alternative routes:

1. From Kuwait, around the southern tip of Africa, and then on to Rotterdam, Marseille, and Naples. The respective transportation costs are $1.80, $2.10, and $2.00 per barrel. At least 20% of the oil must use this route, because of the need to use large tankers to transport this amount of oil.

2. From Kuwait to the city of Suez, through the Suez Canal to Port Said, and then on to Rotterdam, Marseille, and Naples. The transportation cost from Kuwait to the city of Suez is $0.45 per barrel, and the additional cost of transporting through the canal is $0.30 per barrel. From Port Said to Rotterdam, Marseille, and Naples, the respective transportation costs are $0.38, $0.30, and $0.23 per barrel.

3. From Kuwait to the city of Suez (as described in item 2), but then through a pipeline from Suez to Alexandria. The pipeline has a capacity of 10 million barrels and the transportation cost is $0.22 per barrel. From Alexandria to Rotterdam, Marseille, and Naples, the respective transportation costs are $0.33, $0.25, and $0.21 per barrel.

The objective is to transport the oil from Kuwait to the European ports at minimum cost.

(a) Draw the network representation of this problem.

(b) Suppose the total amount shipped from Port Said to the European ports must be at least 5 and at most 9 million barrels. What modifications to part (a)'s network are necessary?

(c) Use a network software package to solve the problem, ignoring part (b)'s modification.

8.5. An agricultural cooperative grows wheat on farms at locations A and B, ships it to mills at locations C and D, where it is processed, and sends it to distribution centers E, F, and G, where it is sold to customers. Relevant data are:

■ The maximum possible wheat harvests at farms A and B are 600 and 500 tons, respectively.

■ The cost of growing and harvesting at farms A and B are $2 per ton and $2.25 per ton, respectively.

■ Any wheat not sent to be milled is sold at a wheat auction at a price of $2.50 per ton. In the tables below, the wheat auction's location is denoted by H.

■ The processing capacities of mills C and D are 800 and 600 tons, respectively. Each mill must operate at least 50% of capacity.

■ The cost of milling at mills C and D are $1 per ton and $1.10 per ton, respectively.

■ The demands (that must be met) at distribution centers E, F, and G are 250, 350, and 300 tons, respectively.

■ Shipping costs (in dollars per ton) are given by the following tables:

	To C	To D	To H
From A	.40	.30	.35
From B	.33	.25	.05

	To E	To F	To G
From C	.10	.20	.15
From D	.12	.18	1.7

(a) Draw a network representation of this problem.

(b) Use a network software package to solve the problem.

8.6. The Woodstock Chair Company has 4 plants located around the country. For each plant, the table below displays a chair's unit manufacturing cost (*exclusive* of the necessary wood) and the minimum and maximum production for the upcoming month:

Plant	Unit Manufacturing Cost	Maximum Production	Minimum Production
1	$5	600	0
2	$7	700	400
3	$3	400	200
4	$4	300	100

Woodstock purchases wood from two sources (1 and 2). Contracts with these suppliers stipulate the following for the upcoming month:

- From wood source 1, Woodstock must buy an amount of wood equivalent to at least 400 chairs and at most 900 chairs. The cost for wood equivalent to one chair is $3.
- From wood source 2, Woodstock must buy an amount of wood equivalent to at least 500 and at most 800 chairs. The cost for wood equivalent to one chair is $2.

The table below displays the shipping cost between each wood source and each plant, expressed in terms of dollars per an amount of wood equivalent to one chair:

		Plant			
		1	2	3	4
Wood	1	0.20	0.40	0.80	0.70
Source	2	0.80	0.60	0.40	0.30

Woodstock sells the chairs in three cities (1, 2, and 3). For the upcoming month the tables below display each city's demand for chairs and the transportation cost per chair (in dollars) between each plant-city combination:

City	1	2	3
	600	400	500

		City			
		1	2	3	4
Plant	1	1	1	2	5
	2	3	6	7	3
	3	3	1	5	3
	4	8	2	1	4

Woodstock wants to minimize the total cost of wood purchases, chair production, and wood and chair transportation.

(a) Draw the network representation of this problem.

(b) Now suppose there is no upper limit on the amount of wood Woodstock can buy from either wood source. (The lower limits still apply.) What modifications are necessary to part (a)'s network?

(c) Use a network software package to solve the problem, ignoring part (b)'s modification.

8.7. Six families are coming to a dinner party. The hostess wants to seat the guests at five tables in such a

manner that no two members of the same family are seated at the same table. The tables below display the number of seats at each table and the number of members in each family:

Table	1	2	3	4	5
Number of Seats	5	4	3	3	2

Family	1	2	3	4	5	6
Number of Members	4	4	3	2	2	2

(a) Draw the network representation of the hostess's problem. (*Hints*: Regard the tables as having supplies and the families as having demands. Also, since only a feasible solution is desired, the unit flow costs may be chosen arbitrarily.)

(b) Use a network software package to solve the hostess's problem.

(c) Repeat parts (a) and (b), this time using the following data:

Table	1	2	3	4	5	Family	1	2	3	4	5
Number of Seats	6	5	2	2	2	Number of Members	4	4	4	3	2

(Note that there are now only five families.) When you solve the revised problem, what do you discover?

Exercises 8.8–8.14 test your understanding of four special cases of the minimum-cost network flow problem: the transportation problem, the assignment problem, the shortest-path problem, and the maximum-flow problem.

*8.8. Reconsider the transportation problem in Exercise 4.6. Draw the network representation of the problem.

8.9. In preparation for the upcoming winter's ice and snow, the city of Northville must replenish the four sites (A, B, C, and D) at which it maintains sand and salt stockpiles. The table below displays the number of truckloads each site requires:

Site	A	B	C	D
Demand	80	90	60	70

Northville has asked three suppliers (1, 2, and 3) to bid on contracts to supply the four sites. They have responded as follows:

- Supplier 1 has stated that it can provide Northville with a total of at most 100 truckloads. The

388

cost per truckload delivered to sites A, B, C, and D are $50, $56, $40, and $68, respectively.

- Supplier 2 has stated that it can provide Northville with a total of at most 130 truckloads. The cost per truckload delivered to sites A, B, C, and D are $40, $60, $75, and $58, respectively.
- Supplier 3 has stated that it can provide Northville with a total of at most 120 truckloads. The cost per truckload delivered to sites A, B, C, and D are $46, $36, $50, and $64, respectively.

Northville may award a supplier a contract to provide all or just part of the demand at any site and may also award a supplier contracts for more than one site. Northville wants to award the contracts in a way that minimizes total cost.

(a) Draw the network representation of Northville's problem.

(b) Formulate the corresponding linear program.

(c) Use a network software package to determine the problem's optimal solution.

*8.10. Reconsider the assignment problem in Exercise 4.18.

(a) Draw a network representation of the original version of the problem (that is, ignore the modifications made in parts (b) and (c)).

(b) Now assume that, as described in parts (b) and (c) of Exercise 4.18, a fifth candidate named Harry is available and that Harry must be given a job. What modifications to part (a)'s network are necessary?

8.11. In a swimming competition, the 200-meter medley relay is an event in which four different swimmers each swim 50 meters using one of four different strokes: backstroke, breast stroke, butterfly, and freestyle. The table below displays a coach's best estimate of how fast (in seconds) each of four swimmers can swim each stroke for 50 meters:

Swimmer	Stroke			
	Backstroke	Breast Stroke	Butterfly	Freestyle
Stephanie	37.7	43.4	33.3	29.2
Gwen	32.9	33.1	28.5	26.4
June	33.8	42.2	38.9	29.6
Barbara	37.0	34.7	30.4	28.5

The coach wants to determine the optimal assignment of swimmers to strokes.

(a) Draw a network representation of the coach's problem.

(b) Formulate the corresponding linear program.

(c) Suppose that, besides the above four swimmers, a fifth swimmer named Sara is also under consideration. This means one of the five swimmers will not be a member of the relay team. Sara's estimated times in the four events are 35.4 for the backstroke, 41.8 for the breast

stroke, 33.6 for the butterfly, and 31.1 in the freestyle. What modifications to part (a)'s network are necessary?

(d) Use a network software package to solve the original version of the coach's problem (i.e., with only four swimmers).

8.12. Consider the following network:

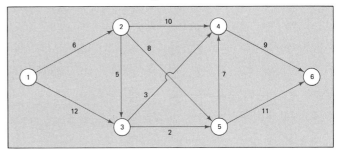

Suppose that the number adjacent to an arc represents the distance between the two nodes it connects. Draw a network representation of the problem of finding the shortest path from node 1 to node 6.

8.13. A state government plans to construct a new freeway connecting two of each major cities, Westtown and Eastville. In the network below, each arc represents an alternative road segment that can be constructed.

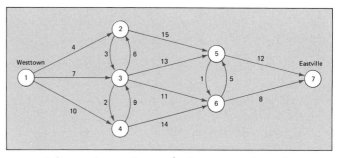

Because of many factors (such as geography and required land purchases), the cost of constructing a road segment varies. The costs (in millions of dollars) are indicated by the numbers adjacent to the arcs.

(a) Draw a network representation of the problem of finding the cheapest route for the road to follow between Westtown and Eastville.

(b) Formulate the corresponding linear program.

(c) Use a network software package to solve the problem.

8.14. Reconsider the network in Exercise 8.12. Now assume that the number adjacent to an arc represents an upper bound on the flow on the arc of a particular commodity. Draw a network representation of the problem of finding the maximum flow from node 1 to node 6.

389

Exercises 8.15 and 8.16 involve manually solving a minimum-spanning-tree problem using the procedure discussed in Section 8.8.

*8.15. Solve the minimum-spanning-tree problem for the network below:

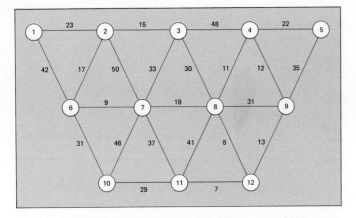

8.16. In the network shown in the next column, each node represents an offshore natural-gas wellhead, and each arc represents a *potential* (not an existing) pipeline connection between two wellheads. The number adjacent to each arc is the cost (in thousands of dollars) of constructing the pipeline the arc represents.

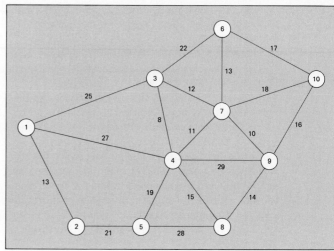

Since the wellhead at node 1 is the closest to shore, it will pump the output of all wells to the on-shore delivery point. The problem is to determine the least expensive way to construct a pipeline connection that will link the wellhead at node 1 to the remaining wellheads. Manually solve this minimum-spanning-tree problem.

INTEGER LINEAR PROGRAMMING

9.1 INTRODUCTION

When some or all decision variables of a linear program (LP) are restricted to be integer-valued, we refer to the resulting problem as an *integer linear program (ILP)*. As illustrated by this chapter's examples and exercises, many important decision problems can be formulated as ILPs.

Of course, a successful application of integer linear programming requires not only the formulation of an ILP but also its solution. Since the early 1960s, management scientists have known of algorithms that guaranteed, in theory, to solve any ILP in a finite number of steps. Practitioners in the 1960s quickly discovered that such guarantees were meaningless, because in the vast majority of cases the limitations on the speed and storage capacity of existing computers precluded the termination of the algorithms. It is fair to summarize the status of integer linear programming in the 1960s, and even into the 1970s, as practitioners formulating ILPs that could rarely be solved and theoreticians devising algorithms that could rarely be used in practice.

The gap between the theory and practice of integer linear programming began to narrow in the mid-1970s and continues to narrow each year. Today's practitioners recognize integer linear programming as a valuable decision-making tool capable of providing insight into the solution of a wide variety of important decision problems, including such strategic problems as capital budgeting and plant location.

In discussing linear programming, we stressed that one or more of the decision variables in an LP's optimal solution might assume noninteger values—that is, values having fractional parts such as $61\frac{5}{7}$ or ₁82.59. In many contexts, a decision variable with a noninteger value has a meaningful interpretation. For example, in a product mix problem, an optimal hourly production rate of $6\frac{1}{4}$ items per hour for a certain product is perfectly acceptable. Also, in a blending problem, it is meaningful to have the optimal blending "recipe" call for 39.75 gallons of a particular ingredient. However, in many other contexts the decision variables represent indivisible items or activities and, thus, must assume integer values in order to have meaningful interpretations. For example, the optimal solution of an airline's capacity expansion problem cannot call for the purchase of $5\frac{4}{9}$ new 727 aircraft and $1\frac{1}{2}$ new 747 aircraft. Also, in a capital budgeting problem in which the nature of the projects requires that each be fully accepted or fully rejected, the optimal decision cannot call for accepting $\frac{3}{5}$ of one project, $\frac{1}{3}$ of another project, and $\frac{7}{8}$ of yet another project. These are but two examples of the wide variety of important decision problems requiring the formulation of an ILP—that is, an LP where some or all decision variables must assume integer values.

We must stress an important aspect of integer linear programming. Simply put:

> While formulating an ILP is generally as easy as formulating an LP, optimally solving an ILP is generally much more difficult than optimally solving an LP that has the same number of decision variables and structural constraints.

The mere addition of the sentence, "All variables must assume integer values," to an LP converts the problem from one that can be efficiently solved by the simplex method into one that will generally require much more time and effort to solve. This phenomenon results from the fact that the algorithms for solving ILPs are quite inefficient in comparison with the simplex method. When solving an LP via a state-of-the-art computer implementation of the simplex method, there is no practical limit on the number of decision variables. As a rule of thumb, the inclusion of 100 structural constraints results in a small problem; 1000, a medium-sized problem; and 10,000, a large problem. In contrast, an ILP with 100 variables and 100 constraints may be quite difficult to solve. Consequently, while we can find optimal solutions for all but a few of the large-scale LPs arising in practice, for many of the large-scale ILPs it is virtually impossible to do so. This limitation does not diminish the importance of integer linear programming as a decision-making tool. Fortunately, when an ILP is too large to solve optimally, we can frequently use a *heuristic*— a method that produces a solution that is rarely optimal but often acceptably close-to-optimal and almost always better than any that we could discover by substituting common sense and intuition for the formulation of the ILP.

In this chapter we will discuss integer linear programming from a managerial perspective. After introducing the fundamental concepts, we will study in detail six of the wide variety of important classes of decision problems that may be formulated as ILPs. For more technically oriented readers, Section 9.14 will discuss an algorithm used to solve ILPs.

9.2 A TAXONOMY FOR INTEGER LINEAR PROGRAMS

In discussing ILPs, we use a number of specific terms. A constraint requiring a decision variable to assume an integer value is an *integrality constraint*. A decision variable required to assume an integer value is an *integer variable*. A decision variable permitted to assume any value (integer or noninteger) is a *continuous variable*. In general, an integer variable may assume any integer value, subject of

TABLE 9.1 A Taxonomy for Integer Linear Programs

	Binary	General
Pure	All variables are binary variables.	All variables are integer variables, but at least one is *not* a binary variable.
Mixed	A specified subset of the variables are binary variables. The remaining variables are continuous variables.	A specified subset of the variables are integer variables, but at least one of this subset is *not* a binary variable. The remaining variables are continuous variables.

course to the ILP's structural and nonnegativity constraints. However, as we will see, it is often desirable to restrict the values to just two, 0 and 1; we will refer to this special type of integer variable as a *binary variable*.

We can classify ILPs in terms of the following characteristics:

- **Pure versus mixed.** In a pure ILP, all variables are integer variables, while in a mixed ILP a specified subset is an integer variable and the remainder are continuous variables.

- **Binary versus general.** In a binary ILP, all integer variables are binary variables, while in a general ILP at least one integer variable is not a binary variable.

In terms of these characteristics, there are four mutually exclusive categories of ILPs: *pure-binary ILPs, pure-general ILPs, mixed-binary ILPs, and mixed-general ILPs*. Table 9.1 summarizes this taxonomy. Most of the LPs encountered in Chapters 4 and 5 can serve as examples of pure-general ILPs or mixed-general ILPs, once the verbal statements of the decision problems are altered to involve indivisible items or activities. In light of this fact, most of the examples and exercises of the present chapter will involve the remaining two categories, pure-binary ILPs and mixed-binary ILPs.

9.3 THE LINEAR PROGRAMMING RELAXATION OF AN INTEGER LINEAR PROGRAM

The *linear programming relaxation* (*LP relaxation*) of an ILP is simply the LP that results from deleting the ILP's integrality constraints. In this section we will discuss the relationship between an ILP and its LP relaxation; in the next, we will discuss how knowledge of the LP relaxation's optimal solution may aid the search for the ILP's optimal solution.

To illustrate the relationship between an ILP and its LP relaxation, we will consider the following example:

Trans Global Airlines (TGA) wants to expand its fleet by purchasing two types of aircraft: AC474 and AC272s. Table 9.2 displays for each aircraft type the net annual contribution to profit (after subtracting capital recovery costs), the purchase price, and the annual maintenance requirement. The board of directors has specified two constraints on the fleet expansion. First, the total purchase price of the new aircraft must not exceed $100 million, and second, the total annual maintenance requirements of the new aircraft must not exceed 4000 hours. Subject to these two constraints, TGA desires to expand its fleet with the maximum net annual contribution to profit.

TABLE 9.2 Data for TGA's Fleet Expansion Problem

Item	AC474	AC272
Net Annual Contribution to Profit ($000)	900	700
Purchase Price ($000,000)	20	10
Annual Maintenance Requirement (hours)	400	500

To formulate TGA's problem as an ILP, let

x_1 = the number of AC474 aircraft purchased by TGA,
x_2 = the number of AC272 aircraft purchased by TGA.

We can then state TGA's problem as the following pure-general ILP:

$$\text{Maximize } 900x_1 + 700x_2 \qquad \text{(maximize profit)}$$

$$\begin{aligned}
\text{subject to } \quad 20x_1 + 10x_2 &\leq 100 \quad \text{(budget constraint)} \\
400x_1 + 500x_2 &\leq 4000 \quad \text{(maintenance constraint)}
\end{aligned}$$

$$\begin{aligned}
\text{and } \quad x_1, x_2 &\geq 0 \qquad \text{(nonnegativity constraints)} \\
x_1, x_2 \text{ integer-valued.} \qquad \text{(integrality constraints)}
\end{aligned}$$

The integrality constraints on x_1 and x_2 are a mandatory part of the formulation, since it is difficult to purchase (let alone fly!) a fractional part of an airplane.

Let us now contrast the optimal solution to TGA's ILP and the optimal solution to the LP relaxation resulting from the deletion of the integrality constraints on x_1 and x_2. Since both the ILP and its LP relaxation contain only two decision variables, we can solve both graphically. Figure 9.1 displays the graphical solution of both problems. (Temporarily ignore the dashed box in the figure.) Observe the following:

- The feasible region of the LP relaxation consists of the shaded area. The isoprofit line $900x_1 + 700x_2 = 6166\frac{2}{3}$ is the highest-valued isoprofit line that intersects the LP's feasible region. Therefore, the LP relaxation's optimal solution occurs at $(x_1, x_2) = (1\frac{2}{3}, 6\frac{2}{3})$ and has an objective value of $6166\frac{2}{3}$.

- The feasible region of the ILP is contained within that of the LP relaxation. It consists only of the isolated small black dots within the shaded area—that is, the points (x_1, x_2) satisfying all the constraints of the LP relaxation and further satisfying the integrality requirements. The isoprofit line $900x_1 + 700x_2 = 6000$, intersecting the ILP's feasible region at the point $(x_1, x_2) = (2, 6)$, is the highest-valued isoprofit line that intersects the ILP's feasible region. Therefore, TGA's maximal profit contribution is only 6000 thousands of dollars and results from the purchase of 2 AC474 aircraft and 6 AC272 aircraft.

Thus, the ILP and its LP relaxation have different optimal solutions and, furthermore, the optimal objective value for the ILP is *worse* than that for the the LP relaxation.

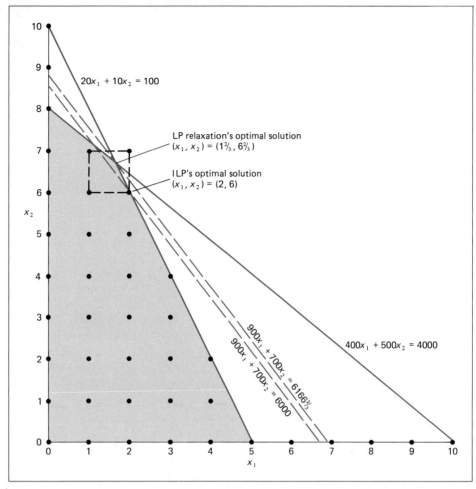

Figure 9.1 Graphical solution of TGA's ILP

Our graphical solutions of TGA's ILP and its LP relaxation illustrate not only the general procedure for graphically solving a two-variable ILP but also the following general relationships:

Relationships
Between an ILP
and Its LP
Relaxation

Relationship 1. Because the ILP's integrality constraints account for the only difference between the constraints of the ILP and its LP relaxation, the ILP's feasible region is always contained within the LP relaxation's feasible region.

Relationship 2. Owing to Relationship 1, the optimal objective value of the ILP can never be better than the optimal objective value of the LP relaxation. In fact, because the optimal solutions usually occur at different points, the ILP's optimal objective value is usually worse than that of the LP relaxation. objective value.

Relationship 3. If, by chance, the optimal solution to the LP relaxation satisfies the ILP's integrality constraints, then it must also be the ILP's optimal solution. If this were not true, Relationship 2 would be contradicted.

We have just seen that the optimal solution to the LP relaxation will not generally be the optimal solution to the ILP. However, the question remains as to whether we can always obtain the ILP's optimal solution by first finding the LP relaxation's optimal solution and then simply rounding to the closest integer any integer variable having a fractional value. In the next section we will see that the answer is "No!"

9.4 ATTEMPTING TO SOLVE AN INTEGER LINEAR PROGRAM BY ROUNDING

At first glance it would appear that the following strategy would always produce an ILP's optimal solution:

1. Using the simplex method, solve the LP relaxation of the ILP under consideration.

2. Having obtained the LP relaxation's optimal solution, find the ILP's optimal solution by simply rounding to the closest integer value any integer variable having a fractional value.

Given the efficiency of the simplex method and the simplicity of the rounding strategy, it would be nice if the rounding strategy would always work. Unfortunately, in the vast majority of cases this rounding strategy will fail to produce the ILP's optimal solution. A slight modification of the strategy, however, will often produce an acceptable close-to-optimal solution.

For example, let us reconsider Trans Global Airlines's ILP and its graphical solution in Figure 9.1. The LP relaxation's optimal solution is $(1\frac{2}{3}, 6\frac{2}{3})$. Rounding each variable to the closest integer results in $(2, 7)$, a point that—as a glance at Figure 9.1 indicates— is not even feasible for the ILP, let alone optimal.

By now, another appealing rounding strategy may have occurred to you. Instead of only rounding to the closest integer value, we could consider each integer variable and sometimes round "up" to the next highest integer and sometimes round "down" to the next lowest integer. This revised rounding strategy results in not just one but several *rounding alternatives*. In Figure 9.1, the four corners of the dashed box enclosing $(1\frac{2}{3}, 6\frac{2}{3})$, the LP relaxation's optimal solution, represent the four rounding alternatives obtained from considering all possible combinations of rounding up and down. For example, the point $(1, 7)$ in the box's northwest corner results from rounding $1\frac{2}{3}$ down and $6\frac{2}{3}$ up. Observe that three of the four rounding alternatives are feasible for the ILP, the other one being the infeasible solution we encountered when rounding only to the nearest integer. In fact, one of the three feasible rounding alternatives, $(2, 6)$, is the ILP's optimal solution. Is this just a coincidence? Unfortunately, the answer is yes. While our revised rounding strategy has produced the optimal solution to TGA's ILP, it will generally fail to do so—for three reasons:

1. For large-scale problems, considering all possible rounding combinations of rounding up and down would result in 2^n alternatives, where n is the number of integer variables assuming fractional values in the LP relaxation's optimal solution. With $n=2$ in TGA's ILP, it is simple to enumerate all $2^2 = 4$ alternatives. However, if n were to equal 25, there would be 2^{25} (over 33 million) rounding alternatives. Even with the aid of a computer, it would be impractical to enumerate each of these rounding alternatives, check each for feasibility, and then identify the feasible alternative with the best objective value.

2. Even if it were possible to enumerate all of the rounding alternatives, all of them may be infeasible.

To illustrate this second reason, consider the following ILP:

$$\text{Maximize} \quad 45x_1 + 100x_2$$

$$\text{subject to} \quad \begin{aligned} -5x_1 + 5x_2 &\leq 9 \\ 5x_1 + 10x_2 &\leq 99 \end{aligned}$$

and $x_1, x_2 \geq 0$

x_1, x_2 integer-valued.

Figure 9.2 displays the graphical solution to both the ILP and its LP relaxation. As before, the four corners of the dashed box represent the four rounding alternatives. Observe, however, that all four rounding alternatives are infeasible. While it is rare that all rounding alternatives are infeasible, it is not uncommon for a vast majority of them to be, especially when the ILP contains many equality constraints.

3. Even if it were possible to enumerate all of the possible rounding alternatives and even if some of the alternatives were feasible for the ILP, these feasible rounding alternatives would not usually include the ILP's optimal solution.

To illustrate this third reason, consider the following ILP:

$$\text{Maximize} \quad 100x_1 + 360x_2$$

$$\text{subject to} \quad \begin{aligned} -4x_1 + 7x_2 &\leq 3 \\ 2x_1 + 7x_2 &\leq 18 \end{aligned}$$

and $x_1, x_2 \geq 0$

x_1, x_2 integer-valued.

Figure 9.3 displays the graphical solution to both the ILP and its LP relaxation. Once again, the four corners of the dashed box represent the four possible rounding alternatives. Observe that only two of the alternatives are feasible for the ILP. Of these two, the point $(3, 1)$ has the higher objective value, namely $100(3) + 360(1) = 660$. However, as indicated in Figure 9.3, the actual optimal ILP solution occurs at $(9, 0)$ with an objective value of 900, a value far greater than 660!

Figure 9.2 Graphical solution of an example illustrating that all rounding alternatives may be infeasible

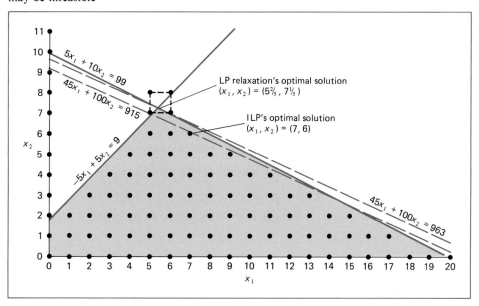

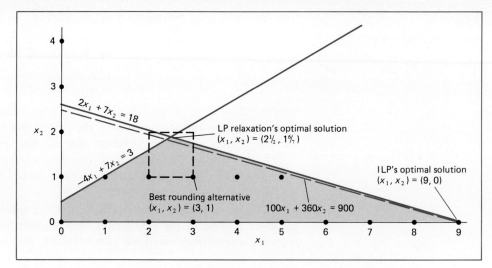

Figure 9.3 Graphical solution of an example illustrating that the set of rounding alternatives need not include the ILP's optimal solution

Many of our examples in subsequent sections will also illustrate that a rounding strategy will not generally produce the ILP's optimal solution.

Although it is unlikely to produce the ILP's optimal solution, rounding the LP relaxation's optimal solution is often an effective way to find an acceptable close-to-optimal solution. To illustrate, let us reconsider Trans Global Airlines's ILP. Let us pretend that TGA's ILP contains many variables and that TGA does *not* know the optimal solution to this "large-scale" ILP. Suppose that TGA first obtains $(1\frac{2}{3}, 6\frac{2}{3})$ with an objective value of $6166\frac{2}{3}$ as the LP relaxation's optimal solution and then determines that the best rounding alternative is $(2, 6)$ with an objective value of 6000. At this point, it is useful for TGA to ask: "What is the *maximum percentage error* that might result if $(2, 6)$ were used as a "proxy" for (i.e., in place of) the actual optimal solution?" Remember that TGA does not know that $(2, 6)$ is actually the ILP's optimal solution and, therefore, cannot answer, "0%." However, TGA does know that the ILP's optimal objective value cannot be better than $6166\frac{2}{3}$, the optimal objective value for the LP relaxation.[1] Therefore, if TGA were to use $(2, 6)$ with its objective value of 6000 rather than solving for the ILP's optimal solution, the maximum percentage error that might result is

$$\frac{6166\frac{2}{3} - 6000}{6166\frac{2}{3}} \times 100\% = 2.7\%.$$

TGA must now decide between the following two courses of action:

1. Attempt to find the ILP's optimal solution, hoping that the cost of doing so is less than the improvement in the objective value over $6000.

2. Forget about searching for the ILP's optimal solution and use the close-to-optimal solution $(2, 6)$ in its place. In doing so, TGA would be accepting the fact that a percentage error as large as 2.7% might result but would be hoping that the actual percentage error would be less.

---

[1] This follows from the second of the three relationships between an ILP and its LP relaxation, as listed in the preceding section.

Given our prior graphical analysis, we know that the second course of action is correct. However, TGA does not know that $(2, 6)$ is the optimal solution; it knows only that the use of $(2, 6)$ can result in a maximum percentage error of 2.7% or, equivalently, a maximum dollar error (in thousands of dollars) of

$$6166\tfrac{2}{3} - 6000 = 166\tfrac{2}{3} \,.$$

Consequently, TGA should attempt to find the ILP's optimal solution only if it estimates that the cost of doing so will be less than \$166,667; otherwise, it should abandon the search for optimality and use the close-to-optimal rounding alternative $(2, 6)$.

As an additional example of the use of the concept of maximum percentage error, reconsider the example and its graphical solution in Figure 9.3. As we did for TGA's ILP, suppose we do not know that $(9, 0)$ with an objective value of 900 is the ILP's optimal solution. Instead, suppose we have used the simplex method to obtain $(2\tfrac{1}{2}, 1\tfrac{6}{7})$ with an objective value of $918\tfrac{4}{7}$ as the LP relaxation's optimal solution and have identified $(3, 1)$ with an objective value of 660 as the best rounding alternative. If we were to abandon the search for ILP's optimal solution and use $(3, 1)$ as its proxy, the maximum percentage error that might result is

$$\frac{918\tfrac{4}{7} - 660}{918\tfrac{4}{7}} \times 100\% = 28.1\% \,.$$

In the face of such a large maximum percentage error, we should consider it unlikely that the actual percentage error is very small, and so we should continue the search for the ILP's optimal solution. In this particular case, our decision will be vindicated by the discovery that, had we simply used the best rounding alternative, the actual percentage error would have been

$$\frac{900 - 660}{900} \times 100\% = 26.7\% \,.$$

It is important to understand, however, that we did run the risk of spending much time and money only to discover that, despite the 28.1% maximum percentage error, the actual percentage error was some acceptably low percentage (even 0%).

For future reference, we now summarize the steps of what we will hereafter refer to as the *naive rounding strategy:*

The Naive Rounding Strategy

1. Use the simplex method to determine the optimal solution of the LP relaxation, and let n denote the number of the ILP's integer variables that assume noninteger values.

2. Given the size of n, enumerate as many of the 2^n rounding alternatives as seems practical.

3. Check each rounding alternative for feasibility, calculate the objective value of each feasible rounding alternative, and identify the feasible rounding alternative with the best objective value.

4. Let OV_{LP} and OV_{ROUND} denote the optimal objective values of the LP relaxa-

tion and the best rounding alternative, respectively. Then, using the formula

$$\frac{OV_{LP} - OV_{ROUND}}{OV_{LP}} \times 100\%,$$

calculate the maximum percentage error that might result from using the best rounding alternative in place of the actual optimal ILP solution. (If the objective function involves minimization rather than maximization, reverse the order of the two terms in the formula's numerator in order to get a nonnegative percentage.)

5. Based upon the size of maximum percentage error, decide whether to continue the search for the ILP's optimal solution or to use the best feasible rounding alternative as an acceptable close-to-optimal solution.

As a rule of thumb, practitioners almost always abandon the search for optimality if the maximum percentage error is 1% or less, almost always continue the search for optimality if the maximum percentage error is 10% or more, and use intuition and past experience to guide their decision when the maximum percentage error is in the range of 1% to 10%. Of course, the unit of measurement for the objective value plays a role in the decision. For example, a maximum percentage error of only 1% might not dissuade a practitioner from continuing the search for optimality if the objective value of the best feasible rounding alternative were $20,000,000; the potential of a $200,000 improvement in the objective value might be too tempting to pass up.

Practitioners often employ the naive rounding strategy because it is easy to understand, it is easy to implement on a computer, and it frequently gives an acceptable result when one is needed in a hurry. The naive rounding strategy works best for pure-general ILPs and mixed-general ILPs. As we shall see in subsequent sections, the naive rounding strategy is usually of little help for pure-binary ILPs or mixed-binary ILPs.

More sophisticated rounding strategies exist for instances when the naive rounding strategy is inappropriate or results in an unacceptable solution. A description of these sophisticated rounding strategies is beyond the scope of this chapter. While these more sophisticated rounding strategies also cannot guarantee to produce the ILP's optimal solution, they will usually yield a solution with a much lower maximum percentage error than that obtained by the naive rounding strategy. Unfortunately, the sophisticated rounding strategies do not enjoy widespread use by current practitioners. The primary reason is that computer implementations of these strategies are not commercially available, and most organizations find "in-house" development of such computer codes impractical owing to a lack of expertise, time, and/or money. Despite this drawback, the sophisticated rounding strategies merit serious consideration by any decision maker who must solve large-scale ILPs on a regular basis.

To summarize:

A rounding strategy will rarely produce the ILP's optimal solution but may well produce an acceptable close-to-optimal solution—that is, a feasible solution with an acceptably low maximum percentage error.

In the next section, we will discuss how to integrate a rounding strategy into an overall strategy for solving an ILP.

9.5 A PRACTICAL PROCEDURE FOR SOLVING AN INTEGER LINEAR PROGRAM[2]

At the outset of this chapter, we stressed the difficulty in optimally solving a large-scale ILP. In light of this difficulty, the following is a highly recommended step-by-step procedure for attempting to optimally solve a large-scale ILP:

A Practical
Procedure For
Solving an ILP

1. By consulting textbooks, journals, and experts, we should first do some research to determine if someone has proven that the ILP under consideration belongs to a class of ILPs with the following property:

    > Every corner point of the LP relaxation's feasible region satisfies the ILP's integrality constraints.

    If this property holds, the ILP's integrality constraints are unnecessary, and we may determine the ILP's optimal solution by simply solving the LP relaxation via the simplex method. How someone might prove that such a property holds is well beyond the scope of this chapter; however, we have already seen examples of such ILPs, including Suny's production and inventory planning problem in Section 4.3, Graham's transportation problem in Section 4.5, and all of the network linear programs of Chapter 8.

2. Even if there is no advance guarantee that the optimal solution to the LP relaxation will satisfy the ILP's integrality constraints, we should "cross our fingers" and solve the LP relaxation anyway. If its optimal solution does in fact satisfy the ILP's integrality constraints, we will consider ourselves fortunate to have solved the ILP as if it were an LP.

3. If at least one of the ILP's integer variables assumes a noninteger value in the LP relaxation's optimal solution, we should next attempt to find an acceptable close-to-optimal solution by employing at least the naive rounding strategy (and possibly even a more sophisticated rounding strategy).

4. If we do not discover an acceptable close-to-optimal solution by rounding, we should do some further research to determine if a *special-purpose method (or heuristic)* exists for finding an optimal solution, or at least an acceptable close-to-optimal solution, to the ILP. Whereas a *general-purpose method* (or *heuristic*) is designed to solve all ILPs belonging to one or more of the four general categories described in Sec. 9.2, a special-purpose method (or heuristic) is specifically designed for use on a narrow class of ILPs, such as all pure-binary ILPs. As we will see throughout the remainder of this chapter, special-purpose methods exist for many important classes of ILPs. Even though their exact natures are beyond the scope of this chapter, it is important to be aware of their existence because they are significantly more efficient, and therefore cheaper, to use than general-purpose methods. This is especially true if the ILP under consideration will need to be resolved repeatedly with alternative data or if similar ILPs will arise frequently in the future. As is true for the sophisticated rounding strategies, computer implementations of special-purpose methods are not yet widely available for purchase or lease, thereby forcing organizations to

---

[2] Although you should read this section now, you will have a clearer understanding of some of its aspects if you reread it after completing the entire chapter.

incur the expense of in-house development. However, in view of the current trends in the availability of computer software, this drawback is unlikely to apply in the future.

5. As a last resort, we should attempt to discover the ILP's optimal solution by employing a general-purpose method, such as the one we will discuss in Section 9.14. In contrast to special-purpose methods, computer implementations of general-purpose methods are available for purchase or lease from many vendors.

This procedure is intended for use on large-scale ILPs. When faced with a small-scale ILP, it is probably safe to bypass Steps 1 through 4 and proceed directly to Step 5, unless variations of the ILP need to be solved now or in the future. In such a case, it would be advisable to perform Steps 1, 4, and then 5.

9.6 AN OVERVIEW OF THE APPLICATIONS OF INTEGER LINEAR PROGRAMMING

We indicated in Section 9.2. that many of the linear programming applications discussed in Chapters 4 and 5 become integer linear programming applications when the decision variables represent items or activities that are indivisible. However, the value of integer linear programming as a modeling device extends far beyond simply adding integrality constraints to LPs.

In the next six sections, we will examine in depth the application of integer linear programming to six classes of decision problems:

- Capital budgeting problems.
- Problems involving fixed charges.
- Contract awards problems.
- Facility location problems.
- Airline crew scheduling problems.
- Clustering analysis in marketing research.

These applications not only illustrate the vastly expanded modeling capability of integer linear programming over linear programming but also provide valuable insight into how to formulate integer linear programming models of other decision problems. Subject to a few minor deviations, our discussion will adhere to the following format:

1. We will verbally state a scenario illustrating the decision problem in a specific context.

2. We will formulate the scenario as an ILP. All but one of our formulations will result in pure-binary or mixed-binary ILPs, reflecting the fact that the majority of practical applications of integer linear programming involve binary variables. As we will see, a binary variable typically represents a decision having a dichotomous nature—that is, a decision involving the choice between two alternatives (yes or no, accept or reject, do something or do not do something, etc.).

3. For some ILPs, we will examine the LP relaxation's optimal solution and attempt to discover an acceptable close-to-optimal solution by rounding; for others, this will be left as an exercise. In one instance (the capital budgeting problems), we will attempt to discover an acceptable close-to-optimal solution not only by rounding but also by using a special-purpose heuristic.

4. We will provide and interpret the ILP's optimal solution.

5. For some decision problems, we will also discuss special cases and/or extensions.

Let us now begin our detailed examination of six applications of integer linear programming.

9.7 CAPITAL BUDGETING PROBLEMS

In a capital budgeting problem, a decision maker must decide how to budget (i.e., allocate) a limited amount of capital (e.g., money or manpower) among several investment proposals in order to maximize the net present value of the budgeted capital. Examples of investment proposals that frequently arise in practice are

- Expansion or remodeling of an existing plant or construction of a new plant.
- Purchase of new equipment or machinery.
- Investment in a financial security or in real estate.
- Acquisition of a new technology.
- Research and development for a new product.
- An advertising campaign or a test marketing program.

The most common type of investiment proposal requires either full approval or full rejection; that is, the proposal requests approval of its budget in full or not at all. For example, it would be meaningless to approve only $\frac{5}{9}$ of a proposal to purchase a new piece of machinery. Another common type of investment proposal requests funding for one of a small number of alternative budgets and corresponding levels of performance. For example, a proposal for the construction of a new plant might request funding of one of three alternative budgets corresponding to three alternative plant sizes. As we will see, it is convenient to regard such multialternative proposals as a set of individual proposals of which at most one can be approved.

To illustrate the capital budgeting problem, consider the following scenario:

Chloe Schwasher, the Vice President of Finance for a major appliance manufacturer, has before her eight investment proposals submitted by various segments of the company for her approval or rejection. The columns of Table 9.3 (except for the last column) summarize each proposal's net present value (NPV) and capital requirements for each of the next five years. Although Chloe finds all of the proposals attractive,

TABLE 9.3 Data for Chloe's Capital Budgeting Problem

		Proposal								Capital
		1	2	3	4	5	6	7	8	Availability
Net Present Value ($000):		151	197	119	70	130	253	165	300	($000)
Capital Requirement	Year 1	20	100	20	30	50	40	50	80	230
	Year 2	20	10	10	30	10	20	40	30	100
	Year 3	20	0	10	30	10	20	10	20	50
	Year 4	20	0	10	20	10	20	10	0	50
	Year 5	10	30	10	10	10	20	10	0	50

she must reject some because of the limited availability of investment capital. As indicated by the last column of Table 9.3, the total capital requirements of the *approved* proposals cannot exceed \$230,000 in Year 1, \$100,000 in Year 2, and \$50,000 in each of Years 3, 4, and 5. Subject to these annual limitations on total cash outflow, Chloe's objective is to maximize the total NPV of the approved proposals.

As we mentioned in the preceding section, a binary variable is an appropriate way to represent a decision involving a choice between two alternatives. In the context of Chloe's capital budgeting problem, this means using a different binary variable to represent the approve-or-reject decision Chloe must make for each investment proposal. More specifically, Chloe defines eight binary variables $x_1, x_2, \ldots, x_8$, where

$$x_j = \begin{cases} 1 \text{ denotes Chloe's approval of proposal } j \\ 0 \text{ denotes Chloe's rejection of proposal } j. \end{cases}$$

With these eight decision variables, Chloe formulates her capital budgeting problem as the following pure-binary ILP:

Maximize $151x_1 + 197x_2 + 119x_3 + 70x_4 + 130x_5 + 253x_6 + 165x_7 + 300x_8$ (total NPV)

subject to
$$20x_1 + 100x_2 + 20x_3 + 30x_4 + 50x_5 + 40x_6 + 50x_7 + 80x_8 \leqslant 230 \text{ (year 1)}$$
$$20x_1 + 10x_2 + 10x_3 + 30x_4 + 10x_5 + 20x_6 + 40x_7 + 30x_8 \leqslant 100 \text{ (year 2)}$$
$$20x_1 + 10x_3 + 30x_4 + 10x_5 + 20x_6 + 10x_7 + 20x_8 \leqslant 50 \text{ (year 3)}$$
$$20x_1 + 10x_3 + 20x_4 + 10x_5 + 20x_6 + 10x_7 \leqslant 50 \text{ (year 4)}$$
$$10x_1 + 30x_2 + 10x_3 + 10x_4 + 10x_5 + 20x_6 + 10x_7 \leqslant 50 \text{ (year 5)}$$

and $x_1, x_2, \ldots, x_8 = 0$ or 1   (integrality)

Chloe's choice of which of the eight proposals to approve is equivalent to the choice of which among the eight binary variables to set equal to 1.

That Chloe's problem is really equivalent to an ILP and not an LP is evident upon an examination of the optimal solution to the ILP's LP relaxation. First, however, a word of caution is in order about the nature of the LP relaxation when the ILP involves binary variables. The binary integrality constraint

$$x_j = 0 \text{ or } 1$$

is actually a concise representation of three separate constraints: a nonnegativity constraint $x_j \geqslant 0$, an upper bound constraint $x_j \leqslant 1$, and an integrality constraint requiring x_j to assume an integer value. Since the LP relaxation results from deleting only the integrality constraints from the ILP, the LP relaxation retains the constraints $x_j \geqslant 0$ and $x_j \leqslant 1$. Consequently, in the LP relaxation, x_j is no longer a binary variable but rather a continuous variable permitted to assume any value between and including the integers 0 and 1.

The first row of Table 9.4 displays the optimal solution to the LP relaxation of Chloe's ILP. Since it is meaningless to approve only a fraction of a proposal, Chloe cannot implement the LP relaxation's optimal solution. However, by employing the naive rounding strategy described in Section 9.4, Chloe hopes to discover an acceptable close-to-optimal solution to her ILP. As you will be asked to verify in one of the end-of-chapter exercises, the best feasible rounding alternative is the one displayed in the second row of Table 9.4. This solution calls for Chloe to approve proposals 2, 6, and 8 and to reject all others, thereby obtaining a total NPV of \$750,000. If Chloe were to abandon her search for the ILP's optimal solution and instead use the best rounding alternative, the maximum percentage error that might result is

TABLE 9.4 Solutions to Chloe's Capital Budgeting Problem

	x_1	x_2	x_3	x_4	x_5	x_6	x_7	x_8	Objective Value
LP relaxation's optimal solution	0	$\frac{2}{3}$	$\frac{2}{9}$	0	0	1	$\frac{7}{9}$	1	$839\frac{1}{9}$
Best rounding alternative	0	1	0	0	0	1	0	1	750
Optimal solution	1	1	1	0	0	0	0	1	767
New optimal solution	0	0	0	0	0	1	1	1	718

$$\frac{839\frac{1}{9} - 750}{839\frac{1}{9}} \times 100\% = 10.6\%.$$

Given the possibility of such a large error, Chloe decides to continue the search for the ILP's optimal solution. Using the general-purpose algorithm described in Section 9.14, Chloe discovers the optimal ILP solution displayed in the third row of Table 9.4. Observe that the total NPV of the ILP's optimal solution exceeds by $17,000 the total NPV of the best rounding alternative. Thus, in contrast to its maximum percentage error of 10.6%, the best rounding alternative's actual percentage error is only

$$\frac{767 - 750}{767} \times 100\% = 2.2\%.$$

Of course, Chloe had no way of knowing the best rounding alternative's actual percentage error until she optimally solved the ILP; therefore, she had to base her decision of whether to continue her search for optimality on the maximum percentage error.

In many practical captial budgeting problems, the presence of nonbudgetary constraints further complicates the decision. Two common occurrences are

- A situation where a group of proposals "conflict" with each other so that approval must be given to at most one, or perhaps exactly one, proposal.

- A situation where one proposal is viable only if another proposal is approved.

To illustrate, consider the following three modifications to Chloe's captial budgeting problem:

1. Suppose proposals 1, 2, and 3 are alternatives for the proposed but not mandatory construction of a new manufacturing plant. The differences among the proposals' NPVs and cash outflow requirements reflect alternative plant sizes and/or locations. Since at most one new plant can be built, Chloe must add to her ILP the *mutually exclusive constraint*

$$x_1 + x_2 + x_3 \leqslant 1.$$

Such a constraint ensures that at most one of the binary variables x_1, x_2, or x_3 will equal 1.

2. Suppose proposals 4, 5, and 6 are alternatives for a mandatory new advertising campaign. The differences among the proposals' NPVs and cash outflow requirements reflect alternative advertising strategies. Since exactly one of the proposals must be approved, Chloe must add to the ILP the *multiple-choice constraint*

$$x_4 + x_5 + x_6 = 1.$$

Such a constraint ensures that exactly one of the binary variables x_4, x_5, or x_6 will equal 1.

3.   Suppose proposal 7 involves the purchase of a new and more powerful computer, and proposal 8 involves the installation of a new computerized inventory control system. Further suppose that the approval of the proposal involving the new inventory control system is contingent upon the proposal involving the new computer; that is, in order to approve proposal 8, Chloe must first approve proposal 7. (Note that Chloe's approval of proposal 7 does not necessarily imply that she will also approve proposal 8.) Since proposal 8 is viable only if Chloe approves proposal 7, Chloe must add to the ILP the *contingency constraint*

$$x_8 \leqslant x_7.$$

Under such a constraint, $x_8 = 1$ (approval of proposal 8) forces $x_7 = 1$ (approval also of proposal 7); however, $x_7 = 1$ (approval of proposal 7) permits either $x_8 = 0$ or $x_8 = 1$ (rejection or approval of proposal 8).

When Chloe adds to the ILP the mutually exclusive constraint, the multiple-choice constraint, and the contingency constraint, the optimal solution to her original ILP (the third row of Table 9.4) is no longer feasible, let alone optimal. The fourth row of Table 9.4 displays the new optimal solution. It calls for the rejection of all the alternative proposals for a new plant, the acceptance of the third alternative for the advertising campaign, and the approval of both the purchase of a new computer and the installation of the new inventory control system.

Other types of nonbudgetary constraints often arise in capital budgeting problems. One other type worthy of mention here is a *k-out-of-n constraint*. Such a constraint is necessary when exactly k, or at most k, of a group of n alternatives must be approved. As an example of a *k-out-of-n* constraint, suppose the five binary variables x_2, x_3, x_4, x_6, and x_9 represent proposals for new plants at five distinct sites. To ensure the construction of exactly three new plants, the ILP must include the 3-out-of-5 constraint

$$x_1 + x_3 + x_4 + x_6 + x_9 = 3.$$

Similarly, to ensure the construction of at most three plants, replace the $=$ by $\leqslant$. As we will see in several other applications discussed in this chapter, mutually exclusive, multiple-choice, *k-out-of-n*, and contingency constraints are useful in contexts other than capital budgeting problems.

Before leaving the subject, we will discuss the general form of the capital budgeting problem and then examine an important special case.

The General Form of the Capital Budgeting Problem

The general form differs from Chloe's capital budgeting problem in two respects:

1.   The general form permits proposals of two types—the type encountered in Chloe's problem, requiring an approve-or-reject decision, and a type for which it is possible to either reject the proposal or approve multiple copies of the proposal. For example, by permitting the approval of multiple copies of a proposal to buy a single share of a particular stock or a single piece of machinery, it becomes possible to model the purchase of any integer amount of stock or machinery. Consequently, in the general form of the capital budgeting problem, a decision variable x_j need not be a binary variable representing an approve-or-reject decision; instead, it may

be a general integer variable representing the number of copies of proposal j that are approved, where $x_j = 0$ represents the proposal's rejection.

2. Instead of involving only one type of capital (such as money in Chloe's problem), the general form of the capital budgeting problem involves several types of capital. Potential types include money, manpower, equipment, and space.

The Knapsack Problem

A special type of capital budgeting problem arises when the problem involves only a single type of capital and a single time period (and in the absence of any mutually exclusive, multiple-choice, k-out-of-n, and contingency constraints). This ILP has received much attention by management scientists and is referred to as the *knapsack problem*, owing to the following facetious scenario, which serves as a prototype for more practical scenarios:

> A hiker packing a knapsack for an upcoming trip is considering including n different types of items. For $1 \leqslant + j \leqslant + n$, each item of type j weighs a_j pounds and, if packed, would provide c_j units of utility to the hiker during the trip. Subject of a weight limitation of b pounds, the hiker must decide how many of each item type to include in the knapsack so as to maximize the knapsack's total utility.

Of course, in the more practical capital budgeting framework, the decision maker is analogous to the hiker, each proposal's NPV and capital requirement are analogous to each item's utility and weight, and the available capital is analogous to the weight limitation on the knapsack.

To illustrate the knapsack problem, consider the following scenario:

> With a budget of $150, Wally Streat is considering the purchase of shares of four different stocks. Table 9.5 displays each stock's estimated annual dividend and current price per share. For diversification purposes, the maximum numbers of shares Wally will purchase of stocks 1, 2, 3, and 4 are 5, 3, 3, and 2. Subject to these diversification requirements and to the budget limitation of $150, Wally wants to find the portfolio of stocks that maximizes total annual dividends.

Letting x_j denote the shares of stock j purchased, Wally formulates his problem as the following knapsack problem:

$$
\begin{aligned}
\text{Maximize} \quad & 5x_1 + 15x_2 + 12x_3 + 18x_4 \\
\text{subject to} \quad & 20x_1 + 40x_2 + 30x_3 + 50x_4 \leqslant 150 \\
& x_1 \leqslant 5 \\
& x_2 \leqslant 3 \\
& x_3 \leqslant 3 \\
& x_4 \leqslant 2
\end{aligned}
$$

and $x_1, x_2, x_3, x_4 \geqslant 0$
x_1, x_2, x_3, x_4 integer-valued.

TABLE 9.5 Data for Wally's Knapsack Problem

	Stock			
	1	2	3	4
Annual dividend per share ($)	5	15	12	18
Price per share ($)	20	40	30	50

TABLE 9.6. Solutions to Wally's Knapsack Problem

	x_1	x_2	x_3	x_4	Objective Value
LP relaxation's optimal solution	0	$1\frac{1}{2}$	3	0	$58\frac{1}{2}$
Best rounding alternative	0	1	3	0	51
"Greedy" solution	1	1	3	0	56
Optimal solution	0	3	1	0	57

Observe that the four upper bound constraints ensure that Wally's portfolio is properly diversified.

The first row of Table 9.6 displays the optimal solution to the LP relaxation of Wally's problem. The only feasible and, therefore, the best rounding alternative results from rounding x_2 down to 1, thereby obtaining the solution displayed in the second row of Table 9.6. The maximum percentage error that might result from using the best rounding alternative as a proxy for the ILP's optimal solution is

$$\frac{58\frac{1}{2} - 51}{58\frac{1}{2}} \times 100\% = 12.8\% .$$

In light of this potentially large error, Wally decides to employ a heuristic specially designed for seeking an acceptable close-to-optimal solution to a knapsack problem. This heuristic is an example of the special-purpose methods referred to in Step 4 of Section 9.5's procedure for solving an ILP. The heuristic proceeds as follows:

1. For each proposal j, compute the ratio c_j/a_j—that is, the ratio of the NPV of one copy of proposal j to the capital requirement of one copy of proposal j.

2. Order the proposals on a list that starts with the one having the highest ratio and continues in decreasing order of the ratio.

3. Starting at the top of the list, successively consider each proposal. For the proposal under consideration, budget for as many copies of it as possible, taking into account both the remaining availability of capital and the maximum number of copies of the proposal permitted by the initial statement of the problem. Then move on to the next proposal on the list.

For obvious reasons, this is often called the *greedy heuristic* for knapsack problems.

In the context of Wally's portfolio problem, the ratio c_j/a_j is the ratio of stock j's annual dividend per share to its price per share. To apply the greedy heuristic to his problem, Wally computes the ratio for each stock as follows:

Stock	Ratio c_j/a_j
1	$5/20 = 0.250$
2	$15/40 = 0.375$
3	$12/30 = 0.400$
4	$18/50 = 0.360$

Given these four ratios, the greedy heuristic will first consider stock 3, then stock 2, then stock 4, and finally stock 1. We can summarize Wally's execution of the greedy heuristic as follows:

■ **Consideration of stock 3.** Since Wally considers stock 3 first, the remaining budget is the initial budget of $150. Although the remaining budget of $150 permits the purchase of 5 shares of stock 3 at $30 per share, stock 3's diversification upper bound limits the purchase to only 3 shares.

■ **Consideration of stock 2.** The remaining budget of $150 − (3)(30) = 60$ dollars permits the purchase of only 1 share of stock 2 at $40 per share, a purchase less than the diversification upper bound of 3 shares.

■ **Consideration of stock 4.** With a remaining budget of $60 − (1)(40) = 20$ dollars, Wally cannot purchase any of stock 4, despite its diversification upper bound of 2 shares.

■ **Consideration of stock 1.** The remaining budget of $20 permits the purchase of only 1 share of stock 1 at $20 per share, an amount less than the diversification upper bound of 5 shares.

The third row of Table 9.6 displays the solution obtained by the greedy heuristic. The maximum percentage error that might result from using the "greedy" portfolio in place of the optimal portfolio is

$$\frac{58\frac{1}{2} - 56}{58\frac{1}{2}} \times 100\% = 4.3\%.$$

—a much lower percentage than that for the best rounding alternative.

If Wally were to use Section 9.14's general-purpose method to optimally solve his knapsack problem, he would discover the optimal solution displayed in the fourth row of Table 9.6. Hence, the actual percentage error for the "greedy" portfolio is only

$$\frac{57 - 56}{57} \times 100\% = 1.8\%.$$

While the greedy heuristic cannot guarantee to produce an acceptable close-to-optimal solution, it is worth trying, especially when no computer is available. It may, however, result in a solution that is far from optimal.

Special-purpose methods exist for optimally solving large-scale knapsack problems. Such methods are capable of solving problems with up to 500 proposals while using less than two minutes of CPU time on a modern mainframe computer. In contrast, a general-purpose method such as that described in Section 9.14 will usually require excessive CPU time to solve a knapsack problem involving more than 50 proposals. As a rule of thumb, then, if the greedy heuristic fails to produce an acceptable close-to-optimal solution, a decision maker attempting to find the knapsack problem's optimal solution should employ a general-purpose method if the number of proposals is less than 50 and a special-purpose method otherwise.

We conclude our discussion of capital budgeting by briefly considering a special type of knapsack problem that occurs when all proposals require only an approve-or-reject decision. We refer to such a problem as the binary knapsack problem, because the decision variables of the resulting ILP are binary variables rather than general integer variables. To illustrate, consider the following scenario:

A firm has 100 thousand dollars available to allocate among five potential projects. Table 9.7 summarizes the NPV of each project as well as the capital outlay required at the outset of each. Subject to the budget limitation, the firm wishes to undertake a set of projects that maximizes the total NPV.

TABLE 9.7 Data for Firm's Binary Knapsack Problem

	Project				
	1	2	3	4	5
Net present value ($000)	26	12	34	4	19
Capital outlay ($000)	40	20	50	10	30

The firm's decision problem is equivalent to the following binary knapsack problem:

$$\text{Maximize } 26x_1 + 12x_2 + 34x_3 + 4x_4 + 19x_5$$
$$\text{subject to } 40x_1 + 20x_2 + 50x_3 + 10x_4 + 30x_5 \leqslant 100$$
$$\text{and } x_1, x_2, x_3, x_4, x_5 = 0 \text{ or } 1.$$

Table 9.8 displays the optimal solution to the ILP's LP relaxation, the best rounding alternative, the solution obtained by applying the greedy heuristic, and the actual optimal solution to the ILP. To obtain the "greedy" solution, it is first necessary to compute the ratios c_j/a_j for $j = 1, 2, \ldots, 5$. These ratios are computed as follows:

Project	Ratio c_j/a_j
1	26/40 = 0.650
2	12/20 = 0.600
3	34/50 = 0.680
4	4/10 = 0.400
5	19/30 = 0.633

Based upon these ratios, the greedy algorithm considers the projects in the order: 3, 1, 5, 2, and 4. In particular, the initial budget of 100 thousand dollars permits the funding of project 3 at a capital outlay of 50 thousand dollars. The remaining budget of $100 - 50 = 50$ thousand dollars permits the funding of project 1 at a capital outlay of 40 thousand dollars. Finally, the remaining budget of $50 - 40 = 10$ thousand dollars precludes the funding of project 5 and project 2 but does permit the funding of project 4 at a capital outlay of 10 thousand dollars.

With respect to when to use a general-purpose method versus a special-purpose method, similar comments apply to the binary knapsack problem as did to the general Knapsack Problem.

TABLE 9.8 Solutions to Firm's Binary Knapsack Problem

	x_1	x_2	x_3	x_4	x_5	Objective Value
LP relaxation's optimal solution	1	0	1	0	$\frac{1}{3}$	$66\frac{1}{3}$
Best rounding alternative	1	0	1	0	0	60
"Greedy" solution	1	0	1	1	0	64
Optimal solution	0	1	1	0	1	65

9.8 A FIXED CHARGE PROBLEM

One of the applications of linear programming discussed in Chapter 2 was the product mix problem, where the decision variables represented the production levels (or rates) of the alternative products. We ignored any fixed charge related to a particular product because it was a "sunk cost," incurred regardless of whether the product's production level was zero or positive. However, as we will see, a fixed charge cannot be ignored if it is incurred for all positive production levels but not for a production level of 0. For example, consider a product for which the total profit from the production and sale of x units is given by:

$$\text{total profit from } x \text{ items} = \begin{cases} 35x - 1000 & \text{if } x > 0, \\ 0 & \text{if } x = 0. \end{cases}$$

In words, if the production level is positive $(x > 0)$, a fixed charge of \$1000 must be subtracted from the total variable profit of $35x$, while if there is no production $(x = 0)$, there is no fixed charge and, of course, no total variable profit. A fixed charge of this type arises when a positive production level results in costs that would otherwise be unnecessary if there were no production at all. Such costs might include one or more of the following:

- The purchase or rental of special equipment.
- The salaries of special personnel.
- The construction of a special production or assembly line.
- The set-up (preparation) cost incurred before a production run can begin (e.g., the energy cost required to heat a blast furnace to the proper temperature).

To illustrate a fixed charge problem, consider the following scenario:

The ABC Company is planning its production for the next month. ABC has the capability to manufacture three different products. Associated with product j $(j = 1, 2, 3)$ are the following quantities:

- The amounts of each of three scarce resources consumed during the production of each unit of product j,
- The unit profit p_j for product j, and
- A fixed charge k_j incurred if and only if the production level of product j is positive.

Table 9.9 summarizes these data as well as the availability of each of the three resources during the next month. ABC estimates it can sell its entire production, regardless of its product mix. Subject to the constraints on resource availabilities, ABC wishes to determine the optimal product mix—that is, the production levels for each of the three products that will maximize next month's total profit.

If there were no fixed charges, ABC could solve its product mix problem by simply defining x_j as the production level of product j and then solving the following LP:

$$\text{Maximize } 35x_1 + 50x_2 + 40x_3 \qquad \text{(total profit)}$$

$$\begin{array}{llll} \text{subject to} & 2x_1 + 3x_2 + 6x_3 \leq 500 & \text{(resource 1)} \\ & 8x_1 + 2x_2 + 3x_3 \leq 400 & \text{(resource 2)} \\ & 4x_1 + 7x_2 + 2x_3 \leq 300 & \text{(resource 3)} \\ \text{and } & x_1, x_2, x_3 \geq 0. & \text{(nonnegativity)} \end{array}$$

411

TABLE 9.9 Data for ABC's Fixed-Charge Problem

		Product			
		1	2	3	
	Unit Profit	35	50	40	Resource
	Fixed Charge:	1000	500	1500	Availability
	Resource 1	2	3	6	500
Consumptions	Resource 2	8	2	3	400
	Resource 3	4	7	2	300

The optimal solution to this LP is

$$\begin{aligned} x_1 &= 20.66, \\ x_2 &= 10.74, \\ x_3 &= 71.07, \\ \text{Profit} &= \$4103.31. \end{aligned}$$

However, the presence of the fixed charges complicates ABC's decision problem. If ABC were to implement the optimal solution to the above LP, its profit would not be \$4103.31. Instead, owing to the accrual of the fixed charges for all three products, ABC's actual profit would be

$$\$4103.31 - \$1000 - \$500 - \$1500 = \$1103.31.$$

ABC may be able to obtain a higher profit by producing less than three products, thereby avoiding at least one of the fixed charges.

To determine the optimal product mix in the presence of the fixed costs, ABC must formulate an ILP, not an LP. Each product j requires, two decisions by ABC: whether or not to produce product j and, if so, how much to produce. Whereas ABC may represent the latter decision by the continuous variable x_j, the former decision is dichotomous (yes or no) and, consequently, requires a binary variable. Thus, in addition to the continuous variables x_1, x_2, and x_3, ABC must define the three binary variables y_1, y_2, and y_3, where

$$y_j = \begin{cases} 0 \text{ denotes that product } j \text{ is not produced,} \\ 1 \text{ denotes that product } j \text{ is produced.} \end{cases}$$

ABC can now express the total profit from product j as

$$p_j x_j - k_j y_j.$$

To ensure that product j's production level is 0 whenever ABC does not incur product j's fixed charge (i.e., $x_j = 0$ whenever $y_j = 0$), ABC must include in its ILP the constraint

$$x_j \leqslant M_j y_j,$$

where M_j is space-saving notation for any large number that exceeds the maximum production level of product j. When $y_j = 0$, this constraint reduces to $x_j \leqslant 0$ which, in conjunction with x_j's nonnegativity constraint, forces $x_j = 0$; furthermore, the total profit from product j will be as it should, namely

$$p_j x_j - k_j y_j = p_j(0) - k_j(0) = 0.$$

When $y_j = 1$, this constraint reduces to $x_j \leqslant M_j$, a constraint that poses no practical limit on x_j; furthermore, the total profit from product j will be as it should, namely

$$p_j x_j - k_j y_j = p_j x_j - k_j(1) = p_j x_j - k_j.$$

Consequently, ABC may formulate its product mix problem as the following mixed-binary ILP:

$$\text{Maximize } 35x_1 + 50x_2 + 40x_3 - 1000y_1 - 500y_2 - 1500y_3 \quad \text{(total profit)}$$

$$
\begin{aligned}
\text{subject to} \quad 2x_1 + 3x_2 + 6x_3 &\leqslant 500 \quad \text{(resource 1)} \\
8x_1 + 2x_2 + 3x_3 &\leqslant 400 \quad \text{(resource 2)} \\
4x_1 + 7x_2 + 2x_3 &\leqslant 300 \quad \text{(resource 3)} \\
x_1 \qquad\qquad &\leqslant M_1 y_1 \quad (y_1 = 0 \text{ implies } x_1 = 0) \\
x_2 \qquad &\leqslant M_2 y_2 \quad (y_2 = 0 \text{ implies } x_2 = 0) \\
x_3 &\leqslant M_3 y_3 \quad (y_3 = 0 \text{ implies } x_3 = 0)
\end{aligned}
$$

$$
\begin{aligned}
\text{and } x_1, x_2, x_3 &\geqslant 0 \quad \text{(nonnegativity)} \\
y_1, y_2, y_3 &= 0 \text{ or } 1 \quad \text{(integrality)}
\end{aligned}
$$

You may be concerned that there seems to be nothing in the ILP to prevent solutions in which $x_j = 0$ but $y_j = 1$ for some product j, — that is solutions in which ABC does not produce product j but still incurs the fixed cost. For example, $x_1 = x_2 = x_3 = 0$ and $y_1 = y_2 = y_3 = 1$ is a feasible solution to ABC's ILP. While it is true that such solutions are feasible, a solution of this type will never be optimal because, whenever $x_j = 0$, setting $y_j = 0$ always results in a higher total profit than setting $y_j = 1$. Thus, while a method seeking the ILP's optimal solution might encounter a solution with $x_j = 0$ and $y_j = 1$, the method will never terminate at such a solution.

Technically, we should rewrite each of the $x_j \leqslant M_j y_j$ constraints as $x_j - M_j y_j \leqslant 0$ in order to follow the convention that no variables should appear on the right-hand side of a constraint. However, in this and other examples of this chapter we will ignore this convention in order to make the interpretation of the constraint more apparent.

Before solving its ILP, ABC must assign values to M_1, M_2, and M_3. Although the only requirement on M_j is that it equal or exceed the product j's maximum production level, research experiments indicate that the computational effort required to obtain the ILP's optimal solution will usually be significantly lower if M_j is kept as small as validly possible rather than arbitrarily assigned a very large value. For example, ABC should not set M_1 equal to 5000 if M_1 equal to 50 would also work.

How, then, should ABC assign values to M_1, M_2, and M_3? If the initial statement of ABC's problem were to state explicitly that the maximum production levels for products 1, 2, and 3 were 60, 40 and 70, ABC would simply use these explicit upper bounds on x_1, x_2, and x_3 as the values for M_1, M_2, and M_3, respectively. However, in the absence of an explicit upper bound on x_j, ABC must determine an implicit upper bound using the ILP's structural constraints. For example, the first, second, and third resource constraints implicitly restrict x_1 to at most 50, the smallest of the quantities[3]

$$\frac{500}{2} = 250, \frac{400}{8} = 50, \text{ and } \frac{300}{4} = 75.$$

---

[3] Note that, in the following expressions, the numerators are the resource availabilities and the denominators are the resource consumptions by each unit of product 1.

Consequently, in the constraint $x_1 \leqslant M_1 y_1$, ABC should assign M_1 a value of 50. A higher value for M_1 would not lead to the incorrect solution but would probably require greater computational effort. Similar analysis for x_2 and x_3 shows that ABC should set M_2 equal to $42\frac{6}{7}$ and M_3 equal to $83\frac{1}{3}$. In subsequent formulations of ILPs, we will continue to use M_j as space-saving notation for a large number that is an upper bound on x_j. While we will not repeat the remarks of this paragraph, keep in mind that they still apply.

In Section 9.4 we stated that it was not generally worthwhile to attempt to find a close-to-optimal solution to a mixed-binary ILP by applying the naive rounding strategy to the LP relaxation's optimal solution. We can now illustrate this statement using ABC's mixed-binary ILP. If ABC assigns M_1, M_2, and M_3 the values 50, $42\frac{6}{7}$, and $83\frac{1}{3}$, respectively, the optimal solution to the ILP's LP relaxation is

$$
\begin{array}{ll}
x_1 = 20.66, & y_1 = 0.41, \\
x_2 = 10.74, & y_2 = 0.25, \\
x_3 = 71.07, & y_3 = 0.85.
\end{array}
$$

There is no simple way to round such a solution because of the interaction between the binary variables, which require rounding, and the continuous variables, which do not require rounding. If, for example, y_1 is rounded down to 0, x_1 must also be set equal to 0 or else the resulting solution will violate the constraint $x_1 \leqslant M_1 y_1$. For this reason (and other reasons we will not discuss here), the naive rounding strategy performs poorly for mixed-binary ILPs.

By employing the general-purpose method of Section 9.14, ABC will discover that the optimal solution to its ILP is

$$
\begin{array}{ll}
x_1 = 0, & y_1 = 0 \\
x_2 = 22.22, & y_2 = 1 \\
x_3 = 77.22, & y_3 = 1 \\
\multicolumn{2}{c}{\text{Profit} = \$2000.}
\end{array}
$$

Thus, in the presence of the fixed charges, the optimal solution to the ILP calls for the production of only two of the three products. Recall that, in the absence of the fixed charges, the optimal solution to the LP called for the production of all three products.

9.9 A CONTRACT AWARDS PROBLEM

While a linear programming approach is satisfactory for some contract awards problems, others require an integer linear programming approach in order to properly model several types of complicating factors often present in the suppliers' bids. For example, a common occurrence is for a supplier's bid to specify that the amount contracted for, if any, must be greater than or equal to a minimum acceptable order quantity. To illustrate this and several other complicating factors in the suppliers' bids that necessitate the formulation of an ILP, consider the following scenario:

Three oil companies (A, B, and C) have submitted bids for satisfying the stated aviation fuel requirements of four Air Force bases (1, 2, 3, and 4). Table 9.10 displays the fuel requirement of each base, the maximum amount each oil company can supply to all bases, and the bid each company has made for supplying each base. For exam-

TABLE 9.10 Data for Air Force's Contract Awards Problem

	Bids ($ per 1000 gallons)				Maximum Supply (000 gallons)
	Base 1	Base 2	Base 3	Base 4	
Company A	500	600	650	450	50
Company B	450	300	500	150	40
Company C	550	450	700	250	60
Fuel Requirements (000 gallons)	45	20	30	30	

ple, base 2 requires 20 thousand gallons of fuel, company B can supply at most 40 thousand gallons of fuel to all four bases, and company B's bid for supplying base 2 is $300 per thousand gallons or 30¢ per gallon. In addition to the above data, the bids by the oil companies include the following complicating factors:

- Company A has specified for each base a minimum acceptable award of 15 thousand gallons; that is, if company A is awarded a contract to supply a particular base, then the size of the award must be at least 15 thousand gallons.

- Company B has specified that at least three of the four amounts it supplies to the four bases must be less than or equal to 10 thousand gallons, or, equivalently, at most one of the amounts may exceed 10 thousand gallons.

- Company C has specified that the total amount supplied to all bases must be a multiple of 10 thousand gallons—that is, 0, 10, 20, 30, 40, 50, or 60 thousand gallons.

John Doe, the Air Force's purchasing officer, is responsible for the evaluation of the oil companies' bids and the awarding of the contracts at minimal cost to the Air Force.

As the first step in formulating his decision problem, John defines (for $i = A, B, C$ and $j = 1, 2, 3, 4$) the decision variable x_{ij}, representing the amount of fuel company i will supply to base j. John's problem *without the three complicating factors* is a transportation problem and, therefore, may be formulated as an LP. The following table displays the LP's optimal solution, where the optimal value of x_{ij} (if it is nonzero) appears in row i and column j.

	To Base 1	To Base 2	To Base 3	To Base 4
From Company A	45		5	
From Company B		15	25	
From Company C		5		30

The total cost to the Air Force of this solution is $52,500. Unfortunately, John cannot implement this solution because it violates all three complicating factors. In particular, $x_{A3} < 15$, both x_{B2} and x_{B3} exceed 10, and $x_{C1} + x_{C2} + x_{C3} + x_{C4}$ is not a multiple of 10. To ensure that all complicating factors are satisfied, John must employ integer linear programming rather than linear programming.

John first considers company A's stipulation that any contract with A to supply base 1 must call for A to supply at least 15 thousand gallons of fuel. A requirement of this type is referred to as a *minimum-batch-size requirement*. John states this requirement mathematically as:

$$\text{either } x_{A1} = 0 \text{ or } x_{A1} \geqslant 15.$$

Since the maximum total amount company A can supply to all bases is 50, John restates the requirement as

$$\text{either } x_{A1} = 0 \text{ or } 15 \leqslant x_{A1} \leqslant 50.$$

Next he defines a binary variable y_{A1} as follows:

$$y_{A1} = \begin{cases} 0 \text{ denotes that company } A \text{ is not awarded a contract to supply base 1,} \\ 1 \text{ denotes that company } A \text{ is awarded a contract to supply base 1.} \end{cases}$$

Using this binary variable, John expresses company A's minimum-batch-size requirement as the following pair of linear constraints:

$$x_{A1} \leqslant 50y_{A1},$$
$$x_{A1} \geqslant 15y_{A1}.$$

When $y_{A1} = 0$, this pair of constraints reduces to $x_{A1} \leqslant 0$ and $x_{A1} \geqslant 0$, thereby forcing x_{A1} to equal 0; when $y_{A1} = 1$, the pair of constraints simply ensure that $15 \leqslant x_{A1} \leqslant 50$ holds.

John requires similar pairs of constraints to enforce company A's minimum-batch-size requirements for bases 2, 3, and 4. In particular, company A's minimum-batch-size requirements are mathematically equivalent to the following four pairs of linear constraints involving the continuous variables x_{A1}, x_{A2}, x_{A3}, and x_{A4} and the binary variables y_{A1}, y_{A2}, y_{A3}, and y_{A4}:

$$x_{A1} \geqslant 15y_{A1} \text{ and } x_{A1} \leqslant 50y_{A1},$$
$$x_{A2} \geqslant 15y_{A2} \text{ and } x_{A2} \leqslant 50y_{A2},$$
$$x_{A3} \geqslant 15y_{A3} \text{ and } x_{A3} \leqslant 50y_{A3},$$
$$x_{A4} \geqslant 15y_{A4} \text{ and } x_{A4} \leqslant 50y_{A4}.$$

Minimum-batch-size requirements arise in contexts other than the contract awards problem. In general, a minimum-batch-size requirement restricting a variable x to either equal 0 or be greater than or equal to some specified minimum value m is equivalent to the following pair of constraints:

$$x \geqslant my,$$
$$x \leqslant My,$$

where y is a binary variable and M is an upper bound on x either explicitly stated in the problem or implicitly derived from the problem's structural constraints.

John next considers company B's stipulation that at least three of the four amounts B supplies to the four bases must be less than or equal to 10. Mathematically, at least three of the following four constraints must hold:

$$x_{B1} \leqslant 10,$$
$$x_{B2} \leqslant 10,$$
$$x_{B3} \leqslant 10,$$
$$x_{B4} \leqslant 10.$$

A requirement of this type is referred to as a *k-out-of-n requirement*, where k is the minimum number of the n constraints that must hold. To express company B's 3-out-of-4 constraint as a set of linear constraints, John defines four binary variables y_{B1}, y_{B2}, y_{B3}, and y_{B4}, where

$$y_{Bi} = \begin{cases} 0 \text{ denotes that the constraint } x_{Bi} \leqslant 10 \text{ must be satisfied,} \\ 1 \text{ denotes that the constraint } x_{Bi} \leqslant 10 \text{ need not be satisfied.} \end{cases}$$

Then, company B's 3-out-of-4 constraint is equivalent to the following set of five linear constraints

$$x_{B1} \leqslant 10 + My_{B1},$$
$$x_{B2} \leqslant 10 + My_{B2},$$
$$x_{B3} \leqslant 10 + My_{B3},$$
$$x_{B4} \leqslant 10 + My_{B4},$$

$$y_{B1} + y_{B2} + y_{B3} + y_{B4} \leqslant 1,$$

where once again M is space-saving notation for a large number. To understand the equivalence, observe that, if $y_{Bj} = 0$, the constraint $x_{Bj} \leqslant 10 + My_{Bj}$ reduces to the original constraint $x_{Bj} \leqslant 10$; However, if $y_{Bj} = 1$, the constraint $x_{Bj} \leqslant 10 + My_{Bj}$ reduces to $x_{Bj} \leqslant 10 + M$, a meaningless constraint that is always satisfied owing to the size of M. Since the last of the above constraints guarantees that at most one of the binary variables will equal 1, at least three of the four binary variables will equal 0. Consequently, at least three of the four original constraints will hold.

In the general k-out-of-n requirement, each of the left-hand sides of the n constraints may be linear functions of several variables, rather than just a single variable as they are in John's problem. Also the constraints may involve a mixture of $\leqslant$, $\geqslant$, and $=$ type constraints. For example, consider the following set of constraints:

$$3x_1 + 5x_2 + 6x_3 \leqslant 4,$$
$$2x_1 + x_2 + 4x_3 \leqslant 3,$$
$$x_1 + 4x_2 + 2x_3 = 7,$$
$$2x_1 + 3x_2 + x_3 \geqslant 1,$$
$$3x_1 + 2x_2 + 5x_3 \geqslant 2.$$

A requirement that at least k of these five constraints hold is equivalent to the following set of seven linear constraints involving the three continuous variables x_1, x_2, and x_3 and the five binary variables y_1, y_2, y_3, y_4, and y_5:

$$3x_1 + 5x_2 + 6x_3 \leqslant 4 + My_1$$
$$2x_1 + x_2 + 4x_3 \leqslant 3 + My_2$$
$$x_1 + 4x_2 + 2x_3 \leqslant 7 + My_3$$
$$x_1 + 4x_2 + 2x_3 \geqslant 7 - My_3$$
$$2x_1 + 3x_2 + x_3 \geqslant 1 - My_4$$
$$3x_1 + 2x_2 + 5x_3 \geqslant 2 - My_5$$

$$y_1 + y_2 + y_3 + y_4 + y_5 \leqslant 5 - k$$

To understand the equivalence, observe the following:

- A quantity My_i is added to the right-hand side of a $\leqslant$-constraint but is subtracted from the right-hand side of a $\geqslant$-constraint. When $y_i = 0$, the modified constraint reduces to the original constraint; however, when $y_i = 1$, the modified constraint becomes a meaningless constraint that is always satisfied, thereby eliminating the requirement that the original constraint be satisfied.

- The third original constraint, an equality constraint, was first replaced by the two inequalities

$$x_1 + 4x_2 + 2x_3 \leqslant 7,$$
$$x_1 + 4x_2 + 2x_3 \geqslant 7.$$

Then, the same quantity, My_3, was added to the right-hand side of the $\leqslant$

constraint and subtracted from the right-hand side of the $\geqslant$ constraint. Consequently, when $y_3 = 0$, the two modified inequalities require

$$x_1 + 4x_2 + 2x_3$$

to be both $\leqslant 7$ and $\geqslant 7$, thereby ensuring that the original $=$ constraint will hold. Alternatively, when $y_3 = 1$, both the inequalities become meaningless, thereby eliminating the requirement that the original $=$ constraint must hold.

■ The right-hand side of the last of the seven constraints is $5 - k$ (not k). Consequently, at most $5 - k$ of the original constraints need not hold, or, equivalently, at least k will hold.

Finally, John considers company $C's$ stipulation that the total amount C supplies to all bases must be a multiple of 10. Mathematically, the expression

$$x_{C1} + x_{C2} + x_{C3} + x_{C4}$$

must assume exactly one of the nonconsecutive values 0, 10, 20, 30, 40, 50, and 60. A requirement of this type is referred to as a *nonconsecutive values requirement*. This is equivalent to the following pair of linear constraints involving the four continuous variables x_{C1}, x_{C2}, x_{C3}, and x_{C4} and the seven binary variables $y_1, y_2, ..., y_7$:

$$x_{C1} + x_{C2} + x_{C3} + x_{C4} = 0y_{C1} + 10y_{C2} + 20y_{C3} + 30y_{C4} + 40y_{C5} + 50y_{C6} + 60y_{C7},$$
$$y_{C1} + y_{C2} + y_{C3} + y_{C4} + y_{C5} + y_{C6} + y_{C7} = 1.$$

Since the second constraint forces exactly one of the seven binary variables to equal 1, the left-hand side of the first constraint will assume a value that is a multiple of 10.

In general, a nonconsecutive-values requirement requires a linear function of several decision variables to assume exactly one of several nonconsecutive values. For example, the requirement that the linear function

$$3x_1 + x_2 + 2x_3$$

assume one of the four values 1, 4, 6, and 9 is equivalent to the following pair of constraints:

$$3x_1 + x_2 + 2x_3 = 1y_1 + 4y_2 + 6y_3 + 9y_4,$$
$$y_1 + y_2 + y_3 + y_4 = 1,$$

where y_i for $1 \leqslant i \leqslant 4$ is a binary variable which, when equal to 1, forces the linear function to assume the ith value.

Now that John has determined how to treat each of the three complicating factors, he may formulate his contract awards problem as the following mixed-binary ILP:

Minimize
$$500x_{A1} + 600x_{A2} + 650x_{A3} + 450x_{A4}$$
$$+ 450x_{B1} + 300x_{B2} + 500x_{B3} + 150x_{B4} \qquad \text{(total cost)}$$
$$+ 550x_{C1} + 450x_{C2} + 700x_{C3} + 250x_{C4}$$

subject to
$$x_{A1} + x_{A2} + x_{A3} + x_{A4} \leqslant 50$$
$$x_{B1} + x_{B2} + x_{B3} + x_{B4} \leqslant 40 \qquad \text{(supply)}$$
$$x_{C1} + x_{C2} + x_{C3} + x_{C4} \leqslant 60$$

$$\begin{array}{lllll}
x_{A1} + & x_{B1} + & x_{C1} & = 45 \\
x_{A2} + & x_{B2} + & x_{C2} & = 20 \\
x_{A3} + & x_{B3} + & x_{C3} & = 30 \\
x_{A4} + & x_{B4} + & x_{C4} & = 30
\end{array}$$

(demand)

$$\begin{array}{ll}
x_{A1} & \geqslant 15y_{A1} \\
x_{A1} & \leqslant 50y_{A1} \\
x_{A2} & \geqslant 15y_{A2} \\
x_{A2} & \leqslant 50y_{A2} \\
x_{A3} & \geqslant 15y_{A3} \\
x_{A3} & \leqslant 50y_{A3} \\
x_{A4} & \geqslant 15y_{A4} \\
x_{A4} & \leqslant 50y_{A4}
\end{array}$$

(minimum-batch-size)

$$\begin{array}{ll}
x_{B1} & \leqslant 10 + My_{B1} \\
x_{B2} & \leqslant 10 + My_{B2} \\
x_{B3} & \leqslant 10 + My_{B3} \\
x_{B4} & \leqslant 10 + My_{B4}
\end{array}$$

(3-out-of-4)

$$y_{B1} + \quad y_{B2} + \quad y_{B3} + \quad y_{B4} \leqslant 1$$

$$x_{C1} + \quad x_{C2} + \quad x_{C3} + \quad x_{C4} = \begin{array}{l} 0y_{C1} + 10y_{C2} + 20y_{C3} \\ \quad + 30y_{C4} + 40y_{C5} \\ \quad + 50y_{C6} + 60y_{C7} \end{array}$$

(nonconsecutive values)

$$y_{C1} + y_{C2} + \cdots + y_{C7} = 1.$$

and $\quad x_{ij} \geqslant 0$ for $i = A, B, C$ and $j = 1, 2, 3, 4$ (nonnegativity)

$y_{A1}, y_{A2}, y_{A3}, y_{A4} = 0$ or 1

$y_{B1}, y_{B2}, y_{B3}, y_{B4} = 0$ or 1 (integrality)

$y_{C1}, y_{C2}, y_{C3}, y_{C4}, y_{C5}, y_{C6}, y_{C7} = 0$ or 1.

When John employs the general-purpose method described in the Section 9.14, he discovers that the optimal values for the binary variables are

$y_{A1} = 1, y_{A2} = 0, y_{A3} = 0, y_{A4} = 0$ $\left(\begin{array}{l}\text{Owing to } A\text{'s minimum-batch-size} \\ \text{constraint, it will supply only base 1.}\end{array}\right)$

$y_{B1} = 0, y_{B2} = 0, y_{B3} = 1, y_{B4} = 0$ $\left(\begin{array}{l}\text{Owing to } B\text{'s 3-out-of-4 constraint,} \\ \text{only } x_{B3} \text{ will exceed 10.}\end{array}\right)$

$\begin{array}{l} y_{C1} = 0, y_{C2} = 0, y_{C3} = 0, y_{C4} = 0, \\ y_{C5} = 1, y_{C6} = 0, y_{C7} = 0 \end{array}$ $\left(\begin{array}{l}\text{The total amount } C \text{ will} \\ \text{supply to all bases will equal 40.}\end{array}\right)$

and the optimal value for x_{ij} is contained in the row i and column j of the following table:

	To Base 1	To Base 2	To Base 3	To Base 4
From Company A	45			
From Company B		10	30	
From Company C		10		30

The total cost of this optimal solution is $52,500.[4]

John's contract-awards problem is a simplification of an actual decision problem that arose at the United States Department of Defense.[5] The actual problem

---

[4] Coincidentally, this is the same minimum total cost that would result if the three complicating factors were absent from the bids submitted by the oil companies. In general, however, the presence of bid complications of this sort will result in an increase in the minimum total cost.

[5] L.M. Austin and W. W. Hogan, "Optimizing the Procurement of Aviation Fuel," *Management Science*, Vol. 22, No. 5 (January 1976), 515–527.

involved approximately 300 bases, 100 oil companies, three types of fuels, and many complicating factors in the bids. Finding the optimal solution to such a large-scale contract-awards problem required the use of a special-purpose method.

9.10 A FACILITY LOCATION PROBLEM

A strategic problem common to many organizations is known as the *facility location problem*. It involves deciding where to locate a limited number of facilities (such as plants or warehouses), given a larger number of potential sites for the facilities. For example, consider a firm having many retail and/or wholesale outlets for its products. In designing a production and distribution system, a fundamental problem for the firm is where to locate its plants in order to strike a balance between the fixed costs of operating the plants and the transportation costs incurred in distributing the products from the plants to the outlets. One extreme solution is to operate many plants, one plant adjacent to each outlet; such a solution is usually unappealing because, although transportation costs are low, fixed operating costs are high. Another extreme solution is to build a single plant that will distribute the products to all outlets; such a solution is usually unappealing because, although fixed operating costs are low, transportation costs are high. The optimal solution, lying somewhere between the two extremes, may be found by integer linear programming.

As an illustration of the facility location problem, consider the following scenario:

The Special Motors Corporation (SMC) specializes in the production of a single type of car. SMC currently has five plants that manufacture and assemble the cars and then distribute them to six regional warehouses (for subsequent distribution to individual dealers).

Figure 9.4 displays the current locations of the plants (indicated by "P") and the warehouses (indicated by "W"). The top management of SMC feels that the closing of one or more plants would reduce fixed operating costs by more than the resulting increase in transportation costs from the remaining plants to the warehouses. To formally study this issue, SMC has formed a team of staff members from various corporate groups within SMC. Jeff Freon is the team's leader.

Jeff has collected the data summarized in Table 9.11. For example, plant 2 has an annual production capacity of 24 thousand cars and an annual fixed operating cost of 140 thousand dollars (including estimated depreciation costs), warehouse 5 requires 7 thousand cars per year, and the transportation cost from plant 2 to warehouse 5 is 20 thousand dollars per thousand cars.

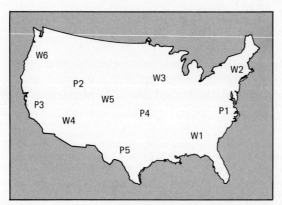

Figure 9.4 Locations of SMC's plants and warehouses

TABLE 9.11 Data for SMC's Facility Location Problem

	Transportation Costs ($000)						Annual Production Capacity (000 cars)	Annual Fixed Operating Costs ($000)
	Warehouse							
	1	2	3	4	5	6		
1	67	16	27	65	46	112	18	306
2	58	78	39	4	20	48	24	140
Plant 3	17	96	57	20	38	32	27	200
4	15	54	22	42	27	93	22	164
5	37	66	28	20	12	72	31	88
Annual Demand (000 cars)	10	8	12	6	7	11		

The current distribution pattern for SMC is summarized by Table 9.12, where the entry in row i and column j represents the thousands of cars SMC currently transports from plant i to warehouse j. The total annual cost of the current distribution pattern is $1,900,000, the sum of annual transportation costs of $1,002,000 and annual fixed operating costs of $898,000. The fact that four of the five plants are operating well below capacity seems to support the general feeling that SMC can achieve a lower total annual cost by closing one or more plants. Jeff's team must now decide which of the plants should remain open and, for each open plant, how many thousands of cars the plant should distribute to each warehouse.

To formulate SMC's problem as an ILP, Jeff defines (for every conbination of i and j) a continuous decision variable x_{ij}, representing the thousands of cars SMC distributes from plant i to warehouse j; in addition, he defines five binary variables $y_1, y_2, ..., y_5$, where

$$y_i = \begin{cases} 1 \text{ denotes that plant } i \text{ remains open,} \\ 0 \text{ denotes that plant } i \text{ closes.} \end{cases}$$

Jeff then expresses SMC's problem as the following mixed-binary ILP:

$$\begin{aligned}
\text{Minimize} \quad & 67x_{11} + 16x_{12} + 27x_{13} + 65x_{14} + 46x_{15} + 112x_{16} \\
& + 58x_{21} + 78x_{22} + 39x_{23} + 4x_{24} + 20x_{25} + 48x_{26} \\
& + 17x_{31} + 96x_{32} + 57x_{33} + 20x_{34} + 38x_{35} + 32x_{36} \quad \text{(transportation costs)} \\
& + 15x_{41} + 54x_{42} + 22x_{43} + 42x_{44} + 27x_{45} + 93x_{46} \\
& + 37x_{51} + 66x_{52} + 28x_{53} + 20x_{54} + 12x_{55} + 72x_{56} \\
& + 306y_1 + 140y_2 + 200y_3 + 164y_4 + 88y_5 \quad \text{(fixed costs)}
\end{aligned}$$

TABLE 9.12 SMC's Current Distribution System

	To Warehouse					
	1	2	3	4	5	6
1		8				
2				6		
From Plant 3						11
4	10		12			
5					7	

subject to

$$
\begin{array}{llllllll}
x_{11} + & x_{12} + & x_{13} + & x_{14} + & x_{15} + & x_{16} & \leqslant & 18y_1 \\
x_{21} + & x_{22} + & x_{23} + & x_{24} + & x_{25} + & x_{26} & \leqslant & 24y_2 \\
x_{31} + & x_{32} + & x_{33} + & x_{34} + & x_{35} + & x_{36} & \leqslant & 27y_3 \\
x_{41} + & x_{42} + & x_{43} + & x_{44} + & x_{45} + & x_{46} & \leqslant & 22y_4 \\
x_{51} + & x_{52} + & x_{53} + & x_{54} + & x_{55} + & x_{56} & \leqslant & 31y_5
\end{array}
$$

(capacity constraints)

$$
\begin{array}{llllll}
x_{11} + & x_{21} + & x_{31} + & x_{41} + & x_{51} & = 10 \\
x_{12} + & x_{22} + & x_{32} + & x_{42} + & x_{52} & = 8 \\
x_{13} + & x_{23} + & x_{33} + & x_{43} + & x_{53} & = 12 \\
x_{14} + & x_{24} + & x_{34} + & x_{44} + & x_{54} & = 6 \\
x_{15} + & x_{25} + & x_{35} + & x_{45} + & x_{55} & = 7 \\
x_{16} + & x_{26} + & x_{36} + & x_{46} + & x_{56} & = 11
\end{array}
$$

(demand constraints)

and $\quad x_{ij} \geqslant 0$ for $i = 1, 2, ..., 5$ and $j = 1, 2, ..., 6$ (nonnegativity)

$y_1, y_2, y_3, y_4, y_5 = 0$ or 1 . (integrality)

Let us discuss the validity of the plants' capacity constraints by considering plant 1; similar comments apply to the other four plants. Note the appearance of y_1 on the right-hand side of the capacity constraint for plant 1. If $y_1 = 0$, plant 1's capacity constraint reduces to

$$x_{11} + x_{12} + x_{13} + x_{14} + x_{15} + x_{16} \leqslant 0,$$

thereby forcing $x_{11}, x_{12}, ..., x_{16}$ to all equal 0; in words, the closure of plant 1 implies SMC cannot distribute any cars from plant 1 to any warehouse. Furthermore, if $y_1 = 0$, the term $306y_1$ in the objective function equals 0; that is, if plant 1 is closed, SMC will no longer incur any fixed costs at plant 1. In contrast, if $y_1 = 1$ (plant 1 remains open), plant 1's capacity constraint reduces to

$$x_{11} + x_{12} + x_{13} + x_{14} + x_{15} + x_{16} \leqslant 18,$$

thereby requiring the total number of cars SMC distributes from plant 1 to be less than the plant's capacity of 18 thousand cars. Furthermore, if $y_1 = 1$, the term $306y_1$ in the objective function equals 306; that is, if plant 1 remains open, SMC will continue to incur a fixed cost of 306 thousand dollars at plant 1. When Jeff employs the general-purpose method described in Section 9.14, he discovers that the optimal values of the binary decision variables are

$$
\begin{array}{ll}
y_1 = 1 & \text{(plant 1 remains open)} \\
y_2 = 0 & \text{(plant 2 closes)} \\
y_3 = 1 & \text{(plant 3 remains open)} \\
y_4 = 0 & \text{(plant 4 closes)} \\
y_5 = 1 & \text{(plant 5 remains open)}
\end{array}
$$

and that the optimal value of x_{ij}, if nonzero, is the entry appearing in row i and column j of the following table:

	To Warehouse					
	1	2	3	4	5	6
1		8	10			
2						
From Plant 3	10			6		11
4						
5			2		7	

The total annual cost of the optimal solution is $1,774,000, the sum of annual transportation costs of $1,180,000 and annual fixed costs of $594,000. Thus, by closing plants 2 and 4 and distributing cars optimally from the plants remaining open, SMC can lower its total annual costs by $126,000.

Although SMC's problem involved keeping open or closing each of several existing plants, the general facility location problem involves locating or not locating a facility at each of several potential sites. Depending upon the context of the problem under consideration, locating a facility at a potential site may correspond to keeping open an existing facility or constructing a new one; similarly, not locating a facility at a potential site may correspond to closing an existing facility or not constructing a new one.

Although the general-purpose method described in Section 9.14 will find an optimal solution to a small-scale facility location problem such as SMC's, the optimal solution of a large-scale facility location problem requires the use of a special-purpose method. For very large-scale problems, practitioners usually do not even attempt to find an optimal solution but instead attempt to find an acceptable close-to-optimal solution by employing a special-purpose heuristic such as that described in Section 18.3.

Our formulation of SMC's facility location problem is somewhat simpler than those usually arising in practice. Fortunately, with appropriate modifications to our formulation, we can incorporate the following realistic features:

- **Specification of an exact number or bounds on the number of facilities actually located at the potential sites.** For example, suppose that facilities must be located on exactly five of the nine potential sites. Then we must add to the formulation the 5-out-of-9 constraint

$$y_1 + y_2 + \cdots + y_9 = 5.$$

  If 5 instead represents an upper bound (or lower bound) on the number of facilities, we need only change the = to a $\leqslant$ (or a $\geqslant$).

- **Mutually exclusive, multiple-choice, or contingency requirements (similar to those encountered in Section 9.7's discussion of the capital budgeting problem).** For example, suppose that the proximity of sites 1, 3, and 7 precludes the location of more than one facility at these sites. Then we must add to the formulation the mutually exclusive constraint

$$y_1 + y_3 + y_7 \leqslant 1.$$

  Also, if a facility cannot be located at site 5 unless a facility is also located at site 3, we must add the contingency constraint

$$y_5 \leqslant y_3.$$

- **Unlimited capacity at a potential facility.** For example, suppose that a potential facility at site 3 has, for all practical purposes, unlimited capacity. Then we should change the capacity constraint for site 3 to

$$x_{31} + x_{32} + \cdots + x_{3n} \leqslant My_3,$$

  where M is space-saving notation for a large number.

- **Expansion or contraction of an existing facility.** For example, suppose that a facility with a current capacity of 8000 items already exists at site 7, and we must make a decision as to whether or not to expand facility 7's capacity by

500 items at an incremental annual fixed cost of $10,000. Then we must change the capacity constraint for site 7 to

$$x_{71} + x_{72} + \cdots + x_{7n} \leqslant 8000 + 500y_7;$$

the term $10,000y_7$ would continue to appear in the objective function. In the case of contraction of an existing facility at site 7 by 500 items, we must change the right-hand side of the above constraint to $8000 - 500y_7$ and, in addition, change the objective-function coefficient of y_7 to $-\$10,000$.

- **Specification of a prescribed range for the capacity of a potential facility.** For example, suppose that, if a facility is located at site 4, its capacity must be at least 3000 items but at most 7000 items. Then we must retain the constraint

$$x_{41} + x_{42} + \cdots + x_{4n} \leqslant 7000y_4$$

and add the constraint

$$x_{41} + x_{42} + \cdots + x_{4n} \geqslant 3000y_4.$$

In a manner similar to the minimum-batch-size requirement in Section 9.9's contract-awards problem, this pair of constraints ensures that the size of the facility at site 4 will be either 0 or in the range of 3000 to 7000 items.

- **Meeting a desired level of service.** For example, suppose that a facility located at site 5 cannot provide the desired level of service to demand center 2 because the transit time between the two locations is too long. Then we must force x_{52} to be 0. To accomplish this, we change the objective-function coefficient of x_{52} to a large number M, thereby ensuring that x_{52} will not assume a positive value in the optimal solution. Alternatively, we could simply exclude the variable x_{52} from the formulation. However, the former approach makes it much easier to alter the input to a computer software package if the desired level of service should subsequently change sufficiently to permit x_{52} to assume a positive value.

- **A fixed charge for using a particular shipping route.** Suppose that, in addition to the fixed cost of locating a facility at site 6 with a capacity of 5000 items, there is an annual fixed charge incurred for utilizing the shipping route between site 6 and demand center 2. In particular, suppose that the annual transportation cost of shipping x_{62} units between site 6 and demand center 2 is 0 if $x_{62} = 0$ and $9000 + 25x_{62}$ if $x_{62} > 0$. Then we must define a binary variable z_{62}, where

$$z_{62} = \begin{cases} 1 \text{ denotes that the shipping route between site 6 and demand center 2 is used,} \\ 0 \text{ denotes that the shipping route between site 6 and demand center 2 is not used.} \end{cases}$$

We can incorporate this additional fixed charge into the model in a manner identical to that described in Section 9.8's fixed-charge problem. More specifically, we must retain the constraint

$$x_{61} + x_{62} + \cdots + x_{6n} \leqslant 5000y_6$$

and add the constraint

$$x_{62} \leqslant M_{62}z_{62},$$

where M_{62} is space-saving notation for an (explicit or implicit) upper bound on x_{62}. Furthermore, we must add the term $9000z_{62}$ to the objective function. Observe that, although $x_{62} > 0$ implies that both $y_6 > 0$ and $z_{62} > 0$ will hold, $y_6 > 0$ but $z_{62} = 0$ can occur if the facility at site 6 does not ship items to demand center 2 but does ship items to at least one other demand center.

Often it is necessary also to incorporate the following three more complex features into the formulation:

- **A multiproduct framework.** Our formulation involved the distribution of a single product; however, most organizations distribute several products using a common distribution system.

- **A multiechelon framework.** Our formulation involved direct shipments between facilities and demand centers. However, in many distribution systems, an item originates at one of several plants, undergoes shipment to one of several warehouses, and then undergoes shipment to one of several customer outlets. The design of such a distribution system may require decisions regarding the location of the plants and/or the location of the warehouses.

- **A single-sourcing framework.** Our basic model permitted *split-sourcing*—that is, the filling of a demand center's demand by more than one facility. However, some distribution systems require *single-sourcing*—that is, the filling of demand center's demand by exactly one facility.

Each of the above frameworks requires substantial modifications to our formulation, including a redefinition of the decision variables.

SMC's facility location problem is a simplification of an actual facility location problem arising at a large producer and distributor of food products.[6] The nature of the food company's distribution system necessitated incorporating many of the realistic features just discussed. In particular, the facility location problem involved the design of a distribution system that would distribute 17 product groups from 14 plants (at fixed locations) to warehouses located at some number (to be determined) of the 45 potential sites and then on to 121 customer zones. The resulting large-scale mixed-binary ILP involved over 24,000 continuous variables and over 700 binary variables and contained over 10,000 structural constraints. The ILP's optimal solution (determined using a special-purpose method) provided the food company with answers to many important logistical questions, including

- How many warehouses should there be, and in what cities should they be located?

- What should be the size of each warehouse, and which of the products should it process?

- Which distribution center, under a single-sourcing environment, should service each demand center?

- How much of each plant's output of each product should be distributed to each warehouse?

By repeatedly solving the model under different scenarios, the food company was

---

[6] A. M. Geoffrion and G. W. Graves, "Multicommodity Distribution System Design by Benders' Decomposition," *Management Science*, Vol. 20, No. 5 (January 1974), 822–844.

able to answer a number of important "what if" questions, including

- What if a strike knocks out a key facility?
- What if a certain regional product goes national?
- What if increasing fuel costs or changes in federal regulatory policies significantly alter the current rate structures of the truck or rail carriers used to transport the products?

Development of the model and its associated data required about six calendar months of work by a project team involving personnel from accounting, data processing, marketing, management science, production, and other areas of the company. Additional expenses resulted from the repeated computer solutions of the large-scale ILP using alternative data. Fortunately, however, the effort and expense were fully justified by annual cost savings attributed to the model of over $1,000,000.

9.11 A CREW SCHEDULING PROBLEM

There exist many applications of integer linear programming to decision problems arising in the airline industry. Such applications include the selection of the mix of aircraft types (e.g., 727, 747, and 767) that will comprise an airline's fleet, the routing of aircraft to meet the airline's flight schedule, and the scheduling of crews to meet an airline's flight schedule. We will illustrate the latter application by considering the following scenario:

Walt Dumbo is responsible for the routing of aircraft and the scheduling of flight crews for Flying Elephant Airlines (FEA), an air cargo carrier serving three cities (A, B, and C). FEA operates 18 flights daily: a morning, an afternoon, and an evening flight in each direction between each pair of cities. Table 9.13 summarizes FEA's flight schedule. (For simplicity, we assume all flights are two hours long.) To meet FEA's schedule, Walt must solve two problems:

1. the optimal routing of aircraft, and
2. the optimal scheduling of flight crews,

where each flight requires a crew of two pilots. As is typical in the airline industry, Walt solves these problems separately because aircraft requirements (e.g., for maintenance) are quite different than crew requirements (e.g., for rest). In general, then, a crew does not spend its entire day with the same aircraft.

Table 9.14 displays Walt's solution to the aircraft routing problem. To meet the 18 scheduled flights, FEA will use six aircraft routes, each consisting of three flights. (You may wish to verify that each route permits at least two hours between each landing and subsequent takeoff in order to unload cargo, refuel the aircraft, perform necessary maintenance, and load new cargo.) Although each of the six aircraft routes originates in the morning at a city different from the one at which it terminates at night, two aircraft always terminate the day in each city. Consequently, the same six routes may be repeated daily, although a particular aircraft will not always fly the same route.

Unfortunately, Walt is unable to solve FEA's crew scheduling problem by assigning one crew to each of the six aircraft routes. Such a crew schedule would violate a labor agreement with the pilots' union stipulating that a crew must always start and end its day at the same city (A, B, or C), hereafter referred to as the crew's *base*.

TABLE 9.13 FEA's Flight Schedule

	Flight Number	Departure From	Time	Arrival At	Time
Morning departures	1AB	A	10:00 a.m.	B	12:00 p.m.
	1AC	A	11:00 a.m.	C	1:00 p.m.
	1BA	B	7:00 a.m.	A	9:00 a.m.
	1BC	B	6:00 a.m.	C	8:00 a.m.
	1CA	C	8:00 a.m.	A	10:00 a.m.
	1CB	C	9:00 a.m.	B	11:00 a.m.
Afternoon departures	2AB	A	5:00 p.m.	B	7:00 p.m.
	2AC	A	12:00 p.m.	C	2:00 p.m.
	2BA	B	2:00 p.m.	A	4:00 p.m.
	2BC	B	3:00 p.m.	C	5:00 p.m.
	2CA	C	4:00 p.m.	A	6:00 p.m.
	2CB	C	1:00 p.m.	B	3:00 p.m.
Evening departures	3AB	A	6:00 p.m.	B	8:00 p.m.
	3AC	A	11:00 p.m.	C	1:00 a.m.
	3BA	B	9:00 p.m.	A	11:00 p.m.
	3BC	B	7:00 p.m.	C	9:00 p.m.
	3CA	C	8:00 p.m.	A	10:00 p.m.
	3CB	C	10:00 p.m.	B	12:00 a.m.

TABLE 9.14 FEA's Aircraft Routing

Route Number	Originates at City	Flight Sequence	Terminates at City
1	A	1AB→2BA→3AB	B
2	A	1AC→2CA→3AC	C
3	B	1BA→2AB→3BA	A
4	B	1BC→2CB→3BC	C
5	C	1CA→2AC→3CA	A
6	C	1CB→2BC→3CB	B

Thus, the labor agreement bars a crew from sleeping overnight in a city other than its base.

As a preliminary step to solving FEA's crew scheduling problem, Walt has generated 30 potential daily schedules an individual crew might follow. In airline parlance, each of these is called a *rotation.* Each rotation calls for a crew to fly two or more flights during the day, always starting and ending the day at the same base. Serving as a crew for a flight involves one-half hour of preflight duty, two hours of inflight duty, and one-half hour of postflight duty. On-duty time costs FEA $40 per hour per two-member crew. Upon completion of postflight duty, a crew must have a rest period of one hour before its next preflight duty. Under the labor agreement with the pilots' union, this rest period is regarded as on-duty time and, therefore, costs FEA $40 per hour per two-member crew. Time in excess of this one-hour rest period that precedes the crew's next preflight duty is referred to as *layover time.* Layover time costs FEA $20 per hour per two-member crew. Some rotations involve the common industry practice of *deadheading,* whereby a crew is repositioned for later use by flying as passengers on one of FEA's flights.[7] Time spent deadheading is regarded as layover time and, therefore, costs FEA $20 per hour per two-member crew. Table 9.15 sum-

TABLE 9.15 Potential Rotations for FEA's Crews

Rotation Number	Flight Sequence	On-duty Time† (hours)	Layover Time‡ (hours)	Total Cost ($)
* 1	1AB→2BC→3CA	11	2	480
2	1BA→2AC→3CB	11	7	580
3	1CB→2BA→3AC	11	6	560
4	(1BA)→1AB→2BA→3AB	11	2.5	490
5	1AB→2BA→3AB→(3BA)	11	2.5	490
6	(1CA)→1AC→2CA→3AC	11	6.5	570
* 7	1BC→2CB→3BC→(3CB)	11	7.5	590
8	1CA→2AC→3CA→(3AC)	11	6.5	570
9	(1BC)→1CB→2BC→3CB	11	7.5	590
10	1AB→2BA	7	0	280
* 11	1AC→2CA	7	1	300
12	1BA→2AB	7	6	400
13	1BC→2CB	7	3	340
* 14	1CA→2AC	7	0	280
15	1CB→2BC	7	2	320
* 16	2AB→3BA	7	0	280
17	2AC→3CA	7	4	360
* 18	2BA→3AB	7	0	280
19	2BC→3CB	7	3	340
20	2CA→3AC	7	3	340
21	2CB→3BC	7	2	320
22	(1AB)→2BC→3CA	7	5.5	390
23	1AB→(2BC)→3CA	7	6	400
24	1AB→2BC→(3CA)	7	5.5	390
25	(1BA)→2AC→3CB	7	10.5	490
* 26	1BA→(2AC)→3CB	7	11	500
27	1BA→2AC→(3CB)	7	10.5	490
28	(1CB)→2BA→3AC	7	9.5	470
* 29	1CB→(2BA)→3AC	7	10	480
30	1CB→2BA→(3AC)	7	9.5	470

† Includes rest periods.
‡ Includes deadheading.
* Corresponding decision variable equals 1 in the ILP's optimal solution.

marizes the 30 potential crew rotations, where parentheses around a flight number indicate the crew is deadheading on the flight. (For the moment, ignore the asterisks that precede some rotations.) For example, rotation 29 calls for the following crew schedule and cost:

Time Period	How Spent	Cost ($)
8:30 a.m. - 9:00 a.m.	Preflight duty on Flight 1CB	$\frac{1}{2} \times 40 =$ 20
9:00 a.m. - 11:00 a.m.	Inflight duty on Flight 1CB	$2 \times 40 =$ 80
11:00 a.m. - 11:30 a.m.	Postflight duty on Flight 1CB	$\frac{1}{2} \times 40 =$ 20
11:30 a.m. - 12:30 p.m.	Rest period	$1 \times 40 =$ 40
12:30 p.m. - 2:00 p.m.	Layover time	$1\frac{1}{2} \times 20 =$ 30
2:00 p.m. - 4:00 p.m.	Deadheading on Flight 2BA	$2 \times 20 =$ 40
4:00 p.m. - 10:30 p.m.	Layover time	$6\frac{1}{2} \times 20 =$ 130
10:30 p.m. - 11:00 p.m.	Preflight duty on Flight 3AC	$\frac{1}{2} \times 40 =$ 20
11:00 p.m. - 1:00 a.m.	Inflight duty on Flight 3AC	$2 \times 40 =$ 80
1:00 a.m. - 1:30 a.m.	Postflight duty on Flight 3AC	$\frac{1}{2} \times 40 =$ 20
		Total Cost = 480

---

[7] Although our example does not allow for the possibility, in practice an airline may permit deadheading on the scheduled flights of another airline.

(You may wish to verify the data for some of the other rotations.) Rotations not appearing in Table 9.15 are absent because they are infeasible, either because they are physically impossible or because they violate federal regulations, company policy, or the labor agreement with the pilots' union.

Walt must now decide which of the 30 rotations to assign crews to in order to meet FEA's eighteen-flight schedule at minimal cost.

To formulate his decision problem as an ILP, Walt first defines 30 binary variables $x_1, x_2, \ldots, x_{30}$, where

$$x_j = \begin{cases} 1 \text{ denotes that a crew is assigned to rotation } j, \\ 0 \text{ denotes that a crew is not assigned to rotation } j. \end{cases}$$

Walt then formulates FEA's crew scheduling problem as the following pure-binary ILP:

Minimize $480x_1 + 580x_2 + 560x_3 + 490x_4 + 490x_5 + 570x_6 + 590x_7 + 570x_8 + 590x_9 + 280x_{10}$
$+ 300x_{11} + 400x_{12} + 340x_{13} + 280x_{14} + 320x_{15} + 280x_{16} + 360x_{17} + 280x_{18} + 340x_{19} + 340x_{20}$
$+ 320x_{21} + 390x_{22} + 400x_{23} + 390x_{24} + 490x_{25} + 500x_{26} + 490x_{27} + 470x_{28} + 480x_{29} + 470x_{30}$

subject to

$x_1 + x_4 + x_5 + x_{10} + x_{23} + x_{24}$					$= 1$	(1AB)
$x_6 + x_{11}$					$= 1$	(1AC)
$x_2 + x_{12} + x_{26} + x_{27}$					$= 1$	(1BA)
$x_7 + x_{13}$					$= 1$	(1BC)
$x_8 + x_{14}$					$= 1$	(1CA)
$x_3 + x_9 + x_{15} + x_{29} + x_{30}$					$= 1$	(1CB)
$x_{12} + x_{16}$					$= 1$	(2AB)
$x_2 + x_8 + x_{14} + x_{17} + x_{25} + x_{27}$					$= 1$	(2AC)
$x_3 + x_4 + x_5 + x_{10} + x_{18} + x_{28} + x_{30}$					$= 1$	(2BA)
$x_1 + x_9 + x_{15} + x_{19} + x_{22} + x_{24}$					$= 1$	(2BC)
$x_6 + x_{11} + x_{20}$					$= 1$	(2CA)
$x_7 + x_{13} + x_{21}$					$= 1$	(2CB)
$x_4 + x_5 + x_{18}$					$= 1$	(3AB)
$x_3 + x_6 + x_{20} + x_{28} + x_{29}$					$= 1$	(3AC)
x_{16}					$= 1$	(3BA)
$x_7 + x_{21}$					$= 1$	(3BC)
$x_1 + x_8 + x_{17} + x_{22} + x_{23}$					$= 1$	(3CA)
$x_2 + x_9 + x_{19} + x_{25} + x_{26}$					$= 1$	(3CB)

and $x_1, x_2, \ldots, x_{30} = 0$ or 1.

The 18 constraints ensure that each of the 18 flights has exactly one crew on duty. To see this, observe that there is one constraint corresponding to each of the 18 daily flights, and that the left-hand side of the constraint corresponding to a particular flight contains only the binary variables corresponding to the rotations whose crews would be on-duty for that flight. Requiring these binary variables to sum to exactly 1 ensures that the flight will have exactly one crew on-duty. For example, requiring in the first constraint that x_1, x_4, x_5, x_{10}, x_{23}, and x_{24} sum to exactly 1 ensures that Flight 1AB will have exactly one crew on duty, the crew assigned to either rotation 1, 4, 5, 10, 23, and 24.. Observe that x_{22} does not appear in the first constraint because a crew assigned to rotation 22 would be deadheading on Flight 1AB.

When Walt solves the LP relaxation of his ILP, he receives a pleasant surprise. All decision variables assume integer values! Thus, Walt is fortunate enough to have found his ILP's optimal solution by simply solving its LP relaxation—something that, while still rare, occurs with more frequency for airline crew scheduling problems than for the "average" ILP. The asterisks at the extreme left of Table 9.15 indicate the eight rotations that correspond to the only binary variables assuming the value of 1 in the ILP's optimal solution; the optimal objective value is $3190. As indicated by the asterisks, the optimal solution calls for the assignment of eight crews, one to each of the rotations 1, 7, 11, 14, 16, 18, 26, and 29. Consequently, FEA will employ eight crews: three crews will be based in city *A* and fly rotations 1, 11, and 16; three crews will be based in city *B* and will fly rotations 7, 18, and 26; and two crews will be based in city *C* and fly rotations 14 and 29. Observe that the same crew need not fly the same rotation each day. For example, the two crews based in city *C* can alternate on a daily basis between rotations 14 and 29, thereby equalizing the workloads between crews.

FEA's crew scheduling problem is a simplification of an actual crew scheduling problem that arose at the Flying Tiger Line (FTL), a cargo airline headquartered in Los Angeles.[8] A typical crew scheduling problem at FTL was more complex than our example for several reasons, including

- A weekly (rather than a daily) planning horizon.
- A complex flight schedule.
- The possibility of a crew overnighting at a city other than its base.
- The possibility of deadheading on the scheduled flights of several passenger airlines.
- Complex federal regulations, company policies, and labor agreements with the pilots' union governing such things as a crew's maximum hours on-duty and minimum hours of rest.

As a result of these complexities in FTL's problem, the integer linear programming formulation of a typical crew scheduling problem had 78 structural constraints (corresponding to flights) and over 14,000 decision variables (corresponding to rotations). To solve such a large-scale ILP, FTL had to use a special-purpose algorithm. Even so, obtaining the ILP's optimal solution required over 30 minutes of CPU time on a large IBM computer. Fortunately, the large computer bill proved to be a wise investment. FTL's implementation of the optimal solution resulted in annual savings of over $300,000. Furthermore, FTL enjoyed several indirect benefits, such as the ability to quickly evaluate (during negotiations) the impact of proposed changes in the pilots' labor contract.

The crew scheduling problems of the Flying Tiger Line are small in comparison with those for a large passenger airline. It would not be unusual for one of those to result in an ILP having over 3000 constraints and over 15,000 variables. Consequently, a large passenger airline will usually not attempt to optimally solve the resulting ILP but will instead seek an acceptable close-to-optimal solution using a special-purpose heuristic. Alternatively, the airline may seek an acceptable close-to-optimal solution by decomposing the crew scheduling problem into several subproblems (e.g., one subproblem for each aircraft type) and then optimally solving each subproblem.

The crew scheduling problem is just one of many diverse applications that give rise to three important classes of ILPs: the *set partitioning problem*, the *set-covering problem*, and the *set-packing problem*. The context in which the set partitioning problem arises can be broadly described as follows:

> A set of *m* requirements (e.g., the flights in the crew scheduling problem) must be satisfied. There exist *n* alternative activities (e.g., the rotations in the crew scheduling problem), each of which satisfies at a known cost a different subset of the requirements. The objective is to choose the minimal-cost combination of activities that will satisfy each requirement exactly once, thereby partitioning (dividing) the set of requirements among the various activities.

[8] R. E. Marsten, M. R. Muller, and C. L. Killion, "Crew Planning at Flying Tiger: A Successful Application of Integer Programming," *Management Science*, Vol. 25, No. 12 (December 1979), 1175–1183.

Upon letting x_j denote a binary variable that equals 1 if and only if activity j is chosen, the set-partitioning problem can be expressed as the following pure-binary ILP:

$$\text{Minimize } c_1 x_1 + c_2 x_2 + \cdots + c_n x_n$$
$$\text{subject to } a_{i1} x_1 + a_{i2} x_2 + \cdots + a_{in} x_n = 1 \quad \text{for } i = 1, 2, ..., m$$
$$\text{and } x_j = 0 \text{ or } 1 \quad \text{for } j = 1, 2, ..., n,$$

where c_j denotes the cost of alternative j and where the coefficient a_{ij} equals 1 if activity j satisfies requirement i and equals 0 otherwise. As with Walt's formulation of FEA's crew scheduling problem, each of the m structural constraints ensures that the corresponding requirement will be satisfied exactly once.

The set-covering problem is identical to the set-partitioning problem except the relationships in all structural constraints are $\geq$ rather than $=$. The presence of the $\geq$ constraints permits a requirement to be "oversatisfied"—that is, satisfied by more than one activity. Exercise __ involves a simplification of an actual set-covering problem.[9] The problem involved the selection (from 112 potential sites) of a combination of sites for the location of fire companies to serve 246 geographical subdivisions of the city of Denver. In contrast to FEA's crew scheduling problem, where each flight requires exactly one crew, it is permissible (and even desirable) for a geographical subdivision to be covered (served) by more than one fire company.

Set-packing problems differ from set-partitioning problems in that the relationships in the structural constraints are all of the $\leq$ type and the objective function involves maximization.

As we have seen, the formulation of a set-partitioning, a set-covering, or a set-packing problem results in an integer linear program. However, as illustrated by FEA's crew scheduling problem, computational experience by practitioners suggests that the optimal solution of the LP relaxation results in an all-integer solution with a frequency greater than that for the "average" ILP. Even if the LP-relaxation's optimal solution has a fractional value for some decision variables, a rounding strategy can often produce an acceptable close-to-optimal solution.

9.12 CLUSTER ANALYSIS FOR MARKETING RESEARCH

A fundamental tool in marketing research (and, indeed, many other diverse disciplines such as biology and linguistics) is known as *cluster analysis*. Cluster analysis is a generic label applied to a set of techniques that partition a set of objects into distinct clusters (groups), where two objects in the same cluster have a high degree of similarity and two objects in different clusters have a low degree of similarity. Marketing applications of cluster analysis include the clustering of customers into different market segments.

A wide variety of cluster-analysis techniques exist, each differing from the others in the way it measures the similarity between two objects and/or in the way it uses the measure of similarity to form the clusters. Research by Mulvey and Crowder established that integer linear programming deserved to be on the list of cluster-analysis techniques.[10] To illustrate, we will consider the following scenario:

---

[10] J. M. Mulvey and H. P. Crowder, "Cluster Analysis: An Application of Langrangian Relaxation," *Management Science*, Vol. 25, No. 4 (April 1979), 329–340.
[9] D. R. Plane and T. E. Hendrick, "Mathematical Programming and the Location of Fire Companies for the Denver Fire Department," *Operations Research*, Vol. 25, No. 4 (July–August 1977), 563–578.

Mark Eting is in charge of a test marketing program for a new product. Its purpose is to estimate the first-time sales of the new product, both with and without an introductory price discount. Mark has identified six cities (1, 2, 3, 4, 5, 6) as potential test markets. However, owing to budget limitations, he can select only four cities from this list.

Mark plans to use cluster analysis to design a more reliable test marketing program. He will first partition the six cities into two clusters, where any two cities in the same cluster are similar and any two cities in different clusters are dissimilar with respect to several size and demographic characteristics. Then, to reflect the fact that the two clusters are, in effect, two different market segments, Mark plans to choose one pair of cities from each cluster. He will use one city in each pair for "treatment," test marketing the product in that city with the introductory price discount. He will use the other city in each pair for "control," test marketing the product in that city without the price discount. By designing the program in this way, Mark will reduce undesired variability between the city used for treatment and the city used for control. He will thereby obtain more reliable estimates of the effects the price discount will have on sales in each market segment, and, after aggregating the estimates for each segment, he will achieve a more reliable estimate of the overall effect of the price discount.

To measure the similarity between every pair of cities, Mark performed the following steps:

1. Mark characterized each city by obtaining values for each of three attributes: the number of households in the city, the median age of the city's population, and the proportion of the city's population that is nonwhite.

2. Next Mark computed the six-city mean and the six-city standard deviation of each of the three attributes.

3. Mark then computed the "normalized" value of each of the cities' attributes by using the formula

$$\frac{\text{(attribute's actual value)} - \text{(attribute's six-city mean)}}{\text{(attribute's six-city standard deviation)}}$$

For city i, Mark let h_i, g_i, and p_i denote the normalized value of the city's number of households, median age, and proportion nonwhite, respectively. For example, a value of 1.3 for h_3 indicates that the number of households in city 3 is 1.3 standard deviations *above* the six-city mean; a value of -0.9 for p_5 indicates that the proportion nonwhite in city 5 is 0.9 standard deviations *below* the six-city mean.

4. Finally, Mark defined d_{ij} as the measure of similarity between city i and city j, and he computed d_{ij} according to the formula

$$d_{ij} = \sqrt{(h_i - h_j)^2 + (g_i - g_j)^2 + (p_i - p_j)^2}.$$

In words, d_{ij} is the square root of the sum of the squared differences between the two cities' normalized values for each attribute. For example, Mark obtained the following values for the normalized attributes of city 1 and city 2:

Attribute	Normalized Value	
	City 1	City 2
Number of households	3	−1
Median age	0	1
Proportion nonwhite	−1	2

TABLE 9.16 "Distance" d_{ij} Between City i and City j

	$j=1$	$j=2$	$j=3$	$j=4$	$j=5$	$j=6$
$i=1$	—	5.10	0.78	1.96	1.96	0.78
$i=2$	5.10	—	1.96	6.28	0.78	6.67
$i=3$	0.78	1.96	—	1.96	0.39	1.57
$i=4$	1.96	6.28	1.96	—	3.92	0.39
$i=5$	1.96	0.78	0.39	3.92	—	3.53
$i=6$	0.78	6.67	1.57	0.39	3.53	—

Given these data, he computed

$$d_{12} = \sqrt{[3 - (-1)]^2 + [0 - 1]^2 + [-1 - 2]^2} = \sqrt{26} = 5.10 .$$

Table 9.16 summarizes the values of d_{ij} for all possible pairs of cities. Of course, $d_{ij} = d_{ji}$. Hereafter, we will refer to d_{ij} as the *distance between city i and city j*. The closer the value of d_{ij} is to 0, the more similar are city i and city j. Consequently, Mark may now compare city i with city j by looking at the single number d_{ij} rather than by subjectively comparing the original multiattribute characterization of the two cities.

Having computed the distances between all pairs of cities, Mark next turns his attention to the problem of partitioning the six cities into two clusters. He regards this as a two-part problem. First, he must select two cities to serve as the so-called *cluster medians*, each of which will be the "focal point" for a different cluster. Then he must form two clusters by "assigning" each of the remaining cities to one of the two cluster medians. In selecting the cluster medians and assigning the remaining cities to a cluster median, Mark's objective is to minimize the sum over both cluster medians of the distances from each remaining city to the cluster median to which it is assigned. For example, suppose that city 2 serves as the cluster median for a cluster consisting of cities 2 and 5 and that city 6 serves as a cluster median for a cluster consisting of cities 1, 3, 4, and 6, then the resulting objective value is

$$(d_{52}) + (d_{16} + d_{36} + d_{46}) = (0.78) + (0.78 + 1.57 + 0.39) = 3.52 .$$

With respect to this objective function, Mark's goal is to find the optimal selection of cluster medians and assignments of the remaining cities to the cluster medians.

To formulate his cluster analysis problem as an ILP, Mark defines six binary variables $y_1, y_2, ..., y_6$, where

$$y_i = \begin{cases} 1 \text{ denotes that city } i \text{ is a cluster median,} \\ 0 \text{ denotes that city } i \text{ is not a cluster median.} \end{cases}$$

He also defines 30 additional binary variables x_{ij} for $1 \leqslant i \leqslant 6$ and $1 \leqslant j \leqslant 6$ and $i \neq j$, where

$$x_{ij} = \begin{cases} 1 \text{ denotes that city } i \text{ is assigned to a cluster median at city } j, \\ 0 \text{ denotes that city } i \text{ is not assigned to a cluster median at city } j. \end{cases}$$

Mark then formulates his problem as the following pure-binary ILP:

Minimize
$$5.10x_{12} + 0.78x_{13} + 1.96x_{14} + 1.96x_{15} + 0.78x_{16}$$
$$+ 5.10x_{21} + 1.96x_{23} + 6.28x_{24} + 0.78x_{25} + 6.67x_{26}$$
$$+ 0.78x_{31} + 1.96x_{32} + 1.96x_{34} + 0.39x_{35} + 1.57x_{36}$$
$$+ 1.96x_{41} + 6.28x_{42} + 1.96x_{43} + 3.92x_{45} + 0.39x_{46}$$
$$+ 1.96x_{51} + 0.78x_{52} + 0.39x_{53} + 3.92x_{54} + 3.53x_{56}$$
$$+ 0.78x_{61} + 6.67x_{62} + 1.57x_{63} + 0.39x_{64} + 3.53x_{65}$$

(Minimize the sum of the distances from each city to its respective cluster median.)

subject to

$$x_{21} + x_{31} + x_{41} + x_{51} + x_{61} \leqslant 5y_1$$
$$x_{12} + x_{32} + x_{42} + x_{52} + x_{62} \leqslant 5y_2$$
$$x_{13} + x_{23} + x_{43} + x_{53} + x_{63} \leqslant 5y_3$$
$$x_{14} + x_{24} + x_{34} + x_{54} + x_{64} \leqslant 5y_4$$
$$x_{15} + x_{25} + x_{35} + x_{45} + x_{65} \leqslant 5y_5$$
$$x_{16} + x_{26} + x_{36} + x_{46} + x_{56} \leqslant 5y_6$$

(Unless city j is a cluster median, no cities can be assigned to it; that is, $y_j = 0$ implies that $x_{ij} = 0$ for all j.)

$$x_{21} + x_{31} + x_{41} + x_{51} + x_{61} \geqslant y_1$$
$$x_{12} + x_{32} + x_{42} + x_{52} + x_{62} \geqslant y_2$$
$$x_{13} + x_{23} + x_{43} + x_{53} + x_{63} \geqslant y_3$$
$$x_{14} + x_{24} + x_{34} + x_{54} + x_{64} \geqslant y_4$$
$$x_{15} + x_{25} + x_{35} + x_{45} + x_{65} \geqslant y_5$$
$$x_{16} + x_{26} + x_{36} + x_{46} + x_{56} \geqslant y_6$$

(If city j is a cluster median, at least one other city must be assigned to it; that is, $y_j = 1$ implies that $x_{ij} = 1$ for at least one j.)

$$y_1 + x_{12} + x_{13} + x_{14} + x_{15} + x_{16} = 1$$
$$y_2 + x_{21} + x_{23} + x_{24} + x_{25} + x_{26} = 1$$
$$y_3 + x_{31} + x_{32} + x_{34} + x_{35} + x_{36} = 1$$
$$y_4 + x_{41} + x_{42} + x_{43} + x_{45} + x_{46} = 1$$
$$y_5 + x_{51} + x_{52} + x_{53} + x_{54} + x_{56} = 1$$
$$y_6 + x_{61} + x_{62} + x_{63} + x_{64} + x_{65} = 1$$

(Either city i is a cluster median or it is assigned to a cluster median at another city; that is either $y_i = 1$ or $x_{ij} = 1$ for some j.)

$$y_1 + y_2 + y_3 + y_4 + y_5 + y_6 = 2$$

(There must be 2 clusters.)

and

$x_{ij} = 0$ or 1 for $i = 1, 2, \ldots, n$ and $j = 1, 2, \ldots, n$ and $i \neq j$
$y_1, y_2, y_3, y_4, y_5, y_6 = 0$ or 1.

(integrality)

The verbal comments to the right of the formulation should suffice as an explanation of the formulation, especially given the ILP's similarity to the ILP arising in the facility location problem of Section 9.10.

Mark may find the actual optimal solution to his ILP using either the general-purpose method described in the Section 9.14 or the special-purpose method described by Mulvey and Crowder.[11] In the ILP's optimal solution,

$$y_5 = y_6 = 1 \quad \text{(cities 5 and 6 are cluster medians)},$$
$$x_{25} = x_{35} = 1 \quad \text{(cities 2 and 3 are assigned to the cluster median at city 5)},$$
$$x_{16} = x_{46} = 1 \quad \text{(cities 1 and 4 are assigned to the cluster median at city 6)},$$

and all other decision variable equal 0; the corresponding optimal objective value is 2.34. Such a solution corresponds to the following clusters:

{city 2, city 3, city 5*},
{city 1, city 4, city 6*},

where the asterisks indicate the cluster medians. After Mark obtains these "optimal" clusters, he may then select a pair of cities from each cluster and, within each pair, test market the product with the price discount in one city and without it in the other.

Mark's problem is a simplification of one of the first marketing applications of cluster analysis.[12] The actual problem involved the partitioning of 88 cities in 18 clusters on the basis of the cities' similarity with respect to 14 attributes.

In the general cluster-analysis problem, the objects to be clustered need not be potential cities for test marketing. Other possibilities include customers, product

---

[11] *Ibid.*

[12] P. E. Green, R. E. Frank, and P. J. Robinson, "Cluster Analysis in Test Market Selection," *Management Science*, Vol. 13, No. 8 (April 1967), 387–400.

brands, advertisements, television programs, and magazines. Regardless of the nature of the objects, the goal of cluster analysis is to partition them into similar clusters, where the similarity between a pair of objects is defined in terms of a single number that summarizes the likeness between the multiattribute characteristics of the objects.

In a manner similar to that for the facility location problem of Section 9.10, we can easily incorporate the following features into a formulation of a cluster-analysis problem.

- An upper bound and/or lower bound on the number of clusters to be formed, instead of a specification of the exact number,

- An upper bound and/or lower bound on the number of objects in any one cluster, and

- An upper bound on the distance from any object to the cluster median to which it is assigned, thereby preventing the assignment of any object to a cluster whose cluster median is quite dissimilar from the object.

9.13 SOLVING INTEGER LINEAR PROGRAMS USING A COMPUTER SOFTWARE PACKAGE

For the benefit of those readers who do not intend to proceed to the next section, we shall now comment briefly on the solution of integer linear programs using a computer software packatge. The next section contains the details of the solution method used by most commercially available software packages.

As we have seen, an ILP is simply an LP with the added restrictions that some or all of the decision variables must assume integer values. Consequently, except for the specification of which decision variables must assume integer values, the computer input necessary to solve an ILP is identical to that described in Section 3.7 for solving an LP. In fact, most commercially available software for solving ILPs is part of a "package" of software designed to solve both LPs and ILPs. The input to such a software package consists of the following two parts, the second of which is optional:

I. Part I, the most complex part, involves specifying the data for the LP or the ILP. These data include the objective-function type (maximize or minimize), the names of each decision variable, the coefficient of each decision variable in the objective function, the type of each constraint ($\leqslant$, $\geqslant$, or $=$), the coefficient of each decision variable in each constraint, and the right-hand side of each constraint. We illustrated a typical format for providing these data in Section 3.7's discussion of the hypothetical LINPRO.

II. Part II, the optional part, involves specifying which decision variables (if any) must assume integer values. Although varying somewhat according to the particular software package in use, the format for Part II usually consists of a simple command or set of commands specifying the names of the integer variables.

If Part II is absent, the software package assumes the input pertains to an LP and employs the simplex method to obtain the optimal solution. If Part II is present, the computer package assumes the input pertains to an ILP and finds the optimal solution using a general-purpose method such as the one described in the next section.

Regardless of whether the problem under consideration is an LP or an ILP, the output from the computer package will, of course, provide the optimal values of the objective function and the decision variables. However, there is one important distinction between the output from the computer package for an LP and that for an ILP. As we saw in Section 3.7, the output for an LP includes (perhaps as an option) some sensitivity analysis, such as the shadow price for the right-hand side for each constraint. Such sensitivity analysis is absent from the output for an ILP, because there is no formal methodology for performing sensitivity analysis for an ILP.[13] Unfortunately, the user can answer questions asking "What if ...?" only by inputting revised data and resolving the ILP.

To summarize:

> Although a software package will generally take much longer to solve an ILP than an LP of the same size, the input the user must provide to the software package in order to solve an ILP is virtually identical. The only additional information required is the names of the variables that must assume integer values.

9.14 SOLVING AN INTEGER LINEAR PROGRAM USING THE BRANCH-AND-BOUND METHOD[14]

In this section we learn how to solve an ILP using what is known as the *branch-and-bound method,* hereafter abbreviated as the *B&B method.* The B&B method is currently the most efficient general-purpose method for solving an ILP and is used by almost all commercially available software packages.

We will first learn the B&B method in the context of a pure-general ILP whose objective function involves maximization, postponing until later a discussion of the modifications necessary to solve other types of ILPs. Throughout our discussion we will use the terminology *all-integer solution* when all decision variables required by the ILP to have integer values actually have integer values. Conversely, we will use the terminology *fractional solution* when at least one decision variable required by the ILP to have an integer value has a noninteger value.

As our example, consider the ILP displayed in Figure 9.5. Figure 9.5 also

---

[13] A software package designed to solve both LPs and ILPs might use the same format to report an ILP's optimal solution as it does for an LP's optimal solution. If so, you must remember to ignore any sensitivity analysis in the context of an ILP. It is meaningless!

[14] This section may be omitted without significant loss of continuity.

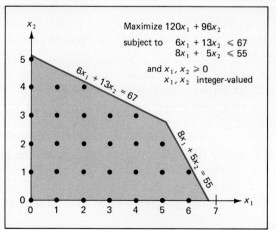

Figure 9.5 The example ILP and its feasible region

displays the feasible region for this ILP and its LP relaxation. As usual, the shaded region represents the LP relaxation's feasible region, and the 29 isolated dots within the shaded region represent the ILP's feasible region. (Before proceeding, verify the correctness of Figure 9.5's graph.)

The B&B method consists of an *initialization step* followed by as many repetitions as necessary of a sequence of *iterative steps*. Each repetition of the iterative steps comprises an *iteration* of the B&B method.

Let us now apply the B&B method to our example ILP. Throughout our commentary, we make repeated references to Figures 9.6, 9.7, and 9.8, which summarize our analysis in a format known as a *tree*.[15] Each figure consists of interconnected rectangles which we refer to as *nodes*. At the tops of the nodes are the labels 0, 1A, 1B, 2A, 2B, and so on. We use each label to simplify reference to a specific node and its associated ILP. Dashed lines divide each figure into six portions. As we discuss each portion in turn (from top to bottom), pretend that all portions below do not yet exist.

Initialization

The B&B method's initialization step begins with the solution of the LP relaxation of the ILP. If we are lucky, the LP relaxation has an all-integer optimal solution. If so, then Relationship 3 in Section 9.3 implies that the LP relaxation's optimal solution must also be the ILP's optimal solution.

In general, we must use the simplex method (discussed in Chapters 6 and 7) to solve the LP relaxation. However, because our example ILP has only two decision variables, we may graphically solve its LP relaxation. Of course, we could also graphically solve our example ILP. We will not do so, however, since our goal is to learn the B&B method.

Figure 9.6's topmost node displays our example ILP (hereafter called ILP 0), and Figure 9.7's topmost node displays the graphical solution of the LP relaxation of ILP 0 (where the graph's dashed line represents the objective function's optimal isoquant line). Observe that the LP relaxation's optimal solution lies at the intersection of the two boundary equations

$$6x_1 + 13x_2 = 67,$$
$$8x_1 + 5x_2 = 55.$$

You should verify that the solution to this system of equations is

$$(x_1, x_2) = (5\tfrac{5}{37}, 2\tfrac{29}{37}.)$$

Substituting this solution into the objective function, we obtain an objective value of

$$120(5\tfrac{5}{37}) + 96(2\tfrac{29}{37}) = 883\tfrac{17}{37}.$$

Unfortunately, since the decision variables' values are not integer, we have not solved ILP 0. However, our solution of the LP relaxation has not been in vain. Although we do not yet know ILP 0's optimal solution, we know from Relationship 2 in Section 9.3 that the ILP's optimal objective value cannot exceed $883\tfrac{17}{37}$, the LP relaxation's optimal objective value.

---

[15] This terminology is motivated by the resemblances of Figures 9.6–9.8 to trees that have been turned upside-down.

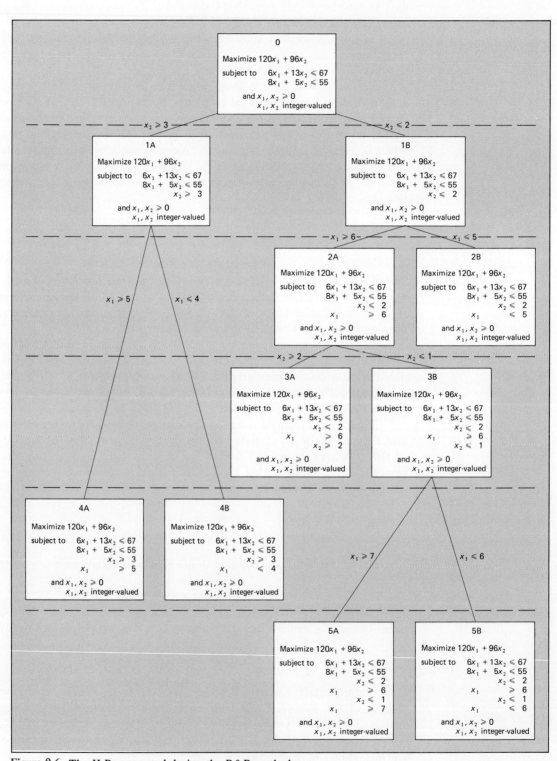

Figure 9.6 The ILPs generated during the B&B method

438

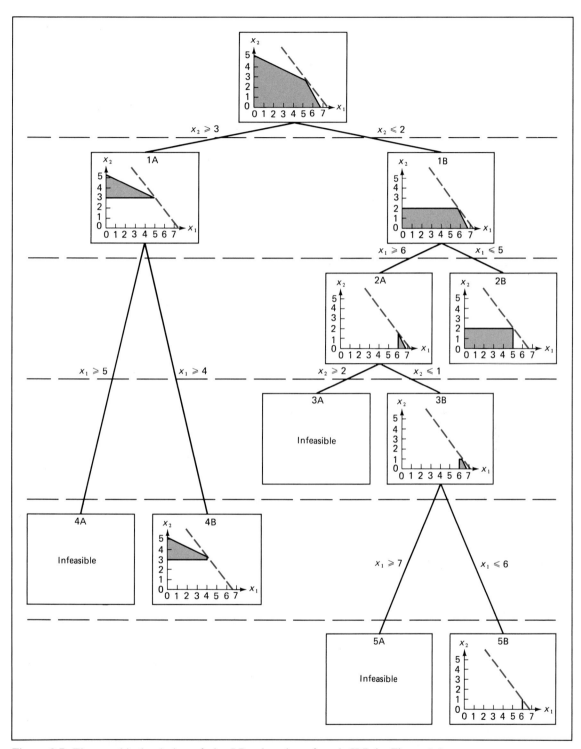

Figure 9.7 The graphical solution of the LP relaxation of each ILP in Figure 9.6

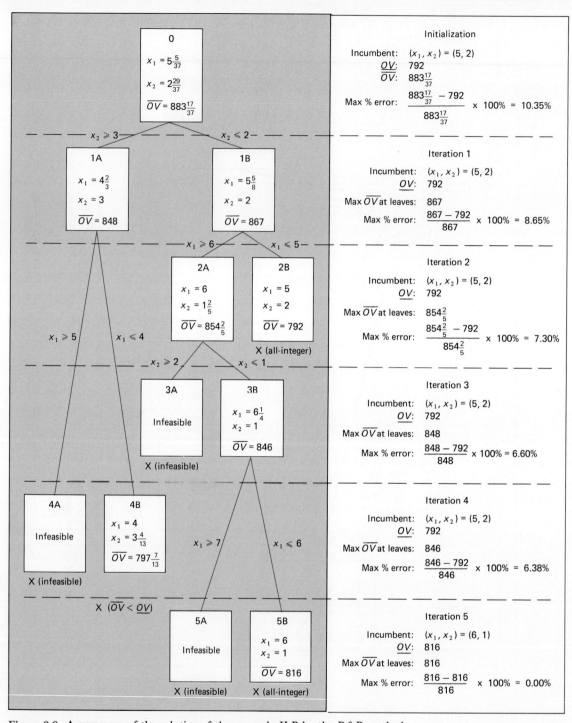

Figure 9.8 A summary of the solution of the example ILP by the B&B method

Besides providing an upper bound on ILP 0's optimal objective value, the LP relaxation's optimal solution provides a good starting point for an attempt to use rounding to obtain an acceptable close-to-optimal solution. Examination of Figure 9.5 shows that, of the four rounding alternatives for $(x_1, x_2) = (5\frac{5}{37}, 2\frac{29}{37})$, only $(x_1, x_2) = (5, 2)$ is feasible. This rounding alternative has an objective value of

$$120(5) + 96(2) = 792$$

Although it is unlikely that this rounding alternative is ILP 0's optimal solution, its objective value of 792 is a lower bound on ILP 0's optimal objective value.

Throughout our execution of the B&B method, we call the feasible solution to ILP 0 having the best objective value thus far encountered the *incumbent*. At this point, $(x_1, x_2) = (5, 2)$ is the only feasible solution to ILP 0 we have encountered and, hence, by default, is the incumbent.[16] At any point during the B&B method, we always have the option of terminating and using the incumbent as a "proxy" for ILP 0's optimal solution. If we were to do so now, the maximum percentage error would be

$$\text{maximum percentage error} = \frac{\begin{pmatrix}\text{objective value of} \\ \text{optimal solution for} \\ \text{LP relaxation}\end{pmatrix} - \begin{pmatrix}\text{objective value} \\ \text{of} \\ \text{incumbent}\end{pmatrix}}{\begin{pmatrix}\text{objective value of} \\ \text{optimal solution for} \\ \text{LP relaxation}\end{pmatrix}} \times 100\%$$

$$= \frac{883\frac{17}{37} - 792}{883\frac{17}{37}} \times 100\%$$

$$= 10.35\%.$$

Let us assume that a maximum percentage error of 10.35% is unacceptable and proceed with the B&B method. Before doing so, we summarize the initialization step in node 0 of Figure 9.8. Node 0 contains the optimal solution and the optimal objective value of the LP relaxation of ILP 0. Observe within node 0 that we have denoted the LP relaxation's optimal objective value by $\overline{OV}$, where the line above the OV reminds us that this is an upper bound on ILP 0's optimal objective value. To the right of node 0 are four lines we hereafter call the *incumbent summary*. The first line displays the incumbent; the second line displays the incumbent's objective value, denoted by $\underline{OV}$ to remind us that it is a lower bound on ILP 0's optimal objective value; the third line displays the $\overline{OV}$ value from node 0; the fourth line displays the maximum percentage error computed from $\overline{OV}$ and $\underline{OV}$.

Iteration 1

We now begin a sequence of steps that comprise the first iteration of the B&B method. The iteration's first step is known as *branching*.[17] Branching consists of "dividing" ILP 0 into two smaller ILPs, smaller in the sense that each ILP has fewer feasible solutions. In particular, branching at iteration 1 consists of the following steps:

1. We arbitrarily select a decision variable having a noninteger value in the optimal solution to the LP relaxation of ILP 0. We refer to this variable as the *branching variable*. Looking at node 0 in Figure 9.8, we see that both x_1 and x_2 have noninteger values. Let us arbitrarily select x_2 as the branching variable.

---

[16] You may be wondering why we say we have not yet encountered the feasible solutions represented by the other 28 dots in Figure 9.5. As we execute the B&B method, keep in mind that a graph such as Figure 9.5 is possible only because our example ILP has two decision variables. In general, we do not have a graph available and, therefore, know only what we discover through the B&B method.

[17] Some refer to branching as *partitioning*.

2. Based on x_2's optimal value of $2\frac{29}{37}$, we create two new ILPs from ILP 0, one by adding the structural constraint $x_2 \geqslant 3$ and another by adding $x_2 \leqslant 2$. Note that the constraints' right-hand sides (2 and 3) are the two integers obtained by rounding x_2's optimal value ($2\frac{29}{37}$) up to the nearest integer and down to the nearest integer.

We refer to these two new ILPs as ILP 1A and ILP 1B ("1" for the first iteration and "A" and "B" to differentiate between them). To pictorially represent that ILP 1A and ILP 1B are each obtained by adding a constraint to ILP 0, we return to Figure 9.6 and draw two so-called *branches* emanating from node 0. These branches end at nodes 1A and 1B, which respectively display ILP 1A and ILP 1B. We call node 0 the *parent* of nodes 1A and 1B, and we call nodes 1A and 1B the *children* of node 0.

You may be wondering what we gain by branching. It appears that all we accomplish is to replace one unsolved ILP (the parent) by two unsolved ILPs (the children)! Although the precise benefits of branching will not become apparent until later, Figure 9.9 at least provides some insight by illustrating the following facts:

- Branching has divided ILP 0's feasible solutions into two pieces and eliminated from consideration a third piece containing no feasible solutions. In particular, the 9 dots in Figure 9.9's upper shaded region represent ILP 1A's feasible region—that is, the portion of ILP 0's feasible region that also satisfies the additional constraint $x_2 \geqslant 3$. Similarly, the 20 dots in Figure 9.9's lower shaded region represent ILP 1B's feasible region—that is, the portion of ILP 0's feasible region that also satisfies the additional constraint $x_2 \leqslant 2$. Furthermore, the absence of any dots in Figure 9.9 lying between (but not on) the lines $x_2 = 2$ and $x_2 = 3$ indicates that this region labeled "Excluded," contains no feasible solutions to ILP 0.

- Since all feasible solutions to ILP 0 are now feasible solutions to either ILP 1A or ILP 1B and since the objective functions for ILP 0, ILP 1A, and ILP 1B are identical, ILP 0's optimal solution is either ILP 1A's optimal solution or ILP 1B's optimal solution, whichever has the highest objective value. It follows that we may forget about solving ILP 0 and instead solve ILP 1A and ILP 1B.

- The optimal solution to the LP relaxation of ILP 0 is not a feasible solution (let alone optimal) to the LP relaxation of either ILP 1A or ILP 1B. Can you see why? The reason is that we have added to the structural constraints

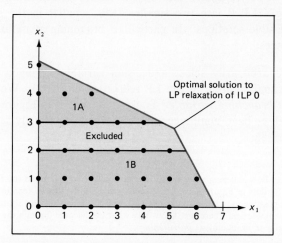

Figure 9.9 Graphical illustration of branching

of ILP 0 either $x_2 \geqslant 3$ or $x_2 \leqslant 2$. Either constraint precludes x_2 from equaling $2\frac{29}{37}$, as it did in the optimal solution to the LP relaxation of ILP 0. Hence, if we solve the LP relaxation of ILP 1A or ILP 1B, we are guaranteed not to obtain $(x_1, x_2) = (5\frac{5}{37}, 2\frac{29}{37})$ as the optimal solution. To obtain a graphical confirmation of this guarantee, note in Figure 9.9 that $(x_1, x_2) = (5\frac{5}{37}, 2\frac{29}{37})$ lies in the "Excluded" region eliminated from further consideration.

To summarize, branching "divides" the parent, ILP 0, into two children, ILP 1A and ILP 1B. When solving the children's LP relaxations, we are guaranteed not to obtain the optimal solution to the parent's LP relaxation. If we are lucky, each child's LP relaxation will have an all-integer optimal solution. If so, we may terminate the B&B method; if not, we must continue by repeating the branching process at least once more.

After branching, the second step within an iteration of the B&B method is known as *bounding*. Bounding consists of solving the LP relaxations of ILP 1A and ILP 1B, the children created by the branching at ILP 0. The graphical solutions of these LP relaxations are displayed in nodes 1A and 1B in Figure 9.7. From these graphs, observe that the respective optimal solutions for the LP relaxations of ILP 1A and ILP 1B lie at the intersection of the following boundary equations:

For LP Relaxation of ILP 1A	For LP Relaxation of ILP 1B
$6x_1 + 13x_2 = 67$	$8x_1 + 5x_2 = 55$
$x_2 = 3$	$x_2 = 2$

You should verify that the solution to each system of equations is

For LP Relaxation of ILP 1A	For LP Relaxation of ILP 1B
$(x_1, x_2) = (4\frac{2}{3}, 3)$	$(x_1, x_2) = (5\frac{5}{8}, 2)$

Substituting these solutions into the objective function results in objective values of

For LP Relaxation of ILP 1A	For LP Relaxation of ILP 1B
$\overline{OV} = 120(4\frac{2}{3}) + 96(3) = 848$	$\overline{OV} = 120(5\frac{5}{8}) + 96(2) = 867$

Observe that we have once again used the notation $\overline{OV}$ as a reminder that an LP relaxation's optimal value is an upper bound on the ILP's optimal objective value. We complete iteration 1's bounding step by returning to Figure 9.8, creating nodes 1A and 1B as children of node 0, and recording in these nodes the results of our solution of the LP relaxations of ILP 1A and ILP 1B.

We are now ready to perform the iteration's third step, a step known as *updating*. Updating consists of revising the incumbent, if possible, and revising the incumbent's maximum percentage error. Since the LP relaxation of neither ILP 1A nor ILP 1B has an all-integer optimal solution, the incumbent remains unchanged. At least, however, we can reduce the incumbent's maximum percentage error. To explain how, we need to introduce the concept of a *leaf*. In a tree such as that in Figure 9.8, any childless node is a leaf. The current tree consists only of the portion in Figure 9.8 above the second dashed line. Hence, the tree has two leaves, node 1A and node 1B. The $\overline{OV}$ value written within each leaf is an upper bound on the optimal objective value of the leaf's ILP.

In Figure 9.8, node 1A's $\overline{OV}$ value and node 1B's $\overline{OV}$ value are both less than node 0's $\overline{OV}$ value. This is no coincidence! Since the feasible region of a child's LP relaxation is always a subset of the feasible region for the parent's LP relaxation, a child's $\overline{OV}$ value will always be less than or equal to (usually strictly less than) its parent's $\overline{OV}$ value. Thus, in Figure 9.8's tree, we henceforth ignore node 0's $\overline{OV}$ value and focus instead on the leaves' $\overline{OV}$ values. Although node 1A's $\overline{OV}$ value of 848 is an upper bound on ILP 1A's optimal objective value and node 1B's $\overline{OV}$ value of 867 is an upper bound on ILP 1B's optimal objective value, only the *maximum* of these two $\overline{OV}$ values is an upper bound on ILP 0's optimal objective value. This maximum $\overline{OV}$ value, then, is the one we must use when computing the incumbent's maximum percentage error.

We summarize the update step in Figure 9.8's incumbent summary for iteration 1. Since the incumbent has not been changed, the first two lines are identical to those in the initialization step. However, on the third line, we record the maximum $\overline{OV}$ value at the tree's leaves, node 1B's $\overline{OV}$ value of 867. Then, on the fourth line, we use the bounds on the second and third lines to compute the incumbent's maximum percentage error. Comparing the maximum percentage errors from the initialization step and iteration 1 (10.35% versus 8.65%), we see that we have made some progress. Although we have not yet identified ILP 0's optimal solution, we have reduced the maximum percentage error associated with terminating the B&B method and using the incumbent as a proxy for ILP 0's optimal solution. Let us assume that a maximum percentage error of 8.65% is unacceptable and perform another iteration.

Iteration 2

Like iteration 1, iteration 2 begins with branching and continues with bounding followed by updating. However, these three steps are followed by two additional steps that were unnecessary in iteration 1. The following commentary, in conjunction with Figures 9.6–9.8, summarizes iteration 2:

Branching. At the start of iteration 1, there was no uncertainty over where to branch because our tree had only one leaf, node 0. However, at the start of iteration 2, our tree has two leaves, node 1A and node 1B. We must select one at which to branch, the so-called *branching leaf*.

To select the branching leaf, we will always follow the rule of selecting the leaf having the maximum $\overline{OV}$ value. This rule is known as the *best bound rule*. To understand the rationale for it, recall from iteration 1 that a child's $\overline{OV}$ value is never higher and almost always lower than the parent's $\overline{OV}$ value. Thus, after branching according to the best bound rule, the leaf having the highest $\overline{OV}$ value is replaced by two leaves whose $\overline{OV}$ values will almost always be lower. Hence, when we subsequently revise the incumbent's maximum percentage error in the updating step, it will almost always be lower than before.

Applying the best bound rule to the tree at the start of iteration 2, we select node 1B, since its $\overline{OV}$ value of 867 exceeds node 1A's $\overline{OV}$ value of 848. Looking at node 1B in Figure 9.8, we see that x_1 is the only decision variable having a noninteger value. Hence, by default, x_1 becomes the branching variable. Branching now proceeds as summarized below and as diagrammed in Figure 9.6 between the second and third dashed lines:

We draw two branches emanating from node 1B. The branches end at ILP 2A and ILP 2B, children of ILP 1B obtained by respectively adding the constraints $x_1 \geqslant 6$ and $x_1 \leqslant 5$. Note that the constraints' right-hand sides of 6 and 5 are the integers on either side of $5\frac{5}{8}$, x_1's value in the optimal solution to the LP relaxation of ILP 1B (see node 1B in Figure 9.8).

Bounding. Bounding consists of solving the LP relaxations of ILP 2A and ILP 2B, the children created by the branching at ILP 1B. The graphical solutions of these LP relaxations are displayed in nodes 2A and 2B in Figure 9.7. Using these graphs, you should verify that the respective optimal solutions and optimal objective values for the LP relaxations of ILP 2A and ILP 2B are

<table>
<tr><td>For LP Relaxation of ILP 2A</td><td>For LP Relaxation of ILP 2B</td></tr>
<tr><td>$(x_1, x_2) = (6, 1\frac{2}{5})$</td><td>$(x_1, x_2) = (5, 2)$</td></tr>
<tr><td>$\overline{OV} = 854\frac{2}{5}$</td><td>$\overline{OV} = 792$</td></tr>
</table>

We complete iteration 2's bounding step by returning to Figure 9.8, creating nodes 2A and 2B as children of node 1B, and recording in these nodes the results of our solution of the LP relaxations of ILP 2A and ILP 2B. (Note that we have not yet added to the tree the "X" and the parenthetic remark below node 2B.)

Updating. We summarize the update step in Figure 9.8's incumbent summary for Iteration 2. Since the LP relaxation of ILP 2B has an all-integer optimal solution, we must check to see if it should become the new incumbent, by virtue of having a higher objective value than the current incumbent. Unfortunately (and coincidentally), the optimal solution to the LP relaxation of ILP 2B is identical to the incumbent. Hence, the first two lines of iteration 2's incumbent summary are identical to those in iteration 1. Despite our inability to change the incumbent, we can at least reduce the maximum percentage error. To see why, note that our current tree (the portion in Figure 9.8 above the third dashed line) has three leaves: node 1A with $\overline{OV} = 848$, node 2A with $\overline{OV} = 854\frac{2}{5}$, and node 2B with $\overline{OV} = 792$. Since the maximum of the leaves' $\overline{OV}$ values is $854\frac{2}{5}$, this is the value we record on the third line of the incumbent summary. Then, on the fourth line, we use the bounds on the second and third lines to compute the incumbent's maximum percentage error. Comparing the maximum percentage errors from iteration 1 and iteration 2 (8.65% versus 7.30%), we see that we have again made some progress.

Pruning. We now introduce a fourth step (unnecessary until this iteration) known as *pruning.*[18] A leaf is said to be *pruned* when we can conclude that further branching at the leaf is unnecessary. Such a conclusion is valid if one of the three conditions listed in Table 9.17 occurs. Pruning Condition 1 has occurred at node 2B in Figure 9.8. We indicate the pruning of this leaf by placing below it an "X" followed by a brief parenthetic explanation of the reason for the pruning. In later iterations, we will encounter examples of Pruning Conditions 2 and 3.

Termination Check. The fifth and final step of a typical iteration of the B&B method is known as the *termination check.* We terminate the B&B method if either of the conditions listed in Table 9.18 occurs. In our example, let us assume that we will settle for nothing less than the optimal solution to ILP 0; that is, we will continue performing iterations until the occurrence of Termination Condition 2.

---

[18] Some refer to pruning as *fathoming.*

TABLE 9.17 The B&B Method's Three Pruning Conditions

1. The LP relaxation of the leaf's ILP has an all-integer optimal solution. Since this solution must also be optimal for the leaf's IPL, further branching from the leaf is unnecessary.

2. The LP relaxation of the leaf's ILP has no feasible solution (let alone an optimal one). Since this in turn implies that the leaf's ILP has no feasible solution, further branching from the leaf is unnecessary.

3. The LP relaxation of the leaf's ILP has an optimal objective value that is less than or equal to the incumbent's objective value. With $\overline{OV} \leqslant \underline{OV}$, further branching from the leaf is unnecessary, since it could never discover a feasible solution to ILP 0 that is better than the incumbent. (Note that, if we want to find all optimal solutions should multiple optimality occur, then $<$ replaces $\leqslant$ in this condition.)

TABLE 9.18 The B&B Method's Two Termination Conditions

1. The incumbent's maximum percentage error has been reduced to a value acceptable to us (say, for example, less than 5%). When terminating in this manner, we use the incumbent as a proxy for ILP 0's optimal solution.

2. All leaves in the tree have been pruned, thereby making further branching unnecessary. When terminating in this manner, we are guaranteed that the incumbent is ILP 0's optimal solution.

After concluding our example, we will comment on why Termination Condition 1 is often used when solving a real-world ILP.

The current tree now has three leaves: node 1A, node 2A and node 2B. Of these leaves, only node 2B has been pruned. Hence, we must perform at least one more iteration.

Iteration 3

The following commentary, in conjunction with Figures 9.6–9.8, summarizes iteration 3's branching, bounding, updating, pruning, and termination check:

Branching. We must first select the branching leaf from among the tree's unpruned leaves. As we have noted, there are only two unpruned leaves: node 1A and node 2A. Using the best bound rule, we select as the branching leaf node 2A. We must now select the branching variable. Looking at node 2A in Figure 9.8, we see that x_2 is the only variable having a noninteger value. Hence, by default, x_2 becomes the branching variable. As diagrammed in Figure 9.6 between the third and fourth dashed lines, branching now proceeds by creating ILP 3A and ILP 3B, children of ILP 2A obtained by respectively adding the constraints $x_2 \geqslant 2$ and $x_2 \leqslant 1$. Note that the constraints' right-hand sides of 2 and 1 are the integers on either side of $1\frac{2}{5}$, x_2's value in the optimal solution to the LP relaxation of ILP 2A (see node 2A in Figure 9.8).

Bounding. Bounding consists of solving the LP relaxations of ILP 3A and ILP 3B, the children created by the branching at ILP 2A. The former has no feasible solution (let alone an optimal one). To see why, look at the graph in Figure 9.7's node 2A (the parent of node 3A) and observe that the entire feasible region lies below the line $x_2 = 2$. Hence, the addition of the constraint $x_2 \geqslant 2$ leads to infeasibility. We now turn to the solution of the LP relaxation of ILP 3B. Using the graph in Figure 9.7's node 3B, you should verify that the optimal solution is $(x_1, x_2) = (6\frac{1}{4}, 1)$ and the optimal objective value is $\overline{OV} = 846$. We complete iteration 3's bounding step by summarizing these results in nodes 3A and 3B in Figure 9.8. (Note that we have not yet added to the tree the "X" and the parenthetic remark below node 3A.)

Updating. We summarize the update step in Figure 9.8's incumbent summary for iteration 3. Since the LP relaxation of neither ILP 3A nor ILP 3B has an all-integer optimal solution, the first two lines of iteration 3's incumbent summary are identical to those in iteration 2. Despite our inability to change the incumbent, we can at least reduce the maximum percentage error. To see why, note that our current tree (the portion in Figure 9.8 above the fourth dotted line) has three unpruned leaves, only two of which have $\overline{OV}$ values: node 1A with $\overline{OV} = 848$ and node 3B with $\overline{OV} = 846$. Since the maximum of the leaves' $\overline{OV}$ values is 848, this is the value we record on the third line of the incumbent summary. Then, on the fourth line, we compute the incumbent's maximum percentage error as 6.60% (a reduction of 0.70% from the previous iteration).

Pruning. The current tree has three unpruned leaves: node 1A, node 3A, and node 3B. Applying Table 9.17's pruning conditions to each leaf, we see that Pruning Condition 2 has occurred at node 3A. In Figure 9.8, we indicate the pruning of this leaf by placing below it an "X" followed by a brief parenthetic explanation.

Termination Check. The current tree now has two unpruned leaves: node 1A and node 3B. Hence, we must perform another iteration (assuming we are unwilling to accept a maximum percentage error of 6.60%).

Iteration 4

The following commentary, in conjunction with Figures 9.6–9.8, summarizes iteration 4:

Branching. We must first select the branching leaf from among the tree's unpruned leaves. As we have noted, there are only two unpruned leaves: node 1A and node 3B. Using the best bound rule, we select as the branching leaf node 1A. We must now select the branching variable. Looking at node 1A in Figure 9.8, we see that x_1 is the only variable having a noninteger value. Hence, by default, x_1 becomes the branching variable. As diagrammed in Figure 9.6 between the fourth and fifth dashed lines, branching now proceeds by creating ILP 4A and ILP 4B, children of ILP 1A obtained by respectively adding the constraints $x_1 \geqslant 5$ and $x_1 \leqslant 4$. Note that the constraints' right-hand sides of 5 and 4 are the integers on either side of $4\frac{2}{3}$, x_1's value in the optimal solution to the LP relaxation of ILP 1A (see node 1A in Figure 9.8).

Bounding. Bounding consists of solving the LP relaxations of ILP 4A and ILP 4B, the children created by the branching at ILP 1A. To see why the former LP relaxation has no feasible solution, look at the graph in Figure 9.7's node 1A (the parent of node 4A) and observe that the entire feasible region lies to the left of the line $x_1 = 5$. Hence, the addition of the constraint $x_1 \geqslant 5$ leads to infeasibility. We now turn to the solution of the LP relaxation of ILP 4B. Using the graph in Figure 9.7's node 4B, you should verify that the optimal solution is $(x_1, x_2) = (4, 3\frac{4}{13})$ and the optimal objective value is $\overline{OV} = 797\frac{7}{13}$. We complete iteration 4's bounding step by summarizing these results in nodes 4A and 4B in Figure 9.8. (For both node 4A and 4B, note that we have not yet added to the tree the "X" and the parenthetic remark below each node.)

Updating. We summarize the update step in Figure 9.8's incumbent summary for Iteration 4. Since the LP relaxation of neither ILP 4A nor ILP 4B has an all-integer optimal solution, the first two lines of iteration 4's incumbent summary are identical to those in iteration 3. Despite our inability to change the incumbent, we can at least reduce the maximum percentage error. To see why, note that our current tree (the portion in Figure 9.8 above the last dotted line) has three unpruned leaves, only two of which have $\overline{OV}$ values: node 3B with $\overline{OV} = 846$ and node 4B with $\overline{OV} = 797\frac{7}{13}$. Since the maximum of the leaves' $\overline{OV}$ values is 846, this is the value we record on the third line of the incumbent summary. Then, on the fourth line, we compute the incumbent's maximum percentage error as 6.38% (a reduction of 0.22% from the previous iteration).

Pruning. The current tree has three unpruned leaves: node 3B, node 4A, and node 4B. Applying Table 9.17's pruning conditions to each leaf, we see that Pruning Condition 2 has occurred at node 4A. In Figure 9.8, we indicate the pruning of this leaf by placing below it an "X" followed by a brief parenthetic explanation. (Note that we have not yet added the "X" and the parenthetic remark below node 4B; we will do so in the next iteration.)

Termination Check. The current tree now has two unpruned leaves: node 3B and node 4B. Hence, we must perform another iteration (assuming we are unwilling to accept a maximum percentage error of 6.38%).

Iteration 5

The following commentary, in conjunction with Figures 9.6–9.8, summarizes iteration 5:

Branching. We must first select the branching leaf from among the tree's unpruned leaves. As we have noted, there are only two unpruned leaves: node 3B and node 4B. Using the best bound rule, we select as the branching leaf node 3B. We must now select the branching variable. Looking at node 3B in Figure 9.8, we see that x_1 is the only variable having a noninteger variable. Hence, by default, x_1 becomes the branching variable. As diagrammed in Figure 9.6 beneath the last dashed line, branching now proceeds by creating ILP 5A and ILP 5B, children of ILP 3B obtained by respectively adding the constraints $x_1 \geqslant 7$ and $x_1 \leqslant 6$. Note that the constraints' right-hand sides of 7 and 6 are the integers on either side of $6\frac{1}{4}$, x_1's value in the optimal solution to the LP relaxation of ILP 3B (see node 3B in Figure 9.8).

Bounding. Bounding consists of solving the LP relaxations of ILP 5A and ILP

5B, the children created by the branching at ILP 3B. To see why the former LP relaxation has no feasible solution, look at the graph in Figure 9.7's node 3B (the parent of node 5A) and observe that the entire feasible region lies on the line $x_1 = 6$. Hence, the addition of the constraint $x_1 \geqslant 7$ leads to infeasibility. We now turn to the solution of the LP relaxation of ILP 5B. Using the graph in Figure 9.7's node 5B, you should verify that the optimal solution is $(x_1, x_2) = (6,1)$ and the optimal objective value is $\overline{OV} = 816$. We complete iteration 5's bounding step by summarizing these results in nodes 5A and 5B in Figure 9.8.

Updating. We summarize the update step in Figure 9.8's incumbent summary for iteration 5. Since the LP relaxation of ILP 5B has an all-integer optimal solution, we must check to see if it should become the new incumbent, by virtue of having a higher objective value than the current incumbent. Looking at Figure 9.8's node 5B, we see that this is true.[19] Hence, in iteration 5's incumbent summary, we record on the first line that $(x_1, x_2) = (6,1)$ is now the incumbent, and we record on the second line that the incumbent's objective value is now $\underline{OV} = 816$. Besides changing the incumbent, we can also reduce the maximum percentage error. To see why, note that our current tree (the entire tree in Figure 9.8) has three unpruned leaves, only two of which have $\overline{OV}$ values: node 4B with $\overline{OV} = 797\frac{7}{13}$ and node 5B with $\overline{OV} = 816$. Since the maximum of the leaves' $\overline{OV}$ values is 816, this is the value we record on the third line of the incumbent summary. Then, on the fourth line, we compute the incumbent's maximum percentage error as 0.0%, an indication that we have finally identified ILP 0's optimal solution.

Pruning. Although the maximum percentage error of 0.00% indicates we can terminate the B&B method, let us verify this "officially" by completing the pruning and termination check. The current tree has three unpruned leaves: node 4B, node 5A, and node 5B. Applying Table 9.17's pruning conditions to each leaf, we observe the following:

- We can prune node 4B using Pruning Condition 3. In particular, node 4B's $\overline{OV}$ value of $797\frac{7}{13}$ exceeded the incumbent's objective value in iteration 4. However, after iteration 5's incumbent change, node 4B's $\overline{OV}$ value is less than the incumbent's objective value of $\underline{OV}$ of 816. With $\overline{OV} < \underline{OV}$, further branching at node 4B cannot discover a feasible solution to ILP 0 that has a higher objective value than the incumbent.
- We can prune node 5A using Pruning Condition 2.
- We can prune node 5B using Pruning Condition 1.

In Figure 9.8, we indicate the pruning of these three leaves by placing below each leaf an "X" followed by a brief parenthetic explanation.

Termination Check. Our current tree has no unpruned leaves. Hence, we can finally terminate the B&B method. The incumbent $(x_1, x_2) = (6, 1)$ and its objective value of 816 are optimal for ILP 0, our original ILP.

---

[19] We should stress that obtaining an all-integer optimal solution for an LP relaxation need not lead to a change in the incumbent. Unlike this iteration, the newly discovered all-integer solution may have an objective value that is lower than the incumbent's objective value. If this occurs, the incumbent remains the same.

Why an ILP Is Difficult to Solve

The just-completed example illustrates why solving an ILP is much more difficult than solving an LP having the same number of decision variables and structural constraints. The 11 nodes in Figure 9.8's tree imply that the solution of our example ILP required us to solve 11 LPs. In general, then, solving an ILP requires the solution of one LP for every node in the tree constructed during the B&B method.

Obviously, we must use a computer implementation of the B&B method to solve most real-world ILPs. Unfortunately, owing to the complexity of today's business problems, even state-of-the-art computers are sometimes incapable of solving an ILP. When the ILP has a large number of decision variables and/or structural constraints, the size of the tree (as measured by the number of nodes) can become so large that excessive usage of CPU time or memory precludes execution of the B&B method until obtaining the optimal solution. If this limit should be reached, we hope that the B&B method has made enough progress to reduce the incumbent's maximum percentage error to an acceptable value. For example, if excessive usage of CPU time or memory results in termination without an optimal solution, most decision makers would not be upset if the incumbent's maximum percentage error were only 2%. On the other hand, a maximum percentage error of 25% would be disappointing.

As indicated by Termination Condition 1 in Table 9.18, it is possible (and sometimes advisable) to voluntarily terminate the B&B method before obtaining the optimal solution. In our example, we terminated only after all leaves had been pruned. Suppose, however, that we decide before beginning the B&B method that we are willing to terminate the first time the incumbent's maximum percentage error falls below 7%. Looking at Figure 9.8's incumbent summaries, we see that this occurs after three iterations. If we terminate after iteration 3 and use the incumbent $(x_1, x_2) = (5, 2)$ as a proxy for ILP 0's optimal solution, we know that the maximum percentage error is 6.60%. Of course, if we do terminate after iteration 3, we will never learn whether the incumbent is actually ILP 0's optimal solution. However, two factors work in our favor:

1. As illustrated several times in Section 9.4, the *actual* percentage error is usually less than the *maximum* percentage error. For example, the actual percentage error if we use iteration 3's incumbent as a proxy for ILP 0's optimal solution is

$$\text{actual percentage error} = \frac{\left(\begin{array}{c}\text{objective value of} \\ \text{optimal solution for} \\ \text{ILP 0}\end{array}\right) - \left(\begin{array}{c}\text{objective value} \\ \text{of} \\ \text{incumbent}\end{array}\right)}{\left(\begin{array}{c}\text{objective value of} \\ \text{optimal solution for} \\ \text{ILP 0}\end{array}\right)} \times 100\%$$

$$= \frac{816 - 792}{816} \times 100\%$$

$$= 2.94\%$$

well under iteration 3's maximum percentage error of 6.60%. Of course, at the end of iteration 3, we do not know the value of the incumbent's actual percentage error. We simply hope (with no guarantee) that it is significantly less than the maximum percentage error.

2. Experts have decades of computational experience with the B&B method.

450

They have found that, when Table 9.18's Termination Condition 1 is disallowed, then a frequent occurrence is that the ILP's optimal solution, which is the incumbent at termination, has been the incumbent for a significant number of prior iterations. In other words, although it was not known at the time, the actual percentage error was 0% for many iterations, even though the maximum percentage error was greater than 0%. This did not occur in our example, since termination occurred coincidentally at the very same iteration that the ILP's optimal solution became the incumbent. If, however, the $\overline{OV}$ value for Figure 9.8's node 4B had exceeded node 5B's $\overline{OV}$ value, at least one additional iteration would have been necessary. For a large-scale ILP, it may be necessary to perform a large number of additional iterations. For example, the ILP's optimal solution may become the incumbent at iteration 100, but we may not yet know it is the optimal solution because its maximum percentage error is, say, 20%. We may have to perform an additional 50 iterations to reach a point where the tree has no unpruned leaves, thereby enabling us to conclude the incumbent is optimal. Had we only known, we could have saved ourselves 50 iterations. If we decide to terminate the first time the maximum percentage error falls below, say, 5%, then we hope (with no guarantee) that further iterations are unnecessary because the incumbent is actually the ILP's optimal solution.

To summarize:

Either by our choice or because of excessive usage of CPU time or memory, it is possible for the B&B method to terminate when the maximum percentage error is greater than 0%. When this occurs, we hope the maximum percentage error is misleading in the sense that the actual percentage error is significantly less, possibly even equal to 0%.

Using the B&B Method to Solve a Pure-Binary ILP

Use of the B&B method to solve a pure-binary ILP requires an understanding of the following points:

- A pure-binary ILP has binary integrality constraints of the form

$$x_j = 0 \text{ or } 1.$$

This is actually a concise representation of three separate constraints: a nonnegativity constraint $x_j \geqslant 0$, an upper bound constraint $x_j \leqslant 1$, and an integrality constraint requiring x_j to have an integer value. We obtain the LP relaxation by deleting only the integrality constraint. Therefore, the LP relaxation retains not only the constraint $x_j \geqslant 0$, but also the constraint $x_j \leqslant 1$. Failing to include the latter constraint in the LP relaxation is a common mistake by first-time students of the B&B method.

- Because of the inclusion of the constraints $x_j \geqslant 0$ and $x_j \leqslant 1$, the value of x_j in the LP relaxation's optimal solution will lie in the interval [0, 1]. Now suppose that we select x_j as the branching variable and that it has a value of, say, $\frac{5}{8}$ in the optimal solution of the LP relaxation corresponding to the branching leaf. Then, one child's ILP has the added constraint $x_j \geqslant 1$ and the other child's ILP has the added constraint $x_j \leqslant 0$ (where the constraints' right-hand sides of 1 and 0 are the integers on either side of x_j's value of $\frac{5}{8}$). Since $x_j \leqslant 1$ is already a constraint in the LP relaxation, adding $x_j \geqslant 1$ is equivalent to adding the constraint $x_j = 1$. Similarly, since $x_j \geqslant 0$ is already a constraint in the LP relaxation, adding $x_j \leqslant 0$ is equivalent to adding the constraint $x_j = 0$. Thus, when applying the B&B method to a pure-binary ILP, branching always adds the constraint $x_j = 1$ to obtain one child's ILP and the constraint $x_j = 0$ to obtain the other.

Using the B&B Method to Solve a Mixed-General or a Mixed-Binary ILP

Use of the B&B method to solve a mixed-general or a mixed-binary ILP requires one modification. Recall from Section 9.2 that a mixed ILP has two types of variables: integer variables and continuous variables. Since a continuous variable is permitted to have a noninteger value, we should never select one as the branching variable. More specifically, in selecting the branching variable, we choose arbitrarily from only the integer variables having noninteger values.

The following is a summary of the B&B method, where it is assumed that we are constructing a tree similar to that in Figure 9.8. We also assume that the ILP's objective function involves maximization, postponing until after the summary a discussion of the modifications necessary for minimization.

A Summary of the Branch-and-Bound Method

Initialization. Initialization consists of the following steps:

1. We solve the LP relaxation of the ILP (remembering to include in the relaxation the constraint $x_j \leqslant 1$ for any binary variable). If we are lucky enough to obtain an all-integer optimal solution, it must also be the ILP's optimal solution; otherwise, we proceed to the next step.

2. Using the LP relaxation's optimal solution, we determine the best rounding alternative and use it as the first incumbent.

3. We compute the incumbent's maximum percentage error. If it is acceptable to us, we terminate and use the incumbent as a proxy for the ILP's optimal solution; otherwise, we proceed to the iterative step.

Iterative Step. Each iteration consists of the following steps:

1. **Branching.** Using the best bound rule, we first select as the branching leaf that unpruned leaf with the maximum $\overline{OV}$ value. We refer to the corresponding ILP as the *parent ILP*. We then select the branching variable by arbitrarily choosing a decision variable having a noninteger value in the optimal solution to the parent's LP relaxation (remembering, when solving a mixed ILP, to consider only integer variables). Finally, we branch from the parent ILP by creating two child ILPs. Letting x_j denote the branching variable, the child ILPs differ from the parent ILP in that one has the added constraint $x_j \geqslant v_A$ and the other has the added constraint $x_j \leqslant v_B$, where v_A and v_B are the integers on either side of x_j's value in the optimal solution to the parent's LP relaxation. (When the branching variable is a binary variable, one added constraint is $x_j = 1$ and the other is $x_j = 0$.)

2. **Bounding.** For each of the two child ILPs created when branching, we solve the LP relaxation and denote its optimal objective value by $\overline{OV}$.

3. **Updating.** If an LP relaxation in the bounding step has an all-integer optimal solution, we must check to see if the corresponding $\overline{OV}$ value exceeds the incumbent's objective value, which we denote by $\underline{OV}$. If so, this newly discovered all-integer solution becomes the incumbent and its optimal objective value becomes the new value of $\underline{OV}$; if not, the incumbent and $\underline{OV}$ remain unchanged. Regardless of whether we have changed the incumbent, we can revise the incumbent's maximum percentage error using the formula

$$\text{maximum percentage error} = \frac{\left(\begin{array}{c}\text{maximum of}\\ \overline{OV} \text{ values}\\ \text{at leaves}\end{array}\right) - \underline{OV}}{\left(\begin{array}{c}\text{maximum of}\\ \overline{OV} \text{ values}\\ \text{at leaves}\end{array}\right)} \times 100\%$$

4. **Pruning.** Using Table 9.17's three pruning conditions, we attempt to prune any unpruned leaf, thereby eliminating the need to branch from the leaf at a subsequent iteration.

5. **Termination Check.** Using Table 9.18's two termination conditions, we decide whether to terminate or to perform another iteration.

We conclude our discussion of the B&B method with six further observations:

- When the ILP's objective function involves minimization, we simply reverse the roles of $\overline{OV}$ and $\underline{OV}$. More specifically, we denote the optimal objective value of an LP relaxation by $\underline{OV}$ (since it is now a lower bound on the corresponding ILP's optimal objective value), we denote the incumbent's objective value by $\overline{OV}$ (since it is now an upper bound on the original ILP's optimal objective value), and, when computing the incumbent's maximum percentage error, we use the formula

$$\text{maximum percentage error} = \frac{\overline{OV} - \left(\begin{array}{c}\text{minimum of}\\ \underline{OV} \text{ values}\\ \text{at leaves}\end{array}\right)}{\left(\begin{array}{c}\text{minimum of}\\ \underline{OV} \text{ values}\\ \text{at leaves}\end{array}\right)} \times 100\%$$

- Besides rounding, we can use a heuristic to find the initial incumbent. For example, before using the B&B method to solve a knapsack ILP, we can determine the initial incumbent by using the greedy heuristic discussed in Section 9.7. In fact, we can use both the greedy heuristic and rounding, selecting as the initial incumbent the better of the two solutions obtained.

- An initial incumbent with an objective value that is close to the optimal objective value can significantly reduce the number of iterations required to solve the ILP. The reason is that the incumbent's objective value, which we denote by $\underline{OV}$ (when maximizing), is used in Table 9.17's Pruning Condition 3. The better the initial incumbent's objective value, the more likely it is that we can prune leaves from which we might otherwise perform unnecessary branching. Thus, expending effort in the initialization step to find the initial incumbent (via rounding or a heuristic) is usually a worthwhile investment.

- There are many variants of our version of the B&B method. Most differ with respect to the branching step's selection of the branching leaf (which we select using the best bound rule) and/or the branching variable (which we select by arbitrarily choosing an integer variable having a noninteger value). There exist other selection rules for both the branching leaf and the branching variable. Although we will not discuss these rules here, we should note that no selection rule performs better (in the sense of requiring fewer iterations) on all or even a majority of ILPs. However, experts have found that one rule may perform better on the majority of ILPs of a certain class (e.g., facility location ILPs).

- Our version of the B&B method is a general-purpose method capable (at least in theory) of solving any ILP. Experts have created many special-purpose B&B methods, each designed to solve a specific class of ILPs (e.g., pure-binary ILPs or facility location ILPs). Although our general-purpose method can in theory solve any ILP, some real-world ILPs are too large to be solved to optimality without using a special-purpose method.

- The B&B method is used by almost all commercially available software packages. However, it is only one of several methods for solving an ILP. Those not discussed here include the *cutting plane method*, the *Lagrangian relaxation method*, and *Bender's decomposition method*.

9.15 CONCLUDING REMARKS

At this chapter's outset, we discussed the continual narrowing of the gap between the theory and practice of integer linear programming. We conclude here with an overview of the trends responsible for the narrowing of this gap.

- Owing to the increased storage capacity and increased computational speed of successive generations of computers, there have been continual dramatic increases in the size of the ILPs practitioners can expect to solve.

- Although continuing to improve the efficiency of general-purpose methods, theoreticians have recognized that general-purpose methods currently are (and will probably always be) incapable of optimally solving many of the large-scale ILPs that arise in practice. Consequently, theoreticians have devised special-purpose methods, each specially designed to solve a different class of ILPs. For example, we indicated the existence of special-purpose methods for each of the following special classes of ILPs: the knapsack problem, the contract-awards problem, the facility location problem, the airline crew scheduling problem, and the cluster-analysis problem. More important to the practitioners, the theoreticians have not been content to just prove that their special-purpose methods converge to the optimal solution in a finite number of steps; in addition, they have demonstrated the practical viability of their methods by solving either actual real-world problems or "simulated" problems with realistic data.

- Theoreticians have also recognized that practitioners often formulate ILPs so large that even special-purpose methods are useless. Consequently they have devised both general-purpose and special-purpose heuristics that attempt to find an acceptable close-to-optimal solution, thereby eliminating the need for a costly, and possibly futile, search for the ILP's optimal solution.

■ Theoreticians have also discovered that, when there are alternative formulations of a decision problem, one alternative is frequently better than the others. By better, we mean that it will usually result in a significantly lower execution time than the other alternatives when input to a computer for optimal solution. (Of course, the optimal solution must be the same regardless of which of the alternative formulations is used.) A surprising fact is that the best formulation may actually contain more constraints and/or variables than the other formulations or may even contain redundant (unnecessary) constraints. Although an explanation of this phenomenon and the reasons behind it are beyond the scope of this chapter, your awareness of it may prove valuable in the future. If you ever need to solve a large-scale ILP, remember that a literature survey or consultation with an expert may lead to the discovery of the existence of a better formulation, one that may save you significant time and money and that may even be the difference between being able to solve the ILP or not.

There is every reason to believe that these trends will continue, thereby further narrowing the gap between the theory and practice of integer linear programming. Although successful applications of integer linear programming will probably always require more time, money, and expertise than successful applications of linear programming, today's practitioners recognize the value of using integer linear programming as an aid in the decision-making process.

9.16 CHAPTER CHECKLIST AND GLOSSARY

Quickly review this chapter by rereading the material highlighted by a vertical line in the left margin. You should then be familiar with the concepts, techniques, and terminology in the Checklist and Glossary that follow. If you need "help" with a particular item, consult the section or sections indicated for a more detailed discussion.

Checklist of Concepts and Techniques

☐ The taxonomy for integer linear programs. [9.2]

☐ The relationship between an ILP and its LP relaxation. [9.3]

☐ Why rounding the optimal solution to the LP relaxation does not usually produce the ILP's optimal solution but may produce a feasible solution with an acceptably low maximum percentage error. [9.4]

☐ A practical procedure for solving an ILP. [9.5]

☐ Formulating as a binary ILP the following classes of decision problems:

    ☐ a capital budgeting problem (including a knapsack problem) [9.7],

    ☐ a problem involving fixed charges [9.8, 9.10],

    ☐ a contract awards problem [9.9],

    ☐ a facility location problem [9.10],

☐   a crew scheduling problem [9.11],

☐   a cluster-analysis problem [9.12].

☐   Formulating the following types of constraints and requirements:

     ☐   a mutually exclusive constraint [9.7, 9.10],

     ☐   a multiple-choice constraint [9.7, 9.10],

     ☐   a k-out-of-n constraint [9.7, 9.10],

     ☐   a contingency constraint [9.7, 9.10],

     ☐   a minimum-batch-size requirement [9.9],

     ☐   a k-out-of-n requirement [9.9],

     ☐   a nonconsecutive-values requirement [9.9].

☐   Solving an ILP using a computer software package. [9.13]

☐   Solving an ILP using the branch-and-bound method. [9.14]

Glossary

Integer linear program (ILP). A linear program in which some or all decision variables are restricted to be integer-valued. [9.1]

Integrality constraint. A constraint requiring a specific decision variable to be integer-valued. [9.2]

Integer variable. A decision variable required to be integer-valued. [9.2]

Continuous variable. A decision variable not required to be integer-valued. [9.2]

Binary variable. An integer variable whose value must be either 0 or 1. [9.2]

Pure ILP. An ILP involving only integer variables. [9.2]

Mixed ILP. An ILP involving both integer variables and continuous variables. [9.2]

Binary ILP. An ILP in which every integer variable is a binary variable. [9.2]

General ILP. An ILP in which at least one integer variable is not a binary variable. [9.2]

Linear programming relaxation (LP relaxation). The linear program that results from deleting an ILP's integrality constraints. [9.3]

Rounding alternative. A solution obtained from the LP relaxation's optimal solution by considering each integer variable that has a noninteger value and rounding this value "up" to the next highest integer or "down" to the next lowest integer. [9.4]

Feasible rounding alternative. A rounding alternative that satisfies all constraints of the ILP. [9.4]

Best rounding alternative. The feasible rounding alternative with the best objective value. [9.4]

Maximum percentage error. Given a feasible (but not necessarily optimal) solution to an ILP, the solution's maximum percentage error is an upper bound on the percentage error that results if the solution is used as a "proxy" for the actual optimal solution. [9.4, 9.14]

Heuristic. A method that produces a solution to a problem that is rarely optimal but frequently close-to-optimal. [9.1, 9.5, 9.7]

General-purpose method (or heuristic). A method (or heuristic) that determines the optimal solution (or a close-to-optimal solution) to an ILP. [9.5]

Special-purpose method (or heuristic). A method (or heuristic) that determines the optimal solution (or a close-to-optimal solution) to only a specific type of ILP (e.g., a pure-binary ILP or a facility location ILP). [9.5]

Mutually exclusive constraint. A constraint ensuring that the sum of two or more binary variables is at most one. [9.7, 9.10]

Multiple-choice constraint. A constraint ensuring that the sum of two or more binary variables is exactly one. [9.7, 9.10]

k-out-of-n constraint. A constraint ensuring that the sum of n binary variables is at most k or exactly k (depending on whether $\leqslant$ or $=$ is used). [9.7, 9.10]

Contingency constraint. A constraint ensuring that a specified binary variable cannot equal one unless another specified binary variable also equals one. [9.7, 9.10]

Minimum-batch-size requirement. A requirement that a continuous variable either equals zero or is greater than or equal to some specified minimum value. [9.9]

k-out-of-n requirement. A requirement that any feasible solution satisfies at least k of a set of n constraints. [9.9]

Nonconsecutive-values requirement. A requirement that a specified linear function of the decision variables assumes exactly one of several nonconsecutive values. [9.9]

Branch-and-bound method (B&B method). A general-purpose method for solving an ILP that is based on dividing the set of feasible solutions into smaller and smaller subsets until discovering the ILP's optimal solution. [9.14]

Incumbent. During the execution of the B&B method, the incumbent is the feasible solution to the original ILP having the best objective value thus far encountered. [9.14]

Tree. The tree-like format for summarizing the execution of the B&B method. [9.14]

Node. A rectangle in the tree which contains a summary of the corresponding LP relaxation's optimal solution. [9.14]

Branch. A line in the tree which connects a parent node to one of its two child nodes and represents the addition of a constraint to the corresponding parent ILP. [9.14]

Leaf. A node in the tree from which no branches emanate. [9.14]

Branching. The step in the B&B method which selects a leaf in the tree and "divides" the corresponding ILP into two child ILPs. [9.14]

Bounding. The step in the B&B method that solves the LP relaxation of each child ILP created during branching. [9.14]

Updating. The step in the B&B method that revises the incumbent, if possible, and then revises the maximum percentage error associated with terminating the B&B method and using the incumbent as a "proxy" for the ILP's optimal solution. [9.14]

Pruning. The step in the B&B method that uses Table 9.17 to determine whether further branching from a leaf is unnecessary. [9.14]

Termination check. The step in the B&B method that uses Table 9.18 to determine whether the B&B method can terminate. [9.14]

Iteration of the B&B method. The performance of one repetition of branching, bounding, updating, pruning, and the termination check. [9.14]

EXERCISES

Exercises 9.1–9.7 illustrate what can happen when we attempt to solve an integer linear program by first solving its LP relaxation and then determining the best rounding alternative.

*9.1. Consider the following ILP:

$$\text{Maximize} \quad 30x_1 + 50x_2$$

$$\text{subject to} \quad 5x_1 + 8x_2 \leqslant 60$$
$$x_1 \qquad\quad \leqslant 8$$
$$x_2 \leqslant 4$$

$$\text{and} \quad x_1, x_2 \geqslant 0$$
$$x_1, x_2 \text{ integer-valued.}$$

(a) On the same graph, display the LP relaxation's feasible region and the ILP's feasible region.
(b) Use part (a)'s graph to determine the LP relaxation's optimal solution.
(c) Determine the best feasible rounding alternative by identifying the one with the best objective value.
(d) Compute the maximum percentage error that could occur if we were to use part (c)'s best feasible rounding alternative as a proxy for the ILP's optimal solution. [Note: Skip this part if there was no feasible rounding alternative in part (c).]
(e) Use part (a)'s graph to determine the ILP's optimal solution.
(f) Compute the actual percentage error that would have occurred if we had used part (c)'s best feasible rounding alternative as a proxy for the ILP's optimal solution. [Note: Skip this part if you also skipped part (d).]

9.2. Redo Exercise 9.1, this time using the following ILP:

$$\text{Maximize} \quad 300x_1 + 500x_2$$

$$\text{subject to} \quad 3x_1 + 6x_2 \leqslant 50$$
$$x_1 + x_2 \leqslant 10$$
$$x_1 \qquad\quad \leqslant 8$$

$$\text{and} \quad x_1, x_2 \geqslant 0$$
$$x_1, x_2 \text{ integer-valued.}$$

9.3. Redo Exercise 9.1, this time using the following ILP:

$$\text{Maximize} \quad x_1 + 5x_2$$

$$\text{subject to} \quad -4x_1 + 3x_2 \leqslant 6$$
$$3x_1 + 2x_2 \leqslant 18$$

and $\quad x_1, x_2 \geqslant 0$
$\qquad x_1, x_2$ integer-valued.

9.4. Redo Exercise 9.1, this time using the following ILP:

$$\text{Maximize} \quad x_1 + 5x_2$$

$$\text{subject to} \quad x_1 + 10x_2 \leqslant 20$$
$$10x_1 + x_2 \leqslant 20$$

and $\quad x_1, x_2 \geqslant 0$
$\qquad x_1, x_2$ integer-valued.

*9.5. Consider the following integer linear program:

$$\text{Maximize} \quad 6x_1 + 10x_2 + 9x_3$$

$$\text{subject to} \quad x_1 + x_2 + x_3 \geqslant 10$$
$$2x_1 + \qquad\quad 3x_3 \leqslant 35$$
$$3x_2 + 2x_3 \leqslant 28$$

and $\quad x_1, x_2, x_3 \geqslant 0$
$\qquad x_1, x_2, x_3$ integer-valued.

Accept as a fact that the LP relaxation of this ILP has an optimal solution of

$$(x_1, x_2, x_3) = \left[17\tfrac{1}{2}, 9\tfrac{1}{3}, 0 \right].$$

(a) Determine the best feasible rounding alternative by identifying the one with the best objective value.
(b) Compute the maximum percentage error that could occur if we were to use part (a)'s best feasible rounding alternative as a proxy for the ILP's optimal solution.

9.6. Consider the following integer linear program:

$$\text{Maximize} \quad 4x_1 - 2x_2 + 7x_3$$

$$\text{subject to} \quad x_1 + \qquad 5x_3 \leqslant 10$$
$$x_1 + x_2 - x_3 \leqslant 1$$
$$6x_1 - 5x_2 \qquad \leqslant 0$$

and $\quad x_1, x_2, x_3 \geqslant 0$
$\qquad x_1, x_2, x_3$ integer-valued.

Accept as a fact that the LP relaxation of this ILP has an optimal solution of

$$(x_1, x_2, x_3) = \left[1\tfrac{1}{4}, 1\tfrac{1}{2}, 1\tfrac{3}{4} \right].$$

458

(a) Verify that each of the 8 rounding alternatives is infeasible.

(b) What does this illustrate about hoping to find an ILP's optimal solution by rounding the LP relaxation's optimal solution?

9.7. The first row of Table 9.4 displays the optimal solution to the LP relaxation of the ILP for Chloe's capital budgeting problem in Section 9.7. In discussing Chloe's problem, we stated without verification that Table 9.4's second row contained the best feasible rounding alternative for the LP relaxation's optimal solution. Verify that this is so by considering all rounding alternatives.

As illustrated by the next exercise, it is possible (in theory) to reformulate any general ILP as a binary ILP.

9.8. Reconsider the ILP in Exercise 9.5.

(a) Reformulate this pure-general ILP as a pure-binary ILP (*Hint*: Any number can be expressed as the weighted sum of the powers of 2, where the weights are either 0 or 1. For example, $5 = (2^0)(1) + (2^1)(0) + (2^2)(1)$. Use this fact to replace each decision variable by a weighted sum of the powers of 2, where the weights are binary decision variables. For example, if we knew, say, that a decision variable x_j had an upper bound of 8, we could replace it with $1y_{j0} + 2y_{j1} + 4y_{j2} + 8y_{j3}$.)

(b) What is the disadvantage of the reformulation procedure illustrated in part (a)?

The next exercise illustrates that, when there are alternative integer linear programming formulations of a decision problem, the one containing more constraints and/or variables may require significantly *less* time to solve on a computer.

*9.9. Reconsider SMC's facility location problem in Section 9.10. In the formulation of this problem, the first of the five capacity constraints is

$$x_{11} + x_{12} + x_{13} + x_{14} + x_{15} + x_{16} \leqslant 18y_1$$

(a) Explain why we still have a correct formulation if we replace the above constraint by the following seven constraints:

$$
\begin{aligned}
x_{11} + x_{12} + x_{13} + x_{14} + x_{15} + x_{16} &\leqslant 18 \\
x_{11} &\leqslant 18y_1 \\
x_{12} &\leqslant 18y_1 \\
x_{13} &\leqslant 18y_1 \\
x_{14} &\leqslant 18y_1 \\
x_{15} &\leqslant 18y_1 \\
x_{16} &\leqslant 18y_1
\end{aligned}
$$

(b) Suppose we carry out a replacement similar to the one above for each of the five capacity con-

straints in the original formulation in Section 9.10. In comparison to the original formulation, how many more constraints will the revised formulation have?

(c) Repeat part (b), this time assuming that the problem involves 10 plants and 50 warehouses.

(d) Surprisingly, in comparison to the original formulation, the revised formulation of any facility location problem usually requires *less* time to solve on a computer. If you have access to an ILP software package that, when reporting the optimal solution, also reports a measure of the computational effort (e.g., CPU time or number of iterations), then solve the original and revised formulations of SMC's problem and compare the computational effort each requires.

Exercises 9.10–9.22 test your ability to formulate an integer linear program. Exercises 9.10–9.14 involve scenarios that closely resemble those discussed in the chapter. Exercises 9.15–9.22 illustrate a variety of other applications of integer linear programming. If you have access to a computer package, you should use it to solve the ILPs you formulate. This not only will give you experience with the software, but also, after close examination of the computer output, may reveal a flaw in your formulation that would otherwise go undetected.

9.10. *Capital Budgeting With Two Types of Capital.* A manager of a firm's research and development is currently reviewing a set of proposals prepared by her staff. She must soon decide which proposals to fund. The table below displays each proposal's net present value (NPV) and, for each of the next three years, each proposal's requirements for cash and labor:

Proposal	NPV ($000,000)	Cash Requirements ($000)			Labor Requirements (man-years)		
		Year 1	Year 2	Year 3	Year 1	Year 2	Year 4
1	5.0	200	300	300	1	2	2
2	2.8	200	200	0	2	2	0
3	4.8	300	300	0	2	2	0
4	6.0	0	300	300	0	1	2
5	5.4	100	500	400	1	3	3

The manager wants to maximize the total NPV of the approved proposals, subject to the following restrictions:

- The total cash requirements for the approved proposals cannot exceed $700,000 in the first year, $800,000 in the second year, and $900,000 in the third year.
- The total labor requirements for the approved proposals cannot exceed 4 man-years in year 1, 6 man-years in year 2, and 7 man-years in year 3.

(a) Formulate an appropriate ILP.

459

(b) What modifications to part (a)'s ILP are necessary under each of the following assumptions (where, as you consider each assumption, you should ignore the others):

(i) At most two of proposals 1, 3, and 5 can be approved.

(ii) Exactly one of proposals 1, 2, and 4 must be approved.

(iii) Proposal 2 cannot be approved unless proposal 4 is also approved.

(iv) Proposal 3 cannot be approved unless both proposals 1 and 5 are also approved.

(v) If proposals 2 and 3 are both approved, then proposal 4 must also be approved.

9.11. *A Product Mix Problem With Fixed Charges.* Reconsider the product mix problem of the Big-Bang Novelty Company in Exercise 2.28. Besides using the information given there, make the following assumptions:

- If the company produces any Toots, it incurs a fixed cost of $15.
- If the company products any Wheets, it incurs a fixed cost of $25.
- If the company products any Honks, it incurs a fixed cost of $10.

Reformulate the revised problem as an ILP.

9.12. *Contract Awards.* (Note that, although this exercise refers to an exercise in Chapter 8, you can work it even if you did not read Chapter 8. Just read the problem as if it were restated here.) Reconsider Northville's contract awards problem in Exercise 8.9. Besides the assumptions made there, assume the following:

- Supplier 1 has specified that if Northville awards it one or more contracts, the total amount delivered to all contracted sites must be at least 75 truckloads, and the amount delivered to each contracted site must be at least 17 truckloads.
- Because of an existing contract with Northville, supplier 2 must supply one site (the choice is Northville's) with at least 23 truckloads. (Note that Northville can also award additional contracts to supplier 2.)
- Supplier 3 has specified that the total amount it supplies to all bases must be a multiple of 20 truckloads (including 0).

Formulate Northville's revised problem as an ILP.

9.13. *Facility Location.* A manufacturer currently operates a single plant from which it ships its only product to its customers. For simplicity, assume there are only three customers: A, B, and C. Because the current plant is too old, the manufacturer intends to replace the plant with one or more new plants. Five potential plant sites (1 through 5) have been identified. The relevant information is summa-

rized in the table below:

		Transportation Costs ($) Customer			Annual Production Capacity	Annual Fixed Operating Costs
		A	B	C		
	1	50	20	30	10,000	$325,000
	2	40	30	40	20,000	$350,000
Plant Site	3	90	70	40	30,000	$300,000
	4	00	40	10	40,000	$200,000
	5	80	30	20	30,000	$300,000
Annual Demand		30,000	20,000	20,000		

For example, a plant at site 2 would have an annual production capacity of 20,000 units and an annual fixed operating cost of $350,000 (including the amortized construction costs); customer A has an annual demand of 30,000 units; and the transportation cost from site 2 to customer A is $40 per unit.

(a) Given an objective of minimizing the total annual transportation and operating costs, formulate an ILP the manufacturer can use to determine where to locate its plants and how to distribute its product from the plants to the customers.

(b) What modifications to part (a)'s ILP are necessary under each of the following assumptions (where, as you consider each assumption, you should ignore the others):

(i) If a plant is built at a site, it cannot operate at less than 60% of its capacity (as measured by the total units shipped to customers).

(ii) Besides the unit transportation cost of $10, any shipment from a plant at site 4 to customer C will incur a fixed charge of $25,000. For example, the total cost of transporting 15,000 units along this route is

$$(25,000) + (15,000)(10) = 175,000$$

(iii) If a plant is built at site 5, the three alternatives summarized below are possible:

Alternative	Annual Production Capacity	Annual Fixed Operating Costs
1	10,000	$150,000
2	20,000	$250,000
3	30,000	$300,000

9.14. *Cluster Analysis.* A company plans to advertise a

new product in 8 different magazines. Because the magazines' readerships have different characteristics, the company wants to first use cluster analysis to partition the magazines into three clusters and then design three distinct advertisements, one for each cluster's magazines.

As the first step in measuring the similarity between every pair of magazines, the company characterized each magazine by obtaining the magazine's percentage of readers with an annual income of at least $50,000, the percentage who graduated from college, and the percentage that are under 35 years old. The company then proceeded in a manner similar to that described in Mark Etting's cluster analysis problem in Section 9.12. This resulted in a "distance" d_{ij} between magazines i and j for each i-j combination. (We will not specify the values of the distances, but you should assume they are known.)

(a) Assuming the company wants each cluster to contain at least 2 magazines, formulate an appropriate ILP.

(b) What modifications to part (a)'s ILP are necessary if the company also wants each cluster to contain at most 3 magazines?

*9.15. *Capital Budgeting With Shared Fixed Costs.* A firm has the opportunity to undertake seven projects (1 through 7), each of which (if undertaken) requires the performance of a different subset of six activities (A through F). The requirements are displayed in the table below:

Project	1	2	3	4	5	6	7
Required Activities	{A,B}	{A,E}	{B,C,D}	{C,D}	{C,D,E}	{D,F}	{E,F}

Note that, if the firm undertakes two or more projects that require the same activity, the common activity must be performed only once. Thus, for example, if a firm undertakes projects 3, 4, and 5, the common activities C and D (as well as the activities not in common) must be performed only once. The tables below display the fixed cost of performing each activity and the fixed profit of undertaking each project, *exclusive* of the fixed costs of performing the activities the project requires:

Activity	A	B	C	D	E	F
Fixed Cost ($000)	4	5	17	10	7	5

Project	1	2	3	4	5	6	7
Fixed Profit ($000), Excluding Fixed Costs of Required Activities	7	10	9	3	8	6	8

For example, if the firm undertakes projects 1 and 2 and rejects the others, its total net profit is the fixed profits of projects 1 and 2 minus the fixed costs of the required activities A, B, and E; that is, $(7 + 10) - (4 + 5 + 7) = 1$. Assuming an objective of maximizing the total net profits, formulate an ILP the firm can use to determine which projects to undertake.

9.16. *A Lot Size Problem.* For planning purposes, the XYZ firm divides the calendar year into 13 four-week periods. Based on its production schedule for the next four-week period, XYZ has the following requirements for an important raw material that it obtains from a vendor:

Week n	Requirement r_n (00)
1	5
2	1
3	2
4	3

At the start of any week, the vendor will only deliver a *lot* or *batch* whose size is 0, 1, 2, 3, 4, or 5 hundred items. The vendor charges $200 per hundred items and, in addition, imposes a fixed charge of $25 in any week a delivery is made. Thus if XYZ requests the vendor to deliver a lot of x hundred items at the start of a particular week, the lot's total cost (fixed cost plus item cost) is $0 if $x = 0$ and $25 + 200x$ if $x = 1, 2, 3, 4,$ or 5. If at the end of a particular week XYZ has items of the raw material in inventory, it's inventory cost for that week will be $10 per hundred items. XYZ plans on having an inventory level of 1 hundred items when the next four-week planning period starts but wishes to have an inventory level of 0 when the four-week period ends. XYZ will not permit a shortage of raw material at any time during the four-week period. With the goal of minimizing cost, XYZ must now decide how many items of the raw material to order for delivery at the start of each of the next four weeks. Formulate XYZ's problem as an ILP.

*9.17. *Cargo Loading.* Reconsider the cargo loading problem in Exercise 4.20. In that exercise, we assumed that the shipowner could place more than one commodity in each hold.

(a) Now assume that the shipowner can place at most one commodity in each hold but can place the same commodity in more than one hold. Formulate an appropriate ILP.

(b) What modifications to part (a)'s ILP are necessary if we *replace* part (a)'s assumption with the assumption that the shipowner can place at

461

most one commodity in each hold and can place each commodity in at most one hold.

(c) What modifications to part (a)'s ILP are necessary if we *add to* part (a)'s assumption the assumption that, if the shipowner decides to carry any of commodity 1, he must carry at least 2000 tons.

9.18. *Facility Location Under a Single-Sourcing Requirement.* Reconsider SMC's facility location problem in Section 9.10. In the formulation of this problem, we permitted split-sourcing—that is, the satisfying of a warehouse's demand by more than one plant. Now assume a single-sourcing environment in which exactly one plant must satisfy all of a warehouse's demand. Reformulate SMC's problem under this new assumption. (*Hint:* Your formulation should include only binary decision variables.)

*9.19. *Set Covering.* The city of Safedale wants to redesign its fire protection services. Safedale has already done the following:

■ Divided the city into 10 fire service districts.
■ Selected 7 potential sites for the fire stations.
■ Computed the annual expense of locating a fire station at each site.
■ Defined "safe coverage" for a district as having at least one fire station close enough to respond to a fire in the district in less than five minutes (on average).
■ Determined for each site which districts a fire station at the site could safely cover.

This information is summarized in the table below:

Potential Site	Annual Expense of Locating a Station at Site ($000)	Districts a Station at the Site Could Safely Cover
1	410	1, 3, 5, 7, 8, 10
2	100	4, 7, 9, 10
3	300	1, 2, 3, 4
4	500	1, 3, 4, 5, 8, 9
5	200	3, 6, 8, 10
6	440	1, 2, 4, 6, 8, 10
7	400	2, 5, 8, 9

Safedale wants to determine the set of sites at which to locate fire stations. In doing so, it wants to minimize the total annual cost, subject to the restriction that every district is safely covered by at least one fire station.

(a) Formulate an appropriate ILP.

(b) Suppose that the objective is to minimize the number of fire stations. What modifications to part (a)'s ILP are necessary?

(c) Suppose that district 3 has so many fires that at least two fire stations are necessary to safely cover it. What modifications to part (a)'s ILP are necessary?

9.20. *Set Packing.* Holiday International Corporation (HIC) operates two types of motels. One, called a Motel 33, is family-oriented and has a room charge of $33 per night. The other, called an Executive Inn, is oriented toward business persons who are willing to pay more for quieter and more luxurious rooms. HIC is planning the expansion of its operations into the San Francisco Bay Area and has already done the following:

■ Identified 10 potential sites, each of which can accommodate a Motel 33 or an Executive Inn, but not both. (HIC can also decide not to locate a motel at a site.)
■ Estimated, for each site, the net present value (NPV) of the cash flows that would result from locating at the site either a Motel 33 or an Executive Inn.
■ Determined those sites within 20 miles of each site, since this is the minimum distance HIC permits between two Motel 33s.
■ Determined those sites within 25 miles of each site, since this is the minimum distance HIC permits between two Executive Inns.

This information is summarized in the table below:

Site	Other Sites Within 20 Miles	Other Sites Within 25 Miles	NPV of Motel 33 at Site ($000,000)	NPV of Executive Inn at Site ($000,000)
1	2, 3, 4	2, 3, 4	11.3	15.7
2	1, 3, 5	1, 3, 5	12.8	13.3
3	1, 2, 4	1, 2, 4, 5	18.5	14.1
4	1, 3	1, 3	17.3	11.9
5	2	2, 3, 10	9.5	13.2
6	–	7	15.6	19.5
7	8	6, 8	12.8	10.3
8	7	7	18.3	14.7
9	10	10	16.7	15.4
10	9	5, 9	13.9	16.3

Formulate an ILP that HIC can use to determine the set of sites at which to locate a Motel 33 and the set of sites at which to locate an Executive Inn. (Note that HIC need not locate a motel at each site. In fact, it may be impossible for HIC to do so, given the minimum-distance restrictions.)

9.21. *Selection of Gymnastics Competitors.*[20] Jim Nastix is a coach of a women's intercollegiate gymnastics

[20] This exercise is based on an actual application reported in the following reference: P. M. Ellis and R. W. Corn, "Using Bivalent Integer Programming to Select Teams for Intercollegiate Women's Gymnastic Competition," *Interfaces*, **14**, 3 (May–June 1984), pp. 41–46.

team consisting of 10 gymnasts. In NCAA competition, there are four events: vaulting, uneven bars, balance beam, and floor exercise. The table below contains the scores expected by Jim for each gymnast in each event (10 is a perfect score):

Gymnast	Event 1 (Vault)	Event 2 (Bars)	Event 3 (Beam)	Event 4 (Floor)	Total
1	9.3	9.3	9.2	9.5	37.3
2	9.1	9.0	8.8	8.7	35.6
3	9.2	9.0	9.2	9.0	36.4
4	9.0	8.6	8.6	8.65	34.85
5	8.8	8.7	8.5	8.5	34.5
6	8.7	7.5	7.5	8.7	32.4
7	8.5	8.8	8.7	8.5	34.5
8	9.1	9.0	9.0	9.2	36.3
9	9.2	7.0	7.0	9.1	32.3
10	8.9	8.9	9.1	8.7	35.6

In determining the participants for an upcoming meet, Jim must adhere to the following NCAA rules:

- At least four gymnasts must be designated as "all-arounders," that is, gymnasts who will compete in all four events.
- Six gymnasts must compete in each event. Of course, at least four of these gymnasts will be all-arounders; the remaining gymnasts in an event will be "specialists" in the event (and in up to two other events).

(a) For simplicity, assume (unrealistically) that the team's final score is determined by summing the scores of all competing gymnasts. Formulate an ILP Jim can use to select the participants in the upcoming meet.

(b) Now assume (as specified by NCAA rules) that the team's final score is determined by discarding the lowest score in each event and summing the remaining scores. In other words, only the five highest scores in each event count. What modifications to part (a)'s ILP are necessary?

9.22. *Real Estate Development*.[21] Over a period of seven years, Real Estate Development, Incorporated (REDI) plans to build three office buildings on a parcel of land it owns. At issue is when REDI should finish the construction of each building and how many square feet to rent in each building in each year after its opening. If a building were opened too soon, profits would suffer because of inadequate demand to fill the building. On the other hand, if a building were opened too late, profits

would suffer because rentals would be lost to competing developments. REDI has compiled the following data and made the following assumptions:

- The table below displays the nearby area's new demand in each year for office space of the type REDI's three buildings will contain:

Year	1	2	3	4	5	6	7
Demand (square feet)	200,000	220,000	242,000	266,000	293,000	322,000	354,000

REDI assumes that any demand it does not meet in a given year is lost to competing developments.

- The following table displays the planned size of each building:

Building Number	1	2	3
Square Footage	350,000	450,000	350,000

Note that the buildings' sizes cannot be changed.

- Construction costs for a building ready for occupancy at the beginning of year 1 will be $104 per square foot. REDI estimates that these costs will increase at the rate of 8% per year. For simplicity, REDI assumes that if a building is ready for occupancy at the beginning of a particular year, the entire cost of construction is incurred at the *beginning* of that year.
- Net operating income (NOI) received from office space rented in year 1 will be $13.25 per square foot. REDI estimates NOI will also increase at the rate of 8% per year. For simplicity, REDI assumes that the entire NOI from office space rented during a particular year is received at the *end* of that year.
- At the end of year 7, REDI will sell all three buildings. A building's selling price will be ten times the NOI it generates in year 7.
- Using a discount factor of 20%, REDI wants to maximize the present value of the cash flows resulting during the seven years from the construction of the buildings, the rental of office space, and the sale of the buildings.

To begin formulating REDI's problem as an ILP, define the following two types of decision variables:

x_{ij} = a continuous variable equal to the number of square feet rented in building i in year j

y_{ij} = a binary variable equal to 1 if building i is first ready for occupancy in year j and equal to 0 otherwise

Using these decision variables, complete the formulation of REDI's problem as an ILP. Given the size of the formulation, you should not write it out in

[21] This exercise is based on actual application reported in the following reference: R. B. Peiser and S. G. Andrus, "Phasing of Income-Producing Real Estate," *Interfaces*, **13**, 5 (October 1983), pp. 1–9.

full. Instead, you should provide an example of each type of constraint and, in the objective function, you should provide an example of each type of term. (*Hint*: Your formulation should have four types of constraints and an objective function with three types of terms.)

Exercises 9.23–9.30 involve manually solving an integer linear program using the branch-and-bound method discussed in Section 9.14. As you do so, keep in mind the following:

- You will need to solve several LP relaxations. When the LP involves only two decision variables, you may solve it graphically, as we did in Section 9.14, or by using an LP software package. The latter option is the only one available when the LP involves more than two variables.
- When there is more than one choice for the branching variable, always select the variable with the *lowest* subscript. This will ensure that your analysis proceeds exactly as that of others.

*9.23. Reconsider the ILP in Exercise 9.1.
   (a) Use the branch-and-bound method to determine the ILP's optimal solution. Summarize your iterations in a format similar to that in Figure 9.8.
   (b) Now suppose you are willing to terminate the branch-and-bound method the first time the incumbent's maximum percentage error falls below 4.5%. At which iteration in part (a) do you now terminate? When you terminate, what is the incumbent and the incumbent's maximum percentage error? Compute the incumbent's actual percentage error, and compare it to the maximum percentage error. (Note: You can compute the incumbent's actual percentage error only because you found the ILP's optimal solution in part (a). In reality, when you terminate the branch-and-bound method early, you are unable to compute the incumbent's actual percentage error.)

9.24. Redo Exercise 9.23 with the following modifications:
   - Solve the same ILP (i.e., the one in Exercise 9.1) but change the objective function to $20x_1 + 50x_2$.
   - In part (b), terminate the branch-and-bound method the first time the incumbent's maximum percentage error falls below 3%.

9.25. Redo Exercise 9.23 with the following modifications:
   - Solve the ILP in Exercise 9.2.
   - In part (b), terminate the branch-and-bound method the first time the incumbent's maximum percentage error falls below 2%.

9.26. Redo Exercise 9.23 with the following modifications:
   - Solve the ILP in Exercise 9.3.
   - In part (b), terminate the branch-and-bound method the first time the incumbent's maximum percentage error falls below 6%.
   (Note: As you discovered in Exercise 9.3, there is no feasible rounding alternative for the optimal solution to the LP relaxation of the ILP. Hence, you must begin the branch-and-bound method without an incumbent.)

9.27. Redo Exercise 9.23 with the following modifications:
   - Solve the ILP below:

$$\text{Maximize} \quad x_1 + 3x_2$$
$$\text{subject to} \quad 22x_1 + 34x_2 \leqslant 105$$
$$8x_2 \leqslant 15$$
$$\text{and} \quad x_1, x_2 \geqslant 0$$
$$x_1, x_2 \text{ integer-valued.}$$

   - In part (b), terminate the branch-and-bound method the first time the incumbent's maximum percentage error falls below 20%.

9.28. Redo Exercise 9.23 with the following modifications:
   - Solve the ILP in Exercise 9.5.
   - In part (b), terminate the branch-and-bound method the first time the incumbent's maximum percentage error falls below 2%.

*9.29. Redo Exercise 9.23 with the following modifications:
   - Solve the ILP below:

$$\text{Maximize} \quad 90x_1 + 100x_2 + 70x_3 + 40x_4 + 45x_5$$
$$\text{subject to} \quad 30x_1 + 40x_2 + 35x_3 + 25x_4 + 30x_5 \leqslant 100$$
$$\text{and} \quad x_1, x_2, x_3, x_4, x_5 = 0 \text{ or } 1.$$

   (Note that this is a pure-binary ILP.)
   - In part (b), terminate the branch-and-bound method the first time the maximum percentage error falls below 15%.

9.30. Redo Exercise 9.23 with the following modifications:
   - Solve the ILP below:

$$\text{Maximize} \quad 80x_1 + 40x_2 + 50x_3 + 30x_4$$
$$\text{subject to} \quad 5x_1 + 2x_2 + 3x_3 + x_4 \leqslant 30$$
$$2x_1 + 6x_2 + 10x_3 + 8x_4 \leqslant 100$$
$$x_1 + x_2 + x_3 + x_4 \leqslant 16$$
$$8x_1 + 8x_2 + 12x_3 + 12x_4 \leqslant 161$$
$$\text{and} \quad x_1, x_2, x_3, x_4 \geqslant 0$$
$$x_1, x_2 \text{ integer-valued}$$
$$x_3, x_4 \text{ continuous.}$$

   (Note that this is a mixed ILP.)
   - In part (b), terminate the branch-and-bound method the first time the maximum percentage error falls below 1%.

PROJECT MANAGEMENT: FUNDAMENTAL TOPICS

10.1 INTRODUCTION

Frequently, a manager must plan and execute a project that entails a large number of diverse but interdependent activities. Two examples are the construction of a new plant and the research and development effort associated with a new product. Typically, a large-scale project requires an organization to commit large amounts of resources (money, labor, equipment, raw materials, etc.) in pursuit of an important goal. Consequently, successful project management is vital to the economic well-being of the organization (and to the career of the project manager!).

Successful project management asks and answers the following questions:

1. What is an estimate of the project's duration?

2. Among the activities comprising the project, which are likely to be "bottleneck" activities in the sense that they will directly affect the project's duration? (While the project is still in the planning phase, the project manager may take actions that will speed up bottleneck activities, thereby shortening the project's duration. Furthermore, once the project begins, the project manager should closely monitor the bottleneck activities in order to prevent delays that would in turn delay the project's completion.)

3. What should be the scheduled starting time and finishing time of each of the project's activities?

4. What are the resource implications of the schedule for the activities?

5. Because a project never proceeds exactly as planned, how can the project manager quickly recognize and react to surprises that might otherwise unfavorably affect the project?

Two methodologies for answering these and other related questions emerged in the late 1950s: the *Program Evaluation and Review Technique* (*PERT*) and the *Critical Path Method* (*CPM*). Although developed concurrently and independently, PERT and CPM had much in common. Their major differences resulted from differences between the two types of projects that motivated their development.

PERT was developed jointly by representatives from the United States Navy, Lockheed, and the management consulting firm of Booz, Allen, and Hamilton. Their motivation was the research and development associated with one of the Navy's "new products," the Polaris nuclear missile, designed to be launched by a submarine beneath the ocean's surface. Thus, PERT was designed for projects (such as R&D efforts) where there is little or no experience on which to base estimates of the durations of the activities and where many activity durations contain elements of randomness over which there is little or no control. For example, the duration of an activity requiring a technological invention depends not only on the skill of the scientists and engineers involved but also on luck. In order to capture this uncertainty about an activity's duration, PERT requests the project manager to specify a range of possible durations for each activity and to associate a probability with each. PERT then translates this information about the uncertain durations of the project's activities into information about the uncertain duration of the entire project.

CPM was developed by representatives from both Du Pont and Remington-Rand. Their motivation was Du Pont's wish to improve the planning and execution of both the construction of new production facilities and the maintenance shutdowns of existing facilities. In contrast to PERT, then, CPM was designed for projects consisting primarily of commonly performed activities, each of whose duration is not random but rather a function of the amount of resources allocated to the activity. For example, the time required to perform electrical work for a new plant is a function of the number of electricians used. CPM requests the user to specify for each of the project's activity's a functional relationship between the activity's duration and the dollar value of the resources allocated to it. CPM then determines how to optimally allocate a budget among the various activities in order to achieve the desired project duration at minimal cost.

To summarize,

> The original versions of PERT and CPM treated activity durations differently. PERT regarded each activity duration as uncertain and uncontrollable, while CPM regarded each as a controllable function of the resources allocated.

Although traditionalists continue to distinguish between PERT and CPM, most practitioners today use the acronyms interchangeably or, as we will, combine them into the single acronym PERT/CPM. This chapter discusses the basic PERT/CPM model. The next chapter discusses extensions of the basic model that are similar to the original versions of PERT and CPM, respectively.

The applications of PERT/CPM are numerous and diverse. They include the following:

- Construction or renovation of a plant, an office complex, a residential housing plan, a highway, or a sports stadium
- Research and development associated with a new product
- Relocation of a major facility such as a plant or a hospital
- Manufacture, maintenance, or repair of a large item such as an airplane or a nuclear reactor

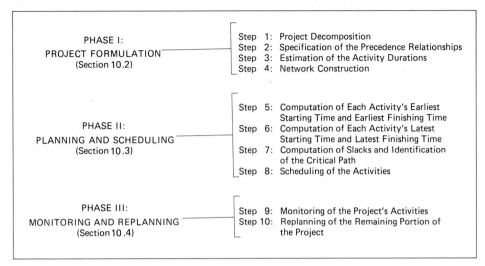

Figure 10.1 The three phases and ten steps of PERT/CPM

- Installation of a new accounting system or management information system
- Making of financial arrangements to start a new business venture or to issue a revenue bond
- Raising of funds for charity purposes
- Conducting an advertising campaign or a political campaign
- Performing complex medical surgery
- Filming a major motion picture
- Countdown for the launch of a rocket

Not all applications of PERT/CPM are successful. However, close inspection of those that fail usually reveals that the blame lies not with PERT/CPM but instead with persons who misused it or believed it could guarantee the project's success. Consequently, we will stress not only the methodology but also the operational problems.

Figure 10.1 summarizes the phases and steps involved in using PERT/CPM. The next three sections discuss in detail each step of each phase.

To illustrate our discussion of PERT/CPM, we will consider the following scenario:

> Designer Genes (DG), a rapidly expanding genetic engineering firm, is relocating to a new office building. Jean Ettic, the project manager, has already leased a vacant office building and approved architectural plans for renovating it. To save money and to gain more control over the project, Jean herself will act as the general contractor for the renovation. She has already selected the subcontractors she will employ. The move to the new building is complicated by the fact that DG will use this opportunity to purchase a computer and establish an in-house Computer Services Department. The present decentralized computer capacity is simply inadequate to meet the future needs of DG.

10.2 PHASE I: PROJECT FORMULATION

The goal of Phase I is a precise description of the project. As indicated in Figure 10.1, Phase I consists of four steps, the first of which is Project Decomposition.

Step 1: Project Decomposition

In any application of PERT/CPM we must first decompose the project into its individual activities. After careful consideration, Jean decomposes the relocation of DG into the 14 individual activities listed in the second column of Table 10.1. To facilitate reference to these activities, she associates each with the alphabetic code listed in the table's first column. (Temporarily ignore the table's third and fourth columns.) Observe that activities *B*, *C*, *F*, *G*, *H*, *I*, *K*, *M*, and *N* comprise the renovation of the building, while activities *A*, *D*, *E*, *J*, and *L* comprise the establishment of the Computer Services Department.

Jean's list includes both "hard" and "soft" activities. A "hard" activity, such as the structural modifications of activity *B*, is difficult to overlook because it involves physical labor and produces tangible results. In contrast, a "soft" activity, such as the personnel training of activity *L*, is easier to overlook because it requires more mental than physical effort and because the result is not as tangible as a new window. A common error during project decomposition is to overlook soft activities that require time and consume resources in ways that, while less obvious, have just as much impact on the project's duration as do hard activities.

In decomposing the project, Jean must achieve an appropriate balance between a "fine" decomposition providing too much detail and a "coarse" decomposition providing too little detail. For example, Jean could have achieved a finer decomposition by splitting activity *B* into several subactivities, one for each distinct structural modification. However, Jean regarded this additional detail as unnecessary. As another example, Jean could have achieved a coarser decomposition by combining activities *F*, *G*, and *H* into one activity described as "utility modifications." However, Jean chose to regard these three activities as distinct, because each involves a different subcontractor. When decomposing the project, choosing the appropriate level of detail is more "art" than "science." Therefore, the initial project decomposition might require revision when subsequent steps of PERT/CPM indicate that there is too little or too much detail.

The creativity and insight required for project decomposition suggest the need for involvement of more than one person. Jean recognizes this and appoints an Advisory Committee, consisting of persons who collectively are more knowledgeable

TABLE 10.1 Project Formulation for Designer Genes' Relocation

Code	Description of Activity	Estimated Duration (days)	Predecessors
A	Hiring of Manager of Computer Services Department	10	None
B	Structural Modifications	19	None
C	Enlarging and Resurfacing of Parking Lot	13	None
D	Hiring of Staff of Computer Services Department	8	*A*
E	Purchase and Receipt of Computer	14	*A*
F	Electrical Modifications	4	*B*
G	Heating and Cooling Modifications	1	*B*
H	Plumbing Modifications	3	*B*
I	Exterior Painting and Installation of Exterior Fixtures	5	*B*
J	Installation of Computer	4	*E*, *F*, *G*
K	Sheetrocking of Walls and Ceiling	6	*F*, *G*, *H*
L	Training of Staff of Computer Services Department	8	*D*, *J*
M	Interior Painting and Interior Decorating	9	*K*
N	Landscaping	7	*C*, *I*

468

about the project than Jean is alone. Each committee member has or shares responsibility for one or more of the project's activities. We assume that the Advisory Committee concurs with Jean's project decomposition.

In practice, one of the first actions of the project manager should be the appointment of an Advisory Committee. The project manager should consult the Advisory Committee during all steps of the PERT/CPM procedure, not just during project decomposition. Many applications of PERT/CPM have been unsuccessful because the project manager neglected early and continual consultation with those directly responsible for the project's execution. The appointment of an Advisory Committee serves a dual purpose. Active participation of committee members not only provides the project manager with valuable advice but also creates a healthy work environment in which everyone regards the use of PERT/CPM as a team effort and shares a commitment to make it successful.

Step 2: Specification of the Precedence Relationships

After decomposing the project, the project manager must specify the *precedence relationships* that exist among the activities. Once the project begins, it is extremely unlikely that all activities can proceed concurrently. Usually, some activities cannot begin until others have finished. The project manager makes this notion precise by specifying the *predecessors* of each activity. The predecessors of activity X are those activities that must completely finish before activity X can begin. In our example, the fourth column of Table 10.1 contains the precedence relationships that result from Jean's consultation with her Advisory Committee. Since activities A, B, and C have no predecessors, they can begin once the project begins. Activity K, however, has predecessors F, G, and H, because sheetrocking cannot begin until the completion of the electrical, heating/cooling, and plumbing modifications. Also, activity N has predecessors C and I because the landscaping cannot begin until after the completion of the parking lot and exterior painting. Before continuing, you should convince yourself that the predecessors of the remaining activities make sense.

By excluding all but "immediate" predecessors, Jean has kept each activity's list of predecessors as small as possible. For example, because A is a predecessor of E, and E is a predecessor of J, A is implicitly a predecessor of J and thus need not be explicitly specified as such. Its explicit specification would be an example of a *redundant precedence relationship*. It would not be wrong but simply unnecessary. As we will see, redundant precedence relationships unnecessarily clutter the project network drawn in Step 4, which in turn adds time and expense to the computations of Steps 5 and 6. Consequently, redundancy should be minimized. In practice, a project manager usually can eliminate most if not all redundancy by simply checking and rechecking for its presence. A project manager suspicious that much redundancy remains undetected may wish to employ a formal method guaranteed to eliminate all redundancies.[1] Well-designed computer implementations of PERT/CPM automatically eliminate redundancy inadvertently specified by the user.

In addition to checking for redundancy, a project manager should check the list of predecessors to ensure that there are no *cyclic precedence relationships,* —that is, that no activity is implicitly a predecessor of itself. An example of cyclic

---

[1] Consult pages 22–25 of J. D. Wiest and F. K. Levy, *A Management Guide to PERT/CPM*, 2nd ed. (Englewood Cliffs, NJ: Prentice Hall, 1977).

precedence relationships is:

X is a predecessor of Y,

Y is a predecessor of Z,

Z is a predecessor of X.

If these precedence relationships were all valid, X could not begin until it ended! Although no project manager would intentionally make such logically inconsistent statements, cyclic precedence relationships can inadvertently occur in large projects. As with redundancy, a project manager can usually detect the presence of cyclic precedence relationships by carefully checking and rechecking the predecessor lists. If necessary, however, the project manager may use the formal method suggested in Exercise 10.12 to detect any cyclic precedence relationships and then make the appropriate corrections. Well-designed computer implementations of PERT/CPM automatically detect cyclic precedence relationships and terminate with a request to the user to resolve the inconsistencies.

The specification of the predecessor lists in a complex project is a formidable task. It would be unwise for the project manager to attempt it without frequently consulting the Advisory Committee. A committee member might point out a subtle aspect of an activity that necessitates changing its predecessor list, or a committee member might point out several viable alternatives for an activity's predecessor list and help the project manager choose among them.

We should introduce here the concept of a *successor,* a concept required in later steps. If activity X is a predecessor of activity Y, then Y is a successor of X. Table 10.1 does not explicitly list the successors of each activity, because this information is implicit in the predecessor lists. When necessary, Jean can quickly determine all successors of activity X by simply noting the activities whose predecessor lists contain X. For example, since F appears only on the predecessor lists of J and K, the only successors of F are J and K. Activities L, M, and N appear on no predecessor lists and, therefore, have no successors. When these activities are all finished, the project is over!

Step 3: Estimation of the Activity Durations

The next step is to carefully estimate *with a single number* the duration of each activity—that is, the time that will elapse between its start and finish. For the DG project, the third column of Table 10.1 contains the estimates of the activity durations that evolved from Jean's consultation with her Advisory Committee. These estimates rely on a combination of experience, intuition, and common sense. As we will see, these estimates are crucial to the analysis to follow in Phase II.

Making a single number estimate of an activity's duration may be difficult for one of the following reasons:

- An activity's duration may be subject to *uncontrollable* random variation. For example, the durations of the exterior work involved in activities C, I, and N may depend on weather, and the durations of the personnel actions of activities A and D may depend on the size and qualifications of the pool of applicants. To make a single-number estimate of the duration of such an activity, the project manager may use the mean, median, or mode of the random duration. The mean is the most common estimate. If the project contains many activities with random durations, the project manager should use the extension of the basic PERT/CPM model discussed in Section 11.2.

- An activity's duration may be subject to *controllable* variation, depending upon the amount of resources allocated to it. For example, the duration of activity *B* (structural modifications) depends partly on the size of the workforce. Consequently, to make a single-number estimate of *B*'s duration, Jean must ascertain the subcontractor's workforce size. If the project contains many activities with controllable durations, the project manager should use the extension of the basic PERT/CPM model discussed in Section 11.3.

Despite the difficulties involved, the basic PERT/CPM model requires a single-number estimate of each activity's duration.

A recommended procedure for obtaining the estimate of an activity's duration is to request a *worst-case estimate* and a *best-case estimate* before requesting and using a *most-likely estimate*. There are two advantages to this procedure. First, forcing the estimator to think about the two extremes will probably result in a more thoughtful most-likely estimate. Second, the difference between the worst-case and best-case estimates provides an informal measure of the estimator's confidence in the most-likely estimate. Large differences between the worst-case and best-case estimates for many activities indicate considerable uncertainty about the durations. In this event, the project manager should use one of the extensions to the basic PERT/CPM model in Sections 11.2 and 11.3.

After obtaining estimates of the activity durations and recording them in Table 10.1, Jean augments this table with two additional columns. To conserve space, Table 10.1 does not display these two columns; however, we will describe their contents. The fifth column displays the name and phone number of the person directly responsible for each activity (e.g., the electrical subcontractor for activity *F*). This information facilitates communication among the persons responsible for the project's activities. The sixth column displays each activity's special requirements for such things as personnel, equipment, materials, and weather conditions. For example, the three-day duration of activity *H* (plumbing modifications) presumes the use of two full-time plumbers, and the five-day duration of activity *I* (exterior painting, etc.) includes at most one day of idle time due to rain. As we will see, the resource and environmental requirements recorded in the sixth column are useful in Step 8, when the project manager must schedule the project's activities.

At the conclusion of Step 3, the project manager has satisfied all the information requirements of PERT/CPM and has summarized them in a table similar to Table 10.1 (augmented with the two additional columns just discussed). Many project managers believe that such a table is one of the biggest benefits of PERT/CPM. The systematic planning required to construct the table forces the manager and the Advisory Committee to resolve, or at least anticipate, crucial issues *before* the project begins.

Step 4: Network Construction

After completing Steps 1–3, the project manager is ready to represent the project as a *network*. Figure 10.2 displays the network for the DG project. Rectangles (referred to as *nodes*) represent the project's activities, and arrows (referred to as *arcs*) represent the predecessor relationships. The number within a node is the duration of the activity represented by the node. To construct the project network, Jean used the information in Table 10.1 and obeyed the following conventions:

Conventions for Constructing the Project Network

- For each activity, there is a corresponding node in the network. In particular, activity *X* corresponds to a node labeled *X*. In addition, the network contains two additional nodes, *START* and *FINISH*, representing the project's start and finish, respectively. *START* and *FINISH* have no durations associated with them.

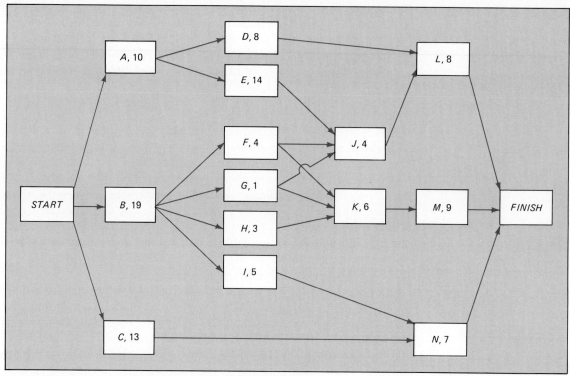

Figure 10.2 Project network for relocation of Designer Genes

- For each of the project's precedence relationships, there is a corresponding arc in the project network. In particular, if activity X is on the predecessor list of activity Y, an arc points from node X to node Y. In addition, there is an arc pointing from *START* to any node representing an activity having no predecessors, and there is an arc pointing to *FINISH* from any node representing an activity having no successors.

For example, the arcs pointing from nodes F, G, and H to node K in Figure 10.2 represent the appearance (in Table 10.1) of F, G, and H on the predecessor list of activity K. Observe that arcs point from *START* to nodes A, B, and C, the only activities having no predecessors. As soon as the project starts, these activities can all begin simultaneously. Also, arcs point to *FINISH* from L, M, and N, the only activities having no successors. When these activities have all finished, the entire project has finished.

The benefits of representing the DG project as a network extend far beyond its use in the numerical analysis to follow in Phase II. For example, Jean and her Advisory Committee will probably find it easier to recognize and correct mistaken or forgotten predecessor relationships by examining the project's pictorial representation in Figure 10.2 as opposed to the project's tabular representation in Table 10.1. Because the project network displays in a simple and direct fashion the complex interrelationships among the activities, Jean will also find it an effective visual aid in meetings and reports. A manager responsible for one of the activities quickly understands from the project network how his or her activity affects, and is affected by, other activities. Once the project begins, Jean plans to visually display its progress by fastening an enlargement of the network to her wall and periodically updating each node in one of three different colors, indicating whether the activity represented by the node has been completed, is in progress, or has yet to begin.

The construction of the project network is something of an art, frequently requiring a first draft and several redrawings. The key to making the final project network as pleasing to the eye as possible is to locate the nodes so that the arcs indicating the precedence relationships will have a left-to-right orientation, no wide variation in their lengths,[2] and no unnecessary crossings of each other. In particular, if activity X is a predecessor of activity Y, then the location of node X should be to the left of, and close to, the location of node Y; otherwise, the arc pointing from X to Y will be excessively long and may have to cross other arcs. By the same reasoning, the *START* node should be located to the extreme left of, and close to, the locations of the nodes representing activities having no predecessors. Similarly, the *FINISH* node should be located to the extreme right of, and close to, the nodes representing activities having no successors.

Before approving the final draft of the network, the project manager should attempt to recognize and eliminate any redundant precedence relationships not discovered in Step 2. This will improve the appearance of the network and, as we will see, reduce the computations required in Steps 5 and 6. For example, if Jean fails to notice in Step 2 that she has redundantly included activity A on the predecessor list of activity J, then Figure 10.2 will contain an arc pointing from node A to node J, an arc that will convey the same information as the sequence of two arcs pointing from A to E and E to J. Perhaps, after she has drawn the project network, Jean will recognize and eliminate the redundant arc that is unnecessarily cluttering the network.

There are two alternative approaches to representing a project as a network: *Activity-On-Node (AON)* and *Activity-On-Arc (AOA)*. AON uses nodes to represent activities and arcs to represent precedence relationships. As illustrated by the project network of Figure 10.2, our discussion has focused so far on AON. Although we will continue to employ AON, we will pause briefly to discuss AOA, an equally popular approach that you may encounter outside this textbook. As its name suggests, AOA uses arcs to represent the activities as well as the precedence relationships. In AOA, network construction proceeds according to the following conventions:

- Activity X is represented by exactly one arc labeled X.
- If activity X is a predecessor of activity Y, then arc X must terminate at the same node at which arc Y originates.
- No two arcs can originate at the same node and terminate at the same node.

Although the AOA conventions are just as easy to state as those of AON, an AOA network is usually much more difficult to construct. To illustrate, consider Figure 10.3, which contrasts AON and AOA for six different cases of fundamental precedence relationships. While AON is straightforward in all cases, AOA is not. In particular, an AOA network representation of Cases (e) and (f) is impossible without the use of *dummy arcs,* the dashed arcs in Figure 10.3. A dummy arc does not represent a real activity. Its sole purpose is to indicate precedence without violating the AOA conventions for network construction. In Case (e), activities B and C have the same predecessor and the same successor. The AOA portion of Figure 10.3 first displays an incorrect representation of Case (e) — incorrect because AOA conventions preclude two arcs from originating at the same node *and* terminating at the same node. The correct AOA representation uses a dummy arc to indicate that C precedes D.[3]

---

[2] The length of an arc has no significance.
[3] Alternatively, the dummy arc and the arc representing C could be interchanged, or the dummy arc could be used with B rather than C.

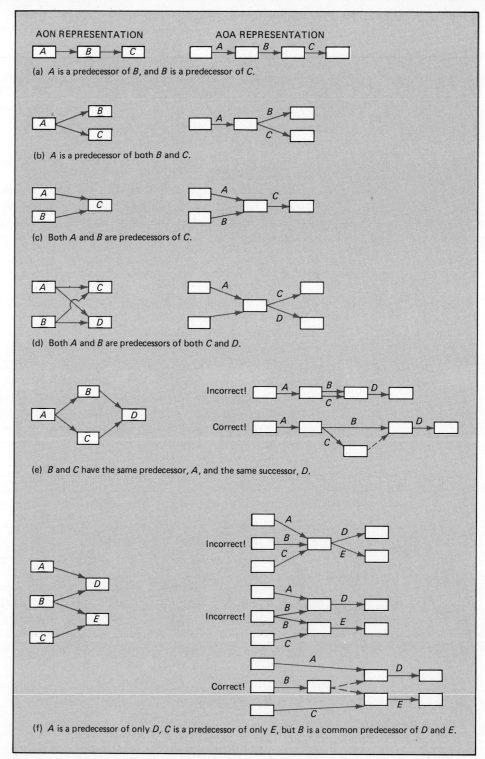

Figure 10.3 Contrast between AON and AOA representations.

In Case (f), B is a common predecessor of both D and E, A is a predecessor of only activity D, and C is a predecessor of only activity E. The AOA portion of Figure 10.3 first shows two incorrect AOA representations of Case (f). The first representation is incorrect because it falsely indicates that A, B, and C (rather than just *B*) are all common predecessors of *D* and *E*. The second representation is incorrect because AOA conventions preclude two arcs from representing the same activity. The correct AOA representation requires two dummy arcs emanating from the terminal node of the arc representing activity *B*. One dummy arc indicates that *B* is a predecessor of *D*, and the other indicates that *B* is also a predecessor of *E*.

Cases (e) and (f) of Figure 10.3 are examples of the following two general situations necessitating the use of dummy arcs:

1. Two or more activities have the same predecessors *and* the same successors [Case (e)].

2. Two or more activities have *some but not all* of their predecessors in common [Case (f)].

Figure 10.4 displays the AOA network representation of the DG project. You should contrast it with the AON representation displayed in Figure 10.2. Observe that the dummy arc labeled d_1 is necessary because activities *F* and *G* have the same predecessor and the same successors; the dummy arcs labeled d_2 and d_3 are necessary because activities *J* and *K* have some but not all of their predecessors in common.

Although AOA and AON have both been in use for over 25 years, there is still no clear-cut answer as to which is better. Proponents of AON (including this author) argue that it is superior for the following reasons:

-   Construction of an AON project network is easier. Construction of an AOA network requires more time and effort because of the insight and creativity required for proper use of dummy arcs to convey certain types of predecessor relationships.

Figure 10.4 AOA project network for relocation of Designer Genes

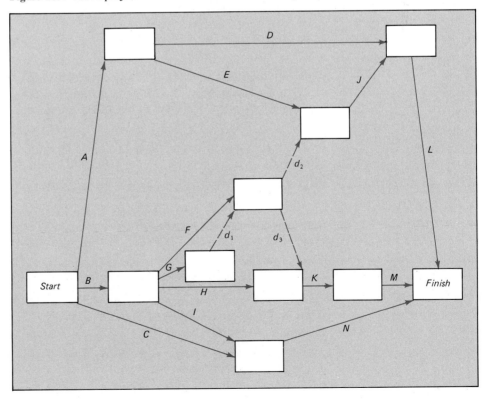

- AON is more easily understood by first-time users, again because of the subtleties associated with the use of the dummy arcs required by AOA. (Keep this in mind if at some future date you find yourself the teacher rather than the student.)

- Once constructed, an AON project network adapts easily to subsequent changes in the project that necessitate adding to or deleting from the list of activities or the predecessor lists. For example, in an AON network, the addition (or deletion) of a forgotten (or mistaken) predecessor relationship simply requires the addition (or removal) of an arc from the network. This is in sharp contrast to an AOA network, where even a single modification to an activity's predecessor list can require the addition to the network of a new node and several dummy arcs.

Throughout the remainder of this chapter, we will employ only AON.

10.3 PHASE II: PLANNING AND SCHEDULING

The primary goals of Phase II are to answer the following questions:

1. What is the project's shortest possible duration?

2. In order to achieve the project's shortest possible duration, which activities are critical in the sense that their actual durations must not exceed their estimated durations?

3. In order to achieve the project's shortest possible duration, what should be the scheduled starting and finishing times for each activity?

Before presenting the formal methodology for answering these questions, let us introduce some concepts and terminology.

The Concept of a Critical Path

A *path* in a project network is a sequence of nodes (activities) interconnected by arcs that lead from the *START* node to the *FINISH* node. For example, in DG the project network (Figure 10.2), one of the many paths is

$$START \rightarrow B \rightarrow F \rightarrow J \rightarrow L \rightarrow FINISH.$$

The *length of a path* is the summation of the durations of the activities on the path. For example, the length of the path displayed above is the sum of the durations of activities B, F, J, and L—namely $19 + 4 + 4 + 8 = 35$. Owing to the small size of the DG project, we can easily identify all nine paths and compute their respective lengths as follows:

Path	Length	
$START \rightarrow A \rightarrow D \rightarrow L \rightarrow FINISH$	$10 + 8 + 8$	$= 26$
$START \rightarrow A \rightarrow E \rightarrow J \rightarrow L \rightarrow FINISH$	$10 + 14 + 4 + 8$	$= 36$
$START \rightarrow B \rightarrow F \rightarrow J \rightarrow L \rightarrow FINISH$	$19 + 4 + 4 + 8$	$= 35$
$START \rightarrow B \rightarrow G \rightarrow J \rightarrow L \rightarrow FINISH$	$19 + 1 + 4 + 8$	$= 32$
$START \rightarrow B \rightarrow F \rightarrow K \rightarrow M \rightarrow FINISH$	$19 + 4 + 6 + 9$	$= 38$
$START \rightarrow B \rightarrow G \rightarrow K \rightarrow M \rightarrow FINISH$	$19 + 1 + 6 + 9$	$= 35$
$START \rightarrow B \rightarrow H \rightarrow K \rightarrow M \rightarrow FINISH$	$19 + 3 + 6 + 9$	$= 37$
$START \rightarrow B \rightarrow I \rightarrow N \rightarrow FINISH$	$19 + 5 + 7$	$= 31$
$START \rightarrow C \rightarrow N \rightarrow FINISH$	$13 + 7$	$= 20$

To understand the significance of a path and its length, consider path

$$START \rightarrow B \rightarrow F \rightarrow J \rightarrow L \rightarrow FINISH$$

and its length of 35 days. Because the arcs interconnecting the nodes of this path indicate precedence relationships, the path represents a sequence of activities that must be performed one at a time in the order in which they appear on the path—namely, B, then F, then J, then L. The completion of the entire project must take at least as long as the completion of every activity in the nonoverlapping sequence of activities represented by the path. Consequently, the path's length of 35 days is a *lower bound* on the duration of the entire project. It is a lower bound because the 35-day length is the sum of only the durations of the activities comprising the path. It does not include possible delays between the finish of a particular activity on the path and the start of its successor activity on the path. For example, activity J cannot begin until both its predecessors, E and F, have finished. Therefore, if E (which is not on the path) finishes after F, there will be a delay between the finish of F and the start of J. Because this delay, completing the sequence of activities $B \rightarrow F \rightarrow J \rightarrow L$ will require more than 35 days, the length of the corresponding path.

Similarly, we may show that the length of every path is a lower bound on the time required to complete the entire project. Since the project's duration must equal or exceed each of the lower bounds, the shortest possible project duration equals the *greatest lower bound* or, equivalently, the length of the *longest path*. For the DG project, the longest path is

$$START \rightarrow B \rightarrow F \rightarrow K \rightarrow M \rightarrow FINISH.$$

Its length of 38 days, then, equals the DG project's shortest possible duration.

In PERT/CPM terminology, the longest path is the *critical path;* the activities comprising the critical path are *critical activities;* and the activities not on the critical path are *noncritical activities*. Knowledge of the critical path for the DG project is fundamentally important to Jean. Its 38-day length represents the shortest possible project duration. Consequently, the critical activities are those activities on which Jean should focus most (but not all) of her attention. For example, if she wishes to guard against a project duration of longer than 38 days, she must ensure that no critical activity's duration exceeds its estimate. Otherwise, the length of the critical path, and therefore the project's duration, will exceed 38 days. Similarly, if she wishes to reduce the project's duration below 38 days, she must reduce the length of the critical path below 38 days by reducing the durations of one or more critical activities.

Although the critical activities deserve most of Jean's attention, she cannot ignore the noncritical activities. To see this, consider the noncritical activity H. It is a member of only one path.

$$START \rightarrow B \rightarrow H \rightarrow K \rightarrow M \rightarrow FINISH.$$

This path's length is 37 days. If H's duration should exceed its estimate by at least 2 days, the path would have a length of at least 39 days, thereby becoming the new critical path. Consequently, the project's duration would be at least 39 days. Thus, H is "almost critical" and certainly deserves Jean's attention.

Activity H illustrates the following distinction between critical and noncritical activities:

Any increase, regardless of how small, in the duration of a critical activity will always increase the project's duration; however, depending upon its size, an increase in the duration of a noncritical activity may or may not affect the project's duration. In short, noncritical activities are *not* unimportant; they are simply less important than critical activities.

Later in this section we will discuss this issue in greater depth.

The identification of the critical path is relatively easy for the DG project, because Jean has to identify and compute the length of only nine paths. In practice, however, most project networks involve many more nodes (activities) and arcs (precedence relationships) and, hence, many more paths. For a complex network, identifying the critical path by attempting to enumerate every path is time-consuming and error-prone. There is a high likelihood of overlooking a few paths, any one of which might be the critical path. Therefore, we will now discuss an efficient procedure for identifying the critical path. We will see that the procedure not only identifies the critical path but also provides a wealth of additional information unavailable from a simple enumeration of all paths.

Step 5: Computation of Each Activity's Earliest Starting and Earliest Finish Times

We begin by defining two important quantities associated with each activity:

- The *Earliest Starting Time* (*EST*) for an activity is an estimate of the earliest possible time at which the activity can start.

- The *Earliest Finishing Time* (*EFT*) for an activity is an estimate of the earliest possible time at which the activity can finish.

Both the EST and the EFT of an activity are measured in units of elapsed working time after the start of the project. For example, an EST of ten days for a particular activity indicates that the earliest possible time the activity can start is ten working days after the project starts—that is, at the beginning of the eleventh working day. Once a specific calendar date is assigned to the start of the project, it is easy to convert every activity's EST and EFT to specific calendar dates.

To illustrate how to compute an activity's EST and EFT, consider Figure 10.5, which displays the portion of the DG project network containing activity *J* and its three predecessors *E*, *F*, and *G*. Because *J* has more than one predecessor, we refer to *J* as a *merge activity*. The other merge activities in the DG project network are *K*, *L*, *N*, and *FINISH*. Figure 10.5(a) illustrates the PERT/CPM convention of recording an activity's EST and EFT in the activity's upper-left and upper-right corners, respectively. As indicated in Figure 10.5(a), let us assume for the moment that we already know that *E*'s EST is 10 days, *F*'s EST is 19 days, and *G*'s EST is 19 days and that we now wish to compute *E*'s EFT, *F*'s EFT, *G*'s EFT, and *J*'s EST and EFT. Our computations would proceed as follows:

- **Computation of *E*'s EFT.** Knowing *E*'s EST is 10 days and its duration is 14 days, we compute *E*'s EFT as 10 + 14 = 24 days, a value we record in node *E*'s upper-right corner.

- **Computation of *F*'s EFT.** Similarly, knowing *F*'s EST is 19 days and its duration is 4 days, we record an EFT for *F* of 19 + 4 = 23 days.

- **Computation of *G*'s EFT.** Similarly, knowing *G*'s EST is 19 days and its duration is 1 day, we record an EFT for *G* of 19 + 1 = 20 days. Our computations have now reached the stage displayed in Figure 10.5(b).

- **Computation of *J*'s EST.** Given EFTs of 24, 23, and 20 days for *J*'s three predecessors, what is *J*'s EST? Although it is tempting to answer 20 days, the correct answer is 24 days. Remember that activity *J* cannot start until *all*

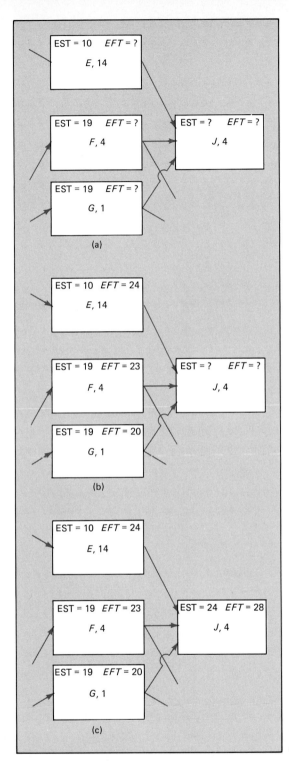

Figure 10.5 Determination of activity
J's EST and EFT

its predecessors have finished. Although *G*'s EFT is 20 days, *E*'s EFT is 24 days. Consequently, we record *J*'s EST as 24 days, the *maximum* of the EFTs of *J*'s three predecessors.

- **Computation of *J*'s EFT.** Having computed *J*'s EST as 24 days and knowing that *J*'s duration is 4 days, we record *J*'s EFT as 24 + 4 = 28 days. Our computations have now reached the stage displayed in Figure 10.5(c).

As we have just illustrated, once we know the EFTs of *all* predecessors of an activity, say activity X, we may compute X's EST according to the following rule:

EST Rule

$$(X\text{'s EST}) = (\text{maximum of EFTs of } X\text{'s predecessors})$$

Of course, if an activity is not a merge activity, its EST simply equals the EFT of its only predecessor. For example, in the DG project, the EST of activity D equals the EFT of D's only predecessor, activity A. Furthermore, once we know X's EST, we may compute X's EFT according to the following rule:

EFT Rule

$$(X\text{'s EFT}) = (X\text{'s EST}) + (X\text{'s duration})$$

The EFT rule and the EST rule suggest a systematic procedure that begins with the *START* node and makes a *forward pass* (i.e., left to right) through the project network, computing an activity's EST and EFT only after doing the same for all the activity's predecessors. It would be convenient if the procedure could consider the activities one at a time in alphabetical order. This would require that the letter code of every predecessor of an activity appear earlier in the alphabet than the letter code of the activity itself. For example, if an activity has a letter code of J, its predecessors should have letter codes drawn from among the letters *A–I*. We call such an assignment of letter codes an *alphabetical ordering of the activities* (with respect to the predecessor relationships). Regardless of the project under consideration, we can always alphabetically order the activities, either informally by inspection or formally by applying the algorithm discussed in Exercise 10.11. Although we have not said so until now, the activities of the DG project are in alphabetical order. To see this, either examine Table 10.1 and observe that an activity always appears below each of its predecessors or, equivalently, examine Figure 10.2 and observe that every arc points from a node with a letter code appearing earlier in the alphabet to a node with a letter code appearing later in the alphabet. Consequently, Jean may compute ESTs and EFTs of all activities by considering them one at a time in alphabetical order. This will mean, for example, that Jean will already know the EFTs for activities E and F before needing them to compute activity J's EST.

Table 10.2 summarizes Jean's computations, which begin by setting the EST of *START* to 0. Then, as the table indicates, the computations continue with repeated applications of the EST rule and the EFT rule until determining that *FINISH*'s EFT is 38 days. Of course, this is the project's shortest possible duration. It is the same duration we determined earlier by the inefficient procedure of enumerating all nine paths, computing the length of each, and identifying the longest path.

Figure 10.6 also summarizes Jean's computations, employing the previously mentioned convention of writing an activity's EST in the upper left corner and the activity's EFT in the upper right corner. (Temporarily ignore the numbers in the lower-left and lower-right corners.) Jean need not wait until her computations are complete to summarize them on the project network. Instead of Table 10.2's tabular approach, she may use the project network as a visual aid to her computations. As soon as she computes an activity's EST and EFT, she can record them directly on the project network and then move to the activity whose letter code is next in the alphabet.

TABLE 10.2 Jean's Computation of Each Activity's EST and EFT

Activity	Duration	Predecessors	EST = max of EFTs of predecessors		EST	+	Duration	=	EFT
START	0	none	EST =		0	0 +	0	=	0
A	10	*START*	EST = max of [0 for *START*] =	0	0	+	10	=	10
B	19	*START*	EST = max of [0 for *START*] =	0	0	+	19	=	19
C	13	*START*	EST = max of [0 for *START*] =	0	0	+	13	=	13
D	8	*A*	EST = max of [10 for *A*] =	10	10	+	8	=	18
E	14	*A*	EST = max of [10 for *A*] =	10	10	+	14	=	24
F	4	*B*	EST = max of [19 for *B*] =	19	19	+	4	=	23
G	1	*B*	EST = max of [19 for *B*] =	19	19	+	1	=	20
H	3	*B*	EST = max of [19 for *B*] =	19	19	+	3	=	22
I	5	*B*	EST = max of [19 for *B*] =	19	19	+	5	=	24
J	4	*E,F,G*	EST = max of $\begin{bmatrix} 24 \text{ for } E \\ 23 \text{ for } F \\ 20 \text{ for } G \end{bmatrix}$ = 24		24	+	4	=	28
K	6	*F,G,H*	EST = max of $\begin{bmatrix} 23 \text{ for } F \\ 20 \text{ for } G \\ 22 \text{ for } H \end{bmatrix}$ = 23		23	+	6	=	29
L	8	*D,J*	EST = max of $\begin{bmatrix} 18 \text{ for } D \\ 28 \text{ for } J \end{bmatrix}$ = 28		28	+	8	=	36
M	9	*K*	EST = max of [29 for *K*] = 29		29	+	9	=	38
N	7	*C,I*	EST = max of $\begin{bmatrix} 13 \text{ for } C \\ 24 \text{ for } I \end{bmatrix}$ = 24		24	+	7	=	31
FINISH	0	*L,M,N*	EST = max of $\begin{bmatrix} 36 \text{ for } L \\ 38 \text{ for } M \\ 31 \text{ for } N \end{bmatrix}$ = 38		38	+	0	=	38

Figure 10.6 Summary of the computations of Steps 5 and 6

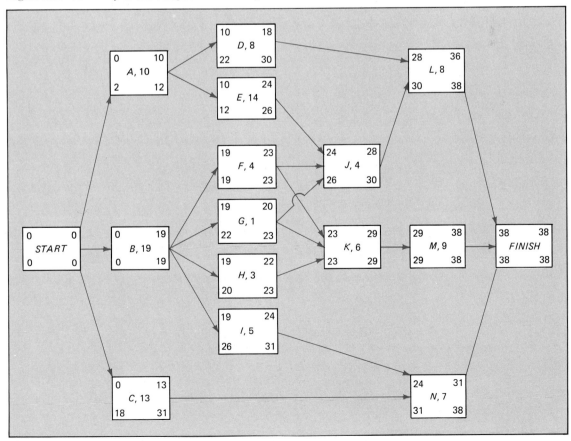

To summarize, Step 5 concludes with the computation of *FINISH*'s EFT, a quantity equal to the project's shortest possible duration and, equivalently, the length of the critical path. Although Jean now knows its length, she does not yet know the activities that comprise the critical path. With a little extra bookkeeping during the computation of the ESTs and EFTs, it would be possible to identify the critical path at the conclusion of Step 5. However, we will soon see that it is easier to identify the critical path at the conclusion of Step 7.

Step 6: Computation of Each Activity's Latest Starting and Latest Finishing Times

The description of Step 6 is essentially a mirror image of the description of Step 5, with "latest" replacing "earliest," "backward pass" replacing "forward pass," "successor" replacing "predecessor," " − " replacing " + ," and "minimum" replacing "maximum." Instead of each activity's EST and EFT, Step 6 computes the following two quantities:

- The *Latest Starting Time* (*LST*) for an activity is an estimate of the latest possible time at which the activity can start without causing the project to finish after its deadline.

- The *Latest Finishing Time* (*LFT*) for an activity is an estimate of the latest possible time at which the activity can finish without causing the project to finish after its deadline.

Unless we state otherwise, assume that the project's deadline is the project's shortest possible duration—that is, the EFT of *FINISH*. In the DG project, then, we will assume the project's deadline equals *FINISH*'s EFT of 38 days. Such an assumption implies that the project manager wants to finish the project as quickly as possible. In some projects, however, the desired or required project deadline may be larger or even smaller than the project's shortest possible duration. For example, even though its shortest possible duration is 50 days, a contract might set the project's deadline at 60 days (to the delight of the project manager) or at 40 days (to the project manager's chagrin). At the conclusion of Step 7, we will discuss the effects of using a project deadline unequal to the EFT of *FINISH*.

To illustrate how to compute an activity's LST and LFT, consider Figure 10.7, which displays the portion of the DG network containing activity *A* and its two successors, *D* and *E*. Because activity *A* has more than one successor, we refer to *A* as a *burst activity*. The other burst activities in the DG project network are *START*, *B*, *F*, and *G*. Figure 10.7(a) illustrates the PERT/CPM convention of recording an activity's LST and LFT in the activity's lower-left and lower-right corners, respectively. As indicated by Figure 10.7(a), let us assume for the moment that we already know that *D*'s LFT is 30 days and *E*'s LFT is 26 days and that we now wish to compute *D*'s LST, *E*'s LST, and *A*'s LFT and LST. Our computations would proceed as follows:

- **Computation of *D*'s LST.** Knowing *D*'s LFT is 30 days and its duration is 8 days, we compute *D*'s LST as $30 - 8 = 22$ days, a value in node *D*'s lower-left corner.

- **Computation of *E*'s LST.** Similarly, knowing *E*'s LFT is 26 days and its duration is 14 days, we record an LST for *E* of $26 - 14 = 12$ days. Our computations have now reached the stage displayed in Figure 10.7(b).

- **Computation of *A*'s LFT.** Given LSTs of 22 days and 12 days for *A*'s two successors, what is *A*'s LFT? Although it is tempting to answer 22 days, the

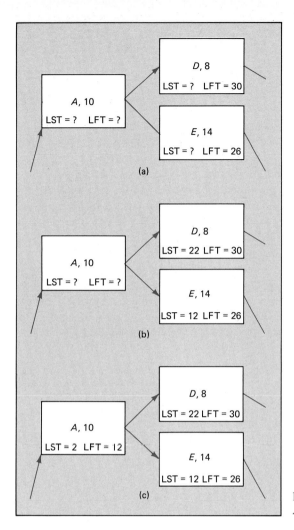

Figure 10.7 Determination of activity
A's LFT and LST

correct answer is 12 days. Remember that *A* must finish before its successors, *D* and *E*, can start. Although *D*'s start can be delayed until its LST of 22 days, *E*'s start must take place no later than its LST of 12 days in order to meet the project deadline. Consequently, we record *A*'s LFT as 12 days, the *minimum* LST between *A*'s two successors.

■ **Computation of *A*'s LST.** Having computed *A*'s LFT as 12 days and knowing that *A*'s duration is 10 days, we can record *A*'s LST as 12 − 10 = 2 days. Our computations have now reached the stage displayed in Figure 10.7(c).

As we have just illustrated, once we know the LSTs of *all* successors of an activity, say activity *X*, we may compute *X*'s LFT according to the following rule:

LFT Rule

$$(X\text{'s LFT}) = (\text{minimum of LSTs of } X\text{'s successors})$$

Of course, if an activity is not a burst activity, its LFT simply equals the LST of its only successor. For example, in the DG project, the LFT of activity *C* equals the LST of *C*'s only successor, activity *N*. Furthermore, once we know *X*'s LFT, we may compute *X*'s LST according to the following rule:

$$(X\text{'s LST}) = (X\text{'s LFT}) - (X\text{'s duration})$$

The LST rule and the LFT rule suggest a systematic procedure that begins with the *FINISH* node and makes a *backward pass* (i.e., right to left) through the project network, computing a particular activity's LFT and LST only after doing the same for all of the activity's successors. Table 10.3 summarizes Jean's computations, which begin by setting *FINISH*'S LFT equal to the project's deadline of 38 days.[4] Then, as Table 10.3 indicates, the computations proceed by considering the activities in reverse alphabetical order and repeatedly applying the LFT rule and the LST rule until determining that *START*'s LST is 0 days.[5] Considering activities in reverse alphabetical order ensures that the computation of each activity's LFT will occur after the computations of the LSTs of all the activity's successors.

Figure 10.6 also summarizes Jean's computations, employing the previously mentioned convention of writing an activity's LST in the lower-left corner and LFT in the lower-right corner. Jean need not wait until her computations are complete to summarize them on the project network. Instead of Table 10.3's tabular approach, she may use the project network as a visual aid to her computations. As soon as she computes an activity's LFT and LST, she can record them directly on

---

[4] Recall our assumption that Jean desires to finish the project as soon as possible and, consequently, uses *FINISH*'s EFT as the project's deadline. At the conclusion of the next subsection, we will discuss the effects of using a project deadline unequal to *FINISH*'s EFT.

[5] You should convince yourself that the LST of *START* will always be 0 if the computations of the backward pass begin by setting *FINISH*'s LFT equal to its EFT.

TABLE 10.3 Jean's Computation of Each Activity's LST and LFT

Activity	Duration	Successors	LFT = min of LSTs of successors		LFT	−	Duration	=	LST
FINISH	0	none	LFT =	38	38	−	0	=	38
N	7	*FINISH*	LFT = min of [38 for *FINISH*] = 38		38	−	7	=	31
M	9	*FINISH*	LFT = min of [38 for *FINISH*] = 38		38	−	9	=	29
L	8	*FINISH*	LFT = min of [38 for *FINISH*] = 38		38	−	8	=	30
K	6	M	LFT = min of [29 for M] = 29		29	−	6	=	23
J	4	L	LFT = min of [30 for L] = 30		30	−	4	=	26
I	5	N	LFT = min of [31 for N] = 31		31	−	5	=	26
H	3	K	LFT = min of [23 for K] = 23		23	−	3	=	20
G	1	J,K	LFT = min of $\begin{bmatrix} 26 \text{ for } J \\ 23 \text{ for } K \end{bmatrix}$ = 23		23	−	1	=	22
F	4	J,K	LFT = min of $\begin{bmatrix} 26 \text{ for } J \\ 23 \text{ for } K \end{bmatrix}$ = 23		23	−	4	=	19
E	14	J	LFT = min of [26 for J] = 26		26	−	14	=	12
D	8	L	LFT = min of [30 for L] = 30		30	−	8	=	22
C	13	N	LFT = min of [31 for N] = 31		31	−	13	=	18
B	19	F,G,H,I	LFT = min of $\begin{bmatrix} 19 \text{ for } F \\ 22 \text{ for } G \\ 20 \text{ for } H \\ 26 \text{ for } I \end{bmatrix}$ = 19		19	−	19	=	0
A	10	D,E	LFT = min of $\begin{bmatrix} 22 \text{ for } D \\ 12 \text{ for } E \end{bmatrix}$ = 12		12	−	10	=	2
START	0	A,B,C	LFT = min of $\begin{bmatrix} 2 \text{ for } A \\ 0 \text{ for } B \\ 18 \text{ for } C \end{bmatrix}$ = 0		0	−	0	=	0

the project network and then move to the activity whose letter code immediately precedes in the alphabet.

Before advancing to PERT/CPM's next step, let us contrast an activity's EST and EFT computed in Step 5 with the activity's LST and LFT computed in Step 6. Consider, for example, activity N in the DG project. N's EST of 24 and EFT of 31 indicate that the earliest interval of time within which N can take place is Day 25 through Day 31. In contrast, N's LST of 31 days and LFT of 38 days indicate that, if the project is to finish in 38 days, the latest interval of time within which N can take place is Day 32 through Day 38. As we will soon see, N is not restricted to a single time interval because it is a noncritical activity. Now consider activity K and observe in Tables 10.2 and 10.3 that

$$EST = LST = 23 \text{ and } EFT = LFT = 29.$$

Thus, if the entire project is to finish in 38 days, the one and only interval of time within which K can take place is Day 24 through Day 29. As we will soon see, K is restricted to a single time interval because it is a critical activity.

Step 7: Computations of Slacks and Identification of the Critical Path

Consider the following question about a particular activity, say activity X:

> *By how much can the duration of X increase without causing the entire project to finish after its deadline?*

In PERT/CPM terminology, the answer is called activity X's *slack*.[6] Knowledge of X's slack is useful to the project manager. For example, suppose X's slack is 0; that is, any increase whatsoever in X's duration will cause the project to finish after its deadline. In this case, the project manager can conclude that X is a critical activity. Now suppose that X has a nonzero slack of six days; that is, X is a noncritical activity whose duration can increase by six days without causing the project to finish after its deadline. The project manager can use this knowledge in either or both of two ways:

- The first alternative will be discussed more formally and in more detail in Section 11.3. Briefly, however, this alternative is to increase X's estimated duration up to six days, thereby reducing the total dollar value of the resources (e.g., labor and equipment) allocated to perform X. This in turn permits the project manager to reduce the project's total budget or to reallocate the resources to one or more of the critical activities in order to shorten the project's duration by shortening the critical path.

- The second alternative for the project manager is to leave the estimated duration of X unchanged but to recognize that, once the project begins, X has a "cushion" of six days to absorb increases in its duration or delays in its start, which might result from unforeseen circumstances (e.g., bad weather) beyond the project manager's control.

In determining how much an activity's duration can be increased without causing the entire project to finish after its deadline, let us respond from the perspective both of an optimist and of a pessimist.

- **The optimist's response.** Expecting that the project will go well prior to X's

---

[6] Some refer to slack as *float*.

start and after X's finish, the optimist believes that X will start at its EST and could finish as late as its LFT. The optimist, then, believes that the amount of time available to perform X will be

$$(X\text{'s LFT}) - (X\text{'s EST}).$$

Consequently, the optimist concludes that X's duration can increase by

$$[(X\text{'s LFT}) - (X\text{'s EST})] - (X\text{'s duration})$$

—that is, the *excess* time currently available to perform X. As an example, consider activity C of the DG project. The optimist believes that C will start at its EST of 0 and could finish as late as its LFT of 31. Considering C's current 13-day duration, then, the optimist believes that there currently are

$$(31 - 0) - 18 = 13$$

excess days to perform C. Consequently, the optimist concludes that C's duration may increase by 18 days without causing the project to finish after its deadline.

■ **The pessimist's response.** Expecting the project to go poorly prior to X's start, the pessimist wants to ensure that the increase in X's duration will not cause a decrease in the LFT of any of X's predecessors. To do so, the pessimist must limit the increase in X's duration to

$$(X\text{'s LST}) - (\text{maximum LFT of } X\text{'s predecessors}).[7]$$

Furthermore, expecting the project to go poorly after X's finish, the pessimist wants to ensure that the increase in X's duration will not cause an increase in the EST of any of X's successors. To do so, the pessimist must limit the increase in X's duration to

$$(\text{minimum EST of } X\text{'s successors}) - (X\text{'s EFT}).[8]$$

Thus, to ensure that the increase in X's duration will neither decrease the LFT of any of X's predecessors nor increase the EST of any of X's successors, the pessimist must limit the increase in X's duration to the smaller of the above two expressions—that is, to

$$\min \text{ of } \begin{cases} (X\text{'s LST}) - (\text{max LFT of } X\text{'s predecessors}), \\ (\text{min EST of } X\text{'s successors}) - (X\text{'s EFT}). \end{cases}$$

As an example, consider once again activity C of the DG project. To ensure that there is no decrease in the LFT of $START$ (C's only predecessor), Jean must limit the increase in C's duration to

$$(C\text{'s LST}) - (\text{LFT of } START, C\text{'s only predecessor}) = 18 - 0 = 18 .$$

Furthermore, to ensure that there is no increase in the EST of N (C's only successor), Jean must limit the increase in C's duration to

---

[7] Some refer to this expression as X's *safety slack*.

[8] Some refer to this expression as X's *free slack*.

$$(\text{EST of } N, C\text{'s only successor}) - (C\text{'s EFT}) = 24 - 13 = 11 \ .$$

Consequently, Jean must limit the increase in C's duration to 11, the minumum of 18 and 11.

In PERT/CPM terminology, the optimist's response is called activity X's *Total Slack* (*TS*) and the pessimist's response is called X's *Unshared Slack* (*US*).

To summarize:

$$(X\text{'s TS}) = [(X\text{'s LFT}) - (X\text{'s EST})] - (X\text{'s duration}),^9$$

$$(X\text{'s US}) = \min \text{ of } \begin{cases} (X\text{'s LST}) - (\max \text{ of LFTs of } X\text{'s predecessors}), \\ (\min \text{ of ESTs of } X\text{'s successors}) - (X\text{'s EFT}). \end{cases}$$

Table 10.4 summarizes the computation of TS and US for each activity of the DG project. Observe that, for every activity, TS $\geq$ US. Such a relationship is intuitive, because the Total Slack is optimistic and Unshared Slack is pessimistic.

The most important use of the concept of slack is to determine, in terms of an activity's TS, whether the activity is critical. For the DG project, Table 10.4 indicates that B, F, K, and M each have a *TS* of 0. Hence, even under the optimistic assumptions used in the computation of *TS*, any increase whatsoever in the duration of any of these activities will result in the project's finishing after its deadline. Because each has a *TS* of 0, B, F, K, and M are the activities that (in addition to *START* and *FINISH*) comprise the critical path. These are the same critical activities we identified earlier by the inefficient procedure of enumerating all nine paths, computing the length of each, and identifying the longest. In identifying the critical path for the DG project, we have illustrated the following general principles:

- A critical activity has a TS of 0.

- Any increase whatsoever in the duration of a critical activity will cause the project to finish after its deadline.

- A noncritical activity has a nonzero TS.

Since TS $\geq$ US always holds, only a noncritical activity may have a nonzero US. Consequently, we need compute an activity's US only if the activity's TS is nonzero. We may automatically set to 0 the US of any activity having a TS equal to 0.

---

9 In addition to this formula, two equivalent formulae for X's TS are

$$(X\text{'s TS}) = (X\text{'s LST}) - (X\text{'s EST})$$

or

$$(X\text{'s TS}) = (X\text{'s LFT}) - (X\text{'s EFT}).$$

To see why, note that the expression

$$[(X\text{'s LFT}) - (X\text{'s EST})] - (X\text{'s duration})$$

may be regrouped as

$$[(X\text{'s LFT}) - (X\text{'s duration})] - (X\text{'s EST})$$

or

$$(X\text{'s LFT}) - [(X\text{'s EST}) + (X\text{'s duration})].$$

These expressions simplify (via the LST rule and the EFT rule, respectively) to

$$(X\text{'s LST}) - (X\text{'s EST})$$

or

$$(X\text{'s LFT}) - (X\text{'s EFT}).$$

TABLE 10.4 Jean's Computation of Each Activity's TS and US

Activity	(LFT − EST) − Duration =	TS	min of	$\begin{bmatrix} \text{LST} - (\text{max of LFTs of predecessors}) \\ (\text{min of ESTs of successors}) - \text{EFT} \end{bmatrix}$	= US
A	(12 − 0) − 10 =	2	min of	$\begin{bmatrix} 2 - \text{max of } (0) & = & 2 \\ \text{min of } (10,10) - 10 & = & 0 \end{bmatrix}$	= 0
B	(19 − 0) − 19 =	0	min of	$\begin{bmatrix} 0 - \text{max of } (0) & = & 0 \\ \text{min of } (19,19,19,19) - 19 & = & 0 \end{bmatrix}$	= 0
C	(31 − 0) − 13 =	18	min of	$\begin{bmatrix} 18 - \text{max of } (0) & = & 18 \\ \text{min of } (24) - 13 & = & 11 \end{bmatrix}$	= 11
D	(30 − 10) − 8 =	12	min of	$\begin{bmatrix} 22 - \text{max of } (12) & = & 10 \\ \text{min of } (28) - 18 & = & 10 \end{bmatrix}$	= 10
E	(26 − 10) − 14 =	2	min of	$\begin{bmatrix} 12 - \text{max of } (12) & = & 0 \\ \text{min of } (24) - 24 & = & 0 \end{bmatrix}$	= 0
F	(23 − 19) − 4 =	0	min of	$\begin{bmatrix} 19 - \text{max of } (19) & = & 0 \\ \text{min of } (24,23) - 23 & = & 0 \end{bmatrix}$	= 0
G	(23 − 19) − 1 =	3	min of	$\begin{bmatrix} 22 - \text{max of } (19) & = & 3 \\ \text{min of } (24,23) - 20 & = & 3 \end{bmatrix}$	= 3
H	(23 − 19) − 3 =	1	min of	$\begin{bmatrix} 20 - \text{max of } (19) & = & 1 \\ \text{min of } (23) - 22 & = & 1 \end{bmatrix}$	= 1
I	(31 − 19) − 5 =	7	min of	$\begin{bmatrix} 26 - \text{max of } (19) & = & 7 \\ \text{min of } (24) - 24 & = & 0 \end{bmatrix}$	= 0
J	(30 − 24) − 4 =	2	min of	$\begin{bmatrix} 26 - \text{max of } (26,23,23) & = & 0 \\ \text{min of } (28) - 28 & = & 0 \end{bmatrix}$	= 0
K	(29 − 23) − 6 =	0	min of	$\begin{bmatrix} 23 - \text{max of } (23,23,23) & = & 0 \\ \text{min of } (29) - 29 & = & 0 \end{bmatrix}$	= 0
L	(38 − 28) − 8 =	2	min of	$\begin{bmatrix} 30 - \text{max of } (30,30) & = & 0 \\ \text{min of } (38) - 36 & = & 2 \end{bmatrix}$	= 0
M	(38 − 29) − 9 =	0	min of	$\begin{bmatrix} 29 - \text{max of } (29) & = & 0 \\ \text{min of } (38) - 38 & = & 0 \end{bmatrix}$	= 0
N	(38 − 24) − 7 =	7	min of	$\begin{bmatrix} 31 - \text{max of } (31) & = & 0 \\ \text{min of } (38) - 31 & = & 7 \end{bmatrix}$	= 0

As the adjectives "total" and "unshared" suggest, the nonzero TS of a noncritical activity consists of two parts:

- An *unshared portion* US that belongs only to *X*, because it exists even under the pessimistic requirement that the LFTs of all *X*'s predecessors and the ESTs of all *X*'s successors remain unchanged.

- A *shared portion* TS − US that is shared with the other activities, because it exists only under the optimistic assumption that *X* will start at its EST and could finish as late as its LFT.

Observe in Table 10.4 that each noncritical activity (one with a nonzero TS) is one of the following types:

1. An activity (such as *A, E, I, J, L,* or *N*) whose TS consists solely of a shared portion; that is, an activity for which $TS > 0$ but $US = 0$.

2. An activity (such as *C* or *D*) whose TS consist of both an unshared portion and a shared portion; that is, an activity for which $0 < US < TS$.

3. An activity (such as *G* or *H*) whose TS consists solely of an unshared portion; that is, an activity for which $US = TS$.

Thinking of a noncritical activity's TS in terms of its unshared portion US and its shared portion TS − US is useful if the project manager intends to increase the duration of more than one noncritical activity. To illustrate, consider activity *D* of the DG project. D's TS of 12 consists of an unshared portion $US = 10$ and a shared portion $TS - US = 2$. Let us successively examine the effects of increasing D's duration by three differents amounts:

- **An increase exceeding D's TS of 12 days.** Increasing D's duration by this amount must cause the project to finish after its deadline, since, by definition, D's TS of 12 days is the maximum (most optimistic) amount by which D's duration may increase without causing the project to finish after its deadline.

- **An increase equal to D's TS of 12 days.** Increasing D's duration by this amount necessitates some revisions to the computations summarized in Figure 10.6. These revisions are displayed in Figure 10.8(a). During Step 5's forward pass, D's EFT increases 12 days, thereby adding 12 days to the EST and EFT of D's successor, L. Furthermore, during Step 6's backward pass, D's LST decreases 12 days, thereby causing a 12-day decrease in the LFT and LST of D's predecessor, A. Because of these changes, there is a 12-day reduction in D's TS from 12 to 0. In addition, because 2 days ($TS - US$) of D's TS are "shared" with A and L, the TS of A and of L decreases from 2 to 0. In other words, whereas A, D, and L, were formerly noncritical, they now comprise an additional critical path, namely,

$$START \rightarrow A \rightarrow D \rightarrow L \rightarrow FINISH.$$

Consequently, if Jean increases D's duration by an amount equal to D's TS, she must forego any increases whatsoever in the durations of activities A and L.

- **An amount equal to D's US of 10 days.** Increasing D's duration by this amount also necessitates some revisions to the computations summarized in Figure 10.6. These revisions are displayed in Figure 10.8(b). During Step

Figure 10.8 Necessary revisions to Figure 10.6 when activity D's duration increases

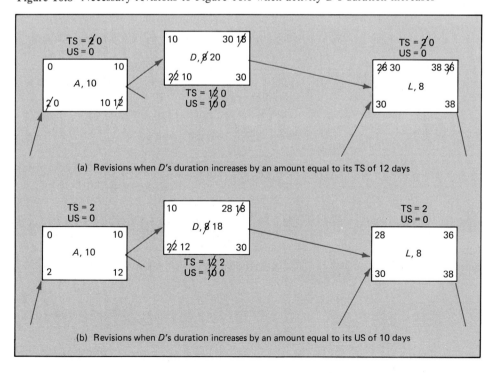

(a) Revisions when D's duration increases by an amount equal to its TS of 12 days

(b) Revisions when D's duration increases by an amount equal to its US of 10 days

5's forward pass, the only revision is the 10-day increase in D's EFT; during the backward pass, the only revision is the 10-day decrease in D's LST. The only consequences of these changes are the 10-day decreases in D's US from 10 to 0 and in D's TS from 12 to 2. Because D's US is not shared with any other activity, the EST, EFT, LST, LFT, TS, and US of every other activity remain unchanged. Therefore, if Jean increases D's duration by an amount equal to D's US of 10 days, she still retains whatever options she previously had for increasing the durations of all other activities.

We have just used activity D of the DG project to illustrate the following general principles that apply to any noncritical activity X:

- An increase in X's duration by an amount exceeding its TS causes the project to finish after its deadline.

- An increase in X's duration by an amount less than or equal to its US does not affect any other activity. In particular, an increase in X's duration by an amount equal to its US results only in an increase in X's EFT, a decrease in X's LST, the reduction of X's US to 0, and the reduction of X's TS to the former value of $TS - US$. The EST, EFT, LST, LFT, US, and TS of every other activity remain unchanged. Consequently, the project manager retains whatever options she formerly had with respect to increasing the durations of other activities.

- An increase in X's duration by an amount less than or equal to its TS but greater than its US usually affects at least one other activity. In particular, an increase in X's duration by an amount equal to its TS creates an additional critical path, a path always containing X. If (before the increase in X's duration) X's TS exceeds its US, then the additional critical path also contains some other formerly noncritical activities. In such a case, increasing X's duration by an amount equal to its TS precludes any increase whatsoever in the durations of these other formerly noncritical activities.

To gain an even better understanding of these principles, you may wish to verify the following three examples:

1. Activity C's TS of 18 days consists of an unshared portion $US = 11$ and a shared portion $TS - US = 7$ (i.e., $0 < US < TS$). If Jean increases C's duration by an amount equal to its TS of 18 days, then

$$START \rightarrow C \rightarrow N \rightarrow FINISH$$

becomes an additional critical path, thereby precluding any increase whatsoever in the duration of activity N, an activity that was formerly noncritical. In contrast, if Jean increases C's duration by an amount equal to its US of 11 days, C's EFT increases by 11 to 24, C's LST decreases by 11 to 7, C's US decreases to 0, and its TS decreases to 7; however, the EST, EFT, LST, LFT, US, and TS of every other activity remain unchanged. Thus, by increasing C's duration by only 11 days, Jean retains the option of increasing N's duration.

2. Activity E's TS of 2 days consists solely of a shared portion of 2 days (i.e., $US = 0$). If Jean increases E's duration by an amount equal to its TS of 2 days, then

$$START \rightarrow A \rightarrow E \rightarrow J \rightarrow L \rightarrow FINISH$$

becomes an additional critical path, thereby precluding any increase whatsoever in the duration of A, J, and L, activities that were formerly noncritical. Since E's US equals 0, Jean cannot increase E's duration by any amount whatsoever without affecting at least one other activity.

3. Activity G's TS of 3 days consists solely of a US of 3 days (i.e., $US = TS$). If Jean increases G's duration by its TS of 3 days, then

$$START \rightarrow B \rightarrow G \rightarrow K \rightarrow M \rightarrow FINISH$$

becomes an additional critical path. However, among the activities that comprise this new critical path, only G is a formerly noncritical activity. Therefore, in the special case where $US = TS$, an increase in the activity's duration by an amount equal to its TS will have no effect on any other activity.

In summary,

> The optimism inherent in the concept of TS makes it an appropriate concept for identifying the critical path. However, owing to the same optimism, an activity's TS is a "risky" measure of the degree to which the activity is noncritical. When considering increases in the durations of more than one noncritical activity, a risk-averse (cautious) project manager would prefer the inherent pessimism of the concept of US.

For example, suppose that the project manager wishes to operate in a decentralized fashion, permitting the supervisors of the individual activities to independently decide the extent to which they will increase the durations of their respective activities. In such a case, the project manager should instruct each supervisor to base the decision on his or her activity's US, not its TS. This ensures that no supervisor's decision adversely affects another activity, even if each supervisor decides to increase the duration of his or her activity by the full amount of its US. After observing the results of the decentralized decisions, the project manager can recompute the new values of each activity's TS and US and, if desired, make a "centralized" decision to increase further the duration of one or more activities.

At this point we should discuss the effects of using a project deadline that is unequal to the project's shortest possible duration—that is, unequal to $FINISH$'s EFT. For convenience, let Δ denote the project's deadline minus the project's shortest possible duration. Until now, we have assumed $\Delta = 0$. However, the desired or required deadline for a project may be strictly greater or strictly less than $FINISH$'s EFT, resulting respectively in a strictly positive or a strictly negative value of Δ. For example, if $FINISH$'s EFT is 38 days but a contract sets the project deadline at 40 days, $\Delta = 40 - 38 = 2$; alternatively, if $FINISH$'s EFT is 38 days but a contract sets the project deadline at 35 days, $\Delta = 35 - 38 = -3$.[10] When $\Delta \neq 0$, no modifications need to be made to the forward pass computations of Step 5, and only the following minor modifications need to be made to the backward-pass computations of Step 6 and the computations of the slacks in Step 7:

1. At the start of Step 6, instead of being set equal to $FINISH$'s EFT, $FINISH$'s LFT should be set equal to the project's desired or required dead-

---

[10] When $\Delta < 0$, the project manager has two options. First, he may renegotiate the deadline so that it is at least as great as $FINISH$'s EFT. Alternatively, he may employ the concepts introduced in Step 10 and made formal in Section 11.3 to reduce the length of the critical path to at least as low as the project's deadline.

line. The computations of each activity's LFT and LST then proceed exactly as before.

2. In Step 7, the formulae for computing each activity's TS and US remain unchanged. However, the critical path will now consist of those activities with a TS of Δ rather than 0. (Exercise 10.8 requests you to redo the computations for the DG project using a project deadline of 40 days rather than 38. If you work this exercise, you will see that each critical activity has a TS of 2 days.)

Step 8: Scheduling the Activities

Before the project begins, the project manager must schedule the activities; that is, she must specify a starting time and a finishing time for each activity. The computation of each activity's EST, EFT, LST, and LFT has identified two extreme schedules: the *ES schedule* and the *LS schedule*. The ES schedule calls for every activity to start at its EST and finish at its EFT. At the other extreme, the LS schedule calls for every activity to start at its LST and finish at its LFT.

A convenient way to represent a schedule is by using a *schedule diagram*. Figures 10.9(a) and (b) are the schedule diagrams for the DG project's ES schedule and LS schedule, respectively.[11] Observe that the bottom of each of these schedule diagrams consists of a time scale ranging from time 0 to the project's deadline at time 38. Above the time scale are line segments representing each of the project's activities. The left endpoint of the line segment representing a particular activity appears above the activity's scheduled starting time, and the right endpoint appears above the scheduled finishing time. Therefore, the length of the line segment equals the activity's duration. For example, in the ES schedule of Figure 10.9(a), the line segment representing activity *I* has its left endpoint above *I*'s EST of 19 and its right endpoint above *I*'s EFT of 24. In contrast, in the LS schedule of Figure 10.9(b), the line segment representing *I* has its left endpoint above *I*'s LST of 26 and its right endpoint above *I*'s LFT of 31.

The two schedule diagrams of Figures 10.9(a) and (b) illustrate two guidelines for deciding upon the vertical placement of the line segments. First, the line segments representing the critical activities are always placed on the same vertical level, thereby displaying the critical path as a connected sequence of line segments. This placement emphasizes that, in any schedule, each critical activity must start immediately after the finish of the preceding activity on the critical path. A second guideline is that the line segment representing a particular noncritical activity should be placed at a vertical level that keeps it as near as possible to the line segment representing the activity's predecessors and successors.

Residing at opposite ends of the spectrum of schedules, the ES schedule and the LS schedule are easy to identify. However, there are many other feasible schedules for completing the project by its deadline. Because a critical activity's EST equals its LST, there is no flexibility with respect to the starting times of the critical activities. However, there is flexibility with respect to the starting times of the noncritical activities. Provided no noncritical activity starts until all its predecessors have finished, an activity can start at any time between its EST and LST. For the DG project, Figure 10.9(c) is a schedule diagram for one of the many *hybrid schedules*. In this schedule, the critical activities *B*, *F*, *K*, and *M* start (as they must) at the same times as in the ES schedule and the LS schedule. How-

---

[11] For the moment, ignore the numbers appearing in brackets next to the activities' letter codes; we will explain and use these numbers later.

ever, the noncritical activities *A*, *D*, and *G* start at their ESTs, the noncritical activities *E*, *H*, *J*, and *L* start at their LSTs, and the noncritical activities *C*, *I*, and *N* start after their ESTs but before their LSTs. (You should verify the feasibility of this schedule by checking that no activity starts until all its predecessors have finished.)

Figure 10.9 Three alternative schedule diagrams

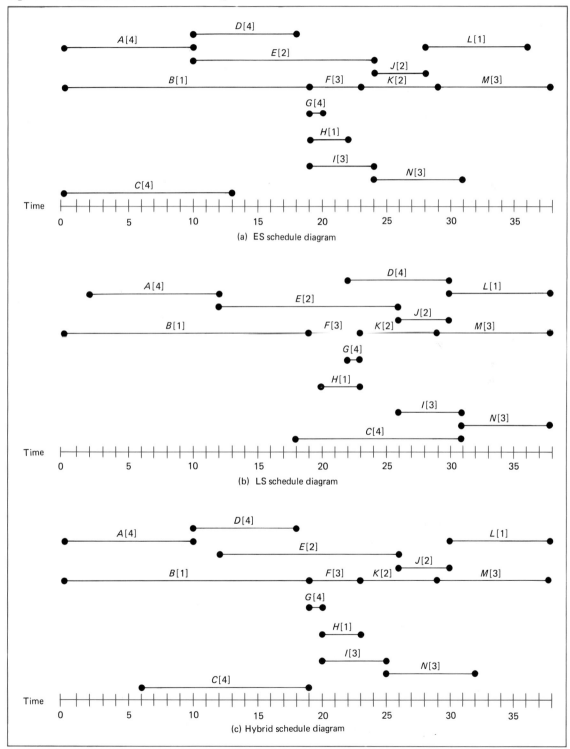

Observe that it is possible to obtain the hybrid schedule diagram of Figure 10.9(c) either by starting with the ES schedule diagram and sliding line segments *C*, *E*, *H*, *I*, *J*, *L*, and *N* to the right by 6, 12, 1, 1, 2, 2, and 1 days, respectively, or by starting with the LS schedule diagram and sliding line segments *A*, *C*, *D*, *G*, *I*, and *N* to the left by 2, 12, 12, 3, 6, and 6 days, respectively. Thus, by starting with the ES schedule diagram and sliding line segments to the right or by starting with the LS schedule diagram and sliding line segments to the left, the project manager can identify many other hybrid schedules. Of course, in sliding a line segment representing a particular activity, the project manager must ensure that it lies somewhere between the activity's EST and its LFT, and that the entire line segment always lies to the right of the end of every line segment representing a predecessor of the activity and to the left of the beginning of every line segment representing a successor of the activity. Theoretically, the project manager could identify every feasible schedule using this procedure. However, in practice, it is impossible to do so in a reasonable amount of time, even with the aid of a computer. Consequently, the project manager must usually be content with generating a limited number of hybrid schedules. To facilitate the use of this sliding procedure, magnetic schedule diagrams are commercially available. Alternatively, the project manager may construct a crude version of a magnetic schedule diagram with strips of paper and tape.

How, then, does the project manager choose among the many feasible schedules? She bases the choice on a comparison of the resource requirements of the alternative schedules.

To illustrate, let us (unrealistically) assume that, in the DG project, the same type of skilled laborers perform all activities. More specifically, we will assume that Table 10.5 displays the size of the daily workforce of these skilled laborers required to perform each activity.[12] For example, Table 10.5 indicates that activity *A* requires a workforce of 4 laborers during every day of its 10-day duration.

Now reconsider the three schedule diagrams in Figure 10.9. Earlier, we ignored the numbers appearing in brackets next to the line segment's letter codes. Observe, now, that these bracketed numbers are the activities' daily workforce requirements, as displayed in Table 10.5. Given a schedule diagram that displays each activity's daily workforce requirement, the project manager can readily compute the entire project's total workforce requirements for each day of the project's duration. For example, to determine the requirements on the 21st day of the project's duration under the ES schedule, Jean examines the portion of Figure 10.9(a) between time 20 and time 21 and observes that the only activities in progress will be *E*, *F*, *H*, and *I*, having respective daily workforce requirements of 2, 3, 1, and 3 laborers. Consequently, under the ES schedule, the entire project's workforce requirement on the 21st day will be $2 + 3 + 1 + 3 = 9$ laborers. With the aid of the schedule diagram, the project manager can perform similar computations to obtain the resource requirement for every day of the project. Such computations are best summarized by the construction of a *resource loading diagram,* a graph showing the entire project's resource requirements during each day of the project's

---

[12] For illustrative purposes, we have assumed that an activity's daily requirement for labor remains constant during the activity's duration.

TABLE 10.5 Daily Workforce Requirements for the Designer Gene Project

Activity	A	B	C	D	E	F	G	H	I	J	K	L	M	N
Size of Daily Workforce (laborers)	4	1	4	4	2	3	4	1	3	2	2	1	3	3

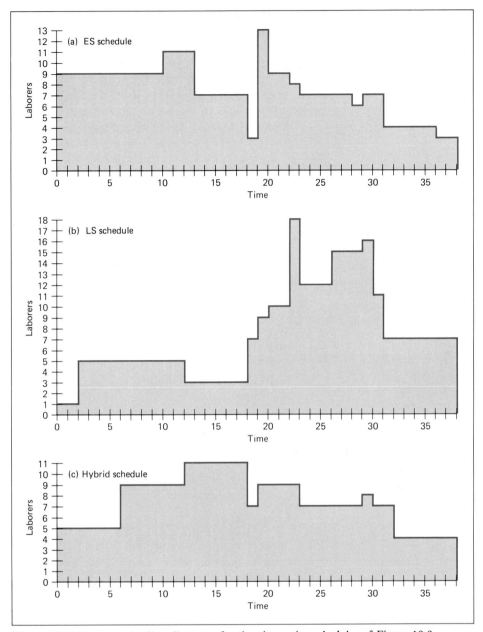

Figure 10.10 Resource loading diagrams for the alternative schedules of Figure 10.9

duration under a particular schedule. Figure 10.10 displays the resource loading diagrams for the three schedule diagrams of Figure 10.9. (Using the schedule diagrams of Figure 10.9, you should verify the correctness of Figure 10.10.)

For simplicity, we have assumed that the DG project requires only one type of resource. Consequently, for each alternative schedule diagram, Jean has to construct only one resource loading diagram. Of course, since most projects require many different resources (e.g., several types of labor, equipment, and raw materials), the project manager will usually have to construct several resource loading diagrams for each alternative schedule diagram, one for each different type of resource.

Resource loading diagrams are often used to display the project's cash requirements. For example, suppose the data of Table 10.5 do not represent each activity's daily workforce requirement but instead represent each activity's daily cash requirements (for such things as payments to subcontractors, purchase of raw materials, and equipment rental). In this case, the resource loading diagrams of Figure 10.10 would display how the entire project's total cash requirements vary over time for each of the three alternative schedules. These graphs would be useful to the project manager, who must ensure that sufficient funds are available to the project in time to satisfy the cash requirements.

Resource loading diagrams provide valuable information to the project manager. By highlighting the resource implications of each alternative schedule, they provide the basis for rationally selecting from among the alternative schedules. Furthermore, after the selection of the schedule, the resource loading diagram provides valuable information to the person responsible for ensuring that sufficient resources are available when needed. For example, given the choice among the three resource loading diagrams of Figure 10.10, Jean should choose the one corresponding to the hybrid schedule, because it has the following appealing characteristics:

- **Low peak requirements.** The peak workforce requirement for the hybrid schedule is 11 laborers. This contrasts with peak requirements of 13 laborers for the ES schedule and 18 laborers for the LS schedule. Knowledge of a schedule's peak resource requirement is important, since an otherwise feasible schedule may be infeasible if its peak requirement exceeds the maximum amount of the resource available on a daily basis.

- **Relatively level requirements.** In contrast to the "high peaks" and "deep valleys" in the resource loading diagrams of the ES schedule and the LS schedule, the resource loading diagram is relatively "level". In other words, in contrast to the extreme variation in the resource requirements over time for both the ES schedule and the LS schedule, the resource usage over time for the hybrid schedule is relatively stable. A relatively stable usage of resources over time is, in most cases, less costly and more efficient than a sharply varying resource usage over time.

To summarize:

In deciding upon an acceptable schedule, the project manager usually has two goals for the schedule's resource loading diagram:

1. Keeping the peak requirement as low as possible

2. *Resource leveling*—that is, keeping the variations as "level" (stable) as possible.

When faced with a moderate-size project involving only one or two important resources, the project manager can usually find an acceptable schedule manually. To do so, she should first construct the schedule diagrams and the resource loading diagrams for the easily identified ES schedule and LS schedule. If neither of these schedules proves acceptable, she can repeatedly reschedule noncritical activities by sliding them to the left or right on a schedule diagram until she obtains a hybrid schedule that results in an acceptable resource loading diagram. In searching for an acceptable hybrid schedule, the project manager may simply use a trial-and-error method, guided somewhat by intuition and common sense. Alternatively, if the project is sufficiently complex, she may employ one of several formal methods to guide the search for an acceptable schedule. The nature of these more formal methods is beyond the scope of this text.

When faced with a large and complex project involving multiple types of resources, the project manager can best conduct the search for an acceptable schedule by employing one of the wide variety of commercially available computer software packages for PERT/CPM. When the project has multiple resource types, even a computer software package may have difficulty finding an acceptable schedule. A particular schedule may result in acceptable resource loading diagrams for some of the resources but unacceptable ones for the other resources. Finding a single schedule that simultaneously leads to acceptable resource loading diagrams for all resource types is at best difficult and in some cases impossible.

Our brief discussion has provided much insight into the problem of selecting a schedule for a project's activities. Unfortunately, space limitations preclude a more detailed discussion of this important topic.[13]

10.4 PHASE III: MONITORING AND REPLANNING

Upon the conclusion of Phase II, the project manager has computed the project's shortest possible duration, has identified the critical path, has computed the Total and Unshared Slacks of the noncritical activities, and has scheduled the starting and finishing times for each activity. In short, PERT/CPM has provided the project manager with a plan for how the project *should* progress.

Of course, a project rarely progresses exactly as planned. Consequently, PERT/CPM does not end with Phase II's planning. Instead, once the project begins, PERT/CPM continues with Phase III, during which the plan undergoes periodic revision as the project progresses and new information becomes available. Phase III consists of two steps: monitoring the project's activities and periodically replanning the remaining portion of the project.

Step 9: Monitoring of the Project's Activities

As the project progresses, the project manager must closely monitor the project's activities, comparing the planned progress to the actual progress. Such monitoring will enable the project manager to quickly recognize and react to unpredictable events that may significantly alter the estimated durations of one or more activities. Examples of events that would lengthen the estimated durations of some activities in the DG project are bad weather, a labor strike, an unanticipated resource shortage, and an unforeseen complication in the structural modifications. Events opposite in nature would shorten some activity durations.

Step 10: Replanning of the Remaining Portion of the Project

When an unforeseen event occurs that may significantly alter the estimated durations of one or more activities, the project manager should begin the process of determining the precise effects of the event. First, considering all available information, the project manager should revise the estimate of every activity duration. At the time of revision, there is no uncertainty about the durations of activities that have already finished, and recently acquired information should lead to more accurate estimates of the durations of activities in progress or not yet started. Second, using the actual durations of activities already finished and the revised estimated

---

[13] If you are ever a project manager, you may read more about this topic by consulting pages 103–132 of Wiest and Levy.

durations of the activities not yet finished, the project manager should repeat Phase II's planning and scheduling; that is, she should determine a revised plan and schedule by recomputing the project's shortest possible duration, the critical activities, and the slacks of the noncritical activities and then rescheduling the starting and finishing times of every activity not yet finished.

At this point, the project manager has two options:

1. If the revised estimate of the project's shortest possible duration is acceptable, the project manager will usually choose to implement the revised plan during the remainder of the project.

2. If the revised estimate of the project's shortest possible duration is unacceptable, the project manager may choose to counteract the effects of the event by repeatedly allocating additional resources to the activities on the revised critical path until the sum of their durations, and therefore the project's duration, decreases to an acceptable level. Such additional resources may be previously uncommitted resources or resources transferred from noncritical activities. Section 11.3 discusses the concepts and methodologies involved in such a process.

To illustrate, suppose that after the DG project has begun, Jean receives information that indicates that she must revise the durations of activities E, K, L, and M as follows:

Activity	Original Duration	Revised Duration
E	14	12
K	6	5
L	8	13
M	9	6

You should verify that such revisions change the critical activities from B, F, K, and M to B, F, J, and L and the length of the critical path from 38 to 40 days. Jean now has two alternatives;:

1. She may accept the fact that the project will now finish two days later than originally planned and attempt to determine an acceptable schedule for those activities not yet finished.

2. She may attempt to reduce the durations of one or more critical activities, thereby reducing the project's duration below the revised 40-day estimate.

Regardless of the alternative Jean chooses, the monitoring and replanning of Phase III permits her to quickly react to surprises that might otherwise have an unfavorable impact.

This concludes our discussion of the basic PERT/CPM model. In the next two sections we will discuss extensions to the basic model that are necessary when it is inappropriate to specify an activity's duration by a single number. Before proceeding, you should return to Figure 10.1 and review its summary of the three phases and ten steps of PERT/CPM.

10.5 COMPUTER IMPLEMENTATION OF PERT/CPM

A wide variety of PERT/CPM software packages are commercially available for both mainframe and personal computers. These software packages are capable of performing not only the fundamental PERT/CPM analysis we have discussed in this chapter but also more sophisticated refinements and extensions beyond the scope of this text. Briefly, some features commonly available with today's software packages include:

- The ability to handle projects with thousands of activities
- The ability to consider resource requirements for dozens of different types of resources
- The ability to generate automatically reports and graphs (such as schedule diagrams and resource loading diagrams).
- The ability to automatically detect cost overruns by maintaining a cost accounting system.

Although computer software is necessary when the project is large and complex, it is not needed when the project is small, say no more than 20 activities. In such a case, the project manager can manually perform the analysis required by PERT/CPM.

10.6 CONCLUDING REMARKS

We have now completed our introduction to project management. If you do not intend to continue to the advanced topics in the next chapter, you should at least read the concluding remarks in Section 11.5.

10.7 CHAPTER CHECKLIST AND GLOSSARY

Quickly review this chapter by rereading the material highlighted by a vertical rule in the left margin and by reexamining Figure 10.1. You should then be familiar with the concepts, techniques, and terminology in the Checklist and Glossary that follow. If you need "help" with a particular item, consult the section or sections indicated for a more detailed discussion.

Checklist of Concepts and Techniques

- ☐ The historical distinction between PERT and CPM. [10.1]
- ☐ The diverse applications of PERT/CPM. [10.1]
- ☐ Phase I: Project Formulation. [10.2]
- ☐ Phase II: Planning and Scheduling. [10.3]
- ☐ Phase III: Monitoring and Replanning. [10.4]
- ☐ Computer implementations of PERT/CPM. [10.5]

Glossary

PERT. An acronym for Program Evaluation and Review Technique, a method developed in the late 1950s for managing projects with activities whose durations depend on random events over which there is little or no control. [10.1]

CPM. An acronym for the Critical Path Method, a method developed in the late

1950s for managing projects with activities whose durations are controllable by varying the resources allocated to them. [10.1]

PERT/CPM. Our terminology for the basic method of project management discussed in this chapter. [10.1]

Project decomposition. Listing the individual activities that comprise the project. [10.2]

Predecessors. The predecessors of activity X are those activities that must finish before X can begin. [10.2]

Redundant precedence relationship. The unnecessary inclusion of an activity on another activity's list of predecessors. [10.2]

Cyclic precedence relationship. An incorrect specification of the activities' lists of predecessors that implies that an activity is a predecessor of itself. [10.2]

Successors. The successors of activity X are those activities for which X is a predecessor. [10.2]

Project network. A pictorial representation of a project. [10.2]

Nodes. The rectangles in a project network. [10.2]

Arcs. The lines interconnecting the nodes of a project network. [10.2]

Activity-On-Node (AON). A method for depicting a project as a network in which the nodes represent activities and the arcs represent the precedence relationships. [10.2]

Activity-On-Arc (AOA). A method for depicting a project as a network in which the arcs represent the activities as well as the precedence relationships. [10.2]

Path. A sequence of nodes in the project network interconnected by arcs that lead from the *START* node to the *FINISH* node. [10.3]

Path length. The sum of the durations of the activities on the path. [10.3]

Critical path. A path with the longest length, a length equal to the project's minimum duration. [10.3]

Critical activity. An activity on the critical path. [10.3]

Noncritical activity. An activity not on the critical path. [10.3]

Earliest Starting Time (EST). The earliest possible time at which an activity can start. [10.3]

Earliest Finishing Time (EFT). The earliest possible time at which an activity can finish. [10.3]

Latest Starting Time (LST). The latest possible time at which an activity can start without causing the project to finish after its deadline. [10.3]

Latest Finishing Time (LFT). The latest possible time at which an activity can finish without causing the project to finish after its deadline. [10.3]

Alphabetical ordering of activities. Assigning letter codes to activities in such a way that the letter code of every predecessor of an activity appears earlier in the alphabet than the letter code of the activity itself. [10.3]

Total slack of an activity. The maximum amount that the activity's duration can increase without increasing the project's duration. [10.3]

Unshared slack of an activity. The maximum amount that the activity's duration can increase without decreasing the LFT of any predecessor and without increasing the EST of any successor. [10.3]

ES schedule. The schedule that calls for every activity to start at its EST and finish at its EFT. [10.4]

LS schedule. The schedule that calls for every activity to start at its LST and finish at its LFT. [10.4]

Hybrid schedule. A feasible schedule that is neither the ES schedule nor the LS schedule. [10.4]

Schedule diagram. A graphical representation of a schedule for the project's activities that uses line segments to represent the time interval during which an activity takes place. [10.4]

Resource loading diagram. A graph showing how the usage of a resource varies over time. [10.4]

Peak resource usage. The highest usage in a resource loading diagram. [10.4]

Resource leveling. The attempt to identify a schedule for the project's activities that has a relatively flat resource loading diagram for every resource. [10.4]

EXERCISES

The first exercise illustrates the difficulty in specifying the precedence relationships that exist among a project's activities.

10.1.[14] Presentation of a stage play involves a number of activities which precede the opening night "curtain-up" call. Listed below in a random fashion is a collection of activities that must be completed before a play's opening night. (Other activities could have been included; however, assume the list is complete.)

Activity Code	Description of Activity
A	Design of scenery
B	Tryouts for actors
C	Selection of stage manager
D	Publicity (posters, mail advertisements)
E	Selection of director
F	Initial rehearsals
G	Arrangements for hall
H	Selection of play
I	Selection of business manager
J	Final dress rehearsal
K	Constructing and painting scenery
L	Sale of tickets
M	Opening night performance
N	Publicity (newspaper story)
O	Advanced rehearsals (with props and scenery)
P	Making or renting costumes
Q	Obtaining props (set furnishings, items used by actors, etc.)
R	Erection of scenery

(a) Add a third column to the above table that specifies your opinion of the predecessors of each activity. (Since differences of opinion will exist, compare your precedence relationships with those of others.)
(b) Draw the project network corresponding to your precedence relationships. (After seeing this network, you may want to change one or more precedence relationships.)

Exercises 10.2–10.7 test your understanding of the various steps in a PERT/CPM analysis of a project. (Note: In each project, we assume for simplicity that all activities involve the same type of labor.)

10.2. Consider the project described below:

Activity Code	Estimated Duration (days)	Predecessors	Daily Manpower Requirement (persons)
A	3	–	4
B	1	–	8
C	5	–	2
D	1	A	6
E	6	C	1
F	1	E	7
G	2	B,D,F	5
H	8	G	3

(a) Draw the project network.
(b) Compute each activity's EST, EFT, LST, and LFT.
(c) Compute each activity's total slack and unshared slack.
(d) Identify the project's critical path(s).
(e) Draw the ES schedule diagram and the LS schedule diagram.

---

[14] Reprinted with permission from Wiest and Levy (*Ibid*).

(f) Draw the resource loading diagrams for the ES schedule and the LS schedule. Identify the peak requirement for each schedule.

(g) Using trial and error, identify (if possible) a hybrid schedule whose resource loading diagram has a lower peak requirement than do the resource loading diagrams of both the ES schedule and the LS schedule.

*10.3. Redo Exercise 10.2, this time using the project described below:

Activity Code	Estimated Duration (days)	Predecessors	Daily Manpower Requirement (persons)
A	2	–	7
B	7	–	1
C	3	A	3
D	1	B	6
E	2	B	2
F	5	C,D	5
G	6	E	4

10.4. Redo Exercise 10.2, this time using the project described below:

Activity Code	Estimated Duration (days)	Predecessors	Daily Manpower Requirement (persons)
A	4	–	10
B	6	A	9
C	8	–	14
D	9	A	13
E	5	B,C	8
F	4	B,C	12
G	7	D,E	11
H	3	F	7

10.5. Redo Exercise 10.2, this time using the project described below and, in part (g), identifying a hybrid schedule whose resource loading diagram is perfectly level:

Activity Code	Estimated Duration (days)	Predecessors	Daily Manpower Requirement (persons)
A	4	–	9
B	2	–	3
C	2	–	6
D	2	–	4
E	3	B	8
F	2	C	7
G	3	D,F	2
H	4	E,G	1

10.6. Redo Exercise 10.2, this time using the project described below:

Activity Code	Estimated Duration (days)	Predecessors	Daily Manpower Requirement (persons)
A	2	–	9
B	9	–	1
C	5	–	4
D	3	C	7
E	7	C	8
F	8	B	3
G	1	D,E	6
H	4	A,F	10
I	3	F,G	5
J	2	G	2

10.7. Redo Exercise 10.2, this time using the project described below:

Activity Code	Estimated Duration (days)	Predecessors	Daily Manpower Requirement (persons)
A	6	–	11
B	1	A	3
C	4	A	8
D	1	A	9
E	9	C	1
F	2	C	13
G	4	C,D	7
H	3	D	2
I	7	B,E	10
J	13	F,G,H	4
K	2	J	6
L	5	J	12
M	2	K,L	5

The next exercise illustrates the effect of not using the project's shortest possible duration (i.e., FINISH's EFT) as the project's deadline.

10.8. In Section 10.3, we began the process of computing the LFT and LST for each activity in the Designer Genes project by assuming that the project's deadline was its shortest possible duration; that is, we set FINISH's LFT equal to its EFT of 38 days. Now assume that the project's deadline is 40 days.

(a) Recompute each activity's LFT, LST, total slack, and unshared slack.

(b) Compare the revised values in part (a) to those obtained in Section 11.3, in which the project's deadline was 38 days.

(c) Explain how to identify the critical path by using part (a)'s revised values for total slacks.

502

(d) Without doing the actual computations, predict what would happen in part (a) if you were to use a project deadline of 35 days.

The next exercise tests your understanding of the distinction between total slack and unshared slack.

10.9. Reconsider the project in Exercise 10.6. Using the total slacks and unshared slacks you computed in Exercise 11.6, answer the questions below in terms of the effects on (1) the project's shortest possible duration, (2) each activity's EST, EFT, LST, LFT, total slack and unshared slack, and (3) determining which activities are the critical activities.

(a) What is the effect of an increase in activity D's duration from 3 to 14 days?
(b) What is the effect of an increase in activity D's duration from 3 to 12 days?
(c) What is the effect of an increase in activity D's duration from 3 to 9 days?
(d) What is the effect of an increase in activity D's duration from 3 to 7 days?
(e) What is the effect of an increase in activity E's duration from 7 to 13 days?
(f) What is the effect of an increase in activity E's duration from 7 to 10 days?
(g) What is the effect of an increase in activity A's duration from 2 to 15 days?
(h) What is the effect of an increase in activity A's duration from 2 to 14 days?

The next exercise illustrates the concept of a redundant precedence relationship.

*10.10. Consider a project with the following list of activities and precedence relationships:

Activity Code	Predecessors
A	
B	–
C	A
D	A,C
E	A,B
F	B
G	B
H	B,D,E,F
I	F,G,H
J	F,G,H

After closely examining this list, identify four redundant precedence relationships.

The next exercise illustrates a formal procedure for obtaining an alphabetical ordering of a project's activities.

10.11. As defined in Section 10.3, an *alphabetical ordering* of a project's activities is an assignment of letter codes to the activities such that the letter code of every predecessor of an activity appears earlier in the alphabet than the letter code of the activity itself. To alphabetically order the activities, we can use a formal procedure. We begin the procedure by arbitrarily assigning *lower-case* letter codes to the activities. We then repeat the following three-step procedure until every activity has been reassigned an *upper-case* letter code:

1. Identify an activity that has no predecessors. (If there are several, select one arbitrarily.)
2. Assign to the selected activity the next upper-case letter code in the alphabet. (If this is the first time this step has been performed, the "next" letter is A.)
3. Delete the selected activity from every activity's predecessor list on which the selected activity now appears.

After repeating these steps as many times as necessary, the activities will be alphabetically ordered. Verify the above procedure by applying it to the following list of activities and precedence relationships:

Activity Code	Predecessors
a	b,c,j
b	i
c	g
d	a,f
e	–
f	i
g	e
h	a,f
i	–
j	e

The next exercise illustrates a formal procedure for determining if a set of precedence relationships contains a subset of cyclic precedence relationships.

10.12. Besides using the procedure in Exercise 10.11 to alphabetically order the activities, we can use it to determine if there are cyclic precedence relationships. In particular, cyclic precedence relationships exist if, after one or more repetitions of steps 1–3, we find it impossible to perform step 1 because every activity has at least one predecessor. To verify that we can use this procedure to identify the existence of cyclic precedence relationships, redo Exercise 10.11, except this time add activity d to activity b's predecessor list.

11

PROJECT MANAGEMENT: ADVANCED TOPICS

11.1 INTRODUCTION

Since this chapter is a continuation of the previous one, we will limit our introduction to the following preview of its contents:

- In Section 11.2 we will discuss a variation of the basic PERT/CPM model in which the project has activities with *stochastic* (i.e., random) durations.
- In Section 11.3 we will discuss a variation of the basic PERT/CPM model called the *time-cost trade-off model*. In this model, each activity's duration is not fixed at a single value but instead is a controllable function of the dollar value of the resources allocated to the activity.
- In Section 11.4 we will discuss two applications of linear programming to project management.

11.2 AN APPROACH TO PROJECTS WITH STOCHASTIC ACTIVITY DURATIONS

Until now, we have assumed that the project consists solely of activities with deterministic durations—that is, durations known with certainty. Hereafter, we refer to such a project as a *deterministic project*. When at least one of the project's activities has a *stochastic duration* (that is, a random duration), we call the project a *stochastic project.* In this section we discuss quantitative aids to the management of stochastic projects. One such aid is the original version of PERT, as discussed briefly in Section 10.1.

The basic PERT/CPM model discussed in Chapter 10 assumes that the project is a deterministic project and, hence, requires a single-number estimate of each activity's duration. For many projects this is an unreasonable assumption. For example, suppose that the project is the R&D effort associated with a new product and that one particular activity involves the development of a new and complex technology. For this activity, there would be much uncertainty about its duration. Those responsible for the activity might state that, if all goes well, the technology might be available in six months; on the other hand, if all goes poorly, the technology might not be available for 18 months. When this occurs, using a single number for the activity's duration can yield misleading results. As another example, consider a large construction project with a particular activity (such as exterior painting or concrete work) that requires a period of dry weather. Any uncertainty about the weather translates into uncertainty about the activity's duration.

To capture its stochastic nature, we must estimate the activity's duration not by a single number but rather by a probability distribution. Thus, for each activity, we must specify a set of possible values that its duration may assume and associate with each value a probability. Of course, the sum of the probabilities associated with the possible values of the duration must sum to 1. For example, we might describe a stochastic activity duration by the following probability distribution:

The duration will be 4 months with probability $\frac{1}{6}$.
The duration will be 7 months with probability $\frac{3}{6}$.
The duration will be 9 months with probability $\frac{2}{6}$.

Theoretically, there is no limit to the number of possible values the duration may assume, but in practice it is recommended that the number be limited to at most three. There are two reasons for this recommendation:

1. Those responsible for the activity will usually find it relatively easy to associate probabilities with a pessimistic estimate, an optimistic estimate, and a most-likely estimate of the activity's duration. However, those same individuals may balk if asked to agree upon ten possible values for the activity's duration and to associate a probability with each.

2. The computational effort required to analyze the project increases rapidly as the number of possible values assumable by each activity duration increases. This fact will be more apparent by the end of this section.

As discussed earlier, PERT was introduced in the late 1950's to aid the managing of the U.S. Navy's Polaris missile project, a project consisting of many activities with stochastic durations. The approach proposed then is still widely used today and will hereafter be referred to as *the original version of PERT.* It has long been recognized that the original version of PERT, despite its widespread use, has many significant shortcomings. In fact, as we will see, a project manager who applies the original version of PERT in spite of or in ignorance of its shortcomings is likely to obtain misleading results. Today, many authors (including this one) believe that the original version of PERT has outlived its usefulness. In light of this, the primary purpose of the remainder of this section will *not* be to provide a detailed description of the original version of PERT. Instead, we will use a small example to illustrate the shortcomings of the original version of PERT and to show why the technique of computer simulation is a preferred alternative approach.[1]

Consider the stochastic project represented by the network in Figure 11.1. The table within each node specifies the probability distribution of the duration of the activity represented by the node. In particular, the column headed "d" contains the possible durations and the column headed "Pr$\{d\}$" contains the associated probabilities. For example, the duration of activity D will be 2 days with probability $\frac{1}{6}$, 5 days with probability $\frac{4}{6}$, and 14 days with probability $\frac{1}{6}$. To simplify our discussion, we will assume that the activity durations are probabilistically independent of each other.

The essence of the approach taken by the original version of PERT is to convert the stochastic project into a deterministic project. It removes the uncertainty associated with each activity duration by replacing its probability distribution with a single number—namely, the mean (expected value) of the duration. Then, it employs the basic PERT/CPM methodology described in Section 10.3 to determine the length of the critical path in the converted deterministic project, and it uses this length as an estimate of the duration of the initial stochastic project.

For example, the application of the original version of PERT to the project network of Figure 11.1 proceeds as follows:

1. We first compute the mean duration of each activity. The following list summarizes these computations:

Activity	Mean Duration			
A	$(10 \times \frac{2}{6})$ + $(15 \times \frac{2}{6})$ + $(20 \times \frac{2}{6})$	= 15
B	$(6 \times \frac{4}{6})$ + $(18 \times \frac{2}{6})$	= 10
C	$(1 \times \frac{3}{6})$ + $(13 \times \frac{3}{6})$	= 7
D	$(2 \times \frac{1}{6})$ + $(5 \times \frac{4}{6})$ + $(14 \times \frac{1}{6})$	= 6

2. Because of the network's simplicity, we can identify the critical path by simply enumerating all paths, computing the length of each, and identifying the longest.[2] The four paths in the project network and their respective lengths are:

Path	Length
$START \rightarrow A \rightarrow C \rightarrow FINISH$	$15 + 7 = 22$
$START \rightarrow A \rightarrow D \rightarrow FINISH$	$15 + 6 = 21$
$START \rightarrow B \rightarrow C \rightarrow FINISH$	$10 + 7 = 17$
$START \rightarrow B \rightarrow D \rightarrow FINISH$	$10 + 6 = 16$

For simplicity, we hereafter refer to these four paths as AC, AD, BC, and BD, respectively. With its length of 22 days, AC is the critical path.

3. We use the 22-day length of the deterministic project's critical path as an estimate of the duration of the initial stochastic project. Furthermore, we regard A and C as the project's critical activities.[3]

---

[1] For a detailed description olf the original version of PERT, consult pages 41–52 of Wiest and Levy. For more about the shortcomings of the original version of PERT, consult R. J. Schonberger, "Why Projects are 'Always' Late: A Rationale Based on Manual Simulation of a PERT/CPM Network," *Interfaces*, **11**, 5 (October 1981), 66–70.

[2] Of course, if the project network were large and complex, we would have to employ the more formal PERT/CPM methodologies discussed in Section 10.3.

[3] Although we will not do so here, the original version of PERT then goes on to calculate a *confidence interval* for the project's duration.

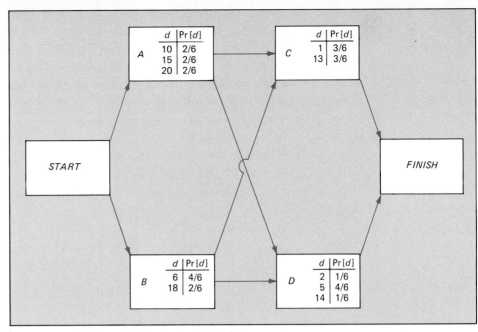

Figure 11.1 An example of a stochastic project

To help us illustrate the shortcomings inherent in the original version of PERT, Table 11.1 provides a summary of all possible *realizations* of the stochastic project network in Figure 11.1. By the term "realization" we mean a particular assignment of values to each of the activity durations. Because the durations of activities *A*, *B*, *C*, and *D* may assume 3, 2, 2, and 3 possible values, respectively, Table 11.1 lists $3 \times 2 \times 2 \times 3 = 36$ possible realizations. When the project is complete, we will observe that exactly one of these realizations has occurred. However, in planning the project, we do not know in advance which one it will be. For example, the first row of the table summarizes the realization of the project in which the durations of *A*, *B*, *C*, and *D* are 10, 6, 1, and 2, respectively. Because of the assumption of probabilistic independence among the activity durations, the probability of this realizations occurring is the product of the probabilities associated with values of the durations of *A*, *B*, *C*, and *D*—namely,

$$\frac{2}{6} \times \frac{4}{6} \times \frac{3}{6} \times \frac{1}{6} = \frac{24}{1296}.$$

This probability appears in the table's sixth column. The seventh through tenth columns indicate that Realization 1 results in a path length of 11 for path *AC*, 12 for path *AD*, 7 for path *BC*, and 8 for path *BD*. As indicated by the circle in the eighth column, the critical path for this realization is *AD* with a length of 12 days. Before reading any further, you should verify other rows of Table 11.1 until you are satisfied that you understand the table's contents.

We can use Table 11.1 to construct the three additional tables:

- Table 11.2 displays the probability that each path is the critical path. For example, to compute the probability that *BC* is the critical path, we need only scan the ninth column of Table 11.1 and observe that circles appear in the rows for Realizations 10, 11, 22, and 23. Summing the probabilities of these realizations, we obtain

$$\frac{12 + 48 + 12 + 48}{1296} = \frac{120}{1296} = 0.093$$

as the probability that BC is the critical path. You should verify the remaining entries in Table 11.2.

- Table 11.3 displays the probability that each particular activity is a critical activity—that is, is a member of the critical path. For example, to compute the probability that B is a member of the critical path, we need only scan Table 11.1's ninth and tenth columns (the only two columns corresponding to

TABLE 11.1 Summary of 36 Possible Realizations
of the Example Stochastic Project

Realization	Activity Durations				Probability of Occurrence	Path Lengths *			
	A	B	C	D		AC	AD	BC	BD
1	10	6	1	2	$\frac{2}{6} \times \frac{4}{6} \times \frac{3}{6} \times \frac{1}{6} = \frac{24}{1296}$	11	⑫	7	8
2	10	6	1	5	$\frac{2}{6} \times \frac{4}{6} \times \frac{3}{6} \times \frac{4}{6} = \frac{96}{1296}$	11	⑮	7	11
3	10	6	1	14	$\frac{2}{6} \times \frac{4}{6} \times \frac{3}{6} \times \frac{1}{6} = \frac{24}{1296}$	11	㉔	7	20
4	10	6	13	2	$\frac{2}{6} \times \frac{4}{6} \times \frac{3}{6} \times \frac{1}{6} = \frac{24}{1296}$	㉓	12	19	8
5	10	6	13	5	$\frac{2}{6} \times \frac{4}{6} \times \frac{3}{6} \times \frac{4}{6} = \frac{96}{1296}$	㉓	15	19	11
6	10	6	13	14	$\frac{2}{6} \times \frac{4}{6} \times \frac{3}{6} \times \frac{1}{6} = \frac{24}{1296}$	23	㉔	19	20
7	10	18	1	2	$\frac{2}{6} \times \frac{2}{6} \times \frac{3}{6} \times \frac{1}{6} = \frac{12}{1296}$	11	12	19	⑳
8	10	18	1	5	$\frac{2}{6} \times \frac{2}{6} \times \frac{3}{6} \times \frac{4}{6} = \frac{48}{1296}$	11	15	19	㉓
9	10	18	1	14	$\frac{2}{6} \times \frac{2}{6} \times \frac{3}{6} \times \frac{1}{6} = \frac{12}{1296}$	11	24	19	㉜
10	10	18	13	2	$\frac{2}{6} \times \frac{2}{6} \times \frac{3}{6} \times \frac{1}{6} = \frac{12}{1296}$	23	12	㉛	20
11	10	18	13	5	$\frac{2}{6} \times \frac{2}{6} \times \frac{3}{6} \times \frac{4}{6} = \frac{48}{1296}$	23	15	㉛	23
12	10	18	13	14	$\frac{2}{6} \times \frac{2}{6} \times \frac{3}{6} \times \frac{1}{6} = \frac{12}{1296}$	23	24	31	32
13	15	6	1	2	$\frac{2}{6} \times \frac{4}{6} \times \frac{3}{6} \times \frac{1}{6} = \frac{24}{1296}$	16	⑰	7	8
14	15	6	1	5	$\frac{2}{6} \times \frac{4}{6} \times \frac{3}{6} \times \frac{4}{6} = \frac{96}{1296}$	16	⑳	7	11
15	15	6	1	14	$\frac{2}{6} \times \frac{4}{6} \times \frac{3}{6} \times \frac{1}{6} = \frac{24}{1296}$	16	㉙	7	20
16	15	6	13	2	$\frac{2}{6} \times \frac{4}{6} \times \frac{3}{6} \times \frac{1}{6} = \frac{24}{1296}$	㉘	17	19	8
17	15	6	13	5	$\frac{2}{6} \times \frac{4}{6} \times \frac{3}{6} \times \frac{4}{6} = \frac{96}{1296}$	㉘	20	19	11
18	15	6	13	14	$\frac{2}{6} \times \frac{4}{6} \times \frac{3}{6} \times \frac{1}{6} = \frac{24}{1296}$	28	㉙	19	20
19	15	18	1	2	$\frac{2}{6} \times \frac{2}{6} \times \frac{3}{6} \times \frac{1}{6} = \frac{12}{1296}$	16	17	19	⑳
20	15	18	1	5	$\frac{2}{6} \times \frac{2}{6} \times \frac{3}{6} \times \frac{4}{6} = \frac{48}{1296}$	16	20	19	㉓
21	15	18	1	14	$\frac{2}{6} \times \frac{2}{6} \times \frac{3}{6} \times \frac{1}{6} = \frac{12}{1296}$	16	29	19	㉜
22	15	18	13	2	$\frac{2}{6} \times \frac{2}{6} \times \frac{3}{6} \times \frac{1}{6} = \frac{12}{1296}$	28	17	㉛	20
23	15	18	13	5	$\frac{2}{6} \times \frac{2}{6} \times \frac{3}{6} \times \frac{4}{6} = \frac{48}{1296}$	28	20	㉛	23
24	15	18	13	14	$\frac{2}{6} \times \frac{2}{6} \times \frac{3}{6} \times \frac{1}{6} = \frac{12}{1296}$	28	29	31	㉜
25	20	6	1	2	$\frac{2}{6} \times \frac{4}{6} \times \frac{3}{6} \times \frac{1}{6} = \frac{24}{1296}$	21	㉒	7	8
26	20	6	1	5	$\frac{2}{6} \times \frac{4}{6} \times \frac{3}{6} \times \frac{4}{6} = \frac{96}{1296}$	21	㉕	7	11
27	20	6	1	14	$\frac{2}{6} \times \frac{4}{6} \times \frac{3}{6} \times \frac{1}{6} = \frac{24}{1296}$	21	㉞	7	20
28	20	6	13	2	$\frac{2}{6} \times \frac{4}{6} \times \frac{3}{6} \times \frac{1}{6} = \frac{24}{1296}$	㉝	22	19	8
29	20	6	13	5	$\frac{2}{6} \times \frac{4}{6} \times \frac{3}{6} \times \frac{4}{6} = \frac{96}{1296}$	㉝	25	19	11
30	20	6	13	14	$\frac{2}{6} \times \frac{4}{6} \times \frac{3}{6} \times \frac{1}{6} = \frac{24}{1296}$	33	㉞	19	20
31	20	18	1	2	$\frac{2}{6} \times \frac{2}{6} \times \frac{3}{6} \times \frac{1}{6} = \frac{12}{1296}$	21	㉒	19	20
32	20	18	1	5	$\frac{2}{6} \times \frac{2}{6} \times \frac{3}{6} \times \frac{4}{6} = \frac{48}{1296}$	21	㉕	19	23
33	20	18	1	14	$\frac{2}{6} \times \frac{2}{6} \times \frac{3}{6} \times \frac{1}{6} = \frac{12}{1296}$	21	㉞	19	32
34	20	18	13	2	$\frac{2}{6} \times \frac{2}{6} \times \frac{3}{6} \times \frac{1}{6} = \frac{12}{1296}$	㉝	22	31	20
35	20	18	13	5	$\frac{2}{6} \times \frac{2}{6} \times \frac{3}{6} \times \frac{4}{6} = \frac{48}{1296}$	㉝	25	31	23
36	20	18	13	14	$\frac{2}{6} \times \frac{2}{6} \times \frac{3}{6} \times \frac{1}{6} = \frac{12}{1296}$	33	㉞	31	32

* indicates each realization's critical path.

TABLE 11.2 Probability that Each Path is the Critical Path

Path	Probability that Path is the Critical Path
AC	$\frac{420}{1296} = 0.324$
AD	$\frac{588}{1296} = 0.454$
BC	$\frac{120}{1296} = 0.093$
BD	$\frac{168}{1296} = 0.130$

TABLE 11.3 Probability that Each Activity is a Critical Activity

Activity	Probability that Activity is a Critical Activity
A	$\frac{1008}{1296} = 0.778$
B	$\frac{288}{1296} = 0.222$
C	$\frac{540}{1296} = 0.417$
D	$\frac{756}{1296} = 0.583$

paths containing B) and observe that circles appear in one of these two columns in the rows for Realizations 7 through 12 and 19 through 24; summing the probabilities of these realizations, we obtain

$$\frac{12 + 48 + 12 + 12 + 48 + 12 + 12 + 48 + 12 + 12 + 48 + 12}{1296}$$

$$= \frac{288}{1296} = 0.2222$$

as the probability that B is a member of the critical path. You should verify the remaining entries in Table 11.3.

■ Table 11.4 displays the probability distribution for the project's duration. For example, to compute the probability that the project has a duration of 20 days, we need only scan the last four columns of Table 11.1 and observe that a circle encloses the number 20 in one of these four columns in the rows for

TABLE 11.4 Probability Distribution of Project's Duration

Project Duration	Probability of Occurrence
12	$\frac{24}{1296} = 0.0185$
15	$\frac{96}{1296} = 0.0741$
17	$\frac{24}{1296} = 0.0185$
20	$\frac{120}{1296} = 0.0926$
22	$\frac{36}{1296} = 0.0278$
23	$\frac{216}{1296} = 0.1667$
24	$\frac{48}{1296} = 0.0370$
25	$\frac{144}{1296} = 0.1111$
28	$\frac{120}{1296} = 0.0926$
29	$\frac{48}{1296} = 0.0370$
31	$\frac{120}{1296} = 0.0926$
32	$\frac{48}{1296} = 0.0370$
33	$\frac{180}{1296} = 0.1389$
34	$\frac{72}{1296} = 0.0556$

Realizations 7, 14, and 19. Summing the probabilities of these realizations, we obtain

$$\frac{12 + 96 + 12}{1296} = \frac{120}{1296} = 0.0926$$

as the probability that the project's duration will be 20 days. You should verify the remaining entries in Table 11.4.

Let us now compare the information provided by the original version of PERT with the information provided by Tables 11.2–11.4. Recall that the original version of PERT estimates the stochastic project's duration as 22 days, the length of the critical path AC in the deterministic network resulting from replacing the probability distribution of each activity duration with its mean duration. Consequently, the project manager would plan on a project duration of 22 days and, when the project began, would closely monitor and control the progress of A and C, even perhaps to the extent of giving less attention to B and D. A somewhat cautious manager might even plan on a project duration in excess of 22 days to take into account the uncertainty removed from the activities' durations when converting the initial stochastic network into a deterministic one.

Now consider a project manager who had access to Tables 11.2–11.4. This project manager would have the following advantages over one who had access only to the information obtained from the original version of PERT:

- Whereas the original version of PERT identified AC as the single critical path, Table 11.2 indicates that each of the four paths has some probability of being the critical path. In fact, the path with the highest probability of being critical is AD, not AC! A table such as Table 11.2 allows the project manager to rank the paths according to their probabilities of being critical and then to closely monitor those paths whose probabilities are high relative to those of the others. In our example project, the project manager should closely monitor both path AC and path AD.

- Whereas the original version of PERT identified A and C as the critical activities, Table 11.3 shows that each of the four activities has some probability of being critical. In fact, although the original version of PERT identified C as being critical, D actually has a higher probability of being critical than does C. A table such as Table 11.3 allows the project manager to rank the activities according to their probabilities of being critical and then to closely monitor the durations of those activities whose probabilities are high relative to those of the others. In our example project, the project manager should closely monitor the durations of A, C, and D.

- Whereas the original version of PERT uses 22 days as an estimate of the project's duration, we can use Table 11.4 to compute a more reliable estimate. In particular, by summing the product of the two terms in each row of Table 11.4, we obtain

$$\left(12 \times \tfrac{24}{1296}\right) + \left(15 \times \tfrac{96}{1296}\right) + \cdots + \left(33 \times \tfrac{180}{1296}\right) + \left(34 \times \tfrac{72}{1296}\right) = \tfrac{33{,}444}{1296} = 25.81$$

as the exact value of the mean duration of the project. Thus, the original version of PERT provides an estimate of the project's duration that is

$$\frac{25.81 - 22}{25.81} \times 100\% = 14.76\%$$

below the actual value of the mean project duration! This is *not* a coincidence. It can be shown that the original version of PERT will *always* produce an *optimistic* estimate of the project's duration—that is, an estimate that is *always lower* than the true mean of the project's duration. Furthermore, the original version of PERT gives us no way of knowing how optimistic the estimate is. The estimate might be 5%, 15%, or even 50% lower than the actual value of the mean project duration. Most managers are risk-averse and, given the choice, do not prefer the optimistic estimate that the original version of PERT always provides. Instead, they prefer an estimate of project duration that is always pessimistic or one that has approximately equal likelihoods of being optimistic or pessimistic.

- Table 11.4 enables the manager not only to compute the exact value of the mean project duration but also to incorporate an acceptable level of "risk" into her estimate of the stochastic project's duration. If the actual duration exceeds the project manager's estimate, the project will be late with respect to the estimate. If the project manager is unwilling to bear any risk that the project will be late with respect to her estimate, Table 11.4 indicates that she must use an estimate of 34 days, the highest duration in the table. Now suppose that the project manager will accept up to a 35% chance that the project will be late or, equivalently, that she wants at least a 65% chance that the project will finish by her estimate. To obtain such an estimate, the project manager moves downward from the top of Table 11.4 and sums the entries in the second column until the sum exceeds 0.65. You should verify that this summation process results in an estimated project duration of 29 days, an estimate having a 67.59% chance of being met or, equivalently, a 32.41% chance of being exceeded. In a similar fashion, the project manager could set any acceptable level of risk and determine the corresponding estimate of the project's duration. Observe that if she plans on a project duration of 22 days, the estimate furnished by the original version of PERT, the summation procedure indicates that this estimate has a 76.85% chance of being exceeded!

By now this section should have instilled within you a mistrust for the original version of PERT—a mistrust that will lead you to avoid its use or at least question its results. If a project manager cannot trust the original version of PERT, what can she do when faced with a project whose activities have uncertain durations? In theory, she should construct tables similar to Tables 11.2–11.4. In practice, however, this is impossible for even moderate-sized projects. For example, if a project consists of 20 activities and each activity duration could assume any one of three possible values, there would be 3^{20} (over 3 billion) possible realizations of the project network. The computational effort required to enumerate all realizations (in a manner similar to Table 11.1) would be excessive, even for today's generation of computers.

Although, for most stochastic networks, it is impossible to compute the *exact* values of the entries for tables similar to Table 11.2–11.4, it is possible to compute *close approximations* via the technique of computer simulation. In Section 17.5, we will see how to use computer simulation to construct approximations of such tables by randomly sampling from the set of all possible realizations. While it requires more computational effort than the original version of PERT, this use of computer simulation yields more reliable information.

We may summarize this section as follows:

- The original version of PERT replaces each activity having a stochastic duration with an activity having a deterministic duration equal to the mean. This always yields an optimistic estimate (i.e., an underestimate) of the true mean of the project duration and often provides misleading indications about the critical activities.

- If you are ever a project manager, you will do well to avoid the original version of PERT and instead use the computer simulation technique described in Section 17.5.

11.3 TIME-COST TRADEOFFS

In this section we will discuss a variation of the basic PERT/CPM model called the *time-cost trade-off model*. This variation is similar to the original version of CPM, as discussed briefly in this chapter's introduction. In the time-cost trade-off model, each activity's duration is not fixed at a single value but instead is a controllable function of the dollar value of the resources allocated to the activity. Our goal will be to investigate the trade-off between time and cost. More specifically, we will construct a graph showing how the project's total cost changes as a function of the project's duration. A project manager may use such a graph to answer such questions as, "What is the total cost of a particular project duration?" or "What project duration minimizes total cost?" As we will see, the analysis used to construct the time-cost trade-off graph will also provide the project manager with insight into the proper allocation of the project's budget among the activities.

A project's total cost consists of three components: *direct costs, indirect costs,* and *penalty costs.* We will discuss these three components in turn. To illustrate their nature and simultaneously introduce the fundamental concepts of the time-cost trade-off model, we will consider a very simple project consisting of only a single activity. Thus, the entire project's duration is simply the single activity's duration.

Below is a discussion of the project's total cost and the three components that comprise it:

- **Direct costs.** Direct costs are associated with the project's individual activities. The performance of each activity requires the use or consumption of specific resources, such as labor, equipment, fuel, and raw materials. The total cost of all resources is the direct cost of the activity. Suppose that the duration of our example project's only activity is not fixed but instead may vary between 13 days and 19 days, depending upon the direct cost of the resources the project manager allocates to the activity. Figure 11.2 summarizes (both tabularly and graphically) the relationship between the activity's duration and its direct cost. Observe that as the activity's duration *decreases,* the activity's direct cost *increases at an increasing rate.* In particular, the respective increases in the activity's direct cost as the project's duration decreases one unit at a time from 19 to 13 days are $1000, $2000, $4000, $8000, $8000, and $10,000. Such a relationship between an activity's duration and its direct cost is typical and is usually the result of the interaction of many factors.[4] Because the project consists of only one activity, the graph and table of Figure 11.2 represent not only the relationship between the activity's duration and its direct cost but also the relationship between the entire

---

[4] If you are disturbed by the form of the relationship between the activity's duration and its direct cost, accept it as a fact for the moment. Relief is just a few paragraphs away! After completing this example, we will examine two of the factors primarily responsible for this relationship.

project's duration and its total direct costs. In multi-activity projects, the project's total direct costs are obtained by summing the direct costs of the individual activities.

- **Indirect costs.** Rather than being attributable to any individual activity, indirect costs (often referred to as overhead costs) are associated with the project as a whole. Examples are the salary of the project manager and other supervisory personnel, the cost of equipment rented for the duration of the

Figure 11.2 Time-cost tradeoff graphs for example project

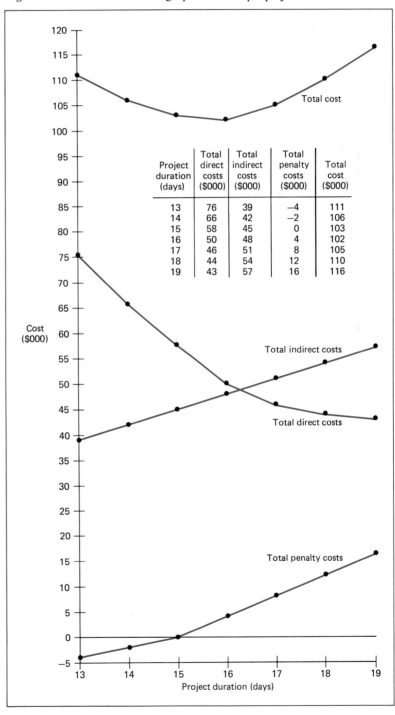

Project duration (days)	Total direct costs ($000)	Total indirect costs ($000)	Total penalty costs ($000)	Total cost ($000)
13	76	39	−4	111
14	66	42	−2	106
15	58	45	0	103
16	50	48	4	102
17	46	51	8	105
18	44	54	12	110
19	43	57	16	116

project, and the premium for property and liability insurance acquired for the duration of the project. Suppose that in our example project indirect costs accrue at the rate of $3000 per day from the project's inception to its completion. Figure 11.2 summarizes this linear relationship between the project's duration and its total indirect costs. Observe that as the project's duration *decreases,* the total indirect costs also *decrease.*

- **Penalty costs.** Penalty costs are common when the project is being performed, under contract, for a second party. In such cases the contract may contain a clause specifying a daily penalty cost (e.g., $4000 per day) paid by the contractor for each day the project's duration exceeds some fixed deadline and a daily bonus revenue (e.g., $2000 per day) paid to the contractor for each day the project's duration falls below some fixed deadline.[5] Alternatively, the contract may call for a fixed penalty cost (e.g., $15,000) paid by the contractor if the project's duration exceeds some fixed deadline by any amount whatsoever and a fixed bonus revenue (e.g., $10,000) paid to the contractor if the project's duration falls below some fixed deadline by any amount whatsoever. Hereafter, we will not use the terminology "bonus revenue". Instead, we will regard a bonus revenue as a *negative* penalty cost. Suppose that in our example project there is a daily penalty cost of $4000 for every day the project's duration exceeds 15 days and a daily penalty cost of −$2000 for every day the project's duration falls below 15 days. Figure 11.2 illustrates this relationship between the project's duration and its total penalty costs. Observe that as the project's duration *decreases,* the total penalty costs also *decrease.*

- **Total cost.** As illustrated in Figure 11.2, the three components of total cost behave differently. As the project's duration decreases, its total direct costs increase, whereas its total indirect costs and total penalty costs both decrease. For each alternative project duration we can obtain the total cost by summing the three components. Figure 11.2 graphs the relationship between the project's duration and its total cost. Hereafter, we will call such a graph a *time-cost trade-off graph.* Observe the graph's shape. The total cost is high if the project's duration is too long or too short. For short project durations, the high total cost is due primarily to high total direct costs; for long project durations, the high total cost is due to the high total indirect costs and high total penalty costs.

Using the time-cost trade-off graph, the project manager can strike a proper balance among the three components of total cost. In our small example, Figure 11.2 indicates that the optimal (minimum-cost) project duration is 16 days, even though such a duration will result in a total penalty cost of $4000. Figure 11.2 also indicates the increase in total costs that would result from planned or unplanned deviations from the optimal project duration.

Before considering a more complex example, we will examine two factors that explain why the relationship between an activity's duration and its direct cost has the form depicted in Figure 11.2. Although we will discuss these two factors in terms of the resource of labor, our remarks remain valid for other types of resources, such as equipment or raw materials.

We can briefly state the first factor as follows:

It becomes increasingly expensive to obtain the *same* number of person-hours of labor in a shorter and shorter interval of time.

---

[5] The fixed deadline that triggers the penalty cost may be higher than the fixed deadline that triggers the bonus revenue. For example, the contract may call for a penalty cost if the project's duration exceeds 45 days and a bonus revenue if the project's duration falls below 40 days.

We can illustrate this factor with a small example. Consider an activity whose completion requires a single (though not necessarily the same) laborer to work three eight-hour workshifts, a total of 24 person-hours of labor. Suppose there are three types of workshifts: a day-shift for which the laborer's pay is $200, an evening-shift for which the laborer's pay is $240, and a night-shift for which the laborer's pay is $260. Also, assume that the nature of the work precludes any of the eight-hour workshifts from being concurrent but does permit periods of inactivity between any pair of eight-hour workshifts. Thus, the activity's duration will be at least one day but may be longer if there are periods of inactivity between one or more pairs of eight-hour workshifts. Let us now compute the respective direct costs of activity durations of three days, two days, and one day:

- An activity duration of three days permits the use of three day-shifts to complete the activity; the resulting direct cost is $200 + 200 + 200 = 600$ dollars.

- An activity duration of two days necessitates the use of two day-shifts and one evening-shift; the resulting direct cost is $200 + 200 + 240 = 640$ dollars.

- An activity duration of one day requires the use of one day-shift, one evening-shift, and one night-shift; the resulting direct cost is $200 + 240 + 260 = 700$ dollars.

Observe that a one-day reduction in the activity's duration from three days to two days *increases* direct costs by $40, and a one-day reduction in the duration from two days to one day *increases* direct costs by $60. Thus, as the time interval for obtaining the same 24 person-hours of labor becomes shorter and shorter, the activity's direct cost increases at an increasing rate, because increasingly expensive types of workshifts have to be used.

The above principle is sufficient to produce the typical relationship (displayed in Figure 11.2) between an activity's duration and its direct cost. However, a second factor is frequently partly responsible for the increase of an activity's direct cost as its duration decreases. Informally, we can state this factor as follows:

> Halving an activity's duration requires a workforce of more than double its former size.[6]

At first glance, this may seem surprising. For example, suppose that an activity duration of 20 days requires 4 persons on each of the 20 days, a total of 80 person-days of labor. It is tempting to conclude that halving the activity's duration from 20 to 10 days would simply require doubling the size of the workforce from 4 to 8 persons, thereby maintaining the use of 80 person-days of labor (i.e., 8 persons working 10 days instead of 4 persons working 20 days). Unfortunately, such a relationship between an activity's duration and the size of workforce required is not common. In most cases, 8 persons working for 10 days are *less productive* than 4 persons working for 20 days. Reasons for this phenomenon include the following:

- Perhaps some aspects of the activity cannot be worked on simultaneously by more than 4 persons, so that a workforce of 8 persons results in periods of idleness (unproductivity) by some of the workers.

- Perhaps the reduction in the activity's duration from 20 to 10 days results in increased mental stress and tension, which in turn results in more errors by the workers.

---

[6] More formally, dividing an activity's duration by a number k ($k > 1$) requires multiplying the size of workforce by a number *greater than* k. In our informal statement, $k = 2$.

- Perhaps a workforce of 8 persons, as opposed to 4 persons, increases the likelihood of a loss of productivity due to personality clashes among the workforce.

Whatever the reason, it is very likely that halving an activity's duration requires a workforce of more than double its former size. Suppose that in our example, halving the activity's duration from 20 to 10 days requires increasing the size of the workforce from 4 to 9 persons, thereby increasing the labor required to perform the activity from $4 \times 20 = 80$ person-days to $9 \times 10 = 90$ person-days. As we have discussed, the direct cost of employing 80 person-days of labor over a period of 10 days is typically higher than the direct cost of employing 80 person-days of labor over a period of 20 days. The fact that the 10-day duration requires 10 additional person-days (i.e., 90 rather than 80) increases the direct cost of a 10-day duration even more.

Having justified the typical relationship between an activity's duration and its direct cost, let us now illustrate how to determine the time-cost trade-off graph for a multi-activity project. When the project consists of a single activity (as it did in our first example), the determination of the project's time-cost trade-off graph is quite simple. However, as we will now see, when the project consists of several activities, determination of the time-cost trade-off graph requires much more effort, because we must systematically compute the minimum total direct cost for every possible project duration. As our example, we will use the six-activity project represented by the network in Figure 11.3. Let us place ourselves in the role of the project manager attempting to determine the time-cost trade-off graph for this project. To do so, we must compute the total direct costs, the total indirect costs, and the total penalty costs of every possible project duration. As we will see, the former

Figure 11.3 Project network for illustration of time-cost trade-off model

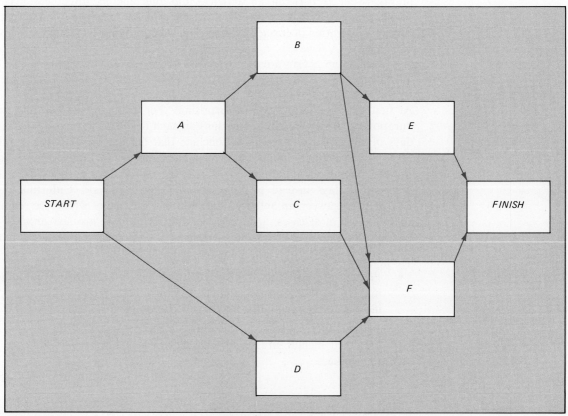

TABLE 11.5 Data for Six-activity Project

Activity	Max. Duration, D_{max} (days)	Max. Duration's Direct Cost, C_{max} ($000)	Min. Duration D_{min} (days)	Min. Duration's Direct Cost, C_{min} ($000)	Direct Cost of a Duration of d Days ($000)	Unit Reduction Cost ($000)
A	6	5	3	14	$23 - 3d$	3
B	4	11	1	29	$35 - 6d$	6
C	8	6	4	10	$14 - 1d$	1
D	13	6	10	21	$71 - 5d$	5
E	7	10	3	26	$38 - 4d$	4
F	5	5	3	9	$15 - 2d$	2

is the most difficult. Once we obtain the total direct costs for a particular duration, it is simple to add the total indirect costs and the total penalty costs to the total direct cost, thereby obtaining the duration's total cost

We begin our example by specifying for each activity the relationship between its duration and its direct cost. Table 11.5 summarizes these relationships. Let us use activity A to illustrate the meaning of the data contained in Table 11.5. The table's second and third columns indicate that A's duration cannot exceed a *maximum duration* of $D_{max} = 6$ days and that the direct cost of the resources necessitated by the 6-day duration is $C_{max} = 5$ thousand dollars. Similarly, the table's fourth and fifth columns indicate that A's duration cannot fall below a *minimum duration* of $D_{min} = 3$ days and that the direct cost of the resources necessitated by the 3-day duration is $C_{min} = 14$ thousand dollars.[7] Thus, the second through fifth columns identify two endpoints on the graph relating A's duration to its direct cost—namely, the two points

$$(D_{max}, C_{max}) = (6, 5) \text{ and } (D_{min}, C_{min}) = (3, 14).$$

For reasons discussed earlier, it is typical that a decrease in an activity's duration results in an increase in its direct cost. Consequently, we should not be surprised to see C_{min} exceed C_{max}. As did the original version of CPM, we will assume that a linear relationship exists between an activity's duration and its direct cost.[8] Figure 11.4 depicts this linear relationship, obtained by plotting the two endpoints (6, 5) and (3, 14) and then connecting them with a straight line. Given two points on the straight line, we may compute the straight line's slope as

$$\frac{C_{max} - C_{min}}{D_{max} - D_{min}} = \frac{5 - 14}{6 - 3} = \frac{-9}{3} = -3.$$

Note that the slope is negative because A's direct cost *decreases* as its duration *increases*. The negative of the straight line's slope, 3, has a special meaning. Hereafter, we will refer to it as A's *unit reduction cost*, since each unit (one-day) reduction in A's duration increases A's direct cost by $3000. We can compute the straight line's intercept on the cost axis as

$$C_{min} + [(\text{unit reduction cost}) \times D_{min}] = 14 + [3 \times 3] = 23$$

---

[7] In future work with the time-cost trade-off model outside this text, you may find an activity's maximum duration and associated direct cost referred to as its *normal time* and *normal cost* and the activity's minimum duration and associated direct cost referred to as its *crash time* and *crash cost*. Such terminology was used in the original version of CPM.

[8] We will comment on the validity (or lack thereof) of this assumption in the next paragraph.

or, alternatively, as

$$C_{max} + [(\text{unit reduction cost}) \times D_{max}] = 5 + [3 \times 6] = 23.$$

Given the slope and intercept of the straight line, we can compute its equation as

$$(\text{direct cost}) = (\text{intercept}) + (\text{slope})d = 23 - 3d.$$

Table 11.5's sixth column contains this linear equation relating A's duration to its direct cost, and the table's seventh column contains A's unit reduction cost. This completes our explanation of the row of Table 11.5 pertaining to activity A. The data in the table pertaining to other activities are similar. First, we specify the activity's minimum and maximum durations and their respective direct costs. Then, assuming a linear relationship, we use these two endpoints to compute the linear equation relating the activity's duration to its total direct cost.

Before proceeding with our example, we should comment on the validity of our assumption of a linear relationship between an activity's duration and its direct cost. Observe that a linear relationship such as that displayed in Figure 11.4 is a simplification of the more general relationship displayed in Figure 11.2. In particular, as the activity's duration decreases, its direct cost in the more general relationship (Figure 11.2) increases at an *increasing rate,* whereas its direct cost in the linear relationship (Figure 11.4) increases at a *constant rate* equal to the activity's unit reduction cost. As did the developers of the original version of CPM, many of today's project managers continue to assume a linear relationship because it simplifies the computations necessary to determine the time-cost trade-off graph. However, a project manager would be foolish to assume a linear relationship if one were not appropriate. Although the computations would be simple, the results would be meaningless! Consequently, a project manager should always question the validity of the linearity assumption for each of the project's activities. Rather than simply connecting the endpoints obtained by estimating the direct costs of the activity's minimum and maximum durations, the project manager should also estimate the direct costs of several durations between the minimum and maximum. Such a procedure provides the project manager with several (rather than just two) points on the graph relating the activity's duration to its direct cost. It is unlikely that these points will all lie exactly on the same straight line. However, if the points form a pattern that suggests that a linear approximation is appropriate (if not entirely accurate), then the project manager can obtain a linear approximation by "fitting" a straight line to the points either visually or by employing the technique of linear regression. If, however, the points form a pattern that suggests that a linear approximation is inappropriate, then the project manager must proceed as illustrated in Exercise 11.7.

Now that we understand the meaning of the data in Table 11.5, let us compute the total cost of each possible project duration, thereby generating the points on the time-cost trade-off graph. Our first and most difficult task will be the computation of the total direct costs—that is, the sum of the direct costs of the project's individual activities. To this total direct cost, we will then add both indirect costs of $3000 for each day of the project's duration and penalty costs of either $4000 for each day the project's duration exceeds 15 days or −$2000 for each day the project's duration falls below 15 days.

We now begin a step-by-step description of the analysis necessary to compute the total cost of each possible project duration. Table 11.6 summarizes our analysis.

■ **Step 1: Computation of the total cost of the project's maximum duration.** We first compute the minimum total direct costs for the project's longest possible duration. To do so, we set the duration of each activity equal to its maximum duration—that is, the duration appearing in Table 11.5's second column. Then, owing to the small size of the project, we can determine the critical

Figure 11.4 The linear relationship between activity A's duration and its direct cost

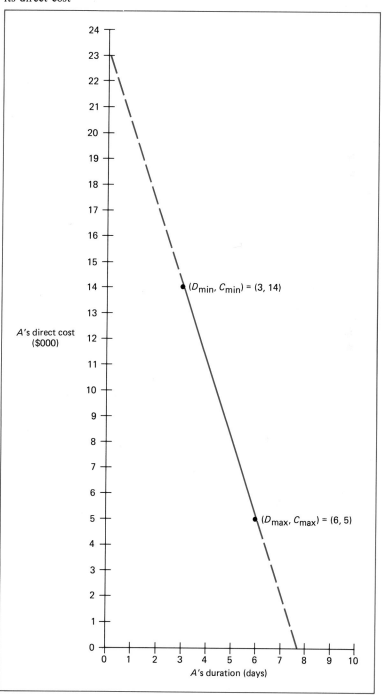

TABLE 11.6 Determination of Time-cost Tradeoff Graph for Example Project

Step	Activity Durations at Step's Start (days) A B C D E F	Path Lengths at Step's Start (days) ABE ABF ACF DF	Alternatives for Simultaneously Reducing the Common Length of the Critical Paths by One Day — Alternative	Cost ($000)	Project's Duration at Step's End (days)	Total Direct Costs ($000)	Total Indirect Costs* ($000)	Total Penalty Costs† ($000)	Total Cost ($000)
1	6 4 8 13 7 5	17 15 19 18	not applicable		19	43	57	16	116
2	6 4 8 13 7 5	17 15 19 18	1. Reduce A 2. Reduce C 3. Reduce F	3 1 2	18	44	54	12	110
3	6 4 7 13 7 5	17 15 18 18	1. Reduce A & D = $3+5=8$ 2. Reduce C & D = $1+5=6$ 3. Reduce F = 2		17	46	51	8	105
4	6 4 7 13 7 4	17 14 17 17	1. Reduce C & D & E = $1+5+4=10$ 2. Reduce B & C & D = $6+1+5=12$ 3. Reduce A & D = $3+5=8$ 4. Reduce A & F, Increase C $3+2-1=4$ 5. Reduce B & F = $6+2=8$ 6. Reduce E & F = $4+2=6$		16	50	48	4	102
5	5 4 8 13 7 3	16 12 16 16	1. Reduce C & D & E = $1+5+4=10$ 2. Reduce B & C & D = $6+1+5=12$ 3. Reduce A & D = $3+5=8$		15	58	45	0	103
6	4 4 8 12 7 3	15 11 15 15	1. Reduce C & D & E = $1+5+4=10$ 2. Reduce B & C & D = $6+1+5=12$ 3. Reduce A & D = $3+5=8$		14	66	42	−2	106
7	3 4 8 11 7 3	14 10 14 14	1. Reduce C & D & E = $1+5+4=10$ 2. Reduce B & C & D = $6+1+5=12$		13	76	39	−4	111
8	3 4 7 10 6 3	13 10 13 13	No feasible alternatives						

* $3000 for each day of the project's duration
† $4000 (or −$2000) for each day the project's duration exceeds (or falls below) 15 days

path and its length by simply enumerating all paths in the project network (Figure 11.3) from *START* to *FINISH*, computing the length of each, and identifying the longest path.[9] There exist four paths in the project network from *START* to *FINISH*:

$START \to A \to B \to E \to FINISH$ (hereafter referred to as path *ABE*)
$START \to A \to B \to F \to FINISH$ (path *ABF*)
$START \to A \to C \to F \to FINISH$ (path *ACF*)
$START \to D \to F \to FINISH$ (path *DF*).

Upon setting the durations of *A*, *B*, *C*, *D*, *E*, and *F* to their respective maximum values of 6, 4, 8, 13, 7, and 5, we may calculate the lengths of the four paths as follows:

Path	Path Length
ABE	$6 + 4 + 7 = 17$
ABF	$6 + 4 + 5 = 15$
ACF	$6 + 8 + 5 = 19$
DF	$13 + 5 \quad = 18$

With the activity durations at their respective maximums the critical path is *ACF*, and the project's duration is 19 days. The total direct costs of this 19-day project duration are the sum of the direct costs associated with each activity's maximum duration. These direct costs appear in Table 11.5's third

[9] Of course, if the project were more complex, we would have to employ the formal methodologies of PERT/CPM discussed in Section 10.3.

column and sum to

$$5 + 11 + 6 + 6 + 10 + 5 = 43$$

thousand dollars. To the total direct costs of $43,000, we add total indirect costs of $57,000 ($3000 for each day of the project's 19-day duration) and total penalty costs of $16,000 ($4000 for each day the project's 19-day duration exceeds 15 days). The resulting total cost is $116,000. Thus, we have identified (19, 116) as the rightmost point on the time-cost trade-off graph.

- **Step 2: Computation of the total cost of a project duration of 18 days.** We first compute the minimum increase in total direct costs necessary to reduce the project's duration from 19 to 18 days. To reduce the project's duration by one day, we must reduce the length of the critical path by one day. Since activities *A*, *C*, and *F* comprise the critical path, we must reduce the duration of one of these critical activities. Table 11.6's summary of Step 2 displays a list of the three alternatives available to us. The table also shows the costs of each alternative, obtained from the unit reduction costs appearing in Table 11.5's last column. Our choice is clear. With its cost of $1000, Alternative 2 minimizes the increase in total direct costs. Selecting Alternative 2 increases total direct costs from $43,000 to $44,000. To the total direct costs, we add total indirect costs of $54,000 ($3000 for each day of the project's 18-day duration) and total penalty costs of $12,000 ($4000 for each day the project's 18-day duration exceeds 15 days). The resulting total cost is $110,000. Thus, we have identified (18, 110) as another point on the time-cost trade-off graph.

- **Step 3: Computation of the total cost of a project duration of 17 Days.** We first compute the minimum increase in total direct costs necessary to reduce the project's duration from 18 to 17 days. Observe that, because of the prior step's one-day reduction in *C*'s duration, the length of path *ACF* decreased from 19 to 18. However, because *C* is not a member of paths *ABE*, *ABF*, and *DF*, the lengths of these paths remained unchanged at 17, 15, and 18, respectively. Consequently, at the start of Step 3, there are two critical paths, *ACF* and *DF*, having a common length of 18. Because both *ACF* and *DF* are now critical, we can no longer reduce the project's duration by simply reducing *C*'s duration. Doing so would have no effect on the critical path *DF*. Instead, we must simultaneously reduce the common length of *both* critical paths by choosing one of the three alternatives listed in Table 11.6's summary of Step 3. With its cost of $2000, Alternative 3 minimizes the increase in total direct costs. Selecting Alternative 3 increases total direct costs from $44,000 to $46,000. To the total direct costs, we add total indirect costs of $51,000 ($3000 for each day of the project's 17-day duration) and total penalty costs of $8000 ($4000 for each day the project's 17-day duration exceeds 15 days). The resulting total cost is $105,000. Thus, we have identified (17, 105) as another point on the time-cost trade-off graph.

- **Step 4: Computation of the total cost of a project duration of 16 days.** We first compute the minimum increase in total direct costs necessary to reduce the project's duration from 17 to 16 days. Observe that, because of the prior step's one-day reduction in *F*'s duration, the lengths of two critical paths *ACF* and *DF* and the noncritical path *ABF* decreased from 18 to 17, from 18 to 17, and from 15 to 14, respectively. However, because *F* is not a member of the path *ABE*, its length remained unchanged at 17. Consequently, at the start of Step 4, there are three critical paths, *ABE*, *ACF*, and *DF*, having a common length of 17. Because F is not a member of all three critical paths, we can no longer reduce the project's duration by simply reducing F's duration. Instead, we must simultaneously reduce the common length of ABE, ACF, and DF. The six alternatives are listed in Table 11.6's summary of Step 4. Alternative 4 merits discussion, since it is easy to overlook the part calling for an increase in C's duration. To see why Alternative 4 is viable, first note that, since C's duration underwent a decrease in Step 2, it is now eligible for an increase. Also note that Alternative 4 has the following effects on the three critical paths:

Path	Change in Path's Length (given one-day reductions in A and F and a one-day increase in C)
ABE	Reduction from 17 to 16 (since only A is on the path)
ACF	Reduction from 17 to 16 (since A, C, and F are all on the path)
DF	Reduction from 17 to 16 (since only F is on the path)

Hence, Alternative 4 is a legitimate way to simultaneously reduce the common length of the critical paths. Unfortunately, Alternative 4 is easy to overlook. Even more unfortunately, overlooking this alternative would lead to a serious error, because it is coincidentally the optimal alternative. Selecting Alternative 4 increases total direct costs from $46,000 to $50,000, the minimum increase among the six alternatives. To the total direct costs, we add total indirect costs of $48,000 ($3000 for each day of the project's 16-day duration) and total penalty costs of $4000 ($4000 for each day the project's 16-day duration exceeds 15 days). The resulting total cost is $102,000. Thus, we have identified (16, 102) as another point on the time-cost trade-off graph.

- **Step 5: Computation of the total cost of a project duration of 15 days.** We first compute the minimum increase in total direct costs necessary to reduce the project's duration from 16 to 15 days. Observe that, because of the prior step's one-day reductions in the durations of both A and F and the one-day increase in C's duration, the common length of the critical paths ABE, ACF, and DF has decreased from 17 to 16. However, because both A and F are members of the noncritical path ABF, its length has decreased from 14 to 12 days. Consequently, the critical paths at the start of Step 5 are the same as they were at the start of Step 4. Only their common length has changed, from 17 to 16 days. However, because the successive one-day reductions of F's duration in Steps 3 and 4 have left F's duration at its minimum duration of three days (consult Table 11.5), only the first three alternatives listed in Step 4 remain viable. With its cost of $8000, Alternative 3 minimizes the increase in total direct costs. Selecting Alternative 3 increases the total direct costs from $50,000 to $58,000. To the total direct costs, we must add total indirect costs of $45,000 ($3000 for each day of the project's 15-day duration) and total penalty costs of $0 ($4000 for each day the project's 15-day duration exceeds 15 days). The resulting total cost is $103,000. Thus, we have identified (15, 103) as another point on the time-cost trade-off graph.

- **Step 6: Computation of the total cost of a project duration of 14 days.** We first compute the minimum increase in total direct costs necessary to reduce the project's duration from 15 to 14 days. Observe that, because of the prior step's one-day reductions in the durations of both A and D, the common length of the three critical paths has decreased from 16 to 15 days. In addition, because A is a member of the noncritical path ABF, its length has decreased from 12 to 11 days. Consequently, the critical paths at the start of Step 6 are the same as they were at the start of Step 5. Only their common length has changed, from 16 to 15 days. Because the critical paths have remained unchanged and because the durations of both A and D still exceed their minimums, we may achieve a one-day reduction in the project's duration by simply repeating our action of Step 5. This increases total direct costs from $58,000 to $66,000. To the total direct costs, we add total indirect costs of $42,000 ($3000 for each day of the project's 14-day duration) and total penalty costs of −$2000 (−$2000 for each day the project's 14-day duration falls below 15 days). The resulting total cost is $106,000. Thus, we have identified (14, 106) as another point on the time-cost trade-off graph.

- **Step 7: Computation of the total cost of a project duration of 13 days.** We first compute the minimum increase in total direct costs necessary to reduce the project's duration from 14 to 13 days. Observe that, because of the prior step's one-day reductions in the durations of both A and D, the common length of the critical paths ABE, ACF, and DF has decreased from 15 to 14. In addition, because A is a member of the noncritical path ABF, its length has decreased from 11 to 10 days. Consequently, the critical paths at the start of Step 7 are the same as they were at the start of Step 6. Only their common length has changed, from 15 to 14 days. However, because the successive one-day reductions in Steps 4–6 have left A's duration at its minimum of three days, we can no longer reduce the project's duration by repeating our action of Step 6. Among those alternatives first listed in Step 5, only Alternatives 1 and 2 remain viable. With its cost of $10,000, Alternative 1 minimizes the increase in total direct costs. Selecting Alternative 1 increases total direct costs from $66,000 to $76,000.[10] To the total direct costs, we add total indirect costs of $39,000 ($3000 for each day of the project's 13-day duration) and total penalty costs of −$4000 (−$2000 for each day the project's 13-day duration falls below 15 days). The resulting total cost is $111,000. Thus, we have identified (13, 111) as another point on the time-cost trade-off graph.

- **Step 8: Computation of the total cost of a project duration of 12 days.** We first compute the minimum increase in total direct costs necessary to reduce project's duration from 13 to 12 days. Observe that, as a result of the prior step's one-day reductions in the durations of C, D, and E, the common length of the critical paths ABE, ACF, and DF has decreased from 14 to 13. However, because neither C, D, nor E is a member of the noncritical path ABF, its length has remained unchanged at 10. Consequently, the critical paths at the start of Step 8 are the same as they were at the start of Step 7. Only their common length has changed, from 14 to 13. Because the reductions in prior steps of the durations of D and F have left them at their minimum values, we are unable to reduce path DF's length below its current length of 13. Consequently, a project duration of 12 days (or lower) is impossible,

Finally, we may terminate our analysis![11]

Compare the last five columns of Table 11.6 with the table appearing in Figure 11.2. You will find them identical! Thus, Figure 11.2 summarizes the time-cost relationships not only for the single-activity project we used to introduce the

---

[10] It is interesting to note that we decreased C's duration in Step 2, increased it in Step 4, and are now decreasing it again in Step 7.

[11] Note that, when the project's duration is at its lowest value of 13 days, not all activity durations are at their minimum values, and not all paths are critical.

time-cost trade-off model but also for the six-activity project we used to illustrate the complexities of the time-cost trade-off model. Observe that, even though we assumed a linear relationship between an activity's duration and its direct cost, the entire project's total *direct* costs are not linear. Instead, as indicated in Figure 11.2, as the project's duration decreases, the project's total direct costs increase at an increasing rate. The time-cost trade-off graph of Figure 11.2 provides the project manager of the six-activity project with a variety of useful information, including the following:

1. The project duration that minimizes total cost is 16 days, even though the resulting total cost of $102,000 includes a penalty cost of $4000.

2. Total cost increases if there is a planned or unplanned deviation from the optimal 16-day project duration. For example, if the project's contract calls for the project to finish within 15 days, the project manager can see from Figure 11.2's time-cost trade-off graph that meeting the contract's deadline will cost $1000 more than finishing one day later.

3. For any specific project duration the project manager can determine the activity durations that minimize the total *direct* costs. For example, if the project manager decides upon a project duration of 15 days, Figure 11.2 indicates that the budget for total *direct* costs should be $58,000. Reference to the row of Table 11.6 summarizing Step 6 then indicates that, to achieve these total direct costs of $58,000, the durations of *A*, *B*, *C*, *D*, *E*, and *F* should be set to 4, 4, 8, 12, 7, and 3 days, respectively.[12] Finally, by "plugging" these durations into the linear relationships appearing in the sixth column of Table 11.5, the project manager obtains the following allocation of the project's $58,000 budget for total direct costs:

Activity	Direct Cost ($000)		
A	$23 - (3 \times 4)$	=	11
B	$35 - (6 \times 4)$	=	11
C	$14 - (1 \times 8)$	=	6
D	$71 - (5 \times 12)$	=	11
E	$38 - (4 \times 7)$	=	10
F	$15 - (2 \times 3)$	=	9

In generating the time-cost trade-off graph, we repeatedly applied the following procedure:

To reduce the project's duration by one unit of time, use the following procedure:

1. Identify every critical path.

2. Enumerate every alternative for simultaneously reducing the common length of the critical paths by one unit of time (being careful not to overlook alternatives such as Alternative 4 in Step 4 of Table 11.6).

3. Compute the cost of each alternative.

4. Select the alternative with the lowest cost.

---

[12] We look at the row of Table 11.6 summarizing Step 6 because, although the row summarizing Step 5 contains the total direct cost of 58, the row summarizing Step 6 contains the associated activity durations.

This is an important procedure to know when faced with the problem of how best to reduce the project's duration. However, the procedure is difficult to apply to a very large project, where there may be several critical paths consisting of many different critical activities. In such cases, it would be extremely difficult to identify all the alternatives for simultaneously reducing the lengths of all critical paths by one unit. Step 4 of our analysis above indicates the difficulties that may arise in even a six-activity project.

In summary, then, this section's example has informally illustrated the steps of a formal method for determining the time-cost trade-off graph. However, when the project is large and complex, performing the method's computations manually is virtually impossible. One alternative is to program a computer to perform them (or at least assist with them). In practice, however, the determination of a large project's time-cost trade-off graph is most efficiently accomplished via linear programming. This is the subject of the next section.

11.4 LINEAR PROGRAMMING APPLICATIONS TO PROJECT MANAGEMENT[13]

This section will discuss two applications of linear programming to project management:

1. A linear programming model for performing the analysis of the basic PERT/CPM model—that is, for determining the shortest possible project duration and the critical activities for a project in which every activity duration is a known constant.

2. A linear programming model for performing the analysis required by the time-cost trade-off model discussed in the preceding section—that is, for generating the time-cost trade-off graph for a project in which every activity duration is not fixed but rather depends on the dollar value of the resources allocated to the activity.

Rather than using complex notation to discuss these models, we will illustrate them with specific examples.

A Linear Programming Model of the Basic PERT/CPM Model

To illustrate the linear programming model, we will reconsider the project network of Figure 11.3, the project network used in the previous section to illustrate the time-cost trade-off model. For the purposes of this subsection, we will temporarily assume that the activity durations are the following known constants:

Activity	A	B	C	D	E	F
Duration	6	4	8	13	7	5

Our goal is to determine, via linear programming, the project's shortest possible duration and its critical path. To this end, we define the decision variables

$$t_{START}, \ t_A, \ t_B, \ t_C, \ t_D, \ t_E, \ t_F, \ t_{FINISH},$$

---

[13] This section presumes an understanding of linear programming, including sensitivity analysis.

which denote starting times of the respective activities. Observe that t_{FINISH} not only denotes the starting time of *FINISH* but, since *FINISH*'s duration is 0, also denotes the project's finishing time. Consequently, we may express the project's duration as $t_{FINISH} - t_{START}$. Our linear programming model will minimize $t_{FINISH} - t_{START}$, subject to constraints that ensure that no activity starts until all its predecessors have finished. To illustrate the nature of the constraints, consider activity *F*, which has the three predecessors *B*, *C*, and *D*. Since the finishing time of an activity is simply the sum of its starting time and its duration, we may express the finishing times of *B*, *C*, and *D* as $t_B + 4$, $t_C + 8$, and $t_D + 13$, respectively. Thus, to ensure that *F* does not start until *B*, *C*, and *D* have all finished, our linear program must include the following set of three constraints:

$$t_F \geqslant t_B + 4$$
$$t_F \geqslant t_C + 8$$
$$t_F \geqslant t_D + 13$$

We can rewrite these constraints (with all decision variables appearing on the left-hand sides of the constraints) as

$$t_F - t_B \geqslant 4$$
$$t_F - t_C \geqslant 8$$
$$t_F - t_D \geqslant 13.$$

The complete linear program, then, is

$$
\begin{array}{llccr}
\text{Minimize} & t_{FINISH} & - & t_{START} \\
\text{subject to} & t_A & - & t_{START} & \geqslant & 0 \\
& t_B & - & t_A & \geqslant & 6 \\
& t_C & - & t_A & \geqslant & 6 \\
& t_D & - & t_{START} & \geqslant & 0 \\
& t_E & - & t_B & \geqslant & 4 \\
& t_F & - & t_B & \geqslant & 4 \\
& t_F & - & t_C & \geqslant & 8 \\
& t_F & - & t_D & \geqslant & 13 \\
& t_{FINISH} & - & t_E & \geqslant & 7 \\
& t_{FINISH} & - & t_F & \geqslant & 5 \\
\end{array}
$$

and $t_{START}, t_A, \ldots, t_F, t_{FINISH} \geqslant 0$.

The linear program consists of eight variables, one for each activity (i.e., node), and ten structural constraints, one for each precedence relationship (i.e., arc). As we have illustrated, each constraint simply ensures that a particular activity does not start before the finish of one of its predecessors.

The linear program's optimal solution, which provides starting times for all of the activities, is

$$
\begin{array}{rcl}
t_{START} & = & 0 \\
t_A & = & 0 \\
t_B & = & 8 \\
t_C & = & 6 \\
t_D & = & 1 \\
t_E & = & 12 \\
t_F & = & 14 \\
t_{FINISH} & = & 19.
\end{array}
$$

The corresponding optimal objective value, equal to the project's shortest possible duration, is 19 days.

To identify the critical activities, we must examine the shadow prices of the structural constraints. Consider, for example, the constraint $t_F - t_C \geq 8$. Recall that this constraint's right-hand side of 8 is activity C's current duration. If *both* C and F are members of the critical path, a one-day increase in the constraint's right-hand side from 8 to 9 must result in a one-day increase in the project's shortest possible duration and, equivalently, a one-day increase in the linear program's optimal objective value. This implies that the shadow price for the constraint must have a value of -1. Alternatively, if either C or F is *not* a member of the critical path, a one-day increase in the constraint's right-hand side from 8 to 9 would have no effect on the linear program's optimal objective value (i.e., the project's shortest possible duration). Consequently, the constraint's shadow price must equal 0. Applying a similar argument to the linear program's other constraints, we reach the following conclusion:

> The shadow price for any particular constraint will equal either 0 or -1, -1 if the critical path contains *both* activities whose starting time variables appear in the constraint and 0 otherwise.

In our example, an examination of the shadow prices would indicate shadow prices of -1 for the following four constraints:

$$
\begin{array}{rcl}
t_A & - \; t_{START} & \geq \; 0 \\
t_C & - \; t_A & \geq \; 6 \\
t_F & - \; t_C & \geq \; 8 \\
t_{FINISH} & - \; t_F & \geq \; 5.
\end{array}
$$

From these shadow prices, we may conclude that the critical path is

$$START \rightarrow A \rightarrow C \rightarrow F \rightarrow FINISH.$$

We should comment on the advantages the PERT/CPM approach presented in Chapter 10 has over the linear programming approach.

- With respect to computational efficiency, PERT/CPM is much quicker than linear programming, regardless of whether the computations are performed by hand or by a computer. To illustrate, reconsider the Designer Gene project summarized by Figure 10.2. Whereas we can analyze the DG project network via PERT/CPM with manual computations performed directly on Figure 10.2, analysis via linear programming would require the solution by a computer of a linear program having 16 variables (one for each node in Figure 10.2) and 23 constraints (one for each arc in Figure 10.2).

- With respect to the information provided, the PERT/CPM approach is more informative than the linear programming approach. Both approaches provide the project manager with the project's shortest possible duration and the critical path. However, the PERT/CPM approach provides two extreme activity schedules for achieving the project's shortest possible duration, the ES schedule and the LS schedule. The PERT/CPM approach also provides the Total and Unshared Slacks of each activity. In contrast, the linear programming approach produces no information regarding slacks and produces only one activity schedule for achieving the project's shortest possible duration—a schedule not guaranteed to be either the ES schedule of the LS schedule.[14]

---

[14] The reason is that the ES schedule and the LS schedule are just two of the many schedules that will achieve the project's shortest possible duration. Consequently, the linear program has multiple optimal solutions.

In short, if the appropriate software is available, the PERT/CPM approach is always preferred to the linear programming approach.

A Linear Programming Model of the Time-Cost Trade-off Model

To illustrate a second and more useful application of linear programming to project management, let us continue to use the example used in Section 11.3 to illustrate the time-cost trade-off model. Figure 11.3 displays the project network for this example and Table 11.5 summarizes the relevant project data. Recall the time-consuming nature of the procedure we used in Section 11.3 to generate the seven points on the time-cost trade-off graph. We commented there on the difficulties of formalizing this procedure for application to a complex project and stated that a linear programming approach is a preferred alternative.

To illustrate this linear programming approach, suppose that we want to determine the minimum total *direct* cost and the associated activity durations necessitated by a project duration of exactly 16 days. To formulate the appropriate linear program, we must define the decision variables

$$t_{START}, \ t_A, \ t_B, \ t_C, \ t_D, \ t_E, \ t_F, \ t_{FINISH},$$

which denote (as in our earlier linear program) the starting times of the respective activities. Furthermore, because the activities' durations are not fixed but under our control, we must also define the additional decision variables

$$x_A, x_B, x_C, x_D, x_E, x_F,$$

denoting the respective durations of each activity. The sixth column of Table 11.5 summarizes the linear relationship between each activity's duration and its direct cost. Using these relationships, we may express the objective of minimizing total direct costs as

$$\text{Minimize } (23 - 3x_A) + (35 - 6x_B) + (14 - 1x_C) + (71 - 5x_D) + (38 - 4x_E)$$
$$+ (15 - 2x_F).$$

When all constants are added together, this objective function simplifies to

$$\text{Minimize } 196 - (3x_A + 6x_B + 1x_C + 5x_D + 4x_E + 2x_F)$$

Since we have no control over the constant 196 but can control the remaining portion of the expression, an equivalent objective function is

$$\text{Maximize } 3x_A + 6x_B + 1x_C + 5x_D + 4x_E + 2x_F;$$

that is, whatever values of $x_A, x_B, \ldots, x_F$ maximize the expression

$$3x_A + 6x_B + 1x_C + 5x_D + 4x_E + 2x_F$$

also minimize 196 minus this expression.

Our linear program, then, will maximize

$$3x_A + 6x_B + 1x_C + 5x_D + 4x_E + 2x_F$$

subject to constraints that ensure the following:

1. The project's duration equals 16 days; that is,

$$t_{FINISH} - t_{START} = 16.$$

2. The duration of each activity must not fall below its minimum duration nor above its maximum duration, as specified by the fourth and second columns of Table 11.5, respectively. For example, Table 11.5 specifies that C's minimum duration is 4 days and its maximum duration is 8 days. Consequently, the linear program must include the following pair of constraints:

$$x_C \geqslant 4 \text{ and } x_C \leqslant 8.$$

3. No activity can start until all its predecessors have finished. For example, consider activity F, which has the three predecessors B, C, and D. Since the finishing time of an activity is simply the sum of its starting time and its duration, we may express the finishing times of B, C, and D as $t_B + x_B$, $t_C + x_C$, and $t_D + x_D$, respectively. Thus, to ensure that F does not start until B, C, and D have all finished, our linear program must include the following set of three constraints:

$$t_F \geqslant t_B + x_B$$
$$t_F \geqslant t_C + x_C$$
$$t_F \geqslant t_D + x_D.$$

We can rewrite the constraints (with all decision variables appearing on the left-hand sides of the constraints) as

$$t_F - t_B - x_B \geqslant 0$$
$$t_F - t_C - x_C \geqslant 0$$
$$t_F - t_D - x_D \geqslant 0.$$

The complete linear program, then, is

Maximize $3x_A + 6x_B + 1x_C + 5x_D + 4x_E + 2x_F$

subject to $t_{FINISH} - t_{START} = 16$,

$x_A \geqslant 3,$	$x_A \leqslant 6,$	$t_A - t_{START} \geqslant 0$
$x_B \geqslant 1,$	$x_B \leqslant 4,$	$t_B - t_A - x_A \geqslant 0$
$x_C \geqslant 4,$	$x_C \leqslant 8,$	$t_C - t_A - x_A \geqslant 0$
$x_D \geqslant 10,$	$x_D \leqslant 13,$	$t_D - t_{START} \geqslant 0$
$x_E \geqslant 3,$	$x_E \leqslant 7,$	$t_E - t_B - x_B \geqslant 0$
$x_F \geqslant 3,$	$x_F \leqslant 5,$	$t_F - t_B - x_B \geqslant 0$
		$t_F - t_C - x_C \geqslant 0$
		$t_F - t_D - x_D \geqslant 0$
		$t_{FINISH} - t_E - x_E \geqslant 0$
		$t_{FINISH} - t_F - x_F \geqslant 0$

and $t_{START}, t_A, t_B, t_C, t_D, t_E, t_F, t_{FINISH} \geqslant 0$
$x_A, x_B, x_C, x_D, x_E, x_F \geqslant 0$.

As we have illustrated, the constraint in the first column simply ensures that the project's duration is 16 days; the 12 constraints in the second and third columns (two for each activity) ensure that each activity's duration is greater than or equal to its minimum duration and less than or equal to its maximum duration; the constraints in the fourth column (one for each precedence relationship) ensure that no activity starts until all its predecessors have finished.

The linear program's optimal solution is

$$
\begin{aligned}
t_{START} &= 0 \\
t_A &= 0, & x_A &= 5 \\
t_B &= 5, & x_B &= 4 \\
t_C &= 5, & x_C &= 8 \\
t_D &= 0, & x_D &= 13 \\
t_E &= 9, & x_E &= 7 \\
t_F &= 13, & x_F &= 3 \\
t_{FINISH} &= 16.
\end{aligned}
$$

The corresponding optimal objective value is 146, which we must remember to subtract from the constant 196 to obtain the minimum total direct cost of 50. A comparison of this minimal total direct cost and the associated activity durations with those appearing in Table 11.6 will show that they are equal.[15] Thus, we can let the linear programming do the work we painstakingly performed by hand in Section 11.3.

We have seen how to use linear programming to determine the minimum total direct cost for the specific project duration of 16 days. In order to use linear programming to generate the entire time-cost trade-off graph, we must proceed as follows:

1. We must obtain the minimum total direct cost for every possible project duration by repeatedly solving the linear program, using the constraint

$$
t_{FINISH} - t_{START} = (desired\ project\ duration).
$$

in place of the constraint

$$
t_{FINISH} - t_{START} = 16.
$$

More specifically we need to solve the linear program 7 times, once with a desired project duration of 13 days, again with a desired project duration of 14 days, and so on, until we solve the linear program a final time with a desired project duration of 19 days.[16] (Actually, unless we set the durations of all activities first to their minimums and then to their maximums and compute the resulting minimum project durations of 13 days and 19 days, respectively, we may mistakenly try a desired project duration less than 13 or greater than 19, only to discover that the linear program is infeasible.)

2. After repeatedly solving the linear program to obtain the minimal total direct cost for every possible project duration, we may generate the time-cost trade-off graph by adding to the minimum total direct cost of each duration the corresponding indirect costs and penalty costs.

---

[15] Remember that although the row of Table 11.6 summarizing Step 4 contains the total direct cost of 50, the row summarizing Step 5 contains the associated activity durations.

[16] For our purposes, we will assume that we actually solve seven linear programs. However, there exists a more efficient means of solving a series of linear programs in which the right-hand side of a particular constraint is systematically changing. The technique, called *parametric programming,* is discussed in most texts containing advanced material on linear programming.

We conclude with the following brief summary of this section:

> To generate the time-cost trade-off graph of a large project, we may replace the cumbersome procedure described in the previous section with the linear programming approach described in this section.

11.5 CONCLUDING REMARKS

This chapter has only touched the surface of the body of knowledge commonly referred to as "project management." As a summary, we list the major features of PERT/CPM that make it a valuable tool for project management:

1. Unlike so many quantitative methods, the fundamental concepts of PERT/CPM are easily understood, even by persons with little technical education.

2. In the project formulation stage, use of PERT/CPM forces those involved in the project to identify its major activities, assign responsibilities, establish precedence relationships, and estimate activity durations and resource requirements.

3. The project network concisely displays the complex interrelationships among the project's activities.

4. The planning and scheduling phase of PERT/CPM identifies critical activities and, through the concept of slack, provides a measure of the degree to which the other activities are noncritical. Furthermore, schedule diagrams and resource loading diagrams provide a basis for rationally selecting one of the many alternative activity schedules.

5. Once the project begins, the monitoring and replanning phase of PERT/CPM ensures quick reaction to surprises that might otherwise adversely effect the project.

Throughout this chapter we have stressed that, in order to successfully apply PERT/CPM, a project manager must pay attention to its qualitative as well as its quantitative aspects. The important qualitative aspects of using PERT/CPM include the following:

- Throughout the project, the project manager should work in close consultation with an Advisory Committee consisting of a cross section of those personnel having major project responsibilities. In short, the application of PERT/CPM should be a team effort.

- Anyone who will be asked to provide input to PERT/CPM (such as estimates of activity durations) or who will directly receive output from PERT/CPM (such as schedule diagrams) should attend a workshop on the fundamental PERT/CPM concepts. Familiarity with PERT/CPM, rather than fear or mistrust, will greatly improve the accuracy of the input and increase the likelihood of proper use of the output.

- PERT/CPM bases all its calculations on the estimates of the durations of the activities. Of course, any inaccuracies in this input will lead to inaccuracies in the output. Consequently, the project manager should exercise great care in deciding upon the proper estimates of activity durations. Such care includes (1) making any person asked to provide an estimate aware of its importance and (2) adjusting the estimate appropriately up or down to take into account any inherent optimism or pessimism of the estimator. For example, the person directly responsible for an activity might overstate its duration to decrease the likelihood he or she will later be blamed for the activity's taking too long to complete.

Of course, use of PERT/CPM does not guarantee a project's success. Unfortunately, overzealous advocates can sometimes lead a project manager to expect too much from PERT/CPM. Then, when the project is unsuccessful, all too often the project manager blames PERT/CPM and vows never to use it again. This scenario was prevalent in the late-1960s and early-1970s when many persons treated PERT/CPM with almost religious reverence. When PERT/CPM failed to live up to the expectations, there was widespread disenchantment. Today, disenchantment has been replaced with enlightened recognition of what PERT/CPM can and cannot do. PERT/CPM cannot manage a project. However, if the project manager judiciously combines her own experience, intuition, and common sense with the valuable information and insight provided by PERT/CPM, the project will have a higher likelihood of success than if PERT/CPM were not used. If, unfortunately, the project should turn out unsuccessful, the project manager should not blame PERT/CPM but should take consolation in the fact that, without it, the outcome would probably have been much worse.

11.6 CHAPTER CHECKLIST AND GLOSSARY

Quickly review this chapter by rereading the material highlighted by a vertical line in the left margin. You should then be familiar with the concepts, techniques, and terminology in the Checklist and Glossary that follow. If you need "help" with a particular item, consult the section or sections indicated for a more detailed discussion.

Checklist of Concepts and Techniques

☐ How to analyze a project whose activities have stochastic durations, and why the original version of PERT is not recommended. [11.2]

☐ The time-cost trade-off model. [11.3]

☐ How to formulate the basic PERT/CPM model as a linear program. [11.4]

☐ How to formulate the time-cost trade-off model as a linear program. [11.4]

☐ The features of PERT/CPM that make it a valuable tool for project management. [11.5]

☐ The important qualitative aspects of using PERT/CPM. [11.5]

Glossary

Stochastic project. A project in which at least one activity has a stochastic duration. [11.2]

Time-cost trade-off model. An extension to the basic PERT/CPM model in which the duration of each activity depends on the dollar value of the resources allocated to it. [11.3]

EXERCISES

Exercises 11.1–11.3 involve the analysis of a project with stochastic activity durations.

11.1. Consider the stochastic project below:

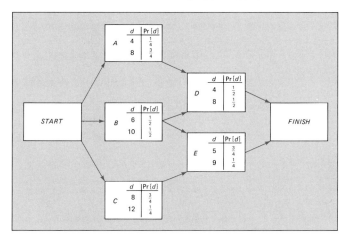

In the table within each activity, the column headed "d" contains the activity's possible durations and the column headed "Pr{d}" contains the associated probabilities.

(a) In this part only, convert the stochastic project into a deterministic project by replacing the probability distribution of each activity duration with a single duration equal to the mean (expected value) duration. Then identify this deterministic project's duration and critical path(s).

(b) Analyze the stochastic project by constructing tables similar to Tables 11.1–11.4.

(c) Use the tables from part (b) to answer the following questions:
   (i) Which path has the highest probability of being the critical path? Compare your answer here to that in part (a).
   (ii) Which activity has the highest probability of being critical?
   (iii) What is the mean duration of the project? If we were to use the project duration computed in part (a) as an estimate for this mean, by what percentage would we underestimate? Also, what is the probability that the project's actual duration will exceed part (a)'s estimate?
   (iv) If you were asked for an estimate of the project's actual duration that had no more than a 25% chance of being exceeded, what estimate would you provide?

*11.2. Redo Exercise 11.1, this time using the stochastic project at the top of the next column:

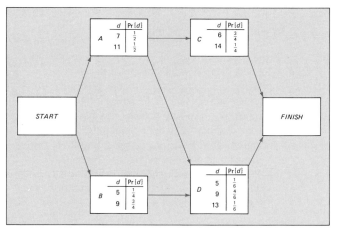

11.3. Redo Exercise 11.1, this time using the stochastic project below:

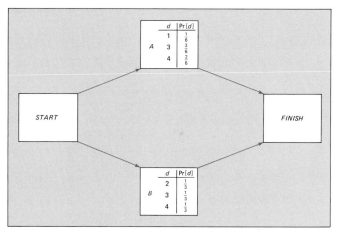

Exercises 11.4–11.6 test your ability to determine a project's time-cost trade-off graph.

11.4. Reconsider the project in Exercise 10.2. In that exercise, each activity's duration is specified by a single number. Now assume that each activity's duration is a linear function of its direct cost. In particular, assume the data below:

Activity	Maximum Duration (days)	Maximum Duration's Direct Cost ($000)	Minimum Duration (days)	Minimum Duration's Direct Cost ($000)	Direct Cost of a Duration of d Days ($000)	Unit Reduction Cost ($000)
A	6	15	2	31	39–4d	4
B	10	8	1	17	18–1d	1
C	5	10	4	13	25–3d	3
D	3	11	1	15	17–2d	2
E	6	13	4	23	43–5d	5
F	2	12	1	20	28–8d	8
G	4	9	1	30	37–7d	7
H	9	6	7	18	60–6d	6

Also assume the following:

- Indirect costs accrue at the rate of $5000 per day from the project's inception to its completion.
- There is a daily penalty cost of $600 for each day the project's duration exceeds 22 days and a daily penalty cost of −$400 for each day the project's duration falls below 22 days.

(a) Given the above data, use the procedure illustrated in Section 11.3 to determine the project's time-cost trade-off graph. Summarize your computations in a table similar to Table 11.6, and display your graph (and its three components) in a manner similar to Figure 11.2.

(b) What is the project's optimal duration, and what is each activity's optimal duration and corresponding direct cost?

* 11.5. Redo Exercise 11.4, this time using the project in Exercise 10.3 and the data below:

Activity	Maximum Duration (days)	Maximum Duration's Direct Cost ($000)	Minimum Duration (days)	Minimum Duration's Direct Cost ($000)	Direct Cost of a Duration of d Days ($000)	Unit Reduction Cost ($000)
A	2	10	1	16	22−6d	6
B	7	17	5	21	31−2d	2
C	3	20	2	24	32−4d	4
D	1	7	1	7	–	–
E	2	8	1	15	22−7d	7
F	5	10	2	19	25−3d	3
G	6	12	3	27	42−5d	5

Daily Indirect Costs = $7000

$$\text{Daily Penalty Cost} = \begin{cases} \$3000 \text{ if project is over 13 days} \\ -\$2000 \text{ if project is under 13 days} \end{cases}$$

(Note that activity D's duration and direct cost must be 1 day and $7000, respectively.)

Redo Exercise 11.4, this time using the project in Exercise 10.4 and the data below:

Activity	Maximum Duration (days)	Maximum Duration's Direct Cost ($000)	Minimum Duration (days)	Minimum Duration's Direct Cost ($000)	Direct Cost of a Duration of d Days ($000)	Unit Reduction Cost ($000)
A	4	21	3	28	49−7d	7
B	6	50	4	60	80−5d	5
C	8	40	6	56	104−8d	8
D	9	54	7	60	81−3d	3
E	5	15	4	24	60−9d	9
F	4	50	1	110	130−20d	20
G	7	60	6	75	165−15d	15
H	3	15	3	15	–	–

534

Daily Indirect Costs = $10,000

$$\text{Daily Penalty Cost} = \begin{cases} \$5000 \text{ if project is over 20 days} \\ -\$3000 \text{ if project is under 20 days} \end{cases}$$

(Note that activity H's duration and direct cost must be 3 days and $15,000, respectively.)

The next exercise illustrates the data and computations necessary to determine a time-cost trade-off graph when there is a nonlinear relationship between an activity's duration and it's direct cost.

11.7. Reconsider Exercise 11.5. In that exercise, we assumed that each activity's duration is a linear function of its direct cost. Now assume the data below:

Activity	Maximum Duration (days)	Maximum Duration's Direct Cost ($000)	Minimum Duration (days)	Unit Reduction Cost
A	2	10	1	$6000 to reduce from 2 days to 1.
B	7	17	5	$2000 to reduce from 7 days to 6. $6000 to reduce from 6 days to 5.
C	3	20	2	$4000 to reduce from 3 days to 2.
D	1	7	1	–
E	2	8	1	$7000 to reduce from 2 days to 1.
F	5	10	2	$3000 to reduce from 5 days to 4. $4000 to reduce from 4 days to 3. $6000 to reduce from 3 days to 2.
G	6	12	3	$5000 to reduce from 6 days to 5. $8000 to reduce from 5 days to 4. $9000 to reduce from 4 days to 3.

To illustrate the difference between the data in this table and the table in Exercise 11.5, consider activity F. In Exercise 11.5, we assumed that each successive one-day reduction in activity F's duration increases F's direct cost by the same amount ($3000). In this exercise, we assume that each successive one-day reduction in F's duration is increasingly expensive ($3000 for the first one-day reduction, $4000 for the second, and $6000 for the third). In other words, we now assume a *nonlinear* relationship between an activity's duration and its direct cost. Given this new data, redo parts (a) and (b) of Exercise 11.5. (Assume the same data for the daily indirect costs and the daily penalty cost.)

Exercises 11.8–11.11 test your understanding of how to apply linear programming to project management.

* 11.8. Reconsider the project in Exercise 10.3.

(a) Formulate a linear program that can be used to analyze the project.

(b) If you have access to a software package, solve part (a)'s linear program and use the optimal solution to identify the project's shortest possible duration, the project's critical path, and a feasible starting time for each activity.

11.9. Redo Exercise 11.8, this time using the project in Exercise 10.4.

*11.10. Reconsider Exercise 11.5. In that exercise, you manually determined the time-cost trade-off graph. In this exercise, you will illustrate how to determine the time-cost trade-off graph by repeatedly solving a linear program.

    (a) Formulate a linear program whose solution will identify the minimum total direct cost and the associated activity durations if a project duration of exactly 13 days is desired.

    (b) What modifications are necessary to part (a)'s linear program if the desired project duration is exactly 12 days?

    (c) If you have access to a software package, solve part (a)'s linear program and use the optimal solution to identify the minimum total direct cost for the desired project duration. Verify that this point on the time-cost trade-off graph is the same one you obtain manually in Exercise 11.5.

11.11. Redo Exercise 11.10, this time using the project in Exercise 11.6 and using a desired project duration of 20 days in part (a) and 19 days in part (b).

12

DECISION ANALYSIS: FUNDAMENTAL TOPICS

12.1 INTRODUCTION

In most real-world decision problems the consequences of the decision that is to be made are uncertain. For example:

- When you buy an insurance policy, you are uncertain whether the hazard you are insuring against will or will not occur, and, should it occur, you are uncertain about the dollar amount of the financial loss you will sustain.

- When a corporation introduces a new product into the marketplace, it is uncertain about the market share the new product will ultimately attain.

- When a department store's buyer orders a new fashion item, she is uncertain about the total consumer demand for the item.

- When a portfolio manager invests in a particular security, she is uncertain about the annual return on investment.

- When an oil company bids for the drilling rights at a particular site, it is uncertain about the quantity of oil (if any) it will discover.

A manager's career advancement depends heavily on decisions made in scenarios such as those above. Consequently, he or she will benefit by learning a logical framework for analyzing problems in which decisions have uncertain outcomes. Such a framework is known as *decision analysis*.

Before looking into decision analysis, let us recall how we dealt with uncertainty in the context of linear programming. Consider, for example, a product mix linear program (such as the one introduced in Chapter 2 for the Orange Microcom-

536

puter Corporation). To formulate the LP's objective function, we had to specify a unit profit for each alternative product. We could not specify, for example, that the decision to produce one unit of a particular product resulted in a contribution to total profit of $20, $25, or $30. We had to specify only one of these three values. Similar comments apply to the LP's remaining data. Thus, before we formulate and solve a linear program, we must eliminate any uncertainty about the data, even if doing so requires making some "tough choices" among some estimates having nearly equal credibility.[1]

In contrast to linear programming, decision analysis does not require the elimination of all uncertainty. Instead, it deals with the uncertainty in a logical way that reduces the role of "luck" in the eventual outcome that a decision produces.

We should stress at the outset that decision analysis does *not* guarantee a good outcome. To illustrate, consider the following scenario:

> You have been invited to participate in the roll of a pair of dice. If the sum of the dice is anything but 2 or 12, you win $1000. If the sum of the dice is 2 or 12, you lose $50.

Suppose you decide to participate in the dice roll. Since the odds are in your favor, most individuals would agree that you have made a good decision. Unfortunately, this good decision does not guarantee a good outcome. Although you will probably win $1000, there is a small chance you may lose $50. If the dice roll should result in your losing $50, it would be unfair for someone to criticize you. Your decision to participate in the dice roll was a good decision, but, owing to circumstances beyond your control, you obtained a bad outcome. The distinction between a *good decision* and a *good outcome* is important. Decision analysis is a logical framework for obtaining good decisions, not for guaranteeing good outcomes. Even after a good decision has been made, luck will play a role in determining whether the decision results in a good or bad outcome. However, if one decision maker consistently uses decision analysis to make good decisions and another decision maker does not, the former will obtain good outcomes more frequently than the latter.

We can summarize this section's overview of decision analysis as follows:

> Decision analysis is a logical framework for making decisions when decisions have uncertain outcomes. Although decision analysis results in good decisions, it does not guarantee good outcomes.

12.2 A PAYOFF MATRIX APPROACH FOR A SINGLE-STAGE DECISION-ANALYSIS PROBLEM

The simplest structure for a decision-analysis problem is known as a *single-stage decision-analysis problem*. Such a problem has the following characteristics:

- A manager must choose one of several alternative decisions.

- After the manager makes her decision, she knows that one of several alternative events will occur. However, she is uncertain about which event will occur because this depends on circumstances and forces beyond her control.

---

[1] Of course, after solving the linear program, we can partially compensate for the elimination of all uncertainty by using the technique of sensitivity analysis to investigate how changes in the data affect the optimal solution.

- The precise consequences of any decision will not be known until the uncertain event occurs.

In brief, the manager must choose one of several alternative decisions *before* the occurrence of one of several alternative uncertain events determines the decision's consequences.

It is customary to refer to the alternative uncertain events as the *alternative states of Nature.* Nature is used here in a metaphoric sense to represent the entity that decides which event actually occurs.[2] In any particular scenario, Nature may or may not be the appropriate metaphor. For example, if the uncertainty is about the weather on a particular day or about how much oil is under a particular tract of land, it is appropriate to think of Nature as controlling the outcome. If the uncertainty is about the price of a stock or the market share of a product, it is inappropriate to think of Nature as controlling the outcome. Regardless of the scenario, we will continue to use the term state of Nature. The central idea is that the decision maker is an "innocent bystander" in the determination of which uncertain event actually occurs.

Table 12.1 provides some examples of a single-stage decision-analysis problem by listing the alternative decisions and the alternative states of Nature that will be observed *after* the decision is made. Observe in Table 12.1's examples that a common practice in decision analysis is to restrict the set of decisions and the set of states of Nature to a manageable size. Thus, although a new product's market share might ultimately be almost any percentage, we might assume, (in a problem to be analyzed with manual computations) that, say, only four market shares are possible or (in a problem to be analyzed with a computer software package) that only ten market shares are possible.

Let us now turn to a specific example of a single-stage decision-analysis problem—an example that we will use throughout the chapter:

Ever since a city announced it would build a new convention center at either site *A*, *B*, or *C*, land near those sites has been selling rapidly. Holly Dayin is the real estate manager of a hotel chain that wants to construct a new hotel near the convention

---

[2] Some readers might prefer to attribute the outcome to fate or a deity rather than Nature.

TABLE 12.1 Examples of a Single-Stage Decision-Analysis Problem

Alternatives for the Decision	Alternatives for the State of Nature Observed after the Decision
Whether to introduce a new product	The alternatives percentages for the product's market share (e.g., 5%, 10%, 15%, and 20%)
The quantity of a new fashion item a deparment store's buyer should order	The alternatives for the total consumer demand (e.g., 10 items, 25 items, and 50 items)
Whether to drill for oil at a particular site	The alternatives for the millions of barrels of oil underground (e.g., 0, 50, 200, 500)
The alternatives for the amount of the deductibility on an insurance policy (e.g., $0, $100, $500, and $1000)	The alternatives for the financial loss that might occur from the hazard being insured against (e.g., from $0 to $10,000 in multiples of $500)

TABLE 12.2 Financial Data for Holly's Decision-Analysis Problem; (in millions of dollars)

Site	Current Purchase Price	Present Value of Future Cash Flow If Convention Center Is Adjacent	Present Value of Future Resale Price If Convention Center Is Not Adjacent
A	20	45	10
B	30	50	20
C	25	35	20

center. Holly has identified the most suitable plot of land near each convention center site. She has given the potential hotel sites convenient labels; that is, hotel site *A* is near convention-center site *A*, and so on.

Although the city council will not select the convention-center site for at least 9 months, Holly feels she must act immediately or else the land will be sold to other buyers. To aid her analysis, Holly has compiled Table 12.2, which displays the following data for each potential hotel site:

■ The land's current purchase price.

■ The present value to the hotel chain of the future cash flow it will receive if it builds a hotel on the site and the convention center is subsequently located near the hotel.

■ The present value of the land's future resale value if the convention center is not located near the site.

Holly must now decide the site or sites at which she should purchase land.

The most common way to evaluate a single-stage decision-analysis problem such as Holly's is to display the structure of the problem in what is known as a *payoff matrix*. A payoff matrix is a rectangular array of numbers that specifies the financial outcome or "payoff" of each possible combination of decision and state of Nature. To construct the payoff matrix for her decision problem, Holly first identifies the alternative decisions and the alternative states of Nature as follows:

The Seven Alternative Decisions	The Three Alternative States of Nature
1. Buy land only at site *A*	1. Convention center at site *A*
2. Buy land only at site *B*	2. Convention center at site *B*
3. Buy land only at site *C*	3. Convention center at site *C*
4. Buy land at sites *A* and *B*	
5. Buy land at sites *A* and *C*	
6. Buy land at sites *B* and *C*	
7. Buy land at sites *A*, *B*, and *C*	

Holly then lists the alternative decisions and the alternative states of Nature in the rectangular fashion displayed in Table 12.3(a). Each row corresponds to an alternative decision and each column to an alternative state of Nature. Holly must now consider the intersection of each row and column and enter the payoff of the corresponding decision and state of Nature. To illustrate, consider the "?" displayed in Table 12.3(a) at the intersection of the fourth row and the second column. Holly must replace this "?" with the payoff if she selects the fourth decision (buy *A* and

TABLE 12.3 Payoff Matrix for Holly's Decision-Analysis Problem

Land Purchase Decisions	States of Nature for Convention Center's Site			Land Purchase Decisions	States of Nature for Convention Center's Site		
	A	*B*	*C*		*A*	*B*	*C*
A	?	?	?	*A*	25	−10	−10
B	?	?	?	*B*	−10	20	−10
C	?	?	?	*C*	−5	−5	10
A & B	?	(?)	?	*A & B*	15	10	−20
A & C	?	?	?	*A & C*	20	−15	0
B & C	(?)	?	?	*B & C*	−15	15	0
A, B, & C	?	?	?	*A, B, & C*	10	5	−10
(a) With Payoffs Missing				(b) With Payoffs Entered			

B) and subsequently observes the second state of Nature (convention center at site *B*). The computation of this payoff proceeds as follows (where a negative payoff is a cost):

$$
\begin{array}{rl}
-20 & \text{(site } A\text{'s purchase price)} \\
-30 & \text{(site } B\text{'s purchase price)} \\
+10 & \text{(value of site } A \text{ with no convention center nearby)} \\
+50 & \text{(value of site } B \text{ with convention center nearby)} \\
\hline
10 & \text{(payoff)}
\end{array}
$$

Table 12.3(b) displays Holly's payoff matrix after she has entered the payoff for each possible combination of decision and state of Nature. Before proceeding, you should verify for yourself several other entries in the payoff matrix.

Table 12.3 illustrates the following general principle:

A payoff matrix is a rectangular array of numbers in which the value in the *i*th row and *j*th column equals the payoff that results if the decision maker selects the *i*th decision and then the *j*th state of Nature occurs.

12.3 NONPROBABILISTIC DECISION-MAKING CRITERIA

Let us now consider some alternative criteria for making a decision based on Table 12.3's payoff matrix. We can divide these alternative decision-making criteria into two categories—those that do not and those that do require probabilities to be assigned to the alternative states of Nature. We refer to the former as *nonprobabilistic* and to the latter as *probabilistic decision-making criteria*. In this section we consider nonprobabilistic decision-making criteria.

The Maximax Criterion

Consider first how Holly would analyze Table 12.3's payoff matrix if she were an eternal optimist. She would optimistically assume that, if she chooses a particular decision, Nature will be "on her side" and provide her with the state of Nature that yields the maximum payoff. For example, if she chooses the fourth decision (buy *A* and *B*), she optimistically assumes that the first state of Nature (convention center at site *A*) will occur, since its payoff of 15 is higher than those of 10 and −20 for

TABLE 12.4 Applying the Maximax Criterion to Holly's Problem

Land Purchase Decisions	States of Nature for Convention Center's Site			Each Decision's Maximum Payoff	
	A	B	C		
A	25	−10	−10	25	← maximum
B	−10	20	−10	20	
C	−5	−5	10	10	
A & B	15	10	−20	15	
A & C	20	−15	0	20	
B & C	−15	15	0	15	
A, B, & C	10	5	−10	10	

the second and third states of Nature. This optimistic approach is summarized in Table 12.4, where each decision's maximum payoff is listed in the last column. If Holly truly believes that Nature will always grant her the highest payoff her decision permits, which of the seven decisions in Table 12.4 should she make? The answer is the first decision (buy *A*), the decision that corresponds to the maximum among the maximum payoffs in Table 12.4's last column. Table 12.4 illustrates the *maximax criterion,* whereby one first identifies the maximum payoff for each decision and then selects the decision that maximizes these maximum payoffs.

The major criticism of the maximax criterion is that it considers only each decision's highest payoff and ignores all other payoffs (by assuming they won't occur). This may be risky. To illustrate, consider Table 12.3's payoff matrix. Although the first decision leads to a profit of 25 (the highest possible payoff) if the first state of Nature occurs, it leads to a loss of 10 if either of the remaining states of Nature occurs. It takes an eternal optimist to believe that, when two of the three states of Nature lead to losses, the one state of Nature that yields a profit will occur. The example payoff matrix below makes this point even more dramatically.

	States of Nature		Each Decision's Maximum Payoff	
	1	2		
Decision 1	9	10	10	
Decision 2	11	−10,000	11	← maximum

A decision maker using the maximax criterion would choose the second decision, although the first decision is much less risky and almost as profitable. A decision maker using the maximax criterion, then, must be willing to bear the risk of sustaining a large loss if she is wrong in assuming that only the best will occur.

The Maximin Criterion

In contrast to the the maximax criterion's extreme optimism, the maximin criterion is based on extreme pessimism. To illustrate, consider how Holly would analyze Table 12.3's payoff matrix if she were an eternal pessimist. She would assume that, if she chooses a particular decision, Nature will be "against her" and provide her with the state of Nature that yields the minimum payoff. For example, if she chooses the fourth decision (buy *A* and *B*), then the third state of Nature (convention center at *C*) will occur, since its payoff of −20 is lower than those of 15 and 10 for the first and second states of Nature. This pessimistic assumption is summarized in Table 12.5, where each decision's minimum payoff is listed in the last

TABLE 12.5 Applying the Maximin Criterion to Holly's Problem

Land Purchase Decisions	States of Nature for Convention Center's Site			Each Decision's Minimum Payoff
	A	B	C	
A	25	-10	-10	-10
B	-10	20	-10	-10
C	-5	-5	10	-5 $\leftarrow$ maximum
A & B	15	10	-20	-20
A & C	20	-15	0	-15
B & C	-15	15	0	-15
A, B, & C	10	5	-10	-10

column. If Holly truly believes that Nature will always provide the minimum payoff, which of the seven decisions in Table 12.5 should she make? The answer is the third decision (buy C), which corresponds to the maximum among the minimum payoffs in Table 12.5's last column. Thus, as its name suggests, the maximin criterion first identifies the minimum payoff for each decision and then selects the decision that maximizes these minimum payoffs.

The major criticism of the maximin criterion is that it considers only each decision's minimum payoff and ignores all other payoffs (by assuming they won't occur). This may be overly cautious. To illustrate this point in a dramatic fashion, consider the following payoff matrix:

	States of Nature		Each Decision's Minimum Payoff
	1	2	
Decision 1	9	10,000	9
Decision 2	11	10	10 $\leftarrow$ maximum

A decision maker using the maximin criterion would choose the second decision, although the first decision is only slightly less profitable if the first state of Nature occurs but significantly more profitable if the second state of Nature occurs. A decision maker using the maximin criterion, then, might forego an opportunity for a large gain.

The Minimax Regret Criterion

Suppose now that Holly is concerned about how the decision she makes might be viewed in the future after the state of Nature is known with certainty. Someone with "20-20 hindsight" might unfairly criticize her for not making the "obvious" decision.

If Holly is concerned about an evaluation of her decision based on what might have been, the so-called *minimax regret criterion* might appeal to her. To employ this criterion, Holly must transform Table 12.3's payoff matrix into a *regret matrix*[3] by replacing every payoff in a column of the payoff matrix with the difference obtained by subtracting the payoff from the column's maximum payoff. Table 12.6 displays this transformation. Observe that the regret matrix always has nonnegative entries, and each column has an entry equal to 0, corresponding to the column's maximum payoff.[4] Let us use the notation r_{ij} to denote the entry in the

---

[3] The regret matrix is sometimes called the *opportunity loss matrix* or the *opportunity cost matrix*.

[4] If there is a tie for a column's maximum payoff, the column will have more than one entry equal to 0.

TABLE 12.6 Computing the Regret Matrix for Holly's Problem

Land Purchase Decisions	States of Nature for Convention Center's Site		
	A	B	C
A	$25 - (25) = 0$	$20 - (-10) = 30$	$10 - (-10) = 20$
B	$25 - (-10) = 35$	$20 - (20) = 0$	$10 - (-10) = 20$
C	$25 - (-5) = 30$	$20 - (-5) = 25$	$10 - (10) = 0$
$A \& B$	$25 - (15) = 10$	$20 - (10) = 10$	$10 - (-20) = 30$
$A \& C$	$25 - (20) = 5$	$20 - (-15) = 35$	$10 - (0) = 10$
$B \& C$	$25 - (-15) = 40$	$20 - (15) = 5$	$10 - (0) = 10$
$A, B, \&$	$25 - (10) = 15$	$20 - (5) = 15$	$10 - (-10) = 20$

regret matrix's ith row and jth column. From Table 12.6, we see that r_{ij} is the difference obtained by subtracting the payoff obtained if the ith decision is made and the jth state of Nature occurs from the maximum possible payoff if the jth state of Nature occurs, that is, from the payoff corresponding to the decision Holly will regret not making once she learns the jth state of Nature has occurred. Thus, the higher r_{ij} is, the more Holly will regret making the ith decision if the jth state of Nature occurs, and the more open she will be to criticism by someone evaluating her on the basis of what might have been.

Once the transformation of the payoff matrix into the regret matrix is complete, the minimax regret criterion is used in the same extremely pessimistic fashion as the maximin criterion. Holly assumes that, after she makes a decision, Nature will be against her and provide the state of Nature that yields the maximum regret. For example, if she chooses the third decision (buy C), then the first state of Nature (convention center at A) will occur because its regret of 30 in Table 12.6's third row is higher than those of 25 and 0 for the second and third states of Nature. This pessimistic approach is summarized in Table 12.7, where each decision's maximum regret is listed in the last column. If Holly truly believes Nature will oppose her by providing the maximum regret, she should make the seventh decision, the decision that has the minimum among the maximum regrets. Thus, as its name suggests, the minimax criterion first identifies the maximum regret for each decision and then selects the decision that minimizes these maximum regrets. Observe that, although the maximin criterion and the minimax regret criterion are both pessimistic criteria, they select different decisions (the third decision for the maximin criterion and the seventh decision for the minimax regret criterion).

TABLE 12.7 Applying the Minimax Regret Criterion to Holly's Problem

Land Purchase Decisions	States of Nature for Convention Center's Site			Each Decision's Maximum Regret
	A	B	C	
A	$25 - (25) = 0$	$20 - (-10) = 30$	$10 - (-10) = 20$	30
B	$25 - (-10) = 35$	$20 - (20) = 0$	$10 - (-10) = 20$	35
C	$25 - (-5) = 30$	$20 - (-5) = 25$	$10 - (10) = 0$	30
$A \& B$	$25 - (15) = 10$	$20 - (10) = 10$	$10 - (-20) = 30$	30
$A \& C$	$25 - (20) = 5$	$20 - (-15) = 35$	$10 - (0) = 10$	35
$B \& C$	$25 - (-15) = 40$	$20 - (15) = 5$	$10 - (0) = 10$	40
$A, B, \& C$	$25 - (10) = 15$	$20 - (5) = 15$	$10 - (-10) = 20$	20 ← minimum

The minimax regret criterion can be criticized for being too conservative. However, there is a more subtle reason to criticize it. To illustrate, consider the two payoff matrices below:

	States of Nature	
	1	2
Decision 1	8	0
Decision 2	2	4

	States of Nature	
	1	2
Decision 1	8	0
Decision 2	2	4
Decision 3	1	7

Observe that the right-hand payoff matrix differs in that a third decision has been added; the payoffs for the first and second decisions are identical in both matrices. You should verify for yourself that the above payoff matrices yield the following two regret matrices:

	States of Nature	
	1	2
Decision 1	0	4
Decision 2	6	0

	States of Nature	
	1	2
Decision 1	0	7
Decision 2	6	3
Decision 3	7	0

Applying the minimax regret criterion, we obtain the following analysis:

	States of Nature		Each Decision's Maximum Regret
	1	2	
Decision 1	0	4	4 ← minimum
Decision 2	6	0	6

	States of Nature		Each Decision's Maximum Regret
	1	2	
Decision 1	0	7	7
Decision 2	6	3	6 ← minimum
Decision 3	7	0	7

Thus, when the third decision is not an alternative, the first decision is chosen over the second decision; however, when the third decision is an alternative, the second decision is chosen over the first (and third) decision. It is bothersome that the presence or absence of an irrelevant decision (i.e., a decision that is not chosen) affects whether the decision maker selects the first or second decision. After all, how much faith would you have in someone who prefers a hamburger over a hot dog but, when given the additional option of a fish sandwich, prefers a hot dog? In the terminology of decision analysis, the minimax regret criterion is *incoherent*.

We can summarize this section as follows:

A Summary of Three Nonprobabilistic Decision-Making Criteria

- The maximax criterion is an optimistic criterion that first identifies each decision's maximum possible payoff and then selects the decision that maximizes these maximum payoffs.

- The maximin criterion is a pessimistic criterion that first identifies each decision's minimum possible payoff and then selects the decision that maximizes these minimum payoffs.

- The minimax regret criterion is a pessimistic criterion that first transforms the payoff matrix into a regret matrix, then identifies each decision's maximum regret, and finally selects the decision that minimizes these maximum regrets.

- For each of these nonprobabilistic decision-making criteria, it is possible to construct examples that demonstrate a flaw in the criterion.

Since all three nonprobabilistic decision-making criteria are flawed, let us now turn our attention to probabilistic decision-making criteria—criteria which require the assignment of probabilities to the alternative states of Nature.

12.4 PROBABILISTIC DECISION-MAKING CRITERIA

In this section we focus on decision-making criteria that require probabilities to be assigned to the alternative states of Nature. We discuss first how to assign these probabilities and then how to incorporate them into the decision-making process.

Assessing Probabilities

The probability of an event is a measure of how likely it is that the event will occur. For example, if an event has a probability of $\frac{1}{2}$, it is equally likely to occur as not occur; if it has a probability of $\frac{3}{4}$, it is three times likely to occur as not occur; if it has a probability of $\frac{1}{5}$, it is one-fourth as likely to occur as not occur. In general, if an event has probability p; it is $p/(1-p)$ times as likely to occur as not occur. Assigning a probability to a particular event is known as *assessing the event's probability*.

There are two types of probabilities: objective and subjective. An *objective probability* is based on historical data, statistical experimentation, and/or scientific analysis. For example, the following are objective probabilities:

- The probability that a coin flip will result in heads.
- The probability that the sum of two dice will equal 7.
- The probability that a fast-food restaurant will sell a specified number of hamburgers between 5:00 and 9:00 on a Saturday night.
- The probability that a television set of a particular brand will fail to operate at least once during its warranty period.
- The probability that a weather forecaster's prediction of rain will be correct.

In each of these examples, a combination of historical data, statistical experimentation, and scientific analysis enables a decision maker to assess a probability with a reasonable degree of confidence.

In contrast, a *subjective probability* is based on personal belief or experience. The following are subjective probabilities:

- The probability in Holly's decision problem that the city council will select site A for the convention center.
- The probability that a new business venture will be successful.
- The probability that a business competitor will react in a certain way.
- The probability the political environment in a country will be stable.

In each of these examples, the decision maker must assess a probability based on her personal beliefs or experiences (although some objective evidence may exist that provides a reference point from which she subjectively makes an upward or downward adjustment).

Extensive psychological research has shown that great care must be exercised when assessing a subjective probability. As a consequence, the following is a method for assessing a probability that is popular with many consultants and computer software packages. Imagine that we must elicit from Holly her assessment of the subjective probability that the city council will select site A for the convention center. We could simply ask Holly to think about it carefully and then give us her probability assessment. However, we can obtain a more reliable assessment by using a device known as a *probability wheel*. As illustrated by the examples displayed in Figure 12.1, a probability wheel consists of a circle divided into two sectors, one shaded and one unshaded. Attached to the circle's center is a spinner, which, after being set in motion, comes to a stop with its point lying in either the shaded or unshaded sector.

To illustrate the use of a probability wheel, imagine we have the following dialogue with Holly:

Us: Holly, suppose we offer you the opportunity to participate in one of the following two bets:

Bet #1	Bet #2
If the city council selects site A for the convention center, you win a new car; otherwise, you win nothing.	If the spinner in Figure 12.1(a)'s probability wheel is set in motion and then stops in the shaded sector, you win a new car; otherwise, you win nothing.

In which bet would you rather participate?

Holly: That's easy! My chance of winning a new car is clearly better with second bet. I'll take my chances with the probability wheel.

We now know that Holly's assessment of the probability that the city council will select site A is less than 0.75, the fraction of the circle that is shaded in Figure 12.1(a). Therefore, we substitute a probability wheel in which the shaded sector is a decreased fraction of the total area.

Us: Holly, suppose you have the same choice of bets as before, except that now we

Figure 12.1 Examples of a probability wheel

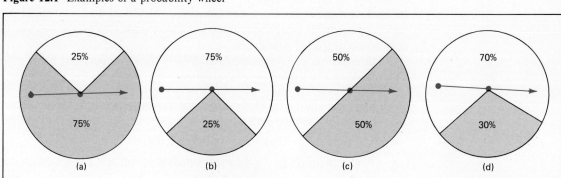

will use Figure 12.1(b)'s probability wheel. In which bet would you now rather participate?

Holly: That's easy, too! Now the first bet maximizes my chance of winning the car. I'd rather take my chances that the city council will select site *A*.

We now know that Holly's assessment of the probability that the city council will select site *A* is greater than 0.25, the fraction of the circle that is shaded in Figure 12.1(b). Therefore, we substitute a probability wheel in which the shaded sector's area is an increased fraction of the total area.

Us: Holly, suppose you have the same choice of bets as before, except that now we will use Figure 12.1(c)'s probability wheel. In which bet would you now rather participate?

Holly: Now I'd switch back to the second bet; that is, I'd take my chances with the probability wheel.

We now know that Holly's assessment of the probability that the city council will select site *A* is less than 0.50, the fraction of the circle that is shaded in Figure 12.1(c).

By now the process should be clear. We continue to adjust the area of the probability wheel's shaded sector (increasing it when Holly selects Bet #1 and decreasing it when Holly selects Bet #2) until we reach a point where Holly says, "That's too close to call! I'm indifferent!" For example, if this occurred when we presented Holly with Figure 12.1(d)'s probability wheel, we would conclude that Holly assesses the probability the city council will select site *A* as 0.3. Research has shown that a subjective probability assessment obtained with the aid of a probability wheel (or a similar device) is much more accurate than an assessment obtained as the response to the direct question "What is your estimate of the probability that ____ will occur?"

Unfortunately, space constraints preclude a more detailed discussion of subjective probability assessment. The important lesson here is that a decision maker should exercise great care when assessing subjective probabilities. As we will soon see, these probabilities are the foundation for all subsequent analysis. Consequently, our analysis is only as reliable as our probability assessments.

The Expected-Monetary-Value Criterion

The decision-making criterion used most often in practice is known as the *expected-monetary-value (EMV) criterion*. The EMV criterion selects the decision whose payoff has the largest expected value (i.e., mean value). To illustrate, suppose Holly has assessed the following probabilities:

State of Nature	Holly's Probability Assessment
City council will select site *A*	0.3
City council will select site *B*	0.5
City council will select site *C*	0.2

Of course, since exactly one of these alternatives must occur, the probabilities add to 1.

Table 12.8 displays Holly's payoff matrix with the probabilities of the alternative states of Nature written at the bottom of each column. We can compute each decision's EMV (i.e., expected payoff value) by summing the products obtained by

TABLE 12.8 Holly's Payoff Matrix
with Probabilities
for the States of Nature

Land Purchase Decisions	States of Nature for Convention Center's Site		
	A	*B*	*C*
A	25	−10	−10
B	−10	20	−10
C	−5	−5	10
A & B	15	10	−20
A & C	20	−15	0
B & C	−15	15	0
A, B, & C	10	5	−10
	0.3	0.5	0.2

multiplying each state of Nature's payoff value by the corresponding probability the state of Nature will occur. For example, if we use EMV_7 to denote the EMV of the seventh decision in Table 12.8 (buy *A*, *B*, and *C*), we compute EMV_7 as follows:

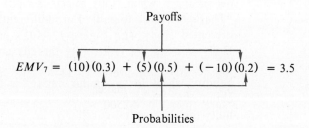

Payoffs

$$EMV_7 = (10)(0.3) + (5)(0.5) + (-10)(0.2) = 3.5$$

Probabilities

It is important to understand what EMV_7 represents. It does *not* represent a payoff Holly will ever receive. As we see in the seventh row of the payoff matrix, the only payoffs for the seventh decision are 10, 5, and −10. What EMV_7 does represent is the average payoff Holly would receive if she were to encounter the identical decision problem a very large number of times (e.g., 1000 times) and were to make the seventh decision in every case. Given Table 12.8's probabilities for the alternative states of Nature, her payoff would be 10 in 30% of the cases, 5 in 50% of the cases, and −10 in 20% of the cases, thereby resulting in an average payoff of $EMV_7 = 3.5$.

Table 12.9 displays the computation of the EMVs for all seven decisions. We have already verified $EMV_7 = 3.5$. Before proceeding, you should verify the computations of the remaining six EMVs. Given the EMVs displayed in Table 12.9, the EMV criterion selects the fourth decision, the decision with the highest EMV. Summarizing:

To employ the EMV criterion, we proceed as follows:

1. We use a probability wheel to assess the probability of each alternative state of Nature (making sure that these probabilities sum to 1).

2. For each decision, we compute its EMV by summing the products obtained by multiplying the payoff for each state of Nature by its associated probability.

3. We select the decision with the highest EMV.

TABLE 12.9 Applying the EMV Criterion to Holly's Decision Problem

Land Purchase Decisions	States of Nature for Convention Center's Site			Each Decision's EMV
	A	B	C	
A	25	-10	-10	$EMV_1 = \quad (25)(0.3) + (-10)(0.5) + (-10)(0.2) = \quad 0.5$
B	-10	20	-10	$EMV_2 = (-10)(0.3) + \quad (20)(0.5) + (-10)(0.2) = \quad 5.0$
C	-5	-5	10	$EMV_3 = \quad (-5)(0.3) + \quad (-5)(0.5) + \quad (10)(0.2) = -2.0$
A & B	15	10	-20	$EMV_4 = \quad (15)(0.3) + \quad (10)(0.5) + (-20)(0.2) = \quad 5.5 \leftarrow$ maximum
A & C	20	-15	0	$EMV_5 = \quad (20)(0.3) + (-15)(0.5) + \quad (0)(0.2) = -1.5$
B & C	-15	15	0	$EMV_6 = (-15)(0.3) + \quad (15)(0.5) + \quad (0)(0.2) = \quad 3.0$
A, B, & C	10	5	-10	$EMV_7 = \quad (10)(0.3) + \quad (5)(0.5) + (-10)(0.2) = \quad 3.5$
	0.3	0.5	0.2	

Criticism of the EMV Criterion

Despite the popularity of the EMV criterion, we can easily construct examples where the decision it selects is not the most appealing one. Table 12.10 displays three such examples. Let us consider each of these in turn.

Given Table 12.10(a)'s payoff matrix, the EMV criterion selects decision 1. This is clearly the best decision if the decision maker will encounter the identical decision problem a very large number of times and, therefore, can afford to "play the averages." However, suppose the decision problem will be encountered only once. A decision maker who is averse to taking risks would prefer decision 2's "sure thing" of $2500 to decision 1's uncertainty. This example illustrates the EMV criterions failure to take into account the decision maker's attitude toward risk, especially when the decision is a one-time decision.

Given Table 12.10(b)'s payoff matrix, the EMV criterion selects decision 1. However, a decision maker unable or unwilling to absorb a large financial loss would prefer decision 2. This example illustrates that the EMV criterion's failure to take into account the decision maker's current financial status, which in turn affects the decision maker's willingness to expose herself to the possibility of a large loss.

Given Table 12.10(c)'s payoff matrix, the EMV criterion selects decision 1. This is clearly the best decision if the decision maker will encounter the identical decision problem a very large number of times and is concerned only about maximizing the average payoff. However, a decision maker who desires a stable cash flow for planning purposes would prefer decision 2, since its payoffs are approximately equal regardless of the state of Nature. This example illustrates the EMV's failure to take into account the variance among a decision's potential payoffs.

We can summarize this subsection as follows:

- The EMV criterion is most appropriate when the decision maker will encounter the identical decision problem a very large number of times and, therefore, can afford to play the averages (i.e., can survive large losses or widely varying payoffs as long as the average payoff is maximized).

- However, the EMV criterion is inappropriate when the decision maker will encounter the decision problem only once or a small number of times, when a large loss would be catastrophic, or when the variance of the potential payoffs is important.

549

TABLE 12.10 Examples Where the EMV Criterion
May Be Inappropriate

	States of Nature		
	1	2	
Decision 1	11,000	-1000	$EMV_1 = 5000 \leftarrow$ maximum
Decision 2	2500	2500	$EMV_2 = 2500$
	0.5	0.5	

(a)

	States of Nature		
	1	2	
Decision 1	10,000	$-10,000$	$EMV_1 = 9800 \leftarrow$ maximum
Decision 2	5000	0	$EMV_2 = 4950$
	0.99	0.01	

(b)

	States of Nature		
	1	2	
Decision 1	5000	0	$EMV_1 = 2500 \leftarrow$ maximum
Decision 2	2100	1900	$EMV_2 = 2000$

(c)

In Chapter 13, we will learn a decision-making criterion that is appropriate in situations when the EMV criterion is not. Until then, we will continue to employ the EMV criterion, recognizing that it may not always be appropriate.

The Expected Regret Criterion

The *expected regret criterion* proceeds in a manner identical to the EMV criterion, except that computations are based on the regret matrix instead of the payoff matrix. Table 12.11 summarizes the computation of each decision's expected regret using Table 12.6's regret matrix in place of Table 12.8's payoff matrix. Observe in Table 12.11 that the decision with the *minimum* expected regret is the fourth decision, the same decision in Table 12.9 that had the *maximum* EMV. Rather than being a coincidence, this is an example of the following general principle (whose proof is beyond the scope of this text):

> The criterion of minimizing expected regret and the criterion of maximizing expected monetary value *always* select the identical decision.

Although the two criteria are equivalent, the EMV criterion is used more frequently, probably because the expected-regret criterion requires the additional step of transforming the payoff matrix into the regret matrix. Hence, in subsequent sections, we will focus our attention on the EMV criterion (although the concept of expected regret will reappear briefly in Section 12.6).

TABLE 12.11 Applying the Expected-Regret Criterion to Holly's Decision Problem

Land Purchase Decisions	States of Nature for Convention Center's Site			Each Decision's Expected Regret
	A	B	C	
A	0	30	20	(0)(0.3) + (30)(0.5) + (20)(0.2) = 19.0
B	35	0	20	(35)(0.3) + (0)(0.5) + (20)(0.2) = 14.5
C	30	25	0	(30)(0.3) + (25)(0.5) + (0)(0.2) = 21.5
A & B	10	10	30	(10)(0.3) + (10)(0.5) + (30)(0.2) = 14.0 ← minimum
A & C	5	35	10	(5)(0.3) + (35)(0.5) + (10)(0.2) = 21.0
B & C	40	5	10	(40)(0.3) + (5)(0.5) + (10)(0.2) = 16.5
A, B, & C	15	15	20	(15)(0.3) + (15)(0.5) + (20)(0.2) = 16.0
	0.3	0.5	0.2	

12.5 A DECISION TREE FOR A SINGLE-STAGE DECISION-ANALYSIS PROBLEM

There is an alternative to using a payoff matrix to analyze a single-stage decision analysis problem. The alternative is known as a *decision tree*. Instead of a tabular representation of the decision problem, a decision tree provides a pictorial representation.

"Growing" a Decision Tree

Figure 12.2 displays the decision-tree representation of Holly's problem. It illustrates the following general characteristics of a decision tree used to represent a single-stage decision-analysis problem:[5]

- A decision tree is so named because a counter-clockwise rotation of 90 degrees produces a structure that resembles a tree. It is customary to orient the tree in a left-to-right fashion.

- A decision tree consists of *nodes* (either circles or squares) interconnected by *branches* (lines).

- A decision is represented by a square node from which one branch emanates for each alternative decision. For example, in Figure 12.2, the only square node has seven branches emanating from it, one for each of Holly's seven alternative decisions. Hereafter, we refer to a square node as a *decision node*. As illustrated in Figure 12.2, it is customary to label each branch emanating from a decision node with a brief description of the decision it represents. To facilitate identification, it is also customary to label the decision node itself with a Roman numeral. In Figure 12.2, the decision node has the label *I*.

- The first node in a decision tree (i.e., the node at the extreme left) is known as the decision tree's *root*. In Figure 12.2's decision tree, the root is decision node *I*.

- An uncertain event is represented by a circular node from which one branch emanates for each alternative state of Nature. For example, in Figure 12.2, three branches emanate from each circular node, one for each alternative convention center site. Hereafter, we refer to each circular node as a *chance*

---

[5] In Section 12.9 we will learn how a decision tree can represent more general decision-analysis problems.

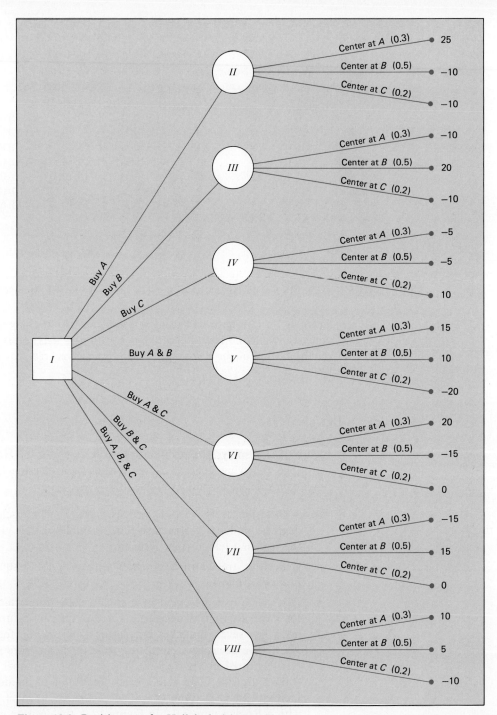

Figure 12.2 Decision tree for Holly's decision problem

node.[6] As illustrated in the figure, it is customary to label each branch
emanating from a chance node not only with a brief description of the state of
Nature it represents but also with the probability that the state of Nature will
occur. To facilitate identification, it is also customary to label each chance
node with a Roman numeral. In Figure 12.2, the chance nodes have the
labels *II* through *VIII*.

---

[6] A chance node is sometimes called an *event node*.

- At the end of the branches at the decision tree's extreme right are small black dots called *leaves*. Each leaf represents one of the possible ways the decision problem can terminate. Consequently, we label each leaf with the payoff received for the particular form of termination. For example, in Figure 12.2, the lowermost leaf corresponds to Holly's making the seventh decision and subsequently observing the third state of Nature. Consequently, we label the lowermost leaf with the payoff of -10, the payoff previously computed and recorded in the lower-right corner of Table 12.8's payoff matrix. Before proceeding, you should convince yourself that the remaining twenty leaves in Figure 12.2 correspond to the remaining twenty payoffs in Table 12.8's payoff matrix.

- We refer to the construction of a decision tree as *growing a decision tree*. When growing a decision tree, it is important that the tree properly represent the chronology of the decision-making process. In particular, if a decision among alternatives D_1, D_2, and D_3 must be made *before* the occurrence of an uncertain event with alternative states of Nature S_1 and S_2, then a portion of the tree looks like

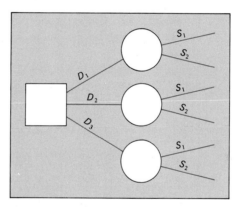

Conversely, if the uncertain event will occur before the decision must be made, a portion of the tree looks like

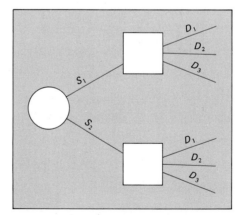

When the decision tree has been grown, it provides a representation of the decision problem that most managers find more appealing than the tabular representation provided by the payoff matrix. As we will now see, the usefulness of a decision tree extends beyond its ability to provide a pictorial representation. It is possible to use a decision tree to identify the optimal decision under the EMV criterion (or any other criterion).

"Pruning" a Decision Tree

The process of identifying the optimal decision for each of decision tree's decision nodes is known as *pruning the decision tree*.[7] Throughout this subsection, we will assume that the decision-making criterion is the EMV criterion. The end-of-chapter exercises will demonstrate that any criterion discussed in Sections 12.3 and 12.4 can be used.

To explain the pruning process, it will be convenient to mix metaphors. In particular, let us imagine that the decision maker is located at the tree's root and will travel along a sequence of branches until finally reaching a leaf, whereupon she will receive the indicated payoff. Which leaf is reached is only partially under the decision maker's control. More specifically, when located at a decision node, the decision maker can select which branch to travel on next; however, when located at a chance node, the branch on which she must next travel is dictated by Nature (i.e., by circumstances or persons over which the decision maker has no control).

The pruning process differs depending on whether we are pruning at a chance node or a decision node. To illustrate the former, consider the portion of Figure 12.2's tree to the immediate right of chance node *VIII*. This portion is displayed in Figure 12.3(a). Chance node VIII represents the point in the decision-making process just after Holly has made the seventh decision and just before the city council makes its uncertain site selection for the convention center. Since Holly has no control over which branch she will follow out of a chance node, the pruning process does not remove any branches emanating from a chance node. Instead, it simply computes the EMV of the uncertain event and writes this value within (or near) the circle representing the event. The computation of the EMV for chance node

---

[7] Some instructors, textbooks, and computer packages find this extension of the tree metaphor a bit much and, consequently, refer to pruning the decision tree as *folding back* or *rolling back* the decision tree.

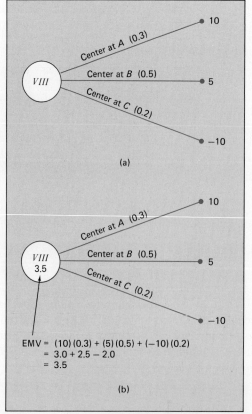

Figure 12.3 Pruning chance node *VIII*

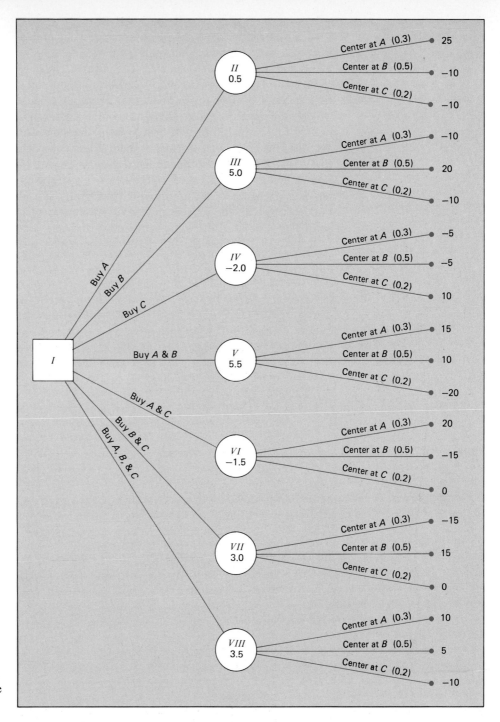

Figure 12.4 Decision tree after pruning of all chance nodes

VIII in Figure 12.3(a) proceeds as follows:

$$(\text{EMV for chance node } VIII) = (10)(0.3) + (5)(0.5) + (-10)(0.2) = 3.5$$

This portion of the decision tree now appears as displayed in Figure 12.3(b).[8] Proceeding in a similar fashion for the remaining six chance nodes results in the decision tree displayed in Figure 12.4.

555

[8] If, for example, we were using the maximin decision-making criterion instead of the EMV criterion, the number written within chance node *VIII* would be −10, the number obtained by ignoring the probabilities and simply identifying the minimum possible payoff.

Now that we understand how the pruning process treats a chance node, we can learn what happens when it encounters a decision node. Let us consider Figure 12.2's only decision node, node *I*. The portion of the decision tree to its immediate right is displayed in Figure 12.5. For pruning purposes, we pretend that this is all that exists, even though we know that branches emanate from the chance node to which each decision leads. Holly has complete control over the chance node in Figure 12.5 to which she will travel from decision node *I*. By making the first decision, she can travel to chance node *II* and subsequently receive a payoff whose EMV is 0.5, by making the second decision, she can travel to chance node *III* and subsequently receive a payoff whose EMV is 5.0; and so on. Given the EMVs written within chance nodes *II* through *VIII*, Holly should select the fourth decision, the decision with the maximum EMV. As illustrated in Figure 12.6, we write the optimal decision's EMV within (or near) decision node *I*. Figure 12.6 also illustrates that, to indicate the inferiority of the remaining six decisions, we place two

Figure 12.5 Pruning decision node *I*

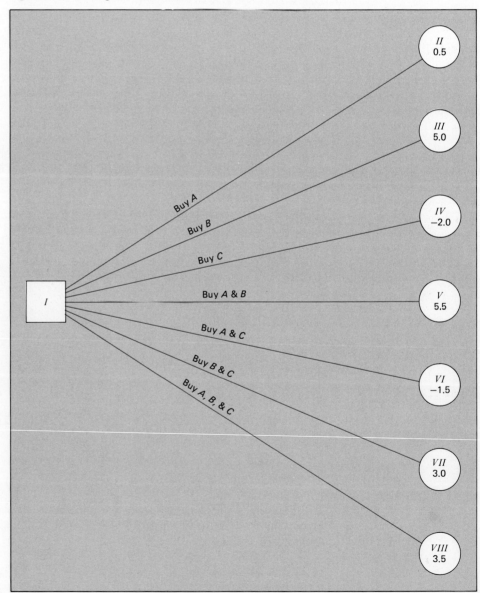

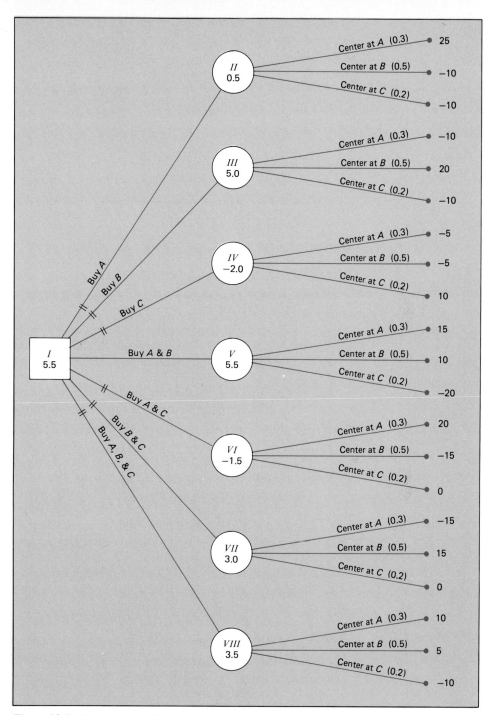

Figure 12.6 Decision tree after pruning of decision node *I*

vertical bars (‖) across each of the branches representing these suboptimal decisions, thereby signifying that we have pruned (i.e., removed) these branches from the tree.

It is helpful to imagine that when a branch is pruned, it falls off, thereby taking with it nodes and branches subsequently connected to it. After the removal of the pruned branches, the remaining portion of the decision tree appears as in Figure 12.7. This remaining portion is a pictorial representation of Holly's optimal

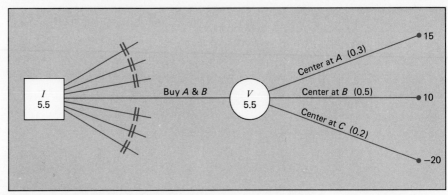

Figure 12.7 Decision tree after removal of pruned branches

strategy—namely, that of making the fourth decision and then waiting for Nature to send her to one of the three leaves remaining in the pruned tree, where she will receive the indicated payoff. Observe that this is the same optimal strategy identified previously using the payoff-matrix approach illustrated in Table 12.9.

To summarize:

- A decision tree provides a pictorial representation of a decision problem. We grow the decision tree in chronological order from left to right. We represent each decision by a square decision node, from which one branch emanates for each alternative decision. We represent each uncertain event by a circular chance node, from which one branch emanates for each alternative state of Nature. The process of constructing a decision tree from the verbal description of the decision problem is known as growing the decision tree.

- The process of using the decision tree to identify the optimal strategy is known as pruning the decision tree. We start pruning at the leaves and work in reverse chronological order (i.e., right to left) toward the root. When we encounter a chance node, we write within the circle the computed EMV, which is the sum of the products we obtain by multiplying the probabilities written along the branches emanating from the node by the corresponding payoffs at the branches' ends. When we encounter a decision node, we write within the square the EMV corresponding to the maximum of the EMVs led to by the branches emanating from the decision node; furthermore, we prune the branches corresponding to suboptimal decisions, signifying their removal from the tree by drawing || across the branches.

We have now learned two approaches for analyzing a single-stage decision analysis problem: a tabular approach employing a payoff matrix and a pictorial approach employing a decision tree. Although the two approaches are equivalent, practitioners and software packages prefer the decision-tree approach unless the decisions and states of Nature are so numerous that the resulting decision tree would be confusingly "bushy"; in that case the compact tabular representation provided by the payoff matrix approach is preferable.

12.6 THE EXPECTED VALUE OF PERFECT INFORMATION

In many decision problems, a manager is given an opportunity to acquire additional information that would permit more accurate assessments of the probabilities for the alternative states of Nature. For example:

- A corporation considering the introduction of a new product on a national level might first test market the product on a regional level.
- An oil company considering bidding for the rights to drill at a particular site might first conduct a geological survey of the site.
- A bank considering whether to grant a loan might first supplement its own application forms with a report on the applicant from a credit agency.
- A contractor planning how fast to proceed with work on a particular outdoor job might first acquire a long-range weather forecast.

In these examples, the decision on whether to acquire the additional information is based on a comparison of the information's acquisition cost versus the increased payoff resulting from being able to make a better decision.

In this section we will learn how a decision maker using the EMV criterion can place a value on an ideal type of information—information that allows a *perfect prediction* (i.e., 100% accurate) of the state of Nature. Such information is called *perfect information,* and the value of perfect information to a decision maker using the EMV criterion is known as the *expected value of perfect information (EVPI).* Of course, perfect information is rarely available. However, we must first learn how to compute the EVPI before we can learn how to compute the expected value of imperfect information—that is, of information that is less than 100% accurate.

To illustrate how to compute the EVPI, we will use Holly's decision-analysis problem. The sequence of events here is as follows:

1. First, Holly decides where to buy land.
2. Then, the city council decides where to build the convention center.

Holly's uncertainty about where to buy land stems from her uncertainty about the location of the convention center (i.e., about the state of Nature that will occur *after* she makes her decision). Let us make the unrealistic assumption that Holly has the opportunity to hire a consultant named Claire Voyant, who can provide a perfect prediction of the location of the convention center *before* Holly has to decide where to buy land. The sequence of events would then proceed as follows:

1. Claire Voyant provides Holly with a prediction guaranteed to be 100% accurate of where the city council will decide to locate the convention center.
2. Using Claire's prediction, Holly decides where to buy land.
3. The city council decides to locate the convention center at the site predicted by Claire.

The question we wish to answer is: "What is the largest fee Holly should be willing to pay for the services of Claire Voyant?" The answer to this question is the EVPI.

Before we compute the EVPI, it is important to understand the following:

- Holly must decide whether to hire Claire *before* knowing what Claire's prediction will be; that is, Holly knows only that, whatever prediction Claire makes, it will be 100% accurate.
- Claire does not control the city council's decision on where to locate the convention center. She only has the power to see into the future and, therefore, to predict what the city council's decision will be.

Computing the EVPI

To compute the EVPI, let us again refer to Table 12.8 and observe that, in terms of Holly's subjective probablity assessments:

- There is a 30% chance that Claire will predict that the first state of Nature will occur. In this case, we look at the values in the payoff matrix's first column and see that Holly maximizes her payoff by making the first decision, thereby obtaining a payoff of 25.

- There is a 50% chance that Claire will predict that the second state of Nature will occur. In this case, we look at the second column and see that Holly maximizes her payoff by making the second decision, thereby obtaining a payoff of 20.

- There is a 20% chance that Claire will predict that the third state of Nature will occur. In this case, we look at the third column indicates and see that Holly maximizes her payoff by making the third decision, thereby obtaining a payoff of 10.

Table 12.12 summarizes these observations by encircling the maximum payoff corresponding to each state of Nature—that is, the maximum payoff in each column. Multiplying each encircled value by the probability of the corresponding state of Nature and then summing the resulting products, we obtain

$$\begin{pmatrix} \text{maximum EMV attainable} \\ \text{with perfect information} \end{pmatrix} = (25)(0.3) + (20)(0.5) + (10)(0.2) = 19.5$$

In Section 12.4, we used Table 12.9 to compute the maximum EMV attainable with no additional information as

$$\begin{pmatrix} \text{maximum EMV attainable} \\ \text{with no additional information} \end{pmatrix} = 5.5$$

The expected value of perfect information or EVPI is the amount by which the maximum EMV attainable with perfect information exceeds the maximum EMV attainable with no additional information; that is,

$$\begin{aligned} \text{EVPI} &= \begin{pmatrix} \text{maximum EMV attainable} \\ \text{with perfect information} \end{pmatrix} - \begin{pmatrix} \text{maximum EMV attainable} \\ \text{with no additional information} \end{pmatrix} \\ &= \qquad\quad 19.5 \qquad\qquad - \qquad\qquad 5.5 \\ &= \qquad\quad 14 \end{aligned}$$

The value of 14 represents the maximum fee Holly should be willing to pay for Claire Voyant's services. If Claire charges more than 14, she is overpriced in the sense that the increase in EMV enabled by Claire's perfect information is less than the cost of the perfect information.

The Relationship of the EVPI to the Expected Value of Imperfect Information

Is the EVPI useful when the additional information that can be acquired is imperfect (i.e., less than 100% accurate). The answer is, "Only if the cost of the additional information exceeds the EVPI." By determining that EVPI = 14, Holly knows she should never pay more than 14 for imperfect information, since imper-

TABLE 12.12 Computing the Maximum EMV Attainable
With Perfect Information

Land Purchase Decisions	States of Nature for Convention Center's Site		
	A	B	C
A	25	−10	−10
B	−10	20	−10
C	−5	−5	10
A & B	15	10	−20
A & C	20	−15	0
B & C	−15	15	0
A, B, & C	10	5	−10
	0.3	0.5	0.2

$$\binom{\text{maximum EMV attainable}}{\text{with perfect information}} = (25)(0.3) + (20)(0.5) + (10)(0.2) = 19.5$$

fect information can never be worth more than perfect information. However, acquiring imperfect information at a cost of, say, 9 may or may not be worthwhile. To decide whether it is, we need to know the value of the imperfect information. In Sections 13.2–13.4, we will learn how to compute the expected value of imperfect information.

Computing the EVPI Using a Decision-Tree Approach

We have seen how to compute the EVPI using a tabular approach based on the payoff matrix. We can also compute the EVPI using a pictorial approach based on a decision tree.

Figure 12.8(a) is a copy of Figure 12.6's pruned decision tree, which we used in Section 12.5 to compute the maximum EMV attainable without perfect information. Since the decision without perfect information is made *before* the state of Nature is known, Figure 12.8(a)'s decision tree starts growing from a root that is a decision node and then branches into the various chance nodes. In contrast, with perfect information, the decision is made *after* the state of Nature is known. Consequently, Figure 12.8(a)'s decision tree is inappropriate for computing the maximum EMV attainable with perfect information. Instead, we must use Figure 12.8(b)'s decision tree, which starts growing from a root that is a chance node and then branches into the various decision nodes.

Figure 12.9 displays the two stages of the pruning of Figure 12.8(b)'s decision tree. In the first stage, Figure 12.9(a), we consider each decision node, identify the decision that maximizes the payoff, write this maximum payoff in the square, and draw ‖ across the branches representing suboptimal decisions. In the second stage, Figure 12.9(b), we multiply the payoffs written in the decision nodes by the corresponding probabilities on the branches entering the decision nodes, sum the resulting products to obtain the EMV for the chance node, and write this EMV in the circle. This EMV of 19.5 represents the maximum EMV attainable with perfect information. Referring again to Figure 12.8(a), we are reminded that pruning this decision tree results in a value of 5.5 for the maximum EMV attainable with no additional information. Combining the results in Figures 12.8(a) and 12.9(b), we compute the EVPI as follows:

$$EVPI = \begin{pmatrix} \text{maximum EMV attainable} \\ \text{with perfect information} \end{pmatrix} - \begin{pmatrix} \text{maximum EMV attainable} \\ \text{with no additional information} \end{pmatrix}$$

$$= \begin{pmatrix} \text{EMV written within} \\ \text{chance node } I \\ \text{in Figure 12.9(b)} \end{pmatrix} - \begin{pmatrix} \text{EMV written within} \\ \text{decision node } I \\ \text{in Figure 12.8(a)} \end{pmatrix}$$

$$= \qquad 19.5 \qquad - \qquad 5.5$$

$$= \qquad 14$$

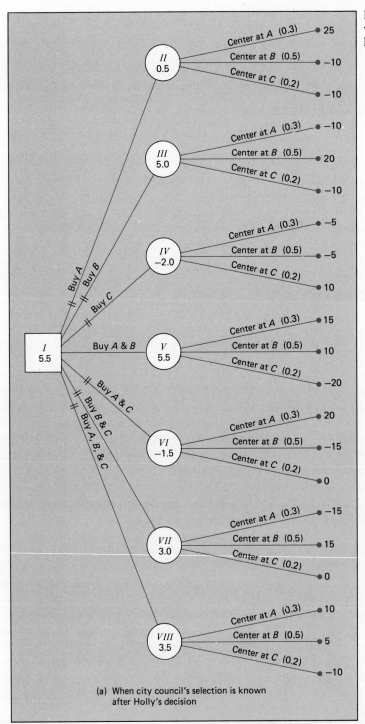

Figure 12.8(a,b) How the time at which the city council's selection is known affects the decision tree

(a) When city council's selection is known after Holly's decision

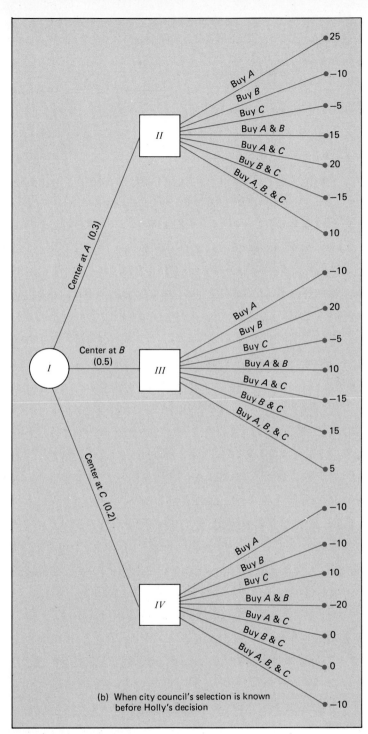

Figure 12.8 (continued)

Of course, this is the same value we computed earlier using the tabular approach based on the payoff matrix.

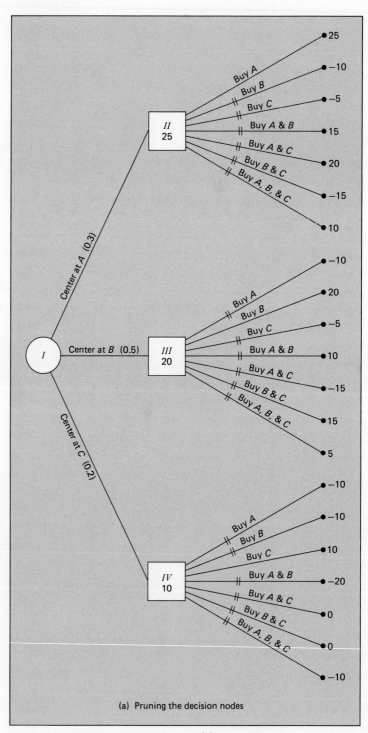

Figure 12.9(a,b) Pruning Figure 12.8(b)'s decision tree

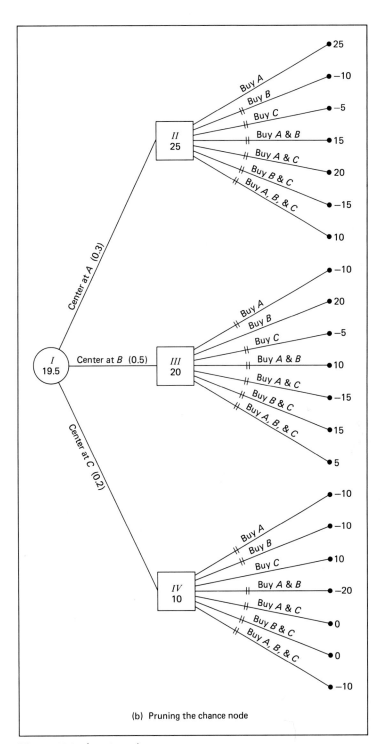

(b) Pruning the chance node

Figure 12.9 (continued)

Yet Another Method for Computing the EVPI

We have computed that, in Holly's decision problem, the EVPI is 14. Referring to Table 12.11, we see that the decision that minimized expected regret (which we know from Section 12.4 is the same decision that maximizes EMV) has an expected regret of 14, a value equal to the EVPI. This is no coincidence! The following is a general principle:

> The EVPI *always* equals the expected regret of the decision that minimizes expected regret (and also maximizes EMV).

A formal proof of this general principle is beyond the scope of this text. We will have to be satisfied by the numerical examples provided by Holly's decision-analysis problem and by the end-of-chapter exercises.

Section Summary

We can summarize the concept of the EVPI as follows:

- The EVPI is a measure of the value of being able to make a decision *after* learning the state of Nature rather than before.

- We compute the EVPI using the formula

$$
\text{EVPI} = \begin{pmatrix} \text{maximum EMV attainable} \\ \text{with perfect information} \end{pmatrix} - \begin{pmatrix} \text{maximum EMV attainable} \\ \text{with no additional information} \end{pmatrix}
$$

  We compute the first term by summing the products obtained by multiplying the maximum payoff for each state of Nature by the state's probability; we compute the second term in the manner described in Section 12.4.

- The computations required to determine the EVPI may be performed with the aid of a payoff matrix (as illustrated in Table 12.12) or with the aid of a decision tree (as illustrated in Figures 12.8 and 12.9).

- The EVPI is the maximum fee a decision maker should pay to obtain a perfect prediction of the state of Nature *before* the decision must be made. If the perfect information's cost exceeds the EVPI, the information is overpriced; if the cost is less than the EVPI, the information is worth purchasing.

- The EVPI is an upper bound on the maximum fee a decision maker should pay for imperfect information; that is, imperfect information costing more than the EVPI should not be acquired. (In Sections 13.2–13.4 we will learn how to decide whether to acquire imperfect information costing less than the EVPI.)

12.7 A SIMPLIFICATION OF HOLLY'S DECISION ANALYSIS PROBLEM

We will continue to use Holly's decision-analysis problem to illustrate our discussions. However, to simplify the computations we must perform, let us henceforth assume that the city council is considering locating the convention center only at site *A* or site *B* (site *C* is no longer under consideration). Holly now estimates that

that the city council will select each site with probability 0.4 for site A and 0.6 for site B. Table 12.13(a) displays the payoff matrix for this simplified problem; the payoffs were taken from the portions of Table 12.8's payoff matrix that apply to sites A and B. Table 12.13(b) displays the computation of the EMV for each of the three alternative decisions and the identification of the third decision (buy A and B) as the decision that maximizes EMV. Table 12.13(c) displays the computation for the simplified problem of EVPI = 10. Before proceeding, you should verify for yourself the computations summarized in Table 12.13.

TABLE 12.13 Payoff Matrix, Optimal Decision, and EVPI for the Simplified Version of Holly's Problem

Land Purchase Decisions	States of Nature for Convention Center's Site	
	A	B
A	25	−10
B	−10	20
A & B	15	10
	0.4	0.6

(a) The Payoff Matrix

Land Purchase Decisions	States of Nature for Convention Center's Site	
	A	B
A	25	−10
B	−10	20
A & B	15	10
	0.4	0.6

Each Decision's EMV

$EMV_A = (25)(0.4) + (-10)(0.6) = 4$
$EMV_B = (-10)(0.4) + (20)(0.6) = 8$
$EMV_{A\&B} = (15)(0.4) + (10)(0.6) = 12 \leftarrow$ maximum

(b) Computing the Optimal Decision

Land Purchase Decisions	States of Nature for Convention Center's Site	
	A	B
A	25	−10
B	−10	20
A & B	15	10
	0.4	0.6

(c) Computing the EVPI

$$\left(\begin{array}{c}\text{maximum EMV attainable} \\ \text{with perfect information}\end{array}\right) = (25)(0.4) + (20)(0.6) = 22$$

$$\left(\begin{array}{c}\text{maximum EMV attainable} \\ \text{with no additional information}\end{array}\right) = 12$$

$$\text{EVPI} = 22 - 12 = 10$$

12.8 SENSITIVITY ANALYSIS

In Chapter 3, we discussed *sensitivity analysis* in the context of linear programming. Now we will learn how to use sensitivity analysis in the context of decision analysis. Regardless of context, sensitivity analysis may be defined as the investigation of how a decision problem's optimal solution changes in response to changes in the data. In a decision-analysis problem, there are two types of data:

1. The probabilities assigned to the alternative states of Nature for each uncertain event (e.g., the probabilities assigned in Holly's problem to alternative sites for the convention center).

2. Cash flow data that enable the computation of the payoffs (e.g., the data for Holly's problem displayed in Table 12.2).

To illustrate the concept of sensitivity analysis, let us consider the simplification of Holly's problem summarized in Table 12.13 (in which site C has been ruled out). Table 12.13(b) indicates that, given the current data, the third decision (buy A and B) maximizes EMV. As a specific example of sensitivity analysis, we will answer the following question:

> *By how much can Holly's probability assessment that the city council will select site A vary from its current value of 0.4 without affecting the optimality of the third decision?*

To answer this question, let us use p_A and p_B to denote Holly's assessments of the probability that the city council will select site A and site B, respectively. Since $p_A + p_B = 1$, we can express p_B as $1 - p_A$. If, in Table 12.8, we substitute p_A for 0.4 and $1 - p_A$ for 0.6 and then compute each decision's EMV as a function of p_A, we obtain the results displayed in Table 12.14. Observe that each of the three EMV expressions in Table 12.14's right margin is a linear function of p_A and, therefore, has a graph that is a straight line. For example, let us graph $EMV_A = 35p_A - 10$. When $p_A = 0$, $EMV_A = -10$; when $p_A = 1$, $EMV_A = 25$. Hence, $(0, -10)$ and $(1, 25)$ are two points on the graph of $EMV_A = 35p_A - 10$. Figure 12.10 displays the graph resulting from plotting these two points and connecting them with a straight line. Proceeding in a similar fashion for EMV_B and $EMV_{A\&B}$ and then displaying all three straight lines on the same graph, we obtain Figure 12.11. Since the optimal decision is the one with the maximum EMV, we can use Figure 12.11 to identify the optimal decision for any specified value of p_A. As examples, Figure 12.11 indicates the following:

- When $p_A = 0.1$, decision B is optimal because EMV_B exceeds EMV_A and $EMV_{A\&B}$.

- When $p_A = 0.4$, decision $A\&B$ is optimal because $EMV_{A\&B}$ exceeds EMV_A and EMV_B.

TABLE 12.14 Sensitivity Analysis on the Probability of the Selection of Site A

Land Purchase Decisions	States of Nature for Convention Center's Site		Each Decision's EMV
	A	B	
A	25	-10	$EMV_A = \quad (25)(p_A) + (-10)(1-p_A) = \quad 35p_A - 10$
B	-10	20	$EMV_B = (-10)(p_A) + \quad (20)(1-p_A) = -30p_A + 20$
$A \& B$	15	10	$EMV_{A\&B} = \quad (15)(p_A) + \quad (10)(1-p_A) = \quad 5p_A + 10$
	p_A	$1 - p_A$	

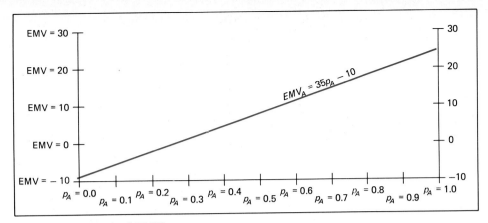

Figure 12.10 Graph of EMV_A

- When $p_A = 0.9$, decision A is optimal because EMV_A exceeds EMV_B and $EMV_{A\&B}$.

These three examples clearly illustrate that the optimal solution depends on the value Holly assigns to p_A.

Some important information is missing from Figure 12.11. In particular, looking at Figure 12.11, it is easy to see that, as p_A increases from 0 to 1, decision B is optimal for low values of p_A, then decision $A\&B$ is optimal for medium values of p_A, and decision A is optimal for high values of p_A. Missing from Figure 12.11 are the precise values of p_A at which the optimal decision changes—values known in as *breakpoints*.

To determine the first breakpoint (which we can see occurs somewhere between $p_A = 0.2$ and $p_A = 0.3$), we observe that it occurs when the graphs of EMV_B and $EMV_{A\&B}$ intersect or, equivalently, when EMV_B equals $EMV_{A\&B}$. To determine the value of p_A at which this intersection occurs, we set equal the expressions for EMV_B and $EMV_{A\&B}$ and solve for p_A. These computations proceed as follows:

$$
\begin{aligned}
EMV_B = EMV_{A\&B} \;\longrightarrow\; -30p_A + 20 &= 5p_A + 10 \\
\longrightarrow\; -35p_A &= -10 \\
\longrightarrow\; p_A &= \frac{10}{35} \\
\longrightarrow\; p_A &= \frac{2}{7} = 0.286
\end{aligned}
$$

Figure 12.11 Graphs of EMV_A, EMV_B, and $EMV_{A\&B}$

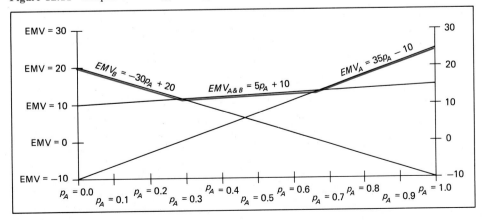

By proceeding in a similar fashion, you should verify that the second breakpoint occurs at $p_A = \frac{2}{3} = 0.667$. Figure 12.12 summarizes our graphical sensitivity analysis. From Figure 12.26, we see that

Range for p_A	Optimal Decision
$0.000 \leqslant p_A \leqslant 0.286$	Decision B
$0.286 \leqslant p_A \leqslant 0.667$	Decision $A\&B$
$0.667 \leqslant p_A \leqslant 1.000$	Decision A

Since Holly's current assessment of $p_A = 0.4$ falls well within the second interval, Holly is confident that decision $A\&B$ is optimal. It would remain optimal even if her assessment that $p_A = 0.4$ were too high by $0.400 - 0.286 = 0.114$ or too low by $0.667 - 0.400 = 0.267$. On the other hand, if Holly's assessment of p_A were to lie close to a breakpoint, she should carefully reassess p_A, since a slight change would lead to a different optimal solution.

We should note that performing sensitivity analysis would have been much more complicated if there had been more than two alternative states of Nature. With only two states, $p_B = 1 - p_A$, thereby allowing us to express each decision's EMV as a function of p_A. Unfortunately, this is impossible when there are three or more states of Nature, unless some specific assumptions are made about how a change in one probability affects the other probabilities. Consequently, sensitivity analysis of the probability assessments for three or more states of Nature is much more complicated than this section's example. This complexity is illustrated in part by some of the end-of-chapter exercises; however, a detailed discussion is well beyond the scope of this text.

We can also conduct sensitivity analysis on how the optimal solution is affected by a change in the financial data used to compute the payoffs. For example, Table 12.2 specifies that Holly currently estimates that site A's purchase price is 20. How does the optimal solution change in response to a decrease or increase in this purchase price? Exercise 12.12 requests you to answer this question.

Summarizing:

> In the context of decision analysis, sensitivity analysis investigates how the optimal solution changes in response to a change in the probability assessments of the states of Nature or the financial data used to compute the payoffs.

Figure 12.12 Graphs of EMV_A, EMV_B, and $EMV_{A\&B}$ with breakpoints displayed

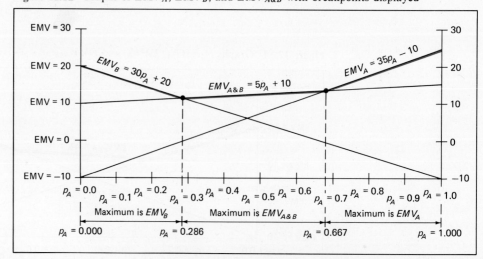

12.9 MULTISTAGE DECISION-ANALYSIS PROBLEMS

Thus far we have been considering a single-stage decision-analysis problem, where a single decision is made and then the outcome of an uncertain event is observed. Now we focus on a problem consisting of a sequence of decisions and uncertain events, in which a decision is made, the outcome of an uncertain event is observed, another decision is made, the outcome of another uncertain event is observed, and so on. Such a problem is known as a *multistage decision-analysis problem.*

An Example

As our example of a multistage decision analysis problem, consider the following scenario:

> MBI Corporation manufactures computers. Its product line includes a personal computer whose sales currently represent a 20% share of the total market. (For simplicity, we will assume that only three market shares are possible: 10%, 20% and 30%.) MBI believes that its current 20% market share is likely to fall dramatically unless it can introduce an improved model in about a year. Consequently, MBI must now select one of the following options:

> 1. Keep selling the current model without making any improvements. If this is done, MBI estimates its market share will either remain at 20% with probability 0.4 or fall to 10% with probability 0.6. MBI also estimates that the present value of future sales of an unimproved model is $1.5 million per percent of market share (e.g., a 20% market share has a value of $1.5 \times 20 = 30$ million).

> 2. Develop a model with one (but not both) of two types of improvements — hereafter referred to as improvement A and improvement B. Research and development costs are $20 million for improvement A and $25 million for improvement B. Each type of improvement will result in either a significant or a slight improvement. For improvement A, MBI believes the probability of significant improvement is 0.8, and of slight improvement is 0.2. For improvement B, the probability of significant improvement is 0.5, and of slight improvement is 0.5. MBI estimates that the present value of future sales for a significantly improved model is $3 million per percent of market share and for a slightly improved model is $2 million per percent of market share.

> If MBI chooses to begin development of either type of improvement, it will subsequently face another decision. After learning whether its research and development has led to a significantly improved or slightly improved model, MBI must then decide whether to launch (i.e. begin selling) the improved model or to keep selling the current model. If MBI decides to launch an improved model, it will incur additional costs of $15 million, regardless of whether the improvement has been significant or slight. With an improved model, MBI estimates that the respective probabilities of market shares of 10%, 20%, and 30% are:

> - 0.2, 0.4, and 0.4 if the model is a significant improvement of type A.
> - 0.5, 0.4, and 0.1 if the model is a slight improvement of type A.
> - 0.0, 0.2, and 0.8 if the model is a significant improvement of type B.
> - 0.2, 0.5, and 0.3 if the model is a slight improvement of type B.

TABLE 12.15 Data for MBI's Multistage Decision Analysis Problem

R&D costs for improvement A = 20
R&D costs for improvement B = 25

Launch costs for improved product = 15

Profit per percentage of market share
for current model = 1.5
for slight improvement = 2.0
for significant improvement = 3.0

(a) Cost and Profit Data ($000,000)

	Significant	Slight
A	0.8	0.2
B	0.5	0.5

(b) Improvement Probabilities

	Market Shares		
	10%	20%	30%
Current Model	0.6	0.4	0.0
Significantly Improved A	0.2	0.4	0.4
Slightly Improved A	0.5	0.4	0.1
Significantly Improved B	0.0	0.2	0.8
Slightly Improved B	0.2	0.5	0.3

(c) Market Share Probabilities

To summarize, MBI must now decide whether to keep selling the current model, begin development of improvement A, or begin development of improvement B. If MBI chooses to develop an improved model, it must subsequently decide, based on whether the improvement is significant or slight, whether to launch the improved model or keep selling the current model. To aid its decision-making process, MBI has prepared the data summary displayed in Table 12.15. Using these data, MBI wishes to determine its optimal strategy under the EMV criterion.

We see that MBI's problem is not a single-stage but rather a multistage decision-analysis problem, since it involves a sequence of decisions and uncertain events. Consequently, we cannot analyze it using the payoff-matrix approach. Fortunately, the decision tree approach remains viable for a multistage decision-analysis problem.

Growing MBI's Decision Tree

As illustrated in Figure 12.13, there are five steps to growing MBI's decision tree:

1. **Representing the decision on whether to improve the model.** As illustrated in Figure 12.13(a), the tree's root is decision node I. This decision node represents the decision on whether to improve the model. Three branches emanate from the node. The upper branch represents the decision to keep selling the current model, the middle branch, the decision to develop improvement A, and the lower branch, the decision to develop improvement B.

2. **Representing the uncertainty over whether the improvement will be significant or slight.** As illustrated in Figure 12.13(b), the tree continues growing with the attachment of chance nodes II and III to the lower two branches emanating from the root node. Each of these chance nodes represents the uncertainty over whether the improvement will be significant or slight. Consequently, two branches emanate from each chance node. The upper branch represents a significant improvement, the lower branch a slight improvement.

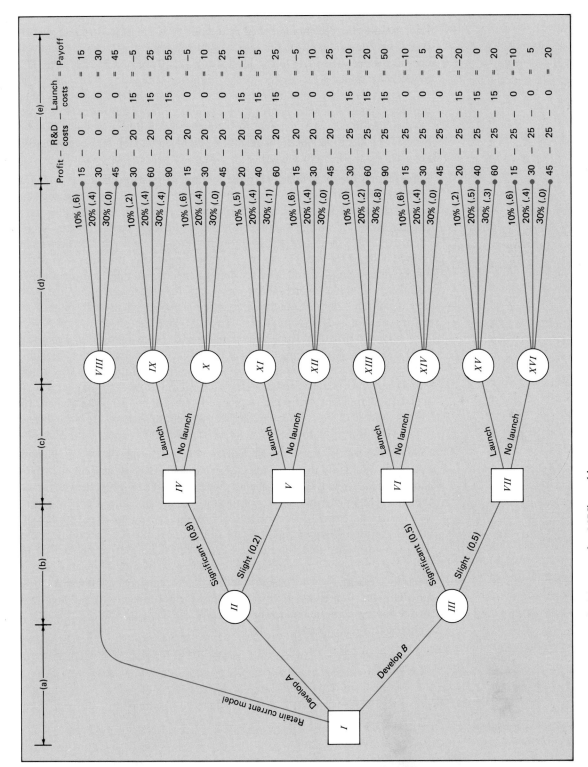

Figure 12.13 Growing the decision tree for *MBI*'s problem

Since these branches emanate from chance nodes, we must write a probability adjacent to each branch. In Table 12.15(b) the first row provides the probabilities for the branches emanating from chance node *II*, and the second row the probabilities for the branches emanating from chance node *III*.

3. **Representing the decision on whether to launch the improved product.** As illustrated in Figure 12.13(c), the tree continues growing with the attachment of decision nodes *IV* and *V* to the branches emanating from chance node *II* and of decision nodes *VI* and *VII* to the branches emanating from chance node *III*. Each decision node represents the decision on whether to launch the improved model. Consequently, two branches emanate from each: the upper branch represents the decision to launch the improved model, the lower branch the decision not to launch the improved model (or, equivalently, to keep selling the current model).[9]

4. **Representing the uncertainty over the market share percentage.** As illustrated in Figure 12.13(d), the tree continues to grow with the attachment of chance nodes: chance node *VIII* to the upper branch emanating from decision node *I*, chance nodes *IX* and *X* to the branches emanating from decision node *IV*, chance nodes Ξ and *XII* to the branches emanating from decision node *V*, chance nodes *XIII* and *XIV* to the branches emanating from decision node *VI*, and chance nodes *XV* and *XVI* to the branches emanating from decision node *VII*. Each of these chance nodes represents the uncertainty over the percentage of market share. Consequently, three branches emanate from each. The upper, middle, and lower branches represent that the uncertain market-share percentage is 10%, 20% and 30%, respectively. Since these branches emanate from chance nodes, we must write a probability adjacent to each branch. In Figure 12.13(c) the first row provides the probabilities for the branches emanating from chance nodes *VIII*, *X*, *XII*, *XIV*, and *XVI* (which all correspond to a decision to continue selling the current model); the second, third, fourth, and fifth rows provide the respective probabilities for the branches emanating from chance nodes *IX*, *XI*, *XIII*, and *XV*.

5. **Computation of the payoffs to be written adjacent to the leaves.** As illustrated in Figure 12.13(e), the tree stops growing with the attachment of leaves to each branch emanating from chance nodes *VIII–XVI*. These leaves represent the end of the decision analysis problem, the point in time when MBI knows its market share and, hence, collects its payoff. As summarized by the headings at the top of Figure 12.13(e), we compute each payoff by adding the contribution to profit from the market share, subtracting research and development costs (if any), and subtracting launch costs (if any). To illustrate, consider the leaf at the end of the middle branch emanating from chance node *XI*. This leaf represents a 20% market share resulting from the launch of a model having a slight improvement of type *A*. Using Table 12.15's data, we compute this leaf's payoff as follows:

$$
\left[\begin{pmatrix} \text{contribution to profit} \\ \text{per percentage of} \\ \text{market share} \end{pmatrix} \times \begin{pmatrix} \text{percentage of mark-} \\ \text{et share received at} \\ \text{leaf} \end{pmatrix} \right] - \begin{pmatrix} \text{R\&D costs for im-} \\ \text{provement } A \end{pmatrix} - \begin{pmatrix} \text{launch costs for an} \\ \text{improved model} \end{pmatrix}
$$

$$
(2 \quad \times \quad 20) \quad - \quad (20) \quad - \quad (15) \quad = 5
$$

---

[9] If you are puzzled by a branch representing a decision not to launch an improved model, remember that a launch entails additional costs of \$15 million and, therefore, may not be advisable if the improvement has been slight.

Before proceeding, you should compute for yourself several of the other payoffs.

Figure 12.13's decision tree is a useful visual aid to any managerial discussion of MBI's decision-analysis problem. To see why, imagine yourself as the manager who must address a group of other managers. Would you rather repeatedly refer the managers to a verbal statement of the problem or to Figure 12.13's decision tree? The answer is obvious! Many managers who have studied decision analysis claim that the most important concept they learned was how to represent a multistage decision-analysis problem by growing a decision tree.

Pruning Figure 12.13's Decision Tree

Having grown Figure 12.13's decision tree, we are now ready to prune it to determine MBI's optimal strategy. As illustrated in Figure 12.14, our pruning proceeds in reverse chronological order (i.e., right to left) and consists of the following four steps:

1. Our pruning first considers the chance nodes *VIII-XVI*. We compute each chance node's EMV by proceeding as follows:
   - We multiply the probabilities adjacent to the three branches emanating from the chance node by the corresponding payoffs adjacent to the leaves at the branches' ends.
   - We sum the three products obtained in the above multiplications.
   - We record this sum within the circular chance node.

   For example,

   $$(\text{EMV for chance node } IX) = (-5)(0.2) + (25)(0.4) + (55)(0.4) = 31.$$

2. Our pruning next considers decision nodes *IV*, *V*, *VI*, and *VIII*. For each, we identify the best decision by examining the two branches emanating from the node and identifying the maximum of the EMVs written within the chance nodes at the branches' ends. For example, examining decision node *IV*, we see that the upper branch (representing a launch) leads to chance node *IX* with an EMV of 31, and the lower branch (representing no launch) leads to chance node *X* with an EMV of 1. Since the upper branch leads to the maximum EMV, the optimal decision at decision node *IV* is to launch. To signify our identification of the best decision at each decision node, we draw ‖ across the branches corresponding to suboptimal decisions.

3. Our pruning next considers chance nodes *II* and *III*. We compute each chance node's EMV by proceeding as follows:
   - We multiply the probabilities adjacent to the two branches emanating from the chance node by the corresponding EMVs within the decision nodes at the branches' ends.
   - We sum the two products obtained in the above multiplications.
   - We record this sum within the circular chance node.

   For example,

   $$(\text{EMV for chance node } II) = (31)(0.8) + (1)(0.2) = 25$$

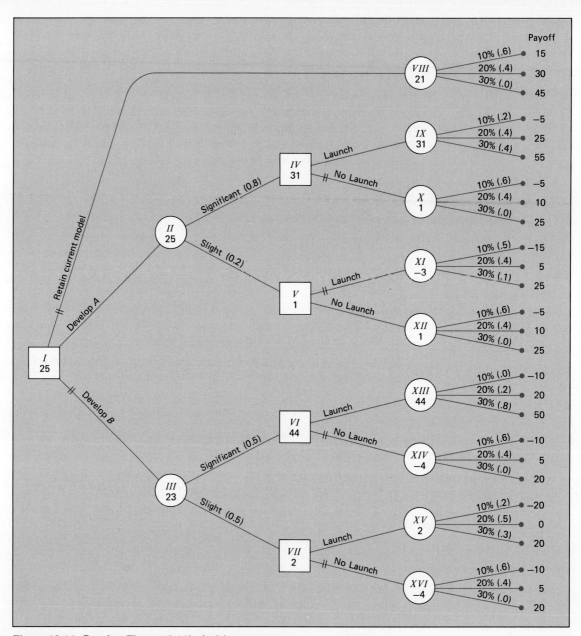

Figure 12.14 Pruning Figure 12.13's decision tree

4. Our pruning concludes by considering decision node *I*. Examining its three branches, we see that the upper branch (representing the retention of the current model) leads to chance node *VIII* with its EMV of 21, the middle branch (representing development of improvement *A*) leads to chance node *II* with its EMV of 25, and the lower branch (representing development of improvement *B*) leads to chance node *III* with its EMV of 23. Since the middle branch leads to the maximum EMV, the optimal decision at decision node *I* is to develop improvement *A*. To signify this, we draw || across the upper and lower branches emanating from decision node *I*, thereby emphasizing their suboptimality.

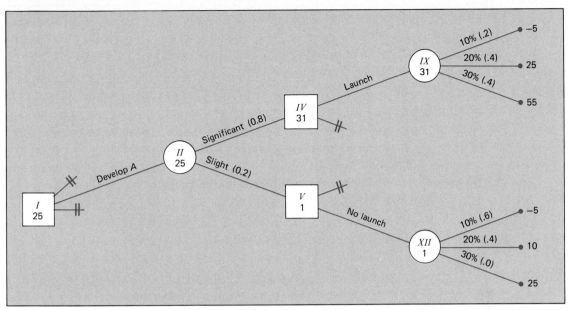

Figure 12.15 Figure 12.14's decision tree after removal of pruned branches

Our pruning has identified MBI's optimal strategy under the EMV criterion. We can better visualize this strategy by removing from Figure 12.14's decision tree those branches corresponding to pruned (i.e., suboptimal) decisions. Figure 12.15 displays the result. From Figure 12.15, we see that MBI's optimal strategy is not a single decision but a set of decisions. In particular, MBI's optimal strategy can be summarized as follows:

Develop improvement *A*. If this development leads to a significant improvement, launch the improved model; if to a slight improvement, do not launch the improved model.

Section Summary

We can summarize this section as follows:

- The decision tree for a multistage decision-analysis problem pictorially represents a sequence of decisions and uncertain events.

- We grow the decision tree in chronological order from left to right. We represent each decision by a square decision node with branches emanating from it for each alternative decision, and we represent each uncertain event by a circular chance node with branches emanating from it for each alternative state of Nature.

- After growing the decision tree, we identify the optimal strategy by pruning the decision tree in reverse chronological order. When pruning at a chance node, we write within the circle the computed EMV, which is the sum of the products we obtain by multiplying the probabilities adjacent to each emanating branch by the payoff or EMV that the branch leads to. When pruning at a decision node, we examine the EMV or payoff led to by each emanating branch, identify the maximum, write this maximum within the square, and draw || across the branches representing suboptimal decisions.

12.10 CONCLUDING REMARKS

Sophisticated decision-analysis software packages are now commercially available for both mainframe and personal computers. These software packages enable rapid analysis of the large decision trees that arise in the real world, where it is common to have hundreds of nodes and thousands of branches. They perform the "number crunching" necessary to prune a decision tree. Many packages also provide color-graphics display of the decision tree. Some even facilitate interactive probability assessment by providing color-graphics display of a probability wheel (as discussed in Section 12.4).

We have now completed our introduction to decision analysis. If you do not intend to continue to the advanced topics in the next chapter, you should at least read the concluding remarks in Section 13.10.

12.11 CHAPTER CHECKLIST AND GLOSSARY

Quickly review this chapter by rereading the material highlighted by a vertical line in the left margin. You should then be familiar with the concepts, techniques. and terminology in the Checklist and Glossary that follow. If you need "help" with a particular item, consult the section or sections indicated for a more detailed discussion.

Checklist of Concepts and Techniques

- ☐ The distinction between a good decision and a good outcome. [12.1]

- ☐ Constructing a payoff matrix for a single-stage decision-analysis problem. [12.2]

- ☐ Determining the optimal decision under the maximax criterion. [12.3]

- ☐ Determining the optimal decision under the maximin criterion. [12.3]

- ☐ Transforming a payoff matrix into a regret matrix. [12.3]

- ☐ Determining the optimal decision under the minimax regret criterion. [12.3]

- ☐ The flaws in the maximax, maximin, and minimax regret criterion. [12.3]

- ☐ The distinction between an objective probability and a subjective probability. [12.4]

- ☐ Assessing a subjective probability with the aid of a probability wheel. [12.4]

- ☐ Determining the optimal decision under the expected-monetary-value (EMV) criterion. [12.4]

- ☐ Scenarios where using the EMV criterion may not be appropriate. [12.4]

- ☐ Determining the optimal solution under the expected-regret criterion. [12.4]

- ☐ That the EMV criterion and the expected-regret criterion both yield the same optimal decision. [12.4]

- ☐ Growing a decision tree for a single-stage decision-analysis problem. [12.5]

- ☐ Determining a single-stage decision-analysis problem's optimal decision by pruning the decision tree. [12.5]

- ☐ Computing and interpreting the expected value of perfect information (EVPI). [12.6]

- [ ] Conducting sensitivity analysis in the context of a decision-analysis problem. [12.8]

- [ ] Growing a decision tree for a multistage decision-analysis problem. [12.9]

- [ ] Determining a multistage decision-analysis problem's optimal strategy by pruning the decision tree. [12.9]

Glossary

Decision analysis. A logical framework for making decisions when the decisions have uncertain outcomes. [12.1]

State of Nature. One of several alternative outcomes for an uncertain event. [12.2]

Single-stage decision-analysis problem. A decision problem in which a manager must choose one of several alternative decisions *before* the occurrence of one of several alternative states of Nature determines the decision's consequences. [12.2]

Payoff matrix. A rectangular array of numbers in which the value in the ith row and the jth column equals the payoff that results if the decision maker selects the ith decision and then jth state of Nature occurs. [12.2]

Nonprobabilistic decision-making criterion. A decision-making criterion which does not require probabilities to be assigned to the alternative states of Nature. [12.3]

Probabilistic decision-making criterion. A decision-making criterion which requires probabilities to be assigned to the alternative states of Nature. [12.3]

Maximax criterion. An optimistic criterion that first identifies each decision's maximum possible payoff and then selects the decision that maximizes these maximum payoffs. [12.3]

Maximin criterion. A pessimistic criterion that first identifies each decision's minimum possible payoff and then selects the decision that maximizes these minimum payoffs. [12.3]

Regret matrix. The transformation of the payoff matrix obtained by replacing every payoff in a column of the matrix with the difference obtained by subtracting the payoff from the column's maximum payoff. [12.3]

Minimax regret criterion. A pessimistic criterion that first transforms the payoff matrix into a regret matrix, then identifies each decision's maximum possible regret, and finally selects the decision that minimizes these maximum regrets. [12.3]

Objective probability. A probability based on historical data, statistical experimentation, and/or scientific analysis. [12.4]

Subjective probability. A probability based on personal beliefs or experiences. [12.4]

Assessing a probability. Assigning a probability to a state of Nature. [12.4]

Probability wheel. A device used to improve the accuracy of the assessment of a subjective probability. [12.4]

Expected monetary value (EMV) for a decision. The decision's expected payoff equal to the summation of the products obtained by multiplying the decision's payoff for each alternative state of Nature by the corresponding probability the state of Nature will occur. [12.4]

EMV criterion. A criterion that first computes each decision's EMV and then selects the decision with the maximum EMV. [12.4]

Expected regret for a decision. The summation of the products obtained by multiply-

579

ing the decision's regret for each alternative state of Nature by the corresponding probability the state of Nature will occur. [12.4]

Expected regret criterion. A criterion that first computes each decision's expected regret and then selects the decision with the minimum expected regret (the same decision as would be selected under the EMV criterion). [12.4]

Decision tree. A pictorial representation of a decision-analysis problem. [12.5]

Decision node. A square node in a decision tree from which branches emanate to represent alternative decisions. [12.5]

Chance node. A circular node in a decision tree from which branches emanate to represent alternative states of Nature. [12.5]

Root. The first (i.e., leftmost) node in a decision tree. [12.5]

Leaves. The last (i.e., rightmost) portion of a decision tree, representing the alternative ways the decision-analysis problem can terminate. [12.5]

Growing a decision tree. The process of constructing a decision tree from the verbal statement of a decision-analysis problem. [12.5]

Pruning a decision tree. The process of determining a decision-analysis problem's optimal strategy by analyzing the decision tree in reverse chronological order, writing within each chance node the EMV of the payoffs or EMVs led to by the emanating branches and writing within each decision node the maximum EMV or payoff led to by the emanating branches. [12.5, 12.9]

Perfect information. A perfect prediction of the state of Nature that is received *before* the decision must be made. [12.6]

Expected value of perfect information (EVPI). The maximum fee a decision maker should be willing to pay for perfect information. [12.6]

Sensitivity analysis. A mathematical investigation of how the optimal strategy changes in response to changes in the probability assessments of the states of Nature or the financial data used to compute the payoffs. [12.8]

Multistage decision-analysis problem. A decision analysis problem consisting of a sequence of decisions and uncertain events. [12.9]

EXERCISES

Exercises 12.1–12.9 involve a single-stage decision-analysis problem. After reading each exercise, you should proceed as follows:

(a) Construct an appropriate payoff matrix. (Note: In Exercises 12.1 and 12.2, the payoff matrix is already constructed.)

(b) Using the maximax criterion, identify the optimal decision.

(c) Using the maximin criterion, identify the optimal decision.

(d) Using the minimax regret criterion, identify the optimal decision.

(e) Using the EMV criterion, identify the optimal decision.

(f) Using the expected regret criterion, identify the optimal decision and verify that it is the same one identified in part (e).

(g) Grow a decision tree for the problem, prune the decision tree using the EMV criterion, and verify that you have obtained the same optimal decision as in part (e).

(h) Using the payoff matrix approach illustrated in Table 12.12, compute the expected value of perfect information (EVPI).

(i) Using the decision-tree approach illustrated in Figures 12.8 and 12.9, compute the EVPI and verify that you have obtained the same answer as in part (h).

(j) Verify that the EVPI obtained in parts (h) and (i) equals the expected regret of the decision identified in part (f) as the one that minimizes expected regret.

*12.1. Consider a single-stage decision-analysis problem where one of seven decisions (1, 2, . . . , 7) must be made before the occurrence of one of three states of nature (A, B, C). The payoff matrix is displayed below:

| | State of Nature | | |
Decision	A	B	C
1	−9	0	12
2	−3	6	−3
3	3	−6	6
4	12	−6	−6
5	9	0	−9
6	6	−12	9
7	−6	−6	15

Assume that the following probabilities have been assessed:

State of Nature	A	B	C
Probability	0.5	0.2	0.3

12.2. Consider a single-stage decision-analysis problem where one of five decisions (1, 2, ... , 5) must be made before the occurrence of one of four states of nature (A, B, C, D). The payoff matrix is displayed below:

| | State of Nature | | | |
Decision	A	B	C	D
1	0	5	20	−10
2	−5	10	15	0
3	25	−20	10	−5
4	5	10	−10	10
5	10	15	−25	5

Assume that the following probabilities have been assessed:

State of Nature	A	B	C	D
Probability	0.3	0.4	0.1	0.2

12.3. The football team of Central State University (CSU) has just received a bid to play in the Banana Bowl. CSU estimates that after paying expenses, its profit from playing in the Banana Bowl would be $200,000. Although CSU finds the Banana Bowl appealing, it cannot decide whether to accept the bid. The reason is that CSU might also get invited to a more prestigious and more profitable bowl, the Berry Bowl. Whether CSU receives a bid to play in the Berry Bowl depends on the result of an upcoming game between two other teams, North State University (NSU) and South State University (SSU). If NSU wins or ties, CSU will receive a Berry Bowl bid; however, if NSU loses, CSU will not receive a Berry

Bowl bid. CSU estimates that after paying expenses, its profit from playing in the Berry Bowl would be $900,000. Although CSU would prefer to play in the Berry Bowl, it unfortunately must accept or reject the Banana Bowl bid before the game between NSU and SSU. CSU feels certain that if it rejects the Banana Bowl bid and then does not get invited to the Berry Bowl, it will not receive any other bowl bid. CSU estimates that the probability NSU will beat SSU is 0.25 and the probability NSU will tie SSU is 0.05.

12.4. Mobon Oil Company owns a lease that entitles it to explore for oil on a parcel of offshore land in California. Since the lease is about to expire, Mobon must now decide whether to drill for oil at the site or to sell the lease to Exxil Oil Company, which has just offered Mobon $50,000. Mobon estimates it would cost $100,000 to drill at the site. If the well were dry, all this cost would be lost. If the well were successful, its value to Mobon would depend on the extent of the oil discovered. For simplicity, Mobon assumes there are only two types of successful wells: a minor success and a major success. Mobon estimates that a minor success would result in revenues of $200,000 in excess of the drilling cost, whereas a major success would result in revenues of $600,000 in excess of the drilling cost. Mobon has assessed the following probabilities:

Type of Well	Dry	Minor Success	Major Success
Probability	0.7	0.2	0.1

*12.5. Even though Valentine's Day is one month away, Bud's Flower Shop must now decide how many roses to have its supplier deliver on the morning of February 14. For simplicity, Bud is considering only two order quantities, which he refers to as small and large. In past years, Bud has observed that his profits are heavily dependent on the Valentine's Day weather. Based on historical records of the weather on Valentine's Day, Bud has made the following probability assessments:

Valentine's Day Weather	Rainy	Cloudy	Sunny
Probability	0.6	0.3	0.1

(It never snows.) Bud has also made the following estimates:
- If he places a small order, his profit will be −$500 if it is rainy, $500 if it is cloudy, and $2000 if it is sunny.
- If he places a large order, his profit will be −$2500 if it is rainy, $1000 if it is cloudy, and $5000 if it is sunny.

581

12.6. Innovative Products Corporation (IPC) is considering whether to introduce a new product. The major factor that will determine the product's profitability is whether competitors will introduce similar products. IPC believes that the number of competitors who do so will be either 0, 1, 2, or 3. For each case, IPC has estimated the probability and the net present value of the cash flows the new product will generate. These estimates are displayed in the table below:

Number of Competing Products	0	1	2	3
Probability	0.1	0.3	0.4	0.2
Net Present Value ($000)	900	300	100	−200

12.7. The Paulbilt Corporation has just completed a sale of construction equipment to a Japanese corporation. Under the terms of this sale, the Japanese corporation must pay Paulbilt 180 million yen in 30 days. Paulbilt is considering the following two options:

- Paulbilt can immediately sell 180 million yen "forward" 30 days at the current exchange rate of 150 yen per dollar, thereby obtaining $1.2 million. It would then invest these funds in a 30-day treasury bill whose monthly interest is 0.75%.
- Paulbilt can wait until it receives the payment of 180 million yen 30 days from now and then convert the yen into dollars. For simplicity, Paulbilt estimates that the exchange rate 30 days from now will be either 140, 145, 150, 155, or 160 yen per dollar. Paulbilt assesses the respective probabilities of these exchange rates as 0.05, 0.25, 0.40, 0.20, and 0.10.

*12.8. The Alpha Beta Corporation (ABC) must decide how much fire insurance to carry in the upcoming year. For simplicity, ABC assumes that fire damage in the upcoming year will have a total value of 0, 20, 40, 60, 80, or 100 thousand dollars. ABC has assessed the following probabilities:

Dollar Value of Year's Losses ($000)	0	20	40	60	80	100
Probability	0.25	0.25	0.20	0.15	0.10	0.05

ABC has the following three options:
- ABC can self-insure (i.e., not buy any insurance).
- For an annual premium of $50,000, ABC can buy an insurance policy with 100% coverage (i.e., ABC would be fully reimbursed for any loss).
- For an annual premium of $10,000, ABC can buy an insurance policy with a $50,000 deductible

clause (i.e., ABC would be reimbursed only by the amount, if any, that its total losses for the year exceeded $50,000).

12.9. The Markhall Card Company (MCC) is a wholesaler of greeting cards and novelty items. MCC is about to launch a special promotion related to the restoration of a national landmark. As part of the promotion, MCC will purchase miniature replicas of the landmark from a manufacturer at a unit cost of $5 and resell them to independent retailers at a unit price of $9. MCC must decide tomorrow how many items to purchase from the manufacturer. MCC's decision is complicated by uncertainty about the demand for the replica by MCC's customers. Using records of past sales of comparable merchandise and intuition about the replica's sales potential, MCC has estimated that its customers' total demand will be 7, 8, 9, 10, 11, 12, or 13 thousand items and has assessed the following probabilities:

Demand (000)	7	8	9	10	11	12	13
Probability	0.05	0.10	0.20	0.30	0.15	0.15	0.05

MCC's decision is further complicated by the fact that the landmark's restoration will be completed by July 4, which is only 3 months away. The July 4 date has two implications:
- If demand is high, there is insufficient time to reorder the replica. Thus, the order MCC will place tomorrow is its one and only chance to acquire the replica.
- If demand is low, MCC will have to "dump" any replicas unsold after July 4 to a discount chain. The discount chain will pay MCC $3 for each unsold replica.

The next exercise involves a modification of the previous exercise.

12.10. Reconsider MCC's problem in Exercise 12.9. In that exercise, MCC had one and only one chance to acquire the replica. Hence, the excess of demand over MCC's order quantity represented lost sales. Now assume that MCC may place two orders for the replica, one before demand is known and another afterwards. More specifically, if demand exceeds MCC's initial order quantity, MCC will place a second order for the excess amount. Since the manufacturer will expedite production and shipment of this second order, MCC's unit cost for items in the second order will be $5.75, an increase of $0.75 over the unit cost of items in the initial order. Furthermore, as compensation to those of its customers who have to wait, MCC will reduce the selling

582

price of a replica in the second order to $8.75, a decrease of $0.25 from the unit price of replicas in the initial order. Given these new assumptions, construct a revised payoff matrix and use it to determine what order quantity is optimal for MCC under the EMV criterion. (Note: Continue to assume that a discount chain will pay MCC $3.00 for each unsold replica.)

Throughout this chapter, we used the EMV criterion to prune a decision tree. The next exercise illustrates that other decision-making criteria can be used to prune a decision tree.

12.11. Reconsider Figure 12.2's decision tree for Holly's problem.
  (a) Prune this decision tree using the maximax criterion.
  (b) Prune this decision tree using the maximin criterion.
  (c) Prune this decision tree using the minimax regret criterion.
  (d) Prune this decision tree using the expected regret criterion.

Exercises 12.12–12.15 test your ability to perform sensitivity analysis on the data for a decision analysis problem. In these exercises, assume the decision-making criterion is the EMV criterion.

*12.12. Reconsider the simplification of Holly's problem summarized by the payoff matrix in Table 12.13(a). The values in this payoff matrix are based on the financial data in Table 12.2 (where the data for site C are ignored in the simplified problem). Table 12.2 specifies that site A's purchase price is $20 million. Assuming all other data remain unchanged, perform sensitivity analysis on site A's purchase price. Summarize your analysis in a graph similar to Figure 12.26.

12.13. Reconsider CSU's problem in Exercise 12.3.
  (a) Assuming all other data remain unchanged, perform sensitivity analysis on CSU's estimate of its profit from playing in the Banana Bowl. Summarize your analysis in a graph similar to Figure 12.26.
  (b) Assuming all other data remain unchanged, perform sensitivity analysis on CSU's assessment of the probability that NSU will beat or tie SSU. Summarize your analysis in a graph similar to Figure 12.26.

12.14. Reconsider Mobon's problem in Exercise 12.4.
  (a) Assuming all other data remain unchanged, perform sensitivity analysis on the amount Exxil offers to buy the lease. Summarize your analysis in a graph similar to Figure 12.26.

  (b) Assuming all other data remain unchanged, perform sensitivity analysis on Mobon's estimate of the cost to drill for oil at the site. Summarize your analysis in a graph similar to Figure 12.26.
  (c) Assuming all other data remain unchanged, perform sensitivity analysis on Mobon's estimate of the probability of a dry well. In performing this sensitivity analysis, assume that if Δ represents the change in the probability of a dry well, then the compensating changes in the probabilities of a minor success and a major success are $-\frac{2}{3}\Delta$ and $-\frac{1}{3}\Delta$, respectively. Summarize your analysis in a graph similar to Figure 12.26.

12.15. Reconsider MCC's problem in Exercise 12.9. Assuming all other data remain unchanged, perform sensitivity analysis on the unit cost at which MCC purchases replicas from the manufacturer. Summarize your analysis in a graph similar to Figure 12.26.

Exercises 12.16–12.20 test your ability to grow and prune a decision tree for a multistage decision-analysis problem. In these exercises, assume the decision-making criterion is the EMV criterion.

12.16. EXP Corporation has recently decided to begin manufacturing its product in Europe. It must now decide what size plant to build. For planning purposes, EXP assumes the plant will have a lifetime of 10 years. EXP is considering two options: a large plant or a small plant that can be expanded two years later into a large plant. The decision depends primarily on the European demand for EXP's product. For simplicity, EXP assumes that European demand will be one of two levels: high or low. As input to its decision, EXP has made the following additional assumptions:
  ▪ The cost to build a large plant is $5 million.
  ▪ The cost to build a small plant is $1 million, and the present value of the additional cost to expand this small plant two years later into a large plant is $3 million. EXP will not consider expanding the plant unless it experiences a high level of demand in the first two years.
  ▪ During the first two years, the probability of high demand is 0.8, and the probability of low demand is 0.2. The level of demand in subsequent years will be the same as in the first two years (e.g., if it is high in the first two years, it will continue to be high in the next eight years).
  ▪ If EXP builds a large plant, then the present value of the profits generated by the plant over the ten-year period will be $8 million if demand

583

is high and $4 million if demand is low. (Note: These profits, as well as those described below, *exclude* construction costs.)

- If EXP builds a small plant now, then the present value of profits generated by the plant over the first two years will be $0.4 million if demand is high and $0.3 million if demand is low.
- If EXP builds a small plant now and decides two years later not to expand the plant, then the present value of the profits generated by the plant over the next eight years will be $1.2 million if demand is high and $0.9 million if demand is low.
- If EXP builds a small plant now, experiences high demand in the first two years, and decides to expand the small plant into a large one, then the present value of the profits generated by the plant over the next eight years will be $6 million.

Using the available information, grow and prune a decision tree for EXP's problem.

*12.17. The 3N Corporation, a manufacturer of copying machines, has recently altered its credit-granting policy. In the past, 3N has granted credit only to customers with an excellent credit rating. However, because of increased sales competition and excess production capacity, 3N now considers granting credit to customers who have a significant chance of being a bad credit risk. 3N has just received a credit request from a new customer who wants to purchase a copying machine. The machine sells for $8000 and costs 3N $5000 to manufacture. As input to its decision of whether to grant credit, 3N has made the following estimates and assumptions:

- If 3N denies the customer credit, there is a probability of 0.2 that the customer will buy the copying machine anyway on a C.O.D. basis.
- If 3N grants credit, the customer will be either a good credit risk or a bad credit risk. The probability of the former is 0.7.
- If 3N grants credit and the customer is a good credit risk, 3N will collect 100% of the $8000 owed.
- If 3N grants credit and the customer is a bad credit risk, 3N has two options. Under the first option, 3N would continue to send the customer a bill and hope it was eventually paid. Under this option, 3N will collect 100% of the amount owed with probability 0.1, 50% with probability 0.2, and 0% with probability 0.7. Under the second option, 3N would vigorously pursue the collection of the amount owed. To do so would

cost 3N 25% of the amount owed, regardless of the amount eventually collected. Under this second option, 3N will collect 100% of the amount owed with probability 0.3, 50% with probability 0.5, and 0% with probability 0.2.

Using the available information, grow and prune a decision tree for 3N's problem.

12.18. No later than one year from now, Meresman Computer Products (MCP) needs to complete the research and development (R&D) for a new product. MCP has identified two alternatives for conducting the necessary R&D. For convenience, MCP refers to these methods as A and B.

Method A can be conducted on either a normal basis or an accelerated basis. If conducted on a normal basis, method A would take 8 months to complete and would cost $600,000. If conducted on an accelerated basis, method A would take 4 months to complete and would cost $800,000. Regardless of whether method A is conducted on a normal or accelerated basis, it is sure to succeed.

Method B consists of two independent steps, which MCP refers to as steps B1 and B2. To complete method B, MCP must complete both steps. MCP can conduct these steps in either order but cannot conduct them concurrently. Neither step is guaranteed to succeed. The probability of success is 0.9 for step B1 and 0.75 for step B2. Each step requires 4 months to complete successfully or to determine that success is impossible. Regardless of whether they succeed, step B1 costs $100,000 and step B2 costs $320,000.

Since method B's total cost is less than that of method A (conducted on either basis), MCP finds method B appealing. However, if MCP uses method B and subsequently discovers it cannot succeed, it will then have to switch to method A (using either the normal basis or accelerated basis, depending on how much time remains until the one-year deadline). Using the available information, grow and prune a decision tree that MCP can use to determine its optimal R&D strategy.

12.19. Triad, Incorporated, manufactures a product that consists of three independent components (A, B, C). Before shipment to customers, each component undergoes its own quality-assurance test. Given the nature of the product, if any component fails its test, it is cheaper to scrap the entire product than to isolate the specific problem and repair it. For each component, Triad has estimated the cost to test the component and the probability that the component will fail the test. This information is summarized in the table below:

Component	Test Cost	Failure Probability
A	$1.10	0.175
B	$1.25	0.100
C	$1.50	0.200

Triad can test the components in any sequence. Once it determines a component has failed, Triad need not perform any further testing, because any failure is sufficient reason to scrap the product. Using the available information, grow and prune a decision tree that Triad can use to determine the testing sequence that minimizes the expected cost of performing the tests.

12.20. Beta Corporation is being threatened by XYZ Corporation with a lawsuit for patent infringement. XYZ has already begun the trial for a similar lawsuit against Alpha Corporation, a corporation with much greater sales than Beta. Consequently, Beta is now considering two basic options: (1) settle out of court now, before XYZ's trial with Alpha is over or (2) wait to see if XYZ wins its lawsuit against Alpha and then decide how to proceed. As input to its decision, Beta has made the following estimates and assumptions:

- The trial involving XYZ and Alpha is too far along for an out-of-court settlement. XYZ will either win or lose the trial. The probability XYZ will win is 0.6.
- If XYZ loses its lawsuit against Alpha, it will not pursue a lawsuit against Beta. However, if XYZ wins its lawsuit against Alpha, the probability is 0.9 that XYZ will sue Beta. (There is no chance XYZ will sue Beta before its lawsuit against Alpha is over.)
- Any settlement (in-court or out-of-court) with XYZ will be based on a percentage of XYZ's average annual revenue over the past five years. This average is $20 million.
- If XYZ sues Beta, Beta has three options: (1) settle out of court with a payment that is likely to be higher than that if a settlement were reached before the lawsuit, (2) go to trial and

contest the alleged patent infringement, and (3) go to trial and concede the patent infringement but contest the amount of the payment to XYZ.

- If Beta settles with XYZ now, the percentage of XYZ's average annual sales revenue that Beta pays XYZ will be 9% with probability 0.3, 10% with probability 0.4, and 11% with probability 0.3.
- If Beta reaches an out-of-court settlement after XYZ has filed a lawsuit, the percentage of XYZ's average annual sales revenue that Beta pays XYZ will be 19% with probability 0.2, 20% with probability 0.6, and 21% with probability 0.2.
- If Beta goes to trial and contests the alleged patent infringement, the probability it will win is 0.2. If Beta wins, there will be no payment to XYZ. However, if it loses, the percentage of XYZ's average annual sales revenue that Beta pays XYZ will be 24% with probability 0.3, 25% with probability 0.4, and 26% with probability 0.3.
- If Beta goes to trial and concedes the patent infringement but contests the percentage of XYZ's average annual sales revenue that Beta pays XYZ, the percentage will be 14% with probability 0.2, 15% with probability 0.6, and 16% with probability 0.2.
- The legal fees and/or court costs for each of Beta's options are displayed in the table below:

Option	Legal Fees and/or Court Costs
Immediate out-of-court settlement	$75,000
Out-of-court settlement after lawsuit is filed	$150,000
Go to trial and contest patent infringement	$800,000
Go to trial and contest only the amount of payment	$300,000

Using the available information, grow and prune a decision tree that Beta can use to determine its optimal legal strategy. (Note: For simplicity, you should assume that it is impossible to appeal a court ruling and impossible to go to trial if Beta does not like the results of attempting to settle out of court.)

13

DECISION ANALYSIS: ADVANCED TOPICS

13.1 INTRODUCTION

Since this chapter is a continuation of the previous one, we will limit our introduction to the following preview of its contents:

- In Section 12.6 we learned how to compute the expected value of perfect information. In Sections 13.2–13.4 we will learn how to compute the expected value of imperfect information—that is, information that results in a prediction of the state of Nature that is *not* guaranteed to be 100% accurate.

- In Section 12.4 we saw three examples where the use of the EMV criterion resulted in a decision that some persons might view as inappropriate. In Sections 13.5–13.9 we will learn a decision-making criterion that accounts for a decision maker's attitude toward risk.

13.2 THE AVAILABILITY OF IMPERFECT INFORMATION IN HOLLY'S PROBLEM

To illustrate imperfect information, we reconsider Section 12.7's simplification of Holly's decision-analysis problem (i.e., the simplification in which site *C* is no longer under consideration). We modify this simplification as follows:

Besides the alternatives of immediately purchasing land at site *A*, site *B*, or both sites *A* and *B*, Holly has a fourth alternative. She can purchase six-month options on both sites *A* and *B* for a total cost of $1 million. (For simplicity, we assume it is impossible to take an option on one site but not the other.) The options' cost of $1 million is non-refundable and cannot be credited to any future land purchase. However, by paying $1 million now, Holly receives an exclusive guarantee that, six months from now, she can purchase the land at site A and/or site B at the current purchase prices specified in Table 12.2 (20 for site A and 30 for site B). Holly finds the options appealing because a planning commission studying the two potential sites for the convention center will recommend one of them to the city council within the next six months. Consequently, purchasing the options enables Holly to delay her purchase decision until after the planning commission makes its recommendation. However, Holly would still have to make her purchase decision before the city council makes its decision, since (as indicated in Section 12.2's statement of Holly's problem) the city council will not make its decision for nine months. Of course, there is no guarantee the city council will follow the planning commission's recommendation. Holly has assessed the following probabilities (based on historical records):

$P(A_{PC} | A_{CC}) = .8$

- If the city council ultimately decides on site A, the planning commission will have recommended site A with probability 0.8 or site B with probability 0.2.
- If the city council ultimately decides on site B, the planning commission will have recommended site A with probability 0.3 or site B with probability 0.7.

Based on these probabilities, Holly must now decide whether the options' $1 million cost is sufficiently compensated for by her knowing the planning commission's recommendation before having to make her purchase decision.

We can analyze Holly's revised problem by growing and pruning a multistage decision tree. To grow the decision tree, we proceed as illustrated in Figure 13.1 and as described below:

1. **Representing the decision on whether to purchase the options.** As illustrated in Figure 13.1(a), the tree's root is decision node I, representing Holly's decision on whether to purchase the options. Consequently, two branches emanate from decision node I: the upper branch represents the decision not to purchase the options and the lower branch the decision to purchase the options.

2. **Representing the uncertainty over the planning commission's recommendation.** As illustrated in Figure 13.1(b), the tree continues growing with the attachment of chance node II to the lower branch emanating from decision node I. This chance node represents the uncertainty over the planning commission's recommendation. Consequently, two branches emanate from chance node II: the upper branch represents a planning commission recommendation for site A, and the lower branch a recommendation for site B. Eventually we will write probabilities adjacent to these branches; however, they require some computations that we will postpone. Therefore, we now indicate the missing probabilities with question marks.

3. **Representing the land purchase decision.** As illustrated in Figure 13.1(c), the tree continues growing with the attachment of decision node III to the upper branch emanating from decision node I and the attachment of decision nodes IV and V to the branches emanating from chance node II. Each of these nodes represents Holly's land purchase decision. Consequently, three branches emanate from each decision node. The upper, middle, and lower branches represent the respective decisions to purchase land only at site A, only at site B, and at both sites A and B. What distinguishes decision nodes III, IV, and V is the information available to Holly. Her land purchase decision at node III occurs immediately after she decides not to purchase the

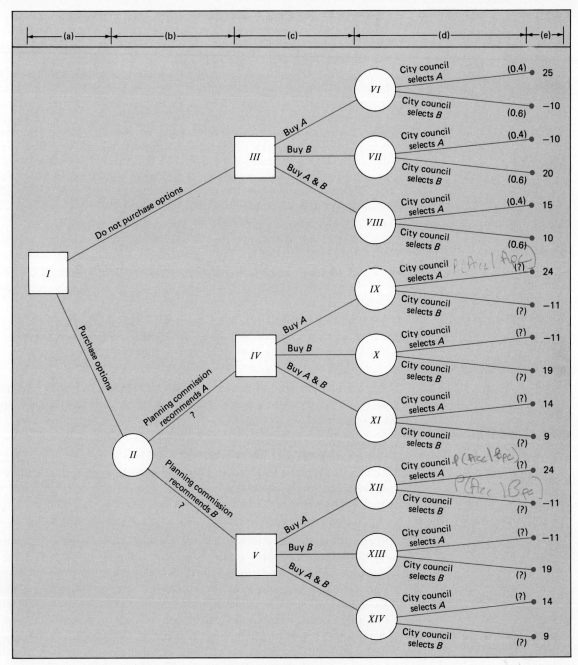

Figure 13.1 Growing the decision tree for Holly's revised

options; at node *IV*, after she decides to purchase the options and subsequently learns the planning commission recommends site *A*; at node *V*, after she decides to purchase the options and subsequently learns the planning commission recommends site *B*.

4. **Representing the uncertainty over the city council's site selection.** As illustrated in Figure 13.1(d), the tree continues growing with the attachment of chance nodes—chance nodes *VI*, *VII*, and *VIII* to the branches emanating from decision node *III*, chance nodes *IX*, *X*, and *XI* to the branches emanating from decision node *IV*, and chance nodes *XII*, *XIII*, and *XIV* to the

588

branches emanating from decision node *V*. Each of these nodes represents the uncertainty over the city council's site selection. Consequently, two branches emanate from each: the upper branch represents the city council's selection of site *A*, and the lower branch the selection of site *B*. We need to write probabilities adjacent to these branches. This is easy for the branches emanating from chance nodes *VI*, *VII*, and *VIII*, since the corresponding probabilities pertain to the situation where Holly does not know the planning commission's recommendation. These probabilities were specified in Table 12.13(a) as 0.4 for the probability the city council will select site *A* and 0.6 for the probability the city council will select site *B*. In contrast, for the branches emanating from chance nodes *IX–XIV*, the probabilities pertain to the situation where Holly knows the planning commission's recommendation. Intuitively, she should then be able to revise her assessments of the probability that the city council will select site *A* and the probability that it will select site *B*. For example, if the planning commission recommends site *A*, Holly's original assessment of 0.4 for the probability that the city council will select site *A* should be revised upward, and her assessment of 0.6 for the probability that it will select site *B* should be revised downward. We will learn the formal method for revising these probabilities in the next subsection. Until then, we write question marks next to the branches.

5. **Computing the payoffs to be written adjacent to the leaves.** As illustrated in Figure 13.1(e), the tree stops growing with the attachment of 18 leaves to the branches emanating from chance nodes *VI-XIV*. These leaves represent the point in time where Holly knows the site selected by the city council and, hence, collects her payoff. We can divide this set of 18 leaves into three groups of six. The upper six leaves are at the ends of the branches emanating from chance nodes *VI*, *VII*, and *VIII*, the middle six at the ends of the branches emanating from chance nodes *IX*, *X*, and *XI*, and the lower six at the ends of the branches emanating from chance nodes *XII*, *XIII*, and *XIV*. We obtain the payoffs for the upper six leaves directly from the Table 12.13(a)'s payoff matrix. However, as illustrated in Figure 13.1(e), we obtain the payoffs for the middle six and the lower six leaves by subtracting the options' $1 million cost from the corresponding payoffs in the upper six leaves.

This completes the growing of the decision tree for Holly's revised problem. The tree still lacks the probabilities now indicated by question marks. We learn next how to compute these missing probabilities.

13.3 REVISING PROBABILITIES IN RESPONSE TO ADDITIONAL INFORMATION

We now illustrate the formal procedure for revising the probability assessments for the alternative states of Nature in response to additional information. We will need the following notation and terminology:

- A_{PC} denotes the event that the planning commission will recommend site *A*, and B_{PC} the event that it will recommend site *B*.

- A_{CC} denotes the event that the city council will select site *A*, and B_{CC} the event that it will select site *B*.

- $Pr\{\cdots\}$ denotes the probability of the occurrence of the event described within the braces. For example, $Pr\{A_{PC}\}$ denotes the probability the planning commission will recommend site *A*.

- With the symbol $\cap$ read as "and", $Pr\{\cdots \cap \cdots\}$ denotes the probability that the two events described before and after $\cap$ will both occur. For example, $Pr\{A_{PC} \cap B_{CC}\}$ denotes the probability that the planning commission will recommend site A and the city council will select site B. This is known as the *joint probability* of the two events separated by $\cap$.

- With the symbol $|$ read as "given", $Pr\{\cdots | \cdots\}$ denotes the probability that the event described before $|$ will occur *given* that we know with certainty the event described after $|$ will occur. For example, $Pr\{A_{CC} | A_{PC}\}$ denotes the probability that the city council will select site A given that we know with certainty the planning commission will recommend site A. This is known as the *conditional probability* of the event preceding the $|$ given the event following the $|$.

We can use the above notation to describe the probabilities we already know and the probabilities we wish to compute. First, let us consider the former. From Table 12.13(a) we know

$$Pr\{A_{CC}\} = 0.4 \text{ and } Pr\{B_{CC}\} = 0.6.$$

From the verbal statement of the modification to Holly's problem given at the beginning of this section, we also know

$$Pr\{A_{PC} | A_{CC}\} = 0.8 \text{ and } Pr\{B_{PC} | A_{CC}\} = 0.2$$

$$Pr\{A_{PC} | B_{CC}\} = 0.3 \text{ and } Pr\{B_{PC} | B_{CC}\} = 0.7.$$

Table 13.1(a) summarizes these known probabilities in a tabular format that we will find useful. These are not the probabilities that are missing from Figure 13.1's decision tree. To see this, observe the following:

- Whereas Table 13.1(a)'s bottom margin displays $Pr\{A_{CC}\}$ and $Pr\{B_{CC}\}$, what is missing in Figure 13.1 from the branches emanating from chance node *II* are $Pr\{A_{PC}\}$ and $Pr\{B_{PC}\}$. In other words, we know the probabilities for the alternative states of Nature for the city council's site selection, but we need to know the probabilities for the alternative states of Nature for the planning commission's recommendation.

- Whereas the four conditional probabilities in Table 13.1(a) are

$$Pr\{A_{PC} | A_{CC}\}, Pr\{B_{PC} | A_{CC}\}, Pr\{A_{PC} | B_{CC}\}, \text{ and } Pr\{B_{PC} | B_{CC}\},$$

what is missing from the branches emanating from chance nodes *IX*, *X*, and *XI* are the conditional probabilities

$$Pr\{A_{CC} | A_{PC}\} \text{ and } Pr\{B_{CC} | A_{PC}\},$$

and what is missing from the branches emanating from chance nodes *XII*, *XIII*, and *XIV* are the conditional probabilities

$$Pr\{A_{CC} | B_{PC}\} \text{ and } Pr\{B_{CC} | B_{PC}\}.$$

That is, we know the conditional probabilities in which the planning commission's recommendation appears before the $|$ and the city council's selection appears after the $|$, but we need to know the conditional probabilities in which the order of appearance is reversed.

TABLE 13.1 Probability Calculations for Holly's Problem

(a) Known Probabilities

Alternative States of Nature for Planning Commission's Recommendation	Alternative States of Nature for City Council's Selection	
	A_{CC}	B_{CC}
A_{PC}	$Pr\{A_{PC} \mid A_{CC}\} = 0.8$	$Pr\{A_{PC} \mid B_{CC}\} = 0.3$
B_{PC}	$Pr\{B_{PC} \mid A_{CC}\} = 0.2$	$Pr\{B_{PC} \mid B_{CC}\} = 0.7$
	$Pr\{A_{CC}\} = 0.4$	$Pr\{B_{CC}\} = 0.6$

(b) Joint Probability Table

Alternative States of Nature for Planning Commission's Recommendation	Alternative States of Nature for City Council's Selection	
	A_{CC}	B_{CC}
A_{PC}	$Pr\{A_{PC} \cap A_{CC}\} = (0.8)(0.4) = 0.32$	$Pr\{A_{PC} \cap B_{CC}\} = (0.3)(0.6) = 0.18$
B_{PC}	$Pr\{B_{PC} \cap A_{CC}\} = (0.2)(0.4) = 0.08$	$Pr\{B_{PC} \cap B_{CC}\} = (0.7)(0.6) = 0.42$
	$Pr\{A_{CC}\} = 0.4$	$Pr\{B_{CC}\} = 0.6$

(c) Joint Probability Table with Row Sums

Alternative States of Nature for Planning Commission's Recommendation	Alternative States of Nature for City Council's Selection		
	A_{CC}	B_{CC}	
A_{PC}	$Pr\{A_{PC} \cap A_{CC}\} = (0.8)(0.4) = 0.32$	$Pr\{A_{PC} \cap B_{CC}\} = (0.3)(0.6) = 0.18$	$Pr\{A_{PC}\} = 0.32 + 0.18 = 0.5$
B_{PC}	$Pr\{B_{PC} \cap A_{CC}\} = (0.2)(0.4) = 0.08$	$Pr\{B_{PC} \cap B_{CC}\} = (0.7)(0.6) = 0.42$	$Pr\{B_{PC}\} = 0.08 + 0.42 = 0.5$
	$Pr\{A_{CC}\} = 0.4$	$Pr\{B_{CC}\} = 0.6$	

(d) Conditional Probabilities

Alternative States of Nature for Planning Commission's Recommendation	Alternative States of Nature for City Council's Selection	
	A_{CC}	B_{CC}
A_{PC}	$Pr\{A_{CC} \mid A_{PC}\} = \dfrac{0.32}{0.50} = 0.64$	$Pr\{B_{CC} \mid A_{PC}\} = \dfrac{0.18}{0.50} = 0.36$
B_{PC}	$Pr\{A_{CC} \mid B_{PC}\} = \dfrac{0.08}{0.50} = 0.16$	$Pr\{B_{CC} \mid B_{PC}\} = \dfrac{0.42}{0.50} = 0.84$

Fortunately, by proceeding as described below, we can use Table 13.1(a)'s probabilities to compute the probabilities missing from Figure 13.1's decision tree.

Our first goal is to compute the joint probabilities

$$Pr\{A_{PC} \cap A_{CC}\}, \; Pr\{A_{PC} \cap B_{CC}\}, \; Pr\{B_{PC} \cap A_{CC}\}, \text{ and } Pr\{B_{PC} \cap B_{CC}\},$$

and the unconditional probabilities

$$Pr\{A_{PC}\} \text{ and } Pr\{B_{PC}\}.$$

To do so, we consider the probabilities displayed in Table 13.1(a) on a column-by-column basis. Table 13.1(a)'s first column consists of

$$\begin{aligned} Pr\{A_{PC} \mid A_{CC}\} &= 0.8 \\ Pr\{B_{PC} \mid A_{CC}\} &= 0.2 \\ \hline Pr\{A_{CC}\} &= 0.4 \end{aligned}$$

Multiplying each conditional probability above the line by the unconditional proba-

592

bility below the line, we obtain

$$Pr\{A_{PC} \mid A_{CC}\} \times Pr\{A_{CC}\} = (0.8)\ (0.4) = 0.32$$
$$Pr\{B_{PC} \mid A_{CC}\} \times Pr\{A_{CC}\} = (0.2)\ (0.4) = 0.08.$$

Those who have studied probability theory, should recall the following general principle:

> When a conditional probability of one event given another is multiplied by the unconditional probability of the second event, the product equals the joint probability of the two events.

Hence, the probabilities of 0.32 and 0.08 computed above are actually the respective probabilities that the planning commission's recommendation will be site A or site B; that is,

$$Pr\{A_{PC} \cap A_{CC}\} = 0.32$$
$$Pr\{B_{PC} \cap A_{CC}\} = 0.08.$$

You should verify for yourself that proceeding in a similar manner for Table 13.1(a)'s second column yields:

$$Pr\{A_{PC} \cap B_{CC}\} = 0.18$$
$$Pr\{B_{PC} \cap B_{CC}\} = 0.42.$$

Table 13.1(b) is a tabular summary of our computations of the joint probabilities. Such a table is known as a *joint probability table*. A joint probability table has the following properties:

1. A joint probability table contains m rows and n columns, with each row corresponding to a state of Nature for one uncertain event and each column corresponding to a state of Nature for a second uncertain event. [For example, in Table 13.1(b), the planning commission's recommendation and the city council's selection both have two alternative states of Nature, so the joint probability table has $m = 2$ rows and $n = 2$ columns.]

2. The number at the intersection of row i and column j of the joint probability table equals the joint probability of the occurrence of the first event's ith state of Nature and the second event's jth state of Nature. [For example, in Table 13.1(b), the entry of 0.18 at the intersection of row 1 and column 2 equals $Pr\{A_{PC} \cap B_{CC}\}$.]

3. Since the probabilities in a joint probability table correspond to all possible combinations for the first event's state of Nature and the second event's state of Nature, the probabilities must sum to 1. [For example, in Table 13.1(b), observe that the four probabilities sum to 1.]

4. A joint probability table's row sums provide the unconditional probabilities for the first event's alternative states of Nature, and the column sums provide the unconditional probabilities for the second event's alternative states of Nature. [For example, in Table 13.1(b), if we sum the first row, we get $Pr\{A_{PC}\} = 0.32 + 0.18 = 0.5$; if we sum the second column, we get $Pr\{B_{CC}\} = 0.18 + 0.42 = 0.6.$]

Table 13.1(c) displays Table 13.1(b)'s joint probability table with the row sums in the right margin and the column sums in the bottom margin. The unconditional probabilities appearing in the bottom margin do not provide us with new information, since $Pr\{A_{CC}\} = 0.4$ and $Pr\{B_{CC}\} = 0.6$ already appeared in Table 13.1(a). In contrast, the unconditional probabilities appearing in Table 13.1(c)'s right margin, $Pr\{A_{PC}\} = 0.5$ and $Pr\{B_{PC}\} = 0.5$, provide new information. In fact, these are precisely the probabilities missing in Figure 13.1's decision tree from the branches emanating from chance node II.[1]

We must still compute the probabilities missing in Figure 13.1 from the branches emanating from the chance nodes $IX–XIV$; that is, the conditional probabilities

$$Pr\{A_{CC} \mid A_{PC}\} \text{ and } Pr\{B_{CC} \mid A_{PC}\}$$

$$Pr\{A_{CC} \mid B_{PC}\} \text{ and } Pr\{B_{CC} \mid B_{PC}\}.$$

To compute these probabilities, we consider the ones displayed in Table 13.1(c)'s joint probability table on a row-by-row basis. The first row is

$$Pr\{A_{PC} \cap A_{CC}\} = 0.32 \quad Pr\{A_{PC} \cap B_{CC}\} = 0.18 \mid Pr\{A_{PC}\} = 0.50.$$

Dividing each joint probability to the left of the vertical line by the unconditional probability to the right of the line, we obtain

$$\frac{Pr\{A_{PC} \cap A_{CC}\}}{Pr\{A_{PC}\}} = \frac{0.32}{0.50} = 0.64 \text{ and } \frac{Pr\{A_{PC} \cap B_{CC}\}}{Pr\{A_{PC}\}} = \frac{0.18}{0.50} = 0.36.$$

Those who have studied probability theory should recall the following general principle:

> When the joint probability of two events is divided by the unconditional probability of the first event, the quotient equals the conditional probability of the second event given the first event.

Hence, the probabilities of 0.64 and 0.36 computed above are actually the respective conditional probabilities that, given the planning commission will recommend site A, the city council will select site A or site B, respectively; that is

$$Pr\{A_{CC} \mid A_{PC}\} = 0.64 \text{ and } Pr\{B_{CC} \mid A_{PC}\} = 0.36.$$

You should verify for yourself that proceeding in a similar manner for Table 13.1(c)'s second row yields

$$Pr\{A_{CC} \mid B_{PC}\} = 0.16 \text{ and } Pr\{B_{CC} \mid B_{PC}\} = 0.84.$$

Table 13.1(d) displays a tabular summary of our computation of the conditional probabilities of the city council's selection given the planning commission's recommendation. The first row contains the probabilities missing in Figure 13.1 from the pair of branches emanating from the chance nodes IX, X, and XI, and the second row the probabilities missing from the pair of branches emanating from the chance nodes XII, XIII, and XIV. When these missing probabilities are added, the decision tree in Figure 13.2 results. Observe in Figure 13.2 that

- The probabilities previously missing from the branches emanating from

---

[1] It is a coincidence that the unconditional probabilities in Table 13.1(c)'s right margin both equal 0.5.

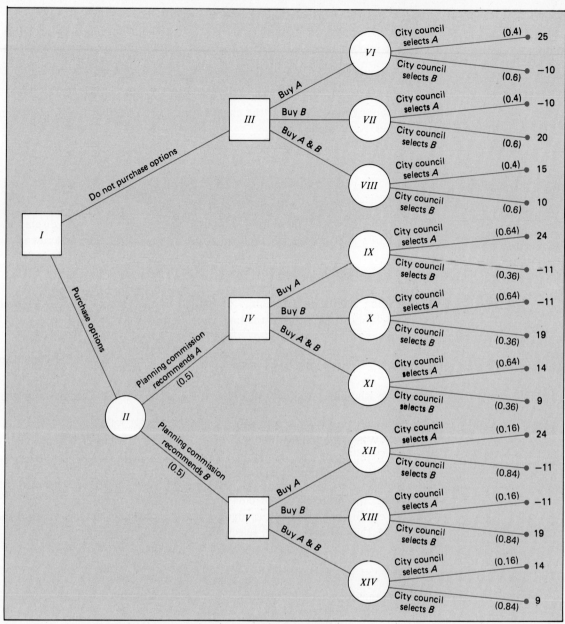

Figure 13.2 The decision tree after adding the missing probabilities

chance node *II* are provided by the unconditional probabilities displayed in Table 13.1(c)'s right margin.

- The probabilities previously missing from the pair of branches emanating from each of the chance nodes *IX*, *X*, and *XI* are provided by the conditional probabilities displayed in Table 13.1(d)'s first row.

- The probabilities previously missing from the pair of branches emanating from each of the chance nodes *XII*, *XIII*, and *XIV* are provided by the conditional probabilities displayed in Table 13.1(d)'s second row.

We will shortly prune Figure 13.2's decision tree to determine Holly's optimal strategy.

At this point let us pause and summarize what we have accomplished. The probabilities in Table 13.1(a)'s bottom margin are known as the *prior probabilities* of the alternative states of Nature for the uncertain event of the city council's site selection. These are Holly's probabilities for the alternative city council selections "prior to" her knowing the planning commission's recommendation. If we were to ask Holly to reassess these same probabilities six months from now, after she knows the planning commission's recommendation, she should respond with revisions of these prior probabilities that account for the planning commission's recommendation in the following manner:

- If the planning commission recommends site *A*, then Holly should revise the prior probabilities displayed in Table 13.1(a)'s bottom margin to the conditional probabilities displayed in Table 13.1(d)'s first row.

- If the planning commission recommends site *B*, then Holly should revise the prior probabilities displayed in Table 13.1(a)'s bottom margin to the conditional probabilities displayed in Table 13.1(d)'s second row.

The conditional probabilities of Table 13.1(d)'s rows are known as the *posterior probabilities* of the alternative states of Nature for city council's site selection. These are Holly's probabilities for the alternative city council selections "posterior to" her knowing the planning commission recommendation. Thus, Table 13.1 provides a tabular representation of a formal procedure for revising prior probabilities into posterior probabilities. Observe that, to compute Table 13.1's posterior probabilities, we had to know not only the prior probabilities displayed in Table 13.1(a)'s bottom margin but also the square array of conditional probabilities displayed in Table 13.1(a) directly above the prior probabilities.

Let us summarize the process of revising prior probabilities into posterior probabilities:

**A Formal
Procedure for
Revising Prior
Probabilities
into Posterior
Probabilities**

Let $B_1, B_2, \ldots, B_n$ denote the verbal descriptions of n alternative states of Nature for an uncertain event, and let $A_1, A_2, \ldots, A_m$ denote the verbal descriptions of m alternative states of Nature for a second uncertain event, an event whose occurrence provides additional information about the first uncertain event. (Note that it is not necessary that $m = n$, as was the case in Holly's example.) Suppose we know the following probabilities:

- The prior probabilities $Pr\{B_j\}$ for $j = 1, 2, \ldots, n$
- The conditional probabilities $Pr\{A_i \mid B_j\}$ for the $m \times n$ combinations of i and j

Furthermore, suppose we wish to compute the following probabilities:

- The unconditional probabilities $Pr\{A_i\}$ for $i = 1, 2, \ldots, m$.
- The posterior probabilities $Pr\{B_j \mid A_i\}$ for the $m \times n$ combinations of i and j.

Then our computations proceed as follows:

1. **Summary of the known probabilities.** We summarize the known probabilities in the tabular format displayed in Table 13.2(a).

2. **Computation of the joint probability table.** Using Table 13.2(a)'s known probabilities, we compute the joint probability table displayed in Table 13.2(b) by executing the following two steps:

   (a) For each combination of i and j, we compute the joint probability $Pr\{A_i \cap B_j\}$ by multiplying each conditional probability in Table

13.2(a)'s rectangular portion by the unconditional probability in the bottom margin of the same column. Symbolically, we perform the computation

$$Pr\{A_i \cap B_j\} = Pr\{A_i \mid B_j\} \times Pr\{B_j\}.$$

As illustrated in Table 13.2(b), we record these joint probabilities within the joint probability table's rectangular portion. (A quick check that we have correctly performed these computations is that the sum of all joint probabilities must equal 1.)

TABLE 13.2 Summary of Tabular Procedure for Revising Prior Probabilities into Posterior Probabilities

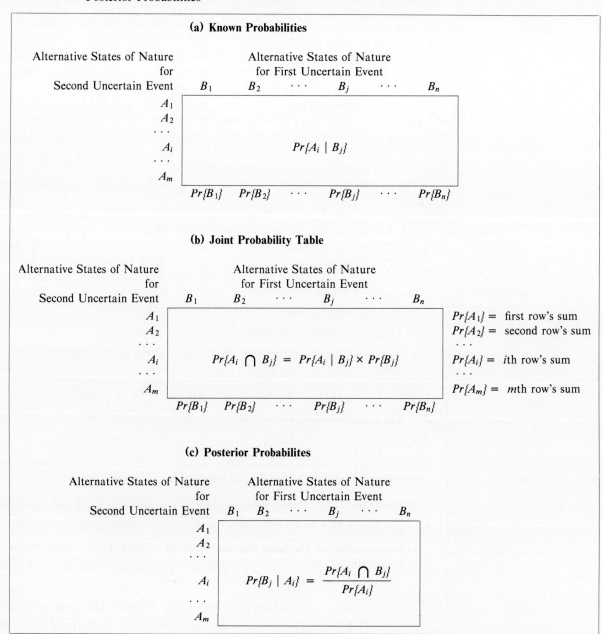

(a) Known Probabilities

Alternative States of Nature for Second Uncertain Event	B_1	B_2	$\cdots$	B_j	$\cdots$	B_n
A_1						
A_2						
$\cdots$						
A_i				$Pr\{A_i \mid B_j\}$		
$\cdots$						
A_m						
	$Pr\{B_1\}$	$Pr\{B_2\}$	$\cdots$	$Pr\{B_j\}$	$\cdots$	$Pr\{B_n\}$

(b) Joint Probability Table

Alternative States of Nature for First Uncertain Event

Alternative States of Nature for Second Uncertain Event	B_1	B_2	$\cdots$	B_j	$\cdots$	B_n	
A_1							$Pr\{A_1\} =$ first row's sum
A_2							$Pr\{A_2\} =$ second row's sum
$\cdots$							$\cdots$
A_i		$Pr\{A_i \cap B_j\} = Pr\{A_i \mid B_j\} \times Pr\{B_j\}$					$Pr\{A_i\} = i$th row's sum
$\cdots$							$\cdots$
A_m							$Pr\{A_m\} = m$th row's sum
	$Pr\{B_1\}$	$Pr\{B_2\}$	$\cdots$	$Pr\{B_j\}$	$\cdots$	$Pr\{B_n\}$	

(c) Posterior Probabilites

Alternative States of Nature for First Uncertain Event

Alternative States of Nature for Second Uncertain Event	B_1	B_2	$\cdots$	B_j	$\cdots$	B_n
A_1						
A_2						
$\cdots$						
A_i	$Pr\{B_j \mid A_i\} = \dfrac{Pr\{A_i \cap B_j\}}{Pr\{A_i\}}$					
$\cdots$						
A_m						

(b) For $i = 1, 2, \ldots, m$, we compute the unconditional probability $Pr\{A_i\}$ by summing the ith row of the joint probabilities computed in step (a) above. Symbolically, we perform the computation

$$Pr\{A_i\} = Pr\{A_i \cap B_1\} + Pr\{A_i \cap B_2\} + \cdots + Pr\{A_i \cap B_n\}$$

As illustrated in Table 13.2(b), we record this unconditional probability in the joint probability table's right margin. (A quick check that we have correctly performed these computations is that the unconditional probabilities in the table's right margin should sum to 1.)

3. **Computation of the posterior probabilities.** Using Table 13.2(b)'s joint probability table, we compute the table of posterior probabilities displayed in Table 13.2(c). For each combination of i and j, we compute the posterior probability $Pr\{B_j \mid A_i\}$ by dividing each joint probability in Table 13.2(b)'s rectangular portion by the unconditional probability in the right margin of the same row. Symbolically, we perform the computation

$$Pr\{B_j \mid A_i\} = \frac{Pr\{A_i \cap B_j\}}{Pr\{A_i\}}$$

We should note that the above three-step procedure is equivalent to repeated application of an important theorem of probability known as *Bayes' theorem.* Space constraints preclude a formal statement and proof of Bayes' theorem. However, those readers already familiar with it should have no difficulty establishing the equivalence between our three-step procedure and repeated application of Bayes' theorem.

13.4 COMPUTING THE EXPECTED VALUE OF IMPERFECT INFORMATION

Having computed the probabilities formerly missing from Figure 13.2's decision tree, we are now ready to prune the decision tree. Since Sections 12.5 and 12.9 contained detailed explanations and examples of the pruning process, we omit the details of pruning here. Instead, before proceeding, you should verify for yourself that pruning yields the pruned decision tree displayed in Figure 13.3. If we remove from Figure 13.3 those branches corresponding to suboptimal decisions (i.e, branches marked with ||), we obtain Figure 13.4. From Figure 13.4, it is easy to see that Holly's optimal strategy can be summarized as follows:

> Take the options now. Then, six months from now, if the planning commission recommends site *A*, buy land at both sites *A* and *B*; if the planning commission recommends site *B*, buy land only at site *B*.

Figure 13.3's pruned decision tree enables us to place a value on the imperfect information provided by the planning commission recommendation. To see how, observe the following:

1. If Holly does not purchase the options, the maximum EMV she can attain is 12, the EMV written in Figure 13.3 within decision node *III*.

2. If Holly purchases the options at a cost of $1 million, the maximum EMV she can attain is 13.2, the EMV written in Figure 13.3 within decision node *II*.

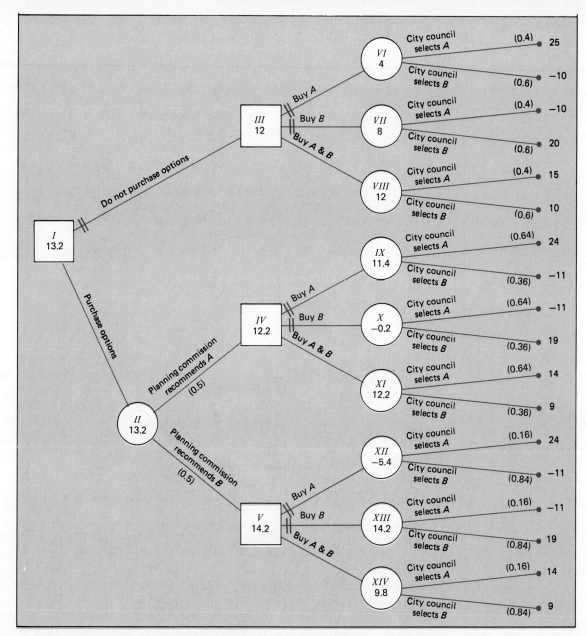

Figure 13.3 Pruning Figure 13.2's decision tree

However, this EMV of 13.2 includes the options' $1 million cost, since we subtracted 1 when computing the payoffs for the lower twelve leaves in Figure 13.3's decision tree. If we now add back the $1 million to decision node *II*'s EMV of 13.2, we obtain 13.2 + 1.0 = 14.2 as the maximum EMV attainable if Holly could purchase the options *at zero cost*.

Subtracting the EMV computed in item (1) from the EMV computed in item (2), we obtain

$$
\left(\begin{array}{l} \text{expected value of imperfect information} \\ \text{provided by planning commission's} \\ \text{recommendation} \end{array} \right) = \left(\begin{array}{l} \text{maximum EMV attainable} \\ \text{if options purchased \textit{at zero cost}} \end{array} \right) - \left(\begin{array}{l} \text{maximum EMV attainable} \\ \text{if options not purchased} \end{array} \right)
$$

$$
= \quad 14.2 \quad - \quad 12.0
$$

$$
= \quad 2.2
$$

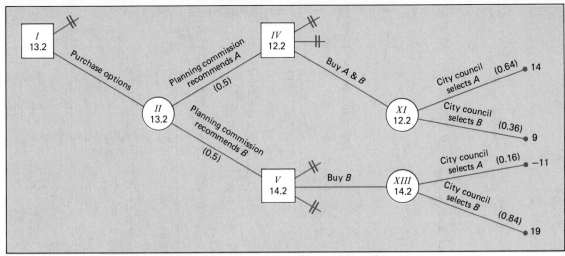

Figure 13.4 Figure 13.3's decision tree after the removal of pruned branches

The value 2.2 is known as the *expected value of imperfect information.*[2] Hereafter, we abbreviate the expected value of imperfect information as EVII. We can interpret the EVII of 2.2 as the maximum price Holly should be willing to pay for the options. If the options cost more than 2.2, they are overpriced in the sense that the increase in EMV enabled by knowledge of the planning commission's recommendation is less than the cost of the options. For example, if the options' cost were to increase by 1.5 from 1.0 to 2.5, the EMV written within decision node *II* of Figure 13.3's decision tree would decrease by 1.5 from 13.2 to 11.7. Since this revised EMV would be less than the EMV of 12 in decision node *III*, Holly's optimal strategy would no longer include the purchase of the options.

It is interesting to compare the EVII of 2.2 to the EVPI of 10 computed earlier in Table 12.13(c). We see the former is significantly less than the latter, because the planning commission's recommendation is not a perfect prediction of the city council's site selection. As you will see in Exercise 13.7, the closer the commission's recommendation is to being a perfect prediction of the council's selection [as reflected by the conditional probabilities in Table 13.1(a)], the closer the EVII is to EVPI.

We conclude our discussion of imperfect information with the following summary of Sections 13.2–13.4:

> To decide whether it is advisable to acquire additional information, we proceed as follows:
>
> **1.** We grow a multistage decision tree whose root is a decision node representing the decision to acquire additional information. Two branches emanate from this decision node. The upper branch represents the decision not to acquire the additional information, the lower branch the decision to acquire the additional information. When growing the decision tree, it is necessary to employ the tabular procedure summarized in Table 13.2 to revise the prior probabilities for the alternative states of Nature into the posterior probabilities.
>
> **2.** The pruning of the decision tree will indicate whether the acquisition of the additional information is part of the optimal strategy.

---

[2] The expected value of imperfect information is sometimes called the *expected value of experimental information* or the *expected value of sample information.*

3. After pruning the decision tree, we can compute the EVII (the expected value of imperfect information) using the following formula

$$
\text{EVII} = \begin{pmatrix} \text{maximum EMV attainable} \\ \text{assuming additional information} \\ \text{is purchased } \textit{at zero cost} \end{pmatrix} - \begin{pmatrix} \text{maximum EMV attainable} \\ \text{assuming additional information} \\ \text{is not purchased.} \end{pmatrix}
$$

The EVII is the maximum fee a decision maker employing the EMV criterion should be willing to pay to acquire the additional information. The EVII is always less than the EVPI (and usually significantly less).

13.5 AN OVERVIEW OF UTILITY AS A BASIS FOR DECISION MAKING

In Section 12.4, we saw three examples where the use of the EMV criterion resulted in a decision some persons might view as inappropriate. By way of introduction to a new decision-making criterion, let us repeat one of these examples. Figure 13.5 displays the decision-tree representation of Table 12.10(a)'s payoff matrix. The decision maker must choose either decision A, which pays \$11,000 with probability 0.5 and $-$ \$1000 with probability 0.5, or decision B, which pays \$2500 with certainty (i.e., with probability 1). Decision A's EMV is

$$(11,000)(0.5) + (-1000)(0.5) = 5000,$$

an EMV twice that of decision B's EMV of 2500. If you knew you were going to choose either decision A or decision B at the beginning of each week for the next year, you could afford to play the averages and, consequently, would choose decision A each week. However, suppose you were faced with a one-time-only choice. Which decision would you make? Your choice clearly depends on such factors as how enticing you find a "sure thing" of \$2500 and how financially able you are to withstand a loss of \$1000. Faced with such a one-time-only choice, many persons, including perhaps yourself, would select decision B. Are persons who select a decision with an EMV that is 50% less than another decision irrational? No! They are simply expressing a personal preference that, at least in this situation, they find decision A too risky in comparison to decision B's sure thing.

This example illustrates the desirability of having a decision-making criterion that takes into account the decision maker's attitude toward risk. The basis for developing such a criterion is provided by the topic of *utility theory*. A detailed

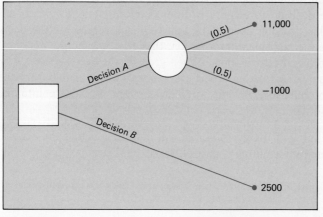

Figure 13.5 Decision-tree representation of Table 12.10(a)'s payoff matrix

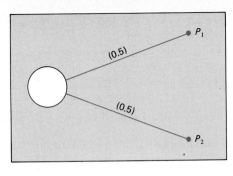

Figure 13.6 A reference lottery with payoffs of P_1 and P_2

and rigorous discussion of the assumptions and principles of utility theory is well beyond the scope of this text. Instead, Sections 13.6–13.9 provide a broad survey of the topic.

13.6 A REFERENCE LOTTERY AND ITS CERTAINTY EQUIVALENT

We begin our survey of utility with two fundamental concepts. The first is that of a *reference lottery* —that is, an uncertain event that results in one of two alternative payoffs, each having probability 0.5. Figure 13.6 is a pictorial representation of a reference lottery, where P_1 denotes one payoff and P_2 the other. Hereafter, we denote a reference lottery by $L(P_1; P_2)$, where P_1 is the larger of the two payoffs and P_2 is the smaller.

The second fundamental concept is that of a reference lottery's *certainty equivalent,* hereafter abbreviated by the acronym CE. A reference lottery's CE is the payoff that makes the decision maker indifferent between participating in the lottery and receiving a certain payment of CE. To illustrate this concept, refer to Figure 13.7, where the decision maker must select either decision A or decision B. Decision A represents a decision to participate in the reference lottery $L(11,000; -1000)$, and decision B represents a decision to accept a certain payoff P. Observe the following:

- If $P = 10,999$, any rational decision maker prefers decision B, since a 50% chance of receiving \$1 more than decision B's certain payoff of \$10,999 is hardly worth the risk of losing \$1000.

- If $P = -999$, any rational decision maker prefers decision A, since the risk

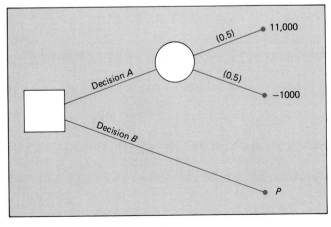

Figure 13.7 Decision-tree representation of the decision to participate in the reference lottery $L(11,000; -1000)$ or to receive a certain payoff of P

of losing $1 more than decision B's certain loss of $999 is more than compensated by the 50% chance of receiving a payoff of $11,000.

■ As P decreases from the reference lottery's maximum payoff of 11,000 to the minimum payoff of -1000, there is some value of P, known as the *certainty equivalent (CE)*, such that the decision maker prefers decision B when P is greater than CE, prefers decision A when P is less than CE, and is indifferent between decisions A and B when P equals *CE*.

Of course, a reference lottery's CE varies according to the decision maker. If we asked fifty decision makers to assess a CE for the reference lottery $L(11,000; -1000)$, we might get almost fifty different responses, because each decision maker has a different attitude toward risk.

We can use a decision maker's CE for a particular reference lottery to classify the individual as either *risk-averse, risk-neutral,* or *risk-seeking.* To illustrate, suppose that, when we ask three decision makers named Tom, Dick, and Harry to each specify his CE for the reference lottery $L(11,000; -1000)$, the responses are as follows:

Decision Maker	Decision Maker's Certainty Equivalent
Tom	2000
Dick	5000
Harry	9000

Considering that the reference lottery $L(11,000; -1000)$ has an EMV of

$$EMV = (11,000)(0.5) + (-1000)(0.5) = 5000$$

can you identify which of the individuals is risk-averse? The answer is Tom. To avoid the risk inherent in participating in the reference lottery, Tom will accept a certain payoff up to $3000 *below* the lottery's EMV. In contrast, Harry is so eager to accept the risk inherent in participating in the lottery that he will do so unless offered a certain payoff at least $4000 *above* the lottery's EMV. We can formally classify a decision maker's attitude toward the risk inherent in participating in a reference lottery by defining the lottery's *risk premium* as the value obtained by subtracting a decision maker's CE from the lottery's EMV; that is,

$$risk\ premium = EMV - CE$$

For example, computing the risk premiums for Tom, Dick, and Harry, we obtain the following:

Decision Maker	EMV	−	CE	=	Risk Premium
Tom	5000	−	2000	=	3000
Dick	5000	−	5000	=	0
Harry	5000	−	9000	=	−4000

Since the risk premium is positive, zero, or negative when the CE is respectively less than, equal to, or greater than the lottery's EMV, the risk premium's sign is an indicator of the decision maker's attitude toward risk. A positive risk premium indicates risk-averse; a zero risk premium, risk-neutral; and a negative risk premium, risk-seeking.

Let us summarize what we have learned thus far:

- A *reference lottery* $L(P_1; P_2)$ is an uncertain event whose payoff is P_1 with probability 0.5 or P_2 with probability 0.5.

- A decision maker's *certainty equivalent* for a reference lottery is the payoff CE that results in indifference between a certain payoff of CE and participation in the reference lottery, preference for participation in the lottery over any certain payoff less than CE, and preference for any certain payoff greater than CE over participation in the lottery.

- A decision maker's *risk premium* for a reference lottery is defined as

$$\begin{pmatrix} \text{decision maker's} \\ \text{risk premium} \\ \text{for the lottery} \end{pmatrix} = \text{(lottery's EMV)} - \begin{pmatrix} \text{decision maker's} \\ \text{certainty equivalent} \\ \text{for the lottery} \end{pmatrix}$$

- With respect to a particular reference lottery, a decision maker is *risk-averse, risk-neutral,* or *risk-seeking,* depending on whether his risk premium is positive, zero, or negative, respectively.

13.7 ASSESSING A UTILITY FUNCTION

We now focus on how the concepts of reference lottery and certainty equivalent can be used to assess what is known as a decision maker's *utility function,* a function that transforms every payoff P into a utility $U(P)$. To illustrate, let us reconsider MBI's decision-analysis problem from Section 12.9. Suppose that the manager responsible for determining MBI's strategy is Mike Roechip.

To begin our assessment of Mike's utility function, we refer to the column of payoffs written in Figure 12.13's decision-tree representation of MBI's problem and observe that the maximum possible payoff is 55 and the minimum possible payoff is -20. In assessing a utility function, it is customary to assign the minimum payoff a utility of 0.0 and the maximum possible payoff a utility of 1.0. Thus, in our example,

$$U(-20) = 0.0 \text{ and } U(55) = 1.0.$$

As P increases from -20 to 55, $U(P)$ increase from 0.0 to 1.0. Figure 13.8 displays this graphically.[3]

To determine the precise nature of how $U(P)$ increases from 0.0 to 1.0 as P increases from -20 to 55, we need to make the following assumption, which we hereafter refer to as the *Equivalence Assumption:*

Equivalence Assumption: The expected utility of any reference lottery $L(P_1;P_2)$ equals the utility of the lottery's certainty equivalent CE; that is,

$$U(CE) = 0.5U(P_1) + 0.5U(P_2)$$

---

[3] Our use of 0.0 and 1.0 as the minimum and maximum utilities is arbitrary. Although we could use any two values, utilities ranging from 0.0 to 1.0 (or from 0 to 100) are clearly more convenient than utilities ranging from, say, 36 to 741.

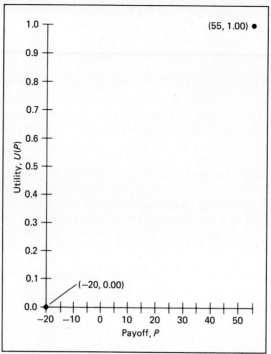

Figure 13.8 Two points on Mike's utility function

The Equivalence Assumption is intuitive since, if a decision maker is indifferent between receiving a certain payoff of CE and participating in a reference lottery that pays P_1 with probability 0.5 and P_2 with probability 0.5, it is reasonable to assume that

$$\underbrace{U(CE)}_{\text{utility of CE}} = \underbrace{0.5U(P_1) + 0.5U(P_2)}_{\text{expected utility of lottery}}$$

Although space constraints preclude us from going into detail, a rigorous development of utility theory requires more than just the Equivalence Assumption.

We already know two points on Mike's utility function, namely, $U(-20) = 0.0$ and $U(55) = 1.0$. To determine a third point, we create a reference lottery whose two payoffs are -20 and 55, the only two payoffs whose utility we already know. Figure 13.9 displays this reference lottery. After explaining to Mike the concept of a certainty equivalent, we request him to tell us his CE for Figure 13.9's reference lottery. After careful consideration, he responds that

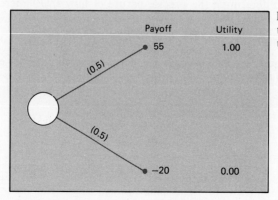

Figure 13.9 The reference lottery used to determine the third point on Mike's utility function

CE = 4.6. Using the Equivalence Assumption, we can now compute Mike's utility for a payoff of 4.6 as follows:

$$\frac{\text{utility of CE}}{U(4.6)} = \frac{\text{expected utility of lottery}}{0.5U(55) + 0.5U(-20)}$$
$$= 0.5(1.0) + 0.5(0.0)$$
$$= 0.5$$

Thus, $U(4.6) = 0.5$ is a third point on Mike's utility function.

We now know the following three points on Mike's utility function:

P	$U(P)$
-20.0	0.0
4.6	0.5
55.0	1.0

Figure 13.10 graphically displays these three points.

Our next goal is to find two additional points on Mike's utility function. To achieve this goal, we create the two reference lotteries displayed in Figure 13.11. Observe the following:

- In Figure 13.11(a)'s reference lottery, the payoffs are 55 and 4.6, whose respective utilities we know to be 1.0 and 0.5.

- In Figure 13.11(b)'s reference lottery, the payoffs are 4.6 and -20, whose respective utilities we know to be 0.5 and 0.0.

Suppose Mike informs us that his CE for Figure 13.11(a)'s reference lottery is 23.2. Then, using the Equivalence Assumption, we compute Mike's utility for 23.2 as follows:

$$\frac{\text{utility of CE}}{U(23.7)} = \frac{\text{expected utility of lottery}}{0.5U(55) + 0.5U(4.6)}$$
$$= 0.5(1.0) + 0.5(0.5)$$
$$= 0.75$$

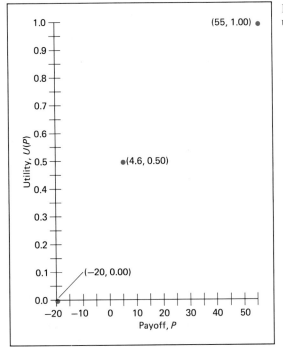

Figure 13.10 Three points on Mike's utility function

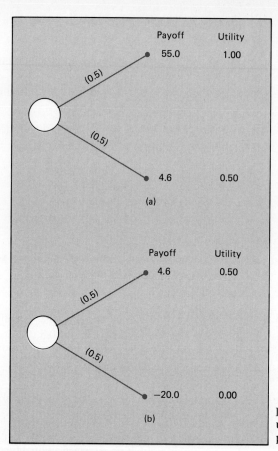

Figure 13.11 The reference lotteries used to determine the fourth and fifth points on Mike's utility function

Also, suppose Mike informs us that his CE for Figure 13.11(b)'s reference lottery is −9.2. Then, using the Equivalence Assumption, we compute Mike's utility for −9.2 as follows:

$$
\frac{\text{utility of CE}}{U(-9.2)} = \frac{\text{expected utility of lottery}}{0.5U(4.6) \; + \; 0.5U(-20)}
$$
$$
= 0.5(0.5) \;\;\; + \;\; 0.5(0.0)
$$
$$
= 0.25
$$

We now know the following five points on Mike's utility function:

P	U(P)
−20.0	0.00
−9.2	0.25
4.6	0.50
23.7	0.75
55.0	1.00

Figure 13.12 graphically displays these five points. If we connect them by a smooth curve, we can approximate Mike's utility function by the graph displayed in Figure 13.13.

We can summarize our procedure as follows:

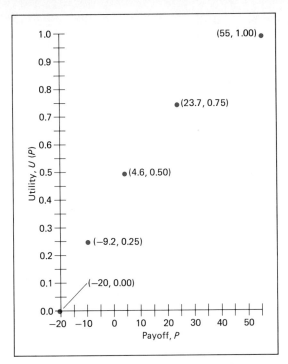

Figure 13.12 Five points on Mike's utility function

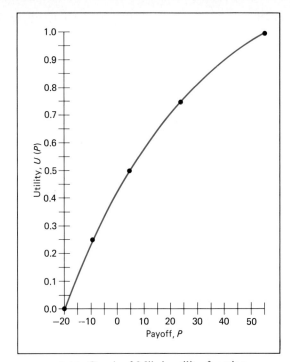

Figure 13.13 Graph of Mike's utility function

Procedure for Determining Five Points on a Utility Function

Suppose the decision problem under consideration has a minimum payoff of $P_{\min}$ and a maximum payoff of $P_{\max}$. Then, to determine five points on the decision maker's utility function, we proceed as follows:

1. We set the utility of $P_{\min}$ to 0.0 and the utility of $P_{\max}$ to 1.0; that is,

$$U(P_{\min}) = 0.0 \quad \text{and} \quad U(P_{\max}) = 1.0.$$

2. To determine a third point on the utility function, we first create a reference lottery whose payoffs are $P_{\max}$ and $P_{\min}$. We next request the decision maker to tell us his certainty equivalent, CE, for this reference lottery. Then, using the Equivalence Assumption, we compute the CE's utility as follows:

$$
\begin{aligned}
U(CE) &= 0.5U(P_{\max}) &&+ 0.5U(P_{min}) \\
&= 0.5(1.0) &&+ 0.5(0.0) \\
&= 0.50
\end{aligned}
$$

3. To determine a fourth point on the utility function, we first create a reference lottery whose payoffs are $P_{\max}$ and step 2's CE, whose utility we computed in step 2 to be 0.5. We next request the decision maker to tell us his CE for this new reference lottery. Then, using the Equivalence Assumption, we compute the CE's utility as follows:

$$
\begin{aligned}
U(CE) &= 0.5U(P_{\max}) &&+ 0.5U(CE \text{ specified in step (2)}) \\
&= 0.5(1.0) &&+ 0.5(0.5) \\
&= 0.75
\end{aligned}
$$

4. To determine a fifth point on the utility function, we first create a reference lottery whose payoffs are P_{min} and step 2's CE, whose utility we computed in step 2 to be 0.5. We next request the decision maker to tell us his CE for this new reference lottery. Then, using the Equivalence Assumption, we compute the CE's utility as follows:

$$
\begin{aligned}
U(CE) &= 0.5U(CE \text{ specified in step 2}) &&+ U(P_{min}) \\
&= 0.5(0.5) &&+ 0.5(0.0) \\
&= 0.25
\end{aligned}
$$

At the conclusion of these steps, we know the payoffs that have utilities of 0.0, 0.25, 0.50, 0.75, and 1.0. Connecting these five points with a smooth curve, we obtain a graph that approximates the decision maker's utility function.

In contrast to the four-step procedure we use in this text, a real-world assessment of a decision maker's utility function is much more complicated. Accurate assessment is complicated by the need to determine more than just five data points, the need to employ statistical curve-fitting techniques to determine the smooth curve that best fits the data points, and the need to employ what is known as *consistency checks*. To illustrate this latter concept, recall that Mike stated that his certainty equivalent for the reference lottery $L(55; -20)$ is 4.6. This enabled us to compute

$$
\begin{aligned}
U(4.6) &= 0.5U(55) &&+ 0.5U(-20) \\
&= 0.5(1.0) &&+ 0.5(0.0) \\
&= 0.5
\end{aligned}
$$

In words, we determined the payoff whose utility is 0.5 using a reference lottery whose payoffs had utilities of 0.0 and 1.0. The Equivalence Assumption implies that, if two reference lotteries have the same expected utilities, they must have the same certainty equivalents. Hence, to check for consistency, we can now request Mike to tell us his CE for another reference lottery whose expected utility also equals 0.5. Such a reference lottery is $L(23.7; -9.2)$. To see why, recall that, during our determination of five points on Mike's utility function, we established $U(23.7) = 0.75$ and $U(-9.2) = 0.25$. Hence, the reference lottery $L(23.7; -9.2)$ has an expected utility of

$$
0.5U(23.7) + 0.5U(-9.2) = 0.5(0.75) + 0.5(0.25) = 0.50
$$

This is the same expected utility as the reference lottery $L(55; -20)$. Since the reference lotteries $L(55; -20)$ and $L(23.7; -9.2)$ both have expected utilities of 0.5, the Equivalence Assumption implies both lotteries must have the same certainty equivalents. When we earlier asked Mike to tell us his CE for the reference lottery $L(55; -20)$, he responded with 4.6. Consequently, he had better respond that his CE for the reference lottery $L(23.7; -9.2)$ is also 4.6. If not, his responses are inconsistent. How to resolve such an inconsistency is beyond the scope of this text. The purpose of raising (but not resolving) the issue of consistency is to illustrate that the real-world assessment of a decision-maker's utility function is not as simple as it might seem.

Despite our simplification of a complex process, you should now "have a feel" for how to assess a utility function. Let us see how to use a utility function to determine the decision maker's optimal strategy.

13.8 USING UTILITY AS A DECISION-MAKING CRITERION

To illustrate how a decision maker can use his utility function to determine the optimal strategy, let us reconsider Figure 12.13's decision-tree representation of MBI's problem. In Section 12.9, we determined MBI's optimal strategy by pruning Figure 12.13's decision tree using the EMV criterion. Will MBI's optimal strategy change if Mike Roechip bases his decisions on expected utility instead of expected monetary value? To answer this question, we must first compute the utility of each payoff adjacent to the leaves in Figure 12.13. For example, Figure 12.13's topmost leaf has an associated payoff of 15. Using Figure 13.13's graph of Mike's utility function, we see that $U(15) = 0.65$. Continuing in this fashion for every other payoff, we obtain the utilities displayed in Table 13.3. Having computed the utility of each payoff, we can now use these utilities in place of the payoffs when pruning the decision tree. For example, when pruning chance node *IX* in Figure 12.13, the value we write within the chance node is not the EMV but the expected utility obtained from the following computation:

$$
\begin{aligned}
\binom{\text{expected utility}}{\text{for chance node } IX} &= (0.2)U(-5) + (0.4)U(25) + (0.4)U(55) \\
&= (0.2)(0.33) + (0.4)(0.76) + (0.4)(1.00) \\
&= 0.07 + 0.30 + 0.40 \\
&= 0.77
\end{aligned}
$$

Figure 13.14 displays the result of pruning Figure 12.13's decision tree using expected utility instead of expected monetary value. Before proceeding, you should verify the pruning for yourself.

Observe from Figure 13.14 that basing the pruning on the payoffs' utilities rather than the payoffs themselves has resulted in a new optimal strategy. Pruning Figure 12.13's decision tree using the EMV criterion resulted in the optimal stra-

TABLE 13.3 Table of Payoffs and Corresponding Utilities

Payoff	Utility (from Figure 13.13)
−20	0.00
−15	0.12
−10	0.23
−5	0.33
0	0.42
5	0.51
10	0.58
15	0.65
20	0.71
25	0.76
30	0.81
35	0.86
40	0.90
45	0.94
50	0.97
55	1.00

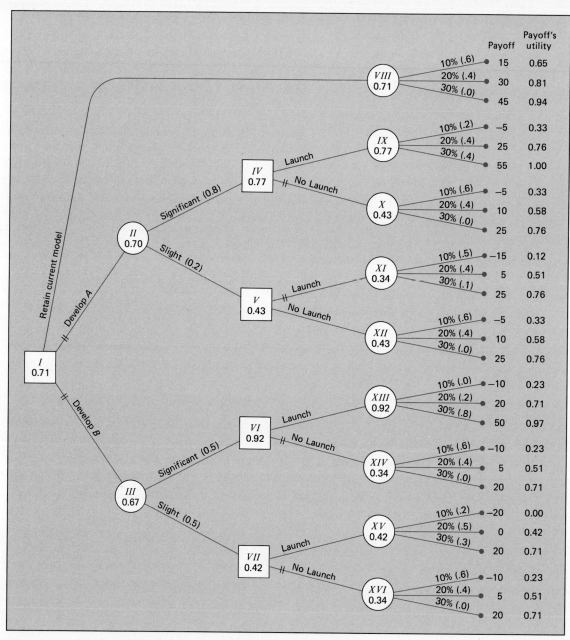

Figure 13.14 Pruning MBI's decision tree using Mike's utility function

tegy displayed in Figure 12.15. In contrast, removal of the pruned branches from Figure 13.14's decision tree results in the optimal strategy displayed in Figure 13.15; that is, MBI should retain the current model and "take its chances" in the marketplace.

It is important to understand that, whereas the strategy that maximizes expected monetary value is the same for all decision makers, the strategy that maximizes expected utility is not. If two decision makers have two different utility functions, their respective optimal strategies may differ. This raises the issue of whose utility function should be used to determine the optimal strategy. For example, in MBI's decision problem, we have (at least) the following three alternatives for the utility function:

610

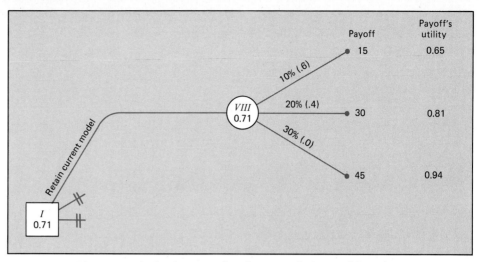

Figure 13.15 Figure 13.14's decsion tree after the removal of pruned branches

- A utility function reflecting the attitude toward risk of Mike Roechip, the individual responsible for making the decision.
- A utility function reflecting the attitude toward risk of MBI's chief executive officer, the person ultimately responsible for the outcome of the decisions.
- A utility function reflecting the attitude toward risk of MBI's stockholders (although such a utility function would be difficult to assess).

Space constraints preclude a detailed discussion of the debate over whose utility function should be used. The most common practice is to use the utility function of the individual directly responsible for making the decision. The purpose in raising (but not fully discussing) the issue is to once again make you aware of the complexities that arise when utility theory is applied in a real-world setting.

> In summary:
>
> To determine the optimal strategy for a decision maker who wishes to maximize expected utility, we replace each payoff with its utility and proceed exactly as if we were maximizing expected monetary value—recognizing, of course, that we are now computing expected utility values.

13.9 CHARACTERIZING A DECISION MAKER''S ATTITUDE TOWARD RISK BY THE SHAPE OF THE UTILITY FUNCTION

Figure 13.16 displays the utility functions for decision makers who are respectively risk-averse, risk-neutral, and risk-seeking. To verify this, let us compute the risk premiums associated with the following three arbitrarily chosen reference lotteries:[4]

$$L(50; -10), \ L(30; -10), \ \text{and} \ L(10; -10)$$

To illustrate these computations, we first consider the reference lottery $L(50; -10)$

---

[4] Recall from a previous section that a reference lottery's risk premium equals the lottery's EMV minus the lottery's certainty equivalent.

and Figure 13.16(a)'s utility function. Regardless of the utility function being used, the EMV for $L(50; -10)$ is

$$0.5(50) + 0.5(-10) = 20.$$

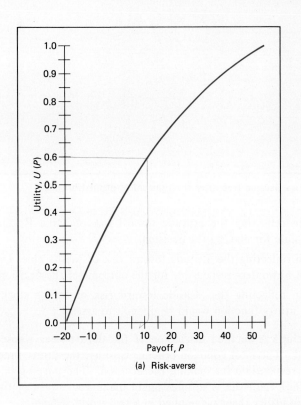

(a) Risk-averse

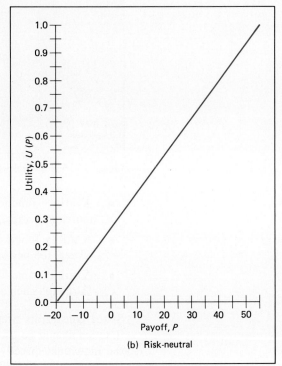

(b) Risk-neutral

Figure 13.16 Three utility functions

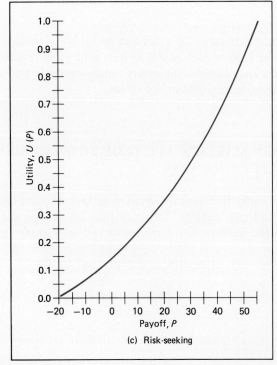

(c) Risk-seeking

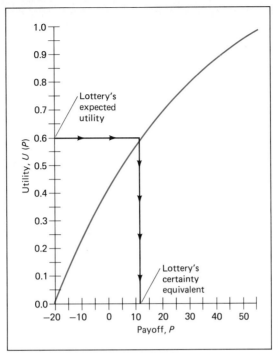

Figure 13.17 Determining the certainty equivalent for the reference lottery $L(50; -10)$

To determine the certainty equivalent CE of $L(50; -10)$ for a decision maker with Figure 13.16(a)'s utility function, we first compute the lottery's expected utility. This computation proceeds as follows:

$$
\begin{aligned}
\text{lottery's expected utility} \;&=\; 0.5U(50) \;+\; 0.5U(-10) \\
&=\; 0.5(0.97) \;+\; 0.5(0.23) \\
&=\; 0.60
\end{aligned}
$$

Then, to obtain the lottery's CE, we use Figure 13.16(a)'s utility function "in reverse," as illustrated in Figure 13.17 and as described below:

1. We start on the vertical axis at the utility value of 0.60 and move horizontally until we "bump into" the utility function's graph.

2. We then make a 90-degree turn downward and proceed until we bump into the horizontal axis at the payoff value of 11.5.

Thus, for a decision maker with Figure 13.16(a)'s utility function, the reference lottery $L(50; -10)$ has a certainty equivalent of CE = 11.5. Substituting CE = 11.5 and EMV = 20 into the formula for risk premium, we obtain

$$
\begin{aligned}
\text{risk premium} \;&=\; \text{EMV} \;-\; \text{CE} \\
&=\; 20.0 \;-\; 11.5 \\
&=\; 8.5
\end{aligned}
$$

Table 13.4 summarizes the computation of the risk premium for each combination of reference lottery and utility function. We have verified the computation summarized in the upper-left corner. Before proceeding, you should verify several of the other computations. Observe in Table 13.4 that, regardless of the lottery,

- The risk premium is always positive for Figure 13.16(a)'s utility function, thereby indicating the decision maker is risk-averse.

TABLE 13.4 Risk Premium for Each Combination of Utility Function
and Reference Lottery

EMV − CE = Risk Premium

Reference Lottery	Utility Function		
	Risk-Averse [from Figure 13.6(a)]	Risk-Neutral [from Figure 13.6(b)]	Risk-Seeking [from Figure 13.6(c)]
$L(-10; 50)$	20 − 11.5 = 8.5	20 − 20 = 0	20 − 28.5 = −8.5
$L(-10; 30)$	10 − 6 = 4.0	10 − 10 = 0	10 − 14 = −4.0
$L(-10; 10)$	0 − (−1) = 1.0	0 − 0 = 0	0 − 1 = −1.0

- The risk premium is always zero for Figure 13.16(b)'s utility function, thereby indicating the decision maker is risk-neutral.

- The risk premium is always negative for Figure 13.16(c)'s utility function, thereby indicating the decision maker is risk-seeking.

The above observations are no coincidence. The same would be true for every reference lottery we might try (although the proof of this is beyond the scope of this text). The computations summarized in Table 13.4 illustrate the following general principle:

- If a decision maker is always risk-averse, his utility function will be "bowed upward" as in Figure 13.16(a). The more risk-averse the decision maker is, the more of an upward bow his utility function will have.

- If a decision maker is always risk-neutral, his utility function will be a straight line as in Figure 13.16(b).

- If a decision maker is always risk-seeking, his utility function will be "bowed downward" as in Figure 13.16(c). The more risk-seeking the decision maker is, the more of an downward bow his utility function will have.

Before proceeding, we briefly note that mathematicians have formal terminology to describe the curvature of the utility functions displayed in Figures 13.16(a) and (c). A utility function with an upward bow is a *concave* utility function, and one with a downward bow is a *convex* utility function.

The characteristic shapes of risk-averse, risk-neutral, and risk-seeking utility functions imply different rates of increase in utility per unit increase in payoff. To illustrate, let us compute for each of Figure 13.16's utility functions the increase in utility that results as we start with a payoff of −20 and successively add 15 to the payoff. These computations are summarized in Table 13.5. Observe the following:

- For Figure 13.16(a)'s risk-averse utility function, each time we add 15 to the payoff, the utility increases, but the increase is *smaller* each time. We say that the utility function has *decreasing marginal utility*. We would expect this behavior from a risk-averse decision maker, since the addition of 15 to a given payoff is worth more when the payoff is low than when it is high. Equivalently, for a risk-averse individual, the increase in utility when 15 is added to a given payoff is less than the decrease in utility when 15 is subtracted from the same payoff.

- For Figure 13.16(b)'s risk-neutral utility function, each time we add 15 to the payoff, the utility increases by the same amount each time. We say that, the utility function has *constant marginal utility*. We would expect this behavior from a risk-neutral decision maker, since the addition of 15 to a given payoff is worth the same when the payoff is low as when it is high. Equivalently, for a risk-neutral individual, the increase in utility when 15 is added to a given payoff is equal to the decrease in utility when 15 is subtracted from the same payoff.

- For Figure 13.16(c)'s risk-seeking utility function, each time we add 15 to the payoff, the utility increases, but the increase is *larger* each time. We say that, the utility function has *increasing marginal utility*. We would expect this behavior from a risk-seeking decision maker, since the addition of 15 to a given payoff is worth less when the payoff is low than when it is high. Equivalently, for a risk-seeking individual, the increase in utility when 15 is added to a given payoff is more than the decrease in utility when 15 is subtracted from the same payoff.

Two additional observations are of interest:

1. A decision maker's attitude toward risk need not always be the same over the entire range of payoff values. For example, it is common that an individual buys insurance (a risk-averse decision) and also buys a lottery ticket (a risk-seeking decision). Figure 13.18 displays a utility function of a decision maker who is risk-averse for payoffs in the range −20 to 5, risk-seeking for payoffs in the range 5 to 30, and once again risk-averse for payoffs in the range 30 to 55. Figure 13.18 illustrates that a utility function can incorporate any type of attitude toward risk.

2. A determination that a decision maker is risk-averse, risk-neutral, or risk-seeking is valid only at the time of the utility function's assessment. At a later point in time, the decision maker's utility function may undergo significant changes due to intervening changes in the decision maker's financial conditions. For example, suppose a decision maker currently assigns the reference lottery $L(11{,}000; -1000)$ a certainty equivalent of 2000, thereby exhibiting risk-averse behavior (since 2000 is less than the lottery's EMV). If this same individual were to subsequently acquire a large sum of money, he could afford to be less risk-averse. Consequently, his certainty equivalent for $L(11{,}000; -1000)$ would be higher than its previous value of 2000. The lesson to be learned here is that a utility function must be reassessed periodically.

TABLE 13.5 Each Utility Function's Increase in Utility as Payoff Is Successively Increased by 15

	Utility Function		
	Risk-Averse [from Figure 13.16(a)]	Risk-Neutral [from Figure 13.16(b)]	Risk-Seeking [from Figure 13.16(c)]
Payoff Increase			
From −20 to −5	0.33 − 0.00 = 0.33	0.20 − 0.00 = 0.20	0.10 − 0.00 = 0.10
From −5 to 10	0.58 − 0.33 = 0.25	0.40 − 0.20 = 0.20	0.24 − 0.10 = 0.14
From 10 to 25	0.76 − 0.58 = 0.18	0.60 − 0.40 = 0.20	0.42 − 0.24 = 0.18
From 25 to 40	0.90 − 0.76 = 0.14	0.80 − 0.60 = 0.20	0.67 − 0.42 = 0.25
From 40 to 55	1.00 − 0.90 = 0.10	1.00 − 0.80 = 0.20	1.00 − 0.67 = 0.33

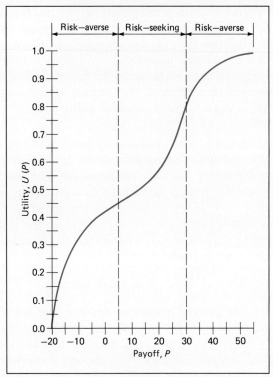

Figure 13.18 Utility function for an individual who switches from risk-averse to risk-seeking to risk-averse

---

13.10 CONCLUDING REMARKS

Our discussion of decision analysis has just "scratched the surface." Entire texts have been devoted to the subject, and consulting firms exist that deal exclusively with decision analysis. Two notable topics in decision analysis that we were unable to consider are:

- **Multiple-criteria decision analysis.** We considered decision-analysis problems in which only a single criterion (i.e., dollars) was used to evaluate alternative decisions. For many real-world decision problems the use of a single criterion is inappropriate. For example, when selecting one of several potential sites for a new airport, the selection criteria must include cost, noise impact on local residents, potential fatalities if a crash were to occur, ecological impact, accessibility from city center, and so on. It is impossible to convert these multiple criteria into dollars and cents. Faced with such a decision problem, a decision maker must use a body of knowledge known as *multiple-criteria decision analysis.*

- **Competitive decision making.** We considered decision-analysis problems involving only a single decision maker. In many real-world decision problems a decision maker competes with other decision makers. An oil company, for example, bids against other oil companies for the drilling rights for a particular site, or a firm's management negotiates with a labor union over a labor contract. Such competition adds another layer of uncertainty to the analysis. Now there is uncertainty not only about what Nature will do but also about what each competitor will do. For example, when bidding for oil drilling rights at a site, a decision maker is uncertain not only about how much oil

Nature has placed underground at the site but also about how much each competitor will bid. Faced with such a problem, a decision maker must use a body of knowledge known as *competitive decision analysis*.

13.11 CHAPTER CHECKLIST AND GLOSSARY

Quickly review this chapter by rereading the material highlighted by a vertical line in the left margin. You should then be familiar with the concepts, techniques, and terminology in the Checklist and Glossary that follow.

Checklist of Concepts and Techniques

☐ Growing a decision tree to represent a multistage decision- analysis problem where the first decision is whether to acquire imperfect information about an uncertain state of Nature. [13.2]

☐ Revising prior probabilities into posterior probabilities. [13.3]

☐ Computing and interpreting the expected value of imperfect information. [13.4]

☐ Using reference lotteries and their certainty equivalents to assess a decision maker's utility function. [13.6 and 13.7]

☐ Determining a decision-analysis problem's optimal strategy when the goal is to maximize expected utility. [13.8]

☐ Using the shape of the utility function to determine whether a decision maker is risk-averse, risk-neutral, or risk-seeking. [13.9]

Glossary

Imperfect information. A less-than-perfect prediction of the state of Nature that is received *before* the decision must be made. [13.2]

Prior probabilities. The probability assessments for the alternative states of Nature before knowing the imperfect information. [13.3]

Posterior probabilities. The probability assessments for the alternative states of Nature after knowing the imperfect information. [13.3]

Expected value of imperfect information (EVII). The maximum fee a decision maker should be willing to pay for imperfect information. [13.4]

Utility theory. A body of knowledge used to quantify a decision maker's attitude toward risk. [13.5]

Reference lottery. An uncertain event that results in one of two alternative payoffs, each having probability 0.5. [13.6]

Certainty equivalent for a reference lottery. A payoff CE that makes the decision maker indifferent between a certain payoff of CE and participation in the reference lottery. [13.6]

Risk premium for a reference lottery. The lottery's EMV minus the decision maker's certainty equivalent for the lottery. [13.6]

Utility function. A function that transforms every payoff P into a utility $U(P)$ between 0.0 and 1.0. [13.7]

Equivalence Assumption. The fundamental assumption for assessing a decision maker's utility function, which states that the expected utility of a reference lottery equals the utility of the lottery's certainty equivalence. [13.7]

Expected utility criterion. A criterion that first computes each decision's expected utility and then selects the decision with the maximum utility. [13.8]

Risk-averse decision maker. A decision maker that has a positive risk premium for every reference lottery or, equivalently, has a utility function that is "bowed upward." [13.9]

Risk-neutral decision maker. A decision maker that has a zero risk premium for every reference lottery or, equivalently, has a utility function that is a straight line. [13.9]

Risk-seeking decision maker. A decision maker that has a negative risk premium for every reference lottery or, equivalently, has a utility function that is "bowed downward." [13.9]

EXERCISES

Exercises 13.1–13.6 each involves a decision-analysis problem where it is possible to pay a fee to acquire imperfect information about an uncertain event. In these exercises, assume the decision-making criterion is the EMV criterion.

13.1. Printus-Hill (PH) is considering whether to publish a manuscript for a textbook in management science. If published, the book will be either a success or a failure. PH estimates that there is a probability of 0.5 that the book will be a success. If it is a success, the present value of the profit the book will generate is $100,000; if it is a failure, the present value of the profit is −$40,000. For a fee of $5000, PH can send the manuscript to a well-known professor who will carefully review it and issue her opinion about whether the book will be a success or failure. Since PH has used this professor many times before, it has records that indicate how accurate the professor's opinion is likely to be. In particular, these records indicate the following:

- When a book has ultimately proved to be a success, the professor had predicted a success 80% of the time.
- When a book has ultimately proved to be a failure, the professor had predicted a failure 90% of the time.

(a) By growing and pruning an appropriate multi-stage decision tree, determine PH's optimal strategy (including whether or not PH should obtain the professor's opinion).

(b) What is the maximum fee PH should pay for the professor's opinion?

*13.2. Reconsider Bud's problem in Exercise 12.5. Now assume that Bud can retain the services of Lowell Prezure, a meteorologist who specializes in long-range weather forecasts. For a fee of $100, Lowell will predict one month in advance what the weather will be on Valentine's Day. When Bud asked about the accuracy of the forecasts Lowell makes one month in advance, Lowell replied that his records indicated the following:

- On days when it has been rainy, Lowell's forecast one month earlier had predicted rain 70% of the time, clouds 20% of the time, and sun 10% of the time.
- On days when it has been cloudy, Lowell's forecast one month earlier had predicted rain 20% of the time, clouds 60% of the time, and sun 20% of the time.
- On days when it has been sunny, Lowell's forecast one month earlier had predicted rain 10% of the time, clouds 30% of the time, and sun 60% of the time.

(a) By growing and pruning an appropriate multi-stage decision tree, determine Bud's optimal strategy (including whether or not Bud should obtain a forecast from Lowell).

(b) What is the maximum fee Bud should pay Lowell for his forecast?

13.3. Reconsider CSU's problem in Exercise 12.3. Now assume that for a fee of $15,000, CSU can obtain a prediction from Pete the Prognosticator about who will win the game between NSU and SSU. Pete will predict that either NSU will win the game or NSU will lose the game. (He never predicts a tie.) After reviewing Pete's past predictions, CSU has compiled the following data:

- When a team has won, Pete had correctly predicted the win 70% of the time.

- When a team has tied, Pete had incorrectly predicted a win 50% of the time.
- When a team has lost, Pete had correctly predicted the loss 70% of the time.

(a) By growing and pruning an appropriate multi-stage decision tree, determine CSU's optimal strategy (including whether or not CSU should obtain a prediction from Pete).

(b) What is the maximum fee CSU should pay Pete for his prediction?

13.4. Reconsider Mobon's problem in Exercise 12.4. Now assume that for a fee of $25,000, Mobon can hire a consulting firm to conduct a test known as a seismic survey. Using seismic soundings, this survey determines whether a site's underlying rock formations are bowed up into a dome. If a dome structure exists, the chances of finding oil are substantially better than if no dome structure exists. The consulting firm has furnished Mobon with data on how well seismic surveys have performed in the past. Based on this data, Mobon has assessed the following probabilities:

- If the well is dry, the seismic survey will indicate a dome structure with probability 0.2.
- If the well is a minor success, the seismic survey will indicate a dome structure with probability 0.6.
- If the well is a major success, the seismic survey will indicate a dome structure with probability 0.9.

(a) By growing and pruning an appropriate multi-stage decision tree, determine Mobon's optimal strategy (including whether or not Mobon should obtain a seismic survey).

(b) What is the maximum fee Mobon should pay the consulting firm for a seismic survey?

*13.5. Reconsider 3N's problem in Exercise 12.17. Now assume that for a fee of $500, National Credit Service (NCS) will furnish 3N with its opinion of the customer's credit rating, classified as either a good credit risk or a bad credit risk. When 3N asked about the accuracy of NCS's credit ratings, NCS replied that its records indicated the following:

- When a firm has ultimately proved to be a good credit risk, NCS had rated the firm a good credit risk 90% of the time.
- When a firm has ultimately proved to be a bad credit risk, NCS had rated the firm a bad credit risk 60% of the time.

(a) By growing and pruning an appropriate multi-stage decision tree, determine 3N's optimal strategy (including whether or not to obtain a credit rating from NCS).

(b) What is the maximum fee 3N should pay NCS for its credit rating?

13.6. Acme Machinery is preparing to deliver one of its machines to a customer. All that remains is for Acme to decide whether to subject the machine to a testing procedure to determine if it meets design specifications. If the machine meets specifications, Acme will earn a profit of $31,000. If testing reveals a failure to meet specifications, the machine will be completely reworked before delivery, thereby *guaranteeing* that the machine will be satisfactory. If rework is done, the profit will be only $16,000. If the machine is delivered to the customer and is *then* found to be unsatisfactory, rework costs and a heavy penalty clause in the sales contract will cause Acme to take a $9000 loss on the deal. Acme will always act in accordance with a test result—deliver if the machine passes the test and rework before delivery if it fails the test. Acme's problem is that it must decide whether to test the unit and, if so, must then choose which of two testing procedures to use. Without testing, Acme estimates that the probability of its machine meeting specifications is 0.6. Both tests cost $2000. (Note that the tests' costs are not reflected in the profit figures given above.) The tests differ only in their accuracy. Test 1 does a better job of identifying a machine that meets specifications. In particular, if a machine actually meets specifications, Test 1 will correctly indicate the machine to be "satisfactory" 80% of the time, whereas Test 2 will correctly indicate "satisfactory" only 60% of the time. On the other hand, Test 1 does a worse job than Test 2 of identifying a machine that fails to meet specifications. In particular, if a machine actually fails to meet specifications, Test 1 will falsely indicate the machine to be "satisfactory" 30% of the time, whereas Test 2 will falsely indicate "satisfactory" only 10% of the time.

(a) By growing and pruning an appropriate decision tree, determine Acme's optimal strategy (including whether or not to test the machine and, if so, which test to use).

(b) For each test, determine the maximum cost Acme should incur to conduct the test.

The next exercise illustrates that, as the accuracy of imperfect information increases, the EVII gets closer to the EVPI.

13.7. Reconsider Holly's problem from Sections 13.2–13.4. In analyzing this problem, we assumed that, based on historical records, Holly had assessed the following probabilities:

- If the city council ultimately decides on site *A*, the planning commission will have recommended site *A* with probability 0.8 or site *B* with probability 0.2.

- If the city council ultimately decides on site *B*, the planning commission will have recommended site *A* with probability 0.3 or site *B* with probability 0.7.

Using these probabilities and the other available information, we computed in Section 13.4 that the expected value of imperfect information (EVII) was $2.2 million. This EVII of $2.2 million was much less than the expected value of perfect information (EVPI) of $10 million, which we had computed earlier in Table 12.13(c).

Now assume that the historical records lead Holly to the following probability assessments:

- If the city council ultimately decides on site *A*, the planning commission will have recommended site *A* with probability 0.95 or site *B* with probability 0.05.
- If the city council ultimately decides on site *B*, the planning commission will have recommended site *A* with probability 0.1 or site *B* with probability 0.9.

(a) Explain why this revised pair of assumptions (in contrast to the original pair) corresponds to the planning commission's recommendation being a more accurate prediction of the city council's ultimate site selection.

(b) Using the revised pair of assumptions, compute the EVII for the planning commission's recommendation and compare it to the EVII of $2.2 million computed originally.

(c) For each pair of assumptions (the original and the revised) compute the ratio of EVII to EVPI. This ratio is often called the *efficiency* of the imperfect information.

(d) What general principle do you think is illustrated by this exercise?

Exercises 13.8–13.12 test your understanding of certainty equivalents for a reference lottery, of how to assess a decision maker's utility function, and of how to characterize a decision maker's attitude toward risk.

13.8. When asked to provide their certainty equivalents for the reference lottery L($7000;−$3000), five managers respond as follows:

Name	Certainty Equivalent
Alex	$2000
Jonathan	$3000
Andrew	$1000
Ian	$5000
Heather	$500

(a) If Heather were given the opportunity either to participate in the reference lottery or to receive a certain payoff of $750, which would she choose?

(b) If Jonathan were given the opportunity either to participate in the reference lottery or to receive a certain payoff of $2500, which would he choose?

(c) Compute each manager's risk premium for the reference lottery.

(d) With respect to the reference lottery, who among the managers is risk-averse, who is risk-neutral, and who is risk-seeking?

(e) Of those managers identified in part (d) as being risk-averse, who is the most risk-averse?

(f) Of those managers identified in part (d) as being risk-seeking, who is the most risk-seeking?

*13.9. Suppose you are assessing a manager's utility function for payoffs ranging from −$2000 to $8000. The table below displays the manager's certainty equivalents for three reference lotteries you present to her:

Reference Lottery	Certainty Equivalent
L($8000;−$2000)	$5200
L($8000;$5200)	$6800
L($5200;−$2000)	$2800

(a) Using the above table, determine five points on the manager's utility function.

(b) Using graph paper, plot the five points from part (a) and connect them with a smooth curve.

(c) Is the manager risk-averse, risk-neutral, or risk-seeking? Why?

(d) Use part (b)'s graph to determine the manager's risk premium for each of the following three reference lotteries: L($8000;$4000), L($3000;$0), and L($3000,−$2000).

(e) What general principle is illustrated by part (d)?

(f) Use part (b)'s graph to fill in the table below:

Payoff Increase	Utility Increase
From −$2000 to $0	?
From $0 to $2000	?
From $2000 to $4000	?
From $4000 to $6000	?
From $6000 to $8000	?

(g) What general principle is illustrated by part (f)?

13.10. Redo Exercise 13.9, this time assuming the manager's certainty equivalents for the reference lotteries you present to her are as follows:

Reference Lottery	Certainty Equivalent
$L(\$8000; -\$2000)$	$3000
$L(\$8000; \$3000)$	$5500
$L(\$3000; -\$2000)$	$500

13.11. Redo Exercise 13.9, this time assuming the manager's certainty equivalents for the reference lotteries you present to her are as follows:

Reference Lottery	Certainty Equivalent
$L(\$8000; -\$2000)$	$900
$L(\$8000; \$900)$	$3200
$L(\$900; -\$2000)$	-$800

13.12. Use the procedure discussed in Section 13.7 to assess a friend's utility function for payoffs ranging from −$1000 to $9000. Does your friend appear to have the same attitude toward risk throughout the interval from −$1000 to $9000, or does his or her attitude change at least once in the interval?

Exercises 13.13–13.17 involve pruning a decision tree using the criterion of maximizing expected utility (and comparing the resulting decision to that obtained earlier using the EMV criterion).

13.13. Reconsider CSU's problem in Exercise 12.3. (Note: Ignore the modification to this problem made in Exercise 13.3.) Now assume that Woody Haze, the person responsible for making the decision, has the utility function displayed below:

Payoff ($000)	Utility
0	0.000
100	0.247
200	0.440
300	0.590
400	0.707
500	0.798
600	0.868
700	0.924
800	0.967
900	1.000

(a) Is Woody risk-averse, risk-neutral, or risk-seeking?

(b) Prune the decision tree you grew in Exercise 12.3, this time using the criterion of maximizing expected utility.

(c) Compare part (b)'s optimal strategy with the optimal strategy determined in Exercise 12.3, in which the criterion was to maximize the EMV. Do the optimal strategies differ? If so, explain why in terms of Woody's attitude toward risk.

13.14. Reconsider Mobon's problem in Exercise 12.4. (Note: Ignore the modification to this problem made in Exercise 13.4.) Now assume that Gus O'Lean, the person responsible for making the decision, has the utility function displayed below:

Payoff ($000)	Utility
−100	0.000
−50	0.028
0	0.060
50	0.096
100	0.136
200	0.235
300	0.361
400	0.524
500	0.732
600	1.000

(a) Is Gus risk-averse, risk-neutral, or risk-seeking?

(b) Prune the decision tree you grew in Exercise 12.4, this time using the criterion of maximizing expected utility.

(c) Compare part (b)'s optimal strategy with the optimal strategy determined in Exercise 12.4, in which the criterion was to maximize the EMV. Do the optimal strategies differ? If so, explain why in terms of Gus's attitude toward risk.

13.15. Reconsider ABC's problem in Exercise 12.8. Now assume that Paul Issi, the person responsible for making the decision, has the utility function displayed below:

Payoff ($000)	Utility
−100	0.000
−90	0.210
−80	0.381
−70	0.522
−60	0.637
−50	0.731
−40	0.808
−30	0.871
−20	0.923
−10	0.965
0	1.000

(a) Is Paul risk-averse, risk-neutral, or risk-seeking?

(b) Prune the decision tree you grew in Exercise 12.8, this time using the criterion of maximizing expected utility.

(c) Compare part (b)'s optimal strategy with the optimal strategy determined in Exercise 12.8, in which the criterion was to maximize the EMV. Do the optimal strategies differ? If so, explain why in terms of Paul's attitude toward risk.

(d) Assuming an insurance company always expects to make a profit, use ABC's problem to illustrate why someone who uses the EMV criterion will never buy insurance.

*13.16. Reconsider 3N's problem in Exercise 12.17. (Note: Ignore the modification to this problem made in Exercise 13.5.) Now assume that Grant Ornot, the person responsible for making the decision, has the utility function displayed below:

Payoff ($000)	Utility
−7	0.000
−6	0.009
−5	0.023
−4	0.043
−3	0.074
−2	0.119
−1	0.187
0	0.288
1	0.439
2	0.664
3	1.000

(a) Is Grant risk-averse, risk-neutral, or risk-seeking?

(b) Prune the decision tree you grew in Exercise 12.17, this time using the criterion of maximizing expected utility.

(c) Compare part (b)'s optimal strategy with the optimal strategy determined in Exercise 12.17, in which the criterion was to maximize the EMV. Do the optimal strategies differ? If so, explain why in terms of Grant's attitude toward risk.

13.17. Reconsider Beta Corporation's problem in Exercise 12.20. Now assume that Prudence Juris, the person responsible for making the decision, has the utility function displayed in Figure 13.19.

(a) Is Prudence risk-averse, risk-neutral, or risk-seeking?

(b) Prune the decision tree you grew in Exercise 12.20, this time using the criterion of maximizing expected utility.

(c) Compare part (b)'s optimal strategy with the optimal strategy determined in Exercise 12.20, in which the criterion was to maximize the EMV. Do the optimal strategies differ? If so, explain why in terms of Prudence's attitude toward risk.

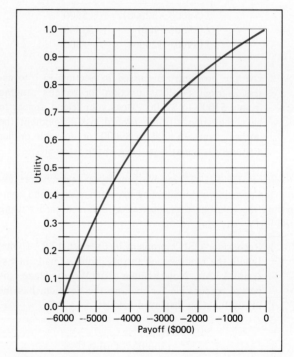

Figure 13.19

Exercises 13.18–13.20 each illustrates a situation where a decision maker can reduce his exposure to risk by forming a *partnership*, by *diversifying*, or by *hedging*.

13.18. Wally Street has the opportunity to invest in a project whose payoff (including Wally's investment) will be as follows:

Payoff ($000)	200	50	−50	−100
Probability	0.25	0.25	0.25	0.25

Besides investing in the project alone, Wally can form a partnership with another investor. The other investor has offered to let Wally have a 75%, 50%, or 25% share of the project. If Wally has a 75% share, for example, he would receive 75% of the payoff and the investor would receive the remaining 25% (even if the payoff is negative). Thus, Wally must make one of five decisions: (1) invest in the project alone, (2) invest in the project with a 75% share, (3) invest in the project with a 50% share, (4) invest in the project with a 25% share, or (5) do not invest in the project.

(a) Grow a decision tree that represents Wally's problem.
(b) If Wally wants to maximize his decision's EMV, which decision should he make?
(c) Suppose Wally has the following utility function for payoffs ranging from −$100,000 to $200,000:

Payoff ($000)	Utility
−100.0	0.000
−75.0	0.191
−50.0	0.350
−37.5	0.418
−25.0	0.481
−12.5	0.538
0.0	0.590
12.5	0.637
25.0	0.680
37.5	0.719
50.0	0.755
75.0	0.817
100.0	0.868
125.0	0.911
150.0	0.946
175.0	0.976
200.0	1.000

If Wally wants to maximize his decision's expected utility, which decision will he make?

(d) Compare your answers to parts (b) and (c). What general principle do you think is illustrated by the difference between your answers?

13.19 Wally Street has the opportunity to invest in three *independent* projects (A, B, and C). For simplicity, assume that each project has the following identical characteristics:

- Each project will be either a failure with probability 0.6 or a success with probability 0.4.
- To fully invest in each project, Wally must put in $100,000. If the project is a failure, Wally loses his entire investment. However, if the project is a success, Wally will earn a profit of $200,000.
- Wally need not fully invest in a project. He may own just a share of a project. For example if he owns a one-half share in project A, he would lose $50,000 if the project is a failure and earn a profit of $100,000 if the project is a success.

Suppose that Wally must choose one of the following three decisions: (1) own a full share of project A and no share of projects B and C, (2) diversify by owning a one-half share in each of projects A and B and no share of project C, or (3) diversify even more by owning a one-third share in each of projects A, B, and C.

(a) Grow a decision tree that represents Wally's problem.
(b) If Wally wants to maximize his decision's EMV, which decision should he make?
(c) Suppose Wally has the same utility function specified in part (c) of Exercise 13.18. If Wally wants to maximize his decision's expected utility, which decision will he make?
(d) Compare your answers to parts (b) and (c). What general principle do you think is illustrated by the difference between your answers?

*13.20. Wally has the opportunity of investing in neither, in one, or in both of two projects (A and B). For simplicity, assume that the payoff from either project depends on whether the current prime interest rate rises or falls during the next month. Project A does well if the prime rate rises, whereas project B does well if the prime rate falls. In particular, assume the following:

- If the prime rate rises, project A's payoff will be $200,000; if it falls, project A's payoff will be −$100,000.
- If the prime rate rises, project B's payoff will be −$50,000; if it falls, project B's payoff will be $150,000.

Wally estimates the prime rate will rise with probability 0.8 or fall with probability 0.2. (He believes there is no chance it will remain unchanged.) Wally must now decide whether to invest in neither project, to invest in project A only, to invest in project

B only, or to "hedge his bets" by investing in both projects A and B.

(a) Grow a decision tree that represents Wally's problem.

(b) If Wally wants to maximize his decision's EMV, which decision should he make?

(c) Suppose Wally has the same utility function specified in part (c) of Exercise 13.18. If Wally wants to maximize his decision's expected utility, which decision will he make?

(d) Compare your answers to parts (b) and (c). What general principle do you think is illustrated by the difference between your answers?

14

INVENTORY MANAGEMENT UNDER DETERMINISTIC DEMAND

14.1 INTRODUCTION

Broadly defined, an *inventory* is a quantity of items being held in storage in order to meet some future need. *Depletion* is the removal of items from inventory for their intended use, and *replenishment* is the addition of items to inventory. In this chapter and the next, we will discuss mathematical models to help manage the depletion and replenishment of inventory, a problem known as *inventory management*.[1]

Inventories are an integral part of most organizations. As examples,

- An automobile manufacturer has inventories of raw materials and parts, inventories of partially built autos awaiting further work, and inventories of fully built autos awaiting shipment.

- A department store has inventories of clothing, furniture, televisions, and so on.

- A hospital has inventories of pharmaceuticals, blood, food, and so on.

- A government agency has inventories of office supplies.

- A financial institution has an inventory of cash awaiting expenditure or investment.

---

[1] If you have read Chapters 4 and 5, then you have already learned a mathematical model for inventory management. In Sections 4.3 and 5.3 we learned to use linear programming to solve two versions of Suny's production and inventory planning problem.

Inventories such as these usually represent a large portion of an organization's assets, sometimes as much as 30% to 40%. Consequently, inventory management is a problem that most managers will confront at least once during their careers.

The fundamental dilemma of inventory management is the simultaneous presence of compelling arguments both for and against having a high inventory level. Let us briefly discuss these arguments.

The Case Against Having a High Inventory Level

The argument cited most often against having a high inventory level is that unnecessary inventory is equivalent to "idle" cash. To illustrate, consider an automobile manufacturer who has 200 autos in inventory at the end of a particular month. If the average cost to manufacture an auto is $5000, an inventory of 200 autos has a cash value of

$$(200)(5000) = \$1,000,000$$

Hence, we can think of parking 200 autos in a storage lot for one month as equivalent to placing a box containing one million dollars in the lot for one month.

By letting one million dollars stand idle for one month, the manufacturer must forego two opportunities: (1) The manufacturer could have invested the idle cash, thereby earning one month's interest on one million dollars, and (2) the manufacturer could have used the idle cash to reduce the amount of its debt, thereby saving one month's interest on one million dollars. The loss of one month's interest on one million dollars is the so-called *opportunity cost* of having an inventory of 200 autos for one month.

It is customary to compute the opportunity cost by multiplying the inventory's cash value by a percentage known as the *cost of capital* per unit of time. For example, if an organization's cost of capital is 1.5% per month, then the opportunity cost of one auto in inventory for one month equals 1.5% of the auto's cash value of $5000—that is, $75 per month per auto. Hence, holding 200 autos in inventory for one month has an opportunity cost of $(200)(75) = \$15,000$ per month. Before leaving the concept of cost of capital, we note that, in some applications, the unit of time is one year rather than one month. In this case, we simply use the annual cost of capital. For example, if the cost of capital is 20% per year, then the opportunity cost of one item in inventory for one year is simply 20% of its equivalent cash value.

Other arguments against having a high inventory level include the following:

- Storage of inventory requires space. Regardless of whether this space is owned or leased by the organization, its cost increases as the inventory level increases.

- Inventory requires maintenance. The nature of the maintenance depends on the item. It may involve some or all of the following: insurance, security guards, an alarm system, a special environment (e.g., heating or refrigeration). Regardless of its nature, maintenance cost increases as the inventory level increases.

- Inventory may spoil or become obsolete. *Spoilage* is possible for an item (e.g., milk in a grocery store or blood in a hospital) that deteriorates in quality the longer it remains in inventory, eventually becoming unusable. In contrast, *obsolescence* is possible for an item (e.g., a particular style of clothing or a computer) whose value would be much lower if there were to be a sudden change in what is in vogue or what is state-of-the-art. As the inventory level increases, so does the potential magnitude of the loss due to spoilage or obsolescence.

The Case for Having a High Inventory Level

The argument cited most often in favor of a high inventory level is that it protects against an unexpected surge in demand. For example, a manufacturer with a low inventory of raw materials might have to refuse an unexpected large order for its product, and a wholesaler or retailer with a low inventory of merchandise might have to do the same.

Other arguments in favor of a high inventory level include the following:

- Items an organization purchases in a large quantity may have a lower unit cost because of discounts in the vendor's pricing structure. Similarly, items an organization produces in a large quantity may have a lower unit cost because of economies of scale in its production process. A large purchase quantity or production quantity results in a high inventory level.

- A gradual build-up of inventory may be the only way for a manufacturer to prepare for a period of peak demand. For example, a manufacturer of VCRs cannot wait until December to produce all it will sell during the peak demand that occurs in the weeks before Christmas. It must increase its inventory level throughout summer and fall so that it may draw on this inventory in December.

- A high inventory level protects against an anticipated shortage of an item. For example, a manufacturer who will be involved in labor negotiations in three months might want to begin increasing its inventory level now as a hedge against a strike.

The Goal of Inventory Management

We can summarize our introduction to inventory management as follows:

> On one hand, an organization should maintain a low inventory level, primarily to avoid incurring the opportunity cost of inventory. On the other hand, the organization should maintain a high inventory level, primarily to provide good service to its customers. An appropriate balance between these conflicting goals can be achieved by using the mathematical models we will discuss in this chapter and the next.

14.2 CHARACTERISTICS OF THE INVENTORY ENVIRONMENT

Before discussing specific mathematical models for inventory management, we must discuss ten general ways to characterize the *inventory system*—that is, the environment in which inventory is being depleted and replenished. By varying these characteristics, we can describe virtually any inventory system.

Single Item Versus Multiple Items

Inventory management is much easier when it involves only a single item instead of a collection of related items. Although we will focus on the former, the latter is more common. Most organizations carry inventories of many distinct items. Rarely are these items totally unrelated. For example, if two items share the same warehouse, a high inventory level for one necessitates a low inventory level for the other. As another example, if two items are ordered from the same vendor, there might be a price discount that depends on the total quantity ordered of both items. In all but Section 14.7, we will assume the inventory system involves a single item. Although somewhat unrealistic, a single-item system serves to introduce the topic of inventory management. Furthermore, the concepts and techniques we will learn provide a foundation for future study outside this text.

Perishable Items Versus Nonperishable Items

An item in inventory is *perishable* if it can spoil or become obsolete (as discussed in the previous section). Examples of perishable items include some types of food in a grocery store, blood in a hospital, clothing, or high-tech products. Except in Sections 15.8–15.12, we assume items are nonperishable.

Ordering Versus Production

There are two ways to replenish inventory: ordering items from a vendor or producing items internally. An important distinction between an ordering environment and a production environment is the manner in which inventory is replenished. In an ordering environment, there is an instantaneous upward "jump" in the inventory level at the discrete points in time when orders arrive. In a production environment, the inventory level rises gradually throughout the period of time in which production occurs.

Single-Echelon Versus Multiechelon System

An inventory system is either a *single-echelon* or a *multiechelon system*. In a single-echelon system, all inventory is stored at a single location. Hence, when an item is withdrawn from inventory, it is used directly to satisfy demand. Examples include the inventory systems for a retail store whose only inventory is on-site, a manufacturer with a single plant that ships directly to its customers, and a hospital that maintains its own inventories of medical supplies.

In a multiechelon system, inventories are stored at various locations. Hence, when an item is withdrawn from inventory, it is not always used directly to satisfy demand; it may simply be transferred from the inventory at one location to the inventory at another location. Examples include the inventory system for a retailer having a central warehouse and several stores and a manufacturer with several plants, several warehouses, and several retail outlets. A multiechelon inventory system is really several single-echelon systems combined into one system. Because of their complexity, multiechelon systems are not discussed in this text.

628

TABLE 14.1 The Four Types of Planning Horizons (assuming time is measured in weeks)

When Decisions Affecting Inventory Can Be Made	The Number of Weeks for Which Plans Are Being Made	
	A Specific Number of Weeks	An Indefinite Number of Weeks
Once per week	Discrete-time finite-period planning horizon	Discrete-time infinite-period planning horizon
Any time	Continuous-time finite-period planning horizon	Continuous-time infinite-period planning horizon

The Nature of the Planning Horizon

The *planning horizon* is the number of time periods (e.g., the number of weeks) over which inventory decisions must be made. Based on how frequently we can make a decision affecting inventory and on how long such decisions will continue to be made, Table 14.1 defines the four types of planning horizons, assuming time is measured in weeks.[2] For example, Suny's production and inventory planning problem in Section 4.3 has a discrete-time finite-period planning horizon. We will see examples of other types of planning horizons in this chapter and the next.

Deterministic Demand Versus Stochastic Demand

There are two types of demand:

- An item has *deterministic demand* when we know with certainty the demand for every period in the planning horizon.

- An item has *stochastic demand* when its demand is not deterministic but instead governed by a specified probability distribution (e.g., a normal distribution with a specified mean and variance).

In this chapter we consider only deterministic demand; in the next chapter we discuss stochastic demand. For only a very few items is demand truly deterministic. However, many mathematical models for inventory management assume deterministic demand, using forecasts of uncertain demands as if they were 100% accurate. The higher the degree of confidence in the forecasts, the more appropriate it is to assume a deterministic demand.

Dependent Demand Versus Independent Demand

Besides characterizing demand as deterministic or stochastic, there is a second characterization:

- An item has *dependent demand* when we can accurately calculate its demand from known plans or schedules. Dependent demand is typical when an item is a component in a finished good, such as transmissions for an automobile or memory chips for a computer. Once we know the production schedule for the finished good, we can calculate the demand for the component.

---

[2] Similar definitions apply if time is measured in days or months.

■ An item has *independent demand* when its demand arises from plans or schedules that are unknown to us. Independent demand is typical when an item is a finished good, such as cameras at a retail store or blood at a hospital. If we sell a finished good, its demand arises from plans and schedules known to our customers but usually not to us.

The distinction between dependent and independent demand is important because, as we will see in Section 14.7, it affects the approach to inventory management.

The Ordering (or Production) Policy[3]

The inventory policy an organization follows depends primarily on how closely it monitors an item's inventory level. Two common policies are described below:

■ A *periodic review policy* occurs when the precise level of an item's inventory is known only after checks made at predetermined fixed intervals of time (e.g., every three months). Each periodic check of inventory computes the net effect of all depletions that occurred since the most recent check. Only at the times of these periodic checks is it possible to place an order. Under these circumstances, it is common to vary the size of the orders. In particular, the current inventory level is compared with a predetermined "target" inventory level, and the difference between these two levels is the quantity ordered.

■ A *continuous review policy* occurs when every depletion of an item's inventory is recorded immediately. Thus, the precise inventory level is known at all times, thereby enabling the placement of an order at any time. Under these circumstances, it is common to order a predetermined fixed quantity each time the inventory level decreases to a predetermined level.

Since a continuous review policy requires much more record keeping than a periodic review policy, it was rare until the widespread commercial availability of computers. Today, it is the rule rather than the exception. Consequently, we will devote most of our attention to the continuous review policy.

It is interesting to note that, for the periodic review policy we described, the time between orders is fixed but the size of an order varies. Just the opposite is true for the continuous review policy we described. There are many variations of these two basic policies. For example, one variation fixes both the time between orders and the order quantity (e.g., always order 100 items every two weeks).

Deterministic Lead Time Versus Stochastic Lead Time

Lead time is the elapsed time between the initiation of an activity that will replenish inventory (either placing an order or deciding to produce) and the receipt of the items. As with demand, lead time can be either deterministic (i.e., known with certainty) or stochastic (i.e., governed by a specified probability distribution). An example of a deterministic lead time is an environment where an order is always received one week after it is placed. Of course, a lead time of exactly one week for every order would be rare. More commonly, the lead time would be one week for most orders but occasionally one or two days less or more. In this environment, it

---

[3] In this subsection, we assume an ordering environment. Our comments remain valid if "production" is substituted everywhere for "ordering."

would still be safe for planning purposes to assume a deterministic lead time of one week. However, if lead time were one week for 50% of the orders, two weeks for 30% of the orders, and four weeks for 20% of the orders, assuming a deterministic lead time equal to the average would be inappropriate. In this chapter we consider only a deterministic lead time; in the next chapter we discuss a stochastic lead time.

The Treatment of a Stockout

A *stockout* occurs when a demand for an item cannot be satisfied because the inventory level has dropped to zero. In some environments (e.g., a hospital's inventory of blood) a stockout has such drastic consequences that the inventory manager must ensure that the probability of a stockout is virtually zero. In these environments a stockout is said to be *disallowed*. In most environments, however, a stockout is allowed, although stockouts are usually accidental rather than planned. If allowed, a stockout may have one of two outcomes (or a combination thereof):

- **Backlogging**. In a *backlogging* environment, all demand for an item that occurs while there is no inventory is accumulated and filled at a later date when inventory has been replenished. In short, backlogged demand leads to a negative inventory level. As we will soon see, backlogged demand has costs associated with it. These costs can be explicit, such as the cost of expediting shipment by a vendor, or implicit, such as a loss of customers' goodwill. Continual erosion of goodwill could result in the eventual loss of customers.

- **Lost Sales**. In a *lost sales* environment, it is impossible for the organization to backlog demand, because customers refuse to wait or because the organization has a policy of turning away all demand when it has no inventory. Lost sales are costly, not only because of the loss of revenue but also because of the loss of goodwill.

To summarize:

To describe an inventory system, we must specify the following characteristics:

1. Whether the inventory system involves a single item or multiple items.

2. Whether items are perishable or nonperishable.

3. Whether items are ordered from a vendor or produced internally.

4. Whether the inventory system is a single-echelon or a multiechelon system.

5. Which of the four planning horizons listed in Table 14.1 is appropriate.

6. Whether demand is deterministic or stochastic.

7. Whether demand is independent or dependent.

8. Whether the inventory policy to be used is a periodic review or a continuous review policy.

9. Whether lead time is deterministic or stochastic.

10. Whether a stockout is disallowed or allowed and, if allowed, whether it results in backlogging or lost sales.

By varying these characteristics, we can describe virtually any inventory system. Although this chapter and the next consider only a few elementary inventory systems, this section has given you an overview of more complex ones.

14.3 COST CRITERIA

When comparing alternative inventory policies, the most common criterion is cost, which consists of three components. We now discuss each component in turn.

Ordering Cost (When Ordering) and Production Cost (When Producing)

In an ordering environment, the *ordering cost* is the cost incurred each time an order is placed. It has two subcomponents:

- **The variable component of ordering cost**. The *variable ordering cost* consists of those costs that change if the quantity ordered changes. Hereafter, we use Q to denote the quantity ordered and C_i to denote the unit cost of an item, where C_i includes not only the unit price paid to the vendor but also internal costs that change as the quantity ordered changes (e.g., inspection costs once the items arrive).[4] Using this notation,

$$\text{variable ordering cost} = C_i Q.$$

- **The fixed component of ordering cost**. The *fixed ordering cost* consists of those costs that do not change if the quantity ordered changes.[5] Hereafter, we use C_o to denote the fixed ordering costs. C_o includes the clerical and administrative costs of processing an order, any mailing or phone expenses incurred while placing the order, and the fixed portion of delivery fees. For example, suppose a vendor's delivery fee consists of a flat $100 plus an additional $2 per item. In this case, C_o would include the $100 flat fee, and C_i would include the $2-per-item fee.

In a production environment, the cost analogous to the ordering cost is the *production cost*—the cost incurred each time a production run is made. The production cost consists of two subcomponents: *variable production cost* and *fixed production cost*. Because these subcomponents are analogous to their counterparts in an ordering environment, we will not discuss them in detail. However, we should note that the fixed production cost consists primarily of the fixed costs of labor, materials, and energy used in "setting up" the machinery for the production run.[6] For example, if production entails heating a furnace from room temperature to some specified high temperature, the energy cost of doing so should be included in the fixed production cost.

---

[4] If the vendor has a price structure for which the unit cost decreases as the quantity ordered increases, then we must indicate that the unit cost is a function of Q by denoting it by $C_i(Q)$. However, except in Section 14.5, we will assume the unit cost does not depend on Q.

[5] Some refer to the fixed ordering cost as the *transaction cost*.

[6] For this reason, some refer to the fixed production cost as the *set-up cost*.

Holding Cost

Once an item is added to inventory, there is a cost associated with keeping it there. The *annual holding cost per item* is the cost of "holding" one item in inventory for one year.[7] Hereafter, we use C_h to denote this quantity. Note that the definition of C_h does not imply that every item remains in inventory for one year. We assume that, if an item remains in inventory for less than one year, then the cost is proportionately lower (e.g., the monthly holding cost per item is one-twelfth of C_h).

As discussed in Section 14.1, C_h consists primarily of the opportunity cost of holding one item in inventory for one year. For example, if an item's unit cost is C_i = \$100 and the organization's annual cost of capital is 20%, then C_h is *at least* $(0.20)(100)$ = \$20. C_h is larger because it also includes an item's share of other annual costs associated with inventory. These additional costs consist of the annual costs of acquiring and maintaining the storage space, of the personnel and equipment that handle the replenishment and depletion of inventory, of items spoiling or becoming obsolete, and so on.

Some organizations find it convenient to express all components of an item's annual holding cost as a percentage of the item's unit cost. For example, C_h might be expressed as 25% of C_i, where the major portion of the 25% consists of the item's annual opportunity cost and the remaining portion consists of the item's share of the other annual costs associated with inventory. Thus, although we will usually denote an item's annual holding cost by C_h, we will sometimes denote this cost by pC_i, where p is the decimal fraction equivalent to the percentage being applied to C_i (e.g., when the percentage is 25%, p = 0.25).

Stockout Cost

An item's *stockout cost* is the cost incurred when an item is demanded but there is no inventory.[8] An item's stockout cost depends on whether a stockout results in backlogging or a lost sale.

In a backlogging environment, one component of an item's stockout cost is the cost associated with the loss of a customer's goodwill. Although difficult to estimate, this cost should not be ignored, because a customer who continually experiences stockouts might eventually take his business to a competitor. Of course, if customers are extremely loyal or have few or no alternatives, the loss of goodwill is not a factor. Besides the cost associated with the loss of goodwill, other costs are usually associated with a stockout in a backlogging environment. Fortunately, they are much easier to estimate. As an example, consider the following:

- Suppose that, when a stockout occurs, the backlogged item is acquired via an expedited shipment from the vendor. In this case, an item's stockout cost is the amount by which the cost of an expedited shipment exceeds the cost of a normal shipment. (A similar comment applies for the use of overtime in a production environment.)
- Suppose that a customer who experiences a backlog is given a price reduction. In this case, an item's stockout cost is the amount by which the normal price exceeds the reduced price.

---

[7] Some refer to the holding cost as the *carrying cost* or the *storage cost*.

[8] Some refer to stockout cost as *shortage cost* or *penalty cost*.

In a lost sales environment, an item's stockout cost consists primarily of the profit foregone because a sale is not made. To this must be added the cost associated with the loss of goodwill.

Hereafter, we use C_s to denote the stockout cost per item. Note, however, that in some environments an item's stockout cost depends on the length of time the item is backordered. For example, suppose that a customer who experiences a stockout is given a price reduction of 1% for each week the item remains backlogged. In such cases it is necessary to specify the stockout cost per item *per unit of time*. We will not consider this type of stockout cost.

A Warning About Computing Costs

Cost accounting systems are often an inadequate means of obtaining values for C_i, C_o, C_h, and C_s, because they often allocate fixed costs in ways that are not appropriate for computing C_i, C_o, C_h, and C_s. To illustrate, suppose inventory is patrolled each night by a security guard whose annual salary is \$30,000. If the average daily inventory level is 10,000 items, it is tempting to include $30,000/10,000 = \$3$ as a portion of C_h, the annual holding cost per item. To see why this is wrong, ask the question, "If the average daily inventory were to drop from 10,000 items to 7,500 items, would the security guard accept a 25% cut in pay?" Since the answer is obviously no, C_h should not include any allocation of the security guard's salary. This example illustrates that, in computing C_i, C_o, C_h, and C_s, we should exclude costs that remain the same regardless of the inventory policy.

We can summarize this section as follows:

When comparing alternative inventory policies, we must consider three cost components:

1. The ordering (production) cost, which, for an order of size Q, is

$$C_o + C_i Q,$$

where C_o is the fixed ordering (production) cost and $C_i Q$ is the variable ordering (production) cost.

2. The annual holding cost per item, C_h.

3. The stockout cost per item, C_s.

In computing these costs, we must exclude any costs that remain the same regardless of the inventory policy.

14.4 THE ECONOMIC ORDER QUANTITY MODEL

In 1915, F. W. Harris developed what has become known as the *economic order quantity (EOQ) model*. The EOQ model was not only the first mathematical model for inventory management but also among the earliest models in the entire field of management science. Despite its age, the EOQ model still plays a fundamental role in inventory management. Hence, we will devote most of this chapter and the next to examining the EOQ model, as well as variations and extensions of it.

Inventory Management at St. Andrew's Hospital

To illustrate an inventory environment to which the EOQ model applies, consider the following scenario:

> The nursery for newborn infants at St. Andrew's Hospital uses disposable diapers purchased from a vendor in boxes of 100 diapers. Over the past year, demand for diapers has averaged 10 boxes per day. Although the demand is not the same each day, it rarely exceeds or falls below the average by much. Consequently, St. Andrew's feels confident using 10 boxes as its estimate for daily demand for the foreseeable future. For planning purposes, St. Andrew's assumes there are 360 days per year. Hence, the daily demand of 10 boxes is equivalent to an annual demand of 3600 boxes.
>
> Because of its long-standing relationship with the vendor, St. Andrew's receives excellent delivery service, almost always receiving an order five days after placing it. In cooperation with its accountants, St. Andrew's estimates that an order of Q boxes from the vendor costs $75 + 16Q$ dollars. St. Andrew's also estimates that, if it held a box of diapers in inventory for one year, the holding cost would be \$4, 25% of a box's unit cost.
>
> St. Andrew's current policy calls for an order of 600 boxes to arrive every 60 days. Since daily demand does not vary greatly from 10 boxes, the arrival of 600 boxes every 60 days has led to very few stockouts. However, St. Andrew's is unsure whether its current policy is optimal. Perhaps it should order less frequently but in larger quantities (e.g., 1200 boxes every 120 days) or more frequently in smaller quantities (e.g., 150 boxes every 15 days). St. Andrew's is willing to change its current ordering policy but wants to ensure that stockouts under the new policy are also infrequent.

The Assumptions of the EOQ Model

Using the ten characteristics summarized at the end of Section 14.2, we can summarize the assumptions of the EOQ model as listed below. As you read them, try to identify those assumptions that accurately describe St. Andrew's problem and those that only approximately describe it.

1. The inventory system involves a single item.
2. The item is nonperishable.
3. The item is ordered from a vendor.
4. The inventory system is a single-echelon system; that is, all inventory is held at a single location. At this location, an item's annual holding cost equals the known value C_h.
5. There is a continuous-time infinite-period planning horizon (i.e., orders can be placed anytime and will continue indefinitely).
6. The item's demand is deterministic and occurs at a known constant rate of d items per day, a rate that results in an annual demand of D items.
7. The item's demand is independent.
8. The ordering policy is a continuous review policy that orders the same fixed quantity Q every time an order is placed. The cost of an order quantity of Q items is $C_o + C_i Q$, where C_o is the known fixed ordering cost and C_i is the item's known unit cost.
9. Lead time is deterministic and equal to the known value of t days.
10. Stockouts never occur.

635

Which of these ten assumptions did you identify as being not entirely accurate for St. Andrew's problem? They are assumptions 6, 9, and 10. Fortunately, however, although these assumptions are not entirely accurate in St. Andrew's problem, it would be unfair to characterize them as unrealistic. In particular

- Although not occurring at a constant rate, daily demand does not vary by much from 10 boxes.
- Although not the same for each order, the lead time does not vary by much from 5 days.
- Although stockouts do occur, they are rare.

Hence, while not entirely accurate, the assumptions of the EOQ model are close approximations to reality.[9]

The How-Much-to-Order Decision

In most ordering environments, inventory management requires answers to two fundamental questions:

1. How much of the item should be ordered each time?
2. When should the order be placed?

To begin answering the first of these questions for the EOQ model, let us examine St. Andrew's current inventory policy, which calls for the vendor to deliver 600 boxes every 60 days.

Because we assume that demand occurs at a constant rate of 10 boxes per day, it is easy to graph how St. Andrew's inventory level varies over time. Figure 14.1(a) displays this graph. Observe that the inventory level follows a cyclical pattern that repeats itself every 60 days, which is equivalent to 6 cycles per year. At the beginning of each cycle, an order for 600 boxes arrives, thereby causing the inventory level to "jump" from 0 to 600. Then, because we assume that demand occurs at a constant rate of 10 boxes per day, the inventory level decreases at this same constant rate. After exactly 60 days, the 600 boxes delivered at the start of the cycle have been depleted and the inventory level has reached 0. However, a stockout is avoided because, just as the inventory level reaches 0, another order arrives and a new cycle begins. Note that, as indicated by the dashed line in Figure 14.1(a), St. Andrew's current policy leads to an average inventory level of 300 boxes, one-half of the order quantity.

What would the graph of inventory level over time look like if St. Andrew's were to change to a policy calling for either an order of 1200 boxes to arrive every 120 days or an order of 300 boxes to arrive every 30 days? The respective graphs are displayed in Figures 14.1(b) and (c). Before proceeding, convince yourself these graphs are correct.

We can summarize Figure 14.1 as follows:

Order Quantity	Orders per Year	Average Inventory Level
300	12	150
600	6	300
1200	3	600

---

[9] In Sections 15.2–15.7 we will learn how to analyze a variation of St. Andrew's problem where assumptions 6, 9, and 10 are inappropriate.

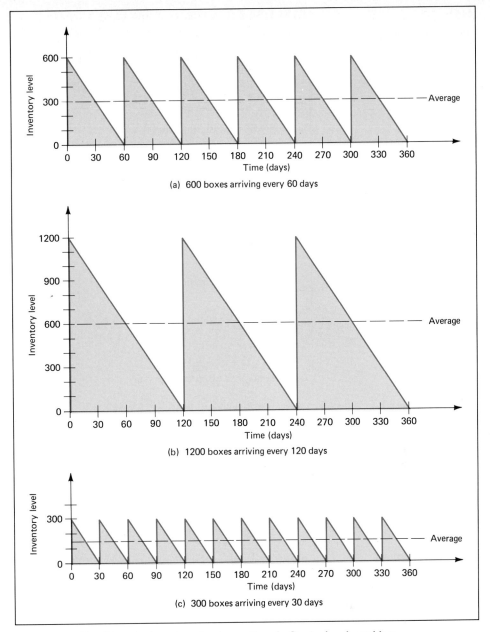

Figure 14.1 Graphing the inventory level over time in St. Andrew's problem

This tabulation and Figure 14.1 illustrate the following general principle:

> Increasing the order quantity decreases the number of orders per year but increases the average inventory level. Decreasing the order quantity has the opposite effect.

This principle embodies the fundamental dilemma of the EOQ model. On one hand, there is an incentive for St. Andrew's to *increase* the order quantity, thereby lowering the annual total of ordering costs. On the other hand, there is an incentive for St. Andrew's to *decrease* the order quantity, thereby lowering the annual total of holding costs. To resolve this dilemma, St. Andrew's must determine the so-called *economic order quantity* — that is, the order quantity that is most economi-

TABLE 14.2 A Summary of the EOQ Model

Definition	Symbol	Value in St. Andrew's Problem
Daily demand rate	d	10 boxes per day
Annual demand	D	3600 boxes per year
Fixed ordering cost	C_o	\$75 per order
Item's unit cost	C_i	\$16 per item
Item's annual holding cost	C_h	\$4 per item per year
Lead time (in days)	t	5 days
Order quantity	Q	Unknown

(a) Summary of Notation

Definition	Formula
Annual total cost	$TC(Q) = \dfrac{C_o D}{Q} + C_i D + \dfrac{C_h Q}{2}$
Optimal order quantity	$Q^* = \sqrt{\dfrac{2 C_o D}{C_h}}$
Optimal number of orders per year	$N^* = \dfrac{D}{Q^*}$
Optimal cycle time	$T^* = \dfrac{Q^*}{D}$ years $= \dfrac{Q^*}{d}$ days
Optimal annual total cost	$TC(Q^*) = C_i D + \sqrt{2 C_o D C_h}$
Ratio of the annual total cost for a nonoptimal Q to the annual total cost for Q^* (excluding the annual total of variable ordering costs in both the numerator and the denominator)	$R(Q) = \dfrac{1}{2}\left(\dfrac{Q^*}{Q} + \dfrac{Q}{Q^*}\right)$
Reorder level for an order quantity Q	$RL = dt$ modulo Q

(b) Summary of Formulae

cal because it minimizes the sum of the annual total of ordering costs and the annual total of holding costs.[10]

Before we determine the economic order quantity, we should pause to review the notation we have thus far introduced. Table 14.2(a) summarizes the definitions of the notation, as well as the specific values for each symbol in St. Andrew's problem.

Using Table 14.2(a)'s notation, we can express the annual total cost as a function of Q by proceeding as follows:

---

[10] Since stockouts never occur in the EOQ model, we can omit the annual total of stockout costs, the third cost component discussed in Section 14.3.

- **Computing the annual total of the fixed ordering costs**. The number of orders per year is D/Q. For example, since the annual demand of $D = 3600$ boxes occurs at a constant rate throughout the year, $Q = 600$ results in $(3600/600) = 6$ orders per year, but $Q = 300$ results in $(3600/300) = 12$ orders per year. The fixed ordering cost of each of the D/Q orders is C_o. Hence,

$$\begin{pmatrix} \text{annual total of} \\ \text{fixed ordering costs} \end{pmatrix} = \begin{pmatrix} \text{fixed cost} \\ \text{per order} \end{pmatrix} \begin{pmatrix} \text{number of orders} \\ \text{per year} \end{pmatrix}$$

$$= (C_o)\left(\frac{D}{Q}\right)$$

$$= \frac{C_o D}{Q}.$$

As we expect, this cost decreases as Q increases.

- **Computing the annual total of variable ordering costs**. There are D/Q orders per year, each having a variable ordering cost of $C_i Q$. Hence,

$$\begin{pmatrix} \text{annual total of} \\ \text{variable ordering costs} \end{pmatrix} = \begin{pmatrix} \text{variable cost} \\ \text{per order} \end{pmatrix} \begin{pmatrix} \text{number of} \\ \text{orders per year} \end{pmatrix}$$

$$= (C_i Q)\left(\frac{D}{Q}\right)$$

$$= C_i D.$$

Note that this cost does not depend on Q, since, regardless of the order quantity, D items must be purchased per year at a cost of C_i per unit.

- **Computing the annual total of holding costs**. As illustrated in Figure 14.1, the average inventory level is $Q/2$. It costs C_h dollars to hold one item in inventory for one year. Hence,

$$\begin{pmatrix} \text{annual total of} \\ \text{holding costs} \end{pmatrix} = \begin{pmatrix} \text{annual holding cost} \\ \text{per item} \end{pmatrix} \begin{pmatrix} \text{average inventory} \\ \text{level} \end{pmatrix}$$

$$= (C_h)\left(\frac{Q}{2}\right)$$

$$= \frac{C_h Q}{2}.$$

Let us use $TC(Q)$ to denote the annual total cost as a function of Q. Summing the above three cost components, we get

$$TC(Q) = \frac{C_o D}{Q} + C_i D + \frac{C_h Q}{2}.$$

For future reference, this formula is summarized in Table 14.2(b). This table also summarizes all subsequent formulae we derive.

Note that, as Q increases, the first term in $TC(Q)$ decreases, the second term remains constant, and the last term increases. This is mathematical confirmation of our earlier observation that Q is being "pulled" in opposite directions.

Our goal is to determine the value of Q that minimizes

$$TC(Q) = \frac{C_o D}{Q} + C_i D + \frac{C_h Q}{2}.$$

Let us see how to achieve this goal in St. Andrew's problem.

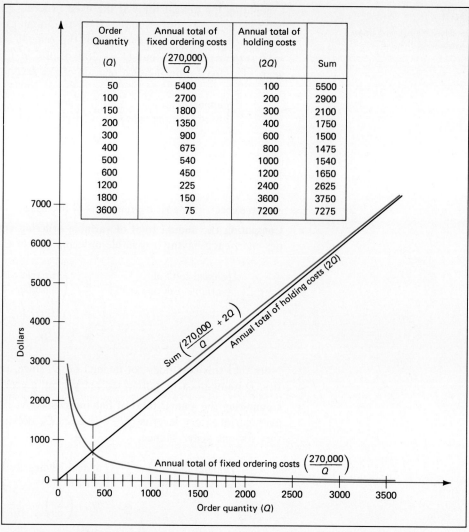

Order Quantity (Q)	Annual total of fixed ordering costs $\left(\frac{270{,}000}{Q}\right)$	Annual total of holding costs (2Q)	Sum
50	5400	100	5500
100	2700	200	2900
150	1800	300	2100
200	1350	400	1750
300	900	600	1500
400	675	800	1475
500	540	1000	1540
600	450	1200	1650
1200	225	2400	2625
1800	150	3600	3750
3600	75	7200	7275

Figure 14.2 Graph of sum of annual totals of fixed ordering costs and holding costs as a function of order quantity

Substituting Table 14.2(a)'s data for St. Andrew's problem into the general expression for $TC(Q)$, we get

$$
\begin{aligned}
TC(Q) &= \frac{C_o D}{Q} + C_i D + \frac{C_h Q}{2} \\
&= \frac{(75)(3600)}{Q} + (16)(3600) + \frac{4Q}{2} \\
&= \frac{270{,}000}{Q} + 57{,}600 + 2Q.
\end{aligned}
$$

Since the middle term is independent of Q, let us temporarily ignore it and focus our attention on only the first and last terms. Using both a tabular format and a graphical format, Figure 14.2 summarizes these two terms and their sum for alternative values of Q. Note the following:

- When Q is too low (e.g., $Q = 50$), the annual total of fixed ordering costs is high and the annual total of holding costs is low, thereby yielding a high sum.

- When Q is too high (e.g., $Q = 1800$), the annual total of fixed ordering costs is low and the annual total of holding costs is high, thereby yielding a high sum. In particular, St. Andrew's current policy of $Q = 600$ is a poor choice, because of excessive holding costs.

■ The optimal value of Q occurs somewhere between $Q = 300$ and $Q = 400$ at the point where the graph of the annual total of fixed ordering costs intersects the graph of the annual total of holding costs.

Let us use Q^* to denote the optimal value of Q. We could obtain a closer approximation of Q^* by expanding Figure 14.2's table to include rows for 310, 320, . . . , 390. Fortunately, this is unnecessary, because it is possible to use differential calculus to prove that the value of Q that minimizes $(C_oD/Q) + (C_hQ/2)$ is given by

$$Q^* = \sqrt{\frac{2C_oD}{C_h}} \ .$$

We omit the derivation of Q^* here, leaving it as an end-of-chapter exercise for those readers familiar with calculus.

Applying the formula for Q^* to St. Andrew's problem, we obtain

$$Q^* = \sqrt{\frac{2C_oD}{C_h}} = \sqrt{\frac{(2)(75)(3600)}{(4)}} \approx 367 \ .$$

where the symbol "$\approx$" means "approximately equal to." To confirm that this is correct, let us compute the annual totals of the fixed ordering costs and the holding costs for $Q^* = 367$. Using the formulae in the headings of the table displayed in Figure 14.2, we proceed as follows:

Annual Total of Fixed Ordering Costs	Annual Total of Holding Costs
$\dfrac{270,000}{Q} = \dfrac{270,000}{367} \approx 735.69$	$2Q = (2)(367) = 734$

The approximate equality of these costs confirms that $Q^* = 367$ is the approximate point of intersection between the respective graphs of the annual totals of fixed ordering costs and holding costs.[11]

St. Andrew's vendor might balk at delivering an order quantity as odd as 367 boxes. For example, the vendor might insist that the order quantity be a multiple of 100. For the moment, however, we will assume that the vendor will deliver any amount. With this assumption, we can derive formulae for the following expressions related to Q^*:

■ **The optimal number of orders per year**. We have noted previously that, if the order quantity is Q, the number of orders per year is D/Q. Hence, if we let N^* denote the optimal number of orders per year,

$$N^* = \frac{D}{Q^*} \ .$$

■ **The optimal cycle time**. The *cycle time* is the time between the arrival of successive orders. The cycle time is simply the inverse of the number of orders

---

[11] While the annual totals of fixed ordering costs and holding costs are equal in the *EOQ* model, their equality is not a general principle.

per year. For example, if there are 12 orders per year, the cycle time is 1/12 of a year. Hence, if we let T^* denote the optimal cycle time,

$$T^* = \frac{Q^*}{D}.$$

- **The optimal annual total cost.** To obtain a formula for the optimal annual total cost, we refer to Table 14.2(b) and substitute the formula for Q^* into the formula for $TC(Q)$. The algebra proceeds as follows:

$$
\begin{aligned}
TC(Q^*) &= \frac{C_o D}{Q^*} + C_i D + \frac{C_h Q^*}{2} \\[2mm]
&= \frac{C_o D}{\sqrt{\dfrac{2C_o D}{C_h}}} + C_i D + \frac{C_h \sqrt{\dfrac{2C_o D}{C_h}}}{2} \\[2mm]
&= \sqrt{\frac{C_o D C_h}{2}} + C_i D + \sqrt{\frac{C_o D C_h}{2}} \\[2mm]
&= C_i D + \sqrt{2 C_o D C_h}.
\end{aligned}
$$

Applying Table 14.2(b)'s formulae for N^*, T^*, and $TC(Q^*)$ to St. Andrew's problem, we get

$$
\begin{aligned}
N^* &= \frac{D}{Q^*} \\[2mm]
&= \frac{3600}{367} \\[2mm]
&\approx 9.8 \text{ orders per year,}
\end{aligned}
$$

$$
\begin{aligned}
T^* &= \frac{Q^*}{D} \\[2mm]
&= \frac{367}{3600} \\[2mm]
&\approx 0.102 \text{ years} \\[2mm]
&\approx 36.7 \text{ days (assuming 360 days per year),}
\end{aligned}
$$

$$
\begin{aligned}
TC(Q^*) &= C_i D + \sqrt{2 C_o D C_h} \\[2mm]
&= (16)(3600) + \sqrt{(2)(75)(3600)(4)} \\[2mm]
&\approx 57{,}600 + 1469.69 \\[2mm]
&\approx 59{,}069.69.
\end{aligned}
$$

The Effects of Using a Nonoptimal Q

If St. Andrew's were to follow precisely the recommendations of the *EOQ* model, its optimal ordering policy would call for $Q^* = 367$ boxes to arrive $N^* = 9.8$ times per year at equally spaced intervals of $T^* = 36.7$ days. Of course, no vendor would agree to this delivery schedule. Thus, St. Andrew's must convert the true optimal policy into a close-to-optimal policy that its vendor will find more acceptable.

To illustrate, suppose St. Andrew's vendor balks at delivering orders at equally spaced intervals of 36.7 days, but will agree to intervals of 40 days. Since the daily demand is 10 boxes, the total demand during a cycle having a length of 40 days is 400 boxes. Hence, to avoid a stockout, St. Andrew's order quantity must be $Q = 400$ instead of $Q^* = 367$. Before using this nonoptimal Q, St. Andrew's would like to answer the question, "How does the annual total cost for $Q = 400$ compare to that for $Q^* = 367$?"

Instead of answering this question for a specific value of Q, we will derive a formula valid for any value of Q. To do so, let us use $R(Q)$ to denote the ratio of the annual total cost for a nonoptimal Q to the annual total cost for Q^*, where we *exclude* in both the numerator and denominator the annual total of variable ordering costs $(C_i D)$, since it is the same for all values of Q. Using the formulae in Table 14.2(b), we can derive a formula for $R(Q)$:

$$R(Q) = \frac{\text{annual total cost for a nonoptimal } Q, \text{ excluding } C_i D}{\text{annual total cost for } Q^*, \text{ excluding } C_i D}$$

$$= \frac{\text{Table 14.2(b)'s formula for } TC(Q), \text{ ignoring } C_i D}{\text{Table 14.2(b)'s formula for } TC(Q^*), \text{ ignoring } C_i D}$$

$$= \frac{\dfrac{C_o D}{Q} + \dfrac{C_h Q}{2}}{\sqrt{2 C_o D C_h}}$$

$$= \frac{C_o D}{Q \sqrt{2 C_o D C_h}} + \frac{C_h Q}{2 \sqrt{2 C_o D C_h}}$$

$$= \frac{\sqrt{\dfrac{2 C_o D}{C_h}}}{2Q} + \frac{Q}{2 \sqrt{\dfrac{2 C_o D}{C_h}}}$$

$$= \frac{1}{2} \left(\frac{Q^*}{Q} + \frac{Q}{Q^*} \right) .$$

Table 14.3 tabulates $R(Q)$ for alternative values of the ratio Q/Q^*. This table shows that we can use a Q that deviates significantly from Q^* without incurring a significant cost increase. As examples, consider the following:

- If instead of Q^* we use a Q that is 50% higher (i.e., $Q/Q^* = 1.5$), the annual total cost that depends on Q increases by only 8.3%.
- If instead of Q^* we use a Q that is 25% lower (i.e., $Q/Q^* = 0.75$), the annual total cost that depends on Q increases by only 4.2%.

We can use the formula for $R(Q)$ to determine the effect in St. Andrew's problem of using $Q = 400$ (corresponding to a cycle time of 40 days). The ratio Q/Q^* is given by

$$\frac{Q}{Q^*} = \frac{400}{367} = 1.09 .$$

TABLE 14.3 $R(Q)$ for Alternative Values of Q/Q^*

Q/Q^*	0.50	0.75	0.90	0.95	1.00	1.05	1.10	1.25	1.50	2.00
$R(Q)$	1.250	1.042	1.006	1.001	1.000	1.001	1.005	1.025	1.083	1.250

Since this ratio does not appear in Table 14.3, we must substitute it into Table 14.2(b)'s formula for $R(Q)$ to obtain a value of

$$\frac{1}{2}\left(\frac{Q}{Q^*} + \frac{Q^*}{Q}\right) = \frac{1}{2}\left(1.09 + \frac{1}{1.09}\right) = 1.004$$

Hence, if St. Andrew's uses $Q = 400$ instead of Q^* (an increase of about 9%), the annual total cost that depends on Q will increase by less than one-half percent. Such a small increase means St. Andrew's should not object to the vendor's request for a cycle time of 40 working days.

The formula for $R(Q)$ is useful for determining the effect not only of an intentional deviation from Q^* (as in the examples above) but also of an unintentional deviation that results from errors in estimating C_o, C_i, C_h, and D. To illustrate, suppose St. Andrew's is confident about the accuracy of its estimates for C_i, C_h, and D but is worried about the accuracy of its estimate of C_o. In particular, suppose St. Andrew's believes that, although the best estimate for C_o is $75, C_o might be as low as 60 or as high as 90. To investigate the effect of this uncertainty about the value of C_h, we proceed as follows:

■ If C_o has a true value of 60, the true optimal order quantity is

$$Q = \sqrt{\frac{2C_o D}{C_h}} = \sqrt{\frac{(2)(60)(3,600)}{4}} \approx 329 \ .$$

However, since St. Andrew's uses $C_o = 75$, it obtains the previously computed value of $Q = 367$. Hence, the ratio of Q to Q^* is

$$\frac{Q}{Q^*} = \frac{367}{329} \approx 1.116 \ .$$

Substituting this ratio into Table 14.2(b)'s formula for $R(Q)$, we obtain a value of

$$\frac{1}{2}\left(1.116 + \frac{1}{1.116}\right) \approx 1.006 \ .$$

■ If C_o has a true value of 90, you should verify that proceeding in a similar manner yields a value for $R(Q)$ of 1.004.

Hence, if St. Andrew's estimates $C_o = 75, the increase in annual total costs that depend on Q is only about one-half percent if C_o is actually $60 or $90. This example illustrates that the estimates for C_o, C_i, C_h, and D need only be "in the ballpark."

The examples of this subsection illustrate the following general principle:

■ To obtain an order quantity or a cycle time that is more acceptable to us or our vendor, we might intentionally deviate from Q^*.

■ Because of errors in estimating the data, we might unintentionally deviate from Q^*.

■ Regardless of whether the deviation for Q^* is intentional or unintentional, Table 14.3 illustrates that there will not be a significant cost increase as long as the Q we use is "in the ballpark."

Now that we know how to make the how-much-to-order decision, we can learn how to make the when-to-order decision. It is customary to express the when-to-order decision in terms of a *reorder level*, defined as the inventory level that "triggers" the placement of an order. Hereafter, we use RL to denote the reorder level. For example, $RL = 50$ means that we continuously monitor the inventory level and place an order as soon as the level drops to 50.

The reorder level depends on what is known as the *lead time demand*. As defined earlier, the lead time is the time that elapses between the placement of an order and its arrival. The lead time demand is the total demand during the lead time. In the EOQ model, it is easy to compute the lead time demand. Since we assume that demand occurs at the known constant rate of d items per day and that the lead time always equals the known constant of t days, lead time demand is given by

$$\text{lead time demand} = (\text{daily demand rate})(\text{lead time}) = dt \, .$$

To illustrate, let us reconsider St. Andrew's problem. As summarized in Table 14.2(a), St. Andrew's daily demand rate is $d = 10$ and its lead time is $t = 5$ days. Hence, the lead time demand is $dt = 50$ boxes.

Can you identify the relationship in the EOQ model between the reorder level and the lead time demand? Intuitively, if we want an order to arrive at the precise instant the inventory level reaches 0, we should place an order when the inventory level equals the lead time demand. Hence, it is tempting to conclude that

$$\text{reorder level} = \text{lead time demand} = dt$$

As we will see, however, this formula is valid only in the first of the following mutually exclusive cases:

1. The lead time demand is less than the order quantity (i.e., $dt < Q$).

2. The lead time demand is greater than or equal to the order quantity (i.e., $dt \geqslant Q$).

In the latter case, the formula requires a slight modification.

Let us first see why setting the reorder level equal to lead time demand is correct when $dt < Q$. St. Andrew's problem is an example of this case. To see why, recall that St. Andrew's new policy calls for an order of $Q = 400$ boxes to arrive every 40 days (a policy obtained by modifying the true optimal policy, which calls for an order of $Q^* = 367$ boxes to arrive every 36.7 days). Hence, under St. Andrew's new policy, $Q = 400$ boxes. The lead time demand is 50 boxes, the product of the daily demand rate of $d = 10$ and the lead time of $t = 5$. Since $dt < Q$, St. Andrew's can begin each cycle with $Q = 400$ boxes and wait to place an order until the inventory level drops to the lead time demand of 50 boxes. By using $dt = 50$ boxes as its reorder level, St. Andrew's is guaranteed that, while it waits for the order to arrive, it will have the exact amount of inventory needed to satisfy the lead time demand. Figure 14.3 diagrams this situation.

To see why setting the reorder level equal to the lead time demand is incorrect when $dt \geqslant Q$, let us modify St. Andrew's problem by changing the lead time from 5 days to 90 days (an unrealistic value we use only for illustration). The lead time demand is now $dt = (10)(90) = 900$ boxes. If St. Andrew's were to

645

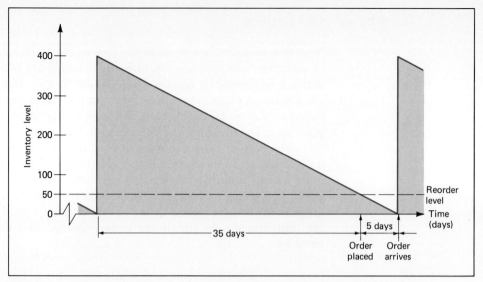

Figure 14.3 Setting the reorder level when lead time demand is less than the order quantity

wait to place an order until the inventory level dropped to 900 boxes, it would be waiting forever, because the maximum inventory level is $Q = 400$. Hence, in this case, St. Andrew's cannot set its reorder level equal to lead time demand.

Figure 14.4 will help us resolve St. Andrew's dilemma. Starting at the figure's right-hand side, we see that the 90-day lead time consists of two complete 40-day cycles plus the last 10 days of another cycle. Hence, we can divide the lead time demand of 900 as follows:

$$
\underset{\begin{pmatrix}\text{lead time} \\ \text{demand}\end{pmatrix}}{900} = \underset{\begin{pmatrix}\text{demand during} \\ \text{Cycle E,} \\ \text{satisfied by} \\ \text{order placed} \\ \text{during Cycle B}\end{pmatrix}}{400} + \underset{\begin{pmatrix}\text{demand during} \\ \text{Cycle D,} \\ \text{satisfied by} \\ \text{order placed} \\ \text{during Cycle A}\end{pmatrix}}{400} + \underset{\begin{pmatrix}\text{demand during} \\ \text{the last 10} \\ \text{days of Cycle C,} \\ \text{satisfied by} \\ \text{inventory} \\ \text{remaining when} \\ \text{Order C is} \\ \text{placed}\end{pmatrix}}{100}
$$

The last term provides the reorder level. Rather than equalling the lead time demand of 900, the reorder level of 100 equals the remainder obtained by subtracting from the lead time demand as many multiples of $Q = 400$ as is possible. Let us now see how to express this method for computing the reorder level in a concise formula.

To understand the general formula for the reorder level that applies both when $dt < Q$ and when $dt \geqslant Q$, we must define an algebraic operation known as *modulo*, an operation you may recall from prior study of college algebra. Given two integers x and y, x modulo y is defined as the remainder when x is divided by y. For example, 20 modulo 3 = 2, since 20 divided by 3 equals 6 with a remainder of 2. Other examples of the modulo operation are 39 modulo 6 = 3, 51 modulo 19 = 13, 15 modulo 3 = 0, and 3 modulo 5 = 3.

The general formula for the reorder level is

$$RL = dt \text{ modulo } Q.$$

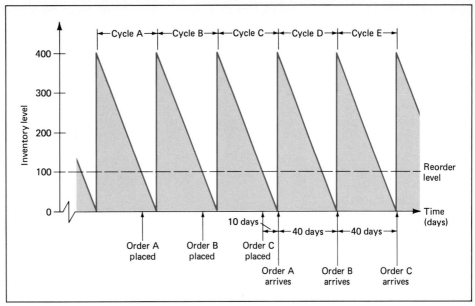

Figure 14.4 Setting the reorder level when lead time demand is greater than the order quantity

In words, the reorder level equals the lead time demand modulo the order quantity. To better understand the formula, let us consider the following two cases:

- When $dt < Q$, dt modulo Q equals dt, so that $RL = dt$. St. Andrew's problem with its original lead time of 5 days is an example of this case. We previously computed the reorder level as

$$RL = dt = (10) (5) = 50.$$

The general formula yields the same value for RL—that is,

$$RL = dt \text{ modulo } Q = 50 \text{ modulo } 400 = 50.$$

- When $dt \geqslant Q$, dt modulo Q equals the remainder obtaining by subtracting from dt as many multiples of Q as possible. St. Andrew's problem with the modified lead time of 90 days is an example of this case. We previously computed the reorder level as

$$RL = 900 - 400 - 400 = 100.$$

The general formula yields the same value for RL; that is,

$$RL = dt \text{ modulo } Q = 900 \text{ modulo } 400 = 100.$$

We now know how to make both the how-much-to-order and the when-to-order decisions. To summarize:

To determine the inventory policy for an EOQ model, we proceed as follows:

1. We estimate the data summarized in Table 14.2(a).

2. To make the how-much-to-order decision, we use the formulae in Table

14.2(b) to compute the optimal order quantity (Q^*), the optimal number of orders per year (N^*), and the optimal cycle time (T^*).

3. If we or our vendor find Q^*, N^*, and T^* unacceptable, we must determine modified values (as illustrated in the previous subsection).

4. We make the when-to-order decision by computing the reorder level using Table 14.2(b)'s formula for RL, where the Q in the formula is either Q^* or its modified value from step (3).

Two Caveats

By paying attention to the following caveats, you will avoid making two common mistakes:

- Although the unit of time measurement is arbitrary, it must be the same for both D and C_h. In St. Andrew's problem, we chose to measure time in units of one year. Therefore, D was the annual demand and C_h was an item's annual holding cost. Alternatively, if we had specified D as a monthly demand, then, to avoid obtaining an erroneous value for Q^*, we would have had to specify C_h as the cost of holding one item in inventory for one month.

- Because C_i does not appear in the formula for Q^*, it is tempting to conclude that Q^* does not change if C_i changes. Can you see why this is a wrong conclusion? Recall from Section 14.3 that the primary component of C_h is the opportunity cost, a cost expressed as a percentage of C_i. Hence, as C_i changes, C_h changes, which in turn leads to a change in Q^*. Thus, although C_i does not explicitly appear in the formula for Q^*, it is there implicitly as part of C_h. In fact, as an alternative to Table 14.2(b)'s formula for Q^*, some instructors, textbooks, and software packages use

$$Q^* = \sqrt{\frac{2C_o D}{pC_i}} \, ,$$

where p is the decimal fraction equivalent to the percentage being applied to C_i to obtain C_h (e.g., when the percentage is 25%, $p = 0.25$).

The Importance of the EOQ Model

Although very few real-world inventory systems satisfy all its assumptions (especially the assumptions that the daily demand rate and the lead time are constant), the EOQ model still plays an important role in inventory management. As the most basic of all inventory models, the EOQ model serves as the foundation for most of our remaining study of inventory management. In the next two sections we will consider two variations of the EOQ model. In one, the item's unit cost decreases as the order quantity increases; in the other, the items are produced internally instead of ordered from a vendor. In the next chapter we examine how to adapt the EOQ model to a situation where the demand and/or the lead time are stochastic.

14.5 AN EOQ MODEL WITH QUANTITY DISCOUNTS

To provide customers with an incentive to order in large quantities, many vendors have a cost structure in which the unit cost decreases as the customer's order quantity increases. In this section we discuss how to adapt the EOQ model when quantity discounts are available.

As our example, we will continue to use St. Andrew's problem, subject to one modification. In the previous section we assumed that, besides a fixed cost of $75 per order, St. Andrew's paid $16 per box of diapers, regardless of the order quantity. In this section we assume that St. Andrew's vendor continues to charge $75 per order but now discounts the unit cost according to the schedule displayed in Table 14.4. The discount schedule provides St. Andrew's with another incentive for a large order quantity, besides the incentive of lowering the annual total of the fixed ordering costs. However, since larger order quantities lead to higher annual holding cost, the discounts may not be as attractive as they seem at first glance. St. Andrew's must base its ordering policy on an analysis of the annual total of all costs.

As the first step in this analysis, we develop three distinct formulae for annual total cost, one for each discount category. Let us adopt the following notation:

$$TC_j(Q) = \text{annual total cost using the unit cost for the } j\text{th discount category.}$$

We need a different formula for each discount category because an item's unit cost (C_i) and, hence, its annual holding cost (C_h) differ by discount category. Table 14.5 summarizes how C_i and C_h differ by category, assuming (as we did in the previous section) that C_h is 25% of C_i.

TABLE 14.4 Vendor's Discount Schedule for St. Andrew's Problem

Discount Category	Values of Q That Qualify	Discount	Item's Unit Cost (C_i)
1	$0 \leqslant Q < 900$	0%	$16.00
2	$900 \leqslant Q < 1800$	2%	$15.68
3	$1800 \leqslant Q$	3%	$15.52

TABLE 14.5 An Item's Unit Cost (C_i) and Annual Holding Cost (C_h) by Discount Category

Discount Category	C_i	C_h
1	$16.00	$4.00
2	$15.68	$3.92
3	$15.52	$3.88

649

If we substitute Table 14.5's values for C_i and C_h and Table 14.2(a)'s values for C_o and D into Table 14.2(b)'s formula for TC(Q), we obtain:

$$TC_1(Q) = \frac{(75)(3600)}{Q} + (16.00)(3600) + \frac{4Q}{2} = \frac{270,000}{Q} + 57,600 + 2.00Q$$

$$TC_2(Q) = \frac{(75)(3600)}{Q} + (15.68)(3600) + \frac{3.92Q}{2} = \frac{270,000}{Q} + 56,448 + 1.96Q$$

$$TC_3(Q) = \frac{(75)(3600)}{Q} + (15.52)(3600) + \frac{3.88Q}{2} = \frac{270,000}{Q} + 55,872 + 1.94Q$$

Recall that, in each formula, the first term represents the annual total of fixed ordering costs; the second, the annual total of variable ordering costs; and the third, the annual holding costs. For future reference, these formulae are summarized in Table 14.6.

Let Q_j^* denote the value of Q that minimizes $TC_j(Q)$ over all values of Q, not just over those values of Q in the jth discount category. Using Table 14.2(b)'s formula for Q^*, we obtain

$$Q_1^* = \sqrt{\frac{(2)(75)(3600)}{4}} \approx 367$$

$$Q_2^* = \sqrt{\frac{(2)(75)(3600)}{3.92}} \approx 371$$

$$Q_3^* = \sqrt{\frac{(2)(75)(3600)}{3.88}} \approx 373$$

It is not surprising that Q_1^*, Q_2^*, and Q_3^* are approximately equal, since the values substituted into the formula are identical except for slight differences in the value of C_h.

Figure 14.5 plots $TC_1(Q)$, $TC_2(Q)$, and $TC_3(Q)$ on the same graph. Observe the following:

1. The curve for Category 1 lies above the curve for Category 2, which in turn lies above the curve for Category 3. To see why this occurs, refer to Table 14.6's formulae and note that the corresponding terms decrease or stay the same as the discount increases (e.g., the term for annual holding cost decreases from 2.00Q to 1.96Q to 1.94Q).

2. Only the bold portions of each curve are feasible. For example, since Category 2 applies when $900 \leqslant Q < 1800$, the portion of the curve above this interval is bold and the portions on either side are not.

TABLE 14.6 Formulae for Annual Total Cost by
Discount Category

Discount Category	Formula for $TC(Q)$
1	$TC_1(Q) = \dfrac{270,000}{Q} + 57,600 + 2.00Q$
2	$TC_2(Q) = \dfrac{270,000}{Q} + 56,448 + 1.96Q$
3	$TC_3(Q) = \dfrac{270,000}{Q} + 55,872 + 1.94Q$

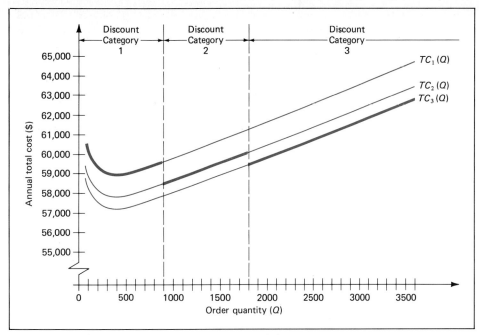

Figure 14.5 Graphs of $TC_1(Q)$, $TC_2(Q)$, and $TC_3(Q)$

Using Figure 14.5, we can identify the optimal value of Q for each discount category and from them select the overall optimum. We proceed as follows:

- **Discount Category 1.** $Q_1^* = 367$ is feasible, since it lies below the bold portion of $TC_1(Q)$. Hence, the optimal order quantity for Category 1 is $Q = 367$.

- **Discount Category 2.** $Q_2^* = 371$ is not feasible, since it lies to the left of the bold portion of $TC_2(Q)$. Hence, the optimal order quantity for Category 2 is $Q = 900$, the smallest order quantity necessary to qualify for Category 2's discount.

- **Discount Category 3.** $Q_3^* = 373$ is not feasible, since it lies to the left of the bold portion of $TC_3(Q)$. Hence, the optimal order quantity for Category 3 is $Q = 1800$, the smallest order quantity necessary to qualify for Category 3's discount.

To summarize, the optimal order quantity is $Q = 367$ for Category 1, $Q = 900$ for Category 2, and $Q = 1800$ for Category 3. Which of these three order quantities is the overall optimum? From Figure 14.5's graph, we can see that $Q = 900$ minimizes the annual total cost. To be sure, however, let us compute the total cost of each category's optimal order quantity by substituting the value into the appropriate cost formula in Table 14.6. Table 14.7 summarizes the computations. Examining this table, we see that the order quantity that minimizes total cost is $Q = 900$, the lowest quantity that qualifies for Category 2's discount of 2%. The smallest order quantity necessary to qualify for Category 3's discount of 3%, $Q = 1800$, is not the overall optimum because of its excessive holding costs. (Exercise 14.13 requests you to show that $Q = 1800$ would be optimal if the discount for Category 3 were 5% instead of 3%.)

It is instructive to compare St. Andrew's optimal order quantity without and with the quantity discounts specified in Table 14.4. We determined (in the previous section) that the former is $Q = 367$ and (in this section) that the latter is $Q =$

TABLE 14.7 Comparison of the Annual Total Cost of Each Discount Category's Optimal Order Quantity

Discount Category	Optimal Value of Q	Annual Total of Fixed Ordering Costs	Annual Total of Variable Ordering Costs	Annual Total of Holding Costs	Annual Total Cost
1	$Q = 367$	$\frac{270,000}{Q} = 735.69$	57,600.00	$2.00Q = 734.00$	$59,069.69
2	$Q = 900$	$\frac{270,000}{Q} = 300.00$	56,488.00	$1.96Q = 1764.00$	$58,512.00
3	$Q = 1800$	$\frac{270,000}{Q} = 150.00$	55,872.00	$1.94Q = 3492.00$	$59,514.00

900. This illustrates that quantity discounts can have a significant impact on the optimal order quantity.

St. Andrew's problem has illustrated the following general procedure:

The Procedure for Analyzing an EOQ Model with Quantity Discounts

1. Let $TC_j(Q)$ denote the annual total cost using the unit cost for the jth discount category. For each discount category, determine the formula for $TC_j(Q)$ by substituting the appropriate values into Table 14.2(b)'s formula for $TC(Q)$. (Only the values of C_i and C_h change.)

2. Let Q_j^* denote the order quantity that minimizes $TC_j(Q)$ over all values of Q, not just over those values of Q in the jth discount category. For each discount category, compute Q_j^* by using Table 14.2(b)'s formula for Q^*.

3. To determine the optimal order quantity for each discount category, proceed as follows:

   - If Q_j^* qualifies for category j's discount, then it is the category's optimal order quantity.

   - If Q_j^* is too small to qualify for category j's discount, then the category's optimal order quantity is the smallest Q that does qualify.

   - If Q_j^* is too large to qualify for category j's discount, then the category's optimal order quantity is the largest Q that does qualify.[12]

4. To identify the overall optimum, use the formulae from step 1 to compute the annual total cost of each category's optimal order quantity.

Note that, while a graph similar to that of Figure 14.5 is a visual aid to understanding the procedure, it is not needed to identify the optimal order quantity.

14.6 THE ECONOMIC PRODUCTION QUANTITY MODEL

There are two ways to replenish inventory: ordering items from a vendor or producing items internally. For an ordering environment, the EOQ model is appropri-

---

[12] Although this case did not occur in St. Andrew's problem, it is possible. In fact, when this case does occur, we can ignore this discount category because, as Exercise 14.15 illustrates, the category's optimal order quantity can never be the overall optimum.

ate. For a production environment, the analogous model is known as the *economic production quantity (EPQ) model.*

Given our knowledge of the EOQ model, we can easily state the assumptions of the EPQ model. In particular, of the ten assumptions for the EOQ model listed near the beginning of Section 14.4, all remain unchanged except the third and eighth. Since these pertain to an ordering environment, they are replaced by the following assumption:

- Items are produced internally. The production policy is a continuous review policy that produces the same fixed quantity Q every time a production run occurs. The cost of a production quantity of Q items is $C_o + C_i Q$, where C_o is a production run's known fixed cost[13] and C_i is an item's known unit production cost. During a production run, items are produced and added to inventory at a known constant rate of p items per day, a rate that is equivalent to an annual production capacity of P items.

To illustrate an inventory environment to which the EPQ model applies, let us consider the following scenario for the manufacturer of the diapers used by St. Andrew's and many other hospitals:

Dockter and Gamble (D&G) manufactures disposable diapers for newborn infants. Among D&G's customers are vendors of medical supplies, who purchase the diapers from D&G in specially packaged boxes of 100.

D&G's plant operates 250 days per year, producing several sizes of diapers. When D&G does devote its plant to the exclusive production of newborn-sized diapers, the production rate is not the same each day. However, it averages 1600 boxes per day, rarely exceeding or falling below the average by much. This daily production rate is equivalent to an annual production capacity of 400,000 boxes.

Each day the plant is open, demand for newborn-sized diapers varies little from day to day and averages 400 boxes per day. This daily demand rate is equivalent to an annual demand of 100,000 boxes.

D&G estimates that a production run of Q boxes costs $120 + 8Q$ dollars. D&G also estimates that, if it held a box of diapers in inventory for one year, the holding cost would be $2, 25% of a box's unit product cost.

In the past, when a production run was about to take place, its size has been determined somewhat arbitrarily. Now, D&G wants to determine the production quantity Q that minimizes the total cost of producing and storing the newborn-sized diapers.

Table 14.8(a) summarizes the notation for the EPQ model, as well as the specific values of each symbol in D&G's problem. Note that, for the EPQ model to make sense, the production rate must exceed the daily demand rate. Otherwise, the inventory level would quickly reach 0 and remain there forever!

Figure 14.6 displays for the EPQ model a graph of how inventory level varies over time if the production run size is Q items. We can use this graph to derive a formula for the annual total cost as a function of Q. Before doing so, we must understand the following facts about the graph:

1. The inventory level follows a cyclical pattern. Each cycle consists of a replenishment portion followed by a depletion portion.

---

[13] As we indicated in Section 14.3, a production run's fixed cost is sometimes called the *set-up cost.*

TABLE 14.8 Summary of the EPQ Model

Definition	Symbol	Value in D&G's Problem
Daily production rate	p	1600 boxes per day
Annual production capacity	P	400,000 boxes per year
Daily demand rate	d	400 boxes per day
Annual demand	D	100,000 boxes per year
Fixed production cost	C_o	$120 per production run
Item's unit production cost	C_i	$8 per item
Item's annual holding cost	C_h	$2 per item per year
Production run size	Q	Unknown

(a) Summary of Notation

Definition	Formulae
Annual total cost	$TC(Q) = \dfrac{C_o D}{Q} + C_i D + \dfrac{C_h\left(1 - \dfrac{D}{P}\right)Q}{2}$
Optimal production run size	$Q^* = \sqrt{\dfrac{2C_o D}{C_h\left(1 - \dfrac{D}{P}\right)}}$
Optimal number of runs per year	$N^* = \dfrac{D}{Q^*}$
Optimal cycle time	$T^* = \dfrac{Q^*}{D}$ years $= \dfrac{Q^*}{d}$ days
Optimal annual total cost	$TC(Q^*) = C_i D + \sqrt{2C_o D C_h\left(1 - \dfrac{D}{P}\right)}$

(b) Summary of Formulae

2. The primary difference between the cycles in Figure 14.6 and those in Figure 14.1 (the counterpart for the EOQ model) is the way in which inventory replenishment occurs. In the EOQ model, the arrival of an order causes the inventory level to "jump" instantaneously from 0 to Q. In the EPQ model, however, there is a gradual rise in the inventory level as items come off the production line and are added to inventory. More specifically, during a production run, items are added to inventory at the rate of p items and removed from inventory at the rate of d items per day. The net effect is an increase at the rate of $p - d$ items per day. For example, in D&G's problem, $p = 1600$ and $d = 400$. Hence, the inventory level's rate of increase in Figure 14.6 is $p - d = 1200$ boxes per day.

3. When a production run ends, there is a gradual fall in the inventory level as items are removed from inventory at the rate of d items per day. In D&G's

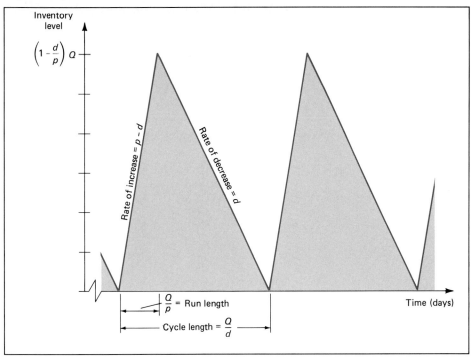

Figure 14.6 Graph of inventory level over time for the EPQ model

problem, the inventory level's rate of decrease in Figure 14.6 is $d = 400$ boxes per day.

4. Since the daily production rate is p and since each production run size is Q, the replenishment portion of a cycle has a length of Q/p days. In D&G's problem, since $p = 1600$ boxes per day, the replenishment portion of a cycle with a production run size of, say, $Q = 4800$ boxes has a length of $Q/p = 4800/1600 = 3$ days.

5. Since the total production in each run is Q items and since the daily demand rate is d, each cycle has a total length of Q/d days. In D&G's problem, since $d = 400$ boxes per day, a cycle with a production run size of $Q = 4800$ boxes has a total length of $Q/d = 4800/400 = 12$ days.

6. The maximum inventory level (occurring at the end of each production run) is not Q. The reason is that, as the Q items from a production run are gradually added to inventory, some items are withdrawn. Facts 2 and 4 permit us to calculate the maximum inventory level as follows:

$$\begin{pmatrix}\text{maximum inventory} \\ \text{level}\end{pmatrix} = \begin{pmatrix}\text{rate at which} \\ \text{additions to inventory} \\ \text{occur during a} \\ \text{production run}\end{pmatrix}\begin{pmatrix}\text{length of a} \\ \text{production run}\end{pmatrix}$$

$$= (p - d)\frac{Q}{p}$$

$$= \left(1 - \frac{d}{p}\right)Q .$$

Note that, since $0 < d < p$, $0 < \left(1 - \dfrac{d}{p}\right) < 1$. Thus, the maximum inventory level is less than Q.

Understanding the above facts enables us to develop an expression for the annual total cost. We proceed as follows:

- **Computing the annual total of the fixed production costs.** The number of production runs per year is D/Q. For example, in D&G's problem, satisfying the annual demand of $D = 100,000$ boxes with production runs of size $Q = 20,000$ requires $D/Q = 100,000/20,000 = 5$ runs, whereas production runs of size $Q = 5000$ require $D/Q = 100,000/5000 = 20$ runs. The fixed production cost of each of the D/Q runs is C_o. Hence,

$$\begin{pmatrix} \text{annual total of the} \\ \text{fixed production} \\ \text{costs} \end{pmatrix} = \begin{pmatrix} \text{fixed cost per} \\ \text{production run} \end{pmatrix} \begin{pmatrix} \text{number of runs} \\ \text{per year} \end{pmatrix}$$

$$= (C_o) \left(\frac{D}{Q} \right)$$

$$= \frac{C_o D}{Q}$$

- **Computing the annual total of variable production costs.** There are D/Q production runs per year, each having a variable cost of $C_i Q$. Hence,

$$\begin{pmatrix} \text{annual total of} \\ \text{variable production} \\ \text{costs} \end{pmatrix} = \begin{pmatrix} \text{variable cost} \\ \text{per production} \\ \text{run} \end{pmatrix} \begin{pmatrix} \text{number of runs} \\ \text{per year} \end{pmatrix}$$

$$= (C_i Q) \left(\frac{D}{Q} \right)$$

$$= C_i D \ .$$

Note that this cost does not depend on Q, since, regardless of the production run size, D items must be produced each year at a cost of C_i per unit.

- **Computing the annual total of holding costs.** As illustrated in Figure 14.6, the maximum inventory level is $Q[1 - (d/p)]$. Since the average inventory level equals one-half of this maximum, the average inventory level is $Q/2[1 - (d/p)]$. It costs C_h dollars to hold one item for one year. Hence,

$$\begin{pmatrix} \text{annual total of} \\ \text{holding costs} \end{pmatrix} = \begin{pmatrix} \text{annual holding} \\ \text{cost per item} \end{pmatrix} \begin{pmatrix} \text{average inventory} \\ \text{level} \end{pmatrix}$$

$$= (C_h) \left[\frac{Q}{2} \left(1 - \frac{d}{p} \right) \right]$$

$$= \frac{C_h \left(1 - \frac{d}{p} \right) Q}{2}$$

Since we expressed the annual totals of fixed production costs and the variable product costs in terms of D (not d), we should do the same for the annual total of holding costs. To do so, we simply replace d/p in the above expression by D/P, since the two ratios are equal. Thus, our final expression is

$$\text{annual total of holding costs} = \frac{C_h \left(1 - \frac{D}{P} \right) Q}{2}$$

As in the EOQ model, let us use $TC(Q)$ to denote the annual total cost as a function of Q. Summing the above three cost components, we get

$$TC(Q) = \frac{C_o D}{Q} + C_i D + \frac{C_h \left(1 - \frac{D}{P}\right) Q}{2}$$

For future reference, this formula is summarized in Table 14.8(b). This table also summarizes all subsequent formulae we derive.

Our goal is to determine the value of Q that minimizes $TC(Q)$. We denote this optimal production quantity by Q^*. We can derive the formula for Q^* in the EPQ model from the corresponding formula for the EOQ model. To see how, let us compare Table 14.8(b)'s formula for $TC(Q)$ in the EPQ model to Table 14.2(b)'s formula for $TC(Q)$ in the EOQ model. We see that only their last term differs, with the role of C_h in the EOQ formula now being played by $C_h[1 - (D/P)] Q$ in the EPQ formula. Hence, to obtain the formula for Q^* in the EPQ model, we simply modify Table 14.2(b)'s formula for Q^* in the EOQ model by substituting $C_h[1 - (D/P)]$ for C_h. This substitution yields

$$Q^* = \sqrt{\frac{2 C_o D}{C_h \left(1 - \frac{D}{P}\right)}}$$

as the formula for the optimal production quantity.[14] Other relevant formulae for the EPQ model are also summarized in Table 14.8(b). Those formulae in the table that we did not derive in our discussion of Figure 14.6 are either identical to the corresponding EOQ formula in Table 14.2(b) or identical with $C_h \left(1 - \frac{D}{P}\right)$ replacing C_h.

Let us apply these formulae to D&G's problem. Substituting Table 14.8(a)'s data into the formulae, we obtain

$$Q^* = \sqrt{\frac{(2)(120)(100{,}000)}{(2)\left[1 - \frac{100{,}000}{400{,}000}\right]}} = 4000 \text{ boxes}$$

$$N^* = \frac{D}{Q^*} = \frac{100{,}000}{4000} = 25 \text{ production runs per year}$$

$$T^* = \frac{Q^*}{d} = \frac{4000}{400} = 10 \text{ days per cycle}$$

$$TC(Q^*) = (8)(100{,}000) + \sqrt{(2)(120)(100{,}000)(2)\left[1 - \frac{100{,}000}{400{,}000}\right]} = \$806{,}000$$

Note that Figure 14.6's graph enables us to see that each 10-day cycle consists of a replenishment portion with a length of $Q^{*/p} = 4000/1600 = 2.5$ days and a depletion portion of 7.5 days. Of course, rather than keeping the production line idle during each cycle's depletion portion, D&G will devote it to other sizes of diapers.

---

[14] This formula can also be derived by applying differential calculus to Table 14.8(b)'s formula for $TC(Q)$. An end-of-chapter exercise requests readers familiar with calculus to do so.

In D&G's problem, we are fortunate that Q^*, N^*, and T^* are such "nice" integers. If $Q^* = 4367.58$ had occurred, then N^* and T^* would also have had noninteger values. In this case, it would have been necessary for us to adjust Q^*, N^*, and T^* to more acceptable values. The procedures for making such adjustments and for evaluating the effect on the annual total cost are identical to those illustrated for the EOQ model in Section 14.4.

We conclude our discussion of the EPQ model by posing the following question:

> Two firms, A and B, sell the same item, but firm A operates in an EOQ environment whereas firm B operates in an EPQ environment. For each firm, the values for D, C_o, C_i, and C_h are identical. Is the optimal order quantity for firm A more than, equal to, or less than the optimal production quantity for firm B?

Before proceeding, try to answer this question on your own.

The answer is *less than*. More specifically, assuming the data are identical, Q^* for the EOQ model is always less than Q^* for the EPQ model. To see why, compare Table 14.2(b)'s formula for Q^* in the EOQ model to Table 14.8(b)'s formula for Q^* in the EPQ model. The only difference is the appearance of $\left(1 - \dfrac{D}{P}\right)$ in the denominator of the EPQ formula. Since $0 < D < P$, $\left(1 - \dfrac{D}{P}\right)$ is less than 1, which in turn implies that Q^* in the EOQ model is always less than Q^* in the EPQ model. Can you provide an intuitive justification for this relationship between the two models? Exercise 14.22 asks you to investigate a related connection between the two models—namely that, as the daily production rate in the EPQ model gets larger and larger, the limiting value of Q^* in the EPQ model is Q^* in the EOQ model.

14.7 MATERIAL REQUIREMENTS PLANNING

Independent Versus Dependent Demand

An assumption of the EOQ and EPQ models is that the item has *independent demand*, defined in Section 14.2 as demand arising from unknown plans or schedules. Independent demand is typical when an item is a finished good, such as the diapers ordered in St. Andrew's EOQ problem or manufactured in D&G's EPQ problem. Other examples of finished goods are automobiles and computers.

A finished good usually consists of many raw materials, parts, and/or subassemblies. For example, an automobile consists of steel, tires, transmissions, and so on. Hereafter, rather than distinguishing between a raw material, a part, or a subassembly, we will use the term *component* to refer to all three. A component in one or more finished goods usually has *dependent demand*, defined in Section 14.2 as demand that can be calculated from known plans or schedules. The reason is that, once we know the production schedules for all finished goods that need the component, we can calculate the demand for the component.

The EOQ and EPQ models are appropriate for inventory management of items with independent demand. However, inventory management of an item with dependent demand requires use of a technique known as *material requirements planning* (MRP).

Equally important to understanding how to use MRP is understanding why to use MRP. To illustrate the rationale for MRP, we consider the following extension of D&G's problem:

> The newborn-sized diapers D&G sells to vendors of medical supplies are packaged in special cardboard boxes that D&G orders from a nearby vendor. The lead time for delivery of an order of boxes from the vendor is 1 day.
>
> D&G produces diapers according to the policy determined in Section 14.6 using the EPQ model. Recall that this policy calls for 10-day cycles consisting of $2\frac{1}{2}$ days during which production of $Q^* = 4000$ boxes of diapers occurs at a rate of 1600 boxes per day followed by $7\frac{1}{2}$ days during which no production occurs.
>
> Since D&G orders the boxes for the diapers, it uses the EOQ model to determine the optimal order quantity and the reorder level. Let us assume that the optimal order quantity is coincidentally $Q^* = 4000$ boxes, the same as the production run size for the diapers themselves.[15] According to the EOQ model, an order for $Q^* = 4000$ boxes should arrive at D&G just as its inventory level for boxes reaches 0. Since the demand for boxes during a production run is equal to the production rate of 1600 boxes per day and since the lead time is 2 days, D&G uses $(1600)(2) = 3200$ as the reorder level.

Our goal is to show that D&G has made an error in using the EOQ model to determine its ordering policy for boxes. Before reading on, see if you can spot the error.

We can obtain our first hint that D&G's ordering policy for diapers is wrong by examining Figure 14.7, which displays graphs for the daily demand over time for both full boxes of diapers awaiting shipment to customers and empty boxes of diapers awaiting use during a production run. In Figure 14.7(a), customer demand for full boxes fluctuates around an average of 400 boxes per day, the value assumed to be the constant daily demand rate in the EPQ model. In Figure 14.7(b), D&G's internal demand for empty boxes fluctuates widely. During a production run, demand occurs at a rate equal to the production rate of 1600 boxes per day; however, between production runs, daily demand is 0. What accounts for the continuous demand in Figure 14.7(a) versus the "lumpy" demand in Figure 14.7(b)? The answer is that the demand for full boxes arises from the continual arrival of orders from D&G's customers, whereas the demand for empty boxes depends on the production schedule for diapers. In short, full boxes have an independent demand and empty boxes have a dependent demand. Thus, while an EPQ model is appropriate for determining the production run size for full boxes, the EOQ model, with its assumption of a constant demand rate, is inappropriate for determining the order size for empty boxes.

To further emphasize this point and to introduce the rationale for MRP, Figures 14.8(a) and (b) display graphs of the inventory level of both full and empty boxes which vary over time under D&G's current policies. Observe the following:

- Figure 14.8(a)'s graph of the inventory level of full boxes follows the typical pattern for the EPQ model displayed earlier in Figure 14.6. During a cycle's

---

[15] We make this assumption to simplify the discussion that follows. Of course, since D, C_o, C_i, and C_h that apply to producing diapers differ from those that apply to ordering boxes, the production run size obtained from the EPQ model would probably differ from the order size obtained from the EOQ model.

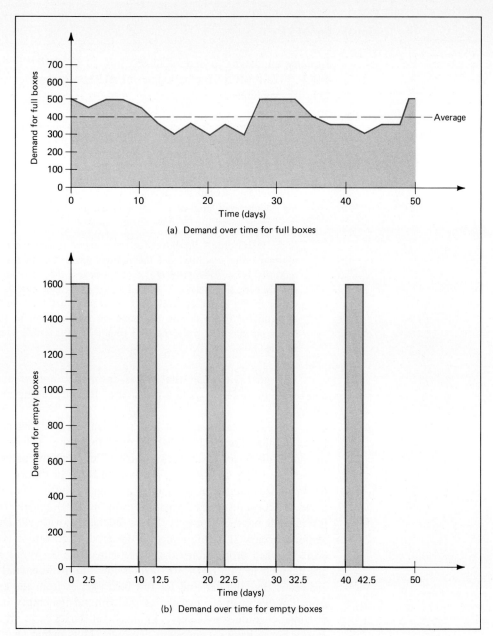

Figure 14.7 Demand over time for full and empty boxes

$2\frac{1}{2}$-day replenishment phase (point A on the time axis to point B), the inventory level of full boxes rises at the rate of 1200 boxes per day (the daily production rate minus the daily demand rate); during the $7\frac{1}{2}$-day depletion phase (point B to point C), the level falls at a rate of 400 boxes per day.

- Figure 14.8(b)'s graph of the inventory level of empty boxes also follows a cyclical pattern with phases that correspond to those in Figure 14.8(a). Each cycle begins with an inventory level of 4000 empty boxes. Then, from time A to time B, the production of diapers at the rate of 1600 boxes per day causes the inventory level of empty boxes to fall at the same rate. The inventory level crosses the reorder point of 1600 one day (i.e., the lead time) before the inventory level reaches 0 at point B. Hence, at point B, the inventory level jumps from 0 to 4000, the order quantity. Since no production occurs from

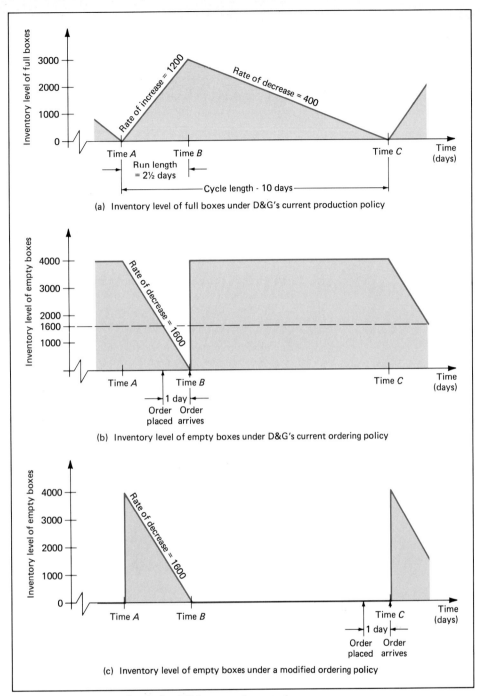

Figure 14.8 Inventory levels for full boxes and empty boxes

point B to point C, the inventory level of empty boxes remains at 4000 until a new cycle begins at point C.

Figure 14.8(b) demonstrates the flaw in D&G's current ordering policy for empty boxes. Maintaining an inventory level of 4000 empty boxes is clearly unnecessary. Since D&G knows it will not need these boxes until the next production run, it can determine when to place the order by "backing up" from point C by the lead time of 1 day. Following this policy leads to the graph displayed in Figure

14.8(c). Whereas the inventory level is 4000 boxes 75% of the time in Figure 14.8(b), it is 0 boxes 75% of the time in Figure 14.8(c). Thus, without increasing the number of orders per year, D&G can dramatically decrease its average inventory level of empty boxes by recognizing that the demand is dependent.

Figure 14.8 illustrates the underlying philosophy of MRP. When an item has dependent demand, we manage its inventory by working backward from the production schedules of all the finished goods in which the item is a component.

The Details of MRP

Now that we understand why to use MRP, let us discuss how to use it. Since entire books have been written about MRP, we can provide only a simplified overview here. To illustrate an inventory management problem to which MRP applies, consider the following scenario:

> The Orange Microcomputer Corporation (OMC) manufactures two models of personal computers: a desktop model with two floppy disk drives and a portable model with a single disk drive. Hereafter we refer to these models as A and B, respectively, and we refer to the disk drive as component C.
>
> Each disk drive consists of several subcomponents. To simplify our discussion, we will consider only one, which we hereafter refer to as subcomponent D. Each disk drive contains three of subcomponent D.
>
> We can summarize the stages involved in the production of models A and B using a diagram known as a *bill of materials*. Figure 14.9 displays a simplified bill of materials for models A and B, simplified because it specifies only those items in which we are interested. The arrows emanating from the circle that represents an item lead to the components that comprise the item, and the number in parentheses next to an item indicates how many of that component go into each item.
>
> OMC assembles the disk drives in-house. If OMC wants to have a batch of component C ready to install in model A or B, two days prior notification must be issued to the manager responsible for assembling component C. OMC purchases subcomponent D from a vendor. To ensure delivery of a batch of D on a specific day, OMC must place the order one day earlier. Table 14.9 summarizes the lead times for C and D as well as their current inventory levels.

Figure 14.9 Bill of materials for models A and B

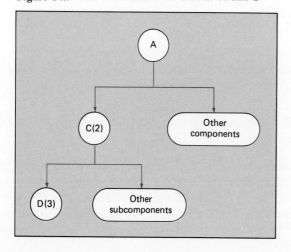
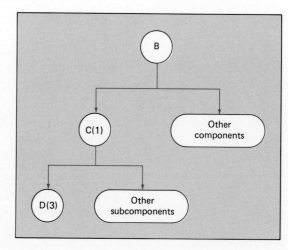

TABLE 14.9 Lead Times and Current Inventory
Levels for Component C and Subcomponent D

Item	Lead Time (days)	Current Inventory Level
C	2	120
D	1	500

Over the next six days, OMC wants to produce 100 of model A on days 3 and 6 and 50 of model B on days 2, 4, and 6. Table 14.10 summarizes this production schedule. Based on this schedule for its finished goods, OMC wants to determine what actions it should schedule for component C and subcomponent D.

The demand for subcomponent D depends on the demand for component C, whose demand in turn depends on the production schedule for models A and B. Hence, by working backward from Table 14.10's schedule, we can manage the daily inventory level of items C and D.

Table 14.11 summarizes the calculations for component C, using a format typical for the MRP technique. An explanation of each row of the table follows:

- **Gross requirements.** In MRP terminology, it is customary to refer to an item's demand as its *requirements*. Table 14.11's first row provides a day-by-day summary of the requirements for component C necessary to meet the production schedules for models A and B. To obtain this amount for a particular day, we refer to that day in Table 14.10 and add twice the production quantity of A to the production quantity for B (since each A contains 2 of C and each B contains 1 of C). For example,

TABLE 14.10 Production Schedules
for Models A and B

	Week					
	1	2	3	4	5	6
Model A	0	0	100	0	0	100
Model B	0	50	0	50	0	50

TABLE 14.11 MRP Calculations for Component C

	Week					
	1	2	3	4	5	6
Gross requirements	0	50	200	50	0	250
Remaining initial inventory (120)	120	70	0	0	0	0
Net requirements	0	0	130	50	0	250
Planned orders	130	50	0	250	X	X

$$\begin{pmatrix} \text{gross requirements} \\ \text{for C on day 6} \end{pmatrix} = 2 \begin{pmatrix} \text{scheduled} \\ \text{production of} \\ \text{model A on} \\ \text{day 6} \end{pmatrix} + \begin{pmatrix} \text{scheduled} \\ \text{production of} \\ \text{model B on} \\ \text{day 6} \end{pmatrix}$$

$$= 2(100) + (50)$$

$$= 250$$

Before proceeding, verify the gross requirements for the other days.

- **Remaining initial inventory**. Table 14.11's second row provides a day-by-day summary of how much of C's initial inventory remains in inventory, where the entry of 120 at the row's beginning is C's initial inventory level from 14.9. To obtain this amount for a particular day, we first subtract the day's gross requirements from the *previous* day's remaining initial inventory and then, if this difference is negative, we reset it to 0. For example,

$$\begin{pmatrix} \text{initial inventory} \\ \text{of C that remains} \\ \text{on day 2} \end{pmatrix} = \begin{pmatrix} \text{initial inventory} \\ \text{of C that remains} \\ \text{on day 1} \end{pmatrix} - \begin{pmatrix} \text{gross} \\ \text{requirements for} \\ \text{C on day 2} \end{pmatrix}$$

$$= 120 - 50$$

$$= 70.$$

Before proceeding, verify the remaining initial inventory for the other days.

- **Net requirements**. Table 14.11's third row provides a day-by-day summary of the portion of a day's gross requirements that cannot be satisfied by remaining initial inventory and, thus, must be satisfied by new assemblies of component C. To obtain this amount for a particular day, we first subtract the *previous* day's remaining initial inventory from the day's gross requirements and then, if this difference is negative, we reset it to 0. For example,

$$\begin{pmatrix} \text{net requirements} \\ \text{for C on day 3} \end{pmatrix} = \begin{pmatrix} \text{gross requirements} \\ \text{for C on day 3} \end{pmatrix} - \begin{pmatrix} \text{initial inventory of C} \\ \text{that remains on day 2} \end{pmatrix}$$

$$= 200 - 70$$

$$= 130.$$

Before proceeding, verify the net requirements for the other days.

- **Planned orders**. Table 14.11's fourth row provides a day-by-day summary of how much of C must be ordered on a particular day to satisfy the net requirements two days later, a length of time equal to C's lead time. Thus, the fourth row is simply the net requirements row shifted to the left by two days, where the Xs for days 5 and 6 indicate the absence of net requirements for days 7 and 8.

By working backward from the planned orders for component C, we can calculate the planned orders for subcomponent D. Table 14.12 summarizes these calculations. Since each C contains three of subcomponent D, we obtain the gross requirements row for D by multiplying C's planned orders row by 3. We obtain Table 14.12's remaining rows using the similar logic to that used for Table 14.11. Before proceeding, verify all entries in Table 14.12.

The planned orders rows of Tables 14.11 and 14.12 indicate the specific actions OMC must take to meet Table 14.10's production schedule for models A and B. To summarize,

TABLE 14.12 MRP Calculations for Subcomponent D

	Day					
	1	2	3	4	5	6
Gross requirements	390	150	0	750	X	X
Remaining initial inventory (500)	110	0	0	0	X	X
Net requirements	0	40	0	750	X	X
Planned orders	40	0	750	X	X	X

- Table 14.12 indicates that, to meet the requirements component C has for subcomponent D, OMC must place an order for 40 of D on day 1 and 750 of D on day 3. These orders will arrive one day later in time for use in C.

- Table 14.11 indicates that to meet the requirements models A and B have for component C, the manager responsible for assembling C must be notified on day 1 that 130 of C will be needed 2 days later, on day 2 that 50 of C will be needed 2 days later, and on day 4 that 250 of C will be needed 2 days later.

We conclude our overview of MRP with the following observations:

- If an MRP were to work precisely as we described it, component inventory levels would be low. Each batch of components would arrive just in time to be used in the next stage of production and, thus, would spend little time in inventory. Of course, in the real world, nothing goes exactly as planned. For example, an unanticipated large order might arrive and cause a significant modification to the planned production schedule for finished goods, a particular order's lead time might be much larger than usual, or a particular order might contain a higher-than-usual percentage of items that must be scrapped because of poor quality. Fortunately, a real MRP system is designed to operate in a way that minimizes the impact of surprises such as these. Space constraints preclude a discussion of the details.

- Although MRP's calculations involve only simple arithmetic, an enormous number of calculations must be performed to apply MRP to most real manufacturing environments. Given our small example, you can appreciate the volume of calculations necessary for an automobile manufacturer to manage the inventories at one of its assembly plants.

- Fortunately, today's computer technology makes MRP feasible, even for small-sized manufacturers who have access only to personal computers. With a computerized MRP system, it is easy to evaluate the effects of changes, such as a change in the production schedule for an end product or a change in a component's lead time.

- We have provided only a simplified overview of MRP. One simplification that merits discussion is the interpretation of the planned orders rows in Tables 14.11 and 14.12. We have assumed that each entry in the planned orders row generates an order of that size. This is known as *lot-for-lot ordering*. To illustrate why lot-for-lot ordering is not always desirable, suppose that a component's planned orders row for the next four days is

Day	1	2	3	4
Planned orders	500	100	400	300

If the vendor imposes little or no fixed cost to deliver an order and offers no quantity discounts, lot-for-lot scheduling makes sense. However, if either condition is not true, then it might be cheaper to combine several planned orders into a single order. For example, we might combine the planned orders for days 1 and 2 into a single order of 600 on day 1 and the planned orders for days 3 and 4 into a single order of 700 of day 3. This would be cheaper only if the increased holding costs were offset by lower fixed costs and/or a lower unit cost because of quantity discounts. The problem of whether or not to combine orders is known as the *lot-size problem*. Computerized MRP systems offer the user the option of using lot-for-lot scheduling or of using the planned orders row as data for a lot size problem.

Despite our simplified presentation, we have gained much insight into MRP's underlying philosophy and computational framework. To summarize:

> When an item has dependent demand, it is wrong, if the item is ordered from a vendor, to determine the order quantity using the EOQ model or, if the item is produced in-house, to determine the production run size using the EPQ model. Instead, the item's inventory should be managed using MRP, which (as illustrated by Tables 14.10–14.12) works backward from the production schedules of all finished goods in which the item is a component.

14.8 CONCLUDING REMARKS

In this chapter we have surveyed a few inventory models applicable when demand is deterministic. In the next chapter we will survey two models for use when demand is stochastic.

Although every manager should have a general understanding of the most common inventory models, the most important lesson to be learned from this chapter is qualitative, not quantitative:

> Proper inventory management requires the notification of anyone with responsibility for inventory that job performance will be measured by the *total* cost of his or her inventory policy, not just a portion of this cost.

To illustrate, consider a plant manager who gets reprimanded by the company's vice president of manufacturing only when the manager fails to meet a scheduled shipment date to a major customer. How will this plant manager react? The obvious answer is that the manager will attempt to avoid late shipments by maintaining excessive inventory levels for every item used in the production process. Although this decreases the costs associated with stockouts, it increases the holding costs, especially the opportunity cost of having too many dollars tied up in inventory instead of being put to better use elsewhere. To provide the plant manager with the right incentives, the vice president should make sure the plant manager understands that the plant's inventory levels will be closely monitored and that there will be reprimands not only when inventory levels are too low but also when they are too high. Although we have used a plant manager in our example, the same principle applies to all managerial levels, down to the clerk responsible for office supplies.

14.9 CHAPTER CHECKLIST AND GLOSSARY

Quickly review this chapter by rereading the material highlighted by a vertical line in the left margin. You should then be familiar with the concepts, techniques, and terminology in the Checklist and Glossary that follow. If you need "help" with a particular item, consult the section or sections indicated for a more detailed discussion.

Checklist of Concepts and Techniques

☐ The arguments both for and against having a high inventory level. [14.1]

☐ The ten characteristics that we must specify to describe an inventory system. [14.2]

☐ The three components of cost:

☐ the ordering or production cost (consisting of fixed and variable subcomponents),

☐ the holding cost, and

☐ the stockout cost. [14.3]

☐ The EOQ model, including

☐ computing the optimal order quantity and related quantities,

☐ analyzing the effects of using a nonoptimal order quantity, and

☐ computing the reorder level. [14.4]

☐ The EOQ model with quantity discounts. [14.5]

☐ The EPQ model. [14.6]

☐ Why the EOQ model and the EPQ model are inappropriate when an item has dependent demand. [14.7]

☐ The use of MRP to manage the inventories of components of finished goods with known production schedules. [14.7]

Glossary

Perishable item. An item that may suffer a loss in value because of spoilage or obsolescence. [14.2]

Multiechelon inventory system. An inventory system where inventories are stored at several geographically dispersed locations. Instead of being used to satisfy demand, an item withdrawn from inventory may be transferred from the inventory at one location to the inventory at another location. [14.2]

Planning horizon. The number of time periods over which decisions must be made. Table 14.1 displays the four types of planning horizons. [14.2]

Deterministic. Known with certainty. [14.2]

Stochastic. Governed by a probability distribution. [14.2]

Dependent demand. Demand arising from plans or schedules known to the organization that must satisfy the demand. [14.2]

Independent demand. The antonym of dependent demand. [14.2]

Periodic review policy. A policy based on checking an item's inventory level only at predetermined fixed intervals of time. [14.2]

Continuous review policy. A policy based on continuously monitoring an item's inventory level. [14.2]

Lead time for an order (or a production run). The elapsed time between the placement of an order and its delivery (or between the decision to produce and the start of a production run). [14.2]

Stockout. The situation when there is demand for an item but its inventory level is zero. [14.2]

Backlogging. Postponing the delivery of an item until inventory can be replenished. [14.2]

Lost sales. Sales that do not occur because backlogging is impossible. [14.2]

Variable costs of an order (or production run). Those costs that change if the quantity ordered (or produced) changes. [14.3]

Fixed costs of an order (or production run). Those costs that remain the same regardless of the quantity ordered (or produced). [14.3]

Holding cost per item. The cost to store one item in inventory for a specified interval of time. [14.3]

Opportunity cost portion of holding cost. The major component of holding cost, incurred because the funds tied up in inventory could be used for investments or to reduce debt. [14.3]

Stockout cost per item. The cost incurred when demand for an item cannot be satisfied because the inventory level is zero. This cost is often difficult to estimate because it must account for the loss of the customer's goodwill. [14.3]

EOQ model. A model that determines the optimal order quantity, assuming a constant demand rate. [14.4]

Cycle time. The elapsed time between the delivery of consecutive orders or between the start of consecutive production runs. [14.4, 14.6]

Lead time demand. The demand that occurs between the placement of an order and its delivery or between the decision to produce and the start of a production run. [14.4]

Reorder level. The inventory level that "triggers" the placement of an order or the decision to produce. [14.4]

Quantity discount. A means by which a vendor encourages large order quantities by decreasing the unit cost to the buyer as the order quantity increases. [14.5]

EPQ model. A model that determines the optimal order quantity, assuming a constant production rate during a production run and a constant demand rate. [14.6]

Bill of materials. A pictorial representation of the components that comprise a finished good, the subcomponents that comprise each of these components, and so on. [14.7]

Material requirements planning (MRP). A technique for managing the inventory levels of the raw materials, parts, components, and/or assemblies that comprise a finished good. [14.7]

EXERCISES

The first exercise tests your understanding of the arguments both for and against having a high inventory level.

14.1. Consider each of the three job titles listed below in parts (a)-(c). For each, specify whether a person

with that job title is likely to prefer a high inventory level or a low inventory level (as judged by which makes his or her job easier). Give a brief justification for each of your answers.
(a) Plant Manager
(b) Marketing Manager
(c) Financial Vice President

The next exercise tests your understanding of the costs in an inventory management problem.

14.2. Consider each of the eight costs listed below in parts (a)–(h). For each, specify whether the cost affects the value of C_o (the fixed component of the ordering or production cost), C_i (the variable component of the ordering or production cost), or C_h (an item's annual holding cost). Give a brief justification for each of your answers. Note that, in some parts, the correct answer might be "none" or "more than one" of C_o, C_i, and C_h.
(a) The salary of the clerk who places orders.
(b) The cost of inspecting each item in an order that has just arrived.
(c) The cost of sterilizing the equipment used during a production run of a particular flavor of ice cream.
(d) The state or local taxes that must be paid based on the value of the inventory.
(e) The cost of insuring the inventory against damage or theft.
(f) The phone expenses incurred during the placement of an order.
(g) The cost of the electricity used by a refrigeration system used to cool all items held in inventory.
(h) The cost of attaching machine-readable tags to each item in an order that has just arrived.

Exercises 14.3–14.6 involve the analysis of an EOQ model. Note that Exercises 14.5 and 14.6 illustrate that an item held in inventory can be something other than a product.

*14.3. JoAnn Froyo owns a shop that sells frozen yogurt and ice cream. The shop is located in an indoor shopping mall that is open 360 days per year. JoAnn orders cartons of the frozen yogurt mix from a vendor who charges $21.33 per carton. In addition, the vendor charges $25 to make a delivery to JoAnn's shop, regardless of the number of cartons delivered. Over the past year, daily demand at JoAnn's shop has rarely deviated by much from an average of 15 cartons per day. JoAnn estimates that if she held a carton of frozen yogurt mix in inventory for one year, the holding cost would be 25% of a carton's unit cost. Under JoAnn's current ordering policy, an order of 450 cartons arrives every 30 days.

(a) Draw a graph (similar to that in Figure 14.2) that displays the sum of the annual totals of JoAnn's fixed ordering costs and holding costs as a function of the order quantity.
(b) What is JoAnn's optimal order quantity?
(c) Draw a graph (similar to those in Figure 14.1) that displays how JoAnn's inventory level will vary over time if she orders the optimal quantity.
(d) Under the optimal ordering policy, how many orders does JoAnn place per year and how many days elapse between the arrival of successive orders?
(e) Under the optimal ordering policy, what is the annual total of fixed ordering costs, the annual total of variable ordering costs, the annual total of holding costs, and the sum of these three components of annual cost?
(f) Compare your answers in part (e) to the corresponding costs under JoAnn's current ordering policy. How much does JoAnn save per year by using the optimal ordering policy?
(g) If JoAnn always receives an order exactly 5 days after placing it, what reorder level should she use?
(h) If JoAnn always receives an order exactly 25 days after placing it, what reorder level should she use?

14.4. Bay Area Transit (BAT) is reevaluating its ordering policy for the tires used on its fleet of buses. Under BAT's current policy, an order of 1440 tires arrives every 90 days. As input to its ordering decision, BAT has made the following assumptions and estimates:

■ There are 360 days per year.
■ Demand for new tires rarely deviates by much from an average of 16 tires per day.
■ The vendor that supplies tires to BAT charges $115 per tire. In addition, the supplier charges $250 to make a delivery, regardless of the number of tires delivered.
■ Besides the vendor's fixed delivery charge of $250, BAT incurs a fixed cost of $70 to process and receive an order.
■ The annual holding cost per tire is 20% of its cost.

(a) Draw a graph (similar to that in Figure 14.2) that displays the sum of the annual totals of BAT's fixed ordering costs and holding costs as a function of the order quantity.
(b) What is BAT's optimal order quantity?
(c) Draw a graph (similar to those in Figure 14.1) that displays how BAT's inventory level will vary over time if it orders the optimal quantity.
(d) Under the optimal ordering policy, how many orders does BAT place per year and how many

days elapse between the arrival of successive orders?

(e) Under the optimal ordering policy, what is the annual total of fixed ordering costs, the annual total of variable ordering costs, the annual total of holding costs, and the sum of these three components of annual cost?

(f) Compare your answers in part (e) to the corresponding costs under BAT's current ordering policy. How much does BAT save per year by using the optimal ordering policy?

(g) If BAT always receives an order exactly 7 days after placing it, what reorder level should it use?

(h) If BAT always receives an order exactly 60 days after placing it, what reorder level should it use?

14.5. At one of its assembly plants, MBI Computer Corporation experiences a high turnover rate among its assembly-line workers. During the 250 days per year that the plant is open, assembly-line workers quit at a rate that rarely deviates by much from an average of 6 workers per day. To ensure that its plant always operates at full capacity, MBI maintains a pool of trained workers who are "on call" in the sense that they do *not* report for work immediately after finishing training. Instead, each on-call worker waits until MBI needs him or her to replace a worker who has just quit. While on call, a worker receives 25% of the salary of a full-time worker, whose annual salary is $31,200 per year. On-call workers are trained by a consulting firm hired by MBI. The consulting firm's fee is $9600 per training session (regardless of the number of trainees) plus $1000 per trainee. The number of trainees that drop out of a training session or subsequently quit before being called for full-time work is insignificant. Given this information, MBI wants to determine the optimal size of a training class.

(a) Assume that when MBI evaluates an item's annual holding cost, a portion of this cost always includes an opportunity cost equal to 20% of the item's cost. Under this assumption, what is the annual cost of "holding" someone in the pool of on-call workers?

(b) What is the optimal size of a training class?

(c) If MBI uses the optimal training class size, how many training sessions does MBI have per year and how many working days elapse between the completion of successive training sessions?

(d) Assume that the consulting firm requires an advance notice of 2 working days to prepare for a training session and that the training session lasts 5 working days. How many on-call workers should be in the pool when MBI notifies the consulting firm it wants a new training session to begin?

(e) Redo part (d), this time assuming that the consulting firm requires an advance notice of 5 working days and that the training session lasts 7 working days.

14.6. For the foreseeable future, Newco, Inc., intends to finance its operations by borrowing from the Second National Bank (SNB). For planning purposes, Newco assumes there are 250 working days per year. Newco estimates that its demand for borrowed cash will rarely deviate by much from $20,000 per day. Newco's line of credit with SNB has the following terms:

- Newco can borrow cash at an annual interest rate of 10%.
- At the end of each fiscal year, Newco must repay all the cash it borrowed during the year plus all accrued interest.
- During any fiscal year, Newco can originate any number of loans.
- At the time of the origination of any loan, Newco will pay SNB a loan-origination fee of $945 plus 2 points—that is, $945 plus 2% of the total amount borrowed. (Note: Assume that Newco pays this fee using its own funds rather than using the proceeds of the loan.)

Given this information, Newco wants to determine its optimal loan amount.

(a) Assume that when Newco evaluates an item's annual holding cost, a portion of this cost always includes an opportunity cost equal to 25% of the item's cost. Under this assumption, what is the annual cost of "holding" a dollar borrowed from SNB?

(b) What is Newco's optimal loan amount?

(c) Under the optimal borrowing policy, how many loans does Newco originate per year and how many working days elapse between the origination of successive loans?

(d) If SNB requires 10 working days to process a loan request, at what level of borrowed (but unspent) cash should Newco initiate a loan request?

(e) Redo part (d), this time assuming that SNB requires 20 working days to process a loan request.

Exercises 14.7–14.10 require you to analyze the effect in an EOQ model of using an order quantity that differs from the optimal order quantity.

* 14.7 Reconsider JoAnn's problem in Exercise 14.3. In that exercise, we assumed that the vendor placed no restriction on JoAnn's order quantity. Now assume

that the vendor packs the frozen yogurt in cases of 12 cartons and requires that JoAnn's order quantity be a multiple of 5 cases. In other words, JoAnn's order quantity must be a multiple of 60 cartons.

(a) What should JoAnn use as her order quantity?

(b) If JoAnn uses the order quantity computed in part (a) instead of the one computed in Exercise 14.3, what is the percentage increase in the portion of the annual total cost that depends on the order quantity (i.e., the annual total cost excluding the annual total of variable ordering costs)?

14.8. Reconsider BAT's problem in Exercise 14.4. In that exercise, we assumed that the vendor placed no restriction on BAT's order quantity. Now assume that the vendor ships tires in truckloads of 256 tires and, hence, requires that BAT's order quantity be a multiple of 256.

(a) What should BAT use as its order quantity?

(b) If BAT uses the order quantity computed in part (a) instead of the one computed in Exercise 14.4, what is the percentage increase in the portion of the annual total cost that depends on the order quantity (i.e., the annual total cost excluding the annual total of variable ordering costs)?

14.9. Reconsider MBI's problem in Exercise 14.5. In that exercise, we assumed that assembly-line workers quit at the rate of 6 workers per day. Now assume that the true turnover rate is 12 workers per day. Further assume that since MBI is unaware of this true value, it continues to compute the size of a training class using a turnover rate of 6 workers per day, an estimate that is 50% lower than the true value.

(a) What is the true optimal value of the size of a training class?

(b) If MBI uses the training class size computed in Exercise 14.5 instead of the one computed in part (a), what is the percentage increase in the portion of the annual total cost that depends on the order quantity (i.e., the annual total cost excluding the annual total of variable ordering costs)?

14.10. Consider an EOQ model in which there is uncertainty about the values of C_o (an order's fixed cost) and C_h (an item's annual holding cost).

(a) Assume that the estimate of C_o is 25% *higher* than its true value, and the estimate of C_h is 25% *lower* than its true value. Let Q^* denote the optimal order quantity that would be obtained using the true values of C_o and C_h and let Q denote the optimal order quantity that is obtained using the estimates for the values of

C_o and C_h. If an order quantity of Q is used instead of Q^*, what is the percentage increase in the portion of the annual total cost that depends on the order quantity (i.e., the annual total cost excluding the annual total of variable ordering costs)?

(b) Redo part (a), this time assuming that the estimates of C_o and C_h are both 25% *higher* than their respective true values.

(c) Redo part (a), this time assuming that the estimate of C_o is 25% lower than its true value, and the estimate of C_h is 25% *higher* than its true value.

(d) Redo part (a), this time assuming that the estimates of C_o and C_h are both 25% *lower* than their respective true values.

Exercises 14.11 and 14.12 require you to identify an error that has been made during the analysis of an EOQ model.

14.11. A firm has an inventory management problem that fits the assumptions of the EOQ model. As input to its decision, the firm has made the following assumptions and estimates:

- Demand occurs at a constant rate of 200 items per day.
- The cost to order Q items is $900 + 20Q$ dollars.
- An item's annual holding cost is $4.

Using this information, the firm computes its optimal order quantity as follows:

$$\sqrt{\frac{(2)(900)(200)}{(4)}} = 300 \text{ items.}$$

Explain why the firm's computation is wrong.

14.12. Using the EOQ model, a firm has computed that an item's optimal order quantity is 500 items. After using this optimal order quantity for a year, the firm receives a notice from the item's vendor that the item's unit cost is going up by 20%. On examining the formula for the optimal order quantity in an EOQ model, the firm observes that the only data in the formula are the item's annual demand, the item's annual holding cost, and an order's fixed cost. Consequently, the firm concludes that the optimal order quantity is unaffected by the 20% increase in the item's unit cost. Explain why the firm's conclusion is wrong.

Exercises 14.13–14.16 involve the analysis of an EOQ model with quantity discounts.

14.13 Reconsider the quantity-discount version of St. Andrew's problem in Section 14.5. Using the discount schedule displayed in Table 14.4, we computed in Section 14.5 that the optimal order quantity was $Q = 900$. Now assume that the discount schedule is the one displayed below:

Discount Category	Values of Q That Qualify	Discount	Unit Cost
1	$0 \leqslant Q < 900$	0%	$16.00
2	$900 \leqslant Q < 1800$	2%	$15.68
3	$1800 \leqslant Q$	5%	$15.20

Observe that the only change from Table 14.4 is that the discount for Category 3 is now 5% instead of 3%.

(a) Under the new discount schedule, what is the optimal order quantity? Summarize your analysis in a table similar to Table 14.7.
(b) Compare part (a)'s optimal order quantity to the one computed in Section 14.5. Provide an intuitive explanation of the reason for the difference.

14.14. Reconsider Newco's problem in Exercise 14.6. In that exercise, we assumed that Second National Bank (SNB) charged 2 points, regardless of the loan amount.
(a) Now assume that SNB's loan-origination fee is $945 plus 2 points for any loan amount less than $500,000 but is $945 plus 1.75 points for any loan amount equal to or greater than $500,000. Under this discount structure, what is Newco's optimal loan amount? Summarize your analysis in a table similar to Table 14.7.
(b) Redo part (a), this time assuming that the minimum loan amount that qualifies for 1.75 points is $1,000,000 instead of $500,000.

*14.15. Reconsider JoAnn's problem in Exercise 14.3. In that exercise, we assumed that the unit cost of a carton of frozen yogurt was $21.33, regardless of the order quantity Q.
(a) Now assume that JoAnn's vendor discounts a carton's unit cost according to the schedule displayed below:

Discount Category	Values of Q That Qualify	Discount	Unit Cost
1	$0 \leqslant Q < 200$	$0.00	$21.33
2	$200 \leqslant Q < 400$	$0.13	$21.20
3	$400 \leqslant Q$	$0.33	$21.00

Under this discount structure, what is JoAnn's optimal order quantity? Summarize your analysis in a table similar to Table 14.7.
(b) Redo part (a), this time using the following discount schedule:

Discount Category	Values of Q That Qualify	Discount	Unit Cost
1	$0 \leqslant Q < 200$	$0.00	$21.33
2	$200 \leqslant Q < 1000$	$0.13	$21.20
3	$1000 \leqslant Q$	$0.33	$21.00

14.16. Reconsider BAT's problem in Exercise 14.4. In that exercise, we assumed that unit cost of a tire was $115, regardless of the order quantity Q.
(a) Now assume that BAT's vendor discounts a tire's unit cost according to the schedule displayed below:

Discount Category	Values of Q That Qualify	Discount	Unit Cost
1	$0 \leqslant Q < 100$	0%	$115.00
2	$100 \leqslant Q < 250$	1%	$113.85
3	$250 \leqslant Q < 500$	2%	$112.70
4	$500 \leqslant Q < 1500$	3%	$111.55
5	$1500 \leqslant Q < 2000$	4%	$110.40
6	$2000 \leqslant Q$	5%	$109.25

Under this discount structure, what is BAT's optimal order quantity? Summarize your analysis in a table similar to Table 14.7.
(b) Redo part (a), this time using the following discount schedule:

Discount Category	Values of Q That Qualify	Discount	Unit Cost
1	$0 \leqslant Q < 100$	0%	$115.00
2	$100 \leqslant Q < 250$	1%	$113.85
3	$250 \leqslant Q < 500$	2%	$112.70
4	$500 \leqslant Q < 1000$	3%	$111.55
5	$1000 \leqslant Q < 2000$	4%	$110.40
6	$2000 \leqslant Q$	5%	$109.25

(c) Redo part (a), this time using the following discount schedule:

Discount Category	Values of Q That Qualify	Discount	Unit Cost
1	$0 \leqslant Q < 100$	0%	$115.00
2	$100 \leqslant Q < 250$	1%	$113.85
3	$250 \leqslant Q < 500$	2%	$112.70
4	$500 \leqslant Q < 1000$	3%	$111.55
5	$1000 \leqslant Q < 1500$	4%	$110.40
6	$1500 \leqslant Q$	5%	$109.25

Exercises 14.17–14.19 involve the analysis of an EPQ model.

*14.17. Wilsun Sporting Goods (WSG) manufactures several types of golf balls at a plant that operates 250 days per year. One of the types of golf balls is

672

called the Gofar. When WSG devotes its plant to the exclusive production of Gofar golf balls, the production rate averages 40,000 dozen balls per day. Every day the plant is open, demand for Gofar golf balls averages 8000 dozen balls per day. WSG estimates that a production run of Q dozen Gofar golf balls costs $640 + 10Q$ dollars. WSG also estimates that if it held a dozen Gofar golf balls in inventory for one year, the holding cost would be $2. Under its current policy, WSG produces Gofar golf balls in runs having a size of 200,000 dozen balls.

(a) What is the optimal size for a production run of Gofar golf balls?

(b) Draw a graph (similar to that in Figure 14.6) that displays how WSG's inventory level of Gofar golf balls will vary over time if WSG uses the optimal production policy.

(c) Under the optimal production policy, how many production runs take place per year, what is the length (in working days) of a production run, what is the inventory level at the end of a production run, and how many working days elapse between the start of successive production runs?

(d) Under the optimal production policy, what is the annual total of fixed production costs, the annual total of variable production costs, the annual total of holding costs, and the sum of these three components of annual cost?

(e) Compare your answers in part (d) to the corresponding costs under WSG's current production policy. How much does WSG save per year by using the optimal production policy?

14.18. Specific Electric Company (SEC) manufactures appliances at a plant that operates 250 days per year. One of the appliances made at the plant is a refrigerator known as the Hasitall. SEC wants to determine the optimal size for a production run of Hasitall refrigerators. As input to its decision, SEC has made the following assumptions and estimates:

- When SEC's plant is manufacturing Hasitall refrigerators, the production rate is 200 refrigerators per day.

- Every day the plant is open, SEC must ship a total of 80 Hasitall refrigerators to its regional warehouses.

- A production run costs $960 (regardless of its size) plus $500 per refrigerator.

- The annual holding cost for a Hasitall refrigerator is $100.

(a) What is the optimal size for a production run of Hasitall refrigerators?

(b) Draw a graph (similar to that in Figure 14.6) that displays how SEC's inventory level of

Hasitall refrigerators will vary over time if SEC uses the optimal production policy.

(c) Under the optimal production policy, how many production runs take place per year, what is the length (in working days) of a production run, what is the inventory level at the end of a production run, and how many working days elapse between the start of successive production runs?

(d) Under the optimal production policy, what is the annual total of fixed production costs, the annual total of variable production costs, the annual total of holding costs, and the sum of these three components of annual cost?

14.19. Wagner Winery operates a plant that produces several varieties of wine, including Chardonnay. Wagner wants to determine the optimal size for a production run of Chardonnay. As input to its decision, Wagner has made the following assumptions and estimates:

- Wagner's plant operates 250 days per year.

- When the plant is producing Chardonnay, the production rate is 4000 bottles per day.

- Every day the plant is open Wagner must ship a total of 1000 bottles of Chardonnay to its customers.

- A production run of Q bottles of Chardonnay costs $864 + 12Q$ dollars.

- The annual holding cost for a bottle of Chardonnay is $4.

(a) What is the optimal size for a production run of Chardonnay?

(b) Under the optimal production policy, how many production runs take place per year, what is the length (in working days) of a production run, what is the inventory level at the end of a production run, and how many working days elapse between the start of successive production runs?

(c) Under the optimal production policy, what is the annual total of fixed production costs, the annual total of variable production costs, the annual total of holding costs, and the sum of these three components of annual cost?

Exercises 14.20–14.22 require you to derive a formula or a relationship that was stated without proof in the chapter. Note that Exercises 14.20 and 14.21 require knowledge of differential calculus.

*14.20. In Section 14.4, we stated without proof that the optimal order quantity in an EOQ model can be computed using the formula for Q^* in Table 14.2(b). Use differential calculus to derive this formula.

673

14.21. In Section 14.6, we stated without proof that the optimal order quantity in an EPQ model can be computed using the formula for Q^* in Table 14.8(b). Use differential calculus to derive this formula.

14.22. Two firms, A and B, sell the same item, but firm A operates in an EOQ environment whereas firm B operates in an EPQ environment (i.e., firm A orders the item whereas firm B produces the item). For each firm, the values for D, C_o, C_i, and C_h are identical. Show that as firm B's daily production rate gets larger and larger, firm B's optimal production quantity gets closer and closer to firm A's optimal order quantity.

Exercises 14.23–14.25 test your understanding of material requirements planning (MRP).

14.23. Reconsider the Orange Microcomputer Corporation's MRP problem in Section 14.7. In discussing this problem, we considered only one of the subcomponents that comprise component C, subcomponent D. Now assume the following:
- Another of the subcomponents that comprise component C is subcomponent E.
- Each component C contains 1 of subcomponent E.
- Subcomponent E is purchased from a vendor. To ensure delivery of a batch of subcomponent E on a specific day, an order must be placed 2 days earlier.
- The current inventory level of subcomponent E is 200.

Using the format of Tables 14.11 and 14.12, perform the MRP calculations for subcomponent E.

* **14.24.** Consider an MRP problem with the following data:
- A company manufactures three models of a particular product—models A, B, and C.
- Over the next nine days, the production schedules for models A, B, and C are as follows:

	Day								
	1	2	3	4	5	6	7	8	9
Model A	0	0	100	0	0	100	0	0	100
Model B	25	25	25	25	25	25	25	25	25
Model C	50	0	50	0	50	0	50	0	50

- Models A, B, and C consist of several components. One of these is component D. Each model A contains 3 of component D; each model B contains 2 of component D; each model C contains 1 of component D.
- Component D consists of several subcomponents.

One of these is subcomponent E. Each component D contains 4 of subcomponent E.
- The company assembles component D in-house. If the company wants to have a batch of component D ready on a specific day to install in model A, B, or C, the manager responsible for assembling component D must be notified 1 day in advance.
- The company purchases subcomponent E from a vendor. To ensure the vendor delivers a batch of subcomponent E on a specific day, the company must place the order 2 days earlier.
- The current inventory levels for component D and subcomponent E are 170 and 1600, respectively.

Given this data, the company wants to determine what actions it should schedule for component D and subcomponent E in order to meet the production schedules for models A, B, and C.
- (a) For each model, draw a bill of materials similar to those displayed in Figure 14.9.
- (b) Using the format of Tables 14.11 and 14.12, perform the MRP calculations for component D and subcomponent E.

14.25. Consider an MRP problem with the following data:
- A company manufactures two models of a particular product—models A and B.

- Over the next eight days, the production schedules for models A and B are as follows:

	Day							
	1	2	3	4	5	6	7	8
Model A	50	50	50	50	50	50	50	50
Model B	0	75	0	75	0	75	0	75

- Models A and B consist of several components. One of these is component C. Each model A contains 3 of component C; each model B contains 2 of component C.
- Component C consists of several subcomponents. One of these is subcomponent D. Each component C contains 1 of subcomponent D.
- Subcomponent D consists of several parts. One of these is part E. Each subcomponent D contains 2 of part E.
- The company assembles component C in-house. If the company wants to have a batch of component C ready on a specific day to install in model A or B, the manager responsible for assembling component C must be notified 2 days in advance.
- The company assembles subcomponent D in-

674

house. If the company wants to have a batch of subcomponent D ready on a specific day to install in component C, the manager responsible for assembling subcomponent D must be notified 1 day in advance.

- The company purchases part E from a vendor. To ensure the vendor delivers a batch of part E on a specific day, the company must place the order 3 days earlier.
- The current inventory levels for component C, subcomponent D, and part E are 500, 150, and 1600, respectively.

Given this data, the company wants to determine what actions it should schedule for component C, subcomponent D, and part E in order to meet the production schedules for models A and B.

(a) For each model, draw a bill of materials similar to those displayed in Figure 14.9.

(b) Using the format of Tables 14.11 and 14.12, perform the MRP calculations for component C, subcomponent D, and part E.

(c) Now assume that, before being placed in inventory, part E must be inspected for defaults. On average, only 80% of a batch of part E is found to be usable. How does this new assumption affect your MRP calculations?

INVENTORY MANAGEMENT UNDER STOCHASTIC DEMAND

15.1 INTRODUCTION

In the preceding chapter we assumed that both demand and lead time were deterministic. These assumptions are often unrealistic. An item's demand may vary widely from day to day, and a vendor may deliver an item well after its promised date. To model such situations, we assume in this chapter that demand and lead time are stochastic.

We will consider two distinct stochastic models:

- In Sections 15.2–15.7 we learn how to adapt the EOQ model to a situation where the demand and lead time are stochastic.

- In Sections 15.8–15.12 we consider a classic management science problem known as the newsboy problem. This problem involves a single time period and involves an item whose demand is stochastic and whose value is lower at the end of the period than at the beginning.

15.2 AN OVERVIEW OF THE EFFECT STOCHASTIC DEMAND AND LEAD TIME HAVE ON THE REORDER LEVEL

In the EOQ model, lead time demand is constant, since we assume that demand occurs at a constant daily rate and lead time is constant. For example, since the daily demand at St. Andrew's for disposable diapers is always 10 boxes per day and an order's lead time is always 5 days, the lead time demand is always 50 boxes.

If lead time demand is constant, we learned in Section 14.4 that stockouts can be avoided by setting the reorder level equal to the lead time demand (modulo the order quantity if necessary). Figure 14.3 illustrated this for St. Andrew's problem. With the reorder level equal to the lead time demand of 50, an order always arrived just as the inventory level reached 0.

When the daily demand is stochastic and/or the lead time is stochastic, the lead time demand is stochastic and, thus, a stockout is possible. To illustrate, consider the following scenarios for St. Andrew's problem:

- **Stochastic daily demand and constant lead time**. Suppose the daily demand fluctuates among 9, 10, and 11 boxes per day and the lead time is always 5 days. Then the lead time demand is stochastic, falling somewhere in the interval between 45 and 55 boxes.

- **Constant daily demand and stochastic lead time**. Suppose the daily demand is always 10 boxes per day, and the lead time fluctuates among 4, 5, and 6 days. Then the lead time demand is stochastic, fluctuating among 40, 50 and 60 boxes.

- **Stochastic daily demand and stochastic lead time**. Suppose the daily demand fluctuates among 9, 10, and 11 boxes per day, and the lead time fluctuates among 4, 5, and 6 days. Then the lead time demand is stochastic, falling somewhere in the interval between 36 and 66 boxes.

In each of these scenarios, if St. Andrew's continues to use 50 boxes as the reorder level, a stockout will occur whenever the lead time demand exceeds 50 boxes. These scenarios illustrate the following general principle:

> When demand is stochastic and/or lead time is stochastic, lead time demand is stochastic. Hence, a stockout occurs whenever lead time demand exceeds the reorder level.

Recall from the previous chapter that stockouts are costly. In a backlogging environment, there may be a cost incurred for expediting the receipt of backlogged items; in a lost sales environment, the profit from a potential sale is lost. Also, regardless of the environment, repeated stockouts may cause customers to turn to a competitor who provides more reliable service.

At first glance, there seems to be an easy way to avoid stockouts. We can simply set the reorder level higher than the maximum value for lead time demand. For example, if the daily demand never exceeds 13 and the lead time never exceeds 7 days, then using 91 as the reorder level precludes a stockout. Can you spot the fallacy in such a policy? It is that, because the reorder level is so high, there is usually a high inventory level when an order arrives. Hence, although the policy precludes costly stockouts, it increases holding costs. In fact, if minimizing holding costs were our only concern, we would set the reorder level to 0. Although this policy guarantees a stockout, (except in the unlikely event that lead time demand is 0) it also guarantees an inventory level of 0 when an order arrives.

The reorder level, then, is being "pulled" in opposite directions. On one hand, raising the reorder level precludes costly stockouts. On the other hand, lowering the reorder level reduces holding costs. Resolution of this dilemma is the focus of Sections 15.3–15.7.

15.3 THE ORDER-QUANTITY REORDER-LEVEL INVENTORY POLICY

When demand and/or lead time are stochastic, it is common to use the so-called *order-quantity reorder-level inventory policy*. Hereafter, we abbreviate this policy as the (Q, RL) policy, where Q denotes the order quantity and RL denotes the reorder level. A (Q, RL) policy is easy to describe:

Continuously monitor the inventory level and, when it decreases to the level RL, place an order for Q items.

Our analysis of the EOQ model in Section 14.4 led to a (Q, RL) policy, where Q and RL are determined from the formulae in Table 14.2. Because of the EOQ model's assumption that daily demand and lead time are constant, the graph of the inventory level over time consists of identical cycles, each having the form displayed in Figure 14.3 for St. Andrew's problem.

When demand and lead time are stochastic, use of a (Q, RL) policy results in a graph for the inventory level over time that does not consist of identical cycles. To see what this graph does look like, let us adopt the following notation:

$$LT_j = \text{the lead time for the } j\text{th order,}$$
$$LTD_j = \text{the demand during the lead time for the } j\text{th order.}$$

Using this notation, Figure 15.1 displays a typical graph of the inventory level over time for a (Q, RL) policy used when demand and lead time are stochastic. Observe the following aspects of this graph:

Figure 15.1 Graph of the inventory level over time for a (Q, RL) policy used when demand and lead time are stochastic

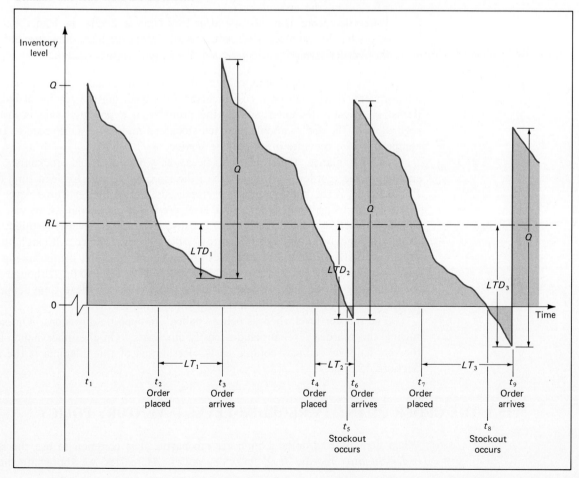

- The graph begins at time t_1 with an inventory level of Q. As demand occurs, the inventory level decreases. However, because demand is stochastic, the daily demand varies and, hence, the inventory level does not decrease at a constant rate.

- At time t_2, the inventory level drops to RL, thereby triggering the placement of an order for Q items. Because the lead time is stochastic, we are uncertain about when this order will arrive. We hope it arrives in time to avoid a stockout. To do so, the RL items in inventory when we place the order must be sufficient to satisfy the lead time demand. There is no guarantee. The lead time demand might exceed RL if the lead time is excessively long and/or the daily demand during the lead time is consistently higher than normal.

- At time t_3, the order arrives. The interval between t_2 and t_3 is the first lead time, LT_1; the decrease in the inventory level between t_2 and t_3 is the first lead time demand, LTD_1. Because LTD_1 is less than RL, a stockout does not occur. With the arrival of Q items, the inventory level jumps upward by Q and a new cycle begins.

- At time t_4, the inventory level drops to RL, thereby triggering the placement of the second order. Unfortunately, before this order arrives, daily demand increases sharply, thereby causing a rapid drop in the inventory level. At time t_5, a stockout occurs when the inventory level reaches 0. Assuming a backlogging environment, the inventory level continues to decrease, taking on increasingly negative values as more and more items are backlogged (e.g., an inventory level of -15 indicates 15 items are backlogged).[1]

- At time t_6, the order finally arrives and the inventory level jumps upward by Q items. Note that we use a portion of the order to satisfy backlogged demand and the remainder to replenish inventory. Also note that LT_2 is less than LT_1. Despite this lower lead time, the second cycle had a stockout because of the sudden surge in demand.

- The cycle that begins at time t_6 is similar to the previous cycle. In this cycle, however, the stockout is caused not by a surge in demand but because of an excessively long lead time.

Figure 15.1 is a visual representation of the previously stated general principle that, when demand and lead time are stochastic, lead time demand is stochastic and, thus, a stockout occurs whenever the lead time demand exceeds the reorder level.

15.4 A STOCHASTIC VERSION OF ST. ANDREW'S PROBLEM

As our example of the use of a (Q, RL) policy when demand and lead time are stochastic, we will use a stochastic version of St. Andrew's problem. In the previous chapter, we assumed that the daily demand for disposable diapers is always 10 boxes per day and that an order's lead time is always 5 days. We now replace these two assumptions with the following scenario:

> Although daily demand has averaged 10 boxes per day over the past year, the demand on any particular day can be well above or well below this average. Similarly, although lead time has averaged 5 days over the past year, lead time for any particular order can be well above or well below this average.

---

[1] In a lost sales environment, the inventory level would remain at 0 instead of taking on negative values.

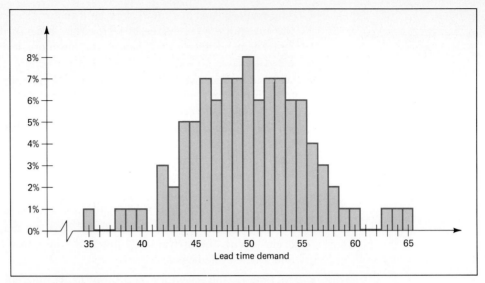

Figure 15.2 Histogram for lead time demand in St. Andrew's problem

The uncertainty about daily demand and lead time results in uncertainty about lead time demand. St. Andrew's has maintained accurate records of lead time demand. Analysis of this data yields Figure 15.2's histogram. For example, historically, lead time demand has been 42 boxes 3% of the time, 50 boxes 8% of the time, and 65 boxes 1% of the time. St. Andrew's believes that Figure 15.2's histogram will apply to future lead time demands as well.

When a stockout does occur, St. Andrew's temporarily uses an old supply of cloth diapers until the next order of disposable diapers arrives. When this happens too frequently, the staff and parents complain. St. Andrew's wants to determine an appropriate (Q, RL) policy to use in this stochastic environment.

Before we consider the when-to-order decision, let us discuss the how-much-to-order decision. Despite the fact that demand does not occur at a constant daily rate, we use the EOQ model to determine the order quantity Q. Recall that, in the EOQ model, the formula for the optimal order quantity contains the symbol D, the annual demand. Since we no longer assume daily demand is constant, we are uncertain about the value of D. However, we can estimate D by simply multiplying the average daily demand of 10 by 360, the number of days per year assumed by St. Andrew's for planning purposes. This estimate of $(10)(360) = 3600$ is probably a good approximation to annual demand because, over the course of an entire year, we expect the days where demand exceeds 10 by a particular amount to be offset by an approximately equal number of days where demand falls below 10 by the same amount.

The estimate of $D = 3600$ is the same as that in the previous chapter's deterministic version of St. Andrew's problem. The cost data is also the same. Hence, when we use Table 14.2's formula for Q^*, we once again obtain $Q^* = 367$. As we did in the deterministic version of St. Andrew's problem, we assume that, because its vendor finds an order quantity of 367 unacceptable, St. Andrew's instead uses $Q = 400$.

15.5 BASING THE WHEN-TO-ORDER DECISION ON A HISTOGRAM

Now that St. Andrew's knows how much to order, it wants to determine when to order. In particular, St. Andrew's wants to determine the reorder level RL that triggers the placement of an order. In this subsection, we assume that St. Andrew's will determine RL under the assumption that Figure 15.2's histogram is also valid for future lead time demands.

Using Figure 15.2, we can compute the average lead time demand by multiplying each lead time demand by the percentage of times it occurs and summing the resulting products. When we do so, we obtain

$$(35)(0.01) + 36(0.00) + \cdots + (50)(0.08) + \cdots + (64)(0.01) + (65)(0.01) = 50.$$

It is tempting to conclude that St. Andrew's should use the average lead time demand of 50 as the reorder level. To see why this is a wrong conclusion, observe that, if $RL = 50$, a stockout occurs whenever the lead time demand exceeds 50. Summing the percentages in the rectangles in Figure 15.2 corresponding to lead time demands ranging from 51 to 65, we obtain

$$6 + 7 + \cdots + 1 = 46\%$$

Thus, if $RL = 50$, there is a 46% chance of a stockout. St. Andrew's would probably find this unacceptable.

To decrease the likelihood of a stockout, St. Andrew's must set the reorder level above the average lead time demand. The amount by which the reorder level exceeds the average lead time demand is called the safety stock;[2] that is,

$$(\text{safety stock}) = (\text{reorder level}) - (\text{average lead time demand}).$$

The safety stock serves as a "cushion" in case lead time demand exceeds its average. The higher the safety stock, the less likely it is that a stockout will occur.

Before deciding on the size of its safety stock, St. Andrew's must decide on the so-called *service level*. The service level is the probability that a stockout will not occur or, equivalently, that the lead time demand is less than or equal to the reorder level. For example, if $RL = 50$, we saw that there is a 46% chance of a stockout. Hence, if $RL = 50$, the service level is 0.54. For all values of RL ranging from 50 to 65, Table 15.1 displays the corresponding safety stock and service level. (Temporarily ignore Table 15.1's last column.) Note that, to obtain the service level for each RL, we: (1) sum the percentages in Figure 15.2 corresponding to lead time demands that exceed RL, (2) convert this sum from a percentage to a probability, and (3) subtract this probability from 1.[3] For example, suppose $RL = 56$. The percentages in Figure 15.2 corresponding to demands ranging from 57 to 65 sum to 10%. This is equivalent to a probability of 0.10, which we subtract from 1 to obtain a service level of 0.90. Before proceeding, verify several of the remaining service levels in Table 15.1.

Table 15.1 confirms the intuitive observation that, as the reorder level increases, the service level increases (or, equivalently, the probability of a stockout decreases). Once St. Andrew's decides on a service level, it can use Table 15.1 to determine the corresponding reorder level.

Why should St. Andrew's settle for anything less than a service level of 100%? We provided a qualitative answer in Section 15.2 when we observed that increasing the reorder level increases the average inventory level, which in turn increases holding costs. Using the concept of safety stock, we can now provide a quantitative answer.

---

[2] Safety stock is sometimes called *buffer stock*.

[3] The last step is necessary because the second step yields the probability of a stockout, whereas the service level is the probability a stockout will not occur.

TABLE 15.1 The Effect the Reorder Level Has on the Service Level
and Holding Costs (based on Figure 15.2's histogram)

Reorder Level (RL)	Safety Stock (RL − 50)	Service Level (probability of no stockout)	Average Increase in the Annual Total of Holding Costs [4(RL − 50)]
50	0	0.54	0
51	1	0.60	4
52	2	0.67	8
53	3	0.74	12
54	4	0.80	16
55	5	0.86	20
56	6	0.90	24
57	7	0.93	28
58	8	0.95	32
59	9	0.96	36
60	10	0.97	40
61	11	0.97	44
62	12	0.97	48
63	13	0.98	52
64	14	0.99	56
65	15	1.00	60

Safety stock is the amount by which the reorder level exceeds the average lead time demand. During some lead times, no safety stock will be needed because lead time demand is below average; during other lead times, some or all of the safety stock will be needed because lead time demand is above average. Thus, safety stock is a good approximation to the average inventory level when an order arrives. This contrasts to the ideal situation where an order arrives at the precise moment when the inventory level reaches 0. Hence, the use of safety stock increases average inventory level by an amount approximately equal to the safety stock. If C_h denotes an item's annual holding cost, we can express the average increase in the annual total of holding costs as

$$(C_h) \text{ (safety stock)}$$

For example, since $C_h = \$4$ in St. Andrew's problem, the annual total of holding costs increases by an average of \$4 for every unit the reorder level exceeds the average lead time demand.

We have now quantified the effects the reorder level has on both the service level and the annual total of holding costs. The previously ignored last column in Table 15.1 summarizes these effects for St. Andrew's problem.

Table 15.1 does not provide a clear answer to what reorder level St. Andrew's should use. It only helps St. Andrew's to quantify the increased holding costs that necessarily accompany increased service levels. The management of St. Andrew's must still decide on the reorder level. If, instead of diapers, the problem involved a pharmaceutical used to treat heart attack victims in the emergency room, St. Andrew's would probably decide that a $60 increase in the annual total of holding costs is a small price to pay for a service level of 100%. However, given that cloth diapers serve as a substitute for disposable diapers during a stockout, St. Andrew's might decide on a reorder level of 56. Using $RL = 56$ results in a service level of 90% and saves $36 per year when compared with a 100% service level. If the savings seem too small to worry about, remember that this savings applies to only one of the thousands of items St. Andrew's holds in inventory. If St. Andrew's uses similar analysis to manage all items in inventory, its total savings will be substantial.

15.6 BASING THE WHEN-TO-ORDER DECISION ON A PROBABILITY DISTRIBUTION

Most computer software packages for inventory management assume that lead time demand is governed by a probability distribution. In St. Andrew's problem, this means we must determine which probability distribution best "fits" the data in Figure 15.1's histogram. Although there are formal statistical techniques for doing so, we will proceed in an informal manner.

Using a Normal Distribution

The approximately symmetrical and two-tailed nature of Figure 15.2's histogram suggests that the normal probability distribution governs lead time demand. We now need to specify values for the two parameters of the normal distribution: the mean, μ, and the standard deviation, σ. Since we previously computed the average lead time demand as 50, we can use this as our estimate of μ. To estimate σ, we can use the fact that over 99% of data arising from a normal distribution lies in an interval ranging from 3 standard deviations below the mean to 3 standard deviations above. In Figure 15.2, then, the difference between the largest lead time demand and the smallest equals approximately 6 standard deviations. Hence, our estimate for the standard deviation is

$$\sigma = \frac{65 - 35}{6} = 5.$$

To summarize, we now assume that lead time demand is governed by a normal probability distribution with $\mu = 50$ and $\sigma = 5$. Figure 15.3 displays this dis-

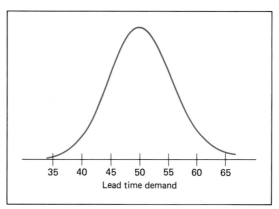

Figure 15.3 A normal probability distribution with $\mu = 50$ and $\sigma = 5$

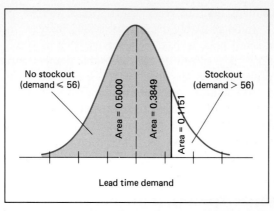

Figure 15.4 Computing the service level when the reorder level is $RL = 56$ and lead time demand has a normal distribution

tribution. Software packages prefer such an assumption because storing μ and σ requires much less computer memory than storing a histogram.

The assumption that lead time demand has a normal distribution enables St. Andrew's to compute the service level provided by a particular reorder level. For example, to compute the service level when $RL = 56$, we proceed as illustrated in Figure 15.4 and as described below:

The number of standard deviations by which RL exceeds μ is given by

$$\frac{RL - \mu}{\sigma} = \frac{56 - 50}{5} = 1.20 \, .$$

Consulting Table 15.2, we see that a lead time demand lying 1.20 standard deviations above its mean occurs with a probability of

$$0.5000 + 0.3849 = 0.9849 \, .$$

Note that we must add 0.5000 to 0.3849 because Table 15.2 only provides the probability of a value between the mean and a z value of 1.20.

By reversing the above procedure, we can also compute the reorder level necessary to provide a desired service level. For example, suppose St. Andrew's wants a service level of 0.95. To compute the required reorder level, we first subtract 0.5 from 0.95 to obtain 0.4500 as the probability we must find in Table 15.2. Although 0.4500 does not appear in the table, we see that 0.4495 and 0.4505 do. These probabilities correspond to respective z values of 1.64 and 1.65. Interpolating between these two z values, we obtain a z value of 1.645. Hence, to provide a service level of 0.95, the reorder level must be 1.645 standard deviations above μ; that is,

$$RL = 50 + (1.645)(5) = 58.225 \, .$$

Table 15.3 is analogous to Table 15.1, except that the service levels are computed using a normal probability distribution with $\mu = 50$ and $\sigma = 5$ instead of using Figure 15.2's histogram. We have already verified the row for $RL = 56$. Before proceeding, verify several of the other rows.

Using a Uniform Distribution

It is necessary to exercise caution when choosing the probability distribution that governs lead time demand. A common mistake is to assume a normal distribution

TABLE 15.2 Areas for the Standard Normal Distribution

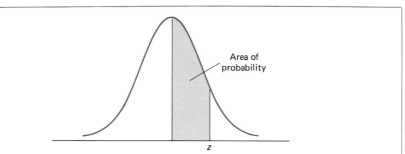

Area of probability

Entries in the table give the area under the curve between the mean and z standard deviations above the mean. For example, for $z = 1.25$ the area under the curve between the mean and z is 0.3944.

z	0.00	0.01	0.02	0.03	0.04	0.05	0.06	0.07	0.08	0.09
0.0	0.0000	0.0040	0.0080	0.0120	0.0160	0.0199	0.0239	0.0279	0.0319	0.0359
0.1	0.0398	0.0438	0.0478	0.0517	0.0557	0.0596	0.0636	0.0675	0.0714	0.0753
0.2	0.0793	0.0832	0.0871	0.0910	0.0948	0.0987	0.1026	0.1064	0.1103	0.1141
0.3	0.1179	0.1217	0.1255	0.1293	0.1331	0.1368	0.1406	0.1443	0.1480	0.1517
0.4	0.1554	0.1591	0.1628	0.1664	0.1700	0.1736	0.1772	0.1808	0.1844	0.1879
0.5	0.1915	0.1950	0.1985	0.2019	0.2054	0.2088	0.2123	0.2157	0.2190	0.2224
0.6	0.2257	0.2291	0.2324	0.2357	0.2389	0.2422	0.2454	0.2486	0.2518	0.2549
0.7	0.2580	0.2612	0.2642	0.2673	0.2704	0.2734	0.2764	0.2794	0.2823	0.2852
0.8	0.2881	0.2910	0.2939	0.2967	0.2995	0.3023	0.3051	0.3078	0.3106	0.3133
0.9	0.3159	0.3186	0.3212	0.3238	0.3264	0.3289	0.3315	0.3340	0.3365	0.3389
1.0	0.3413	0.3438	0.3461	0.3485	0.3508	0.3531	0.3554	0.3577	0.3599	0.3621
1.1	0.3643	0.3665	0.3686	0.3708	0.3729	0.3749	0.3770	0.3790	0.3810	0.3830
1.2	0.3849	0.3869	0.3888	0.3907	0.3925	0.3944	0.3962	0.3980	0.3997	0.4015
1.3	0.4032	0.4049	0.4066	0.4082	0.4099	0.4115	0.4131	0.4147	0.4162	0.4177
1.4	0.4192	0.4207	0.4222	0.4236	0.4251	0.4265	0.4279	0.4292	0.4306	0.4319
1.5	0.4332	0.4345	0.4357	0.4370	0.4382	0.4394	0.4406	0.4418	0.4429	0.4441
1.6	0.4452	0.4463	0.4474	0.4484	0.4495	0.4505	0.4515	0.4525	0.4535	0.4545
1.7	0.4554	0.4564	0.4573	0.4582	0.4591	0.4599	0.4608	0.4616	0.4625	0.4633
1.8	0.4641	0.4649	0.4656	0.4664	0.4671	0.4678	0.4686	0.4693	0.4699	0.4706
1.9	0.4713	0.4719	0.4726	0.4732	0.4738	0.4744	0.4750	0.4756	0.4761	0.4767
2.0	0.4772	0.4778	0.4783	0.4788	0.4793	0.4798	0.4803	0.4808	0.4812	0.4817
2.1	0.4821	0.4826	0.4830	0.4834	0.4838	0.4842	0.4846	0.4850	0.4854	0.4857
2.2	0.4861	0.4864	0.4868	0.4871	0.4875	0.4878	0.4881	0.4884	0.4887	0.4890
2.3	0.4893	0.4896	0.4898	0.4901	0.4904	0.4906	0.4909	0.4911	0.4913	0.4916
2.4	0.4918	0.4920	0.4922	0.4925	0.4927	0.4929	0.4931	0.4932	0.4934	0.4936
2.5	0.4938	0.4940	0.4941	0.4943	0.4945	0.4946	0.4948	0.4949	0.4951	0.4952
2.6	0.4953	0.4955	0.4956	0.4957	0.4959	0.4960	0.4961	0.4962	0.4963	0.4964
2.7	0.4965	0.4966	0.4967	0.4968	0.4969	0.4970	0.4971	0.4972	0.4973	0.4974
2.8	0.4974	0.4975	0.4976	0.4977	0.4977	0.4978	0.4979	0.4979	0.4980	0.4981
2.9	0.4981	0.4982	0.4982	0.4983	0.4984	0.4984	0.4985	0.4985	0.4986	0.4986
3.0	0.4986	0.4987	0.4987	0.4988	0.4988	0.4989	0.4989	0.4989	0.4990	0.4990

when a close examination of available data would indicate otherwise. To illustrate, suppose that, when St. Andrew's analyzes the historical records of lead time demand, it obtains the histogram in Figure 15.5 instead of that in Figure 15.2. Figure 15.5's histogram suggests that there is little difference between the probability of one value for lead time demand and another. Hence, instead of assuming that

TABLE 15.3 The Effect the Reorder Level Has on the Service Level and Holding Costs (based on Figure 15.3's normal distribution)

Reorder Level (RL)	Safety Stock $(RL - 50)$	Service Level (probability of no stockout)	Average Increase in the Annual Total of Holding Costs $[4(RL - 50)]$
50	0	0.5000	0
51	1	0.5793	4
52	2	0.6554	8
53	3	0.7257	12
54	4	0.7881	16
55	5	0.8413	20
56	6	0.8849	24
57	7	0.9192	28
58	8	0.9452	32
59	9	0.9641	36
60	10	0.9772	40
61	11	0.9861	44
62	12	0.9918	48
63	13	0.9953	52
64	14	0.9974	56
65	15	0.9986	60

Figure 15.5 An alternative histogram for lead time demand in St. Andrew's problem

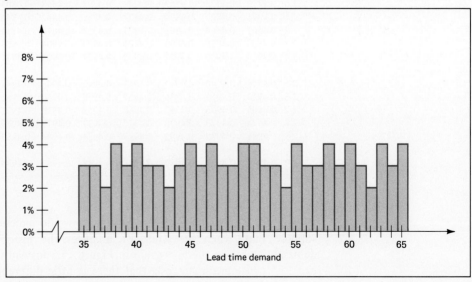

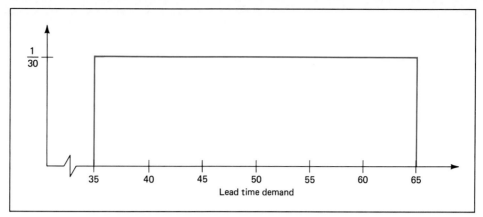

Figure 15.6 A uniform probability distribution over the interval ranging from 35 to 65

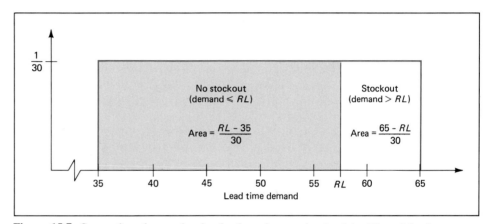

Figure 15.7 Computing the service level when the reorder level is RL and lead time demand has a uniform distribution

lead time demand is governed by a normal distribution, we should assume the uniform probability distribution displayed in Figure 15.6. With this assumption, we compute the service level provided by a particular reorder level by proceeding as illustrated in Figure 15.7 and as described below:

> The probability that lead time demand is less than or equal to RL equals the area of the shaded rectangle in Figure 15.7. Since the rectangle's height is 1/30 and its width is $RL - 35$, the service level equals $(RL - 35)/30$.[4]

Table 15.4 is analogous to Table 15.3, except that the service levels are computed using a uniform probability distribution instead of a normal distribution. Comparing these two tables, we see that the two assumptions yield quite different service levels for the same reorder level.

---

[4] In general, if the lead time demand has a uniform distribution over the interval between the integers a and b, the service level for a reorder level of RL is

$$\frac{RL - a}{b - a}.$$

TABLE 15.4 The Effect the Reorder Level Has on the Service Level and Holding Costs (Based on Figure 15.6's Uniform Distribution)

Reorder Level (RL)	Safety Stock $(RL - 50)$	Service Level (probability of no stockout)	Average Increase in the Annual Total of Holding Costs $[4(RL - 50)]$
50	0	0.5000	0
51	1	0.5333	4
52	2	0.5667	8
53	3	0.6000	12
54	4	0.6333	16
55	5	0.6667	20
56	6	0.7000	24
57	7	0.7333	28
58	8	0.7667	32
59	9	0.8000	36
60	10	0.8333	40
61	11	0.8667	44
62	12	0.9000	48
63	13	0.9333	52
64	14	0.9667	56
65	15	1.0000	60

The Need for Caution When Choosing the Probability Distribution

The differences between Tables 15.3 and 15.4 illustrate the following general principle:

> The probability distribution that we assume governs the lead time demand significantly affects the service level corresponding to a particular reorder level. Hence, we should base our choice of the probability distribution on a careful analysis of available data.

A well-designed software package will ask the user to select from several alternative distributions.

15.7 A SUMMARY OF THE (Q, RL) POLICY WHEN DEMAND AND LEAD TIME ARE STOCHASTIC

To summarize Sections 15.2–15.6:

> When demand and lead time are stochastic, we determine the (Q, RL) policy using the following procedure:

1. **Determining the order quantity Q.** After using the average daily demand to estimate the annual demand, we compute Q just as we do in an EOQ model.

2. **Determining the reorder level RL.** To determine the reorder level RL, we specify either the histogram or probability distribution that governs lead time demand. Using either the histogram or the probability distribution, we compute for each alternative reorder level the corresponding service level and average increase in the annual total of holding costs. After summarizing these computations in a table similar to Table 15.4, we select the reorder level based on a subjective judgment of the trade-off between service level and cost.

We should emphasize that, although the above procedure is commonly used in practice, it is based on the simplest definition of the service level. We defined the service level as the probability that a stockout will not occur during a lead time. In some environments, it might be more appropriate to use one of the following definitions:

- The service level is the average number of lead times per year without a stockout.
- The service level is the average percentage of annual demand that is not backlogged in a backlogging environment or not lost in a lost sales environment.

Either of these definitions complicates the selection of the reorder level. Space constraints preclude our discussing the details of the procedures used to select the reorder level under these alternative definitions of service level.

15.8 AN OVERVIEW OF THE NEWSBOY PROBLEM

A classic management science problem is known as the *newsboy problem*. As an example, consider the following scenario:

Randy Hurst sells copies of a daily newspaper for 25 cents each at a street corner newsstand. At the beginning of each day, Randy buys papers from the local distributor for 10 cents each. According to his contract with the distributor, if Randy runs out of papers during the day, he cannot reorder; furthermore, if he ends the day with a surplus, his rebate from the distributor is only 4 cents per unsold paper. Because Randy is uncertain about how many papers he will sell, he is unsure about how many to buy from the distributor. If he buys more papers than he sells, he loses money because the rebate for each unsold paper is less than he paid. If he runs out of papers, he loses money because of lost sales. Assuming Randy estimates that the total number of papers he will sell each day has a normal probability distribution with a mean of 500 and a standard deviation of 30, how many papers should he buy?

We call any problem analogous to Randy's problem a newsboy problem, even if it does not involve the sale of newspapers. The newsboy problem arises in many other contexts. As examples, consider the following:

- A restaurant that has a particular type of fresh fish on its menu must decide how many to have delivered at the beginning of each day.
- A florist must decide how many freshly cut roses to have delivered at the beginning of each day.

TABLE 15.5 MCC's Estimate of the Probability Distribution of Demand

Demand (000)	7	8	9	10	11	12	13
Probability	0.05	0.10	0.20	0.30	0.15	0.15	0.05

- A retailer of Christmas trees must decide how many to have delivered on December 4 for sale between then and Christmas.

- A department store buyer must decide how many of a new line of women's bathing suits to have delivered at the beginning of Spring for sale over the next four months.

The distinguishing characteristics of the newsboy problem are

1. The problem involves only a single time period (e.g., a one-day period in our restaurant example, a three-week period in our Christmas tree retailer example, and a four-month period in our department store buyer example).

2. The item is purchased at the beginning of the period and there is no opportunity to reorder the item if a stockout occurs.

3. The problem involves a perishable item (an item that spoils or becomes obsolete). Because of their perishability, items unsold by the end of the period have less value than they did at the beginning of the period. An item's value at the end of the period is called its *salvage value*.

4. Demand for the item is stochastic.

We will leave the solution of Randy's newsboy problem to the end-of-chapter exercises. In its place, we will use as our example the following newsboy problem:[5]

The Markhall Card Company (MCC) is a wholesaler of greeting cards and novelty items. MCC is about to launch a special promotion related to the restoration of a national landmark. As part of the promotion, MCC will purchase miniature replicas of the landmark from a manufacturer at a unit cost of $5 and resell them to independent retailers at a unit price of $9. MCC must decide tomorrow how many items to purchase from the manufacturer. MCC's decision is complicated by uncertainty about the demand for the replica by MCC's customers. Using records of past sales of comparable merchandise and intuition about the replica's sales potential, MCC has summarized its estimate of consumer demand in Table 15.5. For example, MCC estimates that there is a 30% chance that demand will be 10 thousand items. MCC's decision is further complicated by the fact that the landmark's restoration will be completed by July 4, which is only three months away. The July 4 date has two implications:

1. If demand is high, there is insufficient time to reorder the replica. Thus, the order MCC will place tomorrow is its one and only chance to acquire the replica.

2. If demand is low, MCC will have to "dump" any replicas unsold after July 4 to a discount chain. The discount chain will pay MCC $3 for each unsold replica.

Using the available information, MCC must now determine how many replicas to order from the manufacturer.

---

[5] This scenario is adapted from F.H. Barron, "Payoff Matrices Pay Off at Hallmark," *Interfaces*, **15**, 4 (July–August 1985), pp. 20–25.

15.9 SOLVING A NEWSBOY PROBLEM

Solution by Computing the Expected Total Profit for Each Alternative Ordering Quantity

Let us use Q to denote MCC's order quantity, measured in thousands of items. MCC has seven choices for Q: $Q = 7$, $Q = 8$, ..., $Q = 13$. Because demand is stochastic, the total profit if MCC orders Q items is also stochastic. To illustrate, suppose MCC orders $Q = 10$ thousand items and experiences a demand of 7 thousand items. This results in a total profit obtained by subtracting the purchase cost of 10 thousand items from the revenue from the sale of 7 thousand items to customers and 3 thousand items to the discount chain. Table 15.6 summarizes the computation of this total profit, as well as those for the other possible demands. Note that, as demand ranges from 7 to 13 thousand items, total profit ranges from 22 to 40 thousand dollars.

Matching the total profits in Table 15.6 with their corresponding probabilities in Table 15.5, we obtain Table 15.7. From this table, we see that, if $Q = 10$, there is a 5% chance that total profit is 22, a 10% chance it is 28, and so on. As indicated at the base of Table 15.7, if we multiply each total profit by its corresponding probability and sum the resulting products, we obtain 36.7 as the expected total profit when $Q = 10$ (i.e., the average total profit if MCC were to face the identical problem many times and always choose $Q = 10$).

Table 15.8 displays the expected total profit for each alternative value of Q. We have verified only the entry for $Q = 10$. Before proceeding, verify several of the remaining entries by constructing tables similar to Tables 15.6 and 15.7.

TABLE 15.6 Computing the Total Profit When $Q = 10$ (profit measured in units of $1000)

	Demand (000)						
	$D = 7$	$D = 8$	$D = 9$	$D = 10$	$D = 11$	$D = 12$	$D = 13$
Revenue from sales to customers at $9 each	$(9)(7) = 63$	$(9)(8) = 72$	$(9)(9) = 81$	$(9)(10) = 90$	$(9)(10) = 90$	$(9)(10) = 90$	$(9)(10) = 90$
Revenue from sales to discount chain at $3 each	$(3)(3) = 9$	$(3)(2) = 6$	$(3)(1) = 3$	$(3)(0) = 0$	$(3)(0) = 0$	$(3)(0) = 0$	$(3)(0) = 0$
Purchase cost of $Q = 10$ thousand items at $5 each	50	50	50	50	50	50	50
Total profit	22	28	34	40	40	40	40

TABLE 15.7 Total Profits from Table 15.6 with Their Corresponding Probabilities from Table 15.5

	Demand						
	$D = 7$	$D = 8$	$D = 9$	$D = 10$	$D = 11$	$D = 12$	$D = 13$
Total Profit	22	28	34	40	40	40	40
Probability	0.05	0.10	0.20	0.30	0.15	0.15	0.05
Sum of products	$= (22)(0.05) + (28)(0.10) + (34)(0.20) + (40)(0.30 + 0.15 + 0.15 + 0.05) = 36.7$						

691

TABLE 15.8 Expected Total Profit for Each Alternative Order Quantity

Order quantity (000)	$Q = 7$	$Q = 8$	$Q = 9$	$Q = 10$	$Q = 11$	$Q = 12$	$Q = 13$
Expected total profit (\$000)	28.0	31.7	34.8	36.7	36.8	36.0	34.3

Let us use Q^* to denote MCC's optimal order quantity under the criterion of maximizing expected total profit. From Table 15.8, we see that $Q^* = 11$ thousand items.

A Shortcut for Solving MCC'S Newsboy Problem

Although the computations that led to Table 15.8 involve only simple arithmetic, they are tedious.[6] You can imagine how cumbersome it would be to produce a similar table if there were 100 possible values for demand and, thus, 100 alternative values for Q. Fortunately, there is a shortcut for solving a newsboy problem.

To use this shortcut, we must first identify the two unit costs summarized in Table 15.9. Let us determine C_{under} and C_{over} for MCC's problem.

- **Determining C_{under}.** If MCC fails to order a replica that it could have sold to a customer, then its profit decreases by $9 - 5 = \$4$, the difference between a replica's selling price and its purchase cost.

- **Determining C_{over}.** If MCC orders an item that it cannot sell to a customer, then its profit decreases by $5 - 3 = \$2$, the difference between a replica's purchase cost and its "dumping" price to the discount chain.

To summarize, $C_{under} = \$4$ and $C_{over} = \$2$.

Besides C_{under} and C_{over}, solving a newsboy problem requires knowledge of the probability distribution of demand. In MCC's problem, Table 15.5 provides this distribution. Let us use D to denote the uncertain value for the demand and $\Pr\{D = v\}$ to denote the probability that D equals the value v. Similarly, we will use $\Pr\{D \leqslant v\}$ to denote the probability that D is less than or equal to v. For example, in MCC's problem, we see from Table 15.5 that $\Pr\{D = 9\} = 0.20$ and

---

[6] Those who have read Chapter 12 should recognize that our computations here are similar to those we would perform if we analyzed MCC's single-stage decision-analysis problem using either the payoff-matrix approach or the decision-tree approach. In fact, Exercise 12.9 requests you to solve MCC's problem using one of these approaches.

TABLE 15.9 The Two Cost Components in a Newsboy Problem

Terminology	Notation	Definition
Unit cost of underordering	C_{under}	The profit decrease that results from failing to order an item that could have been sold at its normal price.
Unit cost of overordering	C_{over}	The profit decrease that results from ordering an item that cannot be sold at its normal price.

$$\begin{aligned} \Pr\{D \leqslant 9\} &= \Pr\{D + 7\} + \Pr\{D + 8\} \\ &= 0.05 + 0.10 + 0.20 \\ &= 0.35 . \end{aligned}$$

Before we describe how to use C_{under}, C_{over}, and D's probability distribution to determine the optimal order quantity, we need one further definition. In a newsboy problem, the *service level* provided by an order quantity of Q items is the probability a stockout does *not* occur when Q items are ordered. In general, the service level provided by an order quantity of Q equals $\Pr\{D \leqslant Q\}$. For example, in MCC's problem, the service level when $Q = 9$ is $\Pr\{D \leqslant 9\}$, which we computed in the preceding paragraph as 0.35, the sum of the entries in Table 15.5 for demands of 9 or less. Using Table 15.5's probability distribution, we can compute the service level for each alternative value of Q. Table 15.10 displays the results. We have verified the service level for $Q = 9$. Before proceeding, verify the service level for the remaining values of Q.

We are now ready to describe how to determine the optimal order quantity, Q^*. We do so according to the following rule (whose proof is beyond the scope of this text):

In a newsboy problem, the optimal service level is

$$\frac{C_{under}}{C_{under} + C_{over}}$$

Hence, the optimal order quantity Q^* is the smallest quantity for which

$$\text{PR}\{D \leqslant Q\} \geqslant \frac{C_{under}}{C_{under} + C_{over}} .$$

Hereafter, we refer to this rule as the *newsboy ordering rule*.

Although we cannot prove the optimality of the newsboy ordering rule, we can at least verify that applying the rule to MCC's problem leads to the same order quantity we determined earlier by using Table 15.8 to maximize the expected total profit. In MCC's problem, $C_{under} = \$4$ and $C_{over} = \$2$. Hence, the optimal service level is given by

$$\frac{C_{under}}{C_{under} + C_{over}} = \frac{4}{4 + 2} \approx 0.6667 .$$

To provide this service level, we must determine the smallest value of Q for which $\Pr\{D \leqslant Q\} \geqslant 0.6667$. Examining Table 15.10, we see that $Q = 11$, $Q = 12$, and $Q = 13$ all provide service levels of at least 0.6667. Since $Q = 11$ is the smallest of these values, the optimal order quantitiy is $Q^* = 11$. This is the same value we determined earlier by using Table 15.8 to maximize the expected total profit.

The following observations provide further insight into how the newsboy order rule works:

TABLE 15.10 The Service Level for Each Alternative Order Quantity
(Based on Table 15.5's Probability Distribution)

Order quantity (000)	$Q = 7$	$Q = 8$	$Q = 9$	$Q = 10$	$Q = 11$	$Q = 12$	$Q = 13$
Service level ($\Pr D \leqslant Q\}$)	0.05	0.15	0.35	0.65	0.80	0.95	1.00

- If C_{under} is much greater than C_{over}, then intuitively we should avoid a stockout. This is precisely what the newsboy ordering rule indicates since, when C_{under} is much greater than C_{over}, $[C_{under}/(C_{under} + C_{over})]$ is close to 1. To provide this service level, the order quantity must be close to the maximum demand.

- If C_{under} is much less than C_{over}, then intuitively we should not worry about a stockout. This is precisely what the newsboy ordering rule indicates since, when C_{under} is much less than C_{over}, $[C_{under}/(C_{under} + C_{over})]$ is close to 0. To provide this service level, the order quantity must be close to the minimum demand.

- If C_{under} is close to C_{over}, then intuitively we should be indifferent between a stockout occurring and not occurring. This is precisely what the newsboy ordering rule indicates since, when C_{under} is close to C_{over}, $[C_{under}/(C_{under} + C_{over})]$ is about 0.5. To provide this service level, the order quantity must be close to the median of the probability distribution for demand.

Given our omission of the proof that the newsboy ordering rule is optimal, it is comforting to see that it yields an order quantity that conforms to our intuition.

15.10 SOLVING THE NEWSBOY PROBLEM WHEN DEMAND HAS A NORMAL OR UNIFORM DISTRIBUTION

Using a Normal Probability Distribution

Suppose that, instead of Table 15.5's probability distribution, MCC estimates that demand is governed by a normal probability distribution with a mean of $\mu = 10$ thousand and a standard deviation of $\sigma = 1$ thousand. Figure 15.8 displays this distribution.

Since C_{under} and C_{over} remain unchanged, the optimal service level is still 0.6667. To determine the smallest order quantity that provides this service level, we proceed as diagrammed in Figure 15.9 and as described below:

We first subtract 0.5 from 0.6667 to obtain 0.1667 as the probability we must find in Table 15.2. Although 0.1667 does not appear in the table, we see that 0.1664 and

Figure 15.8 A normal probability distribution with $\mu = 10$ and $\sigma = 1$

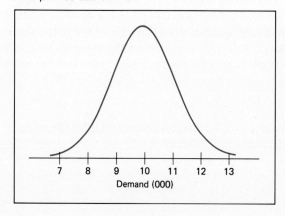

Figure 15.9 Solving MCC's newsboy problem when demand has a normal distribution

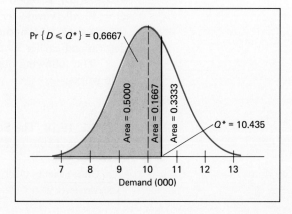

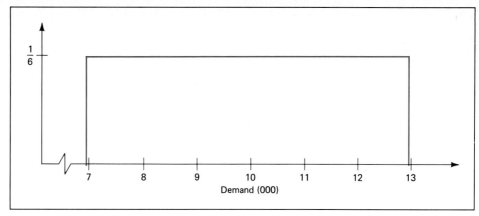

Figure 15.10 A uniform probability distribution over the interval ranging from 7 to 13

0.1700 do. These values correspond to respective z values of 0.43 and 0.44. Interpolating between these z values, we obtain a z value of 0.435. Hence, the optimal service level of 0.6667 corresponds to an optimal order quantity Q^* that lies 0.435 standard deviations above μ; that is,

$$Q^* = \mu + 0.435\sigma = 10 + (0.435)(1) = 10.435 \,.$$

Using a Uniform Distribution

Now suppose that MCC estimates that demand is governed by the uniform probability distribution displayed in Figure 15.10. Since C_{under} and C_{over} are still the same, the optimal service level remains 0.6667 or, equivalently, 2/3. To determine the corresponding optimal order quantity Q^*, we simply start in Figure 15.10 at the distribution's minimum value 7 and move two-thirds of the way toward its maximum of 13. Doing so results in

$$Q^* = 7 + \tfrac{2}{3}(13 - 7) = 11 \,.$$

The Need for Caution When Choosing the Probability Distribution

We have solved MCC's problem with the probability distributions in Table 15.5, Figure 15.8, and Figure 15.10. In doing so, we obtained respective optimal order quantities of 11, 10.435, and 11. The closeness of these three quantities is a coincidence. In general, different distributions may lead to widely different order quantities. Hence, we should choose the probability distribution that governs an item's demand only after carefully examining all relevant data and surveying all persons who might have insight into the item's demand.

15.11 VARIATION OF THE NEWSBOY PROBLEM

A Newsboy Problem with the Possibility of Backlogging

In the classic version of the newsboy problem, the item is purchased at the beginning of the period and there is no opportunity to reorder if a stockout occurs.

Hence, all unsatisfied demand represents lost sales. We now consider a modified version of the newsboy problem that permits backlogging. To illustrate, consider the following modification to MCC's problem:

> If demand exceeds MCC's initial order quantity, MCC has made arrangements for the manufacturer to satisfy the backlogged demand using expedited production and shipment. Because of this expediting, MCC's unit cost for a backlogged item is $5.75, an increase of $0.75 over the unit cost of items in MCC's initial order. Furthermore, as compensation to those customers whose orders are backlogged, MCC will reduce its unit selling price to $8.75, a decrease of $0.25 from the unit price of items not backlogged.

We can still use the newsboy ordering rule to solve this modified problem. However, since the modification may have changed MCC's unit cost of underordering and unit cost of overordering, we should recompute C_{under} and C_{over}. These computations proceed as follows:

- **Determining C_{under}.** If MCC's initial order does not include a replica that it could have sold to a customer without backlogging, then its profit decreases by

$$(5.75 - 5.00) \qquad + \qquad (9.00 - 8.75) \qquad = 1.00$$

$$\uparrow \qquad\qquad\qquad\qquad \uparrow$$

$$\begin{pmatrix} \text{increase in unit cost for} \\ \text{backlogged items} \end{pmatrix} \quad \begin{pmatrix} \text{decrease in unit selling price} \\ \text{for backlogged items} \end{pmatrix}$$

- **Determining C_{over}.** If MCC's initial order includes an item that it cannot sell to a customer, its profit decreases $5 - 3 = \$2$, the difference between a replica's purchase cost and its "dumping" price to the discount chain. (This is unchanged from the original version of MCC's problem.)

To summarize, $C_{under} = \$1$ and $C_{over} = \$2$.

Applying the newsboy ordering rule, we obtain an optimal service level of

$$\frac{C_{under}}{C_{under} + C_{over}} = \frac{1}{1 + 2} \approx 0.3333 .$$

The corresponding optimal ordering quantity Q^* is the smallest value of Q for which $\Pr\{D \leqslant Q\} \geqslant 0.3333$. Examining Table 15.10, we see that $Q^* = 9$. Q^* in this modified version of MCC's problem is much lower than Q^* in the original version because the corresponding value of the ratio $[C_{under}/(C_{under} + C_{over})]$ is much lower ($\frac{1}{3}$ versus $\frac{2}{3}$).

A "Disguised" Newsboy Problem

Sometimes a problem is stated in a way that "disguises" its analogy to the newsboy problem. However, with proper interpretation, we can see through the disguise to recognize that the problem is in fact a newsboy problem. To illustrate, consider the following scenario:

> Mark Post is the manager of the California "hub" of the U.S. Postal Service's Express Mail Division. Each day, all express mail received by 5:00 P.M. at post offices

throughout California is sent to the hub for sorting and subsequent distribution to other hubs.

Mark is currently reevaluating the size of the staff that does the sorting. A sorter works an eight-hour shift, unless the volume of mail is so high that the sorter is asked to work overtime. Records kept over the past year indicate that the number of eight-hour shifts needed each night to process a day's volume of mail has a normal probability distribution with a mean of $\mu = 300$ and a standard deviation of $\sigma = 10$.

During the regular eight-hour shift a sorter's wages and fringe benefits amount to $21 per hour. When a day's mail volume is too high for the staff to process during the regular eight-hour shift, Mark has four persons each work two hours of overtime for every eight-hour shift the hub is understaffed. For example, if Mark sets the staff size at 300 and the processing for a particular day needs 310 persons working eight-hour shifts, Mark has 40 persons from the staff of 300 work a regular eight-hour shift plus two hours of overtime. During overtime, a sorter's wages and fringe benefits amount to $35 per hour. Using the available information, Mark must now determine how large the staff of sorters should be.

Can you see why Mark's problem is a newsboy problem? Mark's staff size is analogous to the order quantity, with understaffing and overstaffing analogous to underordering and overordering. We will leave the solution of Mark's newsboy problem to the end-of-chapter exercises, where you will also encounter another newsboy problem in disguise.

15.12 A SUMMARY OF THE NEWSBOY PROBLEM

Summarizing Sections 15.8–15.11:

To solve a newsboy problem, we proceed as follows

1. We estimate C_{under} and C_{over} using the definitions in Table 15.9. According to these definitions, in a lost sales environment,

$$C_{\text{under}} = \begin{pmatrix} \text{item's unit} \\ \text{selling price} \end{pmatrix} - \begin{pmatrix} \text{items's unit} \\ \text{purchase cost ,} \end{pmatrix}$$

$$C_{\text{over}} = \begin{pmatrix} \text{item's unit} \\ \text{purchase cost} \end{pmatrix} - \begin{pmatrix} \text{items's unit} \\ \text{salvage value} \end{pmatrix}.$$

In a backlogging environment,

$$C_{\text{under}} = \begin{pmatrix} \text{increase in unit} \\ \text{purchase cost for} \\ \text{backlogged items} \end{pmatrix} + \begin{pmatrix} \text{decrease in unit} \\ \text{selling price for} \\ \text{backlogged items} \end{pmatrix}$$

$$C_{\text{over}} = \begin{pmatrix} \text{item's unit} \\ \text{purchase cost} \end{pmatrix} - \begin{pmatrix} \text{items's salvage} \\ \text{value} \end{pmatrix}.$$

2. We specify the probability distribution that governs demand.

3. We compute the optimal service level as

$$\frac{C_{\text{under}}}{C_{\text{under}} + C_{\text{over}}}.$$

4. The optimal ordering quantity Q^* is the smallest quantity Q such that

$$\Pr\{D \leqslant Q\} \geqslant \frac{C_{\text{under}}}{C_{\text{under}} + C_{\text{over}}}.$$

15.13 CONCLUDING REMARKS

Inventory management has benefited greatly from the widespread commercial availability of computer software packages. Gone are the days when the time and expense of manually recording each depletion or replenishment of inventory meant that an organization was usually unaware of an item's inventory level until a physical count was made every so often (e.g., every three months). Today, with the aid of computer hardware and software, an organization can monitor an item's inventory level on at least a daily basis. For example many department stores and grocery stores are equipped with cash registers connected electronically to a computer. Besides preparing a customer's receipt, these cash registers automatically notify the computer to decrease the inventory levels of the items purchased by the customer.

To illustrate the effect computers have had on inventory management, let us consider the (Q, RL) policy we discussed in Sections 15.2–15.7. Before the widespread commercial availability of computers, implementing a (Q, RL) policy required use of what is called the *two-bin system*. Under this system, an item's inventory is segregated into two bins, say, bin 1 and bin 2. Bin 1 contains RL items, and bin 2 contains the inventory in excess of RL. To satisfy demand, items are first withdrawn from bin 2. When bin 2 is empty, the inventory level is equal to the RL items in bin 1. This is the signal that it is time to place an order for Q items. As a reminder, it is customary to attach a "flag" to the item at the top of bin 1. The person who withdraws this flagged item is responsible for initiating the order. During the lead time, demand is satisfied using the RL items in bin 1. A stockout occurs if bin 1 becomes empty before the order arrives. When the order arrives, items are first added to bin 1 to refill it to the level of RL, and then the remaining items are placed in bin 2. The process now repeats itself.

With a computerized implementation of a (Q, RL) policy, there is no need to segregate an item's inventory into two bins. Since each depletion or replenishment of inventory is automatically recorded, the computer knows the precise inventory level at all times. As soon as an item's inventory level decreases to RL, the computer issues a warning to place an order for Q items.

Our contrast between implementing a (Q, RL) policy with a two-bin system versus a computerized system illustrates that computerized systems simply automate what formerly had to be performed manually. This automation has many benefits, including increased speed, fewer errors, and lower cost. Perhaps automation's greatest benefit is that it has expanded the scope of inventory management to virtually every item held in inventory.

In closing, we note that the greatest simplification made during our survey of inventory management is that, with the exception of Section 14.7's overview of MRP, we have treated each item as if it were unrelated to other items. This is usually not the case. For example, two distinct items may share the same storage space, the same vendor, or the same production facility. This necessitates coordinating the inventory policies for the two items. Learning how to achieve this coordination should be the first step if you wish to go beyond our overview of inventory management.

15.14 CHAPTER CHECKLIST AND GLOSSARY

Quickly review this chapter by rereading the material highlighted by a vertical line in the left margin. You should then be familiar with the concepts, techniques, and terminology in the Checklist and Glossary that follow. If you need "help" with a particular item, consult the section or sections indicated for a more detailed discussion.

Checklist of Concepts and Techniques

☐ Why the reorder level is being "pulled" in opposite directions when lead time demand is stochastic. [15.2]

☐ How the inventory level varies under a (Q, RL) policy when demand and lead time are stochastic. [15.3]

☐ Determining Q when demand and lead time are stochastic. [15.4]

☐ For a given reorder level, how to determine the corresponding safety stock, service level, and average increase in the annual total of holding costs when lead time demand

    ☐ is summarized by a histogram. [15.5]

    ☐ has a normal probability distribution. [15.6]

    ☐ has a uniform probability distribution. [15.6]

☐ The need for caution when choosing the probability distribution that governs lead time demand. [15.6]

☐ The characteristics of a newsboy problem. [15.8]

☐ The variety of contexts in which the newsboy problem arises. [15.8, 15.11]

☐ Solving a newsboy problem by computing the expected total profit of each alternative order quantity. [15.9]

☐ Computing in a newsboy problem the unit cost of underordering (C_{under}) and the unit cost of overordering (C_{over}). [15.9, 15.11, 15.12]

☐ Solving a newsboy problem based on C_{under}, C_{over}, and the probability distribution of demand. [15.9–15.12]

☐ The need in a newsboy problem to exercise caution when choosing the probability distribution than governs demand. [15.10]

☐ Solving the variation of the newsboy problem that permits backlogging of demand. [15.11]

☐ Recognizing a "disguised" newsboy problem. [15.11]

Glossary

Order-quantity reorder-level inventory policy. An inventory policy that continuously monitors the inventory level and, when it decreases to the level RL, places an order for Q items. [15.3]

Safety stock. The amount by which the reorder level exceeds the average lead time demand. [15.5]

Service level for a (Q, RL) **policy.** The probability that a stockout will not occur during the lead time (i.e., that the lead time demand will not exceed the RL items in inventory when an order is placed). [15.5]

Newsboy problem. A classic management problem that involves a single time period and an item whose demand is stochastic and whose value is lower at the end of the period than at the beginning. [15.8]

Salvage value. An item's value in a newsboy problem at the end of the time period. [15.8]

Unit cost of underordering in a newsboy problem. The profit decrease that results from failing to order an item that could have been sold at its normal price. [15.9]

Unit cost of overordering in a newsboy problem. The profit decrease that results from ordering an item that cannot be sold at its normal price. [15.9]

Service level in a newsboy problem. The probability that a stockout will not occur (i.e., that demand will be less than or equal to the order quantity). [15.9]

EXERCISES

Exercises 15.1–15.9 test your understanding of how to use an order-quantity reorder-level inventory policy when demand and/or lead time are stochastic.

*15.1. Reconsider JoAnn's problem in Exercise 14.3. In that exercise, we assumed that demand occurred at a constant rate of 15 cartons per day and also that the lead time was constant. Now assume the following:

- Although daily demand has averaged 15 cartons per day over the past year, the demand on any particular day can be above or below this average.

- Although lead time has averaged 5 days over the past year, lead time for any particular order can be above or below this average.

This uncertainty about daily demand and lead time results in uncertainty about lead time demand, thereby making it possible for a stockout to occur. When a stockout does occur, JoAnn tries to convince her customers to order ice cream instead; however, she is often unsuccessful and thus loses potential sales. JoAnn's records of past lead time demands are summarized in the histogram displayed below:

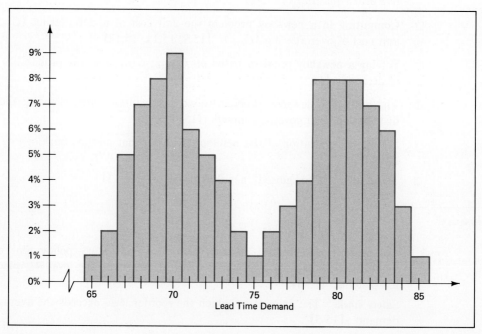

Exercise 15.1

JoAnn believes that this histogram will apply to future lead time demands as well. She wants to determine an appropriate (Q, RL) inventory policy to use in this stochastic environment. (Assume that the other aspects of JoAnn's problem remain the same as described in Exercise 14.3.)

(a) What order quantity should JoAnn use?

(b) Use the histogram to verify that the average of the past lead time demands is about 75 cartons. If JoAnn uses 75 as the reorder level, what is the service level?

(c) For each of the alternative reorder levels in the interval from 75 to 85, compute the corresponding safety stock, service level, and average increase in the annual total of holding costs. Summarize your analysis in the format of Table 15.1.

(d) What service level is provided by a reorder level of 80 cartons?

(e) What reorder level should JoAnn use if she wants a service level of at least 80%?

(f) What reorder level should JoAnn use if she wants a service level of at least 95%?

*15.2. Redo Exercise 15.1, this time assuming that lead time demand is governed by a normal probability distribution with $\mu = 75$ and $\sigma = 4$.

*15.3. Redo Exercise 15.1, this time assuming that lead time demand is governed by a uniform probability distribution over the interval from 65 to 85.

15.4. Reconsider BAT's problem in Exercise 14.4. In that exercise, we assumed that demand occurred at a constant rate of 16 tires per day and also that the lead time was constant. Now assume the following:

- Although daily demand has averaged 16 tires per day over the past year, the demand on any particular day can be above or below this average.
- Although lead time over the past year has usually been 1 day, it has occasionally been 2 days.

This uncertainty about daily demand and lead time results in uncertainty about lead time demand, thereby making it possible for a stockout to occur. When a stockout does occur, BAT must remove buses from use and cancel some scheduled service. BAT's records of past lead time demands are summarized in the histogram displayed below.

BAT believes that this histogram will apply to future lead time demands as well. It wants to determine an appropriate (Q, RL) inventory policy to use in this stochastic environment. (Assume that the other aspects of BAT's problem remain the same as described in Exercise 14.4.)

(a) What order quantity should BAT use?

(b) Use the histogram to verify that the average of the past lead time demands is about 15 tires. If BAT uses 15 as the reorder level, what is the service level?

(c) For each of the alternative reorder levels in the interval from 15 to 30, compute the corresponding safety stock, service level, and average increase in the annual total of holding costs. Summarize your analysis in the format of Table 15.1.

(d) What service level is provided by a reorder level of 18 tires?

(e) What reorder level should BAT use if it wants a service level of at least 80%?

(f) What reorder level should BAT use if it wants a service level of at least 90%?

15.5. Redo Exercise 15.4, this time assuming that lead time demand is governed by a normal probability distribution with $\mu = 15$ and $\sigma = 5$.

15.6. Redo Exercise 15.4, this time assuming that lead time demand is governed by a uniform probability distribution over the interval from 0 to 30.

15.7. Reconsider MBI's problem in Exercise 14.5. In that exercise, we assumed that turnover occurred at a constant rate of 6 workers per day and also that the time needed by the consulting firm to prepare for

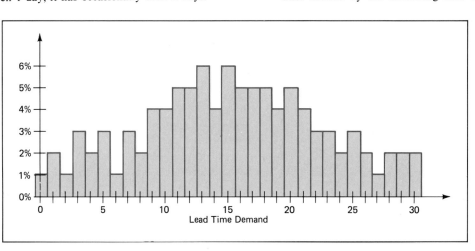

Exercise 15.4

and conduct a training session was constant. Now assume the following:

- Although daily turnover has averaged 6 workers per day over the past year, the turnover on any particular day can be above or below this average.
- Although the lead time needed by the consulting firm to prepare for and conduct a training session has almost always been 7 days, it has sometimes been 8 days.

This uncertainty about daily turnover and lead time results in uncertainty about lead time turnover, thereby making it possible for MBI to find the pool of on-call workers empty. When this occurs, MBI's plant must operate at less than full capacity. MBI's records of past lead time turnovers are summarized in the histogram displayed below:

MBI believes that this histogram will apply to future lead time turnovers as well. It wants to determine an appropriate (Q, RL) inventory policy to use in this stochastic environment. (Assume that the other aspects of MBI's problem remain the same as described in Exercise 14.5.)

(a) What training class size should MBI use?

(b) Use the histogram to verify that the average of the past lead time turnovers is 42 workers. If MBI uses 42 as the "reorder" level (i.e., the level of on-call workers when MBI notifies the consulting firm it wants a new training session to begin), what is the service level?

(c) For each of the alternative reorder levels in the interval from 42 to 50, compute the corresponding values of the safety stock of on-call workers, the service level, and the average increase

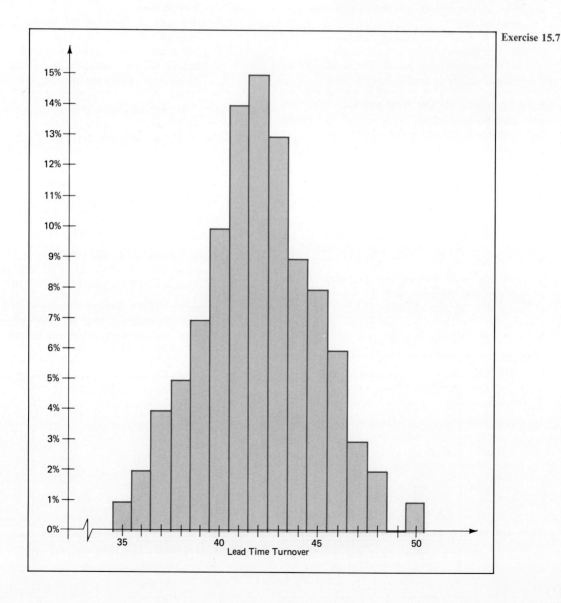

Exercise 15.7

702

in the annual total of "holding" costs for on-call workers. Summarize your analysis in the format of Table 15.1.

(d) What service level is provided by a reorder level of 44 workers?

(e) What reorder level should MBI use if it wants a service level of at least 70%?

(f) What reorder level should MBI use if it wants a service level of at least 85%?

15.8. Redo Exercise 15.7, this time assuming that lead time turnover is governed by a normal probability distribution with $\mu = 42$ and $\sigma = 2.5$.

15.9. Redo Exercise 15.7, this time assuming that lead time turnover is governed by a uniform probability distribution over the interval from 35 to 50.

Exercises 15.10–15.25 involve the analysis of a newsboy problem.

*15.10. At the beginning of each day, Sharon must decide how many baguettes to bake for sale at her boulangerie. Sharon bakes baguettes at a cost of $0.80 each and sells them for $2.00 each. If any baguettes remain unsold at the end of the day, Sharon sells them to a local "day old" bakery for $0.40 each. Sharon's estimate of the daily demand for her baguettes is summarized by the following probability distribution:

Demand	170	180	190	200	210	220	230
Probability	0.40	0.30	0.15	0.07	0.05	0.02	0.01

(a) What is the optimal service level in Sharon's problem?

(b) What is the optimal number of baguettes Sharon should bake?

(c) If Sharon bakes the optimal number of baguettes, what is the probability of a stockout?

*15.11. Resolve Sharon's problem in Exercise 15.10, this time assuming that demand for baguettes is governed by a normal probability distribution with $\mu = 200$ and $\sigma = 10$.

*15.12. Resolve Sharon's problem in Exercise 15.10, this time assuming that demand for baguettes is governed by a uniform probability distribution over the interval from 170 to 230.

15.13. Cindy is planning the twenty-fifth reunion of the St. Mark's Nursery School. Her plans include trying to raise some funds for the school by selling pennants imprinted with

St. Mark's Nursery School
25th Reunion

The pennants cost $2 each, and Cindy will resell them for $5 each. Because the pennants will have "25th Reunion" printed on them, Cindy feels that very few, if any, can be sold after the reunion. The printer requires Cindy to place her order for the pennants now, one month in advance of the reunion. Unfortunately, Cindy does not yet know how many families will attend the reunion and, of those families that do attend, how many will want to buy a pennant. Her estimate of the number of pennants she can sell is summarized by the following probability distribution:

Demand	Probability
600	0.04
625	0.08
650	0.12
675	0.17
700	0.18
725	0.17
750	0.12
775	0.08
800	0.04

(a) What is the optimal service level in Cindy's problem?

(b) What is the optimal order quantity?

(c) If Cindy orders the optimal quantity, what is the probability of a stockout?

15.14. Resolve Cindy's problem in Exercise 15.13, this time assuming that demand for pennants is governed by a normal probability distribution with $\mu = 700$ and $\sigma = 70$.

15.15. Resolve Cindy's problem in Exercise 15.13, this time assuming that demand for pennants is governed by a uniform probability distribution over the interval from 600 to 800.

15.16. Reconsider Cindy's problem in Exercise 15.13. In that exercise, we assumed that Cindy had only one opportunity to order the pennants. Now suppose that if demand for the pennant at the reunion exceeds Cindy's initial order quantity, she can satisfy the excess demand by placing a second order with the printer. The printer will charge Cindy $2.50 for each pennant in the second order, $0.50 more than a pennant in the first order. Cindy will not pass this additional cost on to those who buy the pennants in the second order; that is, she will sell them for the same price as those in the first order.

(a) What is the optimal service level in Cindy's revised problem?

(b) What is the optimal initial order quantity?

(c) If Cindy orders the optimal initial quantity, what is the probability she will have to place a second order?

703

15.17. At the beginning of Section 15.8, we stated but did not solve Randy Hurst's newsboy problem.
 (a) What is the optimal service level in Randy's problem?
 (b) What is the optimal order quantity?
 (c) If Randy orders the optimal quantity, what is the probability of a stockout?

15.18. Resolve Randy's problem in Exercise 15.17, this time assuming that demand for newspapers is governed by a uniform probability distribution over the interval from 475 to 525.

15.19. Resolve Randy's problem in Exercise 15.17, this time assuming that demand for newspapers is governed by the probability distribution in the table below.

Demand	Probability
475	0.05
480	0.10
485	0.15
490	0.10
495	0.05
500	0.10
505	0.05
510	0.10
515	0.15
520	0.10
525	0.05

15.20. At the end of Section 15.11, we stated but did not solve Mark Post's "disguised" newsboy problem.
 (a) What is the optimal size for the staff of sorters?
 (b) If Mark uses the optimal staff size, what is the probability that overtime will be needed?

15.21. Resolve Mark's problem in Exercise 15.20, this time assuming that demand for sorters is governed by a uniform probability distribution over the interval from 275 to 325.

15.22. Resolve Mark's problem in Exercise 15.20, this time assuming that demand for sorters is governed by the probability distribution in the table below.

Demand	Probability
275	0.03
280	0.06
285	0.09
290	0.12
295	0.13
300	0.14
305	0.13
310	0.12
315	0.09
320	0.06
325	0.03

15.23. The Alpha Beta Corporation (ABC) has just purchased a new copying machine. The machine's vendor has offered ABC the following maintenance contract:
 ■ ABC can prepurchase any number of service calls now at a cost of $100 each.
 ■ If prepurchased service calls have not been used by the end of the year, the vendor will not rebate any money to ABC and will not credit ABC toward next year's contract.
 ■ If ABC needs service calls beyond the number prepurchased, it can simply pay for them individually as needed throughout the year. For such a service call, the vendor will charge $130, $30 more than a prepurchased service call.

ABC's estimate of the number of service calls it will need during the upcoming year is summarized by the following probability distribution:

Demand	Probability
10	0.30
11	0.20
12	0.14
13	0.08
14	0.07
15	0.06
16	0.05
17	0.04
18	0.03
19	0.02
20	0.01

 (a) How many service calls should ABC prepurchase?
 (b) If ABC prepurchases the optimal number of service calls, what is the probability that it will need more than this number during the year?

15.24. Resolve ABC's problem in Exercise 15.23, this time assuming that demand for service calls is governed by a normal probability distribution with $\mu = 15$ and $\sigma = 2$.

15.25. Resolve ABC's problem in Exercise 15.23, this time assuming that demand for service calls is governed by a uniform probability distribution over the interval from 10 to 20.

704

16

QUEUEING ANALYSIS

16.1 INTRODUCTION

A waiting line or *queue* forms whenever the current demand for some type of service exceeds the current capacity to provide that service. Hardly a day goes by when we do not wait in at least one queue. Examples include

- Waiting in a queue at a bank to make a deposit or withdrawal.
- Waiting in a queue at a post office to mail a package or buy stamps.
- Waiting in a queue at a grocery store to be checked out.
- Waiting in a queue at a gas station to purchase gas.
- Waiting in a queue at a toll bridge to pay the toll.
- Waiting in a queue at an administrative office to register for courses at the start of an academic term.

A queue need not consist of people. It might consist of ships awaiting an unloading dock, failed machines awaiting repair, or computer programs awaiting execution. Nor does a queue need to be a physical one forming in front of a physical structure that provides service. For example, consider a company that repairs failed duplicating machines dispersed throughout some geographical area. The failed machines do not physically join a queue; instead the queue "forms" on a sheet of paper that lists the locations of the failed machines in the order in which they are to be repaired. As another example, consider the callers to an airline's phone reservation system who are put "on hold." Such callers do not physically join a queue; instead, they are in an electronic queue that records the order in which the calls are received.

The mathematical study of queues is known as *queueing analysis* or *queueing theory*. The field of queueing analysis traces its roots to 1917 and the Danish telephone engineer A. K. Erlang, who investigated the problems callers encountered at a telephone switchboard. Since that time, queueing analysis has grown to become one of the most studied fields in all management science.

Queueing analysis has received so much attention because queues are so commonplace in a wide variety of profit-making and not-for-profit organizations. Here are some additional examples:

- Memorandums awaiting typing in a secretarial pool.
- Airplanes waiting to land or take off at an airport.
- Medical emergencies dispersed throughout a geographical area awaiting the arrival of an ambulance.
- Patients awaiting treatment in a hospital's emergency room.
- Criminal cases awaiting trial in a federal court district.

Unfortunately for a survey text such as this one, queueing analysis is a highly mathematical area. To fully understand it, one must first understand advanced concepts in probability and calculus. Rather than provide a mathematically rigorous introduction, then, this chapter provides a qualitative introduction to the topic. We will learn the type of information that queueing analysis provides and how a manager can interpret and apply this information. We will leave to the experts (or to your future study) the mathematical details of how this information is derived.

We will discuss queues not from the perspective of a someone waiting in a queue but from the perspective of a manager who has responsibility for providing the service desired by the queue's members. To a manager, the formation of queue is both "good news" and "bad news." The good news is that the manager has not overstaffed the facility with employees or equipment that are idle a high percentage of the time. The bad news is that members of the queue are being kept waiting. Keeping members of a queue waiting can be costly to an organization in a variety of ways, including the following:

- When an airline's phone reservation system consistently provides callers with a busy signal or a significant wait on hold, some callers will eventually take their business to a competitor.
- When a hospital consistently has a long queue in its emergency room, a long patient wait may aggravate the injury or illness, thereby increasing the likelihood of a costly lawsuit.
- When a business's secretaries consistently have to wait in a long queue to use a duplicating machine, secretarial productivity drops significantly.

To summarize:

Providing too much service capacity is costly (owing to idle employees or equipment) and providing too little service capacity is costly (owing to waiting members of the queue). The purpose of queueing analysis is to provide information a manager can use to determine an acceptable level of service.

16.2 THE FUNDAMENTAL STRUCTURE OF A QUEUEING SYSTEM

As depicted in Figure 16.1, we will assume that a *queueing system* has the following fundamental structure:

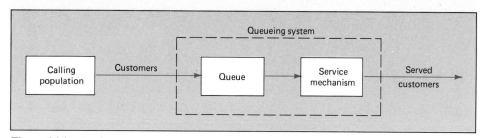

Figure 16.1 The fundamental structure of a queueing system

- *Customers* from a *calling population* arrive from time to time at the queueing system. (We will use the term *customers* regardless of whether the arrivals are people or inanimate objects.)
- Arriving customers join a *queue* (which may at times be empty).
- At certain times, a group of one or more customers is chosen from the queue for service according to some rule known as the *service discipline*.
- A *service mechanism* then performs the customer's required service, after which the customer leaves the queueing system.

Let us discuss each of these components. We will see that, by making different assumptions about them, we can describe a variety of queueing systems.

To describe a queueing system, we must specify the following nine characteristics:

Size of the Calling Population

The calling population's *size* is the total number of customers that require service from time to time. We may assume the size to be either *finite* or *infinite*. The assumption of infinite size is preferable, because it leads to mathematical results that are easier to derive and more complete. It is usually safe to assume an infinite calling population whenever the average rate at which customers arrive at the queueing system is not significantly affected by the number of customers already there. For example, the size of a bank's calling population is so large that the average rate at which customers arrive is virtually the same whether the number of customers already in the bank is 5 or 25. Consequently, a queueing analysis of a bank could safely assume an infinite calling population. In contrast, if the calling population's size is, say, less than 200, we must assume a finite calling population or run the risk of obtaining inaccurate results.

Probability Distribution Governing the Interarrival Times

The time between consecutive arrivals to the queueing system is known as the *interarrival time*. For most queueing systems, the interarrival time differs for each successive pair of customers. For example, suppose we sat outside a bank and observed the arrivals of customers. If we used a stopwatch to record the elapsed time between the arrivals of the first and second customers, the second and third customers, the third and fourth customers, and so on, we might find that the first interarrival time was 1 minute, the second was 2 minutes, the third was $\frac{1}{2}$ minute, and so on. To account for these unequal interarrival times, we assume that they are governed by a specific probability distribution. There are several choices for this probability distribution; Section 16.4 will discuss them.

Queue Capacity

A queue's *capacity* is the maximum number of customers it can contain at any one time. We may assume the queue's capacity is either *finite* or *infinite*. The assumption of a finite queue capacity creates undesirable complications in the mathematical analysis. Therefore, it is customary to assume an infinite queue capacity whenever the queue capacity is a large finite number. For example, a queueing analysis of a bank could safely assume an infinite queue capacity. In contrast, the queue to an airline's telephone reservation system cannot exceed the capacity to put callers on hold when all agents are busy. This capacity is usually sufficiently small that any queueing analysis must assume a finite queue capacity.

Unusual Customer Behavior

Customers may exhibit "unusual" behavior on arrival at the queueing system or after joining the queue. Possibilities include the following:

- *Balking* occurs when a customer arrives at the queueing system, decides that the number of customers already in the queue is too large, and immediately leaves. For example, balking is a common phenomenon at gas stations.

- *Reneging* occurs when a customer joins the queue but subsequently decides that she has been waiting too long and leaves. For example, reneging is a common phenomenon when a customer is put on hold after calling an airline's phone reservation system.

- *Jockeying* occurs when there are several adjacent queues providing the same service and a customer switches queues because he decides his queue is moving too slowly. For example, jockeying is a common phenomenon in grocery-store checkout queues. (For reasons discussed in Section 16.5, banks long ago eliminated jockeying by requiring customers to form a single queue.)

Throughout this chapter, we assume no unusual customer behavior.

Service Discipline

The queueing system's *service discipline* is the rule by which a customer in the queue is selected to be the next to undergo service. Some alternative service disciplines are:

- *First-In, First-Out (FIFO)*. Under a FIFO service discipline, the customer in the queue to begin service next is the one who has waited in the queue for the longest time (i.e., the one who arrived first).

- *Last-In, First-Out (LIFO)*. Under a LIFO service discipline, the customer in the queue to begin service next is the one who has waited in the queue for the shortest time (i.e., the one who arrived last).

- *Random*. Under a random service discipline, the customer in the queue to begin service next is chosen randomly from among all customers in the queue.

- *Priority*. Under a priority service discipline, each arriving customer is assigned to a priority class. The customer in the queue to begin service next is the one belonging to the highest priority class represented in the queue, with ties among the same priority class broken according to the FIFO service discipline.

708

An end-of-chapter exercise requests you to think of real-world examples of each of these service disciplines. The FIFO service discipline is the most common and is the one we assume throughout this chapter.

Configuration of the Service Facilities That Comprise the Service Mechanism

The service mechanism consists of one or more *service facilities*. A queueing system with just one service facility that all customers must pass through is known as a *single-facility queueing system*. For such a queueing system, Figure 16.2(a) illustrates that customers arrive, wait in the queue, receive service, and depart. In contrast, a *multifacility queueing system* consists of a set of service facilities arranged in some configuration, often in such a way that departures from one of them are arrivals to one or more others. Queues may form at any service facility. For example, Figure 16.2(b) illustrates three service facilities linked in parallel. Each arriving customer must pass through only one facility, with the choice perhaps left up to the customer or perhaps dictated by the nature of the service the customer requires. As another example, Figure 16.2(c) illustrates three service facilities linked in series. Every arriving customer must pass through each in sequence, pos-

Figure 16.2 Some examples of the configuration of the service facilities

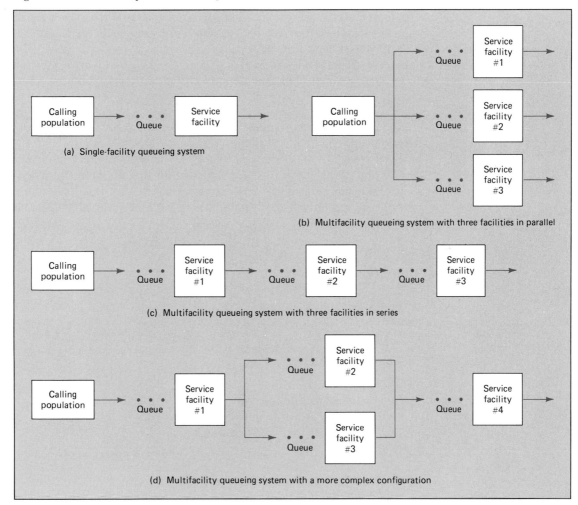

(a) Single-facility queueing system

(b) Multifacility queueing system with three facilities in parallel

(c) Multifacility queueing system with three facilities in series

(d) Multifacility queueing system with a more complex configuration

sibly waiting in a queue at each one. Figure 16.2(d) illustrates four service facilities linked so that a customer completing service at the first one proceeds to either the second or third (depending on some criterion), a customer completing service at the second or third facility proceeds to the fourth, and a customer completing service at the fourth facility departs the queueing system. Multifacility queueing systems are common in manufacturing environments where production takes place in stages, such as an automobile assembly line. Because the analysis of multifacility systems is well beyond the scope of this text, we will restrict our attention to single-facility queueing systems.

The Number of Servers at Each Service Facility

As indicated in the previous subsection, the service mechanism consists of a configuration of service facilities. Each consists of one or more *servers,* each capable of providing all the service required by any customer. A service facility is called a *single-server facility* or a *multi-server facility* depending on whether it has one server or more than one.[1]

Probability Distribution Governing the Service Times

The time a server spends servicing a customer is known as the *service time.* For most queueing systems, the service time differs for each customer. For example, suppose we sat next to a bank teller and observed the time spent with successive customers. If we used a stopwatch to record the elapsed service time for successive customers, we might find that the first customer's service time was 3 minutes; the second customer's, 5 minutes; the third customer's, 1 minute; and so on. To account for these unequal service times, we assume that they are governed by a specific probability distribution. There are several choices for this probability distribution. Section 16.4 will discuss them. In theory, it is possible for each of the facility's servers to have a service time governed by a different probability distribution; in practice, however, it is usually assumed that all servers at a service facility share a common probability distribution (although, in a multifacility queueing system, two servers at different facilities may have different probability distributions governing their respective service times).

Unusual Server Behavior

Servers may exhibit "unusual" behavior while servicing a customer. Possibilities include:

- *Failure.* A server (especially when machinery is involved) may fail while serving a customer, thereby interrupting service until a repair can be made.
- *Changing service rates.* A server may speed up or slow down, depending on the number of customers in the queue. For example, when the queue is long, a server may speed up in response to the pressure or, alternatively, may adopt a "Who cares?" attitude and slow down.
- *Batch processing.* A server may service several customers simultaneously, a

---

[1] *Channel* is sometimes used as a synonym for *server.*

phenomenon known as *batch processing*. Examples include a ski lift, an amusement park ride, and some types of computers.

Throughout this chapter, we assume no unusual customer behavior. Summarizing:

To describe a queueing system, we must specify the following characteristics:

1. Whether the calling population has infinite or finite size.

2. The probability distribution that governs the interarrival time— that is, the time between the arrivals of consecutive customers.

3. Whether the queue has infinite or finite capacity.

4. Any unusual customer behavior.

5. The service discipline used to choose the customer in the queue to begin service next.

6. The configuration of the service facilities that comprise the service mechanism.

7. The number of servers at each service facility.

8. The probability distribution that governs each server's service time—that is, the time required to complete the service required by a customer.

9. Any unusual server behavior.

Considering the number of options available for each of the above characteristics, it is no wonder that the management science literature is filled with so many distinct queueing systems. Although this chapter considers only a few elementary ones, this section has provided an overview of more complicated queueing systems.

16.3 A QUEUEING SYSTEM'S OPERATING CHARACTERISTICS

We now introduce some terminology and notation used to describe the results of an analysis of a queueing system. In such an analysis, the characteristics we would like to compute include:

- The probability (or percentage of time) that a specified number of customers are present in the queueing system. (This includes customers waiting in the queue and undergoing service.)
- The average number of customers in the queueing system. (This includes customers waiting in the queue and undergoing service.)
- The average time each customer spends in the queueing system. (This includes time spent waiting in the queue and undergoing service.)
- The average number of customers in the queue. (This excludes customers undergoing service.)
- The average time each customer spends in the queue. (This excludes time spent undergoing service.)

These are known as a queueing system's *operating characteristics*.

When a queueing system has recently begun operation, its operating characteristics are greatly affected by such factors as the initial conditions (e.g., the number of customers present when the system opened) and the time that has elapsed since the system opened. A recently opened system is said to be in a *transient condition*. After sufficient time has elapsed, a system's operating characteristics may become independent of the initial conditions and the elapsed time since the system opened. When this occurs, the queueing system is said to be in a *steady-state condition*. It takes an expert in queueing analysis to estimate the precise length of time required for a queueing system to attain steady-state (if it ever does). For our purposes, it will be sufficient to assume that any queueing system we analyze has been operating long enough to attain steady-state.

Table 16.1 displays the notation we will use to denote a queueing system's operating characteristics. These characteristics require some interpretation. To illustrate, suppose an analysis of a queueing system produces the result that $L_q = 5$. How can we interpret this result? Does it mean that, after the queueing system has been operating for a long period of time, there will always be 5 customers in the queueing system? No, it does not! To obtain a correct interpretation of $L_q = 5$, imagine that we count the number of customers in the queueing system at the end of 1000 equally spaced, long intervals of time (e.g., at the end of every hour for 1000 hours if the service time is usually well under an hour). Sometimes we might observe 3 customers in the queue, sometimes 8 customers, sometimes 0 customers, and so on. However, if we sum the number of customers in the queue at each of the 1000 observations and divide the sum by 1000, we obtain a number close to $L_q = 5$. Thus, L_q is an average or mean value. It provides the best estimate of how many customers we expect to find in the queue. Note that, because L_q is an average, it will usually have a noninteger value such as 5.71.

Similar interpretations apply to the other operating characteristics. For example, to interpret $W = 3.74$ minutes, imagine that we measure the time spent in the queueing system by 1000 customers who arrive at widely separated times (e.g., the 25th, 50th, 75th, 100th, and so on customers). Each customer would spend a different amount of time in the queueing system. However, the average time spent by each of the 1000 customers would be a value close to $W = 3.74$ minutes.

Knowing P_0, P_1, P_2, and so on enables us to compute other important operating characteristics. For example,

TABLE 16.1 Notation for a Queueing System's Operating Characteristics

Notation	Definition
P_n	The steady-state probability that n customers are present in the queueing system.
L	The steady-state average number of customers in the queueing system.
W	The steady-state average amount of time a customer spends in the queueing system.
L_q	The steady-state average number of customers in the queue.
W_q	The steady-state average amount of time a customer spends in the queue.

- Since P_0 equals the probability that the queueing system has no customers present, it also equals the probability that all servers are idle.

- In a multiserver queueing system, if s represents the number of servers, then

$$P_0 + P_1 + P_2 + \cdots + P_{s-1}$$

equals the probability that at least one server is idle. Hence,

$$1 - (P_0 + P_1 + P_2 + \cdots + P_{s-1})$$

equals the probability that no server is idle or, equivalently, the probability that an arriving customer must join the queue.

16.4 THE EXPONENTIAL PROBABILITY DISTRIBUTION

As discussed in Section 16.2, describing a queueing system requires the specification of two probability distributions:

1. The probability distribution governing the interarrival times.
2. The probability distribution governing the service times.

In choosing a probability distribution, we usually have two conflicting objectives. We want the probability distribution to be complicated enough to accurately reflect the customers' arrivals or the servers' service. We also want it to be simple enough to make the queueing system *mathematically tractable* — which means that we can derive mathematical formulae for the system's operating characteristics. The probability distribution that provides the most acceptable compromise between accurate representation and mathematical tractability is known as the *exponential probability distribution*.

Brief Review of Some Topics in Probability Theory

At this point we need to introduce some notation and terminology and review some concepts that should be familiar to you from your prior study of probability theory:

- We denote by T a random variable representing the uncertain time between consecutive occurrences of some particular kind of incident. In the context of customer arrivals, T denotes the interarrival time (i.e., the uncertain time between the arrival of consecutive customers). In the context of customer service, T denotes the service time (i.e., the uncertain time between consecutive service completions by a continuously busy server).

- For any specified constant t, $Pr\{T \leqslant t\}$ denotes the probability that the value of the random variable T will be less than or equal to t. $Pr\{T \geqslant t\}$ is defined similarly, and, of course,

$$Pr\{T \geqslant t\} = 1 - Pr\{T \leqslant t\}.$$

For example, if T denotes the interarrival time measured in minutes, then $Pr\{T \leqslant 2\}$ denotes the probability that the next customer will arrive within 2 minutes of the most recent customer.

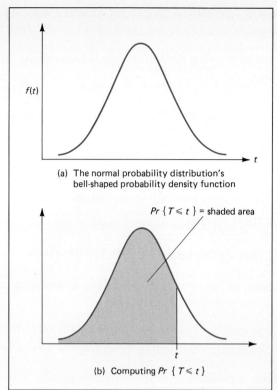

(a) The normal probability distribution's bell-shaped probability density function

(b) Computing $Pr\{T \leqslant t\}$

Figure 16.3 The normal probability distribution.

- With the symbol $\cap$ read as "and", $Pr\{\cdots \cap \cdots\}$ denotes the probability that the two events described before and after $\cap$ will both occur. This is known as the *joint probability* of the two events. For example, if T denotes the interarrival time measured in minutes, then $Pr\{(T \geqslant 2) \cap (T \leqslant 5)\}$ denotes the probability that the next customer will arrive at least 2 minutes after but at most 5 minutes after the most recent customer.

- With the symbol $|$ read as "given", $Pr\{\cdots | \cdots\}$ denotes that probability that the event described before $|$ will occur *given* that we know with certainty that the event described after $|$ will occur. This is known as the *conditional probability* of the first event given the second event. For example, if T denotes the interarrival time measured in minutes, $Pr\{(T \geqslant 5)|(T \geqslant 2)\}$ denotes the probability that the next customer will arrive at least 5 minutes after the most recent customer, *given* that we know with certainty that the next arrival will occur at least 2 minutes after the most recent arrival.

- Associated with the random variable T is a probability density function $f(t)$. For example, Figure 16.3(a) displays the bell-shaped probability density function of the well-known normal probability distribution. The total area under the curve of any probability density function equals 1. As illustrated by the shaded area in Figure 16.3(b), we compute $Pr\{T \leqslant t\}$ by determining the total area under the curve and to the left of t.

Properties of the Exponential Probability Distribution

A random variable T is said to have an *exponential distribution with parameter α* if its probability density function is

$$f(t) = \alpha e^{-\alpha t}.$$

Note that the probability density function involves only one unknown, t. The parameter α (the Greek letter alpha) is a prespecified nonnegative constant, and e represents the "never-ending" constant 2.718. . . . The characteristic shape of the exponential probability density function is illustrated in Figure 16.4, which displays for $\alpha = 5$ the graph of $f(t) = 5e^{-5t}$. Before proceeding, you should convince yourself the graph is correct by verifying several points on the graph. For example,

$$f(0) = 5e^{-5(0)} = 5e^0 = 5 \quad \text{and} \quad f(0.4) = 5e^{-5(0.4)} = 5e^{-2} = 0.677.$$

Note that, although Figure 16.4 stops graphing the function at $t = 1.2$, the graph actually continues indefinitely, approaching but never reaching the horizontal axis. In discussing an exponential probability density function, we will denote its parameter by α when our discussion has no specific context. However, in keeping with convention, we will denote the parameter by λ (the Greek letter lambda) in the context of an interarrival time, and we will denote the parameter by μ (the Greek letter mu) in the context of a service time.

The exponential probability distribution possesses several properties that we will now discuss. Although it is possible to rigorously prove these properties, we will not do so. Instead, we will state each property as a fact, using the minimum mathematics necessary to gain an intuitive understanding of its implication for queueing analysis. Here, then, is a nonrigorous survey of five important properties possessed by an exponential probability distribution with parameter α.

Property 1: For any specified value of t, $Pr\{T \leqslant t\} = 1 - e^{-\alpha t}$ or, equivalently, $Pr\{T \geqslant t\} = e^{-\alpha t}$.

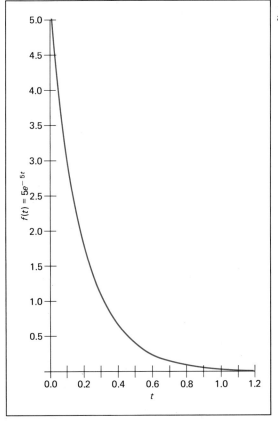

Figure 16.4 Graph of exponential probability density function for $\alpha = 5$

This property results from the fact that, as illustrated in Figure 16.5, the area under the exponential probability density function and to the left of any specified value of t equals $1 - e^{-\alpha t}$. We omit a formal proof. Those readers familiar with integral calculus should have no difficulty constructing their own. Since the total area under any probability density function equals 1, the area under the exponential probability density function and to the right of t equals

$$1 - (1 - e^{-\alpha t}) = e^{-\alpha t}.$$

This property enables us to quickly compute probabilities associated with an exponential random variable. For example, for an exponential random variable with parameter $\alpha = \frac{1}{2}$,

$$
\begin{aligned}
Pr\{T \leqslant 3\} &= 1 - e^{-\alpha t} \\
&= 1 - e^{-(1/2)3} \\
&= 1 - e^{-1.5} \\
&= 1 - 0.223 \\
&= 0.777
\end{aligned}
$$

Property 2: The mean of an exponential random variable with parameter α is $1/\alpha$.

As with Property 1, we omit a formal proof, leaving those readers familiar with integral calculus to construct their own. To gain an intuitive understanding of this property, assume that T represents the interarrival time measured in hours and that T has an exponential distribution with parameter $\alpha = 20$. That an exponential random variable has a mean of $1/\alpha = 1/20$ hours implies that the mean interarrival time is $\frac{1}{20}$ hours or 3 minutes. Equivalently, we can say that customers arrive at the mean rate of 20 per hour. Thus, we have the following interpretation for an exponential random variable used in the context of queueing analysis:

- If we say that the interarrival time has an exponential distribution with parameter λ, then

$$\lambda = \text{the mean arrival rate (i.e., the average number of arrivals per unit of time)}$$

$$\frac{1}{\lambda} = \text{the mean interarrival time (i.e., the average time between arrivals)}$$

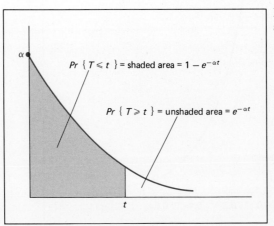

Figure 16.5 Computing $Pr\{T \leqslant t\}$ for an exponential probability distribution

For example, if the interarrival time is measured in hours and $\lambda = 20$, then customers arrive at an average rate of 20 per hour, and the average time between arrivals is $\frac{1}{20}$ hours or 3 minutes.

- Similarly, if we say that the service time has an exponential distribution with parameter μ, then

$$\mu = \text{the mean service rate (i.e., the average number of service completions per unit of time by a continuously busy server)}$$

$$\frac{1}{\mu} = \text{the mean service time (i.e., the average time required by a server to serve a single customer)}$$

For example, if the service time is measured in hours and $\mu = 30$, then service completions by a continuously busy server occur at an average rate of 30 per hour, and the average time between service completions is $\frac{1}{30}$ hours or 2 minutes.

Property 3: An exponential random variable will most likely take on a small value.

We can see this graphically by referring to the exponential probability density function in Figure 16.4 and observing that most of the area under the probability density function is concentrated in the left portion. To illustrate this property mathematically, let us use T to denote an exponential random variable having parameter α, and let us compute the probability that T takes on a value less than or equal to one-half its mean. From Property 1, for any value of t,

$$Pr\{T \leqslant t\} = 1 - e^{-\alpha t}.$$

Substituting $t = \frac{1}{2}(1/\alpha)$ (i.e., one-half the mean from Property 2) into the above expression, we obtain

$$
\begin{aligned}
Pr\{T \leqslant t\} &= 1 - e^{-\alpha t} \\
&= 1 - e^{-\alpha(1/2)(1/\alpha)} \\
&= 1 - e^{-1/2} \\
&= 1 - 0.6065 \\
&= 0.3935
\end{aligned}
$$

Thus, for any exponential random variable T, there is almost a 40 percent chance that T will take on a value less than or equal to one-half its mean. For example, if T denotes an interarrival time measured in hours and T has an exponential distribution with parameter $\lambda = 20$, we know from Property 2 that the mean time between consecutive arrivals is $\frac{1}{\lambda} = \frac{1}{20}$ hours = 3 minutes. Hence, there is about a 40 percent chance that the interarrival time will be less than $1\frac{1}{2}$ minutes.

Property 4: The exponential probability distribution has what is called a *lack-of-memory property*.

To illustrate this property, let T denote a random variable representing the interarrival time, and assume T has an exponential probability distribution with parameter α. Let us compute the following four probabilities:

Mathematical Statement	Verbal Statement
$Pr\{T \geqslant 5\}$	Probability that the next arrival will not occur within the next 5 minutes (given that an arrival has just occurred).
$Pr\{T \geqslant 15 \mid T \geqslant 10\}$	Probability that the next arrival will not occur within the next 5 minutes, given that 10 minutes have already elapsed since the most recent arrival.
$Pr\{T \geqslant 105 \mid T \geqslant 100\}$	Probability that the next arrival will not occur within the next 5 minutes, given that 100 minutes have already elapsed since the most recent arrival.
$Pr\{T \geqslant 1005 \mid T \geqslant 1000\}$	Probability that the next arrival will not occur within the next 5 minutes, given that 1000 minutes have already elapsed since the most recent arrival.

The computation of the first of these probabilities follows directly from Property 1:

$$Pr\{T \geqslant 5\} = e^{-\alpha 5}.$$

To compute the second, third, and fourth probabilities, recall from your prior study of probability theory that, given two events A and B,

$$Pr\{A \mid B\} = \frac{Pr\{A \cap B\}}{Pr\{B\}}.$$

Consequently,

$$
\begin{aligned}
Pr\{T \geqslant 15 \mid T \geqslant 10\} &= \frac{Pr\{(T \geqslant 15) \cap (T \geqslant 10)\}}{Pr\{T \geqslant 10\}} \\
&= \frac{Pr\{(T \geqslant 15)\}}{Pr\{T \geqslant 10\}} \\
&= \frac{e^{-\alpha 15}}{e^{-\alpha 10}} \\
&= e^{-\alpha 5}.
\end{aligned}
$$

Similarly,

$$
\begin{aligned}
Pr\{T \geqslant 105 \mid T \geqslant 100\} &= \frac{Pr\{(T \geqslant 105) \cap (T \geqslant 100)\}}{Pr\{T \geqslant 100\}} \\
&= \frac{Pr\{(T \geqslant 105)\}}{Pr\{T \geqslant 100\}} \\
&= \frac{e^{-\alpha 105}}{e^{-\alpha 100}} \\
&= e^{-\alpha 5}.
\end{aligned}
$$

Before proceeding, you should verify in a similar fashion that

$$Pr\{(T \geqslant 1005) \mid (T \geqslant 1000)\} = e^{-\alpha 5}.$$

To summarize we have shown that

$$Pr\{T \geqslant 5 \qquad\qquad\} = e^{-\alpha 5}$$

$$Pr\{T \geqslant 15 \quad | \; T \geqslant 10 \qquad\} = e^{-\alpha 5}$$

$$Pr\{T \geqslant 105 \quad | \; T \geqslant 100 \qquad\} = e^{-\alpha 5}$$

$$Pr\{T \geqslant 1005 \; | \; T \geqslant 1000 \quad\} = e^{-\alpha 5}$$

—that is, all four probabilities are equal! The equality of the probabilities illustrates the following general principle:

Let T denote a random variable representing the time between consecutive occurrences of a particular type of incident (e.g., a customer arrival or a service completion). If T has an exponential probability distribution, then, for any positive values of t_1 and t_2,

$$\underbrace{Pr\{T \geqslant t_1 + t_2 | T \geqslant t_1\}}_{} \qquad = \qquad \underbrace{Pr\{T \geqslant t_2\}}_{}$$

The next incident will not occur within the next t_2 units of time, given that t_1 units of time have already elapsed since the most recent incident.	The next incident will not occur within the next t_2 units of time, given that an incident has just occurred.

In other words, the probability distribution of the *remaining* time until the next occurrence of an incident is always the same, regardless of how much time has elapsed since the most recent incident. The exponential probability distribution "forgets" when the most recent incident occurred. It may have just occurred, or it may have occurred a long time ago. The "forgetfulness" of the exponential distribution is usually called the *lack-of-memory property*. Experts in the field of probability theory have shown that the exponential distribution is the only probability distribution with the lack-of-memory property.

Property 5: If

$T =$ a random variable representing the time between consecutive occurrences of particular type of incident (e.g., a customer arrival or a service completion)

$N =$ a random variable representing the number of incidents that occur over a specified length of time t,

then the assumption that T has an exponential distribution with parameter α is equivalent to the assumption that N has a Poisson distribution with parameter αt.[2]

You can't have one without the other! Space constraints preclude a detailed discussion of the intimate relationship between the exponential distribution and the Poisson distribution. The purpose of our brief discussion here is to clarify statements you may encounter, such as

Customers arrive at a queueing system according to a Poisson process with parameter λ.

---

[2] If N has a Poisson distribution with parameter αt, then

$$Pr\{N = n\} = \frac{(\alpha t)^n e^{-\alpha t}}{n!}$$

or

Service completions by a continuously busy server occur according to a Poisson process with parameter μ.

These are just equivalent ways of stating that the interarrival time has an exponential distribution with parameter λ, and the service time has an exponential distribution with parameter μ.

We may summarize the above five properties as follows:

**Five
Properties
of the
Exponential
Probability
Distribution**

Let T denote a random variable representing the time between consecutive occurrences of a particular type of incident (i.e., consecutive customer arrivals or consecutive service completions by a continuously busy server). If T has an exponential probability distribution with parameter α, then

1. For any specified value of t, $Pr\{T \leq t\} = 1 - e^{-\alpha t}$.

2. α equals the mean rate at which the incidents occur, and $1/\alpha$ equals the mean time between consecutive incidents.

3. T will most likely take on small values.

4. The probability distribution has the lack-of-memory property; that is, the probability distribution of the *remaining* time until the next occurrence of an incident is always the same, regardless of how much time has elapsed since the most recent incident.

5. The assumption that the time between consecutive occurrences of an incident has an exponential distribution is equivalent to the assumption that the number of occurrences of the incident within a specified interval of time has a Poisson distribution.

Implications of the Exponential Distribution for Interarrival Times and Service Times

What are the implications of assuming that the interarrival time or the service time has an exponential distribution? First, consider the assumption that the interarrival time has an exponential distribution with parameter λ. Such an assumption has the following implications:

- From Property 2, we know that customers arrive at the queueing system at a mean rate of λ customers per unit of time, with the mean time between arrivals being $1/\lambda$ units of time.

- From Property 3, we know that the time between customer arrivals will usually be small; only occasionally will a long interval elapse without a customer arriving.

- From Property 4, we know that the remaining time until the next arrival does not depend on how much time has elapsed since the most recent arrival.

These three implications are ideally suited to a process in which customers arriving according to some mean arrival rate (e.g., 20 per hour) do not arrive at the ends of equally spaced intervals of time but instead arrive at random (i.e., independent of one another).

Now consider the assumption that the time between consecutive service completions by a continuously busy server has an exponential distribution with parameter μ. Such an assumption has the following implications:

- From Property 2, we know that service completions occur at a mean rate of μ completions per unit of time, with the mean time between completions being $1/\mu$ units of time.

- From Property 3, we know that the time between service completions will usually be small; only occasionally will a long interval elapse without a service completion.

- From Property 4, we know that the remaining time until the next service completion does not depend on how much time has elapsed since the most recent service completion.

Although the first of these implications is usually appropriate, the last two are not. When considering service completions by a continuously busy server, it is frequently the case that service times cluster about some mean, with only an occasional few being significantly below or above the mean. For example, if we sat with a stopwatch next to a bank teller and timed his service times for 100 successive customers, we might obtain the frequency distribution displayed in Figure 16.6(a). Most of the service times are close to the mean of 3 minutes, with only an occasional few being significantly above or below the mean. Figure 16.6(a)'s frequency distribution suggests that the service time does not have an exponential distribution. If it did, we would expect a frequency distribution similar to that displayed in Figure 16.6(b).

Figure 16.6 Frequency distribution for the service time of 100 successive customers

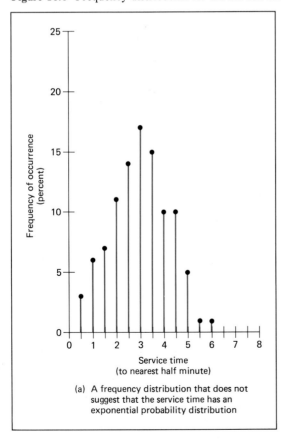

(a) A frequency distribution that does not suggest that the service time has an exponential probability distribution

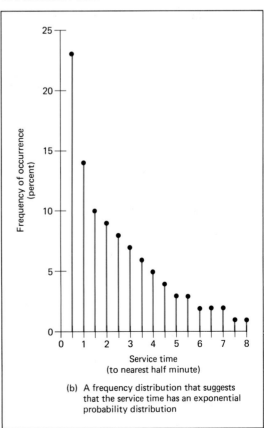

(b) A frequency distribution that suggests that the service time has an exponential probability distribution

To summarize:

> Because of its properties, the exponential probability distribution is usually ideally suited for the interarrival time but is often inappropriate for the service time.

Despite this potential inappropriateness for the service times, we will use the exponential probability distribution throughout this chapter. Space constraints preclude a discussion of alternatives.

16.5 OUR BASIC QUEUEING SYSTEM

We consider now our *basic queueing system,* in which the set of assumptions is the most elementary possible. With reference to the nine characteristics summarized at the end of Section 16.3, we make the following assumptions:

1. The calling population has infinite size.
2. The interarrival time has an exponential probability distribution with a mean arrival rate of λ customer arrivals per unit time (or, equivalently, a mean interarrival time of $1/\lambda$).
3. Customers wait in a single queue having infinite capacity.
4. There is no unusual customer behavior.
5. The service discipline is FIFO.
6. The service mechanism consists of a single service facility.
7. The single service facility has s identical servers, each capable of serving any customer.
8. For each server, the service time has an exponential probability distribution with a mean service rate of μ service completions per unit time (or, equivalently, a mean service time of $1/\mu$).
9. There is no unusual server behavior.

Figure 16.7 depicts our basic queueing system. To illustrate this system, consider the following scenario:

> The Second National Bank has recently begun to receive numerous customer complaints about long waits to use the only automatic teller machine (ATM) located at a shopping mall. Data collected while observing customer transactions indicate the following:

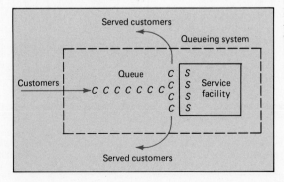

Figure 16.7 Our basic queueing system (with each customer indicated by a C and each server by an S)

- The interarrival time has an exponential probability distribution with a mean arrival rate of $\lambda = 16$ customer arrivals per hour (or, equivalently, a mean interarrival time of $1/\lambda = \frac{1}{16}$ hours = 3.75 minutes).

- The service time has an exponential probability distribution with a mean service rate of $\mu = 20$ service completions per hour (or, equivalently, a mean service time of $1/\mu = \frac{1}{20}$ hours = 3 minutes).

In response to its customers' complaints, Second National Bank is considering the following four options:

1. **The status quo.** Under this option, Second National Bank would maintain the single ATM and simply try to handle customer complaints in a courteous fashion, without promising any dramatic improvement.

2. **Replacement of the current ATM with a faster model.** Under this option, Second National Bank would replace the current ATM with a new ATM containing a state-of-the-art microprocessor control system. With a mean service rate of $\mu = 30$ service completions per hour, the new ATM would be significantly faster than the current model. Second National Bank assumes the mean arrival rate would remain unchanged from its current value of $\lambda = 16$.

3. **Installation of a second ATM at the opposite end of the mall.** Under this option, Second National Bank would install a second ATM at the opposite end of the shopping mall. The second ATM would be identical to the current one. Because of their locations at opposite ends of the mall, Second National Bank believes that customers would be equally likely to choose either ATM. Consequently, Second National Bank assumes that the mean arrival rate at *each* ATM would be half the current mean arrival rate at the current ATM; that is, mean arrival rate at each ATM would be $\lambda = (\frac{1}{2})(16) = 8$.

4. **Installation of a second ATM adjacent to the existing one.** Under this option, Second National Bank would install a second, identical ATM adjacent to the existing one. Signs would be posted requesting customers to form a single queue to wait for the first available ATM. Second National Bank assumes the mean arrival rate at the pair of ATMs would remain unchanged from its current value of $\lambda = 16$.

Before deciding which option to select, Second National Bank would like to compare the following operating characteristics for each option: P_n for $n = 1, 2, 3$, and so on; L; W; L_q; and W_q.

Table 16.2 displays the formulae required to analyze Second National Bank's four options. The formulae are divided into two halves, the first half for use in analyzing the single-server version of our basic queueing system and the second half for analyzing the multiserver version.[3] The derivations of these formulae are well beyond the scope of this text. Consequently, we must accept these formulae as facts and focus instead on how to apply them.

At this point we must issue a warning! Table 16.2's formulae are valid only when $\lambda < s\mu$. If $\lambda \geqslant s\mu$, then the queueing system "explodes" in the sense that the queue keeps growing longer and longer. The requirement that $\lambda < s\mu$ has an intuitive interpretation. Since μ is each server's mean service rate, $s\mu$ equals that maximum rate at which customers can depart from the queueing system. Hence, the requirement that $\lambda < s\mu$ simply states that, on average, the arrival rate cannot exceed the maximum departure rate. There is an equivalent way of stating that $\lambda < s\mu$ must hold. In particular, if we define ρ (the Greek letter size +1 rho) by

---

[3] Observe that the multiserver formulae require the computations be performed in sequence; that is, we must first compute P_0, use P_0 to compute L_q, use L_q to compute W_q, and so on.

TABLE 16.2 Formulae for the Operating Characteristics of Our Basic Queueing System

$$P_0 = 1 - \frac{\lambda}{\mu}$$

$$P_n = \left(\frac{\lambda}{\mu}\right)^n \left[1 - \frac{\lambda}{\mu}\right]$$

$$L = \frac{\lambda}{\mu - \lambda}$$

$$W = \frac{1}{\mu - \lambda}$$

$$L_q = \frac{\lambda^2}{\mu(\mu - \lambda)}$$

$$W_q = \frac{\lambda}{\mu(\mu - \lambda)}$$

(a) Formulae for the single-server version

$$P_0 = \frac{1}{1 + \frac{\lambda}{\mu} + \frac{\left(\frac{\lambda}{\mu}\right)^2}{2!} + \ldots + \frac{\left(\frac{\lambda}{\mu}\right)^{s-1}}{(s-1)!} + \frac{\left(\frac{\lambda}{\mu}\right)^s}{s!\left(1 - \frac{\lambda}{s\mu}\right)}}$$

$$P_n = \begin{cases} \dfrac{\left[\dfrac{\lambda}{\mu}\right]^n}{n!} P_0 & \text{for } n = 1, 2, \ldots, s \\[4mm] \dfrac{\left[\dfrac{\lambda}{\mu}\right]^n}{s! s^{n-s}} P_0 & \text{for } n = s+1, s+2, s+3, \ldots \end{cases}$$

$$L_q = \left[\frac{\left(\frac{\lambda}{\mu}\right)^{s+1}}{(s-1)!\left[s - \frac{\lambda}{\mu}\right]^2}\right] P_0$$

$$W_q = \frac{L_q}{\lambda}$$

$$W = W_q + \frac{1}{\mu}$$

$$L = L_q + \frac{\lambda}{\mu}$$

(b) Formulae for the multiple-server version

$$\rho = \frac{\lambda}{s\mu},$$

then requiring $\lambda < s\mu$ is equivalent to requiring $\rho < 1$. We call ρ the *utilization factor*.[4]

---

[4] Sometimes ρ is referred to as the *traffic intensity*.

Let us now employ Table 16.2's formulae to analyze Second National Bank's four options:

Analysis of option 1: The status quo

The status quo is a single-server basic queueing system with $\lambda = 16$ and $\mu = 20$. Since $\lambda < \mu$, we may analyze the queueing system using the formulae in Table 16.2(a), obtaining the following results:

$$P_0 = 1 - \frac{\lambda}{\mu} = 1 - \frac{(16)}{(20)} = 0.2$$

$$P_n = \left[\frac{\lambda}{\mu}\right]^n \left[1 - \frac{\lambda}{\mu}\right] = \left[\frac{16}{20}\right]^n \left[1 - \frac{16}{20}\right] = (0.8)^n (0.2)$$

$$L = \frac{\lambda}{\mu - \lambda} = \frac{16}{20 - 16} = 4.0$$

$$W = \frac{1}{\mu - \lambda} = \frac{1}{20 - 16} = 0.25 \text{ hours}$$

$$L_q = \frac{\lambda^2}{\mu(\mu - \lambda)} = \frac{16^2}{20(20 - 16)} = 3.2$$

$$W_q = \frac{\lambda}{\mu(\mu - \lambda)} = \frac{16}{20(20 - 16)} = 0.2 \text{ hours}$$

Thus, for example, the probability that no one is using the ATM is $P_0 = 0.2$, and the average number of customers waiting to use the ATM is $L_q = 3.2$. For subsequent comparison to the remaining options, the operating characteristics L_q and W_q are summarized in the first row of Table 16.3.[5]

Analysis of option 2: Replacement of the current ATM with a faster ATM

Like option 1, this option is also a single-server basic queueing system. However, there is an important difference. Although λ remains unchanged from its value of $\lambda = 16$ in option (1), the mean service rate is now $\mu = 30$ instead of $\mu = 20$.

---

[5] Note that Table 16.3 expresses W_q in minutes, the product obtained by multiplying 60 by W_q expressed in hours.

TABLE 16.3 Summary of L_q and W_q for Each of Second National Bank's Options

Option	L_q	W_q (minutes)
1. Status quo	3.200	12.000
2. Faster ATM	0.610	2.286
3. Second ATM at opposite end of mall	0.267	2.000
4. Second ATM adjacent to existing one	0.152	0.572

Since $\lambda < \mu$, we may once again use the formula in Table 16.2(a). Before proceeding, verify for yourself that substituting $\lambda = 16$ and $\mu = 30$ into the formulae results in the operating characteristics summarized in Table 16.3's second row.

Analysis of option 3: Installation of a second ATM at the opposite end of the mall

This option consists of two distinct single-server basic queueing systems, one at each end of the mall. For each queueing system, the mean arrival rate is $\lambda = 8$, half the value used in option 1; furthermore, the mean service rate is $\mu = 20$, the same service rate used in option 1. Since $\lambda < \mu$, we may continue to use the formulae in Table 16.2(a). Before proceeding, verify for yourself that substituting $\lambda = 8$ and $\mu = 20$ into the formulae results in the operating characteristics summarized in Table 16.3's third row. Remember, these operating characteristics apply to each ATM. Thus, for example, $L_q = 0.267$ implies that each ATM has an average of 0.267 customers waiting in the queue, for a total average of 0.534 in both queues.

Analysis of option 4: Installation of a second ATM adjacent to the existing one

In contrast to the first three options, option 4 is a multiserver basic queueing system with $s = 2$ servers, $\lambda = 16$, and $\mu = 20$. Since $\lambda < s\mu$, we may analyze the system using the formulae in Table 16.2(b). Observe that, because they are more complicated, the multiserver formulae require more algebra than their single-server counterparts. Substituting $s = 2$, $\lambda = 16$, and $\mu = 20$ into the formula for P_0, we obtain the following result:

$$P_0 = \cfrac{1}{1 + \dfrac{\lambda}{\mu} + \dfrac{(\frac{\lambda}{\mu})^2}{2!} + \ldots + \dfrac{(\frac{\lambda}{\mu})^{s-1}}{(s-1)!} + \dfrac{(\frac{\lambda}{\mu})^s}{s!(1 - \frac{\lambda}{s\mu})}}$$

$$= \cfrac{1}{1 + \dfrac{16}{20} + \cfrac{\left[\dfrac{16}{20}\right]^2}{2!\left[1 - \dfrac{16}{(2)(20)}\right]}}$$

$$= 0.4286$$

Using $P_0 = 0.4286$, we compute the remaining operating characteristics as follows:

$$L_q = \left[\cfrac{\left(\dfrac{\lambda}{\mu}\right)^{s+1}}{(s-1)!\left[s - \dfrac{\lambda}{\mu}\right]^2}\right]P_0 = \left[\cfrac{\left(\dfrac{16}{20}\right)^{2+1}}{(2-1)!\left[2 - \dfrac{16}{20}\right]^2}\right]0.4286 = 0.1524$$

$$W_q = \frac{L_q}{\lambda} = \frac{0.1524}{16} = 0.009525 \text{ hours}$$

$$W = W_q + \frac{1}{\mu} = 0.009525 + \frac{1}{20} = 0.05952 \text{ hours}$$

$$L = L_q + \frac{\lambda}{\mu} = 0.1524 + \frac{16}{20} = 0.9524$$

The operating characteristics L_q and W_q are summarized in Table 16.3's fourth row.

Table 16.3 provides information useful to Second National Bank when it decides which option to implement. For example, if $W_q \leqslant 3$ minutes is desired, then the bank may choose either option 2, 3, or 4; however, if $W_q \leqslant 1$ minute is desired, then the bank must choose option 4.

Table 16.3 illustrates a general principle:

> The operating characteristics L, W, L_q, and W_q can always be reduced either by increasing each server's mean service rate or by increasing the number of servers.

Unfortunately, this reduction is not free! To implement option 2, 3 or 4, Second National Bank must incur costs. The bank must decide whether these increased costs are compensated by the reduction in L, W, L_q, and W_q. Usually, a manager bases such a decision on a qualitative judgment such as, "A reduction in mean customer waiting time from __ to __ justifies spending __ dollars." Sometimes, however, a manager can base the decision on quantitative analysis, which we will introduce in Section 16.8.

Table 16.3 illustrates a second general principle. In particular, Table 16.3's comparison of options 3 and 4 illustrates the following:

> Suppose the following options are available:
>
> A. A multiserver basic queueing system with s servers, a mean arrival rate of λ customers per unit of time, and a mean service rate for each server of μ service completions per unit of time. (This is option 4 in Second National Bank's problem.)
>
> B. s distinct single-server basic queueing systems, each having a mean arrival rate of λ/s customers per unit of time, and a mean service rate for each server of μ service completions per unit of time. (This is option 3 in Second National Bank's problem.)
>
> Then W_q (or W), the mean time a customer waits in the queue (or the queueing system) is always lower for option A than for option B. That is, from the standpoint of customer waiting time, it is always better to have a single queue serviced by s servers than it is to have s distinct queues, each serviced by their own server.

It is this general principle that leads banks to require customers to form a single queue to wait for the next available teller.

Although W_q is always lower for option A than for option B, there are situations in which option B might be preferable. For example:

- Option B may be preferable if there is insufficient space for a single queue to form. For example, the formation of a single queue would significantly reduce W_q in a grocery store with multiple checkout counters. However, the implementation of a single queue is unlikely because it would result in congested grocery aisles (unless the traditional grocery store layout were radically altered).

■ Option *B* may be preferable if the queueing system's calling population is dispersed over a large geographical area, so that the time required for a customer to travel to and from his point of origin is important. Travel time is unimportant when a bank decides whether to install the two ATMs at a shopping mall either adjacent to each other or at opposite ends of the mall. However, travel time is important when a bank decides where to install the ATMs that will serve an entire town. If W_q were the only consideration, a bank would install all its ATMs at a single centralized location with plenty of parking space. However, a bank would never implement such a policy because many customers would have to travel a long time to reach the centralized location. From such a customer's point of view, this long travel time is equivalent to waiting in a queue. Therefore, rather than install all its ATMs at a single location, a bank will divide them among several geographically-dispersed locations. At a particular location, however, the general principle suggests it is best to locate the ATMs adjacent to each other to permit the formation of a single queue.

At this point we observe that computing any queueing system's operating characteristics by substituting into formulae similar to those displayed in Table 16.2 is time-consuming and error-prone. Such computations are best performed with a software package, where the user simply inputs the data and lets the computer do the work. If a software package is unavailable, some library research should turn up graphs such as the one displayed in Figure 16.8. Let us see how

Figure 16.8 Graphical approach to computing *L* in our basic queueing system

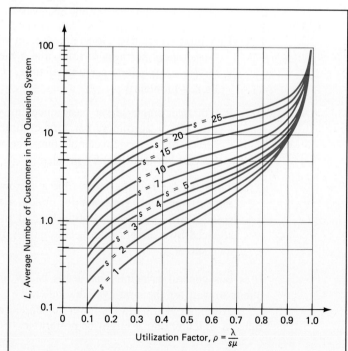

Source: F. S. Hillier and G. J. Lieberman, *Introduction to Operations Research*, 4th ed. (Oakland: Holden-Day, Inc., 1986), p. 549.

easy it is to employ the graph to compute L for option 4 in Second National Bank's problem. For this option, $\lambda = 16$, $\mu = 20$, and $s = 2$. Hence,

$$\rho = \frac{\lambda}{s\mu} = \frac{16}{(2)(20)} = 0.4.$$

Locating $\rho = 0.4$ on the horizontal axis and moving upward until we "hit" the $s = 2$ curve, we see that $L = 0.95$. This is much easier than substituting into Table 16.2's formulae.

While we are considering Figure 16.8's graphs, we should observe how steeply the curves begin to rise once ρ exceeds, say, 0.8. This illustrates the general principle that, when λ is close to $s\mu$ (i.e., the queueing system is operating close to capacity), even a small increase in λ or a small decrease in μ can result in a significant worsening of the queueing system's operating characteristics.

16.6 OUR BASIC QUEUEING SYSTEM WITH A FINITE QUEUE CAPACITY

Section 16.5's basic queueing system assumes that the queue has infinite capacity. In this section, we consider the variation in which the queue has finite capacity; that is, the queue's length cannot exceed a specified finite value of m. We assume that, whenever the queue's length is equal to m, any arriving customer is "blocked" from entering the system. Observe that, if the queueing system has s servers, stating that the queue has a capacity of m customers is equivalent to stating that the entire queueing system has a capacity of $s + m$ customers. The queueing system is filled to capacity when all s servers are busy and the queue length is at its maximum value of m.

The most common example of this situation is a telephone reservation system (e.g., for an airline) having s reservation agents and, if all agents are busy, having the capability to place up to m customers on hold to await the first available agent. A customer who calls when all s agents are busy and m customers are already on hold will receive a busy signal and, thus, will be prevented from entering the queueing system. Consequently, the queue's total length cannot exceed the finite value of m, or, equivalently, the total number of customers in the queueing system cannot exceed $s + m$.

To illustrate a queueing system with a finite queue capacity, consider the following scenario:

During the 9:00 p.m. to 1:00 a.m. time slot, radio station WAIT plays only songs that its listeners request by phone. The telephone system WAIT uses to process its listeners' calls has $s = 2$ operators and, when all operators are busy, has the capability to place up to $m = 4$ callers on hold. An operator asks a caller to state his or her name, the requested song, and a brief reason for the request. The caller's response is recorded on tape and used if the station's DJ subsequently decides to play the song. (Not all requests are played because there are many more requests than can be played in the four-hour time slot.) WAIT estimates that

- The callers' interarrival time has an exponential probability distribution with a mean arrival rate of $\lambda = 25$ calls per hour (or, equivalently, a mean interarrival time of $1/\lambda = \frac{1}{25}$ *hours* = 2.4 minutes).

- Each operator's service time has an exponential probability distribution with a mean service rate of $\mu = 20$ service completions per hour (or, equivalently, a mean time between service completions of $1/\mu = \frac{1}{20}$ *hours* = 3 minutes).

WAIT would like to know the operating characteristics of its phone request system, particularly the percentage of callers who get a busy signal.

As indicated by the scenario's last sentence, the operating characteristic of most importance in a queueing system with a finite queue capacity is the percentage of customers that are blocked from entering the system because the queue is filled to capacity. In the context of a telephone system, a blocked customer is a caller who receives a busy signal.

To begin our analysis of our basic queueing system with a finite queue capacity of m, we observe that the steady-state probabilities for the number of customers in the system are nonzero only for

$$P_0, P_1, P_2, \ldots, P_{s+m}.$$

The remaining probabilities are 0, because the queueing system has a capacity for only $s + m$ customers. For example, since $s = 2$ and $m = 4$ in WAIT's problem, there can never be more than 6 callers in the queueing system. Consequently, only

$$P_0, P_1, P_2, P_3, P_4, P_5, \text{ and } P_6$$

are nonzero.

Table 16.4 displays formulae for

$$P_1, P_2, \ldots, P_{s+m}$$

stated in terms of P_0. These formulae, plus the fact that

$$P_0 + P_1 + \cdots + P_{s+m} = 1,$$

enable us to calculate the queueing system's operating characteristics. To illustrate, let us apply Table 16.4's formulae to WAIT's problem. Substituting $s = 2$, $m = 4$, $\lambda = 25$, and $\mu = 20$ into the formulae, we obtain Table 16.5's expressions for P_1, $P_2, \ldots, P_6$ in terms of P_0. We can now substitute Table 16.5's expressions for P_1, $P_2, \ldots, P_6$ into

$$P_0 + P_1 + \cdots + P_6 = 1,$$

and then solve for P_0. The computations proceed as follows:

$$P_0 + P_1 + P_2 + P_3 + P_4 + P_5 + P_6 = 1 \rightarrow P_0 + (1.2500)P_0 + (0.7812)P_0 + (0.4883)P_0 + (0.3052)P_0 + (0.1907)P_0 + (0.1192)P_0 = 1$$

$$\rightarrow (1.0000 + 1.2500 + 0.7812 + 0.4883 + 0.3052 + 0.1907 + 0.1192)P_0 = 1$$

$$\rightarrow 4.1346 P_0 = 1$$

$$\rightarrow P_0 = \frac{1}{4.1346} = 0.2419$$

TABLE 16.4 Formulae for P_n for Our Basic Queueing System with a Finite Queue Capacity

$$P_n = \begin{cases} \dfrac{\left(\dfrac{\lambda}{\mu}\right)^n}{n!} P_0 & \text{for } n = 1, 2, \ldots, s \\[4ex] \dfrac{\left(\dfrac{\lambda}{\mu}\right)^n}{s! s^{n-s}} P_0 & \text{for } n = s+1, s+2, \ldots, s+m \end{cases}$$

TABLE 16.5 Expressions for $P_1, P_2, \ldots P_6$ in Terms of P_0

$$P_1 = \frac{\left(\dfrac{\lambda}{\mu}\right)^1}{1!} P_0 = \frac{\left(\dfrac{25}{20}\right)^1}{1!} P_0 = 1.2500\, P_0$$

$$P_2 = \frac{\left(\dfrac{\lambda}{\mu}\right)^2}{2!} P_0 = \frac{\left(\dfrac{25}{20}\right)^2}{2!} P_0 = 0.7812\, P_0$$

$$P_3 = \frac{\left(\dfrac{\lambda}{\mu}\right)^3}{s!\, s^{3-s}} P_0 = \frac{\left(\dfrac{25}{20}\right)^3}{2!\, 2^{3-2}} P_0 = 0.4883\, P_0$$

$$P_4 = \frac{\left(\dfrac{\lambda}{\mu}\right)^4}{s!\, s^{4-s}} P_0 = \frac{\left(\dfrac{25}{20}\right)^4}{2!\, 2^{4-2}} P_0 = 0.3052\, P_0$$

$$P_5 = \frac{\left(\dfrac{\lambda}{\mu}\right)^5}{s!\, s^{5-s}} P_0 = \frac{\left(\dfrac{25}{20}\right)^5}{2!\, 2^{5-2}} P_0 = 0.1907\, P_0$$

$$P_6 = \frac{\left(\dfrac{\lambda}{\mu}\right)^6}{s!\, s^{6-s}} P_0 = \frac{\left(\dfrac{25}{20}\right)^6}{2!\, 2^{6-2}} P_0 = 0.1192\, P_0$$

Finally, we substitute $P_0 = 0.2419$ into Table 16.5's expressions, thereby obtaining

$$
\begin{aligned}
P_1 &= 1.2500 P_0 = (1.2500)(0.2419) = 0.3024 \\
P_2 &= 0.7812 P_0 = (0.7812)(0.2419) = 0.1890 \\
P_3 &= 0.4883 P_0 = (0.4883)(0.2419) = 0.1181 \\
P_4 &= 0.3052 P_0 = (0.3052)(0.2419) = 0.0738 \\
P_5 &= 0.1907 P_0 = (0.1907)(0.2419) = 0.0461 \\
P_6 &= 0.1192 P_0 = (0.1192)(0.2419) = 0.0288
\end{aligned}
$$

The last of these probabilities, P_6, has a special interpretation. P_6 equals the probability that both servers are busy and 4 callers are already on hold, or, equivalently, the probability that a caller will get a busy signal. Consequently, $P_6 = 0.0288$ implies that 2.88% of the callers to WAIT will get a busy signal.

For WAIT's problem, it is instructive to compare the percentage of callers who get a busy signal for several alternative values of m. Table 16.6 provides this comparison. We have already verified the computations $m = 4$. An end-of-chapter exercise requests you to verify the computations for several of the remaining values of m. From Table 16.6, WAIT can see how the percentage of callers who get a busy signal is affected by the maximum number of callers who can be placed on hold. For example, if WAIT is willing to have up to 5 percent of its callers get a busy signal, then it can have $m = 3$ hold lines, 1 fewer than it now has. In contrast, if WAIT is willing to have no more than 1 percent of its callers get a busy signal, then it must have $m = 7$ hold lines, 3 more than it now has.

Here is summary of how to compute the percentage of blocked customers:

TABLE 16.6 Percentage of Callers
Who Get a Busy Signal ($P_2 + {}_m$)
for Several Values of m

m	Percentage of Callers Who Get a Busy Signal
$m = 0$	25.8%
$m = 1$	13.9%
$m = 2$	8.0%
$m = 3$	4.8%
$m = 4$	2.9%
$m = 5$	1.8%
$m = 6$	1.1%
$m = 7$	0.7%

Procedure for Computing the Percentage of Blocked Customers in a Basic Queueing System with a Finite Queue Capacity

Let

λ = average arrival rate
μ = average service rate
s = number of servers
m = queue's capacity

To compute the percentage of blocked customers, we proceed as follows:

1. Use the formulae in Table 16.4 to express $P_1, P_2, \ldots, P_{s+m}$ in terms of P_0.

2. Substitute step 1's expressions into

$$P_0 + P_1 + \cdots + P_{s+m} = 1$$

and then solve for the value of P_0.

3. Substitute step 2's value for P_0 into step 1's expressions to obtain values for $P_1, P_2, \ldots, P_{s+m}$.

The percentage of blocked customers equals $P_{s+m} \times 100\%$.

Two observations about our basic queueing system with a finite queue capacity are of interest:

- It is *not* required that $\lambda < s\mu$ for this queueing system to attain a steady-state condition. Consequently, we may use Table 16.4's formulae to obtain steady-state results for any values of λ, μ, and s.

- Although we discussed only the computation of $P_0, P_1, \ldots, P_{s+m}$, the values of the operating characteristics L, W, L_q, W_q would also be of interest. For example, in WAIT's problem, W_q equals the average amount of time a caller spends on hold. Fortunately, there are formulae that enable us to compute these additional operating characteristics. To conserve space, we omit the details. However, a well-designed software package routinely prints the values of all operating characteristics.

16.7 OUR BASIC QUEUEING SYSTEM WITH A FINITE CALLING POPULATION

We consider now the version of our basic model in which the size of the calling population is a specified finite value m. Thus, when the number of customers in the system is m, there can be no further arrivals until at least one customer is served, leaves the queueing system, and subsequently returns.

The most common example of a queueing system with a finite calling population is known as the *machine repair problem*. In this problem, there exist m machines that fail from time to time. A failed machine is repaired by one of a crew of s repair persons. The m machines constitute the calling population, and the s repair persons are the servers. Each failed machine corresponds to a "customer" within the queueing system, whereas each operating machine corresponds to a customer outside the queueing system.

To illustrate a queueing system with a finite calling population, consider the following machine repair problem:

> Däagen Hazs produces ice cream in $m = 5$ machines that are subject to failure. A failed machine is repaired by one member of a crew of $s = 2$ repair persons. Däagen Hazs estimates the following:
>
> - Once repaired, the time until the machine fails again has an exponential probability distribution with a mean failure rate of $\lambda = 0.2$ failures per hour (or, equivalently, a mean time to failure of $1 / \lambda = 5$ hours).
>
> - The time required for a repair person to repair a failed machine has an exponential probability distribution with a mean repair rate of $\mu = 0.5$ repairs per hour (or, equivalently, a mean repair time of $1 / \mu = 2$ hours).

Däagen Hazs would like to know the operating characteristics of its repair system, particularly the average number of failed machines.

To begin our analysis, we note that the number of customers in the queueing system cannot exceed m. Thus, the steady-state probabilities for the number of customers in the queueing system are nonzero only for

$$P_0, P_1, P_2, \ldots, P_m.$$

For example, since $m = 5$ in Däagen Hazs's problem, there can never be more than 5 failed machines. Consequently, only

$$P_0, P_1, P_2, \ldots, P_5.$$

are nonzero.

Table 16.7 displays formulae for

$$P_1, P_2, \ldots, P_m$$

stated in terms of P_0. These formulae, plus the fact that

$$P_0 + P_1 + \cdots + P_m = 1,$$

TABLE 16.7 Formulae for P_n for Our Basic Queueing System with a Finite Calling Population

$$
P_n = \begin{cases} \dfrac{m!}{(m-n)!n!} \left(\dfrac{\lambda}{\mu} \right)^n P_0 & \text{for } n = 1, 2, \ldots, s \\[3ex] \dfrac{m!}{(m-n)!s!s^{n-s}} \left(\dfrac{\lambda}{\mu} \right)^n P_0 & \text{for } n = s+1, s+2, \ldots, m \end{cases}
$$

enable us to calculate the queueing system's operating characteristics. To illustrate, let us apply Table 16.7's formulae to Däagen Hazs's problem. Substituting $s = 2$, $m = 5$, $\lambda = 0.2$, and $\mu = 0.5$ into the formulae, we obtain Table 16.8's expressions for $P_1, P_2, \ldots, P_5$ in terms of P_0. We can now substitute Table 16.8's expressions for $P_1, P_2, \ldots, P_5$ into

$$P_0 + P_1 + \cdots + P_5 = 1,$$

and then solve for P_0. The computations proceed as follows:

$$P_0 + P_1 + P_2 + P_3 + P_4 + P_5 = 1 \rightarrow P_0 + (2.0000)P_0 + (1.6000)P_0 + (0.9600)P_0 + (0.3840)P_0 + (0.0768)P_0 = 1$$

$$\rightarrow (1.0000 + 2.0000 + 1.6000 + 0.9600 + 0.3840 + 0.0768)P_0 = 1$$

$$\rightarrow 6.0208P_0 = 1$$

$$\rightarrow P_0 = \frac{1}{6.0208} = 0.1661$$

Finally, we substitute $P_0 = 0.1161$ into Table 16.8's expressions, thereby obtaining

$$
\begin{aligned}
P_1 &= 2.0000P_0 = (2.0000)(0.1661) = 0.3322 \\
P_2 &= 1.6000P_0 = (1.6000)(0.1661) = 0.2658 \\
P_3 &= 0.9600P_0 = (0.9600)(0.1661) = 0.1595 \\
P_4 &= 0.3840P_0 = (0.3840)(0.1661) = 0.0638 \\
P_5 &= 0.0768P_0 = (0.0768)(0.1661) = 0.0128
\end{aligned}
$$

Recall from the last sentence in the statement of Däagen Hazs's problem that the operating characteristic of most interest is the average number of failed machines. Since each failed machine corresponds to a customer in the queueing system, the average number of failed machines equals, L, the average number of customers in the queueing system. To compute L, it is convenient to summarize P_0, $P_1, \ldots, P_5$ in the following format:

n	0	1	2	3	4	5
P_n	0.1161	0.3322	0.2658	0.1595	0.0638	0.0128

TABLE 16.8 Expressions for $P_1, P_2, \ldots, P_5$ in Terms of P_0

$$P_1 = \frac{m!}{(m-1)!1!}\left[\frac{\lambda}{\mu}\right]^1 P_0 = \frac{5!}{(5-1)!1!}\left[\frac{0.2}{0.5}\right]^1 P_0 = 2.0000P_0$$

$$P_2 = \frac{m!}{(m-2)!2!}\left[\frac{\lambda}{\mu}\right]^2 P_0 = \frac{5!}{(5-2)!2!}\left[\frac{0.2}{0.5}\right]^2 P_0 = 1.6000P_0$$

$$P_3 = \frac{m!}{(m-3)!s!s^{3-s}}\left[\frac{\lambda}{\mu}\right]^3 P_0 = \frac{5!}{(5-3)!2!2^{3-2}}\left[\frac{0.2}{0.5}\right]^3 P_0 = 0.9600P_0$$

$$P_4 = \frac{m!}{(m-4)!s!s^{4-s}}\left[\frac{\lambda}{\mu}\right]^4 P_0 = \frac{5!}{(5-4)!2!2^{4-2}}\left[\frac{0.2}{0.5}\right]^4 P_0 = 0.3840P_0$$

$$P_5 = \frac{m!}{(m-5)!s!s^{5-s}}\left[\frac{\lambda}{\mu}\right]^5 P_0 = \frac{5!}{(5-5)!2!2^{5-2}}\left[\frac{0.2}{0.5}\right]^5 P_0 = 0.0768P_0$$

TABLE 16.9 Average
Number of Failed Machines
(L) for Several Values of s

s	L
$s = 1$	$L = 2.674$
$s = 2$	$L = 1.661$
$s = 3$	$L = 1.457$
$s = 4$	$L = 1.430$
$s = 5$	$L = 1.429$

Summing the products of nP_n for $n = 0, 1, \ldots, 5$, we obtain

$$
\begin{aligned}
L &= \text{(average value of } n) \\
&= 0P_0 + 1P_1 + 2P_2 + 3P_3 + 4P_4 + 5P_5 \\
&= 0(0.1661) + 1(0.3322) + 2(0.2658) + 3(0.1595) + 4(0.0638) + 5(0.0128) \\
&= 1.6609
\end{aligned}
$$

Thus, on average, there are $L = 1.661$ failed machines.

For Däagen Hazs's problem, it is instructive to compare the value of L for several alternative values of s. Table 16.9 provides this comparison. We have already verified the computations for $s = 2$. An end-of-chapter exercise requests you to verify the computations for several of the remaining values of s. From Table 16.9, Däagen Hazs can see how the value of L is affected by the number of repair persons. For example we see that, if Däagen Hazs were to increase the number of its repair persons from $s = 2$ to $s = 3$, a slight reduction in L would result; however, further increases in s result in only negligible reductions in L.

The following is a summary of how to compute average number of customers in the system:

**Procedure for
Computing L in
a Basic Queueing
System with a
Finite Calling
Population**

Let

$$
\begin{aligned}
\lambda &= \text{average arrival rate} \\
\mu &= \text{average service rate} \\
s &= \text{number of servers} \\
m &= \text{calling population's size}
\end{aligned}
$$

To compute L, we proceed as follows:

1. Use the formulae in Table 16.7 to express $P_1, P_2, \ldots, P_m$ in terms of P_0.

2. Substitute step 1's expressions into

$$
P_0 + P_1 + \cdots + P_m = 1
$$

and then solve for the value of P_0.

3. Substitute step 2's value for P_0 into step 1's expressions to obtain values for $P_1, P_2, \ldots, P_m$.

4. Compute L using the formula

$$
L = 0P_0 + 1P_1 + 2P_2 + \cdots + mP_m.
$$

Two observations about our basic queueing system with a finite queue capacity are of interest:

- It is *not* required that $\lambda < s\mu$ for the queueing system to attain a steady-state condition. Consequently, we may use Table 16.7's formulae to obtain steady-state results for any values of λ, μ, and s.

- Although we discussed only the computation of P_0, P_1, ..., P_m and L, the values of the operating characteristics W, L_q, W_q would also be of interest. For example, in Däagen Hazs's problem, W equals the average time that elapses between a machine's failure and its return to operation (i.e., a machine's average downtime). Fortunately, there are formulae that enable us to compute these additional operating characteristics. To conserve space, we omit the details. However, a well-designed software package routinely prints the values of all operating characteristics.

16.8 A COST-MINIMIZING APPROACH TO SELECTING FROM AMONG ALTERNATIVE QUEUEING SYSTEMS

Up to this point, we have focused on how to compute a queueing system's operating characteristics. We will see now that we can sometimes use the operating characteristics to explicitly evaluate the queueing system's hourly (or daily, or whatever) operating costs. When this is possible, we can choose among several alternative queueing systems by computing the hourly operating cost of each and selecting the alternative with the minimum cost.

To illustrate, let us reconsider Däagen Hazs's machine repair problem from Section 16.7. Recall that 5 machines are currently being serviced by 2 repair persons. Suppose Däagen Hazs is willing to consider employing more or less than its current 2 repair persons. What is the best number? To answer this question, Däagen Hazs can adopt either a *service-level approach* or a *cost-minimizing approach*. Let us consider each in turn.

To use a service-level approach, Däagen Hazs specifies a value that must not be exceeded by L, the average number of failed machines. For example, if the average number of failed machines is not to exceed 1.5, then $L \leqslant 1.5$ must hold. Examining Table 16.9, we see that the lowest value of s for which $L \leqslant 1.5$ holds is $s = 3$. Consequently, Däagen Hazs should hire an additional repair person.

The drawback here is that the decision on how many servers to hire is not based on the costs of operating the queueing system. To remedy this drawback, Däagen Hazs must be willing and able to specify the following two costs:

$$C_s = \text{cost of employing one server for one hour}$$

$$C_w = \text{cost of one machine's being failed for one hour}$$

Once Däagen Hazs assigns values to C_s and C_w, it can then compute the queueing system's total hourly operating costs by summing the following two components:

1. **Service cost.** Since employing one repair person for one hour costs C_s, then sC_s is the hourly cost of employing s servers. Using $C_s = 25$, Figure 16.9(a) tabulates and graphs sC_s for alternative value of s. Observe (from either the table or graph) that sC_s increases as s increases.

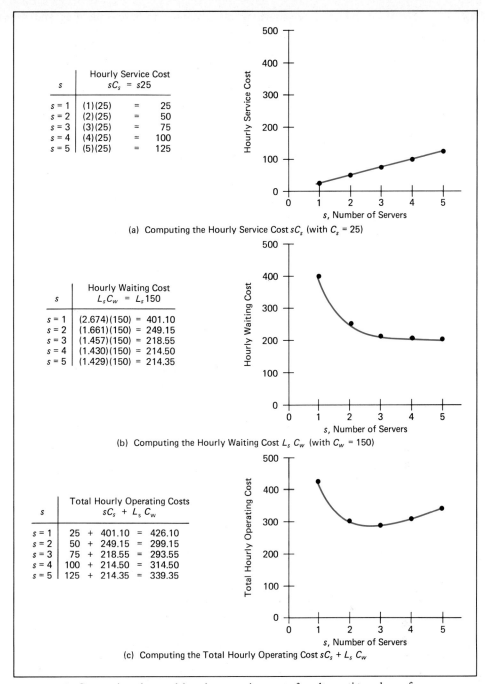

s	Hourly Service Cost $sC_s = s25$		
$s = 1$	(1)(25)	=	25
$s = 2$	(2)(25)	=	50
$s = 3$	(3)(25)	=	75
$s = 4$	(4)(25)	=	100
$s = 5$	(5)(25)	=	125

(a) Computing the Hourly Service Cost sC_s (with $C_s = 25$)

s	Hourly Waiting Cost $L_s C_w = L_s 150$		
$s = 1$	(2.674)(150)	=	401.10
$s = 2$	(1.661)(150)	=	249.15
$s = 3$	(1.457)(150)	=	218.55
$s = 4$	(1.430)(150)	=	214.50
$s = 5$	(1.429)(150)	=	214.35

(b) Computing the Hourly Waiting Cost $L_s C_w$ (with $C_w = 150$)

s	Total Hourly Operating Costs $sC_s + L_s C_w$			
$s = 1$	25	+	401.10	=	426.10
$s = 2$	50	+	249.15	=	299.15
$s = 3$	75	+	218.55	=	293.55
$s = 4$	100	+	214.50	=	314.50
$s = 5$	125	+	214.35	=	339.35

(c) Computing the Total Hourly Operating Cost $sC_s + L_s C_w$

Figure 16.9 Computing the total hourly operating costs for alternative values of s

2. **Waiting cost.**[6] When s repair persons are employed, let L_s denote the average number of failed machines. Since one machine's being failed for one hour costs C_w, then $L_s C_w$ is the average hourly cost of having an average of L_s machines failed. Observe that $L_s C_w$ is an *average* hourly waiting cost. During each hour, the actual hourly cost will fluctuate; however, on average, it will be $L_s C_w$. Using $C_w = 150$ and using Table 16.9 to determine L_s for a

---

[6] Throughout this section, the waiting cost includes the cost of both waiting in the queue and waiting for service to be completed.

given value of s, Figure 16.9(b) tabulates and graphs $L_s C_w$ for alternative value of s. Observe that $L_s C_w$ decreases as s increases.

To summarize, the total hourly operating cost is given by

total hourly operating cost = (hourly service cost) + (hourly waiting cost)

These two cost components behave in the opposite manner. When s is low, the service cost $s C_s$ is low, but the waiting cost $L_s C_w$ is high. Conversely, when s is high, the service cost $s C_s$ is high, but the waiting cost $L_s C_w$ is low. Däagen Hazs's goal is to choose s to minimize $s C_s + L_s C_w$. To achieve this goal, Däagen Hazs adds the tables and graphs in Figure 16.9(a) and (b), obtaining those in Figure 16.9(c). Examining either the table or graph, Däagen Hazs concludes that the number of repair persons that minimizes the total hourly operating costs is $s = 3$.

At this point let us summarize the cost-minimizing approach to selecting the number of servers:

A Cost-Minimizing Approach to Selecting the Number of Servers

1. Estimate C_s, the hourly cost per server, and C_w, the hourly waiting cost per customer in the queueing system.

2. For each alternative value of s, tabulate and/or graph the hourly service cost $s C_s$.

3. For each alternative value of s, tabulate and/or graph the hourly waiting cost $L_s C_w$.

4. For each alternative value of s, sum the results of steps 2 and 3 to obtain a tabular and/or graphical representation of

$$\text{total hourly costs} = s C_s + L_s C_w.$$

5. Using the results of step 4, select the value of s that minimizes the total hourly costs.

Why is the cost-minimizing approach often difficult to implement? The difficulty arises in the estimation of C_w. Given a server's wages and benefits, C_s is usually easy to estimate. In contrast, the estimation of C_w is difficult. What does it cost for one customer to wait one hour in the queueing system? The answer depends on the relationship of the customer to the organization operating the queueing system. There are two cases to consider:

1. The customers are *internal* to the organization operating the queueing system; that is, the organization either employs the customers if they are persons or owns them if they are machines (e.g., a firm's secretaries waiting to use a pool of duplicating machines or a firm's failed personal computers waiting to be repaired by an in-house repair person).

2. The customers are *external* to the organization operating the queueing system; that is, the organization neither employs nor owns the customers (e.g., customers waiting in a queue at a bank, patients waiting in a hospital's emergency room, or students waiting in registration lines).

If the customers are internal to the organization, C_w can usually be estimated accurately by computing the profit foregone when one unproductive employee or machine waits in the queueing system for one hour. However, when the customers are external to the organization, estimating C_w is difficult. For example, consider a bank. A bank incurs costs when it consistently has a long queue, because some customers will be motivated to switch their accounts to another bank. Although a bank can easily recognize that there are costs associated with consistently having a long queue, it is virtually impossible for the bank to estimate the cost per minute per waiting customer. As another example, consider a hospital's emergency room. A hospital incurs costs when its emergency room consistently has a long queue, because a long patient wait may aggravate the injury or illness, thereby increasing the likelihood of a costly lawsuit. Although a hospital can easily recognize that these costs exist, it is virtually impossible for the hospital to estimate the cost per minute per waiting patient. To summarize:

> When a queueing system's customers are external to the organization operating the queueing system, it is difficult to estimate C_w, hence it is difficult to implement the cost-minimizing approach to selecting the number of servers. In such situations, a service-level approach is the only alternative.

16.9 A TAXONOMY FOR QUEUEING SYSTEMS

The variety of queueing systems is virtually endless. To provide a means of concisely specifying the queueing system under consideration, there exists a taxonomy based on the following notation:

$$A/B/s,$$

where A is a code that designates the probability distribution governing the interarrival time, B is a code that designates the probability distribution governing the service time, and s is the number of servers. Some frequently used codes are

M designates that the interarrival time or service time is governed by an exponential probability distribution.

D designates that, instead of being governed by a probability distribution, the interarrival time or service time is a known constant (e.g., always equal to 5 minutes).

GI or G designates that the interarrival time or service time, respectively, is governed by some unspecified probability distribution with a known mean and variance.

For example, an $M/G/3$ queueing system is one in which the interarrival time has an exponential probability distribution, the service time has an unspecified probability distribution, and there are 3 servers. As additional examples, in Second National Bank's problem, options 1, 2, and 3 are each an $M/M/1$ queueing system, and option 4 is an $M/M/2$ queueing system. Although we did not use this taxonomy in prior sections, we have introduced it now because you may well encounter it elsewhere.

16.10 CONCLUDING REMARKS

This chapter's survey of queueing analysis has taken only a small "bite" out of the subject. Space constraints have precluded our discussing anything more complex than our basic queueing system, our basic system with a finite queue capacity, and our basic system with a finite calling population. We have also had to omit the mathematical analysis necessary to derive the formulae for the operating characteristics. Despite these omissions, we have gained insight into how queueing analysis provides information that is useful to a manager responsible for the operation of a queueing system.

We should note that sometimes a queueing system is so complex that mathematicians have been unable to derive formulae for its operating characteristics. It is then necessary to determine the operating characteristics by *simulation,* the topic of the next chapter.

16.11 CHAPTER CHECKLIST AND GLOSSARY

Quickly review this chapter by rereading the material highlighted by a vertical line in the left margin. You should then be familiar with the concepts, techniques, and terminology in the Checklist and Glossary that follow. If you need "help" with a particular item, consult the section or sections indicated for a more detailed discussion.

Checklist of Concepts and Techniques

☐ Real-world examples of queueing systems. [16.1, 16.5, 16.6, 16.7]

☐ The nine characteristics that must be specified to describe a queueing system. [16.2]

☐ The definitions of the operating characteristics P_n, L, W, L_q, and W_q. [16.3]

☐ The properties of the exponential probability distribution. [16.4]

☐ Computing the operating characteristics for our basic queueing system. [16.5]

☐ Computing the operating characteristics for our basic queueing system with a finite queue capacity. [16.6]

☐ Computing the operating characteristics for our basic queueing system with a finite calling population. [16.7]

☐ Selecting from among alternative queueing systems using a service-level approach. [16.8]

☐ Selecting from among alternative queueing systems using a cost-minimizing approach. [16.8]

☐ A taxonomy for queueing systems. [16.9]

Glossary

Queue. A line of waiting customers. [16.1]

Queueing analysis. The mathematical study of queues. [16.1]

Calling population. The set of customers who require the queueing system's service from time to time. [16.2]

Interarrival time. The time between consecutive arrivals to a queueing system. [16.2]

Queue capacity. The maximum number of customers the queue can contain at any one time. [16.2]

Service discipline. The rule by which a customer in the queue is selected to be the one to receive service next. [16.2]

Service mechanism. The portion of the queueing system that provides service to the customers. [16.2]

Service facility. A component of the service mechanism that provides a particular type of service to the customers. [16.2]

Single-facility queueing system. A queueing system whose service mechanism consists of just one service facility that all customers must pass through. [16.2]

Multifacility queueing system. A queueing system whose service mechanism consists of a set of service facilities arranged in some configuration, often in such a way that the departures from one service facility are arrivals to one or more other service facilities. [16.2]

Single-server service facility. A service facility with a single server. [16.2]

Multiserver service facility. A service facility with at least two identical servers, each of whom is capable of providing service to any customer. [16.2]

Service time. The time a server spends servicing a customer. [16.2]

Operating characteristics. The characteristics of a queueing system, such as P_n, L, W, L_q, and W_q. [16.3]

Transient condition. The condition of the queueing system for a period during which operating characteristics depend on the conditions present when the system began operation and on the time that has elapsed since the system began operation. [16.3]

Steady-state condition. The condition of the queueing system after it is no longer in a transient condition—that is, after it has been operating long enough that the operating characteristics are independent of the conditions present when the system began operation and of the time that has elapsed since the system began operation. [16.3]

Exponential probability distribution. A probability distribution used frequently in queueing analysis as the one that governs the interarrival times and/or the service times. [16.4]

Mean arrival rate (λ). The average number of customer arrivals per unit of time. [16.4]

Mean service rate (μ). The average number of service completions per unit of time by a continuously busy server. [16.4]

Lack-of-memory property. A property (unique to the exponential probability distribution) that states that the probability distribution of the *remaining* time until the next occurrence of an incident is always the same, regardless of how much time has elapsed since the most recent incident. [16.4]

Utilization factor (ρ). The ratio of the mean arrival rate (λ) to the product of the number of servers (s) and the mean service rate (μ); that is, $\rho = \lambda/s\mu$. [16.5]

Service-level approach. An approach to selecting from among alternative queueing systems in which a manager rules out any queueing system that does not meet a specified level of service (e.g., $L \leqslant 5$). [16.8]

Cost-minimizing approach. An approach to selecting from among alternative queueing systems in which a manager selects the queueing system that minimizes the total hourly operating costs, including both the hourly service cost and the hourly waiting cost. [16.8]

EXERCISES

The first exercise asks you to provide real-world examples of the various service disciplines discussed in Section 16.2.

16.1. In Section 16.2, we described four alternative service disciplines: FIFO, LIFO, random, and priority. Provide a real-world example of each of these service disciplines.

Exercises 16.2–16.8 test your understanding of the exponential probability distribution.

*16.2. Assume that the interarrival time between consecutive customers at a queueing system has an exponential probability distribution with a mean arrival rate of 2 customers per hour.
   (a) What is the average interarrival time?
   (b) Graph the interarrival time's probability density function (in a manner similar to Figure 16.4).
   (c) Suppose a customer has just arrived. What is the probability that the next customer will arrive within the next 15 minutes?
   (d) Suppose a customer has just arrived. What is the probability that the next customer will not arrive within the next 15 minutes but will arrive within the next 1 hour and 15 minutes?
   (e) Suppose a customer has just arrived. What is the probability that the next customer will not arrive within the next 1 hour and 15 minutes?
   (f) Suppose the most recent customer arrived one-half hour ago. What is the probability that the next customer will not arrive within the next 1 hour and 15 minutes?
   (g) What property of the exponential probability distribution is illustrated by your answers to parts (e) and (f)?

16.3. Assume that the time required by a queueing system's server to serve a customer has an exponential probability distribution with a mean service rate of 8 customers per hour.
   (a) What is the average service time?
   (b) Graph the service time's probability density function (in a manner similar to Figure 16.4).
   (c) Suppose the server has just begun to serve a customer. What is the probability that the server will complete the customer's service within the next 2 minutes?
   (d) Suppose the server has just begun to serve a customer. What is the probability that the server will not complete the customer's service within the next 2 minutes but will do so within the next 10 minutes?
   (e) Suppose the server has just begun to serve a customer. What is the probability that the server will not complete the customer's service within the next 10 minutes?

   (f) Suppose the server began serving a customer one hour ago. What is the probability that the server will not complete this customer's service within the next 10 minutes?
   (g) What property of the exponential probability distribution is illustrated by your answers to parts (e) and (f)?

16.4. A phone company is performing a queueing analysis of its directory-assistance operators. The company wants to assume that the interarrival time between consecutive calls for directory assistance is governed by an exponential probability distribution with parameter λ. To estimate λ, the company notes that 480 calls for directory assistance were made in a particular four-hour period. Based on this information, the company estimates that $\lambda = (4/480) = (1/120)$. Do you agree with this estimate? Explain why or why not.

16.5. A bank is performing a queueing analysis of its tellers. The bank wants to assume that the time a teller requires to serve a customer is governed by an exponential probability distribution with parameter μ. To estimate μ, the bank observes that during a particular four-hour period when five tellers were working, 240 customers were served. Based on this information, the bank estimates that $\mu = \frac{240}{(4)(5)} = 12$. Do you agree with this estimate? Explain why or why not.

*16.6. Suppose a random variable T has an exponential probability distribution with parameter α. In Section 16.4, we computed that the probability that T takes on a value less than or equal to one-half of its mean is 0.3935.
   (a) Compute the probability that T takes on a value less than or equal to one-quarter of its mean.
   (b) Compute the probability that T takes on a value less than or equal to its mean. Also compute the probability that T takes on a value greater than or equal to its mean.
   (c) Compare your answers to part (b) to the corresponding probabilities you would compute if T had a normal probability distribution.

16.7. Angela, Marshella, and Latasha sell tickets at a box office for a theater that holds rock concerts. Let T_A, T_M, and T_L denote random variables representing the respective times required by Angela, Marshella, and Latasha to process a customer's ticket order. Assume the following:

   ■ T_A has an exponential probability distribution with a mean service rate of $\frac{1}{4}$ customer per

742

minute (or, equivalently, with a mean service time of 4 minutes).

- T_M has a normal probability distribution with a mean of 4 minutes and a standard deviation of 1 minute.
- T_L has a uniform probability distribution over the interval from 1 to 7 minutes.

(a) Provide a verbal description of each of the following probabilities:

$$Pr\{T_A \geqslant 2 \,|\, T_A \geqslant 1\}, \; Pr\{T_A \geqslant 4$$
$$|\, T_A \geqslant 3\}, \text{ and } Pr\{T_A \geqslant 6 \,|\, T_A \geqslant 5\};$$
$$Pr\{T_M \geqslant 2 \,|\, T_M \geqslant 1\}, \; Pr\{T_M \geqslant 4$$
$$|\, T_M \geqslant 3\}, \text{ and } Pr\{T_M \geqslant 6 \,|\, T_M \geqslant 5\};$$
$$Pr\{T_L \geqslant 2 \,|\, T_L \geqslant 1\}, \; Pr\{T_L \geqslant 4$$
$$|\, T_L \geqslant 3\}, \text{ and } Pr\{T_L \geqslant 6 \,|\, T_L \geqslant 5\}.$$

(b) Compute each of the above probabilities. (Use Table 15.2 to obtain the probabilities you need for the normal probability distribution.)

(c) Explain why the probabilities computed in part (b) illustrate that the exponential distribution is the only probability distribution with the lack-of-memory property.

16.8. A barber shop has two barbers, Vince and Joe. Three brothers—Andrew, Jonathan, and Alex—enter the barber shop when both barbers are idle. Vince begins to cut Andrew's hair, and Joe begins to cut Jonathan's hair. Alex must wait; he will have his hair cut by either Vince or Joe, whoever finishes first. Assume that the time required by either barber to complete a haircut has the same exponential probability distribution.

(a) What is the probability that Alex is the last of the three brothers to have his haircut completed?

(b) Do you think it is realistic to assume the service time for a barber has an exponential probability distribution? Why or why not?

Exercises 16.9–16.19 test your understanding of our basic queueing system.

*16.9. Melvin's Market has an "express" checkout for customers with twelve items or less. The interarrival time for customers at the express checkout has an exponential probability distribution with a mean time between arrivals of 90 seconds. The checkout time for a customer at the express checkout has an exponential probability distribution with a mean checkout time that depends on whether a cashier has the help of a bagger. With a bagger's help, the average time a cashier needs to check out a customer is 50 seconds; without a bagger's help, the aver-

age time is 72 seconds. Consider the situations in which a cashier has and does not have a bagger's help, and construct a table that compares these situations with respect to the following operating characteristics:

(a) The probability that there are no customers at the express checkout.

(b) The average number of customers at the express checkout.

(c) The average time a customer spends at the express checkout.

(d) The average number of customers waiting to use the express checkout.

(e) The average time a customer spends waiting to use the express checkout.

16.10.[7] The Metropolis Public Housing Authority (MPHA) maintains a waiting list of families who have applied to live in a public housing project that consists of several hundred three-bedroom apartments. MPHA's records indicate the following:

- The interarrival time for new applications has an exponential probability distribution with a mean arrival rate of 58 applications per year.
- The time between consecutive vacancies at the housing project has an exponential probability distribution with a mean rate of 60 vacancies per year.

Because of the desirability of the project's housing units, MPHA has found that an insignificant number of families withdraw their names from the waiting list or refuse to accept the housing offered to them.

(a) What is the probability that the waiting list is empty?

(b) What is the average number of families on the waiting list?

(c) What is the average amount of time a family spends on the waiting list?

16.11.[8] Gus's gas station has only a single pump and, thus, can serve only one car at a time. The time required to service a car at Gus's has an exponential probability distribution with a mean service time of $[3 + (G/4)]$ minutes, where G is the average number of gallons purchased each time a customer stops for gas. Currently, $G = 12$ gallons, and the interarrival

---

[7] This exercise is a simplified version of an actual application reported in the following reference: E. H. Kaplan, "Analyzing Tenant Assignment Policies," *Management Science,* **33**, No. 3 (March 1987), pp. 395–408.

[8] This exercise is a simplified version of the scenario analyzed in the following reference: Warren J. Erikson, "Management Science and the Gas Shortage," *Interfaces,* **4**, 4 (August 1974), pp. 47–51.

time for customers at Gus's has an exponential probability distribution with a mean arrival rate of 4 customers per hour.

(a) Under current conditions, what is the average number of cars waiting to buy gas at Gus's, and what is the average amount of time a car must wait to get to the gas pump?

(b) Now suppose that Gus's customers think there is a gasoline shortage when there really is not. Because of the imagined shortage, customers begin to stop at Gus's three times as often; that is, G now equals 4 gallons (instead of 12), and the mean arrival rate now equals 12 customers per hour (instead of 4). Under these new conditions, what is the average number of cars waiting to buy gas, and what is the average amount of time a car must wait to get to the pump?

(c) Because of the imagined shortage, what has been the percentage increase in the average number of waiting cars and in the average waiting time per car?

*16.12. All trucks traveling on a particular stretch of interstate highway are required by law to stop at a weigh station. The interarrival time for trucks approaching the weigh station has an exponential probability distribution with a mean arrival rate of 15 trucks per hour. The time required to weigh a truck has an exponential probability distribution with a mean weighing time of 3 minutes.

(a) Assuming there is only a single weighing scale, compute the following quantities:
  (i) the average number of trucks at the weigh station,
  (ii) the average time a truck spends at the weigh station,
  (iii) the average number of trucks waiting for their weighings to begin,
  (iv) the average time a truck spends waiting for its weighing to begin.

(b) Redo part (a), this time assuming that there are 2 weighing scales and that trucks form a single queue to wait for the first available scale.

(c) Suppose that, if there are two or more trucks waiting in the queue, an approaching truck driver is tempted to pass the station and risk being caught and ticketed by the state police. For both the case of one scale and the case of two scales, compute the probability a truck driver will be tempted to pass the station.

16.13. At the Lafayette Post Office, the interarrival time between consecutive customers has an exponential probability distribution with a mean arrival rate of 100 customers per hour. For each of the 4 postal clerks, the time required to serve a customer has an exponential probability distribution with a mean service time of 2 minutes. Consider the following two cases:

■ *Four Distinct Queues.* There is a distinct queue in front of each postal clerk (with no jockeying between lines). As customers arrive, they are equally likely to join any of the four queues. Hence, the mean arrival rate at each postal clerk is 25 customers per hour.

■ *A Single Queue.* As customers arrive, they must join a single queue to wait for the first available postal clerk.

(a) For each of these cases, compute the average time a customer waits until his or her service begins.

(b) What general principle does this exercise illustrate?

16.14. The Monroeville city government receives requests for commercial building inspections at a mean rate of 5 per day. The interarrival time between these requests has an exponential probability distribution. The time required to inspect a commercial building has an exponential probability distribution with a mean inspection rate (when continuously busy) of 2 buildings per day. Monroeville is considering maintaining a staff of 3, 4, or 5 commercial building inspectors. Construct a table that compares these three staffing levels with respect to the following operating characteristics:

(a) The probability that all inspectors are idle.
(b) The probability that all inspectors are busy.
(c) The average number of idle inspectors.
(d) The average number of buildings waiting for their inspections to begin.
(e) The average time a building must wait until its inspection begins.

16.15. The 911 number of the city of Turtle Creek receives emergency calls for a life-support vehicle (LSV) at a mean rate of 15 calls per hour. The interarrival time between these calls has an exponential probability distribution. The time that elapses from the dispatch of an LSV in response to a call until the LSV is available to respond to another call has an exponential probability distribution with a mean of 48 minutes. Turtle Creek defines the *average response time* as the average time between the receipt of call and the dispatch of an LSV. Turtle Creek wants an LSV fleet of sufficient size to keep average response time to less than 2 minutes.

(a) Turtle Creek is considering two different sizes for its fleet of LSVs: 15 LSVs or 20 LSVs. For each of these fleet sizes, use Figure 16.8 or an available computer software package to compute the average response time. (*Hint:* If you use Figure 16.8 to determine L, then use the last formula in Table 16.2(b) to determine L_q and then use the second-to-the-last formula in Table 16.2(b) to determine W_q.)

(b) Does either of the fleet sizes meet Turtle Creek's goal of an average response time of less than 2 minutes?

16.16. Consider the formula in Table 16.2(a) for W_q in the single-server version of our basic queueing system. Assuming that the mean service rate μ equals 10, graph how the value of W_q changes as the mean arrival rate λ varies between 0 and 10.

*16.17. Consider the formulae in Table 16.2(a) for L, W, L_q, and W_q in the single-server version of our basic queueing system. Using these formulae, determine what happens to L, W, L_q, and W_q if the mean arrival rate λ and the mean service rate μ are both doubled.

16.18. Reconsider our analysis in Section 16.5 of option 1 (the status quo) in the Second National Bank's problem. In that analysis, we computed that $L = 4.0$ and $L_q = 3.2$. Suppose that, after reviewing this analysis, Cassie, the Vice President for Operations at Second National Bank, says we must have made a mistake. Cassie argues that whereas our computed values for L and L_q differ by $4.0-3.2 = 0.8$, they should differ by 1.0. Her reasoning is that since the total number of persons at the ATM equals the number of persons in the queue plus the one person using the ATM, $L = L_q + 1$ should be true. How would you convince Cassie that she is wrong?

16.19. Consider the formulae in Table 16.2 for the operating characteristics of our basic queueing system.
(a) Use the formula for the single-server model in part (a) of Table 16.2 to derive the following formula:

$$W = W_q + \frac{1}{\mu} .$$

Observe that this formula also appears as the formula for W in the multiserver model in part (b) of the table. Explain why $W = W_q + \frac{1}{\mu}$ makes sense intuitively.

(b) Use the formulae for the single-server model in part (a) and the multiserver model in part (b) of Table 16.2 to derive the following formulae:

$$L = \lambda W$$

$$L_q = \lambda W_q$$

Explain why these two formulae make sense intuitively. (*Note:* These two formulae are known as *Little's formulae;* they apply not only to our basic queueing system but also to many other queueing systems.)

(c) Explain why the three formulae derived in parts (a)–(c) enable us to use a known value for L, L_q, W, or W_q to compute the values of the remaining three.

Exercises 16.20–16.23 test your understanding of our basic queueing system with a finite queue capacity.

16.20. In our analysis of WAIT's problem in Section 16.6, we verified the row in Table 16.6 corresponding to $m = 4$. Verify now the following rows in Table 16.6:
(a) The row corresponding to $m = 0$.
(b) The row corresponding to $m = 2$.
(c) The row corresponding to $m = 6$.

*16.21. Nationwide Rental Car has an 800 number that customers can call to reserve a car. The telephone system Nationwide uses to process calls to the 800 number has 3 reservation agents and, when all agents are busy, has the capability to place up to 3 callers on hold. Nationwide estimates that

■ The interarrival time for callers to the 800 number has an exponential probability distribution with a mean interarrival time of 2 minutes.
■ The time required by an agent to complete a caller's reservation has an exponential probability distribution with a mean service time of 6 minutes.

Assume that a caller who obtains a busy signal reserves a car from one of Nationwide's competitors.
(a) What is the probability all agents are idle?
(b) What is the probability a caller gets placed on hold?
(c) What is the probability a caller gets a busy signal?

16.22. Jackie's is a fast-food restaurant with a drive-up window as well as inside counter service. Cars waiting to use the drive-up window must wait in a special lane which has space for the car at the window plus 4 waiting cars. If a car arrives when the drive-up lane is filled to capacity, it cannot join the queue because it would illegally block traffic on the highway along which Jackie's is located. Assume that, if a car is unable to join the queue, it drives to a competitor of Jackie's. The interarrival time for cars wanting to use the drive-up window has an exponential probability distribution with a mean arrival rate of 20 cars per hour. The time required to serve a car at the drive-up window has an exponential probability distribution with a mean service time of $3\frac{1}{3}$ minutes. What percentage of cars wanting to use Jackie's drive-up window are unable to do so?

16.23. In addition to the traditional labor, delivery, and recovery rooms in the maternity unit of St. Andrew's hospital, there are 4 Alternative Birthing Center (ABC) rooms. Except for a special bed, ABC rooms are furnished much like a bedroom at home (e.g., wallpaper, pictures, and so on). The entire birthing process—labor, delivery, and recovery—takes place in an ABC room. Over the past several years, more and more couples have been requesting to use an ABC room if one is available at the time of admission to the hospital. (If none are available, the couple must use the traditional sequence of a labor room, followed by a delivery room, followed by a recovery room.) St. Andrew's records indicate the following:

- The time between consecutive arrivals of couples who want to use an ABC room has an exponential probability distribution with a mean arrival rate of 1 couple per hour.
- The time a couple (and the eventual child) spend in an ABC room before being transferred to a normal hospital room has an exponential probability distribution with a mean of 5 hours.

(a) What is the probability that a couple who wants to use an ABC room will be unable to do so?

(b) How would the answer to part (a) change if St. Andrew's were to build a fifth ABC room?

Exercises 16.24–16.28 test your understanding of our basic queueing system with a finite calling population.

16.24. In our analysis of Däagen Haz's problem in Section 16.7, we verified the row in Table 16.9 corresponding to $s = 2$. Verify now the following rows in Table 16.9:

(a) The row corresponding to $s = 1$.

(b) The row corresponding to $s = 3$.

(c) The row corresponding to $s = 5$.

*16.25. Zrox employs 3 service technicians to repair 6 copiers it rents to businesses in the area. Once repaired, the time until a copier fails again has an exponential probability distribution with a mean time to failure of 2 days. The time required by a technician to repair a copier (including travel time to the copier) has an exponential probability distribution with a mean repair time of $\frac{1}{2}$ day.

(a) What is the probability that all technicians are idle?

(b) What is the probability that all technicians are busy?

(c) What is the average number of idle technicians?

(d) What is the average number of failed copiers?

16.26. A pool of 3 secretaries provides typing service to 7 managers. Assume that a manager never submits a request for typing until his or her previous request has been returned. Once a manager's typing has been returned, the time until he or she submits a new request has an exponential probability distribution with a mean time until submission of 1 hour. The time required for a typist to complete a manager's typing request has an exponential probability distribution with a mean completion time of $\frac{1}{2}$ hour.

(a) What is the probability that all secretaries are idle?

(b) What is the probability that no secretary is idle?

(c) What is the average number of idle secretaries?

(d) What is the average number of typing requests either currently being typed or waiting to be typed?

(e) What is the average number of typing requests that are waiting to be typed?

16.27. When Jeff's Pizzeria is fully staffed at dinner time, there are 4 waitresses. Unfortunately, waitress turnover is high. Once hired, the time until a waitress quits has an exponential probability distribution with a mean length of employment of 5 months. In almost all cases, a waitress quits with no advance notice. When Jeff's needs to hire waitresses, the time required to do so has an exponential probability distribution with a mean hiring rate of 2 waitresses per month.

(a) What is the probability that Jeff's is fully staffed?

(b) What is the average number of unfilled waitress positions?

(c) Although only 4 waitresses are needed, suppose Jeff's is willing to hire 5 waitresses in recognition of the fact that there will often be at least one unfilled position. Under this new assumption, what is the probability that Jeff's is fully staffed or overstaffed?

16.28. A single machine is maintained by a single service technician. Once the machine has been repaired, the time until it fails again has an exponential probability distribution with a parameter of λ. Once the machine has failed, the time required by the technician to repair it has an exponential probability distribution with a parameter of μ.

(a) What is the probability (in terms of λ and μ) that the machine is failed?

(b) What is the probability that the machine is operational?

Exercises 16.29–16.33 test your understanding of how to use a cost-minimizing approach to select from alternative queueing systems.

*16.29. To promote its reputation for fast service, Earl's While-U-Wait Automotive Tune-up Shop promises to reduce a customer's bill by $0.20 for every minute the customer must wait until his or her car's tune-up is finished. The interarrival time for Earl's customers has an exponential probability distribution with a mean arrival rate of 5 customers per hour. The time required by a mechanic to perform a tune-up has an exponential probability distribution with a mean tune-up rate (when continuously busy) of 2 cars per hour. Earl is considering maintaining a staff of 3, 4, or 5 mechanics. A mechanic's salary is $20 per hour. Define Earl's total hourly cost as the sum of two components: (1) the cost per hour of the mechanics and (2) the profit lost per hour because of reductions of customers' bills. Estimate the total hourly cost if Earl employs 3, 4, or 5 mechanics. Which number of mechanics results in the lowest total? (*Hint:* If you have worked Exercise 16.14, you can save some computational effort by noting that, except for the unit of time measurement, the data for Exercise 16.14 and this exercise are identical.)

16.30. Reconsider Earl's problem in Exercise 16.29. In that exercise, we assume that a mechanic earns $20 per hour and can perform a tune-up in a time that has an exponential probability distribution with a mean tune-up rate (when continuously busy) of 2 cars per hour. Let us call such a mechanic a class B mechanic. In comparison to a class B mechanic, a class A mechanic earns an hourly salary that is 50% higher, and he or she works at a speed that is 50% faster. More specifically, a class A mechanic earns $30 per hour and can perform a tune-up in a time that has an exponential probability distribution with a mean tune-up rate (when continuously busy) of 3 cars per hour. Suppose in this exercise that Earl is considering a staff consisting of either *two* class A mechanics or *three* class B mechanics. In thinking about his staffing decision, Earl observes the following:

- The total hourly salary for two class A mechanics is (2)($30) = $60 per hour. The total hourly salary for three class B mechanics is (3)($20) = $60 per hour, the same as for two class A mechanics.
- Two class A mechanics can perform tune-ups at a total rate of (2)(3) = 6 cars per hour. Three class B mechanics can perform tune-ups at a total rate of (3)(2) = 6 cars per hour, the same as two class A mechanics.

Given these two observations, Earl concludes that he should be indifferent between a staff of two class A mechanics or three class B mechanics. Is Earl correct? If so, why; if not, which alternative should he prefer?

16.31. Reconsider Zrox's problem in Exercise 16.25. Now assume the following:

- It costs Zrox $120 per day to employ a service technician.
- Zrox rents its copiers to businesses at the rate of $150 per day but, under the terms of its rental contract, receives no rental when a copier is failed.

Define Zrox's total daily cost as the sum of two components: (1) the cost per day for the technicians and (2) the rental fees lost per day because of failed copiers. Estimate the total daily cost Zrox will incur if it employs 1, 2, or 3 technicians. Which number of technicians results in the lowest total daily cost?

16.32. Reconsider Nationwide's problem in Exercise 16.21. Now assume the following:

- It costs Nationwide $15 per hour to employ a reservation agent, including the cost of the agent's phone line.
- For each hold line Nationwide has, it incurs a cost of $0.25 per hour.
- Nationwide's average profit per customer is $50.

Define Nationwide's total cost per hour as the sum of three components: (1) the cost per hour for the reservation agents, (2) the cost per hour for the hold lines, and (3) the profit lost per hour because callers receive busy signals and, hence, reserve a car from one of Nationwide's competitors.
(a) Estimate the total hourly cost for Nationwide's current telephone system. (*Hint:* To obtain the average number of callers per hour who get a busy signal, multiply the average number of calls per hour by the probability that a caller gets a busy signal.)
(b) Estimate the total hourly cost if Nationwide adds another agent and keeps the same number of hold lines.
(c) Estimate the total hourly cost if Nationwide keeps the same number of agents and adds another hold line.
(d) Which telephone system—part (a)'s, (b)'s, or (c)'s—results in the lowest total hourly cost?

16.33. Martha's and Erica's Cookie Company (MECC) wants to decide on how large of a crew it should use to load the trucks that pick up its cookies for delivery to customers. The interarrival time for

747

trucks at MECC has an exponential probability distribution with a mean arrival rate of 2 trucks per hour. Since MECC has only one loading dock, only one truck can be loaded at a time. The time required to load a truck has an exponential probability distribution with a mean loading time of $20/n$ minutes, where n is the size of the crew that loads the trucks. For example if $n = 5$, the crew's mean loading time is 4 minutes or, equivalently, the crew's mean loading rate (when continuously busy) is 15 trucks per hour. Assume the following cost data:

- Each member of the loading crew receives a salary of $15 per hour.

- The trucking firm MECC uses to deliver its cookies to its customers charges MECC $160 for each hour a truck spends being loaded or waiting to be loaded.

Define MECC's total hourly cost as the sum of two components: (1) the cost per hour for members of the loading crew and (2) the cost per hour for trucks being loaded or waiting to be loaded. If MECC wants to minimize its total hourly cost, what should be the size of its loading crew? Support your answer with a comparison of the total hourly costs for alternative crew sizes.

17

SIMULATION

17.1 INTRODUCTION

This chapter discusses a management science technique known as *simulation*. Broadly defined,

> A simulation is an experiment in which we attempt to understand how something will behave in reality by imitating its behavior in an artificial environment that approximates reality as closely as possible.

Additional introductory comments about simulation will be more meaningful after we have seen an example. Consequently, we will postpone a general overview of simulation until Section 17.4.

To introduce the concept of simulation, consider the following scenario:

May N. Tayne is responsible for scheduling maintenance of the various mechanical and electrical components of a plant's assembly line. Her immediate concern is a rubber belt that drives the assembly line's conveyer system. Until now, May has replaced this belt only when it broke, a policy she calls a *replace-only-at-failure policy*. She is now having second thoughts about this policy because it appears to be too costly. When the belt breaks, the entire assembly line shuts down until a new one is installed. Furthermore, the breaking of a belt often causes incidental damage to surrounding components, thereby adding further delay and cost to returning the assembly line to operation.

May now wants to consider a policy known as an *age replacement policy*. This policy calls for replacing a belt either when it fails or when it reaches the age of T days, where T is a prespecified constant. For example, if $T = 10$ days, May replaces a belt

TABLE 17.1 The Probability Distributuion that Governs a Belt's Lifetime

Lifetime (days)	8	9	10	11	12
Probability	0.12	0.21	0.34	0.21	0.12

Average lifetime = $(8)(0.12) + (9)(0.21) + (10)(0.34)$
$+ (11)(0.21) + (12)(0.12) = 10$

either when it fails or when it has operated successfully for 10 days, whichever occurs first. Thus, under an age replacement policy, there are two types of replacements: an *unplanned replacement*, which occurs when a belt fails, and a *planned replacement*, which occurs when a belt becomes too old.

A planned replacement is cheaper than an unplanned replacement. The primary reason is that a planned replacement does not require shutting down the production line, because May can "cheat a little" and postpone the replacement slightly so that it occurs during the lunch hour or after working hours. Despite this advantage, it is not obvious to May that an age replacement policy is cheaper than her current replace-only-at-failure policy. The former would consume more belts per year than the latter, and belts are expensive.

To aid her decision making, May has collected the following data:

- She estimates that each unplanned replacement costs $1000. This includes the cost of the belt, the labor cost of an unplanned replacement, the average costs of an idle assembly line during the replacement (e.g., the wages of the workers), and the average cost of any incidental damage caused when the belt breaks.

- She estimates that each planned replacement costs $770. This includes the cost of the belt plus the labor cost of a planned replacement.[1]

- She estimates that a belt's lifetime (i.e., the elapsed time from a belt's installation to its failure) is governed by the probability distribution displayed in Table 17.1.

Based on this data, May wants to determine if she should switch from a replace-only-at-failure policy to an age replacement policy and, if so, what value she should assign to T, the age that triggers a planned replacement. Hence, she must evaluate six policies: the replace-only-at-failure policy and age replacement policies with $T = 7$, $T = 8$, $T = 9$, $T = 10$, and $T = 11$.[2]

May could solve her problem by trying a different policy during each of the next six years and then implementing the policy with the lowest annual cost. This approach has two obvious flaws: (1) it takes six years to determine the optimal policy and (2) the costs incurred during the five years in which the optimal policy is not in use would be unnecessary if May knew the optimal policy now. Instead of conducting this real-life experiment, May would greatly prefer to evaluate alternative policies in an artificial environment where real belts become imaginary belts, years become minutes, and real dollars become "funny money." Let us see how to create such an environment using the technique of simulation.

---

[1] The costs of unplanned and planned replacements must include the cost of the belt to account for the fact that different policies consume belts at different rates.

[2] It is unnecessary to consider an age replacement policy with T less than 7 or greater than 11 because, according to Table 17.1, a belt always lasts at least 7 days and never lasts more than 12 days.

17.2 SIMULATING A STOCHASTIC EVENT USING A RANDOM NUMBER GENERATOR

A *stochastic event* is an event whose outcome is uncertain (e.g., a belt's lifetime in May's problem). To describe a stochastic event, we specify the alternative outcomes and the probability distribution that governs which outcome occurs (e.g., Table 17.1 in May's problem). Using this probability distribution, we can simulate a stochastic event without actually waiting for it to occur.

To illustrate, let us simulate the operation and failure of belts in May's problem. We will simplify matters at the start by temporarily assuming that a belt's lifetime is governed by the probability distribution in Table 17.2 instead of Table 17.1. To simulate this probability distribution, we need a device that generates a 9 with a probability of 0.2, a 10 with a probability of 0.5, and an 11 with a probability of 0.3.

The following is one of many ways to create such a device:

1. Cut out 10 identical slips of paper.
2. Label one slip with the number 0, another with the number 1, another with the number 2, and so on until the last slip is labeled with the number 9.
3. Place the slips of paper in a hat.
4. Shake the hat, select a slip of paper at random, record the number on the slip, and place the slip back into the hat.
5. Using Table 17.3, convert the recorded number into a lifetime.
6. Repeat steps 1–5 as many times as needed. (For example, if we want to simulate the lifetimes of 25 consecutive belts, we perform 25 repetitions.)

Since we have an equal chance of selecting each number and since Table 17.3 assigns 2 of the 10 numbers to a lifetime of 9, we will generate a lifetime of 9 with a probability of 0.2. A similar comment applies to the probability of generating a 10 or an 11. Note that Table 17.3 is not the only assignment of random numbers that simulates Table 17.2's probability distribution. All that is necessary is to assign 20% of the numbers to a lifetime of 9, 50% to 10, and 30% to 11. However, it is customary and convenient to assign consecutive numbers to each outcome.

Steps 1–4 of the above process are an example of what is known as a *random number generator*, a process in which each number in a specified interval (the

TABLE 17.2 A Simplified Probability Distribution for a Belt's Lifetime

Lifetime (days)	9	10	11
Probability	0.2	0.5	0.3

TABLE 17.3 Assignment of Random Numbers to Table 17.2's Probability Distribution

Lifetime (days)	9	10	11
Probability	0.2	0.5	0.3
Random numbers	0–1	2–6	7–9

751

integers from 0 to 9 in our example) has an equal probability of occurring. Although a hat containing 10 slips of paper is a random number generator that is easy to visualize, it is cumbersome to use. A more convenient one is a table of random numbers such as Table 17.4. Observe that

- The table contains 1000 single-digit numbers. The grouping of the digits into sets of five is simply to facilitate reading the table.

- Each digit is a random selection from the ten integers 0, 1, 2, . . . , 9. We can imagine that each digit was generated by randomly selecting from a hat containing ten slips of paper, each labeled with a different integer in the interval from 0 through 9.

- In using the table to generate a sequence of random digits, we can start at any digit. However, once we select the starting digit, we should continue by moving from left-to-right and row-by-row. Haphazardly selecting each digit (e.g., by closing your eyes and pointing) will usually not result in a truly random sequence of digits.

- Although Table 17.4 will be sufficient for our purposes, a real-world simulation would require a table with more digits. Larger tables are readily available.[3]

- When a computer performs a simulation, it has a more efficient way to generate random numbers than by storing a larger version of Table 17.4 in its memory. In Section 17.8 we will discuss how computers generate random numbers, as well as several other topics pertaining to random number generation.

---

[3] For example, consult *A Million Random Digits With 100,000 Normal Deviates* (New York: The Free Press, 1955).

TABLE 17.4 Table of 1000 Random Digits

96420	62515	41296	21912	65481	21626	19243	72395	92319	61543
34413	12081	13203	14957	33406	13637	62110	77462	85465	79933
20232	82459	76877	05673	51651	86542	95319	64943	27406	89450
94271	64016	21127	72920	19076	31783	47749	09640	53395	23021
05192	56204	87516	86414	42653	17270	47466	37688	14459	32340
20501	56096	84158	53637	56468	10802	25683	33635	75682	61104
17359	09629	51959	30652	52355	92487	20823	37214	46293	70137
09059	08719	94854	61534	04917	31885	00255	14711	36667	87229
63029	88662	81803	21932	85185	25560	33292	15427	02488	95799
72947	64714	00862	77100	53478	82686	83497	93471	33347	82763
09906	23853	01467	29083	18342	95077	46030	89966	84289	29889
86502	45166	60362	32844	15847	42262	83946	19889	50990	10751
32827	73654	12191	76379	94550	85727	66332	74902	09335	29993
34417	06623	55222	07047	95034	16545	95228	22204	10047	54205
56808	00372	17510	78362	58936	44202	17423	04918	53600	73473
60597	68315	31312	57741	85109	21615	24365	27684	16124	33888
14966	35303	69921	85774	04920	69672	86816	63027	84470	45605
16732	46740	21680	65999	47520	16217	04174	47462	21938	97990
73498	65812	41065	12509	23607	52680	51702	66541	69455	37258
61794	58872	04115	11416	09631	98974	68157	76101	65273	53814

To illustrate the use of Table 17.4, let us simulate the lifetimes of 10 consecutive belts, assuming that a belt's lifetime is governed by Table 17.2's probability distribution. The first 10 digits in Table 17.4 are

9, 6, 4, 2, 0, 6, 2, 5, 1, 5.

According to Table 17.3, this sequence of random numbers corresponds to the following sequence of lifetimes:

		Belt								
	1	2	3	4	5	6	7	8	9	10
Random number	9	6	4	2	0	6	2	5	1	5
Corresponding lifetime in Table 17.3	11	10	10	10	9	10	10	10	9	10

The probability distribution in Table 17.2 is easy to simulate, not only because there are just three alternative lifetimes but also because the corresponding probabilities are multiples of 0.1. The latter characteristic enables us to simulate a belt's lifetime by generating only a single-digit random number.

To illustrate a case where we must generate two-digit random numbers, let us now assume that a belt's lifetime is governed by the probability distribution in Table 17.1 (the distribution specified in the statement of May's problem). If we were to use only the ten digits from 0 through 9, it would be impossible to assign 12% of them to a lifetime of 8, 21% to a lifetime of 9, and so on. Suppose, however, that we use the two-digit numbers from 00 through 99. We can then simulate Table 17.1's probability distribution using the assignment of random numbers displayed in Table 17.5. Note that, of the 100 random numbers from 00 to 99, Table 17.5 assigns 12% to a lifetime of 8, 21% to a lifetime of 9, 34% to a lifetime of 10, 21% to a lifetime of 11, and 12% to a lifetime of 12. These percentages correspond precisely to the probabilities in Table 17.1.

Let us use Table 17.5 to simulate the lifetimes of 10 consecutive belts. This time, when we use Table 17.4 to generate random numbers, we must use pairs of digits. In Table 17.4, the first 10 pairs of digits (ignoring the spaces after every fifth digit) are

96, 42, 06, 25, 15, 41, 29, 62, 19, 12.

According to Table 17.5, this sequence of random numbers corresponds to the following sequence of lifetimes:

		Belt								
	1	2	3	4	5	6	7	8	9	10
Random number	96	42	06	25	15	41	29	62	19	12
Corresponding lifetime in Table 17.5	12	10	8	9	9	10	9	10	9	9

TABLE 17.5 Assignment of Random Numbers to Table 17.1's Probability Distribution

Lifetime (days)	8	9	10	11	12
Probability	0.12	0.21	0.34	0.21	0.12
Random numbers	00–11	12–32	33–66	67–87	88–99

TABLE 17.6 Probability Distribution Whose Simulation Requires Three-digit Random Numbers

Lifetime (days)	8	9	10	11	12
Probability	0.123	0.199	0.333	0.207	0.138

TABLE 17.7 Assignment of Random Numbers to Table 17.6's Probability Distribution

Lifetime (days)	8	9	10	11	12
Probability	0.123	0.199	0.333	0.207	0.138
Random numbers	000–122	123–321	322–654	655–861	862–999

If the probability distribution we are trying to simulate contains at least one probability that is not a multiple of 0.01, then we must generate a random number that consists of at least three digits. To illustrate, suppose a belt's lifetime is governed by the probability distribution in Table 17.6. Can you devise an appropriate assignment of the 1000 random numbers from 000 to 999 to each lifetime? You will find one such assignment in Table 17.7. When using this table to simulate the lifetimes of consecutive belts, we must use three-digit random numbers obtained by grouping the digits in Table 17.4 into triplets.

In this text, we assume that it is sufficient to approximate any probability to three decimal places (i.e., $\frac{1}{6}$ becomes 0.167). Thus, we will never need more than a three-digit random number.

17.3 USING SIMULATION TO ANALYZE MAY'S BELT REPLACEMENT PROBLEM

We are now ready to use simulation to analyze May's belt replacement problem. Throughout this section, we assume a belt's lifetime is governed by Table 17.1's probability distribution and, hence, we use Table 17.5's assignment of random numbers to the alternative lifetimes. Also, before we begin our simulation, we should recall that an unplanned replacement costs $1000 and a planned replacement costs $770.

Let us first simulate the replace-only-at-failure policy. Table 17.8 displays a simulation of this policy for 25 consecutive belt replacements. The following commentary summarizes the first and second belt replacements:

- In Table 17.4, the first pair of random digits is 96. Using Table 17.5, this corresponds to a belt lifetime of 12 days. At the end of this lifetime, there is a cost of $1000 for an unplanned replacement. The cumulative time (i.e., the elapsed time since the simulation began) is now 12 days, and the cumulative cost (i.e., the total cost since the simulation began) is now $1000.

- In Table 17.4, the second pair of random digits is 42. Using Table 17.5, this corresponds to a lifetime of 10 days. At the end of this lifetime, there is once again a cost of $1000 for an unplanned replacement. The cumulative time is now 22 days, and the cumulative cost is now $2000.

Before proceeding, verify several of the remaining 23 belt replacements.

TABLE 17.8 Manual Simulation of the Replace-Only-At-Failure Policy

Belt	Random Number	Corresponding Lifetime	Cost Associated with Lifetime	Cumulative Time	Cumulative Cost
1	96	12	1000	12	1000
2	42	10	1000	22	2000
3	06	8	1000	30	3000
4	25	9	1000	39	4000
5	15	9	1000	48	5000
6	41	10	1000	58	6000
7	29	9	1000	67	7000
8	62	10	1000	77	8000
9	19	9	1000	86	9000
10	12	9	1000	95	10,000
11	65	10	1000	105	11,000
12	48	10	1000	115	12,000
13	12	9	1000	124	13,000
14	16	9	1000	133	14,000
15	26	9	1000	142	15,000
16	19	9	1000	151	16,000
17	24	9	1000	160	17,000
18	37	10	1000	170	18,000
19	23	9	1000	179	19,000
20	95	12	1000	191	20,000
21	92	12	1000	203	21,000
22	31	9	1000	212	22,000
23	96	12	1000	224	23,000
24	15	9	1000	233	24,000
25	43	10	1000	243	25,000

Using the cumulative time and cumulative cost in the last row of Table 17.8, we can estimate the average daily cost of the replace-only-at-failure policy as follows:

$$\text{average daily cost} = \frac{\text{cumulative cost}}{\text{cumulative time}} = \frac{25,000}{243} = \$102.88 \text{ per day.}$$

Actually, there is no need to use simulation to estimate this average daily cost. We can compute its exact value as follows:

$$\text{average daily cost} = \frac{\text{cost of unplanned replacement}}{\text{average belt lifetime from Table 17.1}}$$

$$= \frac{1000}{10}$$

$$= \$100 \text{ per day.}$$

Although we need not simulate the replace-only-at-failure policy, we did so for two reasons. First, it serves as a simple example. Second, the difference between the average daily cost's exact value (\$100.00) and its simulated value (\$102.88) illustrates explicitly that simulation provides only an estimate. We will discuss this point in more detail later in this section.

Let us now simulate an age replacement policy with $T = 9$ days, one of the five age replacement policies May can use. In conducting this simulation, we will assume that if a belt's lifetime is 9 days, it fails sometime on its ninth day of operation before it reaches the age of 9 days. Thus, a lifetime of 8 or 9 days results in an unplanned replacement at a cost of $1000, whereas a lifetime of 10, 11, or 12 days results in a planned replacement after 9 days at a cost of $770.

Table 17.9 displays a simulation of an age replacement policy with $T = 9$ days for 25 consecutive belt replacements. The following commentary summarizes the first three belt replacements:

- So that our simulation of the age replacement policy uses the same imaginary belts as did our simulation of the replace-only-at-failure policy, we return to the start of Table 17.4 to generate our first random number. The first pair of random digits is 96. Using Table 17.5, this corresponds to a belt lifetime of 12 days. However, because we are using an age replacement policy with $T = 9$, the belt is replaced after 9 days. This is indicated in Table 17.9's third column by the notation "12 → 9." At the end of this reduced lifetime, there is a cost of $770 for a planned replacement. The cumulative time is now 9 days, and the cumulative cost is now $770.

- The second belt replacement is similar to the first. Before proceeding, verify the second row of Table 17.9.

- In Table 17.4, the third pair of random digits is 06. Using Table 17.5, this corresponds to a lifetime of 8 days. At the end of this lifetime, there is a cost of $1000 for an unplanned replacement. The cumulative time is now 27 days, and the cumulative cost is now $2540.

Before proceeding, verify several of the remaining 22 belt replacements. Using the cumulative time and cumulative cost in Table 17.9's last row, we can estimate the

TABLE 17.9 Manual Simulation of an Age Replacement Policy with $T = 9$

Belt	Random Number	Corresponding Lifetime			Cost Associated with Lifetime	Cumulative Time	Cumulative Cost
1	96	12	→	9	770	9	770
2	42	10	→	9	770	18	1540
3	06	8			1000	26	2540
4	25	9			1000	35	3540
5	15	9			1000	44	4540
6	41	10	→	9	770	53	5310
7	29	9			1000	62	6310
8	62	10	→	9	770	71	7080
9	19	9			1000	80	8080
10	12	9			1000	89	9080
11	65	10	→	9	770	98	9850
12	48	10	→	9	770	107	10,620
13	12	9			1000	116	11,620
14	16	9			1000	125	12,620
15	26	9			1000	134	13,620
16	19	9			1000	143	14,620
17	24	9			1000	152	15,620
18	37	10	→	9	770	161	16,390
19	23	9			1000	170	17,390
20	95	12	→	9	770	179	18,160
21	92	12	→	9	770	188	18,930
22	31	9			1000	197	19,930
23	96	12	→	9	770	206	20,700
24	15	9			1000	215	21,700
25	43	10	→	9	770	224	22,470

TABLE 17.10 Summary of a Computer Simulation of May's Problem

	Number of Runs						
	25	50	100	250	500	750	1000
Replace-only-at-Failure	101.21	100.60	101.32	100.77	100.32	100.04	100.07
Age replacement with $T = 7$	110.00	110.00	110.00	110.00	110.00	110.00	110.00
Age replacement with $T = 8$	98.55	99.70	99.99	100.62	99.87	99.82	99.70
Age replacement with $T = 9$	96.64	97.59	97.44	96.59	95.89	95.35	95.54
Age replacement with $T = 10$	99.24	97.93	98.66	97.62	97.34	96.81	96.85
Age replacement with $T = 11$	99.63	98.49	99.73	99.18	98.63	98.44	98.45

average daily cost of an age replacement policy with $T = 9$ days as $22{,}470/224 = \$100.31$ per day.

Our simulations have thus far terminated after 25 belt replacements. Let us call each belt replacement a *run* of the simulation. To obtain an accurate estimate of a policy's average daily cost, we need to perform a large number of runs. How many runs is large enough? Given the introductory nature of this chapter, we will leave this question unanswered.[4] However, we can at least illustrate that the accuracy of the simulated average daily cost increases as the number of runs increases. In particular, Table 17.10 summarizes the results of using a computer program to perform 25, 50, 100, 250, 500, 750, and 1000 runs for the six policies May must analyze.[5] The following aspects of the table merit discussion:

- Looking at the column corresponding to 25 runs, we see that the computer-generated estimates of the average daily cost for the replace-only-at-failure policy and the age replacement policy with $T = 9$ days are $\$101.21$ and $\$96.64$, respectively. These differ from the estimates we obtained via manual simulation ($\$102.88$ and $\$100.31$, respectively). The differences are due to the computer's use of random numbers that differed from those in Table 17.4. The differences between the computer-generated estimates and the manually-generated estimates illustrate that, since a simulation uses random numbers, its results are random. It is important to understand that the computer-generated estimates after 25 runs are not better than our estimates; they are just different.

- Looking at the row corresponding to the replace-only-at-failure policy, we see that, as the number of runs increases, the estimates of the average daily costs get closer and closer to the exact value of $\$100.00$. This illustrates that, the larger the number of runs is, the more accurate the results tend to be. Note that improved accuracy for more runs is an overall trend, not a guarantee. For example, the estimate for the replace-only-at-failure policy is actually slightly worse after 1000 runs than after 750 runs. This slight worsening is once again due to the randomness of results obtained via simulation.

- Looking at the column corresponding to 1000 runs (the column we expect to contain the most accurate estimates), we are tempted to conclude that the optimal policy is an age replacement policy with $T = 9$ days. However, given

---

[4] There are formal statistical techniques for determining how many runs are necessary to obtain a specified degree of accuracy in the estimate of the average daily cost.

[5] There is no need to use simulation to analyze an age replacement policy with $T = 7$ days. Under this policy, there will always be a planned replacement every 7 days (before the belt has a chance to fail). Hence, the average daily cost's exact value is $770/7 = \$110$ per day.

the randomness of results obtained via simulation, we should not be too hasty. Using a more cautious approach, we might proceed as follows:

1. Select the best two policies based on 1000 runs.

2. Simulate another 1000 runs for each of these two policies. (Since these new runs involve different random numbers, their results will differ from the original runs.)

3. Average the results of the new runs with those of the original runs.

4. Implement the policy giving the best results for the average of the new and original runs.

This approach has the advantage of focusing the additional computational effort only on those policies with the highest likelihood of being optimal.

17.4 AN OVERVIEW OF SIMULATION

Our analysis of May's belt replacement problem has illustrated the following general principles:

- A simulation creates an artificial environment that approximates reality.

- Within this artificial environment, a simulation conducts experiments that would be too costly and too time-consuming to perform in reality.

- Because a simulation involves the generation of random numbers, the data it generates are random.

- Because a simulation generates random data, obtaining accurate results requires the simulation to consist of a large number of repetitions or runs. (We have left unanswered the question of how many runs is large enough.)

- Because of the need for a large number of runs, a simulation is best conducted on a computer.

- When the intent of a simulation is to choose from among several policies, a two-stage approach is recommended. The first stage consists of simulating each policy for a specified number of runs; the second stage consists of performing additional runs only for those policies that the first stage indicates have a high likelihood of being optimal. The chosen policy is the one with the best performance averaged over both stages.

- Because a simulation generates random data, there is no guarantee that the chosen policy is actually the optimal policy.

17.5 SIMULATING A PROJECT WITH STOCHASTIC ACTIVITY DURATIONS[6]

At the conclusion of Section 11.2 we noted briefly that simulation is a useful technique for analyzing a project with stochastic activity durations. In this section we provide the details.

---

[6] This section assumes familiarity with Section 11.2. It may be omitted without loss of continuity.

As our example, let us reconsider the stochastic project displayed in Figure 11.1. For ease of reference, Figure 17.1 is a copy of Figure 11.1. Recall that the table within each activity in Figure 17.1 specifies the probability distribution of the activity's duration. In particular, the column headed d contains the possible durations, and the column headed $Pr\{d\}$ contains the associated probabilities. To simplify our discussion, we assume (as we did in Section 11.2) that the durations of the activities are probabilistically independent of each other.

Our simulation will have the following overall logic:

1. Generate four random numbers, one for each activity, and use them to determine the durations of the activities.

2. Use the durations to determine the critical path and its length.

3. Repeat steps 1 and 2 many times and summarize the results.

Let us now discuss the details of these steps.

Table 17.11 displays for each activity an assignment of random numbers that simulates the probability distribution of the activity's duration. Consider, for example, activity B. Of the 1000 numbers from 000 to 999, two-thirds correspond to a duration for B of 6 and one-third to a duration of 18. Before proceeding, verify the assignments of random numbers to activities A, C, and D. Observe that, whereas A, B, and D require a three-digit random number, C requires only a one-digit random number.

By using Table 17.4 to generate random numbers and then using Table 17.11 to convert them to activity durations, we can simulate the project. Let us arbitrarily begin our random number generation in Table 17.4's sixth row, where the first 10 random digits are:

$$\underbrace{205}_{A}\,\underbrace{015}_{B}\,\underbrace{6}_{C}\,\underbrace{096}_{D}$$

Figure 17.1 Stochastic project from Chapter 11

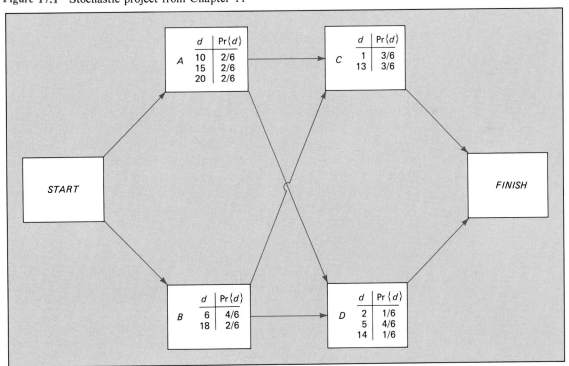

TABLE 17.11 Assignment of Random Numbers to the Probability Distribution of Each Activity's Duration

Activity A			
Duration	10	15	20
Probability	$\frac{2}{6}$	$\frac{2}{6}$	$\frac{2}{6}$
Random numbers	000–332	333–666	667–999

Activity C		
Duration	1	13
Probability	$\frac{3}{6}$	$\frac{3}{6}$
Random numbers	0–4	5–9

Activity B		
Duration	6	18
Probability	$\frac{4}{6}$	$\frac{2}{6}$
Random numbers	000–666	667–999

Activity D			
Duration	2	5	14
Probability	$\frac{1}{6}$	$\frac{4}{6}$	$\frac{1}{6}$
Random numbers	000–166	167–832	833–999

Using Table 17.11, we convert these random numbers to the following durations:

	Activity			
	A	B	C	D
Random number	205	015	6	096
Corresponding duration in Table 17.11	10	6	13	2

Because of the simplicity of Figure 17.1's network, we can identify the critical path by simply enumerating all paths, computing the length of each, and identifying the longest.[7] The network's four paths and their respective lengths are

Path	Length	
START → A → C → FINISH	10 + 13	= 23
START → A → D → FINISH	10 + 2	= 12
START → B → C → FINISH	6 + 13	= 19
START → B → D → FINISH	6 + 2	= 8

For simplicity we shall refer to these four paths as *AC*, *AD*, *BC*, and *BD*. With its length of 23 days, *AC* is the critical path.

Simulating the project just once is of little value. To obtain accurate data, we must perform many runs (i.e., repetitions) of the simulation. Table 17.12 displays 25 runs, the one we already performed and 24 others. For each run, a circle in one of the table's last four columns indicates which path is critical. Before proceeding, verify several other runs. To obtain the random numbers for each run, begin in Table 17.4 where you left off for the previous run.

How do we interpret the results of the simulation runs? The answer is provided by Tables 17.13–17.15. We will discuss each table in turn.

Table 17.13 displays an estimate of the probability that each path is the critical path. For example, to estimate the probability that *BC* is the critical path, we scan the next-to-the-last column of Table 17.12 and observe that circles appear in the rows for Runs 15, 19, and 20. Since *BC* was the critical path in 3 of the 25 runs, we estimate the probability of this occurring as $\frac{3}{25}$. Before proceeding, verify the remaining entries in Table 17.13.

---

[7] Of course, if the project network were large and complex, we would have to employ the formal PERT/CPM technique discussed in Section 10.3.

TABLE 17.12 Manual Simulation of the Stochastic Project

Run	Random Numbers				Activity Durations				Path Length			
	A	*B*	*C*	*D*	*A*	*B*	*C*	*D*	*AC*	*AD*	*BC*	*BD*
1	205	015	6	096	10	6	13	2	㉓	12	19	8
2	841	585	3	637	20	6	1	5	21	㉕	7	11
3	564	681	0	802	15	18	1	5	16	20	19	㉓
4	256	833	3	635	10	18	1	5	11	15	19	㉓
5	756	826	1	104	20	18	1	2	21	㉒	19	20
6	173	590	9	629	10	6	13	5	㉓	15	19	11
7	519	593	0	652	15	6	1	5	16	⑳	7	11
8	523	559	2	487	15	6	1	5	16	⑳	7	11
9	208	233	7	214	10	6	13	5	㉓	15	19	11
10	462	937	0	137	15	18	1	2	1o	17	19	⑳
11	090	590	8	719	10	6	13	5	23	15	19	11
12	948	546	1	534	20	6	1	5	21	㉕	7	11
13	049	173	1	885	10	6	1	14	11	㉔	7	20
14	002	551	4	711	10	6	1	5	11	⑮	7	11
15	366	678	7	229	15	18	13	5	28	20	㉛	23
16	630	298	8	662	15	6	13	5	㉘	20	19	11
17	818	032	1	932	20	6	1	14	21	㉞	7	20
18	851	852	5	560	20	18	13	5	㉝	25	31	23
19	332	921	5	427	10	18	13	5	23	15	㉛	23
20	024	889	5	799	10	18	13	5	23	15	㉛	23
21	729	476	4	714	20	6	1	5	21	㉕	7	11
22	008	627	7	100	10	6	13	2	㉓	12	19	8
23	534	788	2	686	15	18	1	5	16	20	19	㉓
24	834	979	3	471	20	18	1	5	21	㉕	19	23
25	333	478	2	763	15	6	1	5	16	⑳	7	11

○ indicates each run's critical path.

TABLE 17.13 An Estimate after 25 Runs that Each Path Is the Critical Path

Path	Probability That the Path is the Critical Path
AC	$\frac{7}{25} = 0.28$
AD	$\frac{11}{25} = 0.44$
BC	$\frac{3}{25} = 0.12$
BD	$\frac{4}{25} = 0.16$

TABLE 17.14 An Estimate after 25 Runs that Each Activity Is a Critical Activity

Activity	Probability That the Activity is a Critical Activity
A	$\frac{18}{25} = 0.72$
B	$\frac{7}{25} = 0.28$
C	$\frac{10}{25} = 0.40$
D	$\frac{15}{25} = 0.60$

TABLE 17.15 An Estimate after 25 Runs
of the Probability Distribution of the
Project's Duration

Project Duration	Probability of Occurrence
12	$\frac{0}{25}$ = 0.00
15	$\frac{1}{25}$ = 0.04
17	$\frac{0}{25}$ = 0.00
20	$\frac{4}{25}$ = 0.16
22	$\frac{1}{25}$ = 0.04
23	$\frac{8}{25}$ = 0.32
24	$\frac{1}{25}$ = 0.04
25	$\frac{4}{25}$ = 0.16
28	$\frac{1}{25}$ = 0.04
29	$\frac{0}{25}$ = 0.00
31	$\frac{3}{25}$ = 0.12
32	$\frac{0}{25}$ = 0.00
33	$\frac{1}{25}$ = 0.04
34	$\frac{1}{25}$ = 0.04

Table 17.14 displays an estimate of the probability that each activity is a critical activity. For example, to estimate the probability that B is a member of the critical path, we scan Table 17.12's last two columns (the only two columns corresponding to paths containing B) and observe that circles appear in one of these two columns in the rows for Runs 3, 4, 10, 15, 19, 20, and 23. Since B is a critical activity in 7 of the 25 runs, we estimate the probability of this occurring as $\frac{7}{25}$. Before proceeding, verify the remaining entries in Table 17.14.

Table 17.15 displays an estimate of the probability of each alternative project duration.[8] For example, to estimate the probability of a project duration of 20 days, we scan Table 17.12's last four columns and observe that a circle encloses the number 20 in one of these four columns in the rows for Runs 7, 8, 10, and 25. Since the project has a duration of 20 in 4 of the 25 runs, we estimate the probability of this occurring as $\frac{4}{25}$. Before proceeding, verify the remaining entries in Table 17.15.

Tables 17.13–17.15 contain estimates of the exact probabilities displayed in Tables 11.2–11.4. These exact probabilities were computed in Section 11.2 only for the purposes of illustration. In a project having many activities with stochastic durations, it would be impossible to obtain the exact probabilities. We would have to rely on the estimates obtained by simulation.

It is instructive to compare the estimates in Tables 17.13–17.15 to the corresponding exact probabilities in Tables 11.2–11.4. Observe that the estimates are not accurate. The reason is that 25 runs is too few. To obtain accurate estimates, we must perform a large number of runs. How large is large enough? Although

---

[8] To facilitate subsequent comparisons, Table 17.15 includes some project durations that did not occur in our simulation.

TABLE 17.16 An Estimate after 1000 Runs that Each Path Is the Critical Path

Path	Probability That the Path is the Critical Path
AC	$\frac{311}{1000} = 0.311$
AD	$\frac{466}{1000} = 0.466$
BC	$\frac{81}{1000} = 0.081$
BD	$\frac{142}{1000} = 0.142$

TABLE 17.17 An Estimate after 1000 Runs that Each Activity Is a Critical Activity

Activity	Probability That the Activity is a Critical Activity
A	$\frac{777}{1000} = 0.777$
B	$\frac{223}{1000} = 0.223$
C	$\frac{392}{1000} = 0.392$
D	$\frac{608}{1000} = 0.608$

we will once again leave this question unanswered,[9] we can again illustrate that accuracy increases as the number of runs increases. In particular, Tables 17.16–17.18 summarize the results of using a computer program to perform 1000 runs. Comparing these tables to Tables 11.2–11.4, we see that the estimates are much better than after only 25 runs.

We use Tables 17.16–17.18 just as though they were the exact probabilities in Tables 11.2–11.4. Briefly,

- Tables 17.16 and 17.l7 enable us to rank the paths and activities according to their probabilities of being critical. The higher the probability is, the more closely we should monitor the corresponding path or activity once the project begins.

- Table 17.18 enables us to estimate the project's mean duration. We simply multiply each duration in Table 17.18 by its corresponding probability estimate and sum the resulting products. This yields an estimate of the project's mean duration of

$$(12)(0.025) + (15)(0.069) + \cdots + (34)(0.070) = 25.95 .$$

- Table 17.18 also enables us to incorporate an acceptable level of risk into our estimate of the project's duration. For example, suppose we want an estimate of the project's duration for which there is at most a 35% chance of finishing after the estimate or, equivalently, at least a 65% chance of finishing on or before the estimate. To obtain this estimate, we move down from the top of Table 17.18 and sum the probabilities in the second column until the first time the sum exceeds 0.650. You should verify that this summation process results in an estimate for the project duration of 29 days.

---

[9] There are formal statistical techniques for determining how many runs are necessary to obtain a specified degree of accuracy.

TABLE 17.18   An Estimate after 1000 Runs
of the Probability Distribution of the
Project's Duration

Project Duration	Probability of Occurrence
12	$\frac{25}{1000} = 0.025$
15	$\frac{69}{1000} = 0.069$
17	$\frac{14}{1000} = 0.014$
20	$\frac{97}{1000} = 0.097$
22	$\frac{26}{1000} = 0.026$
23	$\frac{157}{1000} = 0.157$
24	$\frac{43}{1000} = 0.043$
25	$\frac{105}{1000} = 0.105$
28	$\frac{83}{1000} = 0.083$
29	$\frac{39}{1000} = 0.039$
31	$\frac{81}{1000} = 0.081$
32	$\frac{49}{1000} = 0.049$
33	$\frac{142}{1000} = 0.142$
34	$\frac{70}{1000} = 0.070$

For a more detailed discussion of the uses of Tables 17.16–17.18, consult Section 11.2's discussion of the uses of Tables 11.2–11.4.

17.6 SIMULATING THE EFFECTS OF ILLEGALLY PARKED CARS ON A CITY'S MECHANICAL STREET CLEANING EFFORTS

Gotham City's Street Cleaning Problem

Public administrators have found simulation to be an effective tool for policy analysis. To illustrate, consider the following scenario:[10]

One of the responsibilities of Gotham City's Department of Sanitation (DOS) is to clean the city's streets. To do so, DOS relies primarily on mechanical street sweeping vehicles.

Since 95% of all street litter accumulates within 18 inches of the curb, it is important that the mechanical sweepers be able to get close to the curb. To provide curb accessibility, Gotham City has instituted special regulations that prohibit parking on one side of an entire street block during the interval of time that a mechanical sweeper is scheduled to clean that side of the block.

[10] This scenario and its analysis are adapted from L. J. Riccio and A. Litke, "Making a Clean Sweep: Simulating the Effects of Illegally Parked Cars on New York City's Mechanical Street-Cleaning Efforts," *Operations Research*, Volume 34, Number 5 (September–October 1986), pp. 661–666.

DOS has noted that, during the past year, there has been a dramatic increase in the number of violations of the special parking regulations. These violations retard DOS's street cleaning. When an illegally parked car blocks the path of a mechanical sweeper, the sweeper must swing out into the middle of the street and thus miss sweeping litter from the gutter.

Unfortunately, DOS does not have the authority to enforce parking regulations. This authority resides with the Department of Traffic (DOT). DOS has repeatedly requested DOT to assign more agents to ticket cars blocking the paths of the mechanical sweepers. DOT has denied these requests, maintaining that it has more important tasks for its agents.

To resolve the impasse between DOS and DOT, Gotham City has retained a consultant named Bruce Wayne. Bruce has been asked to quantify how much more effective street cleaning would be if there were better compliance with the special parking regulations. In what follows, we describe Bruce's approach to Gotham City's street cleaning problem.

To quantify the relationship between the ability to clean a street and the number of illegally parked cars on the street, Bruce decides to use simulation. He realizes his simulation must consist of the following four components:

1. A way to randomly place litter on the street.

2. A way to randomly place illegally parked cars on the street.

3. A way to determine the path the mechanical sweeper will take, given the number and spacing of illegally parked cars on the block.

4. A way to measure how clean a street is, both before and after cleaning.

Let us discuss each component in turn.

Litter Placement

Initially, Bruce decides to assume the following:

■ One side of a city block consists of 8 consecutive parking spaces.

■ Each parking space consists of 8 so-called *litter spaces*.

■ A litter space contains either no litter, a single piece of litter, or a pile of litter (i.e., more than one piece).

Later, after he is convinced that his model is correct, Bruce intends to make the more realistic assumption that one side of a city block consists of 24 parking spaces, each subdivided into 8 litter spaces.

Bruce conducts a study that indicates that, with 8 litter spaces per parking space, there is a 50% chance of no litter in a litter space, a 40% chance of a piece of litter, and a 10% chance of a pile of litter. Table 17.19(a) summarizes Bruce's assignment of random numbers to these three possibilities.

To simulate the placement of litter, Bruce sequentially considers each of the 64 litter spaces. For each litter space, he generates a single-digit random number and then uses Table 17.19(a) to determine how much litter the space contains. For example, if the random number is 7, the space contains a piece of litter.

TABLE 17.19 Random Number Assignments in Gotham City's Problem

Type of litter	No litter	Piece	Pile
Random numbers	0–4	5–8	9

(a) Litter Placement

Parking space	1	2	3	4	5	6	7	8	Meaningless
Random numbers	00–11	12–23	24–35	36–47	48–59	60–71	72–83	84–95	96–99

(b) Parked Car Placement

If space contains a piece:

Effectiveness	Piece picked up	Piece left
Random numbers	0–8	9

If space contains a pile:

Effectiveness	Pile picked up	One piece left
Random numbers	0–8	9

(c) Sweeper Effectiveness

Parked Car Placement

Initially, Bruce assumes that one side of a city block always contains 3 illegally parked cars. Later, after he increases the number of parking spaces per block from 8 to 24, he intends to conduct separate simulations in which the number of illegally parked cars varies from 3 to 17.

To simulate the placement of 3 parked cars on the block, Bruce divides the two-digit random numbers between 00 and 95 into 8 equal intervals and assigns each interval to one of the 8 parking spaces. Table 17.19(b) summarizes Bruce's assignment of random numbers. Note that the random numbers from 96 to 99 are meaningless; if Bruce generates one of these, he will ignore it and generate another random number. To illustrate how Bruce uses Table 17.19(b) to place the 3 parked cars, suppose that the three random numbers he generates are 18, 57, and 74. According to Table 17.19(b), these random numbers correspond to placing cars in the second, fifth, and seventh parking spaces. Note that, if the three random numbers do not correspond to three distinct parking places, then Bruce must continue generating random numbers until he obtains three parked cars.

The Path of the Mechanical Sweeper

The spacing of the parked cars affects the behavior of the mechanical sweeper. Bruce assumes that the sweepers behave according to the rules summarized in Figure 17.2.

Even if a sweeper is able to reach a space, it may not pick up all litter in the space. Studies have found that a sweeper picks up 90% of the litter it encounters. Hence, Bruce assumes the following:

- If a sweeper encounters a space containing a piece of litter, it will pick up the piece 90% of the time.

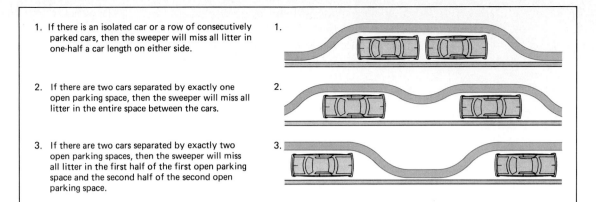

1. If there is an isolated car or a row of consecutively parked cars, then the sweeper will miss all litter in one-half a car length on either side.

2. If there are two cars separated by exactly one open parking space, then the sweeper will miss all litter in the entire space between the cars.

3. If there are two cars separated by exactly two open parking spaces, then the sweeper will miss all litter in the first half of the first open parking space and the second half of the second open parking space.

Figure 17.2 Rules governing the effectiveness of a mechanical street sweeper

■ If the sweeper encounters a space containing a pile of litter, it will pick up the entire pile 90% of the time but will leave a piece 10% of the time.

Table 17.19(c) summarizes how Bruce simulates the cleaning of a space the sweeper can reach.

Measuring the Cleanliness of a Street

Fortunately for Bruce, Gotham City already has in place a scientific litter measurement system that rates a street's cleanliness on a scale ranging from 1 for no litter to 3 for continuous litter along the curb. Table 17.20 displays the cleanliness rating for a block of 64 litter spaces as a function of the number of piles and pieces of litter that are present. Gotham City considers a block "acceptably clean" if its rating is 1.5 or less.

Recall that Bruce subsequently intends to expand his definition of a city block from 64 litter spaces (8 parking spaces) to 192 litter spaces (24 parking spaces).

TABLE 17.20 Cleanliness Rating for a Block of 64 Litter Spaces as Function of the Number of Piles and Pieces of Litter

Number of Piles	Number of Pieces	Cleanliness Rating
0	0	1.0
0	1 to 10	1.2
0	11 to 25	1.5
0	26 to 40	1.8
0	above 40	2.0
1 or 2	0 to 20	1.8
1 or 2	above 20	2.0
3 to 9	0 to 20	2.0
3 to 9	above 20	2.5
10 to 39	any	2.5
40 to 64	any	3.0

When he does so, he will still be able to use Table 17.20 to measure the cleanliness of the expanded block. He will simply divide the expanded block into thirds, use Table 17.20 to rate the cleanliness of each, and average the ratings. If the average rating is 1.5 or less, Bruce will consider the expanded block acceptably clean.

Conducting One Simulation Run

To manually simulate the littering and cleaning of a street block, Bruce proceeds as follows:

- **Initialization**. Figure 17.3(a) depicts one side of an empty street, with the curb adjacent to the figure's base. Each large square represents one of the 8 parking spaces. At the base of each large square are 8 small squares, each representing a litter space adjacent to the curb.

- **Placement of litter**. To simulate the placement of litter, Bruce must generate single-digit random numbers for each of the 64 litter spaces. Beginning arbitrarily in Table 17.4's sixteenth row, Bruce copies the first 64 random numbers to the top of Figure 17.3(b). These random numbers and Table 17.19(a) yield the litter placement diagrammed in Figure 17.3(b), where a dot represents a piece of litter and a square represents a pile of litter. For example, since the sequence of random numbers begins with 6, 0, 5, 9, and 7, Table 17.19(a) indicates that litter space 1 contains a piece, litter space 2 is empty, litter space 3 contains a piece, litter space 4 contains a pile, and litter space 5 contains a piece.

- **Placement of parked cars**. To simulate the placement of the 3 illegally parked cars, Bruce must generate 3 two-digit random numbers. Starting in Table 17.4 where he quit at the end of litter placement, Bruce copies the next 3 two-digit random numbers to the top of Figure 17.3(c). According to Table 17.19(b), these random numbers correspond to placing cars in the second, fifth, and seventh parking spaces. This placement of cars is diagrammed in Figure 17.3(c), where shaded parking spaces have cars and unshaded spaces do not.

- **Determining the path of the sweeper**. According to the rules summarized in Figure 17.2, the mechanical sweeper can only reach the pieces and piles of litter highlighted in color in Figure 17.3(d). Recall, though, that the sweeper is only 90% effective. Hence, to simulate the effectiveness of the sweeper, Bruce must generate a single-digit random number for each of the 6 pieces and 4 piles of litter the sweeper can reach. Starting in Table 17.4 where he quit at the end of car placement, Bruce copies the next 10 random numbers to the top of Figure 17.3(e). These numbers and Table 17.19(c) determine the cleanliness of a litter space after the sweeper has passed by. For example, since the sequence of random numbers begins with 0, 4, and 9, Table 17.19(c) indicates that the sweeper picks up the piece of litter in the first space, picks up the piece in the third space, and leaves one piece from the pile in the fourth space. Figure 17.3(e) displays the litter that remains after the sweeper has passed by, where black denotes litter that the sweeper could not reach and color denotes litter that the sweeper reached but could not pick up.

- **Measuring the cleanliness**. Examining Figure 17.3(b)'s display of the litter before cleaning, Bruce sees 5 piles and 26 pieces. According to Table 17.20, this corresponds to a cleanliness rating of 2.5. After the sweeper has passed

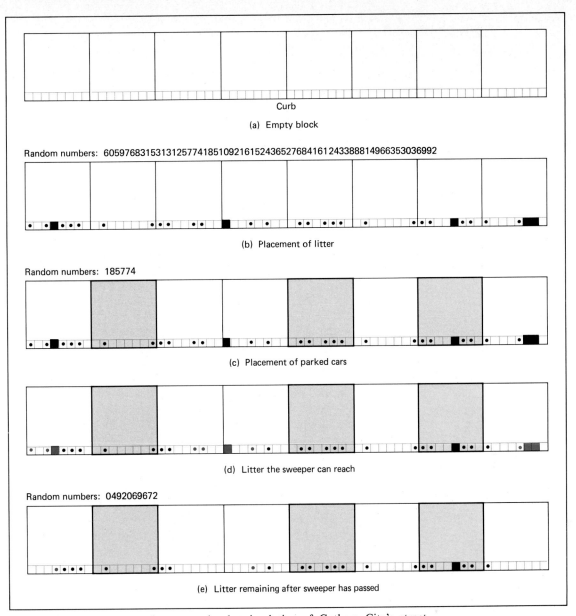

Figure 17.3 A summary of one run in the simulation of Gotham City's street cleaning problem

by, Figure 17.3(e) indicates that 1 pile and 22 pieces of litter are still present. This corresponds to a cleanliness rating of 2.0, more than the 1.5 rating that is the cutoff for being acceptably clean. Note that, if the car in the seventh parking place were not present, the sweeper could have reached the remaining pile of litter in Figure 17.3(e) and, thus, would probably have made the street acceptably clean.

- **Summary**. This concludes one simulation of the effect 3 parked cars have on cleanliness. In this simulation, the sweeper was unable to make the block acceptably clean. Of course, if Bruce were to perform another simulation, different litter and car placements might then lead to an acceptably clean block.

769

Computer Simulation

After manually performing several more runs, Bruce is happy with his model. He describes the mechanics to a computer programmer, who writes a program that automates Bruce's manual simulation.

Bruce's manual simulation considered only a block having 8 parking spaces and 3 illegally parked cars. In the computer simulation, Bruce considers an expanded block having 24 parking spaces and a number of illegally parked cars ranging from 3 to 17. (Fewer than 3 cars rarely prevents the sweeper from making the street acceptably clean, and more than 17 cars rarely occurs.) For each number of illegally parked cars in the interval from 3 to 17, the computer program executes 10,000 simulation runs. Each run proceeds exactly as described earlier, except that the expanded block size increases the computational effort. Table 17.21 summarizes those of the 150,000 runs for which the number of illegally parked cars was between 3 and 10 and the initial cleanliness rating was between 1.6 and 2.0. For example, the entry in Table 17.21's fifth row and third column means that, of those runs that had 7 illegally parked cars on a block with an initial cleanliness rating of 1.8, only 23% ended with the sweeper having made the block acceptably clean.

The simulation demonstrates that small reductions in the number of illegally parked cars often lead to significant increases in a sweeper's ability to make a block acceptably clean. For example, Table 17.21 indicates that:

- If the block has an initial cleanliness rating of 1.9, reducing the number of illegally parked cars from 4 to 3 increases the chance the sweeper will make the block acceptably clean from 53% to 80%.

- If the block has an initial cleanliness rating of 2.0, reducing the number of illegally parked cars from 4 to 3 increases the chance the sweeper will make the block acceptably clean from 18% to 46%.

Bruce's simulation model has quantified the relationship between the number of illegally parked cars and a sweeper's ability to make a block acceptably clean. The Department of Sanitation now has data to support its contention that the Department of Transportation should assign more agents to ticket and perhaps tow cars that block the path of the mechanical sweeper.

TABLE 17.21 A Summary of a Computer Simulation of Gotham City's Problem. (Each entry is the probability that a street block will be made acceptably clean, given its initial cleanliness rating and the number of legally parked cars.)

| | | Initial Cleanliness Rating | | | | |
		1.6	1.7	1.8	1.9	2.0
	3	0.99	0.98	0.97	0.80	0.46
	4	0.99	0.95	0.86	0.53	0.18
Number	5	0.95	0.87	0.65	0.29	0.06
of	6	0.88	0.72	0.40	0.13	0.02
Parked	7	0.78	0.50	0.23	0.07	0.01
Cars	8	0.63	0.36	0.11	0.03	0.01
	9	0.50	0.20	0.06	0.01	0.00
	10	0.36	0.11	0.02	0.01	0.00

17.7 NEXT-EVENT SIMULATION[11]

The environment to be simulated often consists of several stochastic events that take place concurrently rather than sequentially. The most popular approach to simulating such an environment is called *next-event simulation*.

Däagen Hazs' Machine Repair Problem

To illustrate next-event simulation, we will consider the following scenario:[12]

Däagen Hazs (DH) produces ice cream in 5 identical machines that are subject to failure. A failed machine is repaired by one member of a crew of 2 service technicians. DH estimates that

- Once a machine has been repaired, the time until it fails again is governed by the probability distribution in Table 17.22(a)'s first two rows. (Temporarily ignore the third row.)

- The time required for a technician to repair a failed machine is governed by the probability distribution displayed in Table 17.22(b)'s first two rows. (Temporarily ignore the third row.) The repair time excludes any time a machine must wait because both technicians are busy with other machines.

Although DH currently employs 2 technicians, it is not convinced this is the optimal number.

In deciding how many technicians to employ, the primary factor DH will consider is the average *downtime* of a machine—that is, the average amount of time that elapses from the time a machine fails until the time its repair is complete. Obviously, DH can decrease downtime by employing more technicians. However, more technicians means higher payroll costs. DH wants to quantify the effect the number of technicians has on a machine's average downtime.

---

[11] This section, which discusses an advanced topic, may be omitted without loss of continuity.

[12] Those who have read Chapter 16 will recognize this scenario as a variation of the scenario used in Section 16.7 to illustrate a basic queueing system with a finite calling population.

TABLE 17.22 The Probability Distributions in Däagen Hazs' Problem

Machine's lifetime (hours)	4	5	6	7
Probability	0.4	0.3	0.2	0.1
Random numbers	0–3	4–6	7–8	9

(a) Probability Distribution of a Machine's Lifetime

Repair duration (hours)	1	2	3
Probability	0.2	0.6	0.2
Random numbers	0–1	2–7	8–9

(b) Probability Distribution of a Repair Duration

In DH's problem, there are always several stochastic events taking place concurrently. The next event to occur will be either the failure of one of the currently operating machines or the repair of one of the currently failed machines. As we will see, next-event simulation provides a framework for identifying the time at which the next event will occur and advancing the simulation's "clock" to this time. This approach avoids inefficiently having to consider the intervals of time between events when the characteristics of the environment remain unchanged (e.g., the intervals of time during which the same machines are operating, the same machines are undergoing repair, and the same machines are waiting to undergo repair).

A Manual Simulation of DH's Problem

Let us now manually simulate DH's current policy of employing 2 technicians. We will summarize our simulation using Table 17.23. Before beginning the simulation, we will provide an overview of the data we record in each of Table 17.23's columns:

- **Clock time**. This column records the simulation's elapsed time. We initialize the clock to 0 and then increase it each time a failure or repair occurs. To distinguish rows in Table 17.23 with the same clock time, we append plus signs (e.g., 14, 14^+, and 14^{++}).

- **Event description**. This column contains a brief description of which event has just occurred. If the event is a failure, we specify which machine has just failed and either which technician we assign to repair it or, if all technicians

TABLE 17.23 A Manual Simulation of Däagen Hazs' Problem

Clock Time	Event Description	Machine Status* 1	2	3	4	5	Technician Status† 1	2	Queue Status††	Total Number of Repaired Machines	Total Down-time
0	Initialization	5	4	6	7	5	~	~	~	0	0
4	M2 fails and T1 begins its repair.	5	~	6	7	5	(2,4,6)	~	~	0	0
5	M1 fails and T2 begins its repair.	~	~	6	7	5	(2,4,6)	(1,5,8)	~	0	0
5^+	M5 fails and joins queue.	~	~	6	7	~	(2,4,6)	(1,5,8)	(5,5)	0	0
6	M3 fails and joins queue.	~	~	~	7	~	(2,4,6)	(1,5,8)	(5,5) (3,6)	0	0
6^+	T1 completes M2's repair and begins M5"s repair.	~	12	~	7	~	(5,5,8)	(1,5,8)	(3,6)	1	2
7	M4 fails and joins queue.	~	12	~	~	~	(5,5,8)	(1,5,8,)	(3,6,) (4,7)	1	2
8	T1 completes M5's repair and begins M3's repair.	~	12	~	~	12	(3,6,9)	(1,5,8)	(4,7)	2	5
8^+	T2 completes M1's repair and begins M4's repair.	13	12	~	~	12	(3,6,9)	(4,7,9)	~	3	8
9	T1 completes M3's repair and becomes idle.	13	12	13	~	12	~	(4,7,9)	~	4	11
9^+	T2 completes M4's repair and becomes idle.	13	12	13	14	12	~	~	~	5	13
12	M2 fails and T1 begins its repair.	13	~	13	14	12	(2,12,13)	~	~	5	13
12^+	M5 fails and T2 begins its repair.	13	~	13	14	~	(2,12,13)	(5,12,13)	~	5	13
13	M1 fails and joins queue.	~	~	13	14	~	(2,12,13)	(5,12,13)	(1,13)	5	13
13^+	M3 fails and joins queue.	~	~	~	14	~	(2,12,13)	(5,12,13)	(1,13) (3,13)	5	13
13^{++}	T1 completes M2's repair and begins M1's repair.	~	18	~	14	~	(1,13,14)	(5,12,13)	(3,13)	6	14
13^{+++}	T2 completes M5's repair and begins M3's repair.	~	18	~	14	18	(1,13,14)	(3,13,14)	~	7	15
14	M4 fails and joins queue.	~	18	~	~	18	(1,13,14)	(3,13,14)	(4,14)	7	15
14^+	T1 completes M1's repair and begins M4's repair.	21	18	~	~	18	(4,14,16)	(3,13,14)	~	8	16
14^{++}	T2 completes M3's repair and becomes idle.	21	18	18	~	18	(4,14,16)	~	~	9	17
16	T1 completes M4's repair and becomes idle.	21	18	18	20	18	~	~	~	10	19

* This column displays the failure time for each operating machine.

† This column displays, for each technician, the machine undergoing repair, the time when it failed, and the time when its repair will be complete.

†† This column displays each machine in the queue and the time when it failed.

are busy, that the machine joins the queue of machines waiting for repair. If the event is a repair, we specify which technician has just completed a repair and, if there is a queue of machines waiting for repair, we also specify which machine the technician begins repairing next.

- **Machine status**. For each operating machine, this column specifies the clock time at which the machine will next fail. If the machine is currently failed, we indicate so with the symbol "~".

- **Repair person status**. For each busy technician, this column specifies three attributes of the machine currently undergoing repair: (1) the number of the machine, (2) the clock time at which the machine failed, and (3) the clock time at which the machine's repair will be complete. For example, if the status of technician 1 is

$$(3, 10, 12),$$

it indicates that technician 1 is currently repairing machine 3, which failed when the clock time was 10 and will be completely repaired when the clock time is 12. If the technician is idle, we indicate so with the symbol "~".

- **Queue status**. For each machine waiting for repair, this column specifies the number of the machine and the clock time at which it failed. For example,

$$(5, 11)$$
$$(2, 13)$$

indicates that the queue consists of machine 5, which failed when the clock time was 11, and machine 2, which failed when the clock time was 13. If there is no queue, we indicate so with the symbol "~". Note that we add a machine to the bottom of the queue and remove a machine from the top. Hence, the next machine to begin repair is the one that has been in the queue the longest time.

- **Total number of repaired machines and total downtime**. Both columns initially contain a value of 0. Each time a technician completes a repair, we increase the former value by 1 and the latter value by the machine's downtime. Hence, at any clock time, we can obtain the average downtime since the simulation began by dividing the latter value by the former.

This completes our overview of the data contained in each of Table 17.23's columns. We will soon see that these data provide a concise summary of all the information we need to conduct our simulation.

Before we begin the simulation, we need to discuss the rules we will use to break ties when two or more events occur simultaneously. Since the choice of tie-breaking rules is arbitrary, we can use the easily remembered ones that follow:

1. If the clock time at which a machine will next fail equals the clock time at which a technician will complete another machine's repair, we assume the failure occurs first.

2. If the clock times at which two machines will next fail are equal, we assume the lower-numbered machine fails first (e.g., machine 3 would "win" a tie with machine 5).

3. If the clock times at which two technicians will finish a repair are equal, we assume the lower-numbered technician finishes first.

4. If a machine fails when two or more technicians are idle, we assign the machine to the lowest-numbered technician.

In brief, these rules state that, to break a tie, we select a failure over a repair and a lower-numbered machine or technician over a higher-numbered one.

We are now ready to begin the simulation. The previously ignored third rows of Tables 17.22(a) and (b) summarize the assignments of single-digit random numbers we will use to simulate the probability distributions of machine failure and repair. To generate random numbers, we will arbitrarily begin in Table 17.4's twentieth row.

The following commentary, in conjunction with Table 17.23, summarizes the simulation from a clock time of 0 through 6. After carefully reading this commentary, you should be able to verify for yourself the remaining portion of the simulation.

- **Clock time = 0.** To summarize the environment at the start of the simulation, we record in the following information in Table 17.23's first row:

  1. We initialize to 0 the clock time, the total number of repaired machines, and the total downtime.

  2. We use "~" to indicate that both technicians are idle and there is no queue.

  3. To determine when each machine will fail, we note that the first five single-digit random numbers in the twentieth row of Table 17.4 are

  $$6\ 1\ 7\ 9\ 4.$$

  Using Table 17.22(a), we convert these random numbers to respective failure times of 5, 4, 6, 7, and 5. We record these values in the Machine Status column.

We are now ready to advance the clock. To do so, we must identify the next event that will occur. In general, since the next event may be either a failure or a repair, we must examine not only the failure times in the Machine Status column but also the repair times in the Technician Status column. However, at initialization, we need only examine the former column, since the latter contains no repair times. Examining the failure times, we note the next event is the failure of machine 2 at time 4. Before proceeding to this event, observe that, since the next event will not occur until a clock time of 4, the summary in Table 17.23's first row is valid for not just a clock time of 0 but the entire interval between time 0 and time 4. This illustrates the key feature of a next-event simulation—the repeated advancement of the clock from the time of one event to the time of the next event.

- **Clock time = 4.** To update the environment when machine 2 fails, we record the following information in Table 17.23:

  1. We use "~" to indicate that machine 2 is now failed.

  2. Using our tie-breaking rules, we assign technician 1 to repair machine 2.

  3. To determine when this repair will finish, we note that the next random number in Table 17.4 is

  Using Table 17.22(b), we convert this random number to a repair duration of 2. Adding this duration to the current clock time of 4, we obtain 6 as the repair's completion time. Technician 1 is now repairing machine 2, which failed at time 4 and will be completely repaired at

time 6. To summarize this, we record (2, 4, 6) as the technician's status.

We are now ready to advance the clock. Note that the next event is a tie at time 5 between the failures of machines 1 and 5. Using our tie-breaking rules, we assume that machine 1 fails first.

- **Clock time = 5**. To update the environment when machine 1 fails, we record the following information in Table 17.23:

  1. We use "~" to indicate machine 1 is now failed.

  2. We assign technician 2 to repair machine 1.

  3. To determine when this repair will finish, we note that the next random number in Table 17.4 is

  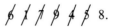 8.

  From Table 17.22(b), this random number corresponds to a repair duration of 3. Adding this duration to the current clock time of 5, we obtain 8 as the repair's completion time. Technician 2 is now repairing machine 1, which failed at time 5 and will be completely repaired at time 8. To summarize this, we record (1, 5, 8) as the technician's status.

We are now ready to advance the clock. Observe that the next event is the failure of machine 5 at time 5. Since we have already used a clock time of 5, we refer to the next clock time as 5$^+$, but we regard it as being the same as time 5.

- **Clock time = 5$^+$**. To summarize the environment when machine 5 fails, we record the following information in Table 17.23:

  1. We use "~" to indicate that machine 5 is now failed.

  2. Since both technicians are busy, machine 5 must join the (now-empty) queue of machines waiting for repair. We indicate that the queue now consists of machine 5, which failed at time 5, by recording (5, 5) in the Queue Status column. We will wait to generate a repair completion time for machine 5 until its repair begins.

We are now ready to advance the clock. Note that the next event is a tie at time 6 between the failure of machine 3 and the repair completion by technician 1. Using our tie-breaking rules, we assume machine 3's failure occurs first.

- **Clock time = 6**. To summarize the environment when machine 3 fails, we proceed almost identically as when the clock time was 5$^+$. The only difference is that machine 3 joins the queue as the second entry rather than the first. We are now ready to advance the clock. Note that the next event is the repair completion by technician 1 at a time we refer to as 6$^+$.

- **Clock time = 6$^+$**. To summarize the environment when technician 1 completes the repair, we record the following information in Table 17.23:

  1. Since a repair completion has occurred, we must increase the values of 0 now appearing in the last two columns. In particular, we increase the total number of repaired machines from 0 to 1, and the total downtime from 0 to 2, the downtime for the just-repaired machine 2. We can easily compute this downtime because the Technician Status column includes the time machine 2 failed as well as the time its repair is completed. Since machine 2 began repair immediately upon failure, its downtime equals the time spent undergoing repair. In general, the downtime may also include time waiting in the queue.

2. Since machine 2 is operating once again, we must determine when it will next fail. To do so, we note that the next random number in Table 17.4 is

$$\not{6}\,\not{1}\,\not{7}\,\not{0}\,\not{4}\,\not{5}\,\not{8}\; 8.$$

Using Table 17.22(a), we convert this random number to a lifetime of 6. Adding this lifetime to the current clock of 6, we obtain 12 as machine 2's next failure time. We record this value in the Machine Status column.

3. Since there is a queue of failed machines, technician 1 does not become idle upon completing the repair of machine 1. Instead, we assign technician 1 to the first machine in the queue, machine 5. We delete machine 5 from the queue and move each remaining machine up one position.

4. Since technician 1 has just begun a repair, we must determine when this repair will finish. To do so, we note that the next random number in Table 17.4 is

$$\not{6}\,\not{1}\,\not{7}\,\not{0}\,\not{4}\,\not{5}\,\not{8}\; 7.$$

Using Table 17.22(b), we convert this random number to a repair duration of 2. Adding this duration to the current clock time of 6, we obtain 8 as the repair's completion time. Technician 1 is now repairing machine 5, which failed at time 5 and will be completely repaired at time 8. To summarize this, we record (5, 5, 8) as the technician's status.

We are now ready to advance the clock. Observe that the next event is the failure of machine 4 at time 7.

■ **Clock times above 6.** Given our detailed explanation of clock times up to 6, you should be able to verify the remainder of Table 17.23 on your own. Table 17.24 provides guidelines for how to proceed in the four cases you will encounter. To finish the simulation, you will need the random numbers from Table 17.4 that are displayed below:

TABLE 17.24 Guidelines for Completing Figure 17.23

If . . .	then . . .
1. The next event is a failure, and there is at least one idle technician.	Proceed as we did when the clock time was 4 and 5.
2. The next event is a failure, and there is no idle technician.	Proceed as we did when the clock time was 5^{+} and 6.
3. The next event is a repair completion, and there is a queue of failed machines.	Proceed as we did when the clock time was 6^{+}.
4. The next event is a repair completion, and there is no queue of failed machines.	Proceed as we did when the clock time was 6^{+}, except that the technician who just completed the repair becomes idle.

ø ı ƚ ɜ 4 ƙ 6 ɼ 2 0 4 1 1 5 1 1 4 1 6 0 9 6 3 1.

At the conclusion of our manual simulation, we see that the total number of repaired machines is 10 and the total downtime experienced by these 10 machines is 19. Hence, we can estimate the average downtime as 19/10 = 1.9 hours.

Because we stopped our simulation after the repair of only 10 machines, we do not expect to obtain an accurate estimate of average downtime. As in our previous simulation examples, greater accuracy requires us to let the simulation "run" longer. This is especially true for our simulation of DH's machine repair problem. The reason is that we began our simulation with all machines operating. For a brief simulation, this starting condition usually leads to an underestimate of average downtime, since there is a high likelihood that a machine failing at an early clock time need not join the queue. An alternative is to begin the simulation with all machines failed. For a brief simulation, this alternative usually leads to an overestimate of average downtime, since there is a high likelihood that a machine failing at an early clock time must joint the queue.

These two examples of the so-called *initial conditions* illustrate an important reason for letting the simulation run a longer time. We want to allow enough time for the effect of the initial conditions to dissipate.

There are several ways to measure how long our simulation has run. One way is to run the simulation until the clock time exceeds a prespecified value (e.g., 5000 hours); another way is to run the simulation until the total number of repaired machines exceeds a prespecified value (e.g., 2500 repairs). We will adopt the latter approach.

The introductory nature of this chapter precludes us from discussing how long we need to run the simulation to obtain an accurate estimate. We will simply assume that 2500 repairs is enough.

To run the simulation this long, we clearly need a computer program to automate our manual simulation. If you have any experience writing computer programs, you can appreciate that it is easy to convert the steps we followed into instructions to a computer. For example, a program written in the BASIC language would consist of less than 100 lines of code. When a computer performs the simulation, it need not store in memory the entire summary of the simulation (e.g., Table 17.23). All that is needed to estimate the average downtime is the summary of the environment at the simulation's ending clock time (e.g., Table 17.23's last row).

Table 17.25 displays the estimates of average downtime obtained using a BASIC computer program to simulate 2500 repairs for a staffing level ranging from 1 service technician to 5.[13] Execution of the program on an IBM PC-AT required less than 3 minutes for each set of 2500 repairs. Using Table 17.25, Däagen Hazs can decide whether it wants to increase or decrease the number of technicians. For example, if DH is unhappy with the average downtime of 2.258 hours currently obtained with 2 technicians, it should consider hiring another technician. In deciding whether to do so, it must answer the question, "Is a reduction in the average downtime from 2.258 hours to 2.029 hours (a reduction of about 14 minutes) worth the increase in payroll costs incurred by hiring another technician?" Regardless of the answer, one thing is clear from Table 17.25. DH should not reduce the number

---

[13] It is unnecessary to simulate the case where there are 5 technicians. Because the number of technicians equals the number of machines, a failed machine must never join a queue. Hence, the exact value of the average downtime is 2 hours, the average repair computed in Table 17.22(b). That the value in Table 17.25 is 2.011 is another indication that simulation provides only an estimate (even after 2500 repairs!).

TABLE 17.25 Average Downtime
Obtained from a Computer Simulation
of 2500 Repairs

Number of Technicians	Average Downtime after 2500 Repairs (hours)
1	5.033
2	2.258
3	2.029
4	2.014
5	2.011

of technicians from 2 to 1, unless it can tolerate an increase of almost 3 hours in average downtime.

We can also use the simulation to estimate the average number of idle technicians, the average number of failed machines, and the average number of machines in the queue.[14] To illustrate, let us use Table 17.23 to estimate the latter quantity. (A similar approach is applicable to the others.) From Table 17.23's Queue Status column, we can quickly identify the queue's size during any interval of time. For example, from the number of machines in the Queue Status column at clock times of 5^+ and 6^+, we see that there was 1 machine in the queue between time 5 and 6. Note that we used a clock time of 5^+ instead of 5 because the change in the queue's size between clock times of 5 and 5^+ was instantaneous and, hence, can be ignored. In general, when there are several rows in Table 17.23 corresponding to identical clock times, we ignore all but the last. Examining Table 17.23's Queue Status column from top to bottom, we see that the queue's size was 0 machines from time 0 to time 5, 1 machine from time 5 to time 7, 2 machines from time 7 to time 8, and 0 machines from time 8 to time 16. Figure 17.4 displays a graph of the queue size as function of time. From this graph, we see that the average queue size during our simulation was the following weighted average

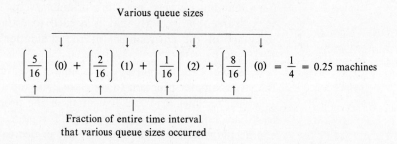

$$\left[\frac{5}{16}\right](0) + \left[\frac{2}{16}\right](1) + \left[\frac{1}{16}\right](2) + \left[\frac{8}{16}\right](0) = \frac{1}{4} = 0.25 \text{ machines}$$

This method of estimating the average queue size is inefficient for a computer. The reason is that the computer would have to store in memory the entire summary of the simulation (e.g., all of Table 17.23) so that it could reexamine the entire Queue Status column at the end of the simulation. Fortunately, the computer can avoid this inefficient use of its memory by performing some additional recordkeeping during the simulation. The computer then can estimate the average queue size

---

[14] Those who have read Chapter 16 will recognize that, in the notation of queueing analysis, the average downtime is W, the average time spent in the queue is W_q, the average number of failed machines is L, and the average number of machines in the queue is L_q.

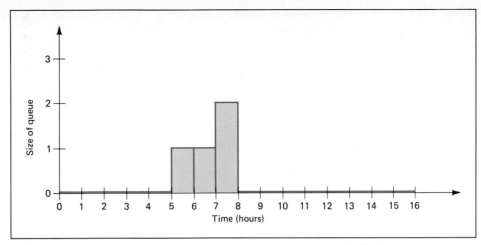

Figure 17.4 Queue size as a function of time during our manual simulation

just as it estimates the average downtime—that is, from the summary of the environment at the end of the simulation (e.g., Table 17.23's last row). Space constraints preclude us from discussing this more efficient way to estimate the average queue size.

We conclude this section by summarizing the important characteristics of a next-event simulation:

- Next-event simulation is applicable when several stochastic events are taking place concurrently rather than sequentially.

- The key feature of next-event simulation is recognition that it is sufficient to summarize the environment only at the discrete times at which an event occurs. Hence, the clock can be advanced repeatedly from the time of one event to the time of the next event.

- Because the initial conditions can greatly affect the estimates obtained from a next-event simulation, it is important to let the simulation run long enough for the effect to dissipate.

17.8 COMPUTER GENERATION OF RANDOM NUMBERS

Throughout this chapter we have generated random numbers by using a table of random numbers. A real-world simulation often requires hundreds of thousands (even millions) of random digits. Storing a table this large in a computer's memory is impractical. For this reason, mathematicians have devised efficient methods for generating random numbers on a computer. These methods are the topic of this section.

Generating $U(0, 1)$ Random Numbers

The foundation of computer generation of random numbers is the generation of decimal fractions (e.g., 0.5173) randomly distributed over the interval from 0 up to but not including 1. Hereafter, we refer to such a random number as a *U(0, 1) random number*. We use this terminology because the random numbers have properties similar to a random variable governed by a uniform probability distribution over the interval from 0 to 1.

The most popular method of generating $U(0, 1)$ random numbers is called the *mixed congruential method (MCM)*. Before we explain the MCM, we need to recall (from Chapter 14) the algebraic operation known as *modulo*. Given two integers x and m, x modulo m equals the remainder when x is divided by m. For example, 26 modulo 7 equals 5, since dividing 26 by 7 yields 3 with a remainder of 5. Other examples of the modulo operation are 42 modulo 8 = 2, 69 modulo 5 = 4, and 24 modulo 6 = 0.

The MCM generates a sequence of $U(0, 1)$ random numbers we will denote by r_0, r_1, r_2, r_3, and so on. The first number in the sequence, r_0, is an arbitrarily chosen decimal fraction between 0 and 1. It is called the *seed* because, as we will see, it starts the "growth" of the entire sequence. Using r_0 to initialize the process, the MCM generates the next random number using the previous random number and the following formula:

$$r_i = \frac{[(mar_{i-1} + c)(\text{modulo } m)]}{m},$$

where m = a prespecified positive integer known as the *modulus*,
a = a prespecified positive integer less than m known as the *multiplier*,
c = a prespecified nonnegative integer less than m known as the *increment*.

To illustrate, if $r_0 = 0.4373$, $m = 16$, $a = 5$, and $c = 3$, Table 17.26 summarizes the generation of r_1 through r_{16}. Before proceeding, you should verify Table 17.26's calculations.

Although the choice of $m = 16$, $a = 5$, and $c = 3$ illustrates how the MCM generates $U(0, 1)$ random numbers, no one would make such a choice in practice. Can you see why? The reason becomes apparent when we compare r_0 and r_{16} and note they are equal. Thus, there is no sense in continuing to generate more random numbers, because the sequence would just repeat itself in the same order. Note

TABLE 17.26 Generating the First Sixteen $U(0,1)$ Random Numbers Using the MCM Method with $r_0 = 0.4375$, $m = 16$, $a = 5$, and $c = 3$

i	r_{i-1}	$(16)(5)r_{i-1} + 3$	$(80r_{i-1} + 3)(\text{modulo } 16)$	$r_i = \dfrac{(80r_{i-1} + 3)(\text{modulo } 16)}{16}$
1	0.4375	38	6	0.3750
2	0.3750	33	1	0.0625
3	0.0625	8	8	0.5000
4	0.5000	43	11	0.6875
5	0.6875	58	10	0.6250
6	0.6250	53	5	0.3125
7	0.3125	28	12	0.7500
8	0.7500	63	15	0.9375
9	0.9375	78	14	0.8750
10	0.8750	73	9	0.5625
11	0.5625	48	0	0.0000
12	0.0000	3	3	0.1875
13	0.1875	18	2	0.1250
14	0.1250	13	13	0.8125
15	0.8125	68	4	0.2500
16	0.2500	23	7	0.4375

that the number of distinct random numbers generated before the "looping" begins is 16, the value of the modulus m. As illustrated by an end-of-chapter exercise, for a given value of m, not every choice of values for a and c leads to m distinct random numbers before the looping begins.

The looping behavior of the MCM is inevitable, regardless of the choice of values for m, a, and c. (Note that the choice of the seed r_0 is arbitrary because it affects only where the sequence begins, not how frequently it loops.) The question is not if the looping will occur but when. Mathematicians have devised rules for choosing m, a, and c that delay the looping as long as possible and also lead to other desirable properties in the sequence of random numbers. (These rules, as well as the other desirable properties, are beyond the scope of this text.) For example, a recommended choice when the computer has 32-bit words is

$$m = 2^{31}, \quad a = 314{,}159{,}169, \quad c = 453{,}806{,}245.$$

This choice generates 2^{31} or over 2 billion $U(0, 1)$ random numbers before looping. Fortunately, as a user of a computer, you need not worry about the choice of m, a, and c. These choices have been made for you by the designer of the computer software you are using.

Strictly speaking, the sequence of numbers generated by the MCM are not random in the sense of being unpredictable and irreproducible. As we have seen, specifying r_0, m, a, and c automatically determines what sequence of numbers we will generate. For this reason, random numbers generated on a computer are often called *pseudorandom numbers*. Although not truly random, pseudorandom numbers behave as if they were. Furthermore, their properties of predictability and reproducibility are advantageous. Predictability (by a mathematical formula) avoids wasting the computer's memory with storage of a large table of random numbers. Reproducibility (by using the same seed over again) enables a simulation to evaluate two distinct policies using the same sequence of random numbers or to repeat the same simulation months later.

A computer needs only to generate $U(0, 1)$ random numbers because they in turn can be used to simulate any desired probability distribution. This is the topic of the remainder of this section.

Using $U(0, 1)$ Random Numbers to Simulate a Stochastic Event Having a Finite Number of Outcomes

In each of our example simulations, the events we simulated had only a finite number of alternative outcomes. For example, in simulating May's belt replacement problem in Section 17.3, we assumed a belt's lifetime was 8, 9, 10, 11, or 12 days. As illustrated throughout the chapter, we can always simulate a stochastic event having only a finite number of outcomes by appropriately assigning to each outcome a subset of the random integers in the interval from 0 to 9, 00 to 99, or 000 to 999 (e.g., Table 17.5).

We need not abandon this approach when writing a computer program to perform a simulation. To illustrate, suppose we wish to generate a random integer in the interval from 00 to 99. We can do so by generating a $U(0, 1)$ random number, multiplying by 100, and truncating (i.e., ignoring) the fractional part. For example, if the $U(0, 1)$ random number is 0.3954, we multiply by 100 to obtain 39.54 and truncate the fractional part to obtain 39 as the random integer. In general, to obtain a random integer in the interval from 0 to $10^n - 1$ (for some specified value of n), we multiply a $U(0, 1)$ random number by 10^n and truncate the fractional part.

Using $U(0, 1)$ Random Numbers to Simulate a Stochastic Event Having an Infinite Number of Outcomes

It is often more realistic to assume a stochastic event has an infinite number of alternative outcomes. For example, in May's belt replacement problem, it would have been more realistic to assume a belt's lifetime could be any of the infinite number of values in the interval from 8 to 12 days (not just the five integers).

When a stochastic event has an infinite number of outcomes, a common assumption is that the outcome is governed by either a uniform probability distribution or a normal probability distribution. Below is an overview of how to simulate these two probability distributions using $U(0, 1)$ random numbers:

■ **Simulating a uniform probability distribution**. Suppose in May's belt replacement problem that a belt's lifetime has a uniform probability distribution over the entire interval from 8 to 12. To simulate this distribution, we generate a $U(0, 1)$ random number, multiply it by 4 (the length of the interval), and add the product to 8 (the interval's left endpoint). For example, if the $U(0, 1)$ random number is 0.3954, we transform it to

$$8 + (4)(0.3954) = 9.5816 .$$

In general, to simulate a uniform probability distribution over the entire interval from a to b, we transform a $U(0, 1)$ random number r using the formula

$$a + (b - a)r.$$

■ **Simulating a normal probability distribution**. Now suppose we wish to simulate a normal probability distribution with a known mean of μ and a known standard deviation of σ. A common way to do so is via approximation. It can be proved that if $r_1, r_2, ..., r_{12}$ are twelve $U(0, 1)$ random numbers, then

$$\mu + [(r_1 + r_2 + \cdots + r_{12}) - 6]\sigma$$

is approximately normally distributed with a mean of μ and a standard deviation of σ. Although the proof of this fact is beyond the scope of this text, we can at least illustrate it, under the arbitrary assumption that $\mu = 75$ and $\sigma = 10$. Figure 17.5 displays a histogram of 10,000 values, each obtained by subtracting 6 from the sum of 12 $U(0, 1)$ random numbers, multiplying the result by $\sigma = 10$, adding this to $\mu = 75$, and then rounding the sum to the nearest integer. (The rounding was done only because the values were to be used for a histogram.) We can see that the histogram has the "bell" shape characteristic of the normal probability distribution and is approximately symmetric around the value of 75. This approximation method is inefficient because it requires 12 $U(0, 1)$ random variables each time. There are more efficient approximation methods, but their explanation is beyond the scope of this text.

Of course, besides the uniform and normal, there are many other probability distributions we might want to simulate. Although we cannot go into detail here, we can say that computers simulate these other probability distributions by using $U(0, 1)$ random numbers in ways similar to those we have described.

To summarize,

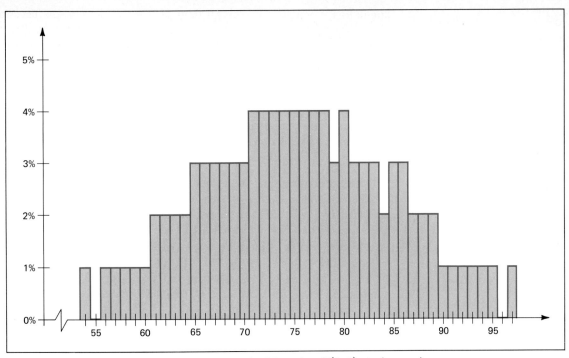

Figure 17.5 A histogram of 10,000 values obtained by using $U(0, 1)$ random variables to approximate a normal distribution with $\mu = 75$ and $\sigma = 10$

- A computer generates random numbers by using a mathematical formula, not by storing a table.

- The foundation of computer generation of random numbers is what we called $U(0, 1)$ random numbers. These are decimal fractions randomly distributed over the interval from 0 up to but not including 1.

- With appropriate transformations of $U(0, 1)$ random numbers, we can simulate any desired probability distribution (although sometimes an approximation is necessary).

17.9 CONCLUDING REMARKS

Owing to space constraints and the introductory nature of this text, we are unable to discuss in detail several important issues that arise in almost every simulation. The following is a brief overview of four issues that merit further study if you ever become involved in a simulation project:

- **Knowing when to simulate**. Because simulation provides only estimated values, it should be used only after a determination that there is no way to compute the exact values. For example, suppose in Däagen Hazs' machine repair problem it is valid to assume that a machine's failure time and its repair duration are each governed by an exponential probability distribution. Then, using the mathematical model described in Section 16.7, we can easily compute the exact value of a machine's average downtime. If we were to use simulation, it might take several days of labor to develop the necessary computer program and to use the program to obtain a table similar to Table 17.23. It would then have taken days to estimate a value we could have computed exactly in minutes. This small example illustrates the importance of doing some research to determine if simulation can be avoided. On the other hand, it is also important not to make simplifying assumptions just to avoid simulation. One of the advantages of simulation is that we are not required to make simplifying assumptions, such as assuming an exponential probability distribution in DH's machine repair problem when all available data and judgment suggests otherwise.

■ **Selecting a language for the computer program**. A computer program to perform a simulation can always be written in a general-purpose language such as BASIC or FORTRAN. Small-scale simulations can even be performed using spreadsheet software such as Lotus 1-2-3.[15] However, large-scale simulations are best written in a special-purpose simulation language such as GPSS, SIMSCRIPT, or SLAM. Different special-purpose languages have different strengths and weaknesses and are designed for different types of simulation. Programs written in a special-purpose language are usually faster and cheaper to develop and are easier to document for both the user and a future programmer who might have to make modifications long after the original programmer is gone. The importance of documentation cannot be overemphasized. The "graveyard" is filled with simulation programs that have died prematurely because no one could understand how to modify them when the need arose.

■ **Improving the accuracy of a simulation's estimates**. In all of our simulation examples, we illustrated that one way to improve the accuracy of an estimate obtained from a simulation is to let the simulation run longer. There has been much research on other ways to improve the accuracy. This body of knowledge is known as *variance-reducing techniques*.

■ **Validation of the simulation**. *Validation* is the process of verifying that a simulation accurately represents the environment it is trying to imitate. This is important if we are to have confidence in the decisions made on the basis of the simulation's results. There are two principal means of validation: (1) comparing examples of the simulated environment to the real environment, and (2) asking those with first-hand knowledge of the real environment to comment on examples of the simulated environment. To illustrate these two validation methods, let us use Gotham City's street cleaning problem. One aspect of this simulation was the use of Table 17.19(a) to simulate litter placement on a street block. To validate this table, Bruce should compare a dozen or so examples of simulated litter placement with the distribution of litter on real street blocks. If the comparison indicated significant disagreement between the simulated and actual litter distribution, he would continue to revise Table 17.19(a) until it passed the validation check. Besides comparing the examples of simulated litter placement to the real thing, Bruce should show the simulated placements to the drivers of the mechanical street sweepers and ask for their comments. Failing to consult persons having first-hand knowledge of the environment is a serious but common error.

---

[15] For an example, consult S. E. Bodily, "Spreadsheet Modeling as a Stepping Stone," *Interfaces*, Volume 16, Number 5 (September–October 1986), pp. 34–52.

17.10 CHAPTER CHECKLIST AND GLOSSARY

Quickly review this chapter by reading the material highlighted by a vertical line in the left margin. You should then be familiar with the concepts, techniques, and terminology in the Checklist and Glossary that follow. If you need "help" with a particular item, consult the section or sections indicated for a more detailed discussion.

Checklist of Concepts and Techniques

- ☐ The distinction between a replace-only-at-failure policy and an age replacement policy. [17.1]
- ☐ Simulating a stochastic event using random numbers. [17.2]
- ☐ Using simulation to analyze an equipment replacement problem. [17.3]
- ☐ The general characteristics of a simulation. [17.4]
- ☐ Simulating a project with stochastic activity durations. [17.5]
- ☐ Simulating the effects of illegally parked cars on a city's mechanical street sweeping efforts. [17.6]
- ☐ Simulating a machine repair problem using next-event simulation. [17.7]
- ☐ The general characteristics of a next-event simulation. [17.7]
- ☐ Using $U(0, 1)$ random numbers using the mixed congruential method. [17.8]
- ☐ Using $U(0, 1)$ random numbers to simulate a stochastic event having a finite number of outcomes. [17.8]
- ☐ Using $U(0, 1)$ random numbers to simulate a stochastic event having a infinite number of outcomes, including an event governed by
  - ☐ a uniform probability distribution. [17.8]
  - ☐ a normal probability distribution. [17.8]
- ☐ Simulation topics for further study. [17.9]

Glossary

Simulation. An experiment in which we attempt to understand how something will behave in reality by imitating its behavior in an artificial environment that approximates reality. [17.1]

Replace-only-at-failure policy. A policy which replaces an item only when it fails. [17.1]

Age replacement policy. A policy which replaces an item either when it fails or when it reaches the age of T, where T is a prespecified constant. [17.1]

Stochastic event. An event whose outcome is uncertain and, thus, governed by a probability distribution. [17.2]

Random number generator. A device or process that generates numbers randomly distributed over a specified interval. [17.2]

Table of random numbers. A table displaying a sequence of digits, each of which is a random selection from the interval from 0 to 9. [17.2]

Run. Each repetition of a simulation. [17.3]

Next-event simulation. A type of simulation that proceeds by repeatedly advancing the clock from the time of one event to the time of the next event. [17.7]

Downtime. The amount of time that elapses from the time a machine fails until the time its repair is complete. [17.7]

$U(0, 1)$ **random numbers.** Computer-generated decimal fractions that are randomly distributed over the interval from 0 up to but not including 1. [17.8]

Mixed congruential method. The most common method used by computers to generate $U(0, 1)$ random numbers. [17.8]

Pseudorandom numbers. A term often used to describe computer-generated random numbers (since they are generated using a mathematical formula instead of being truly random). [17.8]

GPSS, SIMSCRIPT, and SLAM. Special-purpose computer languages for simulation. [17.9]

Variance-reducing techniques. A body of knowledge relating to how to improve the accuracy of estimates obtained by simulation. [17.9]

Validation. The process of verifying that a simulation accurately represents the environment it is trying to simulate. [17.9]

EXERCISES

Exercises 17.1–17.6 test your understanding of simulation in the context of variations of the four scenarios we used to illustrate simulation in Sections 17.1-17.7. Note that Exercises 17.5 and 17.6 involve next-event simulation and, hence, should be worked only if you have read Section 17.7.

*17.1 Reconsider May Tayne's problem in Sections 17.1-17.3. Table 17.9 summarized our simulation of an age replacement policy with $T = 9$. Construct a similar table for the simulation of an age replacement policy with $T = 10$. Begin your random number generation at the start of Table 17.4's tenth row.

17.2. Reconsider May Tayne's problem in Sections 17.1–17.3. Now suppose that, besides a repair-only-at-failure policy and an age replacement policy, May wants to consider a third type of policy known as a *block replacement policy*. This policy calls for replacing the belt when it fails and also at any time that is a multiple of T days, where T is a prespecified constant. For example, if $T = 25$, the belt undergoes an unplanned replacement when it fails and planned replacements at the end of days 25, 50, 75, and so on. (Note that a planned replacement occurs regardless of the current belt's age.)

(a) Using the format of Table 17.9, simulate 25 consecutive belt replacements under a block replacement policy with $T = 25$ days. Begin your random number generation at the start of Table 17.4's tenth row.

(b) Suppose it turns out that the average daily cost for the best age replacement policy is only slightly better than the average daily cost for the best block replacement policy. Why might May prefer to use the block replacement policy? (*Hint:* Consider the record-keeping requirements.)

17.3. Reconsider the stochastic project in Exercise 11.3.

(a) Using the format of Table 17.12, simulate 20 runs of this stochastic project. Begin your simulation at the start of Table 17.4's first row.

(b) Using the formats of Tables 17.13–17.15, summarize the results of part (a)'s simulation.

(c) Based on your simulation, estimate the project's mean duration.

(d) Based on your simulation, provide the smallest estimate of the project's duration for which there is at least a 65% chance of finishing on or before the estimate.

17.4. Reconsider Gotham City's problem in Section 17.6.

(a) Using the format of Figure 17.3, perform

another simulation run, this time beginning the random number generation at the start of Table 17.4's sixth row.

(b) Using Table 17.20, compute the street's cleanliness rating before cleaning and after cleaning.

17.5. Reconsider DH's problem in Section 17.7. Table 17.23 summarized our simulation of DH's current policy of employing 2 service technicians. We stopped this simulation when the total number of repairs reached 10.

(a) Continue the simulation until the total number of repairs reaches 20. Begin your random number generation at the point in Table 17.4 where we ended our simulation in Section 17.7; that is, your first random number should be the "9" that appears in Table 17.4's twentieth row and twenty-sixth column. (If you run out of numbers in Table 17.4's twentieth row, continue with the table's first row.)

(b) Based on your simulation, estimate a machine's average downtime.

(c) Based on your simulation, estimate the average number of idle technicians, the average number of failed machines, and the average number of failed machines in the queue.

(d) Based on your simulation, estimate the probability that at most 2 machines are failed, and estimate the probability that neither technician is idle.

17.6. Reconsider DH's problem in Section 17.7. Table 17.23 summarized our simulation of DH's current policy of employing 2 service technicians.

(a) Using the format of Table 17.23, simulate a policy of using 1 service technician. Begin your random number generation at the start of Table 17.4's twentieth row. Stop your simulation when the total number of repaired machines reaches 10.

(b) Based on your simulation, estimate a machine's average downtime.

(c) Based on your simulation, estimate the average number of failed machines and the average number of failed machines in the queue.

(d) Based on your simulation, estimate the probability that at most 2 machines are failed, and estimate the probability that the technician is idle.

Exercises 17.7–17.15 test your understanding of simulation in the context of scenarios different from those encountered in Sections 17.1–17.7. Note that Exercise 17.15 involves next-event simulation and, hence, should be worked only if you have read Section 17.7.

*17.7. Suppose you are offered a chance to play a game with the following rules:

- You will repeatedly flip a biased coin whose probability of heads is 0.6 and probability of tails is 0.4.
- The game ends the first time that the number of heads tossed exceeds the number of tails tossed by three.
- You pay $1 for each coin flip but receive $10 at the end of the game.

By simulating 10 plays of the game, estimate the average amount *per game* you would win or lose if you played the game a very large number of times. Begin your random number generation at the start of Table 17.4's fifteenth row.

17.8. For those who have never played the game of craps, the following is a summary of the rules:

- The player rolls two dice.
- If the first throw results in a sum of 7 or 11, the player wins.
- If the first throw results in a sum of 2, 3, or 12, the player loses.
- If the first throw results in a sum of 4, 5, 6, 8, 9, 10, this sum becomes the player's *point*. The player continues to roll the two dice until the sum is either the point or a 7. In the former case, the player wins; in the latter case, the player loses.

By simulating 10 plays of the game, estimate the probability of winning a single game of craps. Begin your random number generation at the start of Table 17.4's seventh row.

17.9. For those who have never played the game of bowling, the following a summary of the rules:

- A game consists of ten *frames*.
- In each of the first nine frames, the bowler gets two chances to knock over ten pins with a bowling ball. If the first ball knocks over all ten pins, it is a *strike* and the frame is over. If the bowler does not get a strike but knocks over the remaining pins with the second ball, it is a *spare* and the frame is over. Even if pins remain standing after the second ball, the frame is over, and the next frame begins with ten pins.
- In each of the first nine frames, a bowler's score is computed as follows:

  1. If no spare or strike occurs, the score equals the number of pins knocked over.
  2. If a spare occurs, the score equals 10 plus the number of pins knocked over with the next ball (in the next frame).
  3. If a strike occurs, the score equals 10 plus the number of pins knocked over with the next two balls (even if a strike in the next frame means the second of the balls occurs two frames later).

- The tenth frame is slightly different than the first nine. The following rules determine the number of balls rolled and the bowler's score:

  1. If neither a spare nor a strike occurs, the game is over, and the score in the tenth frame equals the number of pins knocked over.

  2. If a spare occurs, the bowler gets to roll an extra ball, and the score in the tenth frame equals 10 plus the number of pins knocked over with the extra ball.

  3. If a strike occurs, the bowler gets to roll two extra balls, and the score in the tenth frame equals 10 plus the number of pins knocked over with the two extra balls.

- A bowler's game score equals the sum of the scores in the ten frames. (The maximum game score is 300, which results from a strike in each of the first nine frames and three strikes in the tenth frame.)

Suppose Andy and Anne are bowling together. The table below displays each bowler's probability distribution for the number of pins he or she will knock over with the first ball in any frame and with any extra ball in the tenth frame.

	0–5	6	7	8	9	10
Andy's probabilities	0.00	0.02	0.03	0.10	0.15	0.70
Anne's probabilities	0.00	0.05	0.05	0.05	0.05	0.80

Depending on the number of pins knocked over with the first ball, the tables below display each bowler's probability distribution for the number of pins he or she will knock over with the second ball in any frame (except for an extra ball in the tenth frame):

Andy's Probabilities

Pins Knocked Over With First Ball	Pins Knocked Over With Second Ball				
	0	1	2	3	4
6	0.01	0.03	0.06	0.10	0.80
7	0.01	0.05	0.09	0.85	~
8	0.02	0.08	0.90	~	~
9	0.05	0.95	~	~	~

Anne's Probabilities

Pins Knocked Over With First Ball	Pins Knocked Over With Second Ball				
	0	1	2	3	4
6	0.01	0.04	0.05	0.15	0.75
7	0.02	0.06	0.12	0.80	~
8	0.05	0.10	0.85	~	~
9	0.10	0.90	~	~	~

Simulate a game of bowling between Andy and Anne and specify who wins and the score of each bowler. Begin your random number generation at the start of Table 17.4's tenth row.

*17.10. The United States Senate will soon vote on the confirmation of the President's nominee to the Supreme Court. As of now, there have been firm declarations by 44 senators that they will vote for the confirmation and by 46 senators that they will vote against the confirmation. Assume none of these 90 senators will change his or her mind. The remaining ten senators are undecided. Based on conversations with these undecided senators, the President has estimated the following probabilities:

	Undecided Senator									
	A	B	C	D	E	F	G	H	I	J
Probability of Voting For Confirmation	0.9	0.5	0.8	0.1	0.7	0.4	0.9	0.1	0.5	0.7
Probability of Voting Against Confirmation	0.1	0.5	0.2	0.9	0.3	0.6	0.1	0.9	0.5	0.3

Assume that each undecided senator's vote is probabilistically independent of the votes of the other undecided senators. If the vote should end in a tie, the Vice President (as the Senate's presiding officer) must vote to break the tie. The Vice President will definitely vote for the confirmation. To avoid political embarrassment, the President is considering withdrawing the nomination before the vote occurs. Before deciding whether to withdraw the nomination, the President would like to estimate the probability that the nominee will be confirmed. Estimate this probability by simulating 10 repetitions of the outcome of the votes of the undecided senators. Begin your random number generation at the start of Table 17.4's thirteenth row.

17.11. In the network below, each node (i.e., circle) represents a computer, and each arc (i.e., line) represents a two-way communication link between the corresponding pair of computers:

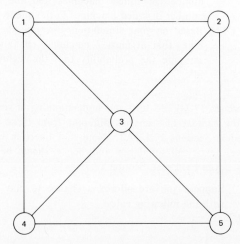

At any point in time, the communication link between computers i and j, denoted by i–j, is either operating or failed. The table below displays each link's operating probability:

Link i-j	1-2	1-3	1-4	2-3	2-5	3-4	3-5	4-5
Operating Probability	0.9	0.6	0.7	0.5	0.8	0.7	0.9	0.8

For simplicity, assume that the operation of each link is probabilistically independent of the operation of every other link, and assume that the computers themselves never fail. The *reliability* of the entire communication network is the probability that all computers can communicate with each other—that is, the probability that every pair of computers is connected by at least one path of operating links. By simulating the network at 10 distinct points in time, estimate the network's reliability. Begin your random number generation at the start of Table 17.4's eighteenth row.

17.12. Stattick Electric Company (SEC) manufactures a special type of battery used by a large number of customers in a major metropolitan area. Since it costs $60 for SEC to manufacture a battery and since SEC currently sells a battery for $100, SEC's profit is $40 per battery. Once installed, a battery operates continuously until it fails. A battery's lifetime (i.e., the elapsed time between a battery's installation and its failure) is governed by the probability distribution displayed below:

Lifetime (days)	6	7	8	9	10	11	12
Probability	0.05	0.10	0.20	0.30	0.20	0.10	0.05

Although SEC currently offers no warranty, it believes a warranty might attract new customers. Consequently, SEC is considering offering a type of warranty known as a *ten-day pro rata warranty*. This warranty would operate as follows:

- If a battery's lifetime is less than 10 days, the customer obtains a replacement battery for a reduced price of $(d/10)(\$100)$, where d is the battery's lifetime. For example, if the battery's lifetime is 8 days, the customer pays $80 instead of $100 for a replacement battery.
- If a battery's lifetime is at least 10 days, the customer pays the normal price of $100 for a replacement battery.

SEC would trust that a customer would report the true lifetime of a failed battery when purchasing a replacement battery. It would audit any customer with an abnormal number of warranty claims. In what follows, assume a customer uses only one battery at a time.

(a) Without using simulation, compute SEC's average daily profit per customer under its current no-warranty policy. (*Hint:* First compute a battery's average lifetime.)
(b) By simulating 20 consecutive battery lifetimes, estimate SEC's average daily profit per customer if it offers a ten-day pro rata warranty. Begin your random number generation at the start of Table 17.4's third row.
(c) Using your answers to parts (a) and (b), estimate the minimum percentage increase in SEC's number of customers that would be necessary to compensate for the profit lost from switching from no warranty to a ten-day pro rata warranty.

*17.13. Wilcox and Wilcox (W&W) is a pharmaceutical company. One of its products is Rayban, a sun block packaged in eight-ounce bottles. W&W wants to estimate the profit it will earn from the sale of Rayban during the upcoming year. This profit depends on five factors: (1) the total size of the annual market for sun block, (2) Rayban's share of the total market, (3) the selling price per bottle, (4) the variable cost per bottle, and (5) the annual fixed costs (i.e., those costs that are independent of the amount of Rayban sold). For each of these factors, W&W has determined a most-likely estimate, a pessimistic estimate, and an optimistic estimate. These estimates are summarized in the table below:

Factor	Most-likely Estimate	Pessimistic Estimate	Optimistic Estimate
1. Total annual market (bottles)	1,000,000	800,000	1,200,000
2. Market share	20%	15%	25%
3. Selling price per bottle	$10	$9	$11
4. Variable cost per bottle	$5	$6	$4
5. Annual fixed cost	$400,000	$500,000	$300,000

W&W has made the following simplifying assumptions:

- Each factor will equal its most-likely estimate with a probability of 0.6, its pessimistic estimate with a probability of 0.2, or its optimistic estimate with a probability of 0.2.
- Each factor is probabilistically independent of every other factor.
- A factor's value will not change during the year.

Since there are many possible combinations of values for the five factors, W&W's annual profit from the sale of Rayban is uncertain. For example, if factor 1 equals its most-likely estimate, factors 2 and 4 equal their pessimistic estimates, and factors 3 and 5 equal their optimistic estimates, then W&W's annual profit will equal

$$(1,000,000)(0.15)(\$11-\$6) - \$300,000 = \$450,000.$$

(a) Simulate 10 combinations of values for the five factors, and, for each combination, compute W&W's annual profit from the sale of Rayban. Begin your random number generation at the start of Table 17.4's fifth row.

(b) Based on your simulation, estimate the mean of the annual profit.

(c) Based on your simulation, provide the largest estimate of the annual profit for which there is at least a 65% chance that the profit will equal or exceed the estimate.

17.14. Hurtz is a small car-rental agency that leases a fleet of cars from a major auto manufacturer and then rents the cars to local customers. Hurtz wants to decide how large its fleet size should be. Based on historical data, Hurtz has estimated the following probability distributions:

Number of Customers Per Day	0	1	2
Probability	0.2	0.3	0.5

Length of Rental Contract (Days)	1	2	3	4
Probability	0.2	0.3	0.3	0.2

Hurtz is open for business seven days per week. The lease cost for each car in its fleet is $10 per day. The net profit on rental contracts (exclusive of the lease cost) is $20 per day. Suppose that Hurtz decides to use a fleet of 3 cars. Simulate 21 days of rental business to estimate the following:

- Hurtz's average daily profit.
- The probability that a potential customer will find no car available.

In conducting your simulation, make the following simplifying assumptions:

1. A rental always occurs at the beginning of the day.
2. A return of a car always occurs at the end of the day, and the returned car is always available to rent at the beginning of the next day.
3. A rental is always paid in full at the beginning of the rental.

Also, in conducting your simulation, begin your random number generation at the start of Table 17.4's fifteenth row.

17.15. The Second National Bank employs 3 tellers to serve its customers. The time between the arrivals of consecutive customers is governed by the following probability distribution:

Time Between Arrivals (Minutes)	1	2	3	4	5
Probability	0.45	0.25	0.15	0.10	0.05

If a customer finds all tellers busy, he or she joins a queue (i.e., a waiting line) that is serviced by all tellers; that is, there is not a distinct queue for each teller but rather a single queue of customers waiting for the first available teller. When a teller finishes serving a customer, he or she next serves the first customer in the queue. The time required to serve a customer is governed by the following probability distribution:

Service Time (Minutes)	2	3	4	5	6	7
Probability	0.05	0.15	0.30	0.30	0.15	0.05

Conduct a next-event simulation of the arrival and service of customers at Second National Bank. In doing so,

- Begin your simulation with no customers present in the bank.
- Begin your random number generation at the start of Table 17.4's second row.
- Stop your simulation when 20 customers have been served.
- Assume that, if the clock time at which the next customer will arrive equals the clock time at which a teller will finish serving a customer, the service completion occurs first.
- Assume that, if the clock times at which two or more tellers will finish serving their respective customers are equal, the lowest-numbered teller finishes first.
- Assume that, if two or more tellers are idle when the queue is empty, the lowest-numbered teller is the first to begin serving a customer when one arrives.

Based on your simulation, estimate the average time a customer waits in the queue, the average number of customers in the queue, and the probability that an arriving customer must join the queue (i.e., the probability that no teller is idle).

Exercises 17.16–17.20 test your understanding of how a computer generates $U(0,1)$ random numbers using the mixed congruential method and how $U(0,1)$ random numbers can be transformed into other types of random numbers.

*17.16. Reconsider Table 17.26, which summarizes the generation of the first sixteen $U(0,1)$ random numbers using the mixed congruential method (MCM) with $r_0 = 0.4375$, $m = 16$, $a = 5$, and $c = 3$. When discussing Table 17.26 in Section 17.8, we noted that, for $m = 16$, using $a = 5$ and $c = 3$ leads to the generation of 16 distinct random numbers before the sequence of random numbers begins to loop. To illustrate that this is not the case for every choice of a and c, change from $c = 3$ to $c = 8$ and (with m, a, and r_0 unchanged) use the MCM to generate $U(0,1)$ random numbers until the sequence begins to loop. In comparison to the generation of 16 distinct random numbers before looping begins when $c = 3$, how many distinct random numbers are generated before looping begins when $c = 8$?

17.17. In this exercise, you will use the mixed congruential method (MCM) to generate $U(0,1)$ random variables with a modulus of $m = 8$ and alternative values for the multiplier a, the increment c, and the seed r_0.

(a) Using the format of Table 17.26, apply the MCM with $m = 8$, $a = 5$, $c = 1$, and $r_0 = 0.625$ to generate $U(0,1)$ random numbers until the sequence begins to loop. How many distinct random numbers are generated before looping begins?

(b) Repeat part (a), this time with $r_0 = 0.125$ and with m, a, and c unchanged from part (a).

(c) Repeat part (a), this time with $c = 2$ and with m, a, and r_0 unchanged from part (a).

(d) Repeat part (a), this time with $a = 3$ and with m, c, and r_0 unchanged from part (a).

(e) What do parts (a)–(d) illustrate about how the choice of values for a, c, and r_0 affect the ability to generate m distinct random numbers before the sequence begins to loop?

17.18. Using the format of Table 17.26, apply the mixed congruential method with $m = 1000$, $a = 201$, $c = 503$, and $r_0 = 0.327$ until you have generated five $U(0,1)$ random numbers.

17.19. When using the mixed congruential method (MCM), the choice for the modulus m, the multiplier a, and the increment c is said to have *full period* if m distinct $U(0,1)$ random numbers are generated before looping begins. Experts have proved that a choice for m, a, and c has full period if and only if all three of the following conditions hold:

1. The only positive integer by which both m and c are divisible is 1.
2. If m is divisible by a prime number p (i.e., a number divisible only by itself and 1), then $a-1$ is also divisible by p.
3. If m is divisible by 4, then $a-1$ is also divisible by 4.

Using this theorem, determine (without actually generating any random numbers) which of the following choices for m, a, and c have full period and, for those that do not, which of the theorem's conditions are violated.

(a) $m = 16$, $a = 5$, and $c = 3$ (as in Table 17.26).
(b) $m = 16$, $a = 5$, and $c = 8$ (as in Exercise 17.16).
(c) $m = 8$, $a = 5$, and $c = 1$ (as in part (a) of Exercise 17.17).
(d) $m = 8$, $a = 5$, and $c = 2$ (as in part (c) of Exercise 17.17).
(e) $m = 8$, $a = 3$, and $c = 1$ (as in part (d) of Exercise 17.17).
(f) $m = 1000$, $a = 201$, and $c = 503$ (as in Exercise 17.18).
(g) $m = 1000$, $a = 191$, and $c = 503$.
(h) $m = 1000$, $a = 193$, and $c = 503$.
(i) $m = 1000$, $a = 181$, and $c = 489$.

17.20. Assume a computer has generated the following twelve $U(0,1)$ random numbers using the mixed congruential method:

0.65452
0.46233
0.02003
0.36567
0.96418
0.58333
0.17808
0.61619
0.32230
0.80013
0.09101
0.26950

(a) Using the procedure described in Section 17.8, transform the first six of these $U(0,1)$ random numbers into six random integers in the interval from 000 to 999.

(b) Using the procedure described in Section 17.8, transform the first six of these $U(0,1)$ random numbers into six random numbers drawn from a uniform probability distribution over the entire interval from 40 to 60.

(c) Using the procedure described in Section 17.8, transform all twelve $U(0,1)$ random numbers into *one* random number drawn from a probability distribution that is approximately normal with a mean of $\mu = 500$ and a standard deviation $\sigma = 100$.

SOLUTIONS
TO SELECTED EXERCISES

Here are solutions (frequently abbreviated) to the end-of-chapter exercises marked with an *. For the complete solution to an exercise, consult the accompanying Instructor's Manual.

Chapter 2

2.2. (a)

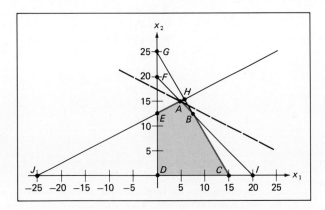

(b) The feasible region has 5 corner points—the points labeled A, B, C, D, and E.

(c) The optimal solution is at point A, whose coordinates are (5, 15). The optimal objective value is 175.

(d)

Constraint	Binding or Nonbinding?
$-x_1 + 2x_2 \leq 25$	Binding
$x_1 + x_2 \leq 20$	Binding
$5x_1 + 3x_2 \leq 75$	Nonbinding
$x_1 \geq 0$	Nonbinding
$x_2 \geq 0$	Nonbinding

(e) $S_1 = 0$, $S_2 = 0$, $S_3 = 5$.

2.6. (a)

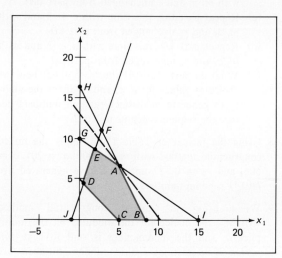

(b) The points labeled A, B, C, D, and E.

(c) The optimal solution is at point A, whose coordinates are $(4\frac{1}{2}, 7)$. The optimal objective value is $50\frac{1}{2}$.

(d)

Constraint	Binding or Nonbinding?
$10x_1 + 15x_2 \leq 150$	Binding
$20x_1 + 20x_2 \geq 100$	Nonbinding
$20x_1 + 10x_2 \leq 160$	Binding
$-3x_1 + x_2 \leq 3$	Nonbinding
$x_1 \geq 0$	Nonbinding
$x_2 \geq 0$	Nonbinding

(e) $S_1 = 0$, $E_2 = 130$, $S_2 = 0$, and $S_4 = 9\frac{1}{2}$.

2.9. Infeasibility has occurred.

2.13. Unboundedness has occurred.

2.17.

Point	Sign of S_1	Sign of S_2	Sign of S_3
A	$S_1 < 0$	$S_2 < 0$	$S_3 > 0$
B	$S_1 < 0$	$S_2 < 0$	$S_3 < 0$
C	$S_1 < 0$	$S_2 = 0$	$S_3 > 0$
D	$S_1 > 0$	$S_2 = 0$	$S_3 = 0$
E	$S_1 > 0$	$S_2 > 0$	$S_3 > 0$

2.20. (a) Consult the graph previously displayed in the solution to Exercise 2.2.

(b) Corner-point solution B.

(c) Corner-point solution C.

(d) There are an infinite number of correct answers. One specific objective function is "Maximize $-10x_1 + 10x_2$."
In general, for a maximizing objective function $c_1 x_1 + c_2 x_2$ to be a correct answer, c_1 must be negative, c_2 must be nonnegative, and $-c_1/c_2$ must be greater than or equal to ½.

2.23. (a)

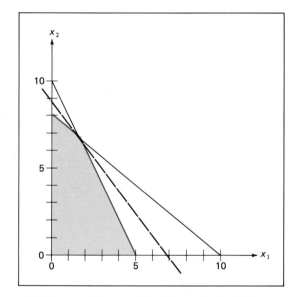

(b) The coordinates of the LP's optimal solution are (1⅔, 6⅔). The LP's optimal objective value is 61⅔.

(c) Substituting (2, 7) into the two structural constraints, we find that this rounded solution violates both constraints. Hence, it is infeasible.

(d) Substituting (2, 6) into the two structural constraints, we find that this rounded solution satisfies both constraints. Hence, it is feasible. Its objective value is 60. Its maximum percentage error is 2.7%.

(e) Since (2, 6) is guaranteed to be within 2.7% of optimality for the integer linear program, it is a good approximation. In fact, after you have read Chapter 9, you can verify that (2, 6) is the true optimal solution (although rounding will not generally yield the optimal solution).

2.25.

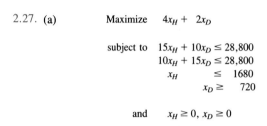

Maximize $5x_1 + 3x_2$

subject to $x_1 + 2x_2 \leq 40$
$2x_1 + x_2 \leq 25$
$3x_1 + 2x_2 \leq 30$

and $x_1 \geq 0, x_2 \geq 0$

2.27. (a)

Maximize $4x_H + 2x_D$

subject to $15x_H + 10x_D \leq 28{,}800$
$10x_H + 15x_D \leq 28{,}800$
$x_H \leq 1680$
$x_D \geq 720$

and $x_H \geq 0, x_D \geq 0$

(b)

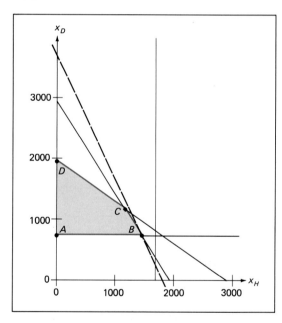

(c) The optimal solution is at point B, whose coordinates are (1440, 720). The optimal objective value is 7200.

(d)

Constraint	Binding or Nonbinding?
$15x_H + 10x_D \leq 28{,}800$	Binding
$10x_H + 15x_D \leq 28{,}800$	Nonbinding
$x_H \leq 1680$	Nonbinding
$x_D \geq 720$	Binding
$x_H \geq 0$	Nonbinding
$x_D \geq 0$	Nonbinding

(e) Since $10x_H + 15x_D \leq 28{,}800$ and $x_H \leq 1680$ are nonbinding constraints, the stuffing machine and the beak sharpening machine are being used for less time than available.

(f) As indicated in part (d), $x_D \geq 720$ is a binding constraint.

(g) The optimal solution remains at point B.

(h) The optimal solution switches to point C.

2.31. $\quad$ Minimize $\quad 1.0x_B + 0.5x_C + 0.7x_L$

$$
\begin{aligned}
\text{subject to} \quad x_B + \quad x_C + \quad x_L &= 100 \\
0.20x_B + 0.15x_C + 0.15x_L &\geq 12 \\
0.20x_B + 0.15x_C + 0.25x_L &\leq 24 \\
0.60x_B + 0.70x_C + 0.60x_L &\leq 64 \\
x_L &\geq 30
\end{aligned}
$$

$$
\text{and} \quad x_B \geq 0, \, x_C \geq 0, \, x_L \geq 0.
$$

Chapter 3

3.2. (a) Consult the previously displayed solution to Exercise 2.2.

(b) The table below summarizes the analysis.

Decision Variable	Current Value of Coefficient	Maximum Allowable Increase	Maximum Allowable Decrease
x_1	5	5	10
x_2	10	∞	5

(c) The tables below summarize the analysis.

RHS_1's Current Value	RHS_1's Maximum Allowable Increase	RHS_1's Maximum Allowable Decrease	Optimal Values x_1	x_2	S_1	S_2	S_3	Objective Value
25	15	$7\frac{1}{2}$	$5 - \frac{1}{3}\Delta$	$15 + \frac{1}{3}\Delta$	0	0	$5 + \frac{2}{3}\Delta$	$175 + \frac{5}{3}\Delta$

RHS_2's Current Value	RHS_2's Maximum Allowable Increase	RHS_2's Maximum Allowable Decrease	Optimal Values x_1	x_2	S_1	S_2	S_3	Objective Value
20	$1\frac{2}{13}$	$7\frac{1}{2}$	$5 + \frac{2}{3}\Delta$	$15 + \frac{1}{3}\Delta$	0	0	$5 - \frac{13}{3}\Delta$	$175 + \frac{20}{3}\Delta$

RHS_3's Current Value	RHS_3's Maximum Allowable Increase	RHS_3's Maximum Allowable Decrease	Optimal Values x_1	x_2	S_1	S_2	S_3	Objective Value
75	∞	5	5	15	0	0	$5 + \Delta$	175

(d) Omitted here.

3.6. (a) Consult the previously displayed solution to Exercise 2.6.

(b) The table below summarizes the analysis.

Decision Variable	Current Value of Coefficient	Maximum Allowable Increase	Maximum Allowable Decrease
x_1	5	3	$2\frac{1}{3}$
x_2	4	$3\frac{1}{2}$	$1\frac{1}{2}$

(c) The tables below summarize the analysis.

RHS_1's Current Value	RHS_1's Maximum Allowable Increase	RHS_1's Maximum Allowable Decrease	Optimal Values x_1	x_2	S_1	E_2	S_3	S_4	Objective Value
150	38	70	$4\frac{1}{2} - \frac{1}{20}\Delta$	$7 + \frac{1}{10}\Delta$	0	$130 + \Delta$	0	$9\frac{1}{2} - \frac{1}{4}\Delta$	$50\frac{1}{2} + \frac{3}{20}\Delta$

RHS_2's Current Value	RHS_2's Maximum Allowable Increase	RHS_2's Maximum Allowable Decrease	Optimal Values x_1	x_2	S_1	E_2	S_3	S_4	Objective Value
100	130	∞	$4\frac{1}{2}$	7	0	$130 - \Delta$	0	$9\frac{1}{2}$	$50\frac{1}{2}$

RHS_3's Current Value	RHS_3's Maximum Allowable Increase	RHS_3's Maximum Allowable Decrease	Optimal Values x_1	x_2	S_1	E_2	S_3	S_4	Objective Value
160	140	$34\frac{6}{11}$	$4\frac{1}{2} + \frac{3}{40}\Delta$	$7 - \frac{1}{20}\Delta$	0	$130 + \frac{1}{2}\Delta$	0	$9\frac{1}{2} + \frac{11}{40}\Delta$	$50\frac{1}{2} + \frac{7}{40}\Delta$

RHS_4's Current Value	RHS_4's Maximum Allowable Increase	RHS_4's Maximum Allowable Decrease	Optimal Values x_1	x_2	S_1	E_2	S_3	S_4	Objective Value
3	∞	$9\frac{1}{2}$	$4\frac{1}{2}$	7	0	130	0	$9\frac{1}{2} + \Delta$	$50\frac{1}{2}$

(d) Omitted here.

3.14. (a) $5 \leq c_2 \leq \infty$.

(b) (5, 15) remains the optimal solution, and the optimal objective value changes to 195.

(c) There is insufficient information.

(d) $17.5 \leq RHS_1 \leq 40$.

(e) Substituting $\Delta = 6$ into the expressions derived in Exercise 3.2(c)'s sensitivity analysis of RHS_1, we obtain a new optimal solution of $x_1 = 3$, $x_2 = 17$, $S_1 = 0$, $S_2 = 0$, and $S_3 = 9$, and a new optimal objective value of 185.

(f) There is insufficient information.

(g) Since the third structural constraint is nonbinding at optimality, the optimal value of S_3 decreases by 3 from 5 to 2, and the optimal values of x_1, x_2, S_1, S_2, and the objective value remain unchanged.

3.18. (a) $2\frac{1}{2} \leq c_2 \leq 7\frac{1}{2}$.

(b) $(4\frac{1}{2}, 7)$ remains the optimal solution, and the optimal objective value changes to $43\frac{1}{2}$.

(c) There is insufficient information.

(d) $80 \leq RHS_1 \leq 188$.

(e) Substituting $\Delta = -20$ into the expressions derived in Exercise 3.6(c)'s sensitivity analysis of RHS_1, we obtain a new optimal solution of $x_1 = 3$, and $x_2 = 8$, $S_1 = 0$, $E_2 = 120$, $S_3 = 0$, and $S_4 = 4$, and a new optimal objective value of 47.

(f) Since the second structural constraint is nonbinding at optimality, the optimal value of E_2 decreases by 100 from 130 to 30, and the optimal values of x_1, x_2, S_1, S_3, S_4 and the objective value remain unchanged.

(g) There is insufficient information to analyze the change.

3.20. (a) (1440, 720) remains the optimal solution, and the optimal objective value changes to 7560.

(b) There is insufficient information to analyze the change.

(c) Because the constraint's shadow price is 0.266667, the optimal objective value changes to 7200 + (0.266667)(1800) = 7680.

(d) Because the constraint's shadow price is 0.00, the optimal objective value remains unchanged at 7200.

(e) Because the constraint's shadow price is −0.666667, the optimal objective value changes to 7200 + (−0.666667)(−120) = 7280.

(f) There is insufficient information to analyze the change.

3.24. (a) (0, 40, 60) remains the optimal solution, and the optimal objective value remains at 62 (since x_B's optimal value is 0).

(b) There is insufficient information to analyze the change.

(c) (0, 40, 60) remains the optimal solution, and the optimal objective value changes to 62 + (0.20)(60) = 74.

(d) Because the constraint's shadow price is 0.00, the optimal objective value remains unchanged at 62.

(e) There is insufficient information.

(f) Because the constraint's shadow price is 2, the optimal objective value changes to 62 − (2)(−2) = 66.

(g) A decrease in the amount of the blend from 100 to 90 pounds causes the right-hand sides of all five structural constraints to change. Since LINPRO's sensitivity analysis output is valid only when one right-hand side changes and the others remain unchanged, there is insufficient information.

3.26. (a)
$$\text{Maximize} \quad 2y_1 + 3y_2 - 5w$$
$$\begin{aligned} \text{subject to} \quad & y_1 + 2y_2 - 3w \leq 12 \\ & y_1 - 4y_2 + 3w \leq 24 \\ & y_1 - y_2 \quad\;\; \geq 1 \end{aligned}$$
$$\text{and} \quad y_1 \geq 0,\, y_2 \geq 0,\, w \geq 0$$

(b) The equivalent LP's optimal solution is $(y_1, y_2, w) = (18, 0, 2)$ with an optimal objective value of 26.

(c) The original LP's optimal solution is $(x_1, x_2) = (16, -2)$ with an objective value of 26.

3.29. (a)
$$\text{Maximize} \quad 2y_1 + 3y_2$$
$$\begin{aligned} \text{subject to} \quad & y_1 + 2y_2 \leq 13 \\ & y_1 - y_2 \geq -4 \end{aligned}$$
$$\text{and} \quad y_1 \geq 0,\, y_2 \geq 0$$

(b) The equivalent LP's optimal solution is $(y_1, y_2) = (13, 0)$ with an objective value of 26.

(c) The original LP's optimal solution is $(x_1, x_2) = (16, -2)$ with an objective value of 26.

Chapter 4

4.3. (a) The objective function becomes

$$\text{Maximize} \quad 1.015A_6 + 1.035B_5 + 1.060C_4 + 1.110D_1$$

The cash balance equations become

$$\begin{aligned} A_1 + B_1 + C_1 + D_1 &= 500{,}000 \\ A_2 - 1.015A_1 &= 0 \\ A_3 + B_3 - 1.015A_2 - 1.035B_1 &= 0 \\ A_4 + C_4 - 1.015A_3 - 1.060C_1 &= 0 \\ A_5 + B_5 - 1.015A_4 - 1.035B_3 &= 0 \\ A_6 - 1.015A_5 &= 0 \end{aligned}$$

The average risk constraints, average maturity constraints, and nonnegativity constraints remain the same.

(b) The right-hand side of the cash balance equation for month 4 becomes 250,000.

$$
\begin{aligned}
a_1 &\geq 40 \\
a_1 &\leq 200 \\
a_2 &\leq 200 \\
0.6a_1 - 0.4a_2 &\leq 0
\end{aligned}
$$

and $\quad a_1, a_2, p_1, p_2, p_3 \geq 0.$

4.8. Let plant 4 be a fictitious plant with a supply of 30, the excess of demand over supply. Besides the decision variables defined in Section 4.5, let $x_{41}, x_{42}, \ldots, x_{45}$ denote the respective amounts shipped from the fictitious plant 4 to warehouses 1, 2, . . . , 5. Since plant 4 is fictitious, x_{4j} represents the unsatisfied demand at warehouse j. The linear program is:

Minimize
$$
\begin{aligned}
& 4x_{11} + 6x_{12} + 5x_{13} + 12x_{14} + 19x_{15} \\
&+ 10x_{21} + 4x_{22} + 8x_{23} + 5x_{24} + 14x_{25} \\
&+ 13x_{31} + 9x_{32} + 3x_{33} + 6x_{34} + 10x_{35} \\
&+ 0.15x_{41} + 0.10x_{42} + 0.25x_{43} + 0.20x_{44} + 0.05x_{45}
\end{aligned}
$$

subject to
$$
\begin{aligned}
x_{11} + x_{12} + x_{13} + x_{14} + x_{15} &= 180 \\
x_{21} + x_{22} + x_{23} + x_{24} + x_{25} &= 250 \\
x_{31} + x_{32} + x_{33} + x_{34} + x_{35} &= 150 \\
x_{41} + x_{42} + x_{43} + x_{44} + x_{45} &= 30
\end{aligned}
$$

$$
\begin{aligned}
x_{11} + x_{21} + x_{31} + x_{41} &= 120 \\
x_{12} + x_{22} + x_{32} + x_{42} &= 100 \\
x_{13} + x_{23} + x_{33} + x_{43} &= 160 \\
x_{14} + x_{24} + x_{34} + x_{44} &= 80 \\
x_{15} + x_{25} + x_{35} + x_{45} &= 150
\end{aligned}
$$

and $\quad x_{ij} \geq 0$ for all i-j pairs.

4.11. Let p_1 and p_2 denote the respective production quantities of sweet pickles and dill pickles.
Let a_1 and a_2 denote the respective amounts spent on the advertising of sweet pickles and dill pickles.
The linear program is

Maximize $\quad 0.85p_1 + 0.90p_2 - a_1 - a_2$

subject to
$$
\begin{aligned}
0.60p_1 + 0.85p_2 + a_1 + a_2 &\leq 16{,}000 \\
p_1 \qquad\qquad - 3a_1 \quad\; &\leq 5000 \\
p_2 \qquad - 5a_2 &\leq 4000 \\
0.4p_1 - 0.6p_2 \qquad\qquad\; &\leq 0 \\
0.7p_1 - 0.3p_2 \qquad\qquad\; &\geq 0
\end{aligned}
$$

and $\quad p_1, p_2, a_1, a_2, \geq 0.$

4.13. Let p_1, p_2, and p_3 denote the respective square yards of cardboard stamped using patterns 1, 2, and 3.
Let a_1 and a_2 denote the respective production quantities of arrangements 1 and 2.
The linear program is

Maximize $\quad 7a_1 + 5a_2 - 10p_1 - 10p_2 - 10p_3$

subject to
$$
\begin{aligned}
8a_1 + 3a_2 - 70p_1 - 60p_2 - 23p_3 &\leq 0 \\
4a_1 + 12a_2 - 20p_1 - 60p_2 - 117p_3 &\leq 0 \\
p_1 + p_2 + p_3 &\leq 1000
\end{aligned}
$$

4.17. (a) Let x_{AY}, x_{AZ}, x_{BY}, x_{BZ}, x_{CY}, and x_{CZ} denote the amounts shipped between the various plant-warehouse combinations.
Let x_{Y1}, x_{Y2}, x_{Y3}, x_{Y4}, x_{Z1}, x_{Z2}, x_{Z3}, x_{Z4} denote the amounts shipped between the various warehouse-customer combinations.
The linear program is

Minimize
$$
\begin{aligned}
& 18x_{AY} + 23x_{AZ} + 19x_{BY} + 21x_{BZ} + 25x_{CY} + 16x_{CZ} \\
&+ 5x_{Y1} + 7x_{Y2} + 14x_{Y3} + 11x_{Y4} \\
&+ 12x_{Z1} + 15x_{Z2} + 10x_{Z3} + 8x_{Z4}
\end{aligned}
$$

subject to
$$
\begin{aligned}
x_{AY} + x_{AZ} &= 25 \\
x_{BY} + x_{BZ} &= 29 \\
x_{CY} + x_{CZ} &= 16 \\
x_{Y1} + x_{Y2} + x_{Y3} + x_{Y4} - x_{AY} - x_{BY} - x_{CY} &= 0 \\
x_{Z1} + x_{Z2} + x_{Z3} + x_{Z4} - x_{AZ} - x_{BZ} - x_{CZ} &= 0 \\
x_{Y1} + x_{Z1} &= 19 \\
x_{Y2} + x_{Z2} &= 24 \\
x_{Y3} + x_{Z3} &= 17 \\
x_{Y4} + x_{Z4} &= 10
\end{aligned}
$$

and $\quad x_{ij} \geq 0$ for all i-j pairs.

(b) Change the $=$ in the first three structural constraints to $\leq$.

(c) Add the following two structural constraints:

$$x_{BY} \geq 7 \quad \text{and} \quad x_{BY} \leq 12$$

4.20. Let x_{F1}, x_{F2}, x_{F3}, and x_{F4} denote the respective tons of commodities 1, 2, 3, and 4 loaded into the forward hold.
Similarly define x_{C1}, x_{C2}, x_{C3}, and x_{C4} for the center hold.
Similarly define x_{R1}, x_{R2}, x_{R3}, and x_{R4} for the rear hold.
The linear program is

Maximize
$$
\begin{aligned}
& 6x_{F1} + 6x_{C1} + 6x_{R1} + 8x_{F2} + 8x_{C2} + 8x_{R2} \\
&+ 5x_{F3} + 5x_{C3} + 5x_{R3} + 7x_{F4} + 7x_{C4} + 7x_{R4}
\end{aligned}
$$

subject to
$$
\begin{aligned}
x_{F1} + x_{F2} + x_{F3} + x_{F4} &\leq 3000 \\
x_{C1} + x_{C2} + x_{C3} + x_{C4} &\leq 4000 \\
x_{R1} + x_{R2} + x_{R3} + x_{R4} &\leq 2500 \\
60x_{F1} + 50x_{F2} + 25x_{F3} + 40x_{F4} &\leq 155{,}000 \\
60x_{C1} + 50x_{C2} + 25x_{C3} + 40x_{C4} &\leq 185{,}000 \\
60x_{R1} + 50x_{R2} + 25x_{R3} + 40x_{R4} &\leq 145{,}000 \\
x_{F1} + x_{C1} + x_{R1} &\leq 5000 \\
x_{F2} + x_{C2} + x_{R2} &\leq 3000 \\
x_{F3} + x_{C3} + x_{R3} &\leq 1000 \\
x_{F4} + x_{C4} + x_{R4} &\leq 1500
\end{aligned}
$$

$$x_{F1} + x_{F2} + x_{F3} + x_{F4} - 1.05x_{R1} - 1.05x_{R2} - 1.05x_{R3} - 1.05x_{R4} \leq 0$$
$$x_{F1} + x_{F2} + x_{F3} + x_{F4} - 0.95x_{R1} - 0.95x_{R2} - 0.95x_{R3} - 0.95x_{R4} \geq 0$$
$$x_{C1} + x_{C2} + x_{C3} + x_{C4} - 1.30x_{F1} - 1.30x_{F2} - 1.30x_{F3} - 1.30x_{F4} \geq 0$$
$$x_{C1} + x_{C2} + x_{C3} + x_{C4} - 1.30x_{R1} - 1.30x_{R2} - 1.30x_{R3} - 1.30x_{R4} \geq 0$$
$$x_{C1} + x_{C2} + x_{C3} + x_{C4} - 0.90x_{F1} - 0.90x_{F2} - 0.90x_{F3} - 0.90x_{F4}$$
$$- 0.90x_{R1} - 0.90x_{R2} - 0.90x_{R3} - 0.90x_{R4} \leq 0$$

and $x_{ij} \geq 0$ for all i-j pairs.

Chapter 5

5.2 (a)–(f) Omitted here.

(g) Let $x_{H1}, x_{H2}, x_{H3},$ and x_{H4} denote the internal variables for hawks.
Let $x_{D1}, x_{D2}, x_{D3},$ and x_{D4} denote the interval variable for doves.
The linear program is

Maximize $7.0x_{H1} + 5.0x_{H2} + 3.0x_{H3} + 1.0x_{H4} + 4.5x_{D1} + 3.5x_{D2} + 2.5x_{D3} + 1.5x_{D4}$

subject to
$$15x_{H1} + 15x_{H2} + 15x_{H3} + 15x_{H4} + 10x_{D1} + 10x_{D2} + 10x_{D3} + 10x_{D4} \leq 28{,}800$$
$$10x_{H1} + 10x_{H2} + 10x_{H3} + 10x_{H4} + 15x_{D1} + 15x_{D2} + 15x_{D3} + 15x_{D4} \leq 28{,}800$$
$$x_{H1} + x_{H2} + x_{H3} + x_{H4} \leq 1680$$
$$x_{D1} + x_{D2} + x_{D3} + x_{D4} \geq 720$$
$$x_{H1} \leq 500$$
$$x_{H2} \leq 500$$
$$x_{H3} \leq 500$$
$$x_{H4} \leq 500$$
$$x_{D1} \leq 500$$
$$x_{D2} \leq 500$$
$$x_{D3} \leq 500$$
$$x_{D4} \leq 500$$

and x_{ij} for all i-j pairs.

(h) Omitted here.

5.5. (a) and (b) Omitted here.

(c) Let $x_{B1}, x_{B2},$ and x_{B3} denote the interval variables for the pounds of barley used in the blend.
Let $x_C, x_W,$ and x_H denote the respective pounds of corn, wheat, and hay used in the blend.
The linear program is

Minimize $60x_C + 40x_W + 30x_{B1} + 35x_{B2} + 45x_{B3} + 5x_H$

subject to
$$2x_C + x_W + 3x_{B1} + 3x_{B2} + 3x_{B3} + 4x_H \geq 25$$
$$2x_C + x_W + 3x_{B1} + 3x_{B2} + 3x_{B3} + 4x_H \leq 100$$
$$20x_C + 15x_W + 15x_{B1} + 15x_{B2} + 15x_{B3} + 10x_H \geq 400$$
$$4x_C + 7x_W + 6x_{B1} + 6x_{B2} + 6x_{B3} + 5x_H \geq 125$$
$$200x_C + 400x_W + 300x_{B1} + 300x_{B2} + 300x_{B3} + 500x_H \geq 6000$$
$$x_C + x_W + x_{B1} + x_{B2} + x_{B3} + x_H = 24$$
$$x_{B1} \leq 5$$
$$x_{B2} \leq 10$$

and $x_C, x_W, x_{B1}, x_{B2}, x_{B3}, x_H \geq 0.$

(d) and (e) Omitted here.

5.9. Let x denote the coordinate of the fire station.
The linear program is

Minimize $100d_A^+ + 100d_A^- + 400d_B^+ + 400d_B^- + 200d_C^+ + 200d_C^- + 300d_D^+ + 300d_D^-$

subject to
$$x - d_A^+ + d_A^- = 0$$
$$x - d_B^+ + d_B^- = 2$$
$$x - d_C^+ + d_C^- = 5$$
$$x - d_D^+ + d_D^- = 9$$

and $x \geq 0$ and $d_i^+, d_i^- \geq 0$ for $i = A, B, C,$ and $D.$

5.13. Minimize $p_1^+ d_1^+ + p_1^- d_1^- + p_2^- d_2^- + p_3^+ d_3^+$

subject to
$$3x_1 + 2x_2 - d_1^+ + d_1^- = 60$$
$$2x_1 + x_2 - d_2^+ + d_2^- = 44$$
$$7x_1 + 3x_2 - d_3^+ + d_3^- = 84$$

and $x_1, x_2 \geq 0$ and $d_i^+, d_i^- \geq 0$ for $i = 1, 2, 3.$

5.19. Define the following decision variables:

Decision Variable	Sex	Minority Status	Job Title
x_m	male	nonminority	manager
x_c	male	nonminority	clerk
y_m	male	minority	manager
y_c	male	minority	clerk
w_m	female	nonminority	manager
w_c	female	nonminority	clerk
z_m	female	minority	manager
z_c	female	minority	clerk

The goal program is

Minimize $p_1^- d_1^- + p_2^- d_2^- + p_3^+ d_3^+ + p_4^+ d_4^+ + p_5^+ d_5^+$

subject to
$$x_m + y_m + w_m + z_m = 50$$
$$x_c + y_c + w_c + z_c = 200$$
$$w_m + w_c + z_m + z_c - d_1^+ + d_1^- = 100$$
$$y_m + y_c + z_m + z_c - d_2^+ + d_2^- = 62.5$$
$$900x_m + 400x_c + 1080y_m + 480y_c + 990w_m + 440w_c + 1170z_m + 520z_c - d_3^+ + d_3^- = 175{,}000$$
$$y_c + z_c - d_4^+ + d_4^- = 120$$
$$w_c + z_c - d_5^+ + d_5^- = 150$$

and $x_m, x_c, y_m, y_c, w_m, w_c, z_m, z_c \geq 0$
$d_i^+, d_i^- \geq 0$ for $i = 1, 2, \ldots, 5$

5.22. Minimize z

subject to
$$1a + b - d_1^+ + d_1^- = 40$$
$$3a + b - d_2^+ + d_2^- = 50$$
$$5a + b - d_3^+ + d_3^- = 80$$
$$8a + b - d_4^+ + d_4^- = 90$$
$$10a + b - d_5^+ + d_5^- = 100$$
$$d_1^+ + d_1^- - z \leq 0$$
$$d_2^+ + d_2^- - z \leq 0$$
$$d_3^+ + d_3^- - z \leq 0$$
$$d_4^+ + d_4^- - z \leq 0$$
$$d_5^+ + d_5^- - z \leq 0$$

and $a \geq 0, b \geq 0, z \geq 0$
$d_i^+, d_i^- \geq 0$ for $i = 1, 2, \ldots, 5$

5.25. Let $x_t, x_s,$ and x_m denote the respective number of beds in major trauma, surgical, and medical.

Let d_{11}^+, d_{12}^+, and d_{13}^+ denote the interval variables for the positive deviation for the first goal.
Let d_1^- denote the negative deviation for the first goal.
Let d_i^+ and d_i^- denote the positive deviation and the negative deviation for goal i ($i = 2, 3, 4$).
The objective function becomes

$$\text{Minimize} \quad 10d_{11}^+ + 15d_{12}^+ + 25d_{13}^+ + 5d_2^- + 3d_3^+ + 1d_4^-$$

The deviation constraint for the first goal becomes

$$474x_t + 542x_s + 438x_m - d_{11}^+ - d_{12}^+ - d_{13}^+ + d_1^- = 15{,}000$$

The deviation constraints for the second, third, and fourth goals remain the same as in Exercise 5.17. The following structural constraints must be added to the deviation constraints: $d_{11}^+ \leq 500$ and $d_{12}^+ \leq 1000$

Chapter 6

6.1. (a) All points.

(b) A, B, D, F, H, K, L

(c) A, C, D, F, G, K, L

(d) A, D, F, K, L

(e)

Point	Nonbasic Variables	Basic Variables
A	x_1, x_2	S_1, S_2, S_3, S_4
D	S_1, S_2	x_1, x_2, S_3, S_4
F	x_1, S_1	x_2, S_2, S_3, S_4
K	S_2, S_3	x_1, x_2, S_1, S_4
L	x_2, S_4	x_1, S_1, S_2, S_3

(f) 1. x_1 is remaining constant at 0; x_2 is increasing.
2. S_1, S_2, and S_3 are decreasing; S_4 is remaining constant.
3. S_1
4. At point A, x_2 is a nonbasic variable, and S_1 is a basic variable. At point F, the opposite is true.

(g) 1. S_1 is increasing; S_2 is remaining constant at 0.
2. x_1 is increasing; x_2, S_3, and S_4 are decreasing.
3. S_3.
4. At point D, S_1 is a nonbasic variable, and S_3 is a basic variable. At point K, the opposite is true.

6.4. (a) Consult the previously displayed graph in Exercise 2.2.

(b) $-x_1 + 2x_2 + S_1 \qquad = 25$
$\quad x_1 + \ x_2 \quad + S_2 \quad = 20$
$\quad 5x_1 + 3x_2 \qquad + S_3 = 75$

(c) Two nonbasic variables.

(d) The basic solutions are summarized in the table below, where the last column should be ignored until part (e):

Point	Nonbasic Variables	Corresponding Basic Solution $(x_1, x_2, S_1, S_2, S_3)$	Objective Value $(5x_1 + 10x_2)$
A	S_1, S_2	$(5, 15, 0, 0, 5)$	175
B	S_2, S_3	$\left(7\frac{1}{2}, 12\frac{1}{2}, 7\frac{1}{2}, 0, 0\right)$	$162\frac{1}{2}$
C	x_2, S_3	$(15, 0, 40, 5, 0)$	75
D	x_1, x_2	$(0, 0, 25, 20, 75)$	0
E	x_1, S_1	$\left(0, 12\frac{1}{2}, 0, 7\frac{1}{2}, 37\frac{1}{2}\right)$	125
F	x_1, S_2	$(0, 20, -15, 0, 15)$	$\sim$
G	x_1, S_3	$(0, 25, -25, -5, 0)$	$\sim$
H	S_1, S_3	$\left(5\frac{10}{13}, 15\frac{5}{13}, 0, -1\frac{2}{13}, 0\right)$	$\sim$
I	x_2, S_2	$(20, 0, 45, 0, -25)$	$\sim$
J	x_2, S_1	$(-25, 0, 0, 45, 200)$	$\sim$

(e) Delete the last five rows from the above table.

(f) Since the basic feasible solution corresponding to point A has the highest objective value, it is optimal.

(g) To determine the optimal solution, the simplex method usually considers only a small subset of the basic feasible solutions.

6.8. (a) Consult the previously displayed graph in Exercise 2.2.

(b) To conserve space, we omit here the complete sequence of simplex tableaux. The optimal simplex tableau is

Equation	Basic Variable	c_j / c_B	5 / x_1	10 / x_2	0 / S_1	0 / S_2	0 / S_3	RHS
I	x_2	10	0	1	$\frac{1}{3}$	$\frac{1}{3}$	0	15
II	x_1	5	1	0	$-\frac{1}{3}$	$\frac{2}{3}$	0	5
III	S_3	0	0	0	$\frac{2}{3}$	$-\frac{13}{3}$	1	5
	z_j		$*$	$*$	$\frac{5}{3}$	$\frac{20}{3}$	$*$	$OV = 175$
	$c_j - z_j$		$*$	$*$	$-\frac{5}{3}$	$-\frac{20}{3}$	$*$	

(c) The optimal basic feasible solution is $(x_1, x_2, S_1, S_2, S_3) = (5, 15, 0, 0, 5)$, and the optimal objective value is 175.

(d) $D \rightarrow E \rightarrow A$.

6.10. (a)

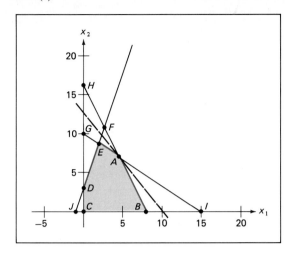

(b) To conserve space, we omit here the complete sequence of simplex tableaux. The optimal simplex tableau is

Equation	Basic Variable	c_j c_B	5 x_1	4 x_2	0 S_1	0 S_2	0 S_3	RHS
I	x_2	4	0	1	$\frac{1}{10}$	$-\frac{1}{20}$	0	7
II	x_1	5	1	0	$-\frac{1}{20}$	$\frac{3}{40}$	0	$\frac{9}{2}$
III	S_3	0	0	0	$-\frac{1}{4}$	$\frac{11}{40}$	1	$\frac{19}{2}$
	z_j		*	*	$\frac{3}{20}$	$\frac{7}{40}$	*	$OV = \frac{101}{2}$
	$c_j - z_j$		*	*	$-\frac{3}{20}$	$-\frac{7}{40}$	*	

(c) The optimal basic feasible solution is $(x_1, x_2, S_1, S_2, S_3) = (9/2, 7, 0, 0, 19/2)$, and the optimal objective value is $50\frac{1}{2}$.

(d) $C \to B \to A$.

6.14. When the first iteration's entering basic variable is x_2, the leaving basic variable is S_3. The pivot results in the following simplex tableau:

Equation	Basic Variable	c_j c_B	9 x_1	6 x_2	0 S_1	0 S_2	0 S_3	RHS
I	S_1	0	$\frac{12}{7}$	0	1	0	$-\frac{1}{7}$	$\frac{52}{7}$
II	S_2	0	$\frac{26}{7}$	0	0	1	$-\frac{1}{7}$	$\frac{136}{7}$
III	x_2	6	$\frac{2}{7}$	1	0	0	$\frac{1}{7}$	$\frac{88}{7}$
	z_j		$\frac{12}{7}$	*	*	*	$\frac{6}{7}$	$OV = \frac{528}{7}$
	$c_j - z_j$		$\frac{51}{7}$	*	*	*	$-\frac{6}{7}$	

In the second iteration, the entering basic variable is x_1 and the leaving basic variable is S_1. The pivot results in the optimal simplex tableau displayed in Figure 6.16(d), except that the equations appear in a different order.

(a) Two iterations.

(b) $A \to E \to D$.

(c) The general principle summarized at the end of Section 6.8.

Chapter 7

7.3. At the end of Phase I (after the transition to Phase II), the simplex tableau is:

Equation	Basic Variable	c_j c_B	30 x_1	20 x_2	0 E_1	0 E_3	0 A_1	0 A_2	0 A_3	RHS
I	x_1	30	1	0	0	$\frac{1}{3}$	0	$\frac{2}{3}$	$-\frac{1}{3}$	7
II	E_1	0	0	0	1	$\frac{1}{3}$	-1	$\frac{2}{3}$	$-\frac{1}{3}$	3
III	x_2	20	0	1	0	$-\frac{2}{3}$	0	$\frac{1}{3}$	$\frac{2}{3}$	6
	z_j		*	*	*	$-\frac{10}{3}$	0	$\frac{40}{3}$	$\frac{10}{3}$	$OV = 330$
	$c_j - z_j$		*	*	*	$\frac{10}{3}$	0	$-\frac{40}{3}$	$-\frac{10}{3}$	

This tableau identifies $(x_1, x_2, E_1, E_3) = (7, 6, 3, 0)$ as a basic feasible solution. Since the objective in Phase II is to minimize and since all nonbasic variables (except the artificial variables) have nonnegative $c_j - z_j$ values, the above tableau is optimal. In other words, the basic feasible solution identified by Phase I is coincidentally the optimal basic feasible solution. The optimal objective value is 330.

7.7. The equivalent linear program is the one summarized previously in the solution to Exercise 3.26. At the end of Phase I (after the transition to Phase II), the simplex tableau is

Equation	Basic Variable	c_j c_B	2 y_1	3 y_2	-5 w	0 S_1	0 S_2	0 E_3	0 A_3	RHS
I	S_1	0	0	3	-3	1	0	1	-1	11
II	S_2	0	0	-3	3	0	1	1	-1	23
III	y_1	2	1	-1	0	0	0	-1	1	1
	z_j		*	-2	0	*	*	-2	2	$OV = 2$
	$c_j - z_j$		*	5	-5	*	*	2	-2	

This tableau identifies $(y_1, y_2, w, S_1, S_2, E_3) = (1, 0, 0, 11, 23, 0)$ as a basic feasible solution. After performing Phase II, we obtain the following optimal simplex tableau:

Equation	Basic Variable	c_j c_B	2 y_1	3 y_2	-5 w	0 S_1	0 S_2	0 E_3	0 A_3	RHS
I	E_3	0	0	0	0	$\frac{1}{2}$	$\frac{1}{2}$	1	-1	17
II	w	-5	0	-1	1	$-\frac{1}{6}$	$\frac{1}{6}$	0	0	2
III	y_1	2	1	-1	0	$\frac{1}{2}$	$\frac{1}{2}$	0	0	18
	z_j		*	3	*	$\frac{11}{6}$	$\frac{1}{6}$	*	0	
	$c_j - z_j$		*	0	*	$-\frac{11}{6}$	$-\frac{1}{6}$	*	0	OV = 26

The optimal basic feasible solution is $(y_1, y_2, w, S_1, S_2, E_3) = (18, 0, 2, 0, 0, 17)$, and the optimal objective value is 26. This corresponds to an optimal solution of the original linear program of $(16, -2, 0, 0, 17)$, and an optimal objective value of 26.

7.11. LP 1 has no optimal solution because of unboundedness. LP 2 has no optimal solution because of infeasibility. LP 3 has multiple optimal solutions. The current tableau corresponds to an optimal basic feasible solution of $(x_1, x_2, S_1, S_2, S_3) = (4, 3, 0, 6, 0)$, and an optimal objective value of 54. To discover another optimal basic feasible solution, we perform a pivot initiated by selecting S_1 as the entering basic variable. The resulting simplex tableau (omitted here) corresponds to an optimal basic feasible solution of $(2, 6, 2, 0, 0)$.

7.16. In performing the sensitivity analysis, we consult the optimal simplex tableau previously displayed in the solution to Exercise 7.3.

(a) The table below summarizes the analysis:

Decision Variable	Current Value of Coefficient	Maximum Allowable Increase	Maximum Allowable Decrease
x_1	30	10	∞
x_2	20	∞	5

(b) The tables below summarize the analysis:

RHS_1's Current Value	RHS_1's Maximum Allowable Increase	RHS_1's Maximum Allowable Decrease	Optimal Values					
			x_1	x_2	E_1	E_3	Objective Value
4	3	∞	7	6	$3 - \Delta$	0	330

RHS_2's Current Value	RHS_2's Maximum Allowable Increase	RHS_2's Maximum Allowable Decrease	Optimal Values				
			x_1	x_2	E_1	E_3	Objective Value
20	18	$\frac{9}{2}$	$7 + \frac{2}{3}\Delta$	$6 - \frac{1}{3}\Delta$	$3 + \frac{2}{3}\Delta$	0	$330 + \frac{40}{3}\Delta$

RHS_3's Current Value	RHS_3's Maximum Allowable Increase	RHS_3's Maximum Allowable Decrease	Optimal Values				
			x_1	x_2	E_1	E_3	Objective Value
19	9	9	$7 - \frac{1}{3}\Delta$	$6 + \frac{2}{3}\Delta$	$3 - \frac{1}{3}\Delta$	0	$330 + \frac{10}{3}\Delta$

7.19. (a) The table below summarizes the analysis:

Decision Variable	Current Value of Coefficient	Maximum Allowable Increase	Maximum Allowable Decrease
x_B	1.0	∞	$\frac{3}{10}$
x_L	0.7	$\frac{3}{10}$	$\frac{1}{5}$

(b) The tables below summarize the analysis:

RHS_3's Current Value	RHS_3's Maximum Allowable Increase	RHS_3's Maximum Allowable Decrease	Optimal Values						
			x_B	x_C	x_L	E_2	S_3	S_4	E_5	Objective Value
24	∞	3	0	40	60	3	$3 + \Delta$	0	30	62

RHS_4's Current Value	RHS_4's Maximum Allowable Increase	RHS_4's Maximum Allowable Decrease	Optimal Values						
			x_B	x_C	x_L	E_2	S_3	S_4	E_5	Objective Value
64	3	3	0	$40 + 10\Delta$	$60 - 10\Delta$	3	$3 + \Delta$	0	$30 - 10\Delta$	$62 - 2\Delta$

(c) $(x_B, x_C, x_L) = (0, 40, 60)$ remains the optimal solution, and the optimal objective value remains at 62 (since x_B's optimal value is 0).

(d) Substituting $\Delta = 2$ into the part (b)'s sensitivity analysis of RHS_4, we obtain a new optimal solution of $x_B = 0$, $x_C = 60$, $x_L = 40$, $E_2 = 3$, $S_3 = 5$, $S_4 = 0$, and $E_5 = 10$, and a new optimal objective value of 58.

7.22 (a) Minimize $\quad 22y_1 + 10y_2 + 7y_3 + 2y_4$

$$\text{subject to} \quad \begin{aligned} 2y_1 - y_2 + 2y_3 + y_4 &\geq 3 \\ 4y_1 + 4y_2 - y_3 - 2y_4 &\geq 2 \end{aligned}$$

$$\text{and} \quad y_1 \geq 0,\ y_2 \geq 0,\ y_3 \geq 0,\ y_4 \geq 0.$$

(b) The dual of the primal's dual is the primal.

(c) If the primal is a max-≤-nonnegative LP or a min-≥-nonnegative LP, the dual of the primal's dual is the primal.

7.25. (a) Maximize $\quad 4y_1 + 20y_2 + 19y_3$

subject to $\quad y_1 + 2y_2 + \quad y_3 \le 30$
$\quad\quad\quad\quad\quad y_2 + 2y_3 \le 20$

and $\quad y_1 \ge 0, y_2$ unconstrained, $y_3 \ge 0$

(b) The dual LP's optimal solution is $(y_1, y_2, y_3, S_1, S_2) = (0, {}^{40}\!/\!_3, {}^{10}\!/\!_3, 0, 0)$ and its optimal objective value is 330.

(c) $E_1 y_1 = (3)(0) = 0$
$A_2 y_2 = (0)({}^{40}\!/\!_3) = 0 \quad x_1 S_1 = (7)(0) = 0$
$E_3 y_3 = (0)({}^{10}\!/\!_3) = 0 \quad x_2 S_2 = (6)(0) = 0$

7.29. (a)

Primal Structural Constraint		Constraint's Shadow Price (from 7.16)	Optimal Value of Constraint's Associated Dual Variable (from 7.29)
x_1	≥ 4	0	0
$2x_1 + x_2$	$= 20$	$-\dfrac{40}{3}$	$\dfrac{40}{3}$
$x_1 + 2x_2$	≥ 19	$-\dfrac{10}{3}$	$\dfrac{10}{3}$

(b) A primal constraint's shadow price and the constraint's associated dual variable always have the same absolute value but may differ in sign.

Chapter 8

8.4. (a) and (c) In the network below, the three numbers adjacent to each arc in parentheses are respectively the arc's unit flow cost, the upper bound on flow on the arc (where ∞ denotes 9999), and the lower bound on flow on the arc. Also, the number adjacent to an arc written beneath an arrow is the arc's optimal flow (when it is nonzero). The minimum total cost is $28.43 million.

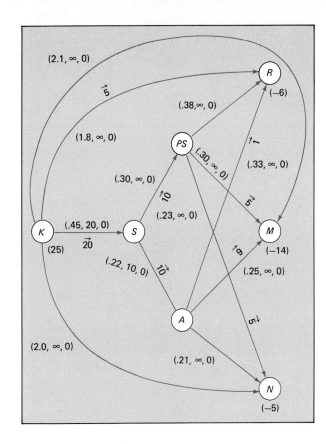

(b) The portion of the network that changes is displayed below, where the node named PS' represents a collection node for Port Said.

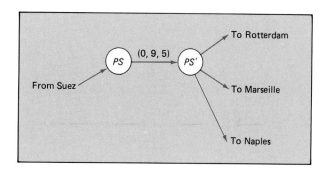

(c) Omitted here.

8.8. In the network below, the number adjacent to each arc is the arc's unit flow cost. The upper and lower bounds on flow have been omitted because all arcs have upper bounds of 9999 and lower bounds of 0.

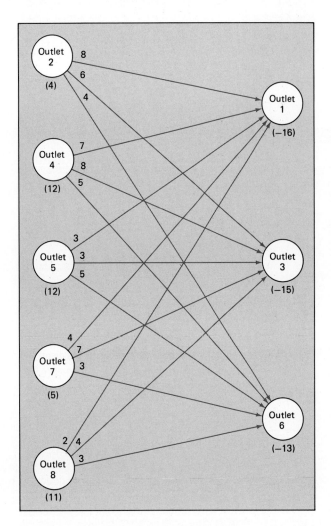

8.10. (a) In the network below, the number adjacent to each arc is the arc's unit flow cost. The upper and lower bounds on flow have been omitted because all arcs have upper bounds of 9999 and lower bounds of 0.

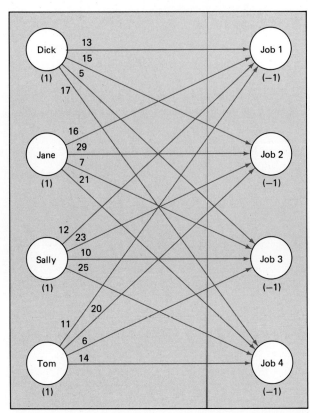

(b) Add a source node named "Harry" to the vertical column of nodes at the network's left, and add a fictitious sink node to the vertical column of nodes at the network's right. To ensure Harry is given a job, the unit flow cost of the arc directed from "Harry" to the fictitious sink node must equal an arbitrarily large number (e.g., 9999); the unit flow costs of all other arcs directed into the fictitious sink node are 0. The unit flow costs for the arcs directed from "Harry" to the nonfictitious jobs are obtained from the data given in part (b) of Exercise 4.18.

8.15. In the network below, the boldface subnetwork is the minimum-spanning tree. Its total cost is 172.

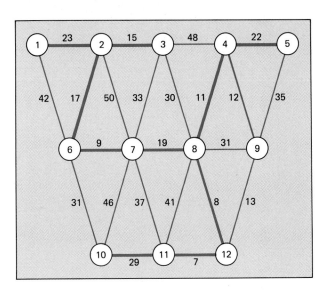

Chapter 9

9.1. (a)

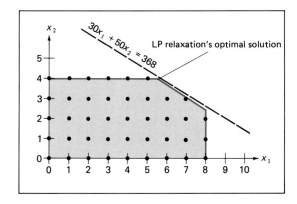

(b) The coordinates of the LP relaxation's optimal solution are $(5\frac{3}{5}, 4)$. The optimal objective value is 368.

(c) $(x_1, x_2) = (5, 4)$ is the best (and only) feasible rounding alternative.

(d) The maximum percentage error is 4.89%.

(e) As the LP relaxation's optimal isoquant line "backs up" in a parallel and southwesterly direction, the first all-integer solution encountered is $(x_1, x_2) = (7, 3)$, a solution whose objective value is 360.

(f) The actual percentage error would have been 2.78%.

9.5. (a) $(x_1, x_2, x_3) = (17, 9, 0)$ is the best (and only) feasible rounding alternative.

(b) Note that the LP relaxation has an optimal objective value of $198\frac{1}{3}$. Hence, the maximum percentage error is 3.19%.

9.9 (a) The first of the seven constraints ensures that the total amount distributed from plant 1 will be at most 18 thousand cars. The remaining six constraints ensure that plant 1 cannot distribute cars unless it remains open.

(b) The revised formulation will have 30 more constraints.

(c) The revised formulation will have 500 more constraints.

(d) Omitted here.

9.15. Let x_j equal 1 if activity j is performed and 0 if it is not (for $j = A, B, \ldots, F$).
Let y_i equal 1 if project i is undertaken and 0 if it is not (for $i = 1, 2, \ldots, 7$).
The ILP is

Maximize $\quad 7y_1 + 10y_2 + 9y_3 + 3y_4 + 8y_5 + 6y_6 + 8y_7$
$\qquad\qquad -4x_A - 5x_B - 17x_C - 10x_D - 7x_E - 5x_F$

subject to $\quad y_1 \le x_A, \; y_1 \le x_B,$
$\qquad\qquad y_2 \le x_A, \; y_2 \le x_E,$
$\qquad\qquad y_3 \le x_B, \; y_3 \le x_C, \; y_3 \le x_D$
$\qquad\qquad y_4 \le x_C, \; y_4 \le x_D,$
$\qquad\qquad y_5 \le x_C, \; y_5 \le x_D, \; y_5 \le x_E$
$\qquad\qquad y_6 \le x_D, \; y_6 \le x_F,$
$\qquad\qquad y_7 \le x_E, \; y_7 \le x_F$

and $\qquad x_A, x_B, \ldots, x_F = 0$ or 1
$\qquad\qquad y_1, y_2, \ldots, y_7 = 0$ or 1.

9.17. (a) Corresponding to each x_{ij} variable defined in the previously displayed solution to Exercise 4.20, define a variable y_{ij} equal to 1 if hold i contains commodity j and equal to 0 if it does not. The ILP is obtained by adding the constraints below to the linear program previously displayed in the solution to Exercise 4.20:

$$x_{F1} \le My_{F1}, \quad x_{C1} \le My_{C1}, \quad x_{R1} \le My_{R1}$$
$$x_{F2} \le My_{F2}, \quad x_{C2} \le My_{C2}, \quad x_{R2} \le My_{R2}$$
$$x_{F3} \le My_{F3}, \quad x_{C3} \le My_{C3}, \quad x_{R3} \le My_{R3}$$
$$x_{F4} \le My_{F4}, \quad x_{C4} \le My_{C4}, \quad x_{R4} \le My_{R4}$$

$$y_{F1} + y_{F2} + y_{F3} + y_{F4} \le 1$$
$$y_{C1} + y_{C2} + y_{C3} + y_{C4} \le 1$$
$$y_{R1} + y_{R2} + y_{R3} + y_{R4} \le 1$$

and $\quad x_{ij} \ge 0$ for all i-j pairs
$\quad\quad y_{ij} = 0$ or 1 for all i-j pairs.

Note that M denotes a large number that must be assigned a specific value (e.g., 5000) before solving the ILP.

(b) Add the following constraints to part (a)'s ILP:

$$y_{F1} + y_{C1} + y_{R1} \le 1$$
$$y_{F2} + y_{C2} + y_{R2} \le 1$$
$$y_{F3} + y_{C3} + y_{R3} \le 1$$
$$y_{F4} + y_{C4} + y_{R4} \le 1$$

(c) Let z_1 equal 1 if commodity 1 is carried anywhere on the ship and 0 if it is not.
Add the following constraints to part (a)'s ILP:

$$y_{F1} + y_{C1} + y_{R1} \le \quad 3z_1$$
$$x_{F1} + x_{C1} + x_{R1} \le \quad Mz_1$$
$$x_{F1} + x_{C1} + x_{R1} \ge 2000z_1$$

and $\quad z_1 = 0$ or 1

9.19. (a) Let x_j equal 1 if a fire station is located at site j and 0 if one is not (for $j = 1, 2, \ldots, 7$).
The ILP is

Minimize $\quad 410x_1 + 100x_2 + 300x_3 + 500x_4 + 200x_5 + 440x_6 + 400x_7$

subject to

$$
\begin{array}{llllllll}
x_1 & & + x_3 + x_4 & & + x_6 & & \ge 1 \\
 & & x_3 & & + x_6 + & x_7 & \ge 1 \\
x_1 & & + x_3 + x_4 + & x_5 & & & \ge 1 \\
 & x_2 + & x_3 + x_4 & & + x_6 & & \ge 1 \\
x_1 & & + x_4 & & & + x_7 & \ge 1 \\
 & & & x_5 + & x_6 & & \ge 1 \\
x_1 + & x_2 & & & & & \ge 1 \\
x_1 & & + x_4 + & x_5 + & x_6 + & x_7 & \ge 1 \\
 & x_2 & + x_4 & & & + x_7 & \ge 1 \\
x_1 + & x_2 & & + x_5 + & x_6 & & \ge 1
\end{array}
$$

and $\quad x_1, x_2, \ldots, x_7 = 0$ or 1.

(b) The objective function changes to

Minimize $\quad x_1 + x_2 + x_3 + x_4 + x_5 + x_6 + x_7$.

(c) The right-hand side of the third structural constraint changes from 1 to 2.

9.23. (a) A summary appears below.

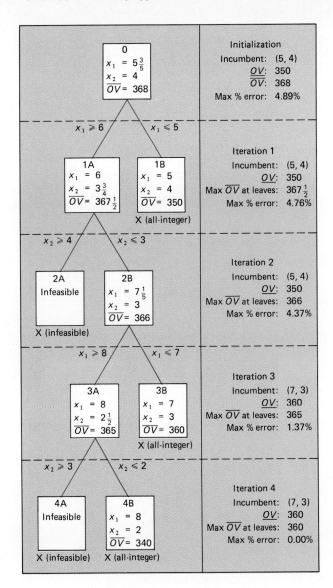

(b) We terminate at the end of Iteration 2. At termination, the incumbent is $(x_1, x_2) = (5, 4)$, and its maximum percentage error is 4.37%. The incumbent's actual percentage error is 2.78%.

9.29. (a) A summary appears on the next page. Note that the pruning of ILP 2B does not occur until Iteration 4.

(b) We terminate at the end of Iteration 3. At termination, the incumbent is $(x_1, x_2, x_3, x_4, x_5) = (0, 1, 1, 1, 0)$, and its maximum percentage error is 11.58%. The incumbent's actual percentage error is 10.64%.

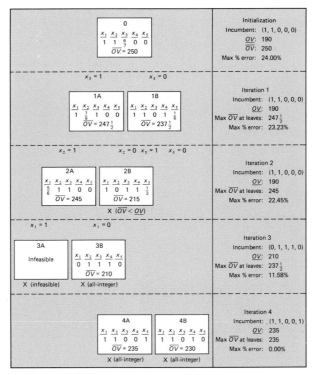

Figure for Exercise 9.29(a).

Chapter 10

10.3. (a) and (b)

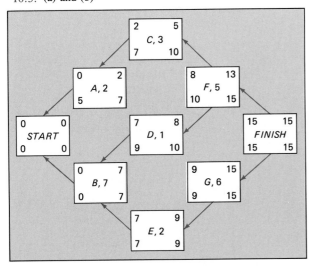

(c) Activity	A	B	C	D	E	F	G
Total Slack	5	0	5	2	0	2	0
Unshared Slack	0	0	0	0	0	0	0

(d) $START \rightarrow B \rightarrow E \rightarrow G \rightarrow FINISH$

(e), (f), and (g) Consult the diagrams on the next page. Note that, because activities F and G must overlap, it is impossible to find a hybrid schedule whose peak requirement is less than 9 persons, the ES schedule's peak requirement.

10.10. The following precedence relationships are redundant: A is a predecessor of D, B is a predecessor of H, F is a predecessor of I, and F is a predecessor of J.

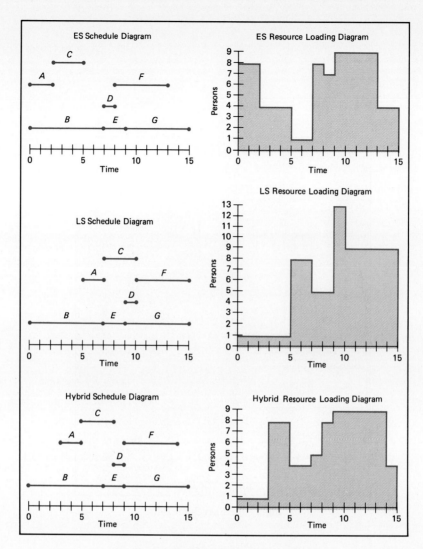

Figure for Exercise 10.3(e), (f), and (g).

Chapter 11

11.2. (a) The table below displays each activity's mean duration:

Activity	A	B	C	D
Mean Duration	9	8	8	9

If these mean durations replace the probability distributions, the resulting deterministic project has a duration of 18 and a critical path of $START \rightarrow A \rightarrow D \rightarrow FINISH$.

(b)

Path	Probability that Path is the Critical Path
AC	(6,480/20,736) = 0.3125
AD	(8,100/20,736) = 0.3906
BD	(6,156/20,736) = 0.2969

Activity	Probability that Activity is a Critical Activity
A	(14,580/20,736) = 0.7031
B	(6,156/20,736) = 0.2969
C	(6,480/20,736) = 0.3125
D	(14,256/20,736) = 0.6875

Project Duration	Probability of Occurrence
13	(324/20,736) = 0.0156
14	(972/20,736) = 0.0469
16	(1,296/20,736) = 0.0625
17	(1,296/20,736) = 0.0625
18	(3,888/20,736) = 0.1875
20	(5,508/20,736) = 0.2656
21	(2,268/20,736) = 0.1094
22	(1,296/20,736) = 0.0625
24	(1,296/20,736) = 0.0625
25	(2,592/20,736) = 0.1250

(c) (i) $START \rightarrow A \rightarrow D \rightarrow FINISH$, the same as in part (a).

(ii) Activity A.

(iii) The mean project duration is
$$(13)(0.0156) + (14)(0.0496) + \ldots$$
$$+ (25)(0.1250) = 19.91$$
The duration computed in part (a) is 18. This underestimates the true mean by 9.59%. The probability that the project's actual duration will exceed this underestimate of the true mean is 0.6250.

(iv) 21 days.

11.8. (a) The linear program is

Minimize $t_{FINISH} - t_{START}$

subject to
$$t_A - t_{START} \geq 0$$
$$t_B - t_{START} \geq 0$$
$$t_C - t_A \geq 2$$
$$t_D - t_B \geq 7$$
$$t_E - t_B \geq 7$$
$$t_F - t_C \geq 3$$
$$t_F - t_D \geq 1$$
$$t_G - t_E \geq 2$$
$$t_{FINISH} - t_F \geq 5$$
$$t_{FINISH} - t_G \geq 6$$

and $t_{START}, t_A, \ldots, t_G, t_{FINISH} \geq 0$.

(b) The LP's optimal objective value is 15. The structural constraints with shadow prices of -1 are the second, fifth, eighth, and tenth. Hence, the critical path is $START \rightarrow B \rightarrow E \rightarrow G \rightarrow FINISH$.

11.10. (a) Note that because activity D's duration must be 1 day, there is no need for a decision variable x_D. The linear program is shown below the table and continues on the next page.

11.5. (a)

Step	Activity Durations at Step's Start								Path Lengths at Step's Start			Alternatives for Simultaneously Reducing the Common Length of the Critical Paths by One Day		Project Duration at Step's End	Total Direct Costs ($000)	Total Indirect Costs ($000)	Total Penalty Costs ($000)	Total Cost ($000)
	A	B	C	D	E	F	G	ACF	BDF	BEG	Alternative	Cost ($000)					
1	2	7	3	1	2	5	6	10	13	15	Not applicable		15	84	105	6	195
2	2	7	3	1	2	5	6	10	13	15	1. Reduce B 2. Reduce E 3. Reduce G	2 7 5	14	86	98	3	187
3	2	6	3	1	2	5	6	10	12	14	1. Reduce B 2. Reduce E 3. Reduce G	2 7 5	13	88	91	0	179
4	2	5	3	1	2	5	6	10	11	13	1. Reduce E 2. Reduce G	7 5	12	93	84	-2	175
5	2	5	3	1	2	5	5	10	11	12	1. Reduce E 2. Reduce G	7 5	11	98	77	-4	171
6	2	5	3	1	2	5	4	10	11	11	1. Reduce E & F 2. Reduce F & G	10 8	10	106	70	-6	170
7	2	5	3	1	2	4	3	9	10	10	1. Reduce E & F	10	9	116	63	-8	171
8	2	5	3	1	1	3	3	8	9	9	No feasible alternatives						

(b) The project's optimal duration is 10 days. The table below summarizes each activity's optimal duration and corresponding direct cost:

Activity	A	B	C	D	E	F	G
Optimal Duration (days)	2	5	3	1	2	4	3
Direct Cost ($000)	10	21	20	7	8	13	27

Maximize $6x_A + 2x_B + 4x_C + 7x_E + 3x_F + 5x_G$

subject to
$$t_{FINISH} - t_{START} = 13$$
$$x_A \geq 1, \quad x_A \leq 2$$
$$x_B \geq 5, \quad x_B \leq 7$$
$$x_C \geq 2, \quad x_C \leq 3$$
$$x_E \geq 1, \quad x_E \leq 2$$
$$x_F \geq 2, \quad x_F \leq 5$$
$$x_G \geq 3, \quad x_G \leq 6$$

$$
\begin{aligned}
t_A &- t_{START} &\geq 0 \\
t_B &- t_{START} &\geq 0 \\
t_C &- t_A &- x_A \geq 0 \\
t_D &- t_B &- x_B \geq 0 \\
t_E &- t_B &- x_B \geq 0 \\
t_F &- t_C &- x_C \geq 0 \\
t_F &- t_D & \geq 1 \\
t_G &- t_E &- x_E \geq 0 \\
t_{FINISH} &- t_F &- x_F \geq 0 \\
t_{FINISH} &- t_G &- x_G \geq 0
\end{aligned}
$$

and $t_{START}, t_A, \ldots, t_G, t_{FINISH} \geq 0$
$x_A, x_B, x_C, x_E, x_F, x_G \geq 0.$

(b) The right-hand side of the first structural constraint changes from 13 to 12.

(c) The LP's optimal objective value is 93. Subtracting this value from the constant of 181, we obtain 88 as the minimum total direct cost for a project duration of 13 days. This cost is the same as that obtained in Exercise 11.5.

Chapter 12

12.1. (a) The payoff matrix appears in the statement of the problem.

(b) Decision 7 is optimal.

(c) Decision 2 is optimal.

(d) Decision 3 is optimal.

(e) With an EMV of 3.3, decision 6 is optimal.

(f) With an expected regret of 8.4, decision 6 is optimal.

(g) The pruned decision tree is displayed at the top of the next column.

(h) EVPI = [(12)(0.5) + (6)(0.2) + (15)(0.3)]
$- 3.3 = 8.4.$

(i) Omitted here.

(j) EVPI = 8.4, and decision 6's expected regret is 8.4.

12.5. (a) The payoff matrix is

Decisions	States of Nature		
	Rainy	Cloudy	Sunny
Small order	−500	500	2000
Large order	−2500	1000	5000

(b) A large order is optimal.

(c) A small order is optimal.

(d) A large order is optimal.

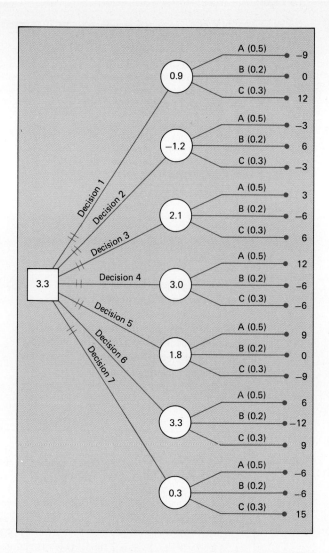

(e) With an EMV of 50, a small order is optimal.

(f) With an expected regret of 450, a small order is optimal.

(g) The pruned decision tree is displayed below:

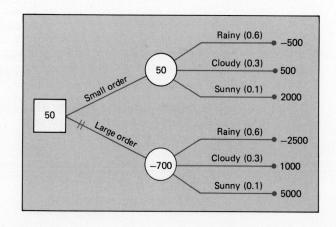

(h) EVPI = [(−500)(0.6) + (1000)(0.3)
                        + (5000)(0.1)] − 50 = 450

(i) Omitted here.

(j) EVPI = 450, and a small order's expected regret is 450.

12.8. (a) The payoff martix (in units of $000) is

| Decisions | States of Nature | | | | | |
	Loss = 0	Loss = 20	Loss = 40	Loss = 60	Loss = 80	Loss = 100
Self-insure	0	−20	−40	−60	−80	−100
100% coverage	−50	−50	−50	−50	−50	−50
$50,000 deductible	−10	−30	−50	−60	−60	−60

(b) Self-insuring is optimal.

(c) 100% coverage is optimal.

(d) $50,000 deductible is optimal.

(e) With an EMV of −35, self-insuring is optimal.

(f) With an expected regret of 7, self-insuring is optimal.

(g) The pruned decision tree is displayed below:

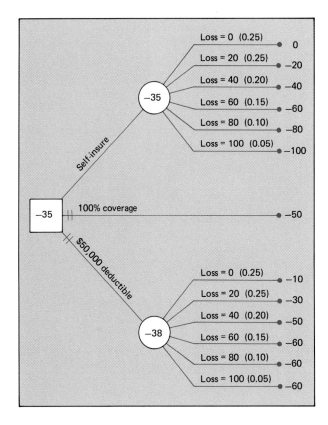

(h) EVPI = [(0)(.25) + (−20)(.25) + (−40)(.20)
                        + (−50)(.15) + (−50)(.10)
                        + (−50)(0.5)] − (−35) = 7

(i) Omitted here.

(j) EVPI = 7, and the expected regret of self-insuring is 7.

12.12. The graph below summarizes the sensitivity analysis:

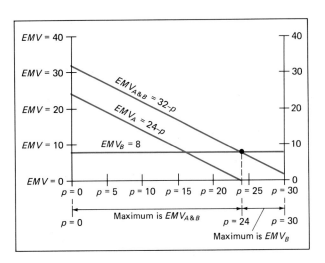

12.17. The pruned decision tree is displayed below:

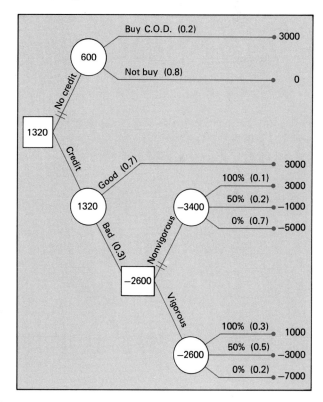

13.2. (a) The pruned decision tree is displayed below:

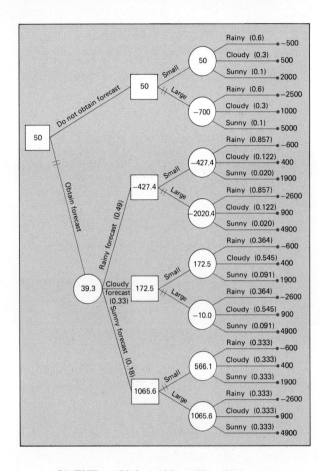

(b) EVII = (39.3 + 100) − 50 = 89.3

13.5. (a) The pruned decision tree is displayed at the top of the next column:

(b) EVII = (1228 + 500) − 1320 = 408

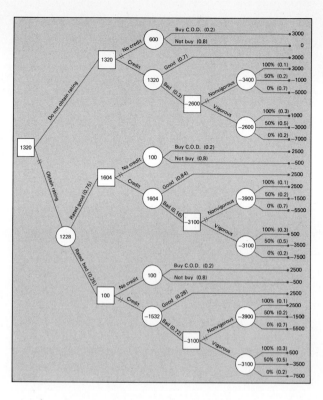

13.9. (a) The five points on the graph are:

P	$U(P)$
−2000	0.00
2800	0.25
5200	0.50
6800	0.75
8000	1.00

(b) Omitted here.

(c) Because the graph is "bowed downward," the manager is risk-seeking.

(d)

Reference Lottery	EMV −	CE	= Risk Premium
$L(8000; 4000)$	6000 −	6400	= −400
$L(3000; 0)$	1500 −	1750	= −250
$L(3000; -2000)$	500 −	1100	= −600

(e) For a risk-seeking decision maker, the risk premium is always negative.

(f)

Payoff Increase	Utility Increase
From −2000 to 0	0.08 − 0.00 = 0.08
From 0 to 2000	0.19 − 0.08 = 0.11
From 2000 to 4000	0.36 − 0.19 = 0.17
From 4000 to 6000	0.60 − 0.36 = 0.24
From 6000 to 8000	1.00 − 0.60 = 0.40

(g) For a risk-seeking utility function, each time we add $2000 to the payoff, the utility increases by a larger amount each time.

13.16. (a) A sketch of Grant's utility function would show it is "bowed downward." Hence, Grant is risk-seeking.

(b) The pruned decision tree is displayed below:

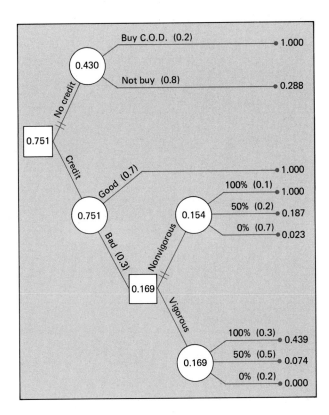

(c) The optimal strategies are the same.

13.20. (a), (b), and (c) In the decision trees in the next column, the upper tree is pruned using the EMV criterion and the lower tree is pruned using the expected utility criterion.

According to these trees, if Wally wants to maximize his decision's EMV, he should invest only in project A; if he wants to maximize his decision's expected utility, he should hedge by investing in both project A and project B.

(d) Suppose a decision maker has three choices: a decision with a positive EMV, a decision with a negative EMV, or a hedging strategy that combines both decisions. A decision maker who wants to maximize EMV will *always* choose the decision with the positive EMV. However, a risk-averse decision

maker who wants to maximize expected utility *may* choose the hedging strategy.

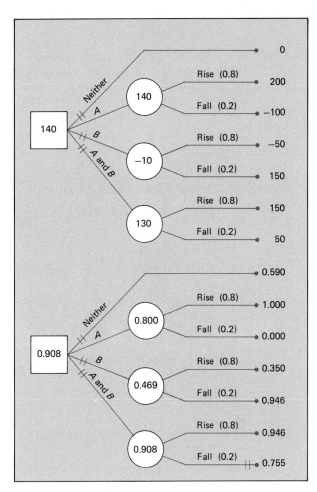

Chapter 14

14.3. $d = 15$, $D = 5400$, $C_o = 25$, $C_i = 21.33$, and $C_h = 5.3325$

(a) Omitted here.

(b) $Q^* = \sqrt{[(2)(25)(5400)]/(5.3325)} \approx 225$

(c) Omitted here.

(d) $N^* = 5400/225 = 24$ and $T^* = 225/15 = 15$ days

(e) and (f)

	Optimal Policy		Current Policy	
Fixed Ordering Costs	(25)(5400/225) =	600	(25)(5400/450) =	300
Variable Ordering Costs	(21.33)(5400) =	115,182	(21.33)(5400) =	115,182
Holding Costs	(5.3325)(225/2) =	600	(5.3325)(450/2) =	1,200
Sum		$116,382		$116,682

By using the optimal policy, the annual savings is $300.

(g) $RL = [(15)(5)]$ (modulo 225) $= 75$

(h) $RL = [(15)(25)]$ (modulo 225) $= 150$

14.7. (a) The two alternatives are the greatest multiple of 60 that is less than $Q^* = 225$ and the least multiple of 60 that is greater than $Q^* = 225$. In other words, the two alternatives are $Q = 180$ and $Q = 240$. Using the formula for $R(Q)$ in Table 14.2(b), we obtain

$R(180) = (1/2) [(225/180) + (180/225)] = 1.025$
$R(240) = (1/2) [(225/240) + (240/225)] = 1.002.$

Hence, $Q = 240$ is better than $Q = 180$.

(b) Since $R(240) = 1.002$, the percentage increase is 0.2%.

14.15. (a)

Discount Category	Optimal Value of Q	Fixed Ordering Costs	Variable Ordering Costs	Holding Costs	Annual Total Cost
1	199	678.39	115,182.00	530.58	$116,390.97
2	226	597.35	114,480.00	598.90	$115,676.25
3	400	337.50	113,400.00	1050.00	$114,787.50

Given the above table, $Q = 400$ is optimal.

(b)

Discount Category	Optimal Value of Q	Fixed Ordering Costs	Variable Ordering Costs	Holding Costs	Annual Total Cost
1	199	678.39	115,182.00	530.58	$116,390.97
2	226	597.35	114,480.00	598.90	$115,676.25
3	1000	135.00	113,400.00	2625.00	$116,160.00

Given the above table, $Q = 226$ is optimal.

14.17. $p = 40,000; P = 10,000,000$
$d = 8000; D = 2,000,000$
$C_o = 640; C_i = 10; C_h = 2$

(a) $Q^* = \sqrt{[(2)(640)(2,000,000)]/[(2)(0.8)]} = 40,000$

(b) Omitted here.

(c) $N^* = 2,000,000/40,000 = 50$
Length of a production run $= 40,000/40,000$
$= 1$ day
Inventory level at end of production run
$= (40,000) (0.8) = 32,000$
$T^* = 40,000/8000 = 5$ days

(d) and (e)

	Optimal Policy	Current Policy
Fixed Ordering Costs	$(640)(2,000,000/40,000) = 32,000$	$(640)(2,000,000/200,000) = 6400$
Variable Ordering Costs	$(10)(2,000,000) = 20,000,000$	$(10)(2,000,000) = 20,000,000$
Holding Costs	$(2)(32,000/2) = 32,000$	$(2)(160,000/2) = 160,000$
Sum	$20,064,000	$20,166,400

By using the optimal policy, WSG's annual savings is $102,400.

14.20. Let $TC'(Q)$ and $TC''(Q)$ respectively denote the first and second derivatives for the function $TC(Q)$ in Table 14.2(b).

$$TC'(Q) = -\frac{C_o D}{Q^2} + \frac{C_h}{2}$$

Setting $TC'(Q)$ equal to 0 and then solving for Q, we obtain the formula for Q^* in Table 14.2(b).

$$TC''(Q) = 2C_o DQ^3$$

Since $TC''(Q) > 0$ for all positive values of Q, Q^* minimizes $TC(Q)$.

14.24. (a) Omitted here.

(b)

MRP Calculations for Component D

	Week								
	1	2	3	4	5	6	7	8	9
Gross Requirements	100	50	400	50	100	350	100	50	400
Remaining Initial Inventory (170)	70	20	0	0	0	0	0	0	0
Net Requirements	0	0	380	50	100	350	100	50	400
Planned Orders	0	380	50	100	350	100	50	400	X

MRP Calculations for Subcomponent E

	Week								
	1	2	3	4	5	6	7	8	9
Gross Requirements	0	1520	200	400	1400	400	200	1600	X
Remaining Initial Inventory (1600)	1600	80	0	0	0	0	0	0	X
Net Requirements	0	0	120	400	1400	400	200	1600	X
Planned Orders	120	400	1400	400	200	1600	X	X	X

Chapter 15

15.1 (a) $Q = 225$ cartons.

(b) Average lead time demand is
$(65)(0.01) + (66)(0.02) + \ldots + (84)(0.03)$
$+ (85)(0.01) \approx 75.$
If $RL = 75$, the service level is 0.50.

(c)

Reorder Level (RL)	Safety Stock ($RL - 75$)	Service Level	Average Increase in the Annual Total of Holding Costs [$5.33(RL - 75)$]
75	0	0.50	0.00
76	1	0.52	5.33
77	2	0.55	10.66
78	3	0.59	15.99
79	4	0.67	21.32
80	5	0.75	26.65
81	6	0.83	31.98
82	7	0.90	37.31
83	8	0.96	42.64
84	9	0.99	47.97
85	10	1.00	53.30

(d) 0.75

(e) RL = 81 cartons

(f) RL = 83 cartons

15.2. (a) and (b) The answers are the same as in Exercise 15.1.

(c)

Reorder Level (RL)	Safety Stock (RL − 75)	Service Level	Average Increase in the Annual Total of Holding Costs [5.33(RL − 75)]
75	0	0.5000	0.00
76	1	0.5987	5.33
77	2	0.6915	10.66
78	3	0.7734	15.99
79	4	0.8413	21.32
80	5	0.8944	26.65
81	6	0.9332	31.98
82	7	0.9599	37.31
83	8	0.9772	42.64
84	9	0.9878	47.97
85	10	0.9938	53.30

(d) 0.8944

(e) RL = 75 + (0.842)(4) = 78.37

(f) RL = 75 + (1.645)(4) = 81.58

15.3. (a) and (b) The answers are the same as in Exercise 15.1.

(c)

Reorder Level (RL)	Safety Stock (RL − 75)	Service Level	Average Increase in the Annual Total of Holding Costs [5.33(RL − 75)]
75	0	0.50	0.00
76	1	0.55	5.33
77	2	0.60	10.66
78	3	0.65	15.99
79	4	0.70	21.32
80	5	0.75	26.65
81	6	0.80	31.98
82	7	0.85	37.31
83	8	0.90	42.64
84	9	0.95	47.97
85	10	1.00	53.30

(d) 0.75

(e) RL = 65 + (0.80)(20) = 81

(f) RL = 65 + (0.95)(20) = 84

15.10. (a) C_{under} = 2.00 − 0.80 = 1.20
C_{over} = 0.80 − 0.40 = 0.40
Optimal service level = [1.20/(1.20 + 0.40)] = 0.75

(b) Q^* = 190

(c) 0.15

15.11. (a) As in Exercise 15.10, the optimal service level is 0.75.

(b) Q^* = 200 + (0.674)(10) = 206.74

(c) 0.25

15.12. (a) As in Exercise 15.10, the optimal service level is 0.75.

(b) Q^* = 170 + (0.75)(230 − 170) = 215

(c) 0.25

Chapter 16

(a) ½ hour

(b) Omitted here.

(c) $Pr\{T \leq 0.25\} = 1 - e^{-(2)(0.25)} = 0.393$

(d) $Pr\{0.25 \leq T \leq 1.25\} = [1 - e^{-(2)(1.25)}]$
$- [1 - e^{-(2)(0.25)}] = 0.525$

(e) $Pr\{T \geq 1.25\} = e^{-(2)(1.25)} = 0.082$

(f) and (g) By the exponential distribution's lack-of-memory property,

$Pr\{T \geq 0.50 + 1.25 \mid T \geq 0.50\} = Pr\{T \geq 1.25\}$.

Hence, the probability is 0.082, the same as in part (e).

16.6. (a) $Pr\{T \leq (0.25/\alpha)\} = 1 - e^{-(\alpha)(0.25/\alpha)} = 0.221$

(b) $Pr\{T \leq (1/\alpha)\} = 1 - e^{-(\alpha)(1/\alpha)} = 0.632$
$Pr\{T \geq (1/\alpha)\} = e^{-(\alpha)(1/\alpha)} = 0.368$

(c) If T had a normal distribution, the probabilities corresponding to those in part (b) would both equal 0.5.

16.9. Melvin's queueing system is a basic queueing system with a single server. We can analyze it using the formulae in Table 16.2(a). Let us use hours as the unit of measurement for time. Regardless of whether a bagger is helping, λ = 40. With the help of a bagger, μ = 72; without the help of a bagger, μ = 50. The table below summarizes the analysis.

	(a) P_0	(b) L	(c) W (minutes)	(d) L_q	(e) W_q (minutes)
With Bagger	0.4444	1.25	1.875	0.69	1.042
Without Bagger	0.2000	4.00	6.000	3.20	4.800

16.12. The weigh station is a basic queueing system with one server in part (a) and two servers in part (b). We can analyze it using the formulae in Table 16.2. Let us use hours as the unit of measurement for time. Regardless of whether there is one or two scales, $\lambda = 15$ and $\mu = 20$. The table below summarizes the analysis:

	(i) L	(ii) W (minutes)	(iii) L_q	(iv) W_q (minutes)
(a) One scale	5.00	20.000	4.25	17.000
(b) Two scales	0.87	3.491	0.12	0.491

(c) When there is one scale, the probability is

$$P_3 + P_4 + \cdots = 1 - (P_0 + P_1 + P_2) = 0.4219.$$

When there are two scales, the probability is

$$P_4 + P_5 + \cdots = 1 - (P_0 + P_1 + P_2 + P_3) = 0.0288.$$

16.17. When λ and μ are both doubled, L and L_q remain the same, but W and W_q decrease to 50% of their former values.

16.21. Nationwide's reservation system is a basic queueing system with a finite queue capacity of $m = 3$, $s = 3$ servers, $\lambda = 30$ calls per hour, and $\mu = 10$ calls per hour. Using the procedure summarized at the end of Section 16.6, we obtain the following results:

P_0	P_1	P_2	P_3	P_4	P_5	P_6
0.0377	0.1132	0.1698	0.1698	0.1698	0.1698	0.1698

(a) $P_0 = 0.0377$

(b) $P_3 + P_4 + P_5 + P_6 = 0.6792$

(c) $P_6 = 0.1698$

16.25. Zrox's repair system is a basic queueing system with a finite calling population of $m = 6$, $s = 3$ servers, $\lambda = 0.5$ failures per day, and $\mu = 2$ repairs per day. Using the procedure summarized at the end of Section 16.7, we obtain the following results:

P_0	P_1	P_2	P_3	P_4	P_5	P_6
0.2603	0.3904	0.2440	0.0813	0.0203	0.0034	0.0003

(a) $P_0 = 0.2603$

(b) $P_3 + P_4 + P_5 + P_6 = 0.1053$

(c) $3P_0 + 2P_1 + 1P_2 + 0(P_3 + P_4 + P_5 + P_6) = 1.8057$

(d) $L = 0P_0 + 1P_1 + \ldots + 6P_6 = 1.2223$

16.29. Earl's shop is a basic queueing system with $\lambda = 5$ customers per hour, $\mu = 2$ customers per hour, and $s = 3$, $s = 4$, or $s = 5$. Using the formula in Table 16.2(b), we obtain the following results:

			Total Hourly Cost
s	P_0	L	$20s + 12L$
$s = 3$	0.0449	6.011	$132.13
$s = 4$	0.0736	3.033	$116.40
$s = 5$	0.0801	2.630	$131.56

The total hourly cost is minimized with $s = 4$ mechanics.

Chapter 17

17.1. In conducting the simulation, we use the assignment of random numbers in Table 17.5. The table below summarizes the beginning and the end of the simulation:

Belt	Random Number	Corresponding Lifetime	Cost Associated With Lifetime	Cumulative Time	Cumulative Cost
1	72	$11 \rightarrow 10$	770	10	770
2	94	$12 \rightarrow 10$	770	20	1540
3	76	$11 \rightarrow 10$	770	30	2310
.	.	.		.	.
.	.	.		.	.
24	27	9	1000	232	21,470
25	63	10	1000	242	22,470

Hence, the estimate of the average daily cost for an age replacement policy with $T = 10$ is $22,470/242 = \$92.85$.

17.7. In conducting the simulation, we use the following assignment of random numbers:

Result of coin flip	Heads	Tails
Probability	0.6	0.4
Random numbers	0–5	6–9

The table below summarizes the beginning and the end of the simulation:

Play	Random Numbers and Corresponding Sequence of Heads and Tails (H = heads; T = tails)	Number of Flips	Winnings	Cumulative Winnings
1	56808003721 HTTHTHHHTHH	11	$10 - 11 = -1$	-1
2	75107836258936442 THHHTTHTHHTTHTHHH	17	$10 - 17 = -7$	-8
3	021 HHH	3	$10 - 3 = 7$	-1
.	.	.	.	.
.	.	.	.	.
.	.	.	.	.
9	9216152 THHTHHH	7	$10 - 7 = 3$	9
10	43652 HHTHH	5	$10 - 5 = 5$	14

Hence, the estimate of the average winnings per game is 14/10 = $1.40.

17.10. In conducting the simulation, we use the following assignment of random numbers where the first row contains the probabilities and the second row contains the corresponding assignment of random numbers:

	Senator								
	A		B		C		D		E
For	Against	For	Against	For	Against	For	Against	For	Against
0.9	0.1	0.5	0.5	0.8	0.2	0.1	0.9	0.7	0.3
0–8	9	0–4	5–9	0–7	8–9	0	1–9	0–6	7–9

	Senator								
	F		G		H		I		J
For	Against	For	Against	For	Against	For	Against	For	Against
0.4	0.6	0.9	0.1	0.1	0.9	0.5	0.5	0.7	0.3
0–3	4–9	0–8	9	0	1–9	0–4	5–9	0–6	7–9

Note that confirmation requires that at least 6 undecided senators vote for the nominee. The table below summarizes the beginning and the end of the simulation:

Repetition	Random Numbers and Corresponding Votes by Senators (F = for; A = against) A B C D E F G H I J	Number of Votes For	Confirmed?	Cumulative Confirmations
1	3 2 8 2 7 7 3 6 5 4 F F A A A A F A A F	4	No	0
2	1 2 1 9 1 7 6 3 7 9 F F F A F A F A A A	5	No	0
3	9 4 5 5 0 8 5 7 2 7 A F F A F A F A F A	5	No	0
.	. . . .	.	.	.
.	. . . .	.	.	.
.	. . . .	.	.	.
9	9 5 2 2 8 2 2 2 0 4 A A F A A F F A F F	5	No	4
10	1 0 0 4 7 5 4 2 0 5 F F F A A A F A F F	6	Yes	5

Hence, the estimate of the probability of confirmation is 5/10 = 1/2.

17.13. (a) In conducting the simulation, we use the following assignment of random numbers for each factor:

Value of factor	Most-likely	Pessimistic	Optimistic
Probability	0.6	0.2	0.2
Random numbers	0–5	6–7	8–9

The table below summarizes the beginning and the end of the simulation, where the values of factors 1, 2, 3, 4, and 5 are denoted respectively by m, s, p, c, and f.

Combination	Random Numbers and Corresponding Values of Factors					Profit $ms(p-c)-f$	Cumulative Profit ($000)
	m	s	p	c	f		
1	0	5	1	9	2		
	1,000,000	20%	$10	$4	$400,000	$800,000	800
2	5	6	2	0	4		
	1,000,000	15%	$10	$5	$400,000	$350,000	1150
3	8	7	5	1	6		
	1,200,000	15%	$10	$5	$500,000	$400,000	1550
.	.	.	.	.	.	.	.
.	.	.	.	.	.	.	.
.	.	.	.	.	.	.	.
9	1	4	4	5	9		
	1,000,000	20%	$10	$5	$300,000	$700,000	3900
10	3	2	3	4	0		
	1,000,000	20%	$10	$5	$400,000	$600,000	4500

(b) The estimate of the mean of the annual profit is 4,500,000/10 = $450,000.

(c) The estimate of the probability distribution of the annual profit is

Profit ($000)	100	200	350	400	450	500	600	700	800
Probability	0.1	0.1	0.1	0.2	0.1	0.1	0.1	0.1	0.1

Hence, $400,000 is the largest estimate of the annual profit for which there is at least a 65% chance of equaling or exceeding the estimate.

17.16. Looping begins after the generation of 4 distinct random numbers.

INDEX

Next event simulation, 771–79
  See also Simulation
Node-arc incidence, 384
Nodes:
  chance, 580
  collection, 360–63, 385
  decision, 346, 351, 384, 580
  fictitious sink, 357–59, 385
  flow balance equations, 348–49
  PERT uses, 473–76
  sink and transshipment, 346, 384,
    580
  See also Matrix; Sinks
Nonconsecutive values requirement,
    418, 457
Noninteger values, 391
Nonlinear constraint, 154
Nonlinear program, 65
Nonlinear NLP decision problems
    solved by, 214
Nonnegative values, 43
Numerical values, nonnegative, 196–
    97

O

Objective function, 67, 209
  coefficients (LP), 76–87
  See also Sensitivity analysis
Objective value, 34–40
  maximal, 35
  optimal, 35
Objectives:
  conflicting, 201, 215
  incommensurate, 200–201, 215
Operational research, 10
Operations research, definition, 20
Operations Research Society of Amer-
    ica (ORSA), 10–11
Optimal objective value (LP), 52, 99–
    100
  definition, 68
Optimal solution (LP):
  coordinates, 97–99, 107–9
  current, 83
  isoprofit plane, 307
  slides, 100–102
Optimality:
  description of unique and multiple,
    298
  distinguishing unique and multiple,
    306–7
  multiple and unique, 59, 62, 68,
    80, 303–7
  ranges for coefficients, 309–12

solutions of multiple and unique,
    64, 305
ORSA (*see* Operations Research Soci-
    ety of America)
Outside purchases, 139–41

P

Path:
  cycle, 385
  shortest problem, 385
  uses in PERT and CPM, 476, 500
Penalty approach:
  assignment of preemptive and uni-
    form, 215
  definition, 201, 215
Personnel scheduling, 138, 174
  illustrated, 165–70
PERT (Program Evaluation and Re-
    view Techniques), 466, 499
PERT and CPM:
  activity distinction, 477–78
  activity estimating, 470–71
  activity times, 478–85
  advantages of, 527, 531
  applications of, 466–67, 525
  immediate predecessors relation-
    ships, 469–70, 500
  LP model of, 525–28
  network diagram, 472
  network project constructing, 471–
    75, 500
  phases involved in using, 466–98
  reason for design, 466
  replanning, 497–98
  scheduling, 492–97, 500–501, 531
  slack, 485–92
  See also Arcs; Nodes; Path; Re-
    source loading diagram
Piecewise linear functions:
  concave, 187, 214
  convex, 214
  definition, 214
  introduction, 184–89
  techniques applied, 193
  types of, 193
Piecewise linear programming:
  applicable, 194
  combining techniques, 214
  convex approximation, 193–94
  description, 215
  introduction, 184–89
  single approximation, 194
  technique illustrated, 184–89, 193
  types of, 193
  See also Interval variables

Pivot:
  definition, 245, 279
  equation and variable, 242–43, 245
  goal, 261
  steps involved in, 260–61, 264
Place holder, 196
Planning horizon, definition, 29
Planning production and inventory,
    143–50, 194–99
  constant production level or chase
    demand, 195
Point of tangency, 38
Poisson distribution, 719–20
Postoptimality analysis, 76*n*
Probability:
  conditional, 714
  density, 717
  exponential distribution, 713–22,
    741
  joint, 714
  theory, 713
Probability assessing, 545–47, 579
  formal procedure for, 589–97
  joint and conditional, 590–95
  prior and posterior, 595–97, 617
  subjective and objective, 579
  wheel, 546–47, 579
Product independence, 31
  definition, 65
Product mix problem, 29
Production and inventory planning,
    194–99
  constant level plan, 195
  optimal solution, 148–50, 198–99
  problem, 138, 143–50, 173
  use of deviation variables, 194–200
  See also Deviation variables
Profit:
  constant, 185
  marginal and decreasing, 186
Project management, 9
  PERT, 465

Q

Quadrant, nonnegative, 35
Quality assurance constraint:
  shadow price of, 103–5
  See also Constraints
Quality assurance labor, 104
Quantitative methods, 21
Quantitative perspective, 1
Quantity discounts, 668
Queue:
  capacity, 708, 740
  definition, 740